ASYNDETON AND ITS INTERPRETATION
IN LATIN LITERATURE

Asyndetic coordination (omission of coordinators such as *but, or, and*) is ancient in Indo-European languages. Most commentaries on Greek and Latin texts index 'asyndeton', but wide-ranging treatments of asyndeton across a variety of literary and non-literary genres are largely lacking, and comments are often impressionistic. This book provides the most comprehensive account of asyndeton of this category in Latin ever attempted, and it also contains material from Greek and Umbrian. It analyses asyndeta in diverse genres from early Latin to the early Empire, including prayers and laws, and aims to identify types, determinants, generic variations and chronological changes. Since coordinators are easily left out or added by scribes, criteria are discussed that might be used by editors in deciding between asyndeton and coordination. External influences on Latin, such as Greek and Italic, are also considered. The book will be essential for all scholars of Latin language and literature as well as historical linguistics.

J. N. ADAMS CBE FBA is an Emeritus Fellow of All Souls College Oxford, an Honorary Fellow of Brasenose College Oxford and an Honorary Research Fellow, University of Manchester. He has published many articles and books on the Latin Language, including *Bilingualism and the Latin Language* (Cambridge 2003), *The Regional Diversification of Latin 200 BC–AD 600* (Cambridge 2007) and *Social Variation and the Latin Language* (Cambridge 2013). He was awarded the Kenyon Medal of the British Academy in 2009.

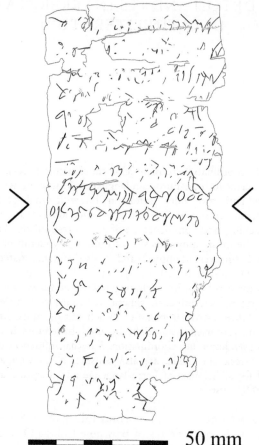

Drawing of an unpublished curse tablet from the temple of Mercury at Uley in Gloucestershire. It contains an unusually long letter written to the god Mercury on both sides of a sheet of lead by a man who has been defrauded of a large sum of money. He 'gives' it to the god, to interest him in recovering it and punishing the defaulter. He represents the verb 'to give' by four Latin verbs in lines 8–9 of face (*a*) illustrated above:

..........................*obd[o]*
of(f)ero destino deputo

Reproduced by permission of Roger S. Tomlin

ASYNDETON AND ITS INTERPRETATION IN LATIN LITERATURE
History, Patterns, Textual Criticism

J. N. ADAMS
All Souls College, Oxford

CAMBRIDGE
UNIVERSITY PRESS

University Printing House, Cambridge CB2 8BS, United Kingdom

One Liberty Plaza, 20th Floor, New York, NY 10006, USA

477 Williamstown Road, Port Melbourne, VIC 3207, Australia

314–321, 3rd Floor, Plot 3, Splendor Forum, Jasola District Centre, New Delhi – 110025, India

79 Anson Road, #06–04/06, Singapore 079906

Cambridge University Press is part of the University of Cambridge.

It furthers the University's mission by disseminating knowledge in the pursuit of education, learning, and research at the highest international levels of excellence.

www.cambridge.org
Information on this title: www.cambridge.org/9781108837859
DOI: 10.1017/9781108943284

© J. N. Adams 2021

This publication is in copyright. Subject to statutory exception and to the provisions of relevant collective licensing agreements, no reproduction of any part may take place without the written permission of Cambridge University Press.

First published 2021

Printed in the United Kingdom by TJ Books Limited, Padstow Cornwall

A catalogue record for this publication is available from the British Library.

ISBN 978-1-108-83785-9 Hardback

Cambridge University Press has no responsibility for the persistence or accuracy of URLs for external or third-party internet websites referred to in this publication and does not guarantee that any content on such websites is, or will remain, accurate or appropriate.

Contents

Preface	*page* xxi
Acknowledgements	xxvii
List of Abbreviations	xxix

PART I INTRODUCTION   1

I Asyndetic and Syndetic Coordination: Definitions and Types   3
1 Coordination and Asyndeton   3
2 Asyndeton with Two Members, Conjunctive, Disjunctive and Adversative   7
3 Ancient Classifications of Asyndeton   10
4 Longer Single-Word Asyndeta in Latin   14
5 Asyndeta Bimembria in Which at Least One of the Coordinates Is a Pair of Words Forming a Unit   16
6 Phrasal Asyndeton with Two Members   17
7 A Mixed Type   19
8 Clausal Asyndeton   20
9 Causal, Explanatory, Explicative (etc.) 'Asyndeton'   27
10 Asyndeton with Anaphora   29
11 Conclusions   32

II 'Asyndeta' That May Not Be Asyndeta: Roles of Adjectives; Appositional Compounds; and 'Asyndetic Hendiadys'   33
1 Introduction   33
2 Juxtaposed Adjectives That Are Not Asyndetic   33
   2.1 Attributive and Predicative Adjectives; Secondary Predicates   33
   2.2 Groups of Adjectives; Other Classifications ('Rank', 'Hierarchy', 'Stacking', 'Layering')   34
   2.3 Poetic Periphrases and Additional Adjectives   35
   2.4 Scholarly Classifications of Adjectival Roles   36
   2.5 Conclusions   44

	3	Quasi-compounds, and Pairs in Which One Term Is a Modifier of the Other	44
		3.1 Appositional Compounds	44
		3.2 Modifier + Modified et al.	46
		3.2.1 *uolens propitius*	46
		3.2.2 Some Pairs in Which One Term Is a (Predicative) Modifier of the Other	49
		3.2.3 Pairs of Uncertain Interpretation	52
		3.2.3.1 Pairs of Verbs	52
		3.2.3.2 Pairs of Nouns	53
		3.2.3.3 Conclusions	54

III Asyndeton Versus Coordination, an Introduction — 55
1. The Antiquity of Asyndeton versus Syndetic Coordination — 55
2. Dvandva Compounds — 57
3. Textual Criticism: Asyndeton versus Coordination — 61

IV Lists of Two Types — 66
1. Introduction — 66
2. Lists as Totalities — 66
3. Open-Ended Lists: 'Illustrations' — 71
4. Open-Ended Lists Comprising Pairs of Adjectives: a Specific Case — 74
5. Conclusions — 75

V Supposed 'Effects' of Asyndeton — 76
1. 'Rapidity' et sim. and the Articulation of Asyndetic Pairs; Some Ancient Evidence — 76
2. 'Pauses for Thought' and Postponed Adjectives in Latin — 79
3. Possible Variability of Articulation — 82

PART 2 'GRAMMATICAL' TYPES — 85

VI Asyndetic Pairs (Mainly of Adjectives) of Which at Least One Member Is a Term with a Negative Prefix (in Latin, Usually *in-*) — 87
1. Introduction — 87
2. Asyndetic Pairs of Which Both Members Are Privatives — 88
   2.1 Greek — 88
   2.2 Latin — 91
      2.2.1 Some Conclusions — 93
   2.3 The Rigveda — 94
3. Asyndetic Pairs with *in-* or alpha at the Start of Both Members, but with at Least One Member That Is Not a Privative Compound — 95
4. Asyndetic Pairs with Just One Member (Usually the Second) That Is a Privative — 96

Contents vii

    4.1 Greek   96
    4.2 Latin   97
  5 Asyndetic Triplets (or Longer Sequences) Comprising Terms That
    All Have a Privative Prefix   99
    5.1 Greek   99
    5.2 Latin   101
    5.3 The Rigveda   101
  6 Oppositions, with a Privative Compound Negating Its Simplex   102
  7 Positive–Negative Pairs in Latin of Which the Negated Term Has
    a Prefix other than Privative *in-*   106
  8 Prefixes other than the Privative That Are Repeated in Asyndetic
    Pairs   108
    8.1 Greek   108
    8.2 Latin   108
  9 Conclusions   109
  Appendix: English   111

VII Simplex + Compound in Asyndeton   113
  1 Evidence   113
  2 Conclusions   120

VIII Juxtaposition of Active and Passive Forms of the Same Verb   121
  1 Evidence   121
  2 Conclusions   124

IX Asyndetic Pairs of Verbs of Different Tense or Mood   125
  1 Evidence   125
  2 Conclusions   127

X Pairs of Imperatives   128
  1 'Go' + Imperative   128
    1.1 Early Latin   128
    1.2 An Official Formula   130
    1.3 A Reversal of Order   131
    1.4 Later Latin   132
    1.5 Italo-Romance Dialects   133
  2 Pseudo-Asyndeton: the Use of *age*   135
  3 Some Special Types of Asyndetic Imperatives   136
  4 Greek: New Comedy and Miscellaneous   136
  5 Conclusions   137

XI Masculine + Feminine Pairs   138
  1 Introduction   138
  2 Gods, Goddesses   138
  3 Men, Women   140

	4 Boys, Girls	141
	5 Miscellaneous Pairs, Mainly in Legal Contexts	141
	6 Conclusions	142
XII	Recapitulation: 'Grammatical' Types and Their Distribution	143

PART 3 SEMANTIC TYPES   147

XIII Pairs of Opposites   149
    1 Introduction   149
    2 Definitions: Complementarities, Antonyms, Converses
      and Directional Opposites   150
    3 Statistics   155
    4 Structures and Uses   156
      4.1 Accumulations: Juxtaposed Asyndetic Pairs of Opposites 156
      4.2 Accumulations: Asyndetic Pairs of Opposites Juxtaposed
        with Syndetic Pairs of Opposites   159
      4.3 Accumulations: Asyndetic Pairs of Opposites Juxtaposed with
        Asyndetic Pairs of Other Types   160
    5 A Few Types of Opposites Worthy of Comment   161
      5.1 'Town' : 'Country' et sim.   161
      5.2 'Public' : 'Private' et sim.   162
      5.3 Pairs Denoting Opposites of Social Status   162
      5.4 Asyndetic Pairs of Adverbs   163
      5.5 Variations on the Type of Asyndetic Pair That Is Composed
        of Explicit Opposites   165
    6 Conclusions   166

XIV Pairs Denoting Family Members   167
    1 Introduction   167
    2 A Selection of Pairs   167
      2.1 Father, Mother   167
      2.2 Brother, Sister   168
      2.3 Women/Wives, Children   168
      2.4 Parent, Children   169
      2.5 Forms of Kinship of Diverse Types   169
    3 Conclusions   170

XV 'Semantic' Types: Some Conclusions   171

PART 4 STRUCTURES   175

XVI Rule of Ascending Length (?)   177
    1 'Behaghel's Law'   177
    2 Statistics   179

	3 Some Other Factors Determining the Order of the Constituents of an Asyndetic Pair	184
	4 Conclusions	187
XVII	**Correlative Distribution**	188
	1 Evidence	188
	2 Conclusions	191
XVIII	**End-of-List Coordination and 'Weak' Asyndeton Bimembre**	192
	1 Introduction	192
	2 Statistics	193
	2.1 Livy 8	193
	2.1.1 Asyndeta	193
	2.1.2 Groups with Internal Coordination (but Not End-of-List Type)	194
	2.1.3 End-of-List Coordination	195
	2.2 Cicero *De officiis* 1.1–100	195
	2.2.1 Asyndeta	195
	2.2.2 Coordinations	196
	2.2.3 End-of-List Coordination	196
	2.3 Cato	197
	2.4 Plautus	197
	3 Internal Unities Expressed by Coordinators	198
	4 Examples of the Structure AB*Cque* That Arguably Do Not Have End-of-List Coordination	200
	5 End-of-List Coordination	204
	6 Special Structures That May Have 'Weak' Asyndeton Bimembre + Third Element	206
	7 Further Ambiguities of Interpretation	209
	8 Conclusions	210
XIX	**Accumulations of Asyndeta: a Few Patterns**	211
	1 Antiquity and Continuity	211
	2 Types, Statistics, Textual Criticism	216
	3 Juxtaposed Asyndeta That Are Open to Misinterpretation	218
	4 Conclusions	218
XX	**Discontinuous Asyndeton and Conjunct Hyperbaton**	220
	1 Conjunct Hyperbaton	220
	2 Discontinuous Asyndeton	221
	3 Discontinuous Asyndeton in Menander	224
	4 Conclusions	224

Contents

XXI Asyndetic Pairs Dependent on a Single Preposition — 225
1. Introduction — 225
2. Structural Patterns — 225
3. Pairs Dependent on a Preposition in Caesar, *Bellum Ciuile* — 227
4. Asyndetic Pairs Dependent on a Single Preposition That Are Not in Significant Structures — 228
5. Conclusions — 230

PART 5 GENRES AND TEXTS — 231

XXII Laws and Prayers — 233
1. Introduction — 233
2. Coordination in the *Lex Cornelia de XX quaestoribus*, *Lex Antonia de Termessibus*, *Senatus consultum de Cn. Pisone patre* — 234
   2.1 *Lex Cornelia de XX quaestoribus* — 234
   2.2 *Lex Antonia de Termessibus* — 237
   2.3 *Senatus consultum de Cn. Pisone patre* — 240
3. Asyndeton and Coordination in Selected Prayers — 241
   3.1 A Spell in Macrobius, *Sat.* 3.9.7–8 — 241
   3.2 Prayers in Cato, *Agr.* 141 — 242
   3.3 Varro *Ling.* 7.8 and the Formula for Taking the Auspices — 242
   3.4 A Prayer for the Devotion of Cities to Destruction, Uttered only by Generals and Dictators (Macr. *Sat.* 3.9.10–11) — 243
   3.5 Quotations from the Books of the *haruspices* Found in Cicero's *Har.* — 245
4. Asyndeton in Umbrian — 246
   4.1 Introduction — 246
   4.2 Nouns — 246
   4.3 Adjectives — 248
   4.4 Verbs — 248
   4.5 'Prepositional' Type — 249
   4.6 Accumulations of Pairs of Different Types — 249
   4.7 Phrasal and Mixed Asyndeta — 251
   4.8 Conclusions — 251
5. Some Legal Pairs, Mainly Old — 252
   5.1 *patres conscripti* — 252
   5.2 *uelitis iubeatis* — 254
   5.3 *sarta tecta* — 256
   5.4 *loca lautia* — 257
   5.5 *ruta caesa* — 258
   5.6 *usus fructus* — 258
   5.7, 8 *emptio uenditio, locatio conductio* — 259
   5.9 *populus Romanus Quirites* (?) — 262
   5.10 *usus auctoritas* — 263

	5.11 Conclusions	263
6	Some Religious Pairs	263
	6.1 *sub diu(o) columine*	263
	6.2 *(Iuppiter) optimus maximus*	264
	6.3 Some Augural Formulae	264
	6.4 *prima postrema*	265
	6.5 *porci sacres sinceri*	265
7	Legal Phrases in Literary Texts	265
	7.1 Proposals in the Senate; Other Contexts	265
	7.2 Offices, Officials, Titles, Honours	266
	7.3 Groups or Individuals within the State of a Defined Status; External Groups Possessing an Official Relationship with the State	267
	7.4 Abstract Terms Denoting Relationships with States	267
	7.5 Types of States and Foundations, Methods of Government	267
	7.6 Activities Regulated by Law	268
8	Religious Phrases in Literary Texts	268
9	Conclusions	268

XXIII Plautus 272

1	Statistics	272
2	Diversity of Types	272
3	Religious and Legal Expressions	274
4	Compounds or Long Suffixal Derivatives, Often Coinages, Juxtaposed	276
5	Verbs	280
	5.1 Imperatives	280
	5.2 Subjunctives	282
	5.3 Non-Imperatival Pairs of Verbs Consisting of a Verb of Motion and Another Verb	282
	5.4 Asyndetic Pairs of Verbs Marked by Assonance of One Type or Another	283
	5.5 Miscellaneous Pairs of Verbs in Asyndeton	286
6	Privatives	289
7	Structures	292
	7.1 Juxtaposed Asyndetic Pairs	292
	7.2 Asyndeton Juxtaposed with Coordinations	294
	7.3 Embedded Pairs	295
	7.4 Anaphora of Prepositions	296
8	Semantic Categories	297
	8.1 Adornment and the Like, Mainly Female	297
	8.2 Decadent or Depraved Behaviour	299
	8.3 'Eat, Drink'	300
	8.4 Vices, Adjectives Applied to Disapproved Behaviour	300
	8.5 Food Lists, Recipes, Shopping Lists etc.	301

8.6	Precious Metals and the Like	301
8.7	Athletic Pursuits	301
8.8	Adjectives to Do with Age and Decrepitude	302
8.9	Numerical Approximations	302
8.10	Pairs of Opposites	303
8.11	Relationships by Blood, Marriage, Alliance and Friendship	304
8.12	Complementary Parts of the Body	304
8.13	Masculine + Feminine Pairs	304
8.14	Some Miscellaneous Pairs That Occur more than Once, in Plautus or in Plautus and elsewhere	305
	uiuo ualeo	305
	opus/opera labor	305
	do dono	305
	frigus fames	305
	iocus ludus	305
9	Conclusions	306
	Appendix: Lists of Asyndetic Pairs of Nouns, Adjectives and Adverbs in Plautus	308

XXIV Virgil and Early High-Style Poetry 313

1 Introduction 313
2 Virgil 314
   2.1 Asyndeta Bimembria Where the Two Parts Consist of a Single Word 314
      2.1.1 Adjectives 314
      2.1.2 Nouns, Names 318
      2.1.3 Adverbs 319
      2.1.4 Verbs 319
      2.1.5 Prepositional Expressions 319
   2.2 Adjectival Asyndeta with Two Members, One of Extended Length 320
   2.3 Conclusions 323
3 Homer 324
4 Conclusions: Homer and Virgil 330
5 Asyndeton Bimembre in Ennius 331
   5.1 The *Annals* 331
      5.1.1 Adjectives 331
      5.1.2 Adjective + Adverb 336
      5.1.3 Nouns 337
      5.1.4 Verbs 338
      5.1.5 Some False or Dubious Examples 338
   5.2 Tragedies 339
      5.2.1 Adjectives 339
      5.2.2 Nouns 340
      5.2.3 Adverbs 341

Contents

5.2.4 Verbs	341
5.2.5 Some False or Dubious Examples	342
5.2.6 Aspects of Coordination and Longer Asyndeta in Ennius	343
5.3 Conclusions: a Comparison of Ennius and Virgil (and Plautus)	345
6 Pacuvius, Tragedies	347
6.1 Adjectives	347
6.2 Nouns	348
6.3 Verbs	349
6.4 Pairs with One Member of Extended Length	351
6.5 Conclusions	352
7 Asyndeton Bimembre in Lucretius	352
7.1 Pairs with Single-Word Members	353
7.1.1 Adjectives	353
7.1.2 Nouns	354
7.1.3 Verbs	356
7.1.4 Prepositional type	358
7.1.5 Adverbs	358
7.2 Type with One Member of Extended Length	358
7.3 Examples That Are Difficult to Classify	359
7.4 Some Long Asyndeta	361
7.5 End-of-List Coordinations in Lucretius	362
7.6 Multiple Coordinations	362
7.7 Conclusions: Some Comparisons of Lucretius with Ennius, Pacuvius and Virgil	363
8 Livius Andronicus, *Odyssea* and Naevius, *Belli Punici Carmen*	364
9 Final Conclusions	367
Appendix: Some Coordinated Pairs with -*que* (mainly) in Lucretius and Virgil	368
XXV Lucilius	**373**
1 Asyndeton Bimembre	373
1.1 Asyndeton Bimembre Consisting for the Most Part of Single Words	374
1.1.1 'Stylised' examples	374
1.1.2 Accumulations	375
1.1.3 Open-ended lists	379
1.1.4 Adjectives	381
1.1.5 Imperatives	384
1.1.6 Other Verb Forms	384
1.1.7 Adverbs	385
1.1.8 Names	385
1.1.9 Nouns	386
1.1.10 Prepositional Type	387
1.2 Conclusions	388
2 Terms with Privative Prefix	389

3	Long Asyndeta	392
4	End-of-List Coordination	398
5	Multiple Coordinations	399
6	Some Stylistic Features of Asyndetic and Coordinated Pairs	400
7	Conclusions	403

XXVI Cicero 405

1 Introduction	405
2 Data: Speeches	406
2.1 Nouns	406
2.2 Names	416
2.3 Adjectives	418
2.4 Verbs	421
2.5 Adverbs	427
2.6 Prepositional Type	428
3 Data: Philosophica	429
3.1 Nouns	429
3.2 Names	437
3.3 Adjectives	438
3.4 Verbs	439
3.5 Prepositional Type	442
4 Data: Letters *Ad Atticum*	443
4.1 Nouns	443
4.2 Names	446
4.3 Adjectives	447
4.4 Adverbs	448
4.5 Verbs	448
4.6 Prepositional Type	450
5 Data: Letters *Ad familiares*	452
5.1 Nouns	452
5.2 Names	455
5.3 Adjectives	456
5.4 Verbs	457
5.5 Prepositional Type	458
6 Some Letters of Caelius	458
6.1 Nouns	458
6.2 Names	459
6.3 Adverbs	459
6.4 Verbs	461
6.5 Prepositional Type	461
7 Conclusions	461
7.1 Distributions	461
7.2 Observations on the Speeches	462
7.2.1 Nouns	462
7.2.2 Adjectives	464

Contents   xv

7.2.3 Verbs	465
7.2.4 Prepositional Type	467
7.2.5 Accumulations: Statistics	467
7.2.6 Pairs of Opposites in the Speeches	467
7.3 Observations on the Philosophica	467
7.3.1 Accumulations and Opposites, of Nouns and Verbs	467
7.4 Observations on the Letters *Ad Atticum*	470
7.4.1 Types and Distributions	470
7.4.2 Accumulations	472
7.4.3 Opposites	472
7.4.4 Further Remarks	472
7.5 Observations on the Letters *Ad familiares*	472
7.5.1 Accumulations	473
7.5.2 Types and Distributions	473
7.5.3 Addressees and Asyndeton	473
7.6 Contexts and Genres as Determinants of Asyndeton	474
7.7 Punctuation, Textual Issues and Some Influences on Asyndeton	475
7.8 Some Semantic Categories	479
7.8.1 Legal and Religious Pairs	479
7.8.2 Miscellaneous Semantic Types	480

XXVII Catullus 482
1 Asyndeta Bimembria	482
1.1 Nouns	482
1.2 Adjectives	484
1.3 Adverbs	485
1.4 Imperatives	487
1.5 Other Verb Forms	488
1.6 Asyndeton Bimembre: Conclusions	489
2 Sequences of Three or More Words: Asyndeton, Coordination and End-of-List Coordination	490
3 Coordinated Pairs	492
4 Conclusions	495

XXVIII Caesar, *Bellum Ciuile*: Asyndeton and Textual Criticism 496
1 Introduction	496
2 Categories	497
2.1 Place Names and Designations of Peoples	497
2.2 Noun Pairs	502
3 Conclusions	506
Appendix 1: Pairs of Nouns or Phrases Dependent on a Preposition	508
Appendix 2: Some Coordinated Military Pairs in Caesar *Civ.*	511

XXIX Horace 512
1 Introduction	512
2 Asyndeton Bimembre	512

Contents

2.1	*Satires*	512
	2.1.1 Privatives	513
	2.1.2 Accumulations	515
	2.1.3 Discontinuous Asyndetic Pairs	516
	2.1.4 Some Other Types	516
	2.1.4.1 Masculine + Feminine Pairs	516
	2.1.4.2 Family Members	517
	2.1.4.3 The City and its Components	517
	2.1.4.4 Pairs of Names	517
	2.1.4.5 Opposites	518
	2.1.4.6 Verbal Pairs with One Member of Extended Length	518
	2.1.4.7 A Special Case	519
	2.1.5 Conclusions	519
2.2	*Epistles*	520
	2.2.1 Conclusions	522
2.3	*Odes*	522
	2.3.1 Conclusions	523
2.4	*Ars Poetica*	523
3 Longer Asyndeta		523
3.1	*Satires*	523
	3.1.1 Conclusions	525
3.2	*Epistles*	525
	3.2.1 Conclusions	527
3.3	*Odes*	527
	3.3.1 Conclusions	527
3.4	*Ars Poetica*	527
4 Forms of Explicit Coordination		528
4.1	Coordinated Pairs	528
	4.1.1 Totalities/Merisms	529
	4.1.2 Masculine + Feminine	529
	4.1.3 Opposites	530
	4.1.4 Adverbial Opposites	530
	4.1.5 Family Members	530
	4.1.6 Different Moods/Tenses	531
	4.1.7 Miscellaneous	531
	4.1.8 Conclusions	531
4.2	End-of-List Coordination	532
	4.2.1 *Satires*	532
	4.2.2 *Epistles*	533
	4.2.3 *Odes*	534
	4.2.4 *Epodes*	534

	4.3 Multiple Coordinations	535
	4.3.1 *Satires*	535
	4.3.2 *Epistles*	536
	4.3.3 *Odes*	537
	4.4 Conclusions: Longer Sequences, Asyndetic and Coordinated	539
	4.5 A Selective Corpus from Pindar	540
5	Conclusions	542

XXX The Annalists, Sallust and Tacitus 544

1 Introduction 544
2 Annalists 544
   2.1 Asyndeta Bimembria with Members Comprising Single Words 545
   2.2 Longer Asyndeta of Single Terms, Possible Embedded Pairs and a Few Complex Types 548
   2.3 Phrasal or Clausal Asyndeta with More Members than Two 552
   2.4 Phrasal or Clausal Asyndeta with Two Members 552
   2.5 Conclusions 552
3 Sallust 553
   3.1 Introduction 553
   3.2 The Evidence 554
      3.2.1 Nouns 554
      3.2.2 Adjectives 570
      3.2.3 Verbs 575
      3.2.4 Adverbs 581
      3.2.5 Prepositional Type 581
   3.3 Sallust: Conclusions 582
      3.3.1 Contexts, Narrative versus Speech 582
      3.3.2 Parts of Speech and Some Aspects of Uniformity 582
      3.3.3 Structural Patterns 584
      3.3.4 Textual Matters 586
4 Tacitus *Histories* 587
   4.1 The Evidence 587
      4.1.1 Nouns 587
      4.1.2 Adjectives 593
      4.1.3 Verbs 595
      4.1.4 Adverbs 599
      4.1.5 Prepositional Type 599
   4.2 Tacitus *Histories*: Conclusions 600
      4.2.1 Narrative versus Speeches 600
      4.2.2 Parts of Speech and Other Features 600
      4.2.3 Semantic Relationships 601
      4.2.4 Structural Patterns 601
5 Tacitus *Annals* 602
   5.1 The Evidence 602
      5.1.1 Nouns 602

			5.1.2 Adjectives	618
			5.1.3 Verbs	621
			5.1.4 Adverbs	627
			5.1.5 Prepositional Type	628
		5.2	Tacitus *Annals*: Conclusions	629
			5.2.1 Distributions	629
			5.2.2 Types: Parts of Speech and Difficulties of Interpretation	630
			5.2.3 Semantic and Structural Features	631
			5.2.4 Some Textual Points	634
	6	Conclusions: Sallust and Tacitus		635
		6.1	Lexical and Syntactic Similarities and Differences	635
		6.2	Some Structural Similarities and Differences	636

XXXI Livy   644

1	Introduction		644
2	Data		645
	2.1	Nouns	645
	2.2	Adjectives	657
	2.3	Verbs	661
	2.4	Adverbs	663
	2.5	Prepositional Type	664
3	Conclusions		667
	3.1	Incidence	667
	3.2	Speeches versus Narrative	667
	3.3	Nouns	668
	3.4	Adjectives	669
	3.5	Verbs	671
	3.6	Pairs of Opposites	671
	3.7	Some Other Features of Distribution and Structure	672
	3.8	Contextual Factors and Other Determinants	674
	3.9	Asyndeton Bimembre and Textual Criticism	675
Appendix: Prepositions with Two Dependent Nouns in Selected Books			678

PART 6 CONCLUSIONS   681

XXXII Asyndeton in Latin   683

1	Some Types of Asyndeton Bimembre	683
2	Asyndetic Tricola (and Longer), versus Asyndeton Bimembre	686
3	Some Determinants of Asyndeton Bimembre	687
	3.1 Accumulations and Structures	687
	3.2 Genre	688
	3.3 Formulae versus ad hoc Asyndetic Pairs Reflecting Intonation Patterns (?)	689

Contents

3.4 A Few Semantic Types — 691
3.5 Personal Taste — 692
3.6 Addressees, Contexts, Circumstances — 692
4 Asyndeton and Latin Literature — 693

Bibliography — 700
Subject Index — 715
Index Mainly of Selected Pairs and Longer Sequences — 721
Selective Index Locorum — 734

Preface

The term 'asyndeton' is constantly used in classical scholarship. Most commentaries on Greek and Latin texts have an entry for asyndeton in the index, often with multiple references. For example, the editions of Tacitus *Histories 2* and *Annals 15* by Rhiannon Ash have 68 and 46 references respectively. Few recent commentaries lack any mention of the phenomenon. Notes in commentaries often have impressionistic remarks on the function of the asyndeton in particular contexts.

Commentators tend to use the term without much (or any) specification of what they mean. In this book 'asyndeton' is used to refer to coordinations that lack explicit coordinators, by which I mean terms corresponding to English *and, or, but*. A distinction is sometimes made by linguists between coordination that is syndetic (with *and, or, but*), and that which is asyndetic. There is a tradition particularly in Greek scholarship of including under the heading 'asyndeton' the omission of sentence particles as well, a phenomenon that often differs from the omission of coordinators. In the juxtaposed sentences *He is hungry. He hasn't eaten for three days* it is not strictly a coordinator that is missing, but a term such as *for* or *because*. Commentators regularly refer to the absence of γάρ as asyndeton, but is that designation satisfactory? It would seem more appropriate to say that it is the equivalent of a subordinating conjunction that is lacking in the above, not a coordinator, an interesting phenomenon to be sure, but is it to be mixed up with asyndetic coordination (see e.g. Quirk et al. 1972: 552 on the ambiguous status of *for*)? The term 'parataxis' may sometimes be more suitable, or absence of 'sentence connectors'.

Some importance clearly is attached to asyndeton by commentators, to judge by the frequency with which it is mentioned. We find in an overview of coordination in Latin by Torrego (2009) a statement that coordination by juxtaposition (asyndeton) was 'almost marginal' from the first texts (452), but the term 'marginal' does not seem fully appropriate once it is realised that, for example, in the *Lex Cornelia de XX quaestoribus* of Sullan date asyndeton far outnumbers overt coordination, or that a speech put into the mouth of Catiline by Sallust has a striking accumulation of asyndetic pairs. What was Sallust's purpose? Interestingly, Cicero's speeches against Catiline also have some accumulations of asyndeta at high points. Asyndeton must have had a role of sorts in late republican political oratory.

Articles have been written on asyndeton in particular authors, but there has never been a systematic account of its use and functions in Latin, though there is a useful old dissertation by Preuss (1881). Nor does asyndetic coordination get much coverage in modern languages, as far as I can see. Eduard Fraenkel once presented an asyndetic sequence in Milton's *Paradise Lost* (2.185 *unrespited, unpitied, unreprieved*) as being imitated from (Greek) tragedy (see Chapter VI, Appendix), but certainly asyndeton (as I would define it), particularly adjectival, is used freely today in English in novels and newspapers, not least in headlines, and not least with the structure of the example in Milton. This commonplace English type, showing either sequences of privative adjectives with the prefix *un-*, or positive–negative pairs, one with the privative prefix, is paralleled widely in e.g. Greek, Latin, Vedic and Umbrian, and is likely to have been inherited. In English it occurs for example in the poetry of George Herbert (1593–1633).

There are numerous types of asyndetic coordination in Latin, phrasal, clausal, that consisting of single words, sequences short, long or with a mixture of different categories. All types receive some coverage in this book, however brief, but the book is mainly about pairs of single words, so-called 'asyndeton bimembre', and evidence for this is collected systematically from a variety of genres and analysed. Asyndeton bimembre is the most interesting type in Latin, and also the most problematic, given the ease with which scribes may omit or add a coordinator. It is ancient, and persistent. It is also a type that has been subject to generalisations deriving from a simplification of the evidence. A favourite descriptive term has been 'sacral', a term that is applicable to just a minute fraction of the evidence. The main period dealt with here spans the early Republic to the Augustan period, but for historiography I have gone beyond the latter to include Tacitus' *Histories* and *Annals*. Later legal language also has a place. The assembling of evidence is an immensely time-consuming task, resistant to technological methods of data collection (as far as I am aware). Pure statistics are not of much help unless contexts are taken into account. Textual issues come up, and analysis of phrase structure is often required. Problems of phrase structure are not eased by the unsystematic and often inconsistent punctuation of texts to be found in many editions, a topic which is discussed in places in the book.

A two-word asyndeton and its effects cannot be assessed merely as a pair of words viewed on the written page next to each other, supposedly for example representing 'rapidity' or 'excitement' (because of the missing term). Asyndetic coordination has a place in speech too, and in speech (in modern languages) it shows variable intonation patterns, which an author will inevitably have in mind when choosing to omit a coordinator in writing. Often in speech an asyndetic pair is articulated, not with rapidity, but with a marked pause after the first element. It cannot be assumed that all such omissions will have the same motivation. Two nouns or verbs in a legal formula are likely to have differed in intonation from a pair of condemnatory adjectives placed at the end of a colon expressing a judgement, with the second word semantically stronger and preceded (in speech) by a 'pause for thought' to highlight the final condemnation. I have started with the assumption that asyndeton bimembre is not a single phenomenon with a single aim, and have tried to demonstrate the varieties, from the mundane to the contrived, in some detail. Although we cannot know much about Latin intonation, it is certainly possible to identify different types and functions of two-word asyndeta. There are moreover in ancient grammarians and rhetoricians some interesting comments on the articulation of asyndeta, and these are collected and discussed in the book.

The book is not only about Latin. There is a detailed account of asyndeton in Umbrian (Iguvine Tables), and Vedic is dealt with (thanks to Elizabeth Tucker of the Oriental Institute, Oxford) in the chapter on negative adjectives. Greek is cited throughout, and not only in the sections in which the term occurs in a heading. An obvious question is whether Greek had much influence on the use of asyndeta bimembria in Latin. Greek may have been influential, for example, in the use of juxtaposed asyndetic pairs of opposites in philosophy, and Virgil was certainly influenced by Homer, but some similarities between Latin and Greek may reflect rather inherited patterns. This point is made in the chapter on alpha- and *in*-privatives, in which semantic differences emerge between the two languages in the use of such pairings. There are comparisons in the book between for example Virgil and Homer, Plautus and Menander, and Horace's *Odes* and Pindar.

A few old or formulaic pairs exist that are always or almost always asyndetic, but the majority of terms attested in asyndeton are also attested with explicit coordination, a point that is illustrated throughout the literary chapters. Wölfflin's extensive collection (1933) of alliterative pairs has full details of the forms of coordination, asyndetic or syndetic, found with each pair. An Umbrian pair attested both with and without a coordinator is noted at Chapter XXII.4. Editors of texts sometimes eliminate an asyndeton on the grounds that the pairing is elsewhere attested with coordinators. That is an unsatisfactory methodology, because many asyndetic pairs are isolated or rare, and if majority usage were to be used as a main criterion in judging an asyndeton much of Latin literature would have to be extensively rewritten. A major aim therefore has been to identify determinants of the omission of coordinators in Latin. Many asyndetic pairs are located in what are called here 'accumulations', which are defined and extensively discussed. Their relevance to textual problems is illustrated. These structural patterns are the most influential determinant of asyndeton bimembre in the Latin of the periods covered here. For example, the legal pair *emptio uenditio*, regularly used as a technical term in modern textbooks of Roman law and given the meaning 'sale', in Latin texts almost always has a coordinator (*et*), unless it is in an accumulation (thus *emptio et uenditio*, but *emptio uenditio, locatio conductio*). Genre, context and addressees come into it too. Asyndeta bimembria, particularly of several types that are given separate chapters, are extremely common in republican laws, but rare in early prayers (despite the use of the term 'sacral' to characterise asyndeton), in which the coordinator *-que* is preferred. Cicero uses asyndeton bimembre infrequently when writing to Atticus, but has it often in certain of his letters *Ad familiares*, notably those addressed to persons with whom his connection was distant or cold. In some historians asyndeta accumulate in speeches. Certain parts of speech or types of terms attract asyndeton, particularly imperatives addressed to subordinates, and judgemental adjectives placed at the end of cola and containing at least one *in*-privative. In both these cases patterns of intonation probably lie behind the omission of the coordinator. In various parts of the book semantic categories that seem to favour asyndeta are identified too. The chapter on Caesar, *Bellum ciuile* (XXVIII), which makes use of the recent critical edition by Cynthia Damon, is not only about asyndeton or its absence in that work, but discusses methodologies that may be used by editors faced with choosing between an asyndeton and an overt coordination. This topic comes up in other chapters too, such as III.3, XIX.2 and XXI.

The interpretation of pairs of adjectives (or of adjective + participle) is especially complex and has sometimes caused problems. Two adjectives without a coordinator are not necessarily in asyndeton. In the phrase *the young criminal lawyer* the insertion of a coordinator would give the wrong

Preface xxv

meaning. There is 'layering' of the two adjectives. Not infrequently pairs of adjectives in Latin differing in this or a similar way have been falsely taken as asyndetic. A classic case is the pairing *uolens propitius*, regularly cited as the sacral asyndeton par excellence. In its earliest use it is not an asyndeton at all, though, with a change of its verbal construction later, it does become asyndetic. A superficially similar pair in Umbrian, which by contrast is a genuine asyndeton and tends to be cited as a parallel to the Latin, differs semantically from the Latin pair in a significant way. Chapter II deals with the problems of analysis that pairs of adjectives raise, and introduces some types of compounds.

The book is loosely speaking in two parts, the first typological, the second literary, this latter dealing with numerous literary genres and also with prayers and laws. The final chapter is an overview of asyndeton bimembre in Latin literature, and its types, chronology and variations.

Here are a few comments on the evidence used in the literary chapters and on its presentation.

First, I have set out to collect every case of asyndeton bimembre in the texts consulted, but inevitably some omissions will have been made. In several places in chapters in which the examples are numbered I have inserted at a later stage omitted passages that I happen to have noticed, usually keeping the original numbering and giving the added examples a number of the type (1a). It would have been out of the question to re-read the whole corpus looking systematically for missed examples, but the evidence presented is I hope tolerably complete.

Second, the chapters are not uniform in format and content. In the chapters on Plautus, Lucilius, Catullus and Horace I have collected and discussed not only asyndeta bimembria but also some other types of asyndeta and forms of explicit coordination. The chapters on long prose works, such as those of Cicero and the historians, are more restricted in scope, in that they concentrate mainly on asyndeton bimembre (though the section on the annalists in Chapter XXX is more comprehensive). As was stated above, the chapter on Caesar is specifically about asyndeton and textual criticism. Textual issues do however come up frequently in other chapters on prose works.

Third, it may seem a simple matter to identify asyndeta bimembria, but that is not always so. For example, semantically unified asyndetic pairs may be placed within much longer asyndetic sequences. If e.g. the positive–negative pair *dignus indignus* were to occur within an asyndetic series of six otherwise miscellaneous adjectives, I would usually classify it as an 'embedded' asyndeton bimembre. Especially hard to categorise are some sequences that superficially are of the type *A, B and C* (cf. *bacon, lettuce and tomatoes*, with what I call 'end-of-list' coordination). How is one to interpret the structure of a case that has a unified pair at the start, followed by an element (attached by a coordinator) of a different semantic type? I have tended to treat such initial pairs as 'weak' asyndeta bimembria within a longer structure, another form of embedding. Apparent end-of-list coordination in Latin is not always what it seems.

Fourth, I have not placed commas between the two members of asyndeta bimembria if they consist of single words. This is an arbitrary decision, given that in some contexts, for example when the second term outdoes the first semantically, there may be reason to think that in speech there would have been a pause before the dramatic stronger term. An editor of a critical text may indeed decide to use variable punctuations, making explicit for example a rising emphasis by inserting a comma before the second member. If on the other hand an asyndeton bimembre consists of a single word + a phrase, or of two phrases, I have marked the division between the two members with a comma, because in some contexts it may not be immediately obvious where the division lies. Longer asyndetic sequences consisting of single words (i.e. tricola and longer cola) have also been left unpunctuated. However, some such sequences are manifestly composed of groups of semantically unified pairs, such as the two juxtaposed Ciceronian pairs of opposites, *uita mors diuitiae paupertas*. In my opinion it is unsatisfactory for an editor to fail to indicate the phrase structure by a comma (*uita mors, diuitiae paupertas*).

Finally, I am aware that anyone looking at the literary chapters is likely to be not so much reading the whole as consulting a chapter on a particular author or passage. I have decided to make each of these chapters as self-contained as possible. The conclusions scattered about within them and at their ends summarise features of the author's use of asyndeton, and may be consulted alongside or in preference to the full collections of data. The typological chapters are in a way a separate work.

Cross references throughout consist mainly of chapter and section numbers (the former in roman numerals). Those comprising an author's name and a number in bold (e.g. 'Cicero **23**') refer to passages numbered in bold in the chapter devoted to that author.

Acknowledgements

I owe a particular debt to Elizabeth Tucker, who generously supplied me with material from Sanskrit, which is used in Chapter VI. She also gave me bibliography on other topics. John Briscoe has answered many questions (usually by return mail), and has directed me around the ever-changing library of Manchester University. He also made detailed comments on the chapter on Livy. Harm Pinkster let me have a copy of the relevant chapter of his *Oxford Latin Syntax* 2 before publication. Wolfgang de Melo read a draft of the whole work and made many acute comments. Roger Tomlin kindly allowed me to use the image from a Uley writing tablet (unpublished) that appears as the frontispiece, as well as providing information about certain pairs. Giuseppe Pezzini has not only given me a lot of information but has also himself produced a draft of a paper or chapter on asyndeton in Terence, which I have drawn on a little, but I have largely passed over Terence in the hope that one day that draft will be converted into an article of his own. Simon Hornblower read a chapter in considerable detail and made a number of very informative comments. Anna Chahoud has answered a multitude of questions and helped so often that I could not possibly catalogue her contributions. Others have supplied me with information, copies of articles, bibliographical information, answers to queries, or read sections of the work. An anonymous referee made some very useful points. I express here my profound gratitude to the following (well aware that I have probably forgotten others): Gualtiero Calboli, Kathleen Coleman, Tony Corbeill, Marcus Deufert, Arthur Emmett, Laurence Emmett, Wolfgang Ernst, Trevor Evans, Patrick Finglass, Adam Gitner, Christa Gray, Nigel Kay, David Langslow, Adam Ledgeway, Roland Mayer, Veronika Nikitina, Stephen Oakley, Sarah Ogilvie, Costas Panayotakis, Lucia Prauscello, Michael Reeve, Richard Thomas, Michael Winterbottom and Tony Woodman.

I would also like to thank Michael Sharp and Sarah Starkey of Cambridge University Press for their usual efficiency and, in this case, patience, and Juliet Wilberforce for her skilled and agreeable copy-editing.

I have been very fortunate to have had the generous academic support of All Souls College even well into retirement, and ready access to the excellent Manchester University Library and the John Rylands Library, Manchester.

Abbreviations

CEL	P. Cugusi, *Corpus epistolarum Latinarum papyris tabulis ostracis servatarum*, 3 vols. (Florence, 1992–2002).
ChLA	A. Bruckner, R. Marichal et al., eds, *Chartae Latinae antiquiores* (Olten, Lausanne etc., 1954–).
CIL	*Corpus inscriptionum Latinarum* (Berlin, 1862–).
CLE	F. Bücheler, A. Riese and E. Lommatzsch, *Carmina Latina epigraphica*, 3 vols. (Leipzig, 1897–1926).
FRH	T. J. Cornell et al., *The Fragments of the Roman Historians*, 3 vols. (Oxford, 2013).
GL	H. Keil (ed.), *Grammatici Latini*, 8 vols. (Leipzig, 1855–80).
ILLRP	A. Degrassi (ed.), *Inscriptiones Latinae liberae rei publicae*, 2 vols. (Florence, I 2nd edn 1965, II 1963).
ILS	H. Dessau (ed.), *Inscriptiones Latinae selectae*, 3 vols. (Berlin, 1892–1916).
Loeb	Loeb Classical Library.
LSJ	H. G. Liddell and R. Scott, *A Greek-English Lexicon* (revised and augmented by H. S. Jones, with a Revised Supplement, 1996) (Oxford, 1996).
NT	New Testament.
OCT	Oxford Classical Texts.
OLD	*Oxford Latin Dictionary* (Oxford, 1968–82).
ORF	H. Malcovati, *Oratorum Romanorum fragmenta liberae rei publicae*, 4th edn (Turin, 1976).
Suppl. Mag.	See Daniel and Maltomini (1990–2).
Tab. Ig.	See Poultney (1959).
TLL	*Thesaurus linguae Latinae* (Leipzig, 1900–).

PART I

Introduction

CHAPTER 1

Asyndetic and Syndetic Coordination: Definitions and Types

1 Coordination and Asyndeton

'Asyndeton' has been used by classicists in mixed ways. In this book I use the term as it is used in modern linguistics, to refer to a form of coordination. Various other phenomena, though interesting in their own right and often labelled 'asyndeta' by classical commentators and others, are left aside, worthy as they may be of study. I start with 'coordination'.

Huddleston, Payne and Peterson (2002: 1275) define coordination as follows:

> Coordination is a relation between two or more elements of syntactically equal status, the **coordinates**; they are usually linked by means of a **coordinator** such as *and* or *or*.

There is a similar definition at Huddleston (2002: 66), where a third coordinator (*but*) is added. Examples are given of clause-coordination, noun phrase-coordination and noun phrase prepositional phrase-coordination. Quirk et al. (1972: 550–2) may be consulted too for definitions along the same lines.

The definition of Haspelmath (2004b: 3–4) is much the same:

> A construction [A B] is considered coordinate if the two parts A and B have the same status (in some sense that needs to be specified further), whereas it is not coordinate if it is asymmetrical and one of the parts is clearly more salient or important, while the other part is in some sense subordinate. In practice, we typically suspect that a construction will be coordinate if it is systematically used to render English constructions with the coordinating particles *and*, *or* and *but*.

I follow here the view that the coordinators of Latin are copulative/ conjunctive, disjunctive and adversative (see e.g. Pinkster 1990: 11–12, Torrego 2009: 444–6). Haspelmath, who accepts this distinction between the three semantic types of coordination (2004b: 5), observes (2004b: 6)

3

that sometimes an additional type, 'causal coordination', is included. I do not treat causal/explicative constructions here as forms of coordination. Torrego (2009: 443) refers in this connection to coordinators on the one hand, and 'discourse connectors' on the other, citing Pinkster (1990: 11–12) for the criteria distinguishing them. See in particular Huddleston, Payne and Peterson (2002: 1321–2), discussing the question whether in English *for* is a coordinator. They state at the outset (1321) that *for* (along with several other terms) lacks most of the properties that mark coordinators, and conclude (1322), after an account of the properties of these terms: 'On balance, we would favour putting them with the prepositions; in the absence of positive coordinator properties the ability to link unlike elements ... can hardly be reconciled with a coordinator analysis.' 'Prepositions' here (sc. 'with clausal complements') is used in a special sense, equivalent to 'subordinating conjunctions' in traditional analysis (see 1321 on this point). Quirk et al. (1972: 552) also argue that *for* is not a pure coordinator. It follows that, if in the sentence *I am hungry, for I have not eaten in three days*, the word *for* were omitted (*I am hungry. I have not eaten in three days*), there would not be asyndeton but, in the traditional terminology of classical scholarship, parataxis (see e.g. Woodcock 1959: 98; also Quirk and Wrenn 1957: 96 on Old English, distinguishing parataxis from coordination), with an element missing that is not strictly a coordinator (*for* can of course be replaced by *because* in English). This book is not about parataxis. I return to this topic below, 9.

Coordination is said to be 'syndetic' when it is overtly marked by a coordinator, but 'asyndetic' when it is not (Huddleston, Payne and Peterson 2002: 1276; see also e.g. Quirk et al. 1972: 550, Haspelmath 2004b: 4). The example given of asyndetic coordination, usually called by classicists 'asyndeton', is: *He invited [all his colleagues, all his students]*. The following distinction is made (2002: 1275–6) between coordination and subordination (see too Haspelmath 2004b: 33–7 on this issue):

> Coordination contrasts with subordination, where the elements are of unequal status. In subordination one element is head, the other(s) dependent, but precisely because coordinates are of equal status the functions of head and dependent are not applicable to coordination.

It would no doubt be possible to collect many definitions of coordination. I restrict myself to just one other, that of Dik (1968: 25):

> A coordination is a construction consisting of two or more members which are equivalent as to grammatical function, and bound together at the same level of structural hierarchy by means of a linking device.

1 Coordination and Asyndeton

Dik expands on various aspects of this definition in the following pages. I comment here just on 'equivalent as to grammatical function' and 'linking device'.

Equivalence of grammatical function does not mean (e.g.) that two or more terms coordinated (whether with coordinator or asyndetically) must be of the same part of speech (see Dik 1968: 27–9, illustrating at 28 for example coordination of an adjective and prepositional phrase: *He was quite happy and at ease in his new surroundings*), though that is usually the case (see further on this issue e.g. Pinkster 1990: 9–10, Huddleston, Payne and Peterson 2002: 1326–9). In Latin it is tempting to interpret the asyndetic pair *ui pugnando* (e.g. Plaut. *Am.* 414 *legiones Teloboarum ui pugnando cepimus*, 'we have captured the legions of the Teloboians by force of arms'), in which *ui* is an ablative noun and *pugnando* an ablatival gerund, as hierarchically different (with *ui* a modifier of *pugnando*), but the pair also occurs with a coordinator (Plaut. *Mil.* 267 *ui pugnandoque hominem caperest certa res*, 'I am determined to capture the man by force and fighting'), and can be taken as coordinated (asyndetically), but composed of different parts of speech (note also *As.* 555 *copiae exercitusque eorum | ui pugnando, periuriis nostris fugae potiti*, with Leo 1960: 175, and see Adams 2005: 76 on *ui expugnando* in the *Bellum Africum* (36.4)). Or again, at Cic. *Fin.* 5.89 *in foro, domi*, a prepositional phrase and a locative are juxtaposed, but the syntactic distinction is natural because in classical Latin *domus* tends to be used without a preposition (thus *domi* = *in domo*). Note too Plaut. *As.* 562 *sciens lubenter peiieraris*, *Rud.* 186 *in usu, experiundo is datur acerbum* (on this last see XXIII.5.4). See also XXIV.5.1.2 on Ennius *Ann.* 192 (9) *prognariter ... prudens*, with additional bibliography. For a pair that has overt coordination but linking different parts of speech see Catull. 31.4 *quam te libenter quamque laetus inuiso*. *Libenter* (adverb) and *laetus* (adjective) are coordinated by the anaphoric construction *quam ... quamque*. Note too XXV.1.1.7 on Lucil. 1320 *clam inprouiso insidiisque*; also Hor. *Sat.* 1.4.18 *raro et pauca loquentis*, 2.6.27 *clare certumque locuto*. Such coordination is possible because predicative adjectives often behave as adverbs (see e.g. Woodcock 1959: 712). For further examples of this type see Hofmann and Szantyr (1965: 172), citing also Sjögren (1900: 61).

One issue has however just been alluded to (on *ui pugnando*) that will come up constantly in this book: in a pair of terms (of the same or different parts of speech) that have usually been interpreted as coordinated asyndetically, one term may in reality be a modifier of the other (see

II.3.2), and in such cases the question arises whether the pair is genuinely an asyndeton.

Dik (1968: 31–2) discusses 'linking device' (see above for his definition of 'coordinatioin') briefly. He says:

> It seems that in all languages the linking device can either consist in the mere juxtaposition of the coordinated members (accompanied, in many cases, by a specific intonation pattern), or in the use of one or more coordinating particles.

Dik here uses 'juxtaposition' instead of 'asyndeton' as favoured by classicists (Torrego 2009 too prefers the former), and he also makes the (undoubtedly correct) point that in the case of coordination by juxtaposition/asyndeton there will usually be some intonational feature that marks out the terms as coordinated (see XX.1). He does not illustrate, but here is an example from a sentence of an English novel (P. D. James, *A Certain Justice*, Penguin, 1998):

> 229 And now, in his Chambers, there was this murder, <u>bloody, obscene</u>, with its overtones of madness and revenge, to demonstrate how fragile was that elegant, complicated bridge of order and reason.

If *bloody obscene* were pronounced without a pause *bloody* would have its slang sense and be an intensifier of *obscene*. If the two words are to be coordinated asyndetically (= *bloody and obscene*), there must be a pause between them. In this postponed position it is usually the second adjective that is the stronger one, and in such phrases it may be implied that the pause is for thought (see V.2), as the speaker seeks to come up with a term that will cap the first. In the pronunciation of the second pair above too (*elegant, complicated*) there would be a pause. Asyndeton (in speech) therefore does not consist of absence of coordination, but of coordination by means not of overt coordinating terms, but of features of pronunciation.

We know hardly anything of intonation in Greek and Latin, but it will be suggested later that there are indeed forms of asyndeton that must have been articulated with a distinctive tone, pause or the like (see V.1–2). See V.1 particularly on Arist. *Rh.* 1413b.29–30 = 3.12.4, where an example of ἀσύνδετα is ἦλθον, ἀπήντησα, ἐδεόμην. Aristotle's comments on the passage imply that there would have been a particular intonation, and similar comments are to be found in Quintilian. For an interesting remark see too Parker (2007: 136) on E. *Alc.* 400 ὑπάκουσον ἄκουσον: 'Where such a special effect occurs in correspondence, it must surely have been reflected in some way in the music.'

2 Asyndeton with Two Members, Conjunctive, Disjunctive and Adversative

Huddleston, Payne and Peterson (2002: 1275) use the term NP-coordination (noun phrase-coordination) of an example showing two single words (names) coordinated ([*Kim and Pat*] *speak excellent French*), but do not, at least at this point, use it of single words asyndetically coordinated. This latter type is common in Latin, and will form the main subject of this book. Classicists have traditionally called it 'asyndeton bimembre', though that is a term that can also be used of other varieties of asyndetic coordination, for example clausal or phrasal; by 'phrasal' I mean in this context that the asyndetic pair comprises not single words but longer units, phrases (see below, 6).

There are so many different types of asyndeton that to collect all the phenomena in a Latin corpus that might loosely be called 'asyndetic' would be a vast, even impossible, task and hardly worth the effort. In some texts there may even be asyndeta of one sort or another in just about every sentence or two, and there is no point in setting out to classify the completely banal. That is why I have decided to concentrate particularly (but not exclusively) on one distinctive and stylistically interesting type, a type with a literary dimension, in that its use and motivations vary across literary genres. It is also of great antiquity, in that it is found in other early Indo-European languages, including other varieties of Italic (on Umbrian see XXII.4), and also in some ancient formulae (e.g. *patres conscripti*) in Latin that must go back to the period before written literature (see XXII.5 on some old formulae). It is a type too that continues in modern languages, not least English, and indeed in certain patterns that are very similar to some of those in Latin (see VI, Appendix). A question that will also come up is whether in some literary genres our type of asyndeton may sometimes have been influenced by the practice of Greek writers in the same genres. I note in passing that, according to Torrego (2009: 452), coordination by juxtaposition (i.e. asyndeton) (in Latin) 'is an almost marginal device from the first texts'. It is added that '[t]wo types of juxtaposed sets can be found in Latin: residual and formularized expressions, and instances where they are used as a marked form of coordination with stylistic intention'. These assertions are misleading on several fronts. First, when a coordinated group has three or more members, juxtaposition is the normal form of coordination (see below, 4, and also XVIII.2.1, 2.2, 2.3, 2.4). Second, there are writers and genres in which asyndetic pairs are very common, and in some laws, for example, such pairs outnumber coordinated pairs (see XXII.2.1).

8   I Definitions and Types

Third, the types of asyndetic pairs vary considerably, from the mundane and everyday (e.g. pairs of imperatives addressed to a subordinate), to the contrived, such as compound coinages in early Latin. The numerous types will be defined in later chapters. The above remark does little justice to the diversity even of asyndeton bimembre in classical Latin.

Also unsatisfactory is Leo's summary (1960: 164) of the distribution of asyndeton bimembre: 'asyndeton autem bimembre notum est italicis linguis familiare esse, graecae non item; unde evenit ut Cicero Caesar Sallustius et sequentes omnes culti sermonis antistites raro eo uterentur ..., cum tricolon a Graecis excultum semper floreret'. It is indeed rare in Caesar, but common in certain of Cicero's works (particularly the philosophica), and in the historians Sallust and Tacitus. On the comparative rarity of asyndeton bimembre in Greek see e.g. Wölfflin (1900: 27–8), Denniston (1952: 105), Dover (1968: 129) on *Nub.* 241. Nor should it be implied that there is a close connection between Latin and Greek in the use of asyndeton. This is a topic that will come up from time to time.

I refer above to asyndeton bimembre consisting of two words as a 'type', but it is many types, which will be identified later, in a preliminary way in this Introduction (see below, this section, and sections 5–10), and then in detail when phenomena are classified in separate chapters, and when specific texts are discussed. It may seem straightforward to identify pairs of juxtaposed words to which a coordinator could be added without changing the meaning, but there are often difficulties of interpretation (see e.g. II.2.3)

An asyndeton with two members in Latin could usually be rewritten with the addition of the Latin equivalent of one of the coordinators referred to earlier, *and, or, but*, and as a preliminary classification I illustrate these three semantic features of asyndetic pairs.

First, at Sall. *Cat.* 51.9 **(15)** *caedem incendia fieri*, 'slaughter and arson are carried out', *caedem* and *incendia* could be linked by *et*, *-que* or *atque*, as these are two manifestations of the savagery of war. Cf. e.g. Cic. *Cat.* 1.3 *caede atque incendiis*, *Cat.* 1.6 *caedis atque incendiorum*, *Dom.* 21 *caedis et incendiorum*, *Har. resp.* 6 *caede incendiisque*, 58, same phrase. The variability of the coordinator in this one phrase when it is syndetically coordinated (a variability typical of established pairs) incidentally makes it clear that neat distinctions between the semantics of the different Latin coordinators are unlikely to bear close inspection. Torrego, for example, states (2009: 459) of *atque* that the 'capacity of presenting a member in an emphatic (or oriented) way is the differentiating property of this coordinator'. Tac. *Ann.*

2 Conjunctive, Disjunctive and Adversative

4.26.2 *regemque et socium atque amicum appellaret* is quoted with the translation 'and he called him king and ally, even friend'. This translation has the effect of associating *regem* and *socium*, and of dissociating *amicum* from *socium*, as if *amicum* were particularly emphatic. But *socius* + *amicus* was an established pair (see on Sall. *Hist.* 4.60.17 Ramsey (47); also XVIII.4), used asyndetically (Sallust 47) or coordinated by *-que* as well as *atque*, and with variable word order (cf. Sall. *Cat.* 16.4 *amicis sociisque* but Livy 38.11.2 *socios amicosque*). We will also see that in legal language *societas* and *amicitia* were associated, asyndetically (see on Sallust 47). Moreover *socius* and *amicus* combined belong to a wider semantic type, of pairs to do with personal or inter-state relationships (see on Sallust 47, with cross references). The phrase structure of *regemque et socium atque amicum* above was not correctly analysed (it is [*regemque*] et [*socium atque amicum*], and that is a constant problem in comments on both syndetic and asyndetic coordination.

Second, at Sall. *Cat.* 14.3 (5) *omnes undique parricidae sacrilegi conuicti iudiciis*, 'everyone everywhere convicted of parricide or sacrilege by the courts', *aut* could be added but *et* would give the wrong meaning. The asyndeton *parricidae sacrilegi* would traditionally be described as 'disjunctive'.

Third, 'adversative asyndeton', that is of the type in which *sed* could be inserted, is not so easy to illustrate from pairs of individual words or pairs of phrases, though the term is used constantly by commentators and others to express a relationship between two clauses. I will discuss clausal adversative asyndeton below (8). Here however are some phrasal adversative examples:

Cic. *Att.* 3.15.7 *fidem eandem, curam maiorem adhibuisses*, 'you would have brought to bear the same loyalty but greater solicitude'.
Cic. *Fam.* 9.26.4 *non multi cibi hospitem accipies, multi ioci*, 'you will receive a guest of not much appetite for food but of much appetite for jokes'.
Livy 3.71.6 *non iuuenem, uicesima iam stipendia merentem*, 'not a youth, but one already performing his twentieth year of military service'.
Tac. *Ann.* 5.3.2 *sed non arma, non rerum nouarum studium, amores iuuenum et impudicitiam nepoti obiectabat*, 'yet the princeps cast against his grandson imputations of neither armed force nor enthusiasm for revolution but of love affairs with young men and immorality' (Woodman 2004; on the adversative asyndeton see Woodman 2017: 62).

The second example above does show an adversative relationship between the two phrases *non multi cibi, multi ioci*, but they are not juxtaposed. For other instances of adversative phrasal asyndeton, see Cic. *Off.* 3.119 (below, 8) and Cic. *Quinct.* 54 (below, 7).

10   I Definitions and Types

Adversative asyndeton comprising just two words is hard to identify, because possible pairs are usually open to another interpretation. Here is a possibility, but it is not straightforward:

Tac. *Ann.* 2.48.1 (118) *bona Aemiliae Musae, <u>locupletis intestatae</u> ... tradidit,* 'the goods of the wealthy but intestate Aemilia Musa ... he handed to ...'.

The translation, by Woodman (2004), treats *locupletis intestatae* as an adversative asyndeton, but one could take *intestatae* as substantival, 'a wealthy intestate woman', or alternatively if both terms are adjectival the (asyndetic) coordination may be copulative ('wealthy and intestate').

The following pair is also problematic:

Caelius ap. Cic. *Fam.* 8.1.4 *sed inter paucos, quos tu nosti, palam secreto narrantur,* 'but among a few – you know who – they are related openly but in secret' (a small group say these things openly among themselves, but not outside the closed circle (?)).

See Cicero 213 on possible interpretations of this passage.

I have restricted myself in this section to the most basic semantic classification of asyndeta bimembria, in line with the usual classification of syndetic coordinations (see e.g. Torrego 2009: 445–6 for the three types illustrated from Latin both with and without coordinators).

In later sections I will go beyond the two-word asyndeton bimembre that is my primary subject, to illustrate some of the other types of asyndeton attested in Latin that will come up. I begin though with a brief account of classifications by the ancients themselves.

3 Ancient Classifications of Asyndeton

Asyndeton is not infrequently discussed in ancient rhetorical works, Greek and also Latin. Lausberg (1998: 315–16), §§709-11 collects numerous passages, and distinguishes (citing ancient sources) between nominal and verbal asyndeton, and within the first category between single words and groups of words (i.e. nominal phrases), and within the second category between single words and groups of words, including clauses lined up one after another. Boccotti (1975) also has a useful collection of ancient evidence, and his discussion deals particularly with the supposed aims and effects of the phenomena, as argued by the sources. See further Calboli (1993: 370–2, 1997a: 800).

The type comprising sequences of single words, usually three or more, comes up quite often, particularly groups of verbs. We saw Arist. *Rh.* 1413b.29–30 ἦλθον, ἀπήντησα, ἐδεόμην above, 1. In the same passage Aristotle cites another example, also consisting of three verbs (ἦλθον,

3 Ancient Classifications of Asyndeton

διελέχθην, ἱκέτευσα, 'I came, I conversed, I sought'), an asyndeton that is said to produce amplification (αὔξησις). Both of these examples are similar to Caesar's *ueni uidi uici*, for which see Suet. *Caes.* 37.2 *Pontico triumpho inter pompae fercula trium uerborum praetulit titulum VENI · VIDI · VICI non acta belli significantem sicut ceteris, sed celeriter confecti notam* ('In his Pontic triumph he displayed among the show-pieces of the procession an inscription of but three words, "I came, I saw, I conquered", not indicating the events of the war, as the others did, but the speed with which it was finished').[1] Suetonius finds the group to be indicative of a war 'quickly completed' (note *celeriter*), and the expression of 'speed' is one of the functions of asyndeton frequently found by modern commentators on ancient texts. It is an idea found too in other ancient sources. Aquila 41 (Halm 1863: 35), equating *solutum* with ἀσύνδετον,[2] puts it thus: *facit autem figura et ad celeritatem et ad uim doloris aliquam significandum*. The example cited by Aquila (Cic. *Verr.* 3.28), *expecto uim edicti, seueritatem praetoris, faueo aratori, cupio octuplo damnari Apronium*, has two types of asyndeton. There are three asyndetic clauses, each with a present tense verb, and within the first clause a pair of asyndetic phrases, each with noun + genitive. On 'rapidity' see also below on 'Longinus' 19.2.

Demetrius *Eloc.* 194 also cites an asyndetic tricolon comprising three verbs, this a fragment of Menander: ἐδεξάμην, ἔτικτον, ἐκτρέφω, 'I conceived, I gave birth, I nurse' (see Boccotti 1975: 39). Demetrius twice in the passage calls asyndeton λύσις. Cf. also *Eloc.* 63 for λύσις (see Montanari 1995, s.v. giving the meaning 'asindeto' for the term in Demetrius). At 194 Demetrius rewrites the tricolon with the coordinator καί, stating that the coordination lowers the emotional level. He makes it clear that the asyndeton is suited to the stage and forces the speaker to be dramatic.

Asyndeton consisting of just two words is also commented on. Demetrius *Eloc.* 64 cites the Homeric κυρτά, φαληριόωντα (*Il.* 13.799) ('high-arched, foam-crested')[3] as an instance of the 'omission of the connective καί' (τῇ ἐξαιρέσει τοῦ "καί" συνδέσμου). This is said to make the passage more impressive. Demetrius had just argued (63) that the use of

---

[1] Cf. too Ter. *Ph.* 103 *imus uenimus uidemus*.
[2] At *Rhet. Her.* 4.41 asyndeton is called *dissolutum* (on the Latin terms for the figure see Boccotti 1975: 45 n. 49; also Calboli 1993: 370–1, Russell 2001: IV.128 n. 103). Quintilian (see Boccotti 1975: 45) calls asyndeton *dissolutio* (9.3.50) (changed by Russell 2001 to *dissolutum*).
[3] These two terms are at the start of a line, a common placement in verse for an asyndetic pair. They are preceded in the line before by κύματα παφλάζοντα πολυφλοίσβοιο θαλάσσης 'surging waves of the loud-resounding sea'. The participle παφλάζοντα is attributive, and the two adjectives cited by Demetrius are predicative adjuncts. On this distinction see II.2.1.

connectives could add to the grandeur of a passage. All such evaluations are subjective, and it is no surprise to find inconsistencies.

An interesting instance of verbs in asyndeton is cited by Longinus 19.1, from Xenophon (*Ages.* 2.12) (see Boccotti 1975: 40–1). The sequence has four verbs, ἐωθοῦντο ἐμάχοντο, ἀπέκτεινον ἀπέθνησκον, 'they pushed and fought, killed and fell'. There are probably two pairs here. The author does not make this point, but the last two verbs are opposites, complementarities, killing and/or being killed, whereas the first two refer to the combat in progress. This then is not a tetracolon, but comprises two asyndetic pairs, a structure that will come up very often in this book (an 'accumulation': see e.g. XIX).

Other comments on asyndetic sequences comprising single words may be found in the sources (see further Lausberg 1998: 316, Boccotti 1975: 45 n. 51), but this was not the only type of asyndeton recognised by ancient rhetoricians. Quintilian (9.3.50) (see Boccotti 1975: 45) says that the figure *dissolutio* (*dissolutum*) is used with individual words, and with *sententiis*, which to judge by the examples given means 'phrases' and probably embraces clauses as well: *ideoque utimur hac figura non in singulis modo uerbis, sed sententiis etiam*. We have already seen that Aquila's illustration of asyndeton from Cicero combines asyndetic clauses with a pair of asyndetic phrases.

A second example cited by Longinus 19.2 is from Hom. *Od.* 10.251–2, and this one consists of two sentences, without connecting particles, each with the verb in first position. The two verbs are ἤλθομεν, εἴδομεν, 'we came ... we saw', again similar to Caesar's *ueni uidi uici*. The author classifies the effects, referring to the phrases as 'rapid', κατεσπευσμένα. See above on 'speed'.

At *Rhet. Her.* 4.41 the two examples given by the author of *dissolutum* = asyndeton both comprise a sequence of four phrases/clauses each with an imperative verb.

Ancient commentators show some interest in asyndetic sequences (verbal, phrasal or clausal) that also have anaphora, that is a repeated word at the start of each member (on such combinations in Latin, see below, 10). At *Eloc.* 268 Demetrius cites a passage with three clauses, and also anaphora, ἐπὶ σαυτὸν καλεῖς, ἐπὶ τοὺς νόμους καλεῖς, ἐπὶ τὴν δημοκρατίαν καλεῖς. He then rephrases it using καί to connect the prepositional phrases, and reducing the repeated verb to a single instance. At 20.1 Longinus refers to the combination of asyndeton with repetition, using the terms 'anaphora' and 'asyndeton', ταῖς ἀναφοραῖς, ... τὰ ἀσύνδετα. The first example given, from a speech of Demosthenes (21.72), has an asyndetic tricolon

3 Ancient Classifications of Asyndeton

(of single words) with repetition of the article, τῷ σχήματι, τῷ βλέμματι, τῇ φωνῇ, 'by his manner, his look, his voice'. The illustration continues at 20.2, and this time contains a repetition of four ὅταν-clauses without any particles.

Then at 21.1 the first passage is rewritten in a different style (described as that of Isocrates), with an abundance of particles. ὡς πολλὰ ἂν ποιήσειεν ὁ τύπτων, πρῶτον μὲν τῷ σχήματι, εἶτα δὲ τῷ βλέμματι, εἶτά γε μὴν αὐτῇ τῇ φωνῇ. There is an indication here that an ancient scholar might regard absence of discourse particles, even if they were not in the strict sense coordinators, as a form of asyndeton. Similarly Demetrius, at *Eloc.* 192, where the term ἀσύνδετον is used, seems to be talking about particles, though examples are not given. Note ἄδηλος γὰρ ἡ ἑκάστου κώλου ἀρχὴ διὰ τὴν λύσιν, 'the beginning of each colon is unclear because of the asyndeton'. Also, Porphyrio on Hor. *Carm.* 1.2.25 maintains that *ergo* has to be understood (*ceterum subaudienda hic est coniunctio 'ergo'*), and he describes the transition as 'asyndetic' (ἀσυνδέτως *transiit*).

Similar to the anaphoric tricolon from Demosthenes above is another example quoted by Quintilian at 9.4.23, where it is stated that words in asyndeton should be in increasing order of impressiveness. The example cited, from Cicero *Phil.* 2.23, combines anaphora with asyndeton, *tu . . . istis faucibus, istis lateribus, ista gladiatoria totius corporis firmitate.*

I refer finally to Aristotle *Rh.* 1414a.2–3, who quotes Homer *Il.* 2.671–3 as a second example of amplification, αὔξησις. The quotation is selective, comprising the name Νιρεύς used three times with different epithets, whereas in Homer the name is at the start of three successive lines of varied structures. Aristotle does not specifically say that this is an asyndeton, but that is implied. Boccotti (1975: 37) interprets the Homeric passage as having both asyndeton and anaphora. Demetrius *Eloc.* 61 (see Boccotti 1975: 39) takes up the passage on Nireus and says that it is made impressive by anaphora (ἐπαναφορά) and absence of connectives (διάλυσις).

For other Greek authors who comment on asyndeton, see Boccotti (1975: 43 n. 39). For a list of Latin passages, see Boccotti (1975: 46 n. 34). For the different types of asyndeton according to a Greek classification, see Boccotti (1975: 44): κατ' ὄνομα, κατὰ κῶλον, κατὰ κόμμα. Finally, Lausberg (1998: 316) has a substantial list of Greek and Latin comments on phrasal and clausal asyndeton.

The main types that we have seen commented on here are sequences of single words, phrases, clauses and sentences. The omission of sentence particles has come up, but not frequently (on this topic see below, 9).

The supposed 'speed' of asyndetic sequences will be discussed at V.1.

4 Longer Single-Word Asyndeta in Latin

Juxtaposed single words forming asyndeta with three or more members far outnumber single-word asyndeta with just two members in prose (on groups of three see particularly Norden 1897: 35–53, dealing with both Greek and Latin, and Leo 1960: 163–84), though not in some forms of verse (see XXV.3 on Lucilius, XXVII.4 on Catullus and XXIX.3.1.1 on Horace's *Satires*, in all of which pairs are more numerous; on prose see also XVIII.2). I have elsewhere (Adams 2016: 81–3) discussed asyndeton in Varro's *Res rusticae*. When Varro lists three or more items he regularly uses asyndeton, but if the list contains just two items a coordinator is the norm. There are only about nine or ten asyndeta bimembria in the whole work. Here are some statistics from Cicero.

In Cicero's *Philippics* book 2 asyndeta (comprising single words) with three or more members occur 22 times, but asyndeta bimembria (with single words) only 5 times. In *Philippics* 3 there are fourteen asyndeta of the longer types, and just three examples with only two members.[4] The latter three are in a senatorial motion by Cicero (see Cicero 23, 24, 25).

One of Cicero's earliest speeches, the *pro S. Roscio* (80 BC) has just one possible instance of an asyndeton bimembre with single words (Cicero 39), apart from the old religious expression (*Iuppiter*) *optimus maximus* (40). Phrasal pairs (or pairs of ascending length) are not common either: 101 *ueniat modo, explicet suum uolumen*, 113 *fama mortui, fortunae uiui*, 152 *ex altera parte egentem, probatum suis filium*. On the other hand groups of three or more terms are often in asyndeton:

15 *cum Metellis Seruiliis Scipionibus erat ei ... hospitium*
16 *opera studio auctoritate defendit*
24 *emptio flagitiosa, possessio furta rapinae donationes*
27 *eius uirtute fide diligentia factum est*
30 *bona adempta possessa direpta*
75 *parsimoniae diligentiae iustitiae magistra est*
76 *pretio gratia spe promissis induxit aliquem*
90 *commemorare Curtios Marios denique Memmios*
110 *isto hortatore auctore intercessore*
117 *induxit decepit destituit, aduersariis tradidit, omni fraude et perfidia fefellit* (the first three single verbs go closely together, and then there is a phrasal pair).
122 *quicquid malefici sceleris caedis erit*
134 *mitto hasce artes uulgares, coquos pistores lecticarios*
149 *ipse adsiduitate consilio auctoritate diligentia perfecit*

---

[4] Consular names, which are regularly asyndetic in the classical period, are not systematically collected here, but see XXII.9.

4 Longer Single-Word Asyndeta in Latin

152 *cum uideatis ex altera parte sectorem inimicum sicarium eundemque accusatorem hoc tempore*.

There are fourteen instances here. Three (or more) single words are not only found in asyndeton but may also be linked by coordinators. Note the following:

35 *crimen aduersariorum et audacia et potentia*
40 *eam quoque iustam et magnam et perspicuam fuisse*
40 *sine causis multis et magnis et necessariis*
50 *quibus rebus et agris et urbibus et nationibus rem publicam atque hoc imperium et populi Romani nomen auxerunt* (here there are first four single-word ablatives linked by *et*, and then three accusatives, mainly phrasal, linked by *atque* and then *et*).
54 *iudicio ac legibus ac maiestate uestra abuti* (note *ac* instead of the usual *et*)
101 *cupiditas et auaritia et audacia*.

I have found only the following six cases of end-of-list coordination (for details of which pattern see XVIII) in the speech: 31 *omnia non modo dicere uerum etiam libenter audacter libereque dicere*, 71 *caelum solem aquam terramque ademerint*, 96 *Ameriae Sex. Rosci domus uxor liberique essent*, 109 *totam uitam naturam moresque hominis ... cognoscite*, 115 *Sex. Roscius cum fama uita bonisque omnibus*, 131 *caelum terra mariaque reguntur*. In a comprehensive discussion of these examples the question would have to be addressed whether some of the lists contain internal unities (i.e. embedded pairs: could the structure at e.g. 96 be of the type [*domus*] [*uxor liberique*], making it an asyndetic dicolon rather than a tricolon?). This is an issue that is taken up below, XVIII.4.

For more systematic statistics from other works for tricola and longer sequences with asyndeton, internal coordination or end-of-list coordination see below, XVIII.2.

The contrasting methods of coordinating pairs and longer sequences of single words (in prose) can also be brought out by some statistics from the first twenty sections of the first book of *De officiis*, a work in which there are constant oppositions and accumulations of terms. Explicitly coordinated pairs of single words occur 53 times (A *et* B 23, *et* A *et* B 5, AB*que* 18, A *ac/atque* B 7), whereas there is only one asyndeton bimembre, of the prepositional kind (on which anaphoric type see below, 10): 9 *ad opes ad potentiam*. Here is a typical short passage (1.15–16) with coordinated pairs underlined:

aut in animi excelsi atque inuicti magnitudine ac robore aut in omnium quae fiunt quaeque dicuntur ordine et modo, in quo inest modestia et temperantia. quae quattuor

16   I Definitions and Types

quamquam inter se conligata atque implicata sunt, tamen ex singulis certa officiorum genera nascuntur, uelut ex ea parte quae prima descripta est, in qua sapientiam et prudentiam ponimus, inest indagatio atque inuentio ueri, eiusque uirtutis hoc munus est proprium. ut enim quisque maxime perspicit quid in re quaque uerissimum sit quique acutissime et celerrime potest et uidere et explicare rationem, is prudentissimus et sapientissimus rite haberi solet.

By contrast in *Off.* 1.1–20 longer groups of single words are almost always asyndetic. Here is the complete list: 2 *apte distincte ornate*, 6 *Stoicorum Academicorum Perpateticorum*, 6 *Aristonis Pyrrhonis Erilli*, 13 *uidere audire addiscere*, 14 *pulchritudinem constantiam ordinem*, 18 *labi autem errare nescire decipi*; add too 6 *firma stabilia coniuncta naturae*, where the third member is of extended length (for asyndeta comprising a combination of single words and short phrases see below, 7). In a later chapter (XVIII.2) in a different context there is a more extensive collection of tricola and longer sequences, from the first 100 sections of the book. Of end-of-list coordinations I have found in 1–20 only a single instance (12 *coniugi liberis ceterisque*), and it is of a problematic type (see XVIII.6 and on Sallust 1); on the interpretation of 13 *uerum simplex sincerumque sit* see XVIII.4.

5 Asyndeta Bimembria in Which at Least One of the Coordinates Is a Pair of Words Forming a Unit

In an official context at Cic. *Phil.* 2.37 the titles *imperator, consul designatus* are twice attached to the name D. Brutus (Cicero 28, 29). The two terms *consul designatus* constitute a single title, and *imperator, consul designatus* must be classified as a 'single-word' asyndeton bimembre. There are other such compounded pairs. At Cic. *Sest.* 33 in a law note the asyndetic titles of two laws: *ut lex Aelia lex Fufia ne ualeret* (Cicero 33). See further Cicero 34, 35, 36. Commonplace terms such as *res publica, res familiaris, tribuni plebis, res gestae* are of course equivalent to compounds.

Two or three names possessed by a single person are a single designation, and these are often in asyndetic coordination with the names of another person. References to pairs of consuls, and not only in statements of the appointment of a pair, are constantly asyndetic, but other officials too may be referred to asyndetically. Note e.g. Caes. *Civ.* 1.2.7 *intercedit M. Antonius Q. Cassius, tribuni plebis*, Livy 42.19.7 *Ti. Claudium Neronem M. Decimium legatos miserunt*, Livy 42.22.5 (quoting a *senatus consultum*) *senatus consultum factum est ut qui Ligurum post Q. Fuluium L. Manlium consules hostes non fuissent, ut eos C. Licinius Cn. Sicinius praetores in libertatem restituendos curarent*, where both the consuls' names and those of the praetors are in asyndeton.

On consular naming and the gradual shift from asyndeton to coordination, see XXII.9. I have decided in this book not to collect asyndetic consuls' names (see also above, n. 4), because such pairs are banal and the changing usage has been demonstrated in detail (see XXII.9 for bibliography).

6 Phrasal Asyndeton with Two Members

Asyndeton consisting of two (or indeed more) juxtaposed phrases is commonplace in Latin, and can be illustrated at random from many texts. For example, in the following sentence there are two pairs comprising adjective + noun: Cic. *Sest.* 143 *cogitemus denique corpus uirorum fortium, magnorum hominum esse mortale*, 'finally, let us contemplate that the body of brave men, of great men, is mortal' (a late manuscript, *s*, has *magnorumque*). There are comparable phrases at *Pis.* 25: *splendidissimorum hominum, fortissimorum uirorum, optimorum ciuium* (where no manuscript variation is reported). In this case the phrases are part of a longer asyndetic sequence. At *Red. Quir.* 17 too (*summos uiros, ornatissimos atque amplissimos homines*) the list also continues (*principes ciuitatis, omnis consularis*, etc.). On the other hand note Cic. *S. Rosc.* 51 *summi uiri clarissimimique homines* and *Red. sen.* 5 *nobilissimi hominis atque optimi uiri*, where two such phrases are linked by *-que* and *atque* (cf. e.g. *Red. sen.* 9). It is incidentally an interesting question why in these expressions both *uiri* and *homines* are used, instead of two coordinated adjectives with just one of the nouns. The two nouns may pile up the categories of people notable for some characteristic or act, whereas with just one noun there might be only one category of persons. *Vir* and *homo* can imply a difference of status (e.g. Cic. *Prov. cons.* 38 *neque solum summo in uiro sed etiam mediocri in homine*), but that is hardly the case in the above passages. Note too in that respect Cic. *Fam.* 7.5.3 (Cicero **199**) *probiorem hominem, meliorem uirum, pudentiorem, esse neminem*, 2.14 *uiro optimo et homine doctissimo*, 15.9.1 *hominibus prudentissimis uirisque optimis*, 2.18.2 *uiros optimos hominesque innocentissimos*, 13.55.2 *gratissimum hominem atque optimum uirum* (much the same at 13.53.1), *Fin.* 2.119 *cum optimos uiros, tum homines doctissimos* (note that the ordering of *uir* versus *homo* varies). A number of these examples point to the formulaic status of *uir optimus*. We see in this paragraph both asyndetic and syndetic phrases, the latter with variations of coordinator, used with apparent indifference, and that is a constant feature of Latin coordination.

Phrasal pairs have differing semantic relationships. Most pairs in this section are conjunctive, but other types occur, as was seen above (2) in the discussion of adversative asyndeton. At e.g. Cic. *Quinct.* 54 there are again two adjective + noun pairs (one further extended by a prepositional phrase): *quicum mihi necessitudo uetus, controuersia de re pecuniaria recens intercedit*, 'a man with whom I have a long-standing intimacy, but a recent dispute about a money matter'. I take both *necessitudo* and *controuersia* to be subjects of *intercedit* (which means simply 'be, exist between': see *OLD* s.v. 1, 2), rather than assuming ellipse of a verb with *necessitudo uetus* ('bonds of friendship', of the type expressed here by *necessitudo*, are particularly often subject of *intercedere* 'exist between' (*OLD* s.v. 2a), and that is why it would be unconvincing to understand another verb with *necessitudo uetus*). The second phrase has an adversative relationship to the first, and there is a double semantic opposition between the two phrases, of *necessitudo* versus *controuersia* and *uetus* versus *recens* (whereas e.g. the phrases at *Sest.* 143 in the last paragraph are near-synonyms). For opposites (here *uetus/recens*, antonyms) embedded in asyndetic phrases/clauses see the next example and e.g. XXV.2 on Lucil. 1058; also below, 8 on Cic. *Red. sen.* 29.

For the type comprising nouns + genitives see Cic. *S. Rosc.* 113 *is cui fama mortui, fortunae uiui commendatae sunt atque concreditae* ('he to whom the reputation of the dead and the fortunes of the living have been committed and entrusted'). *Fama* and *fortuna* are alliterative terms of complementary meanings which are often in asyndeton or coordinated (see Wölfflin 1933: 258 for an extensive collection), and 'alive' and 'dead' are opposites (complementarities: see XIII.2 and Cic. *Off.* 2.37 (120) for the asyndeton *uita mors*). Phrasal pairs offer the possibility of expressing double contrasts or semantic similarities.

In rhetorical prose such as the speeches of Cicero asyndetic phrasal sequences with two or more members are often in the immediate vicinity of asyndetic sequences of other types. The following passage, for example, has two asyndetic sequences with three phrasal members (underlined), two groups of three asyndetic clauses, with anaphora as well (of *nihil*); I use the term 'clauses' because *respondistis* and *declarauit* have to be taken with all three members beginning with *nihil* that precede each), and finally a sequence of four *neque/nec* ... *neque/nec* phrases. A sentence omitted here is similar, as is the first sentence of 8:

7 A Mixed Type

Cic. *Red. sen.* 6–7 *nihil uos ciuibus, nihil sociis, nihil regibus respondistis; nihil iudices sententiis, nihil populus suffragiis, nihil hic ordo auctoritate declarauit; mutum forum, elinguem curiam, tacitam et fractam ciuitatem uidebatis* . . . (7) *reliqui fuerunt quos neque terror nec uis, nec spes nec metus, nec promissa nec minae, nec tela nec faces a uestra auctoritate, a populi Romani dignitate, a mea salute depellerent* (the pattern continues into the next section).

Phrasal asyndeton is not dealt with here systematically, mainly because it is so widespread, but it is structurally important for this book because phrasal asyndeta are often juxtaposed with single-word asyndeta bimembria. That point is constantly made in references to 'accumulations' of asyndetic elements (see e.g. XIX). Phrasal asyndeton often also comes up in other connections, for example in the chapters on Plautus, Lucilius and Catullus (see too the next section).

7 A Mixed Type

A variant on phrasal asyndeton bimembre is a mixed type in which a phrase is juxtaposed with a single word, as at Cic. *S. Rosc.* 152 (41) *cum uideatis . . . ex altera parte egentem, probatum suis filium*, '. . . a son needy, but esteemed by his intimates'.

Here are two Virgilian examples with a literary pedigree (see XXIV.2.2, 26, 27):

Aen. 9.793–4 *at territus ille*, | *asper, acerba tuens, retro redit*
Georg. 3.149 *asper, acerba sonans*

This type (comprising adjectives or equivalent) is well-established in Virgil (see XXIV.2.2). Usually it is the second member that is of extended length. The type (and not only comprising adjectives) is found elsewhere. For example, it is common in Plautus in imperatival pairs (see XXIII.5.1) and in pairs of verbs in general (XXIII.5.3), and is a presence in Lucilius (see XXV.1).

For two comparable examples in Ovid (both with hyperbaton in the extended member) see:

Met. 3.407 *fons erat inlimis, nitidis argenteus undis*, 'there was a spring free from slime, silvery with bright waves'.
Met. 4.261 *sedit humo nuda, nudis incompta capillis*, 'she sat on the ground naked, unkempt with uncovered hair'.

In both there is a privative adjective with *in-*. Adjectives of this type have a prominent place in asyndeton (see VI).

I would not put in this mixed category examples such as Cic. *Phil.* 5.29 (27) *noui hominis insaniam, adrogationem*, 'I know the madness, the arrogance of the man.' There is not a phrase here plus a single noun, because the genitive *hominis* goes with both nouns. The structure is: [*hominis*] [*insaniam adrogationem*]. Similarly, though in a different syntactic structure, at Tac. *Ann.* 15.12.3 (147) (*simul suas legiones adire hortari*, 'at the same time he approached and encouraged his legions') two asyndetic verbs are jointly construed with a single object: [*suas legiones*] [*adire hortari*].

8 Clausal Asyndeton

Clausal asyndeton is more complicated. I use the term 'clausal' of groups of words that have a finite verb (or an infinitive, equivalent in function to a finite verb). Clausal asyndeta may have different subjects, but usually the subject of all verbs is the same. The following passage from an annalist, for example, has three clauses with finite verbs juxtaposed, and is punctuated by the latest editor with commas at the end of each of the units:

Coelius *FRH* II.15.F38 (XXX.2.4, 19) *omnes simul terram cum classi accedunt, nauibus atque scaphis egrediuntur, castra metati signa statuunt*, 'they all reached land with the fleet at the same time, they disembarked from the ships and skiffs, they measured out the camp and set up the standards' (Briscoe, *FRH*).

There is asyndeton in the sense that the units, expressing a sequence of events in the order in which they occurred, do not have coordinators. Some however might prefer to punctuate with full stops, taking the description to contain three short (asyndetic) sentences. There is nothing remarkable in Latin about a narrative that consists of sentences without any formal connection; it is easy to find such sequences, for example, in Caesar (note *Civ.* 1.15.3 *milites imperat. mittunt. interea legio duodecima Caesarem consequitur. cum his duabus Asculum Picenum proficiscitur*; punctuation of Damon, OCT) and Tacitus. On the contrary, it is sentences linked repeatedly by *et* that stand out as odd: in the later period they are particularly a mark of biblical style and of imitators of that (see Adams 2016: 708, index s.v. *et* 'sentence connective'). In many cases it matters little whether one punctuates with commas or full-stops, or whether one uses the term 'clausal asyndeton' or 'sentence asyndeton'. Nor do editors only use full-stops or commas in such cases. Here is the punctuation of the the OCT (Peterson) at Cic. *Prov. cons.* 10: *pactiones sine ulla iniuria factas rescidit; custodias sustulit; uectigalis multos ac stipendiarios liberauit*.

More straightforward as an asyndetic clausal tricolon is Cic. *Red. sen.* 22:

8 Clausal Asyndeton

quem ad salutem meam uoluntas impulit, uis retardauit, auctoritas uestra reuocauit, 'he was driven to my salvation by his will, held up by violence, and recalled by your authority'.

Quem is object of all three verbs, and the clauses could not be separated by full-stops. Each verb has a different subject. Cf. e.g. Catull. 62.41 *quem mulcent aurae, firmat sol, educat imber.*

Such clausal or sentence examples may consist of pairs too. See e.g.:

Sisenna *FRH* II.26.F102 (XXX.2.4, 23) *funis expediunt, claustra foribus inposita periclitantur,* 'they unwind the ropes and test the bolts fitted to the doors' (Briscoe, *FRH*).

While a full-stop would be possible in this last example, that is not the case at Cic. *Red. sen.* 29:

eodemque tempore improbos auctoritate sua compresserit, bonos excitarit, 'and at the same time he checked the wicked by his authority, and roused the good'.

Eodem tempore links the two clauses, such that they are (asyndetically) coordinated: at the same time he did A *and* B. There are two pairs of opposites in the juxtaposed clauses, *improbos/bonos* and *compresserit/excitarit* (see above, 6 on Cic. *Quinct.* 54 for such embedding of opposites).

There are contexts in which it is clear that a writer was deliberately piling up uncoordinated clauses as a stylistic device to create a forceful larger unit that we might call impressionistically a 'sentence'. I refer to extended asyndetic sequences containing different forms of asyndeta, which it would be perverse to split up by the use of full-stops. Note the following passage:

Sall. *Cat.* 12.2 (3) *rapere consumere, sua parui pendere, aliena cupere, pudorem pudicitiam, diuina atque humana promiscua, nihil pensi neque moderati habere.*

First there are two asyndetic historic infinitives. Then come two slightly longer (asyndetic) clauses, each with a historic infinitive, in which the nominal elements (*sua, aliena*) are opposites (complementarities), as are the two verb (phrases), *parui pendere* and *cupere* (antonyms), a pair of contrasts that binds the clauses together (cf. the Ciceronian passage just cited). Finally there is a third asyndetic clause with a single verb, *habere*, at the end, containing first an asyndetic pair of antonyms, *pudorem pudicitiam*, and then a second pair (*diuina atque humana*), this time with a coordinator. These two nominal pairs stand together in asyndeton, their predicate being *promiscua*. *Habere* has two separate (asyndetic) dependent constructions, the first from *pudorem* to *promiscua*, the second from *nihil* to *moderati* (see Ramsey 2007: 91). The three main units, [*rapere consumere*], [*sua parui pendere, aliena cupere*] and [*pudorem pudicitiam, diuina atque humana promiscua, nihil pensi neque moderati habere*], are of ascending length. Splitting this passage up into shorter sentences would obscure its internal unities and cumulative force.

Thus in extended accumulations of asyndeton as found not least in historians but also elsewhere there may be clausal asyndeta juxtaposed with other types of asyndeton, such as single-word juxtapositions and also phrases.

The passages so far quoted have juxtaposed main clauses, but asyndetic subordinate clauses are also common. See particularly Leo (1912: 272–3 n. 4), though not all of his many examples are straightforward (see also Hofmann and Szantyr 1965: 830–1, with further bibliography). Here is one example: Plaut. *Poen.* 1099–1100 *hanc fabricam apparo, | ut te allegemus, filias dicas tuas*, 'I am preparing this trick, that we send you and you say that they are your daughters'; another is at Caes. *Civ.* 1.52.3. Pease (1958: 1024) comments on an example at Cic. *Nat.* 3.30, in which 'the protasis is composed (with asyndeton) of two parts'. Berry (1996: 222) discusses an example in Cicero (*Sull.* 44), observing that in some cases (where the subordination is long) a scribe may have omitted a conjunction, and he himself prints Halm's <*et*>. For another case in which there may be a protasis in two (asyndetic) parts, see Cic. *Att.* 7.9.2 *si per tribunos pl. non patiatur* <*et*> *tamen quiescat, rem adduci ad interregnum*, which is translated by Shackleton Bailey, 'Should he obstruct this by means of Tribunes but not resort to violence, there will be an interregnum.' Lambinus added *et*, and so Shackleton Bailey. The translation however gives the coordination an adversative role. It is frequently hard to be precise about the semantics of an asyndetic coordination (whether e.g. it be conjunctive or adversative), but it is not satisfactory to emend by adding one coordinator but to translate another. *At* would suit the translation better.

I take up now the adversative type of clausal asyndeton, which over a long period has attracted the notice of numerous commentators on Latin texts (and Greek). A study of commentaries gives a good impression of the distribution of the usage, and many of the examples below are from commentators. Works on colloquial Latin tend to disregard the literary evidence.

Here is a typical example (with juxtaposed subordinate, not main, clauses): Cic. *Ac.* 1.16 *ut nihil adfirmet ipse, refellat alios*, 'so that he asserts nothing himself, but refutes others'. Reid (1885: 111) says ad loc.: 'the adversative asyndeton, so common in Cic.; e.g. 2.39'. It is typical here

8 Clausal Asyndeton

that there is a negative in the first clause, and the structure is thus '*non* A, B' (for 'but B'). This is much the same as saying that the first clause is concessive, but without its concessive force marked by *quamquam* or the like. Commentators usually paraphrase cases of what they call adversative asyndeton by understanding *sed* at the start of the second clause, but equally *quamquam* can usually be understood at the head of the first clause. It is however reasonable to call the type 'asyndeton' since a coordinator could be added.

The negative in the first clause above is *nihil*, but the negative in this structure varies. Note the following:

Cic. *Ac.* 2.103 *itaque ait uehementer errare eos, qui dicant ab Academia sensus eripi, a quibus numquam dictum sit aut colorem aut saporem aut sonum nullum esse, illud sit disputatum, non inesse in his propriam, quae nusquam alibi esset, ueri et certi notam*, 'And accordingly he asserts that those who say that the Academy robs us of our senses are violently mistaken, as that school never said that colour, taste or sound was non-existent, but their contention was that these presentations do not contain a mark of truth and certainty peculiar to themselves and found nowhere else' (Rackham, Loeb).

Reid (1885: 299) says on *illud*, 'adversative asyndeton'. Here the negative is *numquam*.

For *non* see Cic. *Att.* 2.2.3:

de lolio, sanus non es; de uino, laudo, 'as regards the darnel, you are not sane, but as for the wine, I approve'.

Different again is the following:

Livy 9.20.3 *itaque de foedere negatum; indutiae biennii . . . impetratae*, 'and so, as for a treaty, it was denied; but an armistice of two years . . . was obtained'.

Here the negative is contained within the verb *negatum*, which is equivalent to *non datum*. Anderson (1928: 162) uses the term 'adversative Asyndeton'.

For another example with *nihil* see:

Cic. *Prov. cons.* 8 *quorum ego nihil dico, patres conscripti, nunc in hominem ipsum: de prouincia disputo*, 'none of these things am I saying now against the man himself, senators, but I am discussing the province'.

Clausal asyndeton is common in Propertius. For an adversative example following a negative in the preceding clause, see:

1.15.11–12 *at non sic Ithaci digressu mota Calypso | desertis olim fleuerat aequoribus: | multos illa dies incomptis maesta capillis | sederat, iniusto multa locuta salo*, 'Not thus was Calypso affected [i.e. moved to improve the appearance of her hair: cf. l. 5] by the Ithacan's departure, when in ages past she wept to the lonely waves: [but] for many days she sat disconsolately with unkempt tresses uttering many a complaint to the unjust sea' (Goold, Loeb). There is another adversative example at 1.15.17–19. See further Fedeli (1980: 104) on 1.2.23.

Whereas the examples so far quoted (as too most of the phrasal adversative examples illustrated above, 2) have a negative in the first clause or part, sometimes in adversative asyndeton it is the adversative clause that contains the negative, as e.g. at Plaut. *Pers.* 44 *quaesiui, nusquam reperi*, 'I sought, but nowhere found', Cic. *Fam.* 9.26.2 *'habeo' inquit, 'non habeor a Laide'*, 'I possess Lais but am not possessed by her', *Att.* 2.2.3 *sed heus tu, ecquid uides Kalendas uenire, Antonium non uenire?*, 'look here, do you see that the Kalends are coming but that Antonius is not coming?'

The following is a more complicated example:

Cic. *Ac.* 2.39 *maxime autem absurdum uitia in ipsorum esse potestate neque peccare quemquam sine adsensione, hoc idem in uirtute non esse*, 'And what is most absurd is that men's vices should be in their own power and that nobody should sin except with assent, but that the same should not be true in the case of virtue' (Rackham, Loeb).

Reid (1885: 225) says on *hoc idem*, 'the juxtaposition of two contrasted sentences, without the second being accompanied by any adversative particle to mark the contrast, is common in Cic.'

The type with a negative in the second clause is also found at Cic. *Ac.* 2.98.

It is not always the case that in one of the two juxtaposed clauses with an adversative relationship there is an explicit negative. Here are some examples of different kinds, taken mainly from commentators:

Cic. *Dom.* 34 *dico apud pontifices, augures adsunt: uersor in medio iure publico*, 'I am speaking before the pontiffs, and augurs are present; yet I am taking my stand upon/I am dealing with a fundamental point of public law.'

This is the interpretation of Nisbet (1939: 96), who says that *uersor* = *tamen uersor*, which he names 'asyndeton aduersativum'. There is an accumulation of asyndeta on Nisbet's interpretation: *dico apud pontifices* and *augures adsunt*.

Nisbet (1939: 114) discusses another adversative example found at *Dom.* 49. Here are some further passages:

8 Clausal Asyndeton 25

Cic. Fin. 2.31 *simul atque natum animal est, gaudet uoluptate et eam appetit ut bonum, aspernatur dolorem ut malum*, 'as soon as an animal is born, it rejoices in pleasure and seeks that as a good, but scorns pain as an evil'.
Livy 9.1.11 *pro certo habete priora bella aduersus deos magis quam homines gessisse, hoc quod instat ducibus ipsis dis gesturos*, 'regard it as certain that, whereas we waged former wars against gods more than against men, this war that is overhanging us we will wage with the gods themselves as our leaders'.

Anderson (1928: 77) states: 'Such coupling of contrasted clauses is often called Adversative Asyndeton.' I have translated the first clause here as an implied concessive clause (= *quamquam priora bella*), making the clause that follows the main clause, but again instead it would be possible to understand *sed* before the second clause.

Anderson (1928: 153) also uses 'adversative Asyndeton' of Livy 9.18.9:

qui eo extollunt quod populus Romanus etsi nullo bello multis tamen proeliis uictus sit, Alexando nullius pugnae non secunda fortuna fuerit, non intellegunt ..., 'those who magnify it for this reason, that although the Roman people have been conquered in no war they have been conquered in many battles, but for Alexander in no battle was his fortune not favourable, do not understand ...'

Here is a Tacitean example:

Ann. 6.28.4 *sed antiquitas quidem obscura; inter Ptolemaeum ac Tiberium minus ducenti quinquaginta anni fuerunt*, 'Now antiquity is of course a dark age; but between Ptolemy and Tiberius there were less than two hundred [and] fifty years' (Woodman 2004; see Woodman 2017: 210 on the adversative asyndeton here).

Adversative asyndeton is particularly common in Tacitus' *Agricola*, to judge from the number of notes on it in the commentary of Woodman and Kraus (2014: see the index, 349, s.v. 'asyndeton'). Sometimes there is no negative in either clause. Here is one example:

Agr. 3.1 *ut corpora nostra lente augescunt, cito extinguuntur* (see Woodman and Kraus 2014: 87; there are two pairs of opposites contrasted in the two clauses).

Another type is that in which, although there is not an overt negative in either clause, one is implied, for example by the semantics of the verb (cf. below on Cic. *Red. sen.* 5). Here is a case, again from Tacitus' *Agricola*:

12.3 *caelum crebris imbribus ac nebulis foedum; asperitas frigorum abest*

Woodman and Kraus (2014: 151) note the adversative asyndeton in the second clause, where *abest* conveys a negative idea (= 'but there is not harsh cold'). Another verb that is an implied negative (*deerant*), but this time in the first clause, is at *Agr.* 18.4:

naues deerant; ratio et constantia ducis transuexit

Woodman and Kraus (2014: 187) render the second clause as '<but> the leader's calculation and resolution conveyed <them> across'.
Note too:

Cic. *Red. sen.* 5 *ut corpus abesset meum, dignitas iam in patriam reuertisset*, 'that my body was absent, but my dignity had already returned to its native land' (another example with juxtaposed subordinate clauses; *abesset* can be taken as negative by implication, = *non adesset*).

Some possible examples are not so straightforward. Sometimes what looks at first sight to be clausal asyndeton bimembre turns out to be of different type. Note the following:

Cic. *Off.* 3.119 (**148**) *non recipit istam coniunctionem honestas, aspernatur repellit*, 'moral rectitude does not accept such a link, but scorns, spurns it'.

This may seem to be the clausal type with a negative in the first clause, given that two finite verbs (*aspernatur, repellit*) provide the adversative part. However, whereas we can paraphrase by understanding *sed* 'but' before *aspernatur, repellit*, we cannot adopt the alternative paraphrase by understanding *quamquam* before *non recipit*: *'although moral rectitude does not accept such a risk, it scorns, spurns it'. In fact *aspernatur, repellit* have the same subject and object as *non recipit*, and are arguably in the same (main) clause as it. *Aspernatur, repellit* form a single-word asyndeton bimembre with an adversative relationship not to a different clause, but to *non recipit* in the same clause, as can be seen if the word order is changed in rewriting: *non recipit, (sed) aspernatur, repellit istam coniunctionem honestas.*

Cic. *Phil.* 2.82 has a problematic sequence of a different type, in that it is open to more than one interpretation: *sortitio praerogatiuae: quiescit. renuntiatur: tacet.* This is translated in the Loeb edition (Shackleton Bailey, Ramsey and Manuwald) as: 'Lots are drawn for the right of first vote; Antonius makes no move. The result is declared; Antonius keeps silent.' On one interpretation there is a series of four events, described in order, the last three by single verbs. But are there rather two pairs here, with the second member of each pair having an adversative relation to the first member? Thus 'lots are drawn for the right of first vote, but Antonius makes no move; the result is declared, but Antonius keeps silent'.

9 Causal (etc.) 'Asyndeton' (?) of Clauses

I conclude with an important point about distribution. The examples of adversative asyndeton quoted in this section are exclusively from high literature, mainly Cicero, Livy, Propertius and Tacitus. On the other hand Hofmann and Ricottilli (2003: 258–9) illustrate the phenomenon from comedy and Cicero's letters, traditionally regarded as a source for colloquial Latin, and their book itself is devoted to that subject. But such clausal asyndeton was ubiquitous in the language, and not restricted to colloquial registers. Fedeli (1980: 104) comments on an example of adversative asyndetron in Propertius as 'proprio del *sermo communis*' (citing some further bibliography with this theme), but the many cases in Cicero, Livy and Tacitus cannot simply be dismissed in this way. It is in their function, not their stylistic level, that the motivation of these structures should be sought. It may suit a poet, for example, not to spell out the relationship between clauses in every instance, given that poetry is often suggestive and elliptical.

9 Causal, Explanatory, Explicative (etc.) 'Asyndeton'

In this section I deal in passing with a form of clausal or sentence 'asyndeton' that some would not give that designation.

It was seen above (1) that *for* in English is regarded by Huddleston, Payne and Peterson (2002) as not having the properties of a coordinator, and it would follow that the omission of *for*, as in *I am hungry. I have not eaten in three days*, would not be treated as a case of asyndetic coordination (see above, 1). The sentence *I am hungry, for I have not eaten in three days* would be interpreted as having in its second part a construction akin to a subordinate clause, with *for* similar to a subordinating conjunction (= *I am hungry, because I haven't eaten in three days*). Classicists, on the other hand, and particularly commentators on Greek texts, regularly interpret the absence of e.g. γάρ as a type of asyndeton, specifying it as 'explanatory, explicative' or the like. I illustrate here, but without committing myself to the use of the term 'asyndeton'. 'Parataxis' may be preferable in some cases. For a wide-ranging account of the omission of particles in Greek ('sentence asyndeton') see now Battezzato and Rodda (2018), with their definition of 'asyndeton' at 4–5 with n. 4; also Maehler (2000). My own view is that omission of sentence particles is an interesting topic well worthy of systematic study, but that it is usually a different phenomenon from asyndetic coordination as that is defined here.

Barrett (1964: 271) on *Hipp*. 591–5 has this rendering: 'You are betrayed, dear lady; what device can I find you now? What was hidden has come to light.' τὰ κρυπτὰ γὰρ πέφηνε of the manuscripts is rejected, and he comments: '... asyndeton is right and is at the same time liable to corruption by the intrusion of this very γάρ'. He prints (594) τὰ κρυπτ' ἐκπέφηνε. Barrett elsewhere comments on the tendency for manuscripts to remove 'asyndeton' by inserting particles (e.g. p. 323 on 834–5, p. 361 on 1070–1, p. 395 on 1280–2). Mastronarde (2002: 92) states: 'When one clause follows another in asyndeton, the second is often explanatory of the first, equivalent to a γάρ-clause.' See too e.g. Schwyzer (1950: 2.632–3), Hesiod *Op.* 434 with West (1978: 268), *Th.* 533 with West (1966: 317), citing *Th.* 770 and numerous passages from Homer; also Fraenkel (1950: 3.834) s.v. 'asyndeton, explanatory', Griffith (1983: 137) on Aeschylus *Pr.* 266, Maehler (2004: 113, 141), Allen (2008: 204) on Euripides *Hel.* 503.

In Latin note for example Petron. 38.2 *parum illi bona lana nascebatur: arietes a Tarento emit*, 'not enough good wool was being produced for him: he bought rams from Tarentum'. The first clause could be rewritten as causal, 'because not enough wool was being produced, he ...' The second clause here is of a type called by Hofmann and Szantyr (1965: 830) 'asyndeton conclusivum'. On the other hand for an explanatory clause that comes second, see Cic. *Phil.* 6.9 *ibitur. non parebit*, 'That is what will happen: he will not obey' (Loeb). Note too Prop. 1.12.11 *non sum ego qui fueram: mutat uia longa puellas* (cf. 1.12.15–16, 1.12.16–17, 1.13.19–20, 1.13.34, 2.23.19–20), Petron. 38.6–7 *reliquos autem collibertos eius caue contemnas: ualde sucos[s]i sunt*, 'be careful not to despise the rest of his freedmen: they are absolutely loaded'. Hofmann and Szantyr (1965: 830) call this type 'asyndeton explicativum'. See further Kühner and Stegmann (1955: 2.158), Adams (2016: 244–5).

G. Williams (1968: 333) on Horace writes: 'it is noticeable in the *Ars Poetica* as in Horace's *Epistles* in general, that a movement to a new topic is often indicated by asyndeton'. In n. 2 the following passages are referred to: *Ars* 24, 38, 73, 99, 153, 251, 275. Williams continues (333–4), 'the abrupt asyndeton at this point indicates a pause and a change of voice'. Cf. Williams (1968: 803, index), 'Asyndeton indicates commencement of new topic.'

No definition is offered of what asyndeton might be. At *Ars* 24, for example (*maxima pars uatum, pater et iuuenes patre digni,* | *decipimur specie recti*), there is a change of topic that might seem abrupt, but that does not constitute asyndeton as that term might be used in linguistic literature. What is missing? Horace might have said something to the effect that 'I will move on now to topic X', and the omission of a transitional remark may be of interest in its own right, but the imprecision of terminology entailed in labelling as 'asyndeton' such a change of topic is unhelpful. Nor would it seem appropriate to speak of parataxis. Williams' use of the term looks to be based on 'asyndeton' as it is commonly used by Greek commentators, to indicate the omission of sentence-connective particles. One can explain precisely what particle might be missing from a particular Greek context, but merely using 'asyndeton' of an abrupt transition in Latin is vague.

10 Asyndeton with Anaphora

An asyndetic sequence may also have anaphora, that is repetition of a term at the head of each member of the sequence. Cases were cited earlier (3) in the account of ancient classifications of asyndeton. For such structures in Greek see Denniston (1952: 106–7), Fehling (1969: 210–11), Thomas (2011: 146), citing alongside Hor. *Saec.* 59 *per damna per caedes*, Hom. *Il.* 10.298 ἂμ φόνον, ἂν νέκυας, and for Latin Leo (1960: 177, 181–2). Commentators also draw attention to specific examples (e.g. Mastronarde 2002: 295 on Euripides *Med.* 765–7). The pattern is found in Umbrian too: e.g. *Tab. Ig.* IIa.25 **tiu : puni : tiu : vinu** '(I invoke) thee with mead (?), (I invoke) thee with wine' (Poultney 1959: 182; on the doubtful meaning of the first noun, denoting it seems some sort of drink offering, see Untermann 2000: 606). The pair **puni vinu** is also in the corpus as a straightforward asyndeton without anaphora (see XXII.4.2).

In Latin a special type is in the old religious expression seen e.g. in a spell at Macr. *Sat.* 3.9.7 *si deus, si dea est,* 'be it god (or) be it goddess' (see Oakley 1998: 242 for examples and bibliography). Curse tablets have variations on this structure, such as *si puer, si puella* (for example in a fragmentary Uley tablet published by Tomlin 2016: 396, no. 11). Cf. e.g. Plaut. *Capt.* 114 *si foris, si intus uolent* (with Lindsay 1900: 151; note that the adverbs are opposites).

Combinations of asyndeton (bimembre or longer) with anaphora are commonplace in Latin and take many forms. Here are some illustrations chosen at random (see also Oakley 1997: 729 for many different instances from Livy). At Cic. *Off.* 1.158 (*tum docere tum discere uellet, tum audire tum dicere*) there are two pairs of verbs of opposite meanings (converses), *docere discere* and *audire dicere*, with each of the four verbs preceded by *tum*. This clause is translated by Miller (Loeb) as 'he would wish to teach, as well as to learn; to hear, as well as to speak'. *Tum . . . tum* here is equivalent to *et . . . et* 'both . . . and' (for which usage see *OLD* s.v. *tum* 10b). See too for some other anaphoric terms Catull. 3.9 *modo huc modo illuc*, 17.21 *talis iste meus stupor nil uidet, nihil audit*, Cic. Dom. 47 *o caenum, o portentum, o scelus*, Fin. 3.63 *ut oculi, ut aures . . . ut crura, ut manus*, 4.46 *quid sequi, quid fugere debeant*, 5.62 *cum pie, cum amice*, Livy 30.28.1 *simul spes simul cura*, 30.32.5 *simul laeta simul tristia obuersabantur* (a pair of opposites (antonyms) again), 30.34.7 *simul cum hostibus simul cum suis*, 34.45.7 *non pedes non manus habentem natum*, 38.9.7 *partim consilio partim precibus*. In several of these cases the repeated terms are like coordinators. *Simul . . . simul* is equivalent to *et . . . et*, and *non . . . non* to *non . . . nec* or *nec . . . nec*; see above on *tum . . . tum*. There may be patterns within such sequences, as at Catull. 63.63 *ego mulier, ego adulescens, ego ephebus, ego puer*. See Fordyce (1961: 269): the four types of human figure are enumerated in descending order of age from adulthood to childhood, a striking reversal. Lee translates (1991) this and the previous line thus: 'What kind of human figure have I not undergone? | A woman I, a young man, an ephebe I, a child.' It should be noted that anaphoric sequences of the above types may also be coordinated: e.g. Catull. 49.2–3 *quot sunt quotque fuere, Marce Tulli, | quotque post aliis erunt in annis*.

One combination of asyndeton with anaphora I have decided to include systematically in this book. I usually refer to it as the 'prepositional type' of asyndeton bimembre, characterised by a preposition repeated with two different nouns, as at Sall. *Cat.* 6.1 (**84**) *sine legibus sine imperio*. Such asyndeta look phrasal, with two pairs of two words juxtaposed, but preposition + noun in Latin was a phonological unit not a pair of separate words, and the type is so distinctive that it deserves special treatment. The type is found in Greek (see above, 3) and also Umbrian (see XXII.4.5). Asyndeta bimembria in which the two members have the same 'fore-element' are very old (see West 1988: 156).

To put this prepositional type in perspective, I have collected from a speech of Cicero, the *Pro Quinctio*, prepositional expressions with more nominal members than one. The examples are arranged in categories according to their structure. The rarity of our prepositional type becomes apparent (see also the evidence from Caesar at XXVIII, Appendix 1):

A (single preposition and coordinator)
5 *contra uim et gratiam*
6 *in dicione ac potestate*
9 *propter uirtutem nobilitatemque*
15 *de tota illa ratione atque re Gallicana*
19 *de rebus rationibusque societatis*
28 *de saltu agroque communi*
33 *de fama fortunisque P. Quincti*

10 Asyndeton with Anaphora

33 *in salute atque auxilio ferendo*
43 *de rationibus et controuersiis societatis*
43 *de uita et ornamentis suis omnibus*
53 *non ad C. Aquilium aut L. Lucilium rettulisti*
55 *cum ista summa sanctimonia ac diligentia*
59 *in tanto metu miser periculoque uersabitur*
64 *per summum dedecus et ignominiam*
65 *inter ipsum Alfenum et Naeuium*
69 *per uim et scelus plurimum*
85 *cum summa sua inuidia maximoque periculo P. Quincti*
91 *per senectutem ac solitudinem suam*
92 *contra luxuriem ac licentiam*
94 *in capite fortunisque hominum honestissimorum*
94 *cum audacia perfidiaque*
94 *contra nutum dicionemque Naeui*
95 *a pari uinci aut superiore.*

B (single prepositon without coordinator, or with a coordinator after a juxtaposition)

10 *in tuam, C. Aquili, fidem ueritatem misericordiam . . . confugerit*
28 *contra ius consuetudinem edicta praetorum*
46 *sine cuiusquam dedecore infamia pernicieque*
59 *cum bonis fama fortunisque omnibus*
90 *ex ceteris dictis factis cogitatisque Sex. Naeui.*

C (preposition repeated, with coordinator)

12 *tollitur ab atriis Liciniis atque a praeconum consessu*
16 *pro fraterna illa necessitudine et pro ipsius adfinitate*
25 *ab atriis Liciniis et a faucibus macelli*
48 *ex offici ratione atque ex omnium consuetudine*
53 *non statim ad C. Aquilium aut ad eorum aliquem*
68 *per ius et per magistratum.*

D (preposition repeated, without coordinator)

90 *per uim, per iniuriam, per iniquitatem iudici*
97 *per fratris sui mortui cinerem, per nomen propinquitatis, per ipsius coniugem et liberos.*

The most common type by far (A) is that in which there is a single preposition and two dependent nouns linked by a coordinator. After a single preposition asyndeton does occur (B), but (in this corpus) only if there are more dependent nouns than two (I have included in this section a few examples in which the nominal elements have the structure ABC*que*). Finally, a preposition is sometimes repeated, but only when there is a coordinator if the sequence has just two nominal elements (C), or when there are more nominal elements than two if coordinators are not present (D). Missing from the list are the types *contra uim gratiam* (cf. A 5) and *per ius per magistratum* (cf. C 68).

But these last two types, absent from this one speech, do occur. The first type is dealt with systematically elsewhere, not least because its authenticity seems to have been doubted by some editors (see XXI; see also e.g. on Cicero 15, Tacitus 91). Of the second type Sallust e.g. has 5 examples, Tacitus' *Histories* have 8, and the *Annals* 14. For the pattern in Livy see XXXI.2.5. Cicero too has the type in other works than the speech above (see XXVI.2.6, 3.5, 4.6, 5.5). Asyndeton of the prepositional type will come up in the discussion of texts, and it will emerge that it often occurs in asyndetic accumulations (see e.g. on Cicero XXVI.7.2.4, and on the historians XXX.6.2a).

11 Conclusions

The definitions and examples offered in this chapter are intended to be introductory. It should however be clear that there has been a lack of precision in the use of the word 'asyndeton' in classical scholarship. I have decided to confine myself to asyndetic coordination as that expression is now used in linguistics, not because I wish to dismiss e.g. sentence particles as uninteresting, but because their absence is usually a different matter from the absence of coordinators between words. It is true that ancient commentators sometimes applied the term 'asyndeton' to the omission of particles, but they also applied it to the omission of coordinators, and in recent times it has become clear that there is a difference between the two types of omission and that they should not be thrown together without distinction, whatever the precedent might be for doing so.

Ancient assertions about the supposed effects of asyndetic coordination have been reported here without comment. I will return to this topic at Chapter V.

CHAPTER II

'Asyndeta' That May Not Be Asyndeta: Roles of Adjectives; Appositional Compounds; and 'Asyndetic Hendiadys'

1 Introduction

If two terms are juxtaposed without a coordinator they need not be in asyndeton, though it is commonly assumed in commentaries that any juxtaposed words of the same part of speech must be asyndetic. There are various relationships between two words that may rule out the insertion of a coordinator. For example, if the two are adjectives, they may differ hierarchically (see e.g. Quirk et al. 1972: 550–1), a distinction sometimes referred to as 'rank'. Or one may be attributive and the other predicative, or a secondary predicate (see below). A pair may form an 'appositional compound'. Again, one term may be a modifier of the other, with overt coordination possibly unnecessary or inappropriate, though this type is rather nebulous. All these categories will be illustrated below. Perhaps most important are the roles of adjectives, such as attributive versus predicative. The distinction is sometimes neglected in literary commentaries.

2 Juxtaposed Adjectives that Are Not Asyndetic

2.1 Attributive and Predicative Adjectives; Secondary Predicates

Pairs of adjectives (in Latin) may differ in their degree of connection to the noun modified, such that asyndetic coordination is out of the question even when the two are together. In this section (2) I discuss the necessity of distinguishing between different functions. I start with an illustration of the difference between attributive and predicative uses, with reference to a phrase of Virgil, and move on to three similar passages of a different kind.

Horsfall (2013: 2.393) on *Aen.* 6.552 (*porta aduersa ingens*) describes the adjectives here as an asyndeton. Aeneas sees to his left fortifications with a triple wall. Horsfall's translation of the phrase (2013.1.39), 'Facing him there was a great gate', does not accord with the idea that the adjectives are in asyndeton. In the sentence *a huge gate was opposite*, *huge* is attributive and *opposite* predicative. Virgil has achieved a juxtaposition of the adjectives by separating *ingens* from *porta*, but they are not asyndetically coordinated (**a gate was huge and opposite*).

At Plaut. *Am.* 1001 (*faciam ut sit madidus sobrius*, 'I will see that he is soaked when sober' (literally, 'I will see that he, sober, is soaked') *madidus* is predicate with the verb 'to be', but *sobrius* has a different function. I do not take such adjectives in this book as precisely attributive (they need not accompany an expressed noun, and tend to express passing and not defining characteristics; they are 'optional constituents' and 'are not part of [a] noun phrase': Pinkster 2015: 30), but rather as secondary predicates/predicative adjuncts (see Pinkster loc. cit. on the terminology; the term 'predicative adjunct' is also used in the present book; see e.g. Matthews 2014: 126–7). Similar (but with separation) is Lucil. 1070 (1020 W.) *serus cum eo medio a*[*c*] *ludo bene potus recessit*, 'when at a late hour he withdrew pretty drunk from the midst of the fun' (*eo* is problematic but irrelevant here). *Serus* has a predicative role with the verb *recessit*, just as *madidus* does with *sit* above ('he withdrew late'), and *bene potus* is a secondary predicate ('he, being well drunk, withdrew late'). Note finally Plaut. *Trin.* 689: *sed ut inops infamis ne sim*. Many pairs of asyndetic adjectives have the prefix *in-* (see VI.2), but this is not an asyndetic pair. The sense is 'so that, in poverty, I am not in ill repute' (cf. de Melo, Loeb: 'to make sure that I won't have a bad reputation in my poverty'). *Inops* is a secondary predicate, *infamis* predicative. One could translate *inops* as 'though in poverty'.

See also XXVII.1.2 on Catull. 32.10–11 (*pransus iaceo et satur supinus | pertundo tunicamque palliumque*), where it is suggested (against commentators) that the pair, like those in the last paragraph, is not necessarily an asyndeton.

Volens propitius in its early use belongs with these pairs on my interpretation, though it has universally been taken as an asyndeton bimembre (see below, this chapter, 3.2.1, where interpretations of the pair are offered).

2.2 Groups of Adjectives; Other Classifications ('Rank', 'Hierarchy', 'Stacking', 'Layering')

There are other terms that have been used, particularly in relation to English, to describe the different status that pairs of adjectives may have, but sometimes these terms amount to the same thing, that is to a distinction between attributes/predicative adjuncts and predicates. Nevertheless it is worthwhile to mention such terminology here.

A revealing example from the literature is *young criminal lawyer*.[1] This could not (except in exceptional circumstances) be rewritten as *The lawyer was young and criminal*, which would almost always give the wrong meaning. A correct rewriting would take the form *The criminal lawyer was young*. The phrase could be set out as [*young*] [*criminal lawyer*], with *criminal lawyer* virtually a compound. This pattern may be referred to as showing 'layering' or 'stacking' of the adjectives,[2] or, in the terminology of Jespersen (1924: 96–7), 'differences of rank'. To Quirk et al. (1972: 550) there would be a hierarchical difference between the adjectives. *Criminal* modifies *lawyer*, whereas *young* modifies the whole compound.

Pairs of adjectives in Latin texts often exhibit layering (henceforth I mainly use the term of Jespersen, 'rank'), such that they would not (usually) be rewritten with a coordinator. Here are some further examples.

2.3 Poetic Periphrases and Additional Adjectives

Latin poetry has abundant examples of types of phrases containing adjectives differing in function. Poetic language makes extensive use, for example, of periphrases, comprising an adjective, often derived from a proper name, and a general noun, the pair standing for a precise noun, unaccompanied, of the ordinary language. At e.g. Plaut. *Mil.* 413 there is a circumlocution for the sea (*mare*), *in locis Neptuniis* 'in the Neptunian places'. *Loca* is so vague that without *Neptunia* its reference would not be clear. For poetic periphrases see for example Jocelyn (e.g. 1967: 352), Lunelli (1980: 43–6), Maurach (1995: 74–80), and particularly West (2007: 81–3) on what he calls 'kennings', with illustrations from various Indo-European languages. For the type in which the adjective is derived from a proper name see too Austin (1964: 208) on *Aen.* 2.543, and also Horsfall (2000: 47) on *Aen.* 7.1 and (2000: 189) on *Aen.* 7.252.

An adjective of whatever type forming such a periphrasis is so closely bound with the noun that its removal would obscure the meaning. If there happens to be another adjective present denoting an incidental feature of, say, the sea, then that adjective will modify the whole periphrasis. This can be put in another way in reference to the example above. *Neptunius* is an adjectival equivalent of a possessive genitive (cf. e.g. *Campus Martius* = *Campus Martis*),

---
[1] See e.g. Matthews (2014: 56–7).
[2] See e.g. Matthews (2014: 87–8), and the index, 191, s.vv. 'sequences of adjectives' and 'stacking'.

and if there were another adjective, as e.g. in *saeua loca Neptunia*, the expression could be paraphrased as *saeua loca Neptuni*: asyndeton is out of the question. Examples of 'genitival' adjectives in such expressions are given separately below (2.4 (4), **a–i**). Here I illustrate just one poetic circumlocution from Lucretius, itself with a genitive-type adjective, and with the pair modified in this case by an adjectival participle. I then cite an example of layering from Sallust.

At 6.387–8 there occurs a periphrasis typical of Lucretius: *alii fulgentia diui | terrifico quatiunt sonitu caelestia templa* ('other gods shake the shining heavenly regions with terrible din'). The underlined phrase is a circumlocution for *caelum*. *Fulgentia* is in agreement, but it modifies the whole phrase (= *fulgens caelum*). Hofmann and Szantyr (1965: 161) cite, alongside this example, Lucr. 5.490–1 *caeli ... fulgentia templa*, which makes it obvious that *caelestia* can also be taken in the genitival sense referred to above. At 6.387–8 (above) the two terms forming the semantic unit are juxtaposed and separated from the epithet, but that is not an invariable order. I return to word order below, 2.5.

For a Homeric example containing a defining (again genitival) adjective derived from a proper name, and an adjective describing an incidental feature, see *Il.* 2.467 ἐν λειμῶνι Σκαμανδρίῳ ἀνθεμόεντι 'in the flowery mead of Scamander'.

Here is a fragment of Sallust's *Histories*: 2.77 Ramsey *pauca piratica actuaria nauigia*. The primary adjective is *actuaria*: *actuariae naues* were 'vessels propelled by both sails and oars' (Ramsey 2015: 183 ad loc.). These 'light vessels' have the additional feature that they were conducted as if by pirates. Finally there is a numerical adjective that modifies the whole phrase. We may represent thus: *pauca [piratica [actuaria nauigia]]*.

2.4 Scholarly Classifications of Adjectival Roles

Scholars have long, if not consistently, recognised that two adjectives associated with the same noun may differ in status. Munro (1886: 2.55) has a good note on Lucr. 1.258 (*candens lacteus umor*). He says that 'the two epithets are quite regular, as *lac. um.* = simply *lac* or *lactis umor*', adding that '*candens* is an epith. ornans'. The two adjectives differ in rank, with *lacteus* restrictive or defining and forming a poetic periphrasis with *umor*, and *candens* modifying the whole phrase. Munro cites expressions of similar structure from Lucretius, Virgil, Catullus and Propertius. The example from Catullus is in the first line of the first poem, *cui dono lepidum*

2 Juxtaposed Adjectives That Are Not Asyndetic

nouum libellum, where *lepidum* 'charming' indicates a subjective quality that he is claiming for the *nouum libellum*.

There is also recognition of differences of rank at Hofmann and Szantyr (1965: 161), though no such technical designation is used. A good example cited is Caes. *Civ.* 1.30.4 *naues longas ueteres* (a *nauis longa* is a type of ship; a similar example is at *Civ.* 1.26.1 *naues magnas onerarias*); see also the above section (2.3), on the similar expression at Sallust *Hist.* 2.77. Timpanaro (1994: 5 n. 8) also takes *naues longas ueteres* from Hofmann and Szantyr, to illustrate the point he makes that one of two adjectives must not be connected more closely to the noun than the other (if there is to be asyndeton).[3]

At Virg. *Aen.* 3.383 a complex expression is found: *longa ... longis uia diuidit inuia terris*. Both *longa* and *inuia* go with *uia* but this is not an asyndeton (see correctly Horsfall 2006: 292 ad loc.). *Via inuia* is a type of oxymoron taken from Greek (see Horsfall with references), and the pairing forms a unit. *Longa* refers to an incidental characteristic of the *uia inuia*: a *uia inuia* may be short or long.

Just occasionally two adjectives differing in rank may be connected by a coordinator, for a special effect. Note Lucil. 445 (467 W.) *Samio curtoque catino* 'on a Samian and broken dish', for 'broken [Samian dish]'.

The different functions of adjectives in pairs have not always been recognised. I take illustrations from various commentators, numbering not the examples but the commentators drawn on. Sometimes the difference consists of a distinction between an attributive and a predicative adjective.

(1) Jocelyn (1967: 169) on Enn. *trag.* 3–4 discusses what he takes to be a special type of asyndeton bimembre, that in which 'the two adjectives in asyndeton (are) split by their noun'. Separation of words 'in asyndeton' has generated some interest among commentators on Latin. Timpanaro (1994: 35–70) for example has a long discussion of terms said to be in asyndeton that are separated in early poetry and later, but most of the examples cited I would not classify as asyndetic: the adjectives usually differ in rank or function.

One passage cited by Jocelyn (cf. Timpanaro 1994: 38) is Plaut. *Rud.* 907 *qui salsis locis incolit pisculentis*. But here the words *salsis locis* 'salty places' form a circumlocution for the sea not unlike that seen earlier (*in locis*

---

[3] Despite this expression of approval of Hofmann and Szantyr, Timpanaro does add that they tend to excessive exclusivity in their interpretation of asyndeta, and he refers to Cic. *Verr.* 5.106, a passage he discusses at (1994: 31).

Neptuniis), and *pisculentis* modifies the whole phrase ('the salty places full of fish'). The sea contains salt, a defining characteristic, but it is not always full of fish.

Another of Jocelyn's examples is Enn. *trag.* 296 *summis saxis fixus asperis*. *Summus* is a locational/restrictive adjective, the meaning of the first three words being 'fixed to the tops of the rocks'. *Asperis* expresses an incidental feature of these rock tops, 'the sharp rock-tops'.[4]

These two examples share a feature of word order. The unitary phrase is before the verb, and the secondary complement is postponed. To describe the noun as separating the two adjectives is misleading, as it is the verb that separates the phrase from its epithet.

Again, in the passage which Jocelyn was discussing, Enn. *trag.* 3–4 (*per ego deum sublimas subices* | *umidas unde oritur imber*), *sublimas* may be taken as a locational/restrictive adjective (the *subices*, 'underlayers', of the gods are high up, and these lofty underlayers are moist (*umidas*) and produce rain). I follow here the interpretation of *subices* (= 'clouds') advanced by Goldberg and Manuwald (2018: 2.7) (their fragment 2) rather than that of Jocelyn (1967: 170), but again I take the phrase as having a different structure from that implied by their translation. The structure I suggest is [*sublimas subices*] *umidas*. Goldberg and Manuwald translate 'by the liquid underlayers of the gods high up', which suggests the structure *sublimas* [*subices umidas*]. In both this passage and the last the locational/defining adjectives, *summis* and *sublimas*, are placed first, adjacent to the noun, and the other adjective is postponed. Timpanaro (1994: 49) assumes an asyndeton of the adjectives *sublimas* and *umidas*, with separation.

At Plaut. *Per.* 707–8 (*longa nomina* | *contortiplicata habemus*) it is straightforward to translate as 'we have long names with parts all twisted up'. It is the long names, not merely the names, that have these complicated elements. The unitary phrase comes first again, and then its epithet. There is no need to see here hyberbaton of two adjectives of the same status (as assumed by Timpanaro 1994: 38, referring to Jocelyn). On the other

---

[4] Warmington (1936: 355), however, translates (his line 366) 'set . . . on sharp steep rugged rocks', which introduces a threefold asyndeton (cf. Timpanaro 1994: 50, who also adds to the end of the words quoted *euisceratus*, which however belongs to the next colon). Goldberg and Manuwald (2018: 2.137) (their fragment 132) render 'fixed to the top of rough rocks', a translation that does give a different rank to the two adjectives, though not of the same structure as that I have adopted. Their rendering makes the primary phrase *saxis asperis*, i.e. *summis* [*saxis asperis*], whereas the structure of my rendering is [*summis saxis*] *asperis*. The word order favours this latter interpretation (see below, 2.5). The punctuation of the two-line fragment by Goldberg and Manuwald does incidentally make clear the correct colon divisions.

2 Juxtaposed Adjectives That Are Not Asyndetic

hand a phrase with the order *nomina longa contortiplicata habemus* might well have an asyndetic coordination. Pairs of adjectives may sometimes be open to more than one interpretation, a point missed by some commentators keen to find a special type of 'asyndeton' with separation. The word order in fact may indicate the roles of the adjectives.

More convincing from Jocelyn's list as an asyndeton is Plaut. *Trin.* 299 *nil ego istos moror faeceos mores, turbidos*, 'I don't care for those filthy, muddy standards.' Both adjectives are judgemental and pejorative, and near-synonyms. Both are attributive. The word order, which suggests a pause after *mores* followed by a repetitious afterthought to strengthen the first adjective, is the same as that of conjunct hyperbaton, minus the coordinator (for this pattern, with asyndeton, see XX.2). I refer to such structures as 'discontinuous asyndeton'.

Jocelyn's final example, from Porcius Licinius 1, is ruled out as an asyndeton below, this section (3).

(2) Horsfall (2000: 423) on *Aen.* 7.643 likewise mentions the 'Ennian use of two separated adjectives in asyndeton applied to a single noun', and refers the reader back to his note on 7.625 (2000: 404), where two adjectives are described as 'separated in a way that will surely have recalled Ennius'. The first Ennian example Horsfall quotes is *Ann.* 141 Skutsch *magnae gentes opulentae*.

It is just possible that the two adjectives here differ in rank. It is clear from *TLL* VI.2.1858.57ff. (with cross references) that *magna* and *maxima* are standard epithets of *gens*, whereas this Ennian passage is the only place cited at 1858.69 of *opulenta* with *gens*, apart from one in the Vulgate. The primary phrase could be taken to be *magnae gentes* 'great tribes', with their wealth an incidental characteristic: they are 'great tribes (being/that are) rich', [*magnae gentes*] [*opulentae*], with *opulentae* a predicative adjunct. Evidence will however be presented in a later chapter that makes it highly likely that there is indeed a hyperbaton here (see XX.2), of the discontinuous type referred to above, (1) on Plaut. *Trin.* 299. The phrase is unambiguously taken by Goldberg and Manuwald (2018: 1.181) as having a discontinuous structure. I mention this passage here because of the tendency to see such structures as 'Ennian'. Discontinuous asyndeton is widespread (see XX), and pairs of adjectives differing in rank applied to the same noun are for their part also common. It is more important to consider whether such a phrase has discontinuous asyndeton, or whether its adjectives differ in rank, than to leave that question open and to speak vaguely of Ennian influence.

(3) Timpanaro (1994) has been referred to several times above, and earlier too he found asyndetic terms separated in early poetry (1954: 157).⁵ He quotes for example *trag. inc. inc.* 74–5 Ribbeck (1871) (= Cic. *Tusc.* 1.37): *per speluncas saxis structas asperis, pendentibus, | maxumis, ubi rigida constat crassa caligo inferum* (see also Timpanaro 1994: 53–4). The punctuation here of *asperis* ... *maxumis* is that of Dougan (1905). In the second line *rigida* and *crassa* are not in asyndeton. Dougan translates *rigida constat* as 'stiffly holds together', which is the same as an expression 'is/stands stiff', with *rigida* predicative. The last three words mean 'the thick darkness of the underworld', and *crassa* is attributive (for the interpretation of the passage see Skutsch 1985: 550, stating that the adjective–noun group *crassa caligo* 'is predicated by *rigida constat*'). Timpanaro (1994: 54) plays down the distinction between attributive and predicative adjectives: 'La distinzione tra uso predicativo e attributivo è molto oscillante nella terminologia dei grammatici odierni.'

Another instance cited by Timpanaro (see also id. 1994: 55) is *trag. inc. inc.* 19 (Ribbeck 1871) (= Cic. *Div.* 2.115) *unde superstitiosa primum saeua euasit uox foras.*⁶ *Superstitiosa* and *saeua* differ in status. *Superstitiosa* may have a genitival role of a type that has come up before (2.3), = *superstitionis*, and thus mean 'the voice of religious exaltation'. In this context it would have come forth 'fierce'. Skutsch (1985: 550) allows a possible separated asyndeton here, but says that '*saeua* could perhaps be taken predicatively'. Alternatively *saeua* may be a modifier of the phrase *superstitiosa uox*. The word order of this example is discussed below ((4) **a**).

Finally Timpanaro quotes a line of Porcius Licinus (1: Courtney 1993: 83) *intulit se bellicosam in Romuli gentem feram*, a fragment that 'has been the subject of infinite disagreement' (Courtney loc. cit.). Courtney (1993: 85) makes a good case that *bellicosam* goes with *se* (see also Skutsch 1985: 550). Even if it does not, the sense could be 'fierce race given to war', = *bellicosam* [*gentem feram*]. There is a long discussion of the passage by Timpanaro (1994: 56–65) tentatively holding on to the view that there is an asyndeton.

(4) Maguinness (1965: 78) (see also Timpanaro 1994: 66) cites various passages from Lucretius, such as 5.32–3 *aureaque* ... *fulgentia mala*, with the following generalisation:

---

⁵ But see Skutsch's scepticism (1985: 550) about most of these examples, and not least about the textual basis of some of them.

⁶ *Foras* is an emendation for *fera*. Skutsch (1985: 550) says that *fera* should be changed to *ferae*, of the Python. See further Timpanaro (1994: 55).

2 Juxtaposed Adjectives That Are Not Asyndetic

It appears that this duplication, and even accumulation in asyndeton, of adjectives and participles with a single noun is, like so much else, a practice chosen by Lucretius and shunned by most other poets.

Maguinness was alluding here to a doctrine that pairs of adjectives were avoided by most poets. But asyndeton bimembre in general is not frequent in poets, and the adjectival type is comparatively well represented, not least in Virgil (see XXIV. 2.1.1; also for Horace see XXIX. 2.1 and particularly XXIX.2.1.5, where it is shown that adjectival asyndeton with two members is represented in the *Satires*; for Lucretius see XXIV.7.1.1). As for the phrase 'in asyndeton', there is not certain asyndeton in this example, as, at least on one interpretation, the adjectives differ in rank. *Aureus* is a regular epithet of apples (e.g. Varro *Rust.* 2.1.6, Virg. *Ecl.* 3.71), and the primary phrase (with dislocation of word order) can be taken to be *aurea mala*. On this view the whole phrase is modified by *fulgentia* (*fulgentia* [*aurea mala*]). Cf. Timpanaro (1994: 66).

There is also a second possibility, that *aurea* and *fulgentia* form a quasi-compound, 'gold-gleaming apples', 'apples gleaming gold', thus [*aurea fulgentia*] *mala*. As it happens, *-eus* adjectives do not have derived adverbs. I discuss below such compound-like groups comprising adjective and participle (see II.3.2), with the adjective predicative.

Here are two of the other groups listed by Maguinness:

5.13 *diuina aliorum antiqua reperta*, 'the divine ancient discoveries of others', = *diuina* [*antiqua reperta*] (Smith 1992: 'the ancient discoveries accounted godlike, made by others'). *Antiqua* locates the discoveries in time, whereas *diuina* expresses a value judgement of these old discoveries. The example is listed by Timpanaro (1994: 66).

5.24–5 *quid Nemaeus enim nobis nunc magnus hiatus*
ille leonis obesset et horrens Arcadius sus?
'For what harm now could that great gaping of the Nemean lion now do us, and the bristling Arcadian boar?'

There are two instances of adjectives layered here (one in each line: *Nemaeus* ... *magnus hiatus* | ... *leonis* and *horrens Arcadius sus*) that are not asyndetic. I take each in turn.

Nemaeus is a transferred epithet, which strictly belongs with *leonis* (see Munro 1886: 2.285 with cross reference to similar examples). It has the role of a genitive, a role that has been alluded to above (see 2.3). *Nemaeus* and *magnus* differ in function, and coordination would be out of the question. For a Greek transferred genitival epithet derived from a proper name (but not in this case accompanied by another epithet), cf. the well-known

Homeric example, *Il.* 2.54 Νεστορέῃ παρὰ νηΐ Πυλοιγενέος βασιλῆος 'by the Nestorean ship of the Pylos-born king', = 'by the ship of the Pylos-born king Nestor'.

In poetry (in particular) phrases containing adjectives with genitival function (and not least adjectives based on names) are prominent (see especially Austin 1964: 208 on *Aen.* 2.543), and, as they may be confused with asyndeta if there is another adjective present, are worth dwelling on. I start with a few genitival adjectives derived from names. The examples in this digression are alphabetically numbered, and then I return to the second line of Maguinness' example above.

(a) First, Lucr. 2.505 *Phoebeaque daedala chordis* | *carmina*, 'Apollo's songs, skilfully worked with strings'. *Phoebea* is equivalent to a possessive genitive. The word order is of note. The noun and the genitival adjective frame the other epithet. This is the same pattern as that seen in a tragic fragment cited by Timpanaro and discussed above, (3) (*superstitiosa ... saeua ... uox*).

Cf. (b) Virg. *Aen.* 2.542–3 *corpusque exsangue sepulchro* | *reddidit Hectoreum*, 'he gave back to the tomb the lifeless body of Hector' (also with framing word order, though the genitival adjective comes last this time), (c) 3.3 *omnis humo fumat Neptunia Troia*, 'all Neptune's Troy smokes from the ground' (with a different word order; the components of the primary phrase are juxtaposed), (d) 3.321 *o felix ... Priameia uirgo*, 'O happy virgin of Priam' (i.e. daughter of Priam; the word order is the same as that in the last example), (e) 3.706 *uada dura lego saxis Lilybaea caecis*, 'I skirt the shallows of Lilybaeum harsh with unseen rocks' (the framing order again, though here the complement of *dura*, *saxis caecis*, is split around the genitival adjective), (f) 11.850–1 *regis Dercenni ... bustum* | *antiqui Laurentis* ('the burial-mound of Dercennius ancient king of Laurentum'; framing order).

(g) Also equivalent to a genitive (though not in this case based on a name) is *fraterna* at *Aen.* 5.24 *litora ...* | *fida ... fraterna Erycis*, 'faithful shores of your brother Eryx', = *fratris Erycis*. Worth comparing with this are some uses of *patrius*, with Austin (1964: 208).

In all these examples there is an adjective in addition to that with genitival function.

(h) It is a moot point whether *corusca* at Virg. *G.* 1.328 could be taken as genitival: *ipse pater media nimborum in nocte corusca* | *fulmina molitur dextra*. See Mynors (1990: 73) ad loc., arguing that *corusca* is ablative and goes with *dextra* ('the father himself, in the midnight of the storm-clouds, with flashing hand wields his thunderbolts'). He thinks that it is impossible

2 Juxtaposed Adjectives That Are Not Asyndetic 43

with *nocte*. But if *corusca* were a transferred epithet with genitival function in agreement with *nocte* the meaning would be 'in the flashing midnight of storm-clouds', i.e. in the midnight of flashing storm-clouds. The traditional interpretation, adopted e.g. by the Loeb as well as Mynors, is simpler.

(i) A complicated case (again with an adjective that is not derived from a name) is at Lucr. 4.313–15 (line numbering of e.g. Deufert 2019), and here one is on surer ground in finding a genitival use: *cum propior caliginis aer | ater init oculos prior ... apertos, | insequitur candens confestim lucidus aer* ('when the black air of darkness, being nearer, has entered our open eyes first ..., there follows immediately a bright clear air': so Smith, Loeb). The translation I believe is not quite right. The black air belongs to darkness (*aer ater*, with a possessive genitive *caliginis*). *Candens*, in a contrast with *ater*, must have one of its established meanings, 'white'. *Lucidus* (< *lux*) has the same role as *caliginis*, and is its opposite: thus, 'the white air of light' (or, in a more concrete sense, 'consisting of particles of light', as suggested to me by Marcus Deufert). Just as the genitive *caliginis* specifies the source of the *aer ater*, so *lucidus*, which is equivalent to *lucis*, specifies the origin of *candens ... aer*, though the word order obscures the exact nature of the contrast. Deufert points out to me in confirmation of the above interpretation that at 319 it is this *lucidus aer* that fills the channels of the eyes with *lux*: *simul atque uias oculorum luce repleuit*. The passage is cited without comment by Timpanaro (1994: 66) in his account of supposed asyndetic pairs interrupted.

I leave these genitival uses and return to the second line of Maguinness' example above (5.24–5), containing the phrase *horrens Arcadius sus*. The Arcadian boar alludes to one of the labours of Hercules. *Arcadius* is the defining adjective and *horrens* a decorative addition modifying the whole phrase. Cf. Lucr. 1.945–6 *suauiloquenti / carmine Pierio*, 'sweet-speaking Pierian song'. In both of these examples the elements of the primary phrase (the defining adjective from the proper name + noun) are juxtaposed, and the decorative epithet is in the initial position.

Another of Maguinness' examples, finally, is 3.405 *uiuit et aetherias uitalis suscipit auras*, 'he lives and receives the vital breezes of the heavens'. Here *aetherias auras* is a poetic circumlocution for 'air', and the phrase is modified by *uitalis*. *Aetherias* could also be translated as genitival.

(5) According to Schierl (2006: 437), Pacuvius 205.1 (*ardua per loca agrestia*) produces an asyndetic combination of two alliterative (synonymous) adjectives (*ardua ... agrestia*) separated from each other by their noun (cf. Timpanaro 1994: 52). There is no asyndeton here, but layering. *Loca*

agrestia are rural places (cf. Varro *Ling.* 7.10), and this phrase is the primary one, with *agrestia* defining (the *loca* are not *urbana*). These particular rural places have an incidental characteristic: they are steep: *ardua* [*loca agrestia*].

2.5 Conclusions

In this section illustrating mainly pairs of adjectives that exhibit layering/ differences of rank, quite a few of the examples come from modern scholars finding adjectives 'in asyndeton' that are separated (and thus presumably manifesting hyperbaton). The adjectives are not clearly asyndetic, and there is no doubt why the separations occur: it is because there was a tendency to mark by word order the primary adjective–noun combination and to keep the secondary adjective apart. I quote below seven examples from the material above, with the primary pair underlined and the secondary epithet in bold:

Plaut. *Rud.* 907 *qui <u>salsis locis</u> incolit* **pisculentis**
Enn. *trag.* 296 *<u>summis saxis fixus</u>* **asperis**
Enn. *trag.* 3–4 *per ego deum <u>sublimas subices</u>* | **umidas** *unde oritur imber*
Plaut. *Per.* 707–8 *<u>longa nomina</u>* | **contorplicata** *habemus*
trag. inc. inc. 74–5 *per speluncas saxis structas asperis, pendentibus,* | *maxumis, ubi* **rigida** *constat <u>crassa caligo</u> inferum*
Lucr. 5.13 **diuina** *aliorum <u>antiqua reperta</u>*
Pacuvius 205.1 **ardua** *per <u>loca agrestia</u>.*

In every case the primary adjective is juxtaposed with the noun. The secondary adjective is either on the other side of the noun, or separated from the primary adjective in other ways. In two places the secondary adjective is also in a separate line from that of the primary adjective. These are not the only patterns, but they are suggestive of the bond within the primary pair.

3 Quasi-compounds, and Pairs in Which One Term Is a Modifier of the Other

3.1 Appositional Compounds

Aristophanes *Ran.* 207 βατράχων κύκνων θαυμαστά is translated by Stanford (1963: 91–2) as (wonderful) 'songs ... of swan-frogs' (with μέλη understood). He then refers to the first two-word phrase as 'asyndeton', citing Radermacher (1954; but see n. 7 below). There is no asyndeton here, because the two nouns are not coordinated ('of frogs and/or swans' is not the meaning).⁷ The songs are of frogs (i.e. an ugly croaking), but they are likened to those of swans, thought to be a thing of beauty. There is an apposition, of the type in which the second term specifies the first, here of swans that resemble frogs, i.e. 'swan-like frogs'. This type has been referred to as an appositional compound that is a 'descriptive determinative' (see B. Bauer 2017: 299 for the term).

Dover (1993: 218) ad loc. cites as a parallel Ar. *Av.* 1559 κάμηλον ἀμνόν, literally 'camel lamb'. Sommerstein (1987) translates as 'camel-lamb', but it is a camel that is sacrificed (see Sommerstein's note, 1987: 301), and 'lamb' is the specifier, a 'camel, as if a lamb': the pair should be reversed in translation into English if the rendering is to be parallel to that of *Ran.* 207 above, 'lamb-camel', i.e. 'lamb-like camel'. Note too Lycophron, *Alexandra* 1291 ναῦται ... κύνες, translated by Hornblower (2015: 455) as 'sailor-dogs' (sailors that in their behaviour resemble dogs: thus, if as above, 'dog-sailors').

A similar pair in French is *bateau-mouche*, a boat that resembles a fly, with the specifier second as in the Greek examples (see B. Bauer 2017: 297 for the French phrase). However, the Budé edition (Coulon and Van Daele 1977) translates *Av.* 1559 above as 'un agneau-chameau', a translation that reverses the order seen in *bateau-mouche*. There is some uncertainty about the order to be used in expressing such appositions in both French and English (see the fourth paragraph below on this variability). For an English pair with the reversed order see the book title *The Crow Girl*, by Erik Axl Sund (2017), which I assume means 'girl who resembles a crow'. *Girl-crow* on the other hand would refer to a young female crow (or to a female crow as it might be described in nursery language). Another compound in English (slang) in which the first term is the specifier is *she-he* (see Green 2010: 3.825), of a male transvestite or trans-sexual.

An appositional pair in Latin is *lapis silex* (Plaut. *Poen.* 290, Cato *Agr.* 18.3), 'flint stone' (see Adams 2016: 104). The specifier is again in second position, and the English equivalent again has that specifier first, as in the terms above. There is a difference between *lapis silex* and the Greek pairs, in that the stone *is* flint, whereas e.g. the camel *resembles* a lamb. This latter is metaphorical, whereas the other is a technical pairing pinning down the reference to a type of stone. For another such technical pair see Cato *Agr.* 157.7 *ex aceto oxymeli* and Adams (2016: 104); the specifier is second again. Of

---

⁷ Radermacher (1954: 167) does not use the term 'asyndeton', and he obviously took the pair to be a type of compound, because he contrasts the form of expression with dvandva compounds.

the same type are expressions containing *arbor* juxtaposed with a (following) term for the species of tree: e.g. Sisenna, *FRH* II.26.F8 *uetus atque ingens erat arbor ilex*, 'there was an old and huge holm-oak tree', Varro *Rust*. 1.7.7 *ut in Epiro arbores alni*, 1.2.20 *arbor olea* (but at 3.16.24 reversed, *ex olea arbore*) (see B. Bauer 2017: 299 on this type). Cf. Plaut. *Cur*. 647 *exoritur uentus turbo* (a whirlwind). Note too *Rud*. 993 *uidulum piscem* (a trunk that is a fish).

In the apposition *lupus femina*, 'wolf, female' (see Adams 2016: 13–14 on this and a few comparable expressions), *lupus* is a specific animal, male or female. The appositional term specifies which of the sexes is referred to. There is no essential difference between this apposition and that of *arbor ilex*, except that trees exist in a huge number of varieties; *ilex* specifies which of those varieties is meant. These appositions are descriptive determinatives, but of a partitive type, and have nothing to do with asyndeton.

In the appositional compounds cited above, the Greek and Latin pairs almost all have the order specified-specifier (βατράχων κύκνων, κάμηλον ἀμνόν, ναῦται κύνες, *lapis silex, arbor olea, uentus turbo, lupus femina, uidulum piscem*), whereas the English and French terms, whether as translations or existing in their own right, have both orders, specifier-specified or specified-specifier. For specifier-specified see 'swan-frog' (Stanford), *Crow Girl, she-he, flint stone, olive tree*, 'agneau-chameau' (Budé), and for specified-specifier, 'camel-lamb' (Sommerstein), 'sailor-dogs' (Hornblower), *bateau-mouche*.

There is potentially another type of appositional quasi-compound, the copulative (see further III.2, on dvandva compounds), as in English *bittersweet* (see B. Bauer 2017: 301, 326). Such pairs in Greek sometimes turn up as full-blown compounds, as in γλυκύπικρος, which Cicero uses at *Att*. 5.21.4 (cf. Plautus' coinage *tragicomoedia* at *Am*. 59: see Oniga 1988: 132). A possible instance in Caelius (*palam secreto* at Cic. *Fam*. 8.1.4 (**213**) 'open secret'?) is discussed at XXVI.6.3, but appositional quasi-compounds (copulative) consisting of opposites do not seem to be found in classical Latin, and various analyses of *palam secreto* are offered. Note however in the later period Tert. *Val*. 10.3 *ibi demum pater, motus aliquando, quem supra diximus Horon per Monogenem Nun in haec promit in imagine sua, feminam marem, quia et de patris sexu ita uariant* (of someone of indeterminate sex; cf. ἀνδρόγυνος, and see the passages at *TLL* VIII.423.55ff.).

3.2 Modifier + Modified et al.

3.2.1 uolens propitius

In early Latin (Cato and Plautus) this pair (see Hickson 1993: 61–2 for numerous examples from different periods; also Oakley 1998: 243 on Livy

3 Quasi-compounds and Pairs

7.26.4) always occurs in the same syntactic structure. It is used with the verb 'to be' or equivalent (see below on this point), and is complemented by a (personal) dative or string of datives. The instances in Cato are of this type: e.g. *Agr.* 134.2 *Iane pater, te hac strue ommouenda bonas preces precor uti sies uolens propitius mihi liberisque meis domo familiaeque meae* (translated e.g. by Dalby 1998 as '. . . I pray with good prayers that you be ready and favourable to me and my children, to my house and household'). The examples at 139 and 141.2 are structurally the same (with *precor uti sies* preceding, and *uolens propitius* complemented by datives). *Volens propitius* is regularly taken as an asyndeton (see e.g. Hofmann and Szantyr 1965: 828, Timpanaro 1994: 5, Courtney 1999: 65).

There is just one example (humorous: addressed to a door) in Plautus, which has a verb synonymous with the verb 'to be'. *Volens propitius* is again accompanied by a personal dative: *Cur.* 89 *potate, fite mihi uolentes propitiae,* 'imbibe, and be favorable and well-disposed toward me' (de Melo, Loeb). For *fite*, juxtaposed with the verb 'to be', in the same structure see *TLL* X.2.2054.30, citing *Act. lud. saec. Aug.* (*CIL* VI.32323 = *ILS* 5050 = Chapot and Laurot 2001, L41) 99 *estote fitote u<olente>s propitiae*. A string of datives follows, as in Cato.

At *TLL* X.2.2053.35 *uolens* is listed as a synonym of *propitius*, but is it? A difference is apparent if one rewrites the formula *precor uti sies . . .* with just one of the adjectives. *Precor uti sies propitius mihi liberisque meis* is acceptable ('I pray that you may be favourable to me and my children'), but that is not so of *precor uti sies uolens mihi liberisque meis*. What meaning does *uolens* have to justify the dative complement? The *OLD* has a separate entry for adjectival *uolens*, and under 1b it cites such religious examples with the description 'of gods, esp. used in invocations', but without any statement of its meaning in such contexts. At 1c it has a category (*alicui*) *uolenti esse*, 'to be welcome (to), accord with the wishes (of)', but this is not relevant to the prayer usage. At the head of the entry (1) the meanings are given 'desiring the action, experience, etc., concerned, willing', but again these do not easily fit the idea that the dative in the prayer formula is a complement of *uolens*. The datives of the old formula seem entirely dependent on *propitius*, and the question arises what the function of *uolens* is.

In classical Latin there is for the most part a change to the syntax of the *uolens propitius* formula, which removes the syntactic oddity of *uolens*. The original structure does not entirely disappear (we saw it above in an inscription; see further the text of Chapot and Laurot loc. cit. for another instance), but note by contrast Livy 24.38.8 *uos, Ceres mater ac Proserpina, precor, ceteri superi infernique di, qui hanc urbem hos sacratos lacus lucosque colitis, ut ita nobis uolentes propitii adsitis.* The verb in the formula is not *sitis* but *adsitis*, and *adsum*, 'am present for/to help', takes a dative (see *OLD* s.v.13b; see Hickson 1993: 67–9 on *adesse* in prayer language). The slight change of wording changes the syntax. The meaning is now 'that you may be present to help us, willing and favourable'. Whereas in the original formula *mihi* etc. had been dependent on (*uolens*) *propitius*, it is now dependent on *adsum*, and *uolens propitius* becomes an asyndetic secondary predicate/predicative adjunct. Once the pair is separated syntactically from *mihi* etc., the use of *uolens* is rendered normal: one can 'do something willing(ly)', *uolens*' in Latin as a matter of course.

In Livy all other uses of the formula are modified such that the addressee is asked, 'willing and favourable', to do something: 1.16.3 *pacem precibus exposcunt uti uolens propitius suam semper sospitet progeniem,* 7.26.4 *precatus deinde, si diuus, si diua esset qui sibi praepetem misisset, uolens propitius adesset,* 24.21.10 *precantes Iouem ut uolens propitius praebeat sacra arma pro patria,* 29.14.13 *precantibus ut uolens propitiaque urbem Romam iniret.* Note too 39.16.11 *omnia dis propitiis uolentibusque faciemus* (see Briscoe 2008: 279 on the text here). In another variant Horace too gives *uolens* the same function as it has in the passages of Livy above: *Odes* 3.30.16 *lauro cinge uolens, Melpomene, comam.*

I return to the original (early) formula, in which the datives complement *uolens propitius*. Since a dative would not fit *uolens* in classical Latin, either *uolens* must be given another meaning, such as 'favourable', or it must have a function in the pairing different from that of a straightforward coordinated element. There is nothing to be said for the first possibility that I know of. As far as I am aware a meaning of the type 'favourable', such that a dative would be a possible addition, is not otherwise attested. Moreover in a lustration formula quoted in one of the passages of Cato above, *uolentibus* applied to *diuis* clearly refers to the gods 'being willing': *Agr.* 141.1 *cum diuis uolentibus quodque bene eueniat* (see the next paragraph).

There are however other ways of construing the formula, first by taking *uolens* as a modifier of *propitius*. On this view the prayer would not be that the god be 'willing and favourable', but that he be 'willing to be favourable', or more literally 'willingly favourable'. See West (1966: 163), in reference to Hesiod *Th.* 28, on the Greek equivalent (ἐ)θέλων (or the like) and its implication: 'a common qualification in telling of a god's powers ... It explains why he does not always do what he is supposed to be able to' (see too Fraenkel 1950: 2.325). *Volens* would tone down the abruptness of a prayer *sies propitius mihi.* Servius Danielis on Virg. *Aen.*

3 Quasi-compounds and Pairs 49

457 seems to have been aware of such an interpretation: *aut 'uolens', quia cogi non potest si nolit: ut in sacrificiis 'uti uolens propitiusque'*.

Alternatively *uolens* may be treated as a secondary predicate with conditional force, = 'may you, (if) willing, be favourable', = 'may you be favourable, (if) willing'. On this interpretation *propitius* would be the primary predicate and *uolens* a secondary predicate. For the structure cf. Plaut. *As.* 568 *ubi sciens fideli infidus fueris*, 'where you were knowingly unfaithful to someone who trusted you', or 'where you, with full knowledge, were unfaithful to someone who trusted you'. The two possible interpretations of the structure here and in *uolens propitius* are difficult to decide between, but it is obvious that neither phrase is asyndetic (if one leaves aside the later development of *uolens propitius*).

In cases where *uolens* and *propitius* are coordinated (see Preuss 1881: 102–3; also Norden 1939: 19 n. 1) they are not in the original formula.

There is an equivalent or near-equivalent of *uolens propitius* in Umbrian, *fons pacer* (see XXII.4.3), which has been translated '(be) favourable (and) propitious' (see Poultney 1959, index s.vv. *fons, pacer* and his renderings of the text; also Untermann 2000: 302, 509–10). It is followed by a string of datives (see e.g. *Tab. Ig.* VIa.42, 50 etc.). Given that *fons* (translated 'merciful' by de Vaan 2008: 205 s.v. *Faunus*) is of the same root as *faueo* (so de Vaan loc. cit.; cf. too Untermann 2000: 302), it differs semantically from *uolens*, and could itself independently take a dative. The Umbrian pair is genuinely asyndetic. Indeed at *Tab. Ig.* VIa.23 both terms are separately used as predicates with the verb 'to be': *fos . sei . pacer . sei*, 'be favourable, be propitious'. The Umbrian pair cannot be used to explain the syntax of the Latin pair; the two pairs are only loosely parallel.

3.2.2 Some Pairs in Which One Term Is a (Predicative) Modifier of the Other

The members of some pairs have a close relationship with each other such that they seem to behave semantically (but not morphologically) as compounds; alternatively one might say that one term acts as an adverbial/predicative modifier of the other. This is particularly so of pairs consisting of adjectives and participles. On the general phenomenon see also Hofmann and Szantyr (1965: 172) and Mynors (1990: 306).

Virgil *G.* 1.163 *tardaque Eleusinae matris uoluentia plaustra* is translated by Fairclough (Loeb) as 'the slow-rolling wains of the Mother of Eleusis', a rendering (with hyphen) that implicitly gives *tarda uoluentia* the status of a compound. A conventional analysis would be that *tarda* is predicative, 'wagons rolling slow(ly)'. Such a predicative (> adverbial) use of an adjective is illustrated in association with a finite verb at e.g. *G.* 1.240–1 *mundus ... arduus ... | consurgit,* 'the celestial sphere rises steep(ly)'. If *consurgit* were converted into a participle, *arduus consurgens,* the pair would become in our terminology a quasi-compound, 'steep-rising'. For *tardus* standing as the first part of a genuine compound before a verbal element cf. *tardiloquus.*

Mynors (1990: 306) on *G.* 4.370 (*saxosusque sonans*) quotes Servius Danielis (at 4.366): *non ut duo intelligendum, 'saxosus et sonans', sed 'ob saxa sonans',* 'not to be understood as two words, "rocky and sounding", but as "rocky-sounding"'. Here Servius rules out coordination (asyndeton) of *saxosus* and *sonans,* and takes *saxosus* as a modifier of *sonans.*

A particularly good example is at Virg. *Aen.* 10.837: *ipse aeger anhelans | colla fouet* (see XXIV.2.1.1, 10). A possible translation would be, 'he himself, in pain, (and) gasping, bathes his neck', with the adjectives agreeing with the subject of the verb. Harrison (1991: 270) ad loc. aptly says 'closely together', and there may well be here a quasi-compound rather than a straightforward asyndeton. *Aeger* in this context means 'painful' (see *OLD* s.v. 5) and, significantly, at 5. 432 it modifies *anhelitus* in the phrase *aeger anhelitus* 'painful gasping'. Just as there *aeger* is adjectival with the verbal noun, in the present passage with the participle of the same root it surely has a predicative (adverbial) role, 'gasping painfully/in pain'.

Aen. 4.32 *solane perpetua maerens carpere iuuenta* could be translated 'will you, alone, sad, pine away for the whole of your youth?' (see XXIV.2.1.1, 4) This translation treats the two terms *sola* and *maerens* as asyndetic (but separated), in that it could be rephrased to include a coordinator. But here too the pair is close to a compound, 'alone-grieving, grieving on your own', with *sola* predicative. *Soli-* can occur as the first element in compounds, followed by a verbal form, as *soliuagus* (several times in Cicero).

For other Virgilian examples of adjective + participle see *G.* 2.182–3 *surgens oleaster ... | plurimus* ('springing up abundantly'), 2.377 *grauis incumbens scopulis arentibus aestas* (Loeb: 'brooding heavily over'), 3.28–9 *magnumque fluentem | Nilum* ('the Nile ... flowing full'), *Aen.* 8.392 *ignea rima micans percurrit ... nimbos* ('a fiery-flashing rift runs through the clouds'), 8.559 *haeret inexpletus lacrimans* ('inconsolably weeping'; the *OLD* s.v. *inexpletus* 2 classifies this with another example as 'quasi-advl.'), 10.696 *ipsa immota manens,* 12.902 *altior insurgens.*

For a possible example in Pacuvius see 239.6 (Schierl 2006) *grando mixta imbri largifico subita praecipitans cadit.* This is translated by Warmington (1936: 295, line 358) as 'sudden hail fell headlong, mingled plenteously with floods of rain'. *Subita* is thus rendered as an attribute of *grando.* But its placement does not support this interpretation. It is postponed by a long way and juxtaposed with *praecipitans*, with which it can be construed as a predicative modifier: 'hail mixed with abundant rain suddenly gushing headlong falls down'.

Here is a possible case from Sallust: *Jug.* 18.2 (55) *uagi palantes, quas nox coegerat sedes habebant* (cf. Livy 7.17.8 *multos populatores agrorum uagos palantes oppressit*, Fronto p. 205.28–9 *uagi palantes, nullo itineris destinato fini*). The force may be 'wandering (*palantes*) aimless(ly) (*uagi*)' or 'aimlessly wandering': note too Livy 5.44.5 *uagique per agros palantur*, where *uagi* seems to be a predicative modifier of a finite form of *palor*. However, in Livy the two words are in one place coordinated (21.61.2 *naualesque socios uagos palantesque per agros*), in which case they are a pair of juxtaposed synonyms. The relationship between the two was possibly variable, with *uagi* shifting between predicative modifier and synonym. On *palari* in general see Skard (1933: 44–5). See also Preuss (1881: 104).

Full compounds often have a present participial second element: for a list see Bader (1962: 438). Some have a first part with adverbial function: note for example *dulcisonans, lenicrepitans* (Bader 1962: 257–8) and *magnisonans* (Bader 258). This last may be compared with *magnum fluentem* in the *Georgics* above.

Timpanaro (1994: 5 n. 8), citing Löfstedt (1956: 2.112) (cf. id. 1911: 214), quotes Plaut. *Per.* 522 *liberalem uirginem furtiuam abductam ex Arabia penitissima* as not a genuine asyndeton, on the grounds that *furtiuam* has an adverbial role (with the perfect participle following). That however is a doubtful interpretation. *Furtiuus* means 'stolen' (see *OLD* s.v. 1, citing this passage), and the next phrase can be taken as explaining it ('stolen – carried off from the depths of Arabia') (see also Woytek 1982: 336–7 ad loc.). De Melo (Loeb), punctuating with commas after *uirginem* and *furtiuam*, translates: '(has brought) a free-born virgin (with him, of desirable appearance), kidnapped, abducted from the heart of Arabia'. Löfstedt however cites (112–13) a few interesting examples from late Latin in which an adjective may be adverbial, such as Amm. 22.15.30 *animalium species innumeras multas* (though *multas* has been subject to emendation). In an earlier period one would have expected the order *multas innumeras*, with the stronger term second and virtually a correction. Löfstedt's various examples are not exactly the same as those above from Virgil, in that the second element is not participial. He treats his cases as showing attraction: an expected adverb is attracted into adjectival form.

Cf. Hom. *Il.* 3.419 ἑανῷ <u>ἀργῆτι φαεινῷ</u>, 'robe bright shining', *Od.* 1.55 τοῦ θυγάτηρ <u>δύστηνον ὀδυρόμενον</u> κατερύκει, 'his daughter keeps him

52   II   Roles of Adjectives; Appositional Compounds; Hendiadys

back, wretched, wailing': is δύστηνον virtually adverbial, 'wretchedly wailing'? Note too Men. *Mis.* 696 ταυτὶ λέγει | ἄ[παν]τα κλάων ἀντιβολῶν, 'All this he said pleading, in tears!' (Arnott, Loeb). Arnott here has reversed the order of the participles in translation. The first may modify the second, 'tearfully entreating'.

It is not only juxtaposed adjectives and participles in Latin that may be so closely associated that one seems to have the role of modifier of the other. Usually however in these cases with other parts of speech a coordinator can be added and the pair classified as an asyndeton. I collect such pairs of less clear-cut interpretation in the next section.

3.2.3   Pairs of Uncertain Interpretation
3.2.3.1   Pairs of Verbs

Cic. *Att.* 2.22.1 (176) *uolitat furit;* nihil habet certi, 'he rushes wildly up and down . . .'

A single action is referred to, of frenzied rushing about. Shackleton Bailey's translation above is equivalent to rewriting as *uolitat furens*.

Cic. *Sest.* 21 (70) *et quod erat eo nomine ut ingenerata familiae frugalitas uideretur, fauebant gaudebant, et ad integritatem maiorum spe sua hominerm uocabant materni generis obliti*

The verbs express simultaneous acts, = *fauebant gaudentes*.

Sall. *Cat.* 6.5 (64) *at Romani domi militiaeque intenti festinare parare, alius alium hortari, hostibus obuiam ire, libertatem patriam parentisque armis tegere*

This pair refers to hasty preparation, with *festinare* easy to rewrite as a modifier (= *festinanter* or *festinantes parare*).

Sall. *Cat.* 31.2 (71) *festinare trepidare, neque loco neque homini quoiquam satis credere, neque bellum gerere neque pacem habere*

The pair could be paraphrased as *festinare trepidanter, trepide, trepidantes*.

Sall. *Jug.* 76.4 (77) *contra haec oppidani festinare parare*
= *festinanter parare* or *festinantes parare*.

Sall. *Hist.* inc. 9, p. 404 Ramsey (2015) (82) *diu noctuque laborare festinare*
= *laborare festinanter* or *festinantes*.

Livy 34.7.4 (48) *sed in purpura, quae teritur absumitur, iniustam quidem sed aliquam tamen causam tenacitatis uideo*, 'purple, which is rubbed away and destroyed'.

Teritur could be replaced by *terendo*, but equally the pair may be be taken to refer to a chronological sequence (= *teritur et absumitur*).

3 Quasi-compounds and Pairs

Tac. *Hist.* 2.70.3 (31) *aggerem armorum, strues corporum* intueri mirari
Another ambiguity. The pair may mean 'to look at in amazement' (*intueri mirantes*), or could refer to a temporal sequence.

Tac. *Ann.* 1.51.3 (129) pergerent properarent *culpam in decus uertere*
Possibly = *pergerent propere* or *properantes*

Tac. *Ann.* 4.50.4 (137) *cum Sabinus* circumire hortari, *ne* ...
There must be simultaneous acts referred to here: the referent went around giving encouragement, = *circumire hortans*.

I conclude this section with an interesting pair of imperatives from the *Lex Coloniae Genetiuae* (Crawford 1996: 1.415): CXXVIII.12–13 *II(uir) aed(ilis) pra<e>f(ectus)* ... *quicumque erit, is suo quoque anno mag(istratu) imperioq(ue)* facito curato, *quod eius fieri poterit, u(ti)* ... This is translated (p. 430): 'Whoever shall be IIvir, aedile or prefect ..., he during his own year, magistracy and *imperium* is to act and see, as far as shall be possible, ... that ...'. There is a relation of dependency between the two verbs, with the pair equivalent to *faciendum curato*. This construction of the two verbs occurs just a few lines later (18): *facienda curent*.

3.2.3.2 Pairs of Nouns

Sisenna, *FRH* II.26.F19 (XXX.2.1, 6) *Bassus,* assiduitate indulgitate *uictus*.
Could be rewritten *assidua indulgitate*.

Cic. *Phil.* 1.26 *denuntio* uim arma (18), 'I warn of armed violence/force of arms.'
The second noun seems to stand in a genitival relationship to *uim*, but there is the usual ambiguity. A few sentences earlier Cicero had written *an eo quod* ui et armis *omne sublatum est?*

Cic. *Sest.* 85 (14) *clamore concursu,* ui manu *gerebantur*.
Vis manus expresses the single idea 'physical force'.

Livy 7.30.23 salutem uictoriam, *lucem ac libertatem*, 'the salvation of victory, light and liberty'.
The second noun could be rewritten in the genitive, dependent on the first (see XXXI.3.7).

Livy 8.33.20 *propter Q. Fabium ciuitatem in* laetitia uictoria, *supplicationibus ac gratulationibus esse*.
One could rewrite with a genitive, as in the last passage, = *in laetitia uictoriae* (see XXXI.3.7).

Tac. *Hist.* 2.29.2 (5) <u>silentio patientia</u>, *postremo precibus ac lacrimis ueniam quaerebant*
Perhaps of 'silent suffering', = *tacita patientia*. A coordinator would however be possible.

3.2.3.3 Conclusions

All of the pairs above are interesting, in that they could be rephrased in the form of a noun + adjective, noun + genitive, or verb + some sort of modifier. However, they could also be rewritten with a coordinator, and are thus asyndetic. One way to classify them would be as cases of 'asyndetic hendiadys'. Hendiadys is a figure in which two terms linked by a coordinator are equivalent to a single term with a modifier (for Latin see Kühner and Stegmann 1955: II.26–7; on English see Huddleston and Pullum: 2002: 1302 n. 21). The pairs above are very similar to pairs that are cited to illustrate hendiadys, except that they lack explicit coordination. Battezzato (2018: 83) in his note on Eur. *Hec.* 70 makes an implicit connection between asyndeton expressing a single concept and hendiadys, by cross-referring to his note on 436–7, which is about (coordinated) hendiadys as expressing a single concept. On *Hec.* 70 δείμασι φάσμασιν he says: 'the two terms in asyndeton ... express a single concept ..., "fearful apparitions", "fearful dreams".' For a coordinated pair of verbs in Latin that could be rewritten with a finite verb and a participle, like some of the asyndetic pairs seen above at 3.2.3.1, see Catull. 83.4 *gannit et obloquitur*, 'nagging talk against me' (Lee 1991), = *ganniens obloquitur* (*gannio* was used of a dog snarling).

CHAPTER III

Asyndeton Versus Coordination, an Introduction

1 The Antiquity of Asyndeton versus Syndetic Coordination

It is sometimes stated or implied that asyndeton is older than syndetic coordination. This is a view that is put bluntly by Timpanaro (1994: 7): 'Senza dubbio l'asindeto è più antico dell'uso di congiunzioni copulative.' He was aware of the frequency of *-que* compared with asyndeton in what he calls *carmina*, and therefore falls back on the idea that the few instances of asyndeton are archaisms of a type that was losing ground (1994: 8). Luiselli (1969: 165–6) likewise says that in *carmina* syndetic coordination is more common than asyndetic, but suggests that asyndeton was probably more ancient and that it was gradually replaced later by syndetic coordination. But why should asyndeton have been more ancient than explicit coordination? It is to be assumed that underlying the belief is a sense that absence of coordinators must be more 'primitive'. In fact the coordinator that in Latin has the form *-que* must be very ancient, as it has cognates in a wide variety of early Indo-European languages (see e.g. De Vaan 2008: 506; also Penney 2005: 40–3, and particularly Dunkel 1982). Dunkel (1982: 141) simply says: 'Oldest were asyndeton and single *-$k^w e$*.'

Discussions of pairs called 'merisms', which are themselves regarded as going back to an early stage of Indo-European, show a mixture of syndetic and asyndetic coordination. See Gonda (1959: 346), stating that such expressions (the chapter is about 'Complementary Word Groups'), 'whether they are "polar" or not, may be syndetic, asyndetic, or anaphoric'. West's examples (2007: 100) from the Rigveda of the merisms 'gods and men' and 'immortals and mortals' = 'all intelligent beings' contain the coordinator *ca*, and he quotes equivalent expressions from the *Iliad* with coordination. He observes (2007: 100), after discussing various cases, that 'in some of these examples there is no "and"', adding that '[f]urther instances of such asyndeton will appear in the following paragraphs'. He does immediately state that the asyndeton must have been early ('It is no doubt an ancient

55

56 III Asyndeton Versus Coordination, an Introduction

traditional feature of these pairings'), but that is not to say that coordination was not ancient too. Early variations between coordination and asyndeton in different languages are implicit in Watkins' examples of merisms (1995: 43–4, and Chapter XVII). For example, 'two-footed and four-footed' creatures is an expression quoted (1995: 210) from the Rigveda with a coordinator and from Umbrian without (*dupursus peturpursus*: see XXII.4.6). The pairs 'men/ livestock' and 'seen/unseen' occur with a coordinator in Latin but without one in the Iguvine tablets (Watkins 1995: 42, 43, 210–11). It is possible to cite asyndetic expressions from Latin that were undoubtedly old, but equally there are old expressions, such as proverbs, that have coordination. The proverbial expression (clearly originating from sacrifices) *inter sacrum saxumque* ('between the sacrificial victim and the knife', with *saxum* denoting the ancient flint knife of priests), occurs only with coordination (Plaut. *Capt.* 617, *Cas.* 970). An early pair is in the formula for the taking of the auspices at Varro *Ling.* 7.8, *templum tescumque/templa tescaque* (see Norden 1939: 16–30, and now de Melo 2019: 2.905–6, who deletes the -*que* with *tesca*. The combination occurs three times, twice in the singular and once in the plural. It either has coordination throughout, or, if de Melo is followed, both a syndetic and an asyndetic form in coexistence. On the coordinated formula *bene ac/atque prospere* see XXIII.3 and Hickson (1993: 70–1). *Ab acia et acu*, 'down to the smallest detail', has coordination (see Otto 1890: 3, s.v. *acus*, and also Schmeling 2011: 322 on Petron. 76.11). Norden (1939: 18–19) collects numerous old pairs with both coordination and asyndeton. At XI.2, *TLL* V.1.915.12ff. is cited on *di deaeque*, which is very common, whereas the asyndetic variant occurs only 'here and there'. In early prayers -*que* is far more common linking pairs than is asyndetic coordination (see XXII.3.5 for statistics). In what must be some of the most ancient Latin extant, the prayers in Cato *Agr.* 141 (see XXII.3.2), -*que* links pairs nine times but there is only one instance of asyndeton bimembre, and that in a significant context (141.2 *fruges frumenta, uineta uirgultaque*). Here we have the structure asyndeton bimembre + coordinated pair favoured by Latin from the earliest times (see e.g. XIX.1). The asyndeton occurs not because it is the 'earliest form of coordination' and this is an early text, but because it suits the ancient structure (and points to the coexistence of asyndeton and coordination at an early period). Similarly (see XXIII.3; also XXII. 4.2, 6.3) in an augural context in Plautus (*As.* 259–60) there are two pairs of bird names almost juxtaposed, one coordinated the other asyndetic (*picus et cornix ab laeua, coruos parra ab dextera*) whereas in an almost identical augural context in the Iguvine tablets (VIa.1 *parfa. curnase. dersua. peiqu. peica. merstu*) both pairs of bird names are asyndetic, and the two pairs are again slightly separated.

2 *Dvandva Compounds* 57

The formulae must have been of ancient type in Italy, but Umbrian religious language was far more asyndetic than that of Latin (see XXII.4 on asyndeton in Umbrian).

Except in some legal texts (see below), explicit coordination of pairs outnumbered asyndetic throughout the history of Latin. For example, at XXIV.9 explicitly coordinated pairs are listed from Lucretius and Virgil, and these far exceed asyndeta in the two writers. Often such pairs (particularly when -*que* is the coordinator), have features of assonance or meaning that tend to be associated by scholars with asyndetic pairs. Such evidence brings out the rarity of asyndeton bimembre, and the need for caution in explaining its motivation. See also XXVII.3 on the extremely frequent coordinated pairs in Catullus. These again include types prone to be seen as typically asyndetic. Lucilius (see XXV.6) had a liking for coordinated alliterative pairs, and coordinated pairs with the same fore-element. Again, asyndeton is outnumbered. Coordinated pairs are also far more frequent than asyndetic in all genres in Horace (see XXIX.4.1), and again are often of the stylistically marked types referred to above.

I stress again that I am not suggesting that asyndeton was not old, but am questioning the implication that a prehistoric transition took place, from asyndeton alone to asyndeton and syndetic coordination in competition. The antiquity of asyndeton, at least in Indic, is established by a class of compounds (dvandvas), but the evidence provided by these, or what have been taken to be these, for Latin is far less satisfactory. I say something now about dvandva compounds (they are alluded to briefly also at II.3.1). For Latin I concentrate particularly on the significance or otherwise of one possible dvandva compound to asyndeton.

2 Dvandva Compounds

I comment briefly on dvandva compounds because the structure (of some of them) is potentially relevant to the early currency of asyndeton bimembre. A typical example of such a compound, from Latin, is *quindecim*, which has two components, denoting 5 + 10 = 15. Would it have originated from an asyndetic pairing? Before coming back to that question I say a little about the (confused) definitions of dvandva compounds, and then turn to two recent discussions that are clear-cut.

Dvandvas have been called 'copulative compounds', 'coordinating compounds' or 'co-compounds' (see Kiparsky 2010: 302). Bader, for example, uses the term 'composés coordonnants' (1962: 333). Leumann (1977: 403) refers to 'Kopulativkomposita', adding that they are also called

'Additionskomposita'. Buck (1933: 354) adopts 'copulative' compounds, with the definition, 'The parts are co-ordinate, and may be more than two.' He refers e.g. to *suouetaurilia*, 'sacrifice of a pig, sheep and bull' (but see further below). See also Oniga (1988: 131–3) for discussion of terminology and bibliography. Definitions, some of them recent, are scattered about in the literature, with varying degrees of precision. Scalisi and Bisetto (2009: 36) make the point that 'dvandva' is often used for indicating coordinate compounds as a whole, with no account taken of the fact that 'coordination in compounding has different outcomes'. Coordination can '(a) associate two individual elements without reference to any of them as a separate entity, as in true *dvandva* compounds', and they allude to the Vedic compound for 'father–mother' = 'parents'. On the other hand coordination can '(b) express two "properties" associated with an entity, as in modern formations such as *poet–novelist*'. Kastovsky (2009: 332) observes that dvandva compounds are also called 'copulative' or 'coordinative', and then in a note (16) says that the 'term "copulative" is misleading, since genuine *dvandvas* are additive and denote a combination of two entities where none is dominant'. In the text he cites e.g. Vedic *páñcaśa* = Lat. *quindecim* = Germ. *fünfzehn* = Eng. *fifteen*, Germ. *taubstumm* 'deaf and dumb', and various compounds denoting complementary family relationships, 'father and son', 'son-in-law and father-in-law' and 'nephew and uncle'. See also for example Wackernagel (1905: 158).

I move on to a recent classification of possible dvandvas in the Rigveda by Insler (1998), which is very precise. He points out (1998: 285) that in the Rigveda there are three distinct types of what might be called dual dvandvas.

Type 1, as in the term (*dyā́vāpr̥thivī́*) for 'Heaven and Earth', has two characteristic features. 'First, each member of the pairing receives dual inflection and second, each term equally receives an udátta accent.'

Type 2, as in the term for 'Indra and Agni' (*indrā́gnī́*), is far less frequent. Insler notes: 'In this type the dual inflection of each member persists, but it is only the final member of the pair that receives the udátta accent, and specifically on the final syllable of the second stem of the dvandva, regardless of the position of the udátta in the underlying word.'

On Type 3 Insler says: 'The third type is found in the Rigveda only in the formation *indravā́yū́* "Indra and Vāyu". It differs from type 2 in that the first member of the dvandva appears in stem form. Thus dual dvandvas of this type have been fully assimilated to the grammatical status of compounds. For later Vedic texts it is in fact this third type that becomes predominant.'

2 *Dvandva Compounds*   59

Insler's conclusions (1998: 285) are worth quoting:

> Western editors and grammarians cite all forms of dual dvandvas as if they were compounds. For the second and third types of Rigvedic dvandvas there is little doubt that this analysis is correct. A single accent is sufficient testimony to the fact that both elements have been integrated into a single word, even though the vestige of original dual inflection survives in the first member of type 2. But in the instances of the first type of dual dvandvas, where each of the composite terms receives inflection and accent, is it correct to consider such formations as compounds? ... [I]t is the purpose of this paper to demonstrate that dual dvandvas of type 1 represent two independent words in the poetry of the Rigveda.

Insler then produces two arguments that the combinations of type 1 are independent words. The point is made, for example, that this older type (1) 'is able to span the caesura' of the verse, whereas 'the younger form, with single accent, is forced into the pre-caesura position' (288).

A more recent discussion of the earliest dvandvas, by Kiparsky (2010), is along much the same lines. He states (2010: 302) that in the earliest Vedic each of the 'two constituents [of a dvandva compound] has a separate word accent and what looks like a dual case ending. These compounds (also known as copulative compounds, coordinating compounds, or co-compounds) are invariably definite, have two members, and refer to conventionally associated pairs of divine or human beings, or to pairs of personified natural and ritual objects.' He cites e.g. from the earliest Vedic pairs for 'rain and wind' (*parjányāvātā*), 'father and mother' = 'parents' (*mātárāpitárā*).

Kiparsky continues (302):

> The type rapidly recedes after the oldest stage of the language recorded in the Rigveda, and is completely superseded in Classical Sanskrit by a highly productive, regularized type of dvandva compound that, like other compounds, has a single accent, no internal case ending, and a singular, dual, or plural case ending on the final member depending on the cardinality of the compound's denotation; can have more than two members; and can be indefinite and inanimate.

One example cited is a different form of the term for 'father and mother', *mātāpitarau* (dual).

Kiparsky (2010: 303) refers to the Vedic dvandvas as 'synchronically problematic'. He says: 'They are a hybrid construction, patterning in some ways like syntactic phrases *built from separate words by asyndetic coordination*, in others like single compound words' (my emphasis). Despite 'their archaic status in Vedic, they are probably an Indic innovation, with no

60   III Asyndeton Versus Coordination, an Introduction

exact counterpart even in Iranian'. He adds in a footnote (303 n. 5) that some 'other Indo-European languages have dvandva compounds, but they do not share the formal peculiarities of the Vedic ones', and goes on to state: 'I assume that they arose independently of the Sanskrit dvandvas.'

It seems to be the case then that Vedic dvandva compounds arose from asyndetic phrases. Given their special character in Indic, as emphasised by Kiparsky, it would not necessarily follow that in other languages their line of development was the same.

Bader (1962: 340–3) argues that there are no true dvandvas in Latin, though she does allow that there is one special type of coordinating compound common to all languages, that is numerals such as *quindecim* (343). The Latin terms (it is argued) usually claimed to be dvandvas, such as *suouetaurilia*, are adjectival and have a suffix, whereas true dvandvas are substantives (341) (the suffix of *suouetaurilia* is adjectival, but such terms were sometimes substantivised in the neuter: see Leumann 1977: 350). Also, the elements of the compound just cited, she suggests, are not themes but ablatival, *su* + *oue* + *tauro* (341): *suouetaurilia* is thus arguably formed by suffixing *-ilia* to the asyndetic ablatival sequence. It is a secondary formation (342), arising from an asyndeton. *Su* may not be the usual ablatival form of *sus*, but it is 'légitimé par le pluriel *sŭbus*' (341) (an argument that is not compelling: could this be the form *sue* with elision?).

Palmipedalis (for which cf. Leumann 1977: 403) for its part also has attested a variant form *palmo-* (Bader 1962: 289: 'la forme authentique'), and it is suggested by Bader that the adjective is formed, in the supposed manner of *suouetaurilia*, from *palmo* + *pede* + *alis* (with *palmi-* a remodelling to bring the term into line with the structure of compounds in Latin). If this is the case, it is to be assumed (cf. Bader 146) that the noun *palmipes* (a measurement of a palm and a foot; first in Vitruvius) is derived from *palmipedalis*. So at TLL X.1.154.59 it is accepted that *palmipes* is 'retrograde a *palmipedalis*'. On this view *palmipes* would not be a real early dvandva compound.

For our purposes it does not matter whether we define e.g. *palmipedalis* as a dvandva compound or not. If it does originate as an ablative phrase (which, it has to be said, remains uncertain given the dubious status of the form *palmopedalis*), need that phrase have been asyndetic? How are such measurements expressed in Latin when the two elements are given a separate identity? Cato at *Agr.* 135.6–7 gives measurements using these and comparable measurement terms by means both of asyndetic and syndetic coordination: 6 *orbis ... crassos pedem et palmum ... trapetum latum p. IIII et palmum, inter miliarium et labrum pes unus digitus unus*, 7 *orbis altos p. III dig. III, crassos p. I et digit. II.* Given this variability, must one assume an earlier system of rigid asyndetic coordination in measurements in Latin to account for the compound, or could the compound have developed out of such pairings whatever the forms of coordination used? The second possibility must be the right one. In determining the origin of such structures one should not go back to the phrasal pairs in the Rigveda, and not least because of Kiparsky's suggestion that Indic might have been exceptional in these formations. There is such constant alternation in Latin between asyndeton and coordination in specific pairs of words (such as those of measurement seen above) that the compound could have been based on the frequent association of the two terms, not on the specific method of their coordination. If, for argument's sake, there was a commonplace coordinated phrase *palmus et pes*, and if through frequency of use its parts tended to coalesce into a compound, that compound would assume the normal structure of Latin compounds and would not have an embedded coordinator.

I conclude that, while in Indic some compounds did originate from asyndetic phrases, the category dvandva is not as straightforward for Latin as might be thought (and indeed needs further assessment), and that certainly in the case of one term of measurement asyndeton is not a necessary precursor of the compound. A compound numeral likewise might have developed from either a coordinated or uncoordinated pairing. Copulative compounds that might attract the label 'dvandva' are not infrequently late, such as *dulcacidus* (see *TLL* s.v.), and these do not require an asyndetic pairing as their precursor. Dvandva compounds are best kept out of the discussion of the antiquity of asyndeton in Latin.

3 Textual Criticism: Asyndeton versus Coordination

In the classical period editors of texts (prose in particular) face a particular problem. Any two terms that tend to occur together may be coordinated with any of the several Latin coordinators, or paired asyndetically. For example, in his large collection of alliterative pairs, Wölfflin (1933) always draws attention to the different forms of coordination (syndetic or asyndetic) attested in any pairing, and Preuss (1881) too, though his main concern is with asyndeta, cites coordinated variants. Throughout this book when collecting asyndetic pairs from different authors I have made a point of citing alternatives with coordinators from the same authors and/ or others. For example, at Cic. *Fam.* 5.8.5 (**197, 198**) (*in omnibus publicis priuatis, forensibus domesticis, tuis, amicorum, hospitum, clientium negotiis*)

III Asyndeton Versus Coordination, an Introduction

two versions of the 'public/private' contrast are juxtaposed in asyndeton. But compare e.g. Cic. *Leg. agr.* 2.64 *quorum sapientiam temperantiamque in publicis priuatisque, forensibus domesticisque rebus perspexeratis*, and see also *Off.* 1.4 *neque publicis neque priuatis neque forensibus neque domesticis in rebus*, *Tusc.* 1.84 *et domesticis et forensibus solaciis ornamentisque priuati*.

Or again, in XXX it is pointed out in the commentaries that the following asyndetic pairs which Sallust allows are also attested with coordinators, in Sallust himself or elsewhere: for nouns see *Cat.* 10.2 (cited before 1) *labores pericula*, 3 *pudor pudicitia*, 15 *caedes incendia*, 17 *patria parentes*, 18 *domus uilla*, 23 *domus patria*, 26 *fama fides*, 27 *urbs ager*, 31 *arma tela*, 32 *equi uiri*, 37 *locus tempus*, 39 *strepitus clamor*, 40 *dextra sinistra*, 43 *uiri arma*, 47 *socius amicus*; for adjectives, 51 *Graecus Latinus*, 55 *uagus palans*, 56 *acer bellicosus*, 58 *iners inbellis*, 59 *uarius incertus*; for verbs, 74 *colo obseruo*, 76, 80 *caedo/occido capio*; and finally, for adverbs, 83 *procul iuxta*.

So at XXVI.7.7 there are listed all the asyndetic pairs in the sample of Cicero for which elsewhere there are coordinated variants (of 209 pairs I found 47 with coordinated equivalents in Cicero himself or other writers).

The problem for editors (particularly of prose texts) alluded to above is this. Since methods of coordination are so variable, a time-honoured procedure of editors faced with a textual problem is all but ruled out. If a pairing attested a number of times with one coordinator or another turns up just once in asyndeton, it is not acceptable to add a coordinator merely because of what looks like 'normal' usage, though editors do indeed sometimes resort to listing coordinated examples to justify emendation. Any conventional pair may be used asyndetically just once ad hoc, and it hardly matters what the majority practice is. If majority usage were to be the decisive criterion for emending, one ought also to be attempting to regularise the coordinators used in particular combinations. Since scribes were given both to omitting coordinators and adding them, the decisions of editors are bound to be arbitrary, at least sometimes. An attempt will be made to establish some criteria for determining whether an asyndeton is likely to be right, and I will return to this question. Cic. *Fam.* 5.8.5 above, for example, is from a letter to the consul Crassus that contains numerous asyndeta, presumably because Cicero was hostile to Crassus and was writing with insincerity, in the words of Shackleton Bailey (see on Cicero 197, 198). The accumulation of asyndeta looks like a distancing device (by contrast Cicero uses asyndeta in the letters to Atticus comparatively rarely), and it would be unconvincing to emend instances away.

Here are some criteria or procedures that will come up and be discussed in detail later. I merely list them here.

3 Textual Criticism: Asyndeton versus Coordination

First, different manuscripts may of course have varying authority, and it is to be assumed that in a good critical edition an editor will take account of that fact. It may (e.g.) be the case that an oddity of coordination is recurrent in one manuscript, and an editor may have to decide whether another manuscript has simply emended away what is taken to be abnormal. On the lack of authority of a particular manuscript see e.g. XXVIII.2.1 on Caes. *Civ.* 1.30.4 *in Lucanis Brutiisque*, with Damon's comments cited there on the manuscript S.

Second, since there is no point quoting against an asyndeton examples of the same pair coordinated, given that any recurrent pair may show varying syndetic and asyndetic coordination (see above), in one chapter in particular (XXVIII, that on Caesar) I have adopted a different method of assessment. Faced with a pair of place names in the *Bellum ciuile* that may be asyndetic, I did not restrict myself to citing the examples of the same pair, with or without coordinator, elsewhere in the work, but instead collected all coordinated place names (whether syndetic or asyndetic) in the text to see if a pattern emerged (XXVIII.2.1). There is indeed a pattern. The vast majority of place names are explicitly coordinated, with the exception of a tiny handful of asyndetic examples, all in significant structures. The pair in question is itself in such a structure, and the asyndeton can stand.

The same procedure is followed in assessing a few other pairs in the work. To judge two possible asyndetic military pairs (6, 11), I collected all military pairs in the *Bellum ciuile* (see XXVIII, Appendix 2) and found only coordination, and since the above two pairs are not in significant structures I decided against asyndeton. On the other hand asyndeton can be defended in the military pair *auxilia equitatum* (5) because of the phrasal structure in which it occurs. Similarly a unique case of anaphoric prepositional asyndeton (14) is defended not only because it is in a direct speech but also because of the structure of the sentence.

Or again, different writers vary in their willingness to admit asyndetic pairs dependent on a single preposition. Merely considering the question whether the terms in question are attested together in asyndeton may lead nowhere, whereas a full collection of the attestations of all pairs of nouns dependent on prepositions in the author or text may help to establish whether an asyndetic phrase with this syntactic feature is likely in that author (see XXVIII, Appendix 1).

Third, as has been implied several times above, asyndetic pairs are often located in certain structures, mainly of the types that I have called 'accumulations' (see XIX). A pair with conflicting forms of coordination in the manuscript tradition embedded within such a structure may well be easy to

III Asyndeton Versus Coordination, an Introduction

defend as asyndetic. Various structures are arguably the most important determinants of asyndeta bimembria. See e.g. XXI.2 on Cicero 159 for a structural sequence in which an asyndeton bimembre is to be expected, yet a coordinator has been added by an editor; an identical structure is quoted from a speech, where editors do not emend. 'Accumulations' are listed or classified in numerous places in this book, for example from Sallust at XXX.3.3.3e, Tacitus *Histories* at XXX.4.2.4e, and the *Annals* at XXX.5.2.3. At XXX.6.2 specific structures in Sallust and Tacitus are identified and compared. At XXVI.7.2.1 there is a classification of the structures in which pairs of nouns in Cicero occur asyndetically, and at XXVI.7.7 further comment is offered on structures that favoured asyndeton (see also XXVI.7.2.3, 7.3.1). Note too, on Plautus XXIII.7, Lucilius XXV.1.1.2, Horace XXIX.2.1.2 (on accumulations in the *Satires*).

Fourth, in Latin at an early period (and to some extent later) genre was one influence on asyndetic versus syndetic coordination, though it is only a weak criterion for an editor addressing a textual problem. In early prayers *-que* was the norm rather than asyndeton (see above), whereas in legal and official language asyndeton remained prominent until the late Republic, and in one or two such texts asyndeton bimembre was used exclusively instead of coordinated pairs (see XXII.2.1). Thereafter it declined (as seen for example in the change in which pairs of consular names were presented: see XXII.9; similarly some old legal asyndetic pairings, such as *ruta caesa, loca lautia, sarta tecta, uelitis iubeatis*, were eventually challenged by syndetic substitutes: see XXII.5). Nor indeed had asyndeton necessarily been the predominating type of coordination even in the earliest official documents: in the decree of L. Aemilius of 189 BC *-que* is the norm (see XXII.1), a fact which suggests that there were changes of taste from time to time (and drafter to drafter), rather than a relentless language history in one direction. One should allow the possibility that syndetic and asyndetic coordination had been in competition from an early period.

Here are a few other generic variations. In Horace's *Odes*, which were influenced by forms of Greek poetry, asyndeton bimembre hardly occurs (XXIX.2.3.1), whereas he allows some mundane types, particularly of adjectives, in the *Satires* (XXIX.2.1, 2.1.5). In Cicero's philosophica asyndetic pairs of opposites are frequent (XXVI.7.3.1), whereas they are hardly found in our sample of the speeches (XXVI.7.2.6). Contrasts of opposites, often asyndetic, were a feature of philosophical discourse (see on Cicero 94–8). And in Cicero's letters to Atticus asyndeton bimembre plays only a moderate part (see XXVI.7.4.1), whereas at high points in major political speeches it is common (XXVI.7.1, 7.6).

3 Textual Criticism: Asyndeton versus Coordination 65

Fifth, certain semantic categories seem to have favoured asyndetic pairings (e.g. verbs denoting violent acts, negative adjectives particularly with the *in*-prefix), and semantics and structures may come together to motivate omission of a coordinator. See e.g. for Cicero, XXVI.7.8, for Sallust, XXX.3.3.2 and for Tacitus, XXX.5.2.3; see in general XV. A disputed asyndeton may sometimes gain support from belonging to a particular semantic type, but we will suggest later (XXXII.3.4) that the semantics of a pairing has only a limited influence in prompting asyndetic coordination of the members.

CHAPTER IV

Lists of Two Types

1 Introduction

The term 'list' is not particularly helpful in characterising asyndeton and its types, though it (or an equivalent) does have a place in the literature. One 'special type' of asyndeton, according to Hofmann and Szantyr (1965: 830), is 'asyndeton enumerativum'. But virtually any asyndetic sequence, particularly of names, nouns or adjectives, may be seen as a list. A series of adjectives describing the physical features or character of a person is a list of personal characteristics, the itinerary of a traveller is a list of places, the names of persons appointed to some organisation for a fixed period make up a list of officials or officers, and so on. When is an asyndetic sequence not a list? A pair or series of verbs describing actions in a temporal sequence (*they stopped, turned, fled*) would not be well described as a list. Pairs of terms with certain semantic relationships, such as opposites of various sorts (*left/right; up/down; good/bad, go/return*), are not list-like. A pair of verbs consisting of a simplex followed by its compound is not a list. It may be more helpful to identify types of lists. One of these, of some importance in relation to asyndeton, I will call 'open-ended' or composed of 'illustrations'. I start however with a different type, which is perhaps more familiar to anyone using the term 'list'. This type expresses a totality or finite set.

2 Lists as Totalities

A list is perhaps most typically a string of names or items that constitute a totality, and may be without any explicit verbal syntax. A shopping list, for example, is the totality of things a person believes he or she must buy, and it may be set out without a verb (one would rarely write *buy A, B, C...*). A menu comprises the items offered at a dinner, and it is (usually) intended as complete. Listed items are not infrequently written one under another. Sometimes in Latin the members of a list may have an implied syntax, in that, for example, they may be expressed in the accusative case, with a verb absent but easily understood (see Adams 2013: 226–34 on the syntax of lists in Latin; also id. 1995a: 114–16). Alternatively, items may be in the nominative, which was the unmarked or neutral ('default') case. Such lists in Latin include names of those cursed in a curse tablet or of those present on an official occasion, and foodstuffs to be eaten or grown. I give some illustrations of asyndetic Latin lists expressing totalities.

A striking example of a dinner list is at Macrobius, *Sat.* 3.13.12, quoted from the fourth digest of Metellus Pius, *pontifex maximus* from 81–64 BC; the banquet can be dated to 70 BC (see Kaster 2011: 92 n. 102): *cena haec fuit: ante cenam echinos ostreas crudas quantum uellent, peloridas sphondylos, turdum asparagos subtus, gallinam altilem, patinam ostrearum peloridum, balanos nigros, balanos albos; iterum sphondylos, glycymaridas urticas ficedulas, lumbos capruginos aprugnos, altilia ex farina inuoluta, ficedulas, murices et purpura. in cena sumina, sinciput aprugnum, patinam piscium, patinam suminis, anates, querquedulas elixas, lepores, altilia assa, amulum, panes Picentes.* Here is the translation of Kaster (Loeb): 'This was the dinner: as a prelude, sea-urchins, raw oysters (as many as they wanted), cockles and mussels, thrush over asparagus, fattened hen, a dish of baked oysters and cockles, white and black acorn-mollusks; mussels again, clams, jellyfish, fig-peckers, loin of roe-deer, loin of boar, fattened fowl wrapped in dough, fig-peckers, murex and purple-shell; for the main courses, sow's udders, boar's cheek, a dish of baked fish, a dish of baked sow's udder, ducks, boiled water-fowl, hares, fattened fowl roasted, gruel, and bread of Picenum.'

The whole menu, with its large number of components, is asyndetic (though the above translation has the usual English 'end-of-list coordination'). Within it there are embedded asyndetic pairs, three of these (underlined) comprising single words. The first (*peloridas sphondylos,* 'cockles and mussels') is established as a unitary pair partly because it is separated from what precedes by an intervening clause, partly by the different structure of the following phrase *turdum asparagos subtus* ('thrush, asparagus beneath'), and partly by its semantics. The second pair (*ostrearum peloridum*) consists of genitives dependent on the same word, *patinam*. The third (*capruginos aprugnos*) consists of adjectives agreeing with the noun preceding, *lumbos* ('loin of roe-deer, of boar'). For adjectives of material in asyndeton, as in this last pair, cf. Cato *Agr.* 37.2 *frondem iligneam querneam.* Other unitary (phrasal) pairs are identifiable, such as *balanos nigros, balanos albos. Turdum asparagos subtus* 'thrush, asparagus beneath' is also a pair, made up of a noun and another noun with an adverbial specifier. There is only one coordinator in the whole

IV Lists of Two Types

menu, *ficedulas, murices et purpuras*. The *murex* and *purpura* were types of shellfish yielding a purple dye. There is not (it seems) end-of-list coordination following *ficedulas*, because the shellfish constitute a unitary pair.

The totality here consists of the complete dinner menu. I stress in passing that lists often have structures or internal unities, as this one does. For this feature discussed in relation to lists in English see Griffiths (2018: 17–20, and the whole of Chap. 1, 'Lists'; also Goody 1977: 74–111, and particularly 103–4 on grouping in lists). For Latin note e.g. Enn. *Ann.* 240–1 *Iuno Vesta Minerua Ceres Diana Venus Mars | Mercurius Iouis Neptunus Volcanus Apollo*, a list of the twelve great gods grouped according to sex (see Skutsch 1985: 424–5 for further details). For a list of types of humans set out in a striking order see Catull. 63.63, cited at I.10. Or again, at Cato *FRH* 5.F76 (*signis statuis elogiis historiis*) there are not four miscellaneous items but two pairs (see XXX.2.2, 8), a fact that is potentially relevant to the punctuation of the text. For prolonged sequences of unitary pairs (opposites) see particularly on Cicero **94–8**. In long sequences variable and even more complicated patterns may be found (see e.g. on Pacuvius **6–8** at XXIV.6.3 and, notably, quoted on Cicero **94–8**, Cic. *Orat.* 131, where a sequence has a particularly contrived pattern). On the other hand a list without identifiable extended patterns may have an occasional embedded pair (see e.g. Cicero **99** on *recta honesta*; note too the list from Robert Burton, *The Anatomy of Melancholy* discussed by Griffiths 2018: 19, which has at least one pair, *lords, ladies*, in a list of categories of persons). I will often in this book comment on 'embedded pairs'.

Asyndetic dinner lists are also found in literary texts. At Hor. *Sat.* 2.8.9–10 (*acria circum | rapula lactucae radices, qualia lassum | peruellunt stomachum, siser allec, faecula Coa*) the six items are split into two groups of three by the intervening descriptive clause. A similar intrusive clause (introduced by *quantum*) is in the menu above. A shorter dinner list is at *Sat.* 2.8.27: *nos, inquam, cenamus auis conchylia piscis*. Note too Plin. *Ep.* 1.15.2 *paratae erant lactucae singulae, cochleae ternae, oua bina, halica cum mulso et niue, ... oliuae betacei cucurbitae bulbi, alia mille non minus lauta*.

Similarly recipes may be asyndetic. Note e.g. Apicius 9.10.2 *teritur piper <cum> ligustico timo origano ruta careota melle*. A 'list of rations' at *CIL* IV.5380 has foodstuffs in asyndeton (three in number) (see Adams 2013: 230). On the other hand variations in the pattern of coordination in such lists may occur. See Apicius 9.10.6 *ius in mugile salso: piper ligusticum cuminum cepa menta ruta calua careota mel acetum sinape et oleum*, where there is end-of-list coordination (a common structure in recipes in Apicius).

2 Lists as Totalities

For an asyndetic shopping list see Plaut. *Cas.* 493–5 *emito sepiolas lepadas lolligunculas | hordeias ... | soleas.* For a list of leftovers (*reliquiae*) see *Cur.* 323 *pernam abdomen sumen sueris glandium.* For asyndetic lists of produce in Greek see Huitink and Rood (2019: 166).

I turn to lists of names, which, as mentioned above, are often asyndetic totalities. The *SC de Bacchanalibus* (*ILLRP* 511) begins with a section containing the following information: *sc(ribundo) arf(uerunt) M. Claudi(us) M. f., L. Valeri(us) P. f., Q. Minuci(us) C. f.* More striking is an edict of Cn. Pompeius Strabo, cos. 89 BC (*ILLRP* 515), in which some *equites Hispani* were made Roman citizens. The bulk of the document, following an introductory phrase *in consilio [fuerunt]*, is made up of many dozens of personal names in asyndeton. There is no need to illustrate at length asyndetic lists of names in curse tablets. The Myconos *defixio* (see Adams 2003: 680, id. 2013: 227), for example, has about twenty names (in a mixture of accusative and nominative forms) in asyndeton. *Tab. Sulis* 9 as it is extant has an asyndetic list of nine names, some of them accompanied by indicators of status (*seruus, uxor*).

It would no doubt be possible to illustrate many other lists of diverse items forming totalities. I mention only Cato *Agr.* 13, which has an asyndetic list of pieces of equipment (with numbers accompanying the items) needed for a pressing room (*torcularium*): see Adams (2013: 230).

An important characteristic of the above examples is that the lists are long. The longer a list that has a completeness to it, the more likely it is to be asyndetic. Note the variation between the following two clauses from a recipe in Apicius (7.4.1): *teres piper ligusticum anetum cuminum silfium, bacam lauri unam,* but *suffundis liquamen et passum modicum.* Cf. 2.3.2 *cepam, porrum concisum, ius crudum misces,* but *adicies liquamen et uinum,* and 3.4.1 *adicies in mortarium piper cuminum silfi modice [id est laseris radicem], rutam modicum, liquamine et aceto temperabis.* Or again, 7.4.3 *piper tritum, condimentum mel liquamen amulum,* but then *sine liquamine et oleo elixantur.* Also, 7.5.2 *petroselini scripulos VI, laser scripulos VI, gingiberis scripulos VI,* etc., but *liquaminis et olei quod sufficit.* Similarly 7.6.6 *piper cuminum ligusticum, rutae semen, damascenas* but *oenomeli et aceto temperabis.* Note finally 9.7 *piper ligusticum petroselinum, mentam siccam, cuminum plusculum, mel liquamen. si uoles, folium et malabatrum addes.* In all these passages when there are two ingredients in a process there is a coordinator, but when there are more than two, asyndeton.

It is not suggested that when a list of two items expresses a totality it will always have a coordinator. The pairs of names of consuls, for example, are a totality, and these are usually asyndetic. However, a change over time has been observed in consular naming, with coordination increasing (see XXII.9 for bibliography and details). Here are a few further instances of pairs that are complete sets. At Tac. *Ann.* 12.2.1 (97) (*haudquaquam nouercalibus odiis uisura Britannicum, Octauiam*) Britannicus and Octavia were brother and sister. And *Ann.* 6.15.1 (*L. Cassium, M. Vinicium legit*) refers to the choice of husbands for two *uirgines*.

Examples of the type just seen in the last paragraph (i.e. finite pairs with asyndeton) are exceptional, and should be put in perspective. I have collected below all pairs of personal names in Caesar's *De bello ciuili* (using Damon's recent edition) that are either asyndetic or syndetic, arranging the coordinated instances according to the coordinator used.

1.2.7 *intercedit M. Antonius Q. Cassius, tribuni plebis*

1.6.5 *Philippus et Cotta priuato consilio praetereuntur*
1.18.1 *a Q. Lucretio senatore et Attio Paeligno prohiberi*
1.18.3 *Lucretius et Attius de muro se deiecerunt*
1.35.4 *principes ... earum partium Cn. Pompeium et C. Caesarem*
1.40.4 *quo cognito a Petreio et Afranio*
2.44.3 *quo in numero erat Ser. Sulpicius et Licinius Damasippus*
3.1.1 *consules creantur Iulius Caesar et P. Seruilius*
3.4.5 *CCC Tarcondarius Castor et Domnilaus ex Gallograecia dederant*
3.5.3 *praeera(n)t ... (nauibus) Asiaticis D. Laelius et C. Triarius*
3.5.3 *Liburnicae atque Achaicae classi Scribonius Libo et M. Octauius (praeerant)*
3.7.1 *erat Orici Lucretius Vespillo, et Minucius Rufus cum Asiaticis nauibus XVIII*
3.15.6 *loquuntur ambo ex nauibus cum M. Acilio et Staio Murco legatis*
3.16.2 *certior ab Acilio et Murco per litteras factus*
3.26.1 *administrantibus M. Antonio et Furio Caleno*
3.42.3 *Q. Tillium et L. Canuleium legatos misit*
3.55.1 *per Cassium Longinum et Caluisium Sabin*um (π omits *et*; *et* is bound to be right, as Caesar's consistent practice shows)
3.55.2 *eique Sabinum et Cassium cum cohortibus adiungit*
3.59.1 *duo fratres, Roucillus et Egus*
3.104.3 *ab Achilla et Septimio interficitur*
3.109.4 *missi Dioscorides et Serapion*

1.42.2 *Afranius Petreiusque*
1.53.1 *Afranius Petreiusque*
1.61.2 *Afranius Petreiusque*
3.80.3 *ad Scipionem Pompeiumque nuntios mittit*
3.83.1 *Domitius Scipio Spintherque Lentulus*

1.7.6 *Saturnini atque Gracchorum casibus*
1.43.1 *Petreius atque Afranius*
1.63.3 *Petreius atque Afranius*

3 Open-Ended Lists: 'Illustrations'

1.67.1 *ab Petreio atque Afranio*
1.72.5 *Petreius atque Afranius*
1.73.4 *Petreius atque Afranius*
1.74.3 *de Petrei atque Afrani uita*
1.87.3 *Petreius atque Afranius*
3.19.1 *bina castra Pompei atque Caesaris*
3.30.1 *haec eodem fere tempore Caesar atque Pompeius cognoscunt*
3.79.6 *Allobroges, Roucilli atque Egi familiares*
3.107.2 *regem Ptolomaeum atque eius sororem Cleopatram*.

There is just a single asyndetic pair (that at the top of the list), and that in the naming of two officials. Against that 37 coordinated pairs are found (20 with *et*, 5 with *-que* and 12 with *atque*). The contexts of all these pairs cannot be analysed in detail here, but it is obvious enough even from the limited contexts cited that the vast majority refer to sets/finite pairs, not to persons chosen at random as illustrations from a potentially longer list. In classical Latin, if one leaves aside consular naming, such pairs were usually coordinated. In a writer such as Tacitus on the other hand the use of asyndeton to express two names forming a set is suggestive of contrived or artificial style.

3 Open-Ended Lists: 'Illustrations'

If coordination is widespread in finite pairs, by contrast in open-ended lists (i.e. those containing two members stated *exempli gratia*, with the implication that the list could be extended at will) asyndeton is frequent. I have found virtually no comment on this type of asyndeton bimembre in the literature, but it was recognised by Marx (1904–5: II.43) in a note on Lucilius 88–91 (see XXV.1.1.8). In the chapters on writers and genres numerous such examples are commented on, and here I merely illustrate the type with a few examples and some cross references.

One of the clearest manifestations of the asyndetic open-ended list of two items is to be seen in comments by grammarians and others on a spelling or grammatical feature, which they illustrate with just two examples, uncoordinated: e.g. Velius Longus *Orth.* VI.4 (ed. Di Napoli 2011: 45) '*ob' praepositio interdum ponitur plena, ut est 'obire' 'oberrare', interdum ad eam litteram transit, a qua sequens uox incipit, ut est 'offu<l>sit' 'ommutuit'* (see further XXV.1.1.3 on the examples numbered there **14** and **15** and **16–17**). The above passage concerns assimilation or non-assimilation of the prefix *ob*, and illustrations of the two phenomena could be extended hugely.

For a different but equally interesting passage see XXVII.1.1 on Catull. 42.13, where Catullus comments on the possibility of adding to an asyndetic pair that he has just used. See also XXII.3.5 on *deteriores repulsos* at Cic. *Har.* 53, and also XXIX.2.1.1 on Hor. *Sat.* 2.7.39, where Horace too recognises that a pair may be added to.

Here is some further evidence for illustrative asyndeton bimembre.

At Livy 4.15.5 (3) (*sed tamen Claudios Cassios consulatibus decemuiratibus, suis maiorumque honoribus, splendore familiarum sustulisse animos, quo nefas fuerit*, 'men like Claudius, Cassius ...') the implication is that there were others who behaved in the same way. Similar is Plaut. *Bac.* 649, where the names are again generalising plurals given as examples: *non mihi isti placent Parmenones Syri, | qui duas aut tris minas auferunt eris*, 'I don't like those Parmenos and Syruses, who take two or three minas away from their masters' (de Melo, Loeb). These are typical slave names of comedy. For other pairs of plural names chosen *exempli gratia* see XXV.1.1.8 on Lucil. 112–13, numbered 33 (also XXV.1.1.3), XXIX.2.1.2 on Hor. *Sat.* 1.7.8.

Pairs of names chosen as illustrations need not be plural. Cic. *Off.* 2.59 (132) (*dicebat idem Cotta Curio*) has two uncoordinated names at the end of a sentence. Cicero has just referred to Lucius Philippus as a man who used to make a certain boast about his performance in the state. Cotta and Curio are then listed as two others who made the same boast. That *Cotta Curio* is not a closed list is made immediately clear by Cicero, who adds that he too might make the same boast of himself. Cotta and Curio are just two examples (expressed asyndetically) from a potentially larger number.

I would take the names in the following passage in the same way: Cic. *Dom.* 35 (32) *non aetas eius qui adoptabat est quaesita, ut in* <u>Cn. Aufidio M. Pupio</u>, *quorum uterque nostra memoria summa senectute alter Oresten, alter Pisonem adoptauit, quas adoptiones sicut alias innumerabilis hereditates nominis pecuniae sacrorum secutae sunt*. For translation and comment see on Cicero 32.

At Tac. *Hist.* 4.42.5 (*ut omnis aetas instructa sit, et quo modo senes nostri,* <u>Marcellum, Crispum</u>, *iuuenes Regulum imitentur*, 'so that every age may be instructed, and so that, just as our elderly imitate Marcellus, Crispus, so the youth may imitate Regulus') Marcellus and Crispus are mentioned as role models, and the list is hardly complete.

The impression should not be given that pairs of asyndetic illustrations consist entirely of names (for different types see on Lucilius at the start of this section and XXV.1.1.3, XXIX 2.1.5 on Horace; there are also frequent selective pairs of various types in Cicero).

Here is a passage from one of the minor declamations attributed to Quintilian, in which a speaker offers up (in the form of questions) several adjectives as possible descriptions of his character (on this and some similar passages see also V.2). There is first a single adjective, and then an asyndetic pair: 328.14 *ego istum si filium meum occidisset defenderem? qualem me patrem iudicatis? asperum? et ego pro filio mentiar? mitem indulgentem?*, 'Would I be defending him if he had murdered my son? What sort of father do you judge me to be? Harsh? And shall I lie for my son? Gentle, indulgent?' (Shackleton Bailey, Loeb) (= *patrem me iudicatis esse mitem indulgentem?*). The adjectives could obviously be added to. Indeed in another passage from the same work we have 286.8 *habes patrem lenem mitem*, 'you have a father gentle, lenient'. The pair *mitem indulgentem* above might have been extended (e.g.) by the addition of *lenem*. This asyndeton bimembre is typical of adjectival asyndeta in these declamations (see V.2). The speakers are sometimes presented as looking for descriptive words, and those they find are mere possibilities.

Some asyndetic pairs are revealed to be selective by a generalisation following. At Cic. *Off.* 1.150 (*adde huc, si placet, unguentarios saltatores totumque ludum talarium*, 'Add to these, if you please, the perfumers, dancers, and the whole *corps de ballet*', Miller, Loeb) the phrase with *totum* shows that *unguentarios, saltatores* express just two members of a larger group. This example is structurally almost identical to Cic. *Phil.* 5.15 (**26**): *saltatores citharistas, totum denique comissationis Antonianae chorum*, 'dancers, harpists, the whole Antonian troupe of carousers'.

And here are two examples (this time with a summarising *omnis*) from Tacitus' *Annals*: 13.16.4 (**103**) <u>*dolorem caritatem,*</u> *omnis adfectus abscondere didicerat*, 'she had learnt to hide pain, affection, every emotion'; 13.42.4 (**105**) <u>*crimen periculum,*</u> *omnia potius toleraturum, quam ueterem ac diu partam dignationem subitae felicitati submitteret*, 'he would endure charge, danger, everything, rather than subject his old status, achieved over a long time, to sudden good fortune'.

The examples in the last two paragraphs are, however, different from those earlier in the section in that there is a third element in the sequence, though it arguably has a detachment from the initial pair. In at least three cases the final element could be introduced in writing by a dash. See further XVIII.6.

Powell (1988: 141) remarks that particular examples to prove a general point are often introduced by Cicero by means of asyndeton. He had in mind sentence asyndeton (i.e. the example is thrown in by a new sentence without any connective), and was not referring to the type discussed here, but the observation is of interest: that which is *exempli gratia* may be asyndetic in one sense or another. Two of the sentences that Powell refers to are introduced by the name of a person (as exemplar).

IV Lists of Two Types

4 Open-Ended Lists Comprising Pairs of Adjectives: a Specific Case

I deal elsewhere (V.2; see also above, 3 on passages from Quintilian's declamations) with pairs of judgemental adjectives placed after the noun (not infrequently at the end of a colon, and usually predicative in some sense), and suggest that a pause would have been likely between them in speech, implying reflection by the speaker on how to strengthen the effect of the first term. Such pairs are not totalities but could be added to. Here I discuss one example that achieved the status of a formula, *Iuppiter optimus maximus* (or *optumus maxumus*).

The postponed asyndetic terms *optimus maximus* may well have originated as two members of a potentially open-ended string of superlatives, even though the pair remained intact over time: 'Jupiter, the best, the greatest, . . .', etc. These two adjectives were certainly not the only ones that could be applied to Jupiter. Note Naevius, *Bellum Punicum* (Strzelecki 1964) 17 *patrem suum supremum optumum appellat*, 'She thus calls on her father, the all-highest and best' (Warmington 1936: 53, frg. 16), and particularly Plaut. *Per.* 251–2 *Ioui opulento incluto, Ope gnato, | supremo ualido uiripotenti*; also Cic. *Fin.* 3.66 *atque etiam Iouem cum optimum et maximum dicimus cumque eundem salutarem hospitalem statorem, hoc intellegi uolumus, salutem hominum in eius esse tutela*. An inscription recently discussed by Macrae (2018), *CIL* XI.4639 = *ILS* 3001, has (4–5) *Ioui opt(imo) max(imo) | custodi conseruatori* (see Macrae 2018: 67 on the implication of this second pair; the general point for our purposes is that an old pair of this type could be extended to match new circumstances). In English it is a pause that gives a postponed pair its extra weight, along with the unstated implication that there could be more, even stronger, terms to follow. The ease with which such a postponed pair may be extended can be seen from the following two similar passages, each with (in this case) condemnatory adjectives (the first with two, the second with three): Quint. *Decl.* 329.9 *occidit tyrannum crudelissimum saeuissimum* 'he killed a tyrant cruel, savage', Cic. *Dom.* 23 *homini taeterrimo crudelissimo fallacissimo*. Each of these adjectival sequences is then followed by a much longer concluding phrase.

The pair at *Il.* 3.298 (Ζεῦ κύδιστε μέγιστε) is comparable to the Latin formula *Iuppiter optimus maximus*, and may in type have inspired it. Cf. 2.412 Ζεῦ κύδιστε μέγιστε (there then follow two further epithets of different types, κελαινεφές, αἰθέρι ναίων, 'lord of the dark clouds, dwelling in heaven'; the first two can be seen as a pair with assonance in a longer list).

Cf. also 3.276 Ζεῦ πάτερ, Ἴδηθεν μεδέων, κύδιστε μέγιστε. Note too Menander *Samia* 641 νὴ τὸν Δία τὸν μέγιστον. Judgemental superlatives could be used on their own or multiplied indefinitely.

Even if the two adjectives *optumus maxumus* originally referred to rank rather than moral excellence (on this possibility see Pease 1958: 713), the pair would still have been selective, given the use of *supremus* by Naevius above.

Finally, Cicero makes a curious semantic judgement about *optumus maxumus*, which raises a feature of asyndeton bimembre that often comes up. According to *Nat.* 2.64, the first word of this pair was the more powerful: *a poetis pater diuomque hominumque dicitur, a maioribus autem nostris optumus maxumus, et quidem ante optumus, id est beneficentissimus, quam maxumus quia maius est certeque gratius prodesse omnibus quam opes magnas habere*, 'the poets call him "father of gods and men," and our ancestors entitled him "best and greatest," putting the title "best,", that is most beneficent, before that of "greatest," because universal beneficence is greater, or at least more lovable, than the possession of great wealth' (Rackham, Loeb). But in reality in asyndetic pairs it is usually the second term that is stronger (see in general XV, but the point is made throughout). Cicero's semantic argument is not compelling, as it gives too precise a meaning to the two terms (see Pease 1958: 713 for bibliography). They probably had much the same weight.

5 Conclusions

In this chapter a distinction has been made between sequences of terms that are selective (forming what we have called an 'open-ended' list or serving as mere illustrations) and those that are a totality. Extended lists (i.e. those with more than two members) of both types are structured in the same way, with asyndeton the norm. It is the pairs of the two types that may behave differently. Asyndetic pairs that express a totality do exist, but they may be formulaic (such as consuls' names) or belong to high style (a few instances of names from Tacitus were listed above, 2). Such finite pairs often have a coordinator. Selective pairs on the other hand are frequently asyndetic, and it was indeed suggested by Marx in a note alluded to above but quoted elsewhere (on Lucilius: see above, 2 for the reference) that the addition of a coordinator to one asyndetic pair in Lucilius would have converted the pair from open-ended to a totality.

CHAPTER V

Supposed 'Effects' of Asyndeton

1 'Rapidity' et sim. and the Articulation of Asyndetic Pairs; Some Ancient Evidence

In an earlier chapter (I.3) various ancient commentators were cited on the supposed 'speed' or 'rapidity' of asyndeta (Long. 19.2, Suet. *Caes.* 37.2, Aquila 41). It is easy to see how such an idea might have come about. An asyndetic sequence as looked at on the written page has fewer words than a syndetic, and fewer words might mean that a shorter time is needed for the articulation.

Modern commentators too not infrequently find rapidity in one sense or another in asyndeta. Rutherford (2012: 179 n. 26), in a generalisation about asyndeton (in Greek), states: 'Two types should be distinguished. In one ... we have a series of sentences without connecting conjunctions or particles ... Often ... this indicates agitation or excitement. In the other, a number of words with parallel function in a sentence are combined without conjunctions: the effect is usually a sense of rapidity or urgency.' It is not stated exactly how rapidity is achieved, but it is to be assumed that the absence of coordinators is felt to speed things up. Huitink and Rood (2019: 165), commenting on Xen. *An.* 3.4.25 ἔβαλλον, ἐσφενδόνων, ἐτόξευον, state that the 'effect here is to convey the sense of a sudden barrage of stones'. Ash (2007: 87) says of one type (comprising historic infinitives) that it features 'especially in historians for rapid sequences of events'. In another place (2007: 111) she remarks: 'historic infinitives in asyndeton ... mirror the brutally methodical attack'. Or again (2007: 118), 'the tricolon + asyndeton mirror the speedy attack'. Ash has similar comments in her edition of Tac. *Ann.* 15: see e.g. (2018: 97) 'historians favour historic infinitives in asyndeton for rapidly unfolding events', and in the same note, 'Rapid-fire syntax aptly mirrors Corbulo's military dynamism'; or (2018: 209), 'the juxtaposition suggests the money-raising's swift centrifugal momentum' (with an implicit reference to word order too).

1 *'Rapidity' and Articulation of Asyndetic Pairs* 77

Woodman with Kraus (2014: 201) on *templa fora domos* quotes Gudeman: the 'cumulative force of the asyndeton well marks the eager haste of the Britons'. Earlier, see Madvig (1876: 244), 'asyndeton celeris et concitatae orationis rei declarandae aptissimum est', id. (1876: 329) 'Asyndeto utitur in celeri magnarum rerum et gravi notatione.' Pease (1963: 196) remarks: 'the asyndeton indicates the quick succession of events.' Denniston (1952: 105) states that asyndeton 'gives pace to a sentence'. Similar impressionistic terminology is also common. Richardson (2010: 239), for example, comments on the use of asyndeton (phrasal) to express agitation. Note too *Rhet. Her.* 4.41: *hoc genus et acrimoniam habet et uehementissimum est et ad breuitatem adcommodatum.*

Mastronarde (2002: 92) has a more comprehensive list of the effects of asyndeton (combining both asyndetic coordination and sentence/clause connection):

> Since Greek in general favours constant connection of clauses, asyndeton stands out more in Greek and normally has a stylistic or rhetorical effect. Adjs. in groups of two or three in asyndeton usually express pathos or vehemence ... Paired verbs in asyndeton likewise have heightened intensity ... When one clause follows another in asyndeton, the second is often explanatory of the first ... Or the asyndeton may reflect emotion or vehemence.

Statements such as most of those quoted above do not pay attention to pronunciation and intonation. Ancient texts were not always read aloud, but even someone reading silently will interpret what is being read in accordance with the expected intonation. An asyndetic utterance is often the opposite of speedy: it may be slow and deliberate, with pauses. We do not know anything about Latin intonation patterns (but see further below for some suggestive ancient evidence about the pronunciation of asyndeta in both Greek and Latin), but there are features of Greek and Latin word order that hint at pauses, and pauses for thought were inevitable in some asyndetic sequences, where the second word capped the first. It was observed earlier (I.1) that in any coordination, including asyndetic, in current languages there are 'linking devices', which in the case of asyndetic coordination are intonational and/or characterised by pauses. One may speculate about (e.g.) Caesar's *ueni uidi uici* (Suet. *Caes.* 37.2) and how it might have been said. In English it is likely that someone reading aloud a formal inscription with the words *I came, I saw, I conquered* would introduce dramatic pauses and a distinctive intonation, rather than rushing through the three phrases. An unexpressive pronunciation would be more likely in a coordinated version, *I came and saw and conquered* or (particularly) *I came, saw and conquered* (with end-of-list coordination, the norm in English). Caesar's three verbs have, as well as asyndeton, alliteration, equal length and the same ending, and it is plausible that they would have been uttered in such a way as to emphasise these features. Moreover semantically the final verb caps the other two, which refer merely to a preliminary assessment of the situation, and in English at least it could be preceded by a distinct pause: *I came, I saw – I CONQUERED*. The version above with end-of-list coordination would be spoken more quickly.

There are also semantic differences between different asyndetic pairs, and it cannot be assumed that all were treated alike. For example, two verbs may express a temporal sequence, or one may act as a modifier of the first, and there may well have been different intonations for the two types. Even in relation to pairs of verbs, 'speed, rapidity' may be inadequate descriptive terms (see below, 3). Something will be said below about adjectives as well in postponed positions as an illustration of the complexity. See too XXXI.3.8 (second paragraph) on the sheer diversity of the asyndetic types in Livy, in relation to many of which rapidity would not be a meaningful concept.

I turn to some ancient *testimonia* (see also I.3). In Greek an interesting passage (see I.1) is at Arist. *Rh.* 1413b.29–30 = 3.12.4, where an example given of ἀσύνδετα is ἦλθον, ἀπήντησα, ἐδεόμην, 'I came, I met, I entreated', a tricolon not unlike Caesar's (cf. too Ter. *Ph.* 104 *imus uenimus | uidemus*). Aristotle says that the words should not be pronounced as if a single thing was being said, with the same character and intonation (ἀνάγκη γὰρ ὑποκρίνεσθαι καὶ μὴ ὡς ἓν λέγοντα τῷ αὐτῷ ἤθει καὶ τόνῳ εἰπεῖν, rendered by Freese (Loeb) as, 'For here delivery is needed, and the words should not be pronounced with the same tone and character, as if there was only one clause'). Boccotti (1975: 35) takes τόνος to refer to intonation. Whatever the exact force of the word (see LSJ s.v. II.2a–b, 'pitch'), clearly the components were, according to Aristotle, to be uttered in varying ways and by implication separated rather than garbled together.

Aristotle continues that the coordinator makes many things one: ὁ γὰρ σύνδεσμος ἓν ποιεῖ τὰ πολλά. If this σύνδεσμος is removed the opposite will be the case, and the one will be many: δῆλον ὅτι τοὐναντίον ἔσται τὸ ἓν πολλά. Asyndeton is the opposite of coordination in its effect, in that it splits the elements up more distinctly, and that can only be because of pauses and intonation patterns. Aristotle calls the effect amplification, αὔξησις.

2 'Pauses for Thought': Postponed Adjectives

Quintilian 9.3.50 has much the same implication: (*figuram ... dissolutio*) *apta cum instantius dicimus: nam et singula inculcantur et quasi plura fiunt*, 'it [asyndeton] is appropriate when we are particularly insistent on something because our points are thus driven home one at a time and also, as it were, made more numerous' (Russell, Loeb, slightly modified). The reference seems again to be to the opposite of speed: each term is given separate, forceful, articulation (*singula inculcantur*) and the sum appears greater. There must be an allusion here to intonation and pauses. At 9.4.23 Quintilian defines asyndeton as 'words taken singly' (*singula sunt quae* ἀσύνδετα *diximus*), using the same word, *singula*, and he also says that a weaker word must not follow a stronger. It is often the case in an asyndetic pair that the second term outdoes the first, as will be seen repeatedly.

Demetrius (*Eloc.* 194), quoting an asyndetic sequence of three verbs, says that the asyndeton will cause anyone saying the words, whether willingly or not, to be dramatic (ὑποκρίνεσθαι), whereas adding a coordinator lowers the emotional level. There is once more little doubt that the reference must be to an intonational pattern suited to asyndeton, with separations. Anyone attempting subjectively to characterise literary asyndeta in Latin should be aware of this ancient view that absence of coordinators between words does not run them together but separates them.

2 'Pauses for Thought' and Postponed Adjectives in Latin

The 'pause for thought' in asyndetic pairs is familiar in modern languages, the aim being particularly to emphasise the final, stronger term. An example from English is the following: Carol Midgley, *The Times*, 19 August 2015 (*Times* 2 p. 2) *As an image it's unflattering, unstatesmanlike* (of the Prime Minister David Cameron). To be called 'unstatesmanlike' is the ultimate indignity for a prime minister, and if this put-down were delivered in speech there would undoubtedly be a pause before the final term, which would be given a special emphasis too, possibly by two falling pitches. As I have stressed, in a dead language such as Latin or Greek one can only make guesses about such pauses, but there is one structure in written texts in which the final term's independence is marked explicitly, and that is when a word intrudes into an asyndetic pair and detaches the second term from the first. I liken this pattern to conjunct hyperbaton, but without the coordinator, as for example if *he is a good man and kind* (conjunct hyperbaton) were to become *he is a good man, – kind*, in which *kind* would be given a special emphasis. Discontinuous asyndeton comes up throughout the later chapters on writers and genres (see also above, II.2.1, II.2.4, 1, and particularly XX), but here are two examples from Menander (with the Loeb translation of Arnott, modified): *Samia* 348 χαμαιτύπη δ' ἄνθρωπος, ὄλεθρος, 'the woman is a whore, – a disaster'; *Sikyonioi* 150 ὄχλος εἶ, φλυάρου μεστός, 'riff-raff you are, – full of drivel'.

A distinctive placement of certain types of asyndetic adjectives hints at a deliberate articulation. If we start with English, postposition of an asyndetic pair (predicate, predicative adjunct/secondary predicate) may have a rather different implication from anteposition (attributive). In the phrase *the big bad wolf* the two adjectives form a complete and formulaic description of the wolf in the fairy tale. If we rewrite predicatively (with asyndeton) as *the wolf was big, bad*, there is necessarily a pause between the two, as if the speaker were thinking of a term to outdo the first. The list is also not necessarily complete. It is as if these terms are chosen *exempli gratia*, with the possibility of adding others: e.g. *the wolf was big, ... bad, ... ugly* (see above, IV.3).

Winterbottom (1984: 322) lists eight asyndetic pairs of adjectives from the minor declamations of Quintilian, remarking that in 'all of these cases the words are at the end of their clause'. Without exception the adjectives are subjective, expressing a judgement, favourable or unfavourable, and it is in the nature of such terms that they could be supplemented by other subjective words to enhance the characterisation (see IV.3). Here are the pairs (printed without commas following the convention of this book, but they should certainly be punctuated in a critical edition; I have sometimes adopted the translation of Shackleton Bailey, Loeb): 254.21 *ex altera parte homo potens gratiosus*, 'on the other hand a man powerful, full of influence' (favourable), 257.12 *duxi puellam honestam locupletem*, 'I married a girl respectable, rich' (favourable), 267.10 *fletus remissi fatigati*, 'weeping is a mark of a person subdued, weary' (in the context unfavourable), 286.8 *habes patrem lenem mitem*, 'you have a father gentle, lenient' (favourable; that the adjectives here belong to a list that could be lengthened is clear from 328.14 below, *mitem indulgentem*: the father here might have been e.g. *lenem mitem indulgentem* (on these examples and some of those below see IV.3)), 293.2 *sed numquid uobis uideor auarus libidinosus?*, 'but do I seem to you greedy, libidinous?' (unfavourable), 328.14 *ego istum si filium meum occidisset defenderem? qualem me patrem iudicatis? asperum? et ego pro filio mentiar? mitem indulgentem?*, 'Would I be defending him if he had murdered my son? What sort of father do you judge me to be? Harsh? And shall I lie for my son? Gentle, indulgent?' (here the speaker is presented as looking for words, and the articulation would have to imply that), 329.9

2 'Pauses for Thought': Postponed Adjectives 81

occidit tyrannum crudelissimum saeuuissimum, 'he killed a tyrant cruel, savage' (unfavourable; see IV.3 on this passage, with an illustration of the ease with which a list of condemnatory superlatives may be extended), 346.2 *hic enim pater, etsi reuera irascitur, dissimilare hoc debet, et agere mitem indulgentem*, 'although this father is truly angry, he should conceal this and act as one gentle, indulgent'. In more than half of these cases the adjectives are near-synonyms; the function of the second word is to strengthen the effect, and the implication that the list is not complete also has that role. Any suggestion that the articulation would have been more rapid than that of explicitly coordinated pairs would not be convincing.

The above examples are listed to suggest the hazards of seeking neat single-word descriptions of the effect of asyndeton based on the written form. Asyndetic pairs of adjectives that form open-ended lists, that are often postponed or have a significant placement (e.g. at the start of a line in verse), that are often secondary predicates and are frequently judgemental, persist throughout Latin, even in writers (such as Petronius) who rarely have asyndeton bimembre (see XXIII, Appendix on Plautus, XXIV.2, after 15 on Virgil, XXV.1.1.4 on Lucilius, XXX.3.2.2 for examples from Sallust, XXXI.3.4 for Livy, XXXII.1 on Petronius). Here is a very small selection of postponed adjectives from various writers, all of them subjective, and all almost certainly pronounced with pauses within. More detailed comment on these passages will be found elsewhere (see the numbers in bold):

Sall. *Cat.* 18.4 (**50**) *erat eodem tempore Cn. Piso, adulescens nobilis, summae audaciae, egens factiosus*

Sall. *Jug.* 44.1 (**58**) *exercitus ei traditur a Sp. Albino proconsule iners inbellis*

Virg. *Aen.* 4. 179–81 (**5**) *Coeo Enceladoque sororem | progenuit, pedibus celerem et pernicibus alis, | monstrum horrendum ingens*

Livy 4.28.4 (**32**) *'hic praebituri,' inquit, 'uos telis hostium estis indefensi inulti?'*

Tac. *Ann.* 4.37.3 (**119**) *ita per omnes prouincias effigie numinum sacra<ri> ambitiosum superbum*

Tac. *Ann.* 6.8.4 (**121**) *abditos principis sensus, et si quid occultius parat, exquirere inlicitum anceps.*

It will be noted that a number of these adjectives are negatives (*in-* privatives). These are not the only types used thus, but asyndeton of privative adjectives is common (see VI.2.2), and clearly if a pair was postpositive, predicative in some sense and contained at least one privative there was a likelihood that it would be asyndetic. A combination of factors contributes to the asyndetic use.

3 Possible Variability of Articulation

It is not my intention to imply here that all asyndetic pairs would have been articulated in the same way as that suggested for adjectives of the type above. I suggest rather that variations existed from type to type, and that a single-word impressionistic formulation explaining the effects of an asyndeton should not be taken too seriously. For example, 'proverbial' pairs of adverbs such as *huc illuc*, *ultro citro* might have been used in their own way. Some legal pairs (e.g. *sarta tecta*) have the appearance of lawyers' shorthand, and there is no knowing how they would have been uttered.

As for pairs of verbs and the view that they occur in asyndeton to represent rapid events, it is again advisable to look at contexts and the semantics of the individual verbs. Here is a pair of historic infinitives at Tac. *Hist.* 4.81.2 (40): *Vespasianus primo inridere aspernari*. The relationship between them is a familiar one. *Inrideo* means 'laugh at, make fun of', whereas *aspernor* is stronger ('scorn, spurn'). Neither verb denotes a single event. Making fun of someone is repetitive, and indeed historic infinitives are often equivalent to imperfect indicatives and imply repetition. Rejection/spurning for its part is an ongoing state of mind or an attitude. This pair in itself is not to do with unfolding events (though *primo* implies that more is to follow), but expresses an attitude of Vespasian in a forceful way by the juxtaposition of two near-synonyms of which the second caps the first. In English an equivalent of such a pair would be pronounced with a pause and emphasis, whereas the same pair coordinated might be uttered in a matter-of-fact way.

At Cic. *Dom.* 137 (69) the opposites (reversives) *dirueris aedificaris*, of pulling down, building up (buildings), tell us nothing about the rapidity of the acts (which would have taken some time): the juxtaposition merely expresses inconsistent behaviour.

Or again, at Sall. *Jug.* 11.8 (75) (*ira et metu anxius moliri parare*, 'under the strain of anger and dread, he laboured, prepared') the two historic infinitives express laborious preparations. There is no suggestion of rapid action. If one wanted to come up with an impressionistic description of the effect of the asyndeton one might more reasonably assert that a probable pause between the two verbs 'would mirror the drawn-out preparations'. The asyndeton is better seen not in such terms but as related to the structure and syntax. Historic infinitives rarely occur singly but are usually in groups of two or more (see Woodcock 1959: 15), and asyndeton, whether of single words, phrases or clauses, was favoured in such groups. In Sallust

3 Possible Variability of Articulation

there are 11 instances of asyndetic pairs of historical infinitives, in Tacitus' *Histories* 7, and in Tacitus' *Annals* 9. One should look in these cases not to the effects of asyndeta as determining the omission of coordinators, but to the fact that the verbs are historic infinitives in groups.

Here is another pair of verbs, this time from Menander. At *Dyskolos* 762–3 Gorgias betroths the girl to Sostratus and hands her over, with the gods called as witnesses: τοιγαροῦν ἔγωγέ σ[ο]ι | ἐγγυῶ, δίδωμι πάντων [τῶ]ν θεῶν ἐναντίον. This is a ritualistic formula, and 'speed', whether of the utterance or the action, would have been out of the question. Similarly at Men. *Samia* 728–9 there are three verbs in asyndeton from the marriage ceremony, ἔχω, | λαμβάνω, στέργω, 'thus I hold, take, cherish her', followed at 730 by three asyndetic nouns: Χρυσί, πέμπε τὰς γυναῖκας, λουτροφόρον, αὐλητρίδα, 'Chrysis, send the women, the bearer, the piper' (in reference to the prenuptial bath). See also XXIII.3.

To conclude. We have commented on a tendency among commentators to see the absence of coordinators as (apparently) in itself suggesting speed, agitation, emotion and so on. But it is the meanings of the words in the asyndetic sequence that convey such ideas. Despite the shortage of information about the manner of articulation of asyndetic pairs and longer groups, we have argued that there are hints that at least some asyndeta would have been pronounced with pauses, and that it is a mistake simply to assume that a lack of coordinators represents in some way rapidity.

PART 2

'Grammatical' Types

CHAPTER VI

Asyndetic Pairs (Mainly of Adjectives) of Which at Least One Member Is a Term with a Negative Prefix (in Latin, Usually in-)

1 Introduction

In Latin, terms with the prefix *in-* occur in numerous asyndetic patterns, some of them of considerable age and stylistic interest. I am mainly concerned with adjectival pairs of which both members have the privative prefix *in-*, but will deal with other patterns as well to demonstrate the range of types. Material from Greek (showing terms with alpha-privative prefixes) will be cited, and reference will be made too to the Iguvine tablets and to the Rigveda. Presumably the type was inherited as distinct from developing independently in different languages. Prefixes other than *in-*/alpha-privative are also not infrequently repeated in asyndetic sequences (see further below, 7), but it is the type with negative prefix that is most distinctive.

These are the seven patterns distinguished here: (1) asyndetic pairs of which both members are privatives (§2); (2) asyndetic pairs with *in-* or alpha at the start of both members, but with at least one member that is not a privative compound (there being other functions, e.g. local, of the Latin prefix *in-*) (§3); (3) asyndetic pairs with just one member (usually the second) that is a privative (§4); (4) asyndetic triplets (or longer sequences) comprising terms which all have a privative prefix (§5).

In addition to these categories there is a different type (5), which has traditionally attracted more interest, that comprising oppositions of the pattern 'worthy, unworthy', with the privative compound negating its simplex (§6); the opposites are either antonyms or complementarities (see XIII.2). This too is an old type.

There are also some positive–negative pairs in Latin (6) of which the negated term has a prefix other than privative *in-* (§7).

As an addendum (7) I will cite a few examples of prefixes other than the privative that are repeated in asyndetic pairs (§8). There is also an Appendix about English.

2 Asyndetic Pairs of Which Both Members Are Privatives

This structure is old (and continues to the present day in, for example, English: see the Appendix). West (2007: 110) cites examples (including some triplets) from the Rigveda and Greek (cf. West 1988: 156). I start in this section with Greek (2.1), then move on to Latin (2.2), and finally quote cases from the Rigveda (2.3), making some comparisons with Greek and Latin types. Such privative pairs are often asyndetic, but sometimes have overt coordination (see e.g. West 2007: 110), in keeping with the constant alternations that occur between asyndetic and syndetic coordinations. In Latin this category is particularly important in some genres, notably historiography, where a significant proportion of adjectival asyndeta bimembria belong to classes (2) and (4) (for statistics, see below, 9).

2.1 Greek

It is sometimes said that asyndetic single-word pairs (of whatever type) are not common in Greek compared with longer sequences (see e.g. Denniston 1952: 105,[1] Mastronarde 2002: 214 on Eur. *Med.* 255, Diggle 2004: 460), but privative adjectives certainly turn up in pairs, from Homer onwards and particularly in tragedy (see in general Fehling 1969: 235–40, dealing with both asyndetic and syndetic groups). Here are a few examples, first from Homer:

Hom. *Il.* 1.98 πρίν γ᾽ ἀπὸ πατρὶ φίλῳ δόμεναι ἑλικώπιδα κούρην | ἀπριάτην ἀνάποινον, 'until we give back to her dear father the bright-eyed maiden, unbought, unransomed'.

Here the privatives are secondary predicates/predicative adjuncts (see II.2.1; I use these terms interchangeably), and the adjective in the preceding line is attributive. The negative adjectives are postponed, following both the verb and the noun with which they agree, and are at the start of a new line. In Greek and Latin the position of such adjuncts is variable, but does tend to be prominent (e.g. at the start of a clause, or the end). Such pairs are not necessarily in agreement with an expressed noun: often the subject to which they are applied is expressed only by the form of the verb. See XXIV.3, 1.

Hom. *Il.* 22.386 κεῖται πὰρ νήεσσι νέκυς ἄκλαυτος ἄθαπτος | Πάτροκλος, 'there lies by the ships a corpse, unwept, unburied, Patroclus'.

---

[1] I quote: '*The number of co-ordinated words or clauses is seldom less than three.* Asyndeton gives pace to a sentence, and if it is over too quickly the result is mere jerkiness.' On the notion of 'pace', see Chap. V. Denniston goes on to say that Demosthenes has perhaps only 'three examples of two-limbed asyndeton'.

2 Pairs with Both Members Privatives 89

Postponed adjuncts again, at the end of the line. The name is appositional. For the verb 'lies' here, in initial position, see *Od.* 4.788 below, and also Eur. *Hec.* 30 below. *Iaceo* is also used with asyndetic adjuncts (see below, 3 for Lucr. 5.223, Tac. *Ann.* 6.19.2, XXXII.1 for Petronius).

Hom. *Od.* 1.242 οἴχετ' ἄϊστος ἄπυστος, 'he is gone, out of sight, unheard of'.
Both this and the next example have the same structural pattern as the examples above. The adjectives are at the end of a colon. We will see (superficial) Latin correspondents to this pair below.

Hom. *Od.* 4.788 κεῖτ' ἄρ' ἄσιτος ἄπαστος ἐδητύος ἠδὲ ποτῆτος, 'she lay there, without food, without taste of food or drink'.
This example has an extended second member. Here and in the previous passage the phrase is not in agreement with an expressed name or noun.

Here are two examples cited by Fehling (1969: 236; see also 237):

Aesch. *Eum.* 565 ὤλετ' ἄκλαυτος, ἄϊστος, 'he perishes, unwept, unseen'.
Again the pair is postponed (secondary predicates). For 'unwept' in such a pair see *Il.* 22.386 above, and for 'unseen', *Od.* 1.242, also above (for the contraction here Sommerstein 1989: 182 ad loc.).

Aesch. *Eum.* 785 ἐκ δὲ τοῦ | λειχὴν ἄφυλλος ἄτεκνος, ὦ Δίκα Δίκα, | πέδον ἐπισύμενος | βροτοφθόρους κηλῖδας ἐν χώρᾳ βαλεῖ, 'And from it a canker causing leaflessness and childlessness – O Justice, Justice! – sweeping over the soil will fill the land with miasmas fatal to humans' (Sommerstein, Loeb).
Here the adjectives are attributes.

Another instance in Aesch. *Eum.* is at 352: παλλεύκων δὲ πέπλων ἄκληρος ἄμοιρος ἐτύχθην, 'and I was made to have no part or share in pure white garments' (Sommerstein, Loeb; Page OCT prefers ἀπόμοιρος ἄκληρος). This asyndetic pairing is an emendation of the unmetrical manuscript reading (see Sommerstein 1989: 142), with the two terms in the reverse order. The adjectives are predicates, with a copular verb (ἐτύχθην).

See too Aesch. *Supp.* 143=153 σπέρμα σεμνᾶς μέγα ματρὸς εὐνᾶς | ἀνδρῶν, ἒ ἔ | ἄγαμον ἀδάματον ἐκφυγεῖν, 'so that the offspring of a most august mother may escape the beds of men – ah, ah! – unwedded and unsubdued' (Sommerstein, Loeb). These are secondary predicates following and at some remove from the subject, but in this case they precede the verb (ἐκφυγεῖν).

Johansen and Whittle (1980: 3.46) comment as follows on Aesch. *Supp.* 681–2 (ἄχορον ἀκίθαριν δακρυογόνον Ἄρη | βίαν τ' ἔνδημον ἐξοπλίζων, 'arming Ares the breeder of tears, with whom is no dance and no lyre, and intestine violence in the community', Sommerstein, Loeb): 'the use of two ἀ-privative compounds as attrs. to a god exemplifies a common type of expression', with a reference to Fehling (1969: 237–8). Note that in his translation

90   VI Asyndetic Pairs (Mainly of Adjectives)

Sommerstein takes δακρυογόνον as an attribute, and the alpha-privative pair as secondary predicates. The asyndetic pair is at the start of the line.

Note also Bacchylides 19.23 Ἄργον ὄμμασι βλέποντα | πάντοθεν ἀκαμάτοις | μεγιστοάνασσα κέλευσε | χρυσόπεπλος Ἥρα | <u>ἄκοιτον ἄϋπνον</u> ἐόν-|τα καλλικέραν δάμαλιν | φυλάσσεν, 'Argus, looking from all sides with tireless eyes, was ordered by the great queen, gold-robed Hera, to guard unresting and unsleeping the lovely-horned heifer' (Campbell, Loeb). The alpha-privative terms are accompanied by the verb 'to be' (in participial form), at some remove from Ἄργον, but are secondary predicates. See Maehler (2004: 215) ad loc., who cites e.g. Soph. *Ant.* 339 θεῶν | τε τὰν ὑπερτάταν, Γᾶν | <u>ἄφθιτον ἀκαμάταν</u> ἀποτρύεται, 'and he wears away the highest of the gods, Earth, immortal and unwearying' (Lloyd-Jones, Loeb) (accusative secondary predicates following the noun). Xen. *Cyr.* 7.5.53 ἄσιτος καὶ ἄποτος, 'without food and without drink', which Maehler also cites, illustrates (if considered alongside e.g. Hom. *Od.* 4.788 above) the coexistence of syndetic and asyndetic coordination in this type of pairing.

For Euripides see first e.g. *Alc.* 173 προσηύξατο ... | <u>ἄκλαυτος ἀστένακτος</u>, she 'prayed, without weeping, without groaning'. This pair is at the end of a clause and the start of a line. The structure is the familiar one, with verb, and then a postponed asyndetic pair of adjuncts/secondary predicates in agreement with the subject of the verb.

Some further examples from Euripides are:

Supp. 966 καὶ νῦν <u>ἄπαις ἄτεκνος</u> | γηράσκω δυστανοτάτα, 'and now, without child, without offspring, I grow old in utter wretchedness' (see Collard 1975: 349 ad loc., taking ἄπαις ἄτεκνος as an asyndetic dicolon, and noting that asyndetic dicola comprising two alpha-privative adjectives are common in tragedy).

Hec. 30 κεῖμαι δ' ἐπ' ἀκταῖς, ἄλλοτ' ἐν πόντου σάλῳ | πολλοῖς διαύλοις κυμάτων φορούμενος, | <u>ἄκλαυτος ἄταφος</u>, 'I lie now near the beach, now amid the high swell of the main, carried to and fro by the waves' constant ebb and flow, unwept, unburied' (Kovacs, Loeb).

The verb and its initial placement and the postponed asyndetic pair (secondary predicates) replicate Hom. *Il.* 22.386, quoted above. Again the adjuncts, though postponed, are at the start of a line.

I quote finally Menander *Epit.* 908–10: ἐγώ τις ἀναμάρτητος, εἰς δόξαν βλέπων | καὶ ... σκοπῶν, | <u>ἀκέραιος, ἀνεπίπληκτος</u> αὐτὸς τῷ βίῳ, 'A faultless man (I), eyes fixed on his good name, a judge (of what is right and what is wrong), in his own life pure and beyond reproach' (Arnott, Loeb).

2 Pairs with Both Members Privatives

Here is another place where the asyndetic secondary predicates are at the start of a line.

In the passages collected above the pairs of alpha-privatives are usually adjuncts/secondary predicates (and not merely predicates with the verb 'to be'). They tend to be in agreement with the subject of a verb, and are distinctively placed, at the start of a line or end of a clause, following the subject and also sometimes the verb. Certain adjectives recur (see the end of the next section, on Latin, for this point).

2.2 Latin

Plaut. *Bac.* 612–14 *petulans, proteruo iracundo animo, indomito incogitato, sine modo et modestia sum, sine bono iure atque honore, incredibilis imposque animi, inamabilis illepidus uiuo.*

Here is a passage (see XXIII.6) with an accumulation of negatives (note the *sine*-phrases in the second line) in a self-characterisation. There are two single-word pairs of privative adjectives. Line 612 has four adjectives with *animo*, but the placement of *animo* divides them into two pairs, the first two near-synonyms and attributive, of angry aggression, and the second two privatives and secondary predicates ('aggressive I am, with a reckless and angry mind, uncontrolled, thoughtless'). In the last line there are again four adjectives, this time predicates with the verb *uiuo* (though *incredibilis imposque animi* might just be taken with the earlier *sum*). The first two are coordinated ('unreliable and irresponsible'), the second two asyndetic (and near-synonyms, 'unlikeable, charmless'), a constant structure in Latin (for the order coordination-asyndeton see e.g. III.1 for the augural passage Plaut. *As.* 259–60). This last line illustrates the fact that privative adjectives occur together both with syndetic and asyndetic coordination (cf. Fehling 1969: 235–40).

Plaut. *Men.* 972a-973 *qui nihili sunt, quid eis preti detur ab suis eris, ignauis improbis uiris*

A slave should remember 'what reward those who are worthless are given to them by their masters, the lazy and shameless ones' (de Melo, Loeb).

The phrase with these adjectives is appositional (to *eris*), but the adjectives themselves are attributes of *uiris*.

Cato *ORF* 59 *decem hominibus uitam eripis indicta causa, iniudicatis incondemnatis*

Secondary predicates at the end of the sentence. See on the next example with the cross reference to Livy.

Cic. *Cat.* 2.14 (42) *non de spe conatuque depulsus, sed indemnatus innocens in exsilium eiectus a consule ui et minis esse dicetur*

A predicative adjunct/secondary predicate. For the phraseology (and general context) see on Livy 35.34.7 below.

Cic. *Dom.* 139 (48) *id quod imperitus adulescens, nouus sacerdos, sororis precibus, matris minis adductus, ignarus inuitus, sine conlegis, sine libris, sine auctore, sine fictore ... fecisse dicatur*
This example is structurally similar to the last. The verb phrase is *fecisse dicatur*, just as above it was *eiectus esse dicetur*. The subject is *adulescens* but the asyndetic pair is only loosely related to the subject (adjunct/secondary predicate). One could also translate adverbially, 'unknowingly, unwillingly'. For a Greek passage in which there are three alpha-privative adverbs used with the same function as the *in*-privative adjectives here, see below (5.1), Soph. *OC* 130. Note also Woodcock (1959: 71): 'a number of adjectives are often used predicatively, i.e. adverbially'. *Inuitus*, he says, 'is regularly so used', citing Cic. *Fam.* 13.63.1. One of Pinkster's examples (2015: 30) of a secondary predicate is Livy 22.14.7 *laeti spectamus*, where the adjective is interchangeable with the adverb *laete*.
This Ciceronian example is also similar to Plaut. *Bac.* 612–14 above, in that alongside the asyndetic adjectives there is an accumulation of *sine*-phrases. We will see some more instances of this pattern below.

Cic. *Phil.* 11.2 *ecce tibi geminum in scelere par, inuisitatum inauditum, ferum barbarum!,* 'And now behold! A pair of twins in crime, unseen, unheard of, wild, barbarous.'
Two asyndetic pairs are juxtaposed here, first the two privatives and then two near-synonyms of different type. Again the adjectives, predicative adjuncts, are at the end of the clause.
The adjective 'unseen' was also illustrated above (2.1) in alpha-privative pairs in Greek. Note particularly Hom. *Od.* 1.242 οἴχετ' ἄιστος, ἄπυστος, and for the same pair in Latin, see below, Livy 5.45.4. The correspondence suggests that the pair was established in both languages. The contexts of the Homeric and Ciceronian examples are however completely different (pathetic in Homer, referring to death, pejorative in Cicero).

Sall. *Cat.* 11.3 (48) *ea (auaritia pecuniae) ... semper infinita insatiabilis est*
The adjectives are predicates with the verb 'to be'.

Sall. *Jug.* 44.1 (58) *exercitus ei traditur a Sp. Albino proconsule iners inbellis, neque periculi neque laboris patiens, lingua quam manu promptior, praedator ex sociis et ipse praeda hostium, sine imperio et modestia habitus*
This pattern was seen in some Greek examples. The asyndetic pair of adjuncts is postponed to the end of its colon, after both the subject with which they agree and the verb. There follows, as in the last example, a pair coordinated by *neque ... neque*, and as in the first passage of Plautus and Cic. *Dom.* 139 there is a *sine*-phrase in the same sentence.

2 Pairs with Both Members Privatives   93

Livy 4.28.4 (32) '*hic praebituri*', inquit, '*uos telis hostium estis indefensi inulti?*'
Adjuncts, at the end of the sentence.

Livy 5.45.4 (35) *(urbis) oppressae ab hoste inuisitato inaudito*

Livy 23.27.5 (42) *ut quisque arma ceperat, sine imperio sine signo, incompositi inordinati in proelium ruunt*
  This is the fourth passage in this section in which the pair of privatives is juxtaposed with or near one or more prepositional phrases with *sine* (cf. Plaut. *Bac.* 612–14, Cic. *Dom.* 139, Sall. *Jug.* 44.1).

Livy 27.43.7 *audendum aliquid improuisum inopinatum*, 'something was to be dared that was unforeseen, unexpected'.
Possibly predicative adjuncts, in final position.

Livy 35.34.7 *singulos uniuersosque obtestantes ne insontem indemnatum consenescere in exsilio sinerent*, 'beseeching one and all that they should not allow him to grow old in exile, innocent, uncondemned'.
  This example is similar to that of Cic. *Cat.* 2.14 above. In both passages the reference is to being in exile, innocent, uncondemned (adjuncts in agreement with the unexpressed subject accustive, and here in the initial position in the clause). The similarity would not be due to Livian imitation of Cicero, but to a standard Latin way of expressing the pathos of being sent into exile, innocent. Cf. Cicero 71, Sallust 24, 52.
  Another similar pair, *iniudicatis incondemnatis*, was seen above in a fragment of a speech of Cato (*ORF* 59), where the reference is to depriving ten men of life, unjudged and uncondemned. This was a context that inspired a particular type of asyndeton bimembre in Latin.

Plin. *Nat.* 28.87 *reliqua intestabilia infanda*
Predicates.

Tac. *Ann.* 14.36.1 (124) *imbelles inermes cessuros statim, ubi ferrum uirtutemque uincentium totiens fusi agnouissent*
The secondary predicates/adjuncts are in initial position again.

Tac. *Ann.* 16.26.3 (125) *proinde intemeratus impollutus, quorum uestigiis et studiis uitam duxerit, eorum gloria peteret finem*
Adjuncts near the start of the clause.

2.2.1 Some Conclusions

Structurally the Greek and Latin pairs collected above are very similar. They are mainly adjuncts/secondary predicates, often in agreement with the subject of the verb (expressed or unexpressed), and are placed at the beginning or end of a clause or colon. Semantically however there is little overlap, which presumably reflects the differing availability of privative adjectives in the two languages, the different subject matter of the works that employ them, and possibly differences of cultural outlook. Both languages have the 'unseen, unheard' type (but for differences in their use see above on Cic. *Phil.* 11.2). Latin (above) has three examples of the type 'innocent, uncondemned', which is missing from the Greek corpus above, and also another distinctive type, with terms such as 'unarmed, unwarlike'. Other Latin pairs also belong to the field of warfare, such as 'undefended, unavenged', 'lacking order, lacking formation' and 'unforeseen, unexpected'. Greek pairs on the other hand (or at least those cited above) are often connected with the emotions, as 'unwept, unburied', 'unhonoured, without city', 'without weeping, without groaning', 'without child, without offspring'. The Latin pairs tend to be pejorative, the Greek pathetic.

2.3 The Rigveda

The following examples from the Rigveda are quoted with the translations of Jamison and Brereton (2014). This section would not exist were it not for the extremely generous help I have received from Elizabeth Tucker, who provided the examples and the translations.

1.164.2 *triṇābhi cakrám ajáram anarváṃ*
'triple-naved is the unaging, unassailable wheel'.[2]

3.1.6 *vavrā́jā sīm ánadatīr ádabdhā*
divó yahvīr ávasānā ánagnāḥ
'He (Agni) wandered toward them, who neither speak falsely nor can be deceived who are the young women of heaven, neither clothing themselves nor naked.'

3.6.4 *mahā́n sadhásthe dhruvā́ ā́ níṣatto*
'ntár dyā́vā mā́hine háryamāṇaḥ
áskre sapátnī ajā́re ámṛkte
'(Agni) taking pleasure, the great one is set down here in his enduring abode between heaven and earth, the two great ones,
who are united as co-wives, unaging and indestructible.'

3.53.15 *ā́ sū́ryasya duhitā́ tatāna*
śrávo devéṣv amṛ́tam ajuryám

---

[2] In translation the order of the adjectives and noun might be reversed, 'the wheel, unaging, unassailable'.

3 Pairs with at Least One Non-privative in- or alpha

'The Daughter of the Sun has stretched
(their) fame, immortal and unaging, to the gods.'
Hom. Il. 2.447 ἀγήρων ἀθανάτην τε is similar (see West 1988: 156), but there is a coordinator.

10.71.5 *ádhenvā carati māyáyaiṣá*
vácaṃ śuśruvā́m̐ aphalā́m apuṣpā́m
'He moves with an artifice which is no milk-cow
having heard Speech without fruit, without flower.'

10.166.2 *ahám asmi sapatnahéndra ivā́riṣṭo (= ivá áriṣṭo) ákṣataḥ*
'I am a smiter of rivals, like Indra, unharmable, invulnerable.'

All the above pairs are predicative adjuncts, usually in agreement with the subject of the verb, and all are postponed to the end of a line. Semantically they tend to stress invulnerability. The emphasis of the Greek and Latin pairs is different (in each case).
There is also an instance in which the pair is an attribute:

6.61.8 *yásyā anantó áhrutas*
tveṣáś cariṣṇúr arṇaváḥ
ámaś cárati róruvat
'(Sarasvatī) whose boundless, unswerving,
turbulent, roving flood,
her onslaught, proceeds ever roaring.'

Again the asyndetic adjectives (embedded in a longer sequence) are at the end of a line. The structural similarity of these privative pairs to those in Greek and Latin is remarkable.

3 Asyndetic Pairs with *in-* or alpha at the Start of Both Members, but with at Least One Member That Is Not a Privative Compound

Hom. Il. 5.9 ἦν δέ τις ἐν Τρώεσσι Δάρης, ἀφνειὸς ἀμύμων, 'there was among the Trojans one Dares, rich, blameless'.
ἀφνειός 'rich' is of uncertain etymology, but it is unlikely to be an alpha-privative compound. Another adjunct, postponed.

Plaut. *As.* 259 *impetritum inauguratum est*, 'I have a favorable omen, a favorable sign' (de Melo, Loeb).
Impetrio 'to seek a favourable omen for' (see *OLD*), *inauguro* 'to practise augury'.

VI Asyndetic Pairs (Mainly of Adjectives)

Lucr. 5.223 (25) *tum porro puer* ... | ... *nudus humi iacet, infans, indigus omni | uitali auxilio*
The second member is extended. The structure is similar to that of the Homeric example *Il.* 22.386 (with κεῖται: see above, 2.1). *Nudus* is the primary predicate, and the postponed privatives are secondary predicates/adjuncts.

Cic. *Att.* 7.20.1 (172) *illi autem adhuc, id est Nonis, nondum uenerant, sed erant uenturi inanes imparati*
Inanis has no certain etymology. Nevertheless this example, with the two predicative adjectives at the end of the clause, is very similar to some of the examples of genuine privative pairs above (2.2).

Tac. *Ann.* 6.19.2 (90) *iacuit immensa strages, omnis sexus, omnis aetas, inlustres ignobiles, dispersi aut aggerati*
Another instance of the verb *iaceo*. *Inlustres* and *ignobiles* are opposites (antonyms), but with the same prefix. They are substantival in this context.

Tac. *Ann.* 12.48.2 (123) *poteretur Radamistus male partis, dum inuisus infamis*
There is only one privative here. The adjectives are predicative, with the verb 'to be' in ellipse.

The examples collected in this section are structurally much the same as those above (2.2) with two definite privative compounds.

4 Asyndetic Pairs with Just One Member (Usually the Second) That Is a Privative

I make a distinction between this type and type (3) above, in which both members begin with alpha or *in-*, but of which at least one is not a privative compound.

4.1 Greek

Eur. *Med.* 255 ἐγὼ δ' ἔρημος ἄπολις οὖσ' ὑβρίζομαι | πρὸς ἀνδρός, 'while I, without relatives or city, am suffering outrage from my husband' (Kovaks, Loeb).
Adjuncts/secondary predicates. For asyndeta in Latin referring to expulsion and isolation see above, 2.2 on Livy 35.34.7 with cross references.

Men. *Heros* 72 ἃ καὶ ποήσω ... | ἱδρώς, ἀπορία 'I am going to do it ... (there will be) sweat, difficulty.'
A pair of asyndetic nouns expressing the difficulty of doing something.

4 Pairs with Just One Privative Member

4.2 Latin

Pacuvius *trag.* 3.3 Schierl
quadrupes tardigrada agrestis humilis aspera, | *breui capite, ceruice anguina, aspectu truci,* | *euiscerata inanima cum animali sono,* 'eviscerated, without life, but with the sounds of life'.
The first term *euiscerata* has the same function as an *in*-privative. This is part of a much longer asyndetic sequence. *Cum animali sono* seems to be a third, adversative, element, providing a paradoxical contrast to the preceding pair (see XXIV.6.4).

Lucr. 1.557 (2) *longa diei* | *infinita aetas,* 'the long, infinite, age of days'.
Attributes.

Cic. *Ac.* 2.125 *et cum in uno mundo ornatus hic tam sit* mirabilis innumerabilis *supra infra, dextra sinistra, ante post,* 'and since in one world this world-order is so marvellous and infinite above and below, right and left, in front and behind'.
Ornatus renders κόσμος (see Reid 1885: 317 on *Acad.* 2.119). The asyndetic adjectives are predicates with the verb 'to be'. This pair is within a sequence of pairs, the others opposites. For such patterns as typical of philosophical discourse see on Cicero 94–8.

Cic. *Phil.* 4.13 (54) *nam cum alia omnia* falsa incerta *sint, caduca mobilia*
The adjectives are predicative, with the verb 'to be'. For *incertus* in such an asyndeton see Sall. *Jug.* 51.1 below (for *mobilis* see Sall. *Jug.* 91.7, also below).

Cic. *Phil.* 5.29 (27) *noui hominis* insaniam adrogationem

Cic. *Red. sen.* 14 (44) *sine sensu sine sapore, elinguem,* tardum inhumanum *negotium, Cappadocem modo abreptum de grege uenalium diceres*
Here we have again *sine*-phrases near the *in*-privative (this phenomenon was seen several times at 2.2), and there is also a different type of negative adjective (*elinguem = sine lingua*; see below, this section, on Livy 4.37.9). *Tardum inhumanum negotium* is a single phrase, with attributive adjectives: see on Cicero 44.

Cic. *Red. sen.* 30 (46) *tribunatus nihil aliud fuit nisi constans perpetua,* fortis inuicta *defensio salutis meae*

Cic. *Sest.* 22 (11) *uidebamus genus uitae,* desidiam inertiam
The nominal type (see also *Phil.* 5.29 above).

Cic. *Sest.* 85 (50) *insigni quadam,* inaudita noua *magnitudine animi*

Sall. *Cat.* 39.2 (53) *ipsi* innoxii florentes, *sine metu aetatem agere*
The presence of *ipse* with a following predicative adjunct is also a feature shared by Virgil (see *Aen.* 1.384 below, and also 10.837 *ipse* aeger anhelans | *colla fouet*: see

VI Asyndetic Pairs (Mainly of Adjectives)

XXIV.2.1.1, 1, 10). The structure of this sentence and of the Virgilian below is much the same. Again there is a *sine*-phrase juxtaposed.

Sall. *Cat.* 48.2 *incendium uero* crudele inmoderatum *ac sibi maxume calamitosum putabat*

The adjectives are predicative, with the verb 'to be' understood. There may be a tricolon here (see after Sallust 53 on the passage).

Sall. *Cat.* 52.13 *malos . . . loca* taetra inculta, *foeda atque formidulosa habere*

It is not certain that there are two attributive pairs here (the second coordinated): see after Sallust 53. For *incultus* in asyndeton see Sall. *Jug.* 89.5 below.

Sall. *Jug.* 17.5 (54) *mare* saeuom importuosum
Predicates with the verb 'to be' understood.

Sall. *Jug.* 20.2 (57) *at is quem petebat* quietus inbellis.
Predicates with the verb 'to be' understood.

Sall. *Jug.* 51.1 (59) *facies totius negoti* uaria incerta, *foeda atque miserabilis*
Predicates possibly again with the verb 'to be' understood. Cf. Cic. *Phil.* 4.13 above, and for the colon structure (with an accumulation) Sall. *Cat.* 52.13 above.

Sall. *Jug.* 89.5 (60) *alia omnia* uasta inculta, *egentia aquae, infesta serpentibus*
Predicates with the verb 'to be' understood.

Sall. *Jug.* 91.7 (61) *genus hominum* mobile infidum
Predicates with the verb 'to be' understood.

Virg. *Aen.* 1.384 (1) *ipse* ignotus egens, *Libyae deserta peragro*
Predicative adjuncts (cf. Sall. *Cat.* 39.2 above).

Virg. *Aen.* 2.67–8 (2) turbatus inermis, | *constitit*
Adjuncts.

Virg. *G.* 1.407 (15) *ecce* inimicus atrox, *magno stridore per auras* | *insequitur Nisus*
Adjuncts.

Livy 4.37.9 (33) (*clamor*) *ab Romanis* dissonus impar, *segnius saepe iteratus* [*incerto clamore*] *prodidit pauorem animorum*

Adjuncts. This is like the example in Pacuvius (*trag.* 3.3, above, this section), in that there are two different 'negative' prefixes (cf. Livy 40.28.2 below, which has *dispersi inordinati*). *Dis-* and *in-* sometimes overlap, as in the synonyms *impar/ dispar* (see the table at *TLL* VII.1.517). For a particularly clear case of a pair of asyndetic negative adjectives of which only one has the prefix *in-* see Plaut. *Cas.* 550 *illius hirqui improbi edentuli*. For another passage with mixed negatives see above, this section, Cic. *Red. sen.* 14, where *elinguem* is equivalent to *sine lingua*; also Plaut. *Mil.* 544 *me fuisse excordem caecum incogitabilem* (*excors* means 'without intelligence').

5 Longer Sequences of Privatives   99

For a (coordinated) pair with both prefixes negatives but neither consisting of *in-* see Lucil. 874 *dissociataque omnia ac nefantia,* 'everything disunited and unspeakable'.

Livy 23.3.2 (41) *clausos omnes in curia accipite, solos inermos*
Predicative adjuncts.

Livy 40.28.2 *dispersi inordinati exibant*
Adjuncts. See on Livy 35.

Tac. *Hist.* 2.11.3 (24) *ante signa pedes ire, horridus incomptus famaeque dissimilis*
Adjuncts, postponed behind the verb. A third term is added of different meaning.

Tac. *Hist.* 3.39.2 (27) *sanctus inturbidus, nullius repentini honoris, adeo non principatus adpetens, parum effugerat, ne dignus crederetur*
These are predicative adjuncts, agreeing with the subject of the verb.

Tac. *Ann.* 1.17.4 (117) *militiam ipsam grauem infructuosam*
Predicates with the verb 'to be' understood.

Tac. *Ann.* 4.36.3 (79) *leues ignobiles poenis adficiebantur*
The two terms are substantival and subject of the verb.

Tac. *Ann.* 6.8.4 (121) *abditos principis sensus, et si quid occultius parat, exquirere inlicitum anceps*
Predicates with the verb 'to be' understood.

Many of the pairs in this section are pejorative or have an unfavourable nuance. Isolation and expulsion come up, as do uncertainty and fickleness, cruelty, ferocity and hostility, harshness of sound, lack of order, illegality, and vulnerability through lack of arms and lack of support. This does not exhaust the varieties, and there are some pairs with favourable meaning, but generally such pairs express strong feeling. They are frequently predicates or secondary predicates.

5 Asyndetic Triplets (or Longer Sequences) Comprising Terms That All Have a Privative Prefix

5.1 Greek

In Greek, tricola comprising alpha-privatives are quite common, particularly in tragedy. See for example Fraenkel (1950: 2.217), Denniston (1952: 101), Stevens (1971: 156) on Eur. *Andr.* 491 (citing about a dozen cases with a comment on their frequency in Euripides and rhetorical prose), Durante (1976: 151), Johansen and Whittle (1980: 2.120) on Aesch. *Supp.* 143 = 153, Allan (2008: 278–9) ('a mannerism in Eur.'). Lists of such terms tend to be

VI Asyndetic Pairs (Mainly of Adjectives)

given without contexts, but the structures in which they occur are of importance because they are capable of showing up contrasts with other languages. Here is a selection, with structural comments.

Hom. *Il.* 9.63 ἀφρήτωρ ἀθέμιστος ἀνέστιός ἐστιν ἐκεῖνος / ὅς, 'A clanless, lawless, hearthless man is he that ...' (Murray, Loeb).
See Griffin (1995: 83–4 ad loc.). Fraenkel (1950: 2.217) finds here an association with 'solemn imprecations'.
Predicative adjectives with the verb 'to be', in initial position in the line.

Hdt. 1.32 ἄπηρος δὲ ἐστί, ἄνουσος, ἀπαθὴς κακῶν, εὔπαις, εὐηδής, 'and he is free from deformity, sickness, and all evil, and happy in his children and his good looks' (Godley, Loeb, modified).
Here there is first a tricolon of adjectives with alpha-privative, and then an asyndetic pair with the same prefix, εὐ-. Note that the tricolon is discontinuous (interrupted, here by the verb 'to be': see XX). This is an accumulation of asyndeta of a type found often in Latin, comprising a triplet followed by a dicolon (the structures 3 + 2 and 2 + 3 will often come up: see e.g. Cicero 61 and XXVI.7.2.1, third point). See Durante (1976: 151) on this example, who sees it as inspired by poetry.
The adjectives are predicative, with the verb 'to be'.

Aesch. *Cho.* 54 σέβας δ' ἄμαχον ἀδάματον ἀπόλεμον τὸ πρίν, 'The reverence – once unconquerable, invincible, impregnable' (Sommerstein, Loeb).
Adjuncts.

Soph. *Ant.* 876 ἄκλαυτος ἄφιλος ἀνυμέναι|ος <ἁ> ταλαίφρων ἄγομαι | τὰν ἑτοίμαν ὁδόν, 'Unwept, friendless, unwedded, I am conducted, unhappy one, along the way that lies before me!' (Lloyd-Jones, Loeb).
There may be two separate adjuncts, but alternatively the privative tricolon could be taken as predicate with the verb ἄγομαι and <ἁ> ταλαίφρων as secondary predicate ('I, unhappy one, am conducted unwept ...').

Soph. *OC* 130 καὶ παραμειβόμεσθ' ἀδέρκτως | ἀφώνως ἀλόγως, 'whom we pass without looking, without sound, without speech' (Lloyd-Jones, Loeb).
The adverbs have the same function as adjectives of the secondary predicate type elsewhere.

Eur. *Andr.* 491 ἄθεος ἄνομος ἄχαρις ὁ φόνος, 'Godless, lawless, graceless is this murder'(Kovacs, Loeb).
See Stevens (1971: 156) ad loc. The adjectives are predicative, with the verb 'to be' understood. The structure of this line is much the same as that of Hom. *Il.* 9.63 above, this section except that there the verb 'to be' is expressed.

Plato *Phdr.* 240a5 ἔτι τοίνυν ἄγαμον ἄπαιδα ἄοικον ὅ τι πλεῖστον χρόνον παιδικὰ ἐραστὴς εὔξαιτ' ἂν γενέσθαι, 'Moreover the lover would wish his beloved to be as long as possible unmarried, childless, and homeless' (Fowler, Loeb).
This group is predicative, subject of a copula verb (γενέσθαι).

5 Longer Sequences of Privatives

Dem. 4.36 ἄτακτα, ἀδιόρθωτα, ἀόρισθ' ἅπαντα, 'everything is ill-arranged, ill-managed, ill-defined' (Vince, Loeb).

The structure is the same as that at Eur. *Andr.* 491 above, with the tricolon of adjectives at the start, followed by the substantive in agreement, with 'to be' understood.

The following passage is cited by Fraenkel (1950: 2.217; see also 353) as a tricolon with alpha-privatives, but the third adjective is translated by Sommerstein (Loeb) as an attribute of a following noun, with the first two adjectives adjuncts/secondary predicates of an earlier noun (thus the pair ἄμαχον ἀπόλεμον is separated from ἀνίερον):

Aesch. *Ag.* 769 δαίμονά τε τὰν ἄμαχον ἀπόλεμον, | ἀνίερον θράσος... | ...Ἄτας, '(An old act of outrage is wont to give birth to ... and to) the deity with whom none can war or fight, the unholy arrogance ... of Ruin' (Sommerstein, Loeb).

Most of the above examples are predicates with the verb 'to be' or equivalents. They tend to be in prominent positions, usually at the start of the line or near the start.

5.2 Latin

Here are some examples from Latin, adjectival and adverbial:

Plaut. *Per.* 168 *satis fuit indoctae inmemori insipienti dicere totiens*

Plaut. *Per.* 408 *oh, lutum lenonium, | commixtum caeno sterculinum publicum, | inpure inhoneste iniure inlex labes popli*

Plaut. *Rud.* 194 *tum hoc mi indecore inique inmodeste | datis di*

Plaut. *Rud.* 652 *legerupa inpudens inpurus inuerecundissimus*

Lucilius 600 *hic cruciatur fame | frigore, inluuie inbalnitie inperfundi<ti>e incuria*

Cic. *Att.* 9.10.2 ἐν τοῖς ἐρωτικοῖς *alienat <quod> immunde insulse indecore fit, sic...* An emotional context. This is an ascending tricolon.

5.3 The Rigveda

10.94.11 *tṛdilā́ átṛdilāso ádrayo*
'śramaṇā́ áśṛthitā ámṛtyavaḥ
anāturā́ ajárā sthā́maviṣṇavaḥ (= *stha ámaviṣṇavaḥ*)
supīvā́so átṛṣitā átṛṣṇajaḥ

VI Asyndetic Pairs (Mainly of Adjectives)

'Drilled or undrilled, you (pressing) stones
are <u>unwearying, unslackened, immortal</u>
<u>unailing, unaging, unbudgeable,</u>
very stout, <u>unthirsty, unthirsting</u>.'

1.143.8 *ádabdhebhir ádṛpitebhir iṣṭé*
'nimiṣadbhiḥ pári pāhi no jáḥ
'With your undeceivable, undistracted, unwinking (protectors), o object of our quest (Agni), protect our kindred all around.'

10.22.8 *akarmā́ dásyur abhí no amantúr*
anyávrato ámānuṣaḥ
'The Dasyu <u>of non-deeds, of non-thought, the non-man</u>, whose commandments are other, is against us.'

I note finally in passing that some asyndetic tricola have two privative compounds and a third term of different type. I have not collected those of this type systematically, but here are a few:

Aesch. *Pers.* 855 ὁ γεραιὸς | <u>παντάρκης ἀκάκας ἄμαχος</u> βασιλεὺς | ... ἆρχε χώρας, 'our old all-sufficing, never harming, invincible king ... ruled the country'.

Men. *Mis.* 803 ἀ[π]όρως ζῆθ', ὀδυνηρῶς ἀσθενῶ[ς, 'Make your life futile, painful, feeble.'
This is another discontinuous example.

Men. *Asp.* 415 ἄπιστον ἄλογον δεινόν, 'Creditless, senseless, dread'.
Possibly a fragment from an unknown tragedy (see Arnott, Loeb ad loc.).

6 Oppositions, with a Privative Compound Negating Its Simplex

West (2007: 101) notes that the 'Indo-European ability to create negative compounds with the prefix **n̥-* made it easy to form polar expressions of the type "X and non-X"', and he cites examples from the Rigveda and Atharvaveda and other languages, some of them asyndetic (e.g. AV *dūnā́ ádūnā* 'burnt or unburnt'), others syndetic. See also Watkins (1995: 43, 221). In Latin, but not, it seems, Greek, such pairs with asyndeton are quite common (see below). The term 'polarity' is normally used in linguistics to refer to an opposition with 'positive' and 'negative' pairs, but most opposites that fall into the category 'antonyms' (for which see XIII.2) can be analysed as having polarity of this sort (see Cruse 1986: 246–7), even (as is usually the case) when the pair does not have a member with a privative prefix. The term 'polar' is constantly used of opposites in classical

6 Privative Compound Negating Its Simplex 103

scholarship, usually, as far as I can see, without definition, and usually without throwing any light on the nature of the opposition.

Another ancient language that has asyndetic pairs of this structure is Umbrian (Iguvine tablets; see also XXII.4). See *Tab. Ig.* IIa.19 **veskla : snata : asnata**, translated by Poultney (1959: 178) as 'wet and dry vessels', but see his note at 179 on the uncertain etymology, and particularly Untermann (2000: 687–8). Both terms are clearly of the same root, with the second having the negative prefix **a-** (see Untermann 2000: 688). The pair occurs elsewhere in the corpus too (see Untermann 2000: 687).

Note too e.g. *Tab. Ig.* VIb.62 (*nerus*) . *sihitir* . *ansihitir* '(chief citizens) in office, not in office', or 'girt, ungirt' (?) (see Poultney 1959: 326; also Watkins 1995: 43, and particularly Untermann 2000: 396). This pair is followed immediately by another of the same type, (*iouies*) . *hostatir* . *anostatir*, translated '(young men) under arms, not under arms' (see Poultney 1959: 309 and Untermann 2000: 336–7 on the uncertainties). The same accumulation is found also at VIb.59–60.

Tab. Ig. VIa.28 *uirseto . auirseto . uas . est* '(if in thy sacrifice) there be any seen or unseen fault' is a pair of a type also in Vedic and Latin, with or without a coordinator (see Watkins 1995: 43 and the prayer at Cato *Agr.* 141.2, with *morbos uisos inuisosque*; also Poultney 1959: 331, Untermann 2000: 854–5).

This type in Greek occurs at Aesch. *Supp.* 862: σὺ δ' ἐν ναὶ ναὶ βάσῃ τάχα, θέλεος ἀθέλεος 'You will quickly board the ship, the ship, willing or unwilling!' (Sommerstein, Loeb), = Lat. *nolens uolens*. Johansen and Whittle (1980: 3.198) ad loc. remark: 'Asyndeton in an expression signifying "nolens volens" appears to be unidiomatic in Greek', adding that the 'only recorded – and not too close – analogy to θέλεος ἀθέλεος appears to be Hp. *Aph.* 2.3 ὕπνος ἀγρυπνίη' (citing Fehling 1969: 252, 276). See also Sommerstein (2019: 320) ad loc., noting that neither word θέλεος/ἀθέλεος occurs elsewhere, and stating that expressions meaning 'whether you like it or not' are common in Greek but not otherwise with asyndeton. See however Pease (1955: 172), cited below, 7.

The implication of this supposed lack of close analogies to θέλεος ἀθέλεος (cf. too Fehling 1969: 276) would seem to be that the positive + alpha-privative type, with asyndeton, is hardly found in Greek. It may be rare, but here are a few near-parallels.

Arist. *Metaph.* 1.5.6 (986a.23) ἕτεροι δὲ τῶν αὐτῶν τούτων τὰς ἀρχὰς δέκα λέγουσιν εἶναι τὰς κατὰ συστοιχίαν λεγομένας, πέρας ἄπειρον, περιττὸν

VI Asyndetic Pairs (Mainly of Adjectives)

ἄρτιον, ἓν πλῆθος, δεξιὸν ἀριστερόν, ἄρρεν θῆλυ, ἠρεμοῦν κινούμενον, εὐθὺ καμπύλον, φῶς σκότος, ἀγαθὸν κακόν, τετράγωνον ἑτερόμηκες. These are all types of opposites. For ἄπειρος and its relation to πέρας see LSJ s.v. B ('limit and the unlimited': see on Cicero 94–8).

Xen. *Mem*.1.1.16 (with anaphora) σκοπῶν, τί εὐσεβές, τί ἀσεβές, τί καλόν, τί αἰσχρόν, τί δίκαιον, τί ἄδικον, τί σωφροσύνη, τί μανία, τί ἀνδρεία, τί δειλία, 'investigating what is pious, what is impious; what is beautiful, what is ugly; what is just, what is unjust; what is prudence, what is madness; what is courage, what is cowardice' (Marchant and Henderson, Loeb).

NT 2 Tim. 4.2 κήρυξον τὸν λόγον, ἐπίστηθι εὐκαίρως ἀκαίρως, ἔλεγξον, ἐπιτίμησον, παρακάλεσον, 'preach the word, be urgent in season and out of season, convince, rebuke, exhort' (see Malherbe 1984).

The pair εὐκαίρως ἀκαίρως, with εὐ- + root opposed to ἀ- + same root, is of some interest. It is a slight variation on the type with root term followed by its alpha-privative compound, but the effect is the same. The same type (but with anaphora), τί εὐσεβές, τί ἀσεβές, is in the passage of Xenophon above. See also Fehling (1969: 252), and XIX.1, last passage. For semantically opposed prefixes, cf. e.g. Ter. *Hau*. 643 *prosit obsit*, 'helpful or harmful', Tac. *Ann*. 12.33 (100) *ut aditus abscessus, cuncta nobis importuna et suis in melius essent*.

Note also at 2 Tim. 4.2 the asyndetic dicolon followed by an asyndetic tricolon (2 + 3, a common asyndetic structure in Latin: see e.g. Cicero 12, 15, 85 and also XIX.1, XXVI.7.2.1).

I turn now to Latin. There is a collection of positive and negative pairs by Wills (1996: 451–4), but the examples overwhelmingly have a coordinator. Coordination would seem to have been the norm by the classical period, a point that Wills (1996: 454) implies thus: 'The evidence of comedy suggests asyndeton was the inherited syntax in some of these formulae.' Donatus on Ter. *Ad*. 990 cites as *prouerbiales elocutiones* the pairs *fanda nefanda, digna indigna, uelis nolis*, and it is then stated that *fuit ueteribus usitatum iusta iniusta, digna indigna, fas nefas* (see further Oakley 1997: 524, citing two other relevant passages of Donatus, *Andr*. 214, *Eun*. 1058, but not this one). Note that such pairs are here associated with the *ueteres* (see also XXVII.1.1). I collect some examples below, mainly from comedy and the historians.

Plaut. *As*. 247 *dignos indignos adire atque experiri certumst mihi*

This example is cited as an asyndeton by Wills (1996: 454), along with *Capt*. 200 *indigna digna habenda sunt, erus quae facit*. This latter is not an asyndeton at all, but the meaning is 'The wrongs a master does must be deemed right' (de Melo, Loeb). Wills (1996: 453) collects examples of the opposition *dignus/indignus*, in which there is usually coordination. See also further below, this section.

6 Privative Compound Negating Its Simplex 105

Plaut. *Bac.* 401 *nunc certamen cernitur | sisne necne ut esse oportet, malus bonus quoiuis modi,* | *iustus iniustus, malignus largus, comincommodus,* '... whether or not you are as you ought to be, ... just or unjust ...' (de Melo, Loeb).
A series of opposites, which includes *iustus iniustus* (antonyms) (see also XXIII. 8.10). The text is doubtful at the final word (B has *com incomodus,* C *commodus incommodus,* which does not scan; *comincommodus* is printed by Lindsay; Leo prints *comis incommodus*). If *com(m)incommodus* happened to be right (on which see Ernout 1935: 64; attributed to Bergk by de Melo, Loeb), it would have to be an ad hoc comic compound representing *commodus incommodus* (cf. Plautus' *tragicomoedia* at *Am.* 59, with II.3.1).
Adjuncts/secondary predicates. For the pair 'just, unjust' see the passage of Terence below.

Plaut. *Cur.* 280 *date uiam mihi, noti [atque] ignoti*
Atque was deleted by Bentley; for the false addition of coordinators in manuscripts of Plautus see Lindsay (OCT) on *Aul.* 784.

Ter. *Ad.* 990 *quia non iusta iniusta prorsus omnia omnino obsequor,* 'because I won't go along with everything you do indiscriminately right or wrong' (Barsby, Loeb).

Cic. *Ac.* 2.29 *constitutionem ueri falsi, cogniti incogniti*
These two pairs, both of opposites but only the second of the type discussed here, are substantival.

Cic. *Tusc.* 5.114 *at uero bona mala, aequa iniqua, honesta turpia, utilia inutilia, magna parua poterat (discernere)*
Cf. for the first pair two of the passages of Livy cited below. Substantivised adjectives again.

M. Antonius ap. Quint. 3.6.45 *paucae res sunt quibus ex rebus omnes orationes nascuntur, factum non factum, ius iniuria, bonum malum,* 'There are only a few things which give birth to all speeches: fact or not; right or wrong; good or bad' (Russell, Loeb).
See below, 7 for the type *factum non factum.*

Livy 2.32.7 *eam per aequa per iniqua reconciliandam ciuitati esse*

Livy 8.34.10 *nec discernatur interdiu nocte, aequo iniquo loco, <iussu> iniussu imperatoris pugnent*
The addition is virtually certain (see Oakley 1998: 741).

Livy 9.3.3 (38) *armati inermes, fortes ignaui, pariter omnes capti atque uicti sumus*
Strictly the pair should have been *armati inermati* to belong here, but I include this one because *inarmatus/inermatus* is unattested in the period covered by the *OLD.*

Livy 9.14.11 (11) *caedunt pariter resistentes fusosque, inermes atque armatos, seruos liberos, puberes impubes, homines iumentaque*

VI Asyndetic Pairs (Mainly of Adjectives)

Livy 38.23.1 (66) *ruunt caeci per uias per inuia; nulla praecipitia saxa nullae rupes obstant*

Tac. Ann. 4.49.3 (82) *cum ingens multitudo bellatorum imbellium uno reliquo fonte uterentur*
Here is another place in which the negative form is not based exactly on the positive.

At *Sat.* 2.3.248 Horace refers to playing a (childish) game, *ludere par impar*, 'to play odd and even', presumably a guessing game (see XXIX.2.1.1). The same phrase is in a letter at Suet. *Aug.* 71.4 *par impar ludere*. The asyndeton may be old in such a formula.

Dignus indignus, which was seen above, is also used in asyndeton by Virgil at *Aen.* 12.811 (XXIV.2.1.2, 18): *nec tu me aeria solam nunc sede uideres | digna indigna pati.* The adjectives have been substantivised here. On this example see Tarrant (2012: 297) ad loc.: '"suffering all kinds of things". *digna indigna* is an asyndetic polar expression, in which opposites are juxtaposed to express a totality ... Here *digna* is not meant literally, since Juno would not wish to imply that any part of her sufferings was deserved.' Tarrant adds that in most instances of this combination 'both terms have full value'. Gonda (1959: 344) indeed comments on the potential for illogicality in positive–negative pairs: 'It is not surprising that these phrases are not rarely heard in emotional and emphatic speech. They may even express a logical absurdity.' He cites Plaut. *Trin.* 360 *quin comedit quod fuit, quod non fuit,* 'you mean the one who ate up what he had and what he didn't have' (though here the phraseology is meant to be funny). Tarrant cites as a parallel to his example Catull. 64.405 (*fanda nefanda*; but giving the negative the form *infanda*), where only the negative aspects 'can have alienated the gods'. Another parallel (with a coordinator) is Tac. *Ann.* 15.37.4 *per licita atque illicita*, where defilement through permitted actions is a 'paradoxical notion' (Ash 2018: 174). See also Cicero 200 on *summis infimis* (antipodals) at Cic. *Fam.* 8.13.4, which cannot be taken literally, and see further XIII.2 on pairs (such as this last) that embrace all that lies between and not only the extremes.

Here finally is a variant in which the two opposites, one of them a privative, are of different root: Hor. *Sat.* 2.1.59 *diues inops, Romae, seu fors ita iusserit, exsul,* 'rich, poor'. See XXIX.2.1.1.

7 Positive–Negative Pairs in Latin of Which the Negated Term Has a Prefix other than Privative *in-*

Positive–negative asyndetic oppositions do not only comprise pairs with an alpha- or *in*-privative as one member. Note for example (see above,

7 Negative Prefixes other than in-

6, second last paragraph) Plaut. *Trin.* 360 *quod fuit quod non fuit*, where in a clausal pair with anaphora one member is negated by *non*. Lucr. 1.1075 (XXIV.7.1.4, 17) *per medium, per non medium* 'through centre or not centre' is more striking, because *non* behaves as a prefix. The same usage is in a fragment of a speech of M. Antonius quoted by Quint. 3.6.45 (see above, 6): *factum non factum, ius iniuria*. Here the *non*-construction is juxtaposed with positive + *in*-. Cf. Lucil. 387 *quid sumam, quid non* 'what I should choose, what not', 520 *quid 'mundum' <atque 'penus'>, quid non*, Hor. *Ep.* 1.2.3 *quid sit pulchrum, quid turpe, quid utile, quid non.*
   A distinctive opposition is the combining of *uolo* and *nolo* in various forms. The earliest occurrence of this asyndeton is at Cic. *Nat.* 1.17: *nolo existimes me adiutorem huic uenisse sed auditorem, et quidem aequum, libero iudicio, nulla eius modi adstrictum necessitate ut mihi <u>uelim nolim</u> sit certa quaedam tuenda sententia*, 'I do not want you to think that I have come as his assistant rather than as a listener, and indeed a fair one, with freedom of judgment, bound by no necessity of the type that would make me defend a specific opinion willy-nilly.' An apparent example earlier in Terence is of different type:

Ph. 950 <u>*nolo uolo;*</u> <u>*uolo nolo*</u> *rursum; cape cedo*
   The reference is to constant changes of mind, and there is not a form of (asyndetic) coordination. Cf. *Eun.* 818 *pergin, scelesta, mecum perplexe loqui? | 'scio, nescio, abiit, audiui, ego non adfui'*, 'Do you persist in talking in riddles, you wretch? "I know ... I don't know ... he's gone ... I heard ... I wasn't there".' This again is not a coordination (i.e. asyndetic), but is meant to express indecision with changes of mind (see also VIII.1 on Thuc. 7.71.4).

   By far the most comprehensive collection of examples and the most wide-ranging discussion of *uolo nolo* and its variants is by Pease (1955: 171–2), in a long note in which he cites all the evidence for this asyndeton in Latin, and also illustrates (172) the variants with coordination. He also collects Greek asyndetic parallels, which include not only Aesch. *Supp.* 862 θέλεος ἀθέλεος quoted at 6 above, but also Arr. *Epict.* 3.9.16 θέλεις οὐ θέλεις, Arr. *Epict.* 3.3.3, M. Aurel. 11.15 θέλει οὐ θέλει, in which there is not alpha-privative but οὐ (cf. e.g. *factum non factum* above), and (similarly) Liban. *Decl.* 36.9 ἄκων ἔκων.
   Nolo originally had the prefix *ne*- (note Plaut. *Trin.* 361 *multa eueniunt homini quae uolt, quae neuolt*, an anaphoric asyndeton bimembre; cf. *Merc.* 7 *quid uelint, quid non uelint*), and this prefix is found in a different asyndetic pair at Catull. 64.405 (see section 6 above): *omnia fanda nefanda malo permixta furore*. Usually *fas/nefas* and *fandus/nefandus* have a coordinator (see XXVII.1.1, and Wills 1996: 451–2, Oakley 1997: 524).

VI Asyndetic Pairs (Mainly of Adjectives)

An opposition 'A not-A' may sometimes be implicitly present in a pair of lexemes without prefix, as at Hor. *Ep.* 1.7.72 *dicenda tacenda locutus* 'having spoken things that should be said and should not be said' (on this passage see XXIX.2.2).

Alternative privative prefixes came up a number of times, above, 4.2 (see there on *euisceratus, elinguis, dissonus, excors, edentulus*; see also XXIX.2.1.1 on *depugis*, and XXV.1.1.2 on Lucilius 10 with cross references).

8 Prefixes other than the Privative That Are Repeated in Asyndetic Pairs

Alpha- and *in*-prefixes are not the only prefixes that are repeated in asyndetic pairs (see e.g. Durante 1976: 152, West 1988: 156, id. 2007: 109). Here is a small collection of examples from Greek and Latin. The Greek pairs here are mainly adjectives used as adjuncts, whereas most of the Latin examples are pairs of verbs.

8.1 Greek

Hom. *Il.* 2.324–5 τόδ' ἔφηνε τέρας μέγα μητίετα Ζεύς, | ὄψιμον ὀψιτέλεστον, 'the counsellor Zeus showed this great sign, late in coming, late in fulfilment'.
Another pair that is postponed but at the start of a line.

Hom. *Il.* 5.613 ὅς ῥ' ἐνὶ Παισῷ | ναῖε πολυκτήμων πολυλήϊος, 'who dwelt in Paesus, rich in substance, rich in corn-land'.

Hom. *Il.* 9.154 ἐν δ' ἄνδρες ναίουσι πολύρρηνες πολυβοῦται, 'in them dwell men rich in flocks, rich in cattle'.

Aesch. *Ag.* 1410 ἀπέδικες ἀπέταμες, 'You have cast them aside, you have cut them off' (Sommerstein, Loeb) (cf. 1553 κάππεσε, κάτθανε).

8.2 Latin

Ennius *trag.* 117 (XXIV.5.2.4, 18) Jocelyn *alia fluctus differt dissupat* | *uisceratim membra*

Cic. *Att.* 2.20.2 (175) *Pompeius adfirmat non esse periculum, adiurat*

Cic. *Dom.* 113 (67) *quibus inspectantibus domus mea disturbaretur diriperetur*

Cic. *Phil.* 5.36 (75) *cumque exercitum tantum ... conscripserit comparant*

Livy 5.30.6 (34) *(orare)* ne exsulem extorrem *populum Romanum ... in hostium urbem agerent*

Tac. *Ann.* 4.2.2 (136) *inrepere paulatim militares animos* adeundo appellando

Tac. *Ann.* 4.69.3 (86) congressus conloquia, *notae ignotaeque aures uitari*

Tac. *Ann.* 5.7.1 (141) *tunc singulos, ut cuique* adsistere adloqui *animus erat, retinens aut dimittens partem diei absumpsit.*

For asyndetic verbs with repeated prefix in Plautus see XXIII.5.4 (about twenty examples).

There are longer sequences too: note Plaut. *Mil.* 191 *domi habet animum falsiloquom falsificum falsiiurium, Trin.* 406 *comesum expotum, exunctum elotum in balineis* (semantically there seem to be two pairs here).

9 Conclusions

I start with privative pairs (and triplets), and then move on to positive–negative oppositions.

At 2.1 above I have quoted 15 alpha-privative asyndetic pairs from Greek, almost all of which of which are adjuncts/secondary predicates. Aesch. *Eum.* 352 is the only exception. Of the adjuncts, 7 are in final position in a colon or line. These Greek pairs seem mainly intended to evoke pathos, referring as they do to death and lack of burial, abandonment and desertion, disappearance, infertility, childlessness and an unmarried state.

A total of 17 pairs of privatives were quoted from Latin (2.2), 13 of them adjuncts/secondary predicates and 3 predicates with the verb 'to be' or comparable verb. There is only one pair of attributes. Placement of adjuncts in final position is again quite common (five or six examples). Sometimes adjuncts precede the verb and may be in initial position, which is also the case in Greek. Semantically, as was stated earlier, the Latin pairs are quite unlike the Greek. Many of them are pejorative or abusive, referring to un-Roman behaviour, such as absence of warlike qualities, military disorder, lack of reputation, friends, wealth. Those pairs that might be labelled 'pathetic' reflect Roman values, notably innocence in a legal sense. Of the pairs, seven are in accumulations: that is, they are juxtaposed with other coordinated terms, whether syndetic or asyndetic.

We saw seven asyndetic privative pairs (a selection) from the Rigveda (2.3), all of them in final position, and six of them adjuncts. Their semantic differences from the Greek and Latin pairs were noted earlier. Most refer to invulnerability and the like. The structures are very similar

VI Asyndetic Pairs (Mainly of Adjectives)

in the three languages, but the semantic character of the terms is contextually and culturally determined. Even pairs that look much the same, such as 'unseen, unheard', may have a different implication in different languages.

I collected at 5.1 eight alpha-privative tricola from Greek. Only two of these were adjuncts, and five subject of the verb 'to be', expressed or understood, or another copular verb. Final position is not the norm either. Just one instance is of that type (comprising adverbs), whereas in six cases the tricolon is in initial position or near the beginning. I cite six such groups from Latin at 5.2.

In two sections above (3, 4.2) Latin pairs with just one privative in *in-* are cited. Some of these have two prefixes in *in-* of which one has a different function from privative, but most comprise an adjective in *in-* combined with an adjective of a different type. There are 33 examples in total. The vast majority are either adjuncts/secondary predicates, or predicates with the verb 'to be', expressed or understood, and very few are attributive. Again we see the rarity of the attributive type, and the frequency of adjuncts. In about ten cases the pair is part of an accumulation.

Some idea of the prominence of asyndetic pairs in *in-* in Latin is given by statistics from the historians. In Sallust 9 of the 16 numbered pairs of adjectives in asyndeton have at least one privative in *in-*. When there is just one privative in such a pair, it is placed second in every case but one. In the eight books of Livy used as a sample in this work, there are 14 pairs of asyndetic adjectives. There are 5 of these in the religious formula (*Iuppiter*) *optimus maximus*. Of the remaining 9, 7 have at least one privative. When there is just one privative in a pair (4 times), it is always in second position. The other 3 instances have two privatives. In Tacitus' *Annals* 6 of the 10 asyndetic pairs of adjectives have at least one privative (3 have one and 3 have two). Tacitus' *Histories* are the odd work out. There are 8 adjectival pairs in total, 3 of which have one privative in *in-*.

Similarly in Horace's *Satires*, which have about 22 asyndeta bimembria, there are 8 adjectival pairs, of which 5 have at least one member that is an *in*-privative, and the remaining 3 have a negative of another type.

Pairs of adjectives in Latin with at least one privative are spread across a variety of genres: comedy, epic, oratory, history. The predominating type is the secondary predicate, which is also the case in Greek, though there most examples seem to be in tragedy (I stress that I have attempted no comprehensive collection). Such pairs in both languages express strong feelings, and presumably had a rhetorical or judgemental feel to them, particularly in Latin, where they are not only in Cicero's speeches but also in speeches in historians.

It must be stressed that pairs with a privative adjective (or two such) are not only asyndetic. In Horace, for example, even in the *Satires* such pairs do not have the field to themselves (see XXIX.4.1). In other genres, notably the *Odes*, asyndetic pairs are absent but syndetic pairs with at least one privative are found. One of these, at 4.9.26–7 (*inlacrimabiles | urgentur ignotique*), is of Greek type. *Inlacrimabilis*, here meaning 'unwept', is confined to Horace in the classical period, and it must be inspired by ἄκλαυτος. We saw above (2.1, this chapter), that in Homer, Aeschylus and Euripides this term is found in asyndetic pairs, yet Horace uses it with a coordinator. Clearly genre as well as the type of pairing was one determinant of asyndeton (and one must look beyond Homer and tragedy for possible influences on Horace in this respect in the *Odes*).

The distribution of opposites with a positive and negative term with privative prefix is different (above, 6). In Greek the type seems to be very rare. In Latin I have found it mainly in the early period and in historiography, whereas in ordinary classical Latin such oppositions are usually given a coordinator. The examples cited above from Cicero and M. Antonius are all in accumulations. It would seem that the asyndetic type was waning, but preserved to a limited extent in the archaising language of history, or in accumulations of elements coordinated in various ways.

Appendix: English

Fraenkel (1950: 2.217) in a note on privative compounds in asyndeton in Greek remarks that the 'figure is one which invites imitation', and he cites e.g. 'in tragic language' *Paradise Lost* 2.185 *unrespited, unpitied, unreprieved*. In English today privative pairs in particular are commonplace even in mundane journalism, and there is certainly no need now to see in them imitation of Greek (or Latin), though the history of such sequences in English would be of interest. They are often predicative adjuncts. Here are a few examples, from George Herbert (1593–1633), the nineteenth century and more recently.

George Herbert, *Love (3)* ('Love bade me welcome'), in *George Herbert, The Complete Poetry*, ed. J. Drury and V. Moul (2015), p. 180 (l. 9) *I the unkind, ungrateful?* (drawn to my attention by Sarah Ogilvie).

George Eliot, *Middlemarch*, III (Penguin Classics) *the unloved, unvenerated old man.*

VI Asyndetic Pairs (Mainly of Adjectives)

George Eliot, *Middlemarch*, 158 *The tinge of <u>unpretentious, inoffensive</u> vulgarity in Mrs Vincy* ...

The last two examples are attributes.

Colin Dexter, *The Daughters of Cain* (1995), 24 *a house which* ... *she'd immediately observed to be still standing there, <u>unburned, unvandalized</u>*.

Robert A. Caro, *The Years of Lyndon Johnson*, Volume 4: *The Passage of Power* (London 2012), 527–8: *The power to investigate, the power to regulate, the power to license – those were not the only powers of government with which Lyndon Johnson, <u>implacable, unyielding</u>, refusing to accept anything less than exactly what he wanted, was, from behind closed doors at the LBJ ranch, threatening the press during that Christmas vacation*. (I owe this example to Patrick Finglass.)

Gillian Flynn, *Gone Girl* (2012), 32 *something hidden away that makes me <u>unsatisfiable, unsatisfying</u>*.

Gillian Flynn, *Gone Girl*, 37 *I despised the women who staffed Comfort Hill: <u>unsmiling, uncomforting</u>. Underpaid, gruellingly underpaid*.

The negatives continue here in the repetition of *underpaid*.

The Times, 15 February 2013, p. 86, on Chelsea FC's <u>unwanted, unloved</u> interim manager.

Sunday Times Culture, 20 October 2013, book review p. 38 with the heading *Undefeated, uncowed*.

R. Galbraith, *The Cuckoo's Calling* (2013), 5 *They wrote that she was <u>unbalanced, unstable, unsuited</u> to the stardom her wildness and her beauty had snared*.

Les Murray, 'When two percent were students' (poem), in *Humanities Australia* 6 (2015), lines 3–4 *then home to be late for meals, | an <u>impractical, unwanted</u> boarder*.

Here the second term is stronger.

The Sunday Times Magazine, 24 May 2015, p. 16, of 'The Lost Innocents': *They were <u>unmourned, unloved</u> – and buried in <u>unmarked</u> graves*.

Carol Midgley, *The Times*, 19 August 2015 (*Times* 2 p. 2) *As an image it's <u>unflattering, unstatesmanlike</u>* (of the Prime Minister David Cameron).

The Times (*Times* 2), 28 September 2016. Heading of fashion article by Anna Murphy, <u>*Belted, unbelted*</u>, *the trench is good*.

An opposition of positive + negative, the latter a privative in *un-*.

CHAPTER VII

Simplex + Compound in Asyndeton

1 Evidence

A compound verb is sometimes placed immediately after its simplex. Such juxtapositions are not all of the same type.

I start with a straightforward type. In the *Lex Cornelia de XX quaestoribus* of Sullan date (Crawford 1996: 1.293–4) *lego* and *sublego* in different forms occur together twelve times (see XXII.2.1). This law has not a single instance of *et* or *aut* but is replete with various types of asyndeton; *-que* is used, but mainly as a clausal connective. At I.41 e.g. note *quasei . . . antea lectei sublectei essent*, 'as if . . . they had previously been chosen or chosen in replacement'. In this pair the compound has a different meaning from the simplex, and the asyndeton is disjunctive.

Another legal pair is in the *Lex Coloniae Genetiuae*, which was probably engraved in the Flavian period though originating in the Caesarian period (Crawford 1996: 1.395): LXX.14, p. 403 *sumere consumere liceto*, 'it is to be lawful to take and spend' (translation p. 423). There is a sequence of events, which is commonly the case in asyndeta bimembria, and the two verbs are again of different meaning.

A different pattern can be seen, first, in a Greek example. Renehan (1976: 22) quotes Alexis fr. 25.4 K πίνωμεν, ἐμπίνωμεν, and also Men. *Dysk.* 818 δίδου, μεταδίδου. He refers to Watkins (1967: 116) as saying that the 'inversion'[1] in these examples is 'either an artificial feature, or more likely a colloquialism'. But see Renehan (1976: 22): 'This language is neither artificial nor exclusively colloquial. Nor is juxtaposition a necessary condition of it. Edmonds' comment at Alexis, *loc. cit.*, is quite correct: "ἐμπίνωμεν apparently goes one better than πίνωμεν, as 'let's drink, let's

---

[1] 'Inversion', because Watkins was writing about a different pattern, in which a simplex followed a compound (though not in asyndeton). The pattern we are discussing here should not be regarded as a variation on 'compound–simplex iteration'. For the asyndetic pattern compound–simplex as an intensification see below, pp. 116–17.

drink our fill'".' Thus the compound is an intensifier of the verb it follows. It is a moot point whether in such cases it is always justified to use the term 'asyndeton', because if the compound corrects the simplex there may not be coordination in any real sense (see further below). But in this example one could certainly translate 'let's drink, and drink our fill'.

In the passage of Menander above there are (817–18) three imperatives in the text printed by Arnott: πόριζε, Σώστρατε· | δίδου, μεταδίδου, though the first is textually dubious (Gomme and Sandbach 1973: 258). Arnott's text and translation (Loeb) do not cohere. He has a semicolon after the name in the Greek text, thus dividing his first imperative from the simplex–compound, but he translates 'Sostratos (?), you may dispose, and give, and share', thereby implying that there is a tricolon (asyndetic). The simplex–compound may be free-standing, or embedded within a tricolon, or the text may be wrong, which does not matter for the semantic relationship between the two verbs at the end.

The addressee, Sostratos, has just told his father Kallippides not to sit on his money but to help others, or it might fall into the hands of someone undeserving. The simplex, which is very general, could be taken to mean either 'give it to someone' or 'give it to more than one', whereas the compound may specify the second meaning (= 'give – give shares of it (to several/many)'). Or the specification may be slightly different: = 'give it (away), – give part of it (away)'. The pair could be taken as disjunctive.

Renehan (1976) lists various patterns showing a compound after a simplex, though most of his examples do not show juxtaposition of the two and are not strictly relevant to asyndeton. His semantic classification is though of some interest (see also Fehling 1969: 254–6, De Meo 1983: 119, Wills 1996: 443–5).

A first type (23) comprises 'cases where both simplex and compound are in common use with little difference in meaning'. A second type, called 'non-examples', consists of those 'where simplex and compound occur each with a separate and quite distinct meaning'. Not infrequently a compound may be used at a remove from its simplex in such a way that a reader would see no connection between them. But juxtaposed single terms are a different matter. Juxtaposed terms often have very different meanings from each other (see above on *lego sublego*), but that does not mean that their juxtaposition cannot be deliberate and functional, and interesting as asyndetic coordination. In the context of asyndeton I would not use the term 'non-examples'. A third type is described (24) thus: 'By far the most interesting category consists of passages in which the compound is used in conscious "correction" of the simplex; the compound, being the stronger word, suggests that the preceding simplex has understated or inadequately emphasized the realities of the situation.' Renehan uses the terms 'correction' and 'intensifying' (24, 25).

An intensification need not be a correction. Many asyndetic pairs have the stronger term second. I am referring not to compounds specifically, but to pairs of near-synonyms of which the second caps the first. It need not overtly correct it, but may add to it, with the utterance made more emphatic by the powerful second term (see the next paragraph). 'Intensification' and 'correction' are however not always easy to separate. For the corrective potential of a compound that is clearly also an intensification (but not in this case in an asyndetic coordination), see Plaut. *Aul.* 764–5 *negas?* :: *pernego immo*, translated by de Melo (Loeb) thus: 'You deny it?' :: 'More than that, I deny it absolutely' (note the presence of *immo* as well as *per-*).

In the category of intensifiers belongs the simplex–compound pair *dico edico* in a passage of Terence: *Eun.* 962 *dico edico uobis nostrum esse illum erilem filium*, 'I say, declare/pronounce that this is our master's son.' A coordinator would certainly have been possible here. Pairs of verbs of saying (near-synonyms) are often coordinated, as *oro atque obsecro*. *Edico* is stronger in that it refers to a public pronouncement, whereas *dico* may refer to a private utterance: hence 'I say and pronounce.'[2]

For a juxtaposed simplex and compound much more weakly associated, which are not near-synonyms and do not show any hint of correction or intensification either, see Cic. *Fam.* 3.13.1 **(194)** (to Appius Pulcher) *sed etiam opera consilio, domum ueniendo, conueniendis meis nullum onus offici cuiquam reliquum fecisse*, 'but in addition, by your labour and advice, by coming to my house, by meeting my household, you left no burdensome duty to anyone else' (my translation). Cicero was certainly conscious of the morphological relationship between the verbs, since he has introduced a chiasmus into the two phrases to achieve the juxtaposition of simplex and compound. However, semantically the connection is not between two verbs, but between the two phrases: at Cicero's house, Appius met those inside it. There is a (phrasal) asyndeton, in that a coordinator could be

---

[2] It was remarked above that Renehan collected mainly instances in which the simplex and compound were separated, whereas I am concerned here rather with asyndetic juxtaposition. It should be stressed that intensification may occur not only when there is juxtaposition, but also when the compound comes somewhat later. For a case of intensification by a following compound which is not juxtaposed with the simplex see Soph. *OT* 575–6 ἐγὼ δέ σου | μαθεῖν δικαιῶ ταῦθ' ἅπερ κἀμοῦ σὺ νῦν. | :: ἐκμάνθαν', 'but I claim the right to learn from you as much as you have just claimed to learn from me. :: You shall learn all you wish' (Lloyd-Jones, Loeb).

added, but the crucial information is that at Cicero's house he met Cicero's household, and the simplex could easily be written out. We do not have an asyndetic simplex–compound unit of two verbs here.

It is particularly in curse tablets that compounds follow their simplex, to intensify the urgency of the request put to the higher being. See for example *Suppl. Mag.* II.53.12–13 δῆσον καταδῆσον 'bind, bind down' (Daniel and Maltomini 1990–92: II.9, with commentary at 11). The compound is more precise than the simplex. The same pair is at *Suppl. Mag.* II.57.34–5 (p. 36). So a curse tablet from Beisan has the plural equivalent δήσατε καταδήσατε (see Youtie and Bonner 1937: 54, line 2, = Youtie 1982: 620). This formula also occurs in a curse tablet from Apamea (see Van Rengen 1984: 215, on lines 1–2), and at Audollent (1904), 16.X.8. For comment on the type see Youtie and Bonner (1937: 58), = Youtie (1982: 624). The same pair is at Audollent (1904), 187.56, but it is followed by a long sequence of other imperatives (seven apart from the first pair). Audollent (1904), 15 (Syrian curse tablet) has δήσατε συνδήσατε at line 19, as well as four instances of λύσατε ἀναλύσατε (4, 7, 9, 14).

For Latin see e.g. Audollent (1904), 219A = Kropp (2008a), 11.1.1/5 *ligo o<b>ligo linguas illoro*, 'I tie, tie up their tongues', Kropp (2008a), 11.1.1/25A *obliges perobliges Maurussum uenatorem*, Kropp (2008a), 11.1.1/13 *uratur Sucesa, aduratur*, Kropp (2008a), 11.1.1/25B *peruersus sit perperuersus sit Maurussus*. The Johns Hopkins *defixiones* (c. 100 BC) have at line 7 *luctent deluctent* 'wrestle, wrestle utterly' (see Adams 2016: 114). On the other hand at Audollent (1904), 217A there is a different type of pairing, *al[li]go deligo linguas*, which suggests that one way to intensify was to repeat the verb root with variations to the prefix. Cf. Kropp (2008a) 11.1.1/25A *obl[i]getis pe[r] obligetis ... apsumatis desumatis consu[m]at[i]s*, 11.1.1/25B *defigite perfigite consu[mite]* (see also Kropp 2008b: 168–70). It would seem that in some of these late Latin curses intensification by adding a compound to its base form has been mixed up with intensification expressed by the piling up of several compounds of the same root. For literary examples of the accumulating of different compounds of the same root see Plaut. *Bac.* 935 *opsignatas consignatas*, *Merc.* 360 *abdidi apscondidi* [*-con-*], *Mo.* 1031 *perii interii*, and also *HA, Tyr. trig.* 9.9 *lacera occide concide* (quoted from an aggressive letter).

Nor is the order simplex–compound invariable in curse tablets. For the reverse order compound–simplex see Kropp (2008a), 11.1.1/32, fr. 1 *col<l>igo ligo*, and also the Johns Hopkins *defixiones* (for which see above), which in the line following that with *luctent deluctent* has *euincant uincant* (Kropp 2008, 1.4.4/9). I would take this latter pattern in curses to be

1 Evidence

a different phenomenon from Watkins' (1967) Indo-European iteration of compounds by their simplex (see above, n. 1). In curses simple verbs and compounds are varied haphazardly, to make the utterance more emphatic, with both orders it seems having that effect.

So in Greek drama juxtapositions of the compound–simplex order are a method of intensification. See e.g. Eur. *Alc.* 399 ὑπάκουσον ἄκουσον 'listen, listen', where a child addresses the dead Alcestis, *Med.* 1252 κατίδετ' ἴδετε (with Mastronarde 2002: 366 ad loc.), Men. *Epit.* 878 ὑπομαίνεθ᾽ οὗτος, νὴ τὸν Ἀπόλλω, μαίνεται. Further examples, from Euripides, may be found in Diggle (1994: 388–90) and Parker (2007: 136) on Eur. *Alc.* 400.

For this pattern in literary Latin see Pacuvius fr. 199.8 Schierl (9) *retinete tenete*, Plaut. *Merc.* 681 *disperii perii misera* = Ter. *Hau.* 404, Ter. *Eun.* 377 *abduc duc* (see Lindholm 1931: 85, De Meo 1983: 119, Wills 1996: 443, Schierl 2006: 414; Lindholm and Schierl also cite parallels from Greek).

The pairs of the structure simplex–compound from curses above may not look definitely like coordinations (i.e. asyndeta), but such pairs in curses do sometimes have a coordinator. Fragment 2.6 of the first tablet from Beisan (see above) edited by Youtie and Bonner (1937: 56) has the same two verbs in a different form, coordinated: ἔ]δησα κ[ὲ] κατέδησα. The writer of the curse clearly felt that 'bind and bind down' was a coordinated pair, but it is possible that the interpretation of pairings varied from case to case (or person to person). Youtie and Bonner (1937: 58) use the term 'asyndeton' themselves in a note: 'Emphatic asyndeton is naturally common in the curse tablets.' They then quote a dissimilar example, a tricolon of single verbs from Audollent (1904), 234.18, each with the prefix ἐκ/ἐξ. Clearly to them 'emphatic asyndeton' did not specifically refer to the structure simplex–compound.

Arnott (1996: 824), on the pair from Alexis (πίνωμεν, ἐμπίνωμεν) cited above, states: 'this kind of repetition, in which a compound *directly* follows the simple verb merely to reinforce the meaning ("let's drink, let's drink up"), is contrary to normal Attic idiom'. He adds that usually if a compound does follow the simplex in an uninterrupted sentence of Attic 'a substantial modification of the verbal meaning is detectable'. He cites the passage of Menander quoted above (*Dysk.* 818) to illustrate this point, and also Antiphanes 146 (148 K).1–2 ἔρχεται, μετέρχετ᾽ αὖ, προσέρχετ᾽ αὖ, μετέρχεται. He also finds two 'very late' parallels for Alexis' πίνωμεν, ἐμπίνωμεν, but one of these, Audollent (1904), 155A.36 (cf. 155B.6) δεδεμένον συνδεδεμένον καταδεδεμένον, which is quoted in this form at 824–5, is an accumulation of compounds of the type seen above. The other is [Aristaen.] *Epist.* 2.4 μεῖνον ἀνάμεινον, of 'a girl to her lover'. For different compounds attached to the same root see e.g. Heraclit. fr. 10 συμφερόμενον διαφερόμενον, συνᾷδον διᾷδον, cited by Denniston (1952: 103).

It is not clear that Arnott's apparent suggestion (?) that juxtapositions of the type in which the compound has a substantially different meaning from that of the simplex are normal Attic idiom, whereas those in which the compound merely reinforces the meaning of the simplex are not normal idiom, is accurate. Neither type is particularly common. Most of Renehan's examples of simplex + compound are rather different, in that there is no juxtaposition, and therefore no asyndeton (the same is true of the Latin examples cited by Wills (1996: 444–5). It would be safer to say that juxtapositions of the structure simplex + compound are attested in Greek mainly in curse tablets.

A question of interest that has been alluded to already is to what extent pairings of the type simplex–compound are asyndetic (i.e. convey a coordination, whether translatable with 'and', 'or' or 'but'). Pairs of which the second member corrects or specifies do tend to be hard to interpret: can 'and/or' be added, or is there a sharp correction such that a coordinator would be inappropriate?

For a literary example in Latin open to this ambiguity see Plaut. *Am.* 551 *sequor, subsequor te*. Christenson (2000: 242) ad loc. translates 'I'm following you, I'm right on your heels', describing the compound as self-correction. *Subsequor* 'follow close behind' (*OLD* s.v. 1a) stresses the closeness and thus is more precise than the simplex, but is hardly a correction. Coordination cannot be ruled out in translation ('I am following, and am following right behind'). Christenson incidentally refers to his note on line 43 (p. 145) for such correction. There however we find *commemoro* at some distance from an earlier *memoro* (41), and I can see no correction or intensification, and would put the example in Renehan's first type (and there is no asyndeton).

Cicero at *Verr.* 3.155 quotes from a letter of Timarchides, a freedman of Verres: *scribas apparitores recentis arripe; cum L. Volteio, qui plurimum potest, caede concide*, 'seize the scribes, the new clerks; along with L. Volteius, who has very great power, crush, destroy them'. The two verbs here have weakened meanings. Used literally they might have meant 'slash and kill'. It seems reasonable to interpret the two as coordinated. In the same passage the writer used an asyndetic pair of nouns (*scribas apparitores*), and in another of Cicero's quotations from the letter (*Verr.* 3.154) there is a second such: *habes uirtutem eloquentiam*. This is a familiar type, a pair of virtues cited *exempli gratia*, and is, it seems, at the end of a colon. The two verbs above are overtly coordinated at *HA, Aurel.* 31.5 *caesum atque concisum*

1 Evidence 119

est, and we saw above a similar pair used asyndetically in the same work in a longer sequence (*HA, Tyr. trig.* 9.9 *lacera occide concide*). The letter from which Cicero was quoting must have been urgent and heated.

I cite finally the few other instances of the pattern simplex + compound that I know of, and propose another by a simple emendation.

Plaut. *Poen.* 219–23, spoken by the *puella* Adelphasium, has two such pairs in a single speech. Another aspect of the accumulation is that the first pair is juxtaposed with a pair that has a different form of assonance: *ex industria ambae numquam concessamus | lauari aut fricari aut tergeri aut ornari, | poliri expoliri, pingi fingi; et una | binae singulis quae datae nobis ancillae, | eae nos lauando eluendo operam dederunt*. This accumulation is moreover preceded by four verbs disjunctively coordinated. The two compounds are intensifications.

Another Plautine pair, *feror differor*, has the same contextual feature as *poliri expoliri* just mentioned: it is juxtaposed with another asyndetic pair, with a different type of assonance. *Cist.* 208 *miser exanimor, | feror differor, distrahor diripior*, 'poor me, I'm being destroyed, driven, driven apart, dragged apart, torn apart' (de Melo, Loeb). The sequence of five passive verbs consists of 1 + 2 + 2 elements. *Differor* is a semantic intensification of *feror*, and it is obvious that the two are asyndetically coordinated.

For a phrasal/clausal pair see Lucilius 679 (645 W.) *ducunt uxores, producunt . . . liberos*, 'they take wives, beget children'.

Consider finally Livy 40.52.6 *classis regis antea inuicta fusa contusa fugataque est*. *Fundere fugare* is a common pair, 'scatter, put to flight' (for the meaning of the first see *OLD* s.v. *fundo* 11b, 'disperse'), found a number of times in Livy himself (see Preuss 1881: 96–7 and Livy 47), and it is odd to have the coordinated variant, for which see e.g. Livy 28.4.6 *fusa ac fugata classis* (also Oakley 2005b: 332), interrupted by a semantically different verb, = 'crush' (crushing does not necessarily imply scattering but rather destruction). I suggest *fusa confusa fugataque est*, with the compound an intensification ('thrown into disorder'). There would not be end-of-list coordination, i.e. three elements (ABC*que*), but rather the three verbs would fall into two groups, [*fusa confusa*] [*fugataque*], the first asyndetic, the second a single word attached by *-que*. The normal pairing *fundere* + *fugare* would be retained rather than interrupted, but the first verb would be intensified by its own compound.

Like so many types of asyndeton, this type too alternates with explicit coordination. For some interesting examples of coordination see Chahoud (2018: 140).

VII Simplex + Compound in Asyndeton

2 Conclusions

Here are types of asyndeton that are fairly rare (unlike e.g. the pairing of privative adjectives). I say 'types' somewhat pedantically. The second verb (the compound) may either have a different meaning from the first, or act as an intensifier with the same basic meaning, but structurally the two types are the same. Simplex–compound asyndeton is to a considerable extent genre-determined. The second type occurs particularly in curse tablets, both in Greek and Latin; the examples cited above from curses could almost certainly be extended. The first type is also used in laws, and again it is likely that the examples could be increased (note that there are a dozen in a single law). Simplex–compound asyndeton is found sometimes outside curse tablets, usually in comedy in Latin, where several times it is in asyndetic accumulations. An example in a letter quoted by Cicero also points to its dramatic quality, as may the possible case in Livy. The reverse type, compound–simplex, is likewise located in Latin mainly in curses and drama. The simplex–compound type is not well represented in Greek, other than in curses.

CHAPTER VIII

Juxtaposition of Active and Passive Forms of the Same Verb

1 Evidence

Asyndeton with an active verb form alongside a passive form of the same verb is rare in Latin. Just five clear-cut (single-word) instances have been noted, as far as I am aware, and to these may be added a slightly extended pair in Tacitus (see the next paragraph but one). Pairings of active and passive forms are more common when there is a coordinator (see Wills 1996: 295–8 for an extensive but mixed collection of material mostly from poetry, a good deal of it comprising not coordinations but actives and passives near each other in different types of clauses; for the coordinated type note e.g. Tac. *Ann.* 3.55.2 *plebem socios regna colere et coli licitum*). Wills states (296) that 'the combination of voices in a "bimembre asyndeton" was possibly idiomatic', a view that is at variance with the evidence, given that such pairs almost always have a coordinator. It will also be seen below that the few asyndetic examples are not a single type, such that the term 'idiomatic' might be appropriate.

Although this morphological category is rare, the semantic categories to which the few instances belong are commonplace among asyndeta: they are types of opposites (see further below).

Note first Tac. *Ann.* 6.35.1 *ut corporibus et pulsu armorum pellerent pellerentur*, where the verbs are rendered by Woodman (2017: 240), 'with the result that they were repelling or were being repelled'. Woodman (2017: 240) ad loc. cites Tac. *Hist.* 3.23.1 *pellunt hostem, dein pelluntur*, a clausal pair which incidentally shows that an asyndeton of the above type need not be disjunctive.

A second instance is at Catull. 45.20: *nunc ab auspicio bono profecti | mutuis animis amant amantur*, 'Now, setting out from this good omen, with mutual feelings they love and are loved.' The pair expresses reciprocity, and a coordinator such as *et* would not change the meaning: cf. Cic. *Cat.* 2.23 *amare et amari ... didicerunt*.

VIII Juxtaposition of Active and Passive Forms

There was a Latin proverb of the type, 'if you want to be loved, love' (see Otto 1890: 17: e.g. Sen. *Epist.* 9.6 *si uis amari, ama*), which makes an asyndeton comprising active and passive of *amo* easy to understand. Pithy remarks about reciprocal love were commonplace, and asyndeton was suited to the idea. Note too Cic. *Att.* 4.4 *qua re aduola ad nos eo animo ut nos ames, te amari scias*, 'therefore hurry to me, reflecting on your love for me and on the knowledge that you are loved (by me)'. See also Spal (2016: 27–8) on *CIL* IV.346 *alter amat, alter amatur*.

On the other hand Catull. 61.47 (*quis deus magis est amatis petendus amantibus?*, 'what god is more to be sought by loved ones who (themselves) love?') does not contain asyndetic coordination. *Amatis* (if the text is accepted) is substantival, and it is modified by *amantibus*. There is a single phrase, and not a coordination. The only similarity between this phrase and that at 45.20 is that active and passive forms of *amo* together express reciprocity of love. Fordyce (1961: 243) makes the point that this is not an asyndeton, and that the genuine asyndeton at 45.20 cannot be cited in support of this text, which embodies a transposition by Bergk.

A third Latin juxtaposition of active and passive forms of the same verb is at Phaedr. 2.2.2: *a feminis utcumque spoliari uiros, | ament amentur, nempe exemplis discimus*, 'That men are always fleeced by women, whether they love them or are loved, is something that we learn, sure enough, from our model tales' (Perry, Loeb). This pair is disjunctive, and does not denote reciprocity.

Fourth, there is an instance at Plin. *Pan.* 21.4: *ut reuersus imperator, qui priuatus exieras, agnoscis agnosceris*, 'You left us as an ordinary citizen, you return as emperor, you recognise your subjects and you are recognised.'

Finally, Ranstrand (1951: 92) cites the following from the *Querolus*: 41.17 (73.18) *adsideo amplector foueo foueor* (not unlike *amo amor*: see *OLD* s.v. *foueo* 4, 'fondle, caress'). This pair is part of an accumulation, in that it is preceded by an alliterative pair expressing a temporal sequence.

Petron. 77.6 (*habes, habeberis*), where the verbs are in different tenses as well as voices, is not an asyndetic coordination but a parataxis (reduced conditional: see Schmeling 2011: 325). Contrast Lucil. 1120 *tantum habeas . . . tantique habearis* (with a coordinator): see XXV.4.

I turn now to the general types of asyndeton that are represented by these examples.

All five of these (single-word) pairs are semantically opposites, but they perhaps belong to two different categories. *Amant amantur* (and the subjunctive correspondent), *agnoscis agnosceris* and *foueo foueor* are converses, of the same type e.g. as *give/receive* (see XIII.2). Cf. e.g. Cic. *Off.* 1.22

1 Evidence 123

(138) *communes utilitates in medium afferre, mutatione officiorum, <u>dando</u> <u>accipiendo</u>, tum artibus, tum opera, tum facultatibus deuincire hominum inter homines societatem.* For active/passives as converses see Lyons (1977: 280).

Pellerent pellerentur on the other hand arguably comprises directional opposites, of the category called by Cruse (1986: 226) 'reversives'. In this class belong e.g. *go/return, arrive/depart*. A pair meaning 'repel, be repelled' is of much the same type as e.g. *advance/retreat, attack/flee*. See again XIII.2, and cf. e.g. Tac. *Ann.* 12.33 (100) *aditus abscessus*, of entry and exit.

A few asyndetic active–passive alternations in Greek too are cited (see e.g. Kühner and Gerth 1898–1904: 2.346. Dover 1993: 300): Ar. *Ran.* 857 σὺ δὲ μὴ πρὸς ὀργήν, Αἰσχύλ', ἀλλὰ πραόνως | ἔλεγχ', ἐλέγχου, 'And you, Aeschylus, give and take arguments not angrily but calmly' (Henderson, Loeb), 861 ἕτοιμός εἰμ' ἔγωγε, κοὐκ ἀναδύομαι, | δάκνειν δάκνεσθαι πρότερος, εἰ τούτῳ δοκεῖ, | τἄπη, τὰ μέλη, 'I'm ready if he is – and I won't back out – to go first in an exchange of pecks at my words, my songs' (Henderson, Loeb) (see Dover 1993: 300 ad loc., noting of the second that it can be understood as 'to bite his verses, and that my verses should be bitten'), X. *Cyr.* 7.1.38 ἐμάχοντο, ἐώθουν ἐωθοῦντο, ἔπαιον ἐπαίοντο, 'they fought, shoved and were shoved, gave and received blows' (Miller, Loeb). Dover (1993) on *Ran.* 857 also quotes two such pairs that are joined by a coordinator (Ar. *V.* 485, Pl. *Grg.* 462A).

An example quoted by Denniston (1952: 103) in his account of asyndeton in Greek is Th. 7.71.4 ὀλοφυρμὸς βοή, νικῶντες κρατούμενοι, 'wailing, shouting, "We are winning," "We are beaten"' (Smith, Loeb), where the active participle is followed by the passive of a different verb. But this is not straightforwardly an asyndeton, that is a coordination without a coordinator. Those shouting out might first have said 'we are winning' and then made a correction, 'no, we are losing', or one group might have said 'we are winning' and another have corrected them. In neither case could a coordinator have been added. Or there might have been chaos, with different people using different verbs at the same or different times. Pairs expressing changes of mind are not coordinations. Cf. Ter. *Eun.* 818 *pergin, scelesta, mecum perplexe loqui?* | *'scio, nescio, abiit, audiui, ego non adfui'*, 'Do you persist in talking in riddles, you wretch? "I know . . . I don't know . . . he's gone . . . I heard . . . I wasn't there"' (Barsby, Loeb). *Scio, nescio* does not have the meaning 'I know and I don't know', but conveys indecision and switches from knowing at one moment to not knowing at the next (see VI.7 on this and another passage). The passage of Thucydides seems to be much the same. Another possibility would be to say that from the perspective of the speakers who are being quoted there is no asyndeton,

124   VIII   Juxtaposition of Active and Passive Forms

but from the perspective of the historian there could be if his narrative meant 'they shouted both that they were winning and that they were being beaten'. Cf. XXIX.2.2 on Hor. *Ep.* 1.6.54.

Cf. in English Gillian Flynn, *Gone Girl* (2012), p. 32 *something hidden away that makes me* unsatisfiable, unsatisfying. This is a pair comprising a passive versus active adjective, = *unable to be satisfied or to satisfy*, but also consists of privatives.

2   Conclusions

This is an unusual and probably artificial type of asyndeton. The idea that it was 'idiomatic' is unconvincing. Contrasting actives and passives are usually coordinated. Three of the asyndetic examples, however, refer to reciprocity of love/affection, and these may be a special case, related to a proverbial idea that is succinctly reflected by means of asyndeton. In this case then one may say that there is a semantic influence. The other two (straightforward) instances are both in Tacitus, and both have the same verb. Tacitus had a particular liking for opposites, and *pellunt/pelluntur* (reversives) is just another (occasional) manifestation of that taste.

CHAPTER IX

Asyndetic Pairs of Verbs of Different Tense or Mood

1 Evidence

Asyndetic juxtapositions of different tenses or moods of the same verb are very much a feature of legal/official language in Latin. At Cic. *Phil.* 5.46 (76) the following occurs in a proposal by Cicero for a senatorial decree: *libertatem populi Romani defendant defe<nde>rint*. By contrast earlier in the same speech two instances of *praesideo* in different tenses are coordinated, but there the pair is not in a formal motion: 5.37 *Galliaque, quae semper praesidet atque praesedit huic imperio*, 'and Gaul, which always protects and has protected this empire'. Even in official language, however, asyndeton is not invariable. In the same speech again (at 5.53) in another such motion we find *qui . . . auctoritatemque huius ordinis defenderint atque defendant*. The order of the same two verb forms has been reversed. The coordination gives a better clausula than either (asyndetic) *defenderint defendant* or *defendant defenderint*.

Repetitions of a verb in a different tense or mood are not uncommon in literary Latin (including Cicero's prose), but outside official contexts or the like overt coordination is the norm. On different tenses/moods of the same verb coordinated see in general Wills (1996: 298–310). For pairs coordinated in Greek see Fehling (1969: 265–6). For an asyndetic pair see Men. *Mis.* 708–9 ἠγάπησά σε, | [ἀγ]απῶ, φιλῶ, 'I loved you, love and cherish you.' ἀγαπῶ forms a pair with ἠγάπησά (σε), showing a contrast of tenses, and it forms a pair with the final verb, in that both are in the same tense and are synonyms. See Gonda (1959: 342–3) on a contrast of tenses (with coordination) in a passage of the Atharvaveda (AV 1.19.2), which he translates as '(let the shafts fly) those that are hurled and those that are to be hurled'.

A different asyndetic type is illustrated by the following: Cic. *Att.* 7.2.7 *Hortensius quid egerit aueo scire, Cato quid agat*. There is clausal asyndeton here, of the anaphoric type (*quid . . . quid*). For this pattern see too *Att.*

125

5.14.3 *quae sint, quae futura sint*, 7.16.2 *quid Caesar acturus sit ... quid Pompeius agat*, 8.12.6 *quid Domitius agat, quid acturus sit*. On the other hand for this anaphoric type but with coordination see 5.18.4 *quid tu agas quidque acturus*. Note the mixture of asyndeton and coordination at Plaut. *Per*. 777 *qui sunt, qui erunt, quique fuerunt quique futuri sunt posthac*. At *Att*. 8.7.2, *qui patriam reliquit, Italiam relinquit* the asyndeton is clausal, but without anaphora.

For the straightforward coordinated type of pairs of verbs, which is very common (e.g.) in Cicero (not least in the letters), see *Att*. 2.1.4 *Metellus impedit et impediet*, 2.20.5 *do operam et dabo*, 3.15.4 *quantum me amas et amasti, tantum amare deberes ac debuisses* (two pairs), 5.19.2 *laetor magisque laetabor*, 6.1.20 *nec enim me fefellisset nec fallet*, 7.10 *quid consili ceperit capiatue nescio adhuc*, 8.15.2 *cruciat cruciauitque*, *Fam*. 1.9.19 *a me ipso laudantur et laudabuntur idem*, 3.10.11 *agimus et agemus*.

Different tenses/moods of the same verb may also be juxtaposed in contexts where there is no coordination: *Fam*. 1.9.22 *quae me mouerunt, mouissent eadem te*.

I return to two-word asyndeta, which are found particularly in legal Latin and other comparable types. In e.g. a senatorial decree we find two such pairs juxtaposed: *SC De Aphrodisiensibus* (Riccobono 1968, text 38, p. 271) *quaeque praemia honores beneficia ... attribuerunt attribuerint concesserunt concesserint*. The same phenomenon is illustrated from a *lex* at XXII.1. For a different but comparable pattern from a senatorial motion in Cicero see *Phil*. 5.53 (77, 78) *utique C. Pansa A. Hirtius consules, alter amboue, si eis uideretur, rationem agri habe<re>nt qui sine iniuria priuatorum diuidi posset, eisque militibus, legioni Martiae et legioni quartae ita <u>darent adsignarent</u> ut quibus militibus amplissime <u>dati adsignati</u> essent*. The asyndetic pair *darent adsignarent* is picked up by the same asyndetic pair in a different tense.

Further examples (as well as single pairs) are in the *Lex Cornelia de sicariis et ueneficis* quoted by Cicero at *Cluent*. 148: *quiue in senatu sententiam dixit dixerit ... qui eorum coiit coierit, conuenit conuenerit quo quis iudicio publico condemnaretur... qui uenenum malum fecit fecerit*.

An old legal formula is *oportet oportebit* (see *TLL* IX.2.744.26ff., without examples). At XXII.2.1 six examples of this pair are cited from the *Lex Cornelia de xx quaestoribus*; see also XXII.2.2 for an example from the *Lex Antonia de Termessibus*. A remarkable accumulation of such pairs is in the *Tabula Heracleensis* (Crawford 1996: 1.363–9), probably of Caesarian date (Crawford 360): e.g. 110 *fecit fecerit*, 113 *erit fuit fuerit*, 113 *iurauit iurauerit*, 114 *renuntiauit renuntiauerit*, 115 *proue quo datum deprensum est erit* (with double asyndeton, and both auxiliaries belonging with both preceding participles), 116 *praefuit praefuerit*, 117 *fecit fecerit*, 117 *possessa proscriptaue sunt erunt*, 118 *condemnatus est erit*, 118 *resti<tu>tus est erit*, 119 *condemnatus est erit*, 120 *iudicatum est erit*, 121 *ademptus est erit*, 121 *ius<i>t iuserit*, and many other examples. At *Lex Coloniae Genetiuae* LXXIX tabl. b, 5–6 (Crawford 1996: 1.404–5) (*qui eum agrum habent possident habebunt possidebunt*) the contrasts are in an interlocking word order (see XVII on correlative orders). The purpose of these pairs in the language of the law was to cover all possible events of specified types over the full time-spectrum. See also Manuwald (2007: 706) for some bibliography. On this sort of opposition, 'what has been, what is, (what is to be)' in early Indo-European (the Rigveda and Atharvaveda), see West (2007: 103), with n. 98 for some bibliography.

In such pairs it is also common in legal Latin to have -*ue*, as *siet fueritue* twice at *Lex repetundarum* 16 and *fuit fueritue* at 74, *Lex agraria* 9, 10, 12 *oportet oportebitue*, 16 *obuenit obueneritue*, 23 *obuenit obueneritue*, *emit emeritue*.

An unusual type is at Pacuvius 217 Schierl: *ut quae egi ago uel axim uerruncent bene*. There are three forms of the verb *ago*, the third attached by *uel*. Do we have here a straightforward tricolon, with end-of-list coordination? An alternative would be to place a comma after *ago*, taking *egi ago* as an indicative asyndeton bimembre, followed by a subjunctive that is a disjunctive addition to the indicatives: 'what I have done or am doing – or may do'. A prayer of Scipio Africanus in Livy (29.27.2) is comparable: *uos precor quaesoque uti, quae in meo imperio gesta sunt geruntur postque gerentur, ea mihi* ... There is a similar problem of interpretation here. The pair in the past and present tenses could be taken as a unit, with the future separated: 'what has been done or is being done – and will afterwards be done'. Both of these examples are in the same context (prayers). The passage of Livy could be brought into line with that of Pacuvius syntactically if *gerentur* were changed to *gerantur*: 'what has been done or is being done – and may afterwards be done'.

2 Conclusions

Here is a category of asyndeton that is almost exclusively determined by genre. Juxtaposed pairs of verbs of different tenses or moods are a feature of legal language (in the classical period), whereas elsewhere such pairs are coordinated, except when there is an anaphoric repetition of a term such as *quid* before the verbs, and even then there may be a coordinator attaching the second anaphoric term.

CHAPTER X

Pairs of Imperatives

1 'Go' + Imperative

1.1 Early Latin

Pairs of imperatives, used asyndetically, are common from early Latin (see e.g. Adams 2016: 558 listing examples from the early Republic; see too XXII.4.4 for asyndetic pairs of imperatives in Umbrian). The significance of the structure (in relation to overt coordination) in the early period may be illustrated with some details about one of its manifestations, that comprising *i* (or *ite*) + imperative (see particularly the discussion of Sjögren 1900: 82–91). In Plautus (and also Terence) this type of asyndeton is commonplace, and it tends to occur in formulae or idioms suggestive of everyday speech. By contrast in Cato *Agr.* coordinated pairs of imperatives (with *-que* the usual connective) far outnumber asyndetic (by about 80:5: see Adams 2016: 80), but a factor is that most imperatives in Cato are of the *-to* form, and it must have been the commonplace present imperative that was usual in ordinary speech. In all examples cited below from Plautus at least one member of the pair is a present imperative.

One such asyndetic structure, addressed particularly to slaves, consists of the imperative of 'go', with or without a vocative, and then another imperative, the whole instructing the addressee to 'go (and) do something, fetch something or someone'. The second part is usually phrasal. In various languages verbs such as 'go' and 'come' followed by another verb tend to lose their full semantic force (see e.g. Cardinaletti and Giusti 2001, Ledgeway 1997: 261–3, id. 2016: 160–4). In Latin itself *age* (so ἄγε in Greek), as will be shown below (2), is weakened into a hortative particle (thus the term 'pseudo-asyndeton'). It may indeed be followed by a plural rather than a singular imperative, and even by a finite verb in a different person. If *i*/*ite* were subject to such weakening it would be inappropriate

1 'Go' + Imperative 129

to speak of its coordination (asyndetic or otherwise) with a following imperative. It is however often obvious that *i* in early Latin (I stress 'early', because as the Republic advanced the monosyllabic forms of *ire* tended to fall out of use, and in later Latin it is *uade* that is used in such imperatival constructions: see below, 1.4) is a full motion verb. If someone such as a slave is instructed to 'go inside and bring something out', *i* is not a mere hortative particle. Such orders have to be seen in the light of the staging of comedies. A slave who is told to go and get something inside will leave the stage, and his return with the object or person is a second event. On the supposed weakening of *i* in Plautus see Adams (2013: 797–9).

Here are some examples, all with a vocative as well as the asyndetic imperatives. Some have a third imperative:

Am. 770 *tu, Thessala, intus pateram proferto foras*
As. 382 *i, puere, pulta | atque atriensem Sauream, si est intus, euocato huc*
Mil. 1301 *i, Palaestrio, | aurum ornamenta uestem, pretiosa omnia | duc* (cf. Caecilius 100 *age age, i, puere, duc me ad patrios fines decoratum opipare*).
Poen. 364 *i, soror, apscede tu a me*
Poen. 1319–20 *ite istinc, serui, foras, | ecferte fustis*
Rud. 798 *i dum, Turbalio, curriculo, adfert<o domo> | duas clauas* (note *i dum*, and compare *agedum*).
St. 150 *eho, Crocotium, i, parasitum Gelasimum hic arcessito.*

The last pattern, with *i* and imperative of *arcesso* with an object, also occurs without vocatives:

Men. 952 *i arcesse homines qui ...*
Ps. 326 *i accerse hostias | uictumas lanios*
Ps. 330 *i accerse agnos.*

At Ter. *Eun.* 624 (*heus, inquit, puer, i, Pamphilam accerse*) the manuscripts have *puer* without *i*, and modern editors (Kauer and Lindsay 1926, Brothers 2000, Barsby 1999, 2001) print *puer<e>* (without *i*), but Bentley was surely right, given the formulaic status of *i accerse*, to add *i* to follow *puer* (see Sjögren 1900: 86–7). It is inevitable that a verb form consisting of a single letter would be subject to corruption (see e.g. Sjögren 1900: 87). Barsby (1999: 204) says that *puere* is metrically necessary, but Sjögren (1900: 87) shows that *puer i* is more in keeping with Terentian metre, and that *puere* is not a Terentian form (86–7).

In the twelve passages quoted so far *arcesse* or an equivalent occurs as the second verb five times, compounds of *fero* three times, and *duc* twice. The structure expresses the idea 'go (and) fetch', and was clearly formulaic, with the asyndeton tending to be conventional (note also Hor. *Carm.*

3.14.17 *i, pete unguentum, puer, et coronas*, also addressed to a slave). There are also similar passages without a vocative: e.g.:

Aul. 767 *i refer* (repeated at 768 in the form *i uero refer*).
Aul. 800 *i intro, exquaere sitne* ...
Aul. 829 *i redde aurum* (note the *re-* compound in the second part of these orders).
Capt. 658 *ite istinc, ecferte lora*
Cist. 284 *i adfer mihi arma.*

Here are a few other expression-types:

'do something (and) don't delay', 'do something, I'm not delaying you'
Mil. 1361 *i sequere illos, ne morere*
Poen. 1229 *ite in ius, ne moramini*
Epid. 305 *i numera, nil ego te moror* ('go and count it, I'm not delaying you').

The first structure is at Catull. 61.193 (*perge, ne remorare*, 'come on, don't delay'), an indication that this expression-type was idiomatic. For the pattern imperative + negated imperative without coordination in Greek see e.g. Battezzato (2018: 126) on Eur. *Hec.* 387 κεντεῖτε, μὴ φείδεσθ', 'stab me, do not spare me'.

'go, see'
Bac. 901 *i uise estne ibi*
Rud. 567 *i uise, si lubet*
Truc. 196–7 *i intro, amabo,* | *uise illam.*

'rise, go'
As. 921, 923, 924, 925 *surge, amator, i domum.*

'go off, announce, etc.', with *abi*
For the similar use of *abi* in such asyndetic pairs, see on Plautus XXIII.5.1, where for example two instances of *abi nuntia* from Livy also (22.3.13, 22.49.10) are cited.

1.2 An Official Formula

Here is a different expression that is indirectly relevant to some of the material above: Cic. *Rab. perd.* 13 *i, lictor, conliga manus*. A lictor is addressed and *i* is followed asyndetically by another imperative. The same formula is at Livy 1.26.7 *i, lictor, colliga manus* and also 1.26.11. Cf. Livy 3.48.3 *i, inquit, lictor, submoue turbam*, 8.7.19 *i, lictor, deliga ad palum*. Oakley (1998: 450) notes that the appearance of this expression in several other places in Livy and at Cic. *Rab. perd.* 13 'shows that it must have been the standard formal address to a lictor by a magistrate'. Cf. Livy 9.11.13 *i, lictor, deme uincla*

Romanis. Nor was it only lictors who were addressed in this way: note Livy 9.4.16 *ite, consules, redimite armis ciuitatem*. These examples have the same structure as that above in the 'go, fetch' formula (et sim.) in comedy: *i* is accompanied by a vocative, and a second imperative follows, usually as part of a longer phrase. The presence of the structure both in comic dialogue (addressed to slaves in particular) and in address of officials shows that it was firmly based in the language (as a means of giving instructions to subordinates) and not an artificial creation of official style. Note that Plautus at one point adopts the asyndetic construction in a quasi-official context: *Per.* 487 *i ad forum ad praetorem, exquire* ...

For a large collection of imperatives of *eo* followed asyndetically by another imperative see *TLL* V.2.631.62ff. The syndetic variant is also found (631.79ff.). It is however pointed out by Sjögren (1900: 89) that *i et* + imperative (in comedy) is not used except where the coordinator cannot be omitted ('non occurrit nisi ubi particula omitti non potest'). Sjögren (1900: 88) is able to list just three examples from Plautus of *i ac* + imperative. He also (1900: 87) lists four instances from Plautus of *i atque* + imperative, and an additional two where it is transmitted but is not metrical. By contrast, in his account of the asyndetic construction in Plautus he first discusses passages where there are textual uncertainties and then lists (1900: 86) twenty-eight examples 'quae nihil fere praebent memoratu digni', followed by three more where *i* is followed by another verb of motion. *Ac* as coordinator (see above) is reflected in some southern Italian dialects (see below, 1.5).

Greek had an equivalent asyndetic construction, ἴθι or ἴτε + imperative (see Montanari 1995: 608, col. a end–col. b, Kühner and Gerth 1898–1904: I.236). A passage of Soph. *Tr.*, translated by Cicero at *Tusc.* 2.21, has (1070) ἴθ', ὦ τέκνον, τόλμησον, which is rendered *perge, aude, nate*, with *perge*, as not infrequently (see *TLL* X.1.1431.13ff., 1435.10ff.), replacing the more commonplace *i* (see e.g. Plaut. *Merc.* 618 *perge excrucia, carnufex*, where the addressee is treated as a subordinate official, and also Catull. 61.193 quoted above). In the Greek, just as we have seen above in Latin (and in Cicero's rendering), the imperative is associated with a vocative.

1.3 A Reversal of Order

I comment on reversals of the structure 'go, do'.

At Plaut. *Truc.* 583 the *meretrix* Phronesium issues an order to the slave Cyamus: *grata acceptaque ecastor habeo. iube auferri intro, i, Cyame*, 'I do regard them (gifts) as welcome and accepted. Have them brought in, go,

Cyamus' (de Melo, Loeb). The phrase *iube auferri intro* and *i* are reversed from their normal order (cf. e.g. *Mil.* 182 *i sis, iube transire*). The reversal of *i* makes it independent of the other imperative and, free-standing, it is probably more peremptory: 'order them to be brought in – go!'.

There is another such reversal in a passage of Livy dealing with the recapture of Sora by the Romans in 314 aided by a deserter (9.24.1–28.2: see Oakley 2005a : 297–9). The deserter, having established a small group of Romans on the citadel, runs down and makes a short and dramatic speech to his fellow citizens, causing chaos and allowing the Romans to break into the town: 9.24.9 *decurrit inde, quanto maxime poterat cum tumultu 'ad arma' et 'pro uestram fidem, ciues' clamitans; 'arx ab hostibus capta est; defendite ite'*, 'Then he ran down, creating as much din as he could, calling "to arms", "help, citizens! The citadel has been taken by the enemy, to the defence – go!"'

Oakley (2005a: 310–11) feels that *defendite ite* cannot be convincingly defended, on the grounds that the reversal of *i(te)* + another imperative is abnormal, and he supports the deletion of *ite*.

But the reversal fits the context, converting a formulaic structure into one in which *ite* has urgent force at the end of the order: 'defend it – go!'. A single imperative at the end of such a dramatic intervention by the deserter looks weak, and in any case the reversal is closely paralleled by the above usage of Plautus. Nor are parallels even needed to support a deliberately emphatic variant of a hackneyed pattern.

1.4 Later Latin

The monosyllable *i* was to disappear from the language, and in later Latin we find it replaced by *uade* (or *ambula*). Even in classical Latin there are signs that in the imperative form of *uado* was tending to lose its semantic function as indicating an 'impressive, terrifying, threatening, rapid, dangerous or showy advance' (see Adams 2013: 812), and acquiring a use much the same as that of *i*. Note particularly Hor. *Ep.* 1.13.19 *uade uale*, 'be off, farewell', and see the comparable examples (without another imperative) from Ovid and Virgil at Adams (2013: 814).

In the late texts that I have looked at coordination after *uade* seems more frequent than asyndeton, but a systematic survey would be needed. For *uade et* + imperative (particularly *uade et dic*) in the *Historia Apollonii regis Tyri* and some of the school exercises edited by Dickey (2012, 2015), see Adams (2016: 520), and in Gregory the Great, Adams (2016: 558; *uade et dic* is again cited once). At *Anon. Val.* II.88 there is *ambula . . . et dic*, a passage

1 'Go' + Imperative

which demonstrates that *ambulo* means simply 'go' (see Adams 2016: 522). Asyndeton is not entirely lacking: see e.g. *Coll. Mon.-Eins.* (Dickey 2012) 9n *uade, dic illi* (Adams 2016: 520). In the Vulgate (New Testament) *uade* is used both asyndetically and syndetically with another imperative, and not always in agreement with the extant Greek. See e.g. on the one hand Jo 4.16 (*uade uoca uirum tuum* = ὕπαγε φώνησον τὸν ἄνδρα) (for ὑπάγω 'go (away)' in the NT see Bauer, Arndt and Gingrich 1952: 844), where both versions have asyndeton, but on the other hand Mt 18.15 (*uade et corripe eum* = ὕπαγε ἔλεγξον αὐτόν), where it seems that the Latin version has introduced a coordinator.

In Petronius, who does not use *uado*, *i/ite* is followed by another imperative (imperatival phrase) three times, always with the coordinator *et* linking the two (115.14 twice, frg. XXXIII.12). Pairs of imperatives are not particularly common in the work, and vary between syndetic and asyndetic: 57.9 *bis prande, bis cena*, 80.4 *conuertite huc manus, imprimite mucrones*, 98.3 *reduc puerum et uel Ascylto redde*, 107.3 *flectite ergo mentes satisfactione lenitas et patimini*, 114.9 *da oscula, . . . ultimum hoc gaudium . . . rape.*

For some brief further details of the increase of coordinators between pairs of imperatives as time went on see Hofmann and Szantyr (1965: 471), but they do cite Meyer-Lübke (1900), §532 for Romance evidence suggesting the persistence of types of asyndeton (see below, 1.5). There is scope for a comprehensive study; Ranstrand (1951: 93), for example, has a list of pairs of imperatives without coordinators from both classical and later Latin (not confining himself to cases with the verb 'go'), but the significance of the list is unclear without evidence for the coordinated variants. For asyndeton in a speech in Tacitus see *Hist.* 4.77.3 *ite nuntiate Vespasiano*.

1.5 Italo-Romance Dialects

In Italo-Romance, in addition to the construction consisting of an imperative (meaning 'go') with a dependent infinitive, there are scattered about three types of coordinated constructions comprising 'go' and another imperative, first, that with asyndeton, second, with coordination by means of ET, and third, with coordination by means of AC (see Ledgeway 1997: 256, and the whole of the appendix, 255–69; on asyndeton, see too Meyer-Lübke 1900, §532, cited at 1.4 above). The verb for 'go' derives from Lat. *uade*. Ledgeway (1997: 256) quotes these three illustrations of coordinated structures, syndetic and asyndetic, meaning 'go and call':

Va chiama (asyndeton)
Va e chiama (ET-coordination)
Va a chiama (AC-coordination)

He notes (256–7) that the distribution of the structures varies in accordance with geographical and diachronic factors: 'asyndeton and ET-co-ordination are generally restricted to the dialects of southern Italy ... whereas AC-co-ordination appears to occur in varying degrees in all Italian dialects'. The reference in this last clause is particularly to imperatival pairs, as it is stated later (267) that fully productive AC-coordination 'occurs only in Sicilian and Crotonese', whereas a great number of other Italo-Romance varieties 'exhibit a restricted type of AC-co-ordination in the 2.sg. imperative'.[1]

Ledgeway adds (1997: 257) that asyndeton in southern Italy is found particularly in the dialects of Calabria and northern Apulia, where it is a 'productive pattern of complementation'. Extensive illustrations are given (257–9) (not only comprising pairs of imperatives). Asyndeton is also reported (259) from Old Sicilian (again, not only consisting of pairs of imperatives). One of the examples cited from Sicilian (259, 48d *va viri siddu t'ama*, 'go and see if he loves you') has an expression seen above (1.1) in Plautus (*Bac.* 901 *i uise estne ibi*). Neapolitan, the main subject of Ledgeway's paper, has a similar asyndetic construction, but it is far more restricted (Ledgeway 1997: 260, and 248–9; id. 2009: 883–6), in that it occurs with the 2.sg. imperative of two verbs, *jì* 'go' and *venì* 'come', as its first element (1997: 260).

An important question is whether these southern Italian constructions genuinely continue the apparent Latin equivalents. Asyndeton, for example, does not seem to be attested in Neapolitan until the early nineteenth century (see Ledgeway 1997: 260–1), and may well derive from a different source (Ledgeway 1997: 265, 'a nineteenth century innovation'). Ledgeway allows (1997: 265) that the ET-coordinations continue an original Latin construction (examples at 264–5, with a summary at 265), but it is argued (2016: 160–4) that AC-constructions in Apulian are 'pseudo-coordinations' (164 'what diachronically and formally appears to be a case of coordination is best analysed synchronically as a case of ... subordination').

In the Latin examples seen earlier, and in most of the Italo-Romance examples quoted by Ledgeway in the places cited above, the two

---

[1] Cf. 266: 'As a productive means of complementation, paratactic structures co-ordinated by means of AC > *a* are limited to Sicilian dialects ... and the Calabrian dialect spoken in Crotone ... where such structures form part of the core grammar, occurring with all six grammatical persons, imperative and indicative verb forms, and with verbs of motion besides the verb "to go".'

imperatives express separate activities, first some sort of displacement of the person, and second the carrying out of an additional act (see Ledgeway 1997: 232). However, Ledgeway also (1997: 261–3) illustrates (from a number of Italo-Romance varieties, including Old Neapolitan) a weakening of this biclausal structure into a monoclausal one, with the initial *va* becoming an invariable hortative particle (and thus not in a genuine asyndetic relationship with the following verb). In Latin *age* suffered the same weakening (see below, 2), but *i*, certainly in Plautus, seems to retain its full force (see above, 1, and Adams 2013: 798–9). In later Latin of course, as noted above (1.4), it disappeared from use.

2 Pseudo-Asyndeton: the Use of *age*

Age (or *agite*) is regularly followed by an imperative without a coordinator in many types of Latin (see *TLL* I.1403.80ff., Kühner and Stegmann 1955: I.200–1 and also 59–60, Hofmann and Szantyr 1965: 471 and 289, Hofmann and Ricottilli 2003: 149). The structure is for example common in Plautus (Lodge 1924–33: I.83) and Virgil: e.g. *Aen.* 3.169, 8.59, 10.241 *surge age*, 3.362, 6.389 *fare age*, 6.531 *age fare*, 3.462, 5.548 *uade age*, 4.569 *age*, *rumpe moras*, 6.629 *iam age, carpe uiam*, *G.* 3.42–3 *en age, segnis* | *rumpe moras*; cf. Hom. *Il.* 1.210 ἀλλ' ἄγε λῆγ' ἔριδος (and often). Such pairs are usually however not genuine asyndeta. *Age* is not only followed by singular imperatives. It may be followed by imperatives in the plural, as at Plaut. *Mil.* 928 *age igitur, intro abite* (cf. Hom. *Il.* 2.331 ἀλλ' ἄγε, μίμνετε πάντες), or by finite verbs in another person, as at Plaut. *As.* 834 *age ergo, hoc agitemus conuiuium* (see particularly Kühner and Stegmann 1955: I.59–60 for usages of this type, with parallels from Greek at 60; cf. too Kühner and Gerth 1898–1904: I.84–5). Servius' explanation of *age* (with imperatives and other verb forms) is no doubt right: *Aen.* 2.707 *'age' autem non est modo uerbum imperantis, sed hortantis aduerbium, adeo ut plerumque 'age facite' dicamus et singularem numerum copulemus plurali*. *Age* functions not as a full verb participating in a temporal sequence with another verb, but as a hortative particle (for a parallel in Italo-Romance see above, 1.5).

It is however suggested at *TLL* I.1404.11ff. that sometimes in such structures *age* is a full verb ('vis verbalis praevalet, cum additur *et*'), as is supposedly shown by the addition of *et* before the second imperative. But the presence of *et* hardly alters the role of *age*. Compare e.g. Virg. *Aen.* 1.753 *immo age et a prima dic, hospes, origine nobis* | *insidias*, 'but come on and tell us, guest, the plot from its first beginning', with *Aen.* 6.531 *sed te qui uiuum casus, age fare uicissim,* | *attulerint*, 'but come, tell in turn what chance has brought you, alive, here'. In both passages, one with *et* and the other without, the addressee is encouraged to tell a narrative explaining something, and the function of *age* in both is the same: it is hortative. For *age dic(e)* in Plautus (without *et*) with the same function as *age et dic* above see e.g. *Cur.* 132, *Epid.* 262. The term 'pseudo-coordination' has been used of various phenomena in other languages (see e.g. Heycock and Petersen 2012, Ledgeway 2016: 160–4), and may be applied to the use of *et* here. Similarly in the numerous cases where there is no *et* one may speak of 'pseudo-asyndetic coordination'.

If *et* were a genuine coordinator it could be substituted in another context by a disjunctive coordinator, such as *aut*. That does not seem to be the case (on this criterion see Ledgeway 2016: 161). For a list of the features of pseudo-coordinations see Heycock and Petersen (2012: 260), stating that such usages are sometimes referred to as verbal/clausal hendiadys. The first term is usually bleached of its full meaning, the tense/aspect of the two verbs must match, and the second never has an overt subject.

3 Some Special Types of Asyndetic Imperatives

Special types of asyndetic imperatives came up in VII, namely those in which a simplex and compound of the same root are juxtaposed, as Pacuvius fr. 199.8 Schierl *retinete tenete*, Cic. *Verr.* 3.155 *caede concide*, or, in the reverse order, Eur. *Alc.* 399 ὑπάκουσον ἄκουσον, 'listen, listen'. The former type is particularly common in curse tablets.

4 Greek: New Comedy and Miscellaneous

In Plautus numerous examples of asyndetic imperative pairs were cited above, and it was shown that at least some of these occur in phrases that would have been current in ordinary speech. Asyndeton bimembre in general is commonplace in Menander, and asyndetic pairs of imperatives are also found. I list some examples below without comment (see further XXIII.5.1), not to imply that Plautus and Terence were necessarily rendering pairs they found in originals, but merely to suggest that the structure probably had a place in both Greek and Latin dialogue:

Dysk. 954 χόρευε, συνεπίβαινε
Dysk. 960 αἴρεσθε τοῦτον, εἰσφέρετε

Pk. 509–10 ἐλθὼν διαλέγου, | πρέσβευσον
Sam. 327 κάτεχε σαυτόν, καρτέρει.

For Greek see also above, 1.2 on ἴθι, ἴτε + imperative. Usher (1978: 161), for example, notes the imperatives in asyndeton at E. *Cyc.* 659 τυφέτω, καιέτω, 661 τόρνευ', ἕλκε, 'expressing urgency and excitement'.

5 Conclusions

This chapter has been mainly about a particular pairing of imperatives, that of the type 'go' + 'do something'. Elsewhere (XXIII.5.1) it is shown that in Plautus asyndetic pairs of imperatives in general are ubiquitous. Here is a syntactic type of asyndeton that, unlike a number of the other syntactic types discussed in earlier chapters, was almost certainly current in ordinary speech (at least in the earlier period), particularly when slaves or subordinates were addressed. Nor was it confined to slangy contexts. It had found its way also into official formulae, but again when the addressee was a subordinate.

There are hints in later Latin texts that the 'go do something' type was increasingly rivalled by coordinated variants, but nevertheless evidence was seen for the survival of the asyndetic type in some southern Italian dialects.

CHAPTER XI

Masculine + Feminine Pairs

1 Introduction

Types of living beings are sometimes expressed by pairing the masculine term for that being with the feminine. For example, the totality of divine beings may be rendered by '(all) gods (and) goddesses'. Such pairings in Latin show variations between syndetic and asyndetic coordination, with the asyndetic variant common in legal language but coordination usually preferred otherwise. I have just used the term 'totality', but it is misleading without specification. 'Men (and) women' may refer to the infinite number of male and female adults in the world, but the phrase is more likely in ordinary narrative to denote a finite, even small, group in a particular context. The term 'merism' is all very well in idealised accounts of Indo-European poetics, but most people in the real world do not speak only in universals. Watkins' definition (1995: 9, 15) of merism is 'a two-part figure which makes reference to the totality of a single higher concept'. West (2007: 99–100), more clearly, refers to 'pairings of contrasted terms, as an emphatic expression of the totality that they make up'. The method of coordination in male–female pairs in Latin seems unaffected by the difference between a finite set and an infinite.
I illustrate various pairs of this masculine + feminine type.

2 Gods, Goddesses

I start with a striking pair in Greek expressing an infinite set by means of adjectives rather than nouns (see also XXII.3): Men. *Kolax* fr. 1 (Körte and Sandbach), at Arnott (1996–2000: 186, lines 3–4): θεοῖς Ὀλυμπίοις εὐχώμεθα | Ὀλυμπίασι, πᾶσι πάσαις.

The context is religious. The cook who is serving the celebrants in the festival of Aphrodite Pandemos is the speaker. There are two masculine + feminine asyndetic pairs of adjectives, Ὀλυμπίοις ... Ὀλυμπίασι, which is

2 Gods, Goddesses

discontinuous (interrupted by εὐχώμεθα: see further below on this feature), and πᾶσι πάσαις, both pairs modifying θεοῖς. The whole embraces the totality of gods and goddesses. For masculine and feminine forms of the adjective 'all' applied to 'gods', see Dem. 18.1 (cited by Gomme and Sandbach 1973: 432, along with an inscription) τοῖς θεοῖς εὔχομαι πᾶσι καὶ πάσαις (note the interchangeability of asyndeton and coordination). Of note too is RV 6.68.4, where a phrase meaning 'all the gods' is reinforced by the phrase 'females and males' (see West 2007: 102, with further remarks on the opposition 'gods and goddesses'; West 103 also cites a Vedic spell translated 'of the he-locust, of the she-locust ... we tie up the mouth'). See too in general Oakley (1998: 242), on Livy 7.26.4 *si diuus si diua esset*, for the motivation of pairs of the 'gods–goddesses' type: 'ever concerned to address deities in the correct way, the Romans did not wish to offend a god by erring as to his or her gender'.

For a Latin nominal asyndetic pair of this type see Ter. *Hau.* 810 *ut te quidem omnes di deae quantumst, Syre,* | ... *perduint* (a totality), 'may all the gods and goddesses, how many there are, destroy you, Syrus'. Here the manuscripts have *deaeque*, which is unmetrical, and deletion of *-que* is the simplest way to solve the problem. It is possible that the construction (with *quantumst*) is relevant to the choice of asyndeton (see below, 3). At Cato *Agr.* 139 (*si deus si dea es quoium illud sacrum est*) asyndeton with anaphora occurs in a prayer, as at Livy 7.26.4 above. Oakley (1998: 242) cites various *si .. si* formulae, a number containing equivalents to *diuus/diua*.

By contrast a prayer of Scipio Africanus at Livy 29.27.2 has coordination in this pair: *diui diuaeque ... uos precor quaesoque uti*. Another coordinated instance is at Livy 27.45.8 *deos omnis deasque precabantur*, where the word order is discontinuous (a pattern which is not infrequently found in merisms (see XX.1): see e.g. Cic. *Fin.* 2.111 *summum pecudis bonum et hominis* (of four-footed and two-footed creatures: see for this pairing Watkins 1995: 15, West 2007: 100), *Fin.* 3.67 *hominum causa et deorum*, *Fin.* 4.25 *ex animo constamus et corpore*; see too on the passage of Menander above).

Indeed in the pair 'gods, goddesses' in Latin coordination is very much the norm. For Plautus, Lodge (1924–33: 1.378) provides statistics that show no instances of asyndeton, but twenty-four of *di deaeque* and one of *di et deae*. *TLL* V.1.909.14ff. on *di deaeque* and its variants states that *et, atque, uel, siue* are used as the coordinator more rarely (than *-que*). It is then added: 'ἀσυνδέτως hic illic in titulis'. Note e.g. *CIL* 6.101 *sacrum deum dearum* | *uoto suscepto dedicauit* | *C. Paetius Rufus*.

See further Gonda (1959: 342).

3 Men, Women

For this asyndetic pair in Greek (tragedy and comedy) see Soph. *Ant.* 1079 φανεῖ γὰρ οὐ μακροῦ χρόνου τριβὴ | ἀνδρῶν γυναικῶν σοῖς δόμοις κωκύματα, 'For after no long lapse of time there shall be lamentations of men and women in your house' (Lloyd-Jones, Loeb), Ar. *Ran.* 157 καὶ μυρρινῶνας καὶ θιάσους εὐδαίμονας | ἀνδρῶν γυναικῶν καὶ κρότον χειρῶν πολύν, 'and myrtle groves, happy bands of men and women, and a great clapping of hands' (Henderson, Loeb). Note too Men. *Dysk.* 921 παῖ, παι] δίον, γυναῖκες, ἄνδρες, παῖ, θυρωρέ. In this series of vocatives γυναῖκες, ἄνδρες is a unit embedded within the long colon. These pairs do not indicate infinite totalities but specific groups of men and women.

For Vedic note particularly Gonda (1959: 342) on Atharvaveda 1.8.1 *yá idáṃ strī́ púmān ákaḥ*, 'whoever, man (or) woman, has done this'. He comments: 'This very obvious "Aufteilung" of human beings into men and women is one of the most favourite instances of "polarity" in many languages' (with examples). West (2007: 103 n. 96) too cites AV 1.8.1.

Amid citations of the *Lex Cornelia de sicariis et ueneficis* by Cicero at *Cluent.* 148 we find two juxtaposed asyndetic pairs (one of them masculine + feminine), an accumulation typical of legal specification: *omnes uiri mulieres, liberi serui in iudicium uocantur.*[1] For masculine + feminine legal pairs see further below.

At Livy 45.24.11 (*omnia libera capita, quidquid Rhodiorum uirorum feminarum est, cum omni pecunia nostra naues conscendemus*), the expression *quidquid est* is similar to *quantumst* at Ter. *Hau.* 810 above, 2 (with *di deae*), in another of these male–female pairs with asyndeton. The expression in Terence refers to a totality, that in Livy to a finite set.

Another possible example of a 'men–women' asyndeton is at Livy 34.5.12 (18): *in rebus ad omnes pariter uiros feminas pertinentibus* (*feminasque* χ, *feminas* B). On the text see Briscoe (1981: 11) and see below on Livy 18; see also Briscoe (1981: 57) ad loc. If *omnes* is taken as substantival and linked to *pariter* ('to all alike, men and women'), *uiros feminas* becomes an appositional adjunct, specified as a totality, and in such a context asyndeton looks right (cf. the passage above with *quidquid est*, and that with *quantumst* referred to). If *omnes* is adjectival, there is still an explicit totality.

The following two examples are both in asyndetic sequences, as in the law above quoted by Cicero:

---

[1] For the second asyndetic pair here see B. *Afr.* 23.1 *expeditoque exercitu seruorum liberorum II milium numero*. *Liber* and *seruus* are constantly opposed (for coordinated examples see e.g. Caes. *Civ.* 3.14.3, 3.32.2, 3.80.3, Livy 39.49.8, 45.14.7; also *TLL* VII.2.1280.67ff.).

Plin. *Nat.* 37.201 *ergo in toto orbe, quacumque caeli conuexitas uergit, pulcherrima omnium est iis rebus, quae merito principatum naturae optinent, Italia, rectrix parensque mundi altera, <u>uiris feminis</u>, ducibus militibus, seruitiis, artium praestantia, ingeniorum claritatibus, iam situ ac salubritate caeli atque temperie, accessu cunctarum gentium facili, portuosis litoribus, benigno uentorum adflatu.*

ps.-Sall. *Rep.* 2.4.2 *luctus gemitus uirorum mulierum.*

The pair 'men, women' is also found with coordination, as at Livy 27.51.8 *eam supplicationem C. Hostilius praetor edixit. celebrata a uiris feminisque est* and 27.45.7 *et hercule per instructa omnia ordinibus uirorum mulierumque undique ex agris effusorum inter uota et preces et laudes ibant*, Plin. *Ep.* 3.16.1 *dictaque uirorum feminarumque* (see Preuss 1881: 93).

4 Boys, Girls

This pairing occurs at Plaut. *Epid.* 210 *tum captiuorum quid ducunt secum! pueros uirgines | binos ternos*, Sall. *Cat.* 51.9 (14) *rapi uirgines pueros*, Hor. *Sat.* 2.3.325 *mille puellarum puerorum mille furores* (see XXIX.2.1.4.1). For coordinated variants see Catull. 34.2 *puellae et pueri integri*, 64.78 *electos iuuenes simul et decus innuptarum*, Hor. *Carm.* 3.14.9 *uirginum matres iuuenumque nuper*, *Carm.* 3.14.10 *o pueri et puellae*, *Sat.* 1.1.85 *pueri atque puellae*, Ov. *Tr.* 3.12.5 *iam uiolam puerique legunt hilaresque puellae*, Gell. 20.7.2 *pueros puellasque*, and see further on Horace, XXIX.4.1.2. For such pairs in asyndetic phrases (with anaphora) see Catull. 62.42 *multi illum pueri, multae optauere puellae*, 62.44 *nulli illum pueri, nullae optauere puellae*. These two lines were imitated by Ovid, with a slight change of terminology: *Met.* 3.353–5 *multi illum iuuenes, multae cupiere puellae* ... *nulli illum iuuenes, nullae tetigere puellae* (see Fordyce 1961: 259).

Coordination is more common than asyndeton in this pairing.

5 Miscellaneous Pairs, Mainly in Legal Contexts

The pair 'men, women' was seen above in a quotation by Cicero of a law. In legal language persons were often classified into types, and if females as well as males were to be specified in a classification, masculine + feminine pairs were juxtaposed, often in asyndeton, to express totalities. A lot of these pairs belong as well under another heading, that is as asyndeta denoting categories of family members, relations, and I deal with them mainly elsewhere (XIV).

At Ter. *Hau.* 142 the *senex* Menedemus states that he has put all his slaves, female and male, on the market and sold them (with some stated exceptions) *ancillas seruos . . . | omnis produxi ac uendidi*. For this pair and equivalents in literary texts see Plaut. *Cas.* 521 *seruos ancillas*, *Men.* 339 *seruolos ancillulas*, *Trin.* 799 *seruos ancillas*, Cato *ORF* XII.73 *serui ancillae* (see also on Plautus, XXIII.8.13, on Lucilius, XXV.1.1.2, 13, and Preuss 1881: 79). A sequence containing a variant is found in a curse tablet: Audollent (1904), 216, Kropp 2008a, 11.1.1/2 *conserui conseruae, amici amicae*. Curses regularly adopted legal and religious language.

Of note is a passage from the praetor's edict: *Dig.* 3.1.1.11 (cf. 2.4.4.1) *deinde adicit praetor: 'pro alio ne postulent praeterquam pro parente, patrono patrona, liberis parentibusque patroni patronae'. de quibus personis sub titulo de in ius uocando plenius diximus. item adicit: 'liberisue suis, fratre sorore, uxore, socero socra, genero nuru, uitrico nouerca, priuigno priuigna, pupillo pupilla, furioso furiosa'* (= Riccobono 1968: 342, *Edictum perpetuum praetoris urbani* VI.16). There are nine asyndetic masculine + feminine pairs here, which mainly indicate family relationships, and belong in another chapter. Note however *patronus patrona* twice, once in the genitive, *pupillus pupilla* and *furiosus furiosa*.

See also XXIX.2.1.4 on Hor. *Sat.* 1.9.26–7 *mater | cognati*.

6 Conclusions

Asyndeton of this type in Latin does not seem to have been commonplace or in ordinary use. The predominance of *di deaeque* over the asyndetic alternative is particularly striking. Asyndeton was seen in legal specifications or language with a hint of legal formality, and notably in accumulations, where one example may be juxtaposed with another masculine + feminine pair or with another asyndetic pair of different type. These accumulations are not only in jurists but also for example in ps.-Sallust and Pliny, and they represent an old and stylised pattern. We saw several cases too where the notion of totality was reinforced by a complement such as *quantumst*, and these may belong to an ancient type. There was a tendency, no more, for masculine + feminine pairs to be used asyndetically, but contextual and structural influences came into it too, such as the presence of anaphora.

CHAPTER XII

Recapitulation: 'Grammatical' Types and Their Distribution

In VI–XI six types of asyndeton have been examined that are marked by a grammatical (usually morphological) feature of both or one of the terms. The diversity of the types, and particularly the variations in their distributions, are already enough to make it clear that there is no point in trying to come up with a single adjective or phrase that might characterise asyndeton bimembre ('sacral', 'tragic', 'reflecting the ancient *carmen*', 'expressing rapidity', etc.). The different types vary particularly in their frequency across genres, literary and non-literary.

At one extreme is the type consisting of an active and passive form of the same verb. Verb forms of opposite voice are often associated in literary Latin (Wills 1996: 295–8), but almost always with coordination or separated in some way. Asyndetic pairings are so rare that they must have been merely an isolated and artificial variant on the coordinated type. Tacitus, who was a great exploiter of asyndetic pairings of opposites, direct or inexplicit ('inexplicit' oppositions will be explained later), has a couple of examples, both with the same verb, and both no doubt adopted ad hoc to suit his view of the context. The type expressing mutual love (e.g. *amant amantur*) does occur several times, and probably reflects a common ideal of what constitutes 'love', though that ideal is usually conveyed in other ways.

Also extremely rare in literary Latin are asyndetic pairings comprising a single verb in two different tenses or moods. Coordinated pairs of this type are commonplace, but the asyndetic variant belongs in a particular genre, legal documents, where it is constantly used.

At the other extreme are pairs of imperatives, particularly of the 'go do something' type. These are widespread in early Latin and also turn up in the classical period. It was seen that they are typically addressed to a slave or other subordinate, and as such they cannot have been artificial but must have been heard in everyday interactions, both informal (when e.g. a slave was given instructions) and formal (when used by an official to an underling). There are signs that the pattern tended to give way to coordinations later (e.g. in Petronius), but further collections of evidence would be needed if generalisations were to be made about later developments. It was seen that the asyndetic type possibly persisted in some southern Italian dialects, and instances can also be found in some late texts, even if outnumbered by coordination. It is a reasonable guess that asyndeton in the 'go do something' expression was peremptory, and therefore functional rather than artificially stylised in the manner of the active–passive type.

Different again are negative adjectives with the *in*-privative prefix, either in both (or all) terms or in just one (usually the second). We illustrated these from a diversity of genres, from e.g. Plautus, Cicero, Horace's *Satires* to the historians. The type was old and inherited. Equivalents were collected from Umbrian, Greek, Vedic and also English. It will be shown later that there are similarities between Virgil's use of such pairs and Homer's (see XXIV.2.1.1 after 15, XXIV.2.3, XXIV.4), but the influence of Greek was certainly not the prime determinant of such asyndeta in Latin, as semantic differences are identifiable between the Greek and Latin pairs. Many such pairs in Latin are postponed in some sense and are predicative adjuncts, and they belong to the type of list that we have labelled 'open-ended', in that they could be added to and there is implied a pause for thought after the first term. Privative adjectives are not the only category of adjectives used thus in asyndeton in Latin (see IV.4). In these different pairings placement and the resultant intonation probably contributed some sort of emphasis or emotion. On the other hand privative adjectives were also used syndetically. The asyndetic type is common and the examples not to be classified as 'occasional' variants (as is the case e.g. with asyndetic active–passive pairs), but it is not obvious what subjective factors might have prompted a writer to choose one pattern rather than the other. Genre was one influence. In Horace's most conversational genre, the *Satires*, pairs with at least one privative are the most prominent asyndetic type (see XXIX.2.1.1), whereas in other genres he uses syndetic pairs but not asyndetic (see XXIX.4.1).

More specifically genre-related is asyndeton consisting of a simple verb followed by its compound. When the compound has a different meaning from the simplex, the type is characteristic of legal Latin. When the compound is an intensification of the simplex, the pattern belongs in both Greek and Latin particularly to curse tablets. This second type is part of a wider category of verbal repetitions in curse tablets. Compounds with different prefixes based on the same verbal root tend to be piled up as a form of intensification, sometimes with a simplex as well, sometimes without, and sometimes with a compound before the simplex instead of

XII Recapitulation

after. Outside curse tablets simplex + compound intensification is not common in either Greek or Latin, and it must have been only an occasional resource. In Latin the pattern is found a few times in comedy, perhaps most notably in several passages of Plautus where the pairing is part of an accumulation of asyndeta. Accumulations of asyndeta of varying length (often accompanied by syndetically linked elements as well) are a favoured location for embedded asyndetic pairs in Latin, with the asyndeton chosen to suit the structure. Ad hoc asyndetic pairs comprising simplex + compound are not entirely restricted to comedy in Latin. What looks like a dramatic letter quoted in part by Cicero in the Verrines has an example, as well as an asyndeton bimembre of another type. Wills (1996: 443–5) discusses the repetition of a simplex by its compound, but in his examples usually the second member is not simply coordinated to the first but stands in a more complicated relationship to it. For coordination see the examples cited by Chahoud (2018: 140).

Finally, we discussed the type whereby complementary masculine + feminine pairs are paired, as in *gods and goddesses*. This is a type that in literary Latin may be asyndetic, but it is the syndetic form that is preferred, as e.g. in *di deaeque*, with the asyndetic an occasional variant and not always obviously motivated. We did however see, first, that such pairs tend to be in accumulations, and second that such accumulations occur in legal texts, phrases or contexts.

We have noted in this short discussion not only differences of type and distribution, but also, first, the frequency of several types in legal Latin, and second the significance of accumulations.

PART 3

Semantic Types

CHAPTER XIII

Pairs of Opposites

1 Introduction

One of the most frequently used terms in this book is 'opposites', and that is a reflection not only of the role that oppositions play in thought and communication, but also of the marked tendency for Latin to express oppositions asyndetically, particularly in certain genres, such as philosophy and historiography.[1] On the first point it is worth quoting Lyons (1977: 277):

> [A]ntonymy reflects or determines what appears to be a general human tendency to categorize experience in terms of dichotomous contrasts.

Earlier (270) Lyons had remarked that from the very beginnings of structural semantics the importance of paradigmatic oppositions has been emphasised, and that there have been claims that during every utterance 'the opposite is in some way present in the mind of the speaker and hearer'. One should steer clear of such sweeping assertions (as Lyons does), but it is certainly the case that, in Latin, narratives and discussions of different types constantly set up sharp oppositions. The multiplicity of these can be deduced from the fact that in the introductory sections, Parts 2 and 3 of this book, no fewer than four chapters (in addition to the present one) deal to some extent with different types of pairs of opposites (for a list of these chapters, see the end of the next section).

It is not the purpose of this chapter to undertake a comprehensive survey of lexical oppositions in Latin. My aims are, first, to give some precision to the term 'opposites', such that types that come up in other chapters and in the sections on different writers and genres may be more easily categorised; second, to bring out the frequency of asyndetic pairs of opposites in comparison with other types of asyndetic pairs; and, third,

---

[1] For some asyndetic pairs of opposites in Greek, sometimes in sequences, see Kühner and Gerth (1898–1904: II.346), Denniston (1952: 103).

to illustrate some of the structures that seem to determine asyndetic versus syndetic coordination of opposites. I start with the definition of opposites.

2 Definitions: Complementarities, Antonyms, Converses and Directional Opposites

Opposites are not easy to define, and fall into various types that are not always discrete. I am indebted here to the classifications of Lyons (1968: 460–70, 1977: 270–87) and Cruse (1986, Chaps. 9–11).

A first type comprises complementaries (Lyons 1968: 460–2, Cruse 1986: 198–204). I quote Cruse (198–9):

> The essence of a pair of complementaries is that between them they exhaustively divide some conceptual domain into two mutually exclusive compartments, so that what does not fall into one of the compartments must necessarily fall into the other. There is ... no possibility of a third term lying between them.

Cruse gives as examples *true* : *false*, *dead* : *alive*, *open* : *shut* (and others).[2] Another, discussed by Lyons (1968: 460–1), is *married* : *single*. If we deny the applicability of one term to a situation, we effectively commit ourselves to the other (Cruse 1986: 199). Thus *He is not dead* implies *He is alive*, and *He is not alive* implies *He is dead*. Complementarities are usually either verbs or adjectives (Cruse 1986: 201).

At Cic. *Off.* 2.37 (**120, 121**) (*uita mors, diuitiae paupertas omnes homines uehementissime permouent*) the first pair *uita mors* comprises complementarities (cf. e.g. Cic. *S. Rosc.* 113 for *mortuus/uiuus* opposed), but the second pair does not: not being rich does not necessarily constitute being poor. Oppositions of different types are often expressed in Latin, as here, by abstract nouns, whereas the nature of the opposition is more easily understood if it is in adjectival form. For another Latin instance of complementarities see Livy 9.3.3 (**38**) *armati inermes*. One who is 'not unarmed' is by implication armed, and vice versa. On the other hand *armed* is gradable in English, with modifiers such as *heavily/lightly* (see the next paragraph on the idea of 'gradable').

A second type are antonyms. Antonyms, which are mostly adjectives, 'denote degrees of some variable property such as length, speed, weight, accuracy, etc.' (Cruse 1986: 204). The denial of one antonym does not

---

[2] It should be emphasised that the last pair must be used literally to be complementarities. Metaphorical uses of such pairs as *aperte* : *tecte* in Latin are of a different type.

mean that one is asserting the other: *This house is not big* does not imply *This house is small*. Antonyms are gradable, as in *This house is bigger than that, and the third is smaller than both* (see e.g. Lyons 1968: 463). Complementarities on the other hand are not gradable, except in derived, metaphorical uses, such as *She is more alive than her husband* (cf. Lyons 1977: 278). Another feature of antonyms is that lying between, or beyond, the antonyms there is a range of values that cannot be accurately expressed by either term (Cruse 1986: 204), whereas, as was noted above, there can be no third term lying between complementarities. Variants on e.g. the *happy : unhappy* opposition might be *exultant, miserable, content, grief-stricken*. Sentences 'containing antonyms are always implicitly, if not explicitly, comparative' (see Lyons 1968: 465). Positive-negative oppositions, with one member a privative adjective, may be antonyms (e.g. *happy : unhappy*), though sometimes such pairs are complementarities, as *married : unmarried* or *armed : unarmed*, which was seen in the last paragraph (on this point see Lyons 1977: 275).

A typical pair of antonyms in Latin is the 'happy : sad' contrast, e.g. at Tac. *Hist.* 1.3.2 (21), *laeta tristia*. Although antonyms are mainly adjectival, we saw above that it is not unusual to have in Latin pairs of abstract nouns derivable from adjectival pairs: e.g. Sall. *Cat.* 61.9 (21) *uarie per omnem exercitum laetitia maeror*. A revealing pair of abstract nouns, this time coordinated, is at Lucr. 2.517 (*omnis enim calor ac frigus mediique tepores | interutrasque iacent*), where it is explicitly noted that there are grades between hot and cold (on this pattern see further below, this section). Some pairs may be difficult to classify, with renderings into English possibly misleading. At Lucr. 1.14 (XXIV.7.1.2, 6) (*inde ferae, pecudes persultant pabula laeta*) the terms denote wild animals on the one hand, and animals that are part of the livestock of a farm on the other. If one were to paraphrase in English as 'wild' versus 'domestic animals', the pair would seem to be antonyms rather than complementarities. An animal that is 'not wild' need not be 'domestic', and both terms (or slight variants) are gradable (*This cat is wilder/more domesticated than that*). In Latin the two are probably not gradable and embrace a totality with no third term in between. *Armentum*, which is sometimes found in such groups, is merely a near-synonym of *pecus*. I am therefore inclined to take *ferae, pecudes* as complementarities (see further on Lucretius 6 at XXIV.7.1.2).

A third type are converses, exemplified by verbal pairs such as *buy : sell, give : take, teach : learn, pursue : flee, attack : defend, precede : follow*, and also active–passives. *Buy* e.g. is the converse of *sell* (Lyons 1968: 467; see further

XIII Pairs of Opposites

on this relationship id. 1977: 280), and *X killed Y* is the converse of *X was killed by Y* (Lyons 1977: 280). Cruse (1986: 231–2) includes under this heading adverbials such as *above : below, in front of : behind, before : after*, as well as noun pairs such as *ancestor : descendant, father : son, husband : wife, master : servant, teacher : pupil, guest : host*. Cruse's test for a converse relationship between certain (adverbial) pairs is expressed thus (1986: 231):

> [T]hese may be diagnosed ... by the fact that when one member of a pair is substituted for the other in a sentence the new sentence can be made logically equivalent to the original one by interchanging two of the noun phrase arguments.

Thus *The house is above the town* may be replaced by *The town is below the house*.

See also Lyons (1977: 279–80) on *husband : wife* as converses. He also remarks (280):

> Converse relations between lexemes ... are especially common in areas of the vocabulary having to do with reciprocal social roles ('doctor' : 'patient' ...) and kinship relations ('father' / 'mother' : 'son' / 'daughter', etc.), on the one hand, and temporal and spatial relations ('above' : 'below', 'in front of' : 'behind', 'before' : 'after', etc.), on the other.

Asyndetic pairs of verbs with a converse relation are particularly common in Latin and will be illustrated later in this chapter (see particularly 4.1). Verbal nouns may have the same relationship, as *raptor largitor* at Tac. *Hist.* 2.86.2 (**9**) (an equivalent to the 'give' : 'take' opposition, but in the reverse order). Relevant pairs of adverbs will also be dealt with below (5.4).

Lyons (1977: 281–7) sets up a fourth type, called 'directional'. This is seen in pairs of (often intransitive) verbs such as *go : return, enter : leave, arrive : depart, ascend : descend, rise : fall, fill : empty*. Note e.g. Cic. *Dom.* 137 (**69**) *dirueris aedificaris* (of knocking down and building up; the same opposition is at Hor. *Ep.* 1.1.100 (XXIX.2.2) *diruit aedificat*), *Phil.* 2.89 (**74**) *irent redirent*, Tac. *Ann.* 12.33 (**100**) *ut aditus abscessus, cuncta nobis importuna et suis in melius essent* (of entry and exit). Such pairs are called by Cruse (1986: 226) 'reversives', a term that certainly suits Cicero **69** just cited. The category includes adverbial pairs such as *up : down, forwards : backwards, left : right* (see Lyons 1977: 281, Cruse 1986: 223–4), that is pairs that denote opposite directions (Cruse 1986: 223).[3]

---

[3] Note (above) that Lyons (277: 280) includes the pair 'above': 'below' among converses, whereas here 'up': 'down' is put in a different category. I take it that the static adverbials are seen as converses, whereas those that express 'motion towards' are directional.

2 Definitions: Types of Opposites

I introduce here a final term, 'antipodals', as it is used by Cruse (1986: 224–5). Antipodals are not an extra type of opposite, but are classified by Cruse as one form of directional opposition. They are worthy of discussion in their own right because they lie behind a few distinctive idioms in Latin (and elsewhere in Indo-European).

Classical scholars in discussing opposites have tended to use such terms as 'polar expressions', 'polar opposites' or 'opposites' itself without definition and without any specification of the different types of opposites referred to (for the usual sense given to 'polar', 'polarity' in linguistics see VI.6). An interesting case in point is a short discussion by West (2007: 103), under the general heading 'Polar expressions ("merisms")', of a pattern that is described as follows:

> Sometimes the effort is made to stop a possible loophole by adding the middle term to the pair of opposites; the opposites are regularly placed first, with the intermediate term following.

The first two examples cited by West are from the Rigveda (4.25.8), translated 'the higher, the lower, the middle-ranking', and Theognis 3, 'I will always sing of thee first and last and in the middle.' I would add three Latin examples, both coordinated and asyndetic. First, Plaut. *Cist.* 512 *di deaeque, superi atque inferi et medioxumi* (see Leo 1960: 174), 'the gods and goddesses, the highest [in the heavens] and lowest [in the underworld] and those in the middle'. Second, Cic. *Fam.* 5.8.5 *uelim ... ad me scribas de omnibus minimis maximis mediocribus rebus*, 'please write to me on matters smallest, largest or in between'. *Mediocribus*, coming last like *medioxumi* above in keeping with West's rule of placement, lies between the smallest and largest. Perhaps it is meant to sound funny here. So, third, *summus* and *infimus* are given such an addition at Cic. *Nat.* 3.34 *quo naturae ui feratur, alia infimum, alia summum, alia medium*, 'to which it is carried by the force of nature, one to the bottom, another to the top, another to the middle'. These three terms are asyndetic with anaphora.

What types of opposites are e.g. *minimis* and *maximis* or *bottom* and *top*? They are not complementarities. 'Not the smallest' does not imply 'the largest'. They are not obviously antonyms, despite the fact that they admit of a term in between. Crucially, they are not gradable.

Cruse's definition (1986: 224–5) of antipodals is as follows:

> Building on the notion of oppositeness of direction, a category of **antipodal** opposites can be defined, in which one term represents an extreme in one direction along some salient axis, while the other term denotes the corresponding extreme in the other direction. For instance, if we go *up* as far as we

can while remaining within the confines of some spatial entity, we reach its *top*, and in the other direction the lower limit is the *bottom*.

Pairs of antipodal opposites in Latin sometimes admit of an idiomatic interpretation. Consider first another instance of the pair *summus/infimus*, at Cic. *Fam.* 8.13.4 (**200**): *priuatis, summis infimis, fueram iucundus*. If taken literally this would mean 'I made myself pleasant to private individuals, the highest and the lowest' (or 'the top people and the bottom'), with reference to an axis stretching between the two extremes of social status. Clearly Cicero did not seek out the highest and the lowest and disregard the middle classes, and the implication can only be that he made himself pleasant to everyone of whatever status, with the antipodal opposites serving as a frame for the totality. Shackleton Bailey translates, '(I) made myself pleasant to private individuals from the highest to the lowest', which captures the force of the pair and is a correct translation, but it is a translation that necessarily does not correspond exactly to the syntax of the Latin. Strictly *summis infimis* is dative ('to private individuals, the highest, the lowest').

A similar example is in the fetial formula at Livy 1.24.7 (*ut illa palam prima postrema ex illis tabulis ceraue recitata sunt*), which I first translate as it stands: 'when those things, the first, the last, from those tablets or wax have been read out openly'. The reference is to a public recitation of laws, and the meaning cannot be that only the first and the last should be read out. 'The first, the last' implies that those in between are also recited.

Antonyms must also often be interpreted as embracing what comes between as well. When (e.g.) 'young and old' charge the Roman column at Tac. *Ann.* 2.19.1 (**67**) (*iuuentus senes agmen Romanum repente incursant turbant*), the meaning can only be that everyone, whatever their age, did so. But pairs such as 'first/last', 'highest/lowest', largest/smallest', i.e. antipodals, expressing as they do the two extreme points on some axis or other, are more starkly contrastive than antonyms such as 'happy/sad', and any idiom that requires that they be taken to include everything in between as well is more striking than the use of a pair of antonyms to embrace a totality. If it is stated that *The first (and) the last shall receive a prize*, the natural meaning would be that just two persons would be awarded a prize, the one who wins the race, and, as a consolation, the one who completes the course last. If the sentence is to mean that everyone shall get a prize, some sort of contextual pointer would be essential. On the other hand a similarly structured sentence containing antonyms, such as *The rich (and) the poor shall pay tax*, would naturally be taken to mean that everyone, whatever their wealth, would be taxed. See also VI.6 on Virg. *Aen.* 12.811 (XXIV.2.1.2, **18**) *digna indigna*.

This survey of types is sketchy, and is intended simply to bring out the diversity of opposites. I have deliberately passed over numerous problems of classification, and have not discussed differences between the classifications of Lyons and Cruse. In dealing with evidence from texts some use will be made of the terms above.

No fewer than four chapters in Parts 2 and 3 of this book (in addition to the present one) deal with opposites in one way or another. I list these.

First, positive–negative pairs of the type *dignus* : *indignus* and *armatus* : *inermis* are dealt with in the chapter on privative adjectives (VI).

Second, masculine + feminine pairs have been given their own chapter (XI). Most speakers would probably see such pairs as *god* : *goddess, man* : *woman* as opposites, but they are not so easy to classify, and vary in type. *God* : *goddess* certainly does not consist of complementarities. *He is not a god* does not imply that he is a goddess, but is more likely to imply that he is merely mortal. Nor are the terms gradable. They may be seen as e.g. 'counterparts' (to adopt the term used by Cruse 1986: 225, who remarks of *male* and *female* and several other pairs that they 'do not satisfactorily reduce to any specific simpler opposition, but embody a number of different elementary notions'). Because of the difficulties of classification, I have simply put masculine + feminine pairs together without attempting to attach any other designation to them.

Third, active–passive pairs, of the type 'they love, they are loved' (converses) are discussed in a separate chapter (VIII).

Fourth, the next chapter (XIV), on family relations, deals with some converses in Latin and Greek, such as 'mother' : 'father', though this too is a pair that is regarded as difficult to classify (see Cruse 1986: 198; also the citation of Cruse below at 5.1).

3 Statistics

I give here some selective statistics to show the variable incidence of asyndetic pairs of opposites in Latin literary genres. The figures, taken from the conclusions to the relevant literary chapters, are approximate, because the classification of opposites is not always straightforward. I have included in the figures pairs that are not overtly opposite but opposite by implication. This is a category that will be discussed below (5.5), and particularly later in the chapter on the historians (XXX).

In Tacitus' *Histories* 19 of the 54 pairs are opposites (35 per cent) (see XXX.4.2.3a). In the *Annals* I noted 37 examples, representing about 32 per cent of the total (113) (see XXX.5.2.3). A writer's own stylistic ideas were one determinant of frequency (for another, see the next paragraph). In Sallust only 8 of the 89 asyndetic pairs comprise opposites (see the list at the end of XXX.3.3.2). Tacitus had independently adopted a stylistic mannerism and not simply followed Sallust. Livy stands midway between Tacitus and Sallust. There are about 10 pairs of opposites in the eight books used here, of a total of 66 asyndetic pairs, about 15 per cent of the total (see XXXI.3.6).

In the selection of Cicero's speeches there are just 3 pairs of opposites, of the total of about 90 asyndetic pairs (see XXVI.7.2.6). In the philosophical works, on the other hand, 18 of the pairs of nouns and verbs are of this kind, comprising about 26 per cent of the 68 asyndetic pairs in the corpus, and 37.5 per cent of the nominal and verbal pairs (18 out of 48) (see XXVI.7.3.1). Reflected here is a feature of philosophical discourse, in which oppositions were constantly discussed: the determinant of this high incidence is the subject matter. In the letters to Atticus, of the 31 asyndeta bimembria in the books considered, just 3 express opposites (see XXVI.7.4.3). The letters *Ad familiares* are different: 7–9 of the 19 asyndeta bimembria in the selection are opposites (see XXVI.7.5.2). There were differences in the ways in which Cicero addressed Atticus, and others with whom his relationship was more distant. The juxtaposition of opposites was perhaps too stylistically marked or pretentious to be overused in intimate exchanges, but was suited to high historical style, philosophy and communication with those to be kept at a distance.

4 Structures and Uses

I move on from the definition of types to an account of some of the ways in which asyndetic pairs of opposites are used. They occur particularly in certain structures, accumulations (see XIX). These vary in type. Three types will be discussed here.

4.1 *Accumulations: Juxtaposed Asyndetic Pairs of Opposites*

Asyndetic pairs of opposites are often in accumulations, juxtaposed with other such pairs. Asyndeton is so constant in such contexts that it seems to be the accumulation rather than the opposition itself that is the determinant of the form of coordination.

4 Structures and Uses 157

A striking example is Cic. *Fin.* 2.36 (94–8) *quid iudicant sensus? dulce amarum, leue asperum, prope longe, stare mouere, quadratum rotundum.* Here there are three pairs of antonyms first ('near' : 'far' will come up below, 5.4), and then *stare mouere* (with which compare the coordinated pair *motu et statu* at *Off.* 1.126 (116)). *Stare* means 'to stand still' (*OLD* s.v. *sto*, 7a), and the pair are complementarities if the second verb as well as the first refers to an animal (man or beast) that is on its feet. *The horse* (on its feet) *is not moving* implies that the horse is standing still. *The horse is not standing still* implies that the horse is moving. The listing of a series of opposites is a consequence of the (philosophical) context. In the commentary on Cicero 94–8 various other such philosophical sequences are quoted from both Greek and Latin.

Another series, superficially similar, is at *Off.* 1.128 (117, 118): *status incessus, sessio accubito, uoltus oculi manuum motus teneat illud decorum.* The two pairs express two different ways of being upright on both feet (standing still/moving forwards), and of not being on both feet (sitting, reclining). The pairs are not complementarities: a denial, for example, that the referent is sitting would not necessarily imply that he was reclining; he might be standing or lying prone. A denial that he was standing still would not necessarily mean that he was moving forward: he might be moving backwards or jumping on the spot. Nor are the pairs gradable. There are many different postures and movements that persons can adopt when either off their feet or on them: they may lie prone, lie supine, lean on one elbow or both, sit up straight with both legs outstretched, sit on a chair, move forwards, backwards or sideways on one or both feet, etc. Various pairings from such an array it may be tempting to see as opposites (see West 2007: 101), but they need not be opposites in any formal sense. A similarly deceptive pair (but not in an accumulation) is at *Fin.* 5.47 (137): *quem ad modum quis ambulet sedeat, qui ductus oris, qui uultus in quoque sit, nihilne est in his rebus quod dignum libero aut indignum esse ducamus?* These two verbs express contrasting activities, but they are not strictly opposites. It might however be said of the first pair in the other passage above, *status incessus*, that Cicero has deliberately replaced the opposite *motus* for stylistic effect, a weakening of overt opposition of a type that will be discussed below, this section, on Tac. *Ann.* 1.7.1, and also at 5.5.

The following, a fragment of M. Antonius ap. Quint. 3.6.45, has three pairs of opposites, two of them of the positive–negative type but of different morphological forms (on which phenomenon see VI.7): *paucae res sunt quibus ex rebus omnes orationes nascuntur, factum non factum, ius iniuria, bonum malum. Factum non factum* comprises complementarities, whereas the second and the third pairs are antonyms. The 'good' : 'bad' opposition is found outside an accumulation at Ter. *Ph.* 556: *una tecum bona mala tolerabimus* (and cf. the first two passages immediately below).

Here are some further asyndetic accumulations of opposites, of differing types:

Plaut. *Bac.* 400–1 *malus bonus* ... | *iustus iniustus, malignus largus* (there was possibly a third such pair following, but the text is uncertain; antonyms).
Ter. *Hau.* 643 *melius peius, prosit obsit, nil uident nisi quod lubet* (antonyms).
Cic. *Fam.* 5.8.5 (**197, 198**) *in omnibus publicis priuatis, forensibus domesticis* (see the next example).
Fam. 16.4.3 (**203**) *tua . . . in me officia, domestica forensia, urbana prouincialia, in re priuata in publica in studiis in litteris nostris* (the first of these pairs is of the 'public' : 'private' type, the second is of the 'town' : 'country' type; these will be discussed below, 5.1, 5.2).
Off. 2.37 (**120, 121**) *uita mors, diuitiae paupertas omnes homines uehementissime permouent* (complementaries, antonyms: see above, 2).
Off. 2.40 (**141, 142**) *iis etiam qui uendunt emunt, conducunt locant contrahendisque negotiis implicantur* (two pairs of converses; cf. with the first Ar. *Ach.* 685 πωλεῖν ἀγοράζειν).
Livy 38.48.4 (**49, 50**) *regna augetis minuitis, donatis adimitis* (reversives).
Tac. *Hist.* 1.3.2 (**21, 22**) *prodigia et fulminum monitus et futurorum praesagia, laeta tristia, ambigua manifesta* (antonyms).
Tac. *Hist.* 2.86.2 (**9**) *strenuus manu, sermone promptus, serendae in alios inuidiae artifex, discordiis et seditionibus potens, raptor largitor, pace pessimus, bello non spernendus* (a long sequence of asyndetic phrases, with the pair *raptor largitor* comprising converses (see above, 2), and the phrasal pairs that follow conveying a double opposition, good versus bad, and peace versus war, antonyms).
Tac. *Ann.* 2.19.1 (**66, 67**) *plebes primores, iuuentus senes agmen Romanum repente incursant turbant* (note that the two pairs of opposites are followed a little later by an asyndetic pair of verbs; moreover this passage is preceded by a phrasal asyndeton, *pugnam uolunt, arma rapiunt*; 'young' and 'old' are antonyms, but *plebes primores* are more difficult to categorise (see below, 5.3)).

The following clause illustrates a variation on the type of asyndeton composed of overt opposites: Tac. *Ann.* 1.7.1 (**56, 57**) *lacrimas gaudium, questus adulatione<m> miscebant.* Tears (of grief) are the opposite of joy, but *lacrimas* is not an explicit antonym of *gaudium*, as *luctum* or *maerorem* might have been (cf. Sall. *Cat.* 61.9, below, 4.2). It was a stylistic device (particularly favoured by Tacitus) to replace one of the antonyms in an opposition with an alternative that was not so directly contrastive (see above, this section, on *status incessus*). We see this pattern in the second pair too. The most obvious antonym of 'flattery, adulation' (*adulatio*) is not 'complaint' but 'abuse' or 'contempt'. Another example of this type of

4 *Structures and Uses* 159

variation comes up at Tac. *Ann.* 2.20.1, below, 4.3; see also below, 5.5. In the passage of Tacitus above the emendation to *adulationem* is supported by the nature of the accumulation.

The accumulations seen so far are made up of two or more asyndetic pairs of opposites juxtaposed. Not all accumulations of opposites have exactly this content.

4.2 Accumulations: Asyndetic Pairs of Opposites Juxtaposed with Syndetic Pairs of Opposites

Of two pairs of opposites together, one may be asyndetic but the other coordinated. At Cic. *Off.* 1.56 (140) (*quae conficitur ex beneficiis ultro et citro datis acceptis*) an asyndetic pair of converses (*datis acceptis*) is preceded by a coordinated pair of directional opposites ('backwards and forwards': on the type, reversives, see above, 2).

Note too Sall. *Cat.* 61.9 (21) (*uarie per omnem exercitum laetitia maeror, luctus atque gaudia agitabantur*). The first pair of antonyms is asyndetic, the second coordinated by *atque*. The two pairs express joy and sorrow (cf. Tac. *Hist.* 1.3.2 (21) *laeta tristia*), and then, with a chiasmus, sorrow and joy.

At Sall. *Hist.* 4.60.17 (47) Ramsey (*socios amicos, procul iuxta sitos, inopes potentisque trahant excindant*) there is an asyndetic pair of terms expressing relationships, an asyndetic pair of antonyms, embedded (*procul iuxta*: see below, 5.4), and then a coordinated pair of antonyms.

At Ter. *Ph.* 687 (*ut tequidem omnes di deaeque, superi inferi, | malis exemplis perdant*) the coordinated masculine + feminine pair *di deaeque* is specified by a juxtaposed adjunct possibly comprising opposites of the converse type, 'those above, below' (see Cruse 1986: 231), though we might take them as meaning 'the highest, the lowest' (antipodals: see above, 2). *Di* and *deae* are not strictly opposites but are strongly contrastive, and the accumulation is very similar to those consisting definitely of opposites.

At Tac. *Ann.* 3.1.4 (72) (*neque discerneres proximos alienos, uirorum feminarumue planctus*) there is first an asyndetic pair of antonyms, *proximos alienos* 'those closely related, strangers', and then follows a 'men' : 'women' contrast, coordinated by *ue*, but these last two terms are dependent in the genitive plural on *planctus* and thus differ syntactically from the asyndetic pair in the accusative plural. This is an established syntactic variation, found particularly in Tacitus, in juxtapositions of two pairs (see XXX.6.2b, end of section, and Sallust 47, above this section). Again I have included one pair that is only similar to a pair of definite opposites.

4.3 Accumulations: Asyndetic Pairs of Opposites Juxtaposed with Asyndetic Pairs of Other Types

A pair of asyndetic opposites may be embedded within or juxtaposed with an asyndetic sequence of a different structure or of different semantic type (i.e. definitely not composed of opposites), as in the following passages:

Plaut. *Am*. 226 *urbem agrum, aras focos seque uti dederent* (the first pair is of the 'town–country' type, which will come up again in this list, and is discussed below, 5.1; for *aras focus*, not opposites, see e.g. Cic. *Sest*. 90 (**16**) *qui ab aris focis ferrum flammamque depellis*).
Cic. *Off.* 1.22 (**138**) *communes utilitates in medium afferre, mutatione officiorum, dando accipiendo, tum artibus, tum opera, tum facultatibus deuincire hominum inter homines societatem* (the asyndetic converses *dando accipiendo* are followed by an asyndetic anaphoric tricolon).
Cic. *Off.* 1.50 (**139**) *ratio et oratio, quae docendo discendo, communicando disceptando iudicando conciliat inter se homines* (a pair of converses, *docendo discendo*, and then an asyndetic tricolon with members of varying semantics).
Sall. *Jug*. 101.11 (**79, 80**) *sequi fugere, occidi capi* (the first two are converses, of pursuit and flight, though in another context they could be reversives, if the same persons at first pursued and then turned and fled).
Tac. *Ann*. 2.20.1 (**69**) *nihil ex his Caesari incognitum: consilia locos, prompta occulta nouerat* (the antonyms *prompta occulta* follow a pair of non-opposites; *prompta* is a variation on the obvious opposite, *aperta*, for which pattern see 5.5).
Tac. *Ann*. 4.67.4 (**85**) *miles nuntios introitus, aperta secreta uelut in annales referebat* (non-opposites, then a similar pair to that immediately above).
Tac. *Ann*. 12.39.2 (**153**) *crebra hinc proelia, et saepius in modum latrocinii per saltus per paludes, ut cuique sors aut uirtus, temere prouiso, ob iram ob praedam, iussu et aliquando ignaris ducibus* (*temere prouiso* 'recklessly, cautiously' is a pair of antonyms, which immediately precedes an asyndetic pair of non-opposites, and follows at a short remove another such asyndetic prepositional pair).

Pacuvius *trag*. frg. 80 Schierl (2006) (XXIV.6.3, **6–8**; see also XVII.1) (*omnia animat format, alit auget, creat | sepelit*) is more complicated. This is not an asyndetic sequence of six verbs. Rather it consists of three pairs, with the first two, 'animates and forms, nurtures and increases', expressing a chronological sequence. The subject is *quidquid est hoc* 'whatever this is'. For the pair *alit auget* see on Lucretius 12 (XXIV.7.1.3). Against *creat* Schierl (233) writes 'Hysteron proteron' (in that it is preceded by *animat format alit auget*, printed without commas), but in fact the third pair, *creat sepelit*, expressing the very beginning and very end of the whole process of creating and consigning to death, is a summarising frame of the other two pairs: the last two verbs are opposites. Pairs such as 'being born/bringing to life' versus 'dying/being consigned to death' are reversives, denoting

5 A Few Types of Opposites Worthy of Comment 161

'change in opposite directions' (see Cruse 1986: 201, who also points out some complications in the interpretation of such pairs).

Not all pairs of opposites occur in accumulations, but I have set out here to show just how common they are in conjunction with other asyndeta. It would be easy to cite examples that are not in the structures seen here (e.g. Lucil. 1157 *durum molle*, Cic. *Leg.* 3.10 *iussa uetita*, Tac. *Ann.* 2.13.1 *per seria per iocos*, etc.).

5 A Few Types of Opposites Worthy of Comment

I conclude with comment on a few semantic or structural types that are problematic or special in some way. This section is by no means comprehensive.

5.1 'Town': 'Country' et sim.

Such oppositions are not uncommon, with variations of terminology and frequent use of asyndeton.

There is however some doubt about the interpretation of the 'town' : 'country' type. Cruse (1986: 198) states:

> One can distinguish ... central, or prototypical, instances [of opposites], judged by informants to be good examples of the category: *good* : *bad*, *large* : *small*, *true* : *false*, *top* : *bottom*, etc.; and more or less peripheral examples, judged as less good, or about whose status as opposites there is not a perfect consensus, such as *command* : *obey*, *mother* : *father*, *town* : *country*, *clergy* : *laity*, etc.

Later (262) he adds:

> One of the reasons why *work* : *play* and *town* : *country* ... are relatively weak opposites is the difficulty of establishing what the relevant dimension or axis is.

The opposition may be difficult to fit into a neat classification, but it was an important one to Romans, with a variety of implications. To Romans the city was central, and outside were rural areas with rustics. The political class had their careers in the city, but country estates outside that could even be refuges at times of political crisis. The contrast between town and country could be expressed in conflicting ways that presented sometimes city dwellers, sometimes country dwellers in the better light. *Vrbani* might be better educated and regarded as speaking a superior form of Latin compared with *rustici*, but on the other hand the city was given over to vice

162   XIII   Pairs of Opposites

whereas *rustici* maintained an old-fashioned morality. The city, of the rulers, could also be contrasted with the distant provinces, of the ruled. This type of opposition is a converse one, similar to 'master' : 'servant' (see above, 2). Here are some asyndetic examples:

Cic. *Att.* 6.1.24 (184) *iam enim sciemus de rebus urbanis de prouinciis*
Cic. *Fam.* 16.4.3 (202, 203) *tua ... in me officia, domestica forensia, urbana prouincialia, in re priuata in publica, in studiis in litteris nostris*
Cic. *Fin.* 2.77 (100) *omnes urbani rustici, omnes, inquam, qui Latine loquuntur.*

A further example cited above, 4.3, is with the opposition *urbs ager* (cf. *agrorum oppidorum* in an accumulation at Cic. *Phil.* 2.35 (19, 20)). See also on Sallust 27.

5.2   'Public' : 'Private' et sim.

Another opposition variable in its forms in Latin is 'public': 'private'. Strictly these terms are antonyms. They are gradable: *She is a very private person*; *One's fantasies should be more private than one's ambitions*; *He made his achievements more public than his failures*. Sometimes the opposition in Latin has a different phraseology from *publicus* + *priuatus* and is specific to political life in the city. The forum, as the place of public activity, is contrasted with the *domus*, as the place of privacy. Here are some asyndetic examples of several types:

Cic. *Fin.* 5.89 (107) *sed tu etiam, Chrysippe, in foro, domi: in schola desinis* ('in public, at home'; *in foro, domi* is equivalent to the adjectival opposites *forensis domesticus*: see the next examples).
Cic. *Fam.* 5.8.5 (198) *in omnibus publicis priuatis, forensibus domesticis, tuis amicorum, hospitum clientium negotiis*
Cic. *Fam.* 16.4.3 (202) *tua ... in me officia, domestica forensia, urbana prouincialia, in re priuata in publica, in studiis in litteris nostris*
Tac. *Ann.* 3.33.4 (76) *nunc uinclis exsolutis domos fora, iam et exercitus regerent* (cf. Cic. *Fin.* 5.89 above, and the next example).
Tac. *Ann.* 15.58.2 (166) *uolitabantque per fora per domus, rura quoque et proxima municipiorum pedites equitesque.*

The last passage also brings in the 'town' : 'country' opposition.

5.3   Pairs Denoting Opposites of Social Status

Such types of opposition sometimes come up. Note:

Livy 9.14.11 (10) *caedunt pariter resistentes fusosque, inermes atque armatos, seruos liberos, puberes impubes, homines iumentaque*

5 A Few Types of Opposites Worthy of Comment

Tac. *Ann.* 2.19.1 (66) *plebes primores, iuuentus senes agmen Romanum repente incursant turbant.*

Seruos liberos are not complementarities. One who was not a slave was not necessarily *liber*, because *liberti* were in between. They are not gradable. They are probably antipodals. The directions *up/down* if applied to an axis representing the extremes of liberty will have *liberi* at the top and *serui* at the bottom. In the second passage the reference is not to Romans but to Germans, and the words *plebes primores* are not to be taken as Roman technical terms. They seem to denote the ruled and the rulers (cf. *master* : *servant*), and look like converses.

5.4 Asyndetic Pairs of Adverbs

Various types of speech have come up in oppositions in this chapter, but it is worth dwelling on adverbs because of the almost formulaic character they may have in asyndetic oppositions.

Donatus on Ter. *Hec.* 315 (*trepidari sentio et cursari rursum prorsum*, 'I can hear sounds of panic and rushing to and fro/backwards and forwards') says that *rursum prorsum* is proverbial, and cites parallels: *est prouerbiale, ut dicimus 'sursum deorsum', 'intro foras', 'hac illac' et similia*. The use of the term 'proverbial' is of interest, as it suggests that asyndetic adverbial opposites were particularly suited to fossilisation, not least because they usually had a fixed form. The same pair is at Enn. *trag.* 116 Jocelyn: *rursus prorsus reciprocat fluctus*. Later it turns up in Varro with a coordinator: *Men.* 28 *rursus ac prorsus meant*; cf. *Ling.* 10.52 *prosus et rosus* (see de Melo 2019: 2.1229 on the spellings). These are directional opposites.

Preuss (1881: 31) on the comment of Donatus observes that he has not found *intro foras* (but note the similar anaphoric asyndeton at Plaut. *Capt.* 114 *sinito ambulare, si foris si intus uolent*; this however is a static rather than directional pair ('let them walk around outside or inside if they wish'), and the terms would be regarded as converses rather than directional opposites: see n. 3). For *sursus/-m deorsum* 'up and down' see e.g. Ter. *Eun.* 278 *ne sursum deorsum cursites*, 'so that you don't run up and down'. For the same pair with anaphora see Lucil. 703 *modo sursum, modo deorsum*. Both this pair in Terence and *rursum prorsum* at *Hec.* 315 in the last paragraph accompany verbs of running in informal contexts, and they have the appearance of current idioms; by contrast at Tubero, *FRH* II.38.F12, there is a coordinated variant of the second pair, in a context that is not mundane: *palpebras quoque eius, ne coniuere posset, sursum ac deorsum diductas insuebant*. Another of Donatus' examples, *hac illac*, is at Ter. *Hau*. 512 (*hac illac circumcursa*), again with a frequentative form of a verb of running (see further Preuss 1881: 28).

The pair *comminus eminus* (Preuss 1881: 31–2, Timpanaro 1994: 4; see e.g. Tac. *Hist*. 2.4 (**45**) *non una pugnae facies: comminus eminus, cateruis et cuneis concurrebant*, 'hand to hand and at a distance'; in this passage there is a familiar juxtaposition of asyndeton with a coordinated pair) belongs to the category of antonyms (cf. *prope longe* and *procul iuxta* in the next paragraph; conceptually such terms are gradable, but in Latin only *prope* and *longe* have comparative forms). The opposition is expressed by prefixes: both terms are compounds with *manus* as base, but with different prefixes. Of similar type is Tac. *Ann*. 12.33 (**100**) *aditus abscessus*, though in that pair it is not only the prefixes that produce the opposition, but also the roots ('go' versus 'withdraw'); the two terms moreover are reversives not antonyms. For a more precise structural parallel to *comminus eminus* see Ter. *Hau*. 643 *prosit obsit*, 'helps, harms' (antonyms).

Asyndetic adverbs are well attested in accumulations. At Cic. *Fin*. 2.36 (94–8), quoted above, 4.1, *prope longe* is in a long sequence of opposites. A similar pair, which also came up above (4.3), is at Sall. *Hist*. 4.60.17 Ramsey (**47**) *socios amicos, procul iuxta sitos, inopes potentisque*, juxtaposed on the one hand with an asyndetic pair of nouns and on the other with a coordinated pair of opposites. Note too Cic. *Ac*. 2.125 *et cum in uno mundo ornatus hic tam sit mirabilis, innumerabilis supra infra, dextra sinistra, ante post*, where after an asyndetic pair of adjectives (*mirabilis innumerabilis*), the second with a privative prefix, there are two asyndetic pairs of converses. *Dextra sinistra* is a classic pair, usually adverbial in function, used in asyndeton for example by Cato, whereas Varro in his agricultural work had switched to coordination (see Adams 2016: 79, 83). Historically both terms have a comparative suffix, which suggests that they are antonyms (there are also hypercharacterised forms such as *dexterior*). The asyndetic use continues, but in rivalry with the syndetic (see further Preuss 1881: 41–2, and also below, XXXII.4 on the practice of Vitruvius), though in a sequence such as that above the asyndetic pairing is not surprising. Cf. Sall. *Jug*. 101.9 (**40**) *dextra sinistra omnibus occisis*, but on the other hand *Jug*. 50.4 *a sinistra ac dextra*. With *ante post* cf. *Tab. Ig*. Ia.1–2 **aves ... pernaies : pusnaes**, of observing the birds, perhaps 'in front, behind' (see Poultney 1959: 157, with the index at 315; Untermann 2000: 537, 538, 622).

The list of adverbial oppositions in asyndeton could be extended. Here are a few more examples.

5 A Few Types of Opposites Worthy of Comment

For *huc illuc* see e.g. Virg. *Aen.* 4.363, 12.764, Tac. *Hist.* 1. 40.1, 1.76.1, 3.3, 3.73.1, 4.46.3, 5.20.1 (see Tacitus 39–44; for the pair coordinated cf. *Ann.* 13.37.1 *hucque et illuc uolitans*, 15.38.3 *hucque et illuc*). For *hinc inde* see Tac. *Hist.* 4.62.2 (46), and for *aperte tecte*, Cic. *Att.* 1.14.4 (see on Cicero 213). Examples of all three pairs can be found in Preuss (1881), index. The first two are directionals, and the third antonyms. Cf. Catull. 68.133 *circumcursans hinc illinc* (again with a frequentative verb of running).

A common asyndetic adverbial pair of directional opposites in Greek is ἄνω κάτω 'up and down' (cf. *supra infra* 'above and below' at Cic. *Ac.* 2.125 above, this section): e.g. Men. *Kith.* fr. 1.3 (2, p. 134 Arnott, Loeb) στρεφομένους ἄνω κάτω 'tossing up and down'. Men. *Mis.* 7 περιπατῶ τ' ἄνω κάτω 'I saunter up and down', Dem. 2.16, 4.41 etc.

5.5 Variations on the Type of Asyndetic Pair that Is Composed of Explicit Opposites

It was noted above (4.1, 4.3) that not all pairs of semantically contrasting asyndetic terms are exact opposites. Terms may be virtual opposites without being precisely so, and such variations were no doubt stylistically deliberate. Many of the pairs of this type express contrasting emotions or personal qualities. Here are a few examples:

Tac. *Hist.* 1.10.2 (1, 2) *luxuria industria, comitate adrogantia, malis bonisque artibus mixtus* (luxury implies idleness, industry hard work).
Tac. *Hist.* 2.5.2 (4) *tribuni centurionesque et uolgus militum industria licentia, per uirtutes per uoluptates, ut cuique ingenium adsciscebantur* (here disciplined hard work is contrasted with loose living; addiction to pleasure may be the opposite of virtue).
Tac. *Ann.* 1.21.2 (59) *nihil reliqui faciunt quo minus inuidiam misericordiam, metum et iras permouerent* ('ill-will and pity').
Tac. *Ann.* 13.44.3 (107) *ut adsolet in amore et ira, iurgia preces, exprobratio satisfactio, et pars tenebrarum libidini seposita* (expressions of reproach versus implied expressions of approval).
Tac. *Ann.* 6.7.3 (160) *neque discerneres alienos a coniunctis, amicos ab ignotis, quid repens aut uetustate obscurum: perinde in foro in conuiuio, quaqua de re locuti incusabantur* ('in the forum, at a feast'; the contrast is almost 'in public at work, in the household at play'; this pair is preceded by two other contrasting pairs).

It may not be due to chance that the above examples are all from Tacitus (and others are commented on at XXX.4.2.3a, 5.2.3). While Tacitus frequently juxtaposes overt opposites, he had a taste for expressing in asyndeton feelings and forms of behaviour that were very different but not strictly opposites.

XIII Pairs of Opposites

6 Conclusions

The sheer frequency of asyndetic pairs of opposites as it emerges in what is a very selective chapter shows that asyndeton was felt to be highly suited to the expression of oppositions, and that is not surprising, given that the absence of a coordinator causes the opposites to be starkly juxtaposed. By contrast some of the other asyndetic types discussed in other sections were far more restricted in use.

The more banal an opposition, such that it might be called 'proverbial' (a term used by Donatus of various adverbial pairs), the more likely it was to be asyndetic (see 5.4). Three adverbial pairs meaning 'up and down', 'to and fro' and 'this way and that' complementing frequentative verbs of running were quoted from Terence with asyndeton, but when the annalist Tubero spoke of eyelids 'pulled apart, upwards and downwards', one of the three adverbial pairs was used with a coordinator (*sursum ac deorsum*) in this unusual context, with a less mundane verb (*diductas*). The asyndetic examples in Terence look colloquial and formulaic.

Two other determinants of asyndeton have come up in this chapter. First, the most striking feature of asyndetic pairs of opposites is that they are so often in accumulations, that is in juxtapositions with other pairs, which may be opposites themselves or complementary in some other way, and either asyndetic or coordinated. Such sequences occur in legal and philosophical sequences, or in narratives of events, in which the writer presents things in such a way as to bring out the contrasts and inconsistencies in human behaviour and in events themselves.

Second, the infrequency of asyndetic pairs of opposites in Cicero's letters to Atticus, and their greater frequency in letters *Ad familiares* and in historians, suggest that they had a formality to them or obtrusive quality that might cause them to be avoided in informal contexts (except in banal formulae).

The antiquity of asyndetic pairs of opposites versus the coordinated variants cannot be determined with any certainty, but there are hints that some asyndetic pairs were early, and subject to variation later. Cato for example prefers the asyndetic *dextra sinistra*, whereas Varro, writing in the same genre a century or so later, prefers coordination. Ennius has *rursus prorsus*, whereas Varro again has coordination. The opposition 'in front, behind' was seen at 5.4 not only in Cicero but also (probably) in Umbrian.

CHAPTER XIV

Pairs Denoting Family Members

1 Introduction

Pairs of certain semantic types show no more than a weak tendency to occur in asyndeton bimembre: overt coordination is more frequent. There may be a unity of some sort to the terms, which makes them susceptible to occasional asyndetic coordination, but that unity is no more than a background to the asyndeton. It is necessary to look at contexts and structures to see if it is possible to identify factors motivating the absence of a coordinator.

Pairs denoting family members belong in this category. It is particularly in legal language and contexts that asyndeton occurs, and as usual asyndetic pairs are to be found embedded in accumulations. The jurists constantly classify categories of persons by masculine + feminine pairs (see XI.5) or by other relationship terms, and they do so often in long sequences (see for example the whole of *Dig.* 38.10). The asyndeton is suited to the length of the sequence, and also reflects traditional legal shorthand. For asyndetic pairs expressing family relationships in literary texts see Cicero 1, Sallust 12, 47, Livy 5, 6, 19, 23. Terms for political relationships (relations between states) also sometimes occur in asyndetic pairs (see on Sallust 47), as do terms for personal relationships that are not to do with the family (see XXIII.8.11).

2 A Selection of Pairs

2.1 Father, Mother

This is a pair (like 'brother, sister' below) that might have been placed elsewhere in these classifications (with pairs showing the opposition masculine + feminine: see XI, and particularly XI.3 on 'men, women'.).

Pater and *mater* almost always have coordinators, except in legal texts: see *TLL* VIII.437.33ff. for the order *pater et mater*, and 437.37ff. for *mater* (*et*) *pater*. The only asyndetic example cited there is at Plaut. *Merc.* 948 *quid parentes mei? ualent mater pater?*, 'What about my parents? Are my mother, father well?' (see XXIII. 8.11), though a case with anaphora also is quoted (41) from Sen. *Dial.* 6.17.1 (*iam matri iam patri*). The whole short speech of Charinus here (946–50) is a report in telegraph style, with no fewer than seven phrasal or clausal asyndeta in addition to this pair. He has been deliberately given a staccato style here, which must have determined the departure from the usual coordination in this pairing. To put it in another way, the asyndetic pair is in a prolonged accumulation.

Here are some asyndetic legal examples: *Dig.* 48.9.1 *si quis patrem matrem, auum auiam, fratrem sororem patruelem matruelem* . . . *occiderit*, 38.10.1.3 *primo gradu sunt supra pater mater, infra filius filia*. In the first passage *patrem matrem* is disjunctive, as are the other pairs ('if anyone shall have killed his father or mother . . .'), and not to be associated with the dvandva compound *mātárāpitárā* 'father and mother' = 'parents', found in the oldest form of Sanskrit. This latter is a copulative compound (see Kiparsky 2010: 302).

2.2 Brother, Sister

This is another pair that turns up with asyndeton in jurists' classifications, as in the first passage in the last paragraph of 2.1 above. See too e.g. *Dig.* 38.10.1.4 *secundo gradu sunt supra auus auia. infra nepos neptis. ex transuerso frater soror*. Contrast 38.10.1.5 *ex transuerso fratris sororisque filius filia*. In this last the coordinator is probably meant to make it clear that the reference is to the son and daughter of a brother and of a sister separately, not to any incestuous relationship.

Tacitus in one place uses asyndeton in referring to a brother and sister by name rather than by terms of relationship: *Ann.*12.2.1 (97) *haudquaquam nouercalibus odiis uisura* Britannicum, Octauiam.

2.3 Women/Wives, Children

This is a pairing that is quite common in literary texts, as distinct from merely legal. See Cic. *Mil.* 87 *liberos coniugem meam uexarat*, Caes. *Gall.* 7.14.10 *liberos coniuges in seruitutem abstrahi*, Livy 34.35.7 (19) *liberos coniuges restitueret*, Livy 38.43.6 (23) *coniuges liberos in seruitium abstractos*, Cic. *Off.* 3.99 *cum uxore cum liberis*. In several of the above passages the women and children are victims of a violent act. The phraseology of Caesar (who rarely admits asyndeton bimembre) is identical to that at Livy

38.43.6, and it is possible that it was an old formula expressing a consequence of war.

The equivalent asyndetic pairing is found in Greek. See Ar. *Pax* 404 παῖδας γυναῖκας, Ar. *Ran.* 587 ἡ γυνή, τὰ παιδία, 1408 τὰ παιδί', ἡ γυνή. Note too Menander, *Asp.* 255 σοὶ μέν ἐστ' ἔνδον γυνή, | θυγάτηρ. 'Wives and children' also often has a coordinator: see Cic. *Cat.* 3.1 *uitamque omnium uestrum, bona fortunas, coniuges liberosque uestros, Cat.* 4.2 *coniuges liberosque uestros, Off.* 3.48 *coniugibus et liberis,* Catull. 64.298 *cum coniuge natisque,* Livy 5.38.5. In the first passage there is again an accumulation of asyndetic phrases, one of them with asyndeton (*bona fortunas*), whereas 'wives and children' is given a coordinator. See further on Livy 19.

2.4 Parent, Children

From the perspective of a *paterfamilias* the most immediate members of the family were his wife and children, and this pairing has just been illustrated. From the perspective of a wife they are husband and children, and for this pair in asyndeton see Sall. *Cat.* 25.2 (12) *haec mulier genere atque forma, praeterea uiro liberis satis fortunata fuit.* From the perspective of a detached observer there are parents and children. This pair occurs with asyndeton in a legal classification (praetor's edict): Ulp. *Dig.* 2.4.4.1 *praetor ait: 'parentem, patronum patronam, liberos parentes patroni patronae in ius sine permissu meo ne quis uocet'* (but cf. *Dig.* 3.1.1.11, quoted at XI.5, which has *liberis parentibusque*).

2.5 Forms of Kinship of Diverse Types

At Livy 5.11.5 (5, 6) (*qui amissis liberis fratribus, propinquis adfinibus lugubres domos habeant*) the four nouns underlined comprise two asyndetic pairs, each pair with a semantic unity. The two pairs are discussed on Livy 5, 6.

Miscellaneous contrastive pairs of relationship terms turn up particularly in laws. Note e.g. *Lex Coloniae Genetiuae* XCV tabl. c., 16–18 (Crawford 1996: 1.407) *cui ei, quae r(es) tum agetur, gener socer, uitricus priuignus, patron(us) lib(ertus), consobrinus <sit> propiusue eum ea cognatione atfinitate{m}ue contingat* (see on Sallust 42 for this passage and the meaning of the pair *cognatio adfinitas,* abstract nouns of relationship that also occur in asyndeton). Inevitably such pairs in legal language often consist of masculine + feminine forms based on the same root (see XI): e.g. Modest. *Dig.* 38.10.10.16 (Mommsen-Krueger p. 626. col. 2, top of page) *patrui magni filius filia: hi sunt aui fratris filius filia, proaui aut proauiae nepos neptis ex filio* (with many other such examples in the same passage).

See in particular the quotation from the praetor's edict at XI.5, which has a long sequence of pairs of different types for family relationships; see further Kalb (1912: 37, 39).

Finally, note Lucilius 12 *ad matrem cognatam*.

It is not only pairs of terms denoting living family members that may be juxtaposed asyndetically. Here for example is an asyndetic sequence expressing members of four generations: Plaut. *Mil.* 373 *ibi mei maiores sunt siti: pater auos proauos abauos*, 'there my ancestors lie: father, grandfather, great-grandfather, great-great grandfather'.

3 Conclusions

Asyndetic pairs of terms designating family members are not a particularly distinctive type. Masculine + feminine pairs of the type 'father, mother' are a special category, because they are mainly in legal texts, where they tend to occur in strings and reflect jurists' style. I have found little sign of such pairs in ordinary literary texts.

In literary texts a number of the examples above are in accumulations. Accumulations, as we have seen, are a typical location of asyndetic pairs. The most noteworthy pair seen in this section is perhaps 'wives/women, children'. It is a pair quite well attested with asyndeton in Greek and Latin, and may well be an old type (in competition with the coordinated variants), expressing (from a male perspective) the primary members of the family of a *paterfamilias*. The verbal correspondences between an example in Caesar and another in Livy are suggestive of some sort of tradition.

CHAPTER XV

'Semantic' Types: Some Conclusions

Part 3 on semantic types is highly selective, dealing as it does only with opposites, itself however a big subject, and with terms asyndetically specifying different family relationships. This second category has some overlap with that dealt with in XI. I have been selective in this part because semantic types are commented on constantly in the chapters on literary texts. I give a few cross references below.

As for the influence of semantics in prompting an asyndetic rather than syndetic coordination, it is true to say that some subjects tend to inspire certain intonation patterns in speech, which a writer may from time to time think would be better conveyed by asyndeton. One thinks, for example, of pairs of verbs describing acts of violence. It is quite possible for a speaker to convey a sense of outrage or horror by a dramatic pause before the second verb, and a writer may sometimes feel that that pause and the intonation pattern would be better represented in a text by an asyndeton than by a matter-of-fact linking term. In other words it is not so much the semantics of the verbs considered in isolation that sometimes prompts asyndetic coordination, but the writer's attitude of the moment to an act he is presenting (cf. V.2–3, XXXII.3.4). If so, the apparently random variation between asyndeton and coordination that is so common in many pairs would reflect the variable attitudes in different contexts of writers to the events, persons and objects they are describing.

For the many semantic categories of asyndetic pairs in Plautus see XXIII.8. I would single out from there e.g. female adornment and luxury, vices and age/decrepitude (see further below), all of which types occur elsewhere, and also personal/family relationships, for which see too on Lucilius at XXV.1.1.2, Sallust 41–2 and on Horace at XXIX.2.1.4.2, as well as the cross references at XIV.1. In Cicero semantic types are summarised at XXVI.7.8, and these include legal pairs, and pairs to do with virtue and vice, acts of violence and banishment/exclusion (see also Cicero 42, 71, Sallust 24 with cross references, 52, XXXII.3.4 and also further below). For

171

acts of violence in Tacitus see XXX.5.2.3 and on Tacitus 132. Pairs denoting virtues and vices are commented on throughout the chapter on historians. In Virgil asyndetic pairs of adjectives tend to be pathetic or to imply that the referent is threatening in some way (see XXIV.2.1.1 after 15). The description of what is pathetic and threatening is bound to inspire in speech expressive intonation patterns, which may be better conveyed in writing by asyndeton.

In many of the categories referred to above it is a semantically stronger term that is placed second, and that pattern is conducive to pauses for thought as the speaker/writer seeks to outdo the first term with an asyndetic addition. The pattern was recognised by ancient commentators. Quintilian at 9.4.23 (see I.3 and V.2) says that a weaker word must not follow a stronger. According to Alfenus ap. Gell. 7.5.1, *putus* (in the pair *purus putus*, found at Enn. *trag.* 65 and Plaut. *Ps.* 989, 1200) means *ualde purus*. Alfenus cannot be entirely trusted, as the word is obscure, but his comment at least reflects the doctrine that the stronger term should come at the end (on *purus putus* see XXIV.5.2.1). Or again, a comparable remark is at Catull. 42.13, where, after using the abusive asyndetic pair *lutum lupanar* of a woman, Catullus in effect invites the reader to come up with a stronger term (see XXVII.1.1). The pattern is commented on throughout the literary chapters, but here are just a few illustrations. For the verb *excindo* (expressing destruction) as the second member of asyndetic pairs in different writers, see Sall. *Hist.* 4.60.17 Ramsey (47) *inopes potentisque trahant excindant*, Tac. Ann. 2.25.2 *populatur excindit non ausum congredi hostem* (133). The first verb in the second passage is itself expressive of violence ('he ravages, destroys the enemy not daring to engage'), but it is outdone semantically by the second, as is *trahant* in the passage of Sallust. If we turn to adjectives, one of the pairs, *uetulus decrepitus*, belonging to the theme old age/decrepitude referred to above, definitely has the more emphatic word in second position (see Plaut. *Ep.* 666, *Merc.* 291, 314 and Adams 2016: 231–2).

I return to XIII and XIV. Again we have seen that legal texts were a major location for asyndetic pairs, and this stylistic feature of the genre was very persistent, even if it tended to fade in laws themselves and *senatus consulta*. Asyndetic pairs expressing family members do sometimes occur in literary texts along with coordinated pairs, but it is in legal texts that such pairs without a coordinator particularly stand out (XIV). Asyndetic pairs of opposites are far more widespread in literature (XIII), but again structures and genres are important determining factors. Pairs occur especially in accumulations, and they were suited to philosophical discourse under the

XV 'Semantic' Types: Some Conclusions

influence of the subject matter. Cicero has hardly any in the speeches, but they are very common in the philosophica, and some long sequences of asyndetic pairs can also be paralleled in Greek philosophy. An individual's style and taste were also a potential influence. Sallust hardly uses asyndetic pairs of opposites, but they are a mannerism of Tacitus, and with his typical liking for variation he not infrequently made the opposition inexplicit. Asyndetic pairs of adverbial opposites on the other hand often acquired a formulaic or proverbial status. Their fixed (non-inflecting) form may have contributed to their fossilisation.

PART 4

Structures

CHAPTER XVI

Rule of Ascending Length (?)

1 'Behaghel's Law'

It is often said, not least in relation to Greek tragedy, that if the two members of an asyndetic pair are not of the same syllabic length the longer term will usually be placed second. The rule for Greek seems to be stated mainly in reference to asyndetic pairs of verbs. Diggle (1994: 99), for example, says: 'When, in his lyrics, Euripides juxtaposes a pair of verbs in asyndeton, he observes the practice of sound rhetoric: he makes the second verb equal in length to the first, so that it may balance it, or he makes it longer, so that it may outweigh it.' Twenty-two examples are quoted, with just one case where the rhetorical tendency is not observed. The pairs quite often have the same fore-element. On p. 100 Diggle states that he has included in the list only passages where the verbs are absolute or have a common object.

The pattern is thought to exemplify Behaghel's law (or one of them). Collinge (1985: 241) describes this thus:

> Where units of equal status are conjoined (or contrasted) the longest comes last in the sequence. This is often called 'Behaghel's law' par excellence, and is usually titled 'das Gesetz der wachsenden Glieder'.

Collinge (242) has some bibliography to do with Latin. The 'law', or tendency, is assumed to apply not only to asyndetic pairs but to longer asyndeta, and also to coordinations (see the examples given by Wilkinson (1963: 175–8), though he does not refer to Behaghel), but certainly a study of the relative length of single asyndetic terms ought to reveal the workings of any such law, and asyndetic pairs have indeed attracted comment and generalisations. The most detailed study of the law is by Lindholm (1931), who devoted a whole book to it. He did not restrict himself to pairs with asyndeton but embraced groups of varying length (particularly two or three members, and with varying modifiers to the terms) and with different types of coordination, and made distinctions between the various parts of speech. Statistics are provided constantly, for example from Plautus and Terence (81, 89), Cicero (119–20), from the poets Lucretius, Catullus, Virgil and Horace (175) and from Tacitus (190). There is a slight decline in its influence in Cicero and particularly Tacitus (see 17). It is the aim of this chapter to see what light is thrown on the history of the tendency by the statistics for asyndetic pairs alone in the writers considered in this book.

Commentators, particularly on Greek texts, have tended to remark on the length of the members of asyndetic pairs (see above). Finglass (2011: 156), on Soph. *Ajax* 60 ὤτρυνον, εἰσέβαλλον εἰς ἕρκη κακά, 'I urged, cast him into the nets of disaster', comments: 'Verbal asyndeton at the start of the trimeter, with the second verb longer (and more violent) than the first, mimetically expresses Athena's vigour (*El.* 719 n., adding Arnott in Alexis fr. 88.3 *PCG*).'

On Soph. *Electra* 719 (referred to above) see Finglass (2007: 320) ad loc., on ἤφριζον, εἰσέβαλλον: 'verbal asyndeton is common in tragic lyric ... and dialogue. The second verb almost never has fewer syllables than the first.' There is another example at *El.* 1380. Finglass cites e.g. Kühner and Gerth (1898–1904: 2.340–1) and Diggle (1994: 99–100).

It is not only in tragedy that asyndetic pairs of verbs occur, with the second usually longer than the first. In Menander for the order shorter–longer see *Dysk.* 954, *Epit.* 905–6, *Mis.* 696, *Per.* 156, 484, *Sam.* 244, *Sik.* 96; for the reverse order *Dysk.* 623, 657–8.

The tendency in Greek is not only noted in relation to verbs. Johansen and Whittle (1980: 3.46) on Aesch. *Supp.* 681–2 (ἄχορον ἀκίθαριν δακρυογόνον Ἄρη) comment on the increasing length of the epithets. On names see West (2007: 117–19). Although in Menander the order is often shorter–longer, note (the nouns) at *Mis.* 50–2 τηρῶ τὸν Δία | ὕοντα πολλῷ νυκτὸς [οὖσ]ης, ἀστραπάς, | βροντάς, 'I'm waiting for a heavy downpour after dark, lightning, thunder', which raise another issue. Lightning precedes thunder, and the natural order seems here to have overruled that of ascending length. Compare the Latin asyndetic augural formula *Ioue fulgente tonante* (Cic. *Nat.* 2.65), whereas English uses the reverse order, *thunder and lightning*. Cf. Hdt. 3.86 for a coordinated pair with the same order 'lightning and thunder': ἀστραπή ... καὶ βροντή. We will see below in Latin several other determinants of order in competition with relative length.

In Latin the length of two verbs comes up at Ennius *trag.* 303 Jocelyn (XXIV.5.2.4, 20) *set me Apollo ipse delectat ductat Delphicus*. Here *delecto* means 'entice, lure' (*OLD* s.v. 1). Jocelyn (1967: 425) states that 'where two nearly synonymous words stand together in asyndeton the shorter normally precedes the longer': this example is implied to be an exception. Jocelyn's statement of the tendency is different from that of Diggle above (note 'words' rather than 'verbs'). But as I note at XXIV.5.2.4, 20, these verbs in Ennius are not genuine synonyms but denote sequential events ('ensnares, leads on', with the initial enticement followed by a leading on of the victim). This is an example that raises difficulties for any simple rule that the longer word (or verb) in a pair will usually come second. If relative length is a factor in determining order, it is certainly not the only one, and it may not even be the most important. Asyndetic pairs in Latin for example often express a sequence of events, and the term that conveys the later event will almost always come second, whatever its length. Note for instance Tac. *Hist.* 2.78.1 (32) *post Muciani orationem ceteri audentius circumsistere hortari*, 'after the speech of Mucianus, the others more boldly gathered around and encouraged (Vespasian)'. The longer verb is first because the gathering around has to precede the giving of encouragement. It is unusual to have examples of the illogical order when there is a temporal sequence. See Enn. *Ann.* 294–6 Skutsch (XXIV.5.1.4, 12) *tonsamque tenentes | parerent obseruarent portisculus signum | quom dare coepisset*, = Warmington (1961: 111), 297–9, who translates 'that, holding the oar forward, they should obey and watch when the boatswain proceeded to give them the signal'. The watching presumably precedes the obeying, though there are other interpretations that could be put on the events here (see XXIV.5.1.4, 12). Note too Men. *Dysk.* 954 χόρευε, συνεπίβαινε, 'dance, get on your feet along with us'. The imperatives are not in a temporal order. On the meaning of the second verb see Gomme and Sandbach (1973: 285).

Jocelyn (1967: 425) provides an unclassified list of pairs in which the longer member is first. A closer look at these shows that they raise additional determinants of order. For example, four of the eight pairs comprise compound + simplex (of the *retinete tenete* type), and this is a pattern in its own right that is dealt with separately (see VII).

2 Statistics

I now give figures from a variety of writers and genres showing the relative incidence in asyndetic pairs of the order shorter–longer compared with that of the reverse order. A third category consists of pairs in which both terms are of equal length, and figures for these are provided too.

XVI Rule of Ascending Length (?)

I start with some figures from **Plautus**, with various parts of speech considered separately. The figures are set out in three columns, showing the frequency of the patterns shorter–longer, identity of length and longer–shorter. In the chapter on Plautus (XXIII) particular parts of speech are divided up in various ways, and I use the same classifications here. For example, pairs of verbs are not treated as a single category but are split up into various types. I take first asyndetic *pairs of verbs marked by assonance* of one kind or another, which are listed at XXIII.5.4:

        shorter–longer   equal length   longer–shorter
            19   23   5

Of the 47 pairs listed in this category, 42 either have the longer term second or are of equal length. Here is striking evidence for avoidance of pairs with the shorter term last. It may be significant too that the pairs have features of assonance.

At XXIII.5.5 *pairs of verbs described as 'miscellaneous'* are listed. 'Miscellaneous' simply means that there is no obvious assonance, and that the verbs are not imperatives or of a related type, listed elsewhere separately. Here is the distribution of these pairs:

            15   10   6

The absence of assonance seems to have had little or no influence. The pairs of equal length or with the second longer predominate again, by 25:6.

At XXIII.5.1, 33 *pairs of imperatives* are listed, a mere selection, as is noted, of what is a very common form of asyndeton. Statistics from a selection have little justification, but I nevertheless give figures based on the examples quoted. Usually the asyndetic terms do not comprise just single words, but at least one of the members is phrasal. If the length of the complete groups is taken into account, almost invariably the longer member comes second: often there is a single imperative, followed by a phrasal group. If only the imperative forms themselves are considered, here is the distribution:

            14   13   4

Once again, the pattern longer–shorter is heavily outnumbered by the other two patterns (by 27:4).

In the Appendix to the chapter on Plautus examples of various types of pairings are listed. I start with the relative lengths of *pairs of nouns*:

            27   29   7

2 Statistics

The pattern longer–shorter is outnumbered by the other two, by 56:7.

Finally from Plautus the figures for single-word *pairs of asyndetic adjectives*, based again on the list in the Appendix:

36   18   11

Once again longer–shorter is outnumbered, by 54:11.

Overall, of the Plautine pairs considered above, 111 have terms with the order shorter–longer, and 33 with the order longer–shorter. In 93 cases the two terms have the same number of syllables. The order shorter–longer exceeds that of longer–shorter in the ratio 3.3:1, and the order longer–shorter is exceeded by the other two patterns combined by 6:1. In the pairs of verbs marked by assonance, the order longer–shorter is outnumbered by the other two patterns in the ratio of about 8:1. Similarly in this same group of verbs with assonance the order shorter–longer outnumbers the reverse by about 4:1.

Next, there follow statistics from four 'early' republican writers (with Lucretius given this classification too), three of them poets, the other a prose writer.

First, **Pacuvius' tragedies**, but the evidence is not always straightforward:

1   4   5

The evidence also from Ennius' *Annals* is often controversial, and I restrict myself here to **Ennius' tragedies**:

2   2   4

Here are figures for asyndetic pairs from **Cato De agricultura**. The examples are collected at Adams (2016: 78–80):

13   20   7

One adjectival pair occurs in both orders (2.5, 3.2 *uinariam oleariam/ oleariam uinariam*). Again the order with descending length is markedly outnumbered (33:7).

Rough figures for **Lucretius** follow. They are based on single-word pairs, but a few pairs with one member of extended length might have been added, and these usually have the longer member second. Some other possible cases in Lucretius are hard to assess, and these have been omitted:

3   6   5

XVI Rule of Ascending Length (?)

In Pacuvius, Ennius and Lucretius the order shorter–longer is actually outnumbered by longer–shorter, but the figures are so low that they have little meaning. In Cato on the other hand pairs with the longer term second or with both terms of the same length are still in the lead, but less markedly so than in Plautus, but again the figures are not high.

The figures for the whole group on the face of it suggest a shift, but one cannot be certain on the basis of such evidence.

I move on to statistics from the prose works considered in this book. The figures embrace all parts of speech, but the figures for juxtaposed verbs will be given separately later because of the tendency reported above that has been noted in Greek tragedy and Plautus. The figures are restricted to include only numbered examples (unnumbered examples are problematic in some way), and for simplicity to single-word pairs (pairs with prepositional anaphora are however included). Names are excluded.

	Shorter–Longer	Equal Length	Longer–Shorter
Cic. speeches	34	24	13
Cic. philosophica	27	20	14
Cic. *Att.*	5	9	5
Cic. *Fam.*	11	5	1
Sallust	40	30	16
Livy	23	25	12
Tac. *Hist.*	24	20	8
Tac. *Ann.*	41	38	31

It will be recalled that in the Plautine evidence used here the two patterns together, shorter–longer + equal length, outnumber longer–shorter in the proportion 6:1, and shorter–longer outnumbers the reverse by 3.3:1. In the four corpora of Cicero taken into account here the first two patterns taken together outnumber longer–shorter by 135:30, or 4:1, and shorter–longer outnumbers longer–shorter by 77:33, or 2.3:1. The figures for the letters are of some interest, though unfortunately they are low. In the letters to Atticus both orders, shorter–longer and longer–shorter, occur the same number of times. On the other hand in the sample from the letters *Ad familiares* shorter–longer is very much preferred, by 11:1. It will be shown elsewhere that these letters are more contrived in their use of asyndeton.

If there is a slight decline in the incidence of the pattern overall in Cicero, decline is rather more marked in Tacitus' *Annals*. There the order shorter–longer only predominates by 41:31, or about 1.3:1. Also, shorter–longer + equal length in the *Annals* predominates only by 79:31, or 2.5:1. This seems to represent a significant decline from the Plautine figure of 6:1. Overall in Tacitus (*Histories* and *Annals*) the order shorter–longer predominates by 65:39, or 1.6:1, and the two patterns shorter–longer + equal length predominate by 123:51, or 2.4:1.

A decline in the incidence of the order shorter–longer is also to be seen in Sallust, though less so, and in Livy. In Sallust the order shorter–longer outnumbers the reverse by 40:16, or 2.5.1, and the two patterns predominate over longer–shorter by 70:16, or 4.3:1. In Livy the order shorter–longer is barely twice as numerous as longer–shorter (23:12). Shorter–longer + equal length predominate by 48:12, or 4:1.

In every corpus above but one (Cicero's letters to Atticus) the figure for the pattern shorter–longer is higher than that for longer–shorter, but there is evidence of a slight decline in the influence of any rule of ascending length, from Plautus through to Tacitus, with Cato apparently showing up a decline too. Overall in the corpora just considered the order shorter–longer outnumbers longer–shorter by 205:100, or 2:1, compared with the predominance of 3.3:1 of the former in Plautus. There continued a tendency for the longer term to be placed second, but it does not qualify for the designation 'law'.

Here finally are the figures for pairs of verbs alone in the above prose corpora:

	Shorter–Longer	Equal Length	Longer–Shorter
Cic. Speeches	9	9	5
Cic. philosophica	4	5	4
Cic. *Att.*	2	4	2
Cic. *Fam.*	1	0	1
Sallust	4	10	3
Livy	6	1	1
Tac. *Hist.*	1	5	3
Tac. *Ann.*	7	7	7

The order shorter–longer hardly outnumbers the reverse order (34:26, or 1.3:1). Pairs of equal length and those with the order shorter–longer outnumber those of the pattern longer–shorter by 75:26, or 3:1. These figures are very different from those for Plautus (i.e. both the overall figures, and those for verbs alone, with assonance or of miscellaneous types), and they underline the diminishing influence of a rule of ascending length in Latin. In Tacitus the order longer–shorter predominates over shorter–longer.

3 Some Other Factors Determining the Order of the Constituents of an Asyndetic Pair

Figures of the above types cannot without reservation be taken at face value. There are factors apart from relative length that may be the primary determinant of the order of an asyndetic pair. For example, in the pair *pellerent pellerentur* the second term is so placed not because of its length but because the pattern active–passive was a natural one. To put relative length in perspective I offer below a few comments on some of the examples buried away in the statistics above, and also on a few other aspects of the figures.

In Cicero's speeches quite a few of the pairs in which the shorter term is second are special cases. At *Phil.* 3.38 (**25**) the pair *municipia coloniae* has what appears to be a standard order, found in coordinated examples as well, which reflects the relative importance historically of the two types of foundation. At *Cat.* 2.6 (**59**) *Catilina ipse pertimuit profugit* the second verb conveys a consequence of the emotion expressed by the first (he 'took fright and fled'). At *Dom.* 70 (**66**) too (*de me rettulisti, legem promulgasti tulisti*) the sequence of events determines the order of the verbs, in that the law is promulgated and then carried. Cf. above, 1 for this factor.

On the other hand it cannot be assumed that whenever the longer term comes second, the determinant of the order was merely the rhetorical ideal of ascending length. For example, in the pair 'go–return', designating a reversal, *redire* is bound to follow *ire* (*Phil.* 2.89 (**74**) *irent redirent*). Two pairs at *Phil.* 5.53 (**77, 78**) are legal phrases (both with *dare + adsignare*) used in a senatorial motion, and Cicero did not himself have a choice of order. Nor did mere relative length necessarily determine the order of the legal formula. There is a move from a banal, semantically vague, term, to one that is more specific and technical.

In the philosophica the figures are such (with the longer term second 27 times and the shorter 14 times) that one could hardly say that any principle of placing the longer term at the end was overwhelmingly influential. It is true that special factors sometimes cause the longer term to be placed first, but on the other hand sometimes one can see a determinant that is at least as likely as length to have motivated the second position of the longer term.

Here are some passages, with the longer term second (a) and then first (b), in which influences separate from mere length were at work.

(a) Giving and receiving are converse acts, with receiving secondary to giving: there cannot be a receiver if there is not a giver. Thus *Off.* 1.22 (**138**) *dando accipiendo*, *Off.* 1.56 (**140**) *datis acceptis*. At *Fin.* 2.109 (**149**) (*in* *gignendo in educando*) giving birth precedes bringing up. At *Fin.* 2.36 (94, 95) (*quid iudicant sensus? dulce amarum, leue asperum*) the positive (or favourable) terms precede the negative terms. Of the precious metals gold ranks more highly than silver, and thus the standard order is *aurum argentum* (*Off.* 2.11 (119). At *Off.* 3.66 (145) (*dare facere*) Cicero was again quoting a law, not writing in his own person.

(b) At *Off.* 2.37 (120, 121) the order of both pairs is semantically determined: *uita mors, diuitiae paupertas omnes homines uehementissime permouent*. The two positives, life and riches, precede their opposites, and life also comes before death. At *Off.* 3.119 (148) (*non recipit istam coniunctionem honestas, aspernatur repellit*) the second verb expresses a consequence of the first: 'honourable behaviour does not accept such a combination, but scorns, rejects it'.

The order of the pair *conducere locare* introduces another factor. See *Off.* 2.40 (141, 142) *iis etiam qui uendunt emunt, conducunt locant*, 'to those also, who sell and buy, pay rent and let out', *Off.* 2.64 (143, 144) *uendendo emendo, conducendo locando, Off.* 3.70 (146, 147) *idque uersari in tutelis societatibus, fiduciis mandatis, rebus emptis uenditis, conductis locatis, quibus uitae societas contineretur*. In the first and second of these passages the longer verb (*conducunt, conducendo*) comes first in its pair, even though it expresses a role comparable to that of the second verbs (*emunt, emendo*) in the preceding asyndetic pairs. A buyer (a customer) is like a person who pays rent (*conducere*: OLD s.v. 4), and a seller (an entrepreneur) is like one who lets out property (*locare*: OLD s.v. 7). Semantic parallelism would produce the orders *uendunt emunt, locant conducunt*, a pattern which in the first and second passages above would cause the longer verb to be in second position. Semantics and any rule of ascending length seem to have been overruled by rhythm here, as the placing of *locant, locando* and *locatis* in final position gives a better clausula.

This survey of asyndetic pairs in Cicero's philosophica suggests that the relative length of the two members is not the only influence on order, and the survey is not comprehensive.

In the corpus of letters to Atticus assessed in this book Cicero rarely uses asyndeton bimembre, and when he does there is no sign of any rhetorical placement of the longer term second. In the *Ad familiares* on the other hand the order shorter–longer strongly predominates. Drawing conclusions from a quite small number of examples overall in the two corpora is hazardous, but there are signs that Cicero was influenced by his level of intimacy with the different addressees. The *Ad familiares* are in some cases more formal.

In Sallust the longer term is usually in second position (40:16). Final placement of the longer term is proportionately more common in the *Catiline* than it is in the *Jugurtha*. In the *Cat.* postposition of the longer term predominates by 22:9, but in the *Jug.* by only 12:9. This type of variation, if it is taken at its face value, again suggests that there was no hard and fast rule of ascending length in literary Latin of this period.

In Livy there is a tendency of sorts for pairs to show ascending length (23:12), but sometimes when the longer member is in second place a semantic factor has determined the order. This may be seen at 38.48.4 (49, 50) *regna augetis minuitis, donatis adimitis*. In the second pairing giving has to precede taking away. In both pairs the term for a positive act is followed by that for its reversal.

The order shorter–longer predominates in Tacitus' *Histories* by 24:8. But 6 of the 24 comprise the formulaic pair *huc illuc*, and there is also one example of the equally formulaic *hinc inde*. These pairs would usually not be meaningful if they had the opposite order. The role of semantics can be seen too at 2.70.3 (31) (*intueri mirari*) and also at 2.78.1 (32), cited above, 1 (*circumsistere hortari*), where it would not be possible to reverse the terms.

In the *Annals* the order shorter–longer is preferred by 41:31. The figure for longer–shorter is relatively high. Four of the 41 instances of the other order are accounted for by *huc illuc*. There are also semantic or other influences on the order in some cases, as at 4.69.3 (86) *congressus conloquia*, 11.17.3 (161) *per laeta per aduersa*. Equally, special factors have prompted the order long + short in places, as e.g. in the second pair at 2.29.1 (66, 67) *plebes primores, iuuentus senes* (the move is from lesser to greater in both pairs), 2.25.2 (133) *populatur excindit* (a verb of destruction completes the violent process), 4.50.4 (137) *circumire hortari*.

Ordering was subject to multiple factors, and the pattern shorter–longer was just one possible influence, *ceteris paribus*.

Here are some further statistics, which are not in the table above. In Virgil there are not many asyndeta bimembria. For example, pairs of verbs, which are common in other genres and in early Latin, do not occur. I have found in the whole of Virgil 15 examples of single-word adjectival asyndetic pairs (see XXIV.2.1.1, where they are numbered). In only three cases does the longer adjective come in second position (6, 10, 11). In eight cases a shorter adjective is second (1, 3, 5, 7, 8, 9, 13, 15). Four times that adjective is *ingens* (3, 5, 7, 8), which, if it is at the end of a line, is metrically useful. This mannerism, whatever its motivation (*ingens* was notoriously a favourite word of Virgil), was clearly more important to Virgil than the relative length of the term when it was in a pair.

4 Conclusions

In the works considered here there is a tendency for the longer term in an asyndetic pair to follow the shorter when the two terms are of different syllabic length, but overall it is not a particularly strong tendency. The tendency is rather less marked in Tacitus than it is in Plautus, and there is a gradual decline in the incidence of the order shorter–longer over time. Assessing the determinants of the order of two terms in asyndeton is far more than a matter of counting syllables, as many other factors have to be taken into account, and in this chapter I have merely scratched the surface. Some further statistics, from Lucilius, may be found at XXV.6, and the 'law' is no more than a weak tendency in that writer. See particularly there the comment on the tetracolon at 1225.

CHAPTER XVII

Correlative Distribution

1 Evidence

A contrived structure with asyndeton is that in which an asyndetic pair is followed by another pair, asyndetic or syndetic, the members of which refer back to the members of the first pair. Usually the first member of the initial asyndetic pair is picked up by the first member of the following pair (and the second member by the second), but there is sometimes chiasmus, such that the second two terms allude to the first two in reverse order.

In a *senatus consultum* the following (underlined) juxtaposed pairs of asyndeta bimembria occur: *SCC De aquaeductibus* (Riccobono 1968, text 41, p. 279 (Chap. 125)) *et ad eas res omnes exportandas earumque rerum reficiendarum causa, quotiens opus esset, per agros priuatorum sine iniuria eorum <u>itinera actus</u> <u>paterent darentur</u>*, 'and for removing all those things and repairing them whenever there should be a need, paths and rights of way should be open and granted through the lands of private individuals without doing any harm to them'. *Actus* means 'rights of way' (cf. *itus actus* in much the same sense as the pair here at *Lex Coloniae Genetiuae* LXXIX tabl. b.2 (Crawford 1996: 1.404)). *Itinera* is resumed by *paterent* in the following pair (paths should be open), and *actus* by *darentur* (rights of way should be granted). This is a pattern, associated particularly with types of poetry in various languages, which is sometimes called 'correlative distribution' (for this term see Wilkinson 1963: 214). Here is a definition of 'correlative verse' by Preminger and Brogan (1993: 242): 'A literary style and subgenre in which lines or stanzas exhibit two (or more) series of elements, each element in the first corresponding to one in the same position in the second, respectively.' Another term used is *versus rapportati*. Brink (1971: 179–80) on Hor. *Ars* 96 (*Telephus et Peleus, cum pauper et exsul uterque | proicit ampullas*) calls such a pattern 'double zeugma', noting that 'Telephus is *pauper*' and 'it is Peleus who is *exsul*'. This example however has two coordinators and does not exactly belong with the example above,

188

where the first pair at least is asyndetic. Brink also notes that '*et*, not *aut*, predominates in this locution'. I have not investigated classical poetry to determine whether asyndetic examples similar to the coordinated one in Horace above are found. There is an extremely common correlative pattern in poetry in so-called 'interlacing' word orders, as e.g. at Catull. 66.58 *Graia Canopeis incola litoribus*, where each noun looks back to one of the adjectives, but there is no coordination here, syndetic or asyndetic, because the two adjectives and the two nouns are in different cases. For such interlacings in poetry see e.g. Norden (1957: 393–6). For Greek see Denniston (1952: 54–5).

A similar legal example to that above is at *Lex Coloniae Genetiuae* LXXIX tabl. b.5–6 *qui eum agrum habent possident habebunt possidebunt, itineris aquarum lex iusque esto*. Here *habebunt* looks back to *habent* and *possidebunt* to *possident*. Note too *Lex Cornelia de XX quaestoribus* (Crawford 1996: 1.296) Col. II. 29 *utei aa cetereis uiatoribus praeconibus uicarios accipei oportebit*. The doubled preposition *aa* may represent *a cetereis uiatoribus, a praeconibus*, with the second *a* looking forward to the second noun, unless it is gemination to mark the length of the vowel.

An exaggerated specimen of the correlative structure can be found in the so-called *Epitaphium super Vergilium* at *Anthologia Latina* 800: *pastor arator eques paui colui superaui | capras rus hostes fronde ligone manu*.[1] Note also Venantius Fortunatus, *Vita S. Martini* 2.79 *quod mare terra polus pisce alite fruge ministrat*, where the first three nouns are picked up by three others stating the produce of the sea, earth and sky (though Venantius has not managed to achieve the correct order of the three ablatives) (see Kay 2020: 365). Another comparable pattern is at Ven. Mart. 2.412 *tardus edax, uelox uigilans, sopor esca sub ictu*, 'late eating, swift waking, sleep, food under his control', where the last asyndetic pair recapitulates the content of the previous two pairs in reverse order. The correlative structure is chiastic. Correlative patterns are particularly common in medieval Latin verse. A list of such verses may be found at Walther (1969: 178 s.v. 'singula singulis'). I quote just one (Walther: 1967: 297), no. 31268 *temporibus nostris, quicumque placere laborat, | det capiat querat: plurima pauca nihil*.

In literary Latin of the pre-medieval period I have noted occasional (or possible) correlative structures, but they differ from those above in that in most cases the resumptive terms differ syntactically from the asyndetic pair.

---

[1] I owe this and the next two examples to Nigel Kay, to whom I am also grateful for bibliography.

A possible example is at Enn. *Ann.* 591 (XXIV.5.1.3, 10) *diuomque hominumque pater rex*. A comparison with 203 (*diuom pater atque hominum rex*) might suggest that at 591 the two elements of the asyndeton look back to separate genitives (*diuom pater* but *hominum rex*). However, cf. Hom. *Il.* 1.544 πατὴρ ἀνδρῶν τε θεῶν τε, which shows that 'father' can be taken with 'men' as well as 'gods': see, for further similar passages, including the next line of Ennius (592), XXIV.5.1.3, 10. Goldberg and Manuwald (2018) translate 'of gods and men father, king'.

A complicated structure, only partly correlative, is at Pacuvius (XXIV.6.3, 6–8) 80.1, on which see also XIII.4: Schierl *quidquid est hoc, omnia animat format, alit auget, creat | sepelit* (see XXIV.6.3 for discussion). As I have punctuated there are three asyndetic pairs of verbs (see the note ad loc.), the first referring to the giving of life, the second to the development of the living creature, and the third, not only to the end of life (*sepelit*) but also to its creation (*creat*). *Creat* resumes or defines *animat format*. *Sepelit* is not resumptive, but with *creat* it forms a frame of the whole passage of life.

At Sall. *Cat.* 27.2 (70) (*dies noctisque festinare uigilare, neque insomniis neque labore fatigari*) *neque insomniis* (*fatigari*) picks up *uigilare*, and *neque labore fatigari* picks up *festinare*. There is a chiastic correlative connection between the two asyndetic verbs and the following coordinated phrases. The basic meaning of *uigilo* is 'to stay/be awake' (see *OLD* s.v., 1–3). Moreover in the first clause *festinare* refers back to *dies* and *uigilare* to *noctis*: this is a very contrived sentence, with two correlative patterns.

Another interesting passage is Tac. *Ann.* 5.7.1 (141): *tunc singulos, ut cuique absistere adloqui animus erat, retinens aut dimittens partem diei absumpsit.* Here I print *absistere* ('stand back, withdraw') rather than the transmitted *adsistere* (see on Tacitus 141). The referent detains or dismisses individuals, depending on whether he is minded to withdraw or address them: *retinens* resumes *adloqui*, and *dimittens adloqui*: chiasmus again.

In the following Tacitean passage (159) the asyndetic pair is second, following, again chiastically, a coordinated pair of verbs: *Ann.* 4.60.2 *seu loqueretur seu taceret iuuenis, crimen ex silentio ex uoce*.

For two juxtaposed pairs of verbs that seem to have both a correlative and a chiastic relationship see on Tacitus 127, 128. Both pairs may consist of opposites.

The following passage, of Cicero (15), is at least suggestive: *Sest.* 88 *ad ferrum faces, ad cotidianam caedem incendia rapinas se cum exercitu suo contulit*. *Caedes* may be seen as a consequence of *ferrum*, and *incendia* as a consequence of *faces*. *Rapinas* does not fit into the correlation.

It was seen above (on Hor. *Ars* 96) that such correlative patterns need not have an asyndetic member or members. For the syndetic type (with chiasmus) see Sall. *Cat.* 2.2[2] *postea uero quam in Asia Cyrus, in Graecia Lacedaemonii et Athenienses coepere urbis atque nationes subigere*. *Vrbis* are subdued by *Lacedaemonii et Athenienses*, whereas *nationes* are subdued by *Cyrus*.

2 Conclusions

Once again an artificial asyndetic structure turns up in legal language. As for literary language, apart from very late and medieval instances, we have found the pattern with asyndeton mainly in Tacitus, though not in abundance. His examples tend to contain opposites, and the structure is thus just one aspect of his taste for oppositions in asyndeton.

---

[2] Pointed out to me by Tony Woodman.

CHAPTER XVIII

End-Of-List Coordination and 'Weak' Asyndeton Bimembre

1 Introduction

In English (for example) when three or more terms are in a coordinated sequence the normal structure is 'AB and C', with what is sometimes called 'end-of-list' coordination (see e.g. Haspelmath 2004: 572, index s.v. 'end-of -list'): e.g. *bacon, lettuce and tomatoes; Friends, Romans and countrymen.* Latin had, up to a point, the same structure (in several forms because of the number of coordinators in the language), but how significant was it, and is it straightforward to interpret? For *et* and *atque* used thus (and associated textual problems) see Pinkster (1969). For *-que* see Adams (2016: 62–4, with some bibliography), with full details for Cato *Agr.* Pinkster (1969: 266), speaking of the different Latin coordinators found in this structure, says: '*Que* seems to have been most normal in "Classical" Latin, followed by zero, *et, atque* respectively.' This follows the generalisation: 'in Latin A B & C is a normal pattern, occurring beside A B C and A B C*que*'. According to Dyck (2010: 101) on Cic. *S. Rosc.*31, citing Pinkster, '*xyzque* appears to be the commonest way of organising three items in Latin'. That is not so. Torrego indeed states (2009: 472) that 'the marked "A, B, & C" pattern' 'is not encountered often in Pre-Classical and Classical Latin, yet it becomes the standard pattern in Romance', and his examples show that his formulation 'A, B & C' was intended to embrace all the Latin coordinators. In fact what Pinkster calls 'zero', that is asyndeton throughout (ABCD etc.), is much more common than the use of *-que*, and also common are what I would call sequences with multiple coordinations, that is with coordinators used within the list, not least to indicate internal unities. I will illustrate this pattern in section 3.

There is also an issue that must be raised in the interpretation of any sequence ABC(D etc.)*que*. A structure ABC*que* may not be what it seems. It may have distinct units within, such that BC*que* forms one unit semantically different from (and in asyndeton with) A, or alternatively AB may be

2 Statistics

an asyndetic unit, with an item of a different type coordinated to it. Such internal unities are particularly marked when there are four members of the sequence, ABCD*que* (see e.g. XIX.3 on such sequences as falling into two pairs, and the examples listed at XXX.6.2b; also XXXI.3.7 on Livy 8.33.20) but they are not confined to longer sequences.

I begin however with some statistics showing the relative frequency of ABC*que* versus alternatives, first in a book of Livy, in whose prayers end-of-list coordination is common (see Adams and Nikitina, forthcoming, 6), then in a work of Cicero, in Cato *Agr.* and in selected plays of Plautus. Elsewhere too in the book statistics are given for end-of-list coordinations, or examples cited, in different connections. At I.4 there is full evidence from Cicero's speech *Pro Roscio Amerino* for the different ways of coordinating groups of three or more members, and end-of-list coordination is very much in the minority. At XXV.4 possible examples of end-of-list coordination in Lucilius are listed, and their small number contrasted with the greater frequency of long asyndeta in Lucilius. In Lucretius end-of-list coordination is about as common as longer asyndeta, but both patterns are outnumbered by multiple coordinations (see XXIV.7.5). There is a full treatment of sequences of three or more terms in Catullus at XXVII.2, and as usual end-of-list coordination is in the minority compared with syndetic and asyndetic sequences. Finally, it is noted (with evidence) at XXIX.4.2 that end-of-list coordination is 'not very frequent in Horace'.

The one genre in which in the early period end-of-list coordination is relatively frequent is that of prayers and related documents. Examples are quoted at XXII.3, and dealt with systematically in Adams and Nikitina (forthcoming).

2 Statistics

I have collected from one book of Livy (8) all instances of groups of three or more terms, whether asyndetic or containing coordinations. The evidence is arranged in categories:

2.1 Livy 8

2.1.1 Asyndeta

6.15 *lingua moribus, armorum genere, institutis ante omnia militaribus congruentes*
8.8 *sexagenos milites, duos centuriones, uexillarium unum habebat uexillum*
8.8 long phrasal tricolon without coordinators

9.8 *exercitu legionibus auxiliis* (from a prayer).
12.2 *Antiates in agrum Ostiensem Ardeatem Solonium incursiones fecerunt*
16.14 *creauerunt K. Duillium T. Quinctium M. Fabium*
19.12 *agros urbem, corpora ipsorum coniugumque ac liberorum suorum in potestate populi Romani esse futuraque*
25.4 *tria oppida in potestatem uenerunt, Allifae Callifae Rufrium*
25.10 *quod bonum faustum felix Palaepolitanis populoque Romano esset*
31.6 *quam tribunis militum, quam centurionibus, quam militibus esse* (asyndeton with anaphora).
32.3 *pareantque ei consules, regia potestas, praetores*
32.7 *imperio meo spreto, incertis auspiciis, turbatis religionibus*
33.12 *ne plebis quidem hominem, non centurionem, non militem uiolatum* (another case with anaphora).
33.19 *si fusus fugatus, castris exutus fuisset*
34.1 *stabat cum eo senatus maiestas, fauor populi, tribunicium auxilium, memoria absentis exercitus*
34.7–9 nine phrases/clauses in asyndeton, all preceded by a negative, *non* or *nemo* (asyndeton with anaphora again).

2.1.2 Groups with Internal Coordination (but Not End-of-List Type)

8.1 *custodiae uigiliaeque et ordo stationum*
10.4 *memores patriae parentumque et coniugum ac liberorum* (see section 3).
10.11 *consuli dictatorique et praetori*
13.1 *Pedum armis uirisque et omni ui expugnandum ac delendum senatus fremit* (see section 3).
13.5 *Aricinos Lanuuinosque et Veliternos*
14.3 *Aricini Nomentanique et Pedani*
14.10 *conubia commerciaque et concilia inter se ademerunt* (it is a moot point whether examples such as this and the preceding two should be regarded as containing an internal unity, or whether Livy has simply used explicit coordinators to join all three terms).
19.5 *Setinum Norbanumque et Coranum agrum . . . consedit*
19.11 *Fundis pacem esse et animos Romanos et gratam memoriam acceptae ciuitatis* (a clear case of three phrases with coordination throughout: see above on 14.10).
23.2 *uicinos populos, Priuernatem Fundanumque et Formianum*
23.8 *campus Campanus . . . et arma et communis Mars belli* (coordination throughout again).
29.4 *Marsi Paelignique et Marrucini*
32.7 *aduersus morem militarem disciplinamque maiorum et numen deorum* (coordination throughout, with variation of coordinator).
33.20 *in laetitia uictoria, supplicationibus ac gratulationibus esse* (on this example see XXXI.3.7).

2 Statistics

33.21 *intuentem Capitolium atque arcem deosque ab se duobus proeliis haud frustra aduocatos* (coordination throughout, with variation again).
34.2 *ex parte altera imperium inuictum populi Romani et disciplina rei militaris et dictatoris edictum pro numine semper obseruatum et Manliana imperia et posthabita filii caritas publicae utilitati iactabantur* (a sequence of phrases linked by *et*).
36.6 *legatis tribunisque et praefectis*
37.6 *Capitolium atque arx moeniaque et portae* (there are probably two coordinated pairs here).
39.4 *ubi respectantes hostium antesignanos turbataque signa et fluctuantem aciem uidit* (coordination throughout, with variation).

2.1.3 End-of-List Coordination

12.7 *Tiburs Praenestinus Veliturnusque populus*
33.23 *haec simul iurgans, querens, deum hominumque fidem obtestans, et complexus filium pluribus cum lacrimis agebat* (not a compelling example because of the change of construction from the sequence of present participles, all verbs of saying, to a perfect participle from a different semantic field).

End-of-list coordinations are greatly outnumbered in this book both by asyndeta (tricola or longer sequences) and by sequences with multiple coordinations There are just two (possible) end-of-list coordinations, compared with about seventeen asyndeta and nineteen multiple coordinations. Livy uses multiple coordination either to link all the elements in a sequence, or to suggest internal unities, and sometimes for this reason what looks like a sequence of three or four terms may have just (e.g.) two units. That does not concern us here. The crucial point is that in book 8 as a whole asyndeta and multiple coordinations outnumber end-of-list coordination by 36:2.

2.2   Cicero De officiis *1.1–100*

I have collected from the first 100 sections of Cicero's *De officiis* 1 (40 pages of text in Winterbottom's OCT) asyndeta with three or more members, and sequences with three or more members that have internal coordination. Examples with anaphora as well as asyndeton or coordination are also included.

2.2.1   Asyndeta

6 *praecepta firma stabilia coniuncta naturae*
6 *Stoicorum Academicorum Peripateticorum*
6 *Aristonis Pyrrhonis Erilli*

196   XVIII   End-of-List Coordination

9 *ad uitae commoditatem iucunditatemque, ad facultates rerum atque copias, ad opes ad potentiam* (with anaphora, as in some of the examples that follow).
11 *ut pastum, ut latibula, ut alia generis eiusdem*
13 *uidere audire addiscere*
14 *pulchritudinem uenustatem conuenientiam partium*
14 *pulchritudinem constantiam ordinem*
18 *labi autem errare nescire decipi*
22 *tum artibus, tum opera, tum facultatibus*
26 *honoris imperii potentiae gloriae cupiditates*
28 *neglegentia pigritia inertia* (note the repeated ending *-tia*).
29 *nihil . . . studii, nihil operae, nihil facultatum*
35 *Tusculanos Aequos Volscos Sabinos Hernicos*
38 *cum Latinis Sabinis Samnitibus Poenis Pyrrho*
49 *animo studio beniuolentia*
50 *docendo discendo, communicando disceptando iudicando*
50 *iustitiam aequitatem bonitatem*
53 *forum fana porticus uiae leges iura iudicia suffragia*
57 *cari sunt parentes, cari liberi propinqui familiares*
58 *consilia sermones cohortationes consolationes* (note the repeated ending).
61 *de Marathone Salamine Plataeis Thermopylis Leuctris*
61 *hinc Decii, hinc Cn. et P. Scipiones, hinc M. Macellus*
82 *punire sontes, multitudinem conseruare, in omni fortuna recta atque honesta retinere*
92 *ratione diligentia parsimonia*
92 *simpliciter fideliter uere*
94 *falli errare labi decipi*
98 *constantiae moderationis temperantiae uerecundiae partes.*

2.2.2   Coordinations

17 *ordo autem et constantia et moderatio*
18 *ad considerandas res et tempus et diligentiam*
23 *parentes aut amicos aut patriam*
28 *aut inimicitias aut laborem aut sumptu.*
53 *consuetudines praeterea et familiaritates multisque cum multis res rationesque contractae*
66 *aut admirari aut optare aut expetere oportere*
69 *tum etiam aegritudine et uoluptate nimia et iracundia*
70 *et facilior et tutior et minus aliis grauis aut molesta uita est*
81 *opera magni animi et excelsi et prudentia consilioque fidentis*
86 *grauis et fortis ciuis ei in re publica dignus principatu.*

2.2.3   End-of-List Coordination

Two possible instances of end-of-list coordination (12 *coniugi liberis ceterisque quos caros habeat*, 13 *uerum simplex sincerumque sit*) are interpreted below

2 Statistics

(sections 6 and 4 respectively) as possible dicola not tricola. There remains just one candidate for an end-of-list coordination, in a complicated and long-winded phrasal sequence: 93 *in qua uerecundia et quasi quidam ornatus uitae, temperantia et modestia, omnisque sedatio perturbationum animi et rerum modus cernitur* (possibly two coordinated pairs in asyndeton, followed by a third coordinated pair introduced by *omnisque*).

There are 28 asyndeta and 10 cases of coordination throughout, against the tiny group of possible end-of-list coordinations. End-of-list coordination is outnumbered by about 38:1.

Livy makes more use of internal coordination to mark unities than does Cicero, at least in this work.

2.3 Cato

In Cato *Agr.* too outside prayers asyndeta (of three or more elements) greatly outnumber end-of-list coordination. For a full collection of examples of the structure ABC*que* see Adams (2016: 62–3). There are 16–18 cases in the whole work (the variation due to several ambiguities of structure), of which about 40 per cent are in prayers, and about 13 or 14 have a stylised appearance. It would be an immense task to count all instances of asyndeta and coordinated groups with three or more members, but they vastly outnumber the 16–18 cases with *-que* at the end. In the first nine chapters alone I have noted nine cases of asyndeton, three cases with coordination throughout, and four with some form of internal coordination of different sorts other than that at the end of the list. There are 162 chapters in the complete work, and the first nine chapters have as many cases of asyndeton or internal coordination as the whole work has cases of end-of-list coordination (with *-que*). I have noticed (from a quick reading of Briggs 1983) very few instances of end-of-list coordination with *et* (10.5 *et lectos III*, 84 *et ouum unum*).

Adams and Nikitina (forthcoming, 7) also deal with sequences of three or more members in the fragments of Cato's speeches, and from these end-of-list coordination is almost absent.

2.4 Plautus

Here are comparative figures from selected plays of Plautus:

Amphitruo
Long asyndeta 10

End-of-list 2
Multiple coordinations 3

Asinaria
Long asyndeta 12
End-of-list 0
Multiple coordinations 5

Aulularia
Long asyndeta 12
End-of-list 0
Multiple coordinations 5

Mercator
Long asyndeta 19
End-of-list 4

Mostellaria
Long asyndeta 15
End-of-list 2
Multiple coordinations 2

Poenulus
Long asyndeta 13
End-of-list 1
Multiple coordinations 6

Also, in Adams and Nikitina (forthcoming, 6), all examples of the three patterns from the *Miles Gloriosus* are listed, and again end-of-list coordination is an insignificant presence.

3 Internal Unities Expressed by Coordinators

It was stated at 1 above that sequences of terms may have internal unities, and that these may be marked by overt coordinators. It might have been added that long asyndetic sequences too may have internal unities, such that the last member could not straightforwardly be marked by the addition of a coordinator. At Tac. *Ann.* 4.25.2 (*pecorum modo trahi occidi capi*) the translation (with addition of a final *-que*) 'they were dragged off, killed and captured' would not work, as is noted on Sallust 76. A disjunctive coordinator such as *aut* would have to be inserted between *occidi* and *capi* if the sequence were to be interpreted by means of additions, but that disjunctive term would only be applicable to the last two verbs and

3 Internal Unities Expressed by Coordinators 199

not to the whole sequence of three. The dragging off is an earlier, separate stage, which could be brought out clearly by the addition of *et* after *trahi*: 'they were dragged off, and killed or taken into captivity'. There is not here an asyndetic tricolon, but rather two asyndeta bimembria, a long one and a short one. The long one, [*trahi*] [*occidi capi*], has as its two components first a single verb, and then a pair of verbs. The short one consists of the disjunctive pair of single verbs in the second set of brackets. See also Leo (1960: 175) on such sequences.

I now move on to a few clear-cut examples of internal unities within sequences containing coordinators (two of them from Livy 8):

Cic. *Fam.* 15.2.4 *eiusque regis salutem et incolumitatem regnumque defenderem*.
This is translated by Shackleton Bailey (105), 'to defend his welfare, security and throne', a rendering that might be taken to imply a tricolon. There are however two coordinators, one connecting the synonyms *salutem* and *incolumitatem*, the other attaching a word of a different semantic field. These two synonyms are often associated: e.g. Cic. *Pis*. 33 *salutem incolumitatem, reditum precentur*, Livy 23.42.4 *te saluo atque incolumi amico*, 29.27.3 *saluos incolumesque*. A translation should ideally mark the phrase structure ('to defend his welfare and security, and throne').

Caelius ap. Cic. *Fam.* 8.16.1 *deos hominesque amicitiamque nostram testificor*.
'Gods and men' is a merism for all intelligent beings (see West 2007: 100; for the commonplace combination in Latin see *TLL* V.1.32ff.), and this pair is distinct from the friendship of an individual. Shackleton Bailey's translation (153.1), 'I call Gods and men and our friendship to witness' again makes the sequence sound like a straightforward tricolon. Perhaps, 'I call gods and men, and our friendship, to witness.' The crucial feature of the sequence is that it is not a tricolon, despite the three terms, but a dicolon, of the structure [*deos hominesque*][*amicitiamque nostram*]. If *deos homines* were asyndetic, could one say that *deos homines amicitiamque nostram* had end-of-list coordination, or would it be more accurate to say that there were two units, an asyndetic pair, and coordinated with it a miscellaneous item?

Livy 8.10.4 *memores patriae parentumque et coniugum ac liberorum*.
Both *patria/parentes* (see on Sall. *Cat.* 52.3 (17)) and *coniux/liberi* (see XIV.2.3, and below, 6, on Cic. *Off*. 1.12) are common pairings, either with asyndeton or with coordination. This is not a tetracolon with three coordinators joining miscellaneous items, but a dicolon with two coordinated pairs, the two parts linked by *et*.

Livy 8.13.1 *Pedum armis uirisque et omni ui expugnandum ac delendum senatus fremit*.
The grouping of *arma*, *uiri* and *equi* or any two of them, with or without coordination, is probably more common than any other set of two/three in the language (see on Sall. *Jug*. 51.1 (31, 32)). The structure here is thus [*armis uirisque*]

[*et omni ui*], with the first element of the dicolon specific and the second generalising (see also the next section, on Sall. *Hist.* 4.60.16, 43).

The obvious question raised by these examples is whether there are comparable sequences with similar internal unities, but with just one coordinator introducing the last element (ABC*que* and the like). Any such internal unit may rule out taking the sequence as having end-of-list coordination. I turn to that question in the next section.

4 Examples of the Structure ABC*que* That Arguably Do Not Have End-of-List Coordination

In this category probably belongs *Lex Antonia de Termessibus* I.7: *leiberi amicei socieique populi Romani sunto*. *Amicilsocii* is an established pair, not least in legal language, and it is used both syndetically and asyndetically, and *amicitia* and *societas* are also found together (see on Sall. *Hist.* 4.60.17 Ramsey (47)). The translation of Crawford (1996: 1.335) expresses convincingly the structure of the sequence: '(all these and their descendants, citizens of Termessus Maior in Pisidia), are to be free, friends and allies of the Roman people'. A comma might be placed after *leiberi*. The structure as just translated is [*leiberi*] [*amicei socieique populi Romani*], with the two members asyndetic rather than coordinated (or perhaps the second pair is appositional). An alternative would be to take *leiberi* as the attribute of *amicei socieique*, but the granting of freedom expressed by the *-to* imperative of *esse* with the predicate *liber* goes back to the XII Tables (IV.2 (b) *filius a patre liber esto*: see Crawford 1996: 2.631). See also XXII.2.2 on the significance of the genitive *populi Romani*.

The following passage has a pair that was seen in the last section: Sall. *Cat.* 6.5 (**64**) *at Romani domi militiaeque intenti festinare parare, alius alium hortari, hostibus obuiam ire, libertatem patriam parentisque armis tegere*, '. . . protecting by arms their freedom and their fatherland and parents'.

Patriam parentisque was an established unit expressing a person's fatherland and parenthood (two types of paternity, as it were, to which an individual's obligations were at their most extreme). Liberty on the other hand is an abstract concept and of a different type. The structure is again [A][BC*que*].

It is worth quoting alongside the above passage Cic. *Fin.* 5.52 (**105**), though a coordinator attaching the final part is lacking: *quid cum uolumus nomina eorum qui quid gesserint nota nobis esse, parentes patriam, multa praeterea minime necessaria*. Here the unitary pair *parentes patriam* is followed by a vague general phrase of a type not infrequent when there is a coordinator after an asyndetic unit (see below, 6). The structure is arguably [*parentes patriam*] [*multa praeterea minime necessaria*]: see on Cicero 105.

At Plaut. *Trin.* 142 (*quod meae concreditum est | taciturnitati clam, fide et fiduciae*, 'what was entrusted to my silence in secret, to my faith and reliability') the alliterative pair *fide et fiduciae* is a formulaic unit (cf. *Trin.* 117 *qui tuae mandatus est fide et fiduciae* and Wölfflin 1933: 259), and it is moreover separated from *taciturnitati* by *clam*.

At Tac. *Ann.* 4.51.1 (**138**) (*eaque prensare detrahere et aduersum resistentis comminus niti*) the first two verbs have the same object, whereas the next one has a different construction. There seem to be two cola, the first with an asyndeton bimembre.

A spell at Macr. *Sat.* 3.9.7 has the following (see also XXII.3.1): *loca templa sacra urbemque eorum* (note that the same text also has at 8 *loca templa sacra urbs*). There would only be end-of-list coordination here if the division were *loca, templa sacra, urbemque*. *Loca* on its own, however, without a specifier, would be problematic. The sequence is translated by Kaster (Loeb) as 'sacred places, temples, and city', a rendering that raises questions about the position of *sacra*. It is translated as if it were juxtaposed with *loca*, but as it is placed it must go with *templa* as well as *loca*, and a more literal translation would be 'sacred places and temples, and city'. On this view there would not be a tricolon, but an asyndetic pair followed by a single term. The position of *sacra* after *templa*, when it is required with *loca* but not necessarily with *templa* if it means 'temples', brings up the sense of *templa*. It probably does not mean 'temples' here, but has its earlier meaning of '(sacred) places marked out on the ground or in the sky, for the purposes of augury' (see *OLD* s.v. *templum* 1–2). Once it is taken thus it forms a unit with *loca*, the two expressing sacred places of different types. Instead of a tricolon the structure would be [*loca templa sacra*] [*urbsque*].

There follows a passage which, despite appearances, cannot have end-of-list coordination: Livy 34.34.7 *segnitiam inuidiam et obtrectationem domi manentium aduersus militantes*, 'the idleness, and the ill-will and disparagement by those staying at home directed at those fighting'. There should be a comma after *segnitiam*. *Aduersus militantes* goes with *inuidiam et obtrectationem* but does not fit with *segnitiam*, which therefore must be a unit separate from the coordinated pair: [*segnitiam*] [*inuidiam et obtrectationem aduersus militantes*]. *Inuidia* and *obtrectatio* are regularly coordinated (*TLL* IX.2.292.40–6; e.g. Cic. *Inv.* 1.16, Vatin. ap. Cic. *Fam.* 5.9.1), and indeed by Livy: see 30.20.3 *uicit ergo Hannibalem non populus Romanus totiens caesus fugatusque, sed senatus Carthaginiensis obtrectatione atque inuidia*, and particularly 28.40.8 *obtrectationis atque inuidiae aduersus crescentem in dies gloriam fortissimi consulis*. In both these passages *inuidia* comes second, and at 28.40.8 it has the *aduersus*-construction immediately following (cf. 42.12.2 *inuidia aduersus Romanos*). Clearly at 34.34.7 above *aduersus* complements both *inuidia* and *obtrectatio*.

I next consider a few passages from Lucretius. First, at 2.921 (*homines armenta feraeque*) *armenta* and *ferae* denote domesticated versus wild animals, and they stand in contrast to humans. This is a well-known merism, two-footed versus four-footed creatures (see West 2007: 100), with the two parts arguably asyndetically coordinated with each other (see XXIV.7.1.2, 6).

In another place Lucretius has an extended contrast between domestic and wild animals that is relevant here not because of its coordination, but because of the terminology: 1.163 *armenta atque aliae pecudes, genus omne ferarum*, 'cattle and other farm animals and every kind of wild creature'. The wild animals are again *ferae*, whereas the domestic animals are denoted by two terms, *armenta* and *pecudes*, which are difficult to distinguish. This passage is relevant to 5.228 *pecudes armenta feraeque*. Again the domestic animals are expressed by *pecudes* and *armenta*, which are arguably an asyndeton bimembre, opposed to *feraeque*: [*pecudes armenta*] [*feraeque*]. Admittedly there is an uncertainty of interpretation here, and I have not listed this as a definite asyndeton in Lucretius in the relevant chapter. However, it is possible that readers familiar with merisms such as 'men/animals' and 'wild/domestic animals' would have seen the semantic contrasts within these sequences and not merely treated them as miscellaneous lists. Another Lucretian opposition (asyndetic) between wild and domestic animals comes up elsewhere (XXIV.7.1.2, 6): 1.14 *inde ferae, pecudes persultant pabula laeta*. Note that here it is *pecudes* that is opposed to *ferae*, whereas above both *armenta* on its own, and *armenta* and *pecudes* together, were seen in this opposition.

Lucr. 3.395 (*concursare coire et dissultare uicissim* 'run together, meet together, and leap apart in turn' (of the 'seeds of soul')) by means of three verbs expresses an opposition of the reversive type (cf. *enter/exit, arrive/depart*). The first two verbs are near-synonyms, and refer to the coming together. The third on its own expresses the reversal, the separation. There are possibly two cola here (see XXIV.7.3, 28), the first consisting of an asyndetic pair, and the second of a verb of opposite meaning to the other two, but the interpretation is doubtful. Compare Livy 5.51.8 *uicti captique ac redempti*, where defeat and capture are linked by

4 ABCque *without (?) end-of-list coordination*

their own coordinator, and the reversal (being bought back) is separated from them by a different coordinator. There are more obviously two cola here, with the internal unity conveyed in this case by *-que*, not asyndeton.

There are many other passages in which in a sequence AB*Cque* two of the juxtaposed terms have a very close relationship that sets them apart from the other term. I quote a few.

Sall. *Hist.* 4.60.16 Ramsey (43) *magnas opes uirorum armorum et auri esse* resembles Livy 8.13.1, discussed in the last section, in which *arma* and *uiri* were coordinated, and separated by another coordinator from a miscellaneous item. Here they are asyndetic, and separated from a term of a completely different semantic type.

B. *Afr.* 89.2 *armis frumento pecuniaque* may be analysed as [*armis*] [*frumento pecuniaque*], because *frumentum/pecunia* is a very common pair, with and without coordination: see on Livy 23.12.4 (16) *magnam uim frumenti pecuniae absumi*. A comma should be after *armis*.

At Cic. *Pis.* 89 (*in sordibus, lamentis luctuque iacuisti*), *lamentis luctuque* is a unit comprising near-synonyms (see *TLL* VII.2.1744.30ff. for such pairs; also Wölfflin 1933: 265), which are also alliterative, and differ semantically from the first term *sordibus*. *Sordes*, the dark clothing of mourning, is concrete, whereas the two alliterative terms are abstract verbal nouns with the second akin to a modifier of the first (= 'lamentations of grief': 'you lay in dark clothes, (and) in grief-stricken lamentation').

Cic. *Off.* 1.13 (*quod uerum, simplex sincerumque sit*, 'what is true, pure and simple') is similar, but not as striking, and there may be end-of-list coordination. *Simplex* and *sincerus* (another alliterative pair, similar semantically) are however elsewhere paired (see Wölfflin 1933: 275).

A special pattern is illustrated by Plaut. *Merc.* 678 (cited by Leo 1960: 172): *ut des pacem propitius,* | *salutem et sanitatem nostrae familiae*. The sequence *pacem, ... salutem et sanitatem* has two distinctive features. First, it is interrupted by an intrusive term, *propitius*, before the final pair (cf. *clam* at Plaut. *Trin.* 142 above, this section). Second, this pair is alliterative and comprises near-synonyms that differ in meaning from *pacem*. *Saluus sanus* was an established formula, used with asyndeton and coordination (see Adams 2016: 200; note too Cato *Agr.* 141.3 *salutem ualetudinemque* for two such near-synonyms coordinated). *Salutem et sanitatem* is also at the beginning of a new line, and thus further detached from *pacem*. There seem to be two separate units rather than a list of three.

Here is another passage with a distinctive intrusive element: Cic. *Fin.* 5.7 *ab his oratores, ab his imperatores ac rerum publicarum principes exstiterunt*. If the second *ab his* were deleted, there would be a tricolon with a coordinator at the end, *ab his oratores, imperatores ac rerum publicarum principes*. In the text as written the second *ab his* cuts off the coordinated pair that follows from *oratores*: ([*oratores*] [*imperatores ac principes*]). There is a semantic plausibility to the division as well, with orators on the one hand and leaders in a more technical sense on the other.

Very similar is Cic. *Cat.* 4.1 *ut omnis acerbitates, omnis dolores cruciatusque perferrem*. Here it is anaphora of *omnis* that has the same effect as *ab his* above.

The clearest examples of asyndetic sequences with a coordinated term at the end that cannot be treated as mere end-of-list coordination are to be found in longer sequences with the structure [AB] [CD*que*]. These often manifestly consist of two juxtaposed pairs, each with its own semantic unity, the first asyndetic and the second coordinated. It is a very old structure (found for example in a prayer in Cato: see e.g XIX.1), but is sometimes missed, to judge both by some punctuations adopted by editors and by explicit comments. It is dealt with in detail elsewhere (see e.g. XIX.3, XXX.6.2b, XXXI.3.7). Here is one instance.

At Cic. *Sest.* 20 (10) (*uino ganeis, lenociniis adulteriisque confectum*) there is not a series of four items of equivalent type, with the last tacked on by a coordinator. The last two nouns refer to sexual activities, brothel-keeping and adulteries. The first two belong to a different semantic field, that of excessive drinking and eating. The sequence has two semantically unified pairs, with asyndetic and then syndetic coordination. See the note ad loc.

Perhaps the most important example in this section is Livy 34.34.7, which looks to have the structure ABC*que* but in which a syntactic feature rules out straightforward end-of-list coordination. In the other examples discussed an internal unity is revealed by a semantic feature and sometimes something else as well, such as an anaphora. In every case there are grounds for taking the sequences not as tricola but as dicola, one having two members, the other one. The possibility that there may be semantic units within a sequence of three or more terms with a coordinator at the end raises questions about the mechanical use of the 'Oxford comma'.

Finally, see XXII.3.4 on *homines, urbes agrosque* in a prayer quoted by Marcobius, which is not a case of end-of-list coordination.

5 End-of-List Coordination

I cite a few genuine cases of this pattern.

Pompeius (*GL* V.304.29–30, = Zago 2017: 1.63, §82) quotes Virg. *Aen.* 4.593–4 (*ite | ferte citi, flammas, date tela, impellite remos*), an asyndetic

5 *End-of-List Coordination* 205

clausal tetracolon (but on the unmetrical text of the first two cola see Zago 2017: 2.344–5), and then adds that Virgil might have had at the end instead *et impellite remos*, but he *maluit inconexam orationem ponere*. I quote this passage merely to show that the grammarian obviously had a concept of end-of-list coordination.

Prayers are notable for this type of coordination. For example, chapter 141 of Cato *Agr*. has no fewer than six of these (see XXII.3.2), in three of which the three nouns *fundus, ager, terra* occur in three different orders, which rules out any possibility that *-que* might indicate a unitary pair differing from the other term: 141.1 *fundum agrum terramque meam*, 141.2 *agrum terram fundumque meum*, 141.3 *fundi terrae agrique mei lustrandi* ... *ergo*.

At Cic. *Fin*. 1.57 (*non posse iucunde uiui nisi sapienter honeste iusteque uiuatur, nec sapienter honeste iuste nisi iucunde*) the three adverbs occur first with coordination at the end and then in the next clause with asyndeton throughout (no textual variants reported by Reynolds, OCT). It could be said that *iusteque uiuatur* gives a better clausula (cretic–trochee) than *iuste uiuatur* (sequence of long syllables). The passage shows that Cicero could treat the two patterns as interchangeable. Reid (1925: 85) on the other hand says that *-que* possibly should be struck out.

A clear instance of *et* as the coordinator attaching the last element is at Catull. 63.60: *abero foro palaestra stadio et gymnasiis?* Fordyce (1961: 268) observes: 'the market-place, the wrestling-ground, the running-track, and the sport-school, the resorts of young manhood in the Greek city'. Three of the terms are Greek, and *forum* represents ἀγορά. The four terms are all of a type, and cannot be split into pairs.

It was seen above (2.2.1) that an anaphoric repetition may split up a group of three into two units. In the following passage on the other hand there is a threefold anaphora (of *tam*), and all three adjectives so modified are of much the same semantic field: Cic. *Cat*. 1.11 *hanc tam taetram, tam horribilem tamque infestam rei publicae pestem*. This is an ascending tricolon with balancing parts, and the third is attached by *tamque*.

Here is a series of three verbs, the last with a coordinator, expressing a sequence of events: Livy 5.50.2 *fana ... restituerentur terminarentur expiarenturque*. The temples should be restored, have their boundaries marked out and be purified. An example such as this could be paralleled by many asyndetic verbs placed in chronological order. Here is just one example: Cic. *Pis*. 93 (*deturbant adfligunt comminuunt dissipant*, 'they overthrew, smashed, ground to powder, scattered'). This is a genuine tetracolon, which cannot be split into internal groups, and the same is true of the series above with end-of-list coordination.

One type found certainly in Plautus consists of a sequence, of pronouns or with at least one pronoun: Plaut. *Cas.* 642 *pectus auris caput teque di perduint*, *Cur.* 74 *me, te atque hos omnes*, *Men.* 174 *mihi, tibi atque illi.*

At Caes. *Civ.* 2.1.1 there is a triplet *aggerem uineas turresque*. Earlier Caesar had paired the last two nouns: 1.36.4 *turres uineasque*. Should they also be taken together here ([*aggerem*] [*uineas turresque*])? It would be unjustified to divide the phrase thus, because at 2.2.6 it is the first and third nouns instead that are coordinated: *aggeri et turribus*. Also, all three are in asyndeton at Cic. *Fam.* 2.10.3. There are no grounds for detaching the last two from the first, or the first two from the last. This is end-of-list coordination.

6 Special Structures That May Have 'Weak' Asyndeton Bimembre + Third Element

There is a common pattern in Latin whereby an uncoordinated pair with a semantic unity is followed by a third element, coordinated or merely juxtaposed, and introduced by one of various key terms such as *denique, ceteri(que), postremo*, which is semantically different from the asyndetic pair and usually expresses a generalisation or summary, often containing a word meaning 'all' (see on Sallust 1 with cross references). Whether such structures should be seen as asyndeta bimembria followed by a detached summary perhaps preceded by a pause, or as tricola of a special type (with or without end-of-list coordination) is a matter for debate. My aim is to present some evidence here, not to adjudicate on the terminology. I use the term 'weak' because if such sequences are taken as containing an asyndeton bimembre, that asyndeton is not free-standing but is embedded within a longer sequence (see also 4 above, where there are unitary pairs, both syndetic and asyndetic, within longer sequences).

I start with two very similar passages of Sallust and Tacitus (see also XXX.6.2c):

Sall. *Cat.* 10.4 (1) *namque auaritia fidem probitatem ceterasque artis bonas subuortit*
Tac. *Ann.* 2.73.3 (discussed after Tacitus 70) *quantum clementia temperantia, ceteris bonis artibus praestitisset.*

In both an asyndetic pair of two semantically overlapping abstract nouns is followed by a generalising expression *ceterae artes bonae*. *Ceterae* has -*que* in one passage but not in the other. Do we have here two straightforward

6 Structures with 'Weak' Asyndeton Bimembre (?)

tricola? If so the first passage certainly has end-of-list coordination, because its structure is identical to the next, which has asyndeton throughout. Alternatively, such patterns may be analysed as containing a 'weak' asyndeton bimembre, with a detached summary following. Cf. Tac. *Hist.* 3.49.1 (13) (*felicitas in tali ingenio auaritiam superbiam ceteraque occulta mala patefecit*) which is similar particularly to the example of Sallust above (see XXX.6.2c). The clause introduced by *ceteraque* has the expression *occulta mala*, a virtual opposite of the 'good arts' above.

The following passage of Cicero brings out the difficulty of interpreting the structure of such series: *Off.* 1.12 *coniugi liberis ceterisque quos caros habeat*. *Coniux/liberi* is a common pair, as was noted above, 3 on Livy 8.10.4), and it may be asyndetic or syndetic (see XIV.2.3). The same question arises: is there a dicolon, comprising first an asyndetic pair and then a longer general phrase ([*coniugi liberis*] [*ceterisque quos caros habeat*]), or a tricolon with end-of-list coordination? I have left the passage out of the chapter on Cicero, possibly wrongly: the first pair is an identifiable asyndeton bimembre and the attached term is less specific.

For other asyndetic single-word lists followed by *ceteraque* (et sim.) cf. Plaut. *Truc.* 318 *blandimentis hortamentis, ceteris meretriciis* (see Leo 1960: 179), Cic. *Mur.* 15 *dignitatem generis integritatis industriae ceterorumque ornamentorum omnium* (note here *omnium*, on which see below), Sall. *Cat.* 13.3 (4) *sed lubido stupri ganeae ceterique cultus non minor incesserat, Jug.* 43.3 *arma tela equos et cetera instrumenta militiae parare*, Tac. *Hist.* 1.22.1 (3) *adulteria matrimonia ceterasque regnorum libidines, Hist.* 4.5.2 (15) *potentiam nobilitatem ceteraque extra animum neque bonis neque malis adnumerant.* See further on Sallust 1, with many cross references.

Similar to *ceteri(que)* is *alii*, which is found in much the same contexts (see on Sallust 1, which is quoted above):

Sall. *Jug.* 60.6 (34) *lapides ignem, alia praeterea tela ingerunt* (note too *praeterea*, on which see Sallust 33 with cross references, and XXX.3.3.3 i).
Sall. *Jug.* 85.41 (38) *sudorem puluerem et alia talia relinquant nobis*
Tac. *Ann.* 1.32.3 (60) *uigilias stationes, et si qua alia praesens usus indixerat, ipsi partiebantur*
Tac. *Ann.* 3.2.2 (73) *atrata plebes, trabeati equites pro opibus loci uestem odores aliaque funerum sollemnia cremabant.*

After a unitary two-word asyndeton bimembre various writers sometimes have an extended or generalising phrase introduced by *denique*. The following example from Cicero also shows another recurrent feature of such sequences: *Quinct.* 48 (1) *is quicum tibi adfinitas societas, omnes denique causae et necessitudines ueteres intercedebant*. The additional phrase is stressed as a summarising generalisation by *omnes*. Here are some further Ciceronian instances with both elements: *Cat.* 2.22 (2) *quantum genus est parricidarum sicariorum, denique omnium facinerosorum* (two categories of murderers are embraced in the general term 'all criminals'), *Phil.* 5.15 (26) *saltatores citharistas, totum denique comissationis Antonianae chorum, Pis.* 23 *consilio fide grauitate uigilantia cura, toto denique munere*. Similar to *Phil.* 5.15 above, but without *denique*, is *Off.* 1.150 *adde huc, si placet, unguentarios saltatores totumque ludum talarium* (see further below). For Greek see Men. *Dysk.* 524 ὡς ἔχω | ὀσφῦν, μετάφρενον, τὸν τράχηλον, ἑνὶ λόγῳ | ὅλον τὸ σῶμ᾽, 'It crucifies my loins, back, neck – in short, my whole body' (see on Cicero 26). For a summarising *omnia* on its own at the end of an asyndetic list, see the examples collected by Fordyce (1961: 138) on Catull. 14.19.

Here are some further passages where the final element is attached by *denique*:

Sall. *Jug.* 15.2 (25) *gratia uoce, denique omnibus modis . . . nitebantur*
Tac. *Ann.* 11.27 (95) *discubitum inter conuiuas, oscula complexus, noctem denique actam licentia coniugali*
Tac. *Ann.* 11.38.3 (96) *ne secutis quidem diebus odii gaudii, irae tristitiae, ullius denique humani affectus signa dedit*.

In one of the passages a word for 'all' is also in the phrase that follows the asyndeton. We also quoted above one case in which *totumque* was without *denique* (Cic. *Off.* 1.150). The pattern whereby 'all' (adjectival or substantivised) follows an apparent asyndeton is a common one (cf. Leo 1960: 180, and see also the reference to Fordyce 1961: 138 above), and I add some further illustrations:

Cic. *Fin.* 4.49 (128) *Aristoteles Xenocrates, tota illa familia non dabit*
Cic. *Phil.* 6.18 (after 31) *eodem incumbunt municipia coloniae, cuncta Italia*
Cic. *Pis.* 37 *Achaia Thessalia Athenae, cuncta Graecia addicta*, 'Achaea, Thessaly, Athens – in fact the whole of Greece'. A tricolon plus summary.
Livy 28.1.8 *ea stationibus uigiliis, omni iusta militari custodia tuta et firma esse*
Tac. *Ann.* 12.33 (100) *ut aditus abscessus, cuncta nobis importuna et suis in melius essent*
Tac. *Ann.* 12.65.2 *ne quis ambigat decus pudorem corpus, cuncta regno uiliora habere*
Tac. *Ann.* 13.16.4 (103) *dolorem caritatem, omnis adfectus abscondere didicerat*
Tac. *Ann.* 13.42.4 (105) *crimen periculum, omnia potius toleraturum*
Tac. *Ann.* 13.57.2 (110) *quo uoto equi uiri, cuncta [uicta] occidioni dantur*
Tac. *Ann.* 15.19.2 (112) *quod multa securitate, nullis oneribus gratiam honores, cuncta prompta et obuia haberent*.

Similar to the type with *denique* is that with *postremo* introducing the final member: Sall. *Jug.* 16.3 (26) *perfecit uti fama fide, postremo omnibus suis rebus commodum regis anteferret.* Here too there is a move from the specific to the general, with *omnes* again. See on Sallust 26 for *postremo* in such structures.

7 Further Ambiguities of Interpretation

I conclude this chapter with a few more illustrations of the tendency, when there is what looks like end-of-list coordination, for the first two terms to differ markedly in some way from the third. Anyone attempting to analyse the colon structure is faced with the usually insoluble problem of deciding whether there is meant to be a sharp break after the second term.

At Cic. *Phil.* 2.62 (21) (*in urbe auri argenti, maximeque uini foeda direptio*) gold and silver go together as the two precious metals par excellence, and the pair is separated from wine not only by the coordinator but by the comparison conveyed by *maxime*. Cf. *Off.* 2.11 (119) (*partim sunt inanima, ut aurum argentum, ut ea quae gignuntur e terra, ut alia generis eiusdem*), where the contrast between gold and silver and the other *inanima* is made clear by the anaphoric construction, *ut . . . ut . . . ut.*

Cic. *Sest.* 21 (70) (*et quod erat eo nomine ut ingenerata familiae frugalitas uideretur, fauebant gaudebant, et ad integritatem maiorum spe sua hominem uocabant materni generis obliti*) has a special type of AB *et* C structure. The two verbs *fauebant gaudebant* are not independent of each other. The pair could be paraphrased as *fauebant gaudentes*, 'they favoured him, rejoicing', = 'they were pleased to favour him', with the second verb a modifier of the first. To this unit a separate clause with the verb *uocabant* is attached by *et* (structure [AB] [*et* C]).

Another passage from the same speech can be analysed along the same lines, though the final element is not introduced by a coordinator: *Sest.* 139 (*cum multis audacibus improbis, non numquam etiam potentibus dimicandum,* 'they must engage in desperate struggles with many who are reckless, wicked, and, sometimes, even powerful', Kaster 2006). The first two terms express a single concept ('recklessly wicked'), with a privative adjective in second position. The third member expresses a different concept. The phrase *non numquam etiam potentibus dimicandum* is possibly (in semantic terms) the second rather than the third member of the structure.

8 Conclusions

The figures and examples given above at 1 and 2 show that, at least in the texts considered here, end-of-list coordination is comparatively rare except in prayers, though it definitely exists, and must have increased in frequency at a later period in anticipation of the Romance languages (note the example from a late grammarian quoted above, 5). I have included a discussion of it here because sequences of three or more elements with coordination at the end not infrequently in Latin contain within a unitary pair semantically separable from the other term, with one of two structures, either [AB] [C*que*] or [A] [BC*que*]. In the first pattern the unit is asyndetic, and in the second syndetic. Both patterns would seem to rule out straightforward end-of-list coordination, and I have used of the first pattern the terms 'weak' or 'embedded' asyndeton bimembre. A colon divider such as an intrusive word or anaphora sometimes contributes to the division between one element of the triplet and the other. Admittedly however these structures raise difficulties of interpretation and classification, and it is often impossible to come up with decisive criteria for ruling out end-of-list coordination. My aim has been rather to show that the pattern ABC*que* is far from straightforward in Latin, regular though it may be in some modern languages.

See Richardson (2010: 241) on *h. Hom.* 5.173–4, on end-of-list connection in Greek: 'This type of asyndeton ("A, B, and C") is rare in Greek.' It is stated that there is only one example in Homer. The examples he has in mind are phrasal/clausal. Richardson cites Denniston (1934: 164).

CHAPTER XIX

Accumulations of Asyndeta: a Few Patterns

1 Antiquity and Continuity

By 'accumulation' I mean the juxtaposition of one asyndetic pair with another pair, or with more than one other, or the placement of an asyndetic pair alongside or within coordinated groups of various lengths and types. An asyndeton bimembre is in an accumulation if it is not free-standing but is part of a sequence of items that are coordinated syndetically or asyndetically, or have a mixture of both types of coordination. Accumulations have come up frequently already in these introductory chapters, and they will come up more extensively in the later chapters dealing with writers and genres. Accumulations are a prominent location for asyndeta bimembria, such that they are one determinant of this type of asyndeton (see XXXII.3.1). Two words that are usually coordinated may well be used for once asyndetically because they are placed in such a sequence. My aim here is simply to introduce accumulations containing asyndeta bimembria with a little more detail than has been provided so far, but the most comprehensive lists and classifications will be found in later chapters, particularly on Cicero and the historians.

I start for completeness with a list of the main places in preceding chapters where the phenomenon has been alluded to. See I.3 (for two juxtaposed pairs, in a Greek text), I.8 (on Sallust 3), III.3 (on the significance of accumulations for textual criticism, and with a list of places in the literary chapters where accumulation comes up), VI.5.1 (on structures of the types described as having 3 + 2 or 2 + 3 components), VI.9 (on privative adjectives in accumulations), VII.1 (on the type combining simplex + compound, particularly in curses), IX.1, XI.3, XI.5 (on various types, showing a mixture of moods or tenses and combinations of masculine and feminine, found especially in laws), XIII.4.1, XIII.4.2, XIII.4.3 (with a detailed classification of accumulations containing pairs of opposites), XIII.5.4 (on asyndetic pairs of adverbs in accumulations), XIV.2.5 (on accumulated pairs of kinship terms in laws). For accumulations as determinants of asyndeton see VII.2, XI.6, XII, XIII.4, XIV.3 (and XXXII.3.1).

Accumulations with asyndeton are very old, and not only in Latin in Italy. At Plaut. *As.* 259–60 in an augural context there are two pairs of bird names almost juxtaposed, the first pair asyndetic, the second coordinated (see XXII.6.3, XXIII.3). In Umbrian in another augural context of identical type (*Tab. Ig.* VIa.1) two pairs of bird names are again almost together, though in this case both pairs are asyndetic (see XXII.4.2, XXIII.3); on this type of variation see below. Accumulations containing asyndetic pairs are common in the Iguvine tablets (see XXII.4.2 and particularly XXII.4.6). The same pattern as that in the Plautine passage above also occurs in an ancient context in Cato, in the prayer to Mars at *Agr.* 141.2: *utique tu fruges frumenta, uineta uirgultaque grandire beneque euenire siris*. There are two (alliterative) pairs here. For the first see Wölfflin (1933: 261), citing Cic. *Verr.* 5.137 *tui milites in prouincia Sicilia frugibus frumentoque caruerunt* (coordinated, and a unit). As for the second, at Cic. *Leg.* 2.21 where tasks of augurs are elaborated a very similar pair to *uineta uigultaque* occurs, *uineta uirgetaque*: *uineta uirgetaque et salutem populi auguranto*. *Virgulta* means 'brushwood', and *uirgeta* (pl.) 'places where brushwood grows'. The context of the Ciceronian passage is again religious (see Dyck 2004: 305 on the text and stylistic features, and for alliterative religious pairs coordinated by *-que* see Norden 1939: 16–20). Another early example of similar structure, with a different form of coordination at the end, is at Plaut. *Ps.* 164 (*uorsa sparsa, tersa strata, lautaque unctaque omnia uti sint*). If this text and punctuation are accepted (see Fraenkel 1960: 138 n. 2 for the divisions; de Melo (Loeb) punctuates with commas after each of the first four words), two juxtaposed asyndetic pairs are followed by a pair with an old type of polysyndeton.

The structure showing an asyndetic pair followed by a syndetic may be old, but it persists strongly in later literary Latin (see e.g. XXVI.7.2.1, 7.3.1 (iii) for Cicero, XXX.6.2b on Sallust and Tacitus). Plautus however does not have the type very often and tends to prefer the order syndetic pair + asyndetic pair (see XXIII.7.1). He also has asyndetic pairs juxtaposed, particularly with forms of assonance, such as *Cist.* 208 *feror differor, distrahor diripior*, *Poen.* 221 *poliri expoliri, pingi fingi* (see XXIII.5.4, and for further such accumulations, including *Am.* 1062 *strepitus crepitus, sonitus tonitrus*, see XXIII.7.1; with this last cf. *Rhet. Her.* 2.8 *strepitus clamor crepitus exauditus*, and also Cic. *Har. resp.* 20 *auditus est strepitus cum fremitu*). With *Am.* 1062 compare Pacuvius *trag.* 263 Schierl *strepitus fremitus, clamor tonituum et rudentum sibilus* (see XXIV.6.2, 5), where the second pair is coordinated.

1 Antiquity and Continuity 213

The two structures, asyndeton + asyndeton, or asyndeton + coordination, are obviously similar and interchangeable.

These are not the only types of accumulations with asyndeta bimembria found in the earlier period. See for example, for a series of pairs, Pac. *trag.* 80.1 Schierl *quidquid est hoc, omnia animat format, alit auget, creat | sepelit* (see XXIV.6.3, 6–8 for the interpretation of this passage; cf. XIII.4.3, XVII.1). Such sequences continue to turn up later, not least in philosophical texts, with Greek precedent also (see Cicero 94–8). Or again, for an early republican asyndetic pair followed by a longer unified asyndeton see e.g. Lucilius 599–600 (XXV.1.1.2, 7) *hic cruciatur fame | frigore, inluuie inbalnitie imperfundi<ti>e incuria*, with an established alliterative asyndetic pair followed by a longer sequence of asyndetic *in*-privatives. Again, the structure (2 + more than 2 asyndetic items) can be paralleled in classical Latin (see the comments on Lucilius ad loc. for examples from Sallust and Tacitus; there are many examples in Cicero: see e.g. Cicero 12, 15, 85, 92–3, 117–18, 136, 139, 177).

Here is a strikingly prolonged asyndetic accumulation in a prayer in Umbrian: *Tab. Ig.* VI b.59–60 *nerf . sihutu . ansihutu . iouie . hostatu . anhostatu . tursitu . tremitu hondu . holtu . ninctu . nepitu . sonitu . sauitu . preplotatu . preuilatu* (= principes cinctos incinctos, iuuenes hastatos inhastatos, terreto tremefacito, pessumdato aboleto, ninguito inundato, sonato sauciato, praeplauditato praeuinculato; thus Buck 1904: 280; see also Fraenkel 1960: 138 n. 2, 342, from whom the punctuation here derives). The passage is translated by Poultney (1959: 278, 280) as follows: 'the chief citizens in office and not in office, the young men under arms and not under arms ... terrify them and cause them to tremble, cast them down to Hondus, to Hola, overwhelm them with snow, overwhelm them with water, deafen them with thunder and wound them, trample them under foot and bind them'. It has to be said, however, that any attempt at translating the passage is bound to be speculative, though the structure is clear. Poultney (279) comments on the alliteration: 'here follows a series of ten verbs indicating the nature of the afflictions to be visited on the enemies of Iguvium. The arrangement of the verbs in five alliterative pairs is the most striking instance of alliteration to be found anywhere in the Tables.' The passage is also discussed by Norden (1958: 160). The pairs vary in type. There are for example possibly two opposites of the structure positive + privative of the same root (complementarities), a pair of near-synonyms, and some complementary pairs. Forms of assonance were also seen in the limited number of Latin examples cited above.

For two alliterative pairs juxtaposed in an Oscan curse tablet note: **fakinss. fangvam biass. biítam** (Rix 2002: 117, Cm13), 'deeds, tongue, strength, life'. For *uires* and *uita* paired in Latin see Ennius *Ann.* 37 Skutsch *uires uitaque corpus meum nunc deserit omne* (see Watkins 1995: 155). For the same varied alliterative pattern in a Latin curse (written retrograde) see text no. 11 from the sanctuary of Isis and Magna Mater in Mainz, in Blänsdorf (2010: 177–8): *mentem memoriam cor cogitatum* (translated 'mind, memory, heart, thinking'). Another curse tablet from the same corpus (no. 8, Blänsdorf 2010: 173–5) has a similar pair, *deuotum defictum illum menbra medullas* (see Adams 2016: 250). Note the pronoun separating the pairs; single words sometimes split pairs, for example in the augural passage at Plaut. *As.* 259–60 (above), where the divider is a noun with preposition. Rather earlier (c. 100 BC), in the Johns Hopkins *defixiones* another asyndetic sequence with two alliterative pairs occurs. I quote 'Plotius' from Kropp (2008), 1.4.4/8, line 3 (see too Adams 2016: 108 with 111): *salutem c[orpus co]lorem, uires uirtutes*. *Vis* and *uirtus* are a unitary pair (see Wölfflin 1933: 280), though the other three terms seem miscellaneous.

It is clear that accumulations of pairs go well back in Italy in varieties of religious language, and that they persisted in similar types of texts into the Empire, but the matter should not be left there. Here are two reservations that must be added.

In the first place, accumulations, whether of the limited types that have been illustrated above or of the other types that are attested, are by no means confined to religious texts or language but are widespread in a diversity of genres and levels of the language. Asyndetic accumulations were probably heard in formulae in very mundane speech: see Petron. 61.9 *per scutum per ocream egi aginaui*, from a freedman's speech. There is suppressed alliteration in the second part, because we now know that *ago agino* was a fossilised asyndeton bimembre (see the Mainz curse tablet no. 8, referred to above (Blänsdorf 2010: 173–5, Adams 2016: 249), line 6 *quit aget aginat*); the *ag-/ag-* jingle has been lost in the perfect tense. Juxtaposed with the asyndetic pair of verbs is an asyndetic pair of nouns with anaphora of a preposition. The double pairing thus has a structure showing mixed syntax in the two parts. For a similar accumulation of an asyndetic pair of anaphoric prepositional expressions with a pair of words of a different part of speech (verbs, this time participles), see the curse tablet from Barchín del Hoyo, Hispania Tarraconensis (Curbera, Sierra Delage and Velázquez 1999, Kropp 2008a, 2.1.2/1): *pro me pro meis deuotos defixos inferis*. The first pair has double alliteration, and the second pair repetition of a prefix. However, mixed combinations, including the type containing an asyndetic

1 Antiquity and Continuity

pair of anaphoric prepositional phrases, as above, are found in literature too: e.g. Plaut. *Poen.* 835 *tenebrae latebrae, bibitur estur,* Cic. *Dom.* 68 (79, 83) *temere turbulente, per uim per furorem,* Sall. *Hist.* 4.60.17 Ramsey (47, 83) *socios amicos, procul iuxta sitos, inopes potentisque trahant excindant* (and note that there is also an asyndetic pair of verbs at the end), Livy 23.27.5 (42) *ut quisque arma ceperat, sine imperio sine signo, incompositi inordinati in proelium runt,* Tac. *Hist.* 2.5.2 (4, 50) *tribuni centurionesque et uolgus militum industria licentia per uirtutes per uoluptates, ut cuique ingenium adsciscebantur.* Such structures are moreover found in laws and the like too: they are thus very widespread. Here are some legal examples: *SCC De aquaeductibus* (Riccobono 1968: 279, text 41, Chap. 125) *itinera actus paterent darentur* (correlative pattern: see XVII), *Lex Cornelia de XX quaestoribuus* Col. II. 15–18 *in eis uiatoribus praeconibus legundeis sublegundeis in eius uiatoris praeconis locum uiatorem praeconem legant sublegant, quoius in locum per leges plebeiue scita uiatorem praeconem legei sublegei non licebit, Tabula Heracleensis* 115 (Crawford 1996: 1.367) *proue quo datum depensum est erit* (two participles and two auxiliary verbs, the latter two belonging with both participles). For an asyndetic prepositional pair juxtaposed with an asyndetic pair of nouns in Umbrian, see *Tab. Ig.* IIa.25–6, quoted at XXII.4.6.

My second reservation is this. Even in early prayers accumulations of the type seen above in a prayer in Cato (asyndeton + coordination) were not the standard means of associating two such pairs. In prayers, including those quoted by Cato, there are indeed groups of two (or more) pairs (sometimes alliterative), but the members of both (or all) pairs are usually linked by *-que*: see Cato *Agr.* 134.2 *precor uti sies uolens propitius mihi liberisque meis, domo familiaeque meae,* 141.2 *morbos uisos inuisosque, uiduertatem uastitudinemque, calamitates intemperiasque,* Macr. *Sat.* 3.9.10 *qui in his locis regionibusque agris urbibusque habitant abducatis ... uti uos eas urbes agrosque capita aetatesque eorum deuotas consecratasque habeatis.*

Greek accumulations of single-word pairs are collected by Denniston (1952: 103–4), a number of them from Plato and Aristotle. One such, with pairs of opposites, is Arist. *Metaph.* 986a32 λευκὸν μέλαν, γλυκὺ πικρόν, ἀγαθὸν κακόν, μέγα μικρόν (see on Cicero 94–8). In Cicero accumulations, especially of opposites, are common in the philosophical works (for some statistics see below, 2), as at *Fin.* 2.36 (94–8) (*quid iudicant sensus? dulce amarum, leue asperum, prope longe, stare mouere, quadratum rotundum*), which is not unlike the passage from Aristotle. Sequences like these are not to be associated with early religious pairs or the like, but reflect the utility of asyndeta in expressing succinctly the types of contraries in which philosophers were interested. Other opposites are to be found in Denniston's collection.

Accumulated pairs are not necessarily composed of opposites. Note e.g. Hom. *Od.* 15.406 εὔβοτος εὔμηλος, οἰνοπληθὴς πολύπυρος '(land) rich in herds, rich in flocks, full of wine, abounding in wheat'. The unity of the first pair (referring to types of livestock) is underlined by the repeated prefix. The second pair has a loose unity too, in that both terms denote an abundance of certain products of the land.

At Hdt. 1.32 an accumulation has a slightly different structure: ἄπηρος δέ ἐστί, ἄνουσος, ἀπαθὴς κακῶν, εὔπαις εὐηδής, 'and he is free from deformity, sickness, all evil, and happy in his children, his comeliness' (Godley, Loeb, slightly modified). These are not two pairs, but an asyndetic tricolon is followed by an asyndeton bimembre. This structure (3 + 2) and its reverse (2 + 3, which is more common) are frequent in Latin (see above on Lucilius 599–600 with cross references). Again the unity of the two groups is indicated by the repetition of two prefixes, alpha-privative and then εὐ-.

For another early accumulation see Aeschylus *Supp.* 794–6 ἢ λισσὰς αἰγίλιψ ἀπρόσ-|δεικτος οἰόφρων κρεμὰς | γυπιὰς πέτρα. See Johansen and Whittle (1980: 3.144): 'The attrs. fall into three pairs, of which the first and the last emphasize the inaccessibility of the crag, the second (ἀπρόσδεικτος οἰόφρων) its loneliness.' See also Sommerstein (2019: 303) ad loc., and XXIII.4.

Much later, in the New Testament, note the example of the 2 + 3 structure at 2 Tim. 4.2: κήρυξον τὸν λόγον, ἐπίστηθι εὐκαίρως ἀκαίρως, ἔλεγξον ἐπιτίμησον παρακάλεσον, 'preach the word, be urgent in season and out of season, convince, rebuke, exhort' (see also VI.6). The structure I refer to begins at εὐκαίρως. There are first two adverbs (modifying the preceding imperative) with semantically contrasting prefixes, and then three asyndetic imperatives. This is another accumulation in which the groups consist of different parts of speech.

2 Types, Statistics, Textual Criticism

I have said quite a lot above about one type of accumulation, that in which an asyndetic pair is followed by a syndetic. The purpose of the discussion was mainly to show what I mean by 'accumulation'. Other types remain unmentioned, but this is not the place to attempt a systematic collection of all types, as considerable detail has been given in some of the literary

2 Types, Statistics, Textual Criticism 217

chapters. Here are the main references. At XXVI.7.2.1 five categories of accumulations containing pairs of nouns in Cicero's speeches are set out (see also 7.2.3 on pairs of verbs in accumulations in the speeches). For full statistics concerning accumulations in the speeches see 7.2.5: 45 out of 91 pairs are in accumulations, or 50 per cent. For accumulations in the philosophica see XXVI.7.3.1, where there is a sixfold classification of types. It is stated that 42 of a total of 68 asyndeta bimembria in the philosophical sample are in accumulations, i.e. roughly two-thirds, a significantly higher figure than that for the speeches, a reflection presumably of a stylistic feature of philosophical discourse. It is pointed out (see 7.3.1 (ii)) that many of these accumulations have pairs of opposites. For Tacitus *Annals* see XXX.5.2.3, with long lists of various patterns of accumulation, and particularly 6.2a, b, d, e, f, where Tacitus and Sallust are compared in their use of a variety of types of accumulations, with extensive collections of the examples. For Sallust see also. XXX.3.3.3a, c, d, e. It is remarked at the end of 3.3.3 that a 'high proportion' of asyndeta bimembria in Sallust occur in certain structures, 'usually marked by an accumulation'. For Tacitus' *Histories* there are similar classifications of the types of accumulation at 4.2.4a, c, d, e. At XXXI.3.8 (end) twenty accumulations in the sample books of Livy are listed with passage numbers, and these are about a third of the 66 numbered asyndeta in the chapter. For types in Plautus see XXIII.7.

In Caesar (*Civ.*) asyndeton bimembre is rare, and accumulations come into their own as settling textual issues. At XXVIII.2.1 on passage **c** (= 2, 3) the manuscript reading (with asyndeton) is supported by the fact that it presents a particular type of accumulation (see also XXI.3). Also at XXVIII.2.1 the rule is stated, based on the evidence of the whole text, that 'pairs of names are not used asyndetically unless they are in certain types of accumulations', and an emendation adopted by Damon (addition of a coordinator in a pair of names) is justified by this rule. In the conclusion (3) to the chapter it is stated: 'Above all, it is particular structures [i.e. accumulations] that generate the asyndeton, not semantic factors. This work of Caesar is important as suggesting criteria that a textual critic might use in deciding between syndetic and asyndetic coordination.'

There are other places where patterns of accumulation support a particular reading. See for example XXX.3.3.4 and the reference to Sallust 8, and particularly XXXI.3.9 and the discussion of the text at Livy 20. See too XIII.4.1 on an emendation of Tacitus 56, 57 which is supported by the nature of the accumulation that it would be in.

3 Juxtaposed Asyndeta That Are Open to Misinterpretation

I comment here briefly on a type of accumulation that may be mistaken as showing end-of-list coordination.

It is stated at XVIII.4 that the 'clearest examples of asyndetic sequences with a coordinated term at the end that cannot be treated as mere end-of-list coordination are to be found in longer sequences with the structure [AB] [CD*que*]'. Editors and commentators have to be careful not to assume without consideration that any sequence ABCD*que* has four terms of equal status, with the last attached by a coordinator. Consider for example the headline of an article by Gideon Haigh, *Sober, drunk, united or disunited, visitors were simply inferior*, in *The Times*, 9 January 2018, p. 67. Here the four adjectives manifestly fall into two pairs of opposites, and *or* only coordinates *disunited* to *united*. At XVIII.4 an example of this type from Cicero (10) is quoted. See too Sall. *Cat.* 61.9 (21) *laetitia maeror, luctus atque gaudia*, where there are two pairs with exactly the same semantic content but expressed differently and with the members in reversed order in the second pair. Another interesting passage is Livy 8.33.20 *ciuitatem in laetitia uictoria, supplicationibus ac gratulationibus esse*, where there is definitely not end-of-list coordination (for discussion see XXXI.3.7). It seems essential in a critical text to add a comma after the asyndetic pair if the four terms fall into two unified groups, as a comma will reveal the editor's interpretation of the phrase structure but its absence will be non-committal about the structure. A comma after the first term as well as the second will on the other hand suggest that the sequence is taken to have end-of-list coordination.

4 Conclusions

Asyndeta bimembria in accumulations go back a long way, but those accumulations we noted in early Latin prayers (unlike those in Umbrian) tend to consist of asyndetic phrases (not single words) with their members (themselves single words) linked internally by *-que*. It would be a mistake to see in accumulations found in literary texts simply the remnants of an old sacral feature of the language. The literary language had developed varied structures in the historical period, probably under Greek influence in the language of philosophy. Drafters of laws found useful the succinct character of juxtaposed near-synonyms intended to rule out possible loopholes, and accumulations are found in laws too. Legal contexts tended to prompt asyndeta in Cicero, and not least in accumulations, as e.g. at *Off.*

4 Conclusions

3.70 (123, 124, 146, 147) *idque uersari in tutelis societatibus, fiduciis mandatis, rebus emptis uenditis, conductis locatis.*

Accumulations were far from being restricted to religious or legal contexts. They obviously had a strong rhetorical flavour, and were suited to dramatic utterances (note Cic. *Cat.* 1.32 (57, 58) *ut Catilinae profectione omnia patefacta inlustrata, oppressa uindicata esse uideatis*). They are also common in historiography, a formal genre, but not excluded from mundane speech, as we saw from a passage of Petronius.

It would be easy to list other types of accumulations (as is done elsewhere), but the few mentioned here are enough to suggest how common such forms of stylisation were. It is noticeable how regular the patterns above are. Personal taste came into it, as will be seen later in Sallust's unusual preference for *atque* in coordinated pairs following asyndetic pairs (see XXX.6.2b), but certain recurrent patterns, spread across various genres, are suggestive of a sort of rhetorical standardisation of the educated language. The component terms vary, but there are many abstract nouns, terms expressing general concepts or aspects of life and terms to do with emotions and professional activities. Accumulations are by no means predominantly used in narrative, and the old idea that asyndeton conveys 'speed' or the like would not fit much of the evidence. At Cic. *Off.* 1.128 (117, 118), for example (*status incessus, sessio accubito, uoltus oculi manuum motus teneat illud decorum*), various actions are listed (standing and walking, sitting and lying down), but these have nothing to do with 'breathless or excited' action on a particular occasion. Rather, they express contrasting forms of human behaviour (some of them marked by inaction).

It was also suggested that accumulations may generate the choice of asyndetic coordination, and that the presence of a pair in an accumulation may be relevant to textual decisions.

CHAPTER XX

Discontinuous Asyndeton and Conjunct Hyperbaton

1 Conjunct Hyperbaton

Frequently a coordinated pair (or longer sequence), of adjectives, nouns or other parts of speech, is split up by the insertion of a word or phrase to follow the first member of the coordination (see e.g. Devine and Stephens 2006: 586–91, calling the pattern 'conjunct hyperbaton'; also Hofmann and Szantyr 1965: 693, Gray 2015: 65–6). A classic example in English is *brave man and true*. In Latin too it is often *homo* (or *uir*) that is the intrusive term, as at Cic. *Har. resp.* 28: *Brogitaro Gallograeco, impuro homini ac nefario*, *Sest.* 56 *Brogitaro, impuro homini atque indigno illa religione* (in both places with the same referent);[1] see further e.g. for *homo*, Cic. *Att.* 5.15.3, 5.21.6, *Fam.* 1.9.19, *Prov. cons.* 15, etc., and for *uir* instead of *homo*, Cic. *Fam.* 7.18.1 *esse fortem uirum et constantem*, *Fin.* 2.80 *et bonum uirum et comem et humanum fuisse*, Livy 8.8.16 *strenuus uir peritusque militiae*. At Catull. 12.8–9 (*est enim leporum | differtus puer ac facetiarum*) *puer* has the same function.

The terms that are split are not infrequently opposites, as at Cic. *Att.* 6.3.4 *stante Pompeio uel etiam sedente*, *Fin.* 1.38 *aut in uoluptate esse aut in dolore*, *Fin.* 2.23 *nec occidentem (solem) umquam uiderint nec orientem*, *Fin.* 3.58 *nec in bonis ponamus nec in malis*, *Fin.* 4.54 *quod aliud alio melius esset aut peius*, *Fin.* 5.15 *quid sit et bonorum extremum et malorum*, *Fin.* 5.39 *et uiuere uitem et mori dicimus*, *Fin.* 5.47 *dignum libero aut indignum*, Catull. 66.2 *qui stellarum ortus comperit atque obitus*, Caes. *Civ.* 3.91.3 *ut aut uiuo mihi aut mortuo gratias agas*, Hor. *Ep.* 1.2.16 *Iliacos intra muros peccatur et extra*.

Another category consists of split pairs expressing a totality (merisms): e.g. Plaut. *Rud.* 346 *si deos decepit et homines*, Cic. *Fin.* 2.111 *summum pecudis bonum et hominis*, *Fin.* 3.67 *hominum causa et deorum*, *Fin.* 4.25

---

[1] Examples from Tony Corbeill.

ex animo constamus et corpore, Nat. 1.95 *et maris deos et feminas esse dicitis.* With this last example, with its masculine/feminine terms defining the totality of gods, compare in Greek Men. *Kol.* fr. 1 (Körte and Sandbach) (Arnott 1996–2000: 186, lines 3–4): θεοῖς 'Ολυμπίοις εὐχώμεθα | 'Ολυμπίασι, πᾶσι πάσαις. Here masculine and feminine adjectives applied to the gods are split also (by a verb), but in this case the two terms are asyndetic rather than coordinated, i.e. they display discontinuous asyndeton of the type that is the subject of this chapter (see XI.2).

Conjunct hyperbaton is also common in Greek. Here are a few instances from Demosthenes and Menander: Dem. 5.2 δυσκόλου δ' ὄντος φύσει καὶ χαλεποῦ τοῦ βουλεύεσθαι, 5.6 διοικοῦντα Φιλίππῳ καὶ πρυτανεύοντα, 6.3 ἔργῳ κωλύειν καὶ πράξεσιν, Men. *Georg.* 78 δυσνουθετήτῳ θηρίῳ καὶ δυσκόλῳ, *Epit.* 716 λόγου δὲ δεῖται ταῦτα καὶ συμπείσεως.

This is not the place to dwell on conjunct hyperbaton, but note that the following two examples share a feature: Cic. *Prov. cons.* 8 *in mentibus uestris oculisque defixit*, 25 *mentis uestras uoluntatesque mutastis.* The placement of *uestris/uestras* after the second nouns (to which they are also applicable) would have produced an undesirable clausula (a sequence of long syllables), whereas with the present word order the clausula is a sought-after one (cretic–trochee: see Nisbet 1961: xvii). At *Fin.* 1.51 (*saepti esse et muniti uidentur*) the position of *esse* avoids a heroic clausula.

The intrusive word is not infrequently a weak term such as a clitic (including the verb 'to be': see above several times, and further below; *homo* is of this type). Cf. Catull. 28.9 *bene me ac diu supinum . . . irrumasti*, with a pronoun, 112.2 *multus es et pathicus*, Hor. *Sat.* 1.8.18 *curae sunt atque labori.* The emphasis lies rather on the disjoined terms. For another weak separating term see e.g. Cic. *Fin.* 1.42 *omnis rectas res atque laudabilis*, Cic. *Mur.* 20 *multas res ac magnas*, Catull. 12.5 *sordida res et inuenusta est.* Cf. Men. *Epit.* 527 ὡς ἀναιδὴς ἦσθα καὶ ἰταμός τις 'so bold you were and brutal', with the verb 'to be'.

2 Discontinuous Asyndeton

It is a variation on conjunct hyperbaton that is the topic of this chapter, namely the pattern in which the coordinator that follows the intrusive term is omitted. This is a form of asyndeton combined with hyperbaton, as for example if *impuro homini ac nefario* above were converted to *impuro homini, nefario* (see above on Men. *Kol.* fr. 1). The structure may be called 'discontinuous asyndeton'. In such cases there would potentially have been a pause, with the final term capable of particular emphasis. Some examples are collected and discussed below.

A semantically distinctive instance is at Lucr. 5.323 (**15**): *deminui debet, recreari, cum recipit res*. The verbs are opposites (reversives), = 'diminished, remade'. For a similar asyndetic pair of opposites (but without hyperbaton), cf. Cic. *Dom.* 137 (**69**) *dirueris aedificaris* (of knocking down and building up). For another example of asyndetic opposites, this time separated again, see Cic. *Orat.* 131: *sed est faciendum etiam ut irascatur iudex, mitigetur*. In this sentence there is a long sequence of pairs of opposed verbs, and in the first pair the subject *iudex* is inserted. The mental state of the referent is reversed. The similarity between this type of discontinuous asyndeton and conjunct hyperbaton can be seen from the presence of pairs of opposites in both structures.

It was pointed out earlier (II.2.2) that not all adjectival asyndeta supposedly showing discontinuous asyndeton prove to be genuinely of this structure, because the adjectives may differ in rank or status (with one attached closely to the noun and the other modifying the whole phrase noun + adjective). Here first is a pair that is difficult to interpret.

Ennius *Ann.* 141 Skutsch (XXIV.5.1.1, 7) (*circum sos quae sunt magnae gentes opulentae*) is printed thus by Goldberg and Manuwald (2018) and translated, 'around them, who are great peoples and wealthy' (I.181). The translation makes it obvious that they have taken the adjectives as asyndetic and with hyperbaton. Indeed we find at Sall. *Jug.* 14.19 precisely this combination as a conjunct hyperbaton: *magni estis et opulenti*. Note too *Jug.* 79.2 *Cyrenenses quoque magni atque opulenti fuere*. These Sallustian coordinated examples give good support for a discontinuous asyndeton in the passage of Ennius (which, if it is thus, would be better conveyed by a comma after *gentes*), as distinct from layering (= [*magnae gentes*] [*opulentae*]). On this latter view the two adjectives would differ in rank, with *magnae* the attribute of *gentes* and *opulentae* a modifier of *magnae gentes*. It has to be accepted that in the fragmentary state of the text the correct interpretation of this phrase does remain uncertain. It is clear from *TLL* VI.2.1858.57ff. (with cross references) that *magna* and *maxima* are standard epithets of *gens*, whereas this Ennian passage is the only place cited at 1858.69 of *opulenta* with *gens*, apart from one in the Vulgate. If *magna gens* is a set phrase, *opulentae* might just differ in rank from the other adjective. I would give greater weight myself to the coordinated pairs with *magni* and *opulenti* in Sallust above, one of them indeed discontinuous.

There is no such uncertainty about Plaut. *Trin.* 299 *nil ego istos moror faeceos mores, turbidos* (see II.2.4, 1)). The two adjectives are both

2 Discontinuous Asyndeton

judgemental and pejorative, and are near-synonyms. The punctuation is that of Leo, Lindsay and de Melo, and it must be right. The hostile judgement would be intensified not only by the second adjective, but also probably by a pause.

For examples from Terence[2] see *Ad.* 846 *fauillae plena, fumi ac pollinis*, *Eun.* 1079 *fatuos est, insulsus tardus*, *Hau.* 1061 *rufamne illam uirginem, caesiam, sparso ore, adunco naso?* In a case such as the second here (and some others in this chapter) another possible determinant has to be acknowledged, mechanical second-position placement of the copula.

I take Lucr. 1.523 (1) *omne quod est, spatium uacuum constaret inane*, 'the whole universe would be a space vacant, empty' as a discontinuous adjectival asyndeton: see XXIV.7.1.1. *Constaret* is equivalent to the verb 'to be' (*esset*). For the verb 'to be' or the like (or a phrase containing it) inserted in this type of discontinuous asyndeton see e.g. Ter. *Eun.* 1079 quoted above, and Cic. *Fin.* 2.12 *inuidiosum nomen est, infame suspectum*. Cf. Men. *Asp.* 88 ἱμάτι' ἔνεστ' ἐνταῦθα, χλαμύδες 'in there there are clothes, cloaks', *Sik.* 150 ὄχλος εἶ, φλυάρου μεστός, 'riff-raff you are, full of drivel'. In some of these cases the verb 'to be' is not the only intrusive term.

At Cic. *Att.* 2.20.2 (175) (*Pompeius adfirmat non esse periculum, adiurat*) the second verb is stronger and a pause for thought is implied (see ad loc.). The intrusive element here is dependent on the first verb.

For the interpretation of Cic. *Fam.* 7.5.3 (*probiorem hominem, meliorem uirum, pudentiorem, esse neminem*) see on Cicero 199. *Vir* was illustrated earlier (1) as an intrusive term in cases of conjunct hyperbaton, and here it is found in the asyndetic variant. Cf. Hom. *Od.* 1.198–9 χαλεποὶ δέ μιν ἄνδρες ἔχουσιν, | ἄγριοι, 'cruel men keep him, savage' (here ἄνδρες is not the only element that intrudes: see above).

At Tac. *Ann.* 1.16.2 (126) (*lasciuire miles, discordare, pessimi cuiusque sermonibus praebere aures, denique luxum et otium cupere, disciplinam et laborem aspernari*) *lasciuire* and *discordare* verbs of the same semantic type ('ran riot and engaged in disputes') seem to be a discontinuous unit within a longer sequence. The intrusive term *miles* is similar to *homo* or *uir*, and *iudex* at Cic. *Orat.* 131 above, where the two verbs in discontinuous asyndeton are again embedded within a much longer sequence.

Finally, an example with a more complicated structure: Lucr. 1.557–8 (2) *longa diei |infinita aetas* (see XXIV.7.1.1). The adjectives *longa* and *infinita* are separated (with the second stronger than the first), but the separating term *diei* is a genitive dependent on *aetas*, from which it is separated. The

---

[2] I am grateful to Giuseppe Pezzini for drawing these to my attention.

hyperbaton in this case is twofold, and the pattern would more suitably be called a poetic interlocking word order.

A few textually uncertain or disputed cases of discontinuous asyndeton are discussed elsewhere: Cic. *Att.* 8.2.3 *oram quidem maritimam iam relinquemus, Afranium exspectabimus <et?> Petreium* (see XXVI after Cicero 171, with reference to another such passage).

3 Discontinuous Asyndeton in Menander

Discontinuous asyndeton is quite common in Menander, who also has conjunct hyperbaton (a few examples of which were cited above, 1). Here are some asyndetic examples (two others were quoted in the last section), with Arnott's translations, sometimes modified:

Asp. 239–40 χρυσίο[ν] | ἔχων τοσοῦτο, παῖδας, ἥκεις δεσπότῃ | ταῦτ' ἀποκομίζων, 'when you had so much money and slaves, you've brought them all back for your master?'

Dysk. 448 κοίτας φέρονται, στραμνί', 'hampers they bring, wine jars'.

Dysk. 662 εὔχεσθε τὸν γέροντα σωθῆναι κακῶς, | ἀνάπηρον ὄντα, χωλόν, 'pray that the old man's rescue may be bungled, leaving him disabled, a cripple'.

Dysk. 963–4 ἐκδότω | στεφάνους τις ἡμῖν, δᾷδα, 'give us garlands someone, a torch'.

Mis. 803 ἀ[π]όρως ζῆθ', ὀδυνηρῶς, ἀσθενῶ[ς, 'make your life futile, painful, feeble'.

Sam. 14–15 κύνας γὰρ ἔτρεφέ μοι, | [ἵππο]υς, 'he kept hounds for me, horses'.

Sam. 348 χαμαιτύπη δ' ἄνθρωπος, ὄλεθρος, 'a whore the woman is, a bitch'.

4 Conclusions

I have deliberately not collected many examples of asyndetic discontinuity in Latin in this chapter, because the phenomenon is well represented in the literary chapters. The aim has been to illustrate some distinctive types, and to relate this form of asyndeton to conjunct hyperbaton. The terms seen above tend to be opposites, or near-synonyms with the second reinforcing or capping the first. There is a unity to the pairs. On the other hand several of the examples in Menander are more miscellaneous. Any attempt to find old poetic patterns in such asyndeta or the influence of Greek would not be convincing, given that conjunct hyperbaton is extremely widespread in Latin.

CHAPTER XXI

Asyndetic Pairs Dependent on a Single Preposition

1 Introduction

Asyndetic pairs dependent on a single preposition have tended to be treated as problematic by editors and scribes, and manuscript variations are not unusual. I have not, however, noted explicit discussions of the issue by editors (see however Preuss 1881: 53). The criteria that may be used by an editor in judging possible cases of asyndeton include structural factors, and an author's practice elsewhere. I start with a structural pattern and variants, and then refer to two possible asyndeta of this type in Caesar's *Bellum ciuile*, which are dealt with in detail in XVIII. Finally, I consider possible examples in several other writers.

2 Structural Patterns

At Tac. *Ann.* 1.61.1 (63) (*ob propinquos amicos, denique ob casus bellorum et sortem hominum*) there is the familiar pattern (see e.g. XIX.1) showing juxtaposition of an asyndetic pair with a coordinated pair (here, of phrases). The coordinated pair is introduced by *denique* (for *denique* see e.g. XVIII.6, XXX.3.3.3g and on Cicero 1 and Sallust 36, and also the next paragraph). On the semantic unity of each of the pairs here see on Tacitus 63.

With the above passage cf. Cic. *Off.* 1.126 (116) *sed quoniam decorum illud in omnibus factis dictis, in corporis denique motu et statu cernitur*. Again we find an asyndetic pair dependent on a preposition, followed by a coordinated pair (of phrases) dependent on the same preposition, repeated, and again introduced by *denique*. Both pairs have a unity.

These two passages are structurally identical, and it would be perverse to emend away the asyndeta, which are appropriate to and determined by the structure.

Similar patterns are also found. Note first Tac. *Ann.* 3.26.1 (75) *uetustissimi mortalium, nulla adhuc mala libidine, sine probro scelere eoque sine poena aut coercitionibus agebant*. The second, coordinated, pair is introduced by a coordinator (*eoque*), just as the second pairs above are introduced by *denique*. The preposition again is the same in both the asyndetic and the coordinated part. See further on Tacitus 75 for details of the coordinations here.

At Cic. *Sest.* 88 (15) (*ad ferrum faces, ad cotidianam caedem incendia rapinas se cum exercitu suo contulit*) a preposition is first used with an asyndetic pair, and then repeated, this time with an asyndetic tricolon of single terms. For pairs dependent on a preposition elsewhere in Cicero see the note on Cicero 15.

Slightly different again is Cic. *Nat.* 2.150 *ad pingendum fingendum, ad scalpendum, ad neruorum eliciendos sonos* (see the apparatus of Pease 1958: 940). An asyndetic pair dependent on a preposition is again at the head of the construction, and the preposition is then repeated, twice, to form an asyndetic pair of phrases. Cf. Plaut. *Poen.* 221 *pingi fingi*.

All the above examples contain an asyndetic pair governed by a single preposition that is part of a longer prepositional sequence in which the preposition is repeated at least once. The following two passages also have asyndetic pairs in long prepositional sequences, but in these the preposition occurs just once, at the head of the construction:

Cic. *Off.* 3.70 (123, 124, 146, 147) *idque uersari in tutelis societatibus, fiduciis mandatis, rebus emptis uenditis, conductis locatis, quibus uitae societas contineretur.*
Four unitary pairs are juxtaposed, all depending on *in*.

Tac. *Ann.* 15.54.1 (113, 114, 115) *sed mirum quam inter diuersi generis ordinis, aetatis sexus, dites pauperes taciturnitate omnia cohibita sint.*
A threefold structure this time, with *inter* at the head. The construction is probably elliptical in its first two parts. *Dites pauperes* is directly dependent on *inter*, but *generis ordinis* and *aetatis sexus* are not: understand 'those of, people of', *homines*. Alternatively the genitives may be dependent on *dites pauperes*, in which case there would be just a single asyndetic pair dependent on the preposition. Woodman (2004) translates in line with the first interpretation ('among people of different lineage, rank, age, and sex, rich and poor'), though the 'Oxford comma' after 'age' obscures the structure. See also Ash (2018: 248).

At Cic. *Dom.* 121 (**9a**) (*nihil loquor de pontificio iure, nihil de ipsius uerbis dedicationis, nihil <u>de religione caerimoniis</u>*) the anaphoric sequence with *nihil* repeated constitutes a special structure, another type of accumulation. For the two asyndetic nouns together in an asyndetic tricolon see *Dom.* 1, cited at Cicero 16.

3 Pairs Dependent on a Preposition in Caesar

In a passage of Livy discussed at XXXI.3.7 there is also just one preposition, but it is followed by an asyndetic and then a coordinated pair rather than another asyndeton: 8.33.20 *propter Q. Fabium ciuitatem in laetitia uictoria, supplicationibus ac gratulationibus esse*. Cic. *Fam.* 5.8.5 (**197, 198**) has a superficial resemblance to *Off*. 3.70 and Tac. *Ann.* 15.54.1 just cited, but it is different syntactically: *in omnibus publicis priuatis, forensibus domesticis, tuis amicorum, hospitum clientium negotiis*. Again the preposition is expressed just once and there are four pairs (the first two with opposites) following, but the pairs are adjectival or genitival, and only a single noun, *negotiis*, depends on *in*.

Finally, note the following passage, in which Shackleton Bailey (1965–70) admits a coordinator in an asyndeton dependent on a preposition: *Att*. 2.23.3 (SB 43) (**159**) *credibile non est quantum ego in consiliis <et> prudentia tua et, quod maximum est, quantum in amore et fide ponam*. This is the text of Shackleton Bailey (*et* add. 5). Note that *tua*, though it is in agreement with *prudentia*, goes with both the nouns preceding. The asyndetic expression is followed by a coordinator (*et*) and then by a coordinated expression in a parallel clause, with the preposition *in* repeated in both expressions. So at Tacitus **75** above (*uetustissimi mortalium, nulla adhuc mala libidine, sine probro scelere eoque sine poena aut coercitionibus agebant*) an asyndetic pair dependent on a preposition is linked by a coordinator (*-que* in this case) to a coordinated expression dependent on the same preposition, repeated. Similarly at Cicero **159** above the final two prepositional expressions are not only linked by *et*, but also the repetition of *quantum* (and of *in*) is paralleled by the repetition of *nihil* and of the preposition *de* at Dom. 121 (**9a**) above (*nihil loquor de pontificio iure, nihil de ipsius uerbis dedicationis, nihil de religione caerimoniis*). Another similar structure to that in **159**, but without preposition, is found at Cic. *Dom*. 23 (**8**) *cuius eximia uirtus dignitas, et, in eo negotio quod gessit, fides et continentia* (for the structural and semantic details see on **159**). The insertion of *et* at **159** does not therefore look necessary.

Not infrequently then asyndeta bimembria with a preposition are located in various similar structures, and recognition of these ought to deter editors from emending in one place but not in another.

3 Pairs Dependent on a Preposition in Caesar, *Bellum ciuile*

I turn now to two passages of Caesar, for full details of which see XXVIII.2.1 (see also XIX.2). First, *Civ*. 3.4.3 *<ex> Creta Lacedaemone, ex Ponto atque Syria reliquisque ciuitatibus*, where *<ex>* is the reading of M after correction by a later hand. This text is certainly right. Even though

Caesar rarely in the *Civ.* uses asyndetic pairs, least of all pairs of proper names with a single preposition (see further below), the structure here was seen above in a number of passages, that is a preposition with a dependent asyndetic pair, then repetition of the preposition, complemented this time by a coordinated phrase. There would be no justification in this structure for adding a coordinator between the first two place names.

The second is *Civ.* 1.30.4 *in Lucanis Bruttiisque per legatos suos ciuium Romanorum dilectus habebat*. The phrase *in Lucanis Bruttiisque* has a manuscript variation: S is without the coordinator and *-que* is in U. The presence of the coordinator is in line with Caesar's practice elsewhere in the work. At XXVIII Appendix 1 pairs of nouns and pairs of noun phrases dependent on a preposition are listed from the whole work, and there is no case of an uncoordinated pair dependent on a single preposition, apart from that at 3.4.3 above, which is introduced by emendation, and is in a significant structure. It is also shown at XXVIII.2.1 that pairs of place or people's names (whether with preposition or not) are not used asyndetically by Caesar in this work unless the asyndeton is structurally determined. The text of S at 1.30.4 must be wrong.

It is worth emphasising again, first, that an asyndeton bimembre may be motivated by the structure in which it is placed, and, second, that whenever possible a textual variation between syndetic and asyndetic coordination should be assessed not simply by comparing the methods of coordination used in other examples of the same two words, but by comparing the methods used in all other examples in the work of the same types of words or phrases. In that way a general rule may be established.

4 Asyndetic Pairs Dependent on a Single Preposition that Are Not in Significant Structures

Several examples are found in Cato's *De agricultura* (see the list containing various types in Adams (2016: 78)): 14.5 *uilla ex calce caementis* (but 14.1 *calce et caementis*), 157.3 *ad omnia uulnera tumores*.

The construction occurs in the *Lex agraria*: see e.g. 27 (Crawford 1996: 1.116–17) *de eo agro loco . . . quo pro agro loco*, 32 *extra eum agrum locu[m*, 34 *de eo agro loco* (the pair translated 'land or piece of land'). See too *Lex Quinctia* (Crawford 1996: 2.795) line 13 *in castella lacus [im]mi<t>tatur*. Kalb (1912: 137) cites several such expressions in legal language, but not with reference to the prepositional structure: *Dig.* 5.1.80 *si in iudicis nomine praenomine erratum est* (with a dependent genitive: see further below), 37.11.8.2 *sed et cum in praenomine cognomine erratum est*.

4 Asyndetic Pairs Dependent on a Single Preposition 229

At Cic. *Dom.* 35 (**32**) (*non aetas eius qui adoptabat est quaesita, ut in Cn. Aufidio M. Pupio*) there are two names in asyndeton at the end of a colon. Pairs of names, cited *exempli gratia*, are not infrequently used thus in asyndeton, with or without a preposition (see IV.3).

At Sall. *Hist.* 4.60.17 Ramsey (**46**) (*conuenas olim sine patria parentibus*) the pairing was an established one (see Sall. *Cat.* 52.3 (**17**) *patriae parentibus, aris atque focis suis bellum parauere*; in this last example there is the familiar structural pattern, asyndetic pair + coordinated pair).

At Tac. *Ann.* 2.26.2 (**30**) (*formido fuit apud fugientes occursantes*) the terms dependent on *apud* are opposites, and Tacitus had a taste for asyndetic pairs expressing opposites (see XIII.3 with cross references).

So too at Hor. *Sat.* 1.2.63 (*quid inter-|est in matrona ancilla peccesne togata?*) the nouns refer to opposites of social class (see XXIX.2.1.4.5).

At Tac. *Ann.* 11.5.3 (**91**) (*cuius de potentia et exitio in tempore memorabo*) neither M nor L has *et*. Various recentiores have *potentia et exitio* (see the apparatus of Malloch 2013). Is there any reason to insert a coordinator? We have just seen two asyndetic pairs of opposites dependent on a single preposition, one in Tacitus himself. Tacitus announces that he will elsewhere deal with the rise and fall of the referent, and asyndeton would not be out of line with his methods. These terms are reversives, but in typical Tacitean manner the reversal is expressed inexplicitly (see XXX.4.2.3a, 5.2.3). See further on Tacitus 91.

An instance that is not emended away is at *Ann.* 1.33.2 (**61**): *mira comitas et diuersa a Tiberii sermone uultu, adrogantibus et obscuris.* This passage is similar to the last in that in both the nouns in the prepositional phrase have a dependent genitive of possession. Far from suggesting emendation, Goodyear (1972: 252–3) treats this pair as an asyndeton bimembre typical of Tacitus, but makes no mention of the preposition.

In Livy asyndeta in prepositional phrases have been subject to textual and editorial variation. I comment in the chapter on Livy (XXXI) on five such examples. As far as I am aware editorial discussions of the text in these cases do not refer to the dependence of each pair on a preposition, but it is of interest that editorial doubt does seem to be generated by this structure. I merely list the passages here. Discussion of the issues will be found in the chapter on Livy at the places corresponding to the numbers in bold, and also at XXXI.3.9: 34.1.6 (**17**) *nam etiam ex oppidis conciliabulis conueniebant*, 34.5.12 (**18**) *in rebus ad omnes pariter uiros feminas pertinentibus*, 34.61.5 (**22**) *in circulis conuiuiis celebrata sermonibus res est*, 42.1.1 (**25**) *L. Postumius Albinus M. Popilius Laenas cum omnium primum de prouinciis exercitibus* *ad senatum rettulissent*, 42.31.8 (**29**) *commeatus classi legionibusque ut ex Sardinia Sicilia subueherentur*.

In several places it is B that omits the coordinator.

There does seem to be an unstated suspicion of asyndeta depending on a preposition. I mention just one further example, from Velleius. Woodman (1977) prints *in summa pace <et> quiete continuit* at Vell. 125.5, citing in the commentary (1977: 233) two examples of the pair from Tacitus that have a coordinator (but see 233 n. 1). He does not, it is true, mention the preposition, but seems concerned to show that *pax* and *quies* are elsewhere attested with coordination. They do however occur in juxtaposed asyndetic phrases at Caes. *Civ.* 3.57.4 and *Octavia* 475.

5 Conclusions

Although asyndeton is avoided by some writers in pairs dependent on a preposition, it is quite well attested in such structures. One is on firm ground in rejecting the insertion of a coordinator if the asyndetic pair is in a structure that elsewhere houses asyndeton, as at Cic. *Att.* 2.23.3 (see above, 2), but even outside these structures the usage occurs. Its rarity in some writers such as Caesar matches the rarity of asyndeton bimembre in general in those same writers. In writers in whom asyndeta dependent on a single preposition occur quite often (e.g. Cicero, Tacitus), so too asyndeta of other sorts are frequent. I have dealt with the type separately here only because there are places where the structure seems implicitly to have caused textual uncertainty or manuscript variation.

PART 5

Genres And Texts

CHAPTER XXII

Laws and Prayers

1 Introduction

In republican laws asyndetic coordination is widespread, whereas in early prayers in Latin, despite assumptions to the contrary, it is uncommon. Umbrian religious language is a different matter: in the Iguvine tablets asyndeton is the normal type of coordination for pairs (see below, 4 for a detailed account of Umbrian).

In laws and legal texts asyndetic pairs tend to be of limited, recurring types, consisting overwhelmingly of pairs of nouns and particularly verbs. Nouns are usually keywords of the type of document, denoting for example types of officials, categories of property, family relationships (see XIV), legal processes and sometimes abstract concepts such as political or social relationships. Pairs of verbs are even more stereotyped. Often the two express a 'grammatical' variation, as when the same verb is repeated in a different tense or mood (see IX), or when a simplex and compound of the same root are juxtaposed (see VII). Another type is that in which the two verbs are near-synonyms and stress slightly different aspects of an action, or opposites (see n. 3 on 'push' and 'pull'). Various pairs turn up constantly. The repetitiveness of these types is suggestive of a sort of legal shorthand, a clipped style intended to cover different possibilities succinctly. It would however be wrong to think that the asyndetic style was used invariably or consistently. Just as writers attempting to follow a certain spelling rule not infrequently lapsed into an alternative spelling, so drafters of legal documents (or the scribes/stonemasons who copied them) tended to mix up asyndeton with coordination, even in the same pairing. I will illustrate below a rigorously asyndetic legal document alongside another that has more variation, and a third, of slightly later date, in which there has been a radical change of practice.

In early prayers on the other hand the two coordinators *-que* and *-ue* are strongly preferred to asyndeton. *Et* and *aut* incidentally are all but non-existent

234   XXII Laws and Prayers

in both prayers and early laws, though occasional lapses into *et* tend to creep in later. Prayers are more discursive than laws. Superior beings are addressed, and a peremptory presentation might have been inappropriate, though some pairs did become formulaic.

It cannot be assumed that the frequency of asyndeton in some of the legal documents considered here necessarily represents early, or the earliest, practice even in the same types of documents. In one of the few dated official inscriptions of the period before 150 BC, the decree of L. Aemilius from Alcalá de los Gazules (Spain) (see Wachter 1987: 278; *CIL* I².614) of 189 BC, there are two significant coordinated pairs. One, *possidere habereque*, occurs in asyndetic form in the *Lex Coloniae Genetiuae*: e.g. LXXIX tab. b, 1–7 *ad eos riuos fontes lacus aquasque stagna paludes itus actus aquae haustus iis item esto, qui eum agrum habebunt possidebunt, uti iis fuit, qui eum agrum habuerunt possiderunt, itemque iis, qui eum agrum habent possident habebunt possidebunt, itineris aquarum lex iusque esto* (Crawford 1996: 1.404–5). This text was probably engraved in the Flavian period but dates back to the late Republic. It is at least a century and a half later than the inscription of Aemilius. We should not be talking of the 'chronology' of asyndeton versus coordination, but of changes in fashion in the ways in which pairs were presented, with coordinated pairs just as likely to be early as asyndeta (see XXXII.1). The other pair in the inscription above is *agrum oppidumqu(e)*, denoting opposites of the 'town/country' type (see XIII.5.1). This pair, with asyndeton, occurs in the late Republic, including Cicero's *Philippics* (see Cicero 19), and its asyndetic equivalent *urbs ager* is also well attested and later than the decree of Aemilius. The decree also contains *poplus senatusque Romanus*. On other early (official mainly) inscriptions with *-que* see Penney (2005: 40–4).

There follows, first, a comparison of the forms of coordination, syndetic versus asyndetic, in two laws and a *senatus consultum*.

2   Coordination in the *Lex Cornelia de XX quaestoribus*, *Lex Antonia de Termessibus*, *Senatus consultum de Cn. Pisone patre*

2.1   *Lex Cornelia de XX quaestoribus*

The *Lex Cornelia de XX quaestoribus* is of Sullan date (see Crawford 1996: 1.293–4). About 40 lines survive as it is printed in Crawford. Asyndetic pairs (of verbs and nouns only) are extremely common (verbs 24, nouns 15). The text contains no instances of either *et* or *aut*. *-Que* is used, but mainly as a clausal connector (13 times). It coordinates

2 Coordination in Three Legal Texts

words or phrases only 9 times, but most of these pairings are not comparable to the 39 asyndetic pairs. Twice *-que* is attached to a demonstrative that precedes a noun: I.32 *eosque uiatores eosque praecones* ... *legunto* (the first instance here is a clausal connective), II.34–5 *is uiator* ... *isque praecox* (with the phrases separated). Twice it is attached to a preposition: I.38 *eis uiatoribus deque eis uiatoribus*, II.2 *eis praeconibus deque eis praeconibus*. In two cases *ius* and *lex* are coordinated, both times in the same formula: I.39 *iuus lexque esto*, II.3 *iuus lexque esto*. These two nouns also occur three times in asyndeton, but only in anaphoric asyndeta: II.9 *quo iure qua lege*, II.12 *eo iure ea lege*, II.13 *quo iure qua lege*. At I.3 *-que* coordinates the plural of a noun to its singular, again a combination not found with asyndeton in this text: *eam pequniam ei scribae scribeisque herediue eius soluito.*[1] Finally, twice two verbs, *esse* and *licere*, are linked by *-que* (II.27, II.27–8). Although asyndetic pairs of verbs are common, this pairing is not used asyndetically.

I move on to the 39 asyndeta bimembria. Pairs of verbs fall into three distinct categories, two of them stylised. First, six times the same verb, *oportet*, is used in two different tenses: e.g. I.11 *apparere oportet oportebit* (so too I.15, 19, 23, 27, 31).

Second, in twelve places a verb is followed by its compound. The verbs are always *lego* and *sublego*, in a variety of forms:

I.41 *lectei sublectei essent*
II.4–5 *lectei sublectei essent*
II.8 *legere sublegere oportebit*
II.9 *legunto sublegunto*
II.10 *legerunt sublegerunt*
II.11–12 *legere sublegere oportebit*
II.13 *legunto sublegunto*
II.14 *legerunt sublegerunt*
II.15–18 *in eis uiatoribus praeconibus legundeis sublegundeis in eius uiatoris praeconis locum uiatorem praeconem legant sublegant, quoius in locum per leges plebeiue scita uiatorem praeconem legei sublegei non licebit* (seven asyndeta bimembria in a massive accumulation; three of these pairs are the verbs *lego sublego*).
II.31–2 *uiatores praecones quei ex hac lege lectei sublectei erunt, eis uiatoribus praeconibus magistratus proue mag(istratu)* ... (another accumulation, with one instance of the verbal pair).

---

[1] Note however *Lex Coloniae Genetiuae* LXIX, tabl. B, 1 (Crawford 1996: 1.402) *redemptori redemptoribus* 'to the contractor or contractors'. This is another 'grammatical' form of asyndeton (singular + plural), of the type seen for example in pairs comprising masculine + feminine, active + passive, simplex + compound.

Third, there are four and two instances respectively of two verbal pairs, *sumere habere* and *dare subdere*:

II.19–20 *sumito habeto*
II.21 *uiatores habere sumere solitei sunt*
II.22–3 *praecones sumito habeto*
II.24 *praecones habere sumere solitei sunt*
II.25–6 *uicarium dare subdere ius esto licetoque*
II.27–8 *uicarium dare subdere iuus erit licebitque*.[2]

There are fifteen asyndetic pairs of nouns, three of which have been commented on already (those with anaphoric coordination of *ius* and *lex*). The remaining twelve pairs are all the same, namely combinations of *uiatores* and *praecones* ('messengers, criers') in various cases. Pairs of titles or of terms denoting types of officials are found in literary texts, and in other laws (see further below, 7.2):

II.15–18 , quoted above, with four instances of the pair.
II.24–6 *itemque eis uiatoribus praeconibus . . uetei ceterei uiatoribus praeconibus* (two instances).
II.31–2 , quoted above in reference to verbs, with two instances of the pair of nouns.
II.33–4 *quantum ei uiator(ei) praeconei darei oporteret*
II.38–40 *quas in decurias uiatorum praeconum consul ex hac lege uiatores praecones legerit, quorum uiatorum praeconum nomina* (three instances).

In this document little overlap occurs between -*que* and asyndeton. The uses of both types of coordination tend to be formulaic, and that is particularly so of asyndetic verbal pairs, eighteen of which consist of two tenses of the same verb or of simplex + compound. As for nouns, terms for two different officials are never directly coordinated (I.3 *scribae scribeisque* refers to just one type of official). In the only two cases where officials are linked by a coordinator (I.32, II.34–5), the coordinator is attached to a demonstrative, not to the noun itself.

The pair *lego sublego* is disjunctive. The disjunctive -*ue* for its part is also used partly in a formulaic way that is different from uses of *lego sublego*:

---

[2] These pairs mainly refer to the activities of official bodies or officials. Asyndeton of this type is common in laws: e.g. *Lex Coloniae Genetiuae* LXIIII.15 (p. 401) *decreuerint statuerint* 'shall have decreed or decided', CI.17–18 (p. 408) *quicumque comitia magistrat<ib>us creandis subrogandis habebit*, CI.21 (p. 409) *nominari creari*, CXXIIII.10 (p. 413) *sententiae dicendae rogandae* 'for speaking his opinion or being asked an opinion', CXXVI.36 (p. 414) *de loco dando atsignando statu<tum> decretum erit*, CXXVIII.21 (p. 415) *statuerint decreuerint*, CXXXI.6 (p. 416) *de quo tum referetur consuletur*.

2 Coordination in Three Legal Texts

I.3 *ei scribae scribeisque herediue*
II.7 *ex lege plebeiue scito*
II.11 *ex lege plebeiue scito*
II.17 *per leges plebeiue scita*
II.32 *magistratus proue mag(istratu)*.

Three of the five instances are in a single phrase.
Here then is a legal text showing an overwhelming preference for the asyndetic coordination of verbs and nouns. Overt coordination, when it does occur, is of special types.

2.2   Lex Antonia de Termessibus

On the date of this statute (probably 68 BC) see Crawford (1996: 1.332).
Asyndeton bimembre is proportionately less common than in the *Lex Cornelia*, though again there are just two types, pairs of nouns and pairs of verbs.
Pairs of nouns are not frequent. If special cases are left aside, namely consular names, a problematic case of *loca aedificia*, and an odd combination at II.6 consisting of a phrase (a coordinated pair of official titles), and then in asyndeton with it a single noun (denoting a type of official), just one pair of nouns remains, denoting types of legal processes (*iudicia recuperationes*). The various examples just listed are quoted below, along with four longer asyndetic sequences (with three to four members), all of them with much the same components.

I.3 *L. Gellio Cn. Lentulo cos.* and II.18-19 *L. Marcio Sex. Iulio cos.*
I.12 *quei agrei quae loca aedificia publica preiuataue* (translated by the editor, p. 335, 'Whatever lands, whatever pieces of land or buildings, public or private', in which case there would be an asyndetic pair *loca aedificia*, separated from *agrei* by the second of the anaphoric pair *quei ... quae*; however, there are doubts over this interpretation: see below).
II.4 *iudicia recuperationes danto*, 'is to appoint trials and procedures for recovery'.
II.6 *nei quis magistratus proue magistratu legatus ne[i] quis alius*, 'No magistrate or promagistrate or legate or anyone else' (there is an asyndeton here, in that *legatus* is in an asyndetic relationship to the coordinated pair).

I.28 *praeter loca agros aedificia*
II.23 *loceis agreis aedificieis oppideis*
II.25-6 *praeter loca agros aedificia*
II.27-8 *loceis agreis aedificieis oppideis*.

In all four of these passages *loca* and *agri* are juxtaposed, and they are indeed a semantic unit of near-synonyms, 'pieces of lands, fields'. *Ager locus* occurs elsewhere in laws as an asyndetic pair, for example several times at *Lex agraria* 22–3 (Crawford 1996: 1.115). *Aedificia oppida* on the other hand in two of the passages looks like a separate pair, again with a semantic unity (buildings, collections of buildings), juxtaposed with the other. If this is accepted, the interpretation of *loca aedificia* at I.12 above as forming a unit separate from *agrei* looks wrong. The structure seems to be *quei agrei quae loca, aedificia publica priuataue*, 'whatever fields, whatever pieces of land, buildings public or private', with another *quae* understood, before *aedificia* (an easy ellipse).

Pairs of verbs in asyndeton are more frequent. There are twelve such, though the text is doubtful in some cases. They fall into categories typical of laws. Three comprise a single verb used in two different tenses. The remaining examples are pairs of near-synonyms, *habere possidere*, which may occur five times, two instances of *dare praebere*, and single cases of *utantur fruantur* (conjectural) and *sint fiant*.[3]

I.5 *prognati sunt erunt*
I.33–4 *uti sunt fuerunt* (this pair also occurs with a coordinator: see the list below at the end of this section).
II.17 *dare praebere oportet oportebit* (accumulation).

I.17–18 *quodque . . . habuerunt possiderunt usei fructeiue sunt*
I.23 *habean]t possideant*
I.24 *utantur fr]uantur*
I.26 *habueru[nt possederunt usei fruct]ei ue sunt* (in this and the preceding two cases the text is doubtful, but the filling out must be right).
I.31 *quodque . . . habuerunt possiderunt usei fructeiue sunt*
I.35 *ea omnia habere possidere uutei frueique liceto*
II.15 *dent praebeant*
II.30 *ita sint fiant.*

The main coordinator in this text is the disjunctive *-ue*, which occurs twelve times linking pairs,[4] compared with six cases of *-que* (joining terms rather than clausal). A single instance of *et* also intrudes. Coordinated pairs are thus just as common as asyndetic pairs. Coordination has also encroached on asyndeton in combinations of the type that are asyndetic in the other law, particularly in pairs of verbs. There are three instances of

---

[3] I note in passing that it is not only verbal near-synonyms that occur in asyndeton in laws. For opposites see e.g. *Tabula Heracleensis* 57 (Crawford 1996: 1.365) *plostrum . . . . neue ante horam decimam diei ducito agito* (a wagon may be drawn or pushed). Cf. 64 *ducei agei*, 65 *ducantur agantur*.

[4] According to Torrego (2009: 461), *aut* 'replaces *-ue* even in the first written texts'. That is not the case in the texts that we have been looking at, including those that are not at all early. See however Torrego (2009: 457) for more details.

2 Coordination in Three Legal Texts 239

a coordinator linking two tenses of the same verb (I.14, I.15, I.28–9), and three instances of the near-synonyms (participles) *usei fructeiue/que sunt* with coordinator (all quoted above; note too the coordinated infinitives of the same verbs at I.35). It has to be said, however, that this pair always occurs as the second part of an accumulation, following an asyndetic combination of another pair of near-synonymous verbs, *habeo/possideo*. For this type of accumulation, which is widespread from the earliest times, for example in an augural context in Plautus and a prayer in Cato (see below, 3.2), and then in literature, see e.g. XIX.1; see also below, 9, on a possible Ciceronian instance of an abnormal asyndeton, *domi militiae*, which is also in such a structure. There are also five pairs of coordinated nouns, all of them of categories in which asyndeton also is commonly found (classifications of classes of person, friends and allies of the Roman people, freeborn and slaves; types of magistrates; components of estates). The document also has two longer sequences, with three terms, in which *-que* is repeated twice. This pattern is in contrast to the longer asyndetic sequences in the other law. One other feature of the *Lex Antonia* is that it has pairs of adjectives coordinated.

The drafters or scribes of the document were clearly aware of a legal tradition of juxtaposing verbs (in particular) of certain types asyndetically, and also nouns, but consistency has not been achieved. The coordinations are listed below, in groups.

-Que and *et* are in bold. Some of the following examples repeat passages above cited there in other connections.

Nouns

I.7 *leiberi amicei socieique populi Romani sunto* (this is not end-of-list coordination, because the genitive only goes with *amicei sociei*; *leiberi* is probably substantival and a separate unit from *amicei socieique*, 'are to be free, (and) friends and allies of the Roman people' (see XVIII.4)).
I.36 *leiberos seruosue*
II.7–8 *in oppidum ... agrumue* (but the two are separated).
II.6 *nei quis magistratus proue magistratu legatus ne[i] quis alius* (for this odd example see above).
I.5–6 *iei omnes postereique eorum* is a phrasal pair.

Verbs

I.14 *sunt fueruntue*
I.15 *quaeque* [clausal] *insulae eorum sunt fueruntue*
I.28–9 *sunt fueruntue*

I.17–18 *habuerunt possiderunt usei fructeiue sunt*
I.26 *habueru[nt possederunt usei fruct]ei ue sunt* (text doubtful, but *ue* seems to be present).
I.31 *habuerunt possiderunt usei fructeiue sunt*
I.35 *habere possidere uutei frueique liceto.*

Adjectives
I.12 *quei agrei quae loca aedificia publica preiuataue*
I.27–8 *publica preiuataue*
II.31 *portorieis terrestribus maritumeisque*
II.19 *inter ciueis Romanos et Termenses* (the only instance of *et* in the text).

Longer sequences
II.18 *quae leges quodque ious quaeque consuetudo*
II.20–1 *eaedem leges eidemque ious eademque consuetudo.*

2.3 *Senatus consultum de Cn. Pisone patre*

This decree is dated to AD 20. I give some statistics based on a reading of the critical text of Potter in Potter and Damon (1999), without citing details. The purpose is to show the sheer extent of the change that had occurred in official practice (or fashion) in the use of coordination. The document starts with the names of those present at the writing. As is to be expected in such a long list of names, coordinators are not used. Thereafter *et* is used 55 times, *-que* 30, *atque* 5, *ac* 4, *aut* 5, *uel* 2 and *-ue* 3. There is just a single asyndeton bimembre, at 108 in Potter's numeration, *tollenda dimolienda curarent*. Even in the naming of the consuls right at the end (175) *et* is used: *Cotta et Messalla cos*. For an asyndetic pair of gerundives in a *senatus consultum* see e.g. *SC De ludis saecularibus* (Riccobono 1968, text 40), p. 276 *inperent, uti eam pecuniam dandam attribuendam* <... *curent*>. For laws see e.g. *Lex Coloniae Genetiuae* LXXI.28 *pecuniam ... dandam adtribuendam curanto* (Crawford 1996: 1.403), CXXIIII.10 *sententiae dicendae rogandae ... esto* (p. 413). Pairs of gerunds in the ablative similarly were often in asyndeton (see XXIII.5.4).

There follows a discussion of asyndeton and coordination in selected early prayers. One hears in the literature of asyndeton bimembre as sacral, but that is a claim that is exaggerated. Prayers will turn out to be different from laws. The evidence below is a selection: for a more extensive discussion of coordination in prayers see Adams and Nikitina (forthcoming).

3 Asyndeton and Coordination in Selected Prayers

3.1 A Spell in Macrobius, Sat. 3.9.7–8

This is a spell described at the start by Macrobius as intended to call the gods forth when a city is surrounded and under siege (see Chapot and Laurot 2001: 237–8). Macrobius quotes it from Serenus Sammonicus, who claimed to have found it in a 'very ancient' book of a certain Furius.

In this text *et* and *aut* do not occur. The normal coordinator is *-que* (eighteen times in total). In nine of these cases it links pairs, including nouns, verbs, adjectives, and a pronoun + substantive:

7 *populus ciuitasque Carthaginiensis*
7 *urbis huius populique tutelam*
7 *precor uenerorque*
7 *populum ciuitatemque Carthaginiensem deseratis*
8 *eique populo ciuitatique . . . iniciatis*
8 *ad me meosque*
8 *acceptior probatiorque sit*
8 *ut sciamus intellegamusque*
8 *uoueo uobis templa ludosque facturum.*

In the following passage *propitii* has three dative complements, with *-que* attaching the second and third; in *mihique* it is a clausal connective: 8 *mihique populoque Romano militibusque meis propitii sitis*. There are six instances of *-que* (including this one) as a clausal coordinator in the text.

Finally, an instance of *-que* as what looks like an end-of-list coordinator (see however the next paragraph): 7 *loca templa sacra urbemque eorum relinquatis*.

By contrast asyndeton bimembre is not definitely found. Asyndetic tricola occur perhaps twice: 8 *metum formidinem obliuionem iniciatis*, 8 *nostraque uobis loca templa sacra urbs . . . sit* (though there is another possible analysis of the phrase structure here, and at 7, quoted in the last paragraph: see XVIII.4: if *sacra* goes with both *loca* and *templa*, there would be an asyndeton bimembre, i.e. [*loca templa sacra*] + [*urbs*]). Finally, at 7 (*si deus si dea est*) the asyndeton is clausal (with anaphora of *si*).

Coordination in the spell is in contrast to that in the *Lex Cornelia de XX quaestoribus*, with *-que* dominant in the spell and asyndeton in the law. The question raised by this discrepancy is whether the spell is typical of early prayers. I turn now to Cato.

3.2 Prayers in Cato, Agr. 141

This chapter has a number of prayers, mainly to Mars, one of which (2–4) is quite long (see Chapot and Laurot 2001: 252–4). It is described by Watkins (1995: 199) as 'the most ancient piece of Latin literature'. I take account here of all the prayers in the chapter.

Et and *aut* are nowhere found. *-Que* is used nine times as a coordinator of two elements, which, as in the spell above, may be verbal (three times), adjectival (once) or nominal (five times):

141.2 *te precor quaesoque*
141.2 *uti tu morbos uisos inuisosque, uiduertatem uastitudinemque, calamitates intemperiasque prohibessis* (three instances).
141.2 *utique tu fruges frumenta, uineta uirgultaque grandire beneque euenire siris* (two instances).
141.3 *pastores pecuaque*
141.3 *bonam salutem ualetudinemque*
141.3 *lustrandi lustrique faciendi ergo.*

Another feature shared (possibly) with the spell is that the chapter of Cato has end-of-list coordination (six times):

141.1 *fundum agrum terramque meam*
141.2 *propitius mihi domo familiaeque nostrae*
141.2 *agrum terram fundumque meum*
141.2 *prohibessis defendas auerruncesque*
141.3 *mihi domo familiaeque nostrae*
141.3 *fundi terrae agrique mei lustrandi . . . ergo.*

What is striking is that three times *fundus*, *ager* and *terra* are combined, always with a different order: see XVIII.5 on the significance of this variation.

Just a single case of asyndeton occurs, in a pair (141.2 *fruges frumenta*) that is juxtaposed, in an accumulation, with a coordinated pair, a structural pattern that comes up constantly, and was seen above in the *Lex Antonia de Termessibus* (2.2). I omit the phrase *uolens propitius*, for which see II.3.2.1.

The passage of Cato is very similar in its avoidance of asyndeton bimembre and in its uses of *-que* to the spell, and very different from the laws.

In three places, finally, *-que* is used as a clausal coordinator.

3.3 Varro Ling. 7.8 and the Formula for Taking the Auspices

I base this section on the text of Chapot and Laurot (2001: 235), taken from Norden (1939: 15–26); see too Linderski (1986: 2267–9) and de Melo (2019:

3 Asyndeton and Coordination in Selected Prayers   243

1.422), printing some emendations, and his commentary on the passage (2019: 2.905–7); also above, III.1. In this document there are (perhaps) three alliterative formulae with the coordinator *-que, templa tescaque* once, and *templum tescumque* twice (on this formula see Norden 1939: 16–30; de Melo 2019: 2.905–6 deletes the coordinator from *templa tescaque*). In *utique* near the end of the text *-que* seems to be a clausal connective. The text has no other coordinator.

In contrast to the coordinated pairs the text contains an asyndetic tricolon, *inter ea conregione conspicione cortumione*, where all three terms have the same prefix and three-syllable rhyme at the end (cf. Plaut. *Am.* 1062 *strepitus crepitus, sonitus tonitrus*, where each pair has a three-syllable rhyme; cf. XXV.7 for a comparable Ciceronian tricolon; also XVIII.2.2.1 for *Off.* 1.50; XXV.1.1.2 for a long asyndeton with assonance in Lucilius, and also Pacuvius *trag.* 17.1). For a discussion of the three terms above see Norden (1939: 71–85), de Melo (2019: 2.906–7).

The coexistence of (a) pairs coordinated by *-que* and (b) asyndeton with more than two members is also a feature of the spell in Macrobius (above, 3.1). In the formula devoting cities to destruction (Macr. 3.9.10–11), discussed next (3.4), there is the same mixture, as well as one or two other phenomena that link the document to other texts discussed in this section.

3.4   A Prayer for the Devotion of Cities to Destruction, Uttered only by Generals and Dictators (Macr. Sat. 3.9.10–11)

This document (see Chapot and Laurot 2001: 239) has 23 instances of *-que*, and 1 of *et* (10 *et qui*: a clausal connective, which looks like a modernism that has crept in).

-Que is most commonly used to link two terms:

10 *illam urbem Carthaginem exercitumque*
10 *aduersum legiones exercitumque nostrum*
10 *arma telaque ferent*
10 *urbes agrosque eorum*
10 *in his locis regionibusque, agris urbibusque habitant* (two examples, in an accumulation).
10 *urbes agrosque eorum quos* ...
10 *uti uos eas urbes agrosque, capita aetatesque eorum* (two examples, in another accumulation).
10 *deuotas consecratasque habeatis*
11 *legiones exercitumque nostrum*
11 *te Tellus mater teque Iuppiter obtestor*.

There are twelve examples of *-que* here, four of them in two accumulations. The prayer also has end-of-list coordination, four times:

10 *eum exercitum, eos hostes, eosque homines* (with anaphora of the demonstrative).
11 *pro me, fide magistratuque meo*
11 *pro populo Romano exercitibus legionibusque*
11 *ut ego sciam sentiam intellegamque.*

I do not accept in the second example above the emendation *<meaque> fide*, which is printed by Kaster in both his Loeb and OCT. In a prayer context at Cicero *Mur.* 1 (Chapot and Laurot 2001: 264, L24) we find the identical formula (in a different case), without this *mea(e)que*: *precatus a dis immortalibus sum ... ut ea res mihi fidei magistratuique meo ... feliciter eueniret.*

I do not interpret 10 *eosque homines, urbes agrosque eorum* as showing end-of-list coordination. This instance of *eosque homines* is taken in the first quotation above as the third, coordinated, element in an end-of-list coordination, and *urbes agrosque* in the phrase just quoted is a separate pair, which occurs three further times in the text. In the coordinated pair *urbes agrosque eorum* above the pronoun refers back to *eosque homines*, and there is thus a phrasal asyndeton bimembre, 'those men, (and) their cities and lands'. The passage does however have an incoherence at this point, in that the verb *abducatis*, of which *homines* is object, is not suited to *urbes agrosque*.

Another use of *-que* is to link all members of a tricolon:

11 *ut me meamque fidem imperiumque* (a phrase presumably taken by Kaster above as supporting the emendation to *meaque* (*fide*), but the phrase here is not the formula seen above and in the passage of Cicero).

Finally, four uses of *-que* are clausal: 10 *quique*, 10 *exercitumque hostium*, 10 *quandoque*, 11 *eosque*.

There is just a single asyndeton bimembre: 11 *do deuoueo* (note that it is alliterative). See Adams (2016: 250) for this type in curse tablets. On the other hand asyndetic tricola occur twice:

10 *Dis pater Veiouis Manes*
10 *fuga formidine terrore compleatis.*

A phrasal asyndetic pair was seen above (10: the example with *urbes agrosque*), and another is in the same section: 10 *exercitumque hostium, urbes agrosque eorum.* For a clausal pair see 11 *quisquis uotum hoc faxit, ubiubi faxit.*

3 Asyndeton and Coordination in Selected Prayers   245

All the religious texts seen here have in common that coordination of pairs by *-que* is very frequent, and asyndeton bimembre either non-existent or extremely rare. The prayer just considered shares with the prayers in Cato accumulations of juxtaposed pairs coordinated by *-que* and also end-of-list coordination. This latter pattern is found in most of the texts discussed. Finally, a few asyndetic tricola occur in this text, in the spell quoted by Macrobius, and in the passage of Varro.

3.5 Quotations from the Books of the haruspices *Found in Cicero's* Har.

Cicero in his speech *De haruspicum responsis* quotes in Latin replies of *haruspices*, the exact source of which is unclear, but they may derive from the Etruscan *libri Etrusci*, possibly translated at the direction of the senate. I collect them here in their entirety (whether or not they have coordinations):

9 *loca sacra et religiosa profana haberi*
20 *quod in agro Latiniensi auditus est strepitus cum fremitu* (cf. Pac. trag. 363 Schierl *strepitus fremitus*).
20 *postiliones esse Ioui Saturno Neptuno Telluri dis caelestibus*
21 *ludos minus diligenter factos pollutosque*
34 *oratores contra ius fasque interfectos*
36 *fidem iusque iurandum neglectum*
37 *sacrificia uetusta occultaque minus diligenter facta pollutaque*
37 *uetusta occultaque*
40 *ne per optimatium discordiam dissensionemque patribus principibusque caedes periculaque creentur auxilioque diuini numinis deficiantur, †qua re ad unum imperium pecuniae redeant exercitusque apulsus deminutioque accedat*
53 *deteriores repulsos*
55 *ne occultis consiliis res publica laedatur*
56 *ne deterioribus repulsisque honos augeatur.*

These passages have eleven instances of *-que*, as well as one of *et*, which again looks like an isolated modernism. In two places (at 37 and notably 40) we find, as in Cato and the prayer above from Macrobius (3.4), accumulations comprising juxtaposed coordinated pairs (three or four in 40). The only asyndeton is in a sequence of five terms (20). There is no asyndeton bimembre. At 53 *deteriores repulsos* (to be punctuated in a critical text with a comma) is not an actual quotation. Cicero says there that the Etruscan books have certain terms that can be applied to a particular class of person, and he illustrates by citing examples, '*deteriores*', '*repulsos*', 'which you are now going to hear' (*quod iam audietis*). When we do hear the pair (56) from the replies of the *haruspices* the terms are coordinated. The asyndeton is Cicero's own, not that of the *haruspices*. When he cites *exempli gratia* two items from a potentially longer list, Cicero not infrequently places the two in asyndeton, usually at the end of a colon (see Cicero 11, 27, 32, 132 and particularly IV.3).

The forms of coordination seen in these citations match those in the prayers discussed above.

In this small selection of five prayers/religious texts -*que* links pairs 41 times, but there are only 2 instances of asyndeton bimembre. Nor are these figures exceptional. Elsewhere (see Adams and Nikitina, forthcoming) in a fuller corpus of fifteen prayers and the like it is shown that there are 59 instances of -*que* linking pairs, compared with 7 or 8 cases of asyndeton bimembre.

In the next section I discuss asyndeton in Umbrian in the Iguvine tablets. Coordination in these documents is very different from that in the Latin prayers above.

4 Asyndeton in Umbrian

4.1 Introduction

The Iguvine tablets, which have prayers as well as instructions to those carrying out religious practices, are full of asyndetic pairs (and longer sequences), unlike the Latin prayers that have been considered here. This section does not collect every example (quite a few pairs recur, and I have not cited multiple examples of the same formulae), but it is intended to bring out the extent of such usages and their different types, which are found too in Latin (other than in prayers). Translations are usually from Poultney (1959), with some minor modifications to reflect the absence of coordination in phrases translated by Poultney with a coordinator. In many cases Poultney's renderings are speculative, and I have quoted them only to show the structure of phrases. Whenever the meaning of a term in a translation is uncertain I have pointed that out in the commentary, with reference mainly to Untermann's comprehensive listings of possibilities (2000).

4.2 Nouns

Ib.32–3 **taçez : pesnimu : ařeper : arves**, 'pray silently with fat, grain'. I adopt Poultney's translation (modified), but the asyndetic terms (the last two) are obscure (Untermann 2000: 125).

IIa.40 **vinu : pune : tertu**, 'He shall distribute the wine, the mead.' On the second term (some sort of drink offering) see Untermann (2000: 606).

IIb.1 **sim : kaprum : upetu**, 'choose a pig, a he-goat'. **Sim** means 'sow, pig' (Poultney 1959: 323, Untermann 2000: 676), and it is followed by the word for 'he-goat'.

III.8–9 **sakre : uvem : uhtur : teitu**, 'The auctor shall designate a young pig, a sheep.' On the meaning of the first word, translated 'young pig', see Poultney (1959: 321), and particularly Untermann (2000: 650) ('Opfertier').

VIa.1 *parfa . curnase . dersua . peiqu . peica . merstu* (with two pairs) 'the *parra* and crow in the west (?), the woodpecker and magpie in the east'.
This passage is very similar to one in Plautus (*As*. 259–60) in an augural context (see below, 6.3; also XIX.1, XXIII.3). Here is the pattern in which two asyndetic pairs (both consisting of bird names) are almost juxtaposed. Untermann (2000: 170) takes *dersua* as meaning (perhaps) 'on the right', a sense that is supported by *ab dextera* in the passage of Plautus just referred to. The meaning of *merstu* is uncertain (Untermann 2000: 473), but might be 'on the left' (cf. Plautus, *ab laeua*). The Plautine passage seems not to be quoted in relation to the Umbrian. For *curnase* 'crow' see Untermann (2000: 420). *Peiqu* and *peica* correspond to Lat. *picus* and *pica* (Untermann 2000: 526).

VIa.52 *uiro . pequo* (on this pair see below, 4.7). This phrase is from a prayer, whereas the examples above are all part of instructions.

VIa. 59 *prosesetir . strusla . ficla . arsueitu* is rendered 'prosectis struem, offam addito' by Buck (1904: 269), and translated by Poultney (1959: 250), 'and add to the parts cut off a *struśla* cake and a *ficla* cake' (see Untermann 2000: 283, 705). This asyndeton bimembre is also found elsewhere, e.g. at VIb.23.

VIb.17 *mefa . uestisia* 'the *mefa* cake, the libation'. The precise meanings are uncertain (Untermann 2000: 463, 849). At VIIa.37 the same pair (in the reverse order) occurs with *et*, another illustration of the fact that there is no rigid distinction between syndetic and asyndetic coordination.

VIb.44 *fasio . ficla . arsueitu* 'add spelt-cakes, a *ficla* cake'. For the first word (accusative plural, neuter) see Untermann (2000: 266). For the verb see Poultney (1959: 298).

4.3 Adjectives

Fons pacer, which is translated '(be) favourable (and) propitious' (see Poultney 1959: 307, 314), is common, accompanied by a string of datives (see e.g. *Tab. Ig.* VIa.42, 50 etc.). At *Tab. Ig.* VIa.23 both terms are separately used as predicates with the verb 'to be': *fos . sei . pacer . sei*, 'be favourable, be propitious', which establishes that both are of the same status and form a genuine asyndetic coordination (unlike *uolens propitius*, a phrase that is often compared to the Umbrian: see II.3.2.1).

This is a prayer formula. The terms are near-synonyms. See Untermann (2000: 302, 509–10).

IIa.18–19 has an asyndeton with about ten members, most notably (19) **veskla : snata : asnata** 'wet, non-wet vessels'. The translation is Poultney's guess, as the meaning of the pair in final position is unknown (see Untermann 2000: 687–8). The type consisting of adjective + its *an-*privative negative is well represented in Umbrian, as well as Vedic, Greek and Latin (see below, and VI.6).

VIb.30 *uirseto . auirseto . uas . est* 'if . . . there be any seen or unseen fault' (Poultney 1959: 262). Cf. Cato *Agr.* 141.2 *uisos inuisosque*. See Untermann (2000: 854–5).

From a prayer. See the example above for the type, and also VI.6 and Watkins (1995: 43).

4.4 Verbs

VIb.15–16 *pesclu semu . uesticatu . atripursatu*, 'In the middle of the prayer he shall pour a libation, dance the *tripudium*.' The pair of verbs is at the end of the quotation. The translation of *uesticatu* is again Poultney's guess, as the meaning is uncertain (Untermann 2000: 847). The second verb corresponds to Lat. *tripodare* (which lacks a prefix) (see Untermann 2000: 62–3). Asyndetic pairs of imperatives are common (see the next example). For the form of the imperative (cf. Lat. *-to*), cf. e.g. Buck (1904: 176).

VIb.40 *endendu . pelsatu* . The first verb (*-du* = *-tu*) probably means 'place in, insert' (Poultney 1959: 304, Untermann 2000: 742); the second is of unknown meaning (Poultney 1959: 315, Untermann 2000: 529).

VIb.56 *arsmahamo . caterahamo . iouinur*. This is part of the ritual of lustration. There are two verbs in asyndeton addressed to the men of

Iguvium, 'Arrange yourselves in priestly ranks, military ranks, men of Iguvium' (the meaning of the verbs, which are second person plural passive imperatives II, is however uncertain: see Poultney 1959: 276, Untermann 2000: 122, 376; for the verb forms see e.g. Buck 1904: 176).

4.5 'Prepositional' Type

At VIa.53–4 (*ocriper . fisiu . totaper . iiouina*) both pairs ('for the Fisian Mount, for the state of Iguvium') are dependent on repeated *per* 'on behalf of', = *pro*, which is postpositive in Umbrian (Untermann 2000: 531–2). Cf. Ia.8 **ukriper : fisiu : tutaper : ikuvina**, and, as part of a longer sequence, III.24–5 **tutape : iiuvina : trefiper : iiuvina**, 'for the state of Iguvium, for the tribe of Iguvium'.

Note too IV.6 **asamař : erec̨lamař** 'at the altar, at the statue'. For the first word see Untermann (2000:43), = *ara*, and for the second, of which the meaning given is a guess, Untermann (2000: 228). **ař** = *ad* is a postpositive, 'at, to' (Untermann 2000: 46).

4.6 Accumulations of Pairs of Different Types

VIb.10–11 *ditu . ocre . fisi . tote . iouine . ocrer . fisie . totar . iouinar . dupursus | peturpursus . fato . fito . perne . postne . sepse sarsite . uou.se . auie . esone*, 'grant to the Fisian Mount, to the state of Iguvium, to the men and beasts of the Fisian Mount, of the state of Iguvium, (success in) word and deed, before and behind, in private and in public, in vow, in augury, in sacrifice' (Poultney 1959: 256, slightly modified).

This is from a prayer. The two references to the Fisian Mount and state of Iguvium are both asyndetic phrasal pairs, but apart from these the passage contains four asyndeta bimembria, and ends with an asyndetic tricolon, which follows three asyndetic pairs in the same case, a structure (2 + 2 + 2 + 3) of a type we have seen in Latin. There immediately follows (not quoted here) the asyndetic 'favourable/propitious' formula. The passage is totally asyndetic and has a striking sequence of asyndetic pairs, of different parts of speech, two of them possibly pairs of opposites.

Dupursus denotes bipeds, i.e. men, and *peturpursus* quadrupeds, i.e. animals (Poultney 1959: 303, 317, Untermann 2000: 192, 551), and the pair is sometimes referred to as a merism (see e.g. West 2007: 100). *Fato fito* may be the expression 'in word, in deed', 'prediction, outcome', 'prediction, happening' (Poultney 1959: 255, 306, 307, Untermann 2000:

267, 280). *Perne postne* seems to be 'before, behind' (Untermann 2000: 538, 623). *Sepse* and *sarsite* are both of uncertain meaning (see Poultney 1959: 323, 322, Untermann 2000: 668, 656–7). Note that the last three pairs are all alliterative, and to some extent rhyming.

A similar accumulation, also from a prayer, is quoted elsewhere (XIX.1). Here without comment is the text, along with Buck's rendering (1904: 280) into Latin, though it has to be stressed that there are many obscurities: VIb.59–60 *nerf . ṡihutu . anṡihutu . iouie . hostatu . anhostatu . tursitu . tremitu hondu . holtu . ninctu . nepitu . sonitu . sauitu . preplotatu . preuilatu* (= *principes cinctos incinctos, iuuenes hastatos inhastatos, terreto tremefacito, pessumdato aboleto, ninguito inundato, sonato sauciato, praeplauditato praeuinculato*). Again alliteration is pronounced.

IIa.25–6 **tiu : puni : tiu : vinu : teitu : berva : frehtef : fertu**, ' "(I invoke) thee with mead, (I invoke) thee with wine", he shall say. He shall take the spits, the boiled portions' (Poultney 1959: 182).

There is first an asyndetic pair of nouns (which were seen earlier) in an anaphoric construction (**teitu** = *deitu* 'say'). That is almost juxtaposed with an asyndetic pair of nouns (**berva frehtef**). The meaning of both is unknown (Untermann 2000: 145, 295). At IIb.9–10 the nouns are separated by **heri, heri** 'either, or' = Lat. *uel . . . uel* (Untermann 2000: 325). For asyndetic anaphoric (prepositional) pairs juxtaposed with asyndetic pairs of other types in Latin see e.g. XIX.1.

IIa.31–2 **vestikatu : ahtrepuřatu: ařpeltu : statitatu**, 'He shall pour a libation, dance the *tripudium*, approach (the altar), stop.'

The first and second verbs are an established pair (for which see above, 4.4), and the third and fourth, despite uncertainties of meaning, probably belong together too (see Untermann 2000: 52, 703 on possible interpretations). There seem to be two juxtaposed asyndetic pairs.

III.12–13 **sakre : uvem : kletra : fertuta : aituta**, 'They shall lift, carry the young pig, the sheep on a litter.'

A double pairing, each pair with different parts of speech, a type found in Latin (see e.g. on Plautus, XXIII.7.1 and also *Poen.* 835, and on Sallust 47 with cross references). The pair of nouns at the start was seen earlier, 4.2. The two verbs at the end are third person plural imperatives II (Poultney 1959: 307, Untermann 2000: 276 on the first, Untermann 71–2 on the second), the meaning of which is not clear-cut. **kletra**, some sort of device for transporting offerings (Untermann 2000: 400), separates the two pairs.

4 Asyndeton in Umbrian

4.7 Phrasal and Mixed Asyndeta

VIa.51–2 *di . grabouie . saluom . seritu . ocrer . fisier | totar . iiouinar . nome . nerf . arsmo . uiro . pequo . castruo . frif . salua . seritu . futu . fons . pacer . pase . tua*, 'Jupiter Grabovius, keep safe the name of the Fisian Mount, of the state of Iguvium, keep safe the magistrates, the priesthoods, the lives of men and of beasts, the fruits. Be favourable and propitious with thy peace ...' (so Poultney 1959: 248).

This is from a prayer. *ocrer . fisier | totar . iiouinar* are a phrasal asyndetic pair (see above, 4.6). There follows, on the interpretation of Poultney, an asyndetic sequence of four items, within which there is embedded an asyndeton bimembre, *uiro pequo*. *Castruo* is taken by Poultney (1959: 300, 'heads, lives'?) to be complemented by two dependent genitive plurals, *uiro pequo* (Poultney 1959: 315, 331, but with a question mark). This interpretation is rejected by Untermann (2000: 527 s.v. *pequo* and 858 s.v. *uiro*). Both words are probably neuter plural accusative collectives, 'men, cattle'. *Castruo* is of uncertain meaning (Untermann 2000: 374–5), but *frif* means *fruges* (Untermann 2000: 297), and there may be a sequence of three pairs, *nerf arsmo, uiro pequo, castruo frif* (on the last pair see Untermann 2000: 374). On *nerf*, strictly 'man', but here used of the politically active citizens, 'patriciate, magistrates, senate', see Untermann (2000: 496). The second word *arsmo* is however of uncertain meaning (Untermann 2000: 123). In the next sentence the 'favourable, propitious' asyndeton bimembre follows.

A similar passage is at VIb.32.

VIb.51 *ennom . stiplatu parfa desua . seso . tote . iiouine*, 'Then he shall demand a *parra* in the west for himself, for the state of Iguvium.'

Cf. Ib.13 **ennumek : steplatu parfam : tesvam : tefe : tute : ikuvine** 'then demand a *parra* in the west for yourself, for the state of Iguvium' (Poultney 1959: 164). The meaning of *desua* came up earlier (4.2).

4.8 Conclusions

The primary aim of this section has been to present Umbrian evidence as offering a contrast with Latin religious language. Poultney (1959: 305) lists 20 instances of the coordinator **et**/*et* from the Iguvine tablets, whereas about twice as many cases of asyndeton have been collected above, and the collection is far from complete, as many of the expressions occur over and over again and only a selection has been listed, and some different pairs have no doubt been missed. Asyndetic coordination was the norm in the Umbrian documents, but syndetic in early Latin prayers. In one sense the tablets are more akin to Latin legal language, in that active imperatives, second-third person singular, of the **-tu** type are extremely common (Poultney 1959: 138), and these correspond to Latin *-to*, a type frequent in Latin laws. Such imperatives in Umbrian are in prayers as well as instructional passages. The Umbrian tablets span a long time, and asyndeton is remarkably persistent, even in those in Latin script.

Types of pairs and patterns that occur in the examples above (as well as in Latin) include opposities of which one is a negative adjective, merisms (men, beasts; two-footed, four-footed creatures), imperatives, two asyndetic pairs together (in some cases the two pairs are of different parts of speech), alliterative pairs, anaphoric asyndeton, long sequences of pairs, mainly alliterative, accumulations comprising different types of asyndeton, pairs followed by an asyndetic tricolon, for which see VIb.10–11 at 4.6 (the structure we have elsewhere called the 2 + 3 type), and a correspondent to the Latin prepositional type, comprising two terms each with a postpositive attached. Some of the similarities between Latin and Umbrian were no doubt inherited in Italic, such as the pair of bird names in augural contexts in both the tablets and Plautus, and the apparent pair of adverbial opposites seen above (*perne, postne*), which recalls similar adverbial pairs in Latin (XIII.5.4).

5 Some Legal Pairs, Mainly Old

We have seen that in the Republic some drafters thought that asyndeton was appropriate in laws. Pairs of verbs, for example, might be peremptory, and laws state rules. When a coordinator is used in the republican documents we looked at, it is *-que* (or *-ue*). These conventions had broken down by the time of the *Senatus consultum de Cn. Pisone patre*, or at least were disregarded by a particular drafter.

Asyndeta bimembria had had some currency in legal and official terminologies since a very early date, to judge from the number of old pairs that survived into the classical period. I discuss the most important ones here.

5.1 *patres conscripti*

The traditional view is that this is a nominal asyndetic pair (*conscripti* a substantival participle), the first member denoting patricians and the second plebeians drafted in to make up numbers:

5 Some Legal Pairs, Mainly Old

Livy 2.1.11 *traditumque inde fertur ut in senatum uocarentur qui patres quique conscripti essent*, 'and (the custom) is said to have been handed down from that time that there were summoned into the senate "those who were patricians and those who had been enlisted"'.

Festus p. 304.24–30 Lindsay *qui patres, qui conscripti uocati sunt in curiam? quo tempore regibus urbe expulsis, P. Valerius consul propter inopiam patriciorum ex plebe adlegit in numerum senatorum C et LX et IIII, ut expleret numerum senatorum trecentorum et duo genera appellaret*, 'who were the *patres* and who the *conscripti* who were called into the senate? At the time when the kings were expelled from the city, the consul P. Valerius, because of a shortage of patricians, recruited from the plebs into the number of the senators 164 men, with the result that he completed the number of 300 senators and named them as two types' (or the final clause may be one of purpose).

Paul. Fest. p. 6.23–5 Lindsay *nam patres dicuntur, qui sunt patricii generis; conscripti, qui in senatu sunt scriptis adnotati*, 'for they are called *patres* who are of patrician rank, and they *conscripti* who were enrolled in the senate in written documents'.

See *TLL* X.1.677.8ff. on this as the traditional distinction between *patres* and *conscripti*. Ogilvie (1965: 236) states the prevailing opinion ('*patres* were the original patricians ..., *conscripti* were plebeians, i.e. non-patricians, introduced into the Senate by Romulus ... or ... by the first consuls'), but then questions this view, on the grounds that 'the proper term for senators drafted in from outside would be *adscripti* and not *conscripti*' (an unconvincing argument: the basic sense of *conscribo* was 'enrol, enlist', and it is outsiders who are enlisted to form e.g. an army). See Cornell (1995: 247), commenting on the alternative idea that *conscripti* might have been an adjective qualifying *patres*: 'this interpretation can be ruled out, not only because tradition treats the *conscripti* as separate from the *patres*, but because the formula used to summon the Senate called upon "those who are fathers and those who are enrolled", ... which puts the matter beyond doubt'. There remains an uncertainty, because tradition cannot necessarily be trusted. This would not be the only nominal use of *conscripti* in asyndeton with a legal meaning. Note *Tabula Heracleensis* 106 (Crawford 1996: 1.367) *neue in senatum neue in decurionum conscriptorum numero legito sublegito coptato*, translated (376), 'nor is he to enrol them or enrol them in substitution or co-opt them into the senate or among the category of decurions or *conscripti*'. Over time the force of the two terms *patres* and *conscripti* was probably lost, because all senators came to be considered *patres conscripti*. Cicero's use at *Phil.* 13.28 of *pater conscriptus* in the singular must be intended as ironical (see Cornell 1995: 445 n. 17), but note Horace *Ars* 314 *quod sit conscripti, quod iudicis officium*, 'what is the duty of a senator, of a judge', a unique use of the singular *conscriptus* of a senator (see Brink 1971: 341 ad loc.).

If we accept that *patres conscripti* was originally a nominal asyndeton bimembre, semantically the two terms together embrace the membership of a body or organisation, a totality rather than part of a whole. A parallel in type would be the asyndetic pairing of consuls' names, a pairing which constitutes the totality of consuls for a year.

But pairs expressing a totality also exist with explicit coordination, and it is not merely the semantic relationship between the terms that determines the asyndeton. The taste for lack of coordination in republican legal contexts and expressions must have been a factor. Perhaps too an old formula of summons into the senate played a part, with the two groups called forth separately, *patres ... conscripti*, and a coordinator not used because of a pause.

5.2   *uelitis iubeatis*

This formula may be illustrated from Livy 38.54.3 (see Livy 52): *fuit autem rogatio talis: <u>uelitis iubeatis</u>, Quirites, quae pecunia capta ablata coacta ab rege Antiocho est quique sub imperio eius fuerunt, quod eius in publicum relatum non est, uti de ea re Ser. Sulpicius praetor urb<an>us ad senatum referat, quem eam rem uelit senatus quaerere de iis qui praetores nunc sunt*, 'but the *rogatio* was along these lines: "Would you wish and order, Quirites, that the money which was captured, removed and gathered from King Antiochus and those who were under his power (i.e. the part of it which has not been transferred into public funds) – (would you wish and order) that, concerning that matter [*re* is used where *pecunia* is expected], the *praetor urbanus* Servius Sulpicius should refer to the senate the question whom of those who are now praetors would (the senate) wish to inquire into it?"'

Velitis iubeatis is an asyndetic formula 'used by the magistrate presiding over an assembly when taking a vote' (Briscoe 1973: 70 on 31.6.1). It introduces a *rogatio*, as this passage makes explicit (on the *rogatio* see Crawford 1996: 1.10).

The syntax of the formula is not straightforward. It seems to introduce a question, as distinct from containing jussive subjunctives: note Livy 22.10.2 *rogatus in haec uerba populus: 'uelitis iubeatisne haec sic fieri?'*, where the formula, preceded by *rogatus populus*, has the question marker *-ne*; cf. Cic. *Dom.* 80 *ut, si tribuno plebis rogante 'uelitis iubeatisne' Fidulii centum se uelle et iubere dixerint*, a passage with the additional interest that in the hypothetical answer *uelle* and *iubere* are given the coordinator *et*.

However, is that question direct, such that the subjunctives are potential, or is it to be taken as indirect, dependent on an implied *rogo*? If it is direct, the meaning is 'would you wish and order that'; if it is indirect, it means 'do you wish and order that'. Opinions have been expressed or implied about this problem, but without systematic or decisive discussion. Daube (1956: 54), for example, translates what he refers to as 'the question *velitis iubeatis*' as 'would you wish and order'. Ogilvie (1965: 187), commenting on *uellent iuberentne*, gives exactly the same translation of *uelitis iubeatis*, but without comment on the syntax, though he does describe *uelitis iubeatis* as the 'direct form'. Briscoe (2008: 190), on the other hand, again without discussion, says: 'The subjunctives are probably not "potential, denoting deferential enquiry" (Walsh), but are dependent on an expressed or unexpressed *rogo*.' R. G. Nisbet (1939: 109–10) has a fuller note. His own opinion is stated at the start: 'it seems best to take the construction as originally indirect question with *rogo* understood'. He then adds: 'some moderns regard it as a direct question, "Would it be your wish?"; others seem to think of *rogo* as "request" followed by jussive subjunctive'. For a collection of examples see Preuss (1881: 94–5).

It is not clear to me that the problem can be solved, in the absence of more information about the presiding magistrate's preamble.

Of more interest here is the nature of the asyndeton, that is the relationship between the two verbs. It seems to be of classic type. Wishing is weaker than ordering. The second verb in general terms is stronger than the first, but it is possible to be more precise about the relationship. One might interpret the ordering (*iubeatis*) as following on from the wishing (*uelitis*) that something be done: 'do you wish it, and consequently/therefore order it?' We will often note pairs in which the second member may be described as expressing a consequence of the first. A literal rendering into English with asyndeton would have a pause between the verbs, with the second emphasised strongly to cap the first ('do you wish, ORDER, that', = 'do you wish, order indeed, that'). Another possibility would be to take the first verb as a modifier of the second, in that one could rewrite as *uolentes iubeatis* 'do you willingly order?' (see II.3.2.1 on *uolens propitius*). Cf. e.g. Sallust 64 *festinare parare*, which could be paraphrased as *festinanter/festinantes parare* (see in general II.3.2.3.1). I prefer the first interpretation above.

5.3   sarta tecta

Here is another formula found in Livy: 42.3.7 *cui sarta tecta exigere sacris publicis et loca<re> tuenda more maiorum traditum esset*, '(the magistrate) to whom had been entrusted, in the manner of the ancestors, the duty of enforcing a good state of repair, below and on top, for public temples and of contracting for their maintenance' (see Livy **26**).

Sarta tecta is translated as 'repairs and roofing' by Briscoe (2012: 161), but as 'wind-tight and water-tight' by Pinkster (forthcoming, 1.3.4, 19.18), sc. *aedificia* (cf. *OLD*, rendering in the same way the form *sartus tectus*). Shackleton Bailey (1977: 2.441) on Cic. *Fam.* 13.11.1, says: 'Of buildings in good repair . . .; hence = repairs or maintenance (of public buildings)'. Watkins (1995: 44) renders *sarcta tecta* as 'whole and roofed'. For examples see Preuss (1881: 107–8).

Sartus is the past participle of *sarcio* 'mend, repair'. With *tectus* it is found in asyndeton in an adjectival role, 'mended, covered', and hence in general 'in good repair', with the second term referring originally to the state of the roof of a building and the other presumably to the state of the lower structure (or rest of the structure). For the adjectival use see e.g. Cic. *Verr.* 1.131 *quaesiuit quis aedem Castoris sartam tectam deberet tradere*, which is found also when the two terms have a metaphorical role (Plaut. *Trin.* 317, Cic. *Fam.* 13.50.2: see Otto 1890: 309). In this last passage (*Fam.* 13.50.2) the form of the phrase is *sartum et tectum* (applied to a person; the phrase is followed by *ut aiunt*, a mark of its proverbial status), an illustration of the fact that an old asyndeton bimembre will not necessarily remain uncoordinated. *Sarta tecta*, which is mistakenly translated by de Vaan (2008: 539) as 'mended roofs' (giving the first the form *sarcta*), must originate from a phrase such as *aedificia sarta tecta* 'buildings mended and roofed' (= 'well repaired/in repaired state below and on top'), with *sarta tecta* then substantivised by ellipse of *aedificia* (or the like: cf. Paul. Fest. p. 429.5 Lindsay, where *opera publica* is the noun phrase to which the pair is applied) and meaning something like 'repaired state below and on top' or, more generally, 'building repair/maintenance'. Thus we might render Cic. *Fam.* 13.11.1 *quibus . . . sarta tecta aedium sacrarum locorumque communium tueri possi<n>t* as 'by which they can preserve the repaired state below and on top of their sacred temples and public places'. Cf. Cic. *Verr.* 1.128 *in sartis tectis uero quem ad modum se gesserit quid ego dicam?*, 'but what am I to say about how he conducted himself in the matter of public building repairs/maintenance'.

Sartus tectus was a legal phrase (repairs to public buildings were commissioned by the censors) in a typical legal asyndeton (see Kalb 1912: 137:

5 Some Legal Pairs, Mainly Old

e.g. Ulp. *Dig.* 7.1.7.2), but when it passed into general use, as in the metaphorical phrase at Cic. *Fam.* 13.50.2 above, it tended to acquire a coordinator. In the passage of the *Digest* just referred to *sarta tecta* is twice a complement of *habeo* (*ut sarta tecta habeat . . . de modo sarta tecta habendi quaerit*), in clauses open to the loose translation 'that he keep them in good repair . . . he considers the method of keeping them in good repair'. The passage has to do with the duty of keeping a house (*aedes*) repaired, and neuter plurals are several times used in the context in reference to such buildings.

It is of interest that the pairing occurs already in Plautus in a metaphorical sense: *Trin.* 317 *sarta tecta tua praecepta usque habui mea modestia*, 'I have always kept your teachings in good repair thanks to my moderate behaviour' (note too the use of *habeo*, as in the *Digest* above). It must by that time have been extremely familiar in commonplace usage if it could be taken beyond its original sphere in this way.

5.4 loca lautia

See e.g. Livy 42.26.5 *ut ex instituto loca lautia acciperent*, 'so that they might receive, in accordance with the custom, lodging, hospitality' (see Livy 28).

The phrase is taken to refer to the lodging and official entertainment/ hospitality/provisions/upkeep accorded envoys (see Walbank 1979: 111–12, and particularly Timpanaro 1967: 432–9). In the *Senatus consultum de Asclepiade* of 78 BC (Sherk 1969, text 22) *locum lautiaque* is rendered (l. 26 = l. 13 of the Latin) τόπον παροχήν τε (the second word = 'furnishing, supply'). Cf. Charisius p. 37.5 Barwick *lautia* ἐνδομενεία *supellex* (the last two terms = 'household goods, furniture'). Note that again the asyndetic form acquired a coordinated variant: cf. Livy 28.39.19 *locus inde lautiaque legatis praeberi iussa* (see Timpanaro 1967: 433 for asyndetic versus syndetic coordination in this expression, referring to the addition of the coordinator as a modernisation). On the possible etymology of *lautia* see de Vaan (2008: 161–2), accepting an original form *dautia* (see Paul. Fest. p. 60.6 Lindsay *dautia, quae lautia dicimus, et dantur legatis hospitii gratia*) from an Indo-European root meaning 'giving'. De Vaan does not refer to Timpanaro's excursus on the etymology of *lautia* (1967: 439–42), which revives an old suggestion of Mommsen, that *lautium* (not attested in the singular) is connected with *lauo-lautum* (with the formation he compares other deverbatives, *exercitium* and *iustitium*), and originally referred to the preparation of a bath as an act of welcome.

Twice in Livy the phrase is preceded by *aedes liberae*: e.g. 35.23.11 *aedes liberae locus lautia decreta* (so 30.17.14), perhaps an asyndeton trimembre (so Briscoe 2012: 238). A 'place and hospitality' is a 'free house', and it is possible that *liberae aedes* has been added as a modernisation to explain the obscure old phrase ('a free house, i.e. *loca lautia*').

Again the asyndeton is in an old official phrase.

5.5   *ruta caesa*

This phrase refers to things dug or cut that did not belong to buildings: see Bannon (2013: 211): 'The category of *ruta caesa* was used in sale by *mancipatio* to designate accessories that belonged to the seller after the sale.'[5] Bannon discusses at length (particularly at 211–14) the legal problems of definition. At 210 n. 17 she lists attestations of the asyndetic phrase and of the variant in which the terms are coordinated by *et*. *Ruta caesa* occurs eight times, *ruta et caesa* three times. Varro (*Ling.* 9.104), commenting on the long *u* in *ruta*, associates the asyndetic phrase with the law of sale of a farm: *ideoque in lege uenditionis fundi 'ruta caesa' ita dicimus, ut u producamus* (see also Festus p. 320.1–3, where again the context is legal). Cicero has the asyndeton at *Part. Or.* 107, *Top.* 100, and the coordinated variant at *De or.* 2.226. This last, coordinated, example is in an argumentative passage in which *ruta caesa* is emphasised by *ne ... quidem*: *ne in rutis quidem et caesis*. The typical placement of *quidem* and the resultant separation of *rutis* from *caesis* make a coordinator almost inevitable.

The long *u* that Varro reports in this phrase is etymologically expected, though some compounds of the verb have a short *u* (e.g. *eruo*). See de Vaan (2008: 531): 'It seems that the derivatives of *ruō* "to rush" and *ruō* "to dig" have become mixed up: we find short-vowel forms meaning "dig", in spite of the PIE etymology.' See too de Melo (2019: 2.1188; also Reinhardt 2003: 367). *Ruta caesa* preserved the original long vowel.

This asyndeton is in an exclusively legal phrase, and it outnumbers the alternative with coordination.

5.6   *usus fructus*

Vsus fructus 'was the right to use and enjoy the fruits of another's property but not to alter its character fundamentally or destroy it' (Watson 1971: 90;

---

[5] I am grateful to Wolfgang Ernst for drawing Bannon's chapter to my attention.

5 Some Legal Pairs, Mainly Old

see also id. 1968: 203–21). Watson loc. cit. (1971) adds that *usus fructus* 'was most frequently used, both originally and much later, to provide for the widow so that she could live in the style she had been accustomed to during her husband's lifetime, and could continue to occupy what had been the matrimonial home' (see further 90–2).

The asyndetic pairing is extremely common, as can be seen from the column of examples collected at *TLL* VI.1.1376, following a much shorter collection of instances (1375.66ff.) in which the two terms are coordinated or separated in some way (see also especially Roby 1884: ccxxx, 27). Most of the asyndetic pairs are in the lawyers but they also find their way into e.g. philosophical and oratorical texts in legal allusions (see e.g. Cic. *Caec.* 94, *Top.* 15, 17, 21, along with Quint. 5.11.32, quoting Cicero). Note particularly Plaut. *Merc.* 832 *usus fructus, uictus cultus iam mihi harunc aedium | interemptust interfectust alienatust: occidi* (with Leo 1960: 174). This example has juxtaposed asyndetic pairs in the manner of later legal usage.

The two verbs *utor* and *fruor* also occur together in legal contexts with and without coordination. Note *Tabula Heracleensis* (Crawford 1996: 1.365) 74 *ut utei fruei liceat*, 75 *quo minus ieis loceis utantur fruantur*. Here is a lawyers' asyndeton bimembre *par excellence*.

5.7, 8 emptio uenditio, locatio conductio

In this section I raise doubts about the status of these expressions as asyndetic technical terms.[6]

Both pairs are regularly used asyndetically in this nominal form by modern Roman lawyers (without, as far as I can see, any comment on the asyndeton as such) to indicate what would be called in the common law 'sale' and 'hire', with the role of both parties in the transaction specified but the pairing expressing a single concept. I quote Buckland (1921: 478), under his heading *EMPTIO VENDITIO*: 'The most important of all contracts. It was essentially sale for a price, the <u>double name</u> [my emphasis] expressing the fact that it was bilateral but the duties on the two sides were different. The only other contract which had this characteristic was hire and that also was called by a double name – *Locatio Conductio*.' Similarly Buckland (1921: 494–5) says of *locatio conductio*: 'This was the contract of letting and hiring for a price, bilateral, and having a double name because the rights and duties of the parties were different, as in *emptio uenditio*.' Other modern legal writers make the same assumption about the currency of

---

[6] I have received help with this section from Arthur Emmett and Wolfgang Ernst.

these 'double names' (e.g. de Zulueta 1945: 4, 6, 7, Nicholas 1962: 171–8, 182–5), Watson 1971: 130, 137, Zimmermann 1996, Chaps. 8–12).

But were there really two established legal terms, comprising two pairs of abstract nouns used asyndetically? In fact both pairs are far more often overtly coordinated (usually by *et*), and the occasional asyndetic pairings that do turn up have a special motivation: they are in accumulations of asyndetic terms or pairs. We have repeatedly seen that such sequences are one of the most common determinants of asyndeton. In other words, an asyndeton *emptio uenditio* in an accumulation need not mean that *emptio uenditio* was a formulaic asyndetic pairing of the legal language, but might merely reflect the fact that the two terms happen to be in a longer list. For such accumulations see e.g. Just. *Inst.* 3.22 *consensu fiunt obligationes in emptionibus uenditionibus, locationibus conductionibus, societatibus, mandatis* (cited by Kalb 1912: 135) (so Gaius 3.135), Nerat. *Dig.* 2.14.58 *ab emptione uenditione, locatione conductione ceterisque similibus obligationibus,* Hermog. *Dig.* 1.1.5 *ex hoc iure gentium introducta bella, discretae gentes, regna condita, dominia distincta, agris termini positi, aedificia collocata, commercium, emptiones uenditiones, locationes conductiones, obligationes institutae.* Moreover usually it is forms of the corresponding verbs, *emere* and *uendere*, and *locare* and *conducere*, that are used asyndetically. Examples have been cited elsewhere from Cicero's philosophical works (Cicero 123, 124, 135, 141, 142, 143, 144, 146, 147). Another question too is raised by such pairs: if e.g. *emptio* and *uenditio* occur together, need they both refer jointly to the same transaction? I move on first to some statistics.

A quick survey of the *TLL* article on *emptio* (V.2.535) turns up no obvious instances of asyndetic *emptio uenditio*, but there are six examples quoted of the pair coordinated (V.2.535.47–61). I have not checked references to jurists in brackets given there without any text. In Justinian's *Institutes* a chapter headed *De emptione et uenditione* (3.23) has the pair about eight times with coordination (usually *et* but twice *-que*) but never with asyndeton. The two words are variously used in the singular and plural, and that variation is not suggestive of terms being fossilised into a compound unit. The asyndetic examples listed by Preuss (1881: 41) seem to be verbal rather than nominal, as for instance at *Dig.* 18.2.16 (Ulpian) *de empti uenditi actione.*

Similarly the *TLL* s.v. *conductio* (IV.162.65–163.16 'de iure') cites (without in every case quoting) thirteen instances of *locatio* and *conductio* coordinated, but only three that are asyndetic, all in accumulations alongside *emptio uenditio*: Ulp. *Dig.* 2.14.7.1 *ut emptio uenditio, locatio conductio, societas, commodatum, depositum et ceteri similes contractus,* Ulp. *Dig.*

5 Some Legal Pairs, Mainly Old 261

50.16.19 *ueluti emptionem uenditionem, locationem conductionem, societatem* (also Gaius 3.135, rerferred to above). Again, in the chapter *De locatione et conductione* in Justinian's *Institutes* (3.24) there are twelve coordinated instances of the pair (one negative, with a *neque . . . neque* construction), but no asyndetic.

Here are a few examples of explicit coordination:

Pompon. *Dig.* 46.3.80 *aeque cum emptio uel uenditio uel locatio contracta est, quoniam consensu nudo contrahi potest, etiam dissensu contrario dissolui potest* (here there is disjunctive coordination, with e.g. *emptio* and *uenditio* treated as separate acts; the singular verbs that follow, *contracta est, potest* twice, refer not to any collectivity, because the intrusive *locatio* is present in the same disjunctive sequence as *emptio* and *uenditio*, but presumably have been made to agree mechanically with the last member of the sequence).
Paul. *Dig.* 19.4.1.2 *item emptio ac uenditio nuda consentientium uoluntate contrahitur*, 'moreover sale is contracted by single consent of the parties' (here on the other hand what is clearly a single transaction with two parties is described by means of the coordinated pair, with a singular verb in this case referring to a collectivity).
Inst. 3.23 *emptio et uenditio contrahitur, simulatque . . .*, 'a sale is contracted as soon as . . .' (see on the last example).
Dig. 18.1.9.2 *Marcellus scripsit libro sexto digestorum emptionem esse et uenditionem, quia . . .*, 'Marcellus wrote in the sixth book of his Digesta that there was a good contract of sale because . . .'

Asyndeta comprising verb forms of *emere/uendere* and *locare/conducere* reflect the legal taste for uncoordinated pairs of verbs. On the evidence found here it is misleading to fasten on to pairs of nouns such as *emptio uenditio* and to imply that they constitute together an asyndetic technical designation for an act of sale. The terms are more frequently coordinated, and these coordinated examples often, as emerges from the context, refer to a single transaction; they may be subject of a singular verb, which in this case should be taken to indicate that together they express a unity.

However, a reference to buying/selling need not always be to a single transaction with two participants, one the buyer, the other the seller. The same person may buy things from one party and sell them to another. When *emo* and *uendo* are used in asyndeton by Cicero in the *De officiis* it is sometimes clear that a single person is engaging in multiple activities of both types: e.g. *Off.* 2.64 (Cicero 143, 144) *conueniet . . . esse . . . uendundo emendo, conducendo locando, uicinitatibus et confiniis, aequum facilem, multa multis de suo iure cedentem, a litibus uero . . . abhorrentem*, 'it will be suitable for one ... in buying and selling, in hiring and letting, in affairs to do with neighbouring properties and common boundaries, to be fair and approachable, conceding much of his own right to many, but shunning litigation' (cf. e.g. *Off.* 2.40: Cicero **141, 142**). Note the singular referent, *aequum facilem*. We also saw an example above in a disjunctive sequence, *emptio uel uenditio uel locatio*, which refers to three different acts.

I conclude that in textbooks of Roman law sale and hire should be described as *emptio et uenditio*, and *locatio et conductio*. Also, it should not be assumed without reference to the context that a pair such as *emptio et uenditio* necessarily denotes a single act with two parties participating.

5.9 *populus Romanus Quirites* (?)

The inclusion of this pair is merely tentative.[7] What looks like an asyndeton is in a fragment of Fabius Pictor ap. Gell. 1.12.14 *sacerdotem Vestalem facere pro populo Romano Quiritibus*, and also in a praetorian formula quoted at Gell. 10.24.3 (= Macr. *Sat.* 1.4.27) *ea uerba haec sunt: Dienoni populo Romano Quiritibus Compitalia erunt*. There is however an alternative formulation, in which *Quirites* is in the genitive plural dependent on *populus Romanus*, as for example at Livy 41.16.1 and 22.10.3 (words of a *pontifex*) *donum duit populus Romanus Quiritium*. The problem of interpretation is based on the meaning of *Quirites*. I quote de Melo (2019: 2.869) on Varro *Ling.* 6.68: *Quirites* 'has no convincing etymology ... and may be a loanword ... There may be something in Varro's connection of the word with *Cures*, an ancient Sabine town about 42 km from Rome.' The Latin adjective based on this can be *Curensis* or *Curetis*. De Melo notes that this etymology was universally accepted in antiquity. According to Varro (6.68) the *Quirites* were the *Curenses* or 'men of *Cures*', who came with king Tatius to receive a share of the state (see de Melo 2019: 2.395). On this view the *Quirites* would originally have been the non-Roman element in Rome, and the pair would have been asyndetic (cf. *patres conscripti*), but with the loss of the original meaning of *Quirites* the word was perhaps converted into the genitive to convey the supposed identity of the two groups. An example in the genitive throughout (*populi Romani Quiritium*) does not reveal the relation between the terms: if there was originally asyndeton, *Quiritium* might have been subject to

---

[7] I am grateful to Adam Gitner for much information.

6 Some Religious Pairs   263

misinterpretation in this phrase as dependent on *populi Romani*. There remains an element of doubt.

5.10   usus auctoritas

This pair at Cic. *Top*. 23 (*usus auctoritas fundi*, use and warranty of a piece of land) seems to go back to the XII Tables (VI.3: see Crawford 1996: 2.658–9). For discussion see Crawford 659, Reinhardt 2003: 250. For *usus* and *utor* as the first member of legal asyndetic pairs see 5.6. Even if the meaning were to be interpreted as 'warranty for the use', that would not entail taking *usus* as a genitive, because in pairs of the type that have been labelled here 'asyndetic hendiadys' one term semantically may have a genitival relationship to the other, even though it is in the same case (see e.g. II.3.2.3.2. for *salutem victoriam* and *laetitia victoria* in Livy).

5.11   Conclusions

The asyndetic use of pairs of keywords, particularly verbs but also nouns, had an obvious appeal to lawyers, presumably because of their curt, no-nonsense flavour. That does not mean that a consistent asyndetic style was achieved. The pairings collected in this section mainly went well back in time, but they are a mere selection of legal asyndetic pairs. Many others are collected by Kalb (1888: 37–41, 1912: 134–9). For another pair in Cicero see *aequum bonum* at Cicero 163.

6   Some Religious Pairs

Asyndetic pairs loosely from the sphere of religion do occur (in addition to the few examples seen earlier in prayers), but they are not particularly frequent. *Volens propitius* is dealt with elsewhere (II.3.2.1).

6.1   sub di(u)o culmine

This phrase occurs in various forms in the *Acta Fratrum Arualium* (of which there are remains from the last quarter of the first century BC well into the Empire; the twelve *Fratres Aruales* formed a priestly college that carried out various religious ceremonies), such as *sub diuo columine* and *sub diuo culmine* (for references to *CIL* VI see *TLL* V.1.1658.51–2, 55), and *sub dio culmine* (*TLL* V.1.1642.71, 82); see also Leo (1898: 273, Scheid 1998, index 393 s.v. *culmen*). The meaning of *sub di(u)o* is 'in the open air' (see *OLD* s.v. *dium*). *Columen* for its part can mean 'roof'. There is possibly an instance of the full phrase at Plaut. *Mo.* 765, where lines 764–5 are printed by Lindsay as: *quia isti umbram aestate tibi esse audiuit perbonam | sub diuo columine usque perpetuom diem*. Leo printed *sub sicco lumine* in his edition (1896), with a reference to *sub sudo columine* in the apparatus criticus, but in 1898 changed his mind and defended *sub diu columine* on the strength of the passages in the *Acta Fratrum Arualium* (see Leo 1898: 274, 275). The reading of the Ambrosianus at this point is very unclear (see Leo 1898: 274–5; cf. *TLL* V.1.1642.83); the Palatine manuscript has *subdiu col perpetuum diem*. *Sub diu columine* may refer to a covered colonnade into which sunlight comes but not rain (see Leo 1898: 277). *Sub diu columine* is accepted by Norden (1939: 18). Scheid (1998: 161) on *sub diuo culmine* (his text numbered 58.30) translates as 'sous la voûte céleste', though referring in his note (163) to Leo.

The asyndeton would be of a (paradoxical) adversative type, 'under the sky but under a roof'. There is a possible structural parallel in the phrase *palam secreto*, used by Caelius at Cic. *Fam.* 8.1.4 ('openly but in secret': see Cicero 213).

6.2 *(Iuppiter) optimus maximus*

This is of a special adjectival type. See IV.4.

6.3 *Some Augural Formulae*

A few asyndetic pairings in augural formulae are attested, one of them remarkable for its antiquity, in that it is paralleled in the Iguvine tablets.

Note first Cic. *Div.* 2.42 *in nostris commentariis scriptum habemus: 'Ioue tonante fulgurante comitia populi habere nefas'* (see Pease 1963: 424 and XVI.1 for a Greek parallel).

Second, there is the augural context at Plaut. *As.* 259–60: *impetritum inauguratumst: quouis admittunt aues, | picus et cornix ab laeua, coruos parra ab dextera consuadent*. Here are two pairs of bird names, the first pair coordinated, the second asyndetic. This passage is similar to one in the Iguvine tablets, VIa.1 (quoted earlier, 4.2), in which both pairs are asyndetic. The combining of asyndeton and coordination in two parallel pairs in the Latin we saw above (3.2) in the prayer to Mars at Cato *Agr.* 141.2. See also XIX.1, XXIII.3.

6.4 prima postrema

This is at Livy 1.24.7 in the formula of the *fetiales* in concluding a treaty, a formula in which Jupiter is addressed. On the passage see Ogilvie (1965: 110–12), Chapot and Laurot (2001: 298–300). A semantic feature of the asyndeton is discussed at XIII.2, on 'antipodals'.

6.5 porci sacres sinceri

Found at Plaut. *Men.* 290. See Gratwick (1993: 169–70), calling it a 'phrase of ritual'. It is impossible to determine its status given that this is the only occurrence.

I turn now to literary texts and to the appearance in them of asyndetic pairs with a legal flavour. I will then add from such texts a few religious pairs.

7 Legal Phrases in Literary Texts

7.1 Proposals in the Senate; Other Contexts

In oratory and the historians there are many asyndetic pairs that fall loosely into the category of legal expressions. The direct influence of this official style on Cicero can be seen in passages in which he proposes a decree of the senate and quotes his proposal. One such motion is at *Phil.* 5.36, and it contains two instances of the asyndetic pair of titles *imperator, consul designatus* (attached to the name D. Brutus), and also the following: *cumque exercitum tantum ... conscripserit compararit* (see Cicero 75). He has linked two verbs (both with the same prefix) asyndetically, a mannerism of *senatus consulta* as well as laws (for which see above, this chapter, 2.1, 2.2). Cf. e.g.

SC de collegiis artificum Graecis (Riccobono 1968, text 34, p. 255) *ut M. Liuium consulem adeant, isque cognoscat decernat.*
SC de Aphrodisiensibus (Riccobono 1968, text 38, p. 271) *quaeque praemia honores beneficia ... attribuerunt attribuerint concesserunt concesserint.*

Another of Cicero's motions is at *Phil.* 5.46 (Cicero 76). It has two instances of asyndetic titles (*pontifex pro praetore*), and also this: *libertatem populi Romani defendant defe<nde>rint.* The pair of verbs in different tenses is of the type seen in the second *senatus consultum* just quoted (see also IX). For examples in the quotation of a law by Cicero see *Clu.* 148 *qui eorum coiit coierit, conuenit conuenerit quo quis iudicio publico condemnaretur.*

Finally, here is the end of a third motion put forward in the same speech: *Phil.* 5.53 (Cicero 77, 78) *utique C. Pansa A. Hirtius consules, alter amboue, si eis uideretur, rationem agri habe<re>nt qui sine iniuria priuatorum diuidi posset, eisque militibus, legioni Martiae et legioni quartae ita darent adsignarent ut quibus militibus amplissime dati adsignati essent.*

The pair *dare adsignare* in asyndeton in laws is illustrated on Cicero 77, 78, as too is the repetition of the pair in a different form seen here.

But Cicero (and others) not only adopt legal-type asyndeta in quotations of official documents. They use them too in other contexts (see e.g. XXVI.7.8.1). Sometimes one can observe the transfer of a structure from legal document to a more general context. A quotation at Cic. *Sest.* 33 (*ut lex Aelia lex Fufia ne ualeret*: Cicero 33) is from a proposal for a law, and the names of the laws are in asyndeton in this official context. On the other hand *Sest.* 135 (*Caeciliam Didiam, Liciniam Iuniam contempsit*: Cicero 34, 35, 36) is part of Cicero's own narrative, and again he has adopted what must have been considered official style in naming the laws. Note too that each law in this last passage has asyndeton in its own two-word title, comprising adjectival forms of personal names.

Similarly at *Phil.* 3.38 (*eum exercitumque, municipia colonias prouinciae Galliae*) Cicero in a proposal for a senatorial decree uses *municipia* and *coloniae* without a coordinator (Cicero 25). But at *Phil.* 6.18 (*eodem incumbunt municipia coloniae, cuncta Italia*) the same asyndetic pair (as part of a tricolon with a summarising phrase at the end) is in an assertion by Cicero (quoted after Cicero 31).

I offer here, largely without comment, some examples of pairs with a legal flavour from prose writers, arranged in semantic categories (see also the cross references in the commentaries on those numbered in bold).

7.2 *Offices, Officials, Titles, Honours*

Cic. *Off.* 2.67 (**122**) *commendantem iudicibus magistratibus*
Cic. *Rep.* 1.47 *ferunt etiam suffragia, mandant imperia magistratus, ambiuntur rogantur*
Livy 34.7.2 (**64**) *purpura uiri utemur, praetextati in magistratibus in sacerdotiis* (note too Sall. *Cat.* 21.2 *tum Catilina polliceri . . . magistratus sacerdotia, rapinas*, with Sallust 11 on the punctuation).

Tac. *Hist.* 3.86.1 (**14**) *consulatum sacerdotia, nomen locumque . . . adeptus*
Livy 4.15.5 (**3, 4**) *sed tamen Claudios Cassios consulatibus decemuiratibus, suis maiorumque honoribus, splendore familiarum sustulisse animos, quo nefas fuerit*
Tac. *Ann.* 1.4.4 (**55**) *congestos iuueni consulatus triumphos*

7 Legal Phrases in Literary Texts 267

Livy 4.4.2 (2) <u>pontifices augures</u> *Romulo regnante nulli sunt*
Pontifex and *augur* are elsewhere associated: see the note ad loc. Note also *Lex Coloniae Genetiuae* LXVI.34 (Crawford 1996: 1.401) *eiq(ue) pon<t>i[fi]ces augur-esque in pontificum augurum conlegio*, and 37–8 *pontificibus auguribusque*, but LXVI.6 (col. III, p. 402) *cum ei pontific(es) augures sacra publica . . . facient*.

7.3 Groups or Individuals within the State of a Defined Status; External Groups Possessing an Official Relationship with the State

Sall. *Hist*. 4.60.17 (47) Ramsey <u>socios amicos</u>, *procul iuxta sitos, inopes potentisque trahant excindant*
For asyndetic parallels in laws see on Sallust 47.

Tac. *Ann*. 13.48 (109) *legationes, quas diuersas* <u>ordo plebs</u> *ad senatum miserant*

Tac. *Ann*. 4.38.3 (80) *proinde* <u>socios ciues</u> *et deos ipsos et deas precor*
Tac. *Hist*. 4.5.2 (16) <u>ciuis senator</u>, *maritus gener amicus, cunctis uitae officiis aequa-bilis, opum contemptor, recti peruicax, constans aduersus metus*.

7.4 Abstract Terms Denoting Relationships with States

For *amicitia societas* see on Sallust 47, from which there is a citation above. Here are a few further pairs.

Sall. *Iug*. 111.1–2 (41) *quem si Romanis tradidisset, fore ut illi plurumum deberetur;* <u>amicitiam foedus</u>, *Numidiae partem quam nunc peteret tum ultro aduenturam*
Livy 38.48.4 (24) <u>libertatem immunitatem</u> *ciuitatibus datis*.

7.5 Types of States and Foundations, Methods of Government

Cic. *Off*. 1.115 (113) *nam* <u>regna imperia</u>, *nobilitas honores, diuitiae opes*
Sall. *Cat*. 20.7–8 (6, 7) *semper illis* <u>reges tetrarchae</u> *uectigales esse,* <u>populi nationes</u> *stipendia pendere*
Sall. *Iug*. 31.20 (29) *quom* <u>regna prouinciae</u>, <u>leges iura iudicia</u>, *bella atque paces, postremo diuina et humana omnia penes paucos erant*.

Cic. *Dom*. 138 (84) *ex rebus palam per magistratus actis ad conlegiumque delatis,* <u>ex senatus consulto ex lege</u>
Livy 9.9.12 (56) <u>cum senatu cum populo</u> *de pace ac foedere agere*
Cic. *Att*. 7.13.1 (187) *quid autem sit acturus aut quo modo nescio,* <u>sine senatu sine magistratibus</u>

Sall. *Cat.* 6.1 (84) *genus hominum agreste, <u>sine legibus sine imperio</u>, liberum atque solutum* (of an anarchic people, the early Aborigines, who lacked the legal apparatus of the later Roman state).

7.6 Activities Regulated by Law

Cic. *Att.* 1.18.3 (183) *facto senatus consulto <u>de ambitu de iudiciis</u>, nulla lex perlata*

Cic. *Off.* 3.70 (123, 124) *idque uersari in tutelis societatibus, fiduciis mandatis, rebus emptis uenditis, conductis locatis, quibus uitae societas contineretur* (for asyndetic pairs of the type *emptio uenditio* and *locatio conductio* in the jurists see above, 5.7, 8).

The categories above are not intended to be exhaustive.

8 Religious Phrases in Literary Texts

I cite now some literary passages that have pairs from the sphere of religion. Again they are not commented on here, as they come up in chapters on the works concerned.

Enn. *Ann.* 591 (10) *diuomque hominumque <u>pater rex</u>*

Cic. *Att.* 4.2.6 (160) *uotiuam legationem sumpsissem prope omnium <u>fanorum lucorum</u>*

Cic. *Cat.* 3.2 (4) *nam toti urbi, <u>templis delubris</u>, tectis ac moenibus subiectos prope iam ignis circumdatosque restinximus*

Cic. *Sest.* 90 (16) *qui <u>ab aris focis</u> ferrum flammamque depellis*

Tac. *Hist.* 1.3.2 (21, 22) *prodigia et fulminum monitus et futurorum praesagia, <u>laeta tristia, ambigua manifesta</u>.*

9 Conclusions

The statistics given above, 3.5 (and see the next paragraph) show that there was a distinction between prayers, in which coordinators are the norm, and laws, where asyndeton is more common, but it is also the case that in laws there is some diversity, and variation does not exclusively take the form of a transition from asyndetic pairs to coordinated over time. It is true that in the imperial period in laws there was some decline in asyndeton bimembre, but that does not mean that in the earliest period asyndeton was exclusively used, or that the later decline was total. The earliest text seen here (see above, 1), the decree of L. Aemilius from Spain, dated 189 BC, has no

9 Conclusions

asyndetic pairs, but two distinctive coordinated pairs, *possidere habereque* and *agrum oppidumqu(e)*, pairs that can later be found in asyndeton. On the other hand, in the *Digest* and Justinian's *Institutes*, asyndeton remains common, as we have seen for example in IX, XI.5, XIV.2.5.

Here is an overview of the distribution of asyndetic versus coordinated pairs in the laws and prayers dealt with here. The first two laws apart from the decree mentioned in the last paragraph, the *Lex Cornelia* (2.1) and the *Lex Antonia* (2.2), are both roughly of the mid-first century BC. The first (2.1) has 39 asyndetic pairs and only 9 coordinated, and it was shown that the 9 coordinated tend to differ in various ways from the asyndetic. Here is a text in which asyndeton was standard. On the other hand in the other (2.2) there are 14 cases of asyndeton bimembre, but 19 of coordinated pairs. Asyndeton is present but no more frequent than coordination. In the third text, *S. C. de Pisone patre* (2.3) of AD 20 a radical change is in evidence. This text has 104 coordinated pairs, but only 1 asyndetic.

In the five prayers (or similar: I include as 'religious' the replies of *haruspices*) considered (3.1–5), some of them probably very old, we noted just two instances of asyndeton bimembre, but 41 of *-que* linking pairs. The difference between prayers and laws is striking, and, as we saw, can be further demonstrated from prayers not considered here.

These figures do not suggest a single historical development, from an earlier, 'ancient' form of coordination (asyndeton) to a later form (syndetic). It does look as if asyndeton was up to a point going out of fashion in legal language during the Empire, but that does not mean that asyndetic coordination was 'more ancient' than asyndetic. In the earliest legal text considered, the decree, coordination with *-que* was the norm, and *-que* is indeed a term with cognates in other early Indo-European languages (see de Vaan 2008: 506) and was itself ancient (see also III.1). Similarly there are some old pairs with a legal or official flavour that always have a coordinator, such as *aqua et igni interdicere* (*TLL* VII.1.2174.47ff.), *per lancem liciumque* (see *OLD* s.v. *lanx* 3, of an ancient method of search for stolen property: see *OLD* loc. cit.), *domi militiaeque* (see *TLL* IV.1974.67ff.). Fashion, chance and genre came into it. Asyndeton seems to have been more acceptable in legal language than in prayers (at least until the Empire), possibly because laws are more peremptory than prayers and near-synonyms were piled up in relentless strings to cover every eventuality. These distributions do not support the idea that asyndeton bimembre was specifically sacral.

The change of fashion in legal language seen in the *S. C. de Pisone patre* was not of course an absolute, because some drafters were bound to stick to old ways, but it can be further demonstrated from a special sphere. I have not dealt with the naming of pairs of consuls for a particular year in this chapter or systematically anywhere else, but such pairs provide a classic illustration not only of official/legal asyndeta bimembria, but also of the weakening of the asyndetic convention as time went on.

Asyndetic naming was undoubtedly the old and official method of reference. Pease (1963: 379) on Cic. *Div.* 2.20 (*L. Iunio et P. Claudio consulibus*) has a long note on asyndeton versus *et* in consular naming, with bibliography (for brief discussion see also Penney 2005: 37–8, who also quotes at 38 a pair of asyndetic aediles' names from an Oscan inscription), in which he draws particularly on Lommatzsch at *TLL* IV.568–9. I quote Pease:

> (Lommatzsch) lays down the rule that in formal public usage up to the first century after Christ consular names are nearly always found without a connective (Ciceronian examples to the contrary being the present and 2 *Verr.* 5, 34 (in some MSS); *Brut.* 72; 109; *Ac.* 2, 137; *de Am.* 96), but that after that date the use of *et* becomes more frequent. In private usage, however, when but a single name of each consul is cited (e.g., *Brut.* 224: *Mario et Flacco consulibus*), *et* may be employed (on p. 569 he collects seventeen cases from Cicero), a custom which later extended to formal public use.

This increasing use of coordination parallels what we found earlier in the chronological survey of selected legal documents.

It is essential in describing features of sacral language to make a clear distinction between coordinations, asyndeta with two members, and those with three or more. There is something of a tradition of finding 'ancient Italic' formulations in 'solemn' and religious Latin, but disparate material tends to be thrown together without specification. Fraenkel, for example (1960: 138 n. 2), citing Plaut. *Ps.* 164 *uorsa sparsa, tersa strata, lautaque unctaque omnia ut sint*, describes it as 'un magnifico esempio di dizione elevata antico-italica', and compares it with the protracted asyndetic sequence in an Umbrian prayer at *Tab. Ig.* VIb.59–60 (cited above in this chapter, 4.6). Sequences of asyndetic pairs are of course widespread in Latin of many varieties, and also found in Greek (see XIX.1). It is not impossible that Plautus in using such language was indirectly or partly influenced by Italian traditions, but certainly the prominent use of asyndetic pairs in Umbrian prayers and religious language has had little effect on the early Latin prayer language that is extant. There is a marked stylistic difference between the two in the use of coordination, and the same difference is to be found between (e.g.) the prayer in Cato and early Latin legal language.

9 Conclusions

This difference raises a question to which a definite answer cannot be given. Is the coordinated style of Latin prayers due to later rewriting, or had a distinction long been felt in Latin between laying down the law and addressing a deity? The second possibility seems the more likely, given the consistency of the evidence provided by prayers.

CHAPTER XXIII

Plautus

1 Statistics

Asyndeton bimembre is common in Plautus but not overwhelmingly so. There is little point in trying to produce definitive figures, because there are so many variations on the basic (single-word) type, such as word + short phrase, word + long phrase, short phrase + word etc., not to mention unitary pairs within longer asyndetic sequences, which may be treated either as asyndeta bimembria or simply as components of long asyndeta. Phrasal pairs are also common. I concentrate in this chapter mainly on the simple type, or types with only minor modifications of that.

Here are some rough figures. I have noted about 71 pairs of adjectives, 8 pairs of adverbs, 67 pairs of nouns, and very many pairs of verbs (200+). See particularly the Appendix to the chapter.

The text of Plautus used for the most part in this chapter is that of de Melo (Loeb).

2 Diversity of Types

The practice of Plautus brings out the complexity of asyndeton bimembre, as multiple types and influences can be seen. This Plautine diversity opens the way to comparisons with other genres later and the identification of developments over time and differing stylistic patterns. A single adjective simply cannot capture the variety of types.

There are religious and legal phrases, but these are not in great abundance. One religious (augural) instance though is of particular significance, because it can be paralleled in an augural context in one of the (Umbrian) Iguvine tablets (see below, 3). It does therefore seem to spring from more general Italic augural usage.

Another category comprises highly stylised pairs of compounds that are usually coinages, and tend to have forms of assonance as well (see 4).

2 Diversity of Types

Similar are pairs which, though they may not be coinages, have marked sound effects and sometimes occur in juxtaposed pairs. Asyndeton is well suited to the highlighting of sound patterns. Similar usages are found in Latin tragic fragments (see below, 4, 5.4), and must represent a high style of the period. At least one type (that consisting of juxtaposed terms with the same prefix) is found in e.g. Greek tragedy and may have been imitated from there (see VI.8). Repeated privative prefixes indeed are not confined to Greek and Latin but probably inherited in a more general sense (see VI.2.3, VI.5.3). For asyndetic sound effects in Umbrian see XIX.1.

As for Greek influence on Plautus in a wider sense, I have looked at the whole of Menander to get some idea of possible connections between New Comedy and Plautus. Asyndeton bimembre is frequent in Menander (as are other types), and there are some similar types, but the similarities are not so striking as to suggest distinctive impact of the Greek genre on Plautus (see 9). Some of the Plautine categories are characteristic of various early Latin genres (see 4 below), and some other categories that can be paralleled in Greek (i.e. Menander) are familiar also throughout Latin. On asyndeton in some plays of Menander see Ferrero (1976), dealing not only with asyndeton bimembre (see particularly 88–9), but with longer sequences and phrasal and clausal asyndeton, and producing statistics from different plays and types of speeches that do not distinguish the asyndetic categories. However, for a long asyndetic series in Terence translated (loosely) from Menander see Ferrero (1976: 86) on *Ad.* 866, the Greek of which survives in a fragment (for details of the rendering see Martin 1976 ad loc.).

I have concentrated so far on what might be seen as artificial or contrived forms of asyndeton, but by far the most frequent types in Plautus come from ordinary speech. There is an extreme frequency of pairs of imperatives (see 5.1), a type that is widespread in Latin, particularly in the republican period. Many examples have a formulaic structure (notably, in the address of subordinates, 'go' + vocative + further instruction) and also repeated components, and these undoubtedly reflect everyday usage (see X.1).

There are also recurring semantic types (see 8). Certain subjects or contexts, such as the description of female adornments of accessories, or eating and drinking, seem to inspire either asyndetic pairs or longer asyndeta, and such types recur later as well.

In the rest of this chapter I deal separately with a variety of types and patterns.

3 Religious and Legal Expressions

The view that asyndeton (bimembre) in Latin is particularly associated with religion and the law is so entrenched that I start with these types. There are indeed in Plautus instances that are religious or legal, but these are no more than incidental relics. For legal/official and religious pairs in literary texts see also e.g. XXII.7.

An interesting case found in an augural context, the Italic credentials of which seem to have been missed, has come up earlier (XIX.1, XXII.6.3): *As.* 259–60 *impetritum inauguratumst, quouis admittunt aues:* | *picus et cornix ab laeua, coruos parra ab dextera* | *consuadent,* 'I have a favourable omen, a favourable sign: the birds let me go in any direction. The woodpecker and the crow on the left and the raven and owl on the right recommend it' (de Melo, Loeb; see Norden 1939: 60).[1] There are two asyndeta here, the first comprising verbs with repeated prefix (on which type see further below, 5.4). The part to do with specific birds is paralleled in Umbrian in a very similar augural context: *Tab. Ig.* VIa.1 *parfa . curnase . dersua . peiqu . peica . merstu* 'the *parra*, crow in the west (?), the woodpecker, magpie in the east' (see XXII.4.2). *Parfa* and *parra* are the same word (see Untermann 2000: 513). In the Umbrian the two pairs of birds are both asyndetic, whereas in the Latin one pair is coordinated and the other asyndetic (see XIX.1, and below, this chapter, 7.2).

Legal asyndeta are in the following two passages:

Merc. 832 *usus fructus, uictus cultus iam mihi harunc aedium,* 'the ability to use, enjoy, live in and inhabit'.

This is a legal context; use of the father's house has been taken away from the speaker (on *usus fructus* see XXII.5.6). Such accumulations are very common in later legal language, and it is interesting to find a double pairing at this period in legal language.

Trin. 317 *sarta tecta tua praecepta usque habui,* 'I have always kept your teachings in good repair' (see XXII.5.3 on *sarta tecta*).

At *Am.* 991 (*eius dicto imperio sum audiens*) the asyndetic pair *dicto imperio* looks to be legal or official. See Livy 41.10.7 for the same asyndeton, where the reference is to obedience to a consul: *cum illi tum consulis imperio dicto audientes futuros esse dicerent.* In Plautus the speaker is Mercury, who refers to obedience to his father, Jupiter.

---

[1] Translations of Plautus in this chapter are taken largely from the Loeb edition of W. de Melo, sometimes with minor modifications. I have not acknowledged them individually.

3 *Religious and Legal Expressions* 275

See also Cicero **163** on the asyndeton *aequom bonum* denoting equity, which is at *Men*. 580 *qui nec leges neque aequom bonum usquam colunt*.

Harioli and *haruspices* are several times in asyndeton, and that may be a reflection of an old usage. See *Am.* 1132 *hariolos haruspices | mitte omnis* (Jupiter is the speaker), *Poen*. 791 *habui hariolos haruspices*. Both terms are in a longer asyndetic list at Cato *Agr*. 5.4 (separated by *augurem*). Note too *Mil.* 693 *quod dem* ... | *praecantrici coniectrici, hariolae atque haruspicae* (with a combination of asyndeton and coordination, as in the augural passage above). The two terms are often together, coordinated or otherwise (*TLL* VI.2.2534.55ff.).

At *Men*. 290 (*porci ueneunt | sacres sinceri*, 'sacred, unblemished pigs', de Melo) the underlined pair is clearly from the sphere of religion (see Norden 1939: 18; above, XXII.6.5).

Volentes propitiae (*Cur*. 89 *potate, fite mihi uolentes propitiae*) is a religious phrase, but not an asyndeton (see II.3.2.1).

Arae foci (*Am.* 226 *urbem agrum, aras focos, seque uti dederent*) occurs elsewhere both in asyndeton (see Cicero **16**), and with coordination (Sallust **17, 87**, in the last passage following an asyndetic pair), and must be a formula for the sacred places of the household. Here, as in the legal accumulation at *Merc*. 832 above, there are two juxtaposed asyndetic pairs (see 7.1).

Cur. 5 (*si status condictus cum hoste intercedit dies*, 'if a court date fixed, settled on with your adversary from outside comes in between') has a legal phrase (see Norden 1939: 18), which is also attested in coordinated form (*status condictusue dies*) in an old formula cited by Cincius, *De re militari*, quoted by Gellius 16.4.4 (see Preuss 1881: 110). An expression in Terence of similar meaning (*An*. 248 *facta transacta*, 'signed and sealed') has asyndeton bimembre too, though it is not a legal phrase (see below, 5.5).

Laetus lubens (see Preuss 1881: 113, Norden 1939: 18) may be an old prayer formula: *Trin*. 821 *Neptuno | laetus lubens laudis ago et gratis*. Usually however in literature it has a coordinator (see Preuss 1881: 113). It was to have a long history, turning up for example in abbreviated form in a British inscription from Mamucium (*RIB* 576 = *CIL* VII.212 *u(otum) s(oluit) l(aetus) (l)ibens m(erito)*). See also *ILS* 9102b (altar from Lambaesis, the expression unabbreviated), and also a curse tablet from Mainz addressed to the Magna Mater, which concludes *ut laetus libens ea tibi referam* (see Blänsdorf 2010: 181, text 16) (information from Roger Tomlin).

Various other pairs that may look religious or official were either in more general use, or were more often coordinated. At *Am*. 463 (*bene prospere* [*que*] *hoc hodie operis processit mihi*) -*que* is a scribal addition, but cf. *TLL* X.2.2216.55f.; Gell. 4.5.4 *ex quo res bene ac prospere populo Romano cessit*.

This is a variant on the *bene ac/atque feliciter* formula (for which see Hickson 1993: 70–1; e.g. *Cic. Mur.* 1). For *prospere* in such expressions see in general Hickson (1993: 71–2 and especially 72 n. 62).

Oro obsecro occurs three times as an asyndetic pair in Plautus (*Am.* 923 *per dexteram tuam te, Alcumena, oro obsecro,* | *da mihi hanc ueniam, ignosce, Cas.* 321 *orat opsecrat* | *ne Casinam uxorem ducam, Rud.* 882 *oro opsecro, Palaestra*), but, despite e.g. *Am.* 1130 (*di, obsecro uostram fidem*), it is in secular contexts (note the following *ignosce* at *Am.* 923 and cf. *Cic. Att.* 11.2.3 *oro obsecro, ignosce*: clearly formulaic in speech). It is widely attested with coordination (see Wölfflin 1933: 269), and indeed in Plautus himself. See further Preuss (1881: 95).

The above collection, which is tolerably complete, represents a tiny proportion of the asyndeta bimembria in Plautus. I have omitted here the apparently ancient alliterative pair *purus putus* (*Ps.* 989, 1200), because its credentials remain obscure (see XXIV.5.2.1, 13).

An interesting case of asyndeton was seen earlier (XI.2) in a religious context at Menander, *Kolax* fr. 1 (Körte and Sandbach), p. 186, lines 3–4 Arnott: θεοῖς Ὀλυμπίοις εὐχώμεθα | Ὀλυμπίασι, πᾶσι πάσαις. The two pairs of adjectives, 'Olympian', 'all', are asyndetic (the first pair discontinuous) and are masculine + feminine, expressing a totality. Masculine + feminine asyndetic pairs do occur in Latin (see XI), but I am not able to parallel in Latin the type here, where the distinction (gods/goddesses) is expressed not by nouns but by adjectives.

For a ritualistic asyndetic pair (of verbs) see *Dysk.* 762–3, where Gorgias betroths the girl to Sostratos and hands her over, with the gods called as witnesses: τοιγαροῦν ἔγωγέ σ[ο]ι | ἐγγυῶ δίδωμι πάντων [τῶ]ν θεῶν ἐναντίον. At Plaut. *Trin.* 573 a single verb, *spondeo*, is used of a betrothal. Cf. *Sam.* 728–9, from the marriage ceremony, where there are three verbs in asyndeton: ἔχω | λαμβάνω στέργω, 'thus I hold, take, cherish her', followed at 730 by three asyndetic nouns in the context of the same ceremony. See also V.3.

4 Compounds or Long Suffixal Derivatives, Often Coinages, Juxtaposed

A striking component of Plautus' asyndeta are long compounds (or suffixal derivatives) juxtaposed in asyndetic pairs (or longer sequences: see below). In many cases the terms seem to be Plautine coinages, and the type was undoubtedly contrived. For compounds in Plautus see in general Lindner (2002: 240–7); also Coleman (1999: 61–2), Fraenkel (2007: 139–41).

4 Compounds or Suffixal Derivatives, Juxtaposed 277

Asyndetic combinations, used for comic effect, may have been imitated from tragedy or high-style poetry (see further below on Aeschylus). Such compounds are alluded to at Horace *Ars* 97 as *sesquipedalia uerba* (see Brink 1971: 180–1) and classified as tragic (see also the whole of Gell. 19.7). For a notable pair in Pacuvius see *trag.* 238 Schierl *Nerei repandirostrum incuruiceruicum pecus* (see XXIV.6.1, 3). Note too Lucil. 540 *calliplocamon callisphyron* (see XXV.1.1.1, 1). In another passage Pacuvius has the compound *tardigrada* (unique to him in the period covered by the *OLD*) at the head of a long asyndetic sequence composed of single words and then phrases: *trag.* 3 Schierl, lines 1–2 *quadrupes tardigrada agrestis humilis aspera,* | *breui capite, ceruice anguina, aspectu truci* (see XXIV.6.4, on Pacuvius 12). For a similar structure cf. Plaut. *Per.* 421 *perenniserue lurcho edax furax fugax*.[2] *Perenniseruus* is only found in Plautus, and it is followed by an asyndetic tricolon of more familiar words, with assonance of *-ax* (for such uses of compound coinages see also the examples from *Truc.* and *Trin.* further below in this section). With *edax furax fugax* cf. *Per.* 410 *procax rapax trahax* (note the asyndetic sequence in the same speech just before this one at 408, quoted in n. 2). Different endings are often repeated in asyndetic sequences (see below, 5.4). For another tricolon of this type cf. e.g. *Rud.* 215 *algor error pauor, me omnia tenent*.

Here is an alliterative pair with homoeoteleuton, each term with five syllables:

As. 34 *ubi flent nequam homines qui polentam pinsitant,* | *apud fustitudinas ferricrepinas insulas*.

These are again comic formations by Plautus. Presumably the striking character of such coinages was enhanced by juxtaposition.

There are other pairs with four, five or even six syllables in each or one word (with at least one word either a coinage or very rare): e.g.

Aul. 509 *caupones patagiarii indusiarii,* 'the dealers in flounces, tunics'.

The *TLL* (X.1.651.13) gives *patagiarius* as a noun, but then allows that it might be an adjective in Plautus. It and the next word seem here to be adjectives.

---

[2] This sequence occupies a whole line, just as that in Pacuvius occupies two lines. Such prolonged asyndeta are common in Plautus; not infrequently they extend for more than a line. Here are a few other instances: *Aul.* 343 *supellex aurum uestis, uasa argentea, Aul.* 346–7 *comprehendite* | *uincite uerberate, in puteum condite, Cist.* 206 *iactor [crucior] agitor* | *stimulor uorsor, Cist.* 208 *feror differor, distrahor diripior, Cur.* 577 *ita me uolsellae pecten speculum calamistrum meum* | *bene me amassint, Merc.* 630 *ad mandata claudus caecus mutus mancus debilis* (note the alliterative arrangement as well), *Per.* 408 *impure inhoneste iniure illex, labes popli, Rud.* 652 *legerupa impudens impurus inuerecundissumus*.

Aul. 512 *propolae, linteones calceolarii,* 'dealers, linen-retailers, shoemakers'.
All three terms are nouns, with the second and third in apposition to the first (= 'dealers').

Aul. 513 *sedentarii sutores, diabathrarii,* 'squatting cobblers, makers of slippers'.

Capt. 471 *nil morantur iam Lacones unisupselli uiros, plagipatidas,* 'they can't be bothered about us Spartan one-bench men any longer, us blow-bearers' (in this pairing the first element is phrasal, with the compound in the genitive).

Mil. 1055 *urbicape, occisor regum,* 'you capturer of cities, you slayer of kings'.

Mo. 356 *ubi sunt isti plagipatidae ferritribaces uiri,* 'where are those sons of the whip, the men who wear out iron chains?'

Mo. 875 *peculi sui prodigi, plagigeruli,* 'wasteful of their possessions, bearing beatings'.
As at *Capt.* 471 above the first element is phrasal, but here contains no artificial compound.

Poen. 510 n*equiquam hos procos mi elegi loripedes tardissumos*

Ps. 1133 *hos huc adigit | lucrifugas damnicupidos*

St. 227 *(unctiones) alias malacas crapularias,* 'other (ointments), mild, against hangover'.

A more complex sequence is at *Trin.* 251–4a: *ducitur familia tota, | uestiplica unctor, auri custos, | flabelliferae sandaligerulae, cantrices cistellatrices | nuntii renuntii, rap|tores panis et peni,* 'the whole establishment is hired, the dress-folder, the masseur, the guardian of jewellery, the fan-bearers, the sandal-carriers, the female singers, the maids with treasure boxes, the ones who bring messages and the ones who bring messages back, the thieves of bread and sustenance'.
The sequence has two other pairs apart from that underlined, with differing forms of artificiality (alliteration and repeated ending, -*trices*, in the next pair, simplex + compound in the one after, opposites of the reversive kind: for -*trix* repeated in an asyndetic pair, cf. *Mil.* 693 *praecantici coniectrici,* quoted at 3 above; for simplex + compound, see below, 5.4). This is a passage that brings up another feature of asyndeta in Plautus. The list is a description of manifestations of luxury, and luxurious excess is often described in Plautus by means of short or long asyndeta (see below, 8.1, 8.2, 8.5, 8.6).

Truc. 435 *sociai unanimantis fidentis,* 'of an ally who was a soul-mate, trusting'.

Truc. 762–3 *uenefica, | suppostrix puerum,* 'you poisoner and smuggler-in of suppositious children'.

4 Compounds or Suffixal Derivatives, Juxtaposed 279

For invented compound names listed asyndetically, see *Per.* 702 *Vaniloquidorus Virginesuendonides* (continues for three lines).

Such asyndeta often have more than two members. Cf. the asyndetic tricolon (*Mil.* 191) *domi habet animum falsiloquom falsificum falsiiurium*, where all three adjectives seem to have been Plautine coinages. Note too the tricolon *Trin.* 1021 *oculicrepidae, cruricrepidae, ferriteri mastigiae*, 'eye-rattlers, leg-clankers, villains wearing out fetters'. The first, second and fourth terms are (masculine) nouns, and *ferriterus* is an adjective with the last noun. The first word has been regarded as corrupt, but the assonance is appropriate in such coinages (cf. several of the passages above). Sometimes a compound coinage (or more than one) is followed in asyndeton by one or more terms that are attested elsewhere (cf. *Per.* 421, quoted in the first paragraph in this section): e.g. *Truc.* 551–2 *damnigeruli | foras egerones, bonorum exagogae* (the first term, and *egerones*, are only in Plautus, whereas *exagogae* is a Greek borrowing), *Trin.* 769–70 *mendaciloquom aliquem ... falsidicum confidentem* (*mendaciloquos* is only in Plautus; *falsidicus* is in Accius as well as Plautus).

Such pairs may be coordinated, but the asyndetic type is particularly common. Compare e.g. *Bac.* 1167 *eunt eccas tandem | probripellecebrae et persuastrices*.

The early republican vogue for asyndetic compound coinages, usually abusive and probably meant to be funny or grandiose, shows up much later in a passage of Petronius. At 55.6, a poem in iambic senarii recited by Trimalchio has an accumulation of long compounds at lines 5–6: *ciconia etiam, grata peregrina hospita | pietaticultrix gracilipes crotalistria*. Trimalchio claims that the piece is by Publilius, but there have been numerous alternative suggestions about the authorship (collected by Schmeling 2011: 225). Schmeling (226) translates the last three words as 'devotion-filled, graceful-stepping, castanet-dancer', and notes that the two Latin compounds are found only here and may have been coined by Publilius. He states: 'Piling up compounds was in vogue among early writers'. See also Courtney (1991: 21): 'A striking accumulation of compounds in the old-fashioned style.'

For an asyndetic accumulation of adjectives, half of them compounds or regarded as such, in Aeschylus see *Supp.* 794–7 (with Sommerstein 2019: 303 ad loc.), quoted at XIX.1: six adjectives, only two of them attested elsewhere, with the same noun πέτρα. Sommerstein, citing five other examples, describes such accumulations as an Aeschylean mannerism.

The asyndeta seen so far have fallen into artificial categories, with high poetic style (or humorous grandiosity) and sound patterns important determinants. Could some of the terms above have stemmed from the language of the fashion trades? I turn now to pairs of verbs (and some longer sequences), which throw a different light on asyndetic coordination.

5 Verbs

The variety of factors that motivate asyndeton (with two members) is in no way better illustrated than by asyndetic pairs of verbs. Plautus has clearly identifiable types, which differ in their stylistic level. Pairs of imperatives are ubiquitous and belonged to ordinary speech (not least address of slaves). A commonplace type was that comprising 'go' + another directive (see X.1). Plautus also often has a variation on this pattern, consisting not of imperatives but of a verb of motion (e.g. 'go') + a verb expressing a subsequent action, in finite forms (or occasionally in the infinitive or participial forms). Semantically such pairs are the same as the imperatival pairs, and closely related to them. They were probably in common use also: *go fetch it* leads to *he goes, fetches it*. Another related type is that consisting of pairs of subjunctives, which are similar in function to imperatives.

A different type again looks artificial and stylised. This is a type in which both verbs have the same prefix or some other feature (or features) of assonance. I discuss below various types separately.

The impression should not be given that coordination is lacking in pairs of the types discussed here, but it is true to say that asyndeton was commonplace.

5.1 Imperatives

Pairs of imperatives (and longer sequences) may consist of single verbs, or verb + phrase, or phrase + verb, or phrase + phrase. I have not done a complete collection but have noted dozens of asyndetic cases. The following brief selection (of 33 examples) will illustrate the diversity of the type. I have excluded here the type with the simplex 'go', which is dealt with elsewhere (X.1).

As. 445 *da, commoda homini amico*
Cist. 502 *abi quaere*
Cur. 89 *potate, fite mihi uolentes propitiae*
Cur. 172 *tene me, amplectere ergo*
Cur. 255 *abi deprome* (two-word type).
Cur. 423 *cape, signum nosce*
Epid. 182 *tacete, habete animum bonum*

Merc. 309 *cape cultrum, [ac] seca*
Merc. 618 *perge excrucia, carnufex* (two-word type).
Merc. 911 *exite, illinc pallium mi efferte*
Mil. 219–20 *consule,* | *arripe opem auxiliumque*
Mil. 463 *abi, machaeram huc effer*
Mil. 773 *utere accipe* (two-word type).
Mil. 864 *abi, actutum redi* (see too *Trin.* 1108: opposites, reversives).
Mo. 22–4 *dies noctesque* bibite pergraecamini, | *amicas* emite liberate; *pascite* | *parasitos, opsonate pollucibiliter* (two pairs, and then what looks like a third unitary phrasal pair).
Mo. 64–5 bibite pergraecamini | este effercite uos, *saginam caedite* (two pairs, and then an additional imperative).
Mo. 523 *fuge, [atque] operi caput*
Per. 147 *propera, abi domum*
Per. 306 *propera, abi domum*
Per. 311 *uenito promoneto*
Per. 586 *indica, fac pretium*
Per. 602 *tace, parce uoci*
Per. 606 *percontare, exquire quiduis*
Per. 667 *abi, argentum effer huc*
Per. 772 *moue manus, propera*
Ps. 249 *reprehende hominem, assequere*
St. 682 *mihi modo ausculta, iube . . .*
Trin. 384 *posce duce* (single words).
Trin. 1010 *adde gradum, appropera*
Truc. 625 *fac quod iussi, mane*
Truc. 676 *dic, impera mi.*

Several times above it is *abi* that is followed by another imperative (cf. Sjögren 1900: 90; also 5.3 below, for non-imperatival uses of this verb in asyndeton). This is a common structure, and not only in Plautus. Note for eample Ter. *Ph.* 777 *abi prae, nuntia*, and cf. in bursts of direct speech in Livy, 22.3.13 *abi nuntia*, 22.49.10 *abi nuntia publice* (also similarly Tac. *Hist.* 4.77.3 *ite nuntiate Vespasiano*). *Nuntia* is sometimes also attached by a coordinator (Ter. *Hau.* 618, *Hec.* 314; cf. Plaut. *Ba.* 592 *abi et renuntia*). Such repeated pairings probably reflect ordinary (assertive) speech.

Merc. 309 and *Mo.* 523 above bring up a recurrent feature: scribes not infrequently added a coordinator to such pairs (see also the following lists, where further such additions are marked by square brackets). The variety of asyndetic pairs of imperatives is obvious from the list.

For an asyndetic pair of imperatives in Menander addressed to slaves, as is often the case in Plautus, see *Dysk.* 960 αἴρεσθε τοῦτον, εἰσφέρετε, 'lift him up, take him in'. Another pair is at *Dysk.* 954: χόρευε, συνεπίβαινε, 'dance, get on your feet along with us'. The imperatives here are not in a logical temporal order (see also XVI.1). On the meaning of the second verb see XVI.1 with reference. See also *Pk.* 509–10 ἐλθὼν διαλέγου, | πρέσβευσον, 'go and talk to her, be my ambassador' (Arnott, Loeb, who is usually quoted here, sometimes with modifications), *Sam.* 327 κάτεχε σαυτόν, καρτέρει, 'control yourself, be strong', *Sik.* 114 ἔστ]ω, δεδόχθω, '[Let's accept it] and agree' (despite the gap in the text, the construction seems clear). See also X.4.

The structure of Plaut. *Per.* 606 above is similar to that at Ter. *An.* 897 *quiduis oneris inpone, impera.*

5.2 Subjunctives

Here are a few asyndetic pairs of subjunctives that resemble imperatives:

As. 40 *fiat, geratur mos tibi,* a formula found also at *Ps.* 559.
As. 618 *circumsistamus ... appellemus*
Mil. 420 *adeamus appellemus*
Poen. 801 *apscedas, sumas ornatum tuom*, 'go and take your get-up'.

Cf. e.g. Eur. *Hec.* 314 σπεύδωμεν, ἐγκόνωμεν (cited by Fraenkel 1960: 344 n. 2 among tautologous pairs from tragedy), and Lucilius 1092 *surgamus eamus agamus* (see XXV.3), alongside the formula *surge, i domum.*

5.3 Non-Imperatival Pairs of Verbs Consisting of a Verb of Motion and Another Verb

In the list above of asyndetic imperatives I have quoted a few instances where the first verb is one of motion, but the number would be greatly extended if cases of *eo* 'go' in one of its three imperatival forms had been included (see X.1). I now cite a selection of non-imperatival asyndetic pairs of verbs, consisting of a verb of motion and another verb. As was noted above, the type may be seen as a variation on the imperatival type with 'go' or the like as the first element.

Aul. 411a–12 *adest | sequitur*
Aul. 517 *cedunt petunt | treceni*
Aul. 527 *itur, putatur ratio*
Cist. 650 *abiit, apstulit | mulierem* (cf. *Cur.* 255 *abi deprome, Mil.* 463 *abi, machaeram huc effer, Per.* 667 *abi, argentum effer huc*).
Cur. 351 *quid si abeamus [ac] decumbamus*

5 Verbs

Men. 550 *abiit, operuit fores* (cf. *Truc.* 758 below).
Men. 845 *ibo adducam qui*; also *Per.* 576 below, this list (cf. *Poen.* 424 *i, adduce testis tecum, Aul.* 767 *i refer*).
Merc. 99 *uenio decumbo*
Merc. 366 *ibo alloquar*
Merc. 672 *ibo orabo* (cf. *Merc.* 787 *i rogato*).
Mil. 420 *adeamus appellemus*
Mo. 1074 *aggrediar hominem, appellabo*
Per. 576 *uenio, adduco hanc ad te*
Poen. 123 *ego ibo ornabor.*
St. 202 *adeunt perquirunt* (cf. *Cist.* 502 *abi quaere, Men.* 736 *i, Deceo, quaere meum patrem, Per.* 487 *i ad forum ad praetorem, exquire*).
Truc. 514 *adsum, adduco tibi exoptatum Stratophanem* (cf. possibly *asom* [= *adsum*?] *fero* on one of the early Praenestine *cistae*, though the first word is debated: see Wachter 1987: 166 for the text, and 169 on *asom*; for *adsum* in asyndeton see also the first example above, and Cic. *Quinct.* 75, quoted after Cicero 55).
Truc. 758 *abiit intro, exclusit* (cf. *Truc.* 696 *i intro, amabo, cedo manum*).

For this type in Terence see *Hau.* 170 *ibo uisam, An.* 528 *conueniam orabo.*

5.4 Asyndetic Pairs of Verbs Marked by Assonance of One Type or Another

The pairs of verbs seen so far, we have suggested, are of types that were almost certainly in ordinary use, particularly in the Republic. There are signs of increased coordination later (see X.1.4). I turn now to what was probably a more artificial type, that comprising two verbs sharing some form of assonance. Asyndeton is particularly suited to the conveying of sound effects or to the underlining of structural parallelism, because the two terms are juxtaposed and the sound pattern not obscured by interruption. Such sound effects with asyndeton are a feature of early poetry (see e.g. Pac. *trag.* 17 Schierl *agite icite uoluite rapite coma | tractate,* 206 *maerore errore macore senet,* 263 *strepitus fremitus, clamor tonitruum et rudentum sibilus*), and not least parts of Plautus (see above, 4 on compound coinages and with the first passage of Pacuvius just quoted cf. *Aul.* 346–7 *comprehendite | uincite uerberate, in puteum condite,* quoted in a different connection at n. 2 above) and *Aul.* 453 *coquite facite festinate*; cf. too Ter. *An.* 334 *facite fingite inuenite efficite,* and particularly XXV.3 on Lucilius 264–5), and also Greek tragedy (e.g. repeated fore-elements: see VI.8) and to some extent Umbrian (see XIX.1). I list first below the extensive examples in this category and then offer some classifications. It must be stressed that here

I am confining myself to verbs, but asyndetic assonance involves other parts of speech as well (see for example below, 6, on negative adjectives, and two of the examples just cited from Pacuvius).[3]

Am. 335 *timeo, totus torpeo*
Am. 651 *tutantur seruantur*
Am. 923 *oro opsecro*; also *Cas.* 321, *Rud.* 882.
As. 169 *ductando amando*
As. 246 *supplicabo exopsecrabo*
As. 259–60 *impetritum inauguratumst*
Aul. 88 *fateor patior*
Bac. 246 *uiuit ualet*; also *St.* 31 *uiuant ualeant*, *Trin.* 1075 *uiuont ualent*.
Bac. 633 *reppuli reieci hominem*
Bac. 743 *comedim [et] congraecem*
Bac. 862 *perii pertimui*
Bac. 935 *opsignatas consignatas*
Bac. 1080 *dedi donaui*; also *Mil.* 1204 *donaui dedi*.
Bac. 1090 *perii pudet*
Capt. 502–3 *restitando | retinendo[que]*
Capt 641 *deruncinatus deartuatus sum*
Cist. 208 *feror differor, distrahor diripior*
Cist. 650 *abiit, apstulit | mulierem*
Cur. 290 *constant, conferunt sermones*
Cur. 291 *opstant opsistunt*
Epid. 118 *differor difflagitor*
Epid. 219 *deamat deperit*
Epid. 613 *senserunt sciunt*
Men. 342 *se applicant agglutinant* (the prefix here should perhaps be written in unassimilated form).
Merc. 192 *complicandis [et] componendis*
Merc. 221 *retinebit rogitabit*
Merc. 360 *abdidi apscondidi*
Merc. 407 *contemplent conspiciant*
Merc. 407 *nutent nictent*
Merc. 681 *disperii perii*
Mil. 201 *curans cogitans*
Mil. 420 *adeamus appellemus*
Mo. 65 *este effercite*
Mo. 1031 *perii interii*
Poen. 221 *poliri expoliri, pingi fingi*
Poen. 223 *lauando eluendo*
Poen. 661 *potare amare*

---

[3] For a few miscellaneous examples see *As.* 565 *artutos audacis*, *Epid.* 256 *calidi conducibilis consili*, *Epid.* 494 *mucidum, minimi preti*, *Men.* 290 *sacres sinceri*, *St.* 376 *eburatos auratos*.

Poen. 1350 *debetur dabo*
Trin. 243 *labitur liquitur*
Trin. 406 *exunctum elotum*
Truc. 252 *apsterret abigit*
Truc. 566a *suffuror suppilo*.

There are 47 pairs with assonance above, a substantial number, and considerable proportion of the (200+) asyndetic pairs of verbs in the corpus. In twenty cases the two verbs have the same prefix. In three cases the two have the same root but different prefixes (*Bac.* 935 *opsignatas consignatas, Merc.* 360 *abdidi apscondidi* [*-con-*], *Mo.* 1031 *perii interii*). There are four combinations of simplex and compound, in both orders (*Cist.* 208 *feror differor, Merc.* 681 *disperii perii, Poen.* 221 *poliri expoliri, Poen.* 223 *lauando eluendo*). About 36 pairs are alliterative, and 16 share the same ending of two or more syllables; some pairs are both alliterative and have the same ending (*Am.* 335 *timeo, totus torpeo, As.* 259–60 *impetritum inauguratumst, Capt.* 502–3 *restitando | retinendo* [*que*], *Merc.* 192 *complicandis* [*et*] *componendis, Merc.* 360 *abdidi apscondidi, Trin.* 243 *labitur liquitur*). Two passages have juxtaposed asyndetic pairs, with each pair having a form of assonance (*Cist.* 208 *feror differor, distrahor diripior, Poen.* 221 *poliri expoliri, pingi fingi*). On the latter, which is part of a much longer accumulation, see also XXV.3 on Lucilius 264–5.

Asyndetic pairs of verbs with types of assonance are also found in Terence: *Hau.* 473 *consusurrant, conferunt | consilia, Ad.* 795 *repressi redii, Eun.* 117 *coepi ... | docere educere, Hau.* 946 *retundam redigam*.

One manifestation of homoeoteleuton is worth dwelling on briefly because it persisted into literary prose, that is the pairing of gerund(ives) in the ablative. In the Plautine list above are *As.* 169 *ductando amando, Capt.* 502–3 *restitando | retinendo*[*que*], *Merc.* 192 *complicandis* [*et*] *componendis* and *Poen.* 223 *lauando eluendo* (on the etymology of *eluo* see De Vaan 2008: 330–1). Note too *Men.* 882 *lumbi sedendo, oculi spectando dolent* (phrasal), *St.* 70 *exorando haud aduersando sumendam operam censeo* (adversative). Cf. *Truc.* 916 *ita miser cubando in lecto hic exspectando obdurui*, 'so still have I become lying wretchedly on the couch here waiting'. The subject lies while waiting and this is not necessarily an asyndeton.

For the gerund type in a legal text see Kalb (1912: 137; cf. XXII.2.3). For the pattern in Cicero, Sallust, Livy and Tacitus see:

Cic. *Off.* 1.22 (**138**) *dando accipiendo*
Off. 1.50 (**139**) *docendo discendo, communicando disceptando iudicando*
Off. 2.64 (**143, 144**) *uendendo emendo, conducendo locando*
Fin. 2.109 (**149**) *in gignendo in educando*
Sall. *Cat.* 42.2 (**72**) *festinando agitando*

Livy 4.48.11 (45) *suadendo monendo pollicendoque*
Tac. *Hist.* 3.20.1 (34) *prouidendo consultando*
Ann. 2.67.1 (134) *monendo suadendo*
Ann. 4.2.2 (136) *adeundo appellando* (note that this same pair of verbs in asyndeton is quoted above from *Mil.* 420, *adeamus appellemus*).

One final type of asyndeton bimembre with an ablative of the gerund that recurs in Plautus is that in which a noun in the ablative is combined with a gerund. *Vi pugnando* (on which see Adams 2005: 76) occurs twice (*Am.* 414, *As.* 555), and note particularly *Rud.* 186 *in usu, experiundo is datur acerbum*, 'bitterness is given to them through experience and practice', where the noun cannot be taken as a modifier of the verb and the pair is certainly an asyndeton.

5.5 Miscellaneous Pairs of Verbs in Asyndeton

Apart from the pairs belonging to the special categories distinguished above, pairs of verbs of more miscellaneous types are quite common in Plautus. Here are examples I have noted:

Aul. 313 *collegit, omnia apstulit praesegmina*
Aul. 318 *infit ibi postulare plorans eiulans*
Aul. 693 *clamat parturit*
Aul. 727 *eiulans conqueritur, maerens?*
Bac. 931 *cepi expugnaui*
Bac. 1080 *duxi, habui scortum*
Cas. 43 *exorat aufert*
Cas. 44 *ut eam curet educet*
Cas. 45 *fecit educauit*
Cas. 931 *supsilit, obtundit os mihi*
Cist. 567 *amplexa est genua plorans opsecrans | ne deserat se*
Cur. 503 *conspicitur uituperatur*
Men. 961 *noui <ego> homines, alloquor*
Merc. 50 *abnuere negitare*
Merc. 55 *trahere exhaurire*
Mil. 137 *adhortatur iuuat*
Mil. 252 *prandet potat*
Mil. 917 *ubi fundata constituta est*
Mo. 22 *bibite pergraecamini*
Mo. 23 *emite liberate*
Mo. 64 *bibite pergraecamini*
Mo. 122 *extollunt parant*
Mo. 235 *estur bibitur*
Mo. 862 *exercent sese . . . fugiunt*

Per. 716 *argentum accepit, abiit* (with a verb of motion, but in second place).
Per. 734 *fateor, habeo gratiam*
Poen. 244 *olent, salsa sunt*
Poen. 653 *salutat respondemus*
Poen. 835 *bibitur estur*
Ps. 283 *dabit parabit*
Ps. 676 *instituta ornata omnia in ordine*
Trin. 285 *turbant miscent*
Trin. 406 *comesum expotum*
Trin. 1005 *mutum est, tacet*
Truc. 598 *auscultat opseruat.*

These pairs would probably be worthy of a detailed semantic classification but I restrict myself to a few observations.

A feature is the frequency of the complementary pairing 'eat/drink': *Mil.* 252 *prandet potat*, embedded in a longer sequence (cf. also *Men.* 476 *prandi potaui, scortum accubui, apstuli | hanc*), *Mo.* 22 *bibite pergraecamini* (also at *Mo.* 64), *Mo.* 235 *estur bibitur*, *Poen.* 835 *bibitur estur*, *Trin.* 406 *comesum expotum*. Note too *Mo.* 64 *este, effercite uos*, 'eat, stuff yourselves' and the longer sequence *Cas.* 248 *bibe es, disperde rem*. Pairs with repetitive semantic content like this (see also Preuss 1881: 98 for a few later examples) are likely to have been quasi-formulaic, and I will come back to semantic categories in a separate section (8), with further allusion to eating and drinking and related activities in other connections (8.2, 8.5). Such asyndeta may well have been very old. Watkins (1995: 209) notes that in Old Hittite 'eat, drink' was equivalent to 'live happily'. For an asyndetic pair (discontinuous) in Menander falling into the category of food and drink (in the context of decadent behaviour) see *Dysk.* 448 κοίτας φέρονται, στραμνί, 'they bring hampers and wine jars'. There is not a close resemblance to the Latin examples, but self-indulgence does seem to have gone on inspiring asyndeta (see below, 8.2).

Pairs of near-synonyms are found: *Merc.* 50 *abnuere negitare*, *Merc.* 55 *trahere exhaurire*, *Trin.* 285 *turbant miscent*, *Trin.* 1005 *mutum est, tacet*. For this type in Greek tragedy see the examples listed by Fraenkel (1960: 344 n. 2).

Ps. 676 (*instituta ornata omnia in ordine*), of a plan that 'was already completely set up and prepared step for step', is similar to *Ter. An.* 248 *facta transacta omnia* ('It's all signed and sealed', Barsby), which may have been proverbial (see Preuss 1881: 110). The Plautine expression looks like a variant (cf. also above, 3 on *Cur.* 5 *status condictus*).

Pairs of present participles stand out: *Aul.* 318 *infit ibi postulare plorans eiulans*, *Aul.* 727 *eiulans conqueritur, maerens* (discontinuous), *Cist.* 567 *amplexa est genua plorans opsecrans | ne deserat*; cf. from an earlier list *Mil.* 201 *seuero fronte curans cogitans*. Most of these express lamentations. Cf., in Menander, *Epit.* 297 δεόμεν[ο]ς ἱκετεύων ἐγὼ | ἔλαβον παρ' αὐτοῦ τοῦτ', 'begging, pleading, I took the child from him'. This pair is similar to that at *Cist.* 567. Note too *Kolax* E230, 2, p. 182 Arnott, 'He'll come with sixty mates that he's enrolled, ... βοῶν ἀπειλῶν 'yelling, threatening' (followed by a quotation of his words); *Mis.* 696 ταυτὶ λέγει | ἅ[παν]τα κλάων ἀντιβολῶν, 'All this he said weeping, entreating' (very similar to both *plorans eiulans* and *plorans obsecrans*). Note too Eur. *Or.* 950 σὺν δ' ὁμαρτοῦσιν φίλοι κλαίοντες, οἰκτίροντες, and Hor. *Sat.* 1.9.64–5 *nutans, | distorquens oculos*.

Poen. 653 *salutat respondemus*, 'he greets, we reply', is a case of a pair of converses (opposites). For the type in Terence see *Ph.* 488 *loquere audio* ('(you) speak, I am listening'), and see also below on Menander.

'Listening and watching' (*Truc.* 598) are complementary verbs alluding to two of the senses.

Some of the other pairs express sequences of events, with the second act following closely on the first (e.g. *Aul.* 693 *clamat parturit*, *Per.* 716 *argentum accepit, abiit*).

Miscellaneous asyndetic pairs of verbs are found in Menander: e.g. *Sam.* 549 τὸ πρᾶγμ' ἀκούσας χαλεπανεῖ, κεκράξεται, 'once he's heard the true position, he'll be furious and scream' (a sequence of events), *Sam.* 606–7 τρέχει πηδᾷ, πολὺ | πράττεται, μέλας περιπατεῖ, 'he runs, jumps, makes his pile, walks about with hair so dark ...' (arguably two pairs, the first comprising single words denoting associated activities, the second comprising phrases that are not closely associated), *Sam.* 703 ἥμαρτον ἐμάνην, 'I made a mistake, I was mad' (but possibly a parataxis, with the second term explanatory, 'because ...'), *Sam.* 717–18 μοιχὸν ὄντ' εἰλημμένον | ὁμολογοῦντ', 'being a seducer caught in the act, self-confessed', *Sikyonioi* 96 ἔδωκ', ἐδέξω, 'I gave, you took' (opposites, of the converse type, of the same structure as *Poen.* 653 *salutat respondemus* above; *dare accipere* occurs in asyndeton (e.g. Cicero 138)), *Sikyonioi* 269–70 ἀνίστ[ατο] | ἐβάδιζε, 'she rose and then began to move' (another temporal sequence; cf. Plaut. *Rud.* 172 *surrexit, horsum se capessit*, 'she has stood up, she is coming here').

6 Privatives

It was shown above (5.4) that pairs of verbs often have assonance of one sort or another, and it was noted in passing (see n. 2) that such sound effects are not confined to pairs of verbs. I partly follow this point up here, by dealing with privative adjectives (mainly) in asyndeton.

Privatives with the prefix *in-*, used in pairs, or singly, juxtaposed in the latter case either with the corresponding positive or with another term of any type, are a presence (about twenty examples; only a few have two juxtaposed terms in *in-*; I also cite below five longer asyndetic sequences with at least two privatives). Most pairs with *in-* comprise adjectives, but there is a nominal and a possible adverbial instance. Some of the pairs that are quoted here do have two privatives, but one of the terms has a negative prefix other than *in-*. Since there are only a little over 60 adjectival asyndeta bimembria in Plautus, the types with a privative make up a significant proportion.

The three instances of privative + positive are at *As.* 247, *Bac.* 401, *Cur.* 280 (see below, 8.10).

Here are the pairs of which both members are privatives:

Bac. 612–14 *petulans, proteruo iracundo animo, <u>indomito incogitato</u>, | sine modo et modestia sum, sine bono iure atque honore, | incredibilis imposque animi, <u>inamabilis illepidus</u> uiuo.*

This passage (on which see also VI.2.2) has an accumulation of a particular kind. As well as the two privative asyndetic pairs it has a coordinated privative pair, and two juxtaposed coordinated pairs of terms dependent on *sine*. These prepositional phrases are a form of privative and may be equivalent to a privative adjective (so here e.g. *sine modo et modestia* is equivalent to *immoderatus et immodestus*, both of which adjectives are well attested). Such combinations of different kinds of negatives are not confined to Plautus. Cf. e.g. Cic. *Red. sen.* 14 (**44**) *sine sensu sine sapore, elinguem, tardum inhumanum negotium*, a passage with several features relevant to the present section. First, there is an asyndetic pair, *tardum inhumanum*, with a privative adjective. Second, almost juxtaposed with this is a pair of phrases with *sine*. Third, the intervening adjective, *elinguem*, is also a privative of sorts, but with a different prefix; it is equivalent to *sine lingua*.

Elsewhere in this book I have noted accumulations that combine privatives with *sine*-phrases (see Cicero **44, 48**, Livy **42**); for the formation with *e-* see below, this section on, for example, *edentulus*.

Men. 973 *ignauis improbis uiris*

Ps. 794 *multiloquom gloriosum, insulsum inutilem*
   I take it that there are two distinct pairs here, the first to do with talkative boasting, the second with stupidity.

290   XXIII Plautus

Rud. 1097 *immo hercle insignite inique* (?)
   This pair is hard to interpret. The phrase follows and picks up *haud iniquom dicit*, 'he says a thing that is not unfair', and it means (in part), 'on the contrary, (it has been said) unfairly'. Is *insignite* ('remarkably, strikingly') a modifier of the following adverb *inique* (= 'strikingly unfairly'), or is it a modifier of the understood verb, and in asyndeton with *inique* ('on the contrary, it is a striking and unfair remark')? The former interpretation raises the question whether an adverb can modify another adverb in Latin. There seems no linguistic reason why such modification should not occur, though it is statistically uncommon.[4]

Cas. 550 *illius hirqui improbi edentuli*, 'of that worthless, toothless goat'.
   In effect two privatives, because *edentuli* is of the same function as a compound with *in-* (see above on *elinguem* in Cicero). See VI.4.2 on Livy 4.37.9, with comparable examples, and also below, this section, for *Mil.* 554 *excordem*; also Lucr. 1.774 *non animans, non exanimo cum corpore*.

Mo. 105–6 *immigrat nequam homo, indiligens[que] cum pigra familia, immundus instrenuos*.
   There are possibly two pairs of privatives here, the second, *immundus instrenuos*, straightforward. The first would be discontinuous, with *homo* intervening between *nequam* and *indiligens cum pigra familia* (for *uir/homo* intervening in such structures see XX.1, 2). *Nequam* 'worthless' has a negative prefix (cf. *Trin.* 361 *quae uolt, quae neuolt*: see VI.7). The prepositional phrase *cum pigra familia* seems to separate the first two negative adjectives from the final two, converting the latter two into secondary predicates. Alternatively there might be a sequence of four negative adjectives of comparable status in asyndeton.

   Here finally are pairs containing one privative:

As. 475–6 *age, impudice | sceleste*

Aul. 786 *perdidi infelix miser*

---

[4] Catull. 71.4 is transmitted as: *mirifice est a te nactus utrumque malum. A te* is usually obelised, but see Kaster (1977) for a defence of the emendation *mirifice . . apte*, 'marvellously appropriately' (see XXVII.1.3 for further bibliography). Kaster (312) cites such examples as Cic. *Att.* 1.14.3 *ualde grauiter* (cf. 6.1.13). For a few similar examples of such modification see Magni (2010: 166). Plaut. *Trin.* 1008 *fac te propere celerem*, 'make yourself really speedy' (de Melo) suggests that at *Rud.* 1323 (*eloquere propere celeriter*) *propere* may modify *celeriter* ('speedily fast'). Note too *Aul.* 188 *perspicue palam est*, 'it's completely out in the open' (de Melo). See also below, Appendix, adverbs, for *misere male* at *Bac.* 934.

6 Privatives

Men. 863 *equos iunctos iubes | capere me indomitos ferocis*

Merc. 47 *perfidiam iniustitiam lenonum expromere*
Nouns.

Per. 686–7 *id metuebas miser, | impure auare*
There does not seem to be a straightforward sequence of three asyndetic adjectives here. For *miser* agreeing with the subject of a verb of fearing see *Bac.* 862 *pertimui miser*, virtually = 'I was wretchedly afraid'. Here perhaps, 'you were wretchedly afraid of that, you filthy, greedy creature', with *impure auare* secondary predicates. The Loeb (de Melo) separates *miser* from the other two adjectives.

Poen. 28 *nutrices pueros infantis minutulos*
See Köhm (1905: 121) on *infantes*.

Rud. 125 *ecquem tu hic hominem crispum incanum uideris, | malum periurum palpatorem*, 'with hair curly, grey, a wrongdoer...'.
An accumulation, with the first two terms (*crispum incanum*) a unit and detached from the following adjectives, which are also semantically unified.

St. 304 *illam augeam insperato opportuno bono*, 'unhoped for, timely good news'.
Bono is an emendation; *modo* is another possibility.

Trin. 751 *adulescenti... | indomito, pleno amoris ac lasciuiae.*

Privatives (asyndetic) are not of course confined to pairs. Cf. for instances in longer sequences:

Per. 168 *satis fuit indoctae immemori insipienti dicere totiens*

Per. 408 *impure inhoneste iniure illex, labes popli*

Rud. 651–2 *fraudis sceleris parricidi periuri plenissumus, | legerupa impudens impurus inuerecundissumus*

Trin. 826 *(te) spurcificum immanem intolerandum uesanum*
This is a tricolon of privatives. See *OLD* s.v. *uē-* and compare *uecors*.

Mil. 544 *me fuisse excordem caecum incogitabilem*
There are two negatives here, with different prefixes (with *excordem* cf. *edentulus*, and also *uecors* cited on the previous passage). *Caecus* too could be paraphrased as *exoculatum*.

Coordinated pairs also occur: e.g. *Am.* 184 *ingrata ea habui atque irrita, As.* 62 *importunam atque incommodam, As.* 136 *ingrata atque irrita, Aul.* 642 *intemperiae insaniaeque.*

7 Structures

It has already been seen constantly (not least in XIX) that asyndeta bimembria often occur not in isolation but in accumulations. Here are some types in Plautus.

7.1 Juxtaposed Asyndetic Pairs

Two (or more) asyndeta bimembria juxtaposed (or almost juxtaposed) potentially have different structures, and the feature that makes a pair a unity may vary too. The most obvious structure is that in which each pair consists of terms of the same part of speech. Alternatively two asyndetic pairs together may each consist of its own part of speech (e.g. two nouns may be juxtaposed with two adjectives). The unifying characteristic of a pair in a juxtaposition is often semantic. For example, the two terms may be near-synonyms, or opposites, or complementary in some way, and the juxtaposed pair may have its own semantic unity. Some Plautine pairs in juxtapositions have a different unifying feature, consisting of a repeated sound pattern with any semantic similarity not distinctive.

Thus at *Am.* 1062 the four nouns *strepitus crepitus sonitus tonitrus* all refer to types of noises and could not be split into two pairs merely on the strength of meaning. But the two repeated sound patterns *-repitus/-onit(r)us* are so distinctive that the sequence can be readily divided into two pairs. On this sequence see Fraenkel (1960: 335), suggesting that there may be an allusion to a lost tragedy. Other juxtaposed pairs marked by separate sound patterns (and sometimes as well by semantic features) are *tenebrae latebrae, bibitur estur* (*Poen.* 835), where the two pairs are of different parts of speech, *poliri expoliri, pingi fingi* (*Poen.* 221), <u>contemplent conspiciant</u> omnes, <u>nutent nictent</u>, sibilent | uellicent uocent, molesti sint (*Merc.* 407). For the final two underlined verbs together in a longer sequence see *As.* 784 *neque illa ulli homini nutet nictet annuat*.

On the other hand for two pairs with unities dependent on their meanings see *Am.* 226 *urbem agrum, aras focos, seque uti dederent.* For *urbem agrum*, of the 'town/country' type, see on Sall. *Jug.* 20.8 (27), and also XIII.4.3, 5.1. For *aras focos* see above, 3. This sequence is typical of many from later periods in prose.

Also semantically influenced and of a type found in some later genres (notably philosophical contexts: see XIII.4.1) are the three juxtaposed pairs

7 Structures   293

of opposites at *Bac.* 400–1: *certamen cernitur | sisne necne ut esse oportet, malus bonus quoiuis modi, | iustus iniustus, malignus largus.*

Below are other juxtaposed pairs that I have noted, first those in which both pairs are of the same part of speech. Some of these passages come up in other connections elsewhere:

Aul. 95 *cultrum securim, pistillum mortarium*, 'as for knife, axe, pestle, mortar'.

Bac. 612 *petulans, proteruo iracundo animo, indomito incogitato*
    Animo belongs with both pairs. See above, 6.

Cist. 208 *feror differor, distrahor diripior*
    The first two verbs consist of simplex + compound, the second two of near-synonyms with repeated prefix.

Merc. 832 *usus fructus, uictus cultus iam mihi harunc aedium*
    See above, 3.

Mo. 22–4 *dies noctesque* bibite pergraecamini, *| amicas* emite liberate; *pascite | parasitos, opsonate pollucibiliter*
    The two pairs here have their own semantic unities. In the second both verbs have the same object. See above, 5.1.

Mo. 64–5 bibite pergraecamini *|* este effercite *uos, saginam caedite*
    There is the same initial pair here as above, and then a unitary pair, 'eat, stuff yourselves', near-synonyms with the second term stronger than the first.

Mo. 105–6 *immigrat nequam homo, indiligens[que] | cum pigra familia, immundus instrenuos*
    See above, 6.

Ps. 794 *multiloquom gloriosum, insulsum inutilem*
    See above, 6.

Trin. 252–4a *uestiplica unctor, auri custos |* flabelliferae sandaligerulae, *|* cantrices cistellatrices *|* nuntii renuntii, *rap|tores panis et peni*
    See above, 4.

Trin. 289 *rape trahe, fuge late*, 'seize and drag off, flee and hide'.
    Separate events are described by each pair.

Trin. 406 *comesum expotum, exunctum elotum in balineis*, 'it's eaten up and drunk up, anointed away and washed away in the baths'.
    The first pair has the familiar juxtaposition of eating and drinking (see above, 5.3), and the second refers to acts in the baths. Note the repeated prefix.

I move on to pairs comprising different parts of speech.

294   XXIII Plautus

Am. 923–4 *per dexteram tuam te, Alcumena,* <u>oro obsecro</u>, | <u>da</u> *mihi hanc ueniam,*
<u>ignosce</u>
   Cf. Cic. *Att.* 11.2.3 *oro obsecro, ignosce.*

As. 245–6 *experiar opibus, omni copia,* | *supplicabo exopsecrabo*
   There is a tricolon here with three future verbs, but the second and third verbs form a unit.

Epid. 210 *tum captiuorum quid ducunt secum! pueros uirgines,* | *binos ternos*
   See below, 8.9, 8.13.

Poen. 819 *is me . . . uerberat incursat pugnis calcibus*

Ps. 580 *duplicis triplicis dolos perfidias,* 'double, triple tricks, deceptions'.
   See 8.9.

Given the size of the Plautine corpus, this type of accumulation is not frequent, but distinctive sub-categories are represented. There are several cases of repeated prefixes and of simplex + compound. Privative adjectives are found, and forms of assonance. There is a legal accumulation typical of the later legal language, and also a sequence of opposites. Also striking are two of the last three examples, in each of which a pair for a numerical approximation is juxtaposed with a pair of nouns (see 8.9). Some of these types were to become typical of particular genres, but in Plautus are merely isolated presences.

7.2   Asyndeton Juxtaposed with Coordinations

This is another old and long-lived type (see e.g. XIX.1).

Am. 650–1 *libertas salus uita, res et parentes, patria et prognati* | <u>tutantur seruantur</u>, 'freedom, safety, life, possessions and parents, homeland and relatives, are protected, preserved'.
   An accumulation with one asyndeton bimembre (of a different part of speech from the other groups), one asyndetic tricolon and two coordinated pairs. For the mixing of coordinated pairs, asyndetic tricola and asyndeta bimembria cf. e.g. Sall. *Jug.* 31.20 (**29**) *quom regna prouinciae, leges iura iudicia, bella atque paces, postremo diuina et humana omnia penes paucos erant,* Livy 9.14.10–11 (**10, 11**) *caedunt pariter resistentes fusosque, inermes atque armatos, seruos liberos, puberes impubes, homines iumentaque.*

Rud. 1020 *mea opera labore, et rete et horia,* 'with my effort, work – and a net and fishing boat'.
   For much the same asyndetic pair cf. *Am.* 170 *ips' dominus diues operis [et] laboris expers.* See Christenson (2000) on the text, where *et* has been falsely added. Cf. Livy 5.2.7 *in opere ac labore.*

7 Structures

Am. 1012 *apud emporium atque in macello, in palaestra atque in foro,* | *in medicinis in tonstrinis, apud omnis aedis sacras* | *sum defessus quaeritando*
   Two pairs of prepositional expressions with *in* repeated in each, the second pair asyndetic.

As. 548–9 *qui aduorsum stimulos lamminas crucesque compedesque* | *neruos catenas carceres numellas pedicas boias,* 'who went against cattle-prods, hot iron-blades, crosses and shackles, neck-irons, chains, prisons, collars, fetters, yokes'.
   A syndetic pair, and then a long asyndeton.

As. 259–60 *impetritum inauguratumst, quouis admittunt aues:* | picus et cornix *ab laeua,* coruos parra *ab dextera* | *consuadent*
   See above, 3.

Bac. 380 *tuom patrem meque una, amicos affinis tuos*

Bac. 615 *incredibilis imposque animi, inamabilis illepidus uiuo*

Mil. 693 *praecantrici coniectrici, hariolae atque haruspicae*

Mo. 235 *dies noctesque estur bibitur*

Ps. 1265 *unguenta atque odores, lemniscos corollas*

Rud. 664–5 *omnium copiarum atque opum,* | *auxili praesidi uiduitas nos tenet.*

7.3 Embedded Pairs

By this term I refer to asyndeta bimembria that are within a longer asyndetic sequence but are, or appear to be, separate units:

As. 222–3 *bene salutando consuescunt, compellando blanditer,* | *osculando, oratione* uinnula uenustula
   The adjectival terms are alliterative and have homoeoteleuton.

Bac. 1080 duxi habui *scortum, potaui,* dedi donaui
   The first two verbs have the same object, and are thus in asyndeton. The final two verbs are alliterative near-synonyms and appear to be distinct from *potaui*.

Capt. 648 *macilento ore, naso acuto, corpore albo, oculis nigris,* | *subrufus aliquantum,* crispus cincinnatus, '... his hair is somewhat reddish, wavy, curly'.
   The final alliterative terms have very similar meanings, and are arguably detachable from the rest of the description.

Cist. 216–17 fugat agit, *appetit raptat retinet,* | *lactat largitur*
   The first pair of near-synonyms of putting to flight and driving away seems separate from the other verbs, which fall into two groups (2 + 3 + 2?). The tricolon as punctuated here has a meaning contrary to that of the preceding pair.

Men. 974–5 *uerbera compedes* | *molae [magna] lassitudo, fames frigus durum.*
This list of hardships possibly has two embedded pairs, *uerbera compedes* and certainly *fames frigus*, which occurs elsewhere, for example embedded in an accumulation in Lucilius but also on its own (see XXV.1.1.1, 7 and Cicero 103). The accumulation in the passage here is greater than this quotation.

Ps. 64–5 *amores mores consuetudines,* | *iocus ludus, sermo suauisauiatio.*
Iocus ludus I take to be an embedded pair. Cf. *Bac.* 116 and also *Merc.* 846 *uitam amicitiam ciuitatem laetitiam, ludum iocum.* See below, 8.14.

7.4 Anaphora of Prepositions

At 7.2 above the following was cited: *Am.* 1012–13 *in palaestra atque in foro,* | *in medicinis in tonstrinis.* The second phrase ('at the doctors', at the barbers") combines asyndeton with anaphora of the preposition *in*. This form of prepositional asyndeton recurs throughout Latin, not infrequently in accumulations, including cases in which the juxtaposed pair is of different syntactic type (see particularly I.10, and also XIX.1). Here the asyndetic pair is combined with a coordinated with the same syntax. For the combining of asyndeton with anaphora in Greek see Denniston (1952: 106–9) (but citing few examples in which the repeated element is a preposition: here is another such case: Aristoph. *Pax* 357 σὺν δόρει σὺν ἀσπίδι; see too I.3 for a grammarian (Greek) on the pattern; XXIV.3, 24 for a Homeric example; Delbrück 1900: 186 cites a Vedic parallel). I quote some further examples from Plautus.

Epid. 198 (*per medicinas per tonstrinas, in gymnasio atque in foro,* | *per myropolia et lanienas circumque argentarias*) is similar to *Am.* 1012–13 above, in that the same asyndetic pair is again juxtaposed with a coordinated prepositional pair. It looks as if the association of *medicinae* and *tonstrinae* was formulaic or proverbial.

Merc. 988 (*cum porcis cum fiscina*, 'with the pigs and with the basket') has a pair of uncertain meaning but the phrase was probably proverbial again (see Enk 1932: 193–4).

Here are some miscellaneous examples:

Cist. 377 (frg. vi) *siquidem imperes pro copiis pro recula*

8 *Semantic Categories* 297

Cur. 289 *qui incedunt suffarcinati cum libris cum sportulis*

Cur. 612 *quin tu is in malam crucem | cum bolis cum bulbis*

Mil. 712 *me ad se ad prandium ad cenam uocant.*

On the other hand *St.* 413 *in cercuro in stega* is not an asyndeton. The second phrase explains or specifies the first, 'on the vessel – on the deck' (see Petersmann 1973 ad loc.).

8 Semantic Categories

Asyndeton, both of pairs and also of longer types, does seem to be influenced to some extent by semantic factors (see also XXXII.3.4). For example, the imperative 'go' is particularly likely to be followed asyndetically by another imperative, 'go, do something' (and not only in Latin: see X.1.5). Certain subjects seem to inspire asyndetic lists. One such is luxury, particularly female luxury. Terms for adornments, accessories, clothing, hair styles tend to be used in pairs or piled up (usually in contexts of disapproval) without coordinators. Such asyndeta are not only a feature of Plautus, as we will see. Was there something about asyndetic listing that enhanced the implication of disapproval? Asyndetic pronunciation allows significant pauses, and asyndetic lists, as we have seen (IV.3), may be open-ended, thereby implying that the decadence may be greater than stated. For the interaction of intonation with semantics see also XXXII.3.3, 3.4.

Within the following categories I have cited longer asyndeta as well as asyndeta bimembria. However, it is the latter that are more revealing, because any long list is likely to be asyndetic in most writers. It is the pairs that are exceptional, and better able to throw up significant semantic categories.

8.1 *Adornment and the Like, Mainly Female*

In the *Asinaria* a contract is drawn up on behalf of Diabolus obliging a *lena* on receipt of a gift of twenty silver minas to guarantee that Philaenium be with him for a year. The contract lays down the behaviour required of the girl. At *As.* 803 (*tum si coronas serta unguenta iusserit | ancillam ferre Veneri aut Cupidini*, 'if she orders her maid to bring garlands, wreaths, perfumes to Venus or Cupid') it is specified that she should be watched by a slave to make sure that she is not giving these adornments to a man. The tricolon expresses accessories associated with amatory behaviour and ordered by the girl.

At *Epid.* 226 a speaker refers to women walking about the streets wearing 'entire estates' (*fundis exornatae*). He adds: 'What about those women who find new names for their dresses every year?': 230–3 *tunicam rallam, tunicam spissam, linteolum caesicium, | indusiatam patagiatam caltulam aut crocotulam, | supparum aut subnimium, ricam, basilicum aut exoticum, | cumatile aut plumatile, carinum aut cerinum,* 'The sheer tunic, the thick tunic, the small embroidered apron, the outer dress, the bordered dress, the marigold or the saffron dress, the mini-shawl or … the maxi-shawl, the hooded dress, the queen's or the foreign dress, the water-coloured or the dishwater-coloured dress, the nut-brown or the waxen dress.' The long list is asyndetic throughout.

Pairs are also found in such contexts (cf. too the passages of Lucretius cited at XXV.3 on Lucil. 71):

Men. 801 <u>ancillas penum</u> | *recte praehibet,* 'he provides you with slave girls and food as he ought'.

These are supposed necessities for a woman. The female referent also receives jewellery and clothes, *te auratam et uestitam bene habet,* in this clause with coordination (cf. the passage of Terence cited on the next example). Similar is the longer sequence at *Men.* 120-1a, before which the speaker remarks that he has spoiled the woman far too much: *ego tibi ancillas penum | lanam aurum uestem purpuram | bene praebeo.*

Mil. 1127 <u>aurum ornamenta</u> *quae illi instruxisti ferat,* 'let her take the gold, the jewellery you furnished her with'.

The pair is in a longer list at *Mil.* 1302: *i, Palaestrio, | aurum ornamenta uestem, pretiosa omnia | duc.* With part of this list may be compared a pair in Terence: *Hau.* 248 *aurum uestem,* 'All that gold and fine clothing!' (Barsby, Loeb); cf. *auratam et uestitam* cited immediately above. *Mil.* 1302 above alongside 1127 makes it obvious that the pair *aurum ornamenta* is an open-ended list.

Ps. 1265 *unguenta atque odores,* <u>lemniscos corollas</u> | *dari dapsilis,* 'when perfumes and scents, ribbons, garlands are given in abundance'.

The reference is not necessarily specifically to women. For the structure see above, 7.2.

Female adornment is not only described by means of asyndetic strings of nouns. Note the verbs at *Poen.* 229 (*ornantur lauantur tergentur poliuntur*), of women making themselves up. The speaker remarks that there is no such thing as female moderation. Here are asyndetic adjectives used by a man of a woman's hair: *Truc.* 287 *istos fictos compositos crispos cincinnos tuos,* | *unguentatos . . . euellam,* 'I will tear out those nicely arranged, fixed-up, curly, perfumed locks.'

Here finally are two other long asyndeta on similar themes:

Aul. frg. i *pro illis corcotis strophiis, sumptu uxorio,* 'instead of those saffron dresses, breast bands and expenses of wives'.

Cur. 577 *ita me uolsellae pecten speculum calamistrum meum* | *bene me amassint,* 'as truly as my depilatory tweezers, comb, mirror, curling tongs love me well'. The passage then continues after the verb with a double coordination, *meaque axitia linteumque,* 'and makeup pot and bath towel'. The speaker is a pimp, who is being threatened by a soldier, and the mock reply emphasises his femininity.

8.2 Decadent or Depraved Behaviour

This section is similar to the last but I illustrate particularly the fact that so-called 'playing the Greek', whoring, drinking, eating excessively tends to be referred to by means of asyndeton. Asyndetic pairs are underlined:

Bac. 1080 <u>duxi habui</u> scortum, potaui, <u>dedi donaui</u>
Men. 170 *furtum scortum prandium*
Men. 476 <u>prandi potaui</u>, *scortum accubui, apstuli* | *hanc*
Mo. 22–3 *dies noctesque* <u>bibite pergraecamini</u>, | *amicas* <u>emite liberate</u>
Mo. 64–5 <u>bibite pergraecamini</u>, | *este effercite uos, saginam caedite*
Mo. 960 *scorta duci, peregraecari,* <u>fidicinas tibicinas</u> *ducere (cf. St.* 380–1 *fidicinas tibicinas* | *sambucas aduexit,* 'he has brought along lyre girls, flute girls, harp girls').
Poen. 661 <u>potare amare</u> *uolt*
Ps. 1134 *edunt bibunt scortantur*
Ps. 1271–2 *illos accubantis potantis, amantis* | *cum scortis reliqui.*

These last two categories might be put under the general heading of luxurious living. They are not alone in being suited to such a classification. See also below, 8.4.

For a similar sequence in Terence see *Eun.* 373 *cibum una capias, adsis tangas ludas, propter dormias.*

8.3 'Eat, Drink'

This is a type that comes up in the preceding section, but see in particular above, 5.5.

8.4 Vices, Adjectives Applied to Disapproved Behaviour

The previous three sections embrace forms of behaviour that speakers openly or by implication were condemning. In a wider sense too nouns for vices or adjectives applied to character defects likely to lead to vices are often used asyndetically, and the type persists into the classical period, not least in historians. Here are some examples:

Am. 897–8 *sed eccum uideo qui <modo> me miseram arguit | stupri dedecoris* (cf. *Am.* 882–3 *ita me probri | stupri dedecoris a uiro argutam meo!*).
As. 475–6 *age, impudice | sceleste*
Aul. 326 *fur trifurcifer*
Bac. 612 *proteruo iracundo animo, indomito incogitato*
Bac. 784 *ego sum sacer scelestus*
Capt. 671 *tuis scelestis falsidicis fallaciis*
Epid. 421 *stolidum combardum me faciebam*
Men. 269 *ego autem homo iracundus, animi perciti*
Men. 583 *rapaces uiri, fraudulenti*
Merc. 47 *perfidiam iniustitiam lenonum expromere*
Mil. 663 *aduocato tristi iracundo*
Mo. 105 *homo ... | ... immundus instrenuos*
Mo. 875 *peculi sui prodigi, plagigeruli*
Per. 686–7 *id metuebas miser, | impure auare*
Ps. 580 *dolos perfidias*
Ps. 794 *multiloquom gloriosum, insulsum inutilem*
Truc. 762–3 *uenefica, | suppostrix puerum.*

In the above collection *iracundus* occurs three times, *scelestus* three times and *perfidia* twice.

For a similar asyndeton (but discontinuous) in Menander see *Sam.* 348 χαμαιτύπη δ' ἄνθρωπος, ὄλεθρος, 'the woman is a prostitute, a disaster'; also *Mis.* 712 βάρβαρος, λ[έ]αινά τις | ἄν[θρωπος], 'the girl's a savage, a beast!'. Another abusive pair is at *Asp.* 242: οὐδὲν ἱερόν, ἀνδρόγυνος 'you're no good, a womanish creature'. See

8 Semantic Categories   301

Gomme and Sandbach (1973: 83) on both terms, the first apparently proverbial and a two-word unit.

8.5 Food Lists, Recipes, Shopping Lists etc.

Aul. 399 (*congrum murenam exdorsua quantum potest*, 'remove the backbone from the conger-eel and the lamprey as quickly as possible') has an asyndetic pair of fish names in a cooking instruction. In a joke at *Men.* 918 (*soleamne esse auis squamosas, piscis pennatos*, of eating birds with scales and fish with feathers) the two mock-culinary phrasal pairs are asyndetic. Other asyndetic lists of foods that I have noted in Plautus are longer (see also IV.2):

Cas. 493 *emito sepiolas lepadas lolligunculas | hordeias* (shopping list).
Cur. 323 *pernam abdomen sumen sueris glandium*
Cur. 366 *aliquid prius opstrudamus, pernam sumen glandium* (there are then some asyndetic phrases from the same sphere).
Mo. 46 *tu tibi istos habeas turtures piscis auis*
Ps. 741 *murrinam passum defrutum mellam mel quoiuis modi* (sweet things).
Ps. 815, 814 *apponunt rumicem brassicam betam blitum, | indunt coriandrum feniculum alium, atrum holus*
Rud. 297–8 *echinos lopadas ostreas balanos captamus, conchas, | marinam urticam, musculos, plagusias striates* (list of fish caught).

For asyndeton bimembre in a medical recipe in Menander see *Phasm.* 31, p. 380 Arnott ἐμβαλὼν ἅλας, φακούς 'add salt, lentils'. See further IV.2 for asyndetic recipes and shopping lists.

8.6 Precious Metals and the like

St. 377 (*lectos eburatos auratos*, 'couches adorned with ivory and gold') should be compared with Enn. *trag.* 91 Jocelyn (Ennius 15) *auro ebore*. The pair *aurum argentum* is well attested (see Cicero 21 with cross reference): note (with anaphora) *Rud.* 1257 *si aurum, si argentum est*. With the adjectival use of *auratus* in asyndeton above cf. *Rud.* 1158 *securicula ancipes, itidem aurea | litterata*, 'a two-headed axe, also gold, lettered.

8.7 Athletic Pursuits

Bac. 428 *ibi cursu luctando hasta disco pugilatu pila | saliendo sese exercebant*

Mo. 152 *arte gymnasticas:* | *disco hastis pila cursu armis equo* | *uictitabam uolup* (cf. Lucil. 641 (688 W.) *cum <in> stadio in gymnasio, in duplici corpus siccasssem pil*[*a*] (see XXV.3, with cross reference)).

8.8 Adjectives to Do with Age and Decrepitude

Three times Plautus combines *uetulus* asyndetically with *decrepitus*, with the stronger term second (see Adams 2016: 231): *Epid.* 666 *nos uetulos decrepitos duo*, *Merc.* 291 *Accherunticus,* | *senex uetus decrepitus*, *Merc.* 314 *uetulus decrepitus senex.* Decrepitude is a topic that inspired asyndeta, with the disparaging adjectives usually at the end of a colon. Note also:

As. 340 *eos asinos praedicas* | *uetulos claudos*
Mo. 275 *nam istae ueteres, quae se unguentis unctitant, interpoles,* | *uetulae edentulae*, 'those old women who apply ointments, furbishing themselves up, ancient, toothless'.

Toothlessness (*edentulae* above) was associated with age, and virtually equivalent to *decrepitus*. Cf. *Men.* 864 *leonem uetulum olentem edentulum*, and also *Cas.* 550 *illius hirqui improbi edentuli* 'of that worthless, toothless goat'. A word for 'old' in such groups tends to be combined with an adjective referring to physical degeneration.

In Menander note *Dysk.* 662 εὔχεσθε τὸν γέροντα σωθῆναι κακῶς, | ἀνάπηρον ὄντα, χωλόν, 'pray that the old man's rescue may be bungled, leaving him disabled, a cripple'. The open-ended list of pejorative adjectives again comes in final position (the asyndeton is discontinuous). See too *Dysk.* 579–80 ἀνῆψα τὴν δίκελλαν ἀσθενεῖ τινι | καλῳδίῳ, σαπρῷ, 'I tied the mattock to a weak piece of rope, rotten.'

On the other hand old age may be venerated (as for example in a wine). For 'old' and 'venerable' in asyndeton (of an old wine) see Men. *Dysk.* 946 Εὔιον γέροντα πολιὸν ἤδη, 'now a hoary patriarchal vintage'.

8.9 Numerical Approximations

Pairs for numerical approximations are scattered about, denoting 'a few, a lot' or the like. In Plautus we have seen (7.1) *Epid.* 211 *pueros uirgines,* | *binos ternos*, *Ps.* 580 *duplicis triplicis dolos perfidias.* Cf. Ter. *Eun.* 332 *mensibus* | *sex septem.* For examples in Horace (*Ep.* 1.1.58) and Laberius (18.2) see on XXIX.2.2. See also Preuss (1881: 48–9) on the formula *ter*

8 Semantic Categories 303

quater, stating that 'saepissime = compluries'. It is found at Scribonius Largus 4.73, quoted at XXXII.4. Scribonius however often coordinates such pairs.

Counting is asyndetic, but ordinals may be coordinated (*the first and the second*). For asyndetic ordinals see *Mo.* 956–7 *heri et nudiustertius,* | *quartus quintus sextus,* 'yesterday and the day before yesterday, three days ago, four days ago, five days ago'. Note too *Per.* 555–6 *perfidia et peculatus ex urbe et auaritia si exulant,* | *quarta inuidia, quinta ambitio, sexta optrectatio, septimum periurium* (the numbering continues).

8.10 Pairs of Opposites

It is remarkable how few pairs of asyndetic opposites there are in Plautus. A few cases of classic types occur, but in such a large corpus they are insignificant, whereas in some forms of literary Latin later they were to become a marked stylistic trait.

I have noted just three instances of the old positive + privative type, one introduced by emendation following scribal insertion of a coordinator (see further VI.6). Here are two of them: *As.* 247 *dignos indignos adire atque experi[ri] certum est mihi, Cur.* 280 *date uiam mihi, noti [atque] ignoti.* The latter is in a peremptory address of a crowd. For asyndeton bimembre in crowd address see *Rud.* 616 *agricolae accolae propinqui qui estis his regionibus* 'you farmers and neighbours who are close to us here' (citizens of Cyrene). *Patres conscripti* seems to belong in this category (see XXII.5.1). The third example is below, next paragraph.

There is just one sequence of pairs of opposites (antonyms), one of them of the positive + privative type: *Bac.* 401 *certamen cernitur* | *sisne necne ut esse oportet, malus bonus quoiuis modi,* | *iustus iniustus, malignus largus* (then a textual problem). This is a pattern of accumulation found in Greek and some genres of Latin (see on Cicero 94–8 and also XIX.1). It must have been familiar to Plautus but was not exploited or needed.

Another pair of antonyms is at *Cist.* 522: *di me omnes, magni minuti* (text not absolutely certain).

The 'town–country' pair occurs in juxtaposition with another asyndetic pair of formulaic character at *Am.* 226: *urbem agrum, aras focos, seque uti dederent.* For *urbem agrum* see above, 7.1, with cross references.

These examples aside, there are just a few instances of the reversive or converse types: *Mil.* 864 *abi, actutum redi* ('go, come straight back', reversives), *Poen.* 653 *salutat respondemus* (converses), *Trin.* 254 *nuntii renuntii* (of those taking and those bringing back messages: reversives).

Cf. *Poen.* 1350 (*debetur dabo*, 'it is owed: I will give': i.e. 'you are owed, I will give').

For the converse type in Menander and Terence see 5.5.

8.11   Relationships by Blood, Marriage, Alliance and Friendship

Such relationships are sometimes expressed in asyndetic pairs or longer sequences (see XIV). One pair is at *Bac.* 380: *tuom patrem meque una, amicos affinis tuos* (note the accumulation). *Affines* are relatives by marriage (see Sallust 41, 42, Livy 6). Cf. Sall. *Jug.* 14.15 *amicos adfinis propinquos ceteros meos*, and Cic. *Quinct.* 26 *amicum socium adfinem*. Tacitus 63 is similar, and an asyndeton bimembre: *ob propinquos amicos*. At Lucil. 994 (1097 W.) (*ad matrem cognatam ad amicam*) there is first an asyndetic pair dependent on the first *ad* ('to her mother, a kinswoman') and then a third element with the second *ad* ('or to a female friend') (see XXV.1.1.2, 12). *Cognatus* refers to a relationship by blood. Note too *Merc.* 948 *ualent mater pater?*

8.12   Complementary Parts of the Body

At *Mo.* 1118 (*cum pedibus manibus, cum digitis auribus oculis labris*) *cum* (twice) is a divider (like *ad* in the passage of Lucilius immediately above), which detaches *pedibus manibus* from the other anatomical terms. For such dividers see also e.g. Cic. *Sest.* 88 (**15**) *ad ferrum faces, ad cotidianam caedem incendia rapinas*.

For 'hands, feet', see possibly *Ps.* 844 *'manibus pedibus' uolui dicere* (Leo and Lindsay print for *manibus* respectively *dimissis* and *demissis*; see however the apparatus criticus of de Melo). The same asyndetic pair is also in Terence: *An.* 676 *conari manibus pedibus, noctesque et dies* (cf. 161 *manibus pedibusque*). *Poen.* 819 (*is me ... uerberat incursat pugnis calcibus*) is of the same type ('fists, heels': the parts of the hands and feet used in a physical assault).

8.13   Masculine + Feminine Pairs

Note on the one hand *Cas.* 521 *seruos ancillas domo | certum est omnis mittere ad te* and *Men.* 339 *ad portum mittunt seruolos ancillulas* (male, female

8 Semantic Categories 305

slaves), and on the other *Epid.* 210 *tum captiuorum quid ducunt secum! pueros uirgines,* | *binos ternos* (boys, girls). There is an embedded pair ('ladies, gentlemen') in Menander: *Dysk.* 921 παῖ, παι]δίον, γυναῖκες ἄνδρες, παῖ, θυρωρέ. Terence has one of the Plautine pairs above: *Hau.* 142 *ancillas seruos.* Cf. Cato *ORF* XII.73 *serui ancillae, si quis eorum centone crepuit,* XXV.1.1.2 on Lucilius 13. See also XI.5.

8.14 Some Miscellaneous Pairs that Occur more than Once, in Plautus or in Plautus and Elsewhere

uiuo ualeo

See *Bac.* 246 *uiuit ualet, St.* 31 *quom ipsi interea uiuant ualeant,* 'whether in the meantime they themselves are alive and in good health', *Trin.* 1075 *uiuont ualent.*

See further, on the semantic development, XXVII.1.4, XXIX.2.2 (on Hor. *Ep.* 1.6.67).

opus/opera labor

Am. 170 (*ips' dominus diues operis* [*et*] *laboris expers*), *Rud.* 1020 *mea opera labore, et rete et horia.* For the pair with coordination see Livy 5.2.7 *in opere ac labore.*

do dono

For this pair of alliterative near-synonyms see *Mil.* 1204 *donaui dedi* | *quae uoluit* and *Bac.* 1080 *duxi habui scortum, potaui, dedi donaui.* I have not found the pair discussed or annotated.

frigus fames

On this pair, which persisted through Lucilius into the classical period, see 7.3.

iocus ludus

Note *Bac.* 116 *Amor Voluptas Venus Venustas Gaudium* | *Iocus Ludus Sermo Suauisauiatio, Capt.* 770 *laudem lucrum ludum iocum festiuitatem ferias, Merc.* 846 *sex sodalis repperi,* | *uitam auaritiam ciuitatem laetitiam ludum iocum, Ps.* 65 *nunc nostri amores mores consuetudines* | *iocus ludus sermo suauisauiatio.* This pair (or with *lusus* for *ludus*) recurs (see *TLL* VII.2.289.9ff.: e.g. Cic. *Verr.* 1.155 *per ludum et iocum,* Hor. *Carm.* 2.19.-25–6), and in the Plautine passages is embedded within longer asyndetic series (containing other pairs, based to some extent on sound). The two terms are near-synonyms, and may be compared with the opposites partly of the same semantic field at e.g. Cic. *Fin.* 2.85 (101) *ioca seria, ut dicitur* (see Preuss 1881: 34–5).

9 Conclusions

The correspondences, mainly imprecise, between asyndeta in Plautus and Menander for the most part are likely to reflect parallel development of the two languages rather than the influence of New Comedy on Plautus. For example, in both languages asyndetic pairs of imperatives were common, and there is no more than a general similarity between the examples cited from Menander and those from Plautus (5.1). Menander's (formulaic) adverbial pair of opposites ἄνω κάτω 'up and down' (*Kitharistes* fr. 1.3 p. 134 Arnott, *Mis.* 7) is not matched in Plautus (but cf. the pair of synonyms, *clam furtim*, at *Poen.* 662), but if it had been the type was well established in Latin too (see XIII.5.4). Both Menander and Plautus quite often have miscellaneous (non-imperatival) pairs of verbs in asyndeton, but the actual pairs are semantically diverse in both writers, and it would not be convincing to suggest that Plautus was in some way imitating Greek, though there are some similarities: note *Sikyonioi* 269–70 ἀνίστ[ατο], | ἐβάδιζε alongside *Rud.* 172 *surrexit, horsum se capessit* (see 5.5). Pairs of adjectives applied to disapproved behaviour are common to both (see 8.4). Both writers have asyndeta in formulaic or ritualistic contexts (3), but this was an ancient inherited type. One of the Plautine examples, of augural type, has antecedents in Umbrian, whereas the most distinctive religious example in Menander (with two pairs of masculine + feminine adjectives in asyndeton) I have been unable to parallel precisely in Latin. The one exact parallel that I have found between Plautus and Menander is in the use of pairs of participles of the same semantic fields (of pleading, begging, weeping: see 5.5), but in Greek the type is not confined to Menander, as we saw.

One influence on Plautus' use of asyndeton was probably early high-style poetry such as tragedy, and that in its turn might have reflected the influence of Greek tragedy (in which sequences of terms with repeated prefix are found: see VI.8.1) or even of an Italic religious style (see the Umbrian passage *Tab. Ig.* VIb.10–11 with prolonged alliteration cited at XXII.4.6). Features of this Plautine high style include whole lines of asyndetic terms, often with assonance (see above, 4 n. 2), compound coinages, often long, in asyndeton (see 4), and asyndetic pairs with diverse forms of assonance (for pairs of verbs showing such features see 5.4, along

9 Conclusions 307

with n. 2, on other parts of speech; also 3, where there are some religious pairs with alliteration).

Plautine asyndetic pairs suggest long continuities of usage. There are on the one hand types that can be linked with the past. It was noted for example in 6 that about a third of Plautus' adjectival pairs have at least one term with a privative prefix (usually with *in-*, but see below), and we have seen that privatives in asyndeton go right back to the earliest Indo-European. The augural type with two asyndetic bird names has earlier Italic connections (see 3). On the other hand many Plautine types of asyndeton persist into the classical period. The privative type above is not only old but goes on into later periods (see e.g. XXV.2 on Lucilius, XXIX.2.1.1 on Horace's *Satires*). A variant, in which negative prefixes other than *in-* are found in asyndeton, is in Plautus and also continues later (see VI.7, XXV.2, XXVII.1.1, XXIX.2.1.1). Pairs of opposites are not particularly common in Plautus, but they do occur (see 8.10). These are both old in type (see e.g. XXII.4.3, 4.6 for Umbrian examples, and Cicero 94–8 for examples from Aristotle) and common later (see XIII). There are asyndetic pairs of imperatives in e.g. Catullus of old types (XXVII.1.4), and a structure in an official formula later can be paralleled in Plautus (see X.1.2). It was also seen above (3) in a slightly different connection that a formula comprising *oro obsecro* and then the imperative *ignosce* is both in Plautus and then a letter of Cicero. Pairs comprising ablative gerunds are well attested in literary Latin later on (see 5.4), as are masculine + feminine pairs (see 8.13). The legal pair *usus fructus* is juxtaposed with another asyndetic pair (see 3), and such accumulations are a feature of later legal language (see e.g. XXII.5.7, 8). Some of the semantic categories that seem to prompt asyndeta in Plautus continued to do so. For example, asyndetic pairs and longer sequences listing female adornments or accessories (see above, 8.1) are also attested e.g. in Lucilius and Lucretius (see XXV.3, on Lucil. 71). Athletic pursuits (8.7), numerical approximations (8.9), relationships by blood or marriage (8.11) may be expressed in the classical period in asyndeton (see the cross references ad locc.).

A section is included above (7) on various structures in which asyndetic pairs occur in Plautus, notably juxtaposed with other such pairs or with coordinated pairs. It was shown earlier (see XIX.1) that such accumulations are old, and it will be shown in subsequent chapters that they are a feature of both high literature and more mundane genres later.

Appendix: Lists of Asyndetic Pairs of Nouns, Adjectives and Adverbs in Plautus

Nouns

Am. 170 *operis* [*et*] *laboris*
Am. 414 *ui pugnando* (mixed parts of speech).
Am. 614 *forma aetate*
Am. 898 *stupri dedecoris* (cf. *Am.* 882–3 *probri* | *stupri dedecoris*).
Am. 991 *dicto imperio*
Am. 1132 *hariolos haruspices*
As. 245 *opibus, omni copia*
As. 260 *coruos parra*
As. 548 *stimulos lamminas*
As, 555 *ui pugnando* (mixed parts of speech).
As. 824 *turbas litis*
Aul. 95 *cultrum securim, pistillum mortarium*
Aul. 326 *fur trifurcifer*
Aul. 399 *congrum murenam*
Aul. 512 *linteones calceolarii*
Aul. 513 *sedentarii sutores, diabathrarii*
Bac. 116 *iocus ludus* (also *Capt.* 770, *Merc.* 846, *Ps.* 65).
Bac. 380 *amicos affinis*
Bac. 732 *morbum mortem*
Capt. 911 *clades calamitasque, intemperies* (there is first a coordinated pair, and that forms an asyndeton bimembre with *intemperies*; for this structure cf. *Vitr.* 1.1.10, quoted at XXXII.4).
Cas. 521 *seruos ancillas*
Cist. 649 *pessulis repagulis*
Cur. 76 *custos ianitrix* (this looks like an appositional compound, a doorkeeper-guard, but it may be an asyndetic coordination).
Epid. 210 *pueros uirgines*
Epid. 523 *fictor condictor*
Epid. 530 *paupertas pauor*
Men. 339 *seruolos ancillulas*
Men. 801 *ancillas penum*
Men. 918 *auis squamosas, piscis pennatos*
Men. 974–5 *uerbera compedes . . . fames frigus*
Men. 1133 *miseriis laboribus* (cf. 'Sen.' *Octauia* 105 *miseriis luctu*).
Merc. 47 *perfidiam iniustitiam*
Merc. 832 *usus fructus, uictus cultus*
Mil. 647 *sputator screator*
Mil. 1055 *urbicape, occisor regum*
Mil. 1127 *aurum ornamenta*

Appendix: Lists of Asyndetic Pairs in Plautus

Mo. 104 *sumptum operam*
Mo. 138 *grandinem imbrem[que]*
Mo. 960 *fidicinas tibicinas*
Mo. 1118 *pedibus manibus*
Per. 566 *fundis familiis* (cf. Cato *Agr.* 141.2–3 [prayer] for the association).
Poen. 791 *hariolos haruspices*
Poen. 819 *pugnis calcibus*
Poen. 835 *tenebrae latebrae*
Poen. 1188 *spes uitae*
Ps. 580 *dolos perfidias*
Ps. 843 *manibus pedibus*
Ps. 1265 *lemniscos corollas*
Rud. 23 *donis hostiis*
Rud. 186 *in usu, experiundo* (mixed parts of speech).
Rud. 616 *agricolae accolae*
Rud. 665 *auxili praesidi*
Rud. 839 *ui uiolentia*
Rud. 930 *agrum atque aedis, mancupia*
Rud. 1020 *opera labore*
Trin. 302 *imperiis [et] praeceptis*
Trin. 317 *sarta tecta*
Trin. 799 *seruos ancillas*
Trin. 253–4 *flabelliferae cistellatrices,* | *nuntii renuntii*
Truc. 762–3 *uenefica,* | *suppostrix puerum.*

There are 67 examples.

Adjectives

As. 34 *fustitudinas ferricrepinas*
As. 223 *uinnula uenustula*
As. 247 *dignos indignos* (substantival).
As. 340 *uetulos claudos*
As. 301 *nudus uinctus* (the meaning is possibly 'tied up naked', with *nudus* predicative, but note Livy 9.8.9 *nudos uinctosque*).
As. 475–6 *impudice* | *sceleste*
As. 565 *artutos audacis*
Aul. 226–1 *diuitem* | *factiosum* (cf. Sall. *Cat.* 18.4 *egens factiosus: egens* is the opposite of *diues*).
Aul. 509 *patagiarii indusiarii*
Aul. 786 *infelix miser*
Bac. 400–1 *malus bonus* . . . | *iustus iniustus, malignus largus*
Bac. 612 *proteruo iracundo* . . . *indomito incognito*
Bac. 615 *inamabilis illepidus*
Bac. 784 *sacer scelestus*

Capt. 406 *dubiis egenis*
Capt. 648 *crispus cincinnatus*
Capt. 671 *scelestis falsidicis*
Capt. 718 *nuperum nouicium* (see Lindsay 1900: 283).
Capt. 722 *ponderosas crassas*
Capt. 814 *quadrupedanti crucianti*
Capt. 956 *bellus lepidus*
Cas. 550 *improbi edentuli*
Cist. 522 *magni minuti*
Cur. 280 *noti [atque] ignoti*
Cur. 472 *dites damnosos*
Epid. 211 *binos ternos*
Epid. 256 *calidi conducibilis*
Epid. 421 *stolidum combardum*
Epid. 494 *mucidum, minimi preti*
Epid. 666 *uetulos decrepitos*
Men. 290 *sacres sinceri*
Men. 580 *aequom bonum*
Men. 583 *rapaces . . . fraudulenti*
Men. 591 *tortas confragosas*
Men. 767 *dote fretae, feroces*
Men. 863 *indomitos ferocis*
Men. 973 *ignauis improbis*
Merc. 291 *uetus decrepitus*
Merc. 314 *uetulus decrepitus*
Mil. 663 *tristi iracundo*
Mo. 105–6 *nequam . . . indiligens*[que] | *cum pigra familia, immundus instrenuos*
Mo. 275 *uetulae edentulae*
Mo. 875 *peculi sui prodigi, plagigeruli*
Per. 438 *probi numerati*
Per. 522 *furtiuam abductam*
Per. 687 *impure auare*
Per. 707–8 *longa . . .* | *contortiplicata*
Poen. 28 *infantis minutulos*
Poen. 510 *loripedes tardissumos*
Poen. 1179 *myrrhinus omnis*
Ps. 580 *duplicis triplicis*
Ps. 677 *certa deformata*
Ps. 697–8 *strenuom* | *beneuolentem*
Ps. 794 *multiloquom gloriosum, insulsum inutilem*
Ps. 989 *purus putus* (also at 1200).
Ps. 1133 *lucrifugas damnicupidos*
Rud. 125 *crispum incanum*
Rud. 695 *lacrumantes, genibus nixae*
Rud. 1158–9 *aurea* | *litterata*

St. 227 *malacas crapularias*
St. 304 *insperato opportuno*
St. 377 *eburatos auratos*
Trin. 299 *faeceos . . . turbidos*
Trin. 751 *indomito, pleno amoris ac lasciuiae*
Trin. 821 *laetus lubens*
Truc. 435 *unanimantis fidentis.*

There are 71 examples.

Many of the adjectival pairs are at the end of cola, and are predicative or secondary predicates (on such placement see V.2): e.g. *Aul.* 226–7 *ted esse hominem diuitem | factiosum, Bac.* 784 *ego sum sacer scelestus, Capt.* 718 *recens captum hominem, nuperum nouicium, Epid.* 211 *pueros uirgines, | binos ternos, Men.* 863 *equos iunctos iubes | capere me, indomitos ferocis, Per.* 522 *adduxit . . . liberalem uirginem, | furtiuam, abductam ex Arabia, St.* 227 *unctiones . . . | uendo uel alias malacas crapularias.*

Adverbs

I comment briefly on a number of these pairs, few of which have come up earlier.

Am. 213 *superbe, nimis ferociter*
Am. 463 *bene prospere[que]*
Am. 1112 *ego cunas recessim rursum uorsum trahere et ducere,* 'I dragged and shoved the cradles backwards' (both *recessim* and *rursum uorsum* mean 'backwards'. A critical text should be punctuated with a comma after *recessim*, thus indicating an asyndeton bimembre).
As. 562 *sciens lubenter peiieraris* (mixed parts of speech; *sciens* is strictly an adjective, but the sense of the pair is 'knowingly, willingly').
Aul. 188 *perspicue palam est* (but the first may be a modifier of the second: see above, 6 n. 4).
Bac. 934 *qui misere male mulcabere* (but does the first adverb, as a modifier of the second, make *male* into a superlative-equivalent? De Melo translates the pair as an asyndeton. Such examples are difficult to judge. See 6 n. 4).
Mil. 177 *ita abripuit repente sese subito* (if this is an asyndeton, it is discontinuous, with a pronoun, as often, the separating element).
Mil. 739 *meae domi accipiam benigne lepide, et lepidis uictibus* (I would take the final noun phrase to be separate from the adverbial pair, and not as a case of end-of-list coordination).
Poen. 662 *at enim hic clam furtim esse uolt* (cf. the possible pair *clam inprouiso* in Lucilius, XXV.1.1.7, 31).
Rud. 1097 *immo hercle insignite inique* (on this problematic pair see above, 6).

Rud. 1323 *eloquere propere celeriter* (*Trin.* 1008 *fac te propere celerem* suggests that *propere* is a modifier of *celeriter:* see 6 n. 4).

About eight examples.

Names

Here finally are names in asyndeton:

Bac. 649 *non mihi isti placent Parmenones Syri.*

CHAPTER XXIV

Virgil and Early High-Style Poetry

1 Introduction

This chapter is diverse, in that it deals with Virgil and Homer, Ennius and some other early poets (Pacuvius, Livius Andronicus, Naevius), and Lucretius. It is about asyndeton, particularly with two members, in poetry of the higher genres (including some tragic fragments) mainly in the earlier Republic. The chapter does not follow a chronological order. It starts with the latest writer of the group, Virgil, because his use of asyndeton can be straightforwardly described, and the description opens the way to comparisons between poets and to discussion of the influence of one writer on another. Was Virgil influenced by Homer, or by Lucretius or Ennius? Where does Lucretius stand in relation to early poetry? Explicit coordination will also be referred to, and will allow asyndetic coordination to be seen for what it is.

Virgil, Ennius and Lucretius all came up in II, where the problem of defining asyndeton, particularly of adjectives, was discussed. The examples there were of marginal types, not necessarily displaying straightforward asyndetic coordination. This chapter deals largely with definite cases of asyndeton, but I have included one or two examples from II because of ambiguities of interpretation. I begin with asyndeta with two members, where each member consists of a single word, and list all examples in Virgil's epic, and also in the *Eclogues and Georgics*. I then collect examples of a slightly extended adjectival type, where one part consists of one word and the other is longer. The section about Homer that follows is based on a reading of five books of the *Iliad* and one of the *Odyssey*, and the main aim is to consider whether there are similarities between Homer and Virgil that go beyond the chance appearance of standard types of asyndeton in both.

2 Virgil

2.1 Asyndeta Bimembria Where the Two Parts Consist of a Single Word

2.1.1 Adjectives

(1) *Aen.* 1.384 *ipse ignotus egens Libyae deserta peragro*, 'I myself, unknown, destitute, wander the wastes of Libya.'

The adjectives here are in agreement with the subject of the verb, and would be translated into English, if their placement in the Latin were kept, with intonation implying a pause before, after and between. A critical edition might employ commas to highlight the pauses, but I follow the usual practice of this book. These are not attributes but predicative adjuncts. One of the adjectives is a privative in *in-* but both have negative connotations. *Egens* is common in asyndeton, and it is found in Tacitus too in juxtaposition with *ignotus* (*Ann.* 1.74.2: see on Sallust 52 for details, and also XXXII.3.4). See also *Aen.* 4.373 (22, below), where *egens* is in asyndeton with a perfect participle, a structure found in the next passage (also *Ecl.* 9.5 (14): see Horsfall 2008: 101).

(2) *Aen.* 2.67–8 *conspectu in medio turbatus inermis* | *constitit*, 'he stood in the middle of the gazing crowd, disturbed, unarmed'.

Both terms are again in agreement with the subject of the verb, and are again predicative adjuncts/secondary predicates. The predicate is the prepositional expression with *in*. Note the *in*-privative *inermis*, which is quite often used in asyndeton bimembre in the historians, and in similar structures to that here: see Sallust 57, 58, Livy 38, 41, Tacitus 124.

(3) *Aen.* 3.618–19 *domus sanie dapibusque cruenta,* | *intus opaca ingens*, 'his house is bloody with gore and feasts, and is within dark, huge'.

Here the adjectives are predicative, in that the verb 'to be' can be supplied (on the text at the end of the first line see Horsfall 2006: 424–5). *Ingens* was favoured by Virgil in asyndeton, as we will see (see e.g. Austin 1977: 120–1). Etymologically *ingens* may not be an *in*-privative adjective (the etymology is uncertain), but it fits the sound pattern of such asyndeta. At 3.658 in a longer asyndeton Virgil hints that for him it was indistinguishable from such a privative (in structure, not meaning), as he has it juxtaposed with a real privative: *monstrum horrendum informe ingens*.

Opaca ingens is also in 7 below. It is placed almost at the start of a line in both places, and in the present passage is at the end of a sentence.

2 *Virgil* 315

(4) *Aen.* 4.32 <u>solane</u> perpetua <u>maerens</u> carpere iuuenta, 'will you, alone, sad, pine away for the whole of your youth?'
Again an adjective and participle are combined. The two terms on the above interpretation are predicative adjuncts agreeing with the subject of the verb, and are separated. There is an interlaced word order (cf. Lucr. 1.557–8 at 7.1.1 below, 2 <u>longa</u> diei | <u>infinita</u> aetas).
Sola maerens was discussed above, II.3.2.2 as a possible quasi-compound. I have included it here as well because some may prefer to see it as a straightforward asyndetic pair, with a separating element. The sense is not straightforward. At least one other interpretation of the phrase structure is possible ('will you, alone, pine away, sad for the whole of your youth?'), and indeed favoured by the word order.

(5) *Aen.* 4. 179–81 *Coeo Enceladoque sororem | progenuit, pedibus celerem et pernicibus alis, | monstrum <u>horrendum ingens</u>*, 'she brought forth a sister to Coeus and Enceladus, swift of foot and with fast wings, a monster awful, huge'.
Monstrum horrendum ingens is an appositional phrase. The adjectives are attributive but postpositive (at the end of a clause).

(6) *Aen.* 5.650–1 *ipsa egomet dudum Beroen digressa reliqui | <u>aegram indignantem</u>, tali quod sola careret | munere*, 'I myself now departing left Beroe behind, sick, resentful, because she alone had no part in such a rite.'
The phrase *aegram indignantem* is postpositive (following both its noun and the verb) and at the end of a clause. The terms are predicative adjuncts. Again the order is adjective + present participle (cf. 4, and 10 below). One of the terms again has the privative prefix *in-*.

(7) *Aen.* 6.283 *in medio ramos annosaque brachia pandit | ulmus <u>opaca ingens</u>*
The adjectives are attributive, but come right at the end, after the verb as well as the noun (cf. 5 above). Cf. 3 above for the same phrase and placement.

(8) *Aen.* 8.621–2 *loricam ex aere rigentem, | <u>sanguineam ingentem</u>*
This is part of a long description of Aeneas' equipment, with the nouns objects of *uersat*. The line is open to more than one interpretation. It is possible that there is an asyndeton with three members. Alternatively *loricam ex aere rigentem* may form a unit referring to the breastplate and its material ('a breastplate of rigid bronze', an attribute), which is then followed by an asyndeton bimembre modifying the whole phrase, describing terrifying characteristics ('blood-red, huge'). On this (likely) view the

postpositive adjectives (at the beginning of a new line) are adjuncts probably set off by pauses.

(9) *Aen.* 9.424 *tum uero exterritus amens* | *conclamat Nisus*

Could the phrase mean 'terrified out of his wits', with *amens* a consequence of being *exterritus*? The phrase is a predicative adjunct. Here is another case of participle + adjective.

(10) *Aen.* 10.837 *ipse aeger anhelans* | *colla fouet*

Possibly 'he himself, in pain, gasping, bathes his neck', with the adjectives agreeing with the subject of the verb and having the role of predicative adjuncts. If so the phrase could be rewritten with a coordinator and would be an asyndeton, but we saw above (II.3.2.2) that the two parts can be interpreted as forming a quasi-compound. I have again included the example here because of possible disagreements of interpretation. The pair consists of an adjective + present participle (cf. on 6 above).

(11) *Aen.* 12.888 *Aeneas instat contra telumque coruscat* | *ingens arboreum*

The adjectives are possibly attributive, but are postponed behind both the noun and the verb, and are at the start of a new line. The second outdoes the first, or further defines it ('huge, huge as a tree').

(12) *Aen.* 12.897 *saxum circumspicit ingens,* | *saxum antiquum ingens*

There is a rhetorical repetition of *saxum ingens*. The second occurrence, early in the second line, has the afterthought *antiquum*, which being 'new', looks emphatic ('a rock, huge, a rock ANCIENT, huge'), and seems to confer awe on what is seen. For a postponed asyndeton containing a repetition cf. 7.2 below, Lucretius 22.

(13) *Aen.* 12.930 *ille humilis supplex oculos dextramque precantem* | *protendens*, 'he, humble, suppliant, casting forth his eyes and right hand begging'.

For the structure (nominative pronoun followed by asyndetic pair) see 1, 10. For the text and interpretation see Tarrant (2012: 330). One manuscript, M, has *supplexque*, but the structure, shared with 1 and 10, and also the pathetic force of the adjectives, so typical of asyndetic pairs in Virgil (see the summary below after 15), favour the asyndeton. These terms are predicative adjuncts again.

(14) *Ecl.* 9.5 *nunc uicti tristes* ... | *hos illi* ... *mittimus haedos*, 'now, defeated, cowed, we send him these kids'.

The adjectives agree with the (unexpressed) subject of the verb, as in some other cases above, and are predicative adjuncts. The second conveys a consequence of the first ('defeated and (therefore) cowed').

2 Virgil 317

(15) G. 1.407 *ecce inimicus atrox magno stridore per auras | insequitur Nisus*, 'look, hostile, savage, with a great whirring Nisus follows through the air'. These are not attributes but adjuncts.

These fifteen examples have striking similarities.

First, a majority of them (ten) have one term with *in*-, either privative (1, 2, 6, 15), or in *ingens* (3, 5, 7, 8, 11, 12). Privative adjectives are often in asyndeton, as we have seen, particularly in VI. In Horace seven of the eight pairs of adjectives in the *Satires* have at least one privative or equivalent adjective (XXIX.2.1.5). In Plautus about 20 of the 70 adjectival pairs have at least one privative in *in*- (see XXIII.6). In seven of the ten pairs above the privative or *ingens* is in second place, the traditional position for the semantically stronger term (exceptions, 1, 11, 15). Five of the six instances of *ingens* (11 is the exception) have this position. It would seem from these figures that Virgil was attributing considerable force to it.

Second, in six cases, at 1, 2, 4, 10, 13, 14, the pairs precede the verb and are in agreement with the unexpressed subject of the verb (or *ipse/ille*), and we have described each as a (predicative) adjunct/secondary predicate. To these can be added two pairs (9, 15) which are in the same preverbal position, but in agreement with an expressed subject of the verb (the same subject, *Nisus*, in both cases). These pairs too are not straightforward attributes, but are adjuncts. In every one of these examples the terms express not inherent features of the subjects but features acquired or adopted from events befalling them, and they almost always have pathetic connotations (15 is the only exception). Rendered into English they would be marked by pauses and possibly postpositive (15 'Nisus follows ..., hostile, fierce').

Third, in contrast to the above preposed groups, there are seven pairs of postpositive adjectives, which follow a noun or verb or both, sometimes coming at the end of the clause or sentence (3, 5, 6, 7, 8, 11, 12). They are usually attributive (6 and 8 are exceptions). A semantic characteristic of six of these is that they indicate abnormal size or some other threatening feature (3, 5, 7, 8, 11, 12).

Fourth, a positional feature of a group of these postpositives is that they come right at the beginning of a second line, following the line which contains the verb or noun with which they agree (6, 8, 11); to these could be added 3, 5, 7 and 12, where a single word precedes at the start of the line. Here are the first three of these passages again:

Aen. 5.650–1 *ipsa egomet dudum Beroen digressa reliqui* | *aegram indignantem*
Aen. 8.621–2 *loricam ex aere rigentem,* | *sanguineam ingentem*
Aen. 12.888 *Aeneas instat contra telumque coruscat* | *ingens arboreum.*

In every case the pair contains an adjective with the prefix *in-*. We will return to this repetitive structure and its significance below (3).

The pathetic and threatening character referred to above marks these adjectival groups out as dramatic, and that feature may well have been brought out by pauses or a distinctive intonation of the type that would be normal in an English rendering, though one can only speculate about Latin.

In only one place are the two adjectives separated (4), and then there is an interlocking word order, with the separating element *perpetua* itself separated from its noun *iuuenta*. Moreover this is not a straightforward asyndeton (see the next paragraph).

10 and 4 have been treated here as asyndeta, but are they really? The possibility that they might be virtual compounds was discussed at II.3.2.2.

Adjectival adjuncts are so semantically distinctive that it would not be appropriate to describe the asyndeton as formulaic: it is functional and was probably of a type current in emphatic speech. I refer thus not to the actual words used by Virgil, but to the structures (see above, V.2). Note the adjectives in Petronius discussed at XXXII.1.

2.1.2 Nouns, Names

(**16**?) *Aen.* 1.600 <u>urbe domo</u> socias, 'you give us a share of city and home'.

Everyone needs a country and a home, and the pair *patria domus* occurs several times in asyndeton in Sallust (**23**, **24**). *Vrbs domus* is potentially similar to *patria domus*: in both cases the first term could designate the larger area in which the *domus* is. Alternatively the *patria* or *domus* might 'be home'. Austin (1971: 188) calls this an asyndeton (needlessly describing it as archaic and suggestive of legal documents), but his paraphrase implies an apposition ('with the underlying implication "in a city, home"') rather than a coordination. Apposition fits the context better. The reference is to the destitute Trojans, for whom a city would be home. The implication of such pairings could vary according to the context. A person, for example, deprived of *patria domus* would in many cases be deprived of country <u>and</u> household.

(**17**?) *Aen.* 3.503 *populosque propinquos,* | <u>Epiro Hesperia</u>, 'allied peoples, in Epirus, Hesperia'.

But the text is doubtful and this cannot be accepted as an asyndeton (for *Hesperiam* see Horsfall 2006: 358 ad loc.).

(**18**) *Aen.* 12.811 *nec tu me aeria solam nunc sede uideres* | <u>digna indigna</u> *pati*.

These are adjectives, but substantivised. On this example see Tarrant (2012: 297) and above, VI.6. It is a type of opposition that is prone to

2 Virgil

illogicality in some contexts (see VI.6): 'Juno would not wish to imply that any part of her sufferings was deserved' (Tarrant).

The remaining examples are not numbered, because they are mainly open to other interpretations or classifications, or are of types that have not been collected systematically. The most distinctive genuinely asyndetic type below is that with prepositional anaphora, and there are some adverbial opposites too.

2.1.3 Adverbs

There is a special type of 'asyndeton', which is probably best described otherwise, as 'gemination', whereby an adverb (in particular) is repeated, e.g. *magis magis*, a form of intensification (see Wills 1996: 106–21 on the adverbial type; see also XXVII.1.3). There are some such geminations in Virgil. Note *G*. 4.311 *tenuemque magis magis aera carpunt*, where Mynors (1990: 299) cites Catull. 64.274 (note too 38.3); cf. in Greek Aristoph. *Nub*. 1287 πλέον πλέον. On this Latin expression and variants with coordinators see Wölfflin (1933: 311–12), Hofmann and Szantyr (1965: 809), Wills (1996: 112–15). Other such geminations are *nunc nunc* (e.g. *Aen*. 8.579; see Wills 1996: 108) and *iam iam*, which is found ten times, in the *Aeneid* only (Wills 1996: 106). This is a pair that also has a coordinator sometimes (e.g. 8.708 *laxos iam iamque immittere funis*: see Wills 1996: 107). Coordinated pairs such as *magis magisque* and *iam iamque* alongside the uncoordinated type suggest the indeterminacy of the category.

A related type of adverbial asyndeton shows directional opposites such as *huc illuc* (4.363, 12.764) (see XIII.5.4).

2.1.4 Verbs

The type found in early Latin and beyond, whereby two verbs (I leave aside participles behaving as adjectives), often near-synonyms, occur in asyndeton (see e.g. XXIII.5.5), is not found in Virgil. The only verbs in what might look like asyndeta are imperatives, usually showing *age* combined with another imperative (for details see X.2).

2.1.5 Prepositional Expressions

The type of asyndeton with prepositional anaphora is well represented in Virgil. *Per* (in more than one use) is particularly frequent (I quote mainly examples with a single word dependent on each preposition but include a few phrasal cases): *Aen*. 2.358 *per tela per hostis | uadimus*, 2.527 *per tela per hostis | ... fugit*, 2.664 *me per tela per ignis | eripis*, 6.461–2 *ire per umbras |*

per loca senta situ, 11.497 *luduntque iubae per colla per armos*, 12.682 *perque hostis per tela ruit*. This structure is also found in oaths and the like (in which it must be very old), where *per* means 'by, in the name of': 6.458–9 *per sidera iuro*, | *per superos* (separated by the verb of swearing). For explicit coordination in such a construction see Sall. *Jug.* 58.5 *per amicitiam perque rem publicam obsecrat*.

For some other prepositions (I do not confine myself to examples in which there are just single words dependent on the preposition) see 4.254–5 *circum litora, circum* | *piscosos scopulos humilis uolat*, 6.431 *sine sorte datae, sine iudice, sedes* (separated), 6.795–6 *iacet extra sidera tellus*, | *extra anni solisque uias* (with separation again), 7.404 *inter siluas, inter deserta ferarum*, 7.583–4 *contra omina bellum*, | *contra fata deum ... poscunt*, 10.677 *in rupes in saxa ... ferte ratem*. On this last Harrison (1991) ad loc. (alluding to Austin 1964 on 2.358) says that the anaphora and asyndeton 'mark breathless excitement', but such an impressionistic judgement does not capture the tone of all the examples (on this issue see V). Note e.g. 6.458–9, 6.795–6, quoted above, and also 12.820 *pro Latio obtestor, pro maiestate tuorum*, 12.839 *supra homines, supra ire deos pietate uidebis*, where breathless excitement is out of the question; pauses, marked by intonation and indicative of effort, are more likely to have been present. Note that the second member at 6.795–6 above is of extended length, and certainly speed of delivery would not be conceivable. It is a traditional structure, which could be used in a variety of contexts.

For an asyndeton with prepositional anaphora in Homer see below, 3, 24.

Asyndeton bimembre where the two members have just a single word is limited in type as used by Virgil. Apart from that with adverbial gemination and the prepositional type, Virgil's main pairing is adjectival, and he uses it in clearly defined ways with stylistic point. Asyndeton of verbs (apart from the *age*-type) does not exist, and that of nouns is very rare. Further conclusions and summaries will be offered below.

2.2 *Adjectival Asyndeta with Two Members, One of Extended Length*

Adjectival asyndeton bimembre in which one member has a single word and the other is of extended length is of possible literary significance (see further below, 3 on Homer). I have noted the following instances in Virgil.

(19?) *Aen.* 1.531 *terra antiqua, potens armis atque ubere glaebae*

This whole expression is appositional to *est locus* in the previous line. It should possibly not be included among asyndeta, because *antiqua* can be

2 Virgil

taken as attributive ('an ancient land'), and the rest as an adjunct. On the other hand the position of *antiqua* is in favour of giving it the same function as the following phrase. Ambiguity of phrase structure is not uncommon in epic, both in Greek and Latin (see below).

(20?) 3.164 is identical to 19 (and the previous line too is identical to 1.530).

(21) 3.392 *litoreis ingens inuenta sub ilicibus sus | triginta capitum fetus enixa iacebit, | alba, solo recubans*, 'a huge sow will be found under holm oaks on the shore, and will be lying (there) having given birth to a litter of thirty, white, reposing on the ground'.

The asyndetic adjuncts (one adjectival, the other participial), are postponed after the verb and, at the start of a new line, are a long way from the noun. The same phrase is at 25 below, and the preceding two lines and the phrase following are identical in the two passages. For present participles as one member of asyndetic pairs, see above, 4, 6, 10, and below, 26, 27; also in Homer, 17, 18, 19. For *iaceo* accompanied by asyndetic adjuncts see XXXII.1 (in e.g. Petronius).

(22) 4.373 *eiectum litore, egentem | excepi*, '(him), cast on the shore, needy, I welcomed'.

This pair agrees with the unexpressed object of the verb, and precedes the verb. The terms (adjuncts) are of that commonplace asyndetic type in Virgil, expressing pathetic consequences of the action, and are alliterative and at the end of a line. One is a past participle. See above on 1 for *egens* in asyndeton, with cross references (see also XXXII.3.4). Cicero has *egens* in an asyndetic pair of which the second member is of extended length (Cicero 41 *egentem, probatum suis*). *Egens* conveys a concept (abandonment, poverty) that inspires asyndeton, probably because of the intonation with which it was pronounced. The terms with which it is juxtaposed are variable, and it is not a matter of a 'formulaic' use, but of a pattern of speech adopted in expressing pathos.

(23?) 6.113–14 *atque omnis pelagique minas caelique ferebat, | inualidus, uiris ultra sortemque senectae*, 'and he endured all the threats of sea and sky, weak, beyond the strength and lot of old age'.

Translators tend to put a comma after the rendering of *inualidus* (and after *inualidus* itself), but the prepositional phrase *uiris ultra* etc. may be a modifier of *inualidus* and not a free-standing element in asyndeton.

(24) 6.237–8 *spelunca alta fuit uastoque immanis hiatu, | scrupea, tuta lacu nigro nemorumque tenebris*, 'a cave there was, deep and huge with vast opening, rocky, sheltered by the black lake and darkness of the groves'.

Here there are four groups of epithets of the *spelunca*, the first pair (probably attributes) joined by *-que*, the second asyndetic. The asyndetic pair is an adjunct, and is placed at the start of a line, with the noun at the start of the previous line. See below, 6 on Pacuvius 2, *scrupea saxea Bacchi | templa*.

(25) 8.45 identical to 3.392 (21).

(26) 9.793–4 *at territus ille, | asper, acerba tuens retro redit*
With this compare the following:

(27) G. 3.149 *est . . . | plurimus . . . uolitans . . . | . . . . | asper, acerba sonans*
These are significant examples. The first, of a lion at bay, is taken directly from Lucretius (5.33, below, 7.2, 24), where it is applied to a snake. The second too alludes to Lucretius, with the participle changed but the syntax retained. In both places it would have been semantically meaningful for the two adjectives *asper* and *acerbus* to be used together in the same case, forming a pair of near-synonyms of equivalent status, but a deliberate syntactic inconcinnity has been introduced by giving the second term of the pair a different case and number (and putting it in a grecising construction, on which see Deufert 2018: 285). For *asper* and *acerbus* coordinated, see Wölfflin (1933: 254).

I take it that in the first passage (26) *territus* is not of the same status as the following pair, and does not form a tricolon with the two terms: 'but he, (though) terrified, comes back fierce, staring sharply'. *Territus* is a secondary predicate. The asyndetic pair (of predicates accompanying the verb *redit*) is at the start of a line. So in the second passage ('there is many a flying creature, fierce, sharply sounding') the asyndetic pair agrees with the subject of the verb, and is a (postponed) predicative adjunct at the start of a line.

For syntactic inconcinnity in an asyndetic pair see e.g. XXX.6.2b (end) on Tacitus: cf. e.g. Lucr. 1.163 (cited below, 7.1.2 on 6) *armenta atque aliae pecudes, genus omne ferarum*, where domesticated and wild beasts are in opposition but *armenta/pecudes* and *ferarum* are given different cases.

Here is a case of literary imitation as a determinant of asyndeta.

(28) *Aen.* 11.85 *ducitur infelix, aeuo confectus Acoetes*
This example resembles many of the single-word adjectival groups. The terms agree with the subject of the verb, are postponed behind the verb, and one is a privative adjective. For decrepitude expressed by asyndetic pairs see XXIII.8.8.

2 Virgil

(29) 11.483 *armipotens, praeses belli, Tritonia uirgo, | frange manu telum*, 'Tritonian virgin, powerful in arms, in charge of the war, break with your hand the weapon.'
The epithets agree with a vocative; strictly one is an adjective, the other a noun. Cf. Hom. *Il.* 1.122 Ἀτρεΐδη, κύδιστε, φιλοκτεανώτατε πάντων; also *Il.* 1.149, with the longer member first.

(30) 12.707–9 *stupet ipse Latinus | ingentis, genitos diuersis partibus orbis, | inter se coiisse uiros*
The adjectival groups are attributes (or adjuncts?) of the subject accusative *uiros*.

I treat all the above as asyndetic pairs for the purpose of the following statistics, though one or two were open to other interpretations.

In almost every instance the longer member is placed second (19, 20, 21, 23?, 24, 25, 26, 27, 28, 29, 30). An exception is 22.

Placement within the line is distinctive. Many of the examples are at the start of a line, usually postponed, in that the verb or noun in agreement is in the preceding line, and there is also a variant on this pattern, with the asyndeton occupying a whole line (21, 23? (whole line), 24 (whole line), 25, 26, 27, 30 (whole line)). Similarly in 19?, 20? and 29 the noun and asyndetic sequence together occupy the whole line. In one case the asyndeton is at the end of a line (22). The one pair that is within a line (28) is postpositive, in that the name and its asyndetic epithets follow the verb. Comparisons will be made below with Homer.

There are few privative adjectives in the above list (see 23?, 28, also 30 *ingentis*).

2.3 Conclusions

First, in Virgil adjectival asyndeton bimembre is the most prominent type. By contrast Timpanaro (1994: 4 with n. 7, 8–9) has suggested that in the early Latin he investigated (so-called archaic *carmina*, mainly prayers) paired adjectives are rare (cf. Deufert 2018: 36). *Carmina* are not typical of the early period. We found numerous (70) asyndetic adjectival pairs in Plautus (see XXIII, Appendix for a list), and the type is also well represented in Lucilius (XXV.1.1.4). See also Adams (2016: 79) for asyndetic adjectival pairs in Cato *De agricultura*.

Second, 'separation' of the two adjectival components of an asyndeton, supposedly an Ennian feature (and indeed an Ennian feature alleged to have been picked up by Virgil: see II.2.4, 2), is all but non-existent. We saw just one case where the two components were single words (4), and a couple in anaphoric prepositional expressions (2.1.5). The use of the word 'separation' is unsatisfactory, as there may be different types of separation. 4 shows an interlocking word order, a phenomenon commonplace in poetry. Are there any separations of that type in Ennius? Another possible type has the pattern adjective + noun + adjective, without interlocking: this is the discontinuous type (see XX). Does this second pattern turn up in Ennius?

Third, in both collections of adjectival asyndeta above postponement (in some sense) of the pairs was seen to be common, as indeed was placement at the start of a line.

The question must be asked whether there is any connection between Virgil's asyndeta and those of Homer.

3 Homer

In Homer postpositive asyndetic adjuncts of the type placed at the start of a line, following the line containing the relevant noun or verb, are not uncommon. In some cases these are pairs of privative adjectives. Note the following (text that of West, Teubner, translations sometimes by Murray, Loeb, but with modifications):

(1) *Il.* 1.98 πρίν γ' ἀπὸ πατρὶ φίλῳ δόμεναι ἑλικώπιδα κούρην, | ἀπριάτην ἀνάποινον, 'until we give back to her dear father the bright-eyed maiden, unbought, unransomed'.

The structure of this is similar to Virg. *Aen.* 8.621–2 *loricam ex aere rigentem,* | sanguineam ingentem (8), where there is likewise in one line a noun with (attributive) epithet, followed at the start of the next by an asyndetic predicative adjunct belonging with the same noun. In the Greek this adjunct consists of two negative adjectives.

(2) 2.42 μαλακὸν δ' ἔνδυνε χιτῶνα, | καλὸν νηγάτεον, 'he put on his soft tunic, fair, ... (?)'.

The same pattern again, though this example is problematic in that the meaning of νηγάτεος is uncertain. Does it outdo καλός semantically? The context is closer to the passage of Virgil just quoted than is the first passage of Homer above, as both here and in Virgil it is bodily equipment/attire that is described.

(3) 2.324–5 τόδ' ἔφηνε τέρας μέγα μητίετα Ζεύς, | ὄψιμον ὀψιτέλεστον, 'Zeus the counsellor showed this great sign, late in coming, late in fulfilment.'

3 Homer

This is a definite asyndeton, with much the same structure, including a separate epithet, μέγα, in the first line. The asyndetic terms have repeated fore-elements, though not alpha-privative this time. Adjuncts again.

(4) 2.403–4 ὃ βοῦν ἱέρευσεν ἄναξ ἀνδρῶν Ἀγαμέμνων | πίονα πενταέτηρον, 'Agamemnon lord of men slew a bull, fat, of five years.'

Once again the two epithets are at the start of a new line following their noun in the previous line, but here they would differ in rank if rendered into normal English ('fat bull of five years'). But should we treat them thus in Greek in this distinctive structure?

(5) 2.765 τὰς Εὔμηλος ἔλαυνε ποδώκεας ὄρνιθας ὥς | ὄτριχας οἰέτεας, 'These (mares) Eumelus drove, swift like birds, with like hair, of like age.'

A postpositive asyndeton (adjuncts), with similar fore-elements and a separate adjective in the first line.

(6) 2.839 ὃν Ἀρίσβηθεν φέρον ἵπποι | αἴθωνες μεγάλοι 'whom his horses, red-brown, large, had borne from Arisbe'.

These are postpositives that are strictly attributive, with the feature again that they are at the start of a new line. In English adjectives of these meanings would be layered (*big* [*red-brown horses*]), but again it is not certain that this structure is intended in the Greek. If translated with pauses and the order of the Greek, μεγάλοι becomes climactic, 'red-brown – big'.

(7) 3.125–6 ἣ δὲ μέγαν ἱστὸν ὕφαινεν | δίπλακα μαρμαρέην, 'she was weaving a great web, double, gleaming'.

Μέγαν is a straightforward attributive, but the other two are postpositive predicative adjuncts at the start of the next line. For μέγαν with this role cf. 3 above. It is a feature of these Homeric examples that an initial epithet close to the noun is often followed in the next line by a loosely attached pair of postpositives. Both the postpositives are descriptive, and do not obviously differ in rank.

(8) 5.193–4 ἕνδεκα δίφροι | καλοί, πρωτοπαγεῖς νεοτευχέες, 'eleven fair chariots, new-wrought, new-furnished'.

Here there are three adjectives, but the general term καλοί seems to belong in the initial phrase as an attribute (along with the numeral), and then come two postpostive asyndetic adjuncts which follow the first word in the line, a pattern seen above in Virgil (3, 5, 7, 12), and also found in Homer, 9 below. This is the interpretation of the (Loeb) translator above. Alternatively we might detach καλοί from ἕνδεκα δίφροι, thereby introducing a postpositive tricolon, 'fair, new-wrought, new-funished'. If so the last two adjectives would still seem to form a pair within a longer series, sharing a semantic unity. The striking feature of this pair is that both terms are compounds with fore-elements of about the same meaning, but these elements are not morphologically identical. For different prefixes with much the same function in juxtaposed words see below, 6.4 on Pacuvius 12; also VI.4.2 on Livy 33.

(9) 5.613 ὅς ῥ' ἐνὶ Παισῷ | ναῖε πολυκτήμων πολυλήϊος, 'who dwelt in Paesus, (a man) rich in substance, rich in corn-land'.

Here the postpositives agree with the subject of the verb. They definitely form an asyndeton (with the same fore-element). They are not right at the start of the new line but follow an initial word (see note on the last example).

(10) *Od.* 1.130–1 αὐτὴν δ' ἐς θρόνον εἷσεν ἄγων ... | καλὸν δαιδάλεον, 'her he led and seated in a chair ..., beautiful, curiously wrought'.

The second adjective is more specific than the first (see above, 2 for what looks like the same pattern). Cf. *Od.* 1.136–7 προχόῳ ... | καλῇ χρυσείῃ. In English there would be layering in this example, 'beautiful ewer of gold'. But with this placement is the conception different in Greek, 'in a pitcher, beautiful, golden'? For the combination 'beautiful' + 'golden' see below, 8 on a passage of Naevius.

In this selective material from Homer in four cases of ten the asyndetic pair consists of terms with the same (or virtually the same) prefix (1, 3, 5, 9), and in another case (8) the prefixes are semantically similar but different in form. In Virgil on the other hand not a single one of the adjectival pairs, whether consisting of two single words or single word + extended element, comprises terms with the same fore-element.

In Homer eight of the ten pairs are at the start of a line and are postpositive. The other two, 8 and 9, are preceded by a single word, and are again postpositive. In Virgil three of the fifteen single-word adjectival pairs are postpositive and at the start of a line (6, 8, 11), and in another four cases (3, 5, 7, 12) the (postpositive) asyndeton is preceded at the start of a line by a single word only. The placement of the pairs is therefore similar in the two writers.

Semantically there is no connection between the pairs in Virgil and those in Homer. In Virgil, it was noted above, pairs of adjectives have for the most part pathetic associations or are threatening in some way, for example by their reference to overbearing size. The Homeric pairs do not have negative implications. Three refer to the beauty of items of clothing or

3 Homer

furniture (2, 7, 10). Another describes the wealth of a man (9). Three are descriptive of fine animals, a bull, horses, mares (4, 5, 6). The remaining two (1, 3) are in no sense pejorative.

It was seen that several of the Homeric pairs are not unambiguously asyndeta, if translated into English in conventional English idiom. We might however generalise and say that postponement of adjectives without a coordinator, such that they were at the start of a line and in agreement with a word in the previous line, was a pattern favoured by Homer, whether or not the adjectives were 'asyndetic' in the strictest sense.

I have concentrated so far on examples where the postpositive adjectives begin (or almost begin) a new line, and have made a loose connection of Homer with Virgil. But asyndetic adjuncts (where both members consist of a single word) in Virgil are not all in that position, and similarly in Homer there are other asyndeta bimembria placed in such a way that they have the look of pairs in English with the pauses/intonation that we have referred to (see V). Here are a few examples.

(11) *Il.* 4.383 Ἀσωπὸν δ' ἵκοντο βαθύσχοινον λεχεποίην, '(when) they came to Asopus, with deep reeds, grassy'.

Two words of the same semantic field, postponed behind noun and verb, and at the end of the line.

(12) 5.9 ἦν δέ τις ἐν Τρώεσσι Δάρης, ἀφνειὸς ἀμύμων, 'there was among the Trojans one Dares, rich, blameless'.

The adjectives are alliterative, and adjuncts, postponed (end of line). There follows a phrase describing Dares as priest of Hephaestus, but that is an apposition and not part of a tricolon.

(13) 9.154 ἐν δ' ἄνδρες ναίουσι πολύρρηνες πολυβοῦται, 'in them dwell men rich in flocks, rich in cattle'.

This example is structurally (and semantically) similar to 9 above. The asyndetic pair is again at the end of the line.

(14) 9.466 εἰλίποδας ἕλικας βοῦς | ἔσφαζον, 'they slew the oxen, rolling, twisted/of shambling gait (?)'.

Are the adjectives synonymous? See LSJ s.v. ἕλιξ on the problematic meaning of the second adjective. These may be attributes.

(15) *Od.* 1.242 οἴχετ' ἄιστος ἄπυστος, 'he is gone out of sight, out of hearing'.

The verb is at the start of the line. Predicates. For a verb of motion accompanied by asyndetic adjectives cf. Virgil 26.

The group of five examples above has two pairs with repeated prefixes, one pair with semantically similar prefixes, and one pair (12) with an alliteration that resembles a repetition of alpha-privatives.

There are also in Homer as in Virgil adjectival asyndeta in which one member is longer than the other. Here are some examples.

(16) *Il.* 2.308–10 δράκων ἐπὶ νῶτα δαφοινός, | σμερδαλέος ... | ὄρουσεν 'a snake, blood-red on the back, terrible ... darted'.

The epithets are postpositive, and split between two lines. The portrayal of the threatening character of the referent in this way is more in keeping with some of Virgil's adjectival asyndeta, such as nos. 26 and 27. The passage of Lucretius (5.33, 24) on which these two Virgilian asyndeta are based also refers to a snake, but in Lucretius the epithets are not postponed as in Homer (*asper, acerba tuens ... serpens*). In this example the longer member is first.

(17) 2.667 ὅ γ᾽ ἐς Ῥόδον ἷξεν ἀλώμενος, ἄλγεα πάσχων, 'he came to Rhodes, wandering, suffering woes' (alliterative).

Both adjuncts here are participial, the second longer than the first, and postpositive. The translation of the Loeb ('he came to Rhodes in his wanderings, suffering woes') in effect eliminates the asyndeton, a possible interpretation (= 'he came wandering to Rhodes, suffering'). We saw a number of participles in asyndeta in Virgil (see on 21; note too the next two Homeric examples).

(18) 2.825 ἀφνειοί, πίνοντες ὕδωρ μέλαν Αἰσήποιο, '(those who dwelt in Zeleia beneath the nethermost foot of Ida), wealthy, drinking the dark water of Aesepus'.

Adjective + participle, the second member longer than the first, at the start of a new line. For adjectives followed by longer participial groups in Virgil, see nos. 21, 26, 27, 28, 30. In the Homeric example the adjuncts occupy a whole line (see further below, 20, 21). The same is true of the Virgilian examples 23?, 24, 30.

(19) 3.293–4 τοὺς μὲν κατέθηκεν ἐπὶ χθονὸς ἀσπαίροντας, | θυμοῦ δευομένους, 'he laid them down on the ground gasping, failing of spirit'.

(20) 3.330–1 κνημῖδας .... ἔθηκεν | καλάς, ἀργυρέοισιν ἐπισφυρίοις ἀραρυίας, 'the greaves ... he fitted, | beautiful, equipped with silver ankle-pieces'.

Again the adjuncts fill the whole line. Here is another place where Homer starts with the vague term καλός and then becomes more specific. καλάς could however be taken as the primary complement of the noun, with ἀργυρέοισιν ἐπισφυρίοις ἀραρυίας the only adjunct (see on 8 above).

(21) 4.281–2 δήϊον ἐς πόλεμον πυκιναὶ κίνυντο φάλαγγες, | κυάνεαι, σάκεσίν τε καὶ ἔγχεσι πεφρικυίαι, 'into furious war moved the thick battalions, dark, bristling with shields and spears'.

The adjuncts, of ascending length, fill the whole second line.

It is clear from this collection of examples that Homer made extensive use of adjectival asyndeta. As well as this general similarity between Homer and Virgil, there are also structural parallels between them, both in the single-word cases and in those with an extended member. There are also differences. Homer had a taste for pairs with the same fore-element, particularly but not exclusively alpha-privative (there are three pairs in the material above with the alpha prefix, and four pairs with one of three other prefixes), but Virgil did not; Virgil did however often use a single privative adjective in such asyndeta. Semantically too Homer and Virgil differ. The single-word pairs in Homer are mainly neutral or laudatory, whereas Virgil favoured the threatening, pathetic or awe-inspiring. Virgil seems to have taken over a pattern of sorts and put it to his own dramatic use. It looks significant that Virgil exploits adjectival asyndeton and not that with other parts of speech, and that in Homer too the adjectival type is a marked presence.

In the extended type there is more diversity in both Homer and Virgil. Homer has a few threatening or pathetic descriptions, whereas Virgil has some of more laudatory or neutral tone (19?, 20?, 21).

I append a few asyndeta of different types.

(22) *Il.* 3.298 Ζεῦ κύδιστε μέγιστε.

This is comparable to the Latin formula *Iuppiter optimus maximus*. Cf. 2.412 Ζεῦ κύδιστε μέγιστε (there then follow two further epithets of different types, κελαινεφές, αἰθέρι ναίων, 'lord of the dark clouds, dwelling in heaven'; the first two can be seen as a unitary pair with assonance embedded in a longer list). Also 3.276 Ζεῦ πάτερ, Ἴδηθεν μεδέων, κύδιστε μέγιστε. On the extended structures here see IV.4.

Here is another vocative type, with an extended member:

(23) 4.339 καὶ σύ, κακοῖσι δόλοισι κεκασμένε, κερδαλεόφρον, 'you that excel in evil wiles, you of crafty mind'.

Finally, for the prepositional type see:

(24) 2.362 κατὰ φῦλα, κατὰ φρήτρας.

4 Conclusions: Homer and Virgil

Of the 21 adjectival pairs cited from Homer, 7 have a repeated prefix. Of the 30 such pairs in Virgil, none has a repeated prefix. Virgil does however have six pairs that have one instance of the privative prefix *in-*, and another seven instances with *ingens*. Asyndetic pairs with repeated prefix are of course found in Latin elsewhere (see e.g. VI.8.2, XXIII.5.4), but this Homeric mannerism was not picked up by Virgil.

Semantically, we have stressed, there is little resemblance between the pairs in Virgil and those in Homer. Only the Homeric examples 16 and 21 have some similarity to the tone of Virgilian examples, but the connection is not close.

The fact that both Homer and Virgil quite frequently have adjectival pairs is definitely of interest, given the view that adjectival asyndeton was not common, at least in some works. We quoted above six instances from Homer of pairs of unequal length (16–21). In five cases the longer member is placed second. Of these, four pairs are at the end of a line, or fill the whole line. From Virgil we quoted thirteen cases in which the two members were of unequal length (19–30). Eleven of these have the longer member second (a fact that cannot necessarily be put down specifically to Virgilian imitation of Homer, given the general tendency in many languages for longer terms to come second: see XVI). Three occupy the whole line (23?, 24, 30), and another three do so in conjunction with the noun modified (19?, 20?, 29), two of these being at the end of a line. 22 is also at the end of a line. Otherwise, however, the Virgilian examples are not infrequently within the line or at the beginning or split between two lines (21, 25, 26, 27, 28, 29).

Another similarity is that Virgil quite often places a postponed pair consisting of two single words at the start of a new line (see the summary after 15), and that is the almost invariable position in the material above of single-word adjectival pairs in Homer.

Both Homer and Virgil, as has been stressed (see also the last paragraph), often have asyndetic adjectives (frequently adjuncts) postponed, whether behind subject or verb or both. This is not however a similarity that can without reservation be attributed to the influence of Homer on Virgil, as it is a common placement in Latin for asyndetic adjectives (see IV.4, and for examples from Plautus, XXIII Appendix), and was probably associated with a distinctive intonation.

The combining of adjectives with participles in asyndeta by both Virgil and Homer was commented on at 21 (Virgil) and 17 (Homer).

Virgil seems to have been influenced structurally by Homer in his use of asyndeton, but without resorting to direct imitation. The similarities between the two do however have to be put in context, by a comparison of Virgil's practice with that of earlier Latin poets, particularly Ennius, who is seen as his forerunner. If these earlier poets used adjectival pairs in much the same way as Virgil, it would not be convincing to associate Virgilian usage specifically with that of Homer. I move on to Ennius.

5 Asyndeton Bimembre in Ennius

In this section I discuss possible examples from the *Annals* and then the tragic fragments. These are set out according to their parts of speech. A question to be addressed is whether there is any connection between Ennius and Virgil. For the *Annals* the numbering is that of Skutsch (1985) (and Goldberg and Manuwald 2018, vol. I), and for the tragedies, of Jocelyn (1967).

I have included some examples which I am not convinced are genuine asyndeta. They are discussed mainly because they have usually been taken as such, and also because the fragmentary state of the text of Ennius causes uncertainties. It is made clear in problematic cases what view I am taking. In a second section I list a few further false examples.

5.1 The Annals

5.1.1 Adjectives

(1) 86 *et simul ex alto longe* <u>*pulcerrima praepes*</u> | *laeua uolauit auis*

In this same passage (72–91) there is another pairing of *pulcer* and *praeses*, just three lines later, with a coordinator: 89 *praepetibus sese pulcrisque locis dant* (on which see below, 2). This would suggest that *pulcerrima praepes* is also a coordination, asyndetic. Skutsch (1985: 233) takes it as such: '*pulcer praepes* is a term of augural language, preserving an archaic feature in the unconnected double attribute' (cf. Timpanaro 1994: 24, 39). He is more explicit on 457 (1985: 615), where the same combination occurs (see further below): 'as a sub-species of asyndeton bimembre the asyndetic use of two attributes with one noun is characteristic of ritual and augural language' (he refers to 192). This last assertion is dubious. The asyndetic use of two adjectives with one noun was not specifically connected with ritual or augural language in Virgil, or indeed Plautus, in whom we saw 70 asyndetic pairs of adjectives of diverse types. Underlying the statement is the usual assumption that asyndeton was sacral.

There is however an ambiguity to 86, caused by the superlative form *pulcerrima* and the preceding *longe*. This would seem to mean 'by far the finest favourable bird', with *longe* modifying the superlative. Warmington (1961: 30, lines 95–6) has: 'just when, winging to the left, there flew from the height a bird, the luckiest far of flying prophets'. If we take *longe* with *pulcerrima* an asyndeton is, if not entirely ruled out, far less likely. There could be layering, with *longe pulcerrima* modifying the whole phrase *praepes auis*, 'by far the finest [favourable bird]', presumably designating a particularly clear-cut favourable omen. Timpanaro (1994: 24) quotes the line without *longe*, an unacceptable omission.

Goldberg and Manuwald on the other hand take *longe* with *ex alto* ('and at once on high from far away a beautifully winged leftward flight advanced'). On this interpretation *pulcerrima praepes* may be an asyndeton, or perhaps even a quasi-compound, 'beautiful(ly)-favourable'. That is the view implied by this translation.

The problem of interpretation is made more difficult by the uncertain meaning of *praepes*. The *OLD* s.v. 1a gives the meaning as 'Flying straight ahead (as giving a good omen . . .)'. The *TLL* (X.2.763.50ff.) stresses the uncertainty of the meaning, but the conjecture is advanced (763.68ff.) that it might originally have meant '*praevolans, volando antecedens*'. Skutsch (1985: 233) writes: 'the precise semantic development of the word, certainly derived from *peto* in the old sense of "flying", is not entirely clear . . . In language connected with augury it applies to the bird of favourable flight.'

As Skutsch concedes, it is natural to take *longe* with the superlative (though he does say that it could mean 'far away'). Also possibly relevant to the interpretation of of *pulcerrima* is Naevius 25 Strzelecki (see below, 8) *immolabat auream uictimam pulcram*, 'and he busied himself in sacrificing a beautiful golden victim' (Warmington 1936: 49, line 4). In English we would take 'beautiful' here ('fine, special'?) as modifying the whole phrase.

5 Asyndeton Bimembre in Ennius

The word order in Naevius (which is different from that of the Homeric examples seen earlier containing καλός) is suggestive of such layering (see the examples cited at II.2.5).

Skutsch (above, first paragraph) finds the supposed asyndeton characteristic of augural language. I know of only two augural pairs with asyndeton, and these are not adjectives (see XXII.6.3). Contrast, from an augural context at Cic. *Leg.* 2.21, the coordinated pair *uineta uirgetaque*. Note too Ennius *Ann.* 71 *auspicio augurioque*, in an augural context.

(2) 457 *Brundisium* [*inquit*] *pulcro praecinctum praepete portu*

There is no context, but the adjectival combination seems to have been generalised out of the sphere of augury (so Warmington 1961: 203 n. *c*, and Skutsch 1985: 615: 'The meaning "auspicious, favourable" is clearly transferred from the birds and their flight to the place where they alight'; also Goldberg and Manuwald, 'Brundisium ... belted by a handsome, hospitable harbour'). But is the meaning 'beautiful, auspicious (?)[1] harbour' (asyndeton), 'beautifully-auspicious harbour', or 'beautiful [auspicious harbour]'? The last interpretation would definitely not show asyndeton.

If there is an asyndeton, the two asyndetic terms are separated, and such separations are supposedly a mark of Ennian asyndeta. One should not however talk of an interruption unless the pairing is definitely asyndetic. If the terms are asyndetic here, there would not simply be hyperbaton, but an interlaced word order (cf. above 2.1.1, Virgil 4): *Brundisium* would go with *praecinctum*, and *pulcro* with *praepete portu*.

There is one other instance of the pair in Ennius (mentioned above on 1) that may be relevant to the question whether they are asyndetic: 89 (of augural birds) *praepetibus sese pulcrisque locis dant* (apparently of the places of good omen where the birds alight). The two terms are linked by *-que*, which points to an asyndetic relationship in the other passages above. But note that here the order of the two words is reversed, and that may be significant (Goldberg and Manuwald however seem to have translated as if *pulcris* came first: 'settling themselves on fine and favourable seats'). Sometimes two adjectives differing in rank are linked with a coordinator (see II.2.4 on Lucilius 445). See Devine and Stephens (2006: 504), for example, on the behaviour of *multi*, which is often a modifier of a whole phrase (of the type 'many [brave men]'), but is sometimes linked with the other adjective, as at Cic. *Verr.* 5.119 *multi et graues dolores*, which we might render, giving special emphasis to the second adjective, 'many griefs, and those severe'. So perhaps in the augural passage above, 'they land in

[1] The meaning of *praepete* in this context is obscure. See Skutsch (1985: 615) for speculation.

favourable places, and those [favourable places] of the fine type'. The reversal of the order suits the interpretation of the phrase just given.

The interpretation of *pulcer* + *praepes* in Ennius, that is whether the pair is asyndetic or not, remains uncertain. Asyndetic coordination does not look right for 1, especially with *longe* immediately preceding the superlative, but the presence of a coordinator in the passage just cited could certainly be taken to support asyndetic coordination elsewhere. The problem is intensified by the obscure meaning of *praepes* (cf. Timpanaro 1994: 25). Skutsch's view (1985: 297) that '*pulcer praepes* is a fixed term of the augural language' is too strongly expressed, given the variability of the phrase and its order.

(3) 385–6 *o ciues, quae me fortuna fero sic | contudit indigno bello confecit acerbo*

See Skutsch (1985: 550): 'the combination of *fero* and *indigno* with *bello* may be tolerable, but the addition of a third adjective, *acerbo*, after a second verb, *confecit*, is difficult to take'. Warmington (1961: 141) 381–2 prints an emendation *indignum*, but he does put a comma after *bello*, a punctuation which may be right (i.e. with the form *indigno* retained). With a comma in that position there would be two clauses, with *acerbo* not part of a group of three adjectives: 'O my countrymen, what fortune has thus crushed me in a war fierce, undeserved, – has destroyed me in (one) that is bitter.' The privative *indigno* would be suited to the second place in an adjectival pair. Goldberg and Manuwald translate as if there were an adjectival tricolon: 'O Countrymen, what fortune has thus bruised me and destroyed me with undeserved, fierce, bitter war' (cf. Timpanaro 1994: 39, who has a long discussion of the passage). This rendering reverses the positions of *fero* and *indigno*, and produces a mixture of adjectival and verbal asyndeta with separations. Skutsch's failure to translate makes it difficult to know what he had in mind, and he has no note on the pair of verbs. Did he consider those to be asyndetic? Warmington's clause division is acceptable, and there could also be something relevant missing after *acerbo*.

There is little point in pronouncing on problems in a fragmentary text (and on possible asyndeta) unless one is prepared to translate the passage to make the interpretation explicit.

(4, 5, 6) 279–81
doctus, fidelis,
suauis homo, iucundus, suo contentus, beatus,
scitus, secunda loquens in tempore, commodus, uerbum
paucum . . .

5 Asyndeton Bimembre in Ennius 335

Here there is a long list of epithets (not quoted in its entirety here), and the question arises whether there are any pairs within the list. For unitary pairs embedded within long asyndetic sequences in (e.g.) Plautus see XXIII.7.3; see also XVIII.4, 6.

Iucundus is Skutsch's plausible emendation (1985: 459) for the transmitted *facundus*, a term which is out of keeping with *uerbum paucum* that follows. If the emendation is accepted we have a pair of near-synonyms, *suauis* and *iucundus*, grouped around *homo*. See XXIII.6 on Plaut. *Mo.* 105–6 for *homo* as the divider in a discontinuous structure; also XX.2 for *uir* so used. Discontinuous asyndeta do occur in long asyndetic sequences. Cf. Cic. *Orat.* 131 *sed est faciendum etiam ut irascatur iudex, mitigetur, inuideat faueat, contemnat admiretur, oderit diligat, cupiat fastidiat, speret metuat, laetetur doleat.* This sentence has a succession of pairs of verbs of opposite meaning, and the subject *iudex* is inserted within one pair.

Goldberg and Manuwald take *doctus, fidelis,* | *suauis* as a unit going with *homo* ('a learned, loyal, accommodating man'), but it is a contention of this book that long asyndetic sequences constantly have units (pairs) embedded within (which are often missed). *Suauis ... iucundus* looks like one (if the emendation is right), and *doctus fidelis* could be another. For learning (*doctus*) combined with a moral quality (*fidelis*), cf. e.g. Cic. *Att.* 10.17.1 *doctum et probum* (cf. *Fam.* 16.21.5), *Fin.* 1.13 *grauis et doctus.* We are about to see a further two unitary pairs in this sequence.

Another embedded pair above is *suo contentus, beatus* (with first member of extended length). Skutsch (1985: 459) states that *beatus* means virtually the same as *suo contentus*. Alternatively the comma could be removed and the two adjectives (in asyndeton) both taken with *suo* (see Timpanaro 1994: 25–6), an interpretation that does not seem convincing: *suo* is better suited to *contentus* alone, which is often complemented by an ablative (see *OLD* s.v. *contentus* b).

There is also *scitus, secunda loquens in tempore* (this time with extended second member). The second member means 'saying the right thing at the right time', and Skutsch remarks: 'The discernment enabling him to do so is described by *scitus*.' Thus the second element expresses a consequence of the first, a common unifying feature of two terms in asyndeton. See e.g. XXX.2.1, 4, with cross references to Sallust and Tacitus, and some of the examples from Virgil earlier in this chapter (9, 14).

(7) 141 *circum sos quae sunt magnae gentes opulentae*

This passage was discussed at XX.2. Layering is possible ([*magnae*] [*gentes opulentae*]), but reasons were advanced for taking the pair as a discontinuous asyndeton. There remains a doubt, not least because another adjective might have followed in the next line.

(8) 22 *quam Prisci, casci populi, tenuere Latini*
This is the text and punctuation of Skutsch. In his note (1985: 181) he states: '*Prisci* is to be taken with *Latini*, not as the first of two adjectives qualifying *populi*. Like later poets he does not combine two adjectives asyndetically, except in imitation of ritual language.' The allusion in the last clause is to *pulcer praeses*.

There are unsatisfactory features of the assertion quoted. First, the statement that later poets did not combine adjectives asyndetically is false. Virgil, as we have seen, has this form of asyndeton more than any other. In Horace's *Satires* asyndeton bimembre of adjectives is, with that of nouns, the most numerous type (see XXIX.2.1.5). Second, there is the usual idea about the special place of asyndeton in 'ritual language'. Third, the view that Ennius did not combine two adjectives asyndetically disregards the presence in the tragedies of an adjectival asyndeton (*purus putus*: see below, 9) that is structurally identical to *prisci casci* (if the latter is accepted at face value). In both cases there are two synonyms with forms of assonance, comprising first a commonplace term (*purus, prisci*), and second an archaic synonym or near-synonym (*putus, casci*: on this feature of *cascus* see Skutsch himself, 1985: 182). *Prisci* states the meaning in a transparent way, and then (probably after a pause) the more colourful term with ancient associations is added, further defining the antiquity of the referents. This would be a case of the second term outdoing the first. Nor does the word division of Skutsch's punctuation look convincing ('ancient, ancient peoples, ... *Latini*'). I believe that commas should be after *prisci* and *tenuere* but not *populi*. See also Timpanaro (1994: 20–3), defending the asyndeton at some length. Goldberg and Manuwald adopt the interpretation and punctuation of Skutsch.

5.1.2 Adjective + Adverb

(9?) 192 *ut pro populo Romano prognariter armis | certando prudens animam de corpore mitto*

This is translated by Warmington (1961: 74–5, lines 200–2) as: 'just as from my body I breathe my last for the Roman people's sake, with foreknowledge and awareness, in arms and battle'. Skutsch (1985: 355–6) argues that for metrical reasons Ennius has varied an old formula, *sciens prudens*, which, where it is attested in literary sources, always has a coordinator, except at Ter. *Eun.* 72 *prudens sciens | uiuos uidensque pereo* (where the order is varied from the expected *sciens prudens* because of the metre, according to Skutsch 1985: 356).[2] Goldberg and Manuwald translate: 'Just as I knowingly send the spirit from my body in contest of arms on behalf of the Roman people', and have the following note (2018: I.209): 'Ennius substitutes *prognariter* ... *prudens* for the metrically intractable *sciens prudens* in the formula for *devotio*.'

Prognariter and *prudens* may both refer to foreknowledge (see *TLL* X.2.1765.28f. for the former) and are near-synonyms, if allowance is made for the fact that one is an adverb and the other an adjective. They may form a sort of asyndeton, comprising different parts of speech. It is not unusual for an adverb to be coordinated with an adjective, asyndetically or syndetically (see above, I.1 on *ui pugnando* and various other pairs, with Kroll 1929 on Catull. 31.4, Brix and Niemeyer 1907 on Plaut. *Trin.* 268, Skutsch 1985: 355–6), and *sciens* and *prudens* are types of adjectives that are often quasi-adverbial. The two members of the asyndeton would be separated.

If there is asyndetic coordination, a coordinator has to be missing. Its expected place would be before *prudens*. If it is understood to be there, the natural meaning of the clause as it is constructed would be, not that stated by Warmington or that by Goldberg and Manuwald, but rather 'just as from my body I breathe my last, by fighting under arms on behalf of the Roman people with foreknowledge and awareness' (of what might happen). In a discontinuous asyndeton the separated terms usually belong closely with the dividing element (but see XXV.1.1.2), i.e. here *armis certando*. The two (Loeb) translations above however take *prognariter* ... *prudens* as modifiers of *animam* ... *mitto*, thereby assuming a radical dislocation of word order. Skutsch does not translate, but he does argue (1985: 356) that 'in republican times the phrase [*sciens prudens*, with or without a coordinator] is applied exclusively to men meeting their end voluntarily and knowingly'. Thus he too takes *prognariter* ... *prudens* with the main verb phrase *animam* ... *mitto*.

5.1.3 Nouns

(10) 591 *diuomque hominumque pater rex*

On this passage see XVII.1. *Pater* and *rex* are in asyndeton, but is there correlative distribution, with *pater* looking back to *diuom* and *rex* to *hominum* (cf. 203 *diuom pater atque hominum rex*)? It is simpler to take both genitives as dependent on both nominatives together. *Diuomque*

---

[2] As for the abnormal asyndeton, that would be justified by the constant structure, asyndetic pair followed by syndetic pair.

hominumque with polysyndeton is a unit: cf. *Ann.* 284 *leges diuomque hominumque*, 592 *patrem diuomque hominumque*, Virg. *Aen.* 1.229 *res hominumque deumque*. See also Skutsch (1985: 730).

(11?) 165 *nauos repertus homo, Graio patre, <u>Graius homo, rex</u>*
Graius homo, rex look asyndetic, as part of a longer asyndetic sequence.

5.1.4 Verbs

(12) 294–6 *tonsamque tenentes | <u>parerent obseruarent</u> portisculus signum | quom dare coepisset*

On the pair see XVI.1. This looks like an asyndeton comprising two juxtaposed verbs. There also seems to be a hysteron proteron, in that the watching presumably precedes the obeying. If so, this feature is obscured in the rendering of Goldberg and Manuwald ('and holding tight the oar they attended, they watched as the timekeeper began to give the signal'). Or is it possible that the obeying and watching for the signal are simultaneous, such that the second verb could be paraphrased with a present participle, *parerent obseruantes . . . signum*, 'they obeyed (by) watching for'? In Sallust this sort of paraphrase is sometimes possible (see Sallust 64, 77, 82). If *obseruarent* were taken along these lines it could also be explanatory (= 'they obeyed, watched for the signal').

When two verbs in asyndeton express sequential acts, that designating the first act usually precedes, but there are occasional reversals (see XVI.1). For reversal of the expected order of imperatives, see X.1.3.

5.1.5 Some False or Dubious Examples

35 *talia tum memorat lacrimans, exterrita somno*

The phraseology might lead one to think that there is asyndeton, given Virg. *Aen.* 9.424 *tum uero <u>exterritus amens</u> | conclamat Nisus*, where the same past participle does occur in a possible asyndeton (see above, 2.1.1, 9). But there is not an obvious coordination here. A possible translation is: 'she then spoke thus in tears, having been terrified out of sleep' (rather than, with coordination, 'then she spoke thus in tears and terrified out of sleep'). Warmington's translation (1961: 15, line 33) captures the meaning: 'then the maid, frightened out of sleep, spoke thus in tears'. Warmington changes the order in translation to make explicit the order of events. Goldberg and Manuwald translate: 'Then, in tears, frightened out of sleep, she recounts these things.' This rendering is acceptable, but non-committal about whether there is asyndetic coordination.

367–8 *uino curatos somnus repente | iam campo passim mollissimus perculit acris*

See Skutsch (1965: 534), taking *acris* to be an accusative plural (so Goldberg and Manuwald 2018: 2.295 n. 1; contrast the long discussion of Timpanaro 1994: 45–8). *Acris* may well however be a nominative singular, as it is taken by Priscian (see Skutsch loc. cit.), but in that case there would not be an asyndeton with separation (*mollissimus ... acris*), but *mollissimus* would be attributive and *acris* predicative with *perculit* ('the softest sleep suddenly struck them sharply'). The word order favours this interpretation.

446–7 *Iuppiter hic risit tempestatesque serenae | riserunt omnes*
Omnes regularly modifies adjective–noun phrases. Here the sense could perhaps be 'all clear weathers', with *serenae* attributive. Goldberg and Manuwald translate as 'Jupiter here laughed and all the weathers at ease laughed', taking *serenae* as a predicative adjunct. Or could it be predicate, with *riserunt*, i.e. as equivalent to an adverb? Skutsch too (1985: 604) takes this adjective to be predicative. See also 'Smiled clear and calm all weathers' (Warmington 1961: 169, lines 450–1).

620 *machina multa minax minitatur maxima muris*
There are uncertainties about this line (see Skutsch 1985: 747, and XXVII.1.2 on a similar passage of Catullus). *Maxima* may be part of an object that is completed in the next line, or *machina* may have three adjectives, one of them separated. The latter seems acceptable to Skutsch (1985: 747). If *multa* and *minax* are simply a pair, they differ in rank, 'many [a threatening machine]'. But cf. Timpanaro (1994: 48–9).

5.2   Tragedies

5.2.1   Adjectives

(13) 65 *purus put<us>*
There is hardly any context here, and one cannot tell what the role, attributive or predicative, of these adjectives is. According to Alfenus ap. Gell. 7.5.1 *putus* means *ualde purus*: do we have an intensification in the second term? Goldberg and Manuwald (2018: II, *trag.* 17) translate, without committing themselves on this point, as 'clean and pure'. So Varro *Ling.* 6.63 says that the ancients used *putus* to mean *purus* (expressing himself in such a way as to allude to the asyndetic pair: *ideo antiqui purum putum appellarunt*). The two words are etymologically connected, though the first has a long vowel and the second a short (see de Melo 2019: 1.865).

The pair occurs twice in comedy, both times as a predicate with the verb 'to be' (Plaut. *Ps.* 989 *Polymachaeroplagides | purus putus est ipsus*, 1200 *purus putus hic sucophantast*). For further details see Preuss (1881: 112–13). At *TLL* X.2.2780.58f. it is noted that 'vox prisca extra asyndeton bimembre *purus - us* ... servata non est', apart from one instance at Varro *Men.* 98 with *ac* between the terms (an example which shows the constant tendency even for fossilised asyndetic pairs to acquire a coordinator from time to time). Elsewhere, at *Men.* 245 (predicates with the verb 'to be' understood) and 432 (where the two terms are part of an asyndetic sequence with six members), Varro has the asyndeton.

Alfenus is unlikely to be authoritative, as the word is obscure, and was hardly in use by the classical period, but his idea about the semantic relation between the parts is at least of interest (see in general XV), though he was perhaps expressing the general doctrine that the stronger term should be placed second (for which see Quint. 9.4.23 and XV).

(14) 89–90 *uidi ego te adstante ope barbarica, | tectis caelatis laqueatis, | auro ebore instructam regifice*

There are two juxtaposed asyndeta bimembria here, a rare accumulation in the fragments of Ennius, the first adjectival/participial, the second nominal (see further below, next example). The description, of a building, is one of luxurious fittings, and references to luxury attract asyndeta in Plautus too (see XXIII.8.1, 8.2. 8.5, 8.6). Goldberg and Manuwald (*trag.* 12–14) translate: 'I saw you [the building], while barbarian might still stood, with carved and fretted ceilings, furnished with gold and ivory in kingly fashion.' Here for once is a juxtaposed pair of (participial) adjectives, postponed, a pattern favoured by Virgil (see above, 2.1.1, 2.2) and Plautus (see XXIII Appendix, *Adjectives*, where many of the pairs listed are postpositive). For an asyndetic pair in Plautus with the same suffix and again applied to luxury, see Plaut. *St.* 377 (XXIII.8.6) *lectos eburatos auratos.* :: *accubabo regie* (note *regie* here and *regifice* in the passage of Ennius, and also that the adjectival pair *eburatos auratos* corresponds exactly to the asyndetic nominal pair in Ennius). For a similar coordinated pair to those asyndetic pairs here see Lucr. 2.28 *laqueata aurataque templa.*

5.2.2 *Nouns*

(15) 91 *auro ebore*

See above on 14, and also XXIII.8.6 for asyndetic listing of precious metals and the like. For *aurum* in asyndetron bimembre see Cicero 21, 119.

5 Asyndeton Bimembre in Ennius

(16) 166 *saeuiter fortuna ferro cernunt de uictoria*
Jocelyn (1967: 301; cf. 175) takes *fortuna* and *ferro* as forming an asyndeton bimembre (*forte fortuna* is offered as a parallel), but he gives no translation. Warmington (1961: 287, line 193) prints *saeuiter fortunam ferro cernunt de uictoria*, 'Right savagely they settle with the sword | Their chance of victory.' *Fortunam* is an emendation by Ribbeck. Vahlen (1903) has the same text as Jocelyn, as do Goldberg and Manuwald (*trag.* 70) (translating, 'ferociously, with luck and steel, do they decide victory by fighting'). Jocelyn does not comment on what would be an absolute use of *cerno*, but cf. Enn. *Ann.* 132 *adnuit sese mecum decernere ferro*, with Skutsch (1985: 288), stating that the '[a]bsolute use of *decerno*, especially with *ferro, armis* etc., is common'. *Fortuna ferro*, comprising an abstract + concrete noun, may be described as an asyndetic hendiadys ('with the luck of the steel', 'chancing the sword'), for which category see II.3.2.3.2–3. Cf. the similar pair at e.g. Cic. *Phil.* 1.26 (18) *denuntio uim arma*, 'I warn of armed violence/force of arms' (where again the abstract precedes, with the following concrete term specifying its sphere).

5.2.3 Adverbs

(17) 116 *rursus prorsus reciprocat fluctus*
An adverbial pair of opposites ('backwards and forwards'). This and other such pairs are dealt with at XIII.5.4; see also XXIII Appendix, *Adverbs* on Plaut. *Am.* 1112.

5.2.4 Verbs

(18) 117 *alia fluctus differt dissupat | uisceratim membra*, 'the waves disperse and scatter other limbs piecemeal' (Goldberg and Manuwald *trag.* 40).
Jocelyn (1967: 266) lists many examples of *dis-* compounds coordinated, but none in asyndeton. For asyndetic pairs with repeated prefix in Plautus, see XXIII.5.4, and particularly *Cist.* 208 *feror differor, distrahor diripior, Epid.* 118 *differor difflagitor*. Both verbs loosely mean 'scatter', but the second is more vigorous: *differo* means 'carry apart', whereas *dissupo* seems to have an idea of throwing apart (see *OLD* s.v. *supo* and the passages cited there; also De Vaan 2008: 601). A similar pair with the same repeated prefix is cited below, 8, from a comic fragment of Naevius.

(19) 9 *mortales inter sese pugnant proeliant*
Jocelyn (1967: 175) cites comparable examples but not necessarily with asyndeton. Note however below, 7.1.2, Lucretius 7 (*proelia pugnas | edere*

(also 8): see Munro 1886: 2.126), where the nouns are used with a support verb and the combinations are equivalent to the verbs above. *Proelium*, of an armed battle, was potentially a stronger word than *pugna*, which need only refer to a fight between individuals, such as boxers, though there was a blurring of the distinction. Goldberg and Manuwald's translation (*trag.* 7) captures the force of the pair, with the second capping the first: 'thus mortals fight among themselves, they engage in battle'. In his note Jocelyn (175) twice refers to the 'official language' as a linguistic influence here, but near-synonymous verbs in asyndeton are widespread, and one should not randomly invoke officialese as the determinant (see XXXII.1). Such pairings are a form of rhetorical emphasis, with strengthening of the first by the second, and they turn up in contexts that cannot be related to official language, as in 18 above. Here are some near-synonyms from Plautus (see XXIII.5.5): *Merc.* 50 *abnuere negitare*, *Merc.* 55 *trahere exhaurire*, *Trin.* 285 *turbant miscent*, *Trin.* 1005 *mutum est, tacet*; cf. Lucil. 882–3 *subblanditur palpatur*. This group suggests that such pairings could be fairly mundane in the early Republic. We saw that pairs of verbs occur asyndetically 200+ times in Plautus (see XXIII.1 and the whole of 5), and there are run-of-the-mill types such as imperatives.

(20) 303 *set me Apollo ipse delectat ductat Delphicus*

Jocelyn (1967: 425) notes that normally the shorter word precedes the longer in asyndeta (with reference to Lindholm 1931: 80–7). But these are not genuine synonyms because the ensnaring precedes the leading on: semantics determines the order. See on this issue XVI, and XVI.1 on this example. Cf. Warmington (1961: 351 on 353), 'and Apollo himself of Delphi charms and draws me on'. The semantic relationship is much the same as that (e.g.) between the pair often found together, *alit auget* (see below, 6.3 on Pacuvius 6–8, 7.1.3 on Lucretius 12, 13). As for increasing length, Jocelyn himself lists numerous exceptions to this tendency; see further XVI and e.g. Cicero 59, and also below, 6.3 on Pacuvius 11. A feature of the present terms is that they are alliterative (cf. 18, 19 above) and have the same ending (*-ctat*).

5.2.5 Some False or Dubious Examples

Various adjectival pairs, some of which came up in II, seem to have layering rather than asyndeton.

For example, on 3–4 (*per ego deum sublimas subices | umidas unde oritur imber sonitu saeuo et spiritu*) see above, II.2.4., 1.

296 (*summis saxis fixus asperis*) is discussed above, II.4, 1.

5 *Asyndeton Bimembre in Ennius* 343

At 237 (*antiqua erilis fida custos corporis*) *antiqua* and *fida* both go with *custos* while *erilis* goes with *corporis*. It may look as if *antiqua* and *fida* form an asyndeton with the parts separated, but the primary complement of *custos* is *fida*, and the phrase is modified by *antiqua*: the woman is a 'faithful guardian', who is old. See Goldberg and Manuwald, *trag.* 96, 'ancient loyal guardian'.

Similarly at 239 (*Athenas anticum opulentum oppidum | contempla*) *opulentum oppidum* is a possible unit with an etymological play (Jocelyn 1967: 379 ad loc.), and *anticum* a modifier of the phrase, but the analysis of the group is difficult (cf. in the *Annals*, 7 above with cross reference, *magnae gentes opulentae*, which is also not straightforward). Goldberg and Manuwald, *trag.* 94 take *anticum opulentum* as a coordination ('look at Athens, an ancient and wealthy city'). Another such problematic phrase, if it is allowed to Ennius, is *matronae opulentae optumates* (at Cic. *Fam.* 7.6.1, 90 in Goldberg and Manuwald; see the discussion of Shackleton Bailey 1977: II.332). There may be layering ('rich matrons of the nobility'), but both Shackleton Bailey (Loeb) and Goldberg and Manuwald translate as if the terms are asyndetically coordinated ('rich and noble dames', 'rich and noble ladies').

On a false interpretation of 36 *me . . . dementem inuitam ciet* see II.2.1.

The line containing *uestitus . . . saeptus* (281) is corrupt (so Jocelyn, Goldberg and Manuwald 2018: 131 n. 1, their line 126; contrast Timpanaro 1994: 50–1).

5.2.6 Aspects of Coordination and Longer Asyndeta in Ennius
There are four asyndetic pairs of nouns in the *Annals* and tragedies, one of them doubtful (11). One is of religious type (10), and another is an artificial asyndetic hendiadys (16). It is asyndeta rather than coordinations that tend to attract comment, but coordinations with *-que* or *-que . . . -que* (polysyndeton) are at least as likely to be interesting in some way, with e.g. assonance or special semantic relationships between the components, and that is so in Ennius. Here are some examples of coordinated nouns in the *Annals*:

73 *auspicio augurioque*
91 *scamna solumque*
203 *diuom pater atque hominum rex*
226 *postes portasque*
314 *dictum factumque*
493 *uos uostraque uolta*

Most of these are alliterative, one is a religious phrase, another is augural and and a third is a formula with complementary terms (*dictum factumque*). In the tragedies 287 *di deaeque* is an alliterative merism of religious type, and 137 *urbem atque agros* a pair of opposites of the 'town–country' type (see XIII.5.1).

The above examples are only a selection of stylised coordinations of nouns, and they outnumber the asyndetic pairs that were collected. To these can be added similar instances of polysyndeton (cited earlier in a different connection), from the *Annals*:

284 *leges diuomque hominumque*
592 *patrem diuomque hominumque.*

Nor are coordinated pairings of such types confined to nouns. Here are some pairs of verbs (from the *Annals*):

253 *rem repetunt regnumque petunt* (a coordinated clausal pair, with compound + simplex and extended alliteration).
334 *uoce sua nictit ululatque* (an onomatopoeic pair, of a dog: it whimpers and whines).
387 *occisi occensique* (with repeated prefix and same ending).

In the tragedies, 246 *sospitent superstitentque* comprises alliterative synonyms with the same disyllabic ending. 270 *dixi et dicam* has the same verb in different tenses (cf. IX). And at *Ann.* 285 (*loquiue tacereue posset*) the two verbs with polysyndeton are opposites (antonyms). Another pair of coordinated opposites (antonyms, this time adjectives) is at *Ann.* 283 *mores ueteresque nouosque* (antonyms).

Ennius has some longer asyndeta too, some of them of interest. Here are examples, first from the *Annals*:

229 *Marsa manus, Paeligna cohors, Vestina uirum uis* (tricolon, whole line).
360–1 *omnes mortales uictores, cordibus uiuis | laetantes, uino curatos* (phrasal).
556 *terra mare caelum* (for a comprehensive treatment of this type of phrase see Schmidt 1975; also Taylor, forthcoming, sect. 5, and below, 7.1.2 on Lucretius 10).
498 *flentes plorantes lacrumantes obtestantes* (whole line, verbs with assonance: see below, 6.4, commentary on Pacuvius 12; also Enn. *trag.* 308 *cogitat parat putat* for assonance).

The following are two asyndetic 'name-lines' (for name-lines, see on Horace, XXIX.4.5):

240–1 *Iuno Vesta Minerua Ceres Diana, Venus Mars | Mercurius Iouis Neptunus Volcanus Apollo* (on the contrived arrangement here see IV.2).

This example has anaphora too:

108 *o pater, o genitor, o sanguen dis oriundum*

Asyndeton bimembre is less prominent in Ennius than it is in Plautus.

5.3 Conclusions: a Comparison of Ennius and Virgil (and Plautus)

In Virgil we saw fifteen instances of single-word adjectival asyndeta bimembria, and another thirteen adjectival cases where one of the terms was of extended length. Many of these in both categories are postpositive, not infrequently coming at the start of a new line following the line with the noun, verb or both. Of the single-word type a significant number have the prefix *in-*.

In Ennius on the other hand doubts were raised about almost every possible adjectival asyndeton bimembre. *Suauis homo, iucundus* (4) would be a case, but *iucundus* is an emendation. In the same passage there are two adjectival asyndeta in which one member is of extended length (5, 6). We accepted *prisci casci* (8) as an asyndeton, but it was not accepted as such by Skutsch. In the tragic fragments there are two definite adjectival cases (13 *purus putus*, 14 *caelatis laqueatis*). The latter is a rare instance in Ennius of a postpositive pair, and the context (a description of luxury) is a typical one in Latin for asyndeta, not least in Plautus, who has a pair with the same repeated suffix in a similar description.

Two negative features stand out of these adjectival pairings in Ennius (whether they are accepted here as genuine asyndeta or not).

First, there is an almost complete absence of privative adjectives in *in-* (in the *Annals* see just the possible instance with *indigno* at 3). Most adjectival pairs in Virgil contain a privative, and Homer uses privative adjectives in pairs, as well as repeating other prefixes in adjectival pairs.

Second, also all but missing (but see the second paragraph above, on 14) is the typical Virgilian and Homeric type that we have called asyndetic predicative adjuncts, which are often postpositive and come at the start of a new line, and tend to express (in Virgil) pathetic circumstances endured by persons that arise from the narrative, or threatening aspects of inanimate objects. Of the two certain cases in Ennius of adjectival asyndeton, both in the tragedies (13, 14), one is in an old formula attested elsewhere in early Latin (*purus putus*), and the other is participial, in an architectural description.

One aspect of Ennius' adjectival asyndeta (or possible asyndeta) is that they tend to have problematic structures and are difficult to analyse,

346   XXIV Virgil and Early High-Style Poetry

though that is sometimes due to the inadequate survival of the text. Possible pairs sometimes have separation of the members (2, 3, 4, 7), and we have had to raise the question several times whether there might be layering, not least in the sections on false or dubious examples.

There is another striking difference between Ennius and Virgil. Ennius admits the type whereby two finite verbs were juxtaposed. This type is not found in Virgil, if the special case *age* (et sim.) is disregarded. Ennius has four instances in his not very extensive fragments, one of them in the *Annals* (12) and the others in the tragedies (18, 19, 20). These various examples have a few recurrent characteristics. The three in the tragedies are alliterative, and two of these (19, 20) have the same endings as well. That at 18 has not merely alliteration but the repetition of a prefix (*dis-*). Two instances in the tragedies are pairs of near-synonyms that are hard to differentiate (18, 19). All of these features (including the repetition of *dis-*) are to be found among the numerous pairs of juxtaposed verbs in Plautus (see XXIII.5.4; see also above on 19 for near-synonyms paired in Plautus). It seems likely that ordinary (rhetorical) language was the inspiration of Ennius, as distinct from 'ritual' or 'official' language or the like.

Also virtually absent from Virgil are unaccompanied nouns in asyndetic pairs. There are four such pairs in Ennius, one a religious phrase (10) juxtaposed with a coordinated pair, which is one of the most common forms of coordinated accumulation, another (15 *auro ebore*) that has an exact semantic parallel in Plautus, and is also juxtaposed with another asyndetic pair, again a commonplace accumulation (see 14), and a third that we have called an alliterative asyndetic hendiadys (16).

Parallelism with Plautus has been raised above several times, and it must be stressed that, though there are some oddities in Ennius and differences from Virgil, there are also some traditional features and features that were commonplace. *Purus putus* must have been an ancient formula (and it is found in Plautus), and *pulcer praepes* probably derived from augury, though it is not certain that it was an asyndeton. The adverbial opposites *rursus prorsus* belong to a category found in Virgil as well as many other genres. *Prognariter . . . prudens* was possibly a variation on an old formula. Accumulations of coordinations, asyndetic and/or syndetic, were old and very persistent, and we referred to two of these in Ennius in the last paragraph, and another was seen at 4, 5, 6. This last consists of a long asyndetic list with three possible embedded unitary pairs; for such embedding in e.g. Plautus, see XXIII.7.4.

It is clear from this summary and the material assembled earlier that there is not a close similarity between Ennius and Virgil in the use of

6 *Pacuvius, Tragedies* 347

asyndeton, and that in some respects Ennian usage resembles that of Plautus. Such similarities must be put down to general features of the language at the time.

It was pointed out above (5.2.6) on Ennius that coordinations are more common than asyndeta and may be just as contrived. I will return to pairs coordinated by -*que* in Lucretius and Virgil below in an appendix.

I conclude that the evidence from Ennius' fragments makes the similarities between Virgil and Homer look very significant.

6 Pacuvius, *Tragedies*

I use here the text and fragment numbers of Schierl (2006).

6.1 Adjectives

(1) 171 *angues ingentes alites, iuncti iugo*

This (here with my punctuation) is translated by Warmington (1936: 255, line 242) as 'Huge winged snakes yoked to a chariot's yoke'. The implication of such a rendering is right. There is an asyndeton bimembre describing inherent features (attributes) of the snakes ('huge, winged'). Then follows an incidental characteristic (a predicative adjunct: the huge winged snakes are joined to a chariot's yoke): *iuncti iugo* is on this interpretation not part of an asyndeton with three members. Schierl (2006: 367) sees here an asyndetic tricolon. In this chapter two asyndeta bimembria applied to snakes turn up, one in Homer (16), the other at Lucr. 5.33 (24; see also on Virgil 26–7).

(2) 221 *scrupea saxea* Bacchi | *templa prope aggreditur*

Warmington (1936: 279, lines 310–11) translates: 'approaches near the rugged rocky precincts of Bacchus'. *Scrupus* means 'A sharp stone or rock' (*OLD* s.v.), and *scrupeus* 'Composed of sharp rocks or projections of rock' (*OLD* s.v.). *Saxeus* is of the same semantic field but less specific, 'made of stones or rock'. It would not be plausible to find layering of the two adjectives here. In this case the first seems to specify the second, and the pair resembles a compound, 'sharp-rocky precincts of Bacchus', which is the implication of Warmington's translation. Schierl (2006: 456) refers to an 'asyndetische Synonymenpaar', and draws attention to the alliteration and the repeated ending. *Scrupeus* appears as the first member of an asyndeton bimembre at Virgil 24.

(3) 238 *Nerei repandirostrum incuruiceruicum pecus*

Translated by Warmington (1936: 293, line 352) as 'The upturnsnouted and roundcrooknecked herd of Nereus'. There is not enough context to determine how these adjectives are used (presumably of dolphins), but it is obvious that the phrase with its invented compounds ('harsh', *dure*, according to Quintilian 1.5.67) is highly artificial. I have commented earlier (XXIII.4) on such asyndetic compound coinages as part of the tragicomic style of Plautus, and they must have had some sort of vogue in early literary circles. See the note of Schierl (2006: 493) on a possible Greek parallel of the first term (see Quint. 1.5.70 for κυρταύχην, an emendation that would be equivalent to *incuruiceruicus*: see Russell, Loeb, ad loc. n. 91), and on Lucilius' parody of the line (212). For a similarly grandiose asyndetic pairing, in Lucilius (540 *calliplocamon callisphyron*) see XXV.1.1.1, 1.

6.2 Nouns

There are only two nominal examples in the fragments.

(4) 76 *postquam prodigium horriferum portentum pauos*
Prodigium horriferum portentum are all genitive plurals dependent on *pauos*. Both Schierl (2006: 228) and Warmington (1936: 201, line 103) take *horriferum* with *prodigium*, in which case a comma should have been placed after the adjective. Schierl (2006: 228) takes the nouns as synonymous and as forming an asyndeton bimembre. The two nouns can certainly be synonyms (see e.g. the *OLD* s.vv.). If they are taken as such here there would be a pause or broken intonation in an English rendering, and that is another reason for punctuating with a comma in the Latin. It is however just possible that a semantic distinction was intended, with *prodigium* referring to certain unnatural events (see *OLD* s.v. 1, 2a), and *portentum* meaning 'portents', i.e. events portending something. The sense would be 'horrific unnatural events: portents', and *portentum* would be a specifying apposition. There would not on this interpretation be an asyndeton.

Schierl (228) sees the asyndetic pair dependent on an abstract as characteristic of sacral language. I have not noticed such a phenomenon in prayers or religious phrases. Here are some genitive asyndetic pairs in prose authors dependent on abstract nouns:

Cic. *Att.* 4.2.6 *uotiuam legationem sumpsissem prope omnium fanorum lucorum*
Att. 5.13.1 *de concursu legationum priuatorum*
Fam. 3.12.1 *plura uirtutis industriae ornamenta*

6 Pacuvius, Tragedies 349

Fam. 5.8.5 (SB 25) *in omnibus publicis priuatis, forensibus domesticis,* tuis amicorum, hospitum clientium *negotiis*
Sall. *Cat.* 13.3 *lubido* stupri ganeae
Cat. 54.5 *studium* modestiae decoris
Tac. *Hist.* 2.91.1 *pari* libertorum amicorum *socordia*
Ann. 4.43.3 uatum annalium *ad testimonia.*

(5) 263 strepitus fremitus, *clamor tonitruum et rudentum sibilus*
The old type of accumulation in which an asyndetic pair is followed by a coordinated pair. The pair is marked by assonance, and may be compared with one of the replies of the *haruspices* quoted by Cic. *Har.* 20: *quod in agro Latiniensi auditus est* strepitus cum fremitu. See also XXIII.7.1 on Plaut. *Am.* 1062 *strepitus crepitus, sonitus tonitrus.*

6.3 Verbs

(6–8) 80.1–2 *quidquid est hoc, omnia* animat format, alit auget, creat | sepelit
I have added the commas from *format* onwards. There are here three independent pairs of asyndeta bimembria, of two different types. The clue to the interpretation lies in the pairing *alit auget*, which occurs in Lucretius as an asyndetic pair (below, 7.1.3, 12, 13), and is quite widespread elsewhere, including in prose, with coordinators or in longer asyndetic sequences. The usual relationship between these two verbs is sequential, with the increasing following the earlier nurture. There is also a chronological relationship between *animat* and *format*, with an initial giving of life followed by forming, shaping. The third pair summarises the entire process, with 'creation' referring to the very beginning and 'burying' to the end of the process. The third pairing comprises opposites (see XIII.4.3). Pease (1968: 638) compares the passage of Pacuvius with Cic. *Nat.* 2.41: *omnia conseruat, alit auget, sustinet sensuque adficit.* There is a structural overlap, but not an exact parallelism. As the passage is translated by Rackham (Loeb), *omnia conseruat* is a generalisation anticipating what follows, rather than a summary at the end: '(the fire of the body) is the universal preservative, giving nourishment, fostering growth, sustaining, bestowing sensation'. Nor is the chronological progression as clear-cut in this passage as it is in the first two pairs in Pacuvius. For a more precise succession of events expressed asyndetically see Velleius 1.7.4 (drawn to my attention by Stephen Oakley) *uix crediderim tam mature tantam urbem creuisse floruisse concidisse resurrexisse.* A comma could be placed after *floruisse*, because the final two verbs

are opposites and go together, and the first two verbs are a unit of sorts too, with the flourishing a state that follows the growth. For a similar sequence cf. Cic. *Nat.* 1.35 *quae causas gignendi augendi minuendi habeat*. On contrived patterns in long asyndetic sequences see IV.2.

(9) 199.8 <u>retinete! tenete!</u> *opprimit ulcus*

The pair compound + simplex of the same root is not a case of the Indo-European iteration of compound by simplex, a pattern in which the prefix of the first verb also acts on another verb following (for which see Watkins 1967). Here is a form of intensification, with the simplex underlining the compound that precedes. Normally in such intensifications the compound comes second (not least in curse tablets, but elsewhere as well), but in both Greek and Latin (including curse tablets again) the order is sometimes reversed. Examples and bibliography may be found in VII.

The fragment continues (10–11) with an asyndetic tricolon of imperatives, of ascending length: *operite! abscedite! iam iam <me> | mittite!* For this type of assonance see below on 12.

(10) 240.2 *undaeque e gremiis* <u>subiectare adfligere</u>

Warmington (1936: 295, line 362) has: 'Billows dashed down the ship and then upcast it [o]ut of their bosoms' (*adfligere* is a conjecture for *adfigere*: see Schierl's apparatus, 2006: 497). *Subiecto* means 'throw up from below' (*OLD* s.v. 1), *adfligo* 'cast down', or 'wreck, of a ship' (see *OLD* s.v. 2, 3b). If *adfligo* is accepted the verbs are reversive opposites (for which type see XIII.2, and particularly XIII.5.5, on near-opposites that are not quite explicitly so; also below, 7.1.3 on Lucretius 15). *Adfigere* does not look right even as an inexplicit reversive, and it would not suit the implication that there was a constant repetition of the tossing up and down. Translate: 'and the waves threw it up from their depths and cast it down'.

(11) 255.1 *ubi poetae pro sua parte falsa* <u>conficta<nt> canunt</u>

Of devising falsehoods, and singing them (if the emendations of *conficta* and *canant* are accepted). Schierl (2006: 514) sees in the emended text a feature of tragic style, namely two asyndetic verbs with the longer preceding, as in Ennius' *delectat ductat* (20). The determinant of the order of verbs is not the length of the words but the order of the events, and in many asyndetic pairs across all genres the longer element sometimes comes first (see XVI). There is not 'tragic' style in this respect in the line of Pacuvius. At the end of XVI.2 figures are given for the frequency of pairs of verbs with the orders shorter-longer versus longer-shorter in numerous prose texts, and the second pattern is almost as common as the first.

6 *Pacuvius, Tragedies* 351

6.4 *Pairs with One Member of Extended Length*

(12?) 3.3 <u>euiscerata inanima</u> *cum animali sono*
This line (about a *testudo*) is preceded by two consisting first of a sequence of four adjectives in asyndeton (*quadrupes tardigrada agrestis humilis aspera*) and second of three asyndetic phrases (*breui capite, ceruice anguina, aspectu truci*). *Euisceratus* means 'deprived of bowels, eviscerated', here presumably 'seemingly gutted', *inanimus* 'deprived of breath, breathless (seemingly)' (on the phrase see Schierl 2006: 109). Both terms are privative, but with different prefixes. On this phenomenon, i.e. the juxtaposition of different types of negatives: see VI.4.2, VI.7, XXIII.6 on Plaut. *Trin.* 826, *Mil.* 544, XXIX.2.1.1, and below, 7.1.2, 6 on Lucr. 1.774 *exanimo*. *Animali* forms a pun with *inanima*, and for that reason the *cum*-expression might just be taken as part of a second member of extended length, but on the other hand it is possible to see here a tricolon, with the third member (*cum animali sono*) adversative.
The extended asyndeton in the first line (*quadrupes tardigrada agrestis humilis aspera*) is worthy of comment (cf. XXIII.4 on Plautus). The asyndeton fills almost the whole line. Similarly in the next line the three phrasal asyndeta occupy the line. Such lines (with varying patterns, sometimes with forms of assonance, and with the accumulation not in every case occupying the complete line) seem to have been a feature of Pacuvius (though not of him alone: for the pattern in Virgil see above, the summary following 30; also Enn. *Ann.* 498 at 5.2.6, and XXIII.4 n. 2, 5.4, 9). Cf. e.g. 17 *agite icite uoluite rapite coma* | *tractate*, 32 *feroci ingenio, toruus, praegrandi gradu*, 55 *quas famulitas uis egestas fama formido pudor*, 59 *hic sollicita, studio obstupida, suspenso animo ciuitas*, 63 *fluctu flaccescunt, silescunt uenti, mollitur mare*, 147.1 *age adsta mane audi*, 196 *aetate integra,* | *feroci ingenio, facie procera uirum*, 203 *metus egestas maeror, senium exiliumque et senectus*, 206 *maerore errore macore senet*, 263 *strepitus fremitus, clamor tonitruum et rudentum sibilus*, 290 *uoce suppressa, minato fronte, uultu turbido*. For a tricolon occupying half a line see 243.3 *lacerasti orbasti extinxti*.

(13) 101 *amplus, rubicundo colore et spectu proteruo ferox*

(14) 262.4 *quia atrox incerta instabilisque sit*
Incerta instabilisque looks like a unit with two privatives differing semantically from *atrox*, in which case there would be an asyndeton bimembre, [*atrox*] [*incerta instabilisque*] and not end-of-list coordination. For *incertus* in such pairs see Cicero 54, Sallust 59.

6.5 Conclusions

Pacuvius, like Ennius, admitted pairs of verbs in asyndeton, and although the examples are not numerous because of the limited fragments, the types are familiar. There is a classic intensifying compound-simplex pair (9) of a sort also found in the early period in Plautus (*Merc.* 681), a pair of opposites of the reversive type (9), also Plautine (*Mil.* 864, *Trin.* 1108), and an alliterative pair (11). 6–8 has a series of pairs almost a line long, and it was noted that such sequences, though not of exactly the same semantic structure, were to become quite common. On 12 there is a note on asyndetic sequences of about a line long, which are also in Plautus and continue in poetry. One of these consists of verb forms with assonance, for which type in Plautus see XXIII.5.4, and cf. Ennius *Ann.* 498 *flentes plorantes lacrumantes obtestantes* (above, 5.2.6). The final pair in 6–8 (*creat sepelit*) also consists of reversives. The three pairs of asyndetic verbs discussed from Ennius' tragedies (18–20) are all alliterative, and one has a repeated prefix.

Pacuvius' adjectival pairs also have some features typical of the period or the genre. *Ingentes* (1) is characteristic of Virgil, and *scrupeus* (2) is also in an asyndeton in Virgil. The Pacuvian instance comes close to a quasi-compound with *saxeus* following. 3, with two compound coinages of considerable length, is suggestive of Plautus. There was a literary taste for such coinages in the early period (cf. Enn. *Ann.* 198 *bellipotentes sunt magis quam sapientipotentes*, though not with asyndeton in this case). 12, whether it is a tricolon or dicolon, has two privative adjectives, one of the usual type in *in-* and the other with a different prefix, a phenomenon that occurs from time to time.

7 Asyndeton Bimembre in Lucretius

Various passages of Lucretius were discussed in II that have pairs of adjectives resembling asyndeta but are not in my view genuine asyndetic coordinations, usually because there is layering of the adjectives (see II.2.3, 2.4, and especially 2.4, 4). I do not include these examples here. Deufert's note (2018: 36–7) listing (asyndetic?) pairs comprising participles + adjectives or adjectives + adjectives contains many of these examples (1.258, 1.945–6, 2.505–6, 4.315, 5.13, 6.387–8), and most of the additional examples have layering too. I use here for the most part Deufert's text (2019), but sometimes with my own punctuation.

7 Asyndeton Bimembre in Lucretius

7.1 Pairs with Single-Word Members

I first list what look like genuine asyndeta with two single-word members, classified according to the part of speech. A few problematic cases are included and discussed as such.

7.1.1 Adjectives

(1) 1.523 *omne quod est, spatium uacuum constaret, inane*, 'then the existing universe would be vacant and empty space'.

This is the translation of Smith (Loeb, 1992, who for the most part is quoted in translations below), but a more literal translation would be 'the existing universe would be vacant space, empty'. This translation is not meant to imply layering, such that *spatium uacuum* were modified by *inane* ([*spatium uacuum*] *inane*). Rather, *inane* is an afterthought, in a discontinuous structure, with the addition of the synonym hammering home the emptiness, 'would be a space vacant – empty' (for discontinuous asyndeton see XX.2, and also e.g. above on Ennius 4). I would punctuate with a comma as above to mark a pause. Bailey (1947: 2.687) ad loc. refers to an asyndeton, but his translation ('the whole universe would be but empty void space') does not capture the force of the Latin word order.

The adjectives here are predicative.

(2) 1.557–8 *longa diei | infinita aetas*

This was commented on by Timpanaro (1978: 172) as an asyndeton 'accrescitivo'. Bailey (1947) translates 'the long limitless age of days'. The two adjectives are of the same semantic field but not synonyms, as the second caps the first. It might even be a correction, 'the long, nay infinite ...' (see Adams 2016: 232 on such corrections). The adjectives are attributive not predicative.

The separation here is of a different type from that above in 1, producing a poetic interlocking word order (for which pattern see above, Virgil 4, Ennius 2).

(3?) 4.623–4 *suauiter omnia tractant | umida linguai circum sudantia templa*, 'sweetly (they) stroke all the wet trickling regions around the tongue'.

Omnia as translated modifies a whole phrase, consisting of a noun and two attributive adjectives (one strictly a present participle), *umida ... sudantia*. However, *umida* may be predicative with *sudantia*, having adverbial force, 'sweating moist(ly)': i.e. is it another near-compound, 'moist-sweating'? For structures of this type (comprising adjective + participle) see II.3.2.2.

(4) 5.1302 *inde boues lucas turrito corpore, taetros | anguimanus*, 'the Lucanian oxen with turreted backs, hideous, snake-handed' (Smith, slightly modified).

This example could be a tricolon. On the other hand there may be first a factual ablative expression describing the elephants, followed by an asyndetic predicative adjunct (of Homeric and Virgilian type: see Virgil 8, 27, Homer 1–3, 8) expressing terrifying characteristics, with the bizarre feature placed at the start of the new line. Deufert (2019) prints *taetros* (see also the app. crit. on 5.1339, with bibliography, and particularly Deufert 2018: 356–8). Other editors print *taetras*: see also de Melo (2019: 2.947).

(5) 6.1188 *tenuia sputa, minuta*, 'fine thin spittle'.

The adjectives are attributive and of similar meaning. Again there is an afterthought in a discontinuous structure, 'fine spittle, thin'.

7.1.2 Nouns

(6) 1.15 *inde ferae, pecudes persultant pabula laeta*

I take this to be an asyndeton embracing wild and domestic animals, that is opposites either of the category 'antonyms' or of 'complementarities' (see XIII.2 on the question of definition in this case). The comma is essential because *ferae* could be an adjective. For *pecus, pecudes* opposed in various ways to *ferae* see now *TLL* X.1.956.49ff. (e.g. Cic. *Tim.* 45 *pecudum et ferarum*, Livy 3.47.7 *pecudum ferarumque*). For the same opposition, phrasal and asyndetic, see Lucr. 1.163 *armenta atque aliae pecudes, genus omne ferarum*: the first phrase embraces domestic animals, the second wild animals. See too, with different terminology, Cicero 150, 154.

Ferae, pecudes above has not always been taken or considered convincing as an asyndeton (see *TLL* X.1.956.50f., Deufert 2018: 2–3). Deufert (3) contemplates the emendation *ferae pecudesque insultant*, having noted that 'polar' asyndeta are scarcely found in Lucretius (the term 'polar', as has been remarked elsewhere, tends to be used in classical scholarship without definition), and that nominal asyndeton is hardly attested in the work ('Sein einziges zweigliedriges Nominalasyndeton begegnet als Versschluss *proelia pugnas*': but see below, 9, 10 for further examples). Asyndeta bimembria are comparatively rare in most writers in relation to coordinations, and are limited in number in Lucretius too, and those examples admitted are bound to contain the odd type that the writer nowhere else has.

Lucretius does too have other pairs of asyndetic opposites. Some of these will be seen below, of the structures comprising either two single words or

7 Asyndeton Bimembre in Lucretius

a single word plus extended member (see **15, 16**?, **17, 23**). Note too the asyndetic phrasal pair at 1.454: <u>tactus</u> corporibus cunctis, <u>intactus</u> inani, '(as is) touch to all bodies, intangibility to the void'. *Intactus*, like *tactus*, is here a noun (see *OLD* s.v. *intactus*²; see also Deufert 2018: 32), and the terms are opposites (complementarities). Another pair of complementarities, this one asyndetic, with anaphora and with second member phrasal, is at 1.774: non <u>animans</u>, non <u>exanimo</u> cum corpore, 'no living entity, no entity with lifeless body'. Here the privative has the prefix *ex-* rather than *in-* (see XXIII.6 on Plaut. *Curc.* 550). At 2.77 there is a clausal asyndeton bimembre, with the two verbs opposites of the reversive kind: <u>augescunt</u> aliae gentes, aliae <u>minuuntur</u>. 2.921 (*homines armenta feraeque*) might possibly be analysed as an asyndeton bimembre expressing the totality of life, humans on the one hand, and domestic and wild animals on the other ([*homines*] + [*armenta feraeque*]: see XVIII.4) (as distinct from having end-of-list coordination). A comma would be needed after *homines*. *Ferae, pecudes* also expresses a totality, of a more restricted type, that is non-human animals, domestic and wild. Of particular interest is the asyndetic clausal pair at 3.753 containing two pairs of opposites, wisdom and lack of wisdom on the one hand (expressed by verbs, one with a privative prefix), and humans and wild animals on the other: *desiperent homines, saperent fera saecla ferarum*, 'humans would lack wisdom, wise would be the fierce tribes of wild beasts'. But the closest asyndetic parallel to **6** above is the pair already quoted in the first paraagraph (1.163), which has exactly the same opposition in phrasal form. For oppositions embedded in clauses or phrases, as in the above examples, see on Lucilius 1058 at XXV.2.

It is a contention of this book that it is not convincing to note that an asyndetic pairing is nowhere else attested and to emend away the odd example (Deufert at the end of his note eventually declines to emend), because any coordinated pairing may occasionally turn up in asyndeton, and if so the asyndeton should not be removed without special reasons. Numerous asyndeta are discussed in the book that are isolated variations on much better coordinated instances. *Ferae, pecudes* is a straightforward asyndetic pair, and the emendation tentatively suggested by Deufert would remove a threefold alliteration of *p*.

(7–8) 2.118 *et uelut aeterno certamine <u>proelia pugnas</u> | edere*, 'as though in some everlasting strife (they) wage war and battle' (Bailey 1947).

The same pair of near-synonyms occurs at 4.1009 **(8)** *proelia pugnas | edere*. The comparable pair of verbs at Enn. *trag.* 9, *mortales inter se pugnant proeliant* (Ennius **19**) has already been seen. See Jocelyn (1967: 175), citing

Plaut. *Cur.* 179 *sibi honores, sibi uirtutes, sibi pugnas, sibi proelia*, where the association of the two terms is obvious in a longer sequence with anaphora as well. Jocelyn also quotes several other examples of the pairing 'fight'/ 'battle', usually with coordination, as at Lucr. 4.967 *pugnare ac proelia obire*. In most of these the 'battle'-term follows the 'fight'- (but not in the present passage), with *proelium/proeliare* stronger than the other pair (see on Ennius 19). See also Munro (1886: 2.126) on our passage.

(9) 4.1129 *et bene parta patrum fiunt <u>anademata mitrae</u>*, the 'well-won wealth of fathers becomes coronets, head-scarves'.

Cf. Paul. *Dig.* 34.2.26 *mitrae et anademata*. This is a classic asyndeton, listing items of female luxury (see XXIII.8.1, XXV.3 on Lucil. 71), and with the lack of coordination probably implying that the list could be extended (see IV.3). Deufert (2019) prints the pair with a comma between, correctly in my opinion in an open-ended list.

(10) 5.418 *fundarit terram et caelum pontique profunda,* | <u>*solis lunai*</u> *cursus*

The passage begins with a multiple coordination listing the features of the world, which might have been asyndetic (see 1.820 *eadem caelum mare terras flumina solem* | *constituunt, eadem fruges arbusta animantis*, Plaut. *Trin.* 1070 *mare terra caelum*, Cic. *Fin.* 5.9, describing the asyndetic triplet as a poeticism; also above, 5.2.6 on Enn. *Ann.* 556, and *OLD* s.v. *mare* 3), and then lists asyndetically the two main components of the sky, which might have been coordinated (see 471 *solis lunaeque*). For the mixed coordination in another list of components of the universe see 2.1083–4 *caelum* ... | *terramque et solem lunam mare, cetera quae sunt*.

7.1.3 Verbs

(11) 1.680 *nil referret enim quaedam <u>discedere abire</u>,* | *atque alia adtribui*, 'for it will be of no use that some should separate and depart, and others be added'.

Both verbs mean 'depart'. Those departing are contrasted with those added, as expressed by a single verb. Both Bailey and Smith translate 'separate and depart', which implies that there is a temporal sequence expressed by the order of the verbs. Bailey (1947: 2.720) refers to 'two stages, the separation of the particle from the main body and its departure from it' (cf. Deufert 2018: 46–7). There is nothing unusual about two verbs, asyndetic or coordinated, expressing a temporal sequence. Munro (1886: 2.86) notes however that *discedere abire* corresponds to the single noun *abitu* at 677, and *adtribui* to *aditu* (*abitu aut aditu*). There may be a subtle

7 Asyndeton Bimembre in Lucretius 357

distinction between the verbs, but it is not clear-cut, since the basic meaning of *discedo* is 'go off in different directions'. For near-synonyms in asyndeton expressing departure (and also arrival) see the commentary at XXX.2,1, 5.

Here again the longer term comes first. It was noted above (2.1.4) that Virgil does not pair synonymous (or near-synonymous) verbs but that others do (see e.g. XXIII.5.5; also on Ennius 19 above).

(12) 1.873 *praeterea tellus quae corpora cumque alit auget*, 'besides, whatever bodies the earth nourishes and increases'.

This line was deleted by Lambinus (see Deufert 2017: 169). I leave aside the textual issues and simply comment on the phrase.

These are verbs of similar meaning (and alliterative), but the second expresses growth consequent upon nurture. If they are reversed there may be a hysteron proteron of sorts (for this phenomenon see on Ennius 12 above), or the two actions may be seen as simultaneous rather than occurring in sequence.

The combining of *alit* and *auget* (in that order; contrast however Cic. *Fin.* 5.39, with reversal, and see the examples from Lucretius cited on 13 below) is commonplace, but in prose the two do not normally occur in asyndeton bimembre. Pease (1958: 623) (cf. Wölfflin 1933: 253) on Cic. *Nat.* 2.33 (*alendo atque augendo*) cites five examples of the combination in Cicero (and also *Nat.* 2.50 *alantur augescantque*), and in every case there is either a coordinator (*Nat.* 2.81 *ali augerique*, 2.83 *alat et augeat*), or else the asyndeton has more members than two (e.g. *Nat.* 2.41 *conseruat alit auget sustinet*, *Fin.* 5.26 *natura alit auget tuetur*). Add too *Att.* 8.3.3 *istum in rem publicam ille aluit auxit armauit*.

An interesting asyndetic example of the pair in verse was seen above in Pacuvius 6. Note Bailey (1947: 3.1369) on Lucr. 5.322: 'It is from Pacuvius that Lucr. gets this frequently repeated combination.'

(13) 5.257 *quodcumque alit auget*

12 and 13 should be compared with 1.56 *auctet alatque*, 1.229 *alit atque auget*, 1.859 *auget corpus alitque*, 1.873 *cumque alit auget*, 5.322, 6.946 *auget alitque*; note too the variant at 2.546, *procrescere alique*. *Augere alere* is not registered by Preuss (1881). On the text and interpretation at 13 see Deufert (2018: 292)

(14) 4.1199 *si non ipsa quod illorum subat ardet abundans | natura*, 'were it not that their own nature, overflowing, is on heat and burning'.

The two verbs are near-synonyms. The first is a technical term for a female animal on heat. The second may be stronger (see *OLD* s.v. 5, of persons, 'To be violently excited or passionate'). On *illorum* (neuter in reference to females) see Deufert (2018: 279). For a semantically similar pair of verbs in asyndeton see Cicero 72.

(15) 5.322–3 *nam quodcumque alias ex se res auget alitque,* | *deminui debet, recreari, cum recipit res,* 'for whatever increases and nourishes other things from itself must be diminished, and remade when it receives things back'.

A discontinuous asyndeton. The verbs are opposites, of the reversive type. Cf., of pulling down and building up, Cic. *Dom.* 137 *dirueris aedificaris* (**69**); also Hor. *Ep.* 1.1.100 *diruit aedificat, mutat quadrata rotundis* (see XXIX.2.2; XIII.2).

(16?) 6.48 *uentorum existant placentur . . . omnia rursum*

There is a serious crux here, with a line missing before *uentorum* and something missing after *placentur* (see Bailey 1947: 3.1561–2, Deufert 2018: 374–7). Bailey prints <*ut*> after *placentur*, whereas Deufert (376–7) makes a case for *placenturque* (K. Müller). The verbs, of rising up and being calmed, are possibly inexplicit opposites, but are probably coordinated.

I refrain from treating as verbal asyndeta examples of the following type: 2.730–1 *nunc age . . .* | *percipe. Age*, as we have seen (X.2), is often followed by another imperative without coordination, but is not truly in asyndeton.

7.1.4 Prepositional Type

Per medium per non medium at 1.1075 (**17**) came up earlier (VI.7). It is a special type parallel to positive–negative pairs such as *dignus indignus*, in which the negative has the prefix *in-*. The two terms are complementarities. Other Lucretian prepositional examples have pairs of synonyms or complementary pairs: e.g. 2.282 (**18**) *cogitur interdum flecti per membra per artus*, 2.964 (**19**) *per uiscera uiua, per artus,* (**20**) 6.229 *transit per saxa per aera,* (**21**) 6.945 *per omnia membra, per artus.*

7.1.5 Adverbs

Lucretius has a few cases of adverbial opposites, accompanied by anaphora:

2.131 *nunc huc nunc illuc*
2.214 *nunc hinc nunc illinc*
2.575 *nunc hic nunc illic.*

7.2 Type with One Member of Extended Length

I have not made a systematic collection of such examples in Lucretius, but here are some.

7 Asyndeton Bimembre in Lucretius 359

(22) 3.13 *aurea dicta,* | *aurea, perpetua semper dignissima uita.*
The postponed asyndetic adjunct, occupying a whole line, repeats a preceding word and expands on it. Cf. Virgil *Aen.* 12.897 (12) *saxum circumspicit ingens,* | *saxum antiquum ingens,* where *antiquum* is added to the repeated phrase.

(23) 4.570 *pars, solidis adlisa locis, reiecta sonorem* | *reddit,* 'some, dashed upon solid places and thrown back, give back a sound'.
Adlisa and *reiecta* are in asyndeton, with the first having a complement. They express sequential actions (dashed onto something, then thrown back), and are opposites of the reversive type. Similar is Pacuvius 10.

(24) 5.33 *asper, acerba tuens ... serpens*
On this pair see above on Virgil 26–7. The words quoted are preceded and followed by participial constructions applied to the snake.

(25) 5.223 *tum porro puer ...* | *... nudus humi iacet, infans, indigus omni* | *uitali auxilio,* 'Then further the child ... lies naked upon the ground, speechless, in need of every kind of vital support.'
Three adjectives/adjectival phrases are in agreement with *puer,* but the last two differ in function from *nudus. Nudus* goes closely with *iacet* and is a predicate, and *infans, indigus omni uitali auxilio* are postponed adjuncts or secondary predicates (for this sort of structural feature in Lucretius, and also in Virgil and Homer, see above on 4; for the verb *iaceo* used thus with a predicate and secondary predicate see XXXII.1; also VI.2.1 for the Greek equivalent). For the ablative with *indigus* see Deufert (2018: 291). This pair is one of those that resemble a pair of privatives in *in-,* but *indigus* is not a privative. For a similar (phrasal) asyndetic juxtaposition cf. Tac. *Hist.* 3.22.1 *indigus rectoris, inops consilii*; cf. also above on Virgil 3 for *ingens* associated in asyndeton with genuine privatives in *in-;* also VI.3 for such mixed pairs. *Indigus* is of the same root and meaning as *egens,* which, as we have seen, is common in asyndeta (see above on Virgil 1).
This is one of the few postponed asyndetic adjectival adjuncts in Lucretius (cf. 4).

7.3 Examples that Are Difficult to Classify

There are also a few examples that are difficult to classify.

Note (26) 1.491 *dissiliuntque fero feruenti saxa uapore,* 'stones split with fierce fervent heat'. *Feruens* can be a technical term of an extreme form of heat. See Pelagonius 168 *in calidam feruentissimam mittes*, Apicius 1.12.2 *in calidam feruentem merge*, where *calida* is a generic term for hot water, and *feruens* the specifying term applied to hot water of the category boiling, extremely hot (in implied contrast with *tepidus*, which is also attested as a modifier of *calida* (*aqua*); see Adams 1995b: 617–18). *Vapor* here means 'heat' (see *OLD* s.v.2). But did Lucretius really intend *feruenti* to have a technical sense and to form a unit with *uapore* (i.e. *fero* [*feruenti uapore*])? It is simpler to take this is an alliterative asyndeton of two adjectives with similar implication, of the type that might be punctuated in English with a comma, 'fierce, fervent heat'. See also Deufert (2018: 36–7).

A second problematic example (27) is at 2.7–8: *nihil dulcius est bene quam munita tenere | edita doctrina sapientum templa serena*. Here the final phrase *templa serena* has in agreement *bene munita* and *edita*. *Editus* 'lofty' is used only absolutely (see Bailey ad loc.), which means that the ablative expression *doctrina sapientum* must complement *bene munita*. Smith (1992) translates as 'nothing is more delightful than to possess lofty sanctuaries serene, well fortified by the teachings of the wise'. *Templa serena* may be the primary unit, with *serena* attributive. The pair would be modified by *edita*, with *munita* (*doctrina sapientum*) a predicative adjunct. Alternatively, could *bene munita* (*doctrina sapientum*) and *edita* be asyndetic modifiers of *templa serena*, with a disrupted word order? On the other hand Bailey (1947: 2.798) says that 'Giussani may be right in taking *munita* and *edita* together, "built up on high"'. On this view *edita* becomes predicative with *munita*, 'well built up aloft by the teachings of the wise', and the asyndeton disappears. Cf. Timpanaro (1994: 65–6).

What is the structure of 3.395 (28): *concursare coire et dissultare uicissim*? Is this a genuine end-of-list coordination, or is there just a coming together, expressed by two asyndetic near-synonyms, and a jumping apart? There is probably enough of a distinction between the first two verbs to support end-of-list coordination. See XVIII.4.

4.1165 (29) is in a passage listing flattering endearments addressed to women who in reality fall far short of the epithets. A *flagrans odiosa loquacula* is called a *lampadium*. This example is also hard to judge. Is *odiosa loquacula* a unit, 'hateful chatterbox', in this case one that is fiery (layering)? Or do we have an attributive adjectival asyndeton?

5.972–3 (30) *nec plangore diem magno solemque per agros | quaerebant pauidi palantes noctis in umbris* is translated thus by Smith: 'Nor did they go seeking the day and the sun with great outcry over the countryside, wandering panic-stricken in the shadows of the night.' In this rendering *pauidi* is given an adverbial/predicative role in juxtaposition with the participle. Bailey's translation is along the same lines. It would not be justifiable to treat the pair as an asyndetic coordination. Cf. Sall. *Jug.* 66.3 *milites palantes inermos* ('wandering unarmed') (see on Sallust 55).

7.4 Some Long Asyndeta

Lucretius has some long asyndeta, usually nouns, and sometimes filling a line. Many of them denote components of the earth or universe or categories of living creatures and body parts. Some lists embrace the behaviour of atoms or other entities. Here are some examples. The list is tolerably complete for the first two books (see also Deufert 2018: 194–5):

1.455–6 *seruitium contra paupertas diuitiaeque,* | *libertas bellum concordia, cetera quorum* (in the first line there is perhaps end-of-list coordination, followed by an asyndetic tricolon and then a symmarising clause; on the other hand there may be instead an asyndetic pairing at the start comprising a single word and then in asyndeton with it a coordinated pair of antonyms, 'poverty and riches': on this opposition see on Tacitus 113).
1.567 *aer aqua terra uapores*
1.685 *concursus motus ordo positura figurae* | *efficiunt ignis,* '(certain bodies, whose) meetings, movements, order, position and shapes make fires' (here however the first two words, of motion, may be a unit, followed by three static terms to do with placement and shape). The same sequence is at 2.1021.
1.744 *aera solem imbrem terras animalia fruges* (whole line).
1.808 *fruges arbusta animantes* (also 1.821, 2.1016).
1.820 *namque eadem caelum mare terras flumina solem* (so 2.1015).
2.669 *ossa cruor uenae calor umor uiscera nerui* (whole line, possibly with two embedded pairs, *cruor uenae* and *calor umor*).
2.726–7 *interualla uias conexus pondera plagas* | *concursus motus* (the last pair looks to be an embedded unit at the start of a line; cf. 1.685 above).
2.896 *motibus ordinibus posituris*
2.905 *uisceribus neruis uenis*
3.217 *per uenas uiscera neruos* (also 3.691).
3.480 *clamor singultus iurgia*
3.1017 *uerbera carnifices robur pix lamina taedae* (whole line; see Deufert 2018: 194–5).
4.458 *caelum mare flumina montis*
4.517 *praua cubantia prona supina atque absona tecta* (adjectives for once, of a house, with end-of-list coordination; there is definitely here an embedded pair of opposites, reversives, 'leaning forward, leaning back').

An unusual arrangement is at 2.1063 *terrai maris et caeli generisque animantium*. This has an uncoordinated pair, followed by a coordinator and then a pair with coordination. This could be an accumulation consisting of an asyndeton bimembre and then a coordinated pair, with the second pair linked to the first by *et* (for this structure in the historians, see on Tacitus 75). Given however that the first three words belong closely together, perhaps their structure is that of end-of-list coordination, with the end of the list consisting of a different element attached by *-que*. Mixed coordination is at 4.124–5: *panaces absinthia taetra | habrotonique graues et tristia centaurea* ('panacea, sickly wormwood, and strongly smelling habrotonum, and bitter centaury'). Another complicated arrangement is at 2.1084–5: *caelum . . . | terramque et solem lunam mare*. This has first a coordinated pair, and then a switch into an asyndetic tricolon.

7.5 End-of-list Coordinations in Lucretius

This form of coordination is quite common in Lucretius. Here are examples that I have noted in books 1–2 (some quoted, some merely listed):

1.455 (?), 2.457, 2.549 *unde, ubi, qua ui et quo pacto*, 2.553–4 *transtra cauernas | antemnas proram malos tonsasque natantis*, 2.596 *fluuios frondes et pabula laeta*, 2.875 *fluuii frondes et pabula laeta*, 2.940, 2.1060 *temere incassum frustraque*.

This structure is almost as frequent as the long asyndeta listed above. More frequent than each of these categories are multiple coordinations.

7.6 Multiple Coordinations

Again these are partly quoted and partly listed:

1.340, 1.715, 1.771, 1.860, 1.862–3, 1.866, 1.871, 1.889, 2.301, 2.343, 2.345, 2.534, 2.557, 2.598–9, 2.661–2, 2.674–5, 2.699 *humanum genus et fruges arbustaque laeta*, 2.889, 2.983–4, 2.994–5 *fruges arbustaque laeta | et genus humanum*, 2.1005–6, 2.1075–6, 2.1106.

Lucretius anticipates Horace in his preference for multiple coordination over asyndeton and end-of-list coordination (see XXIX.4.3–4). Plautus by contrast far prefers asyndeton to the other two forms of coordination, as does Cicero (see XVIII.2.2). It should however be stressed that in both Lucretius and Horace end-of-list coordination is at least a presence. In various prose writers (Cato, Cicero, Livy) it is rare (see XVIII.2). Its considerable frequency in prayers (see XXII.3.2, 3.4, Adams and Nikitina, forthcoming) along with its place in the above poets suggests a high-style character.

7.7 Conclusions: Some Comparisons of Lucretius with Ennius, Pacuvius and Virgil

Lucretius' use of asyndeton is similar to that of Ennius and Pacuvius, and to some extent of early Latin in general, as evidenced in Plautus. Asyndetic pairs are not however frequent.

Pairs of verbs are noticeable (11–16?, 23), as is the case in Ennius and Pacuvius, but given the length of the poem even this type is rare. *Alit auget* (also found with coordination) is a favourite pairing (see on 12, 13), and may have been picked up from Pacuvius, though it had a long currency and may simply have been formulaic. Several times Lucretius uses opposites of the reversive type in asyndeton (15, 16?, 23), and this third example (*adlisa ... reiecta*) is semantically not unlike Pacuvius 10 (*subiectare adfligere*). Virgil avoids pairs of verbs.

Other opposites are at 6 (*ferae, pecudes*, probably antonyms; also, cited at 6, *tactus ... intactus*, phrasal, complementarities, and, with anaphora, *non animans, non exanimo cum corpore*, cited in the same place). The prepositional pair *per medium per non medium* (17) also consists of complementarities. Given the rarity of asyndeta bimembria in Lucretius, opposites are in comparative terms not unusual, and collectively they give support to the reading *ferae, pecudes* and the interpretation of the pair accepted here, particularly since an exactly comparable pair of asyndetic phrasal antonyms is at 1.163. There is a second pair of verbal opposites in Pacuvius 8 (*creat sepelit*, probably reversives again), but the only asyndetic opposites I have found in Ennius and Virgil are adverbial (Ennius 17 *rursus prorsus*, Virgil at 2.1.3, *huc illuc*).

Lucretius' pair *proelia pugnas* (7, 8) is much the same as Ennius' *pugnant proeliant* (19), but there is a similar (anaphoric) pair at Plaut. *Cur.* 179. *Anademata mitrae* (9) is a semantic type of asyndeton (in reference to female accessories) familiar from Plautus and later literature. *Solis lunai* (10) is also of conventional type: components of the earth, universe or heaven may be listed asyndetically.

I found only two certain adjectival asyndeta in Ennius but six in Pacuvius (1–3, 12–14). There are six in Lucretius (1–5, 22), and another four possibilities (25–27, 29). Five of these are discontinuous (1–3, 5, 26).

Two of the others have a literary pedigree: both 4 and 25 have postponed predicative adjuncts, following the noun in agreement, which in each case has with it another adjective of different function. The same structure occurs in Homer and Virgil (see on 4). Virgil, whose most frequent type of asyndeton bimembre was adjectival, was to make considerable use of such adjuncts, whereas in Lucretius they are isolated oddities. That at 25 also has two terms with the prefix *in(d)-*, though one of these is not strictly a privative. There is only one other privative in an asyndeton bimembre in Lucretius (2 *infinita*), whereas pairs with one privative were favoured by Virgil and some others. Lucretius does however have a privative equivalent (17 *per non medium*), and Pacuvius too may have another such (9? *euiscerata*).

The similarities to Ennius, Pacuvius and Plautus alluded to in the first paragraph above should not be taken to imply that the Lucretian types were exclusive to early Latin. Pairs of opposites, of *in*-privatives, asyndetic predicative adjuncts and pairs of verbs had a long history in Latin. It is Virgil's usage that is the most distinctive in this chapter.

8   Livius Andronicus, *Odyssea* and Naevius, *Belli Punici Carmen*

There is not a great deal of relevance in these very fragmentary works (for which I use the texts of Morel 1927 and Strzelecki 1964), and I do not keep them separate here.

Andr. *Od.* 10 (11) has much the same type of adjectival asyndeton as that in the formula *optimus maximus* (for which, with its variants, see IV.4): *ibidemque uir summus adprimus Patroclus* (Warmington 1936: 28, fragment 13), = Hom. 3.110 ἔνθα δὲ Πάτροκλος, θεόφιν μήστωρ ἀτάλαντος, 'there (lies) Patroclus, equal to the gods as a counsellor'.

There is no asyndeton in the Greek. The Latin phrase can be translated 'a man supreme, by far the first, Patroclus'. This rendering of *adprimus* is that of Gellius (6.7.11), who cites the passage: '*adprimum*' *autem longe primum*. The asyndeton that Livius has introduced is of recognisable type. *Summus* is a superlative, but there can be more *summi* than one (see some of the examples at *OLD* s.v. 13a). *Adprimus* is stronger, of first among the finest ('a man the finest – the very first'). A similar combination occurs at Claudius Quadrigarius, *FRH* 24.F10 *qui adprime summo genere gnatus erat*, an example of interest since *adprime* is an adverb and manifestly modifies *summo*, thus confirming the role of *adprimus* above.

There is another such pair at Naevius 17: *patrem suum supremum optumum appellat*, 'She thus calls on her father, the all-highest and best' (Warmington 1936: 53, fragment 16). This is even more obviously a variant on *optimus maximus*.

Andr. *Od*. 30 (34) *uestis pulla purpurea ampla* corresponds to Hom. 19.225 χλαῖναν πορφυρέην οὔλην ἔχε δῖος Ὀδυσσεύς, | διπλῆν, 'goodly Odysseus wore a woolly purple cloak, double'.

Pulla, a colour term (*OLD* 'drab-coloured, dingy, sombre'; *TLL* X.2.2591.49 'colore obscuro praeditus'), has been used for οὔλην 'woolly', but the rendering has a point. *Pullus* was 'l'épithète habituelle d'une certaine qualité de laine dont c'est la teinte naturelle, originaire surtout de Pollentia, en Ligurie ... et de Tarente' (André 1949: 71) (see *TLL* X.2.2592.50ff. for *pullus* used of sheep). André adds that '*pullus* apparaît dans la langue des éleveurs comme l'équivalent de *niger*'. This then was probably a colour term suggested to Livius by the 'woolliness' of the cloak.

I take the first two Greek adjectives to be an asyndeton bimembre. Layering of the sort '[woolly cloak] of purple colour' seems to be ruled out by the word order. Also, the placement of ἔχε δῖος Ὀδυσσεύς after the first two adjectives appears to make διπλῆν into a predicative adjunct, as distinct from a third attribute (so the Loeb translator, Murray). In the Latin on the other hand there is an asyndetic tricolon of adjectives of the same status, unless one were to take *pulla purpurea* as a quasi-compound, with *pulla* specifying *purpurea*, 'drab-purple'. But such a specification would be out of line with the Greek context, which stresses the luxury of the garment (see *TLL* X.2.2591.54f., taking *pulla* as an indication of 'pulchritudo, splendor'). Livius has interpreted the structure of the three Greek adjectives differently from the interpretation offered here.

Warmington (1936: 39, fragment 40) translates the Latin as 'a garment dusky, dark, and wide'.

Naevius 37 has a pair of adverbs: *superbiter contemtim conterit legiones*, 'Haughtily and scornfully he wears out the legions' (Warmington 1936: 65, line 39). This looks like an adverbial asyndeton of two near-synonyms. The 'contempt' of the second perhaps outdoes the 'arrogance' of the first. The phrase *contemptim conteras* is at Plaut. *Poen.* 537 (*ne nos tam contemptim conteras*: see Maurach 1988: 115 ad loc.).

There are uncertainties about what in the Greek Andr. *Od*. 26 (28) (*topper citi ad aedis uenimus Circas*) corresponds to. Morel (1927: 12) cites 10.252, but that correspondence would depend on Livius' having read καλά as Κίρκης. This source is accepted by Mariotti (1952: 48–9, 98–9).

Morel ad loc. says of *citi*: '*citi* vix sanum, siquidem *topper* iam per se celeriter ac mature significat'. This amounts to saying that an asyndeton comprising two near-synonyms cannot stand. But from this semantic field cf. Plaut. *Mil.* 177 *ita abripuit repente sese subito*, *Rud.* 1323 *eloquere propere celere*; also *Cur.* 283 *ita nunc subito, propere et celere obiectumst mihi negotium*. Mariotti (1952: 48–9) by contrast supports the text. *Topper citi* is treated as an asyndeton by Timpanaro (1994: 10, 18). There is no difficulty raised by an asyndetic or coordinated pair comprising adjective + adverb, as was seen above on Ennius 9 (see also I.1).

However, the exact force of *topper* is uncertain. See Fest. p. 482 Lindsay *topper significare ait Artorius cito, fortasse, celeriter tem\<e\>re*. The *OLD* suggests for *topper* 'Quickly, at once; perhaps' [but is *fortasse* really one of the synonyms listed?], but then stresses the uncertainty. If the meaning is 'quickly', there would be an asyndeton, but another possibility might be, 'at once, we came swift(ly) to the house of Circe'. On this interpretation there would not necessarily be (asyndetic) coordination.

Naevius 25.3 has a use of *pulcer* suggestive of an Ennian use seen above (5.1.1, 1): *immolabat auream uictimam pulcram*, 'and he busied himself in sacrificing a beautiful golden victim' (Warmington 1936: 49, line 4). In English, as was noted earlier (on Ennius 1), 'beautiful' would most naturally be taken as modifying the whole phrase, and the word order of the Latin, with separation of the adjectives, favours that interpretation of *pulcram* (see on Ennius 1, and particularly II.2.5). The same problem of interpretation came up over Ennius' use of *pulcer* with *praepes*. See Timpanaro (1994: 19), posing the question whether the above is sacral language. Note too Hom. *Od.* 1.136–7 προχόῳ ... | καλῇ χρυσείῃ, cited above, 3 on Homer 10 (cf. Timpanaro 1994: 37 n. 80). The Homeric word order implies asyndeton, 'beautiful, golden', whereas that of Naevius does not.

There are various other passages of Naevius worthy of note.

32 (*insulam integram urit | populatur uastat, rem hostium concinnat*) arguably has a clausal asyndeton bimembre, with the first clause containing an embedded asyndetic tricolon of verbs, all with the same object, and the second clause a single verb with object. The asyndetic verbs refer to acts of violence, a common feature (see XV with cross references, and for *populatur* in an asyndeton see Tacitus 133). The passage of Naevius is referred to by Timpanaro (1994: 19) as an asyndeton of three terms, with only *urit populatur uastat* given in the quotation.

A comic fragment of Naevius (57 Ribbeck[2]) cited by Timpanaro (1994: 19) has a striking accumulation: *saxa siluas lapides dissicis dispulueras*. For asyndetic verbs with repeated prefixes (including *dis-*) in Plautus, see XXIII.5.4 also Ennius 18 above, *differt dissupat*) and for juxtaposed asyndeta consisting of different parts of speech, see XXIII.7.1, XXII.4.6 (for the pattern in Umbrian), Cicero 87, 88, Sallust 47, Tacitus 4, 50.

For a pair with extended second member in the *Bellum Punicum* see 58 *cum tu arquitenens, sagittis pollens Dea<na>*.

Finally, Timpanaro (1994: 18) cites from a tragic fragment of Livius Andronicus (22 Ribbeck²) an asyndetic pair of imperatives, *porrige opitula*.

9 Final Conclusions

Earlier in this chapter similarities were pointed out between Virgil and Homer, in their use of pairs of adjectives, postpositive in some way, which were not infrequently predicative adjuncts. The similarities are structural and do not extend to much semantic identity. Now that five republican predecessors of Virgil have been assessed, it has become much clearer that Virgil is to be aligned with Homer and not to any extent with his Latin forerunners. All five of the latter considered here have pairs of verbs in asyndeton, of various types, whereas Virgil has no such pairs. These others do have adjectival pairs (a fact which, along with the numerous examples of the type in Plautus, undermines any claim that asyndetic pairs were rare or only based on ritual language in the early period; note for example Ennius 4–6, mundane pairs in a long sequence), but the distinctive postpositive types and adjuncts of Virgil and Homer are largely missing (see however 14 in Ennius, and 4 and 25 in Lucretius).

Throughout the chapter similarities have been noted between the uses of asyndetic pairs in the five writers, and those in Plautus. There has been a persistent tendency to ascribe asyndeton bimembre in the early period to sacral language or, in one of Jocelyn's notes, to the 'official language' (see Ennius 19). It was however argued in the chapter on Plautus that, while he has a few ritual asyndetic expressions, most of his asyndetic pairs vary from the mundane to the artificially 'literary'. The parallels in the other writers suggest that they, too, were following current trends in the language, and not merely falling into fossilised ritual usage. I list a few illustrations.

The pair of adjectives and that of nouns at Ennius 14 (cf. 15) are in a context in which Plautus favoured asyndeta, and they can also be paralleled verbally in Plautus and elsewhere. Lucretius' asyndetic pair of terms denoting female adornments (9) belongs to another category found in Plautus and elsewhere. The adverbial opposites at Ennius 17 are of a type general in the language. Pacuvius' asyndetic pair of compound coinages (3) represents the more artificial side of republican literary Latin; there are many such pairs in Plautus. Also 'literary' are sequences of verbs with assonance, sometimes filling a whole line (see on Pacuvius 12 and also 6.5); these are illustrated from Pacuvius and Ennius, and they also occur in Plautus. Of the fifteen pairs of asyndetic verbs in Ennius (12, 18–20), Pacuvius (6–11) and Lucretius (11–15), many are paralleled in type in Plautus. Alliteration is common (all three examples in the tragedies of Ennius, 18–20, Pacuvius 7, 11, Lucretius 12, 13), there is a pair comprising compound + simplex (Pacuvius 9), and two pairs are opposites (of the reversive kind) (Pacuvius 10, Lucretius 15) (cf. Plaut. *Poen.* 653 at 5.5). The mundane Plautine type in which the first term is a verb of motion is found at Lucretius 11. There are pairs of near-synonyms (Ennius 18, 19, Lucretius 11, 14), pairs with repeated prefix (Ennius 18, Naevius), others consisting of imperatives (Pacuvius 9, Livius Anronicus). For all these categories in Plautus see XXIII.5.

Appendix: Some Coordinated Pairs with *-que* (mainly) in Lucretius and Virgil

Asyndeton bimembre, we have seen, is not particularly frequent in any of the writers discussed here. It is misleading to cite asyndeta in isolation and to stress certain characteristics of such pairs (e.g. forms of assonance), as if these characteristics were exclusive to asyndeta. In this appendix I cite some coordinated pairs from Lucretius and Virgil. Here first is a collection of coordinated pairs (mainly with *-que*) from Lucretius, the members of which display e.g. alliteration, repeated fore-elements and various other relationships such as semantic oppositions and synonymy that one may be tempted to associate particularly with asyndeton. It will be seen that these coordinations far outnumber asyndeta bimembria in Lucretius.

1.559 *disturbans dissoluensque*
1.641 *admirantur amantque*
2.196 *tigna trabesque*
2.200 *emergant exiliantque*
2.291 *ferre patique*
2.690 *uersus ac uerba*
2.728 *terras ac mare*
2.784 *officiunt obstantque*
2.786 *impediunt prohibentque*
2.920 *coetu concilioque*

Appendix: Some Coordinated Pairs with -que

2.953 *discutere ac dissoluere*
3.416 *anima atque animus*
3.638–9 *dispertita* . . . | *et discissa* . . . *dissicietur*
3.803 *disiunctum discrepitansque*
3.815 *discedere dissoluique*
3.958 *imperfecta* . . . *ingrataque*
3.963 *increpet inciletque*
4.533 *uoces uerbaque*
4.897 *uelis uentoque*
4. 961 *diuisior* . . . *ac distractior*
4.967 *pugnare ac proelia obire*
5.718 *occursans officiensque*
5.804 *uictum uitamque*; cf. 5.1080, same phrase
5.1154 *placidam ac pacatam*
5.1360 *membra manusque*
5.1441 *diuisa* . . . *discretaque*
6.215–16 *diducit* . . . | *dissoluitque*
6.490 *tempestas atque tenebrae*
6.543 *subiunctis suppositisque*
6.915 *uim uinclaque*
6.969 *coria et carnem*
6.1027 *prouehat atque propellat*
6.1095 *morbo mortique*; cf. 6.1144 same phrase, 6.771–2 *morbos* | . . . *et mortem*
6.1099 *nubes nebulaeque*; cf. 1121 *nebula ac nubes*
6.1183 *in maerore metuque*.

Particularly striking here is not merely alliteration but also the frequency of repeated fore-elements in coordinated pairs, against a total absence of this phenomenon in asyndetic pairs in Lucretius. If, as has been suggested (see e.g. Dunkel 1982: 140 on 'preverb repetition'), repeated fore-elements were an inherited feature of asyndeta (showing up in Greek for example in Homer), clearly that feature had little or no life for Lucretius (or indeed Virgil), and one must look to factors other than sound patterns as determinants of asyndeton in Latin poetry of the Republic/Augustan period. This is a question to which I will return at the end of this Appendix.

Here now is a selection from Virgil of examples of *-que* (mainly) in similar collocations:

G. 2.95 *purpureae preciaeque*
3.40 *siluas saltusque* (so 4.53, in reverse order)
4.112 *thymum tinosque*
Aen. 1.574 *Tros Tyriusque*
2.293 *sacra suosque*
2.647 *inuisus* . . . *et inutilis*

3.223 *in partem praedamque*
4.4–5 *uultus | uerbaque*
4.18 *thalami taedaeque*
4.72 *siluas saltusque*
4.94 *magnum et memorabile*
4.563 *dolos dirumque nefas*
5.591 *indeprensus et inremeabilis*
8.152 *os oculosque*
8.155 *accipio agnoscoque* (so 12.260)
8.201 *auxilium aduentumque*
8.266 *uultum uillosaque saetis | pectora*
8.350 *siluam saxumque*
8.500 *flos ueterum uirtusque uirum*
9.222 *succedunt seruantque*
9.260 *fortuna fidesque*
9.270 *clipeum cristasque*
9.341 *molle pecus mutumque metu*
11.372 *inhumata infletaque*
11.473 *saxa sudesque*
12.15 *sedeant spectentque.*

Virgil had a particular taste for polysyndeton (*-que . . . -que*), in imitation of Homeric τε . . . τε, linking alliterative pairs or pairs with other forms of assonance:[3]

G. 1.164 *tribulaque traheaeque*
1.227 *si uero uiciamque seres uilemque phaselum*
2.441 *franguntque feruntque*
2.443 *cedrumque cupressosque*
2.509 *plebisque patrumque*
4.222 *terrasque tractusque*
Aen. 1.87 *clamorque uirum stridorque rudentum* (cf. 2.313 *clamorque uirum clangorque tubarum*)
1.399 *puppesque tuae pubesque tuorum*
1.477 *ceruixque comaeque*
1.566 *uirtutesque uirosque*
3.91 *liminaque laurusque*
3.459 *fugiasque ferasque*
4.581 *rapiuntque ruuntque*
5.521 *artemque . . . arcumque*
5.753 *remosque rudentisque*

---

[3] For full details see Christensen (1908), Hofmann and Szantyr (1965: 515), with bibliography, and particularly Dunkel (1982), comparing the frequency of double coordinators versus single in various early Indo-European languages. There are notes too in commentators, as for example Austin (1955) on *Aen.* 4.83, and Williams (1960) on *Aen.* 5.92.

Appendix: Some Coordinated Pairs with -que

6.64 *dique deaeque*
6.277 *Letumque Labosque*
6.415 *uatemque uirumque*
7.165 *cursuque ictuque*
9.192 *populusque patresque*
9.787 *miseretque pudetque*
12.181 *Fontisque Fluuiosque*
12.336 *Iraeque Insidiaeque*
12.833 *uictusque uolensque.*

For further examples linking words with special semantic relationships see, e.g.,

Aen. 1.218 *spemque metumque inter*
1.229 *hominumque deumque*
1.514 *laetitiaque metuque*
1.598 *terraeque marisque*
2.797 *matresque uirosque*
3.139 *arboribusque satisque*
4.83 *auditque uidetque*
4.438 *fertque refertque*
4.605 *natumque patremque*
5.471 *galeamque ensemque*
5.766 *noctemque diemque* (cf. 6.556).

What is it then that motivates the choice of asyndeton rather than coordination (apart of course from metrical factors)? This question has come up before (see e.g. III.3, and see below, XXXII.3), but I comment briefly here with reference to the texts so far studied. First, some asyndetic pairs, or categories of pairs, did achieve a regularity of use, and though they remained in competition with coordinated variants, they were particularly common. Pairs of imperatives in the early period, particularly if the first meant 'go' or the like, were very commonly used in asyndeton, sometimes with a vocative between. Adverbial opposites are another type which, thoughout Latin, were prone to be used asyndetically, even by writers who rarely if ever used certain other types of asyndetic pairs. Virgil is a case in point. He avoids (e.g.) asyndetic pairs of verbs, but has some adverbial pairs.

Alit + auget was a frequent combination denoting a sequence of events (such that an increase was the consequence of the nurture), and it seems that a familiar pair of this kind was more likely to be admitted without a coordinator from time to time than was a completely random pairing.

Asyndetic coordination in English is regularly marked by certain patterns of intonation, or pauses, and these can add a dramatic effect to an utterance or strong emphasis particularly to the final term. Intonation in Latin is largely unknown, but it is noteworthy that judgemental adjectives often occur in asyndetic pairs, postponed in some way. It is a fair guess that such structures were employed for pathos or other emotional purposes. The addition of a coordinator was possible, but would probably make the utterance more matter-of-fact. There was no requirement to juxtapose such adjectives asyndetically: it was a subjective choice.

Another influence was the subject matter. Certain topics, particularly of a type that induced moralising, such as displays of wealth and luxury (particularly female), inspired asyndeta, possibly because pauses between the terms juxtaposed better conveyed the user's disapproval. The assumption often made by commentators that the absence of a coordinator somehow implies speed is in many cases unconvincing (see V).

CHAPTER XXV

Lucilius

In this chapter I deal first with asyndeton bimembre, then with some longer types, and finally say something about other forms of coordination in Lucilius.

1 Asyndeton Bimembre

It has been stressed that asyndetic coordination (including asyndeton bimembre) is not a single phenomenon reducible to a neat adjectival description but falls into various categories, a number of them mundane. A lot of asyndeta bimembria in Lucilius are indeed run-of-the-mill.

I have found about 33 instances of asyndeton bimembre consisting of single words in the fragments (some of them of doubtful interpretation), 8 further instances in which one of the members is of extended length (in every case but one the second member, a common pattern), and some others that might be described as 'phrasal', that is in which both members are more than single words.

I start with the 41 examples comprising either single words, or single word + extended member. The 41 are not listed in order but are put into categories, the aim being to set up distinctions between various types. The numbering of the fragments is first that of Marx (1904–5), followed by that of Warmington) (1967). Translations are basically those of Warmington, but not infrequently these have been modified or replaced. The best text of Lucilius to date is that in the citations in Chahoud's concordance (1998), a work which also has a collection of bibliography line by line. While I have set out first to quote Marx, every passage has been checked in the concordance and numerous changes introduced. I have also regularly consulted Krenkel (1970).

Each of the passages in this section (1) is given a number in bold, and that is because some passages will come up under more than one subheading. Examples in later sections are not numbered in this way.

1.1 Asyndeton Bimembre Consisting for the Most Part of Single Words

1.1.1 'Stylised' Examples

(1) 540–1 (567–8 W.) *num censes calliplocamon callisphyron ullam | non licitum esse uterum atque etiam inguina tangere mammis*, 'surely you don't believe that any woman with lovely curls and lovely ankles could not touch paunch and even groin with her breasts'.

The artificiality of this pair is obvious from the fact that both terms are Greek (Homeric: see Chahoud 1998: 295) with no currency in Latin (καλλιπλόκαμον καλλίσφυρον). Juxtaposed Greek adjectives with the same fore-element are of a type found in tragedy and epic (see VI.8, VI.8.1, and also Fehling 1969: 248). The high tone is undermined by the line that follows (Marx 1904–5: II.203: 'sordido et castrensi sermone dictum est'). Asyndetic pairs of long compounds, often with striking forms of assonance and not infrequently coinages, are a feature of Plautus' comic style (see XXIII.4; for tragedy cf. Pacuvius 238 Schierl = 3 at XXIV.6.1). See also on 10 below.

For asyndetic descriptions of females see on 6 below.

(2?) 447 (473 W.) *cui parilem fortuna locum fatumque tulit fors*, 'to whom chance and fortune have brought a like position and destiny'.

Since *fors fortuna* was an established asyndetic formula (see Wölfflin 1933: 260; note too the coordination at Lucil. 450 (477 W.): *aut forte omnino ac fortuna uincere bello*),[1] it is possible that *fortuna fors* is the subject of *tulit* (with *tulit* agreeing in number with the juxtaposed *fors*). On this view the asyndetic nouns are separated, in hyperbaton. An alternative would be to see two clauses linked by *-que*, each with a different subject: = *cui parilem fortuna locum [tulit] fatumque [parile] tulit fors*, 'to whom fortune brought a like destiny and chance a like fate'. The hyperbaton on the first interpretation is not easy (see the final paragraph), and an additional problem is that the formulaic pairing *fors fortuna* would have to be be reversed. On the other hand it does not seem straightforward to take *parilem* twice.

An epigraphic Saturnian inscription (Kruschwitz 2002: 191, no. 16) has *fatus et fortuna | iniquiter iudicauit*, and the pair *fatum + fortuna* is noted by Wölfflin (1933: 258), though without this Saturnian example. If however *fortuna . . . fatumque* were taken as subject of *tulit*, with *fors* a third subject

---

[1] *Fors Fortuna* was the name of a goddess but the pair could also be used generally of luck: see on the one hand Ter. *Ph.* 841 and on the other *Hec.* 386.

1 Asyndeton Bimembre 375

attached asyndetically, *fors* would be tacked on at the end; this seems to be the interpretation of Poccetti (2018: 95).

I have tentatively placed this example under stylised asyndeta because, on the first interpretation above, the separation of the two nouns is longer than that normally seen in discontinuous asyndeta. The fragment does however raise serious problems of interpretation. See also XXIV.5.1.2 on Ennius 9 for a problem caused by an abnormal separation.

1.1.2 Accumulations

An 'accumulation' (see XIX) is a combination of coordinated elements, whether syndetic ot asyndetic, in the same sentence. We have seen instances in the literary material so far in Plautus (see XXIII.7), Ennius 14 (XXIV.5.2.1) and Naevius (see XXIV.8 for Naevius 57). Here are the accumulations of different types in Lucilius that have an asyndeton bimembre.

(3) 19–22 (24–7 W.) *ut | nemo sit nostrum quin aut pater optimus diuum, | aut Neptunus pater, Liber Saturnus pater, Mars | Ianus Quirinus pater siet ac dicatur ad unum,* 'so that there is not one of us who is not either "father" the best of the gods, or "father" Neptune, "father" Liber, Saturn, "father" Mars, Janus, Quirinus; one and all are called so'.

The accumulation here consists of 1 + 2 + 3 elements. Lists of names are often in asyndeton (see below, 1.1.8; also IV.2 on Enn. *Ann.* 240–1 and XXIX.4.5 on 'name-lines'). The repetition of *pater* acts as a colon divider, a common presence in accumulations. A single intrusive term can also have the same function. Cf. e.g. Cic. *Fin.* 4.3 *ueteres illos Platonis auditores, Speusippum Aristotelem Xenophontem, deinde eorum Polemonem Theophrastum* (names, as in Lucilius above, here with the structure 3 + 2 rather than 2 + 3), Hor. *Sat.* 1.6.31–3 (XXIX.2.1.2) *puellis | iniciat curam quaerendi singula, quali | sit facie sura, quali pede dente capillo* (structure 2 + 3). In the passage of Lucilius the list may be described as open-ended, in that the names are mere examples. I will return to this feature (1.1.3 and also 1.1.8, 32).

(4) 75 (70 W.) *uiuite lurcones comedones, uiuite uentris*

The parts here are marked by anaphora of *uiuite*, with the structure 2 + 1. The nouns are pejorative, with assonance.

(5) 102–4 (143–5 W.) *et saepe quod ante | optasti, freta, Messanam, Regina uidebis | moenia, tum Liparas, Facelinae templa Dianae,* 'and as often

previously you have wanted, you will see the straits, Messana, the walls of Regium and then the Liparae, the temple of Faceline Diana'.

There is an asyndeton bimembre at the end, with extended second member. The asyndetic list of places has the structure 3 + 2 (see further below, sect. 3 on this passage).

(6) 296–7 (324–5 W.) *quod gracila est, pernix, quod pectore puro,* | *quod puero similis*, 'because she is slender, nimble, because she has a pure heart, because she looks like a boy'.

Discontinuous asyndeton, and again the colon structure is indicated by anaphora (of *quod*). Cf. e.g. Hor. *Sat.* 2.3.215 (XXIX.2.1.3) (*si quis*) *huic uestem ut gnatae paret, ancillas, paret aurum*, '(if) one were to provide for it [a lamb] clothes, as for a daughter, maids, and were to provide gold', where the asyndeton is also discontinuous, and where the repetition of *paret* reveals the colon division. In Lucilius the asyndeton is followed by an asyndetic pair of phrases/clauses, also a common pattern (cf. below, 882–3, 904–5 W. (11)).

For asyndetic adjectives in the description of a woman, see Catull. 86.1 *Quintia formosa est multis. mihi candida longa* | *recta est*, and also above, 1.

(7) 599–600 (727–8 W.) *hic cruciatur fame* | *frigore, inluuie inbalnitie inperfundi<ti>e incuria*, 'here she is tortured by cold, hunger, by absence of washing, absence of bathing, absence of drenching – by absence of care'.

Fame frigore is an asyndetic pair embedded within the longer sequence. For this pair in asyndeton see Cicero 103 *frigus famem*, and for many examples with coordination, Wölfflin (1933: 261). There follow four nouns, some of them coinages, with their own unifying feature, the *in*-privative prefix (see VI.5 for strings of privatives, with parallels from Greek; for examples from Latin, including Plautus and Cicero, see VI.5.2). There is said to be parody of Pacuvius here (see Chahoud 2018: 142–3), though extended series of privatives are not found in Pacuvius. Privatives in Lucilius will be dealt with separately below (sect. 2). For asyndeta bimembria followed by longer single-word asyndetic sequences, cf. e.g. Sallust 29 *regna prouinciae, leges iura iudicia*, Tacitus 16 *ciuis senator, maritus gener amicus*. In these last examples the divisions are semantically, not morphologically, determined.

Poccetti (2018: 95) writes of this passage: 'Two, three, or four synonyms joined in a coordinating or asyndetic structure represent a style reminiscent of archaic *carmina* and Saturnian verses.' I have not found parallels for the type of privative sequence here in epigraphic Saturnians, or Livius Andronicus' *Od.* or Naevius' *Bellum Punicum*. As for archaic *carmina*,

1 Asyndeton Bimembre 377

a term traditionally used of early prayers (by e.g. Timpanaro, Luiselli, Calboli), in a selection of fourteen of these taken from Chapot and Laurot (2001) (their numbers L 3, 4, 5, 6, 18, 44, 45, 47, 48, 49, 50, 51, 52, 53), there are just six asyndetic sequences with more than two terms, and not one of these has any privatives or the structural feature, 2 + 3/4 etc. seen above. The same corpus has just eight or nine asyndeta bimembria, and again not one of these has any privative (see Adams and Nikitina, forthcoming, 3). Some of these fourteen or fifteen examples have pairs of near-synonyms, but there is nothing resembling the sequence in Lucilius (and in any case pairs of near-synonyms in asyndeton, or coordinated, are banal and not a specific feature of *carmina*). Long asyndetic sequences, usually with assonance, are characteristic of Pacuvius (see e.g. XXIV.6.4 on Pacuvius 12), but they are also widespread in Latin poetry (see e.g. Plaut. *Per.* 406–10 *oh, lutum lenonium,* | *commixtum caeno sterculinum publicum,* | *inpure inhoneste iniure inlex, labes popli,* | *pecuniai accipiter auide atque inuide,* | *procax rapax trahax*, an abusive tirade with a similarity to Catull. 42.13 [see XXVII.1.1], which suggests that high emotion could be conveyed in this way, whatever the genre; see too XXIII.5.4 on *Cist.* 208; also XXIX.3.1 on Hor. *Sat.* 1.2.1–2, with cross references). They are found in prose too (e.g. Cicero **139**, which has the structure 2 + 3 as well as extensive assonance, Sallust **6–10** with cross references). Krenkel (1970: II.359) cites Pac. *trag.* 8 Schierl *illuuie corporis* | *et coma promissa impexa conglomerata atque horrida* and 9 *perdita inluuie atque insomnia*, but these hardly resemble Lucilius' accumulation.

The first three *in*-privatives in Lucilius above all denote lack of washing, whereas the last, *incuria*, is more general (lack of care). It looks like a generalisation to embrace areas of neglect so far mentioned, and any others as well. The structure of the accumulation would on this view be 2 + 3 + 1. Generalisations often come at the end of an asyndetic sequence. Note e.g. (below, sect. 3) 1113 (617 W.) *armamenta tamen malum uela omnia seruo*, Cic. *Pis.* 23 *consilio fide grauitate uigilantia cura, toto denique munere*, Sall. *Jug.* 15.2 **(25)** *gratia uoce, denique omnibus modis* ... *nitebantur* (see further on Sallust **1** and XVIII.6). See also XXIV.6.3, **6** on the final pair at Pac. *trag.* 80.1–2 Schierl *omnia animat format, alit auget, creat* | *sepelit*.

Note that the asyndetic sequence in Lucilius above occupies a whole line. For this phenomenon in poetry see e.g. XXIV.2.2 after 30, XXIV.6.4, 12, XXIX.3.1 on Hor. *Sat.* 1.2.1–2 with cross references.

(8) 669 (652 W.) *at libertinus tricorius, Syrus ipse ac mastigias*, 'but he is a freedman, thick-skinned, a Syrian, him, and a rascal'.

The old and widespread type of accumulation, showing an asyndetic pair and then another pair linked by a coordinator (*ad* Nonius p. 55 Lindsay, *ac* Scaliger; Marx prints *at*, Warmington *ac*). Such examples with *ac* as the coordinator in Livy are discussed at XXXI.3.7 (see also XXX.6.2b on Tacitus), and a repetition of *at* would have to be explained. *Ipse* interrupts what might otherwise have been an unbroken sequence with end-of-list coordination, and splits the four terms into two pairs ('A Syrian, he/him, and . . .'). For this use of *ac* see also the passage of Horace discussed on 19 below; see also on 10.

(9) 681 (638 W.) *cribrum incerniculum lucernam, in laterem in telam licium* 'a sieve, a sifter, a lamp, a leash for the *later* and for the warp'.

There are four asyndetic nouns here (from *cribrum* to *licium*). The last is modified by an asyndetic prepositional pair, *in laterem in telam*, a sort of embedded asyndeton bimembre. For the prepositional type of asyndeton bimembre (two nouns with anaphoric preposition) see I.10. The type is often in juxtaposition with other types of asyndeton (see e.g. XIX.1 and on Tacitus 4 with cross references).

(10) 682–3 (640–1 W.) *depoclassere aliqua sperans me ac deargentassere,* | *decalauticare, eburno speculo despeculassere*, 'some woman, hoping she will ungoblet and unplate, unshawl, unmirror me of an ivory mirror'.

Here are four infinitives/infinitival phrases, all with the same prefix, dependent on *sperans*. Syntactically (but not semantically) these fall into two pairs. The members of the first pair are linked by the coordinator *ac*, and those of the second pair (single verb + phrase) are asyndetic (for such a structure, but in reverse, see above on 8). The second member of the asyndetic pair is of extended length. For terms with the same prefix coordinated, see below, 6. The prefixes are negative, and negative pairs, with *in-* or an alternative prefix, are often asyndetic. For alternatives to *in-* see e.g. VI.4.2 on Livy 33, VI.7 and particularly, for *de-*, this chapter, sect. 2, where this passage comes up again.

Here we have another case of an early stylised sequence of compound coinages (see XXIII.4 and on 1 above).

(11) 882–3 (904–5 W.) *hic me ubi* | *uidet, subblanditur palpatur, caput scabit, pedes legit*, 'when he sees me, he caresses, pats me, he scratches my head, gathers the lice'.

An asyndeton bimembre of two single verbs (near-synonyms) comes first, followed by two asyndetic clauses. Such structures are common. Cf.

1 Asyndeton Bimembre 379

e.g. Quadrigarius *FRH* 2.24.F84 (XXX.2.1, 5) *uenit accessit, ligna subdidit, submouit Graecos, ignem admouit.*

(12) 994 (1097 W.) *aut apud aurificem, ad matrem cognatam, ad amicam*
A repeated preposition establishes the colon structure: *matrem cognatam* is one unit, *amicam* the other. For *ad* used as a divider in an accumulation (of structure 2 + 3) see Cicero **15** *ad ferrum faces, ad cotidianam caedem incendia rapinas*. Cf., for another preposition used thus, Plaut. *Mo.* 1118 *cum pedibus manibus, cum digitis auribus oculis labris*. *Cognata* means '(female) relation by blood' (whereas *affinis* refers to relationships by marriage): see on Sallust **41**, **42**, Livy **5**, **6**. The same pairing is also at Hor. *Sat.* 1.9.26–7 (XXIX.2.1.4.2), but with the second term masculine (*mater* / *cognati*). For pairs denoting family or personal relationships, see the commentaries just referred to, and also XIV. *Amicus* also occurs in such pairs (see the cross references above).

(13) 1056–7 (1053–4 W.) *curare domi sint | gerdius, ancillae pueri, zonarius textor,* 'to take care that there are at home a linen-webster, female slaves, male slaves, a belt-maker, and a wool weaver'.
An asyndetic sequence with five members, but it has embedded within it a unitary asyndeton bimembre, the masculine–feminine pair (for which type see XI) *ancillae pueri*. An *ancilla* was a female slave (and the usual term for such; on the other hand *serua* belonged to legal rather than everyday usage), and a *puer* a (young) male slave (see *OLD* s.v. 5). Numerous parallels are cited at XI.5.
Krenkel (1970: II.539) cites Plaut. *Trin.* 252–4 for a similar list of members of a *familia*.

In this section types and structures quoted from Lucilius have been paralleled randomly from Catullus, Cicero (philosophica, speeches), Horace (*Satires*), Plautus, Quadrigarius, Sallust, Livy and Tacitus. The diversity of genres is such that one should be wary of single labels. Eleven pairs in accumulations have been quoted above, more than a quarter of the asyndeta bimembria in Lucilius. In Horace's *Satires* about 20 per cent of the asyndeta bimembria are located in accumulations. In Cicero's philosophica the proportion is much higher (see XIX.2).

1.1.3 Open-ended Lists
As has been seen (IV.2, 3), lists may be finite, expressing a totality, or open-ended, in the sense that they could be extended indefinitely. When at 42.13 (*non assis facit? o lutum lupanar, | aut si perditius potes quid esse!*) Catullus

called a woman *lutum, lupanar,* he made it clear in the clause that follows that stronger abusive terms might potentially be added (see XV, XXVII.1.1). Such open-ended lists may consist of names, chosen at random to illustrate for example a form of behaviour or achievement (see e.g. IV.3 and XXIX.2.1.2 on Hor. *Sat.* 1.7.8 *Sisennas, Barros*), or of judgemental adjectives to which other terms could be added.

There are several instances of this type of asyndeton in Lucilius (and see also below, 6 on 1122 for a case at Cic. *Fin.* 2.25):

(**14, 15**) 352–4 (369–71 W.) *nos tamen unum | hoc faciemus et uno eodemque ut dicimus pacto | scribemus 'pacem' 'Pacideianum', 'aridum' 'acetum',* 'but we will spell both with one letter, and as we say now will write in one and the same way *pacem Pacideianum, aridum acetum*' (text and translation of Warmington above: see Chahoud 1998: 311 s.v. *Pacideianus*).

The passage is about the use of a single A to spell words whether they have a long or short form of the vowel. As the text is printed here (see Warmington 1967: 115 n. *e*, and also Biddau 2008: 146 on the emendation *Pacideianum*), there are two pairs, each having one member with a long vowel and one with a short. It is obvious that a list of words with long or short A could be extended indefinitely. For asyndetic pairs of examples in a grammarian, cf. e.g. Velius Longus *Orth.* VI.4 (ed. Di Napoli 2011) *'ob' praepositio interdum ponitur plena, ut est 'obire' 'oberrare', interdum ad eam litteram transit, a qua sequens uox incipit, ut est 'offu<l>sit' 'ommutuit'* (see further e.g. IV.3).

At Hor. *Ep.* 1.6.54 (*'frater' 'pater' adde: | ut cuique est aetas, ita quemque facetus adopta*) two examples of flattering forms of address are cited asyndetically, and that is the same type of asyndeton in an open-ended list as that seen here.

(**16, 17**) 358–61 (384–6) *'meille' hominum, duo 'meilia', item huc e utroque opus, 'meiles' | 'meilitiam'. tenues i: 'pilum' in qua lusimus, 'pilum' | quo piso, tenues*

These pairs are of the same illustrative type. The second pair is discontinuous. Warmington's text differs from that of Marx, quoted here. For *miles/militiam* rather than the diphthongal forms here see Chahoud (1998: 170) s.vv. with bibliography, and also Biddau's text (2008: 27) of the source Terentius Scaurus (VI.3.2).

Sometimes coordination is used in such a grammatical list: e.g. 367 (380 W.) *'mendaci' furi'que addes e, cum dare furei | iusseris.*

1 Asyndeton Bimembre

See also 15–16 (15–16 W.) *porro 'clinopodas' 'lychnos'que ut diximus semnos | ante 'pedes lecti' atque 'lucernas'*, 'and further, the way we said "clinipods" and "lustres" magnifically, instead of "bed-feet" and "lamps"'.

An asyndetic grammatical example also occurs in Lucilius in a list with more than two components (see below, 3 for 365–6 (378–9 W.)).

1.1.4 Adjectives

Adjectives in asyndeton in Lucilius often express judgements of people, particularly pejorative, and they are mainly predicates or predicative adjuncts/secondary predicates. The same will be shown to be the case in Horace's *Satires* (see XXIX.2.1) and Catullus (XXVII.1.2), and we have noted the pattern in Plautus (XXIII, Appendix, *Adjectives*) and in Virgil (XXIV.2.1.1, after 15). *In*-privative adjectives in asyndeton (whether two privatives together, or one juxtaposed with a term of different type) will come up in this section, but their use will be dealt with more systematically below, 2.

Three pairs of adjectives have already been cited (see 1, 6, 8).

(18?) 65 (76 W.) *lustratus piatus*, 'cleansed, made pure'.

Near-synonyms (adjectival uses of participles) with assonance, but the rest of the line is missing, and there can be no certainty that this was an asyndeton bimembre.

(19) 242 (259 W.) *si nosti, non magnus homo est, nasutus macellus*, 'If you know him, he is not a big man, but is big nosed and thin.'

Nasutus macellus is an adversative clausal asyndeton (with *sed est* understood), a fact that is not brought out by Warmington's translation, which is not used here (for adversative clausal asyndeton see I.8, and also 21, 24 below). This type of (clausal) adversative asyndeton regularly follows a negative in the preceding clause (see I.8). The asyndetic pair of adjectives (predicative) is similar to a pair in Horace: *Sat.* 1.2.93 (XXIX.2.1.1) *depugis nasuta, breui latere ac pede longo est*. In the latter passage the two terms are again predicative and pejorative. The big nose (*nasutus*) in both cases is contrasted with a lack of physical distinctiveness in another respect; an adversative rendering might have been, 'big nosed but small framed'. Both pairs imply contrasts of size, and they resemble those pairs that are not strictly explicit opposites but do hint at oppositions (see XIII.5.5). The pair in Horace is in an accumulation of the type seen at 8 above.

(20) 293 (313 W.) *tristis difficiles sumus, fastidimus bonorum*, 'we are glum, hard to please; we are disdainful of our good things'.
Adjectives conveying character defects. Cf. Hor. *Ars* 173 (XXIX.2.4) *uel quod res omnis timide gelideque ministrat, | dilator, †spe longus,† iners <p>auidusque futuri, | difficilis querulus, laudator temporis acti | se puero, castigator censorque minorum* (of an old man; for asyndeton in the description of decrepitude see XXIII.8.8; another accumulation, with an embedded asyndetic pair).

(21) 476 (505 W.) *ipse ecus non formonsus, gradarius optimus uector*, 'the horse itself was not beautiful, (but) a steady-paced, excellent mount'.
Again (cf. 19) there is clausal adversative asyndeton following a negative in the preceding clause (= *ipse ecus non erat formonsus, [sed erat] gradarius optimus uector*. Translated as above the adversative clause has an asyndetic pair of adjectives, both modifying *uector*. But alternatively *optimus uector* may be taken as a unit (= 'but he was steady-paced, an excellent mount'), in which case there is still an asyndeton bimembre, but with the second member of extended length. It is also semantically stronger than the first term. On both interpretations these are judgemental terms in final position, predicates. This, as was mentioned at the start of this section, is a standard type in Catullus and Horace as well, a mundane use of asyndeton bimembre.

(22) 813 (966 W.) *uentrem alienum maestum fouere*, 'they comforted their estranged, starving bellies'.
The adjectives, again with unfavourable meaning, are attributive. For terms to do with symptoms, illness, in asyndeton see below, 3. On *maestum* see Nonius p. 556 Lindsay: *maestum, enectum fame* (also *TLL* VIII.48.13, 'i. querentem').

(23) 1060 (1025 W.) *unus consterni nobis, uetus, restibus aptus*, 'one couch to be spread for us, old, tied with cords'.
The underlined terms are secondary predicates. The second member of the asyndeton is extended, and expresses a consequence of the first. For old age and asyndeton see on 20 above. *Vetus* occurs as the first member of asyndetic pairs in Plautus (see *Merc.* 291 at XXIII.8.8; so too *uetulus*).

978–9 *et circum uolitant ficedula, turdi | curati os cocti*; 1109–10 W. *et circumuolitant ficedulae . . . turdi | curati cocti*, 'and there went fluttering round (on dishes) fig-peckers and fieldfares, dressed and done to a turn'.
Warmington's version might seem to have an asyndetic pair of adjectival participles, but the text is doubtful: see Nonius p. 420 Lindsay *circumuolitant ficetulae, turdi; curatis, coci*. I disregard this fragment.

1 Asyndeton Bimembre 383

(24) 1026 (1077 W.) *omnes formonsi fortes tibi, ego inprobus* 'in your view all are fine-looking, rich, but I am dishonest'.
For this alliterative pair see Wölfflin (1933: 260). The adjectives are judgemental and predicative. *Ego inprobus* is another adversative clause without *sed* (cf. **19**). *Fortes* is said to mean 'rich' (see Nonius p. 476 Lindsay, *TLL* VI.1.1153.12ff.).

(25) 1065–6 (1028–9) *illo quid fiat, Lamia et Bitto oxyodontes | quod ueniunt, illae gumiae uetulae inprobae ineptae*
This is translated by Warmington as follows: 'What may come of him that the sharp-toothed Lamia and Bitto are turning up there, those wretched little gluttonous villainous stupid old hags.' But this translation does not bring out the structure (if the text quoted is accepted: cf. Nonius p. 169 Lindsay, *gumiae illi*, with Chahoud 1998: 128 s.v. *gumia*, and see also the next paragraph). *Gumiae* is a noun, = 'gluttons', and *uetulae* can be taken as its attribute. Then there is a pejorative pair of privatives, = 'dishonest, stupid', forming a secondary predicate or adjunct, 'those old gluttons are coming, dishonest, stupid'. Pairs of privatives that are secondary predicates are widespread (see VI.2.2).
There is more to be said about this passage. It is printed above with the standard conjecture *illae* for *illi*, but in fact *illi* can be retained (in the same position, moved like *illae* one place for metrical reasons). This would be the predominantly early adverb *illi*, 'there, in that place', a term which in Turpilius (9) complements the verb *uenio* (*uenire illi*), and thus means 'to there', i.e. 'to come there' (see Adams 2016: 143). If it is kept in Lucilius it also complements *uenio* ('they are coming there, the old gluttons, dishonest, stupid'). Again there would be an asyndeton bimembre in the context of decrepitude.
This passage is quoted by Poccetti (2018: 117) as one with a string of adjectives 'ironically reminiscent of the high style of archaic poetry'. For a sequence of adjectives, two of them privatives, in a speech of Cicero, see e.g. *Phil.* 11.2 *ecce tibi geminum in scelere par, inuisitatum inauditum ferum barbarum*. Such sequences are common, and not to be tied to archaic poetry, and in any case *uetulae* and *inprobae ineptae* have been interpreted above as differing in function.

(26) 1121 (1184 W.) *baronum ac rupicum squarr<osa incondita> rostra*, 'of blockheads and louts, scaly, rough mugs'.
Festus p. 442.6 Lindsay is incomplete at this point, but Paul. Fest. p. 443.2–3 has *uaronum ac rupicum squarrosa incondita rostra*. Pejorative adjectives, the second privative. For *squarrosa* see Chahoud (1998: 254), with bibliography.

Another possible pejorative pair (alliterative) designating physical defects is at 801 (850 W.): *qua est Maximus Quintus,* | *qua uaricosus uatax*, translated by Warmington as 'from which have sprung Quintus Maximus and the swell-veined splay-footed . . .'. Since the quotation breaks off at *uatax* the structure is unknown.

1.1.5 Imperatives

In early Latin in particular, but also later, asyndetic pairs of imperatives are common, especially in certain structures (see X.1.1, XXIII.5.1). Lucilius has some coordinated imperatives, usually when both members are phrasal: 758 (833 W.) *persuade et transi, <sed> da . . .*, 782 (803 W.) *coice te intro, ac bono animo es*, 817 (897 W.) *lumen auferte atque aulaea obducite*, 890 (892 W.) *perge amabo, ac si pote face dignam me ut uobis putem.*

Here are the asyndetic imperatives.

(27) 816 (948 W.) <u>surge</u>, *mulier,* <u>ducite</u>

This is the text of Marx, but after a singular imperative and a singular vocative a singular imperative is needed: see Chahoud (1998: 101) s.v. *duco* for the emendation *duc te*. Warmington prints *<tu> surge, mulier, duc te*. *Tu* may be used before an imperative when there is a change of addressee and when two addressees are present: see Plaut. *Am.* 743 *tace tu. tu dice*, 853 *tu, Sosia,* | *duc hos intro* (change of addressee). There is no context here to justify such a change. For *surge* + vocative + imperative see below, 3 on 1092 (1007 W.). *Surge, amator, i domum* is a refrain at Plaut. *As.* 921, 923, 924, 925, and the Lucilian passage would have much the same meaning if *duc te* were at the end. *Duce te* would be closer to the transmitted text, but there are metrical uncertainties over this emendation.

(28) 843 (946 W.) *caede ostium, Gnato,* <u>urgue</u>

The name seems to be that of a slave (see Marx ad loc). In this structure the vocative is often addressed to a slave (see X.1.1). Slaves named within such pairs in comedy are often instructed to approach or enter a house, as here (see X.1.1).

1.1.6 Other Verb Forms

(29) 1249 (1209 W.) <u>petis pipas</u>, 'do you ask – chirp?'

Sometimes one term acts as a modifier (or specifier) of the other. Possibly the referent is seen as asking in a chirping manner, = *petis pipans?* Cf. e.g. Sall. *Hist.* inc. 9, p. 404 Ramsey (2015) (**82**) *diu noctuque laborare*

1 Asyndeton Bimembre

festinare (= *laborare festinantes*): see further II.3.2.3.1 and also XXIV.5.1.4 on Ennius 12. Or is the second verb intended as a more offensive correction of the first, converting the referent from human to animal and the voice to something unpleasant? The latter interpretation is more probable. For an onomatopoeic term (see De Vaan 2008: 254–5) capping a verb applicable to ordinary human speech, see Plaut. *As.* 422 *centiens eadem imperem atque ogganiam*, 'a hundred times I have to command and snarl the same things'. Cf. too *Aul.* 446 *pipilo te differam*, 'I will tear up your reputation with my shrill voice.' Anna Chahoud also (in favour of the second possibility) points out to me that Lucilius often dehumanises his victims by e.g. applying animal terms to them (e.g. *rostrum*).

(30) 1021 (1087 W.) *quod tu <nunc> laudes culpes, non proficis hilum* (Warmington prints *tua tu* for *tu <nunc>*; *tua lades* codd.: see Nonius p. 174 Lindsay), 'because you praise, blame your actions, you make no progress at all'.

Opposites (antonyms). The emendation to *laudes* seems certain. For *laudo* and *culpo* opposed (though not in a single asyndetic pair) see TLL IV.1313.7ff., 83. Note Plaut. *Ba.* 397 *illum laudabunt boni, hunc etiam ipsi culpabunt mali*, Quint. 3.4.8 *laudat aut culpat* (see also Krenkel 1970: II.587).

1.1.7 Adverbs

(31?) 1319–20 (1267–8) *uelut olim | auceps ille facit clam inprouiso insidiisque*
Clam is a conjecture by Marx for *cum*. If this were accepted the phrase would not show straightforward end-of-list coordination, because the two adverbs of much the same meaning would be followed by a different part of speech, a noun, with concrete meaning, 'just as the fowler does, secretly, unexpectedly – and with snares' (see OLD s.v. *insidiae* 3 for this meaning). The second term would be a privative again. Cf. Preuss (1881: 58) on the similar asyndetic pair *clam furtim*. *Clam inprouiso* does look plausible.

1.1.8 Names

(32) 88–91 (87–90 W.) *Graecum te, Albuci, quam Romanum atque Sabinum, | municipem Ponti Tritani, centurionum, | praeclarorum hominum ac primorum signiferumque, | maluisti dici* ..., 'you have preferred to be called a Greek, Albucius, rather than a Roman and a Sabine, a fellow-townsman of Pontius and Tritanus, centurions, of famous and foremost men, yes, standard-bearers'.

Pairs of names are often in asyndeton (see above on 3). I take it that the names are cited *exempli gratia*. Note Marx (1904–5: II.43): 'Poterat Lucilius scribere *Ponti et Tritani*, quod non fecit, quia asyndeto etiam plures magnanimos se enumerare posse uiros apte potuit indicare' ('Lucilius could have written *Ponti et Tritani*, which he did not do, because by the asyndeton he was able to indicate aptly that he could list further "noble" men').[2]

(33) 112–13 (104–5 W.) *illud opus durum, ut Setinum accessimus finem,* | *aigilipes montes, Aetnae omnes, asperi Athones*, 'that was a hard business – goat-deserted mountains, all Aetnas and rugged Athones'.

The plural names express a type ('mountains like ...'; cf. the plural personal names at Hor. *Sat.* 1.7.8, *Sisennas Barros*, discussed at 1.1.3 above). The asyndetic pair *Aetnae ..., asperi Athones* is in apposition to *aigilipes montes*. *Omnes* goes both with *Aetnae* and *asperi Athones* and it has intruded into the asyndetic pair *Aetnae, asperi Athones*: a discontinuous asyndeton.

For place names in asyndeton see below, 3, on 102–4 (143–5 W.).

(34) 615–16 (710–11 W.) *contra flagitium nescire bello uinci a barbaro* | *Viriato Annibale*, 'that on the contrary we know not disgrace of defeat in a whole year by barbarians, Viriathus, Hannibal'.

A finite or open-ended list?

1.1.9 Nouns

Pairs of nouns have come up already in this section: see 2 (formula), 4 (personal pejorative terms), 7 (formula), 9 (miscellaneous), 12 (family members), 13 (masculine–feminine pair). See further:

(35?) 256 (289 W.) *praedium emit qui uendit equum musimonem*, 'he who sells a horse, a wild sheep, buys an estate'.

The character of this apparent list of two animals cannot be determined without any context, and there is an uncertainty about the meaning of *musimo* (see Chahoud 1998: 175 s.v.). The word is missing from De Vaan (2008). For miscellaneous animals in asyndeta see Cicero 150, 151. For an asyndetic pair in a reference to a sale/purchase cf. Petron. 76.8 *uenalicia coemo, iumenta* (see XXXII.1).

(36) 292 (317 W.) *solem, auram aduersam segetem immutasse statumque*, 'that the sun, an adverse breeze, wrought a change in the cornfield and sown crop'.

---

[2] I have not seen in commentators any other such comment on this type of list.

The second member is extended. For *sol* in asyndeta see XXIV.7.1.2 on Lucretius 10.

(37) 484–5 (524–5 W.) <u>terriculas Lamias</u>, *Fauni quas Pompiliique | instituere Numae, tremit has*, 'as for scarecrows and witches, which our Fauns and Numa Pompiliuses established, he trembles at these'.
These are examples of objects imagined as having magical powers (see Apul. *Met.* 2.1 and Krenkel 1970: I.297).

(38, 39) 995 (1104 W.) <u>lana, opus omne</u> *perit:* <u>pallor tiniae</u> *omnia caedunt*, 'her wool, all her work goes to ruin; mustiness and clothes-moths make rags of everything'.
Two asyndetic pairs. The presence of *omne* shows that the phrase is a general one, and that the list could be extended.

(40?) 1034 (1071) *quem sumptum facis in lustris,* <u>circum oppida</u> *lustrans* 'the expenses you incur in brothels, roaming the circus, its barriers (?)' (cf. *OLD* s.v. *oppidum* 2).
Parts or features of the city are sometimes listed in asyndeton (see XXIX.2.1.4.3). However, *circum* is at least as likely to be the preposition/preverb (see Chahoud 1998: 77 s.v. *circum*).

1.1.10 Prepositional Type
See above, 9.

(41) 794 (844 W.) *quare pro facie pro statura Accius*
See Krenkel (1970: II.423) on this pairing, citing Cic. *Phil.* 2.41 *L. Turselius qua facie fuerit, qua statura, quo municipio, qua tribu.*

I digress briefly here to list some other manifestations of asyndeton plus anaphora in Lucilius. Some of his examples are of interest. These examples are not numbered.

387 (418 W.) *quid sumam, quid non*, 'what I should choose, what not', 520 (552 W.) *quid 'mundum' <atque ' penum'>, quid non*, 'what is "toilet", "store", what not?'
For this type of positive–negative contrast see VI.7. Cf. Hor. *Ep.* 1.2.3 *quid sit pulchrum, quid turpe, quid utile, quid non.*

609 (712 W.) *quid cauendum tibi censere<m>, quid uitandum maxume*
There are two contrasting verbs within the clauses.

703 (780 W.) *modo sursum, modo deorsum, tamquam collus cernui*, 'now up, now down, like the neck of one stooping'.

'Up–down' directional opposites are one of the formulaic adverbial asyndetic pairs (see XIII.5.4). Cf. Ter. *Eun.* 278 *ne sursum deorsum cursites*, 'so that you don't run up and down'. According to De Vaan (2008: 110–11) *cernuus*, an adjective apparently substantivised here, means 'head foremost'.

1330 (1200 W.) *quae bona, quae mala item*

It will be seen that Lucilius sometimes expresses opposites (in this last case antonyms) within an anaphoric construction.

1.2 Conclusions

There are 41 pairs listed, some of them with a question mark. I will not dwell on questions of interpretation here, but simply give some rough statistics. Of the twelve pairs of nouns, only two comprise abstracts, both of them well-attested alliterative formulae (2 *fortuna fors*, 7 *frigus fames*). There are also several pairs of recognisable types, namely a pair of family members (12), a masculine–feminine pair (13), and 40, denoting possibly features of city life (?). *Formonsus fortis* (24) is another alliterative pair that is attested elsewhere. Otherwise pairs consist of concrete terms usually denoting mundane entities put together ad hoc. There are no pairs of opposites (apart from the anaphoric pairs at the end of the last section. Horace in the *Satires* uses asyndetic pairs of nouns in similar ways. He too, as will be shown, has a masculine–feminine pair (see XXIX.2.1.4.1), two pairs denoting aspects of urban life (XXIX.2.1.2, 2.1.4.3), one embracing family members (XXIX.2.1.4.2) and another close acquaintances (XXIX.2.1.2). He also shows a taste for discontinuous asyndetic pairs (XXIX.2.1.3), which are sometimes in Lucilius too (2, 6, 27, 28) (I refer here not only to pairs of nouns). Horace's noun pairs are not numerous, and few seem highly stylised (the masculine–feminine pair *puellarum puerorum* at *Sat.* 2.3.325 (XXIX.2.1.4.1) is an exception, given the way the line is structured, and he does have one pair of opposites, *bellum pax*, in the *Satires* (see XXIX.2.1.4.5)). Direct influence of Lucilius on Horace is not obvious, but both seem to have had much the same perception of this form of coordination and of the types that were acceptable in the genre in which they were working.

Horace tends to place asyndeta bimembria in the *Satires* in accumulations (see XXIX.2.1.2), and that too is a tendency shared by Lucilius, though it has been stressed that accumulations are found in a variety of genres, and influence of Lucilius on Horace need not have been an important factor, or a factor at all.

2 Terms with Privative Prefix

There are other asyndeta bimembria in Lucilius of run-of-the-mill type, namely those in open-ended lists, the adverbial pair, if it is accepted, the pairs of imperatives, pairs of names and most of the pairs of adjectives. There are twelve pairs of asyndetic adjectives (most of Horace's asyndeta bimembria in the *Satires* are adjectival) listed above, seven of them pejorative or unfavourable in some way (a pair containing *nasutus* is structurally similar to a pair in Horace with the same adjective), and most of them predicative and judgemental. In two cases they occur in descriptions of females (1, 6), and Horace too has asyndeton in such a context (XXIX.2.1.2). The pair in 1 (*calliplocamon callisphyron*) is unusual in being of elevated style, though it seems to be rendered comic by the line that follows.

Most of the adjectival pairs in Horace have at least one privative member (note too the doublet at *Sat.* 2.7.39, *imbecillus iners*), usually in second position (see XXIX.2.1.1). In Lucilius in the examples discussed so far privative adjectives are not so prominent, but see 25 *inprobae ineptiae* and 26 *squarrosa incondita*; note too the sequence of four nouns with the same negative prefix at 7 (for which see further below, 2). It is worth commenting further on privatives in Lucilius, and I turn to that subject.

2 Terms with Privative Prefix

In Horace in all genres pairs with a privative, or two such, are more often explicitly coordinated than juxtaposed in asyndeton, and even in the *Satires* coordination is almost as frequent as asyndeton (see XXIX.4.1). In the fragments of Lucilius on the other hand *in*-privatives with coordination are rare, but several asyndeta in addition to those seen already do occur.

Here first are the coordinated examples: 11 (11 W.) *infamam honestam turpemque odisse popinam* (corrupt, and to be disregarded: see Chahoud 1998: 145 s.v. *infamis*), 395 (425 W.) *lustrum . . . malum infelixque fuisse*, 514 (519 W.) *insanum hominem et cerebrosum*. Note too 874 (886 W.) *dissociataque omnia ac nefantia*, 'all alike repugnant and unspeakable'. Both terms would have negative prefixes if this text were accepted (but see Chahoud 1998: 98 s.v. *dissocio*). With the second term here cf. Catull. 64.405 *fanda nefanda* at XXVII.1.1.

Certain or possible uses of privatives in asyndetic relationships are as follows:

1058 (1048 W.) *inberbi androgyni, barbati moechocinaedi*

Two phrases in asyndeton (but no context), embedded within each of which is one member of a positive–negative opposition, i.e. *inberbi/*

barbati; cf. Cic. *Cat.* 2.22 *aut imberbis aut bene barbatos* (Chahoud 1998: 144 s.v. *inberbus*). The Greek compounds (*moechocinaedi* is presumably Lucilius' own coinage) alongside Latin terms underline the artificiality of this line, which in its mixture of elements if not in its precise details is similar to 1. See on this and similar pairs with Greek elements Poccetti (2018: 116). Embedded oppositions are not uncommon in asyndetic pairs of phrases or clauses. Here are some examples (opposites, but not all with a privative), from Horace, Plautus and Lucilius (see also XXIV.7.1.2 on Lucretius 6).

Hor. *Sat.* 1.3.2–3 (*ut numquam inducant animum cantare rogati*, | *iniussu numquam desistant*) has another positive–negative (privative) contrast ('bidden/unbidden'), with the opposing terms in this case juxtaposed, but in different clauses. For the same pattern in Plautus see *Cur.* 176 *nam bonum est pauxillum amare sane, insane non bonum est*.

At Lucil. 593 (635 W.) (*Persium non curo legere, Laelium Decumum uolo*) and 596 (634 W.) (*Persium<ue> haec legere nolo, Iunium Congum uolo*) the familiar Latin opposition *uolo/nolo*, which is attested in single-word asyndeta bimembria (see VI.7), is expressed within juxtaposed (asyndetic) clauses (with *non curo* in the first passage a substitute for *nolo*; for a different but comparable substitution see Plaut. *As.* 835 *nolo ego metui, amari mauolo*, where *mauolo* replaces *uolo*).

Note too Lucil. 629 (701 W.) *et quod tibi magno opere cordi est, mihi uementer displicet* (with *dis-* as equivalent to a privative: see VI.4.2 on Livy 4.37.9 (33)), and 699 (779 W.) *re in secunda tollere animos, in mala demittere* (with a double opposition, *secunda/mala* and *tollere/demittere*).

385 (418a W.) *inprobus confidens nequam malus <ut> uideatur*, 'that he seems dishonest, bold, worthless, bad' (Lindsay argued that this is a fragment of Pacuvius).

Note that the adjectives are all abusive and predicative, and that there is a privative. For *confidens* in asyndeton see Hor. *Sat.* 1.7.6–7 (XXIX.2.1.2) *durus homo atque odio qui posset uincere Regem*, | *confidens tumidus*, and for *improbus* Plaut. *Men.* 973 (XXIII.6) *ignauis improbis uiris*. *Nequam* and *malus* may occur together: cf. Plaut. *As.* 305 *quin malus nequamque sis*.

1329–30 (1199–1200 W.) *uirtus scire homini rectum utile quid sit, honestum,* | *quae bona quae mala item, quid inutile turpe inhonestum*, 'virtue is knowing what is right and useful and honourable for a man and what things are good and again what are bad, what is shameful, useless, dishonourable'.

In the first line there is a tricolon that is discontinuous, the members of which express positive qualities. In the second line the tricolon

2 Terms with Privative Prefix

is uninterrupted, and in this the terms express the negative correspondents of the those in the first line (in a different order). There are privatives in the first and last positions.

680 (639 W.) *coniugem, infidamque placitam* [?] *familiam, inpuram domum*

The text is uncertain. See Nonius p. 508 Lindsay, who obelises *flaticam* before *familiam*, and puts a comma after rather than before *infidamque*. If there are just two phrases starting with *infidamque*, each has a privative adjective at its head, but cf. Chahoud (1998: 145) s.v. *infidus: coniugem infidamque, flaccam familiam, inpuram domum*. On this interpretation there are three phrases, two with a privative (see too Krenkel 1970, frg. 633).

599–600 (727–8 W.) *hic cruciatur fame | frigore, inluuie inbalnitie inperfunditie incuria.*

This accumulation was seen above, 1.1.2, 7. The privative prefix in these terms is attached to nominal bases (with the second and third terms coinages). For nominal asyndetic privatives see VI.2.2 on Cic. *Fin.* 4.21 (see Cicero after 102), citing from VI.4.2 also two examples from Cicero's speeches.

I mention finally a pair of a different structure:

682–3 (640–1 W.) *depoclassere aliqua sperans me ac deargentassere, | decalauticare, eburno speculo despeculassere*

All these verb forms with the prefix *de-* are negatives/privatives, and the third and fourth verbs stand in an asyndetic relationship (see above, 10). For *de-* with privative force see XXIX.2.1.1 on Horace's *depugis*, which is equivalent to ἄπυγος.

Virtually any utterance may be interpreted as implying a contrast with an opposite of some sort, but in Latin and some other Indo-European languages (see VI) privatives, either in conjunction with other privatives or in opposition to their positive correspondents, tend to be used artistically for special effects. Some of the examples in this section show that Lucilius was well aware of the stylistic potential of such terms, as when he put together a string of four privatives, two of them coinages, or combined a positive–negative pair with two Greek compounds, one of them his own coinage.

Some of the examples in this section, and those quoted above after 41, show that the absence of juxtaposed nominal opposites noted in the conclusions above (1.2) is not a sign that Lucilius had rejected explicit oppositions.

392   XXV Lucilius

3 Long Asyndeta

The passages in this section consist mainly of sequences of single words in asyndeton. I have also included the occasional examples in which a phrase or two is combined with single words. In some genres we have seen that asyndetic tricola and longer groups are far more frequent than asyndetic pairs (see I.4 on various works of Cicero and Varro's *Res rusticae*; cf. IV.2 on recipes in Apicius). On the other hand it will be shown that in Catullus (see XXVII.4) and Horace (see XXIX.3.1.1) such longer asyndeta are not as numerous as asyndeta bimembria, though neither type is common. Where does Lucilius stand in this respect?

Another question to be considered is how otherwise Lucilius coordinates groups of three or more terms. Two methods other than asyndeton were available, end-of-list coordination, and multiple coordination. There is a view that end-of-list coordination was the norm (see XVIII.1). Is that so in Lucilius? Information about these two methods will be given in later sections. The examples below are mainly in the order of their appearance in Marx's edition, but I have also put together examples that share a semantic feature.

44 (37 W.) *uultus item ut facies mors icter morbus uenenum*, 'his expression is like his face, death, jaundice-disease, poison'.

On the text see Chahoud (1998: 139) s.v. *icter*.

494 (532 W.) ... *febris senium uomitum pus*

Another list of illnesses or afflictions. The text before *febris* is doubtful. For similar lists see the following three examples (and cf. 22 above, 1.1.4):

331–2 (354–5 W.) *quod deformis senex arthriticus ac podagrosus | est, quod mancus miserque, exilis, ramice magno*

A tricolon follows *quod*, consisting of two phrases and one single word. Here is another reference to decrepitude (cf. on 20 above), with a pair coordinated by *ac* followed by the asyndetic tricolon (for the structure see above, 10).

545–6 (572–3 W.) Τυρώ *eupatereiam aliquam rem insignem habuisse | uerrucam naeuum †dictum† dentem eminulum unum?*, 'that a well-born Tyro [could not have?] had some distinguishing mark, a wart, a mole, a pock-mark (Marx and Warmington print *punctum* for *dictum*), one little prominent tooth?'

A list of bodily defects that even a high-born woman might have, and these are chosen just as examples. The asyndetic sequence fills a whole line. For the name and adjective following it see Hom. *Od.* 11.235 (Chahoud 1998: 316).

3 Long Asyndeta

1195 (1246 W.) *inguen ne existat, papulae tama, ne boa noxit*, 'lest a groin-swelling appear, lest pimples, a lump, a blister should give pain'.

Where do the the colon divisions lie? Warmington's translation above divides as follows: [*inguen ne existat*], [*papulae, tama, ne boa noxit*]. But usually in asyndetic sequences with anaphora it is the repeated term that marks the colon division, and on these grounds the second *ne* should introduce a new colon: [*inguen ne existat, papulae tama*], [*ne boa noxit*]. Moreover *inguen ne existat, papulae tama* is a banal type of discontinuous asyndeton, whereas *papulae tama, ne boa noxit* would not be. See below, this section for 312 and 347, both of which have the same discontinuous structure as 1195.

71 (60 W.) *chirodytoe aurati, ricae toracia mitrae*, 'golden-buckled sleeved tunics, headveils, bodices, head bands'.

Cf. Lucr. 4.1129 (XXIV.7.1.2, 9) *et bene parta patrum fiunt anademata mitrae* (see the whole passage, 1121–40, with Brown 1987: 240–69; cf. e.g. 4.1132 *unguenta coronae serta parantur*, with Cic. *Tusc.* 5.62 *aderant unguenta coronae* and other passages cited by Brown 1987: 264). On Lucilius' list of luxurious accessories see Poccetti 2018: 115: 'a list of fashionable luxury dresses of eastern origin intended to depict the effeminate behavior of Roman aristocracy'. Or are the items specifically for women? That is so of the first list in Lucretius above. On the other hand for such items worn by effeminate men see Krenkel (1970: I.129) with Virg. *Aen.* 9.616–17 (where *mitrae* occurs again; also *redimicula*, for which see 504–5 below). A striking asyndetic list of luxurious female garments is at Plaut. *Epid* 230–3 (cited at XXIII.8.1 with translation): *tunicam rallam, tunicam spissam, linteolum caesicium,* | *indusiatam, patagiatam, caltulam aut crocotulam,* | *suppurum aut subnimium, ricam, basilicum aut exoticum,* | *cumatile aut plumatile, carinum aut cerinum.* This list is intended to illustrate the point that some women find new names for their dresses every year (229). Here are further asyndetic lists of garments/luxuries/necessities from Plautus: *Epid.* 725 *soccos tunicam pallium tibi dabo, Men.* 120–1 (see XXIII.8.1). The following pair comprises luxurious gifts given to a woman: Plaut. *Mil.* 1127 *aurum ornamenta quae illi instruxisti ferat* (cited at XXIII.8.1, with parallels). See also XXX.2.2, **13** (Cato) for another prolonged list of this type.

For three other such lists in Lucilius see:

409–10 (438–9 W.) *conuentus pulcher: bracae saga fulgere, torques* | †*datis*† *magni,* 'a fine gathering: trousers, cloaks gleaming, necklaces . . .'.

The end of the passage is corrupt, but there seems to be a tricolon that is discontinuous.

446 (468 W.) *adde Syracusis sola, pasceolum, . . . alutam[en]*, 'and besides these, shoe-soles from Syracuse, a bag, a leather purse'.

504–5 (534–5 W.) *uisuri alieni | sint homines, spiram pallas redimicula promit*, 'should other men be coming to see her, she brings out her chin-ribbons, her mantles, her headbands'.

102–4 (143–5 W.) *et saepe quod ante | optasti, freta Messanam, Regina uidebis | moenia, tum Liparas, Facelinae templa Dianae*, translated at 1.1.2 above (5).

The first three places named (an itinerary) are separated from the last two by *tum*, another case of a colon divider. This last pair is an asyndeton bimembre with extended second member (see above, 1.1.2, 5). The structure is 3 + 2. For place names or their derivatives in asyndeton cf. Cic. *Att.* 5.21.9 (**166, 167**) *ex Id. Mart ibidem Synnadense Pamphylium (tum Phemio dispiciam* κέρας), *<Lyc>aonium Isauricum*, Caes. *Civ.* 3.4.3 (XXVIII.2.1) *sagittarios <ex> Creta Lacedaemone, ex Ponto atque Syria reliquisque ciuitatibus*, *Civ.* 3.4.6 (XXVIII.2.1) *huc Dardanos Bessos partim mercennarios partim imperio aut gratia comparatos, item Macedones Thessalos ac reliquarum gentium et ciuitatum adiecerat*. In these three passages, as in that of Lucilius, there are accumulations, with the cola divided by intrusive items.

219 (243 W.) *custodem classis catapultas pila sarisas*, 'the warden of the fleet, bolts for catapults, pikes, spears'.

A list of weapons. Cf., for lists of threatening objects, Plaut. *As.* 548–9 (see XXIII.7.2) *qui aduorsum stimulos lamminas crucesque compedesque | neruos carceres numellas pedicas boias* (with an embedded asyndetic pair at the start), Sall. *Hist.* 2.74.2 Ramsey *saxa pila sudes iacere*, Livy 27.28.12 *saxis sudibus pilis absterrent hostem*. Note too in Menander *Dysk.* 83 βάλλομαι βώλοις, λίθοις, 'earth and stones being thrown at me', 120–1 σφενδονῶν βώλοις, λίθοις, | ταῖς ἀχράσιν ὡς οὐκ εἶχεν οὐδὲν ἄλλ' ἔτι, 'slinging sods and stones, those pears, too, when he'd nothing else left'.

245 (280 W.) *cum bulga cenat dormit lauit*

264–5 (W. 296–7) *rador subuellor desquamor pumicor ornor | expilor <ex>pingor*, 'I am being scraped, underplucked, scaled, rubbed, adorned, polished and painted.'

3 Long Asyndeta 395

The last three verbs, expressing the finishing touches bestowed on the referent, belong semantically together. Whether there are two pairs earlier is open to doubt (Marx punctuates with commas after *subuellor* and *pumicor*). This is the type of asyndeton that occupies more than a whole line (for which see above, 1.1.1 on 7), and it has the ending *-or* throughout (seven times): see XXIII.5.4 (Plautus) and XXIV.6.4 on Pacuvius 12 for similar extended forms of assonance. Marx (1904–5: II.100) quotes a passage of Scipio Aemilianus ap. Gell. 6.12.5 which has a number of Lucilius' verbs in a different order; see the end of Marx's note on the colon division. Krenkel (1970: I.203) refers to Plaut. *Poen.* 219–223, spoken by the *puella* Adelphasium, of her toiletry: *ex industria ambae numquam concessamus | lauari aut fricari aut tergeri aut ornari | poliri expoliri, pingi fingi; et una | binae singulis quae datae nobis ancillae, | eae nos lauando eluendo operam dederunt.*

294 (314 W.) *muginamur molimur subducimur*, 'we hum and ha, we plan, we are dragged under'.

There seems to be a temporal sequence, with the third verb expressing an event following on from the first two (cf. the structure of 23 above). Note again the assonance.

312 (326 W.) *pistrinum adpositum, posticum sella culina*, 'built on to it is a pounding mill, a backhouse, a store-room [reading cella] and a kitchen'.

An architectural list, with hyperbaton. This list is presumably finite.

347 (410 W.) *uersum unum culpat, uerbum entymema locum <unum>*, 'he blames one line, a word, a thought, one passage'.

This list of literary-critical terms is not unlike a grammarian's list of (e.g.) spellings. Lachmann's *locumue* (accepted by Warmington) would introduce a form of end-of-list coordination that I have not noted in the fragments of Lucilius. The discontinuous structure of this example and the last is the same as that of 1195 (above, this section).

365–6 (378–9 W.) *i si facis solum, | 'pupilli' 'pueri' 'Lucili', hoc unius fiet*

This is another open-ended list of spelling examples (see above, 1.1.3).

385 (418a W.) *inprobus confidens nequam malus <ut> uideatur*

For this passage see above, 2.

515–16 (507–8 W.) *paenula, si quaeris, cantherius seruus segestre | utilior mihi quam sapiens*, 'a cloak, if you ask me, – or a nag, a slave, a straw coat – is more useful to me than a wise man'.

This list is manifestly a selection of worthless things that could be extended indefinitely.

599–600 (727–8 W.) *hic cruciatur fame | frigore, inluuie inbalnitie inperfunditie incuria*
On this passage see above, 1.1.1, 7.

641 (688 W.) *cum <in> stadio, in gymnasio, in duplici corpus siccasssem pil[a]*, 'when I had dried my body on the race-course, in the gymnasium, and in the game of double ball'.
Warmington does not add a preposition with *stadio*. For a largely asyndetic list of mainly Greek terms alluding to forms of exercise cf. Catull. 63.60 *abero foro palaestra stadio et gyminasiis?* (see XXVII.2 and XVIII.5 on the end-of-list coordination). See also XXIII.8.7 on Plautus.

902 (874 W.) *fauitorem me tibi, amicum amatorem putes*, 'consider me to be your supporter, friend and lover' (or 'consider me to be your supporter, and friend and lover').
This (see the first translation) is probably an asyndetic tricolon, discontinuous because of the insertion of clitics in second position. On the other hand *amicus* and *amator* do occur together (see Wölfflin 1933: 254: Plaut. *Truc.* 172 *longe aliter est amicus atque amator*, though there admittedly contrasted). *Amicum amatorem* might just be taken as a unitary pair (of rising emphasis, and length) within a tricolon. For a similar ambiguity cf. Ter. *An.* 718 *summum bonum esse erae putabam hunc Pamphilum, | amicum amatorem, uirum in quouis loco | paratum*, 'I used to think Pamphilus was the best thing for my mistress, a friend and lover, a husband ready in any situation.'
Within a tricolon there may be two terms that have an association, but that would not justify saying that they should be analysed as an asyndeton bimembre within a longer series unless the association were very close and their difference from the other term very sharp.

967 (993 W.) *subpilo pullo premo*
These are apparently nouns. Again there is extended assonance. Or could the *pullipremo* of early editors of Lucilius and Ausonius be right (see Chahoud 1998: 217 s.v. *? pullo*)?

990 (1107 W.) *sic laqueis manicis pedicis mens inretita est*, 'thus was his mind tangled in snares, handcuffs, ankle-fetters'.
Marx punctuates *laqueis, manicis pedicis, mens*. It is not clear from his commentary why he does this, unless he was implying that *laqueis* was a generic term, followed by an appositional pair denoting fetters for the hands, fetters for the feet. *Manibus pedibus* is an asyndetic pair attested in comedy (see XXIII.8.12), and some may prefer to see an embedded asyndeton bimembre here.

3 Long Asyndeta

1056–7 (1053–4 W.) *curare domi sint | gerdius ancillae pueri zonarius textor*
On this passage, listing types of household workers, see above, 1.1.2, **13**.

1092 (1007 W.) *nos esse arquatos. surgamus eamus agamus*, 'the idea that we have jaundice! Let us rise, go, act.'
For 'rise, go' see the Plautine refrain *surge, amator, i domum* cited on 27 above (see too X.1.1). Cf. too Virg. *Aen.* 10.241 *surge age*. The jussive subjunctives above are a variant on the imperative formula 'rise, go'. For the relationship between asyndetic pairs of imperatives and asyndetic pairs of jussive subjunctives see XXIII.5 and 5.2.

1113 (617 W.) *armamenta tamen malum uel\<a\> omnia seruo*, 'But I saved the tackle, the mast, the sails, everything.'
Omnia is a summary of what goes before, and potentially embraces other things as well, making the list open-ended.

1197 (1188 W.) *intereunt[i] labuntur, eunt rursum omnia uorsum*, 'everything perishes, slides away and goes backwards again'.
Eunt rursum is an emendation for *euntur*.

1225–6 (1189–90 W.) *nondum etiam \<qui\> haec omnia habebit, | formonsus diues liber rex solus feretur* (*testeturque* codd.), 'not even he who has all this will alone be called handsome, rich, free, a king'.
The most powerful term is at the end. Note that semantics overrules Behaghel's law (see below, 6): the shortest term is at the end.

1329–30 (1199–1200 W.) *uirtus scire homini <u>rectum utile</u> quid sit, <u>honestum</u>, | quae bona quae mala item, quid <u>inutile turpe inhonestum</u>*
On this passage, with its sequence containing privatives, see above, 2.

There are 30 passages in the above collection. Lucilius admitted longer asyndetic series fairly freely, but they are less common than asyndetic pairs, a feature that sets the work apart from the prose texts referred to at the start of this section. Horace too in the *Satires*, as was noted above, has asyndetic dicola more often than tricola and longer cola. Many of the passages in Lucilius have no contexts and are inadequate for judging whether a list is complete or selective. The list of architectural features at 312 (326 W.) is probably a totality, but quite a lot of the other lists of nouns or adjectives are manifestly open-ended, such as the list of defects that an upper-class woman might have (545–6 = 572–3 W.), the illustrations of a spelling (365–6 = 378–9 W.), the list of worthless things (515–16 = 507–8 W.), and the list of equipment from a boat, which is specified as selective (1113 = 617 W.). These asyndeta display some recurrent topics, such as diseases and symptoms, female (and male) garments and decorations, and grammatical/literary features. Two of the lists have two or more privatives, nominal or adjectival. Particularly striking are the asyndetic lists (some of them pairs in the parallels from other writers cited above) of luxury accessories regarded with disapproval by the writers, and similar is the list of verbs denoting aspects of (female) beautification.

I turn now to the question how these long asyndeta compare with end-of-list coordinations and multiple coordinations.

4 End-of-List Coordination

The structure AB *and* C is so standard in English that it is a temptation to interpret any sequence AB*Cque* (or AB *et* C, etc.) in Latin as being of the same type. End-of-list coordinations certainly exist in Latin, notably in prayers (see XXII.3) and presumably in later Latin in anticipation of Romance, but possible examples in classical Latin constantly raise problems of interpretation (see XVIII). Not infrequently it may be argued that the three terms AB*Cque* do not constitute a tricolon but consist of two elements, AB + C*que*, or A + BC*que*. Here are the possible instances of end-of-list coordination in the fragments that I have noted. The list may not be complete but almost certainly reveals the relative incidence of the phenomenon.

88–90 (87–89 W.) *quam Romanum atque Sabinum, | municipem Ponti Tritani, centurionum, | praeclarorum hominum ac primorum signiferumque*

257 (269 W.) *nequitia occupat hoc* [*hos?*], *petulantia prodigitasque*, 'wickedness takes hold of this/them (?), wantonness and prodigality'.

A typical example, in that it is hard to analyse. Are the postponed alliterative terms a separate unit? I would take this as a tricolon with a coordinator at the end. *Petulantia* is not certain (*peculantia, penulentia* codd.).

321 (349 W.) *unde pareutactoe, clamides ac barbula prima*, 'whence comes their name παρεύτακτοι ("in regular training"), and their cloaks and first little beard'.

Probably not a genuine case, because the first term is not concrete, but the final two are and of very different type from the first.

464–5 (495–6 W.) *ad regem legatus, Rhodum, Ecbatanam ac Babylonem | ibo*
It is possible that Ecbatana and Babylon are a unit.

512–13 (516–17 W.) *uilicum Aristocraten, mediastrinum, atque bubulcum | commanducatus conrupit, ad incita adegit*, 'he chewed up and ruined the bailiff Aristocrates, the rustic slave and the cow-man, and reduced them to a standstill'.

745–6 (838–9 W.) *anno uertenti dies | tetri, miseri ac religiosi*, 'in the turning year, days foul, wretched and ill-omened'.
This example seems certain.

854 (917 W.) *manicis catulo collarique*, 'with handcuffs, a dog-fetter and collar'.
Catulus here means a kind of fetter. This is another clear-cut instance.

872 (885 W.) *saxa spargens tabo, sanie et sanguine atro*, 'spattering the rocks with gore, discharge and blood' (from Ennius' *Thyestes*).

918–19 (860–1 W.) *concedat homini id quod uelit, deleniat, | corrumpat prorsus ac neruos omnis eligat*, 'let him yield to the fellow what he wants, soothe him, corrupt him utterly and pick out all his sinews'.

983–4 (1113–15 W.) *inluuies scabies oculos huic deque petigo | conscendere*, 'filth, mange and eczema spread up to his eyes'.
For *inluuies* in Lucilius and two passages of Pacuvius, see 7 above (1.1.2), with the note.

1120 (1195 W.) *tantum habeas, tantum ipse sies tantique habearis*, 'see that you hold so much, are yourself so much, and are held to be worth so much'.

There are 7 or 8 certain examples above, an insignificant number compared with the 30 of long asyndetic lists. Here is further evidence (cf. XVIII.2) against the idea that in Latin the norm in tricola and longer sequences of single terms or phrases was to attach the final element by a coordinator.

5 Multiple Coordinations

I refer by this term to a sequence of three or more items in which each item after the first is attached by a coordinator. For the frequency of multiple coordination in Cato, Cicero and Livy see XVIII.2. It will also be shown that it is common in Catullus (XXVII.2) and Horace (XXIX.4.3).

I have found the following possible instances in Lucilius.

582 (627 W.) *nasum rectius nunc homini est suraene pedes<ne>?*, 'Now is the fellow's nose straighter, or are his calves or feet so?'

There may however be just two members of this sequence (see the translation), the second attached to the first by the first *-ne*, = [*nasum*] [*surae pedes<ne>*]. *Sura* means 'calf of the leg', and it fits easily with *pedes*.

837–9 (938–9 W.) *pluteos ex scutis tectaque et testudines | reddet*

However, if Lachmann's *excutiet* for *ex scutis* is accepted (so by Warmington), the multiple coordination disappears.

982 (1115 W.) *tristem et corruptum scabie et porriginis plenum*

1293 (1261 W.) *saxa et stridor atque furentum [or rudentum?] sibilus infit*

The text however is doubtful. Cf. Pacuvius 263 Schierl (XXIV.6.2, 5) *clamor tonitruum et rudentum sibilus*.

Multiple coordinations are very rare in Lucilius.

6 Some Stylistic Features of Asyndetic and Coordinated Pairs

There is a tradition of highlighting such features of asyndetic pairs as alliteration, assonance and rising length. In this section I consider just single-word pairs.

First, alliteration in asyndetic pairs. Both pairs characterised as 'stylised' (1.1.1), 1 *calliplocamon callisphyron*, 2 *fortuna fors*, are alliterative, as are 7 *fame frigore*, 24 *formonsi fortes*, 25 *inprobae ineptae* and 29 *petis pipas*. There are six such examples here, of a total of 33 pairs. One might at a pinch add the grammatical examples 14–15 and 16–17, which are expressed in alliterative pairs.

Behaghel's 'law' of ascending length is no more than a tendency in single-word asyndetic pairs in Lucilius. The shorter of the two terms is placed second eight times (1, 2, 6, 9, 11, 22, 24, 37), the longer fourteen times (3, 4, 7, 12, 14, 16, 20, 26, 31, 32, 33, 35, 39, 40). In eleven pairs the terms are of equal length (8, 13, 15, 17, 18, 19, 25, 29, 30, 34, 41). See XVI on the question of the significance of this 'law' in Latin.

In the 30 longer asyndeta listed above there is very little sign of increasing length of the constituents, though assessment is made difficult by textual doubts. A revealing example is the tetracolon at 1225, where the only monosyllable, *rex*, comes last, and the longest term, *formonsus*, comes first. *Rex* is placed last because it is the strongest term semantically, and there is no mechanical adherence to ascending length.

6 Stylistic Features of Asyndetic/Coordinated Pairs

We have illustrated semantic force as a frequent determining factor in XVI.

Nor is alliteration much of a presence in the longer asyndeta, one notable exception being the prolonged sequence at 599–600, which has *fame frigore* followed by *inluuie inbalnitie imperfunditie incuria*. From this example it is clear that Lucilius had a conception that alliterations combined with asyndeton might be used in special contexts as a form of stylistic markedness, and it is therefore to be assumed that the absence of alliteration from most of his asyndeta reflects a sense that asyndeta could be rather banal. Other alliterations in the long asyndeta are 294 *muginamur molimur*, 366 *pupilli pueri*, 902 *amicum amatorem* and 967 *subpilo pullo premo*.

It is not only with asyndetic coordination that Lucilius combines sound effects. He had a taste, for example, for explicitly coordinating two terms with the same fore-element, or placing such in adjacent/coordinated clauses. Here are examples.

63 (79 W.) *atque exigo et excanto*

122 (116 W.) *redit ac recipit se* (Warmington prints *et*).

260 (272 W.) *suam enim <rem> inuadere <se> atque innubere censent*

578 (622 W.) *proras despoliate et detundete guberna*

677 (636 W.) *redisse ac repedasse*

737 (740 W.) *deuorare se omnia ac deuerrere* (Warmington has *deuorrere* for the second infinitive).

825 (951 W.) *detrusus tota ui deiectusque Italia*

851–2 (910–11 W.) *ut nostris animos adtendere dictis | atque adhibere uelis*

999 (1103 W.) *fluctus erex<er>it extuleritque*

1004 (1106 W.) *praeseruit, labra delingit, delenit amore*

1037 (1088 W.) *deuellas me atque deuras*

1068 (1031 W.) *contra haec inuitasse aut instigasse uidentur*

1091 (1019 W.) *conficit ipse comestque*

1119 (1194 W.) *specimen uirtutis uirique est* (with *uir* in both words).

There are many more alliterative pairs in Lucilius that are coordinated rather than asyndetic. The list above has fourteen instances. Here are sixteen further alliterative pairs with coordination.

72 (62 W.) *natibus natricem inpressit crassam et capitatam*

76–7 (71–2 W.) *contra | pestem permitiemque*

The usual pair of this type is *pestis* + *pernicies* (Wölfflin 1933: 270). Plautus has *permities* in an asyndetic alliterative sequence at *As*. 133–133a *perlecebrae permities | adulescentum exitium*. Cf. Catull. 76.20 *pestem perniciemque*.

109 (98 W.) *labosum atque lutosum*

163 (153 W.) *taetri tardique caballi*

282–3 (306–7 W.) *uetulam atque uirosam | uxorem*

288 (321 W.) *iactari caput atque comas*

419 (451 W.) *et formosus homo fuit et famosus*

495 (542 W.) *uidet tunica et toga quid sit*

577 (611 W.) *nugator . . . ac nebulo sit maximus multo*

597 (729 W.) *squalitate summa ac scabie*

608 (726 W.) *mirum ac monstrificabile*

689 (792 W.) *totumque hoc studiose et sedulo*

765 (826 W.) *nil parui ac pensi*

997 (1099 W.) *cui sit data deque dicata*

1122–3 (206–7 W.) *bene cocto et | condito*
This phrase is from a longer fragment quoted by Cicero, *Att*. 13.52.1. I note in passing that Cicero also alludes to the fragment at *Fin*. 2.25: '*cocto, condito'; sed cedo caput cenae: 'sermone bono'*, '"with (well) cooked, spiced, food"; but what is the main point of a dinner?: "with good conversation"'. Here Cicero drops the coordinator, presumably because he is stressing that this is just a selection of the features of a dinner. He then makes it clear that there is another, more important, feature. This I take it is asyndeton in a selective list. Cf. above, 1.1.3 on Catullus 42.13 for asyndeton in a similar context.

1229 (1146 W.) *populusque patresque*
1278 (506 W.) *campos collesque*.

Note too the following examples in which a simplex and an associated compound are coordinated:

1136 (212 W.) *ludet et eludet*
1228 (1145 W.) *festo atque profesto*.

It is probably true that commentators on Latin texts have shown more interest in sound effects in asyndetic sequences than in coordinated. The two extensive lists of coordinated alliterative pairs above highlight the importance of not considering asyndeton in isolation.

7 Conclusions

Single descriptive terms cannot capture the diversity of the forms of coordination that we refer to as asyndeton. It is above all the components of an asyndetic coordination, not the asyndetic coordination in itself, that may establish the stylistic tone of a sequence. There would be no point fastening (e.g.) on to a religious passage in Varro and suggesting that an asyndetic tricolon therein (*Ling.* 7.8 *conregione conspicione cortumione*) was sacral. The context may be sacral, and the components of the list too, but this type of tricolon is widespread in numerous genres. Here is a case in Cicero's *S. Rosc.*, with similar assonance to that in the example above: 110 *isto hortatore auctore intercessore*.

At 540–1 (567–8 W.) Lucilius uses a pair of Greek compound adjectives asyndetically (*calliplocamon callisphyron*). There is nothing about adjectival asyndeton bimembre as such that is special. What is special here is that the adjectives had no currency in Latin, are Homeric, and that they have a structure (with repeated fore-element) found in certain high-style Greek genres. Or again, the string of nouns at 599–600 (727–8 W.) (*hic cruciatur fame | frigore, inluuie inbalnitie inperfunditie incuria*) is not remarkable because it is a long nominal asyndeton (dinner menus, for example, have that feature), but because of its contrived structure, with two forms of alliteration, two coinages, the ending *-ie* three times, and four privative nouns. Many of the other asyndeta we have described as run-of-the-mill (see 1.2 above).

It has been suggested in this chapter that there are general similarities between Lucilius and Horace (in the *Satires*). Both have significant numbers of accumulations and of judgemental adjectives. Both have discontinuous asyndeton, open-ended lists, privatives and more asyndetic dicola than tricola. But most of these features are also found for instance in Plautus, and it would not do to disregard that fact and to set up a special tradition of satire. Some types shared by Lucilius and Plautus, such as pairs of imperatives and sequences to do with female luxury and adornment, were widespread and mundane. We saw for example at 3 on Lucil. 71 (60 W.) that asyndetic lists of luxurious accessories and garments implying disapproval are found in Lucretius and Cicero as well.

It has been seen in this chapter (and others) that the structures we have called accumulations were a determinant of the omission of coordinators, and it is shown elsewhere that accumulations were deep-rooted in the language and not restricted to particular genres.

Open-ended lists, whether with two or more components, are a presence in Lucilius (and elsewhere). Whereas at least one type of list expressing a totality (consuls' names) was gradually replaced by coordination (see XXII.9), selective asyndetic lists persisted into the Empire (IV.4), and substantial numbers of asyndeta in the present chapter fall into this class. Asyndetic adjectives, pejorative or complimentary and placed at the end of a colon as adjuncts or secondary predicates, belong to this selective type.

For Lucilius, the normal way of coordinating more than two words was by asyndeton, not by end-of-list coordination or multiple coordination. A change will be seen when we come to Horace (and Catullus), but it was not end-of-list coordination that became dominant.

Asyndetic coordination cannot be discussed in isolation from syndetic. Various writers use overt coordination sometimes in ways at least as contrived as their uses of asyndeton. Lucilius for example as we have just noted far prefers to coordinate explicitly pairs with the same fore-element, despite the association that this structure has been given, in some of the modern literature, with asyndeton.

In this chapter phrasal and clausal asyndeton have come up in passing, but the chapter is mainly about words, or words + phrases, in asyndeton. Lucilius has numerous cases of phrasal and clausal asyndeton apart from those that happen to have been cited here, but the types are so widespread in Latin that I have not dealt with them as a separate category.

CHAPTER XXVI

Cicero

1 Introduction

In this chapter I collect and discuss all instances of asyndeton bimembre in eighteen speeches of Cicero, in two philosophical works and in half of the letters *Ad Atticum* and half of those *Ad familiares*.

The speeches examined, in chronological order, are: (1) *Quinct.*, 81 BC, (2) *S. Rosc.*, 80 BC, (3) *Cat.*, 63 BC, (4) *Red. Quir.*, 57 BC, (5) *Red. sen.*, 57 BC, (6) *Dom.*, 57 BC, (7) *Sest.*, 56 BC, (8) *Prov. cons.*, 56 BC, (9) *Pis.*, 55 BC, (10) *Phil.* 1–6, 44–43 BC. There are ten works here, which comprise eighteen separate speeches, in that the four books of the *Catilinarians* and six of the *Philippics* have been considered. There are 498 pages in the OCT editions of these speeches.

Of the philosophica, I have been through the five books of the *De finibus* and the three books *De officiis*. These works contain 380 pages in the OCT editions.

The account of asyndeton in Cicero's letters to Atticus covers eight of the sixteen books, or in Shackleton Bailey's chronological numbering of the letters, 1–166 (down to Shackleton Bailey 1965–70: IV.120; the remaining letters, 167–426, occupy the rest of vol. IV and also vols. V and VI). The books considered here in Shackleton Bailey's edition contain 296 pages.

Of the *Ad familiares*, letters 1–173 in the numeration of Shackleton Bailey (1977) have been examined, letters from the period 62–47 BC. These occupy about 120 pages of the edition.

The chapter begins with the evidence from the speeches, philosophica, *Ad Atticum* and *Ad familiares*, in that order, with the examples numbered continuously in bold. A few possible asyndeta that are open to other interpretations are included, but not numbered, and question marks are put against a few of the numbered pairs as well. The judgements implied by the numbers, absence of numbers and question marks are not definitive, as we will see, because not all apparent pairs are easy to interpret. Pairs are divided into the categories nouns, names, adjectives, verbs, adverbs and finally prepositional types.

After the evidence there follows a conclusion, which has a statistical comparison of the various genres, and discussion of the types and determinants of the pairs.

2 **Data: Speeches**

2.1 Nouns

(1) *Quinct.* 48 *is quicum tibi adfinitas societas, omnes denique causae et necessitudines ueteres intercedebant*, 'this man between whom and yourself there existed ties of kinship, partnership, in short, all friendly relations and long-standing intimacy'.[1]

Terms for close relationships, whether e.g. by blood, marriage, friendship or alliance, are often in asyndeta, sometimes with two members, sometimes with more than two. The terms may be abstract nouns, as here, or personal nouns (as e.g. *adfinis socius*). See e.g. Sallust 41–2 on *cognatio adfinitas* (and on their semantics), and 47 on *socius amicus*. For *socius* and *adfinis* juxtaposed, but in a longer asyndetic sequence, see Cic. *Quinct.* 26 *amicum socium adfinem*; also 54 *socius et adfinis meus*, 74 *adfinis socius necessarius*.

The analysis of the phrase structure above is not straightforward. Some may prefer to see a tricolon, consisting of two single terms and then a phrase with coordination. I usually classify such examples as having an asyndeton bimembre, followed by a detached, summarising term or phrase with coordination (see particularly on 141, 142), if, that is, the pair has some sort of semantic unity (on such problems of definition see particularly on Sallust 1, where the term 'weak asyndeton bimembre', taken from XVIII and particularly XVIII.6, is used). The final element here is marked by an adverb, *denique*, which sets it apart, and also by *omnes*, which makes it explicit that a summary or generalisation is to follow the two precise terms that precede. Similar uses of *denique* come up throughout this chapter: cf. 2, 26, 116, and see XVIII.6 for a discussion of the type. This third example, 116 (*Off.* 1.126 *sed quoniam decorum illud in omnibus factis dictis, in corporis denique motu et statu cernitur*) has much the same structure as the present passage, in that a coordinated pair follows the asyndeton and is introduced

---

[1] Translations are often, as here, taken from Loeb editions, sometimes modified, and without constant acknowledgement.

2 *Data: Speeches* 407

by *denique*. In this last case the third element (*in corporis* etc.) is clearly separate from *in omnibus factis dictis*, in that the preposition is repeated as a divider, and the preposition introduces coordinated paired opposites that semantically have nothing to do with *factis dictis*. For *denique* in such contexts in the historians (and indeed combined with uses of *omnis* or equivalents) see on Sallust 25.

For equivalents to the use of *omnes* above (*totus* and *cunctus* are also found) in such summaries see 26, 31, 127. For Greek see Men. *Dysk.* 524, quoted on 26. The structure is also common in the historians (see on Tacitus 100, and also XVIII.6). See below on 141, 142, a passage that clearly shows that a summarising element may be felt as detached from a preceding asyndeton. The next numbered example is much the same as the present one.

(2) *Cat.* 2.22 *quintum genus est parricidarum sicariorum, denique omnium facinerosorum*
This passage has two precise terms (having in common that they both denote murderers) and then a generalisation introduced by *denique*, with *omnes* again juxtaposed.

(3) *Cat.* 3.1 *rem publicam, Quirites, uitamque omnium uestrum, bona fortunas, coniuges liberosque uestros atque hoc domicilium clarissimi imperi, fortunatissimam pulcherrimamque urbem, hodierno die deorum immortalium summo erga uos amore, laboribus consiliis periculis meis e flamma atque ferro ac paene ex faucibus fati ereptam et uobis conseruatam ac restitutam uidetis*, 'Citizens, you see the state and the lives of all of you, your property and fortunes, your wives and children and this domicile of a most famous empire, the most fortunate and beautiful city, today by the supreme love towards you of the immortal gods, and by my toils, plans and perils, snatched away from flame and sword and almost from the jaws of doom and for you preserved and restored.'

The opening sentence of the third speech, in which Cicero breaks the news to the assembled crowd of his salvation of the city. The passage is highly rhetorical. The structure has at the start three pairs, two coordinated and one asyndetic: *rem publicam uitamque ... bona fortunas, coniuges liberosque uestros*. The last four nouns (*bona ... liberosque*) consist of two distinct pairs, after which comes a long noun phrase that is attached by a coordinator. For a long accumulation with similar mixed elements see e.g. Livy 9.14.10–11 (10, 11) *caedunt pariter resistentes fusosque, inermes atque armatos, seruos liberos, puberes impubes, homines iumentaque* (two juxtaposed asyndetic pairs, surrounded by coordinated pairs).

Bona fortunas, expressing a person's wealth and possessions, is not unlike *goods and chattels*, in that it could embrace both moveable and immoveable assets (see Watkins 1995: 9 on *goods and chattels*). As such it is a merism, a totality, referring in this context to all the assets of all the citizens present and by implication of those not present. For the pair coordinated, see *Phil.* 5.32 *quibus bona fortunaeque nostrae notatae sunt*, and particularly *Phil.* 14.37 *cumque . . . bona fortunasque omnium liberosque conseruarint*. In this last passage *bona fortunasque* has a coordinator, and the third term, *liberosque* (with which compare *coniuges liberosque* above) stands apart from it with its own coordinator marking its separateness. In a long asyndetic sequence at *Dom.* 1, not quoted here, there is arguably an embedded pair *bona fortunae*, but the two might alternatively be taken as members of a colon with eleven members.

Later in the sentence there is a threefold asyndeton of single words starting at *laboribus*, followed by a coordinated alliterative pair (*e flamma atque ferro*), which is a common phrase (see Wölfflin 1933: 259; at *Cat.* 2.1 also, and see below, 16, where the two terms are again coordinated, and 182, where they are asyndetic with anaphora of a preposition), and then a threefold coordination of participial phrases. Here then is a classic accumulation of coordinations, syndetic and asyndetic, with an embedded single-word pair.

(4) *Cat.* 3.2 *nam toti urbi, templis delubris, tectis ac moenibus subiectos prope iam ignis circumdatosque restinximus*, 'It is I who have quenched the fires which were on the point of being set to the whole city, to its temples, its shrines, its houses and its walls and which were about to engulf them' (Macdonald, Loeb).

This is also from the opening of the speech. There is first the generalising *toti urbi*, and then two pairs expressing components of the whole city, the first pair asyndetic (*templis delubris*), the second coordinated (see *OLD* s.v. *tectum* 2, 'dwelling'). Coordinated pairs with *ac* following an asyndetic pair are found in Tacitus (see XXX.6.2b and Tacitus 5) and Livy (XXXI.3.7), and Lucilius and Horace (see XXV.1.1.2, 8 for Lucilius and XXV.1.1.4 on Lucilius 19 for a cross reference to Horace). This is another of those sequences of the type ABCD*que* (or alternative coordinator), where the structure, with the last term attached by a coordinator, is not the same as that of end-of-list coordination (see also e.g. XVIII.4). For *delubrum* and *templum* together see *TLL* V.1.472.31ff.; *Cat.* 3.22, 4.2, 4.18 *templa atque delubra*. Examples are listed too by Dyck (2008: 169). For *tecta* and *moenia* together see *Cat.* 1.33.

2 Data: Speeches

Templis delubris is a pairing of concrete terms denoting places or edifices of religious significance (with complementary features, according to a grammarian, the first containing statues of gods, the second indicating an area with porticoes: see *TLL* V.1.471.67ff.). Cf. the pair *arae foci*, at **16** below, and also **160** *fanorum lucorum*. Note too from a spell at Macr. *Sat*. 3.9.8, *nostraque uobis loca templa sacra urbs*, where, if *sacra* modifies both *loca* and *templa* (with *templa* in its old sense of 'space marked out in the sky for the purposes of augury'), the two nouns would form a pair indicating different types of sacred places (see XVIII.4, XXII.3.1). It was seen at XXII.3 that asyndeton is not common in surviving prayers, but asyndetic pairs of religious significance such as the above are certainly attested (see XXII.6 and XXIII.3), and the inconsistency may reflect changes of fashion over time.

(?) *Red. Quir.* 13 *cum* <u>senatus, equites Romani</u> *flere pro me . . . uetarentur*.
The OCT (Peterson) prints *senatus equitesque*. *Equitesque* is the reading of *k* and is a correction in *c*, *t*, but the other manuscripts have asyndeton. There is no unproblematic case of asyndeton bimembre in this speech. Elsewhere in the same section 13 the OCT prints an emendation (by Koch): *omnia cum omnibus foedera reconciliationes<que> gratiarum . . . sancirentur*.
An asyndeton *senatus equites* is not impossible. *Senatus/senatores/patres* and *eques/equites* are often coordinated (*TLL* V.2.713.67ff., 716.61ff.), and any coordination may coexist with an asyndeton (note Tac. *Ann*. 1.7.1 *ruere in seruitium consules patres eques*). Asyndetic pairs denoting groups of different status do occur (e.g. Tacitus **66** *plebes primores*, **109** *ordo plebs*: see XIII.5.3), but asyndeton is perhaps out of keeping with the manner of this speech. I can see no other reason for emendation.

(5–7) *Dom.* 17 *quem ad modum discessu meo* <u>*frugum inopia, fames*</u>, *uastitas caedes incendia rapinae, scelerum impunitas, fuga formido discordia fuisset, sic reditu* <u>*ubertas agrorum, frugum copia*</u>, *spes oti, tranquillitas animorum,* <u>*iudicia leges*</u>, *concordia populi, senatus auctoritas mecum simul reducta uideantur*, 'just as at my departure there had been scarcity of provisions and hunger, devastation, slaughter, arson, looting, impunity for crimes, terrified flight and discord, so at my return there seems to have been restored with me fertility of the fields and abundance of provisions, hope of peace, mental tranquillity, justice and the rule of law, popular concord and senatorial authority'.
In this long list of asyndetic words and phrases some smaller units are embedded. *Frugum inopia, fames* is a unified pair, with the second term expressing a consequence of the first (shortage of provisions leads to

hunger). The asyndetic tetracolon that follows is distinct from this pair, denoting forms of violence. A pair similar to the first, consisting in this case of two phrases, is *ubertas agrorum, frugum copia*: fertility of the fields leads to an abundance of provisions. This pair is almost a reversal of *frugum inopia, fames*. An asyndetic pair comprising single words is *iudicia leges*, and this too is semantically distinct from what follows. Cf. Sallust 29 *quom regna prouinciae, leges iura iudicia, bella atque paces, postremo diuina et humana omnia penes paucos erant* (with the punctuation of Reynolds, which is certainly right), Cic. *Dom.* 70 *legum iudiciorumque. Iudicia leges* 'courts, laws' denotes the system of justice, and may be described as a legal pair.

Less clear-cut is *fuga formido*. For these two terms together, usually with a coordinator, see Wölfflin (1933: 261): note e.g. Cic. *Att.* 8.14.1 *post has fugas et formidines*, and, with asyndeton, Tacitus 19 *formidinem fugam famemque ac totiens captis precariam uitam* (two separate pairs, one with coordination). They are semantically related, in that fear leads to flight (see also on the pair of verbs at 59 below), but can they be separated from *discordia* (i.e. with a punctuation *fuga formido, discordia*)? *Discordia* may seem semantically unlike the preceding two terms, and it is in a contrast on its own with *concordia populi*, but it would be artificial not to allow here a tricolon, with discord an accompaniment of the terrified flight.

(8) *Dom.* 23 *sed omitto Catonem, cuius eximia uirtus dignitas, et, in eo negotio quod gessit, fides et continentia tegere uideretur improbitatem et legis et actionis tuae*, 'but I leave aside Cato, whose remarkable valour and worth, and, in that commission that he carried out, loyalty and steadfastness, seemed to conceal the unscrupulousness of the law and of your action'.

Note the alternation of asyndeton bimembre and coordinated pair, with *et* and a parenthetical clause separating them. For the type of accumulation in general, see above, 4, XVIII.4, XXX.6.2b. For the significance in relation to a textual issue of the structure here (with *et* following the asyndetic pair) see below, 159. For the pairing, with coordination, cf. Livy 26.49.15 *uestra quoque uirtus dignitasque facit*. For *uirtus* as one of the terms in an asyndeton bimembre see on Livy 1 *ingenio uirtute*, and below, 7.8.2.

(9) *Dom.* 55 *cum Gabinio Syria dabatur, Macedonia Pisoni, utrique infinitum imperium, ingens pecunia, ut tibi omnia permitterent, te adiuuarent, tibi manum copias, tibi suos spectatos centuriones, tibi pecuniam, tibi familias compararent, ... ne tum quidem uis erat?*, 'when Syria was given to Gabinius and Macedonia to Piso, unlimited authority to both and a huge sum of money, so that they might allow you everything, assist you, and provide

2 Data: Speeches 411

you with retainers and troops, their distinguished centurions, money, gangs of slaves, ... not even then was it violence?'

The anaphoric pronouns *te, tibi*, ... mark off the cola and show that *manum copias* is an asyndetic unit. Cf. Caes. *Gall.* 1.37.4 *si noua manus Sueborum cum ueteribus copiis Ariouisti sese coniunxisset* (near-synonyms): see *TLL* VIII.368.14ff., 40f. The listing asyndetically of forces is seen in its most frequent form in the tricolon *arma equi uiri* and shorter variants.

For the marking of colon divisions by anaphoric repetitions or single dividers see **15** (with cross references), **54, 55, 91**.

(9a) *Dom.* 121 *nihil loquor de pontificio iure, nihil de ipsius uerbis dedicationis, nihil de religione caerimoniis*

On this passage (with the two nouns dependent on a single preposition) see XXI.4, and also below, **16** for the pair in a longer sequence.

(10) *Sest.* 20 *uino ganeis, lenociniis adulteriisque confectum*

This consists of two pairs, the first asyndetic. It is translated 'undone by drink, gambling, whoring, and adultery' by Kaster (2006), but *ganea* means 'gluttonous eating' (*OLD* s.v. b). The first two nouns refer to activities of the tavern, excessive eating and drinking (for the 'eat/drink' asyndeton see on Plautus, XXIII.5.5, 8.2), and the coordinated pair to disapproved forms of sex. *Vino ganeis* expresses the concept of gluttony. Similar pairings also come up in the context of decadent behaviour in Plautus (see XXIII.8.2, 8.4).

Yet again we see the combining of an asynetic pair with a coordinated.

(11) *Sest.* 22 *uidebamus genus uitae, desidiam inertiam*, 'We saw a way of life – sloth, inertia.'

Near-synonyms, postponed and in apposition to *genus uitae*, no doubt spoken with a pause, which would enhance the condemnatory effect. Cf. *Brut.* 8 *non inertiae neque desidiae*, Plin. *Ep.* 2.10.8 *inertiae et desidiae* (see *TLL* VII.1.1314.52ff.). For the adjective *iners* in asyndeton see on Horace, XXIX.2.1.1 (first passage, with cross references), XXIX.3.2 (first passage, with the term this time in a longer asyndeton).

Cf. **27** below for this structure (with again one term with the prefix *in-*). Similarly in the fragments of a letter by Timarchides, freedman of Verres, quoted by Cicero there is the following pair: *Verr.* 3.154 *habes uirtutem eloquentiam*. The terms here denote virtues rather than vices, but structurally the pair is the same as those at **11** above and also **27** below, in that the two terms are at the end of a colon as objects of a verb, and are members of an open-ended list. For pairs of virtues expressed in this way (asyndetically and at the end of a colon), see below, 104.

(12) *Sest.* 40 <u>uim arma</u>, *exercitus imperatores castra denuntiabat*, 'he put me on notice that there would be ... force of arms, commanders and their armies, war' (Kaster 2006).[2]

This may look like a group of five nouns (Peterson, OCT, for example, puts a comma after each of the first four nouns), but the first two are a unit of the type 'asyndetic hendiadys' (see II.3.2.3.3), 'force of arms', serving as a heading or introduction to the next three nouns, all referring to concrete components of armed force. Kaster (above) has taken the first pair in this way, and has also taken *exercitus, imperatores* together, separated from *castra*. I would prefer to see *exercitus imperatores castra* as a unified tricolon with the implication described above. For the structural pattern 2 + 3 (an asyndeton bimembre, followed by an asyndetic tricolon), see e.g. 15 below and XIX.1). For *uim arma* in asyndeton on its own see below, 18 (where the pair is object of the same verb, *denuntio*), and for the coordinated variant, see Tac. *Hist.* 4.23.1 *uis et arma*, 4.68.2 *uim atque arma*. For a similar phrase see XXIV.5.2.2 on Ennius 16 (*fortuna ferro*), and also the next passage. Asyndetic pairs of nouns (or verbs) denoting forms of force or violence are quite common: see 7.8.2, 14, 15 below and 16 for *ferrum flamma*; also on 5–7 above for a tetracolon of terms for violent acts. *Arma* occurs with other terms in asyndeton too: see on Sallust 31.

(13, 14) *Sest.* 85 <u>clamore concursu</u>, <u>ui manu</u> *gerebantur*

There are two pairs here. *Vis manus* is a common combination, not least in Cicero (for lists of examples see *TLL* VIII.354.18ff., 35ff., in the latter place a number of times as part of asyndetic tricola), another asyndetic hendiadys, = 'physical force' (without necessarily the use of weapons: contrast *uim arma* above). Cf. 87 *ad uim ad manus*.

The shouting is an accompaniment of the running about. For this alliterative pair together cf. *Sest.* 134 *uidebat clamores et concursus futuros*, *Att.* 1.16.1 *clamor concursusque*, Hor. *Sat.* 1.9.78–9 *clamor utrimque,* | *undique concursus*, and see *TLL* IV.115.29f.

(15) *Sest.* 88 *ad <u>ferrum faces</u>, ad cotidianam caedem incendia rapinas se cum exercitu suo contulit*

There are two units here, *ferrum faces* and *caedem incendia rapinas* (structure 2 + 3 again: see 12 above). This is suggested, first, by the

---

[2] Translations of passages from the *Pro Sestio* are usually those of Kaster (2006), and I do not necessarily mention this henceforth.

2 *Data: Speeches* 413

placement of the preposition *ad* (cf. 116, and for the marking of cola by anaphora, see 9 above; cf. too *Nat.* 2.150 *ad pingendum fingendum, ad scalpendum, ad neruorum eliciendos sonos*; see further some of the examples discussed at XXIX.2.1.2, 4.2.3). Second, for the alliterative pairing *ferrum fax* see Wölfflin (1933: 259), also listing examples of the similar pair, *ferrum flamma*, which occurs with coordination at 16 below and asyndetically at 182 *de flamma de ferro*; *ferro* and *facibus* are associated also, in anaphoric asyndeton, at *Sest.* 2 *quos ferro, quos facibus, quos ui manu copiis*. Third, *caedes* and *incendia* often occur together, in asyndeton and with coordinators (see Sallust 15). Fourth, for the attachment of *rapinae* to this pair see *Dom.* 89 and also *Dom.* 17 above, 5–7. Finally, the first two nouns are concrete, denoting forms of weaponry, and the final three are verbal abstracts, with *caedes* a consequence of *ferrum* and *incendia* a consequence of *faces*. This structure, with the third noun looking back to the first, and the fourth to the second, is of the type we have called 'correlative distribution' (see XVII).

Note that in both phrases in 15 the asyndetic terms are dependent on a single preposition. There are other such examples in the texts used for this chapter: cf. 16, 32, 116, 123, 124, 190, 191 and also arguably 159. Editors, it is noted elsewhere, have tended to be uneasy about accepting asyndetic pairs dependent on a single preposition, possibly unaware that the pattern is quite common (see XXI.1; also Preuss 1881: 53).

The pairs at 12, 14 and 15 all denote forms of force.

(16) *Sest.* 90 *qui ab aris focis ferrum flammamque depellis*
For *arae* and *foci* coordinated see Sall. *Cat.* 52.3, and for the pair in asyndeton (juxtaposed with another pair), Plaut. *Am.* 226 (see XXIII.3). Note too the longer asyndeta in this speech at 145 *ego pulsis aris focis deis penatibus*, and also at *Dom.* 1 *arae foci di penates* (full sequence not quoted) and 109 *hic arae sunt, hic foci, hic di penates, hic sacra religiones caerimoniae continentur*; cf. *Phil.* 2.75 *deos patrios aras focos larem suum familiarem*; see also Preuss (1881: 77), and below, 85. The *focus* 'hearth' in the atrium was the place of worship of the *Lar familiaris*, and one of the types of altar (*ara*) was that in a private house, with the two terms together the symbol of the sanctity of the home (see Otto 1890: 33, Landgraf 1914: 61, R. G. Nisbet 1939: 67). This is strictly a concrete pair embracing the totality of the household places of worship, but shifting into an abstract concept. For this religious type of asyndetic pair see above, 4, and see in general XXII.6.

For *ferrum flamma* used asyndetically, see below, 182.

Cicero here (as in the previous example) uses just one preposition with the asyndetic pair.

(17) *Prov. cons.* 14 *homini <u>sceleribus flagitiis</u> contaminato nihil esse credendum*
Butler and Cary (1924) and Peterson (OCT) print this text, noting in the app. crit. that editors add *-que*. See too now Grillo (2015), also printing the asyndeton with the same information in the apparatus. *Scelus* and *flagitium* are often together, usually in coordination (*TLL* VI.1.841.2ff.; 841.6 for an asyndetic example, with prepositional anaphora). This is a pair that could be taken as an asyndetic hendiadys, = 'disgraceful crimes'. Terms denoting vices and the like and also virtues are often in asyndeton (e.g. see on Sallust 1 and Tacitus 13; see also above, 11). For a pair semantically similar to this see Tacitus 75 *sine probro scelere*. See also below, this chapter, 7.8.2 for asyndetic pairs designating vices.

(18) *Phil.* 1.26 *denuntio <u>uim arma</u>*
For this pair see above, 12. It is not convincing to separate the terms of a formulaic pairing, as is done by Clark (OCT): *denuntio uim: arma remouete*. Contrast Shackleton Bailey, Ramsey, Manuwald (Loeb): *Denuntio uim, arma. Removete!*, 'I warn of violence, of armed force. Take it away!'

(19, 20) *Phil.* 2.35 <u>*agrorum oppidorum*</u>, <u>*immunitatium uectigalium*</u> *flagitiosissimae nundinae*, 'scandalous market in lands and towns, exemptions and revenues'.
There are two semantically distinct genitival pairs here. Lands and towns are opposites of the 'town/country' type, for which see XIII.5.1. The second two terms refer to specific types of profiteering. With the first pair cf. e.g. Sallust 27 *urbis agros*, and also the prayer, uttered only by dictators and generals, for the devotion to destruction of enemy armies and cities, quoted at Macr. *Sat.* 3.9.10, where *agri* and *urbes* are four times coordinated by *-que*. For a variant cf. Cicero 100 *urbani rustici*.

(21) *Phil.* 2.62 *in urbe <u>auri argenti</u>, maximeque uini foeda direptio*
On the asyndetic pair *aurum argentum* see below, 119. *Aurum argentum* is an old type of asyndeton, whereby terms for precious substances are juxtaposed (see XXIII.8.6, XXIX.3.2 on Hor. *Ep.* 2.2.180–1 with numerous cross references). There looks to be end-of-list coordination here (but see XVIII.7), in that all three nouns are in the genitive dependent on *direptio*, but gold and silver are semantically very different from wine, and *maxime* detaches *uini* from the other two nouns, which I treat as an embedded unitary pair within a longer sequence.

(22) *Phil.* 2.109 <u>*signa tabulas*</u>, *quas populo Caesar una cum hortis legauit, eas ... deportauit*

2 Data: Speeches

Signa tabulas is at Sallust **19** (speech of Cato) *qui semper <u>domos uillas, signa tabulas uostras</u> pluris quam rem publicam fecistis* (the punctuation of the Latin here is that of Reynolds, OCT). See also XXX.2.2, **8** for *signis statuis* in Cato; Cic. *Verr.* 1.58 *signa et tabulas pictas*, and XXIX.3.2 on Hor. *Ep.* 2.2.180–1. Statues and pictures are the two valuable objets d'art of high cultural status that have the feature that they are the products of artists and not of nature, in contrast to silver and gold. Houses and villas accommodate statues and pictures, and the pair *domos uillas* is distinct from *signa tabulas* in the passage of Sallust. On *domus* in asyndeta see below, 7.8.2, and also Sallust **18**. On *signa tabulae* see Preuss (1881: 75).

(**23, 24**) *Phil.* 3.37 *D. Bruti, <u>imperatoris, consulis designati</u> . . . D. Brutum, <u>imperatorem, consulem designatum</u>*

A pair of titles used twice by Cicero in a motion in the senate for a senatorial decree. On the two titles see Manuwald (2007: 454–5). It would be perverse not to punctuate with a comma here, even given the convention that I have adopted.

(**25**) *Phil.* 3.38 *id eum exercitumque, <u>municipia colonias</u> prouinciae Galliae recte atque ordine exque re publica fecisse et facere.*

Again from Cicero's motion in the senate. There is first a coordinated pair, and then the asyndetic. Cf. 3.13 *municipiorum coloniarumque prouinciae Galliae*, where the same phrase has a coordinator. Note too *Red. sen.* 31 *municipia coloniasque*, and below, example after **31**. A *municipium* contained existing inhabitants who were already Roman citizens and were formed into a self-governing community. A *colonia* on the other hand was a new settlement established by Rome outside the *ager Romanus*, and could be either Roman or Latin. See Manuwald (2007: 367–8) on the pair as used here: 'From that time onwards [49 BC], there was no real difference between *municipia* and *coloniae* in Gaul . . .; the double expression reflects the historical origins and is probably intended to illustrate universal agreement shared by all the settlements' (see also Goodyear 1981: 178 on Tac. *Ann.* 1.79.1). As such the pair expresses a totality. The asyndeton is of a quasi-legal type, describing types of states and foundations, methods of government (see XXII.7.5). Sallust's *regna prouinciae* (**29**) is of the same general type.

(**26?**) *Phil.* 5.15 <u>*saltatores citharistas*</u>, *totum denique comissationis Antonianae chorum*, 'dancers, harpists, the whole Antonian troupe of carousers'.

With this example cf. *Off.* 1.150 *adde huc, si placet, unguentarios saltatores totumque ludum talarium*. The *totum*-phrase is summarising, embracing the types named and others unspecified. The type (with *denique*) came up at 1, where the alternative interpretation of such structures was also mentioned, and cross references to comparable examples given. For Greek see Men. *Dysk.* 524 ὦ τρισκακοδαίμων, ὡς ἔχω | ὀσφῦν, μετάφρενον, τὸν τράχηλον, ἑνὶ λόγῳ | ὅλον τὸ σῶμ'. *Off.* 1.150 above, though its components are much the same as those of 26, may arguably be taken as an end-of-list coordination, but the classification of such examples is arbitrary (see on Sallust 1 and also XVIII.6 for the problems).

(27) *Phil.* 5.29 *noui hominis insaniam adrogationem*
This example is similar in type and structure to 11 *uidebamus genus uitae, desidiam inertiam*.

(28) *Phil.* 5.36 D. *Brutus, imperator, consul designatus*
Proposal for decree of senate.

(29) *Phil.* 5.36 D. *Bruti imperatoris, consulis designati*

(30) *Phil.* 5.46 C. *Caesar C. f. pontifex, pro praetore*
A pair of titles again, in a senatorial decree moved by Cicero.

(31) *Phil.* 5.46 C. *Caesarem C. f. pontificem, pro praetore*

(?) *Phil.* 6.18 *eodem incumbunt municipia coloniae cuncta Italia*
For the pair *municipia coloniae* see 25. The third element may be another summarising phrase (cf. 1, 26 above), or the third member of an ordinary tricolon.

2.2   *Names*

I have not dealt systematically with consular names in this book (see below, 7.4.1), though they occur in the corpus. See e.g. *Phil.* 3.37 (from a motion by Cicero in the senate) *C. Pansa A. Hirtius, consules designati*; also 5.53.

(32) *Dom.* 35 *non aetas eius qui adoptabat est quaesita, ut in Cn. Aufidio M. Pupio, quorum uterque nostra memoria summa senectute alter Oresten, alter Pisonem adoptauit, quas adoptiones sicut alias innumerabilis hereditates nominis pecuniae sacrorum secutae sunt*, 'The age of the adopting party was never inquired into, as it was in the case of Gnaeus Aufidius and Marcus Papius, who, as I recollect, in extreme old age, respectively adopted Orestes and Piso, and these adoptions, as in countless other cases, were followed by

2 Data: Speeches

the adopted party inheriting the name, the wealth, and the family rites of his adopter' (Watts, Loeb).

The two asyndetic names are cited *exempli gratia*, as there were others of the same type (note *sicut alias*). For this type of asyndetic pair see IV.3, and also above, 11 and 27. For the single preposition with two asyndetic dependent terms, see on 15 above.

(33) *Sest.* 33 *ut lex Aelia lex Fufia ne ualeret*
From a law. The names of the two laws are in asyndeton. Both *lex Aelia* and *lex Fufia* comprise two words equivalent to a compound unit naming a single law.

(34, 35, 36) *Sest.* 135 *Caeciliam Didiam, Liciniam Iuniam contempsit*
Here the two laws bear the names (in adjectival form) of two men each (with *legem* understood), and coordinators might have been used, as at Cic. *Att.* 2.9.1 *qui Aeliam legem, qui Iuniam et Liciniam, qui Cae<ci>liam et Didiam neglexerunt*.

There are three asyndeta here: first, each of *Caeciliam Didiam* and *Liciniam Iuniam* (= *Caeciliam et Didiam* and *Liciniam et Iuniam*), which I include under names (though they are strictly adjectives) because the terms are equivalent to possessive genitives; second the two law-names (*legem*) *Caeciliam Didiam* and (*legem*) *Liciniam Iuniam*, given that they might have had a coordinator joining them. These again are compound units naming single laws, not real phrases.

(37) *Prov. cons.* 19 *quis plenior inimicorum fuit C. Mario? L. Crassus M. Scaurus alieni, inimici omnes Metelli*, 'Who ever had more enemies than Gaius Marius? Were not Lucius Crassus and Marcus Scaurus ill-disposed towards him? Were not all the Metelli his enemies?' (Gardner, Loeb).

Marius had many enemies, and this cannot be intended as the totality. The pair is *exempli gratia* again, and it is set off from *omnes Metelli* by the presence of separate predicates (*alieni, inimici*) with the two groups of names.

(38) *Prov. cons.* 37 *Ianuario Februario prouinciam non habebit: Kalendis ei denique Martiis nascetur repente prouincia*, 'During January, February he will have no province; all at once, on the first day of March, a province will be found for him' (Gardner, Loeb, modified).

The first two months of the year are listed as examples of province-free months for the referent, to be followed by an arbitrary acquisition of a province in March.

2.3 Adjectives

(39) *S. Rosc.* 19 *homo* tenuis libertinus, *cliens et familiaris istius T. Rosci*

The Loeb translation (Freese) is: 'a man of no means, a freedman, a client and intimate acquaintance of this Titus Roscius'. On this interpretation the division of the first three words is: [*homo tenuis*] [*libertinus*], with *libertinus* used as a noun. The asyndeton would be phrasal rather than of the single-word type. On the other hand *libertinus* is primarily an adjective, and it often modifies *homo* (*TLL* VII.2.1320.39f.). If it is taken as adjectival, the structure becomes [*homo*] [*tenuis libertinus*], with an adjectival asyndeton bimembre. *Cliens* by contrast is a noun, and *familiaris* too is substantival, and it cannot be taken as modifying *homo*. There may thus be two pairs, with the second consisting of two nominal elements linked by *et*. The combination of an asyndeton with a pair coordinated was seen frequently above in uses of nouns (1, 3, 4, 8, 10). I have decided to take *tenuis libertinus* as a pair of asyndetic adjectives, but even if we take *libertinus* as a noun there is still an asyndetic pair, followed by a coordinated pair of different semantic type.

(40) *S. Rosc.* 131 *(Iuppiter)* optimus maximus

(41) *S. Rosc.* 152 *ex altera parte* egentem, probatum suis *filium*, 'on the other side a son needy, but esteemed by his intimates'.

The second member is extended. *Egens* is commonly in asyndeta (see on Virgil 1, which is quoted in the commentary on 42 immediately below, with cross references, and particularly Sallust 52; also, on *indigus*, XXIV.7.2 on Lucretius 25). This asyndeton seems to be adversative.

(42) *Cat.* 2.14 *non de spe conatuque depulsus, sed* indemnatus innocens *in exsilium eiectus*

A pair of privative adjectives, secondary predictes, in agreement with the unexpressed subject of the verb ('... hurled into exile, uncondemned, innocent'). There are similar patterns in Virgil. Here are two examples where just one of the adjectives agreeing with the subject is a privative: *Aen.* 1.384 (1) *ipse ignotus egens Libyae deserta peragro*, *Aen.* 2.67–8 (2) *conspectu in medio turbatus inermis | constitit.*

Cf. Livy 35.34.7 *obtestantes ne insontem indemnatum consenescere in exsilio sinerent* (see VI.2.2 on the type). See also Livy 34. For asyndeton in such contexts (referring to exclusion, etc.) see below, 71 (with further references), Sallust 52 and 7.8.2 below.

2 *Data: Speeches* 419

(43) *Cat.* 3.23 *Iouis* optimi maximi

(44) *Red. sen.* 14 *sine sensu sine sapore, elinguem,* tardum inhumanum *negotium, Cappadocem modo abreptum de grege uenalium diceres*

Elinguem, tardum, inhumanum cannot all modify *negotium* (a derogatory term applied to a person, 'thing' or the like: see *OLD* s.v. 12b), because *elinguem* is of the wrong gender (though it could be emended). If the three adjectives were a tricolon (i.e. all masculine), they would have to be detached from *negotium* ('you would say he was [without feeling, without taste], [tongue-tied, slow, inhuman], [a thing]'). But detaching *negotium* from adjectives that immediately precede it does not look right, particularly since the other examples of *negotium* in this sense cited by the *OLD* are accompanied by an adjective. We could construe either as [*elinguem, tardum*] [*inhumanum negotium*], or as [*elinguem*] [*tardum inhumanum negotium*]. The latter must be right. Two other examples of *negotium* in Cicero (*Att.* 1.13.6, 6.1.13) are modified by *lentum* (e.g. 1.13.6 *Teucris illa lentum negotium est*, 'that Teucris is an infernal slow-coach', Shackleton Bailey 1965–70), and that makes it likely that the synonymous *tardum* goes with *negotium*, and if that is so, *inhumanum* must go with it too. Moreover, asyndetic pairs of adjectives constantly have a negative in *in-* in the second position (see e.g. XXIV.2.1.1 after Virgil **15**). Construed in this way the units *elinguem*, and *tardum inhumanum negotium*, become the first two members of an ascending tricolon (followed by the longer *Cappadocem modo abreptum de grege uenalium*).

Thus, in a series of three adjectives that could in theory be taken as a tricolon comprising three masculine accusatives, there is an embedded asyndetic pair of neuter adjectives. The Loeb (Watts 1923) punctuates *elinguem, tardum, inhumanum negotium* and translates 'tongue-tied, a dull and brutish clod', construing as I suggest (though not making that clear by punctuation), whereas the Budé (Wuilleumier 1952), punctuating in the same way, translates (from *sine sensu*) 'un être stupide, insipide, muet, lourdaud, un objet grossier', thus dividing as [*elinguem, tardum*] [*inhumanum negotium*]. Shackleton Bailey (1991) translates (from *sine*) 'a mindless, colorless [with a note saying 'lit. "flavorless"'], tongue-tied, dull, churlish specimen', thereby not addressing the problem (and in effect translating as if *elinguem* were *elingue*).

Elinguem could be paraphrased as *sine lingua*, and semantically it thus belongs with the preceding pair, and that is another reason for ruling out [*elinguem, tardum*] [*inhumanum negotium*]. For asyndetic phrases with *sine* associated with privative adjectives in asyndeta see **48** below, XXIX.2.1.4.7

and Livy 42 *ut quisque arma ceperat, sine imperio sine signo, incompositi inordinati in proelium ruunt.*

(45, 46) *Red. sen.* 30 *tribunatus nihil aliud fuit nisi constans perpetua, fortis inuicta defensio salutis meae*

The first two adjectives refer to the constancy of the defence of Cicero's safety, the second two to its strength/invincibility. If we take the four adjectives as forming two pairs, in each pair the second caps the first ('constant and indeed everlasting, strong and indeed invincible'). The OCT (Peterson) has no commas, and the Loeb translation (Watts) treats the adjectives as a tetracolon ('a firm, unceasing, brave, and undaunted championship of my well-being').

(47) *Dom.* 14 *Iouis optimi maximi*

(48) *Dom.* 139 *id quod imperitus adulescens, nouus sacerdos, sororis precibus, matris minis adductus, ignarus inuitus, sine conlegis sine libris sine auctore sine fictore . . . fecisse dicatur,* 'what an inexperienced youth, a new priest, led on by the prayers of his sister and threats of his mother, without knowledge, without will, without colleagues, books, without a prompter, an acolyte, is said to have done'.

For *inuitus* opposed to *ignarus* see *TLL* VII.2.235.58f., but only the present example is notable. This does not seem to be a usual pair. On the structure see on 44. I assume that the four terms with repeated *sine* form a tetracolon and do not consist of two pairs, though the final two nouns are marked by assonance. See also VI.2.2.

(49) *Sest.* 1 *uno aspectu intueri potestis eos qui cum senatu cum bonis omnibus, rem publicam adflictam excitarint et latrocinio domestico liberarint, maestos sordidatos reos, de capite de fama de ciuitate de fortunis de liberis dimicantis,* 'you can (on the one hand) see at a glance that those who joined the senate and all patriots in reviving the commonwealth when it was battered and rescuing it from the assault of domestic brigands are now defendants, distraught and clad in mourning, waging desperate struggles in which their lives as citizens, their reputations, their role in the community, their fortunes, and their children are at stake' (Kaster 2006).

Maestos sordidatos, 'distraught and clad in mourning', of associated meanings, I take as semantically detached from the long phrase ending with *dimicantis*. A sequence of five prepositional terms immediately follows the adjectival pair, a type of accumulation seen above in 48. Earlier in the passage there is a phrasal asyndeton bimembre, with prepositional

2 Data: Speeches

anaphora, *cum senatu cum bonis omnibus*, which might have been numbered if such partially phrasal pairs had been systematically collected (for *senatus* in asyndetic pairs see below, 186, 187).

(50) *Sest.* 85 *insigni quadam, inaudita noua magnitudine animi*
Translated by Kaster (2006) as 'with a remarkable, an unprecedented largeness of spirit'. He has taken *inaudita noua* as expressing a single concept.
I agree that *inaudita* and *noua* do not form a tricolon with *insigni* but are detached from and explanatory of it. *Insigni* may be attributive, with the other two predicative adjuncts, 'with, if I might say so [*quadam*], a remarkable largeness of spirit, (of a type) unheard of, novel'. *Nouus* is constantly combined with *inauditus* (usually with a coordinator): see *TLL* VII.1.837.62ff.

(51) *Sest.* 129 *Iouis optimi maximi*

(52, 53?) *Phil.* 1.33 *metui uero et in odio esse inuidiosum detestabile, imbecillum caducum*, '[b]ut to be feared and hated carries ill-will, execration, weakness, insecurity' (Loeb).
If this is a tetracolon, as it is translated here, its members at least have a semantic arrangement. The first two adjectives refer to extreme unpopularity, the second two to weakness. There is a point for debate here: are the two pairs sharply differentiated enough to be regarded as two asyndeta bimembria? With the second pair cf. Cic. *Leg.* 1.24 *quae fragilia essent et caduca*, and the next passage.

(54, 55) *Phil.* 4.13 *nam cum alia omnia falsa incerta sint, caduca mobilia*, '[w]hile all else is false and doubtful, ephemeral and inconstant'.
Two pairs, it seems, separated by the verb 'to be', the first referring to falsity, the second to a transitory character. For intrusive words defining asyndeta see above 9, with cross references. There seems little difference between the structure here and that in the previous passage, except that the copula is positioned differently. The intrusion of the copula here does suggest that Cicero tended to think in terms of pairs within longer sequences.
Cf. Sallust 59 *facies totius negoti uaria incerta, foeda atque miserabilis*; also 61 *genus hominum mobile infidum, ante neque beneficio neque metu coercitum*.

2.4 Verbs

(?) *Quinct.* 75 *omnes . . . adsunt defendunt, fides huius multis locis cognita ne perfidia Sex. Naeui derogetur laborant*, 'all . . . are here to support and defend him, and are doing their utmost to prevent my client's good faith, well known in many places, from being disparaged by the perfidious slanders of Naevius' (Freese, Loeb).

The first two verbs are semantically a unit, and then there is a much more detailed and specific clause. However, I interpret the structure as an ascending tricolon. For *adsunt* in asyndeton bimembre see Berry (1996: 253) on Cic. *Sul.* 61 *qui adsunt laborant*, citing *Div. Caec.* 11 *adsunt queruntur Siculi uniuersi* (add Plaut. *Aul.* 411a–12 *adest | sequitur, Truc.* 514 *adsum, adduco tibi exoptatum Stratophanem*). In the passage from *Quinct.* above *adsunt* is combined with *laborant*, as at *Sul.* 61, but there is an additional verb, *defendunt*, between the two.

(56) *Cat.* 1.20 *ecquid attendis, ecquid animaduertis horum silentium? patiuntur tacent*, 'do you observe, do you notice their silence? They endure, they say nothing.'

The second may look like a modifier: 'they suffer in silence' (cf. Tacitus 5 *silentio patientia*). However, Cicero is suggesting that the silence speaks (cf. a little later, at 21, *cum tacent, clamant*, 'when they are silent, they are shouting out'), and *tacent* above should be given its own independence. On the structure of this sentence see below, 7.2.3.

(57, 58) *Cat.* 1.32 *ut Catilinae profectione omnia patefacta inlustrata, oppressa uindicata esse uideatis*, 'that by the departure of Catiline you see that all has been revealed and made clear, crushed and punished'.

There are definitely two pairs here, the near-synonyms *patefacta inlustrata* (see Dyck 2008 121–2, noting that the two are elsewhere together, as at 3.21 *quae erant contra salutem omnium cogitata, inlustrata et patefacta uidistis*), indicating the revelation of the plot, and *oppressa uindicata*, of its crushing, a chronological sequence. Both the OCT (Clark) and Dyck punctuate with commas after each of the first three participles, mistakenly in my opinion. On inconsistencies of punctuation in such passages, see below, 7.7.

(?, ?) *Cat.* 2.1 *abiit excessit euasit erupit*

This tetracolon might arguably be split into two pairs. The first two verbs are near-synonyms and denote departure in a neutral way, and the second two are stronger and denote escape. For verbs of departure in asyndetic pairs see XXX.2.1, 5, and see below, 60. Quintilian 9.3.46 quotes the passage as an example of an accumulation of synonyms (as pointed out by Dyck 2008: 127), but there is a gradation here. Dyck observes that the final verb is the most violent. I leave the passage unnumbered because others have interpreted it differently.

2 Data: Speeches 423

(59) *Cat.* 2.6 *Catilina ipse pertimuit profugit*
This is a sentence in its own right. The pair has a temporal sequence, with the second verb conveying a consequence of the emotion expressed by the first (he 'took fright and fled'). Semantically the relationship between these two verbs is exactly the same as that between the nominal pair *fuga* and *formido*, on which see above, on 5–7, and here too alliteration is found, achieved by the addition of prefixes. In these verbal pairs in Cicero it is the semantic content that determines the order, and it is a matter of indifference whether the second is longer (in syllables) or not than the first. A pause would surely have occurred in speech, and an editor ought to use a comma, but I have followed my stated practice.

(60) *Cat.* 2.6 *exeant proficiscantur, ne patiantur desiderio sui Catilinam miserum tabescere*
There is probably again a temporal sequence, in that the primary meaning of *proficiscor* is 'start on a journey' (*OLD* s.v. 1a), whereas *exeo* need only mean 'go out'. See above on Cic. *Cat.* 2.1 (after 58) on such verbs in asyndetic pairs.

(61) *Cat.* 3.16 *appellare temptare sollicitare poterat audebat*
The second verb is stronger: he not only had the ability, but he actually dared to do these things. There would surely have been a pause between the two verbs in speech. Note the asyndetic accumulation, 3 + 2 (see XIX.1).

(62) *Red. sen.* 10 *me duo sceleratissimi post hominum memoriam non consules sed latrones non modo deseruerunt, ... sed prodiderunt oppugnarunt, omni auxilio non solum suo sed etiam uestro ceterorumque ordinum spoliatum esse uoluerunt*, 'the two most wicked men in human history, not consuls, but brigands, not only deserted me, but betrayed, attacked me, and they wanted me stripped of all help, not only from them but also from you and the rest of the orders'.

Possibly a clausal asyndetic tricolon starts at *sed prodiderunt*, but on the other hand the third clause (starting at *omni*) could be detached by a full-stop. The two asyndetic verbs *prodiderunt oppugnarunt* form the second part of a *non modo ... sed* construction, of which the following sentence/clause *omni auxilio ... esse uoluerunt* is not a necessary part. This following part is far more specific in content (and has its own *non solum ... sed etiam* construction within). Admittedly it is a subjective decision to treat the underlined pair here as an asyndeton bimembre, but that at *Quinct.* 75 above (after 55) as part of a tricolon.

For two asyndetic verbs forming an adversative clause (introduced here by *sed*) in Cicero, see **148** (but without *sed* expressed).

(63) *Red. sen.* 18 *uno eodemque tempore domus mea <u>diripiebatur ardebat</u>, bona ad uicinum consulem de Palatio, de Tusculano ad item uicinum alterum consulem deferebantur*, 'At one and the same moment my house was being plundered, was ablaze; the contents of that on the Palatine were being made over to the consul, my neighbour, and those of my villa at Tusculum to the other consul, also my neighbour' (Watts, Loeb).

The final verb *deferebantur* has a different subject (*bona*) from the pair *diripiebatur ardebat* (*domus*), and that sets it apart from them (cf. **66** below for a similar separation). The contexts and semantics of the pair are similar to those at **67**, **68** and **69**.

This example and the last (**62**) are similar. There is a pair of verbs at the end of a clause, and then the sentence continues in such a way that strong punctuation could be used.

(64, 65) *Dom.* 44, 47 *uelitis iubeatis*
On this old formula see XXII.5.2.

(66) *Dom.* 70 *de me rettulisti, legem <u>promulgasti tulisti</u>*, '.... you made a proposal about me, and promulgated and carried a law'.

Legem is object only of the last two verbs (the absolute use of *refero de* is illustrated at *OLD* 7b), which constitute an asyndeton detached from the first verb *rettulisti*. The verbs at the end of the sentence express what is seen as a damaging act to Cicero. The order of the final pair is determined by the meaning, not by a principle of ascending length. See XVI.3.

(67) *Dom.* 113 *quibus inspectantibus domus mea <u>disturbaretur diriperetur</u>*, 'who looked on while my house was being demolished and pulled to pieces'.

These have the same fore-element, and are near-synonyms, with the second perhaps more graphic than the first. They are at the end of a clause, and again describe a hostile act. Cf. **63** above for a similar pair in much the same context, and the next two examples. It looks as if asyndeton enhanced the expression of outrage, presumably because of a pattern of intonation that it admitted. For such repetitions of the prefix *dis-* see XXIV.5.2.4 on Ennius **18**, with cross references to Plautus, and Naevius *com.* 57 quoted at XXIV.8. For another two juxtaposed verbs in Cicero sharing the same prefix (*com-*) see below, **75**.

(68) *Dom.* 114 *tuum monumentum consulibus non modo inspectantibus uerum adiuuantibus <u>disturbaret uerteret</u>*, '(a tribune of the people) would

2 *Data: Speeches* 425

demolish, knock down your monument with the consuls not only looking on but helping'.
Similar to the above and to 63, with again the verbs near-synonyms. Note *disturbo* again, and also that the second verb has fewer syllables than the first.

(69) *Dom.* 137 *quod... <u>dirueris aedificaris</u>, religione omni uiolata religionis tamen nomine contaminaris, in uisceribus eius qui urbem suis laboribus ac periculis conseruasset monumentum deletae rei publicae conlocaris,* ..., 'your acts of pulling down and building up, of polluting all religion, and yet defiling your deeds by the name of religion, of planting a monument of the extinction of the republic in the dwelling of him who by his labours had preserved the city at the risk of his life ...' (Watts, Loeb).

The sequence continues with three asyndetic clauses containing similar verb forms, *contaminaris ... conlocaris ... incideris* (the last not quoted). On the construction see Nisbet (1939: 185), whose interpretation differs slightly from that of the above translation. The asyndetic pair comprises opposites (reversives: for the type see XIII.2), and I take it as an embedded pair in a longer sequence. For this same pair, see Hor. *Ep.* 1.1.100 at XXIX.2.2, *diruit aedificat, mutat quadrata rotundis,* and cf. too XXIV.7.1.3 on Lucretius 15.
The pair is at the end of a colon, expressing actions disapproved of.

(70) *Sest.* 21 *et quod erat eo nomine ut ingenerata familiae frugalitas uideretur, <u>fauebant gaudebant</u>, et ad integritatem maiorum spe sua hominem uocabant materni generis obliti.* 'and because his name suggested that sober soundness was innate in his household, they were pleased to back him and in their hopes summoned him to match the uprightness of his ancestors – forgetting his mother's lineage the while', Kaster (2006).

Note that Kaster translates as if the two verbs *fauebant gaudebant* are not independent of each other. They form one of those asyndeta bimembria that are followed by a much longer clause attached by *et*, which has a more precise content than the asyndetic pair.

The pair could be paraphrased as *fauebant gaudentes,* 'they favoured him, rejoicing', = 'they were pleased to favour him', with the second verb a modifier of the first. See II.3.2.3.1 on such pairs.

(71) *Sest.* 29 *ut ex urbe <u>expulerit relegarit</u> non dico equitem Romanum, ... sed ciuem Romanum*
Near-synonyms ('expelled, banished'), but the second is stronger. The next section (30) makes clear that the banishment is the true outrage. For

asyndetic pairs in the context of expulsion or exile see 42 above and 7.8.2 below, and also Sallust 24, Virgil 22 at XXIV.2.2, Livy 34.

(72) *Pis.* 59 *fertur ille uir, mihi crede, gloria:* flagrat ardet *cupiditate iusti et magni triumphi*, 'that fellow, believe me, is carried away with lust for glory: he is ablaze, on fire with desire for a just and great triumph'.

Near-synonyms. Cf. Lucr. 4.1199 (XXIV.7.1.3, 14) *si non ipsa quod illarum* subat ardet *abundans | natura*. On the structure of the sentence see below, 7.2.3.

(73) *Phil.* 2.84 *apparet esse commotum:* sudat pallet

Closely related near-symptoms of disturbance, defining *commotum* ('he sweats, turns pale'). But agitation would be manifested by other features, and this is an open-ended list. Again, for the structure see below, 7.2.3.

(74) *Phil.* 2.89 *cum ceteri consulares* irent redirent, 'while the other consulars were going back and forth'.

Opposites (reversives). For this formula, which is frequent, not least in Cicero, see Preuss (1881: 39). Reversives may express reversals of direction, as here (cf. *rise and fall, rise and set* (of the sun), *come and go, advance and retreat*). See also XXIX.4.2.2 on Hor. *Ep.* 1.7.55 *it redit et narrat*.

(75) *Phil.* 5.36 *cumque exercitum tantum* ... conscripserit compararit, 'whereas he has enrolled and mustered ... such a large army'.

This is from a proposed senatorial decree. There is a temporal sequence in the two verbs. Both verbs have the same prefix (cf. 67). The pair is at the end of the clause.

A significant number of the asyndeta bimembria in our sample of Cicero are in religious and particularly legal/official phrases or contexts (see 7.8.1).

This passage may be compared with the following: *Sest.* 34 *cum uicatim homines* conscriberentur decuriarentur, *ad uim ad manus, ad caedem ad direptionem incitarentur*, 'as street by street people were enlisted, formed up into squads, and incited to violent assault, murder, and plunder' (Kaster 2006). *Decurio* means literally 'form cavalry into units of ten men', and thus the juxtaposed verbs *conscriberentur decuriarentur* refer to enrolment of units and are very similar to the pair in 75. In this case though I take the two verbs as members of a tricolon. The long clause that follows refers to subsequent action, the instigation of the units to acts of violence. It is notable for the two unitary pairs of prepositional asyndeta. This is another passage that raises issues of definition: should we talk of an asyndeton bimembre embedded within a tricolon? Cf. 62 and 69, where the same

2 Data: Speeches

problem is encountered and where, somewhat arbitrarily, I have adopted a different interpretation.

(76) *Phil.* 5.46 *libertatem populi Romani defendant defe<nde>rint* '(legions) are defending and have defended the liberty of the Roman people'.

Cicero moves a senatorial decree, from which these words come. Earlier in the speech there were two examples of *praesideo* in different tenses, but joined by *atque* (5.37). At 5.53 in another such motion there is *qui . . . auctoritatemque huius ordinis defenderint atque defendant*, where the coordinator produces a better clausula (see IX.1).

The asyndetic combination of two verbs in different moods or tenses is dealt with separately (IX). It is a feature in Latin of laws (cf. too XXII.2.1, 2.2, 7.1) and curse tablets.

(77, 78) *Phil.* 5.53 *utique C. Pansa A. Hirtius consules, alter amboue, si eis uideretur, rationem agri habe<re>nt qui sine iniuria priuatorum diuidi posset, eisque militibus, legioni Martiae et legioni quartae ita darent adsignarent ut quibus militibus amplissime dati adsignati essent*, 'further, that the consuls Gaius Pansa and Aulus Hirtius, either or both, if they see fit, take cognizance of lands available for division without prejudice to individuals and do grant and assign such land to the said soldiers, the Martian legion, and the Fourth Legion in terms no less liberal than any hitherto used in such grants and assignments'.

This is another senatorial motion with two pairs of verbs. For *dare adsignare* in asyndeton see *Lex repetundarum* (Crawford 1996: 1.65) 2 *d(andeis) a(dsignandeis)*, *Lex agraria* (Crawford 1996: 1.113) 3, 5, 7 *dedit adsignauit*. In the Ciceronian passage the two verbs in asyndeton are repeated in the same sentence in a different form. For that feature of legal language see *Lex de Gallia Cisalpina* (Crawford 1996: 1.465) XX.43–4 *includ<a>ntur concipiantur, quae includei concipei . . . oporteret*, *Lex de prouinciis praetoribus*, Delphi copy, block C (Crawford 1996: 1.251) ll. 15–19 *quosque facere iurare oportebit, faciunto iuranto*.

2.5 Adverbs

(79) *Dom.* 68 *omnia contra leges moresque maiorum temere turbulente, per uim per furorem esse gesta*

The accumulation of asyndeta (adverbs plus an asyndetic prepositional pair) is not unlike that at Tacitus 153 *crebra hinc proelia, et saepius in modum latrocinii per saltus per paludes, ut cuique sors aut uirtus, temere prouiso, ob iram ob praedam, iussu et aliquando ignaris ducibus.*

Temere is also in an asyndeton in Livy 54: *nec quicquam raptim aut forte temere egeritis*.

(80?) *Sest.* 83 *luce palam a nefariis pestibus in deorum hominumque conspectu esset occisus*

Luce palam is a widespread combination (Preuss 1881: 58), translated here by Kaster (2006) as 'in broad daylight'. Is it really an asyndetic coordination? *Luce* on its own can mean 'in broad daylight' (see *OLD* s.v. *lux* 3b; *luce/luci* alone may = *luci clara*). *Palam* may be an appositional specifier, 'in broad daylight, i.e. openly'. For another pair with *palam* that is of ambiguous interpretation (in a different way) see Plaut. *Aul.* 188 *perspicue palam est* (XXIII Appendix).

2.6 Prepositional Type

(81) *Cat.* 4.18 *de uestra uita, de coniugum uestrarum atque liberorum anima, de fortunis omnium, de sedibus de focis uestris*

The first two (asyndetic) phrases form a semantic unit, denoting in effect 'your lives and those of your families'. *Sedes* and *foci* are near-synonyms, denoting households (cf. *arae foci* at 16, and particularly *in domo in sedibus, in aris in focis* at 85 below). This pair is an asyndeton bimembre within a longer sequence. *De fortunis omnium* is separate from the following pair because it has a different modifier (*omnium* ... *uestris*). *Sedes* and *focus* sometimes occur in asyndetic sequences (*Dom.* 106).

(82) *Red. sen.* 14 *sine sensu sine sapore, elinguem, tardum inhumanum negotium, Cappadocem modo abreptum de grege uenalium diceres*

On this passage see above, 44.

(83) *Dom.* 68 *omnia contra leges moresque maiorum temere turbulente, per uim per furorem esse gesta*

See above, 79.

(84) *Dom.* 138 *ex senatus consulto, ex lege*

(85) *Dom.* 143 *haec restitutio in domo in sedibus, in aris in focis in dis penatibus reciperandis*

A pair of near-synonyms similar to that at 81, and then a tricolon (structure 2 + 3). On *arae foci* with and without *penates* see above, 16. The distinction is between the house as a home, and its religious contents and significance.

(86) *Sest.* 5 *de omni statu P. Sesti, de genere uitae, de natura de moribus, de incredibili amore in bonos, de studio conseruandae salutis communis atque oti*
Natura and *mores* are near-synonyms. Do we have here a prepositional asyndeton bimembre within a long series of prepositional phrases? The last two phrases fit together, in that both denote the remarkable support given by Sestius to worthy causes. The first two phrases also form a unit of sorts, of station in life (see *OLD* s.v. *status*) and way of life. There are arguably three pairs, one of them referring to his character.
For a similar pair containing *mores* see Tacitus 78.

(87, 88) *Sest.* 34 *cum uicatim homines conscriberentur decuriarentur, ad uim ad manus, ad caedem ad direptionem incitarentur*
The prepositional expressions that are part of this final clause fall into two pairs. *Vis manus* is a frequent juxtaposition in Cicero, sometimes in longer sequences (see in this speech 2, 78, 85; see the commentary on the last, above, 14), denoting physical force. *Caedes* and *direptio* express the consequence of the use of force, slaughter and pillage. For this latter combination, again sometimes in longer sequences, see Cic. *Dom.* 25, *Sest.* 46, Livy 32.21.23 (*caedes direptionesque*), *TLL* III.55.51.

(89?) *Pis.* 64 *quae per latrones per seruos de me egeras*
I include this example only tentatively. The asyndeton is in P but otherwise *et per* is written. It is impossible on linguistic grounds to determine what is right in such a case. If the pair had been part of an accumulation, it would have been justifiable to opt for asyndeton.

(90) *Phil.* 1.24 *de prouinciis de iudiciis.*

3 Data: Philosophica

3.1 Nouns

(91) *Fin.* 1.27 *maledicta contumeliae, tum iracundae contentiones concertationesque in disputando pertinaces indignae philosophia mihi uideri solent,* 'abuse, insults, and in addition angry disputes and persistent conflicts in debate generally seem to me unworthy of philosophy'.
The initial asyndetic pair comprises near-synonyms. It is marked off from what follows by *tum* (cf. 138 for *tum* used thus, and also, with different dividers in the philosophica, 116, 119, 127, 133, 151; also above, 9).
On pairs denoting vices or disapproved behaviour in asyndeton see below, 7.8.2.

(92, 93) *Fin.* 2.23 <u>mundos elegantis</u>, *optimis* <u>cocis pistoribus</u>, *piscatu aucupio uenatione, his omnibus exquisitis, uitantis cruditatem*, 'men of taste, elegance – with the best cooks and bakers, fish, birds, game, all these choice things – avoiding indigestion'.

There are two pairs here, in a long asyndetic sequence. The first two terms are near-synonyms, and *cocis pistoribus* denotes preparers of food of closely related types (with an adjective modifying both: [*optimis*] [*cocis pistoribus*]). The structure is 2 + 2 + 3 (for which see below, this section, 117, 118), followed by a summary. See Reid (1925: 133) on the summarising use of *haec omnia* after asyndeton, and on this form of summary in general see further above, 1, and XVIII.6.

(94, 95, 96, 97, 98) *Fin.* 2.36 *quid iudicant sensus?* <u>dulce amarum, leue asperum, prope longe, stare mouere, quadratum rotundum</u>, 'what do the senses adjudicate on? Sweetness and sourness, smoothness and roughness, proximity and distance, standing still and moving, square and round'.

Strictly there are adjectives, adverbs and verbs here, but they are used substantivally and I include them together instead of scattering them about. All pairs (except the last) express opposites (*stare* = 'standing still') of various types, antonyms in the first three cases (see XIII.5.4 on 'near/far'), and virtual complementarities in the fourth (strictly something meaning 'being still' rather than 'standing/sitting still' would be needed to constitute a complementarity). 'Square' and 'round' are contrasting shapes but not strictly opposites. For this opposition see Hor. *Ep.* 1.1.100 *diruit aedificat, mutat quadrata rotundis*. For such series cf. *Nat.* 2.146 *canorum fuscum, leue asperum, graue acutum, flexibile durum* (musical terms: see Pease 1958: 930–1 for commentary), *Ac.* 2.92 *diues pauper, clarus obscurus sit, multa pauca, magna parua, longa breuia, lata angusta*, *Orat.* 131 *sed est faciendum etiam ut irascatur iudex, mitigetur, inuideat faueat, contemnat admiretur, oderit diligat, cupiat fastidiat, speret metuat, laetetur doleat*, *Tusc.* 5.114 *Democritus luminibus amissis alba scilicet discernere et atra non poterat, at uero bona mala, aequa iniqua, honesta turpia, utilia inutilia, magna parua poterat* (cf. too *Ac.* 2.125, quoted at XIII.5.4). Two features of the list at *Orat.* 131 should be noted. First, the first asyndetic pair is discontinuous (split by the noun *iudex*). Second, the order of the terms, with favourable versus unfavourable meaning, is reversed halfway through the series. The first four pairs show the order unfavourable–favourable, the last three favourable–unfavourable. This is a sequence which brings out the stylised character of such accumulated oppositions.

3 Data: Philosophica

On the Vedic merism 'what moves or stands still' see West (2007: 101), and see also below on 112.

Some schools of philosophy found contrary principles or elements at work, and the contraries are sometimes expressed asyndetically in Greek too. Here are two passages from Aristotle's *Metaphysics*:

1.5.6 (986a23) ἕτεροι δὲ τῶν αὐτῶν τούτων τὰς ἀρχὰς δέκα λέγουσιν εἶναι τὰς κατὰ συστοιχίαν λεγομένας, πέρας ἄπειρον, περιττὸν ἄρτιον, ἕν πλῆθος, δεξιὸν ἀριστερόν, ἄρρεν θῆλυ, ἠρεμοῦν κινούμενον, εὐθὺ καμπύλον, φῶς σκότος, ἀγαθὸν κακόν, τετράγωνον ἑτερόμηκες, 'Others of this same school hold that there are ten principles, which they enunciate in a series of corresponding pairs: (i.) Limit and the Unlimited; (ii.) Odd and Even; (iii.) Unity and Plurality; (iv.) Right and Left; (v.) Male and Female; (vi.) Rest and Motion; (vii.) Straight and Crooked; (viii.) Light and Darkness; (ix.) Good and Evil; (x.) Square and Oblong' (Tredennick, Loeb).

1.5.7 (986a32) λέγων τὰς ἐναντιότητας οὐχ ὥσπερ οὗτοι διωρισμένας ἀλλὰ τὰς τυχούσας, οἷον λευκὸν μέλαν, γλυκὺ πικρόν, ἀγαθὸν κακόν, μέγα μικρόν, 'but the contraries which he [Alcmaeon] mentions are not, as in the case of the Pythagoreans, carefully defined, but are taken at random, e.g. white and black, sweet and bitter, good and bad, great and small' (Loeb). Alcmaeon thought that the 'majority of things in the world of men are in pairs'.

Note that asyndetic 'rest and motion' is in the first passage of Aristotle, as well as in that of Cicero. 'Bitter and sweet' is in Cicero and the second passage of Aristotle.

There is a similar series of opposites in Greek in a letter of Fronto, in a context in which a switch of languages from Latin to Greek takes place (p. 41.16–18 van den Hout 1988). For pairs of opposites in Greek, sometimes in sequences, see Kühner and Gerth (1898–1904: II.346), Denniston (1952: 103).

(99) *Fin.* 2.76 *officium aequitatem dignitatem fidem, recta honesta, digna imperio, digna populo Romano, omnia pericula pro re publica, mori pro patria*, 'duty, fairness, worth, loyalty, things right and honourable, that which is worthy of power, worthy of the Roman people, all dangers undertaken for the state, dying for one's country'.

A long asyndetic sequence, comprising, first, four single words before the pair *recta honesta*, and then four phrases, the first two of balanced structure. *Recta honesta* I take as an embedded unitary pair (of substantival adjectives), near-synonyms. See *Fin.* 2.56 for the pairing, with coordinator, in a context in which the terms are adjectival; also *Leg.* 1.37 *qui omnia recta atque honesta per se expetenda duxerunt.*

(100) *Fin.* 2.77 omnes <u>urbani rustici</u>, omnes, inquam, qui Latine loquuntur, 'all city dwellers, all country dwellers, all, I say, who speak Latin'.

This is a pair of opposites expressing a totality. What is interesting here is that by adding 'all, I say, who speak Latin', Cicero seems to define the pair as a merism (*urbani rustici* = 'all Latin speakers'), from the point of view of a Roman. For the 'town/country' opposition, see above, 19, with XIII.5.1.

(101) *Fin.* 2.85 *at quicum <u>ioca seria</u>, ut dicitur, quicum arcana, quicum occulta omnia?*

Antonyms. The pair usually has a coordinator, but cf. Tacitus 156 *per seria per iocos* (Preuss 1881: 34–5). Notable is *ut dicitur.* Occasionally remarks such as this point to the proverbial status of an asyndetic pair (see XIII.5.4 and XXVII.1.1, where Donatus on Ter. *Ad.* 990 is cited).

(102) *Fin.* 2.107 *haec leuiora ponam: <u>poema orationem</u> cum aut scribis aut legis, cum omnium factorum, cum regionum conquiris historiam signum tabula locus amoenus ludi uenatio,* 'I shall now mention a few less serious things, as when you either write or read a poem, a speech, or investigate the history of a set of events or of regions; statue, picture, picturesque place, games, beast hunt.'

This (disjunctive) pair comprises an open-ended list, as there are other genres of writing. Cf. below, 157 *in poematis in picturis* for forms of artistic composition paired asyndetically. The terms from *signum* to *uenatio* would have been expected to be in the accusative, but instead they form a detached nominative list: see Adams 2013: 216–20. For *signum tabula* see above on 22.

(?) *Fin.* 4.21 *omnium <u>insipientiam iniustitiam</u>, alia uitia similia esse, omniaque peccata esse paria,* '(the view that) everyone's folly, injustice and other vices are similar, and all sins equal'.

This might just be taken to be an embedded asyndeton bimembre, comprising a pair of vices with each term having the privative prefix, followed by a generalisation embracing these vices and the others as well. However, all three nouns are subject of the same verb and share the same predicate (*similia esse*), and I classify the structure as an ascending tricolon. See however above, 11, 27 for such nominal pairs with at least one privative prefix.

3 Data: Philosophica 433

(103) *Fin.* 4.69 <u>frigus famem</u> *propulsare possimus necne possimus*, 'whether we are able or not able to ward off cold, hunger'.

These alliterative terms, expressing hardships with an external cause, are often paired, but usually with a coordinator or in a longer sequence (see Wölfflin 1933: 261 for a long list of examples, e.g. Catull. 28.5 *frigoraque et famem*, Livy 21.40.9). At Lucilius 7 (XXV.1.1.2) however an asyndetic pairing is clearly a unit embedded within a longer sequence containing otherwise semantically related *in-*compounds. See also below, 7.8.2, alluding to Plaut. *Men.* 974–5 at XXIII.7.3. These two hardships constitute a selective list. They are often endured together (and the alliteration connects them further), but they are only two of the difficulties confronting those who are abandoned or persecuted (cf. Plato *Euthphr.* 4d ὑπὸ γὰρ λιμοῦ καὶ ῥίγους καὶ τῶν δεσμῶν ἀποθνῄσκει, 'he died of hunger and cold and his bonds'). On this type of pairing see IV.3.

(104) *Fin.* 5.36 *prioris generis est* <u>docilitas memoria</u>; *quae fere omnia appellantur uno ingeni nomine, easque uirtutes qui habent ingeniosi uocantur*, 'in the first category there are learning ability, memory; practically all of which characteristics are called by the single term "talent", and possessors of those virtues are called "talented"'.

Cicero has said that the mind has two *genera uirtutum*, and he now gives just two examples of the first type. Note *quae fere omnia*, which implies that the type has more members than two. This is a classic example of an open-ended list. See above, 11, and the passage from a letter of Timarchides quoted by Cicero, *Verr.* 3.154 *habes uirtutem eloquentiam*. Selective pairs of virtues/attributes and vices are often expressed in this way, asyndetically (see below, 7.8.2) and at the end of a colon. See further IV.3.

(105) *Fin.* 5.52 *quid cum uolumus nomina eorum qui quid gesserint nota nobis esse,* <u>parentes patriam</u>, *multa praeterea minime necessaria*, 'what of our wish to know the names of those who have achieved something, their parents, place of origin, and many unnecessary details besides'.

Another sequence that is difficult to classify (see e.g. above, 1, 2). *Parentes patriam* is a well-established (alliterative) pairing (see on Sallust 17), and the third element of the sequence is detached from it by *praeterea* and also semantically, in that it is a non-specific generalisation. For this use of *praeterea* see on Sallust 33. Arguably there is a unitary asyndeton bimembre within a tricolon (see also XVIII.4, 6).

(106) *Fin.* 5.62 *quis contra in illa aetate pudorem constantiam* ... *non tamen diligat?*, 'but who on the contrary would not admire modesty and steadfastness in those of that age?'

The nouns have the same role as asyndetic adjectives in the previous sentence: *quis est qui non oderit libidinosam, proteruam adulescentiam?* (see below, 134). Immoral and moral youth are contrasted, with immorality expressed adjectivally and morality by abstract nouns. I have kept in this note the punctuation of Reynolds (OCT), who puts commas between the asyndetic adjectives but juxtaposes the asyndetic nouns without punctuation. The point of this variation is not clear. See below, 7.7 on the inconsistent use of commas by editors.

Again we have an asyndetic pair denoting virtues (see e.g. above, this section, 104).

(107) *Fin.* 5.89 *sed tu etiam, Chrysippe, in foro, domi: in schola desinis*, 'but you too, Chrysippus, do so in public, at home; you stop in the lecture room'.

An interesting example, because *in foro, domi* replicates the adjectival asyndeton *forensis, domesticus* (opposites, of the 'public/private' type: see XIII.4.1, 5.2, and below, 160) found elsewhere in Cicero (see 197, 198, 202, 203). Cf. too *domos fora* at Tacitus 76. This pair demonstrates that an asyndeton bimembre need not consist of terms that are grammatically identical (on which point see I.1, XXIV.5.1.2, XXIII.5.4 on Plaut. *Rud.* 186, XXIII Appendix on *As.* 562). Here Reynolds uses a comma, correctly in my opinion because of the grammatical difference.

(108?, 109?, 110, 111) *Off.* 1.53 *forum fana, porticus uiae, leges iura, iudicia suffragia, consuetudines praeterea et familiaritates* (things common to citizens).

There may possibly be a series of five pairs here, the last coordinated. *Leges* and *iura* certainly go together (cf. Preuss 1881: 86), as do *iudicia* and *suffragia* and *consuetudines* and *familiaritates*. *Forum* and *fana* are both public meeting places, secular and religious, and *porticus* and *uiae* are constructions that serve as walkways. Note Tacitus 88 *deseri itinera fora*. The first two pairs are not however sharply defined, and I have included them tentatively.

(112) *Off.* 1.102 *uultus uoces, motus statusque*

There are certainly two pairs here, the second coordinated. For the first in asyndeton, which is a variant on the combination of *uerba* and *uultus*, cf.

Tacitus 77 *non temperante Tiberio quin premeret uoce uultu, eo quod ipse creberrime interrogabat*, and see further Tacitus 58 and the commentary there on comparable pairs.

Status refers to the state of standing still, and is the virtual opposite of *motus*, though it probably has a derived sense here (e.g. 'position adopted'). We saw the asyndetic pair *stare mouere* at 97 above, and it was pointed out that there was a Vedic merism 'what moves or stands still' (West 2007: 101). For the same pair as that here, coordinated, see below, 116. West loc. cit. cites Greek examples of this opposition.

On the punctuation of this pair see below, 7.7.

(113, 114, 115?) *Off.* 1.115 *nam regna imperia, nobilitas honores, diuitiae opes*
These are possibly three pairs (denoting forms of rule, types of distinctions and wealth, the last expressed by near-synonyms), but on the other hand a number of the terms are mixed up at *Tusc.* 5.45 *da diuitias honores imperia opes gloriam* and Tacitus 89 *opes honores*; see also on Sallust 9, 10. *Diuitiae* and *opes* are often together (*TLL* V.1.1633.74ff.: e.g. Cic. *De orat.* 2.342, again in a long asyndetic series). For *nobilitas* in asyndetic pairs see Tacitus 15, 108, and for *honores*, Sallust 10, Tacitus 89, 112. With the first pair cf. Sallust's *regna prouinciae* (29). For power and wealth contrasted in asyndeton see below, 153.

(116) *Off.* 1.126 *sed quoniam decorum illud in omnibus factis dictis, in corporis denique motu et statu cernitur*, 'but since that form of decorum shows itself in every deed and word, and finally in movement and posture of the body'.

First an asyndetic pair, and then a coordinated pair joined by *et* and introduced by *denique* (for *denique* introducing a coordinated pair after an asyndetic, see also above, 1 and XVIII.6). The two pairs are separated by the repetition of *in*, a type of colon division referred to at e.g. 15 and more generally at 91 above. For the complementary pair *facta dicta* see 195. For the second, coordinated, pair see above, 112.

On the interpretation of the second pair here and those in the next passage see XIII.4.1.

(117, 118) *Off.* 1.128 *status incessus, sessio accubito, uoltus oculi manuum motus teneat illud decorum*, 'let our standing or walking, sitting or reclining, our expressions, eyes, movements of the hands, preserve that propriety'.

Two pairs of complementary asyndetic terms, followed by an (ascending) tricolon (structure 2 + 2 + 3, for which see above, 92, 93). *Status* and *incessus* designate two contrasting forms of being on one's feet, motionless or in motion, and *sessio* and *accubito* two contrasting forms of being off one's feet, sitting or lying. Cf. *Fin.* 5.35 *sessiones quaedam et flexi fractique motus*, and below, **137**. West (2007: 101) cites from the *Mahābhārata* 12.161.21 a formula 'sitting and lying, walking and standing'.

Incessus 'moving forward' is not strictly an opposite of standing still. One who is not standing still need not be moving forward: see XIII.4.1.

(**119**) *Off.* 2.11 *partim sunt inanima, ut <u>aurum argentum</u>, ut ea quae gignuntur e terra, ut alia generis eiusdem*

There is first an asyndeton bimembre denoting two precious metals regularly mentioned together, in asyndeton but also coordinated (see Preuss 1881: 79, and also **21** above), and then a phrasal pair. The repetitions of *ut* reveal the phrase divisions (cf. **91**). Note the quotation from a bill at Cic. *Leg. Agr.* 2.59, a regulation that 'concerns the treatment of war booty' (Manuwald 2018: 318): *aurum argentum ex praeda ex manubiis ex coronario ad quoscumque peruenit.* Pease (1963: 362) refers to the title *tresuiri auro argento aere flando feriundo.* Note Hor. *Ep.* 1.1.52 *uilius argentum est auro*, which shows the reason for the usual order of the pair.

(**120, 121**) *Off.* 2.37 *uita mors, diuitiae paupertas omnes homines uehementissime permouent*

Two pairs of opposites, the first complementarities, the second antonyms (see XIII.2). For *diuitiae* and *paupertas* together see *TLL* V.1.455.78f. (e.g. Lucr. 1.455 *paupertas diuitiaeque*). Cf. also Hor. *Sat.* 2.1.59 *diues inops* (XXIX.2.1.1), Tacitus **115** *sed mirum quam inter diuersi generis ordinis, aetatis sexus, <u>dites pauperes</u> taciturnitate omnia cohibita sint*. For a coordination of *uita* and *mors* see Sen. *Dial.* 11.16.2, and cf. the phrase *uitae necisque potestas* (Cic. *Dom.* 77, Caes. *Gall.* 1.16.5).

Winterbottom (OCT) does not indicate the presence of two pairs by putting a comma after *mors*. The two pairs are so obviously units, and it is so likely that there would have been a pause between them in speech, that in my view a comma is essential (see below, 7.7).

(**122**) *Off.* 2.67 *commendantem <u>iudicibus magistratibus</u>*, 'by witnessing to their character before jurors, magistrates'.

Types of officials listed. See below, **186, 187**, and on Tacitus **16** for asyndeta of this type, and XXII.7.2.

(**123, 124**) *Off.* 3.70 *idque uersari <u>in tutelis societatibus, fiduciis mandatis, rebus emptis uenditis, conductis locatis</u>, quibus uitae societas contineretur*, 'for it was employed in trusteeships and partnerships, in trusts and commissions, in buying and selling, in hiring and letting – in a word, in all the transactions on which the social relations of daily life depend' (Miller, Loeb).

Note the summary, in the form of a clause, that comes after a sequence of four asyndeta bimembria (two of them nominal, two verbal, the latter dealt with below, 146, 147). Asyndetic pairs, as we have seen, are often accompanied by summarising or generalising words, phrases or clauses (see above, 1 and XVIII.6). Winterbottom (OCT) punctuates *in tutelis societatibus fiduciis mandatis, rebus emptis uenditis conductis locatis*. Miller (Loeb) punctuates as above.

(125) *Off.* 3.80 *omnibus uicis statuae, ad eas ius cerei*. 'in every street there were statues (of him); before these, incense, candles'.

3.2 Names

(126) *Fin.* 2.62 *contineo me ab exemplis. Graecis hoc modicum est, Leonidas Epaminondas, tres aliqui aut quattuor*, 'I refrain from further examples. For the Greeks this is a modest lot, Leonidas, Epaminondas, some three or four.'

An open-ended list where that feature is made explicit.

(127) *Fin.* 4.3 *ueteres illos Platonis auditores, Speusippum Aristotelem Xenocratem, deinde eorum Polemonem Theophrastum*, '(my view is that) those old disciples of Plato, Speusippus, Aristotle, Xenocrates, and later their pupils Polemo, Theophrastus'.

This is one of those places in which a list is split into two by an intrusive word or phrase. Cf. 164, 166, 167 for names divided like this. The next two passages also have pairs of philosophers listed asyndetically, and cf. Hor. *Sat.* 2.3.12 (XXIX. 2.1.4.4).

(128) *Fin.* 4.49 *Aristoteles Xenocrates, tota illa familia non dabit*, 'Aristotle, Xenocrates, the whole of that group will not give it.'

The names are given as examples, as the following phrase makes clear. For the use of *tota* (and equivalents) see on 1 and see XVIII.6. Once again there is an ambiguity to the phrase structure: tricolon, or dicolon plus appositional generalisation?

(129) *Fin.* 4.49 *quid censes eos esse facturos qui omnino uirtutem a bonorum fine segregauerunt, Epicurum Hieronymum, illos etiam, si qui Carneadeum finem tueri uolunt?*, 'but what do you think they will do, those who completely separated virtue from the supreme good, Epicurus,

Hieronymus, and also any who want to support the supreme good of Carneades?'

The two names paired again do not comprise a closed list, as the generalisation that follows shows.

(130) *Off.* 1.43 <u>L. Sullae C. Caesaris</u> *pecuniarum translatio a iustis dominis ad alienos non debet liberalis uideri*, 'The conveyance of property by Lucius Sulla and Gaius Caesar from its rightful owners to the hands of strangers should, for that reason, not be regarded as generosity' (Miller, Loeb).

This sentence is preceded by one translated 'We must, therefore, take care to indulge only in such liberality as will help our friends and hurt no one.' The acts of Sulla and of Caesar are quoted as disapproved examples, and the list of examples of bad conveyancing could be extended indefinitely. The context is not official.

(131) *Off.* 1.114 *qui gestu (freti sunt, eligunt)* <u>Melanippam Clytaemestram</u>, 'those who rely on gesture, choose the Melanippa or the Clytemnestra' (of actors who choose the plays most suited to their talents).

Before this there is a coordinated pair, *Epigonos Medumque*, chosen by those who rely on the voice. This is one of those passages in which pairs are coordinated in different ways, either with expressed coordinator or asyndetic coordination.

(132) *Off.* 2.59 *dicebat idem* <u>Cotta Curio</u>

The names are listed at the end of the sentence, apparently *exempli gratia* (see IV.3).

3.3 Adjectives

(133) *Fin.* 1.61 *alii autem etiam amatoriis leuitatibus dediti, alii petulantes, alii* <u>audaces proterui</u>, *idem intemperantes et ignaui*, 'but some also are surrendered to amatory frivolities, some are insolent, others bold, reckless, and these too headstrong and lazy'.

The phrase division is marked by the repeated *alii* and then *idem*, with *audaces* and *proterui* in the same phrasal unit. They are followed by a coordinated pair, separated from them by *idem*. *Audaces* and *proterui* are near-synonyms (if *audax* is taken 'in malam partem'), with the latter probably stronger.

(134) *Fin.* 5.62 *quis est qui non oderit* <u>libidinosam proteruam</u> *adulescentiam* 'but who is there who does not hate libidinous, reckless youth'.

3 Data: Philosophica   439

See above, 106, on the punctuation. Adjectives of disfavour are often in asyndeton, and this is the second instance of *proteruus* in second position (cf. 133).

(135) *Off.* 2.64 *conueniet . . . esse . . . uendendo emendo, conducendo locando, uicinitatibus et confiniis <u>aequum facilem</u>, multa multis de suo iure cedentem, a litibus uero . . . abhorrentem*

On this passage see below, 143, 144 (with translation). It is a typical accumulation of asyndeta bimembria, phrasal asyndeta and a coordinated pair. The separateness of the accusative adjectival pair is marked by a switch not merely to a phrasal pair, but a phrasal pair with present participles.

3.4 Verbs

(136) *Fin.* 5.39 *scientia atque ars agricolarum, quae <u>circumcidat amputet</u>, erigat extollat adminiculet*, 'the science and art of husbandry, which trims and prunes, straightens, raises and props' (Rackham, Loeb).

Two unitary groups (as in the translation), with the asyndetic structure 2 + 3. The first pair seems to mean 'make an incision around and cut off'. The asyndetic tricolon that immediately follows describes the reverse process of raising up and supporting the plant (cf. XXIV.6.3 on Pacuvius 6–8 for unities within asyndetic strings of verbs). Reynolds (OCT) has no commas here.

(137) *Fin.* 5.47 *quem ad modum quis <u>ambulet sedeat</u>, qui ductus oris, qui uultus in quoque sit, nihilne est in his rebus quod dignum libero aut indignum esse ducamus?*, 'how each person walks or sits, the appearance of the face, the expression – is there nothing in these things which we consider worthy or unworthy of a free man?'

'Walking' and 'sitting' are often conjoined or disjunctive, but not usually in asyndeton. See, for Cicero, *TLL* I.1871.39ff., and Mart. 3.20.14 *sedet ambulatue* (other examples in the *TLL* article). Cf. the similar oppositions, but in nominal form, at 117, 118, *status incessus, sessio accubito*. For asyndetic pairs attested both in a nominal and verbal form see on 59 *pertimuit profugit*, on 143, 144 *uendendo emendo, conducendo locando*, and cf. 97 *stare mouere* alongside *status incessus*, just quoted, and 162 for *fremit queritur* alongside *fletibus questibus*. See further XIII.4.1.

The asyndetic pair is followed by an asyndetic clausal pair, with anaphora, another accumulation (see the next example).

(138) *Off.* 1.22 *communes utilitates in medium afferre, mutatione officiorum, <u>dando accipiendo</u>, tum artibus, tum opera, tum facultatibus deuincire*

hominum inter homines societatem, 'to contribute to the general good by an interchange of acts of kindness, by giving and receiving, and thus by our skill, our industry, and our talents to cement human society more closely together, man to man' (Miller, Loeb).

Cf. *Off.* 1.52 for the semantic opposition (*quae sunt iis utilia qui accipiunt, danti non molesta*), and below, 140 for these verbs in asyndeton. This pair, of reciprocal actions seen from the opposite perspective of two participants (opposites, converses: see XIII.2), follows an ablatival phrase which it is possibly meant to define, and is followed immediately by an asyndetic tricolon with anaphora. For the combining of an asyndeton bimembre with an anaphoric asyndeton see above, 137, and also 79. For the asyndetic pair 'give, receive' in legal language see Ulp. *Dig.* 2.13.6.3 *rationem autem esse Labeo ait ultro citro dandi accipiendi, credendi <debendi>, obligandi soluendi sui causa negotiationem* [or *-um*] (Kalb 1912: 135), a passage with a notable accumulation of asyndetic opposites of a type found in our corpus from Cicero's philosophica (see 94–8). Cf. Men. *Sik.* 96 for 'give, take' in asyndeton in Greek: ἔδωκ', ἐδέξω, 'I gave, you took.' For Latin see also Preuss (1881: 39–40), and XIII.2.

(139) *Off.* 1.50 *ratio et oratio, quae <u>docendo discendo</u>, communicando disceptando iudicando conciliat inter se homines*, 'reason and speech, which by the process of teaching and learning, of communication, discussing, and reasoning, associate men together' (Miller, Loeb).

Another pair of converses (for which see *TLL* V.1.1751.9ff.), then an additional tricolon also comprising ablatives of the gerund (structure 2 + 3). For ablative gerunds in asyndeton see XXIII.5.4.

(140) *Off.* 1.56 *quae conficitur ex beneficiis ultro et citro <u>datis acceptis</u>*, '(fellowship), which is effected by kind services given and received to and fro'.

Converses (see above, 138). *Vltro et citro* 'to and fro' are also opposites (reversives), coordinated and juxtaposed with the asyndetic pair. In the passage of the *Digest* cited above (138) the asyndetic pair *ultro citro* precedes the same two asyndetic verbs. Cicero was making use of legal language in this work.

(141, 142) *Off.* 2.40 *iis etiam qui <u>uendunt emunt</u>, <u>conducunt locant</u> contrahendisque negotiis implicantur*, 'to those also, who buy and sell, rent and let, and are engaged in commercial dealing generally'.

The two pairs of opposites here, converses, are undoubtedly intended as juxtaposed asyndeta bimembria. The phrase attached by *-que* is

3 Data: Philosophica 441

a generalisation, embracing the activities listed and others not mentioned. It is separate from the two pairs. This is an important passage, because it is not a colon with five balanced parts (of the structure ABCDE*que*: i.e. end-of-list coordination), but has two embedded unitary pairs followed by a different structure, linked by *-que*. This example suggests that a summarising/generalising element may be conceived of as distinct from an asyndeton that precedes.

For *uendunt emunt* see the next example, and in Greek Aristoph. *Ach.* 685 πωλεῖν ἀγοράζειν (see Olson 2002: 234, noting that asyndeton is 'natural when two opposed ideas are set side by side'). For asyndetic pairs of the type *emptio uenditio* and *locatio conductio* in the jurists see on the next passage, and Kalb (1888: 38, 1912: 135), Preuss (1881: 41) and also XXII.5.7, 5.8.

(143, 144) *Off*. 2.64 *conueniet ... esse ... uendendo emendo, conducendo locando, uicinitatibus et confiniis, aequum facilem, multa multis de suo iure cedentem, a litibus uero ... abhorrentem*, 'it will be suitable for one ... in buying and selling, in hiring and letting, in affairs to do with neighbouring properties and common boundaries, to be fair and approachable, conceding much of his own right to many, but shunning litigation'.

The same pairs of converses. Note that there is also an adjectival asyndeton bimembre in the sentence (cf. **135** above), and also that the two pairs of verbs are followed by a coordinated pair of nouns. This is a recommendation of a certain type of just behaviour, and has nothing to do with narrative 'speed' (see in general V).

With the verbal pairs here cf. the following nominal correspondents: Just. *Inst.* 3.22 *consensu fiunt obligationes in emptionibus uenditionibus, locationibus conductionibus, societatibus, mandatis* (cited by Kalb 1912: 135).

(145) *Off*. 3.66 QVIDQVID SIBI DARE FACERE OPORTERET EX FIDE BONA, '(to decide) what indemnity the owner was under obligation "in good faith" to pay and deliver to him' (Miller, Loeb).

Legal example. See Preuss (1881: 99), Kalb (1888: 39).

(146, 147) *Off*. 3.70 *idque uersari in tutelis societatibus, fiduciis mandatis, rebus emptis uenditis, conductis locatis, quibus uitae societas contineretur*
On this passage see also above, **123, 124**.

(148) *Off*. 3.119 *non recipit istam coniunctionem honestas, aspernatur repellit*
A pair of near-synonyms, of rejection. There is a type of adversative asyndeton here, in that after *non recipit ...*, *sed* has to be understood before *aspernatur*. The second verb moves on semantically from the first:

'honourable behaviour does not accept such a combination, but scorns, rejects it' (see I.8).
For asyndetic verbs in an overt adversative clause cf. 62. For the structure of this example see I.8.

3.5 Prepositional Type

(149) *Fin.* 2.109 *ut in gignendo in educando perfacile appareat aliud quiddam iis propositum, non uoluptatem*, 'as in giving birth, in bringing up offspring ...'
Semantically the relationship between the two verbs resembles that between *creat* and *alit auget* at Pacuvius 6–8, for which see XXIV.6.3 (cf. Lucretius 12, 13, at XXIV.7.1.3).

(150) *Fin.* 4.37 *in omni enim animante est summum aliquid atque optimum, ut in equis in canibus*, 'for in every animal, for example in horses, in dogs, there is some supreme excellence'.
For an equivalent pair in asyndeton see Men. *Samia* 14–15 κύνας γὰρ ἔτρεφέ μοι, | [ἵππο]υς, 'he kept hounds for me, horses' (discontinuous). The Ciceronian example is not a totality, but refers to two species chosen as examples. Cf. XXV.1.1.9 for Lucilius 35, *equum musimonem*.

(151) *Fin.* 5.38 *ut in leonibus, ut in canibus <ut> in equis*
Vt is added by 5, and the above is the text printed by Reynolds. But is *ut* necessary? If there is just one *ut*, a distinction is still made between the wild and the domestic animals, a distinction that recurs (cf. Lucr. 1.14 (6) at XXIV.7.1.2, *inde ferae, pecudes persultant pabula*, 1.163 *armenta atque aliae pecudes, genus omne ferarum*). In Cicero the wild and domestic animals mentioned are merely examples of the type, whereas the Lucretian examples are more generalising. Cf. 150 above and 155 below, where there is no repetition of the *ut*. For repeated phrase dividers (here *ut*) separating asyndeta bimembria from single terms or other units see above on 91.

(152) *Fin.*5.73 *saepe ab Aristotele a Theophrasto mirabiliter est laudata per se ipsa rerum scientia*, 'often by Aristotle, Theophrastus, knowledge was admirably praised for its own sake'.

(153) *Off.* 1.9 *tum autem aut anquirunt aut consultant ad uitae commoditatem iucunditatemque, ad facultates rerum atque copias, ad opes ad potentiam, quibus et se possint iuuare et suos, conducat id necne de quo deliberant*

'Resources' and 'power' look like a unit, the pair following a pair of phrasal prepositional asyndeta. See *TLL* IX.2.810.31ff. For power (loosely speaking) and wealth together see above, 113–15.

(154) *Off.* 1.38 *sic cum Celtiberis cum Cimbris bellum ut cum inimicis gerebatur, ... cum Latinis Sabinis Samnitibus Poenis Pyrrho de imperio dimicabatur*

Another combination of an asyndetic pair with a longer asyndetic sequence (2 + 5), though the two groups are not here juxtaposed.

(155) *Off.* 1.50 *ut in equis in leonibus, iustitiam aequitatem bonitatem non dicimus*

An asyndeton bimembre, and then an asyndetic tricolon (2 + 3); there is also a combination of the prepositional type with another type (for such accumulations see 44, 48, 49, 79, 87, 88). Horses represent domestic animals, lions wild animals (see above on 151).

(156) *Off.* 2.87 *de quaerenda de collocanda pecunia*

(157) *Off.* 3.15 *in poematis in picturis*
See above on 102.

(158) *Off.* 3.99 *cum uxore cum liberis*

For this semantic type, see above 3 for *coniuges liberosque*, and also Sallust 12, and in the Catilinarians 4.2, 4.18 and passages cited by Dyck (2008: 167); see too XIV.2.3.

4 Data: Letters *Ad Atticum*

As was pointed out at the start (1), the lists below are from eight books of Cicero's letters to Atticus, or in Shackleton Bailey's chronological numbering of the letters, 1–166 (down to Shackleton Bailey 1965–70: IV.120). Translations of passages from the letters are those of Shackleton Bailey (1965–70), unless it is stated otherwise. The numbers in brackets after references to the text are the numbers of the letters given by Shackleton Bailey.

4.1 Nouns

(159) *Att.* 2.23.3 (43) *credibile non est quantum ego in consiliis <et> prudentia tua et, quod maximum est, quantum in amore et fide ponam,* 'You cannot believe how much I rely on your advice and knowledge of the world, and, most valuable of all, your affection and loyalty.'

The above is the text of Shackleton Bailey (*et* add. 5), but asyndeton looks plausible. For asyndeton bimembre in Cicero after a single preposition, see on 16, and also XXI.

If asyndeton is accepted at 159, the asyndetic expression would be followed, after a coordinator, by a coordinated expression, a constant pattern. This same structure is found at 8, *cuius eximia* uirtus dignitas*, et, in eo negotio quod gessit,* fides et continentia. In this last sentence the terms again denote virtues, and the coordinator that leads to the second, coordinated, pair, is followed by a parenthetical clause, as is also the case in 159. The asyndeton in 159 is supported by the structure in which it would be located. See also XXI.2.

At 192 below Shackleton Bailey prints the following text, with a pair of virtues again, this time in asyndeton: *ut eum meis omnibus* studiis beneficiis *quam ornatissimum domum reducerem*. There is no more, indeed less, reason for accepting asyndeton there than there is at 159.

(160) *Att.* 4.2.6 (74) *uotiuam legationem sumpsissem prope omnium* fanorum lucorum, 'I should have taken a votive commission to practically "every temple and sacred wood".'

Apparently a formal phrase (see Shackleton Bailey 1965–70: II.172, and on the type, above, 4). *Fana* and *luci* are not the only sacred places, but the phrase does express a set. A *fanum* was originally a piece of consecrated ground in the open air, and a *lucus* a sacred grove; together they refer to sacred places in the open air, with or without plants. For religious pairs in literary texts see XXII.8 and XXIII.3.

For the pair coordinated see Plaut. *Aul.* 615 *in tuo luco et fano est situm*, Livy 35.51.2 *in fano lucoque*.

(161) *Att.* 5.13.1 (106) *de concursu* legationum priuatorum *et de incredibili multitudine quae mihi iam Sami . . . praesto fuit*, 'As for the concourse of deputations and individuals and the huge crowds which welcomed me even at Samos'.

The reference is to weak opposites, official groups (delegations) and private individuals (for the antonyms 'public/private' see above, 107, and XIII.5.2). In society as a whole *priuati* are not only in contrast with *legationes/legati*, but with all sorts of officials and official groups. No textual variants are reported.

(162) *Att.* 5.16.2 (109) *audiuimus nihil aliud nisi imperata* ἐπικεφάλια *soluere non posse*, ὠνὰς *omnium uenditas, ciuitatum* gemitus ploratus, *monstra quaedam non hominis sed ferae nescio cuius immanis*, 'I have heard of

nothing but inability to pay the poll-taxes imposed, universal sales of taxes, groans and moans from the communities, appalling excesses as of some savage beast rather than a human being.'

A long series of phrasal asyndeta, within which there is embedded an asyndeton of two near-synonyms (with *ciuitatum* dependent on the pair). Preuss (1881: 89) cites various such asyndetic pairs, comprising terms expressing lamentation, grief, complaint etc., including Livy 22.61.3 *cum magnis fletibus questibus legatos ad portam prosecuti sunt* (see Briscoe 2016 app. crit. on the text; this is an asyndetic hendiadys, = 'with tearful complaints': for this type see II.3.2.3, and note the assonance here and in the other examples). A glance at *TLL* VI.2.1749–50 s.v. *gemitus* shows that *gemitus* is often coordinated with verbal nouns of the same semantic field. Note particularly Sall. *Rep.* 2.4.2 (with a double asyndeton) *luctus gemitus uirorum mulierum* (for *luctus* and *gemitus* coordinated see Cic. *Verr.* 2.51, Ovid *Trist.* 1.3.21). Cf. *Att.* 4.15.7 (**178**) *Pompeius fremit queritur*, 'Pompey is complaining noisily' (cf. too Tacitus **139**). See further on Sallust **39** *strepitu clamore*.

(**163**) *Att.* 7.7.4 (130) *qui totum istuc aequi boni facit*, 'which takes the whole business philosophically'.

An old legal phrase used proverbially in a general context. Shackleton Bailey (1965–70: III.304) cites Ter. *Hau.* 787 and Livy 34.22.13 for the genitives (coordinated in both cases) with *facit* (and in the passage of Terence *istuc* again precedes the pair). *Aequum bonum* referred to equity, e.g. in a judgment concerning the dowry at the end of a marriage (see Watson 1967: 67–8). See particularly Cic. *Top.* 66, which I quote with the translation of Reinhardt (2003: 151): *in omnibus igitur iis iudiciis, in quibus 'ex fide bona' est additum, ubi uero etiam 'ut inter bonos bene agier oportet', in primisque in arbitrio rei uxoriae, in quo est 'quod eius melius aequius', parati esse debent. illi dolum malum, illi fidem bonam, illi aequum bonum ... tradiderunt*, 'So in all those trials in which "in good faith" is added (to the formula), or indeed "as needs be good practice among good men" and in particular in marriage arbitrations, where "what is better and fairer" is added, they have to be prepared. It was they who have taught us the concepts of fraud, good faith, equity ...'. See also on the passage Reinhardt (2003: 335). For an early asyndetic example see Plaut. *Men.* 580 *qui nec leges neque aequom bonum usquam colunt.* See further Preuss (1881: 110–11). It is noteworthy that two of the generalised examples of the expression cited by Shackleton Bailey have coordination, which was presumably later. For *aequus* in asyndeton see above, **135**.

446 XXVI Cicero

4.2 Names

The naming of consuls is not dealt with systematically here. For the old asyndetic style see e.g. 1.13.6 *M. Messala, M. Pisone coss.*, 1.19.4 *P. Mucio L. Calpurnio consulibus*; for coordination see e.g. 5.21.11 *Lentulo Philippoque consulibus*, 5.21.9 *Sulpicio et Marcello consulibus* (note the absence in the last two of the praenomen).

(**164**) *Att.* 4.16.2 (89) *adiunxi adulescentis Q. Tuberonem P. Rutilium, duo Laeli generos, Scaeuolam et Fannium*, 'with the addition of some young men, Q. Tubero, P. Rutilius, and Laelius' two sons-in-law, Scaevola and Fannius'.

Cicero is referring to a dialogue he is writing. *Duo generos* goes with the following names (which Cicero has coordinated), and looking forward as it does it isolates the preceding, asyndetic, pair. For this sort of intrusion in lists of names, see above, **127**, and also **166, 167**.

(**165**) *Att.* 4.17.5 (91) *quid quaeris aliud? iudicia, credo. Drusus Scaurus non fecisse uidentur. tres candidati rei fore putabantur, Domitius* . . ., 'What else would you care to hear about, I wonder? The trials, perhaps. Well, Drusus and Scaurus are found not guilty. Three of the candidates are expected to have to face a prosecution, Domitius . . .'.

The names are listed as of persons so far found not guilty. There might be others who eventually get off. The names are not yet a totality.

(**166, 167**) *Att.* 5.21.9 (114) *ex Id. Mart ibidem Synnadense Pamphylium (tum Phemio dispiciam* κέρας), *<Lyc>aonium Isauricum*, 'from the Ides of March [I have arranged to hold assize], also at Laodicea [*ibidem*], for Synnada, Pamphylia (I'll spy out a *cor* for Phemius then), Lycaonia, and Isauria'.

The parenthesis splits the group of four into two pairs. It has the same effect as *duo Laeli generos* at **164** (see also on **127**, and see XXVIII.2.1 for the present example alongside a passage of Caesar). The names are in adjectival form, agreeing with an earlier *forum*.

(**168**) *Att.* 6.1.4 (115) *praefecturas M. Scaptio L. Gauio, qui in regno rem Bruti procurabant, detuli*, 'I gave M. Scaptius and L. Gavius, who are looking after Brutus' interests in Cappadocia, the Prefectures . . .'.

The two names here are a complete list, but this is information about an official appointment, and the two appointed are given their full names in formal style.

4 *Data: Letters* Ad Atticum   447

(169) *Att.* 6.1.13 (115) <u>*Thermum Silium*</u> *uere audis laudari; ualde se honeste gerunt*, 'What you hear about Thermus and Silius being well spoken about is true enough. They are doing very creditably.'
  Cicero continues immediately: *adde M. Nonium, Bibulum, me si uoles*, 'Add M. Nonius, Bibulus, myself if you will.'
  Thus the first two names are not a totality.

(170) *Att.* 6.3.5 (117) *amicos habet meras nugas,* <u>*Ma<ti>nium Scaptium*</u>, 'He has friends who are utter good-for-nothings – Matinius, Scaptius.'
  The persons share the feature that they are friends of Brutus, but the list is not necessarily complete.

(171) *Att.* 7.21.3 (145) <u>*Dolabella Caelius*</u> *me illi ualde satis facere*, 'Dolabella and Caelius say he is very well satisfied with my behaviour.'
  These too may be examples. Cicero is expressing himself at a loss what to do.

(?) *Att.* 8.2.3 (152) *oram quidem maritimam iam relinquemus, Afranium exspectabimus <et?> Petreium*, 'We shall presently be giving up the coast, we shall wait for Afranius and Petreius.'
  Et is added here by 5. Conjunct hyperbaton (with a coordinator) is very common in Cicero (see XX.1), and one would need a good reason for accepting the asyndetic variant here. For the coordinated type where the separated terms are names see e.g. *Fam.* 8.8.10 (84) (by Caelius) *libertum Philonem istoc misi et Diogenem Graecum*, 4.2.1 (151) *Postumia tua me conuenit et Seruius noster, Fin.* 2.119 *Sironem dicis et Philodemum*, 5.14 *quam eandem Aristoteli fuisse et Polemonis docet*.
  For the discontinuous pattern (i.e. asyndetic, with the order of conjunct hyperbaton), see examples 175 and 186 below, but in neither of these are the elements names, and in both there seems to be a semantic motive for the separation. The names here are not part of an open-ended list, which might have given some support to a (discontinuous) asyndeton, in that it might have implied that Cicero was searching for examples.
  The same textual issue arises below, *Fam.* 15.4.7, where again two names might be in the pattern of conjunct hyperbaton. The passage, unnumbered, is quoted and discussed after 196.

4.3   Adjectives

(172) *Att.* 7.20.1 (144) *illi autem adhuc, id est Nonis, nondum uenerant, sed erant uenturi* <u>*inanes imparati*</u>, 'They have as yet (i.e. on the Nones) not arrived, but are on their way, empty-handed and unprepared.'

This is the only asyndetic pair of adjectives that I have found in the eight books, and there are two typical features. Both terms (predicative adjuncts) have the prefix *in-* (though only the second is a privative), and they are at the end of the sentence, as is not infrequently the case with such adjectives in other writers (see V.2; see also the examples at VI.4.2).

4.4 Adverbs

(173) *Att.* 1.14.4 (14) *et tamen ab illo <u>aperte tecte</u> quicquid est datum libenter accepi*, 'not but what I was glad enough to take whatever tribute Pompey more or less obliquely vouchsafed'.

I would take this as a disjunctive asyndeton, 'openly or obliquely/ privately', but the matter has been complicated by Shackleton Bailey's interpretation. This example and others similar are discussed below in connection with an expression in a letter of Caelius, 213, along with the view of Shackleton Bailey.

4.5 Verbs

(174) *Att.* 1.16.8 (16) *idem, inquam, ego recreaui adflictos animos bonorum, unumquemque <u>confirmans excitans</u>*, 'well, as I say, it was I yet again who revived the drooping courage of the honest men, fortifying and raising them one by one'.

Shackleton Bailey (1965–70: 1.318) says that the 'rise of emphasis in the second word makes *asyndeton bimembre* natural here'.

The rise of emphasis (i.e. with the second verb expressing a more positive act than the first) does not in itself confirm the asyndeton (though it is a common feature of asyndetic pairs), because in coordinated pairs also the second term is often stronger than the first (see XV). But there is an additional justification of asyndeton here. The fact that the verbs refer to actions that are just a selection of those that Cicero must have carried out (he no doubt e.g. 'encouraged', 'urged on'), and that they are placed at the end of the clause, is also characteristic of a certain category of asyndeton (the 'selective list': see IV.3). Also, for pairs of present participles used asyndetically see XXIII.5.5.

(?) *Att.* 1.18.1 (18) *multa sunt enim quae me sollicitant anguntque, quae . . .*, 'There are many things to worry and vex me, which . . .'.

Here Shackleton Bailey's text (that of Z¹) has both *-que* and *quae*, but Σ has only one of the two (either *anguntque* or *angunt qu(a)e*). Since *quae* is

4 *Data: Letters* Ad Atticum   449

essential to the meaning, there is a choice between coordination of the two verbs, as printed above, and asyndeton (*sollicitant, agunt*).

Asyndetic pairs of verbs at the end of a clause in Cicero often describe hostile or troubling actions or events (see the verbal pairs in the speeches earlier, and below, 7.2.3), but I can see no decisive linguistic argument in favour of asyndeton here.

(175) *Att.* 2.20.2 (40) *Pompeius adfirmat non esse periculum, adiurat,* 'Pompey says there is no danger, he swears to it.'

I have throughout treated as two-word asyndeta bimembria pairs which have the same complement (expressed once), and here the acc. + inf. is dependent on both verbs. The complement intrudes between the two verbs, producing a discontinuous order. Both verbs have the same prefix, and the second definitely outdoes the other semantically. The effect of the intrusive element is to suggest a pause for thought, as Cicero seeks a stronger verb than merely 'state, assert'. In English in an equivalent structure the second verb would both follow a slight pause and be pronounced with emphasis. Cf. V.2 and 186 below.

(176) *Att.* 2.22.1 (42) *uolitat furit; nihil habet certi, <multa> multis denuntiat,* 'he ("Pulchellus") rushes wildly up and down, without any definite programme, threatening numbers of folk with this, that, and the other'.

The pair could be rewritten as *uolitat furens* or *furit uolitans*. A single action is referred to, frenzied rushing about (asyndetic hendiadys).

(177) *Att.* 4.5.1 (80) *senseram noram, inductus relictus proiectus ab iis.* 'I had perceived it, I knew it, led on, deserted, discarded by them' (my translation and punctuation).

The second verb is shorter, but conveys a consequence of the first. Note the asyndetic accumulation, with the structure 2 + 3 (and there is an asyndetic tricolon two sentences earlier: *sed ualeant recta uera honesta consilia*); *ab iis* goes with all three participles.

(178) *Att.* 4.15.7 (90) *Pompeius fremit queritur, Scauro studet; sed utrum fronte an mente dubitatur,* 'Pompey is fuming and growling. Ostensibly Scaurus is his man, but does he mean it?'

Shackleton Bailey's punctuation of the text is out of line with his translation. Is there an asyndetic tricolon, or should a full-stop be placed after *queritur*? Certainly the first two verbs are close semantically (cf. on 162 for comparable nouns in asyndeton). The first verb acts as a modifier of the second: he is complaining inarticulately (cf. 176). In favour of asyndeton is the fact that the *utrum* ... *an* clause complements *Scauro studet*, not the other two verbs.

(179) *Att.* 5.20.6 (113) *Ariobarzanes opera mea uiuit regnat*, 'Ariobarzanes owes his life and throne to me.'

Semantically such a pair, of not only living but also succeeding in some way, is reminiscent of the less specific formula seen e.g. at Plaut. *Bac.* 246 *uiuit ualet*, *St.* 31 *uiuant ualeant*, *Trin.* 1075 *uiuont ualent* (see XXIII.8.14, with cross references, and particularly XXVII.1.4, where different meanings of the formula are noted). See also below, 204 on *uiximus floruimus*. Here are three different asyndetic pairs with *uiuo* as the first verb, and the second verb in each case implies a form of success. There seems to be a semantic determinant of the asyndeton, without the pairs being formulaic.

(180) *Att.* 5.21.12 (114) *adsidunt subducunt; ad nummum conuenit*

A sentence in its own right, expressing a sequence: 'So they sat down together and totted everything up. The figures tallied to a penny.'

(181) *Att.* 6.1.12 (115) *Cicerones pueri amant inter se, discunt exercentur*, 'The boys are fond of one another, are learning their lessons and taking their exercise.'

The second and third verbs are a unit denoting aspects of education. Strictly there is a tricolon, with a clausal first component, but the two single verbs are semantically separate.

4.6 *Prepositional Type*

(182) *Att.* 1.14.3 (14) *totum hunc locum, quem ego uarie meis orationibus ... soleo pingere, de flammis de ferro* (*nosti illas* ληκύθους), *ualde grauiter pertexuit*, 'he worked up the whole theme which I am in the habit of embroidering in my speeches one way or another, all about fire, sword, etc. (you ... know my colour-box)'.

Shackleton Bailey's translation (note 'etc.') shows that he takes the prepositional pair as part of an open-ended list. The whole passage is rhetorical, and this sentence is preceded by a description marked by two strings of asyndetic phrases with anaphora. *Flamma* and *ferrum* are commonly paired (Wölfflin 1933: 259), usually with a coordinator (see above, 16). Very similar to the pair here is *ferrum faces* at 15, and also *ferro igni(que)* in Livy (see Oakely 1998: 299). For asyndetic pairs referring to forms of violence, see below, 7.8.2.

4 *Data: Letters* Ad Atticum   451

(183) *Att.* 1.18.3 (18) *facto senatus consulto de ambitu de iudiciis, nulla lex perlata*, 'The Senate passed a decree on electoral bribery and another on the courts, but no law was carried through.'
A report on senatorial proceedings. A legal or official context.

(184) *Att.* 6.1.24 (115) *iam enim sciemus de rebus urbanis de prouinciis*
Shackleton Bailey translates 'we shall know soon about affairs in Rome, including the provinces'. But the city, Rome (in this case 'city affairs'; *res urbanae* is equivalent to a noun), and the provinces were opposites (of the 'home/away', 'town/country' type: see XIII.5.1). For *urbs* or *Roma* opposed to *prouincia(e)* see *TLL* X.2.2342.37ff. See in particular 203 (Cicero to Tiro) *tua... in me officia, domestica forensia, urbana prouincialia, in re priuata in publica, in studiis in litteris nostris.* See too Cic. *Leg.* 3.18 *sed iam, si placet, de prouinciis decedatur, in urbemque redeatur*, and also the note of Dyck (2004: 492).

(185) *Att.* 6.3.4 (117) *huc enim odiosa adferebantur de Curione de Paulo*, 'for some disagreeable reports are coming here about Curio and Paulus'.
Cicero then reports his sorrow about these two, naming them with a coordinator. Cf. 188 below.

(186) *Att.* 7.11.4 (134) *mira hominum querela est... sine magistratibus urbem esse, sine senatu*, 'The public outcry is astonishing... at the thought of the capital without magistrates or Senate.'
The order is discontinuous. Both terms denote official bodies engaged in aspects of rule. Cf. above, 122 with cross references, and 187. For *senatus* in an asyndetic pair see also above, 49, and the next passage.

(187) *Att.* 7.13.1 (136) *quid autem sit acturus aut quo modo nescio, sine senatu sine magistratibus*, 'But what he will do or how he will do it, without Senate or magistrates, I don't know.'
The same pairing as that in 186, but with the nouns in the reverse order. Was *senatus* semantically stronger, placed second in 186 to convey the public outrage? It would be bad enough if Rome were without magistrates, but intolerable if it had no senate.

(188) *Att.* 7.26.1 (150*)* *ego enim nunc <primum> paulum exorior, et maxime quidem iis litteris quae Roma adferuntur de Domitio de Picentium cohortibus*, 'I am plucking up spirit a little... because of the letters I am getting from Rome about Domitius and the Picene cohorts.'
The context is similar to that of 185 above, in which news arriving about two listed persons is referred to.

(189) *Att.* 8.12.5 (162) *memini quid mihi tum suaseris per Theophanem per Culleonem*, 'I remember what you urged upon me at that time through Theophanes and through Culleo.'

5 Data: Letters *Ad familiares*

The following is a collection of two-word asyndeta from letters 1–173 in the numeration of Shackleton Bailey (1977), letters from the period 62–47 BC (120 pages of text).

5.1 Nouns

(190, 191) *Fam.* 5.8.5 (25) (to Crassus) *in omnibus publicis priuatis, forensibus domesticis, tuis amicorum, hospitum clientium tuorum negotiis*, 'in all concerns – no matter whether public or private, business or domestic, your own or your friends' or your guests' or your clients' ...'.

I tentatively take it that *tuis amicorum* is one pair, and *hospitum clientium* another, with the affairs of guests and clients of less intimate concern to the referent than his own and his friends' affairs. *Tuis* is equivalent to a genitive 'of you', and so in effect pronominal rather than strictly nominal. This passage is discussed below, 197, 198.

(192) *Fam.* 7.5.1 (26) (to Caesar) *ut eum meis omnibus studiis beneficiis quam ornatissimum domum reducerem*, 'in order to bring him home again the richer by any and every benefit and mark of good will in my power to bestow'.

No textual variants are noted. The nouns are near-synonyms. This is *studium* in the sense '(act of) goodwill' (*OLD* s.v. 5a). Cf. *Fam.* 15.11.2 (118) *cui me ... studia communia, beneficia paterna tuaque ... coniunxerant*, where the two nouns are in a phrasal asyndeton, though *studia* has a different sense ('(common) pursuits'). As was remarked earlier, there seems no reason why Shackleton Bailey should have removed an asyndeton at 159, but allowed it here. The nouns in the two passages are of similar type.

(?) *Fam.* 13.6.4 (57) *non modo re sed etiam uerbis, uultu denique*

This is translated by Shackleton Bailey (I include the translation of the beginning of the sentence as well, not quoted here) thus: '(To effect this you have only to bring out for the occasion all the manifold generosity that it lies within your good nature and your present power to provide,) not

5 *Data: Letters* Ad familiares 453

only in a practical way but in words and even in looks.' In this rendering *etiam* is disregarded and the meaning it would usually have is given to *denique*. *Sed etiam* introduces both *uerbis* and *uultu*. The question here concerns how to take *denique*. First, it may go only with *uultu* ('but also with words, and finally/moreover looks'), thus playing the part of a coordinator. Second, it may belong with both *uerbis* and *uultu* ('but also with words and looks, finally'; i.e. = 'but also, finally, with words and looks').

The pair *uerba* and *uultus*, and the equivalent pair *uerba* and *uox*, are often closely associated, both in asyndeton and with forms of coordination. For this pair in asyndeton see Tacitus 58 *uerba uultus in crimen detorquens recondebat*, and the collection ad loc. of examples of pairs both in asyndeton and coordinated; see also above, 112 for the similar asyndeton *uultus uoces*, with further cross references. The idea is that one's words and expression together tell a story, with looks perhaps potentially stronger than words. The second interpretation offered at the end of the last paragraph I would rule out. It is easier to take *denique* as adding a second term, and thus as equivalent in function to a coordinator. Cf. *Fam*. 3.11.1 (74) *litteris nuntiis fama denique ipsa*, where *denique* adds *fama*.

(**193**) *Fam*. 3.12.1 (75) (to Appius Pulcher) *plura uirtutis industriae ornamenta in te sunt*, 'the more distinguished you are for virtue and industry' (my translation: Shackleton Bailey in his Loeb edition has a different text (see below)).

Wesenberg suggested adding *ingeni* after *uirtutis*, comparing *Fam*. 3.11.2 (74) *ingenio industriae uirtuti*. Shackleton Bailey prints the asyndeton in his 1977 edition, but says of Wesenberg's *uirtutis <ingeni>* in his apparatus, 'fort. recte'. He emends the text thus in his Loeb. But there can be no guarantee that Cicero used the same three words twice in a tricolon (and see below on the word order). He was capable of varying a tricolon: cf. e.g. *Fam*. 5.17.4 (23) *pietatem uirtutem industriam*. *Industria* may lead to *uirtus* (see *Her*. 4.27, 4.34), or vice versa, and the two nouns do occur together without a third noun. Note *Her*. 4.13 *uirtute et industria*, Cic. *Phil*. 10.25 *opera consilio, industria uirtute* (two pairs: on the first, see below, **194**) Livy 38.23.11 *uirtus et industria*, Vell. 2.43.4 *uirtute atque industria*.

These coordinated examples have *uirtus* before *industria*, as in the possible asyndetic case, **193** above. Wesenberg's emendation would have the effect of splitting the pair, whereas in the tricolon he cites (see above) as a supposed parallel they are together. Note too the longer (anaphoric) sequence at Cic. *Verr*. 3.8 (*si non uirtute, non industria, non innocentia, non* *pudore, non pudicitia*), where they are again juxtaposed. If an insertion is to be made in our passage, it should not split the pair, and Wesenberg's suggestion is unlikely to be right.

There is another asyndeton bimembre in a letter to the same person, Appius Pulcher (see the next example, 194), and numerous asyndetic tricola or the like also addressed to him, some of them in single letters and even sentences. Here is a collection: 3.1.1 (64) *ingeni offici humanitatis*, 3.6.4 (69) *qui te forum Tarsi agere, statuere multa, decernere iudicare dicerent*, 3.8.5 (70) *cum enim Laodiceae, cum Apameae, cum Synnadis, cum Philomeli, cum Iconi essem*, 3.8.6 (70) *Apameae Synnade Philomeli*, 3.9.1 (72) *plenas humanitatis offici diligentiae*, 3.10.1 (73) *neruis opibus sapientia tua*, 3.10.9 (73) *opes ingenium liberi adfines propinqui*,[3] 3.10.10 (73) *patriam liberos salutem dignitatem memet ipsum*, 3.10.10 (73) *cum me consilio cum auctoritate cum armis denique*, 3.11.1 (74) *litteris nuntiis fama denique ipsa*, 3.11.2 (74) *ingenio industriae uirtuti*, 3.12.3 (75) *acrius apertius significantius*, 3.13.1 (76) *non solum auctoritate oratione sententia tua*. This rhetorical, asyndetic style was clearly felt by Cicero to be appropriate to the addressee, with whom his relations were correct but cool, and asyndeta bimembria tend to be in passages or corpora in which other asyndeta are common. The adyndeton bimembre to Appius below also seems to make emendation unnecessary here.

For *industria* in asyndeta bimembria see on Sallust 35.

(194) *Fam.* 3.13.1 (76) (to Appius Pulcher) *sed etiam opera consilio, domum ueniendo, conueniendis meis nullum onus offici cuiquam reliquum fecisse*, 'but in addition, by your labour and advice, by coming to my house, by meeting my household, you left no burdensome duty to anyone else' (my translation).

Syntactically there are two pairs here, first a pair of ablatival abstract nouns of complementary meanings, and then two asyndetic gerundival phrases in the ablative. The simplex *ueniendo* is followed by its compound *conueniendo*, which conveys an action subsequent to that of *ueniendo*. For simplex + compound see VII. For *opera* used with *consilium* see e.g. Cic. *Phil.* 5.36, 10.25 (in a senatorial motion: the latter example is quoted on 193), and particularly the long list of examples from Plautus onwards at *TLL* IV.452.65ff. It is clear from this material that *opera* + *consilium* was a unit (usually coordinated, and also sometimes together in longer sequences).

---

[3] *Liberi adfines propinqui* go together, and *opes ingenium* might be taken as an embedded asyndeton bimembre.

5 *Data: Letters* Ad familiares

The two single-word pairs in this passage and the last are semantically similar, in that both denote virtues or virtuous behaviour. Both occur in sentences with asyndetic accumulations. In the present sentence there is the following phrasal pair *domum ueniendo, conueniendis meis*, referred to above, and in the previous passage (193), earlier in the same sentence, Cicero has an anaphoric phrasal tricolon, *quo melior ciuis, quo uir clarior, quo fortior amicus es*. Combinations of asyndetic tricola and pairs (structure 2 + 3 or the reverse) we have repeatedly seen. It would be odd to emend 193 and leave 194. 193 is a passage in which the phrase structure supports the asyndeton bimembre, which gives the 3 + 2 pattern.

(195, 196) *Fam.* 15.9.1 (101) (to the consul, Marcellus) *omnibus* dictis factis, studiis institutis. Shackleton Bailey translates as a tetracolon: 'in all our words, acts, pursuits, and habits'. He also punctuates with three commas.

But *dicta facta* is a common asyndetic pair, of complementary terms, and *studiis institutis* is a pair of near-synonyms. *Instituta* is often combined with *mores* (*TLL* VII.1.1994.21ff.), and the combination here is similar ('interests and customs'). For *dicta facta* cf. e.g. above, 116 (where the switch from one pair to another pair is marked by the repeated preposition *in*, and also *denique*), and see Preuss (1881: 37–8). See too, for coordination, Ennius *Ann.* 314 at XXIV.5.2.6 (*dictum factumque*).

5.2 Names

(?) *Fam.* 15.4.7 (110) *magnas Parthorum copias <et> Arabum*
Omission of the coordinator (*et* is from 5) would introduce a discontinuous asyndeton. There is a similar textual issue at *Att.* 8.2.3 above, quoted after 171: *oram quidem maritimam iam relinquemus, Afranium exspectabimus <et?> Petreium*. Usually when names are split like this in Cicero there is a coordinator (see on *Att.* 8.2.3), and when there is an asyndetic hyperbaton one expects the second (disjoined) term to be emphatic or special in some way. The two names here, like those in the other passage just referred to, are part of a closed list or totality (joint forces of Parthians and Arabs). Asyndeton by contrast would tend to imply that Cicero was looking for a second example as part of a potentially open-ended list, which would be inappropriate in this context. Conjunct hyperbaton, on the other hand, with an expressed coordinator rather than asyndetic, is often used in the expression of totalities or opposites (see XX.1), for example in the structure 'both A + intrusive element + and B', though not only in that (e.g. *Att.* 8.3.6 *nauis et in Caieta est parata nobis et*

*Brundisi, Fam.*15.4.11 *et rogare solere et rogari scio, Fin.* 2.33 *sunt et in animo praecipua quaedam et in corpore, Fin.* 2.111 *summum pecudis bonum et hominis, Fin.* 3.67 *hominum causa et deorum*; the last three examples are merisms). To match the pattern seen in these last examples, the (finite) totalities *Parthorum* ... *Arabum* and *Afranium* ... *Petreium* in their discontinuous form would need a coordinator. Emendation seems best here.

5.3 Adjectives

(**197, 198**) *Fam.* 5.8.5 (25) *in omnibus publicis priuatis, forensibus domesticis, tuis amicorum, hospitum clientium negotiis* (translated above, **190, 191**).

There are certainly two pairs of opposites in this sequence (the first four terms, underlined: see XIII.5.1, 5.2). Arguably two further pairs follow (see above, **190, 191**). *Omnibus* (< *omnia*) is taken as substantival.

This is a formal letter to Crassus, with a number of asyndetic tricola, as well as these pairs of asyndeta bimembria. Crassus was consul, and Cicero was hostile to him. Shackleton Bailey (1977: I.327) refers to 'conscious insincerity' accounting 'for the verbose and repetitive character of his letter'.

Both of the first two oppositions occur also at **202, 203**. Both are commonplace, but often with coordination or other forms of separation. Note *Leg. agr.* 2.64 *quorum sapientiam temperantiamque in publicis priuatisque, forensibus domesticisque rebus perspexeratis*, where the coordination in the same pairs of opposites highlights the constant interchangeability of asyndeton and coordination. See also *Off.* 1.4 *neque publicis neque priuatis neque forensibus neque domesticis in rebus*, *Tusc.* 1.84 *et domesticis et forensibus solaciis ornamentisque priuati*.

(**199**) *Fam.* 7.5.3 (26) (to Caesar) *probiorem hominem, meliorem uirum, pudentiorem, esse neminem*

Esse neminem is needed with all the comparatives, all of which have to be negated (with *neminem* (*esse*) subject, and *probiorem hominem* etc. predicates). Thus *meliorem uirum, pudentiorem* is a discontinuous asyndeton bimembre. Shackleton Bailey's translation departs from the word order: 'there is no better fellow, no more honest and honourable gentlemen alive'. He has translated as if the Latin read *meliorem uirum, probiorem hominem, pudentiorem, esse neminem*. Translate 'a more honest fellow, a better man and more decent, cannot be found'. For the presence of both *homo* and *uir* in such characterisations see I.6.

5 Data: Letters Ad familiares

In this discontinuous asyndeton *meliorem uirum, pudentiorem,* the first comparative *meliorem* is vague, and *pudentiorem* makes the praise more specific and stronger.

(200) *Fam.* 2.13.4 (93) (to Caelius) *priuatis, summis infimis, fueram iucundus,* '(I) made myself pleasant to private individuals from the highest to the lowest.'

This pair of antipodals is discussed at XIII.2. It, like a few other such pairs, has an idiomatic sense, denoting not only entities at the two extremes, but also those in between.

Summus is often coordinated with *infimus* (e.g. Cic. *Mil.* 17, with *atque,* Livy 1.54.3, with *-que*) or opposed to it in other ways, but I have not noted other cases of asyndeton.

(201) *Fam.* 15.4.12 (110) (to Cato) *in omnibus orationibus, sententiis dicendis, causis agendis, omnibus scriptis Graecis Latinis* 'in all my speeches, whether addressing the Senate or pleading in court, in all my writings, Greek or Latin'.

First an asyndetic phrasal pair that embraces two categories of speeches that a Roman might have delivered, and then a single-word adjectival pair. Cf. Sall. *Cat.* 25.2 (**49**) for the opposition 'Greek/Latin' in asyndeton (but with textual variants). The gerundival phrasal pair *sententiis dicendis, causis agendis* is marked by assonance. For ablative gerunds in literary Latin in asyndeton, see above, **139** and XXIII.5.4.

(202, 203) *Fam.* 16.4.3 (123) (to Tiro) *tua ... in me officia, domestica forensia, urbana prouincialia, in re priuata in publica, in studiis in litteris nostris.* 'Your services to me ... in my home and out of it, in Rome and abroad, in private affairs and public, in my studies and literary work.'

Two asyndetic pairs of adjectives (opposites), then two asyndetic pairs of the prepositional type (see **207, 208**). In the first of the latter two (*in re priuata in publica*) the opposition is adjectival. For the opposition *urbana prouincialia* see on **184**. For *domestica forensia* and 'public/private', see **197, 198**.

Here is another, markedly extended, accumulation.

5.4 Verbs

(204) *Fam.* 14.4.5 (§6 in the Loeb edition) (6) (to his family) *uiximus floruimus; non uitium nostrum sed uirtus nostra nos adflixit,* 'It has been a good life, a great career. The good in me, nothing bad, has brought me down.'

The second could be taken as modifying the first, 'a very successful life'. Cf. *Fam.* 14.1.2 (8) *beatissimi uiueremus*: so the above = *uiximus florentes*. On the other hand the pair resembles the formula *uiuit ualet* (for which see above, 179, on *uiuit regnat*).

(205) *Fam.* 2.10.3 (86) (to Caelius) *multi <u>occisi capti</u>, reliqui dissipati*

In effect a military report, with a conventional military asyndeton bimembre. There are two clauses here, with *multi* the subject in the first and *reliqui* in the second. For the asyndeton see Sallust 76 *multos mortalis <u>captos occisos</u>*. For the pair coordinated see *Fam.* 15.4.8 (110) *qui occisi captique sunt interclusi fuga*. In our example the sense is probably disjunctive, but not necessarily so (see on Sallust 76). These two verbs may be either conjunctive or disjunctive (see on the passage of Sallust just referred to).

5.5 Prepositional Type

(206) *Fam.* 7.32.3 (113) *de rebus urbanis de re publica*

(207, 208) *Fam.* 16.4.3 (123) (to Tiro) *tua ... in me officia, domestica forensia, urbana prouincialia, <u>in re priuata in publica</u>, <u>in studiis in litteris nostris</u>*

This passage was quoted above (202, 203) with translation. In the prepositional pairs a single term agrees with both members of the pair (*re* with the two adjectives, *nostris* with the two nouns). The two adjectives are opposites (complementarities), the two nouns complements or near-synonyms.

6 Some Letters of Caelius

In the selection of letters from the corpus *Ad familiares* taken into account here there are some letters of Caelius, and in this section I present the asyndeta that turn up as a sort of appendix.

6.1 Nouns

(209, 210) *Fam.* 8.1.1 (77) *omnia enim sunt ibi <u>senatus consulta <e>dicta</u>, <u>fabulae rumores</u>*, 'It's all here – the Senate's decrees, the edicts, the gossip, the rumours.'

The first two terms refer to official decisions, the second two to mere talk. The second two nouns are near-synonyms. Cf. Cic. *Mil.* 42 *rumorem, fabulam falsam fictam leuem perhorrescimus*, and also Cato *orat*. (*ORF*) 60 *rumorem famam flocci fecit*.

6.2   Names

(211) *Fam.* 8.8.7 (84) from a senatorial decree quoted by Caelius: *huic s. c. intercessit <C.> Coelius C. Pansa tr. pl.*
Repeated at the end of §8.

(212) *Fam.* 8.11.2 (91) *decrerant quidem [qui] neque transigi uolebant Domitii Scipiones*, 'Domitius, Scipio, and company had indeed voted in favour, without wanting the business to go through.'
This is definitely not a closed list, and the names come at the end of the clause. The two plurals make it clear that there were more than two who voted thus.

6.3   Adverbs

(213) *Fam.* 8.1.4 (77) *sed inter paucos, quos tu nosti, palam secreto narrantur*, '(they are) retailed as an open secret among a small coterie – you know who'.
Of *aperte tecte* at 173 (*et tamen ab illo aperte tecte quicquid est datum libenter accepi*, translated as 'not but what I was glad enough to take whatever tribute Pompey more or less obliquely vouchsafed') Shackleton Bailey says (1965–70: I.309), 'To be taken together, in the sense that Pompey's praise was neither open and direct nor so veiled as to be imperceptible'. But the phrase is of a common type, and can be taken simply as a disjunctive asyndeton, 'and yet I willingly took whatever he vouchsafed openly or in private' (see *OLD* s.v. *secreto* 3a). See further, for straightforward examples from the same semantic field, Tac. *Ann.* 4.67.4, with cross references, at Tacitus 85 (*aperta secreta*), and Preuss (1881: 33) on Cic. *Inv.* 1.41 *quae clam palam, ui persuasione fecerit*, 'the acts which one performed secretly or openly, by the use of force or by persuasion', Hubbell, Loeb). The Tacitean example is equivalent to a coordination ('disclosures, and secrets', Woodman 2004).
Shackleton Bailey says (I.309) on *aperte tecte* that such phrases are 'far harder to find in Latin than in English'. He had in mind pairs (of adjectives or adverbs) referring to a single entity or event that has conflicting features, that is to what might be called an appositive compound or oxymoron. Thus in English *bitter–sweet* (an example cited by Shackleton Bailey) is

applied to a single entity that combines the opposing features of bitterness and sweetness (whereas in a sentence such as *the dinner comprised courses bitter and sweet* the reference is to several entities, some bitter and some sweet: a coordination rather than a compound). An example of such a pairing that has become a compound is Gk. γλυκύπικρος, which is used once by Cicero himself in a letter (*Att.* 5.21.4). *Dulcacidus* turns up in late Latin (Serenus Sammonicus), and is based on the Greek (see Bader 1962: 333–7 for a few other such Latin terms, not all of them convincing). Although asyndetic pairs in which one term is a modifier of the second are common in Latin, it is true that pairs of the *bitter–sweet* type (appositive compounds that are copulative: on the type see B. Bauer 2017: 301, 326) comprising opposites cannot certainly be found in the classical period, and it is far more satisfactory to take the Ciceronian example as a plain disjunctive asyndeton instead of being influenced by what is possible in English. The types of oxymoron discussed by Calboli (1997b) are not, structurally, appositional compounds comprising two terms of the same part of speech, but are usually in juxtapositions made up of adjective + noun.

I come now to *palam secreto* at 213 above, translated by Shackleton Bailey in accordance with English idiom as 'open secret'. A crucial phrase is *inter paucos*. The uncertain reports (*incerta*) are not bandied about in public (*neque . . . uulgo iactantur*), but among a known group of a few. The pair could be taken as an adversative asyndeton, 'openly but in private', in the sense that the coterie spoke of them openly among themselves, but not among others. This meaning would be captured by English 'openly, but in a closed circle'. An alternative however would be to translate 'openly, in private', giving *secreto* the sense that it is given at *OLD* s.v. 3a, and without any need to stress a possible adversative sense. If we take it thus, there is not necessarily asyndeton (i.e. asyndetic coordination, copulative, disjunctive or adversative) at all. In private they spoke about these matters openly. Cf. XXII.6.1 on *sub diuo columine*.

Shackleton Bailey's paraphrase, stated both at (1965–70: I.309) and (1977: I.383), is in effect adversative, but with a reversal of the order of the words of Caelius: *specie secreto, re uera palam*, 'to appearances in secret, but in reality openly'. Despite this apparent adversative interpretation, Shackleton Bailey translates as if the pair were a compound of the *bitter–sweet* type (i.e. 'open secret'). Yet he says (1965–70: I.309) without explanation that Caelius' *palam secreto* is 'not quite analogous' to *aperte tecte* at *Att.* 1.14.4. That may be the case, but both can be taken as mundane types of asyndeton.

7 Conclusions 461

6.4 Verbs

(214) *Fam.* 8.8.6 (84) *senatum existimare neminem eorum qui potestatem habent intercedendi impediendi moram adferre oportere,* 'in the judgement of the senate no one having power of veto or impediment should bring a delay' (my translation).

This is a quotation from a decree of the senate. On pairs of asyndetic gerund(ives) in *senatus consulta* see e.g. XXII.2.3.

(215) *Fam.* 8.8.6 (84) *qui impedierit prohibuerit, eum senatum existimare contra rem publicam fecisse,* 'whosoever offers such bar or impediment shall in the judgement of the Senate have acted against the commonwealth'.

A continuation (in the next sentence) of the same senatorial decree. In both places the two verbs are near-synonyms, with the pleonasm ruling out all forms of obstruction. In the *Philippics* too there are quotations of senatorial proceedings with asyndeta (see e.g. above, 77, 78).

6.5 Prepositional Type

(216) *Fam.* 8.16.1 (153) *per fortunas tuas,* Cicero, *per liberos te oro et obsecro*

This is the use of *per* found in oaths and imprecations. The possessive adjective goes with both nouns. In oaths in which someone swears by more than one entity *per* may be used just once with the dependent terms coordinated, or it may be repeated, with or without a coordinator (see the examples at *OLD* s.v. *per* 10). With the asyndeton contrast Caes. *Civ.* 3.108.5 *per omnes deos perque foedera . . . populum Romanum obtestabatur*; cf. Plaut. *Mil.* 540–2 *te opsecro | per deos atque homines perque stultitiam meam | perque tua genua.*

7 Conclusions

7.1 Distributions

In the eighteen speeches of Cicero 91 instances of asyndeton bimembre are numbered as being certain, though quite a few other possible cases are quoted but not numbered because their status seems controversial. In these speeches there is roughly one instance of asyndeton every five or six pages. It is worth quoting Denniston's remark (1952: 105) about the use of asyndeton bimembre in Demosthenes' speeches, which is in sharp contrast to that of Cicero: 'Demosthenes perhaps affords three examples of two-limbed asyndeton [which are then quoted] but only in the last is the text above suspicion.' This assertion may be generally right, but certainly Demosthenes has the asyndetic pair ἄνω κάτω (e.g. 2.16, 4.41), which Denniston does not mention. Note too 4.46 ὅταν γὰρ ἡγῆται μὲν ὁ στρατηγὸς ἀθλίων ἀπομίσθων ξένων, 'For when your general leads wretched, ill-paid mercenaries' (Vince, Loeb).

There is not an even distribution across the speeches. In the two earliest, *Quinct.* and *S. Rosc.* (92 pages), there are just four examples, or one every 24 pages. In the *Sest.* (73 pages) there are 20 examples, or about one every 3.6 pages. Similarly in the *Dom.* there are eighteen examples, or about one every three to four pages. These two speeches are dated to 57–56 BC, more than twenty years later than *Quinct.* and *S. Rosc.* (81–80), and it is possible that Cicero came to exploit the usage more over time. In the *Philippics* there are 25 examples in 117 pages, or one every 4.7 pages, but a lot of these are legal or official (see below, 7.8.1).

But the subject matter came into it too, with the frequency and types of asyndeta partly determined by the context or addressee. I will return to this subject below (7.6), but I mention here that the speeches against Catiline, which are quite early, have twelve examples in 54 pages, or one every 4.5 pages. The contrast with the two earlier speeches referred to above is due to the content of the Catilinarians (see also on 3 and 4).

In the two philosophical works there are on the interpretations set out here 68 instances of asyndeton bimembre, or about one example every five pages. That is a quite high figure, when compared for example with the letters to Atticus (see below).

Letters 1–166 to Atticus have about 31 examples of asyndeton comprising two single words, that is about one every nine to ten pages. Leaving aside mere statistics, we will see later (7.4.1) that there are limitations to the varieties of the phenomenon in these letters.

Asyndeton of our type is more common in the letters *Ad familiares* than in those *Ad Atticum* (19 instances in 120 pages, or one every six pages), though the figures are not high (I leave aside the letters by Caelius). The types in *Fam.* also differ from those in *Att.*, and are more diverse (7.5.2).

7.2 Observations on the Speeches

7.2.1 Nouns

About 32 asyndetic pairs of nouns are listed from the speeches. It is striking just how few of these are free-standing. Most are in accumulations of various sorts (see below). Another type is that in which a single-word

7 Conclusions

pair with some sort of semantic unity is followed by a third, generalising element. It is admittedly controversial to classify such sequences as having two members. It is a matter of opinion whether the generalising element should be treated as separate from the preceding pair.

The only pairs used on their own are the following: 11 *desidiam inertiam*, 17 *sceleribus flagitiis* (but textually doubtful), 18 *uim arma*, 22 *signa tabulas*, the title *imperator, consul designatus* (23, 24, 28, 29), 27 *insaniam adrogationem*, 30, 31 *pontifex pro praetore* (another title). I leave aside 16 *qui ab aris focis ferrum flammamque depellis*, because, though there are not two syntactically parallel pairs, the asyndeton is followed by a coordinated pair.

There are eleven examples here, or ten if the textually problematic 17 is left out. Six of the ten (eleven) are official titles, which do not reflect Cicero's way of writing but the way in which double titles were usually expressed. Two of the four (five) remaining examples (11, 27) share a characteristic: they are lists of vices placed at the end of a clause or sentence, expressing the idea that the vices are chosen *exempli gratia* (see IV.3).

Four or five instances of free-standing nominal asyndeta bimembria (leaving aside the official titles) among nouns in eighteen speeches by Cicero is a drop in the ocean. Asyndeton of this type was not just another form of coordination to Cicero, but a stylistic device favoured by certain structures, those containing an accumulation of asyndeta and/or other types of coordination.

I now classify the accumulations in which asyndetic pairs of nouns are found in the selection of speeches.

First, two asyndetic pairs may be juxtaposed or at least in the same sentence: 13, 14 *clamore concursu, ui manu*, 19, 20 *agrorum oppidorum, immunitatum uectigalium flagitiosissimae nundinae*.

Second, an asyndetic pair may be followed (or sometimes preceded) by a coordinated pair: 1 *is quicum tibi adfinitas societas, omnes denique causae et necessitudines ueteres intercedebant*, 3 *rem publicam, Quirites, uitamque omnium uestrum, bona fortunas, coniuges liberosque*, 4 *templis delubris, tectis ac moenibus*, 8 *cuius eximia uirtus dignitas, et in eo negotio quod gessit, fides et continentia*, 10 *uino ganeis, lenociniis adulteriisque*, 16 *aris focis ferrum flammamque depellis* (this is not the same as the other examples in this section, in that the coordinated pair is not in the same case as the asyndetic pair, but still an asyndeton is juxtaposed with a coordination), 25 *eum exercitumque, municipia colonias*.

Third, an asyndeton bimembre may be followed (or preceded) by an asyndetic tricolon (structure 2 + 3, 3 + 2): 12 *uim arma, exercitus imperatores castra denuntiabat*, 15 *ad ferrum faces, ad cotidianam caedem incendia rapinas*. For the pattern asyndetic pair + asyndetic tricolon see e.g. Sallust 29 *regna prouinciae, leges iura iudicia*.

Fourth, sometimes an asyndetic pair is part of a sequence of (mainly) phrasal or clausal asyndeta: 7 *sic reditu ubertas agrorum, frugum copia, spes oti, tranquillitas animorum, iudicia leges, concordia populi, senatus auctoritas*.

Fifth, at 9 (*tibi manum copias, tibi suos spectatos centuriones, tibi pecuniam, tibi familias compararent*) an asyndetic pair is part of an anaphoric asyndetic sequence. This passage has a recurrent structural feature. Sometimes when an asyndeton is in a sequence, there may be syntactic markers (such as *tibi* here, or prepositions, or just a single intrusive term) splitting up the sequence: see on 9, 9a, 91, 137, with cross references, and note too the second example in our third category above.

The five categories of accumulations just listed account for 16 of the 32 nominal pairs.

Some of the numbered examples, as noted above (7.2.1, first paragraph), are problematic, in that they might alternatively be regarded as merely two parts of a tricolon: 2 *quantum genus est parricidarum sicariorum, denique omnium facinerosorum*, 21 *in urbe auri argenti, maximeque uini foeda direptio*, 26 *saltatores citharistas, totum denique comissationis Antonianae chorum*, 31 *eodem incumbunt municipia coloniae, cuncta Italia*. Cf. also 1, placed in the second category above.

Here is a quick statistical review of the categories listed above, to bring out Cicero's practice. One of the examples (17) has been treated by editors as textually dubious, and I put it to one side, thus reducing the possible examples to 31. If the controversial examples are also dropped, the number becomes 27. Six examples are pairs of titles, and indeed usually found in senatorial decrees or motions. They belong to official style, not Cicero's. Without these, the number goes down to 21. Of these, as we have just seen, sixteen are in accumulations. Cicero mainly used (at least in the speeches) nominal asyndeta bimembria in accumulations of certain types.

7.2.2 Adjectives

In the speeches the following are certain cases of adjectival asyndeta bimembria with single-word (or virtually single-word) members (though there might be argument about one or two): 39 *tenuis libertinus*, 40, 43, 47, 51 *optimus maximus*, 41 *egentem, probatum suis*, 42 *indemnatus innocens*, 44 *tardum inhumanum*, 45, 46 *constans perpetua, fortis inuicta*, 48 *ignarus inuitus*, 49 *maestos sordidatos*, 50 *inaudita noua*, 52, 53 *inuidiosum detestabile, imbecillum caducum*, 54, 55 *falsa incerta sint, caduca mobilia*.

7 Conclusions 465

There are seventeen examples, four of them the invariable religious formula *optimus maximus*, which can be disregarded here, and so the number reduces to just thirteen. The thirteen adjectival pairs share a characteristic with the nominal. Most (ten) are in accumulations: 39, 44, 45, 46, 48, 49, 52, 53, 54, 55.

Some of the pairs fall into types. About half comprise either a pair of adjectives in *in-* or a pair with at least one such formation: 42, 44, 46, 48, 50, 52, 53, 54. Pairs of near-synonyms are also found, perhaps most notably 45, 46, where in each pair the second term semantically caps the first.

In-privative adjectives (and nouns: see 5, 11, 27) constantly occur in asyndeta: see e.g. XXIII.6 (Plautus), XXV.2 (Lucilius), XXX.3.3.2 (Sallust), XXIV.2.1.3, summary after 15 (Virgil), XXIX.2.1.1 (Horace), XXX.5.2.3 (Tacitus).

7.2.3 Verbs

Twenty-three pairs of verbs have been classified as certain asyndeta bimembria. They are of different types. I have treated as doubtful several instances that might be taken as unitary pairs embedded within a longer sequence.

Six examples do not represent Ciceronian composition but are legal phrases or variants of legal phrases, or are in official contexts: 64, 65 *uelitis iubeatis*, 75 *conscripserit compararit*, 76 *defendant defe<nde>rint*, 77, 78 *ita darent adsignarent ut quibus militibus amplissime dati adsignati essent*.

The following examples are structurally similar to one another:

56 *ecquid attendis, ecquid animaduertis horum silentium? patiuntur tacent*
72 *fertur ille uir, mihi crede, gloria: flagrat ardet cupiditate iusti et magni triumphi*
73 *apparet esse commotum: sudat pallet*.

In all three passages there is an initial sentence, which is then explained. The explanation has the form of a pair of asyndetic verbs in the present tense (in the second passage there is a complement that goes with both verbs). They are near-synonyms. The placement of the pairs, after the initial assertion or question, is similar to the placement in final position of two pairs of nouns I referred to above (7.2.1, third paragraph) representing open-ended lists: 11 *uidebamus genus uitae, desidiam inertiam*, 27 *noui hominis insaniam adrogationem*. In the above three sentences too the pairs do not express a totality: there are other signs, for example, of being *commotus*.

A similar structure will come up in the philosophica at 148: *non recipit istam coniunctionem honestas, aspernatur repellit*.

A semantic category consists of pairs of verbs expressing acts of violence or hostility (for such pairs in Greek see Mastronarde 2002: 92 with cross references): 62 *prodiderunt oppugnarunt*, 63 *diripiebatur ardebat*, 67 *disturbaretur diriperetur*, 68 *disturbaret uerteret*, 69 *dirueris aedificaris*, 71 *expulerit relegarit*. Five of the verbs have the prefix *dis-*. The asyndetic coordination, presumably with a distinctive intonation, may have stressed the sense of outrage felt by Cicero.

In several cases pairs have the same prefix, or consist of simplex + compound or of a repetition: 67 *disturbaretur diriperetur*, 74 *irent redirent*, 75 *conscripserit compararit*, 76 *defendant defe<nde>rint*; note too *Cat.* 2.1 (unnumbered) *abiit excessit euasit erupit*. 59 *pertimuit profugit* is an alliterative pair with members having different prefixes. Such types of verbal pairs we also saw in Plautus (XXIII.5.4), and they must have been old, though one should not exaggerate their frequency.

There are also pairs of near-synonyms (57, 58 *patefacta inlustrata, oppressa uindicata*, 77, 78 *darent adsignarent ... dati adsignati*) and of opposites (69 *dirueris aedificaris*, 74 *irent redirent*), pairs in which the second verb outdoes the first (61 *poterat audebat*, 71 *expulerit relegarit*), pairs expressing a temporal sequence (59 *pertimuit profugit*, 66 *promulgasti tulisti*), and a pair in which the second verb is in effect a modifier of the first (70 *fauebant gaudebant*).

Asyndetic pairs of verbs are not infrequently in accumulations of one sort or another: 56 *ecquid attendis, ecquid animaduertis horum silentium? patiuntur tacent* (a pair of asyndetic clauses with anaphora and then an asyndeton bimembre), 57, 58 *ut Catilinae profectione omnia patefacta inlustrata, oppressa uindicata esse uideatis* (two pairs juxtaposed), 61 *appellare temptare sollicitare poterat audebat* (two asyndetic groups, with 3 + 2 members), 63 *uno eodemque tempore domus mea diripiebatur ardebat, bona ad uicinum consulem de Palatio, de Tusculano ad item uicinum alterum consulem deferebantur* (two asyndetic verbs, followed by two asyndetic clauses), 69 *dirueris aedificaris, religione omni uiolata religionis tamen nomine contaminaris, in uisceribus eius qui urbem suis laboribus ac periculis conseruasset monumentum deletae rei publicae conlocaris, ... incideris* (an asyndetic pair, and then an asyndetic clausal tricolon; there are also phrasal asyndeta in this passage, not printed here), 77, 78 *ita darent adsignarent ut quibus militibus amplissime dati adsignati essent* (two pairs in the same sentence). There are eight pairs here, of the 23.

7 Conclusions 467

7.2.4 Prepositional Type

Ten asyndetic pairs of the prepositional (anaphoric) type were quoted above. Most are in passages that are structurally significant.

First, four cases are juxtaposed with or near an asyndeton bimembre of another or the same type: 82, 83, 87, 88.

Second, the prepositional pair is sometimes part of a longer sequence comprising different types of asyndeta: 81, 86.

85 has the familiar 2 + 3 structure, that is asyndeton bimembre followed by asyndetic single-word tricolon.

A striking passage is 87, 88 *cum uicatim homines conscriberentur decuriarentur, ad uim ad manus, ad caedem ad direptionem incitarentur,* which has three asyndetic pairs (the first comprising verbs) in succession.

Once again we see the tendency for asyndeton bimembre to occur in accumulations.

7.2.5 Accumulations: Statistics

Roughly 45 pairs of the 91 in the speeches are in accumulations, about half.

7.2.6 Pairs of Opposites in the Speeches

In the speeches I have noted the following pairs of opposites (taking into account not only nouns but the other parts of speech): **19** *agrorum oppidorum,* **69** *dirueris aedificaris,* **74** *irent redirent.*

The juxtaposing of opposites was not a trait of Cicero's oratory.

7.3 Observations on the Philosophica

I repeat that the two philosophical works contain 68 asyndeta bimembria, or about one instance every five pages. There are 35 pairs of nouns and 7 pairs of names. Nouns are more prominent than they are in the letters, as we will see. Pairs of verbs occur thirteen times. There are three pairs of adjectives, and ten pairs of the prepositional type.

It is noticeable in the philosophica that the nouns and verbs are used in stylised ways, in certain structures and accumulations, and in a recurrent semantic relationship.

7.3.1 Accumulations and Opposites, of Nouns and Verbs
(i) Two or More Nominal Pairs Together, Juxtaposed or not Far Apart

92, 93 *mundos elegantis, optimis cocis pistoribus* (followed by an asyndetic nominal tricolon: see below, iv).
94–8 *dulce amarum, leue asperum, prope longe, stare mouere, quadratum rotundum*
108–11 *forum fana, porticus uiae, leges iura, iudicia suffragia*
113–15 *regna imperia, nobilitas honores, diuitiae opes*
117, 118 *status incessus, sessio accubito* (followed by an asyndetic nominal tricolon: see below, iv).
120, 121 *uita mors, diuitiae paupertas*
123, 124 *in tutelis societatibus, fiduciis mandatis* (these two pairs of nouns are followed immediately by two pairs of asyndetic (participial) verbs: see below, ii, 146, 147).

There are seven such accumulations here, which embrace 20 of the 35 asyndetic pairs of nouns in the corpus. Pairs of opposites are frequent in the above list (about seven examples; I omit *sessio accubito*). There are other pairs of opposites among nouns not in accumulations (100 *urbani rustici*, 107 *in foro, domi*). Thus about a quarter (nine) of the asyndetic pairs of nouns consist of opposites.

(ii) Juxtaposed Pairs of Asyndetic Verbs

141, 142 *uendunt emunt, conducunt locant*
143, 144 *uendendo emendo, conducendo locando* (see also below, iii).
146, 147 *rebus emptis uenditis, conductis locatis* (with the two pairs of verbs preceded by two pairs of nouns: see above, i, 123, 124).

These three accumulations comprise six pairs, out of the thirteen pairs of verbs. The number of pairs in accumulations thus rises to 26. All six here are pairs of opposites (converses). There are other pairs of opposites too among the verbs:

138 *dando accipiendo*
139 *docendo discendo*
140 *datis acceptis.*

The three pairs of opposites here added to the six above make up nine of the thirteen asyndetic pairs of verbs in the corpus. All nine are converses. In some cases Cicero has made use of legal phrases. The four verbal pairs that are not opposites are: 136 *circumcidat amputet*, 137 *ambulet sedeat* (though this pair too may be seen as a variation on the opposites *mouere/stare*: see

7 *Conclusions* 469

XIII.5.5 on opposites of this inexplicit type), 145 *DARE FACERE*, 148 *aspernatur repellit*.

The pairs of opposites among nouns and verbs comprise eighteen examples, a significant proportion (about 26 per cent) of the total number of asyndetic pairs (68), and an even higher proportion (37.5 per cent) of the nominal and verbal pairs (18 out of 48). By contrast in the speeches we found just three pairs of opposites in the total of 91 asyndetic pairs, or 3.3 per cent.

The accumulations above are not the only types. Here are some others:

(iii) Asyndetic Pair(s) Followed or Preceded by a Coordinated Pair

91 *maledicta contumeliae, tum iracundae contentiones concertationesque in disputando pertinaces*
112 *uoltus uoces, motus statusque*
116 *in omnibus factis dictis, in corporis denique motu et statu*
140 *ultro et citro datis acceptis*
143, 144 *uendendo emendo, conducendo locando, uicinitatibus et confiniis* (see also above, ii).

(iv) Pairs (or Double Pairings) Followed by an Asyndetic Tricolon

92, 93 *mundos elegantis, optimis cocis pistoribus, piscatu aucupio uenatione* (cited also above at i).
117, 118 *status incessus, sessio accubito, uoltus oculi manuum motus* (cited also above at i).
136 *circumcidat amputet, erigat extollat adminiculet*
139 *docendo discendo, communicando disceptando iudicando*
155 *in equis in leonibus, iustitiam aequitatem bonitatem.*

(v) Pairs Embedded in a Longer Asyndetic Sequence

99 *officium aequitatem dignitatem fidem, <u>recta honesta</u>, digna imperio, digna populo Romano, omnia pericula pro re publica, mori pro patria*

(vi) Asyndetic Pairs that Are Part of or Followed by a Sequence of Anaphoric Asyndeta

119 *ut aurum argentum, ut ea quae gignuntur e terra, ut alia generis eiusdem*
137 *quis ambulet sedeat, qui ductus oris, qui uultus in quoque sit*

138 *dando accipiendo, tum artibus, tum opera, tum facultatibus deuincire hominum inter homines societatem.*

In the six categories just listed there are 20 accumulations, which embrace 36 different asyndetic pairs of nouns and verbs; several passages are cited more than once because they belong to more than one category structurally, but no pairs have been counted twice.

There are just three definite adjectival pairs in asyndeton in the philosophica (133–5), and two of these are in accumulations (133, 135). Asyndetic pairs in accumulations rise further to 39. Asyndeta of the prepositional type are also found in accumulations: 153–5.

The total then is 42 pairs in accumulations. To these could be added an example that has not been put into one of the classifications above: 102. In all, 43 examples represent about 63 per cent of the asyndeta bimembria in the two philosophical works. It was noted earlier (7.2.5) that about half of the asyndetic pairs in the speeches are in accumulations.

The most striking difference between the philosophica and the speeches lies in the frequency of pairs of opposites in the philosophica. For the figures comparing the philosophica with the speeches see above, ii. Reflected here is a feature of philosophical discourse, in which opposites are often contrasted, and there was obviously a tendency to express such oppositions asyndetically, presumably to make the contrast sharper.

Another characteristic of the philosophical works is the frequency with which two (or more) asyndetic pairs are juxtaposed: see above, i, ii for the examples of nouns and verbs, all quoted (ten such accumulations). From the numbered citations above it can be seen that the figures for this feature in the speeches are: nouns two accumulations, adjectives three, verbs one, prepositional type one. The proportion is lower in the speeches. The philosophical works also tend to have longer sequences of juxtaposed pairs, as in a number of the passages at i above.

7.4 Observations on the Letters Ad Atticum

7.4.1 Types and Distributions

We saw above (7.1) that the 296 pages of letters 1–166 have about 31 examples of asyndeton comprising two single words, or about one example every nine to ten pages.

Pairs of nouns are conspicuously infrequent. Just 5 of the 31 asyndeta are of this type, or one in about six cases. Of the five, one (**160**) is in what looks like an old formal (religious) phrase (*fanorum lucorum*), expressing

7 Conclusions

a totality of sorts, which Shackleton Bailey translates using quotation marks. Another, 163 *aequi boni*, is a legal pairing used proverbially in a non-legal context. A third, 162 *gemitus ploratus*, is in a familiar structure: it is embedded within a sequence of phrasal asyndeta. It is also of a semantic type (see 7.8.2).

A distinction has been made throughout this chapter between nouns and names (personal and place-). If one leaves aside consular naming (with full names in asyndeton; by contrast, I have quoted at 4.2, first paragraph, two cases of consuls' names coordinated, but in both cases the consuls are given just a single name and the phrases are thus not of the official type), there are eight pairs of names in asyndeton. These are not all of the same type. In one case (168) an official appointment is reported, and those appointed are given full names. The list is thus a totality, of the old official type. In several other cases the lists (of single, not full names) are either certainly or probably not totalities but comprise examples or persons chosen at random (165, 169, 170, 171). Finally, in two places (164 and 166, 167) lists of four names (personal and place-) are split into two groups of two by the insertion of an intrusive parenthesis. In the first of these the asyndetic pair is followed by a coordinated. For intrusive elements as colon dividers in such groups see on 164, with cross reference, and also Livy 57, 58. It is the open-ended pairs that are of most interest.

There is just a single adjectival asyndeton (172 *inanes imparati*). It belongs to a type, consisting of two adjectives with the prefix *in-*, postponed (both with unfavourable connotations).

More common are pairs of verbs. There are eight (I have not included the textually doubtful 1.18.1, discussed after 174), numbered 174–81, just short of a third of the total of asyndeta bimembria in these letters. Six of the eight are in the present tense, and a seventh pair consists of present participles. The semantic relationship between verbs in asyndeton is varied. In three cases (174, 175, 179) the second verb outdoes the first semantically, and that is particularly so at 175 where the structure implies a pause for thought. Another two (176 *uolitat furit*, 178 *fremit queritur*) express simultaneous happenings, with one verb modifying or specifying the other. Finally, at 177 and 180 there is either a temporal sequence, or the second verb conveys a consequence of the first. Pairs of verbs seem to be a mark of vivid narrative.

In only two cases is the second verb longer than the first (178, 181). In another two the longer verb is first (176, 177); otherwise the verbs have the same number of syllables. The ordering is determined by semantic factors, not by a rhetorical principle. For the 'law of ascending length' in Indo-European languages including Latin, see XVI (with statistics).

Pairs of the prepositional type are also found eight times in the letters *Ad Atticum*. They are placed typically at the end of a clause or sentence. In half the cases the context or content of the phrases is official (183, 184, 186, 187). 182 (*de flammis de ferro*) is an alliterative pairing elsewhere attested, though not with asyndeton (16); here it is in a very rhetorical passage.

7.4.2 Accumulations

Asyndetic pairs in accumulations are not particularly common (six cases: 159, 162, 164, 166–7, 177). Only one of these passages would be described as highly rhetorical (162).

7.4.3 Opposites

Of the 31 asyndeta bimembria, just three comprise opposites of a sort: 161 *legationum priuatorum*, 173 *aperte tecte*, 184 *de rebus urbanis de prouinciis*.

7.4.4 Further Remarks

Most of the asyndetic pairs collected here comprise names, verbs and prepositional structures (24 in total). In more stylised Latin, such as that of historians and Cicero himself in the speeches and philosophica, asyndetic pairs of nouns are more common than they are in these letters, and are used in distinctive ways.

Many pairs of nouns and adjectives in Latin literature in general are established groups that recur, with and without coordination, but paired names often express miscellaneous individuals. Cicero's pairs of verbs too (in these letters), though they might have structural characteristics (such as the second outdoing the first, or one modifying the other) found also in stylised literature, have an ad hoc rather than formulaic character.

Discontinuous pairs occur at 175 and 186, with the delayed term presumably emphatic (notably in the first case). I have not accepted the possible case with two names at 8.2.3 (quoted after 171), for want of parallels in Cicero.

7.5 Observations on the Letters Ad familiares

Asyndeton bimembre is a little more common in the letters *Ad familiares* than in those *Ad Atticum* (19 in 120 pages versus 31 in 296), but it is in the types and their uses that *Fam.* differs most conspicuously from *Att.*

7.5.1 Accumulations

Two-thirds (twelve of nineteen) of the asyndetic pairs in *Fam.* are in accumulations of coordinations, asyndetic and syndetic: 190, 191, 194, 195, 196, 197, 198, 201, 202, 203, 207, 208. In *Att.* 6 pairs out of 31 are in accumulations, about 20 per cent.

7.5.2 Types and Distributions

Most of the pairs listed from *Fam.* (fourteen of the nineteen) consist of nouns or adjectives, whereas in *Att.* only six of the 31 are in these categories. In the speeches and philosophica there are also quite high proportions of nominal and adjectival examples considered together (49/91 and 35/68), though it has to be said that of these 35 in the philosophica only three are adjectives.

Cicero's use of adjectives is much more varied in *Fam.* than in *Att.* Seven examples from *Fam.* have been quoted (197–203), against a single instance of commonplace type in *Att.* (172). In *Fam.*, 207, 208 *in re priuata in publica* has been classified as being of the prepositional type, but it is also adjectival. There are accumulations, as at 197, 198 and 202, 203, where two pairs of adjectival opposites are juxtaposed, and are alongside asyndeta of other types. At 201, *Graecis Latinis* consists of complements, if not opposites, making up the totality of the languages of Cicero's writings, and this is in the same sentence as a pair of phrasal asyndeta. *Summis infimis* at 200 also comprises opposites, and is of an ancient type. Of the seven adjectival asyndeta (or eight, depending on how one takes *in re priuata in publica*), five are pairs of opposites, and five occur in asyndetic accumulations. One adjectival pair that is not made up of opposites and is not in an accumulation is that at 199, but this is distinctive in its own right, in that the structure is discontinuous.

Here is the list of pairs of opposites in the selection from *Fam.*: 197, 198 *publicis priuatis, forensibus domesticis*, 200 *summis infimis*, 202, 203 *domestica forensia, urbana prouincialia*, 207, 208 *in re priuata, in publica*. Some might be inclined to classify the following pairs too as containing opposites: 196 *dictis factis*, 201 *Graecis Latinis*.

A feature of the asyndetic nouns is their tendency to occur in accumulations (five of the seven: 190, 191, 194, 195, 196).

7.5.3 Addressees and Asyndeton

The different addressees influenced Cicero's use or avoidance of asyndeton bimembre in the letters. He was on close terms with Atticus (or presented himself thus), and the rarity of asyndeton bimembre in that corpus suggests that, outside certain banal combinations, it was a stylised usage and not overused in personal discourse. At 190, 191 and 197, 198 by contrast we find a sequence of four asyndeta bimembria in a letter to the consul Crassus described by Shackleton Bailey as showing 'conscious insincerity'. Cicero was hostile to Crassus (see on 197, 198). The letter also has various asyndetic tricola. Two nominal instances are in letters to Appius Pulcher (193, 194), a correspondent to whom Cicero uses a lot of longer asyndetic sequences (on which see the commentary on 193). The second nominal example just referred to is followed immediately by a phrasal pair. Two juxtaposed nominal pairs are in a letter to the consul Marcellus (195, 196). There are also asyndeta in letters to Cato (201: an accumulation) and Caesar (192, 199). The accumulation to Tiro (202, 203) is in a powerful expression of gratitude for all the services that Tiro had performed, and there is a formality to it. The one example in a letter to members of his family (204) is a variant on a formula of well-being. As for the pair of verbs *occisi capti* in a letter to Caelius (205), this is determined by the context, in effect a military report. The two verbs occur together in historians in military contexts, and in asyndeton. It seems that a formal, cool or uneasy relationship with an addressee was likely to motivate asyndeta, and that suggests that asyndeton was often stylised, though there were certainly mundane types as well. In Sallust, for example, there are striking accumulations in certain speeches, such as that of Catiline, and in other historiography the usage is disproportionately frequent in speeches. It was suited to a rhetorical and passionate presentation.

7.6 Contexts and Genres as Determinants of Asyndeton

We have seen differences between the speeches and the philosophical works, between the letters *Ad Atticum* and those *Ad familiares*, and beween the *Att.* and all three of the other corpora.

Just as the frequency of asyndeton bimembre was influenced by Cicero's relations with the addressees and by the circumstances of letters (see above), so in other genres context, circumstances and subject matter are factors that have to be considered as determinants of such usages.

In the dramatic opening to the third Catilinarian, in which Cicero boasts to the people of his salvation of the republic, there are two asyndeta bimembria in a short space, amid accumulations of asyndeta of various other types (3, 4). In the second and third Catilinarians, both delivered to the people, there are eight asyndeta bimembria in 27 pages, about the same incidence as that in the *Sest.* (20 examples in 73 pages: see 7.1). As for the

Sest. itself, this is a speech in which reported praise of Cicero has a prominent place, and in which Cicero identifies his interests with those of the commonwealth and dwells on his hardships undergone for the sake of the state (see the introduction to Kaster 2006 on these themes). It was pointed out earlier (7.1) that asyndeton bimembre is hardly found in Cicero's two earliest speeches, the content of which may have been a factor. Cicero seems to have favoured this type of asyndeton (not least in accumulations) on great public occasions when he was in a position of power or prominence. Incidentally, the considerable proportion of examples in official, mainly legal, contexts (see below, 7.8.1) supports the contention of XXII that asyndeton had a significant place in legal language in the Republic.

The snatches of a letter by Timarchides, freedman of Verres, to Apronius quoted by Cicero at *Verr.* 3.154–7, support the view that in particular types of (non-intimate) letters asyndeton was felt to be appropriate. The scanty fragments, which appear to be full of exhortation and passion, contain no fewer than three asyndeta bimembria, one of them a simplex–compound pair (3.155 *caede concide*) of a type hardly found in literary language (see VII) (cf. 3.154 *habes uirtutem eloquentiam*, 3.155 *scribas apparitores recentis arripe*, this last from the same passage as *caede concide*). There was clearly something about the tone and circumstances of this letter that inspired these pairs.

In the two philosophical works there are 35 pairs of nouns (see 7.3), half of the 68 asyndeta bimembria in the eight books. By contrast, in the letters to Atticus we noted just five pairs of nouns (out of 31 asyndeta bimembria) (see above, 7.4.1), one of them in a textually disputed passage (**159**), and another in a religious formula (**160**). Philosophy deals with abstract concepts, and these are often expressed by abstract nouns. Asyndeton is a means of underlining some semantic relationships between two such terms. It was noted earlier (7.3.1 (ii)) that about 37.5 per cent of the pairs of nouns and verbs in the philosophica comprise opposites. Five of these are in a single sentence (**94–8**). For comparison two passages from Aristotle were quoted, which have similar accumulations of opposites. In the speeches and *Att.* pairs of opposites are rare (see 7.2.6, 7.4.3).

7.7 Punctuation, Textual Issues and Some Influences on Asyndeton

Editors face problems in punctuating asyndeta, and are not always consistent. We have, for example, seen many unitary pairs juxtaposed in these texts. Take **120**, **121**, which has the four nouns *uita mors diuitiae paupertas*.

'Life, death' and 'riches, poverty' are manifestly two separate pairs of opposities (complementarities, antonyms), and it is a reasonable guess that in Latin pronunciation, as in English, there would have been a pause or intonational marker after the first pair. How is an editor to punctuate? There are three possibilities: absence of commas, a comma after *mors* or a comma after each of the first three nouns. Winterbottom (1994) opts for complete absence of commas. On the other hand at 143, 144 *uendendo emendo, conducendo locando, uicinitatibus et confiniis* he puts a comma after *emendo* and *locando*, thus marking the distinction between the two pairs of opposites (converses). Yet at 141, 142 *iis etiam qui uendunt emunt conducunt locant contrahendisque negotiis implicantur*, where the same two pairs of verbs are juxtaposed, and in the same order, he has no commas at all.

The third method of dealing with such juxtaposed pairs may be illustrated from another editor, Shackleton Bailey, who is also inconsistent. In his 1977 edition of the *Ad familiares* at 197, 198 he prints *in omnibus publicis, priuatis, forensibus, domesticis tuis*. By contrast in his Loeb edition of the same passage he has *in omnibus publicis priuatis, forensibus domesticis, tuis* . . .

I cite just one further example. Reynolds (1998) was faced by a whole string of opposites at 94–8, and he punctuated thus: *dulce amarum, leue asperum, prope longe, stare mouere, quadratum rotundum*.

It is obvious from the material in this chapter and other chapters that literary Latin has numerous asyndetic sequences, and that embedded within these there may be pairs (such as pairs of opposites) that are units. In my view they should be marked off by punctuation, as in the last passage cited. It is not only editorial convention that is at issue here, but the interpretation of the Latin. Take, for example, 112 *uultus uoces motus statusque*, which I print here as it is in Winterbottom (1994). How is the sequence to be analysed? One possibility is that there might be a miscellaneous list with end-of-list coordination, of the standard English type. But the list is not miscellaneous. *Motus* and *status* are opposites, of movement versus standing still, an old and well-attested combination. *Voltus* and *uoces* for their part are an attested pairing, used by Tacitus in asyndeton. Not only that, but the structure asyndetic pair + coordinated pair is common in Cicero and other writers, as has frequently been shown in this chapter and elsewhere. It is beyond question that there are two units here, and a comma should be placed after *uoces*, which, unlike absence of punctuation, would make it clear how the sequence is to be taken. The Loeb (Miller), by contrast, is punctuated thus: *uoltus, uoces, motus statusque*. The punctuation suggests (?) that Miller found end-of-list coordination here, without using the so-called 'Oxford comma'. The translation fails to make his interpretation clear ('their features, voices, motions, attitudes'). On the other hand at 117, 118 *status incessus, sessio accubito* Miller punctuates as here (whereas Winterbottom has no comma).

The analysis of phrase structure is a recurrent problem where asyndeta are or may be present, and other cases have come up in this chapter. See for example on 44 *sine sensu sine sapore, elinguem, tardum inhumanum negotium, Cappadocem modo abreptum de grege uenalium diceres* (a passage in which the punctuation adopted here is not universal), 50 *insigni quadam, inaudita noua magnitudine animi*. See too on Caelius 213 *palam secreto*: is this an appositional compound, a disjunctive asyndeton or a pair of adverbs that are unconnected?

It has been seen that asyndeta are common in certain structures. These structural patterns have received insufficient attention, not least in relation to textual issues. At 8 the following passage was cited and discussed: *cuius eximia uirtus dignitas, et, in eo negotio quod gessit, fides et continentia*. It was noted to have three features, an asyndetic pair of virtues (*uirtus dignitas*), a coordinator and parenthetical clause, and then a coordinated pair of additional abstract nouns. 159 *credibile non est quantum ego in consiliis <et> prudentia tua et, quod maximum est, quantum in amore et fide ponam* was shown to have the same three features, and yet there the asyndeton tends to be emended away.

Other textual problems are discussed on *Red. Quir.* 13 (after 4), on 151 (where recognition of a contrast of opposites supports asyndeton) and on 193 (where phrase structure tells against an emendation to eliminate an asyndeton bimembre). At *Att.* 8.2.3 (after 171) and *Fam.* 15.4.7 (after 196) a feature of conjunct hyperbaton in Cicero compared with discontinuous asyndeton supports the inclusion of a coordinator.

Quite a lot of the asyndetic pairs listed in this chapter are also illustrated in the commentaries with coordination, a fact which is in line with a point made elsewhere (see e.g. III), that there are few invariable asyndetic pairs in Latin (I am referring to pairs that occur with asyndeton several times, as distinct from those that are one-off oddities: see further below). On the other hand even a pair that is predominantly syndetic may occur once or twice with asyndeton, and it is unacceptable to emend away an asyndeton on the grounds that the pair is elsewhere coordinated. Structural features of a passage are a criterion for an editor in determining whether an asyndeton should be retained or removed. Such a high proportion of asyndeta bimembria occur in accumulations of different types that an unusual or unattested asyndetic pair in one of these structures may well be right.

I list here the (Ciceronian) asyndetic pairs in this chapter that are shown in the commentaries to be attested also with coordination: 1 *adfinitas societas*, 3 *bona fortunae*, 4 *templa delubra*, 5–7 *fuga formido*, 8 *uirtus dignitas*, 12, 18 *uis arma*, 13 *clamor concursus*, 16 *arae foci*, 17 *scelera flagitia*, 19 *agri oppida*, 25, 31 *municipia coloniae*, 50 *inauditus nouus*, 57 *patefacta inlustrata*, 74 *ire redire*, 76 *defendere* in two different tenses/moods, 86 *natura mores*, 88 *caedes direptio*, 99 *recta honesta*, 101 *ioca seria*, 103 *frigus fames*, 105 *parentes patria*, 112 *uultus uox*, 116, 195 *facta dicta*, 119 *aurum argentum*, 120 *uita mors*, 121 *diuitiae paupertas*, 138, 140 *dare accipere*, 139 *docere discere*, 141, 143, 146 *uendere emere*, 142, 144, 147 *conducere locare*, 160 *fana luci*, 182 *flammae ferrum* (see on 16), 193 *uirtus industria*, 197, 207 *publicus priuatus*, 198, 202 *forensis domesticus*, 200 *summus infimus*, 205 *occisi capti*.

Of the total of 209 asyndetic pairs, 47 (at least) are attested as well with coordination (23 per cent). The coordinated variants would probably be more numerous if a more thorough search were made, but it nevertheless emerges that many of the asyndetic pairings (i.e. the 77 per cent not, it seems, found with coordination) must have been ad hoc, as distinct from deriving from formulaic combinations of terms. One can go further. It is suggested by statistics (see below) that asyndetic pairs of adjectives particularly but also to a lesser extent of verbs were especially likely to be put together ad hoc.

Of the 47 pairs with coordinated variants, 28 are nouns, a proportion of just on 60 per cent. This proportion suggests that Cicero, when using asyndetic pairs of nouns, was drawing to a considerable extent on standard pairings and sometimes dropping the coordinator for some reason (as for example if he was putting together an accumulation).

By contrast, only six of the 47 with coordinated variants comprise adjectives, a proportion of between 12 and 13 per cent. As for verbs, 13 of the 47 have coordinated variants, a proportion of about 27 per cent. It would appear that Cicero's asyndetic pairs of adjectives and verbs were more likely to be ad hoc creations than were his asyndetic pairs of nouns.

There is another way of presenting the evidence to do with the different parts of speech, and that is to compare the numbers of nouns, adjectives and verbs that have coordinated variants, with the numbers of nouns, adjectives and verbs in total in the corpus.

The corpus has 79 pairs of nouns. The 28 with coordinated variants represent about 36 per cent of the total. The total of asyndetic adjectives is

7 Conclusions 479

28, of which six have coordinated variants, a proportion of 21 per cent. The total of asyndetic verbs is 46, of which thirteen have coordinated variants, a proportion of 28 per cent.

Both sets of figures suggest that Cicero was more prone to modify a standard pairing of nouns by deleting the coordinator than he was to produce pairings of adjectives (in particular) and verbs in this way. Pairs of adjectives and verbs were more likely to be juxtaposed asyndetically off-the-cuff than were pairs of nouns. In assessing the determinants of asyndeton it follows that one must consider on the one hand what factors might have caused the omission of a coordinator in a formulaic pairing, and on the other hand what might have prompted the absence of coordination when two words were put together ad hoc. It is probably true to say that, when constructing an accumulation, Cicero was given to including a standard pairing (or more than one, sometimes with the two juxtaposed). Unusual pairings occur for example in open-ended lists, which hint that further terms (particularly nouns for vices or judgemental adjectives) might be added. Pairs particularly at the end of a colon or in discontinuous sequences may imply a pause for thought, and if a second term is to outdo another with an element of surprise, it may well not be simply an habitual member of an asyndeton.

Some semantic fields tend to generate asyndeta, and I turn now to semantic factors.

7.8 Some Semantic Categories

7.8.1 Legal and Religious Pairs

Many of the asyndetic pairs in Cicero are legal/official or religious phrases, either in the strict sense (as being established formulae or used in official contexts such as senatorial decrees), or more loosely. Most of these have been classified as such in the commentaries. Here is a list: 3 *bona fortunas*, 4 *templis delubris*, 7 *iudicia leges*, 9a *religione caerimoniis*, 16 *ab aris focis*, 20 *immunitatum uectigalium*, 23, 24 *imperatoris, consulis designati* + same pair in the accusative, 25 *municipia colonias*, 28 *imperator, consul designatus*, 29 *imperatoris, consulis designati*, 30 *pontificem, pro praetore*, 31 *municipia coloniae*, 33 *lex Aelia lex Fufia*, 34, 35, 36 *Caeciliam Didiam Liciniam Iuniam*, 40 *optimus maximus*, 43 *optimi maximi*, 47 *optimi maximi*, 51 *optimi maximi*, 64, 65 *uelitis iubeatis*, 66 *promulgasti tulisti*, 75 *conscripserit comparariti*, 76 *defendant defe<nde>rint*, 77, 78 *darent adsignarent* ... *dati adsignati*, 122 *iudicibus magistratibus*, 123, 124 *in tutelis societatibus, fiduciis mandatis*, 130 *L. Sullae C. Caesaris*, 140 *ultro et citro datis acceptis*, 142, 143

480   XXVI Cicero

uendunt emunt, conducunt locant, 143, 144 *uendendo emendo, conducendo locando,* 145 *DARE FACERE,* 160 *fanorum lucorum,* 163 *aequi boni,* 168 *M. Scaptio L. Gauio,* 183 *de ambitu de iudiciis.* To these might be added Caelius 209 *senatus consulta <e>dicta.*

There are 42 Ciceronian examples listed here, of 209 asyndeta bimembria in the corpus, or about 19 per cent of the total. Of the eight asyndeta in letters of Caelius discussed here, four are in legal/official phrases. The great majority (34) of these 42 Ciceronian pairs are legal/official. Most (four) of the seven 'religious' pairs consist of the formula *optimus maximus* (cf. also 4, 16, 160). The imbalance is mainly due to the fact that Cicero's works are more on political than on religious themes, but it is also true that asyndeton bimembre is much more common in republican laws than in early prayers (see XXII.2–3).

7.8.2 Miscellaneous Semantic Types

Some asyndetic pairs are formulaic and old, such as the alliterative pair denoting two of the hardships of those who are outcasts (103 *frigus fames*). This came up both in Plautus (XXIII.7.3) and Lucilius (XXV example 7).

On the other hand we sometimes find pairs that are variations on formulaic pairs. For example, the nominal alliterative pair *fuga formido* is converted into a verbal alliterative pair at 59 (*pertimuit profugit*). In the latter the second verb expresses a consequence of the first, whereas in the first formula it is the second term which conveys the motivation of the first. *Fuga formido* may be illogical in its order, but ascending length is achieved. Or again, twice Cicero has pairs (179 *uiuit regnat,* 204 *uiximus floruimus*) that can be interpreted as variants on the old pair *uiuit ualet* (see on 179). *Vino ganeis* ('wine, gluttonous eating') at 10 is a variant of the 'eat/drink' pair found e.g. in Plautus (see on 10). Twice (151, 155) Cicero opposes lions to horses/dogs, and these pairs are specific variants on the general opposition wild versus domestic animals, found in Lucretius (see on 151). In one of these passages (151) the underlying semantics undermines a suggested emendation of the text. 149 *in gignendo in educando* is reminiscent of the pair *alit auget* in Pacuvius and Lucretius, a pair that in Pacuvius is once combined with *creat.*

Virtues/merits and vices/misdeeds are often listed in asyndetic pairs (usually of nouns), lists that were presumably of the open-ended type: for virtues see 8, 99, 106, 135, 159, 163, 192, 193, 194, 199, and for vices and the like, 11, 17, 27, 91, 106, 133, 134. *Virtus* itself occurs in several combinations (8, 193; see also on 11 for *uirtutem eloquentiam* in Cicero).

7 Conclusions

At 205 the asyndetic verbs *occisi capti* are of a type found in military narrative or reports. More generally asyndetic pairs (not only verbs, on which see 7.2.3 above, but also nouns) often express forms of force or violence. *Vis* is used in various pairs: 12 *uim arma*, 14 *ui manu*, 83 *per uim per furorem*, 87 *ad uim ad manus*. Cf. 15 *ferrum faces*, 88 *ad caedem ad direptionem*, 182 *de flamma de ferro*. Note too the tetracolon (5–7) *uastitas caedes incendia rapinae* and the tricolon (15) *ad cotidianam caedem incendia rapinas* (with the note ad loc. on the pair *caedes incendia* in historians).

Banishment, exclusion, abandonment are themes that attract asyndetic pairings. See 42 and 71, with the cross references to other authors. Conversely the emotive concept of 'home(land)' (as distinct, for example, from 'outside') also is expressed in asyndeta: see 81 *de sedibus de focis*, 85 *in domo in sedibus*, 105 *parentes patriam*, 107 *in foro, domi*. See also on *arae foci* (16), and Sallust 23. Note too 67 *domus mea disturbaretur diriperetur*, where the destruction of Cicero's house evokes an asyndetic pair with repeated prefix. For an instance of *domus* in an asyndeton bimembre in Sallust, see 23.

Wealth or power and their indicators are sometimes referred to by asyndetic pairs: 3, 22, 114, 115, 121, 153.

Note too the following pairs, to do with shouting, complaint, lamentation: 13 *clamore concursu*, 162 *gemitus ploratus*, 178 *fremit queritur*.

Certain words tend to turn up in asyndeta, not with the same word each time but with a variety of terms. We have seen three such terms above, *uirtus*, *uis* and *domus* (for the second of these, see also Cic. *Inv.* 1.41, cited on 213 above). Others are *arma* (see on 12), *proteruus* (133, 134), *aequus* (135, 163) and *industria* (193, with cross reference to Sallust). At 79 three instances of *temere* in asyndeton are cited.

CHAPTER XXVII

Catullus

1 Asyndeta Bimembria

Catullus' practice reveals a good deal about the status and currency of types of asyndeta.

1.1 Nouns

Asyndeton of nouns is sometimes taken to be the most prominent type. In the whole of Catullus I have found just two or three asyndetic noun pairs, but they are of some stylistic interest.

First, in the long and stylistically elevated poem 64 there is a pair of substantivised adjectives comprising a positive and its negative, the latter with the same base as the positive but a negative prefix: 64.405 *omnia fanda nefanda malo permixta furore*. Preuss (1881: 43) cites the coordination, Livy 10.41.3 *fando nefandoque sanguine*. See too Fordyce (1961: 325) for an equivalent pair, but with polysyndeton, in Ovid: *Met.* 6.585 *fasque nefasque | confusura ruit*; cf. Sen. *Dial.* 4.9.2 *ad fas nefasque miscendum*; also Oakley (1997: 524) on Livy 6.14.10 (*per omne fas et nefas*) refers to Virg. *Aen.* 1.543 *fandi atque nefandi*. Note also Virg. *Georg.* 1.505 *fas uersum atque nefas* (see Thomson 1997: 438). On the semantic illogicality of some such pairs see XIII.2 on *summis infimis* (Cicero 200) and one or two other pairs, and also VI.6 (citing Gonda 1959: 344); note Tarrant (2012: 297) on this one ('only the *infanda* [sic] can have alienated the gods'). The pairings are in elevated genres. In positive–negative pairs the negative term usually has the privative prefix *in-*, but occasionally the negated term has a different prefix (see VI.7, and also XXV.1.1.2 on Lucilius 10 with cross references). This pair would have been felt to be high style and artificial. Donatus on Ter. *Ad.* 990 cites as *prouerbiales elocutiones* the pairs *fanda nefanda, digna indigna, uelis nolis*, and he then associates *fas nefas* with the *ueteres: fuit ueteribus usitatum iusta iniusta, digna indigna, fas nefas* (see also VI.6).

482

1 Asyndeta Bimembria

The second nominal asyndeton bimembre in Catullus is different in structure and style, and underlines the point that asyndeta are variable in their types and intentions: 42.13 *non assis facit? o lutum lupanar, | aut si perditius potest quid esse! Lutum, lupanar* is abusive. Lee (1991) renders: 'She doesn't care tuppence, the filthy trollop or whatever's more depraved than that.' This translation makes the pair into a virtual compound. However, the *si*-clause implies that Catullus would have been happy to come up with a stronger word. To call a woman a 'brothel' is already to outdo calling her mere 'mud'. A pause for thought is hinted at, and then Catullus leaves open the possibility that even *lupanar* might be capped. A similar but more prolonged passage is at Plaut. *Per.* 406–8: *oh, lutum lenonium, | commixtum caeno sterculinum publicum, | inpure, inhoneste, iniure, inlex, labes popli* (the tirade goes on further: see XXV.1.1.2, 7)

This is one of two places where Catullus in effect comments on an asyndeton (cf. 86.1, below, 2; note too Hor. *Sat.* 2.7.39, at XXIX.2.1.1). The abusive terms, probably Catullus' own combination, are alliterative and of increasing length. The *u* in the first syllables of both words is of the same length (short). The pair is at the end of a line. It is a reasonable guess that the intonation pattern of this pair would have been different from that of *fanda nefanda*, with *lupanar* highlighted in some way.

In an abusive poem about Mamurra and his wealth the following sequence occurs: 115.5 *uno qui in saltu tot bona possideat, | prata arua, ingentes siluas saltusque, paludesque* (with disagreements about the text at *saltusque*). This is not a miscellaneous list of terms but an accumulation, with first an asyndetic pair, *prata arua*, then a coordinated pair (*siluas saltusque*), and finally *paludesque* (see Kroll 1929: 287 ad loc.). The first two words are near-synonyms (pastures, ploughland; see Col. 11.2.15 *prata uel arua*; also Ulp. *Dig.* 39.3.3.2, and particularly the first two lines of the present poem, where they are combined: *instar triginta iugera prati, quadraginta arui*). For *siluae* and *saltus* coordinated, see the extensive collection of passages at Wölfflin (1933: 275), a list that includes Catull. 34.10 (with polysyndeton, *-que/-que*). These two terms also have a unity, in that they refer to forms of forest/woodland (for *saltus* see meanings 2, 3, *OLD* s.v.; not the technical meaning 4, despite Ellis 1889: 499). The second and third elements of the accumulation denote wild places, in contrast to the asyndetic first pair. For the structure cf. Hor. *Sat.* 1.6.34 at XXIX.2.1.2. On accumulations see also below, 1.3 on 38.3.

1.2 Adjectives

Pairs of asyndetic adjectives are also rare, or even non-existent. Thomson (1997: 288) on the other hand says that Catullus is 'apt to use asyndeton of adjectives and adverbs'.

The first line of the first poem (1.1 *lepidum nouum libellum*) has a pair of adjectives with a place in the literature (see II.2.4), not because they are asyndetic but because there is layering: *lepidum* [*nouum libellum*]. Thomson (1997: 320) on 46.11 lists the example as having asyndeton.

At 46.11 (*longe quos simul a domo profectos* | *diuersae uarie uiae reportant*) there is manuscript variation between *uariae* and *uarie*, but Kroll (1929), Fordyce (1961), Mynors (OCT), Eisenhut (1993) and Thomson (1997) all print *uarie*. *Diuersus* and *uarius* are attested in coordination (see Fordyce ad loc.), but the adverb looks apt (separate roads bring those who set out together back in different ways).

115.8 *non homo sed uero mentula magna minax* is not straightforward either. Could there be a difference of rank, with the primary phrase *mentula magna* 'big prick' modified by *minax*? Cf. Enn. *Ann.* 620 Skutsch (see XXIV.5.1.5) *machina multa minax minitatur maxima muris*, a line that is also full of uncertainties. *Maxima* may be part of an object that is completed in the next line, or *machina* may have three adjectives, one of them separated. If *multa* and *minax* are simply a pair, they would differ in rank, 'many [a threatening machine]'. Goldberg and Manuwald (2018) take the line in this last way, translating 'many a menacing machine menaces much the muniments'.[1] Adjectives of quantity and size regularly modify an adjective–noun combination (where the adjective designates an inherent quality).

Despite this possibility in the Ennian line, 'a prick – big, threatening' (= 'big and threatening'), with a treble alliteration, looks appropriate with an asyndetic coordination, in which it would probably have had a distinctive intonation (cf. *lutum lupanar* above). The word order suits this interpretation (contrast the word order of the examples with layering cited at II.2.5). The possibility (see e.g. Thomson 1997: 554, and see below, n. 1) that Catullus was parodying Ennius cannot be established, given that the interpretation of the Ennian line is unsure.

At 32.10–11 (*pransus iaceo et satur supinus* | *pertundo tunicamque palliumque*) *satur supinus* is taken by Kroll (1929: 61) and Thomson (1997: 288; also

---

[1] In their note Goldberg and Manuwald (2018: 1.441) refer to Catullus' phrase as an apparent parody of Ennius, but they misquote Catullus by replacing *magna* with *multa*.

1 Asyndeta Bimembria

320) to be an asyndeton, but the phrase structure is not straightforward. If *et* links two clauses, there may be an asyndeton ('well fed I lie, and, full up, on my back, penetrate ...'). But what if *et* is part of a conjunct hyperbaton, *pransus ... et satur*? The two terms are near-synonyms and go well together, 'well fed and full up I lie'. A second clause on this view might start at *supinus*, '(and) on my back I penetrate'. A third possibility is to take *supinus* as the predicate with *iaceo*, = 'I lie on my back', a very plausible collocation (see XXXII.1 on *iaceo* with various types of predicates). If that were the case, the near-synonyms *pransus* and *satur* would be secondary predicates in conjunct hyperbaton, = 'well fed and full up I lie on my back'. *Pransus/satur* on the one hand and *supinus* on the other would differ in function (cf. the passages discussed at II.2.1, starting with Plaut. *Am.* 1001), and there would be no asyndeton. The next clause would start (asyndetically) at *pertundo*: 'well fed and full up I lie on my back, (and) penetrate ...'. This seems the most convincing interpretation to me. Conjunct hyperbaton is common in Catullus (cf. e.g. 12.8–9, 15.4, 22.9, 28.2, 29.14, 30.9 and often), *pransus* and *satur* fit well together in this construction, and *supinus* is a very appropriate complement of *iaceo*. Finally, I return briefly to the first interpretation above. It is not at all certain that, if *satur* and *supinus* are together in the second clause, they are in asyndetic coordination. *Satur* may be a detached incidental characteristic, a secondary predicate, with *supinus* complementing the verb *pertundo*: 'full up, I penetrate in a supine position ...'.

Thomson (1997: 320) also lists *miserae oblitae* at 65.21 as an asyndeton ((*malum*) *quod miserae oblitae molli sub ueste locatum*, of an apple placed under the soft dress of the poor girl, who has been forgetful and it rolls out), but the two terms differ in status. *Miserae* may be taken as substantival (the forgetful wretch), or, better, *miserae* as attributive and *oblitae* predicative. The poor girl was forgetful, and that is why the apple rolled out and caused embarrassment. One would not paraphrase as 'the girl was poor and forgetful', but rather as 'the poor girl was forgetful'.

1.3 Adverbs

It was seen earlier (XIII.5.4 and elsewhere) that a mundane type of adverbial asyndeton was that comprising pairs of opposites. One such in Catullus is at 68.133: *circumcursans hinc illinc*. This pair is quite well attested (see Preuss 1881: 26–7): e.g. Lucr. 5.881. Catullus favoured such pairs in conjunction with anaphora: 3.9 *circumsiliens modo huc modo illuc*,

15.7 *istos qui in platea modo huc modo illuc* | *in re praetereunt sua occupati* (for *huc illuc* in asyndeton see XIII.5.4); cf. 50.5 *numero modo hoc modo illoc*.

I include here the gemination *magis magis* (38.3 *magis magis in dies et horas*, 64.274 *post uento crescente magis magis increbrescunt*) because the pair is usually coordinated (see Hofmann and Szantyr 1965: 809, Wills 1996: 112–15; note e.g. Catull. 68.48 *notescatque magis mortuus atque magis*). Wills (113) cites just one other asyndetic example (Virg. *Georg.* 4.311 *tenuemque magis magis aera carpunt*), and sees a connection between Catull. 64.274 and this, in that 'both Catullus' waves and Virgil's bees are increasing under the action of Zephyr'. He also suggests 'some Greek antecedent for this structure in Catullus', citing e.g. Eur. *IT* 1406 μᾶλλον δὲ μᾶλλον πρὸς πέτρας ᾔει σκάφος. The connection between Catullus and Virgil does not look compelling, and any coordinated pairing may be converted into an asyndetic from time to time. The first example above (38.3), 'more and more, by the day and by the hour', looks like a banal intensification. Kroll (1929: 72) ad loc. cites a similar example from Aristophanes: *Nub.* 1287 κατὰ μῆνα καὶ καθ' ἡμέραν πλέον πλέον τἀργύριον ἀεὶ γίγνεται. *Magis magis in dies et horas* is a classic accumulation, consisting of an asyndetic pair and then a coordinated (see XIX.1, and above, 1.1 on the nominal sequence at 115.5). Kroll notes too that *in dies et horas* is 'volkstümlich', and it is likely that accumulations of this pattern were by no means confined to the high literary language. Cf. Hor. *Serm.* 2.6.47 *subiectior in diem et horam*.

71.4 *mirifice est apte nactus utrumque malum*, where *apte* is an emendation (see e.g. the apparatus of Eisenhut 1983 for details), has caused some discussion. *Apte* is defended by Kaster (1977) and accepted by Nisbet (1978: 109), and is printed by Thomson (1997), whereas some other editors (Kroll, Mynors, Eisenhut) obelise *a te*. *Apte* is convincing, but the pair *mirifice apte* is probably not an asyndeton: *mirifice* would be a modifier of *apte*, 'marvellously appropriately'. Kaster cites a few cases of an adverb modifying another adverb, and there are other instances in Plautus (XXIII.6 n. 4).

On 36.10 (*et hoc pessima se puella uidit* | *iocose lepide uouere diuis*) Fordyce remarks (1961: 180) that 'the asyndeton cannot be regarded as impossible', rejecting Scaliger's *ioco se*. Kroll (1929: 68) and Thomson (1997: 288, 320) accept the asyndeton.

There is little variation in Catullus' use of adverbial asyndetic pairs.

1.4 Imperatives

More common are asyndetic pairs of imperatives, either with a single word as each member or with extensions of one sort or another. Asyndetic pairs of imperatives go back to the earliest period in Latin (Livius Andronicus and comedy: see the selective early examples at Adams 2016: 558), and they definitely had a place in spoken Latin. On Plautus see X.1.1, XXIII.5.1. For a later (conversational) example in a letter of Terentianus see *P. Mich.* VIII.471.28 *ueni interpone te* (Adams 2016: 278).

Catull. 8.11 (*sed obstinata mente perfer, obdura*) has two synonyms, with the second longer than the first. Fordyce (1961: 112) notes that Ovid uses *perfer et obdura* three times (see too *TLL* IX.2.43.7ff.); the *et* achieves a dactyl. On 14.21 *(uos hinc interea ualete abite | illuc)* see Fordyce (1961: 138): 'the two verbs form a single expression, "get away with my blessing from here"' (see Thomson 1997: 246 for much the same phraseology). Described thus the pair may not seem like a genuine coordination, but *ualeo* can form a unit in coordination with another verb (here 'farewell and be off'). See particularly 11.17 *uiuat ualeatque*, 'let her live, and good luck to her' (Fordyce 1961: 128, who cites Hor. *Sat.* 2.5.110 *uiue ualeque* (omitting the *-que* in the citation) ('live and farewell') and Ter. *An.* 889 *ualeat uiuat cum illa*, translated by Barsby (Loeb), 'let him live with her, and good riddance!'). See too Hor. *Ep.* 1.6.67 *uiue uale* and also *Ep.* 1.13.19 *uade uale* (see XXIX.2.2), which is similar to *ualete abite* above. *Viue uale* was a formula of dismissal, according to Kroll (1929: 26). It is reminiscent of the (asyndetic) divorce formula (Plaut. *Am.* 928) *ualeas, tibi habeas res tuas, reddas meas.* However, the asyndetic pairing above was not exclusively used thus, particularly when the verbs were non-imperatival/non-jussive. The three Plautine examples cited at XXIII.8.14 (*Bac.* 246, *St.* 31, *Trin.* 1075), two of them indicatives and the other non-jussive subjunctives, all mean 'is/are alive and well'. One of the three pairs is preceded by *interea* (*St.* 31), as is the case with the Catullan pair 14.21 above. The combination *uiuo ualeo* either changed meaning over time, or else had an idiomatic meaning when used in the imperative or a similar subjunctive. The pair was indifferently used both asyndetically and with coordination.

Two other imperatival pairs are 61.193 *perge, ne remorare,* 'come on, don't delay' (positive + negative) and 63.19 *simul ite, sequimini | Phrygiam ad domum Cybeles* (*simul* goes with both verbs). There is reason to think that both of these expressions were formulaic/colloquial. For the structure 'go, don't delay' in Plautus, see X.1.1, and *i/ite* + imperative for its part is ubiquitous in comedy and elsewhere (see X.1.1, XXIII.5.1). Plaut. *Mil.* 1361 (*i, sequere illos, ne morere*) combines the expressions in both Catullan passages.

In the following two passages there is (as at 63.19 above) first a single imperative and then a phrase with imperative: 61.38–9 *agite, in modum | dicite*, 'come, in tune say', 61.116 *ite, concinite in modum*, 'come, sing together in tune'. However, *agite* (*age*) became so fossilised in such contexts that it was virtually a hortatory term (cf. Gk. ἄγε), well established in the literary language (see X.2 and also *OLD* s.v. *ago* 24a). See further 61.26–7 *quare age, huc aditum ferens, | perge linquere*, 63.12 *agite ite ad alta, Gallae*, 64.372 *quare agite optatos animi coniungite amores*. All examples in this paragraph are in the long poems, and all are of ascending length.

Catullus also has longer sequences of imperatives, or imperatival phrases together:

55.15–16 *dic nobis ubi sis futurus, ede | audacter, committe, crede luci*
63.78 *agedum, inquit, age ferox, fac ut* (then *fac uti* in the next line).
63.81 *age caede terga cauda, tua uerbera patere, | fac cuncta* . . . (in the next line *quate*).
64.195 *huc huc aduentate, meas audite querellas.*

It will be noted that in the long poem 63 *age(dum)* occurs again, twice.

Finally, Catullus sometimes coordinates pairs of imperatives: 24.9 *abice eleuaque*, 25.9 *reglutina et remitte*, 42.10 *circumsistite eam et reflagitate*.

Various patterns are to be seen in the use of imperatives by Catullus. First, asyndetic coordination seems to be preferred to syndetic. Second, Catullus has several imperatival structures found in comedy (and elsewhere), and no doubt colloquial. Third, sequences introduced by *age/agite* are in the longer poems (six times). This was a structure with literary credentials, even if it turns up outside high literature as well.

1.5 Other Verb Forms

There is only one such case, of artificial type, comprising juxtaposed active and passive forms of the same verb: 45.20 *mutuis animis amant amantur* (for the type see VIII). Poem 45 is stylistically a very contrived composition (see the extensive discussion of its features by Fordyce 1961: 202), and *amant amantur* must have been admitted to suit the style.

I mention finally 17.21 *talis iste meus stupor nil uidet, nihil audit*, with two asyndetic verb phrases with anaphora.

1 Asyndeta Bimembria

1.6 Asyndeton Bimembre: Conclusions

Of asyndeta bimembria in the strictest sense there are only eleven clear-cut instances in the whole corpus. These are not a single stylistic class but fall into several categories.

Fanda nefanda (64.405) and *amant amantur* (45.20) both have stylised structures that have been discussed in separate chapters, and both are in literary poems. The first is a variant of a more familiar structure, whereby a positive adjective is juxtaposed with its negative with the suffix *in-*. *Lutum lupanar* (42.13) and (*mentula*) *magna minax* (115.8) are both abusive phrases with alliteration, with the second term capping the first. Both are at the end of a colon or sentence, and at the end of a line of verse. In the first Catullus indirectly hints at the structure, implying that the aim was to go on trying to find a stronger term. I assume that there would have been a distinctive intonation pattern, with a pause between the two terms. The pattern probably turned up in popular invective. 68.133 *circumcursans hinc illinc* has a banal look. Asyndetic pairs of adverbs of opposite meanings are elsewhere attested in combination with frequentative forms of the verb of running (see XIII.5.4). Another pair of adverbs, *magis magis* at 38.3 is in one of the most frequent structures containing asyndeta bimembria, namely that showing an asyndeton bimembre followed by a coordinated pair (here, *in dies et horas*). The latter phrase is colloquial and the context informal, and here is a hint that the stucture asyndeton + coordinated pair was not confined to high literature. A similar structure occurs as well in the poem containing *mentula magna minax* (at 115.8), in which (at 115.5) Catullus puts after *arua prata* a coordinated pair *ingentes siluas saltusque*, followed by a single coordinated term, *paludesque*. There is a more literary feel to this accumulation, and Catullus appears to have adopted a high style in stressing the wealth of Mamurra, the subject of the abuse. Another instance of *magis magis* (64.274) I would see as an ad hoc variant of the coordinated equivalent, but it is possible that Catullus felt the rarer asyndetic form to be suited to the high style of the poem. Other instances of asyndeta bimembria are in pairs of imperatives: 8.11 *perfer obdura*, 14.21 *ualete abite* (with an adverbial addition to *abite*), 61.193 *perge, ne remorare*, 63.199 *ite sequimini*.

Adverbial and imperatival pairs are the most prominent type, though the figures are not high. The examples tend to be run-of-the-mill and formulaic.

2 Sequences of Three or More Words: Asyndeton, Coordination and End-of-List Coordination

It was seen at XVIII.2 that in samples of Cato, Cicero and Livy such triple (or longer) sequences often have asyndeton or multiple coordination, but that end-of-list coordination is rare. It may be useful to put Catullus' limited use of asyndeton bimembre into perspective by looking at some other phenomena.

I take first asyndeta in Catullus. At 9.7 (*audiamque Hiberum | narrantem loca facta nationes,* | *ut mos est tuus*) Catullus looks forward to the return of Veranius from Spain and to his account of the place. The 'places, deeds, races' of the Spaniards looks like a selective list of the topics on which Veranius might have reported. See Kroll (1929: 19), citing Cic. *Q. fr.* 20 (2.16.4) *quos tu situs, quas naturas rerum et locorum, quos mores, quas gentis, quas pugnas . . . habes,* in reference to *iucundas . . . litteras* from Britain. This list is rather fuller. Asyndetic lists, particularly at the end of a colon, are often open-ended (see e.g. IV.3, V.2, XXV.1.1.3, 1.1.8 on Lucilius 32, Cicero 32, 37, 132 etc.).

14.18–19 (*ad librariorum | curram scrinia, Caesios Aquinos | Suffenum, omnia colligam uenena*) is another open-ended list, a fact marked by the commonplace summarising use of *omnia* at the end (on which see XVIII.6), and also by the plural names ('people like . . .').

The following passage is notable for Catullus' comment after the asyndetic tricolon: 86.1 *Quintia formosa est multis; mihi candida longa | recta est. haec ego sic singula confiteor* 'I grant these single points.' The list is presented as stressing individual features of the girl. There are no internal unities, except that the features are all praiseworthy. It is open to a speaker to use pauses and intonation to mark the separateness of the characteristics.

I repeat that asyndetic single-word tricola as above are banal in the literary language (see for example the statistics from Cic. *Off.* 1 at I.4 above). Poccetti (2018: 117) remarks of Lucilius that a 'physically realistic description of characters is frequently obtained by a sequence of three adjectives, ironically reminiscent of the high style of archaic poetry'. His examples are variously syndetic and asyndetic, and some of them have internal structures that make them not genuinely tricola, but that aside they are not to be associated particularly with archaic poetry.

The asyndetic tetracolon at 63.59 (*patria bonis amicis genitoribus abero,* 'shall I be absent from my country, possessions, friends, parents?') has no marked internal structure, except that there is a movement from things to persons. Again the list is selective, as there were other things that might have been missed.

64.197 *cogor inops ardens, amenti caeca furore* has a tricolon of ascending length with a phrasal final element. The tricolon comes after the verb and is in agreement with the subject of the verb. Such postponed predicative adjuncts are illustrated abundantly in e.g. VI, and e.g. from Plautus (XXIII Appendix, *Adjectives*), Virgil (XXIV.2.1.1, 2.2), Lucilius (XXV.1.1.4), Horace (XXIX.2.1). For the privative see Hor. *Sat.* 2.1.59 *diues inops* (XXIX.2.1.1). Thomson (1997: 417) on the above passage says, 'Notice the asyndeton (characteristic of C.)', but we are far from establishing that asyndeton was very marked in Catullus.

I cite finally 63.85–6 *ferus ipse sese adhortans rabidum incitat animo,* | *uadit fremit refringit uirgulta pede uago* ('The beast, urging himself on, rouses himself to rage of spirit; he rushes forth, roars, breaks the undergrowth with roving paw'). There are two stages to the action described here, corresponding to the two lines. First the beast rouses itself, then it goes into action. I take the second line as containing another ascending tricolon.

I turn now to (mainly) single-word sequences with three or more members that are overtly coordinated. I have noted the following examples (which are roughly of the same, limited, frequency as the asyndetic examples just discussed):

13.4–5 *non sine candida puella* | *et uino et sale et omnibus cachinnis*
22.2 *homo est uenustus et dicax et urbanus*
23.14 *sole et frigore et esuritione*
29.2 *nisi impudicus et uorax et aleo*
29.10 *es impudicus et uorax et aleo.*

End-of-list coordination is as usual outnumbered by the syndetic and asyndetic sequences. Here are the examples I have found:

63.60 *abero foro palaestra stadio et gyminasiis?* A certain example (see XVIII.5). Cf. Plaut. *Am.* 1011 *omnis plateas perreptaui, gymnasia et myropolia* (end-of-list coordination in a similar context).
114.3 *qui tot res in se habet egregias –* | *aucupium omne genus, piscis prata arua ferasque.*

115.5 (above, 1.2) has been taken as comprising an asyndetic pair, a coordinated, and a single term coordinated. At 11.11, finally, the text is uncertain (see Fordyce 1961: 127). End-of-list coordination is poorly attested.

In addition to the three types of sequences just discussed, Catullus has a few other types of mixed tricola and longer groups, made up for example of sequences with anaphora, and phrasal sequences. Here are some examples:

22.6–7 *cartae regiae, noui libri,* | *noui umbilici, lora rubra membranae*
63.40 *lustrauit aethera album, sola dura, mare ferum*
63.63 *ego mulier, ego adulescens, ego ephebus, ego puer* (see above, I.10).
64.69–70 *toto ex te pectore, Theseu,* | *toto animo, tota pendebat perdita mente*
64.186–7 *nulla fugae ratio, nulla spes, omnia muta,* | *omnia sunt deserta, ostentant omnia letum* (two different patterns of anaphoric phrasal asyndeton).
84.5–6 *sic mater, sic liber auunculus eius,* | *sic maternus auus dixerat atque auia.*

3 Coordinated Pairs

The poems of Catullus, particularly the shorter ones, abound in coordinated pairs. Syndetic coordination of pairs (as distinct from asyndetic) is the norm in the language, and common (see for example the statistics from Cic. *Off.* 1.1–20 at I.4, where a short passage (1.15–16) is quoted that is full of coordinated pairs). Many of the pairs in Catullus are of types that are not infrequently found in asyndeton. Here are some illustrations.

At 4.14 (*tibi haec fuisse et esse cognitissima* | *ait phaselus*) different tenses of the same verb are coordinated (see IX for asyndeton in such contexts). Cf. 21.2–3 *sed quot aut fuerunt* | *aut sunt aut aliis erunt in annis,* 24.2–3 *sed quot aut fuerunt* | *aut posthac aliis erunt in annis,* 49.2 *quot sunt quotque fuere, Marce Tulli,* | *quotque post aliis erunt in annis.*

5.4 (*soles occidere et redire possunt*) has a pair of verbs that are directional opposites, reversives (see XIII.2). At 6.9 (*puluinusque peraeque et hic et ille* | *attritus*) Kroll (1929: 13) takes *hic et ille* as referring to left and right, and such a pair too expresses directional opposites. At both 6.15 (*quidquid habes boni malique* and 15.10 (*infesto pueris bonis malisque*) the same pair of antonyms is coordinated by *-que*. For this pair see Preuss (1881: 43), and Ter. *Ph.* 556 for asyndeton. Opposites of the converse type are at 110.4: *quod nec das et fers saepe.* Huc et huc at 61.34–5 (*ut tenax hedera huc et huc* | *arborem implicat errans,* 'As clinging ivy entwines the tree, roving here and there', Lee 1991) is equivalent to *huc et illuc* (on this type of usage see Adams 2016: 42–3), adverbial opposites of a type often asyndetic (see XIII.5.4).

Et pater et nouerca (23.3) and *socer generque* (29.24) are terms for family members (see XIV for such pairs with asyndeton). For masculine + feminine pairs (cf. XI) see 34.2 *puellae et pueri integri,* 34.3–4 <*pueri integri*> |

3 Coordinated Pairs 493

puellaeque, 64.78 *electos iuuenes simul et decus innuptarum*. 43.8 (*o saeclum insapiens et infacetum*) has a pair of privatives, and 10.33 (*tu insulsa male et molesta uiuis*), 36.19 (*pleni ruris et inficetiarum*) and 107.4 (*cupido atque insperanti*) have one privative (VI.4).[2] 21.10–11 (*esurire | ... et sitire*) has complementary terms (of hunger and thirst: see XXIX.2.1.1 on Hor. *Sat.* 2.2.14).

The alliterative pair *uiuat ualeatque* (11.17) was seen earlier (1.4), and it was noted that it is attested in asyndeton. Several other pairs with forms of coordination in Catullus come up elsewhere in this book in an asyndetic form: 28.5 *frigoraque et famem* (Lucilius 7 at XXV.1.1.2, Cicero 103), 28.14 *di deaeque* (XI.2), 30.9 *tua dicta omnia factaque* (Cicero 116, 195), 64.44 *auro atque argento* (Cicero 21, 119).

Three of the pairs in the last paragraph are alliterative. Coordinated pairs, and not only asyndetically coordinated, are often alliterative, not least in Catullus. Here are some further instances:

14.10 *bene ac beate*
37.14 *boni beatique* (Wölfflin 1933: 255).
28.15 *opprobria Romuli Remique* (and the line before has *di deaeque*, see above).
29.6 *ille nunc superbus et superfluens*
42.8 *mimice ac moleste* (quoted only from Catullus by Wölfflin 1933: 266).
42.24 *pudica et proba*
68.90 *uirum et uirtutum omnium acerba cinis* (see Wölfflin 1933: 280, but without this example).
76.20 *pestem perniciemque* (see Wölfflin 1933: 270).
84.8 *audibant eadem haec leniter et leuiter* (cf. 64.84 *naue leui nitens ac lenibus auris*; see also Wölfflin 1933: 264).
97.4 *mundior et melior* (for the assonance at the end in a coordinatred pair see e.g. 45.15 *maior acriorque*).

The material collected in this section is not complete. I add more examples of coordinated terms, miscellaneous or with some sort of unity, whether they be complements, near-synonyms or related in some other way:

11.1 *Furi et Aureli, comites Catulli*
12.15–16 *Fabullus | et Veranius*
13.12 *Veneres Cupidinesque* (cf. 36.3 *Veneri Cupidinique*)
14.12 *horribilem et sacrum libellum*
16.1 and 16.14 *pedicabo ego uos et irrumabo*
16.7 *salem ac leporem*

---

[2] Cf. 30.1 *immemor atque unanimis falsis sodalibus*, where the second member is of increased length.

16.8 *molliculi ac parum pudici*
23.21, 22 *faba et lupillis,* | . . . *teras fricesque*
29.5 and 9 *haec uidebis et feres*
29.14 *ducenties comesset aut trecenties*
29.20 *nunc Galliae timetur et Britanniae*
31.1 *paene insularum . . . insularumque*
37.16 *omnes pusilli et semitarii moechi*
38.4 *quod minimum facillimumque est*
41.6 *amicos medicosque*
42.6 *persequamur eam et reflagitemus*
44.12 *plenam ueneni et pestilentiae*
44.19 *grauedinem et tussim* (cf. 44.13 *grauedo frigida et frequens tussis*).
45.6 *in Libya Indiaque*
45.22 *Syrias Britanniasque*
45.24 *delicias libidinesque*
47.1 *Porci et Socration*
47.2 *scabies famesque mundi*
47.3 *Veraniolo meo et Fabullo*
58.4 *in quadriuiis et angiportis*
58a.4 *niueae citaeque bigae*
58a.5 *plumipedas uolatilesque*
68.89 *Asiae Europaeque*
83.4 *gannit et obloquitur*
83.6 *uritur et loquitur*
103.4 *saeuus et indomitus.*

In this section about 78 coordinated pairs have been cited, with *et* the coordinator 47 times, *-que* 25 and *ac/atque* 6. There are no sharp differences discernible between *et* and *-que*, apart from the greater frequency of the former, which is in line with the gradual decline of *-que*, but *ac/atque* is absent from the pairs of opposites quoted in the third paragraph, and from other special types of pairings (as they occur in this section, if not necessarily right across the corpus of Latin literature) that have been the subject of earlier chapters, namely different tenses/moods of the same verb, pairs of family members, masculine + feminine pairs and pairs of privatives. *Ac* does however occur in a few alliterative pairs of near-synonyms.

For a speculative discussion of Catullus' motives in choosing *ac/atque* (in which statistics are given) see Ross (1969: 26–39). Ross cites in this account various examples that are not included here. It is worth noting that Ross (64) also quotes the seven instances of the archaic polysyndeton *-que -que* in the corpus. Four of these are in sexual phrases or contexts (15.19, 17.9, 32.11, 57.2), a deliberate clash of registers.

4 Conclusions

Asyndetic pairs are more common in Catullus than asyndetic triplets, a distribution different from that of literary prose. Asyndetic tricola and longer sequences are also a feature of Greek. They perhaps had a rhetorical status that may not have appealed to some poets.

Asyndeton bimembre is not however frequent (see above, 1.6 for a fuller summary). The examples that do occur do not constitute a single phenomenon. *Fanda nefanda* in 64 is particularly distinctive, a positive–negative pair but of a rare type, and was undoubtedly artificial. Also, the pair is a variant on the usual opposition, that between *fas* and *nefas*. On the other hand *lutum lupanar* and *magna minax* are alliterative, abusive, have a second term that semantically outdoes the first, and come at the end of a line/colon. They must reflect abusive speech.

If there is a type of asyndeton (bimembre, but also longer) that is banal it is that comprising pairs of imperatives. We did not see many cases of coordinated imperatives. A more literary type is that with *age/agite/agedum* at the start.

Also commonplace in Latin were asyndetic adverbial pairs, notably those with the two terms opposites. *Circumcursans hinc illinc* has the additional formulaic feature that the adverbial pair accompanies a frequentative verb of running.

Catullus, however, was a writer who strongly favoured overt coordination, and in shorter poems not infrequently more coordinated pairs than one turn up.

CHAPTER XXVIII

Caesar, Bellum Ciuile: *Asyndeton and Textual Criticism*

1 Introduction

In this chapter I consider asyndeton in Caesar's *Civ.*, of which there is now a reliable text with apparatus (Damon 2015a). My aim is not merely to classify asyndeta but to consider whether there are criteria that may be used by an editor in deciding on the text when manuscripts have variation between coordination and asyndeton; the chapter is mainly about textual criticism. The passages discussed, which embrace the totality of possible asyndeta (bimembria) in the work, are numbered in bold.

Damon refers in her monograph on the text (2015b: 110 n. 15) to the difficulties posed for an editor by asyndeton ('some instances of which could equally be the result of the omission of -*que*, the most commonly omitted word of our tradition'). It was easily missed because often written as *q*. She states the principles she has followed:

> I accepted as asyndeton only those that occur in list-like passages or are formulaic expressions. Thus, e.g., 1.29.3 *ueterem exercitum, duas Hispanias* and *auxilia equitatum*, 2.4.1 *remigum gubernatorum*, 3.4.6 *Dardanos Bessos* and *Macedones Thessalos*, but 3.26.1 *Apollonia Dyrrachium<que>*.

These criteria are vague: what is 'list-like' and its significance, and what is a formula? Both lists (which are of different types) and formulae may have coordinators, and most plausible asyndetic pairs are not formulae. This formulation is not unlike one by Reid (1885: 110), and greater precision is needed. Reid states that Cicero only omits the copula between two connected words '(1) when the two words may be regarded as in some sense forming a pair, as in *manibus pedibus* and the like phrases; (2) in legal or official formulae such as *sarta tecta*'. The trouble is that most coordinated terms 'form a pair', and why is a coordinator sometimes used and sometimes omitted in 'pairs'?

I discuss the examples above (and some others) separately.

2 Categories

2.1 Place Names and Designations of Peoples

(1) 3.26.1 *Apolloniam Dyrrachium<que>* and (2, 3) 3.4.6 *Dardanos Bessos... Macedones Thessalos*

At *Civ.* 3.26.1 Damon prints *atque altero die Apolloniam Dyrrachiumque praeteruehuntur*. In the app. crit. it is noted that *-que* is in the editio princeps (1469) but that ω had *-m*. ω is the reconstructed archetype (Damon 2015a: xxii). On the face of it there seems to be no clear reason from Damon's principles quoted above for departing from ω. Dyrrachium and Apollonia were two important Illyrian cities on the eastern coast of the Adriatic, which together became the base for Roman armies in Greece and the Balkans. They were on the Via Egnatia and not far apart. They must have been associated in Roman thinking, as distinct from random and unconnected place names. At 3.30.1 there is *praeteruectas Apolloniam Dyrrachiumque naues* (see too 3.11.2 *iterque ex Macedonia in hiberna Apolloniam Dyrrachiumque habebat*), but, as we have seen often, constant variation occurs between asyndeton and coordination in recurrent pairs.

One possible way forward is to go beyond stray examples and to collect all instances of coordinated (both syndetic and asyndetic) pairs of place (and peoples') names in the text to see if Caesar's practice can be discerned. Names of peoples and tribes often have the same function as place names. I have also included in the collection pairs of adjectives based on place names. In the following list the examples are arranged by coordinator, and there is a final category of alphabetically numbered examples (including those at 3.4.6 cited at the start of this section, 2, 3) that are special cases. I will return to *Apolloniam Dyrrachiumque* later (end of this section). A rule of sorts can be formulated from the evidence below, including that of the alphabetically numbered cases.

1.12.1 *Pisauri et Arimini*
1.15.7 *Alba, ex Marsis et Paelignis, finitimis ab regionibus*
1.35.4 *agros Volcarum Arecomicorum et Heluiorum* (two names)
1.48.3 *inter flumina duo, Sicorim et Cingam* (river names)
1.60.1 *Oscenses et Calagurritani*
2.40.1 *Hispanorum et Gallorum equitum*
3.2.3 *ex saluberrimis Galliae et Hispaniae regionibus*
3.4.1 *ex Creta et Macedonia*
3.10.5 *amissa Sicilia et Sardinia duabusque Hispaniis et cohortibus <in> Italia atque Hispania*

3.35.1 *Calydone et Naupacto deiectis*
3.102.5 *in Ciliciam et inde Cyprum*

1.4.5 *ab itinere Asiae Syriaeque*
1.7.7 *omnem Galliam Germaniamque*
1.29.2 *ex . . . regionibus Galliae Picenique*
1.29.3 *Galliam Italiamque*
1.30.4 *in Lucanis Bruttiisque* (here S, for which see Damon 2015a: xlvii–liii, an early manuscript but with a large number of innovations, is without the coordinator: see further below, this section).
1.48.4 *ex Italia Galliaque*
2.29.3 *ex Marsis Paelignisque*
3.4.4 *Gallos Germanosque*
3.11.2 *iterque ex Macedonia in hiberna Apolloniam Dyrrachiumque habebat*
3.30.1 *praeteruectas Apolloniam Dyrrachiumque naues*
3.34.2 *ex Thessalia Aetoliaque*
3.78.3 *Apolloniam Oricumque oppugnare*
3.87.1 *Galliam Germaniamque*
3.100.3 *Corcyra Dyrrachioque*
3.104.1 *Alexandriam Aegyptumque occuparet*
3.110.3 *Syriae Ciliciaeque prouinciae*

1.68.1 *ad Hiberum atque Otogesam* (river names)
2.1.2 *ex Gallia atque Hispania*
2.32.3 *prouinciam Siciliam atque Africam*
3.5.3 *Liburnicae atque Achaicae classi*
3.10.5 *<in> Italia atque Hispania*
3.13.1 *Orci atque Apolloniae*
3.40.4 *Byllide atque Amantia*
3.58.4 *Corcyra atque Acarnania*
3.61.2 *in Epiro atque Aetolia*
3.78.4 *per Epirum atque Athamaniam.*

(**a**) 3.3.2 *magnam imperatam Asiae Syriae regibusque omnibus et dinastis et tetrarchis et liberis Achaiae populis pecuniam exegerat*
(**b**) 3.4.3 *<ex> Creta Lacedaemone, ex Ponto atque Syria reliquisque ciuitatibus*
(**c**) = 2, 3 3.4.6 *huc Dardanos Bessos partim mercenarios partim imperio aut gratia comparatos, item Macedones Thessalos ac reliquarum gentium et ciuitatum adiecerat*
(**d**) 3.5.2 *hiemare Dyrrachi Apolloniae omnibusque oppidis maritimis constituerat* (there are textual variants of the locatives).
(**e**) 3.12.4 *sequuntur Byllidenses Amantini et reliquae finitimae ciuitates totaque Epiros*
(**f**) 1.38.3 *Celtiberiae Cantabris barbarisque omnibus.*

I leave aside the last category (**a**–**f**) for the moment and deal with the others. There are 37 pairs coordinated by *et* (11), *-que* (16) and *atque*

2 *Categories* 499

(10). In the last group *atque* is followed by a vowel (or *h*) in every case. I include among the examples of *-que* 1.30.4 *in Lucanis Bruttiisque* (see above) for a structural reason, and not only because the manuscript that has asyndeton is unreliable (see above on S: *-que* is in U, a manuscript of the late eleventh or early twelfth century, which 'does not have any characteristic error types': Damon 2015a; xlvi; see also xli on the date of the manuscript). This pair of names is dependent on a single preposition, and asyndeton bimembre is not common in Latin in this environment, though it does occur in some writers, such as historians (see e.g. on Sallust 13 and Tacitus 46, with cross references, and particularly XXI). In the three categories dealt with here there are (leaving 1.30.4 aside) thirteen instances of a preposition followed by an overtly coordinated pair of names, but no cases in our material (apart from one special example (**b**) discussed in the next paragraph) in which an asyndeton follows a single preposition. If prepositional expressions followed by pairs of dependents as a whole are examined in Caesar (i.e. including those in which the dependent nouns are not place names), the abnormality of asyndeton in this environment (in this writer) becomes even clearer (see below, Appendix 1 for a full collection). Even as it is there is no doubt that 1.30.4 should not be printed with asyndeton. By contrast note e.g. the following three passages: 3.3.1 *ex Asia Cycladibusque insulis Corcyra Athenis Ponto Bithynia Syria Cicilia Phoenice Aegypto classem coegerat*, 3.5.1 *frumenti uim maximam ex Thessalia Asia Aegypto Creta Cyrenis reliquisque ciuitatibus*, 3.42.3 *in Sicilia Gallia Italia*. Two names dependent on one preposition are avoided (except in the special case below), but it is apparent from these examples that by contrast more names than two were allowed by Caesar to depend on one preposition. There is a familiar pattern here: single-word asyndeta with two members are far less frequent than asyndeta with more members than two in many writers.

I come now to the final category above, the six instances numbered alphabetically. These fall into several clear asyndetic types that turn up in other writers discussed in this book.

First, (**d**) 3.5.2 *hiemare Dyrrachi Apolloniae omnibusque oppidis maritimis constituerat*, (**e**) 3.12.4 *sequuntur Byllidenses Amantini et reliquae finitimae ciuitates totaque Epiros* and (**f**) 1.38.3 *Celtiberiae Cantabris barbarisque omnibus* have a very familiar structure. In all three cases there is an uncoordinated pair, followed by a generalisation introduced by a summarising word (*omnibus, reliquae*). In such structures this summarising word may be *ceteri, reliqui* (see Pease 1958: 1066), *omnes, cuncti, alii, totum* (see in general XVIII.6; for the pattern in Cicero see Cicero 1, 26, and for the historians Sallust 1, with cross references to Tacitus, and also XXX.3.3.3b, 4.2.4b). I have treated it as a moot point whether such structures should be regarded as having an asyndetic pair and then a generalisation, or end-of-list coordination. If the former, the 'weak' asyndeta bimembria in these passages of Caesar are special cases, in that they are structurally determined. Incidentally, at 3.42.4 (*Lisso Parthinisque et omnibus castellis quod esset frumenti conquiri iussit*) there is another sequence with a generalisation (marked here by *omnibus*) following, and here the first pair has a coordinator, a fact which makes it at least defensible to say that comparable sequences in which the first pair is without a coordinator have instead asyndeton bimembre. Passage (e) has in another sense a structure that frequently houses asyndetic pairs. The summarising phrase introduced by *et reliquae* is followed by another phrase introduced by *totaque*. The whole sequence therefore has 'multiple coordination', asyndeton + *et* + *-que*, and sequences of this type often contain an asyndeton bimembre (see below).

I turn now to (b) 3.4.3 <*ex*> <u>*Creta Lacedaemone, ex Ponto atque Syria reliquisque ciuitatibus*</u>, where <*ex*> is the reading of M after correction by a later hand. The emendation is certainly right, though the phrase might seem as a result to violate the tendency stated above, for asyndeton to be avoided after a single preposition. But it is the overall phrasal structure that is important here: the asyndetic pair dependent on *ex* is followed by repetition of the preposition and a further group of dependents. Cf. Cic. *Sest.* 88 *ad <u>ferrum faces</u>, ad cotidianam caedem incendia rapinas se cum exercitu suo contulit*, and *Nat.* 2.150 *ad pingendum fingendum, ad scalpendum, ad neruorum eliciendos sonos* (see Cicero 15). In these examples there is an embedded asyndeton bimembre dependent on a preposition at the start of a longer sequence of anaphoric prepositional expressions.

Passage (b) has two other structural features that help to explain the presence of an asyndeton bimembre (dependent on a single preposition) at the start. First, the asyndetic pair is followed by a pair coordinated by *atque*, an established pattern that occurs particularly in Sallust (see XXX.6.2b), and is also common in various writers with other coordinators (see e.g. XIX.1). Second, the whole sequence has multiple coordination: first asyndetic, then by means of *atque*, and finally with *-que*. This final element has the coordinator attached to *reliquis*, a summarising element which, we have just seen, tends to come after an asyndeton.

2 Categories

Passage (c) (= 2, 3) contains two of Damon's examples of asyndeton: 3.4.6 *huc Dardanos Bessos partim mercennarios partim imperio aut gratia comparatos, item Macedones Thessalos ac reliquarum gentium et ciuitatum adiecerat*. Here are two pairs of names of peoples, separated, with the second introduced by *item*. A structural parallel containing two asyndetic pairs of separated place names is found at Cicero 166, 167: *ex Id. Mart ibidem Synnadense Pamphylium* (*tum Phemio dispiciam* κέρας), *<Lyc>aonium Isauricum*. These passages both have the same sort of accumulations of asyndeta bimembria, showing a separation (see further Cicero 127 for two pairs of personal names split). Other such accumulations of a more general type (but still with separations) occur for example in the historians (see Sallust 6, 7, 8, and Tacitus 87, 88 *fuga uastitas, deseri itinera fora*). Moreover the second pair in (c) is followed by a generalising phrase introduced by *ac reliquarum*, and this is a feature that it shares with (e) and (b), discussed above. In Cicero in speeches and philosophica pairs are found in accumulations in about 40–50 per cent of cases (see XXVI.7.2.5, 7.3.1). A structural characteristic here supports the manuscript readings.

There remains (a) 3.3.2 *imperatam Asiae Syriae regibusque omnibus et dinastis et tetrarchis et liberis Achaiae populis pecuniam exegerat*. The pair *Asiae Syriae* is followed by four coordinated nouns/phrases. Structurally the passage shares a feature with (b), namely that it has multiple coordination. It also belongs structurally with those that have a summarising component after the asyndeton. For a multiple coordination of place/tribe names in which the first pair is asyndetic see Tacitus 70 *Libya Aethiopia Medisque et Persis et Bactriano ac Scytha potitum*. The asyndetic character of *Asiae Syriae* may be seen if the passage is compared with *Civ.* 3.10.5 *amissa Sicilia et Sardinia duabusque Hispaniis et cohortibus <in> Italia atque Hispania*, where the structure is similar to that of (a), but in this case with the initial pair of place names coordinated: *Asiae Syriae* is functionally much the same as *Sicilia et Sardinia*.

In (d) *Dyrrachi Apolloniae* is asyndetic, and the question arises whether it might be used to support the reading *Apolloniam Dyrrachium* at 1. It cannot, because in (d) the two words do not occur on their own but are followed by the generalisation *omnibusque oppidis maritimis*. It is the structure that determines the asyndeton, not any particular feature of the names themselves.

The rule holds good then that in Caesar *Civ.* pairs of place names are not used asyndetically unless they are in certain types of accumulations. Damon's text at 1 (*Apolloniam Dyrrachium<que>*) must be right.

2.2 Noun Pairs

(**4, 5**) 1.29.3 *ueterem exercitum, duas Hispanias* and *auxilia equitatum* (two more of Damon's examples).

The passage runs as follows: *interea ueterem exercitum, duas Hispanias confirmari, quarum erat altera maximis beneficiis Pompei deuincta, auxilia equitatum parari, Galliam Italiamque temptari se absente nolebat*, 'meanwhile he did not want the old army and two Spains (one of which had been put under an obligation by the very great benefits conferred by Pompey) to take heart, auxiliaries and cavalry to be acquired, or Gaul and Italy to be disturbed in his absence'. Here are three asyndetic clauses dependent on *nolebat* (with the verbs *confirmari, parari, temptari*), each clause with a coordinated nominal element but with the method of coordination varying. The first has a phrasal asyndeton bimembre, the second a single-word asyndeton bimembre (*auxilia equitatum*), and the third a pair of place names linked by *-que*. The correctness of *-que* is confirmed by the fact that Caesar regularly, as we have seen, joins place names with an overt coordinator, except in special structures (see above, 2.1), and the variation produced by having asyndeton in the other two clauses creates a typical sequence with mixed coordination (see e.g. Cicero 3, Livy 10, 11, Tacitus 99). In this structure the asyndeta are likely to be right. The phrasal asyndeton in the first clause is of mundane type, and *auxilia equitatum* for its part belongs to a semantic category in which asyndeton is common: pairs of components of an army or military terms in general are often expressed asyndetically (see e.g. Livy 13, 20 and particularly XXXI.3.3; also Cicero 12, Tacitus 60, 93, 99, 101, 102, 110). For the pair (or a variant), coordinated but not in a significant structure, see *Civ.* 1.38.3 *his rebus constitutis equites auxiliaque toti Lusitaniae a Petreio ... imperantur*, *Civ.* 1.61.4 *magnos equitatus magnaque auxilia, Gall.* 3.20.2 *auxiliis equitatuque comparato*, Livy 22.3.9 *equitatu auxiliisque*. In the asyndeton the *auxilia* would be those of the *equites*: see *Civ.* 1.79.5 *ab equitum suorum auxiliis*. Here is a phrase that in Caesar would normally be expected to have explicit coordination, but in a phrasal structure such as this the asyndeton looks right.

(**6**) 2.4.1 *remigum gubernatorum* (another of the asyndeta cited by Damon).

This pair is in a short sentence (or parenthetical clause, depending on editorial choice): *remigum gubernatorum magna copia suppetebat* (ω; various emendations have removed the asyndeton: see the app. crit. of Damon). Rowers and helmsmen constituted the main crew members of

2 Categories 503

a ship determining its motion and course, and the two terms are thus complementary and express a set, a common feature of asyndeta bimembria. Note e.g. Quint. 5.11.26 *remiges sine gubernatore . . . nihil ualere* (i.e. you can't have one without the other). Cf. Tac. *Hist.* 5.23.2 *classem . . . usu remigum, gubernatorum arte, nauium magnitudine potiorem* (note the chiasmus that brings the two terms together), Veg. *Mil.* 4.43.2 *in nauarchis diligentia, in gubernatoribus peritia, in remigibus uirtus eligitur* (distinguishing commanders, helmsmen and rowers). An asyndeton bimembre would be possible, but the fact remains that Caesar overwhelmingly prefers coordination in such military pairs (see Appendix 2 and the examples cited on 5 above; cf. *Civ.* 3.8.3 *nautas dominosque nauium*, 3.27.2 *remigum propugnatorumque*). We defended *auxilia equitatum* above, 5, but only because the asyndeton is supported by structural features of the passage. No such case can be made for *remigum gubernatorum*.

(7) 1.24.2 *seruos pastores armat atque iis equos attribuit*
Damon keeps the asyndeton and notes no manuscript variation in the apparatus. There is a unity to the pair, in that *pastores* were not normally free (cf. 1.57.4 *pastoresque Domiti spe libertatis*): thus country slaves and slaves of other types. To an overwhelming extent in pairs of nouns denoting interrelated types of persons (many of them military: see Appendix 2) Caesar has coordination: cf. e.g. 1.56.3 *colonis pastoribusque*; also 1.51.2 *cum seruis liberisque*, 2.5.3 *cum liberis atque uxoribus*, 3.9.6 *pueris muliebribusque*, 3.14.3 *de seruis liberisque omnibus*, 3.32.2 *seruorum ac liberorum*, 3.80.3 *seruorum ac liberorum* (I have excluded from this list military pairs). I can see no more reason for allowing asyndeton here than at 6 above.

(8) 1.74.4 *compluresque tribuni militum <et> centuriones ad Caesarem ueniunt*
Et is added in the editio princeps, and omitted by ω. Damon prints the text as here. The text printed should not be based solely on the same phrase elsewhere (with coordinators: for coordinated examples of this pair in Caesar see the discussion at the end of Appendix 1), but on Caesar's regular habit of coordinating military pairs.

(9) 1.80.4 *pabulatores equitesque reuocari iubet*
There is a split in the manuscripts here, with M omitting *-que*. This is another of those military phrases in which a coordinator is expected.

(10) 3.53.4 *et cum laboris sui periculique testimonium adferre uellent*, 'and since they wanted to produce evidence of their toil and danger'. This is the text printed by Damon.

Here V has the coordinator but it is omitted by μST. The two terms *labor* and *periculum* are attested together, and in military contexts (Pomp. Trog. 38.7.4 *denuntiaretur ingens militiae periculum ac labor*, Val. Max. 2.3.1 *impigre se laboribus et periculis militiae offerendo*; in Caesar himself, *Civ.* 3.6.1 *ad finem laborum ac periculorum*, 3.82.4 *in labore pari ac periculo*; see also Sallust 58). Any recurrent pair with coordination may turn up asyndetically as well (see XXX.3.2.1 on Sall. *Cat.* 10.2 for this pair without a coordinator, and for a further case of coordination). *Periculi* might in theory be read as an intensification or correction of *labor* ('their toil, indeed danger'): the punctuation of the asyndetic reading might be *laboris sui, periculi*, thereby implying a pause and placing emphasis on *periculi*. But everything must depend on Caesar's method of coordinating abstract nouns: he does not use asyndeton in such contexts elsewhere in the work. Contrast e.g. 1.4.5 *ad suam potentiam dominatumque*, 1.23.3 *a contumeliis militum conuiciisque prohibet*, 1.26.4 *magnam partem laudis atque existimationis*, 1.32.4 *iacturam dignitatis atque honoris*, 1.32.6 *crudelitatem et insolentiam*, 1.32.9 *iustitia et aequitate*, 1.33.3 *disputationibus excusationibusque*, 1.45.1 *praeter opinionem consuetudinemque*, 1.56.2 *praemiis pollicitationibusque*, 1.74.7 *laetitia et gratulatione*, 1.85.4 *pertinacia atque arrogantia*, 2.4.3 *precibus et fletu*, 2.16.1 *opere et labore*, 2.18.5 *uerba atque orationem*, 2.41.8 *timoris et luctus*, 3.22.1 *iussu atque imperio*, 3.56.2 *famam opinionemque hominum*, 3.64.2 *terrorem et periculum*, 3.83.1 *gratiam dignitatemque* (I have only included a few cases here where the abstract nouns are dependent on prepositions; others could be added).

(11) 3.44.6 *etsi prohibere Pompeius totis copiis et dimicare non constituerat tamen suis locis sagittarios funditores mittebat*, 'although Pompey had not decided to prevent it with the whole of his forces and to fight it out, nevertheless he put in place archers and slingers'.

V again has *-que*, which is missing in μT. This time Damon does not follow V but prints the asyndeton *sagittarios funditores* as above. The phrase is a military one and asyndeton is a possibility, but there is no structural reason for it here, and we have already drawn attention to military pairs with coordination (see above, 4, 5, 6 with cross references, and Appendix 2). At 3.45.3, for example, the manuscripts agree in having *sagittariis funditoribusque*. I cannot see any reason for inconsistent treatment of 3.53.4 (above, 10) and 3.44.6 (along with 3.45.3), and, in view of the following evidence concerning *funditores/sagittarii*, I would follow V in both places in printing a coordinator.

2 Categories

For the pair cf. e.g. Sisenna, *FRH* 26.F51 *funditores et sagittarios*, and also Sall. *Jug.* 49.6. The *TLL* VI.1.1557.29ff. quotes many examples of the two words paired, including ten from Caes. *Gall.* and *Civ.* (I omit 3.4.3, which is included in the list, though it is not a real pairing). Of these ten pairs, every one has an explicit coordinator (without manuscript variation reported), with the sole exception of 3.44.6 above. Note for example the three examples in a short passage, *Civ.* 3.88.6 *sagittarios funditoresque omnes*, 3.93.7 *omnes sagittarii funditoresque*, 3.94.4 *sagittariorum ac funditorum*, in none of which is there any support for asyndeton. Caesar's practice is so consistent that, given the absence of any structural determinant of asyndeton in this one passage, I can see no alternative but to have *-que* with V.

There is another point to be made. It is stated explicitly that Pompey did not deploy his whole forces (*totis copiis*), but only archers and slingers. The pairing designates in the context a finite group, and is not a selective list of combatants that the writer has put down merely *exempli gratia*. As we have seen constantly, selective lists are particularly likely to generate asyndeta.

(12) 1.4.3 *Scipionem ... impellit .. simul iudiciorum metus [adulatio] atque ostentatio sui et potentium, qui in re publica iudiciisque tum plurimum pollebant*, 'Scipio was driven on at the same time by fear or adulation of the judges, and by the desire to promote himself and the powerful men who at the time held much sway in the state and the courts.'

Adulatio was deleted by Madvig, who is followed by Damon. In her apparatus she mentions a transposition by Vielhaber (*adulatio* placed before *potentium*), and also suggests 'an *adulatioque?*'

Cf. Tac. *Hist.* 2.87.2 *onerabant multitudinem obuii ex urbe senatores equitesque, quidam metu, multi per adulationem*. *Metus* and *adulatio* are contrasting motivations, and might have occurred in a conjunctive or disjunctive asyndeton. One might also interpret the first as a modifier of the second ('fearful adulation').

Asyndeton is just possible because of the structure: there would be two phrases coordinated by *atque*, one containing an asyndeton, the other the coordinator *et*. There would be syntactic imbalance between the two pairs, with the first (*metus adulatio*) comprising nominative nouns, and the second genitives (*sui et potentium*), dependent on the nominative noun *ostentatio*. For this type of imbalance (in a structure with a pair in asyndeton first, and then a second, explicitly coordinated, pair in a different case), see XXX.6.2b on Sallust and Tacitus and XXXI.3.7 on 20 on Livy. The case for asyndeton in the present case is, however, not decisive, because the meaning is not absolutely clear (and Vielhaber's transposition would give very good sense). Also, the structural pattern is not quite the same as the usual combinations of asyndetic and syndetic pairs.

(13) 1.26.3 *Caninium Rebilum legatum, familiarem <et> necessarium Scriboni Libonis*, 'Caninius Rebilus the legate, a friend and intimate of Scribonius Libo'.

The asyndeton is removed by Damon (cf. app. crit. *necessarium<que>* M^{mr}). Words denoting close relationships and intimacies are not infrequently in asyndeton (see e.g. Cicero 1, Sallust 12, 42, Tacitus 97, and XXX.3.2.1). However, Caesar regularly coordinates pairs classifying or characterising types of persons (see e.g. 7 above), and there is no possible structural determinant of asyndeton here.

(14) 2.39.3 *ad praedam ad gloriam properate, ut iam de praemiis uestris et de referenda gratia cogitare incipiamus*, 'hurry to seize booty, glory, so that we may begin to think about your rewards and about voting thanks'.

This is the one clear-cut instance (in a direct speech) of the anaphoric prepositional type of asyndeton bimembre. On Caesar's methods of expressing two nouns dependent on a preposition see Appendix 1. Here the anaphoric asyndeton is followed in the next clause by a coordinated pair: cf. the structures in which prepositional asyndeta occur in the historians in the list at XXX.6.2a. In Sallust four of the six prepositional asyndeta are in speeches (see XXX.3.2.5), and in Tacitus *Histories* four of the eight. The previous section of this speech has a clausal asyndeton bimembre.

(15, 16) 1.26.1 *fundis sagittis reliquisque telis pugnabatur*
1.57.2 *magnoque numero pilorum tragularum reliquorumque telorum*
Both of these examples are of the 'weak' type (with the pair followed by a generalising phrase introduced by *reliquique*): see further above, on 1 (**d**) and also XVIII.6.

3 Conclusions

If all possible asyndeta bimembria collected above were taken at their face value, there would be 21 cases of asyndeton bimembre in the *Civ.* (comprising the sixteen numbered, and another five in the alphabetical list at the end of 1 – 3 above (I do not include in this figure of five the two examples in (c), which are separately numbered as 2, 3)). Four of these five are of the debatable type with a generalising element following, as are the two cases 15

3 Conclusions 507

and 16; these six 'weak' examples could arguably be disregarded, which would take the maximum number of asyndeta bimembria, in a work with 163 pages in Damon's edition, down to fifteen, a figure so low that it is clear that Caesar scarcely admitted this form of coordination. Moreover the figure of fifteen cannot stand, as a number of the possible cases should be rejected.

I have rejected above nine of the possible instances of asyndeton, on the grounds that they do not fit Caesar's usage elsewhere (and in some cases are not well supported by manuscript evidence either): 1 *Apolloniam Dyrrachium*, 6 *remigum gubernatorum*, 7 *seruos pastores*, 8 *tribuni militum centuriones*, 9 *pabulatores equites*, 10 *laboris sui periculi*, 11 *sagittarios funditores*, 12 *metus adulatio*, 13 *familiarem necessarium*.

That leaves just five asyndeta bimembria in the whole text: 2 *Dardanos Bessos*, 3 *Macedones Thessalos* (which, though of the 'weak' type, I include here because of its relationship to 2), **b** (in the list of coordinated place names) *<ex> Creta Lacedaemone*, 5 *auxilia equitatum*, 14 *ad praedam ad gloriam*. The phrasal example numbered 4 could be added as it is listed by Damon (see the Introduction, 1 above), but possible phrasal asyndeta have not been systematically collected in this chapter.

Of these 14, of prepositional type, is in a direct speech. We have just seen (on 14) that it is a type also quite common in speeches in the historians. The remaining four examples are all in significant structures, in which asyndeton bimembre is common. **b** is a pair dependent on a preposition, which is followed by repetition of the preposition and a further sequence of dependents. We cited parallel structures from Cicero. 5 (*auxilia equitatum*) is a member of one of three asyndetic clauses, each with a different form of coordination within. When there is juxtaposition of different forms of coordination, asyndetic coordination is often one of these forms. We illustrated the pair *auxilia equitatum* (or equivalents) with explicit coordination when the terms occur outside significant structures. Finally, 2 and 3 provide an accumulation of asyndeta bimembria in a single passage, and asyndeton bimembre often occurs in accumulations. Moreover the second pair (*Macedones Thessalos*) is itself in a significant structure (followed by the generalising phrase *ac reliquarum gentium*, which makes it a weak asyndeton bimembre). Its presence justifies the other asyndetic pair.

It is not only the small number of asyndeta bimembria that stands out, but also the extreme limitation to the types. All comprise nouns or names. Asyndetic adjectives and verbs, for instance, which have such a significant place in e.g. Plautus, Lucilius, Cicero and historians, are completely absent. Above all, it is particular structures that generate the asyndeton, not semantic factors. This work of Caesar is important as establishing criteria that a textual critic might use in deciding between syndetic and asyndetic coordination.

Appendix 1: Pairs of Nouns or Phrases Dependent on a Preposition

In this section there is a tolerably complete list of noun pairs dependent on prepositions in the *Civ.*, classified according to the coordinator (for comparable data from a speech of Cicero see I.10). Pairs of place names and the like are not included here, because these were listed separately earlier (2.1).

1.6.7 *in urbe et Capitolio*
1.43.2 *ab oppido et ponte et commeatu omni*
1.81.1 *ab aqua et natura*
1.85.9 *ex praetura et consulatu*
2.20.4 *in foro et porticibus*
3.10.4 *pro disciplina et praeceptis*
3.16.3 *ex aedilitate et praetura*
3.37.1 *inter eum et Domiti castra*
3.62.2 *in scaphas et naues actuarias*

1.4.5 *ad suam potentiam dominatumque*
1.20.1 *per tribunos militum centurionesque atque honestissimos sui generis* (different coordinators).
1.22.1 *cum uigiliis custodibusque nostris*
1.23.3 *a contumeliis militum conuiciisque*
1.25.10 *ab impetu nauium incendiisque*
1.27.5 *in muro turribusque*
1.39.3 *a tribunis militum centurionibusque* (here the coordinator is omitted by SV).
1.44.2 *cum Lusitanis reliquisque barbaris*
1.45.1 *praeter opinionem consuetudinemque*
1.51.2 *cum seruis liberisque*
1.54.1 *ab Afranianis militibus equitibusque*
1.69.2 *sine iumentis impedimentisque*
1.75.3 *a caetratis equitibusque*
1.82.1 *in his operibus consiliisque*
1.82.2 *contra opinionem enim militum famamque omnium*
2.10.1 *ad hostium turrim murumque*
2.11.3 *a nostris telis tormentisque*
2.12.4 *magna cum misericordia fletuque*
2.14.5 *ad alteram turrim aggeremque*

Appendix 1: Pairs Dependent on a Single Preposition 509

2.19.3 *in turribus muroque*
2.43.3 *ad officium imperiumque*
3.14.3 *de seruis liberisque omnibus*
3.16.5 *de copiis auxiliisque suis*
3.44.1 *a mari Dyrrachioque*
3.49.1 *in uigiliis colloquiisque*
3.62.2 *ex maximis castris praesidiisque*
3.78.5 *ab ora maritima Oricoque* (but the text is uncertain).
3.79.4 *per omnes prouincias ciuitatesque*
3.84.2 *a castris suis collibusque Pompeianis*
3.88.4 *inter aciem mediam cornuaque*
3.100.3 *ex portu insulaque*
3.101.7 *a legatis amicisque Caesaris*
3.105.3 *ad ualuas se templi limenque*
3.110.3 *ex praedonibus latronibusque*

2.8.1 *pro castello ac receptaculo*
2.9.9 *sine ullo uulnere ac periculo*
2.11.3 *ex muro ac turribus*
2.16.3 *ex muro ac turribus*
2.36.3 *de custodia ac defensione urbis*
3.18.1 *ex frigore ac labore*
3.82.4 *in labore pari ac periculo*

1.1.3 *ad Caesaris gratiam atque amicitiam*
1.40.4 *ex aggere atque cratibus*
1.82.4 *ad incursum atque impetum militum*
2.5.3 *ex castris C. Trebonio atque omnibus superioribus locis*
2.5.3 *cum liberis atque uxoribus*
2.11.4 *ad legatos atque exercitum*
3.42.2 *ab Asia atque omnibus regionibus*
3.103.2 *per suos propinquos atque amicos*
3.103.3 *pro hospitio atque amicitia*
3.109.1 *pro communi amico atque arbitro.*

In this list there are 60 examples (*et* 9, *-que* 34, *ac* 7, *atque* 10). *-Que* was clearly the favoured coordinator. In the list of coordinated place names earlier (2.1) it was seen that *atque* is always before vowels. In the present list every instance of *ac* is before a consonant, and every instance of *atque* but one before a vowel. Thus some might feel that there is a doubt hanging over 1.40.4 *ex aggere atque cratibus*. However, Caesar does occasionally in other contexts have *atque* before a consonant, though it is very much more common for *atque* to precede a vowel. For *atque* + consonant see e.g. 1.5.1 *raptim atque turbate* (where *atque* produces the rhythm cretic–trochee/spondee, a common clausula), 1.20.2 *spe atque fiducia* (in a speech; double cretic, also common), 1.80.1 *lente atque paulatim* (cretic–trochee). The determinant of *atque* at 1.40.4 may have been metrical (cretic–iambus, a quite common clausula).

Clearly the omission of the coordinator by some manuscripts at 1.39.3 *a tribunis militum centurionibusque* must be down to scribal error. There is no case of an asyndetic pair after a single preposition, apart from the structurally significant example 3.4.3 <*ex*> <u>Creta Lacedaemone</u> (see above, 2.1, **b**). For the pair coordinated see e.g. 2.21.1 *tribunis militum centurionibusque*, 1.67.4 *tribunorum militum et centurionum*, 1.76.3 *tribuni militum centurionesque*, 1.77.2 *ex numero tribunorum militum centurionumque*, 3.13.4 *tribuni militum centurionesque*, 3.95.5 *centurionibus tribunisque militum*.

A variant of the structure in which a single preposition is followed by a pair of explicitly coordinated dependent nouns is provided by cases where the preposition is repeated and preceded by a coordinator:

1.5.3 *in ipso urbis incendio atque in desperatione omnium*
1.5.4 *de imperio Caesaris et de amplissimis uiris*
1.72.1 *sine pugna et sine uulnere*
1.73.3 *et sine timore et sine stationibus*
1.86.2 *de loco et de tempore* (this pair is attested in asyndeton: see Sallust 37).
2.39.3 *ut iam de praemiis uestris et de referenda gratia cogitare incipiamus*
3.6.1 *ex uictoria et ex liberalitate sua*
3.10.8 *ab senatu et a populo*
3.16.5 *de causa et de copiis auxiliisque suis*
3.20.1 *de aestimatione et de solutionibus*
3.53.5 *de se meritus et de re publica*
3.82.3 *de praemiis ac de sacerdotiis* (the manuscripts are split here between *ac de* (μT) and *ac* (U^{ac} SV); *ac*, as we have seen, may link two terms dependent on the same preposition, but there are no other cases of *ac* followed by a preposition that has been repeated).
3.108.5 *per omnes deos perque foedera . . . populum Romanum obtestabatur*
3.112.8 *aditusque habebat ad portum et ad reliqua naualia*.

Different again is the following example, which has a single coordinator but anastrophe of the preposition:

3.6.3 *saxa inter et alia periculosa loca*

Finally, there is the one instance of the prepositional type of asyndeton seen above at 14:

2.39.3 *ad praedam ad gloriam properate*
The abnormality of this example is down to the fact that it is in a direct speech.

Appendix 2: Some Coordinated Military Pairs in Caesar *Civ.*

1.17.4 *centurionibus euocatisque*
1.21.3 *uigiliis stationibusque*
1.21.4 *tribunos militum et praefectos*
1.22.1 *cum uigiliis custodibusque nostris*
1.38.3 *equites auxiliaque*
1.54.1 *ab Afranianis militibus equitibusque*
1.75.3 *a caetratis equitibusque*
1.78.1 *caetrati auxiliaresque*
2.19.3 *custodias uigiliasque*
2.26.2 *equitum peditumque*
2.28.1 *ordines manipulique*
2.40.2 *equitum peditumque*
3.8.1 *legiones equitatusque*
3.8.3 *nautas dominosque nauium*
3.14.1 *legionibus equitibusque*
3.16.5 *de copiis auxiliisque suis*
3.19.7 *centuriones militesque nonnulli*
3.27.2 *remigum propugnatorumque*
3.53.1 *euocatos centurionesque*
3.95.5 *centurionibus tribunisque militum.*

To this list should be added the seven coordinated instances of *tribuni militum* and *centuriones* that are found in Appendix 1 above in the discussion of 1.39.3.

CHAPTER XXIX

Horace

1 Introduction

In this chapter the different genres of Horace's work, the *Satires, Epistles, Odes, Epodes* and *Ars poetica*, are kept apart. Striking generic differences in the use of asyndeton will emerge, between on the one hand the *Satires* and first book of the *Epistles*, and on the other the *Odes* (and *Epodes*).

I start with asyndeta bimembria and then move on to asyndetic tricola and longer groups of single words.[1] The use of these purely asyndetic sequences is then compared with that of comparable sequences that have coordination in some form. The coordinated sequences are of several types, first, coordinated pairs, second, tricola or longer sequences with the last member attached by a coordinator (end-of-list coordination), and, third, sequences with three or more members that have multiple coordination. The relationship between asyndetic coordination and syndetic in the various genres is considered, and possible influences on Horace in some genres suggested.

2 Asyndeton Bimembre[2]

2.1 Satires

Horace admits asyndeton with two members, single words or single word + slightly extended term, about 20 times in the *Satires*. These are often of classifiable types and have familiar structures, are often pejorative and slangy in tone and usually do not look like high-style features. We will

---

[1] 'Single-word' asyndeta are interpreted liberally in lists in this chapter, in that pairs or e.g. tricola with members that are mainly single words but that also have a member of slightly extended length are also included.

[2] Some remarks can be found in Ruckdeschel (1910: 157–8), Calboli (1997a: 802).

see that the *Odes* are very different and provide no evidence that asyndeton bimembre was considered a poetic high-style feature.

2.1.1 *Privatives*

Take first *Sat.* 2.7.39 *nasum nidore supinor,* | *imbecillus iners, si quid uis, adde, popino*, 'I curl up my nose at a rich smell, weak, lazy, and, if you want to add anything, a low glutton.'

Here is a typical pair of privatives that are adjuncts/secondary predicates (see VI.3). These postponed terms are presented as a selection of the possibilities, in that it is openly stated that a stronger term might be added. The passage with the possibility that it lays open is very similar to Catull. 42.13 (on which see Catullus 1.1): *non assis facit? o lutum lupanar,* | *aut si perditius potest quid esse*. We have discussed elsewhere (V.2) a text (the minor declamations of Quintilian) in which asyndetic pairs of judgement adjectives come regularly at the end of a colon, and are selective (cf. IV.3). More will be said below about terms listed in asyndeton *exempli gratia*.

The privatives here denote un-Roman characteristics, weakness and laziness, and that is often a feature of pairs of privatives in high-style literature too (see VI.9). For *iners* in such a pair see Sall. *Jug.* 44.1 (**58**) *iners inbellis*, and also the longer sequence at *Ep.* 1.1.38 cited at 3.2 below. Most of the adjectival pairs in the *Satires* have at least one privative (see the conclusions, 2.1.5).

Here is another: *Sat.* 1.2.93 *depugis nasuta, breui latere ac pede longo est*, '(but) she has no buttocks but a long nose, a short side and long foot'. The first adjective is negative but not with *in-*. It is modelled on ἄπυγος (see *TLL* s.v.). For the privative force of *de-* (cf. e.g. *debellis, deformis*) see *OLD* s.v. *de-*. *De-* is one of several prefixes in addition to *in-* that may be used thus (see XXV.1.1.2 on Lucilius 10). Cf. e.g. *e(x)* at e.g. Cic. *Red. sen.* 14 (**44**) *sine sensu sine sapore, elinguem, tardum inhumanum negotium* ('without a tongue').

The phrase structure is a type of accumulation (see e.g. XIX.1): the asyndetic pair is juxtaposed with a coordinated pair, the coordinator being *ac*, as sometimes in Lucilius (see XXV.1.1.2 on **8, 10**), Livy (XXXI.3.7) and Tacitus (**5**). The structure was not confined to high literature. Note that the coordinated pair in Horace has a contrast, of antonyms (short/long). Cf. e.g. Tac. *Ann.* 6.19.2 (**90**) *inlustres ignobiles, dispersi aut aggerati*, where both the asyndetic pair and the coordinated have contrasts of opposites.

The other pairs with a privative or privative-equivalent in the *Satires* are:

Sat. 1.9.52 *magnum narras, uix credibile*

Vix credibile is equivalent to *incredibile*. The context is conversational, and the structure of the asyndeton is discontinuous, with the second term semantically stronger. The adjectives are substantivised here.

Sat. 2.1.59 *diues inops, Romae, seu fors ita iusserit, exsul,* 'whether rich or poor, at Rome or, if chance so bid, in exile'.

Diues inops is a pair of opposites (antonyms) of the type in which a positive is alongside a negative, usually of the same root (e.g. *dignus/ indignus*: see VI.6), though here there is a variation on that pattern in that the two terms are of different roots ('inexplicit' opposites, of a type favoured by Tacitus). For the semantics cf. the asyndeton *diuitiae paupertas* discussed at Cicero 121.

Again there is an accumulation, with two disjunctive pairs, the first asyndetic, the second coordinated (*seu*), and also expressing an opposition, roughly of the 'town/country' type (for which see XIII.5.1).

Sat. 2.2.14 *cum labor extuderit fastidia, siccus inanis | sperne cibum uilem,* 'when hard work has hammered fastidiousness out of you, thirsty, hungry, scorn (if you can) cheap food'.

A typical pair of adjuncts/secondary predicates in agreement with the subject of the verb, with the second member not strictly (it seems) a privative adjective but behaving as one (on which see VI.3 on Cicero 172). 'Thirst/hunger' (*sitis, fames*) are usually overtly coordinated in Latin (see *TLL* VI.1.232.59ff.; cf. Plaut. *Cas.* 725 *esurio et sitio*, Catull. 21.10–11 *esurire | ... sitire*). The uses of *inanis* for 'hungry' (= *ieiunus*) and *siccus* for 'thirsty' are departures from literal or explicit terminology. An analogous pair is 'eat/drink' (see XXIII.5.5, 7.1 for Plaut. *Trin.* 406, *TLL* II.1959.70ff., and also *Ep.* 2.2.79, *Sat.* 1.1.76, both of which passages are cited later in this chapter; note too Andr. *poet.* 45 Morel *affatim edi bibi lusi* (see also below, 4.2.2 on *Ep.* 2.2.14 in connection with this last example)). The etymology of *inanis* is unknown.

Sat. 2.3.236 *segnis ego, indignus qui ...*

Another discontinuous asyndetic pair, the second adjective longer than the first (cf. *Sat.* 2.2.14 above). For a pronoun in this position cf. Men. *Dysk.* 960 αἵρεσθε τοῦτον, εἰσφέρετε.

Sat. 2.3.248 *ludere par impar*

The name of a game, with the adjectives probably substantivised (see VI.6). This pair was an established one, as the same phrase is in Suetonius (in a letter) with the same meaning (*Aug.* 71.4 *par impar ludere*).

2 Asyndeton Bimembre

2.1.2 Accumulations

I take up now two themes that have been mentioned in relation to the above examples. First, accumulations, of which two (*Sat.* 1.2.93, 2.1.59) were noted above. Here are others:

Sat. 1.1.85 *omnes | <u>uicini</u> oderunt, <u>noti</u>, <u>pueri atque puellae</u>*, 'every one hates you, neighbours and acquaintances, boys and girls' (Fairclough, Loeb).

There is not end-of-list coordination here, because *pueri atque puellae* is a unitary masculine + feminine pair, frequently used by Horace with a coordinator (see below, 4.1, and also XI.4). The Loeb (above) takes *omnes* as the subject, with the other terms appositional. For the structure cf. e.g. Sallust 17 *patriae parentibus, aris atque focis* and XXX.6.2b on the type, with *atque* the coordinator in the second pair. *Vicini* and *noti* (discontinuous) belong together semantically.

Sat. 1.6.31–3 *puellis | iniciat curam quaerendi singula, quali | sit <u>facie sura</u>, quali <u>pede dente capillo</u>.*

The list of single anatomical terms that starts with *facie* is split into two groups by the anaphoric *quali* acting as a colon divider, with the structure 2 + 3 (see e.g. Cicero 12 and XIX.1 for this pattern). Note Cic. *Sest.* 88 (**15**) *ad ferrum faces, ad cotidianam caedem incendia rapinas* (with anaphora again: *ad* has the same function as *quasi*). Both the asyndetic pair and the tricolon in Horace have terms that refer to parts at opposite ends of the body: what may look like miscellaneous lists often have internal patterns (see IV.2). Cf. the list at Plaut. *Am.* 444–5: *sura pes statura tonsus, nasum uel labra, | malae mentum barba collus: totus!*

Sat. 1.6.34 *sic qui promittit <u>ciuis urbem</u> sibi curae, <u>imperium fore et Italiam</u>, <u>delubra deorum</u>*, 'he who promises that he will look after his fellow-citizens and the city, the empire and Italy, and the temples of the gods'.

This accumulation has first an asyndetic pair separated from the rest of the sequence by *sibi curae*, then a coordinated pair and finally a single word. The three elements are also semantically distinct and of increasing importance: the city and its inhabitants, Italy and the wider empire, the gods.

For the structure compare Catull. 115.5 *uno qui in saltu tot bona possideat, | <u>prata arua</u>, <u>ingentes siluas saltusque</u>, <u>paludesque</u>* (see XXVII.1.1): 2 + 2 + 1, as above, the only difference being that in this last the final term is attached by a coordinator.

Sat. 1.7.6–8 *durus homo atque odio qui posset uincere Regem, | <u>confidens tumidus</u>, adeo sermonis amari, | <u>Sisennas Barros</u> ut equis praecurreret albis*, 'A harsh man he was, and of the sort who could outdo Rex in hatred, confident, arrogant, so harsh of speech that he could outstrip the likes of Sisenna or Barrus as if by means of white horses.'

In the final *ut*-clause there is an asyndetic pair of names in the plural denoting types. For this category of asyndeton (the names are chosen *exempli gratia*) see e.g. IV.3 on Livy 4.15.5 (3) with further references, and below, 2.1.4.4 on *Sat.* 2.3.12.

Confidens tumidus is an asyndetic unit within the longer sequence, and is of classic semantic type ('confident, more than confident'). The genitival phrase that follows I take as a new element, and it leads to the following *ut*-clause.

2.1.3 Discontinuous Asyndetic Pairs

Horace not infrequently has this type:

Sat. 1.1.85 *omnes | uicini oderunt, noti, pueri atque puellae*
See above, 2.1.2.

Sat. 1.3.58 *illi tardo cognomen, pingui damus*, 'We give him the nickname slow, thick.'
The second term seems stronger.

Sat. 1.9.52 *magnum narras, uix credibile*
See above, 2.1.1.

Sat. 2.3.215 (*si quis*) *huic uestem (ut gnatae) paret, ancillas, paret aurum* '(if) one were to provide for it [a lamb] clothes (as for a daughter), maids, and were to provide gold'.

In the first clause with the first *paret* there is a discontinuous asyndetic pair of objects (*uestem, ancillas*), and then follows another clause with an additional instance of *paret*.

Sat. 2.3.236 *segnis ego, indignus qui* . . .
See above, 2.1.1.

2.1.4 Some Other Types
2.1.4.1 Masculine + Feminine Pairs

Sat. 2.3.325 *mille puellarum puerorum mille furores*

The two genitives are both dependent on *mille furores* (with *mille* repeated in chiasmus). 'Boys' and 'girls' are often coordinated (see XI.4), not least by Horace, usually with an overt coordinator (see above, 2.1.2 on *Sat.* 1.1.85).

The motivation for the uncoordinated juxtaposition of the pair above lies not in the fact that they are a masculine + feminine pair, but in the structure. The repetition of *mille* is similar to anaphora, and asyndeton with anaphora is a combination favoured by Horace (see e.g. *Carm.* 1.5.10, 4.8.8, *Ep.* 1.17.55–6, 1.19.19–20, *Sat.* 1.2.50, 1.2.92).

2.1.4.2 Family Members

Sat. 1.9.26–7 'est tibi mater | cognati, quis te saluo est opus?', 'Have you a mother, blood relatives, who depend on your welfare?'

A conversational context, and again the list is open-ended. For pairs of family members expressed asyndetically see XIV. This same pair, but with the second term in the feminine, occurs in Lucilius (XXV.1.1.2, 12 *ad matrem cognatam*). For the technical sense of *cognatus, cognatio* see on Sallust 42. See also below, 3.1 on *Sat.* 2.3.57–8.

2.1.4.3 The City and its Components

Sat. 1.9.13 *cum quidlibet ille | garriret, uicos urbem laudaret*, 'while the fellow rattled on about everything, praising the streets, the city' (Loeb, modified).

The context shows that these are just examples of what the man rambled on about, a selective list to do with urban life (cf. above, 2.1.2 on 1.6.34 *sic qui promittit ciuis urbem sibi curae*).

2.1.4.4 Pairs of Names

Sat. 2.3.12 *quorsum pertinuit stipare Platona Menandro, | Eupolin Archilochum, comites educere tantos?* 'What was the point of packing Plato with Menander, and of taking away with you Eupolis, Archilochus, such weighty companions?'

There are two infinitives in this sentence, each with its own object, *Platona* with *stipare* and the asyndetic pair with *educere*. For pairs of names in asyndeton (not infrequently chosen as mere examples), see above, 2.1.2, *Sat.* 1.7.6–8.

Cicero not infrequently lists names in asyndeton. Here are some philosophers: *Fin.* 4.3 (**127**) *ueteres illos Platonis auditores, Speusippum Aristotelem Xenophontem, deinde eorum Polemonem Theophrastum*. For other pairs of philosophers listed asyndetically see Cicero **128, 129**.

2.1.4.5 Opposites

Sat. 1.2.63 *quid inter-* | *est* <u>in matrona ancilla</u> *peccesne* <u>togata</u>?, 'what does it matter whether you sin with a matron or slave girl in a gown?'.

Opposites of social class (XIII.5.3). Both terms are dependent on a single preposition (see XXI.4).

Sat. 2.1.59 <u>diues inops</u>, *Romae, seu fors ita iusserit, exsul*

Sat. 2.3.248 *ludere par impar*
On this and the last example see above, 2.1.1.

Sat. 2.3.264 *exclusit, reuocat: redeam? non si obsecret*, 'she shut me out, she calls me back: shall I return? Not if she implores me.'

The first two verbs are opposites of the reversive type. Horace has taken the whole line from Terence, *Eun.* 49: *exclusit, reuocat: redeam? non si me obsecret* (cf. Calboli 1997a: 801).

Sat. 2.3.267–8 *in amore haec sunt mala,* <u>bellum</u> | <u>pax</u> *rursum*, 'in love there are these evils, war, peace again'.

The two opposites (antonyms) are in apposition to *mala*. For peace and war opposed see e.g. *TLL* II.1855.71ff., but without details of forms of coordination. Again Horace has taken the pair from Terence: *Eun.* 59–61 *in amore haec omnia insunt uitia: iniuriae,* | *suspiciones, inimicitiae indutiae,* | *bellum pax rursum* (in which sequence there is also a preceding pair of opposites, *inimicitiae indutiae*, 'hostilities, truces').

Sat. 1.2.93 *depugis nasuta*
See 2.1.1: an implied opposition, small versus big (antonyms).

2.1.4.6 Verbal Pairs with One Member of Extended Length

Sat. 1.9.59 *occurram in triuiis, deducam*, 'in the streets I will come up to him, escort him'.

Another conversational context (from the story of the tedious companion Horace cannot get rid of), and with the verbs expressing selected possibilities, not totalities. The speaker has just said that he will not give up courting Maecenas, and has stated a few things that he will do. For verbs of motion in asyndetic pairs see XXIII.5.3.

2 Asyndeton Bimembre

Sat. 1.9.64–5 *uellere coepi | et pressare manu lentissima brachia,* <u>nutans,</u> | <u>distorquens oculos,</u> *ut me eriperet,* 'I began to pull at and press his unyielding arms with my hand, nodding, winking so that he would snatch me away.' For pairs of present participles in asyndeton see XXIII.5.5, Cicero 174.

2.1.4.7 A Special Case

Sat. 2.5.28 *uiuet uter* <u>locuples sine gnatis,</u> *improbus, ultro | qui meliorem audax uocet in ius, illius esto | defensor,* 'whichever of the parties is rich and childless, villain though he be, who with wanton impudence calls the better man into court, do you become his advocate' (Faircough, Loeb).

The poem is about legacy hunting, and the two crucial features of the man to be courted are that he is to be rich and childless. *Sine gnatis* plays the role of a privative adjective such that along with *locuples* it is a predicate. *Improbus* expresses an incidental characteristic, and has a different role from the preceding phrase (secondary predicate).

For *sine*-phrases acting as alternatives to privative adjectives, see XXIII.6 on Plaut. *Bac.* 612–14, Cicero 44, 48 (also VI.2.2).

2.1.5 Conclusions

A total of 22 asyndetic pairs have been collected above from the *Satires*, comprising eight pairs of nouns, eight pairs of adjectives, three pairs of verbs, two pairs of names and a mixed pair with adjectival function. Many of the contexts in which they occur are conversational or informal in some sense.

The following pairs of adjectives have at least one member that is a privative or the equivalent of a privative: 1.2.93 *depugis nasuta,* 1.9.52 *magnum, uix credibile,* 2.1.59 *diues inops,* 2.2.14 *siccus inanis,* 2.3.236 *segnis indignus,* 2.3.248 *par impar,* 2.5.28 *locuples sine gnatis,* 2.7.39 *imbecillus iners.* These eight examples are the entirety of the adjectival category. When there is just one negative (only the last example has a pair of privatives), that negative term is in second position in every case except *depugis nasuta.* The following pairs are adjuncts/secondary predicates: 1.7.7 *confidens tumidus,* 2.1.59 *diues inops,* 2.2.14 *siccus inanis,* 2.7.39 *imbecillus iners.* The following are predicates/subject complements: 1.2.93 *depugis nasuta,* 2.3.236 *segnis indignus,* 2.5.28 *locuples sine gnatis.* Horace's practice suggests that asyndetic pairs of adjectives, predicates in one sense or another, of which at least one member was a privative, were mundane. Some of them are pairs of opposites (*diues inops, par impar*), and most of the rest are pejorative in some sense. It was seen earlier (VI.2.2.1) that pairs of privatives in Latin tend to be pejorative, whereas such pairs in Greek are often pathetic. That feature of Latin is reinforced by the evidence from Horace's *Satires*.

Several other features of the pairs in Horace's *Satires* are worth noting.

First, some pairs occur not in isolation but as one member of a coordinated sequence. For example, an asyndetic pair may be followed by a coordinated. Asyndeton within a coordinated sequence is deeply rooted in Latin, with structures going back to early prayers. Accumulations are very common in prose, including the works of Cicero, Sallust and Tacitus (see XIX.2 for references). About 25 per cent of asyndeta bimembria in the *Satires* are in accumulations.

Second, the discontinuous structure (see XX), whereby the asyndetic pair is interrupted by another term or phrase, occurs several times. Pairs with rising emphasis are not unusual in this corpus, as e.g. 1.7.7 *confidens tumidus*.

Third, several of the pairs are in effect open-ended lists, to which extra terms might have been added at will (1.7.8 *Sisennas Barros*, 1.9.26–7 *mater cognati*, 1.9.59 *occurram . . . deducam*, 2.7.39 *imbecillus iners*). Pairs of this type, which often come at the end of a colon, were in mundane use (see IV.3, 4, V.2).

Fourth, we have observed several times above that pairs are in conversational contexts. The two pairs taken from a passage of comedy imply a concept of the stylistic level that the usage might have.

A question remains that will be discussed later. To what extent does Horace use coordination in the types of pairs we have collected with asyndeton, and does his practice vary according to genre?

2.2   *Epistles*

Asyndeton bimembre is also not uncommon in the first book of the *Epistles* of Horace. The examples are first cited in order below.

Ep. 1.1.58 *sed quadringentis sex septem milia desunt*, 'but there are six or seven thousands lacking to the four hundred'.

Numerals and the like may be paired disjunctively, as here, sometimes in asyndeton but not invariably so. On the formulaic *ter quater* see Preuss (1881: 48–9), stating that 'saepissime = compluries'; an example from Vitruvius is quoted at XXXII.4. Note too e.g. Plaut. *Epid.* 211 *pueros uirgines*, | *binos ternos*, 'boys, girls, two each, three each' (see XXIII.8.9),

2 Asyndeton Bimembre 521

Laberius 18.2 *simul sub dentes mulieris ueni, bis ter memordit*: see Panayotakis (2010: 201–2) for examples, including coordinated. He states that 'the asyndeton reinforces the vigour of the imagery of "biting"', but a disjunction, expressing a numerical estimate, hardly implies vigour. As Preuss observed, such a pair usually means just 'several times'. Cf. too Plaut. *Poen.* 580 *duplicis triplicis*.

Ep. 1.1.100 <u>*diruit aedificat*</u>, *mutat quadrata rotundis*, 'it pulls down, builds up, changes square for round'.

Two pairs of opposites et sim., the first a pair of verbs (reversives), the second expressed by two nouns referring to the substitution of square for round. The structure is not that of a tricolon, because the third verb phrase is on a different theme from the pair of verbs, and has its own contrast, of opposite shapes, the one shape with square corners the other without. See on Cicero **94–8**.

The pair of verbs in asyndeton is exactly paralleled at Cic. *Dom.* 137 (**69**) *dirueris aedificaris*.

Ep. 1.2.40–1 *sapere aude,* | *incipe*
Imperatives (see X).

Ep. 1.6.54 '*frater,*' '*pater*' *adde:* | *ut cuique est aetas, ita quemque facetus adopta*

A coordinator (disjunctive) would be possible. These are forms of address that might be used to win favour. The list is potentially open-ended. Each of the two vocatives would be uttered at different times, addressed to persons of different ages. The pair is not therefore a quotation of a single utterance but is part of an instruction of what to say when, and it is not the same as a genuine form of address with asyndetic coordination (as in the pair *patres conscripti* used in the vocative). On the problem of interpreting pairs like this see VIII.1 on Th. 7.71.4.

Ep. 1.6.57–8 <u>*piscemur uenemur*</u>, *ut olim* | *Gargilius, qui mane plagas uenabula seruos* | *differtum transire forum populumque iubebat*, 'Let us fish, let us hunt, like Gargilius in the story, who in the morning would order that nets, spears, slaves pass through the packed forum and the people.'

An accumulation (2 + 3, but with the two members not juxtaposed in this case).

Ep. 1.6.67 *uiue uale* (see XXVII.1.4).

Ep. 1.7.72 *ut uentum ad cenam est,* <u>*dicenda tacenda*</u> *locutus* | *tandem dormitum dimittitur*

A positive–negative pair of opposites (things that should be said and not said: see VI.7). See also Preuss (1881: 43). The pair *fanda nefanda* ('the lawful and unlawful') at Catull. 64.405 (see XXVII.1.1) in its original meaning is much the same (literally 'that which may be said, or may not be said').

Ep. 1.13.19 *uade uale*

This is an anticipation of the use of *uade* in later Latin, where it loses its classical nuances and replaces the monsyllable, classical Latin *i*: see X.1.4 and Adams (2013: 814). Cf. Catull. 14.21 *(uos hinc interea ualete abite | illuc)*, on which see Fordyce (1961: 138): 'the two verbs form a single expression, "get away with my blessing from here"' (see further XXVII.1.4).

2.2.1 Conclusions

Eight pairs are listed above from the first book of *Epistles*. There are no single-word asyndetic pairs in the second book, with the possible exception of an embedded pair, *pullos oua*, at *Ep.* 2.2.162–3, for which see 3.2 below. Three of the above cases are pairs of imperatives, and of these two are formulaic expressions (*uiue uale, uade uale*). Two other pairs are of verbs (*diruit aedificat, piscemur uenemur*), and a third pair comprises verbal derivatives (*dicenda tacenda*). Two of these three are opposites (reversives in the case of *diruit aedificat*, and complementarities in *dicenda tacenda*). The numerical estimate *sex septem* is of conventional type, and the same is true of the asyndetic pair *piscemur uenemur*, placed thus within an accumulation. The asyndeta in the *Epistles* are of run-of-the-mill types.

There may be another embedded asyndetic pair in the *Epistles*, *it redit* at 1.7.55, on which see below, 4.2.2.

2.3 Odes

Carm. 2.3.26 *omnium | uerstaur urna <u>serius ocius</u> | sors exitura*, 'The lot of every one of us is tossing about in the urn, destined sooner, later to come forth' (Bennett, Loeb).

Opposites, antonyms, pairs of adverbs, a common type (see XIII.5.4). See Preuss (1881: 48), Nisbet and Hubbard (1978: 65).

Carm. 3.14.17 *i pete unguentum, puer, et coronas*. A formulaic address to a slave comprising two imperatives, with a vocative (for the structure see X.1.1). The objects of *pete* are in conjunct hyperbaton.

See Nisbet and Rudd (2004: 187).

Carm. 4.4.59 *per damna per caedes*
The prepositional type, with anaphora, a stylised type (see XXVIII Appendix 1).

2.3.1 Conclusions

Asyndeta bimembria are hardly found in the *Odes*. The first example looks proverbial, the second is formulaic in structure, and the third is of an artificial type and is not merely an asyndeton.

2.4 Ars Poetica

172 *uel quod res omnis timide gelideque ministrat,* | *dilator spe longus, iners auidusque futuri,* | *difficilis querulus, laudator temporis acti* | *se puero, castigator censorque minorum* (of an old man), 'or because, in all that he does, he lacks fire and courage, is dilatory and slow to form hopes, is sluggish and greedy of a longer life, peevish, surly, given to praising the days he spent as a boy, and to reproving and condemning the young' (Fairclough, Loeb).

From *dilator* there are five descriptive phrases, not linked by coordinators, comprising single phrases without internal coordination (of which there are two), two phrases with internal coordination (*iners auidusque futuri, castigator censorque minorum*), and one asyndeton bimembre (*difficilis querulus*). This last, consisting of semantically similar adjectives, is a classic instance of an asyndeton embedded within a longer asyndetic sequence. On this pairing see Brink (1971: 240), and for *difficilis* in an asyndetic pair see XXV.1.1.4 on Lucilius 20. Another case of asyndeton in the description of decrepitude (cf. XXIII.8.8).

3 Longer Asyndeta

By 'longer asyndeta' I refer here to asyndeta that are structurally the same as the asyndeta bimembria seen above, in that they consist of single words or slight extensions thereof but have more than two members. Asyndetic tricola are probably the most distinctive type. See Lindholm (1931: 183–4) and also Calboli (1997a: 801).

3.1 Satires

Sat. 1.1.39 *neque hiems ignis mare ferrum,* | *nil obstet tibi*
An open-ended list, as is shown by the summarising *nil*.

Sat. 1.1.74 *panis ematur, holus | uini sextarius*
   Discontinuous. A list of things that may be bought, virtually a shopping list though it is open-ended. A summary of the additional possibilities follows: *adde | quis humana sibi doleat natura negatis,* 'add things which, if denied, would be painful to our human nature'.

Sat. 1.1.77 *formidare malos fures, incendia seruos*

Sat. 1.2.1–2 *ambubaiarum collegia, pharmacopolae | mendici mimae balatrones, hoc genus omne*
   This asyndetic list occupies two lines, a common phenomenon, and is again open-ended, with an all-embracing phrase at the end. For asyndeta in Plautus occupying a whole line or thereabouts see XXIII.4 n. 2; in Pacuvius, see XXIV.6.4 on Pacuvius 12; in Ennius, see XXIV.5.2.6; in Lucretius, see XXIV.7.4 and also Deufert (2018: 194–5) on Lucr. 3.1017; in Virgil, see XXIV.2.2 after Virgil 30; and in Homer, see XXIV.3 on Homer 18, 20, 21. For an epigraphic instance see *CLE* 237.2 (epitaph for a woman) *lanifica pia pudica frugi casta domiseda.* Such extended lists are also found in Horace. The examples come up below, but here is a selection to illustrate the point: Ars 121 *si forte reponis Achillem, | impiger iracundus inexorabilis acer | iura neget sibi nata, Ep.* 2.2.180–1 *gemmas marmor ebur, Tyrrena sigilla, tabellas | argentum, uestes Gaetulo murice tinctas | sunt qui non habeant, Ep.* 2.2.203 *uiribus ingenio specie uirtute loco re, Ep.* 2.2.208–9 *somnia terrores magicos, miracula sagas, | nocturnos lemures portentaque Thessala rides?*

Sat. 1.2.98 *custodes lectica ciniflones parasitae* (whole line).

Sat. 1.4.15 *detur nobis locus hora | custodes*

Sat. 2.3.57–8 *clamet amica | mater, honesta soror cum cognatis, pater uxor*
   Soror cum cognatis resembles *Sat.* 1.9.26–7 *mater cognati* (see above, 2.1.4.2), and also Lucilius 994 (12) *ad matrem cognatam, ad amicam* (see XXV.1.1.2).

Sat. 2.3.94–5 *omnis enim res, | uirtus fama decus, diuina humanaque pulchris | diuitiis parent.*
   This is a miscellaneous list, with the summarising *omnis res* and *diuina humanaque* at the end implying that the terms are chosen as examples.

Sat. 2.3.97 *clarus erit, fortis iustus*

Sat. 2.3.127 *periuras surripis aufers / undique*

Sat. 2.3.227–9 *edicit, piscator uti, pomarius auceps | unguentarius ac Tusci turba impia uici, | cum scurris fartor, cum Velabro omne macellum | mane domum ueniant*, 'he decreed that fishmonger, fruitseller, fowler, perfumer, and the Tuscan street's faithless crowd, cook and parasites, the whole market and Velabrum, should come to him the next morning'.

This sentence has two asyndetic sequences, the first with four single words, the second with three asyndetic phrases. The two groups are linked by *ac*.

Sat. 2.3.255 *ponas insignia morbi,* | *fasciolas cubital focalia*, 'will you lay aside the symptoms of your illness, garters, elbow-cushion, neck-wrap'.

Sat. 2.8.9–10 *rapula lactucae radices, qualia lassum* | *peruellunt stomachum, siser allec, faecula Coa*

This is a dinner list. The six items are split into two groups of three by the intervening descriptive clause. Compare the virtual shopping list at *Sat.* 1.1.74, this section, and see IV.2.

Sat. 2.8.27 *cenamus auis conchylia piscis*
Another dinner list.

3.1.1 Conclusions

Just fourteen longer asyndeta have been listed above (or sixteen, if the sequences that are split into two are counted twice). The type is a little less frequent in the *Satires* than asyndeta bimembria, whereas in (e.g.) rhetorical prose asyndetic tricola (and longer asyndetic cola) are far more frequent than the type with two members. In Catullus too (XXVII.4) asyndetic triplets are less numerous than pairs.

Further conclusions will be offered at the end of the chapter.

3.2 Epistles

Ep. 1.1.38 *inuidus iracundus iners uinosus amator,* | *nemo adeo ferus est, ut non mitescere possit*

This is a selective list, as the *nemo*-clause shows. Two of the first three terms are *in*-privatives, and the intervening term also begins with *i-* (see VI.3 for this phenomenon). For a similar sequence, also containing *iracundus*, see *Ars* 121, quoted below, 3.3. For *iners* in an asyndeton see above 2.1.1 on *Sat.* 2.7.39. The whole first line is occupied by the asyndetic list.

Ep. 1.1.91–2 *mutat cenacula lectos* | *balnea tonsores*

Ep. 1.1.106–7 *diues* | *liber honoratus pulcher, rex denique regum*

Ep. 1.2.15 *seditione dolis scelere atque libidine et ira*
   An asyndetic tricolon followed by a coordinated pair (an accumulation of the structure 3 + 2).

Ep. 1.4.10 *cui | gratia fama ualetudo contingat abunde*

Ep. 1.6.57–8 *piscemur uenemur, ut olim | Gargilius, qui mane plagas uenabula seruos | . . . transire forum . . iubebat*
   This accumulation was seen earlier (2.2). There is an asyndetic tricolon in the relative clause.

Ep. 1.13.10 *uiribus uteris per cliuos flumina lamas*
   The three nouns are dependent on a single preposition (see XXI).

Ep. 1.16.75–6 *'adimam bona.' nempe pecus rem | lectos argentum: tollas licet*

Ep. 2.1.121 *detrimenta, fugas seruorum, incendia ridet*

Ep. 2.1.192 *esseda festinant, pilenta petorrita naues* (followed by an asyndetic phrasal pair: 193 *captiuum portatur ebur, captiua Corinthus*).
   The first line is almost entirely occupied by the asyndetic sequence.

Ep. 2.1.211–12 *qui pectus inaniter angit | irritat mulcet, falsis terroribus implet*

Ep. 2.2.56 *eripuere iocos Venerem conuiuia ludum*
   Almost a whole line of asyndeta again.

Ep. 2.2.162–3 *das nummos, accipis uuam | pullos oua cadum temeti*
   A miscellaneous list, but *pullos* and *oua* go together (an embedded pair?): cf. Petron. 46.2 *inueniemus quod manducemus, pullum oua*. The series is again in effect a shopping list. Note that the two asyndetic clauses contain verbs (*das, accipis*) that are opposites (converses: see XIII.2 for 'give/take'). Cf. Lucil. 868–9 *quid si dare uellent? | acciperesne?* For pairs of opposites standing in adjacent clauses see XXV.2 on Lucilius 1058, and XXIV.7.1.2 on Lucretius 6.

Ep. 2.2.180–1 *gemmas marmor ebur, Tyrrena sigilla, tabellas | argentum, uestes Gaetulo murice tinctas | sunt qui non habeant*
   A list of luxurious possessions. Quite a few of the terms here, or related terms, e.g. *ebur, signa* (cf. *sigilla*), *tabulae* (cf. *tabellas*), *argentum*, occur in asyndeton elsewhere: see XXIII.8.6, XXIV.5.2.2 on Ennius 15, XXX.2.2, 8 (Cato: see the note with numerous cross references), Cicero 21, 22, 119, Sallust 19, 65.

Ep. 2.2.203 *uiribus ingenio specie uirtute loco re.*

Both in this line and the preceding one the asyndeta fill the whole line. Note the declining syllabic length of the nouns (cf. XVI).

3.2.1 Conclusions

There are fifteen instances here. Seven of these are in book 2, in which asyndeta bimembria do not occur (with the possible exception of the embedded *pullos oua*). Is the difference between the two books, with both pairs and longer groups in book 1 but only longer groups in book 2, due to chance?

3.3 Odes

Carm. 3.25.7 *dicam insigne recens, adhuc | indictum alio ore*
These are substantivised adjectives (see Nisbet and Rudd 2004: 302, stating that *aliquid* would be expected in prose): 'I shall sing of an exploit remarkable, recent, still unspoken of by another mouth.' The first and last of the terms are privatives, a pattern seen above, 3.3. It is however just possible that the first two terms are the primary object of the verb (and thus an asyndeton bimembre), and that the *adhuc-* phrase is an adjunct expressing an incidental characteristic of the object ('I shall speak of an event remarkable, recent, which is still unspoken of by another mouth').

3.3.1 Conclusions

The *Odes* then are almost lacking in this form of asyndeton too.

3.4 Ars Poetica

121 *si forte reponis Achillem, | impiger iracundus inexorabilis acer | iura neget sibi nata*
The structure of the first three words, with a pair of privatives surrounding *iracundus*, is identical to that at *Ep.* 1.1.38 (*inuidus iracundus iners*) seen above, 3.2. See also Brink (1971: 200).

428 *clamabit enim 'pulchre! bene! recte!'*
The subject of the verb is a hypothetical flatterer to whom a poet's verses have been recited. This is an interesting example, which brings out the potential difference between reported speech and quotation of speech. Someone reporting the applause of the flatterer might say or write, 'he said *pulchre et bene et recte'*. But a public acclamation containing a series of terms of approval would be unlikely to coordinate them. Someone

watching as football match might exclaim, of a goal, *brilliant, sensational!*, but hardly *brilliant and sensational!* Horace is quoting the cry of approval. Here then is a circumstance in which asyndeton is almost inevitable.

This example may be compared with *Ep.* 1.6.54 *'frater,' 'pater'*, discussed above 2.2, where terms from speech are reported, but there is not a quotation of a single utterance.

See also Brink (1971: 406–7).

4 Forms of Explicit Coordination

We have seen an unequal distribution of types of asyndeton in Horace's works. I turn now to explicit coordination, since asyndeton is just one form of coordination, and has to be put in perspective. Asyndetic pairs and longer cola do not exist in isolation but alternate with syndetic variants. I will look at types of overt coordination and their frequency and usage compared with types of asyndeton. In the next three sections (4.1–3) three categories of coordination will be considered, coordinated pairs, end-of-list coordination, multiple coordination.

4.1 Coordinated Pairs

Coordinated pairs far outnumber asyndetic throughout Horace's works, including the *Satires*, in which there are many dozens of examples of coordinations. Note for example the cluster in the following passage: *Sat.* 1.3.99–104 *primis animalia terris,* | <u>mutum et turpe pecus, glandem atque cubilia propter</u> | <u>unguibus et pugnis</u>, *dein fustibus, atque ita porro* | *pugnabant armis, quos post fabricauerat usus,* | *donec* **uerba**, *quibus* <u>uoces sensusque notarent,</u> | **nominaque** *inuenere*. There are five such pairs here in five lines. *Sat.* 1.5 (the journey to Brundisium) has about 18 pairs in 104 lines.

There would be no point in listing every coordinated pair in Horace. The effort would be huge, and the conclusion that would emerge, namely that asyndeton bimembre has only a marginal place even in the *Satires* and *Epistles* 1 (never mind the genres in which it hardly exists), emerges anyway from selective examples such as those already given in the last paragraph.

Many coordinated pairs in Horace are of types that are often asyndetic, in Horace and/or elsewhere. This is a point that it is worth illustrating, because the incidence of the coordinated examples brings out the true significance of the asyndetic alternatives.

For pairs with at least one privative adjective in the *Satires* see 1.3.24 *stultus et improbus hic amor est*, 1.3.49–50 *ineptus* | *et iactantior hic paulo est*,

4 Forms of Explicit Coordination 529

1.4.124 *inhonestum et inutile factu*, 1.6.69 *purus et insons*, 2.3.181 *is intestabilis et sacer esto*, 2.5.6 *nudus inopsque* (*inops* is in an asyndetic pairing at *Sat.* 2.1.59). In the *Satires* asyndetic alternatives are slightly more numerous (see above, 2.1.1).

On the other hand in the *Odes* there is an absence of asyndetic pairs with privatives (unless one accepts that the example at 3.3 above is of this type) or of positive + negative pairs. Contrast the following coordinations: *Carm.* 1.18.10 *fas atque nefas* (cf. *Epod.* 5.87 *non fas nefasque*), 4.9.26–7 *inlacrimabiles | urgentur ignotique* ('unwept and unknown'; cf. Hom. *Il.* 22.386 κεῖται πὰρ νήεσσι νέκυς ἄκλαυτος ἄθαπτος | Πάτροκλος, a usage which Horace probably had in mind; *inlacrimabilis* is only in Horace in the classical period: see *OLD* and also Thomas 2011: 204). In the sample of Pindar considered in this chapter note *Nem.* 7.30–1 πέσε δ' ἀδόκη-|τον ἐν καὶ δοκέοντα, '(the wave of Hades) falls upon the obscure and the famous' (Race, Loeb; alpha-privative + positive, coordinated).

The *Epodes* lack privatives in asyndeton, but note too 1.16 *imbellis ac firmus parum*, where *firmus parum* is equivalent to a privative; *imbellis* is not infrequent elsewhere in asyndetic pairs.

So in the *Epistles* there are no asyndetic pairs with an *in*-privative member, but see 1.14.19 *deserta et inhospita tesqua*, 2.1.117 *indocti doctique*. Such asyndetic pairs are also lacking in the *Ars poetica* (note however the longer sequence at 121, quoted above, 3.4) but cf. 130 *ignota indictaque*, 474 *indoctum doctumque*.

Here is a selection of coordinated pairs in Horace of types that are well attested elsewhere with asyndeton.

4.1.1 Totalities/Merisms

Carm. 1.12.14 *hominum ac deorum*
Carm. 3.4.47 *diuosque mortalesque turmas*
Ep. 1.6.14 *animoque et corpore torpet* (body and soul, the totality of a human; cf. *Sat.* 2.2.109 *mentem corpusque superbum*).

4.1.2 Masculine + Feminine

Carm. 3.1.4 *uirginibus puerisque* (cf. Pind. *N.* 8.2 ἅ τε παρθενηίοις παίδων τ' ἐφίζοισα γλεφάροις, '(Hora), settling upon the eyes of unwed girls and boys'.)
Carm. 3.14.9 *uirginum matres iuuenumque*
Carm. 3.14.10 *uos, o pueri et puellae | iam [non?] uirum expertae*
Carm. 4.6.31–2 *uirginum primae puerique claris | patribus orti*
Ep. 1.18.74 *pueri pulchri caraeue puellae*
Epod. 11.27–8 *aut puellae candidae | aut teretis pueri*

Saec. 6 *uirgines lectas puerosque castos*
Sat. 1.1.85 *pueri atque puellae*
Sat. 2.3.16 *di te, Damasippe, deaeque*
Sat. 2.3.130 *omnes pueri clamentque puellae*

It was seen earlier (2.1.4.1) that there is just one asyndetic instance of the 'boy–girl' pair in the *Satires*. For pairs of this type, asyndetic and syndetic, see XI.4.

4.1.3   Opposites

Carm. 1.28.19 *senum ac iuuenum*
Carm. 4.14.31 *primosque et extremos metendo*, 'mowing down the first and last' (antipodals).
Ep. 1.1.26 *pueris senibusque*
Ep. 1.1.55 *iuuenes . . . senesque*
Ep. 1.1.72 *nec sequar aut fugiam quae diligit ipse uel odit* (two pairs of opposites, reversives, antonyms).
Ep. 1.3.32 *nequiquam coit et rescinditur* (of the closing and opening of a wound, reversives).
Ep. 1.6.12 *gaudeat an doleat, cupiat metuatne* (the first two verbs are antonyms, and the second two contrastive).
Ep. 1.6.13 *melius peiusue*
Ep. 1.17.10 *qui natus moriensque fefellit* (of birth and death).
Ep. 2.1.101 *quid placet aut odio est*
Ep. 2.2.79 *strepitus nocturnos atque diurnos*
Ep. 2.2.189 *albus et ater*
Saec. 10 *diem . . . | promis et celas* ('you bring out and hide the day': reversives).
Sat. 1.1.76 *noctesque diesque*
Sat. 2.3.288 *das adimisque dolores* (cf. Livy 38.48.4 (50) *donatis adimitis*).

4.1.4   Adverbial Opposites

Carm. 4.11.9 *huc et illuc | cursitant* (for this pair used asyndetically see Preuss 1881: 23–4, and for such adverbial pairs used asyndetically with frequentative verbs of running see XIII.5.4).

4.1.5   Family Members

Ars 24 *pater et iuuenes patre digni*
Carm. 3.3.68 *uirum puerosque* (husband and children).
Carm. 3.27.21 *hostium uxores puerique* (wives and children).
Carm. 4.4.55 *natosque maturosque patres* (children and fathers).
Carm. 4.9.24 *pro pudicis | coniugibus puerisque*
Ep. 2.1.109 *pueri patresque*
Sat. 1.1.83 *gnatis carisque propinquis*.

4 *Forms of Explicit Coordination* 531

4.1.6 *Different Moods/Tenses*

Ars 58 *licuit semperque licebit*
Ars 70 *cecidere cadentque*
Ars 179 *agitur . . . aut acta*
Carm. 2.13.20 *rapuit rapietque gentes*
Ep. 1.2.43 *labitur et labetur*
Ep. 1.3.15 *monitus multumque monendus*
Ep. 2.1.160 *manserunt hodieque manent*
Saec. 2–3 *o colendi | semper et culti*.

4.1.7 *Miscellaneous*

Carm. 1.28.1.1 *maris et terrae* (for asyndeton see Preuss 1881: 35–6).
Carm. 1.31.6 *non aurum aut ebur* (cf. XXIV.5.2.2 on Ennius 15 *uidi ego te adstante ope barbarica, | tectis caelatis laqueatis, | auro ebore instructam regifice*).
Ep. 1.12.17 *uagentur et errent* (cf. Sall. *Jug.* 18.2 *uagi palantes*).
Ep. 1.15.17 *possum quiduis perferre patique*
Ep. 1.16.74 *quid me perferre patique | indignum coges* (with this and the last example cf. XXVII.1.4 on Catull. 8.11 *perfer obdura*, and see also *Sat.* 2.5.39 below).
Ep. 1.18.3–4 *dispar erit atque | discolor* (terms with repeated prefix are often asyndetic).
Sat. 1.2.6 *frigus . . . duramque famem* (for this pair without a coordinator see Cicero 103 with cross references, on which it is noted that the coordinated variant is also in Catullus).
Sat. 1.2.52–3 *nec sibi damno | dedecorique foret* (see Wölfflin 1933: 257 for this pair used asyndetically by Cicero).
Sat. 1.2.123 *candida rectaque sit* (on this pair as part of an asyndetic sequence see XXVII.2 on Catull. 86.1 *Quintia formosa est multis; mihi candida longa | recta est*).
Sat. 2.3.142 *argenti positi intus et auri* (cf. e.g. Cicero 21, 119 for the pair in asyndeton).
Sat. 2.5.39 *persta atque obdura*
Sat. 2.5.110 *uiue ualeque* (cf. Ter. *And.* 889 *ualeat uiuat cum illa* and see XXVII.1.4 for such combinations).

4.1.8 *Conclusions*

It is obvious from the above details that the type of pairing is not a primary determinant of asyndeton, because many types that are frequent with asyndeton elsewhere are usually syndetically coordinated in Horace. Genre and stylistic level were influences too. Such asyndeta as there are in Horace are in conversational genres, the *Satires* and first book of the *Epistles*. Various factors may be suggested as contributing to this distribution. First, certain asyndeta or types of asyndeton had a place in speech, such as pairs of imperatives, pairs of adverbial opposites, abusive pairs, particularly adjectives, with the second term stronger than the first, discontinuous pairs, with the second term highlighted and again outdoing the first, and formulaic or proverbial pairs that had taken on a fixed truncated (asyndetic) form, such as the name of the game *par impar*. Pairs with a privative were often abusive. Second, asyndeton (bimembre but also longer) had a rhetorical flavour, as can be seen from its frequency in speeches in historians, and in rhetorical passages in Cicero's speeches. Conversational Latin no doubt made use of popular rhetoric, and some asyndeta in Horace probably reflect that fact. A case in point would be the cry of approval, '*pulchre! bene! recte!*' Another factor that facilitated the use of asyndeton was structural. An old pattern consisted of the juxtaposition of asyndetic pairs with syndetic, and there are a number of such accumulations in the *Satires*.

Horace's avoidance of asyndeton in the higher genres of the *Odes* may well on the other hand have been influenced by early Greek lyric and iambic poetry (see below, 4.5).

4.2   End-of-List Coordination

From this point we move on from syndetic alternatives to asyndeton bimembre, to syndetic (or partly syndetic) alternatives to longer asyndeta. There are two potential alternatives to, say, an asyndetic tricolon, first the structure ABC*que* (or AB *et* C, etc.), i.e. end-of-list coordination, and second multiple coordination, i.e. A *et* B *et* C (with the same or varied coordinators).

The following collection of end-of-list coordinations is tolerably complete, but there are often problems of interpretation because two of the three terms may form a unit, such that the apparent tricolon is really only a dicolon. Omissions there may be in this list, but the fact remains that end-of-list coordination is not very frequent in Horace.

4.2.1   Satires

Sat. 1.1.29 *ille grauem duro terram qui uertit aratro, | perfidus hic caupo, miles nautaeque per omne | audaces mare qui currunt*, 'yon farmer, who with tough plough turns up the heavy soil, our rascally host here, the soldier and the sailors who boldly scour every sea ...' (Fairclough, Loeb, modified slightly).

The relative clause may go only with *nautaeque*, which is at the end of the list.

Sat. 1.4.107–8 *parce frugaliter atque uiuerem uti contentus eo quod mi ipse parasset*, '(he would encourage me) to live thriftily, frugally and content with what he had prepared for me'.

Sat. 1.6.38 *tune Syri, Damae aut Dionysi filius*

Sat. 2.7.53–4 *proiectis insignibus, anulo equestri Romanoque habitu*

Sat. 2.7.99 *uelut si | re uera pugnent, feriant uitentque mouentes | arma uiri*
Of gladiators, three verbs with the same subject *uiri*.

4.2.2 Epistles

Ep. 1.7.53 *abi quaere et refer, unde domo, quis, | cuius fortunae, quo sit patre quoue patrono*
However, *abi quaere* could be a unit (see the examples at XXIII.5.1, notably *abi quaere* at Plaut. Cist. 502).

Ep. 1.7.55 *it redit et narrat*
Again there is a problem of interpretation. *It redit* is an established asyndetic pair (reversives) (see Preuss 1881: 39 and also Cicero 74). The narrating is possibly conceived as a unit separate from the going and coming back.

Ep. 1.7.84–5 *sulcos et uineta crepat mera, praeparat ulmos, | immoritur studiis et amore senescit habendi*
This is end-of-list coordination of clausal type.

Ep. 1.17.46–7 *indotata mihi soror est, paupercula mater, | et fundus nec uendibilis nec pascere firmus*
Clausal again.

Ep. 2.2.208–9 *somnia, terrores magicos, miracula sagas, | nocturnos lemures portentaque Thessala rides?* 'Dreams, terrors of magic, marvels, witches, ghosts of night and Thessalian portents – do you laugh at these?' (Fairclough, Loeb, modified).

Ep. 2.2.214 *lusisti satis, edisti satis atque bibisti*
There is probably not end-of-list coordination here, and I cite the example to show the problems of interpretation that end-of-list coordination may raise. Eating and drinking are a pair possibly separate from the

other verb (see above, 2.1.1 on *Sat.* 2.2.14 for cross references to the 'eat/ drink' asyndeton), with the repetition of *satis* pointing to a twofold structure of the sequence (i.e. 1 + 2). However, Andr. *poet.* 45, cited above on *Sat.* 2.2.14 (*affatim edi bibi lusi*), which has all three verbs and also an equivalent of *satis*, suggests an alternative interpretation that some may favour.

4.2.3 Odes

Carm. 1.11.6 *sapias, uina liques, et spatio breui | spem longam reseces*
Clausal.

Carm. 1.21.13–14 *hic bellum lacrimosum, hic miseram famem | pestemque a populo... | ... aget*
The manner of repetition of *hic* seems to establish that the phrase structure has two components (1 + 2). Semantically too that is the case. *Fames* and *pestis* go together as physical afflictions caused for example by war.

Carm. 4.14.33–4 *te copias, te consilium et tuos | praebente diuos*, 'with you providing the troops, the plan and your gods'.
If one adopted the same criterion as that applied in the last example, one would have to conclude from the single repetition of *te* that there are just two components here, *copias* on the one hand and *consilium et diuos* on the other. But there is no unity to *consilium* and *diuos*, and it is possible that *tuos* has a similar role to *te*.

Most of the examples in this section and that at the end of the last suggest that it may sometimes be difficult to analyse possible end-of-list coordinations.

4.2.4 Epodes

Epod. 2.61–6 *ut iuuat pastas oues | uidere properantes domum, | uidere fessos uomerem inuersum boues | collo trahentes languido | positosque uernas, ditis examen domus, | circum renidentes Lares*, 'what joy to see the sheep hurrying homeward from pasture, to see the wearied oxen dragging along the upturned ploughshare on their tired necks, and the home-bred slaves, troop of a wealthy house, ranged around the gleaming Lares' (Bennett, Loeb).

This passage is not easy to interpret either. There are three accusative phrases that are object of two instances of *uidere*. In this case it does seem reasonable to take *positosque uernas* as a second object of the second *uidere*, in which case there would not be end-of-list coordination.

4   *Forms of Explicit Coordination*   535

4.3   *Multiple Coordinations*

The examples under this heading are quoted almost without comment, to bring out the sheer extent of the category. The list may not be complete, but it is long enough to establish the point. Particularly interesting is the frequency of the type in the *Odes*, a matter to which I will return. The examples consist mainly of three or more terms coordinated, but there may be internal unities within a sequence, such that, for example, four terms coordinated consist of two coordinated pairs rather than of four individual items. This point is illustrated on *Ep.* 1.7.56–9 below.

4.3.1   Satires

Sat. 1.2.109–10 *dolores | atque aestus curasque grauis*

Sat. 1.3.97–8 *sensus moresque repugnant | atque ipsa utilitas, iusti prope mater et aequi*

Sat. 1.4.1 *Eupolis atque Cratinus Aristophanesque poetae | atque alii*
   A 'name-line': see below, 4.5.

Sat. 1.4.4 *quod moechus foret aut sicarius aut alioqui | famosus*
   With conjunct hyperbaton, around an intrusive verb 'to be'.

Sat. 1.4.90 *hic tibi comis et urbanus liberque uidetur*

Sat. 1.5.31–2 *Maecenas aduenit atque | Cocceius Capitoque simul Fonteius*

Sat. 1.5.36 *praetextam et latum clauum prunaeque uatillum*

Sat. 1.5.40 *Plotius et Varius Sinuessae Vergiliusque | occurrunt*
   All three met Horace at Sinuessa. Another name-line.

Sat. 1.6.115 *domum me | ad porri et ciceris refero laganique catinum*
   With conjunct hyperbaton again, which is quite common in these long coordinations.

Sat. 1.6.131 *ac si | quaestor auus pater atque meus patruusque fuissent*, 'as if my grandfather had been a quaestor, and my father, and my uncle'.

Sat. 1.8.34–5 *serpentes atque uideres | infernas errare canes Lunamque rubentem*

Sat. 1.8.39 *Iulius et fragilis Pediatia furque Voranus*

Sat. 2.3.182 *in cicere atque faba bona tu perdasque lupinis*

Sat. 2.3.244 *nequitia et nugis, prauorum et amore gemellum*, 'twins in wickedness and folly, and in perverted fancies' (Fairclough, Loeb).

Sat. 2.4.3 *Pythagoran Anytique reum doctumque Platona*

Sat. 2.7.67 *rem omnem et uitam et cum corpore famam*

Sat. 2.7.96–7 *Fului Rutubaeque | aut Pacideiani . . . miror | proelia.*

4.3.2   Epistles

Ep. 1.1.48 *discere et audire et meliori credere non uis?*

Ep. 1.5.8 *mitte leuis spes et certamina diuitiarum | et Moschi causam*

Ep. 1.5.26–7 *Butram tibi Septiciumque | et . . . Sabinum*

Ep. 1.6.3–4 *hunc solem et stellas et decedentia certis | tempora momentis*

Ep. 1.6.17 *argentum et marmor uetus aeraque et artes*

Ep. 1.6.36–7 *uxorem cum dote fidemque et amicos | et genus et formam*

Ep. 1.6.45–6 *ubi non et multa supersunt |et dominum fallunt et prosunt furibus* Clausal.

Ep. 1.7.46–7 *strenuus et fortis causisque Philippus agendis | clarus*

Ep. 1.7.56–9 *notum | et properare loco et cessare et quaerere et uti, | gaudentem paruisque sodalibus et lare certo | et ludis et post decisa negotia Campo,* '(a man) known to work hard and idle in season, to make money and spend it, taking pleasure in his humble friends and a home of his own and, when business is over, in the games and in the field of Mars' (Fairclough, Loeb).

I quote this passage to show the potential complexity of multiple coordinations. There are not two sequences of four members here, but four sequences of two members. *Properare* and *cessare* form a unit, as do *quaerere* and *uti*, *sodalibus* and *lare* and *ludis* and *Campo*.

Ep. 1.7.94 *per genium dextramque deosque penates*

Ep. 1.10.7 *laudo ruris amoeni | riuos et musco circumlita saxa nemusque*

Ep. 1.11.21 *Romae laudetur Samos et Chios et Rhodos absens*

Ep. 1.14.15 *nunc urbem et ludos et balnea uilicus optas*

Ep. 1.15.31 *pernicies et tempestas barathrumque macelli*

Ep. 1.16.3 *pomisne an pratis an amicta uitibus ulmo*

Ep. 1.16.50 *cautus enim metuit foueam lupus accipiterque | suspectos laqueos et opertum miluus hamum*
  Clausal.

Ep. 1.17.22 *omnis . . . decuit color et status et res*

Ep. 1.17.53 *qui queritur salebras et acerbum frigus et imbres*

Ep. 1.18.6 *asperitas agrestis et inconcinna grauisque*

Ep. 1.18.49–50 *utile famae | uitaeque et membris*

Ep. 2.1.5 *Romulus et Liber pater et cum Castore Pollux*

Ep. 2.1.32–3 *pingimus atque | psallimus et luctamur*

Ep. 2.1.50 *Ennius et sapiens et fortis et alter Homerus*

Ep. 2.1.113 *calamum et chartas et scrinia posco*

Ep. 2.1.129 *asperitatis et inuidiae corrector et irae*

Ep. 2.1.142 *cum sociis operum et pueris et coniuge fida*

Ep. 2.1.163 *quid Sophocles et Thespis et Aeschylus utile ferrent*

Ep. 2.1.184 *indocti stolidique et depugnare parati*

Ep. 2.1.203–4 *ludi spectantur et artes | diuitiaeque pereginae*

Ep. 2.1.251–6 This is a grandiose catalogue of the subjects of a high-style poem, with a succession of coordinated phrases.

4.3.3 Odes

Carm. 1.4.16 *iam te premet nox fabulaeque Manes | et domus exilis Plutonia*

Carm. 1.7.1–4 *laudabunt alii claram Rhodon aut Mytilenen | aut Ephesum bimarisue Corinthi | moenia uel Baccho Thebas uel Apolline Delphos | insignes aut Thessala Tempe*

Carm. 1.7.12–14 *quam domus Albuneae resonantis | et praeceps Anio ac Tiburni lucus et uda | mobilibus pomaria riuis*

Carm. 1.9.18–19 *nunc et campus et areae | lenesque sub noctem susurri*

Carm. 1.10.13–16 *quin et Atridas duce te superbos | Ilio diues Priamus relicto | Thessalosque ignes et iniqua Troiae | castra fefellit*

Carm. 1.12.15 *qui mare et terras uariisque mundum | temperat horis*

Carm. 1.12.37 *Regulum et Scauros animaeque magnae | prodigum Paulum*

Carm. 1.12.41–3 *hunc et intonsis Curium capillis | utilem bello tulit et Camillum | saeua paupertas*

Carm. 1.15.11–12 *iam galeam Pallas et aegida | currusque et rabiem parat*

Carm. 1.16.9–12 *quas neque Noricus | deterret ensis nec mare naufragum | nec saeuus ignis nec tremendo | Iuppiter ipse ruens tumultu*

Carm. 1.24.6–8 *cui Pudor et Iustitiae soror, | incorrupta Fides, nudaque Veritas, | quando ullum inueniet parem?*

Carm. 1.32.9 *Liberum et Musas Veneremque*

Carm. 1.35.9–12 *te profugi Scythae | urbesque gentesque et Latium ferox | regumque matres barbarorum et | purpurei metuunt tyranni*

Carm. 1.35.33–4 *cicatricum et sceleris pudet | fratrumque*

At *Carm.* 2.1.1–8 the subjects of Pollio's work on the civil wars are listed. In Catullus and Cicero such subjects may be listed asyndetically (see XXVII.2 on Catull. 9.7). The passage of Horace has the following: *bellique causas et uitia et modos | ludumque Fortunae grauesque | principum amicitias et arma | nondum expiatis uncta cruoribus? . . . tractas.*

However at 2.1.17–20 there are three asyndetic clauses, but each begins with *iam* (asyndeton + anaphora): *iam nunc minaci murmure cornuum | perstringis auris, iam litui strepunt, | iam fulgor armorum fugaces | terret equos.*

Carm. 2.3.13 *huc uina et unguenta et nimium breues | flores amoenae ferre iube rosae*

Carm. 2.3.15 *dum res et aetas et sororum | fila trium patiuntur atra*

Carm. 2.4.21 *bracchia et uoltum teretesque suras*

Carm. 2.20.13–16 *iam Daedaleo notior Icaro | uisam gementis litora Bosphori | Syrtesque Gaetulas canorus | ales Hyperboreosque campos*

Carm. 2.20.21–2 *absint inani funere neniae | luctusque turpes et querimoniae*

Carm. 3.5.10–11 *anciliorum et nominis et togae | oblitus aeternaeque Vestae*

Carm. 3.6.17–18 *nuptias* | *primum inquinauere et genus et domos*

Carm. 3.6.35–6 *Pyrrhumque et ingentem cecidit* | *Antiochum Hannibalemque dirum*

Carm. 3.27.1–4 *impios parrae recinentis omen* | *ducat et praegnans canis aut ab agro* | *raua decurrens lupa Lanuuino* | *fetaque uolpes*

Carm. 3.28.13–14 *quae Cnidon* | *fulgentesque tenet Cycladas et Paphum* | *iunctis uisit oloribus*

Carm. 3.29.6–8 *ne semper udum Tibur et Aefulae* | *decliue contempleris aruum et* | *Telegoni iuga parricidae*

Carm. 3.29.36–7 *nunc lapides adesos* | *stirpesque raptas et pecus et domos*

Carm. 4.2.22 *uires animumque moresque aureos educit in astra*

Carm. 4.5.13 *uotis ominibusque et precibus.*

Carm. 4.6.1–4 *diue, quem proles Niobea magnae* | *uindicem linguae Tityosque raptor* | *sensit et Troiae prope uictor altae* | *Phthius Achilles*

Carm. 4.8.26 *uirtus et fauor et lingua potentium* | *uatum*

Carm. 4.9.6–9 *non ...* | *... Pindaricae latent* | *Ceaeque et Alcaei minaces* | *Stesichorique graues Camenae*

Carm. 4.15.31–2 *Troiamque et Anchisen et almae* | *progeniem Veneris canemus.*
Saec. 47 *date remque prolemque* | *et decus omne*

Saec. 57 *Fides et Pax et Honor Pudorque.*

4.4 Conclusions: Longer Sequences, Asyndetic and Coordinated

What then was Horace's preferred method in the various genres of putting together three or more terms? We have looked at the use of three different patterns.

First, asyndetic tricola and longer asyndetic sequences, mainly consisting of single words. From the *Satires* fourteen examples are listed, from the *Epistles* fifteen, from the *Ars poetica* two and from the *Odes* just one. It was seen that asyndeta bimembria occur 22 times in the *Satires*, 8 times in the *Epistles*, once in the *Ars poetica*, and 3 times in the *Odes*. In prose, for example that of Cicero, longer asyndeta sequences such as tricola far outnumber asyndetic pairs, but in the *Satires* and *Epistles* asyndeta bimembria are of the same frequency as longer asyndeta. It is not the frequency of pairs that is striking in these two works, but the fact that asyndetic tricola and the like are not particularly common. In the *Odes* on the other hand both asyndetic pairs and tricola and the like are virtually non-existent.

Second, end-of-list coordination. It is made clear above that possible examples are often difficult to interpret. There are about five instances in the *Satires*, three in the *Epistles* and one in the *Odes*. This then is a pattern which, even in a corpus in which asyndeton is not very frequent, is still heavily outnumbered by asyndeton.

Third, multiple coordinations. I refer thus to three or more terms all of which are linked by a coordinator: by definition there will be one coordinator fewer than the number of terms. Mutiple coordination is Horace's preferred method of linking three or more terms, and in the *Odes* as well as the *Satires* and *Epistles*. The examples listed here may not be complete, but even if there are omissions the general point is clear. In the *Satires* I have noted 17 examples, in the *Epistles* 30, in the *Odes* 34 and in the *Carmen saeculare* 2. Horace's preference for this structure in the *Odes* is remarkable, with the 34 instances contrasting with a total of just 4 of the alternatives. There may well be literary precedent for Horace's usage in the *Odes*, in forms of early Greek poetry such as lyric. Some details of Pindar's practice are given below, 4.5.

4.5 A Selective Corpus from Pindar

In Pindar's Nemean Odes the only pattern that I have found resembling asyndeton bimembre is the anaphoric construction:[3]

N. 6.1 ἓν ἀνδρῶν, ἓν θεῶν γένος, 'there is one race of men, one of gods'.

N. 7.2–3 ἄνευ σέθεν | οὐ φάος, οὐ μέλαιναν δρακέντες εὐφρόναν. 'without you we behold neither light nor the darkness of night'.

Pairs of adjectives are sometimes found without a coordinator, but the adjectives differ in rank or role:

N. 4.52 βουβόται τόθι πρῶνες ἔξοχοι κατάκεινται, 'where cattle-grazing jutting forelands descend'.

The primary phrase is πρῶνες ἔξοχοι.

---

[3] Translations are mainly from Race (Loeb), sometimes slightly modified.

N. 6.43–4 δασκίοις | Φλειοῦντος ὑπ' ὠγυγίοις ὄρεσιν, 'beneath the ancient shadowy hills of Phleious'.
Here the primary phrase is 'ancient/primeval hills' (ὠγυγίοις ὄρεσιν), and 'shadowy' is an epithet of that phrase.

N. 7.92 προγόνων εὐκτήμονα ζαθέαν ἄγυιαν, 'the well-built sacred street of his forefathers'.
This example is similar in type to 6.43–4 above. There there were 'ancient hills' with an incidental epithet, and here a 'sacred street' (ζαθέαν ἄγυιαν) with an epithet.

N. 10.71 πυρφόρον πλᾶξε ψολόεντα κεραυνόν, 'he hurled a smoky thunderbolt of fire'.
The primary phrase is πυρφόρον κεραυνόν, 'thunderbolt of fire'. The other adjective modifies the pair.

I have found only two asyndetic (phrasal) tricola in the book:

N. 3.72 ἐν παισὶ νέοισι παῖς, ἐν ἀνδράσιν ἀνήρ, τρίτον | ἐν παλαιτέροισι, 'as a child among young children, man among men, and thirdly among elders'.

N. 8.33 αἱμύλων μύθων ὁμόφοιτος, δολοφραδής, κακοποιὸν ὄνειδος, '(hateful deception existed even long ago,) the companion of flattering tales, guileful contriver, evil-working disgrace'.

Finally, multiple coordinations, particularly of names, are quite common:

N. 3.60–2 δορίκτυπον ἀλαλὰν Λυκίων | τε προσμένοι καὶ Φρυγῶν | Δαρδάνων τε, 'he would withstand the spear-clashing battle cry of the Lykians and Phrygians and Dardanians'.

N. 3.84 Νεμέας Ἐπιδαυρόθεν τ' ἄπο καὶ Μεγάρων δέδορκεν φάος, 'from Nemea, Epidauros, and Megara has shone the light of glory'.

N. 4.9–11 τό μοι θέμεν Κρονίδᾳ τε Δὶ καὶ Νεμέᾳ | Τιμασάρχου τε πάλᾳ | ὕμνου προκώμιον εἴη, 'May I set forth such a word for Kronos' son Zeus and Nemea and for Timasarchos' wrestling, as my hymn's prelude.'

N. 4.25–7 σὺν ᾧ ποτε Τροΐαν κραταιὸς Τελαμών | πόρθησε καὶ Μέροπας | καὶ τὸν μέγαν πολεμιστὰν ἔκπαγλον Ἀλκυονῆ, 'with whom mighty Telamon once destroyed Troy and the Meropes and that giant warrior, awesome Alkyoneus' (note that there is conjunct hyperbaton within this sequence).

N. 4.75 Οὐλυμπίᾳ τε καὶ Ἰσθμοῖ Νεμέᾳ τε, 'at Olympia and the Isthmus and Nemea'.

N. 5.19 εἰ δ' ὄλβον ἢ χειρῶν βίαν ἢ σιδαρίταν ἐπαινῆσαι πόλεμον δεδόκηται, 'but if it is decided to praise happiness, strength of hands, or steel-clad war'.

N. 10.47–8 ὄν τε Κλείτωρ καὶ Τεγέα καὶ Ἀχαιῶν ὑψίβατοι πόλιες | καὶ Λύκαιον πὰρ Διὸς θῆκε δρόμῳ, 'which Kleitor and Tegea and the lofty cities of the Achaians and Lykaion set beside the racecourse of Zeus'.

Tarrant (2012: 181), on Virg. *Aen.* 12.363 (*Chloreaque Sybarimque Daretaque Thersilochumque | et sternacis equi lapsum ceruice Thymoeten*), refers to Homeric-style 'name-lines'. See particularly Wills (1996: 377–82) and also Harrison (1991: 93) on *Aen.* 10.123.

Pindar's patterns of coordination in the sample are much the same as Horace's in the *Odes*. Asyndeton bimembre is absent, and asyndetic tricola hardly exist. Multiple coordinations are well established, often comprising names, of persons, peoples or places. In the *Odes* of Horace three or more names (or variants on straightforward names) with multiple coordination are found in the collection here at 1.7.1–2, 1.10.13–16, 1.12.37, 1.24.6–8, 1.32.9, 1.35.9–10, 2.20.13–16, 3.6.35–6, 3.28.13–14, 3.29.6–8, 4.6.1–4, 4.9.6–9, 4.15.31–2; also *Saec.* 57 (fourteen examples). Moreover in many of these sequences the names are from Greek myth.

It is not multiple coordination as such that is Greek-inspired, as sequences of three-plus terms in Latin prose often have complete coordination. What is striking about the *Odes* is the distribtion of types, ranging from near absence of asyndeta bimembria and asyndetic tricola, to frequency of multiple coordination. Also of note is the frequency in the last category of coordinated sequences of names.

Pindar also has in the book some coordinated pairs of types found in Horace too, such as pairs of opposites, and pairs of family members. Note:

N. 7.19 ἀφνεὸς πενιχρός τε, 'rich and poor'.

N. 9.29 θανάτου πέρι καὶ ζώας (death and life).

N. 9.4 ματέρι καὶ διδύμοις παίδεσσιν, 'mother and twin children'.

5 Conclusions

The distribution of asyndeton bimembre in Horace's works, with most instances in the *Satires* and hardly any in the *Odes* and *Epodes*, throws light on the character of the usage. It is a mistake to speak of a single category and to seek general designations such as sacral, archaic or the like. There are of course fossilised formulae such as *par impar* and *serius ocius*, but asyndetic coordination may be used creatively in mundane contexts, as for example when exclamatory terms of approval or pejorative adjectives

5 Conclusions

are combined, with a stronger term capping the first. Pairs with a privative adjective are particularly in evidence in the *Satires*, and pairs of imperatives in the classical period are often without a coordinator. We have also seen again the appropriateness of asyndeton in open-ended lists, the members of which are merely examples of a category of persons or things. Names in the plural (meaning 'the likes of X') tend to be used asyndetically.

It became obvious in this chapter that, even in a work in which asyndeton is found, such as the *Satires*, it is far outnumbered by coordinations. The character of a particular pairing (e.g. pairs of antonyms or of privatives) is not the primary determinant of asyndeton, as (e.g.) pairs of antonyms or privatives are often coordinated. Structural factors are an influence, in that asyndetic pairs often occur not in isolation but in combination with other forms of coordination, i.e. in sequences of the type that we have called accumulations. Strength of feeling, admittedly a vague notion, also comes into it, as for example when a speaker/writer wants to make a powerful point by piling up near-synonyms, with the second climactic. And then there is genre. Horace clearly felt that asyndeton bimembre was not appropriate in the *Odes*, but that forms of it were suited to the conversational *Satires*.

CHAPTER XXX

The Annalists, Sallust and Tacitus

1 Introduction

Historiography I have split into two chapters, putting Livy in a separate chapter. Sallust and Tacitus are kept together because of the commonplace view that Tacitus was influenced by Sallust, and the pair will be compared at the end of the chapter (6). A brief treatment of the remains of the early annalists precedes that of Sallust.

The evidence from all three corpora is first presented in the form of examples numbered in bold and arranged according to parts of speech. Most examples are given some sort of commentary, with parallels, relationships and semantic features noted. There are brief conclusions after the presentation of each corpus, but the main conclusions are found at the end (3.3, 4.2, 5.2). It is not only the relationship between Sallust and Tacitus that is of interest, but also that between Tacitus' *Histories* and *Annals*, given the possibility that Tacitus' practice changed over time. There are indeed some differences between the uses of asyndeton in the *Histories* and *Annals*, and Tacitus' use of asyndeton bimembre changes in the later books of the *Annals*.

2 Annalists

The fragments of the annalists do not have many examples of asyndeton bimembre, but there are types that can be paralleled in later historians, and these hint at the beginnings of a long tradition. Cato's use of asyndeton in the fragments of the *Origines* is of special interest. In this section references are usually to *FRH* II, and the two numbers given are those of the author and of the fragment.

2 *Annalists* 545

2.1 *Asyndeta Bimembria with Members Comprising Single Words*

(1) Cato 5.F116 <u>ferrareae argentifodinae</u> pulcherrimae, mons ex sale mero magnus, '(there are) iron and silver mines that are beautiful, and a big mountain of pure salt'.

Ferrareae argentifodinae is a nominal asyndeton bimembre (contrast the similar pair, with coordinator, at Livy 34.21.7 *ex ferrariis argentariisque*), and *pulcherrimae* goes with both terms; these form a unit, and then there is an extended phrase *mons . . . magnus*. The structure of the whole is that of a phrasal asyndeton bimembre ([*ferrareae . . . pulcherrimae*] + [*mons . . . magnus*]), with the first phrase containing a single-word asyndeton bimembre (for such embedding see Sallust 23, 24, 27, 83).

For metals (including silver) and related materials used in the construction of luxury objects paired in asyndeton see XXIII.8.6, Cicero 21, 119. Both terms here are what I have called 'long suffixal derivatives', and one is a long compound as well. Long compounds or suffixal derivatives are often in asydeton in early Latin: e.g. Plaut. *As.* 34 *apud fustitudinas ferricrepinas insulas* (see XXIII.4).

(2) Coelius 15.F44 *res publica <u>amisso exfundato</u> pulcherrimo oppido*, '. . . the state, with the most beautiful town lost and razed to the ground'.

This looks like an asyndeton bimembre of two participles expressing a temporal sequence (the town was lost (to the enemy), and then razed (by the enemy)). *Amisso* has caused doubts, and is obelised in *FRH* by Briscoe. He states (*FRH* III.261) that 'Coelius would scarcely spoil the effect of *exfundato* by prefacing it with the weaker *amisso*'. It is however in the very nature of many asyndeta that the climactic term is placed second: the loss of the town is capped by its destruction. This is a pattern of ordering that comes up throughout this book (see e.g. XV), and is also noted by commentators and others. Timpanaro (1978: 172), for example, called the type 'asindeto accrescitivo'. Note too Shackleton Bailey (1965–70: I.318 on Cicero 174): 'The rise of emphasis in the second word makes *asyndeton bimembre* natural here.' See also Adams (2016: 232, 296), and in this chapter (e.g.) Sallust 58, 61, 67, 81, Tacitus 38, 111, 119, 120, 133. Verbal pairs expressing a temporal sequence, and not least those referring to acts of violence, are a recurrent type of asyndeton bimembre in e.g. the historians (see e.g. Tacitus 132, 135, 136, 137, 138, 142, 146, 147; for a list of those to do specifically with violence see below, 5.2.3) and Cicero (see XXVI.7.2.3). At Sallust 67 and 81, for example, verbs of destruction (*iugulare, excindant*) come second, as here (cf. also Tacitus 133). The pair *capere occidere*, which will come up in this chapter (see Sallust 76), conveys when conjunctive rather than disjunctive a very similar sequence of events to that in Coelius, though persons are the object in one case and a town in the other.

The two verbs in our passage have different agents. The city is lost by one side to another, and then destroyed by this other. Asyndetic pairs of converses (XIII.2) by definition have different subjects/agents (*dare/accipere, emere/uendere, docere/discere, locare/conducere*). For asyndetic pairs of verbs with different subjects note e.g. Men. *Sik.* 96 ἔδωκ', ἐδέξω, 'I gave, you took', Plaut. *Poen.* 653 *salutat respondemus*, *Poen.* 1350 *debetur dabo*, 'it is owed: I will give'.

(3) Quadrigarius 24.F40 *conprehensare suos quisque, sauiari amplexare*

Translated by the editor (Briscoe) as a tricolon: 'each man grasped, kissed, and embraced his own people'. But is there an asyndeton bimembre within the series? *Sauiari amplexare* looks like a unit (first the subject grabs *suos*, then kisses and embraces them). For kissing/embracing as a unitary pair expressed by an asyndeton bimembre see Tacitus 95 *discubitum inter conuiuas, oscula complexus, noctem denique actam licentia coniugali*, 140 *concursus ad exanimos complectentium osculantium* (also Preuss 1881: 14). Note too Men. *Pk.* 155–6 εὐθὺ προσδραμών | ἐφίλει, περιέβ[α]λλ', 'running straight up, he kissed and hugged her' (with the participle here cf. *concursus* at Tacitus 140 just quoted; *comprehensare* plays the same initial role in Quadrigarius). On this view there would not be a remarkable hyperbaton (as Briscoe *FRH* III.312 puts it), but *conprehensare suos quisque* would be a separate colon: 'each man grasped his own people, and kissed and embraced them'. The last two verbs in effect express a single act (= 'kissed while embracing', = *sauiari amplexans*; the example in Menander above is very similar). Asyndetic pairs from time to time convey a single idea (see 6 below for cross references) (asyndetic hendiadys: see II.3.2.3, and particularly 3.2.3.3).

(4) Quadrigarius 24.F49 *ut uiderent ne respueret uerminaret*, 'that they should see to it that he/she/it might not reject it (treatment, a medicament?) and become infested with worms (?)'.

This fragment continues with an expression obelised by Briscoe (*litteris addiualis*) and then has: *quod uerminatum ne ad cancer perueniret*, 'lest the part infested by worms should develop to cancer'. This last clause suggests that *uermino* contains a reference to infestation by worms rather than to mere pain (for this meaning 'to be infested with maggots' see *OLD* s.v. 2, though the *OLD* puts the present example into its category 1, of racking pain), as some sort of concrete infestation would be more likely to be seen as leading *ad cancer* than would abstract pain.

There does seem to be an asyndeton with two verbs, though the text is uncertain. If it is an asyndeton, the second verb would express a consequence of the first: the rejection of treatment or a medicament would lead to the infestation, or, on the alternative interpretation of the second verb, to severe pains. See e.g. Sallust 50, Tacitus 87 for this semantic relationship, which is similar to (indeed often indistinguishable from) that in which the verbs express a sequence of events.

(5) Quadrigarius 24.F84 *uenit accessit, ligna subdidit, submouit Graecos, ignem admouit*

Here there is an asyndetic pair containing two verbs of associated meaning (he came from an unspecified distance, and approached/drew near; the second adds a nuance), followed by a tricolon (with double chiasmus) of three short clauses that are more specific than the introductory pair of verbs. The structure (i.e. a two-word asyndeton followed (or preceded) by a longer sequence of asyndeta) can be readily paralleled in Sallust and Tacitus (e.g. Sallust 3, 29, 35, 58, 65, Tacitus 9, 16, 126, 131; see further 3.3.3c, 4.2.3c, 5.2.3) and Cicero (see XXVI.7.2.1).

The two asyndetic verbs of motion refer to arrival. Similarly, for two verbs of motion in asyndeton referring to departure, see XXIV.7.1.3 on Lucr. 1.680 (11) *nil referret enim quaedam discedere abire*, Cicero 60 *exeant proficiscantur*, Tacitus 131 *abire fugere*. See also Cic. *Cat.* 2.1, discussed after Cicero 58.

(6) Sisenna 26.F19 *Bassus, assiduitate indulgitate uictus*, 'Bassus, overcome by continual attention and kindness'.

Assiduitate serves as a modifier of *indulgitate* (= 'by constant indulgence'), again an asyndetic hendiadys (II.3.2.3). For this relationship between two terms in asyndeton in the historians, see above, 3, and e.g. Sallust 64, 71, 77, Tacitus 5, 25, 31, 129, 131. Assonance is achieved by the use of *indulgitas* for the usual *indulgentia*. For assonance over several syllables in asyndetic terms see e.g. XXIII.5.4, and below, 9.

(7) Sisenna, 26.F82 *iumenta pecuda locis trepidare conpluribus*, 'transport and farm animals panicked in numerous places'.

These are two types of domesticated animals linked asyndetically. Perhaps more familiar is the linking of wild versus domestic animals, for which see XXIV.7.1.2 on Lucretius 6. Cicero at 150 has two other species of domesticated animals combined in asyndeton, and at 151 (a passage that has been seen to have a textual problem), he opposes asyndetically one species of wild animals with a pair denoting two types of domesticated animals. With the passage of Sisenna cf. particularly Tacitus 83 *simul equi armenta, ut mos barbaris, iuxta clausa* (virtually the same pairing; but on the text see the note ad loc.). Though asyndeton does occur in such pairings, usually they have explicit coordination, as can be seen from the *TLL* articles on *pecus, -oris*, and *pecus, -udis* (for the form *pecuda* here see X.1.955.9). For the first + *iumenta* see 949.33ff., + *armenta* 949.50ff., and + *equi* 949.46ff.; for the second + *iumenta* see 957.23ff., and + *armenta* 957.29ff. Another similar pairing is 'men (and) animals' (domestic or otherwise). In Umbrian the pair has asyndeton (*Tab. Ig.* VIa.30 and elsewhere, *ueiro pequo*: see Watkins 1995: 15 on the credentials of this phrase; also on Avestan). At Lucr. 2.921 (*homines armenta feraeque*) I do not see end-of-list coordination, but an asyndeton bimembre, embracing humans + domestic and wild animals (see XXIV.7.1.2 on Lucretius 6). A notable variation, again with asyndeton bimembre but of complex form, is at Virg. *G.* 4.223: *pecudes armenta uiros, genus omne ferarum*. The first part, itself an asyndetic tricolon, covers domesticated animals and men (humans, in the context), and the second part, in asyndeton with the first, expresses the totality of wild animals.

The seven pairs of single-word asyndeta bimembria that I have found above in the annalists consist entirely of verbs and nouns. Though limited in number they have some interest. It has been possible to put all of them into semantic or structural types attested in other genres and also in later historians. Asyndetic hendiadys, it was suggested, occurs twice. We noted a pair with triple homoeoteleuton, a pair expressing an act of violence, the second verb climactic and a pair of long suffixal derivatives. The asyndetic historic infinitives in 3 foreshadow a common sequence later (see below, 6.1). Categories of animals, paired, turn up in high literary genres.

2.2   Longer Asyndeta of Single Terms, Possible Embedded Pairs and a Few Complex Types

(9) Cato 5.F76 *omnis Graecia gloriam atque gratiam praecipuam claritudinis inclitissimae decorauere monumentis: signis statuis elogiis historiis aliisque rebus gratissimum id eius factum habuere*

The reference here is to the glorification of the Laconian Leonidas after his achievements at Thermopylae. Cornell (*FRH*) translates: 'all Greece has

2 Annalists 549

adorned his glory and exceptional esteem with memorials of the highest distinction: by pictures, statues, and honorary inscriptions, in their histories, and in other ways, they have treated that deed of his as most deserving of gratitude'. For a stylistic analysis see Cornell (*FRH* III.124).

In one sense there is an ascending tetracolon from *statuis* to *historiis* (with each word one syllable longer than the one before: see Cornell), followed by a typical generalisation attached by a coordinator and containing *alii*: see Sallust 1 and XVIII.6). Cornell's translation is not an exact representation of such a tetracolon. On the other hand it is possible to see a semantic distinction between the first two terms and the second two. The first two refer to luxurious objects, the second two to writings, and one might split the pairs, 'by pictures, statues, by honorary inscriptions, historical accounts, and by other ... '. This is one of those long sequences that is arguably divisible into two unitary pairs.

This is not the only passage in Cato where *signa* and *statuae* are associated. Cf., in a speech (*ORF* 98), the following long asyndetic phrasal sequence, containing both terms: *miror audere atque religionem non tenere, statuas deorum, exempla earum facierum, signa domi pro supellectile statuere*.

A similar asyndetic pair is *signa tabulae*: see Cicero 22 *signa tabulas, quas populo Caesar una cum hortis legauit, eas ... deportauit*, Sallust 18, 19 *qui semper domos uillas, signa tabulas uostras pluris quam rem publicam fecistis*, Sallust 65 *signa, tabulas pictas, uasa caelata*. In these three passages *tabulae* must denote pictures (note *pictas* in the last, and cf. Cic. *Verr.* 1.58 *signa et tabulas pictas*), and *signa* sculptured figures (see *OLD* s.v. *signum* 12a). On the other hand in the historical fragment *signis*, alongside *statuis*, must be given a different sense, 'painted figures, portraits' (see *OLD* s.v. 12c).

Items of luxury have a tendency to be listed in asyndeton (see XXIII.4, 8.1, 8.2, 8.5, 8.6).

(9) Cato 5.F97 *exercitum ... suum pransum paratum cohortatum eduxit foras atque instruxit*, 'he led out his army, fed, prepared, and encouraged, and drew it up'.

Another ascending tricolon (with the second and third terms each with one more syllable than the term before), and in this case there is assonance as well, alliteration in the first two terms, and homoeoteleuton in the second and third. We have already mentioned assonance in an asyndetic group (see above, 6). Here are a few striking examples, from Pacuvius and Plautus, that have come up earlier: Pac. *trag.* 17 Schierl *agite icite uoluite rapite*, *trag.* 206 *maerore errore macore*, Pl. *Am.* 1062 *strepitus crepitus, sonitus tonitrus*, *Per.* 421 *edax furax fugax*, *Per.* 408 *impure inhoneste iniure*, *Poen.* 221 *poliri expoliri, pingi fingi*. Note too Varro *Ling.* 7.8

conregione conspicione cortumione (from an ancient formula for the taking of the auspices).

(10, 11) Two interesting passages are Cato 5.F99 *fluuium Naronem, magnum pulchrum pisculentum* and Cato 5.F111 (of a river) *magnus atque pulcher, pisculentus.*

In 11 Cato has done an unusual thing with the same three adjectives. He has coordinated the first two, and put *pisculentus* at the end again. The coordinator links the two banal adjectives into a unit, and makes of the three words an asyndeton bimembre, of which the first member is a phrase with two coordinated adjectives. The second element is semantically the more informative. An example such as this raises an issue in the interpretation of possible end-of-list coordinations in Latin. If Cato had written instead *pisculentus, magnus et pulcher*, would he have been using end-of-list coordination of the English type? Not necessarily, because he might still have been treating *magnus et pulcher* as a unit, in asyndeton with *pisculentus*. It is essential to look closely at the semantics of apparent end-of-list coordinations in Latin (see in general XVIII.4).

10 has an asyndetic tricolon of adjectives, with the longest (and semantically most specific) at the end.

(12) Cato 5.F104 *anni aetas uox uires senectus*

Gellius (13.25.15) refers to the use here of *conpluribus uocabulis super eadem re*, 'several words concerning the same thing'. Gellius is loosely right in that all five terms allude to features of age, but there are clear semantic distinctions: years and the voice, strength and old age are not the same things. Cornell (*FRH* III.138) puts it slightly misleadingly in referring to 'synonymous or similar words'. *Anni* and *aetas* are alliterative and near-synonyms, and they are treated by Wölfflin (1933: 254) as an alliterative pairing. *Vox* and *uires* are not only alliterative but are coordinated by Cicero (*Verr.* 1.31) in a similar context to that here: *ne uox uiresque deficerent* (see again Wölfflin 1933: 281). Arguably then there are two pairs, with a general term at the end summarising their implication: the vocal weakness of the years, that is old age. For an asyndetic pair summarising the content of two preceding pairs see XXIV.6.3 on Pacuvius **6–8**.

(13) Cato 5.F109 *mulieres opertae auro purpuraque; arsinea rete diadema, coronas aureas, rusceas fascias, galbeos lineos, pelles redimicula*

This is translated by Cornell (*FRH*) as: 'women covered in gold and purple; headdress, hairnet, diadem, gold crowns, red ribbons, linen armlets, furs, hair-bands'. On such moralising disapproval of female excesses see Cornell, *FRH* III.140. Asyndeton in the description of female adornment and extravagance has come up before (see XXIII.8.1, and also XXV.3 on Lucilius 71). The above passage recalls particularly Plaut. *Epid.* 230–5 (see XXIII. 8.1), where there is a similar list (made up of 'new names' for garments: see l. 229 *nomina* . . . *noua*). It is noteworthy that no term occurs in both lists, an indication that fashion required novelties (or new designations). In both lists however there are unusual colour terms (here *rusceas*). The point of asyndeton (as distinct from multiple coordination or end-of-list coordination) in such an asyndetic sequence is that the list is not necessarily complete: it is hinted that there are other excesses that could be added (see IV.3 on selective lists).

(14) Cato 5.F138 *Etruriam Samnites Lucanos* inter se natinari
For an asyndetic list of geographical adjectives in a speech of Cato, see *ORF* 230 *accessit ager quem priuatim habent Gallicus Samnitis Apulus Bruttius.*

(15) Coelius 15.F24 *nullae nationi tot tantas tam continuas uictorias tam breui spatio datas arbitror quam uobis*

(16) Quadrigarius 24.F4 *forma factis eloquentia dignitate acrimonia confidentia pariter praecellebat*, translated by Briscoe, 'at the same time . . . he excelled equally in physical appearance, deeds, eloquence, rank, drive, and confidence'.

There is not a marked structure to the six terms here. However, *acrimonia* and *confidentia* belong together, as they denote overlapping qualities (the so-called 'Oxford comma' in the above translation obscures the connection, as is often its achievement; see *OLD* s.v. *acrimonia* 4 'vigour, energy', citing this passage). *Forma* and *facta* are alliterative, but are not semantically connected. Despite hints of a weak arrangement, Quadrigarius has not constructed a sequence of distinctive pairs.

(17) Quadrigarius 24.F37 *loca munita res omnis habere quae militibus opus sunt, ligna aquam pabulum*
Three nouns for military necessities, the unity of which is defined in the previous clause.

(18) Sisenna 26.F56 *armis equis commeatibus nos magis iuuerunt*
A tricolon of asyndetic single words; all three of the formula *arma equi uiri* or any two are regularly in asyndeton, sometimes with other terms

present, as here: see e.g. Preuss (1881: 70, 74, 92), and Sallust 31, 32 with cross references.

2.3   Phrasal or Clausal Asyndeta with More Members than Two

(19) Coelius 15.F38 *terram cum classi accedunt, nauibus atque scaphis egrediuntur, castra metati signa statuunt*

(20) Coelius 15.F41 *ferit pectus a<d>uorsum, congenuclat percussus, deiecit dominum*

(21) Sisenna 26.F50 *catapultas sedecim, quattuor ballistas, uiginti plaustra scorpiis ac minoribus sagittis onusta*

This is a list of objects (expressing probably a totality) with quantity terms, of a type found e.g. in recipes (see IV.2 for Apicius 7.5.2). For extended asyndetic lists of items accompanied by quantity terms see e.g. Cato *Agr.* 10–12.

2.4   Phrasal or Clausal Asyndeta with Two Members

(22) Quadrigarius, 24.F46 *Fabius de nocte coepit hostibus castra simulare obpugnare, eum hostem delectare*

(23) Sisenna 26.F102 *funis expediunt, claustra foribus inposita periclitantur.*

2.5   Conclusions

The cross references here to Sallust and Tacitus suggest that there are similarities between the annalists and the later historians in the use of asyndetic words and groups. Further parallels could be cited, but I have not attempted a systematic comparison of the annalists with Sallust and Tacitus except in the use of single-word pairs. A third of the listed passages (eight) above are from Cato. But it is not only later historians who can be cited for parallels.

13, an asyndetic list of female accessories (in Cato), is in a tradition well established by the early period, whereby a moralising male speaker or writer expresses disapproval by means of an extended list, which by implication could go on indefinitely. 3 and 6 can both be interpreted as instances of asyndetic hendiadys, with one word acting as a modifier of the other. Such pairs are found in later historians but in other genres as well (II.3.2.3). Semantically 7 (Sisenna: *iumenta pecuda*) belongs to a recurrent type, found particularly with coordination but also sometimes asyndetically, whereby species of animals, domestic or wild or both, are linked, with or without humans. Asyndetic parallels were seen in Lucretius, Virgil and Tacitus, and also Cicero's *philosophica*. In Cato several instances of pronounced assonance were noted, whether in pairs or longer sequences (6 *assiduiate indulgitate*, 9 *pransum paratum cohortatum*). Such phenomena we have illustrated particularly from early literature, though they are not only early. Another pair in Cato with a structural feature found in the early period most notably in Plautus was that consisting of two long suffixal derivatives/compounds (1). 8 and 9 (both again in Cato) illustrate the tendency (it is no more than that) for items in a series to increase in length. One does not expect to find much evidence for asyndetic/coordinated accumulations in short fragments, but there is one such in 5 (an asyndeton bimembre followed by an asyndetic series of phrases). It was also argued that 8 (Cato) has two juxtaposed pairs of asyndeta comprising single words. These are followed by a generalisation containing *alii* (and comparison was made with e.g. Sallust). Note the frequency with which Cato is mentioned in this paragraph.

3 Sallust

3.1 Introduction

Asyndeton bimembre is common in Sallust, in speeches (a speech by Catiline is notable), narrative and moralising passages. I take the *Catiline, Jugurtha* and *Histories* in order, classifying the examples according to the parts of speech. Sallust has a habit of stringing together multiple phrases/terms without coordinators (accumulations), and within these sequences it is often tempting to find single-word asyndeta bimembria that seem to be units and separable from the other members of the sequence on semantic grounds. They are often at the start of a sequence. There are other recurrent patterns, and Sallust emerges as a formulaic writer in some respects; Tacitus too favours certain patterns, though not all of them of the types found in Sallust.

It is a subjective matter distinguishing a tricolon from an asyndetic pair that is followed by a miscellaneous third element introduced by a coordinator, or distinguishing a tricolon from a single first element followed by a coordinated pair, but I have decided to include all possible examples of asyndetic pairs (sometimes with question marks) and leave it to the reader to query some. It is definitely the case that a structure of the type AB*C*que in Latin need not have end-of-list coordination: see e.g. XVIII.4, and some of the examples from Horace discussed at XXIX.4. For alternative analyses of some such sequences see below on Sallust **64** (*libertatem patriam parentisque*), and on Tacitus *Annals* **134**, where Livy 4.48.11 (*suadendo monendo, pollicendoque*) is discussed.

It is stated in each case whether the context is a speech or narrative.

3.2 The Evidence

3.2.1 Nouns

(?) *Cat.* 10.2 *qui* labores pericula, *dubias atque asperas res facile tolerauerant*, 'who had easily endured toils and dangers, doubtful and harsh events'.

This should probably be taken as an ascending tricolon, but it does have a unitary pair at the start. *Labores* and *pericula* are nouns for different types of hardships (for the combination see Cic. *Arch.* 30 *in his uitae periculis laboribusque*, Val. Max. 2.3.1 *laboribus et periculis militiae*, Pomp. Trog. 38.7.4 *ingens militiae periculum ac labor*; for a possible asyndeton see XXVIII.2.2 on Caes. *Civ.* 3.53.4, **10**; cf. Plaut. *Men.* 1133 *miseriis laboribus* for a comparable asyndetic pair), whereas the next phrase is vague and comprehensive, and might indeed embrace the first two terms.

This passage illustrates the difficulty of classification raised by many sequences.

Narrative.

(**1**) *Cat.* 10.4 *namque auaritia* fidem probitatem *ceterasque artis bonas subuortit*

For *probitas* in asyndeta in Sallust see **22** *probitatem industriam* and **35** *industria probitas*. *Fides* too is in an asyndeton bimembre, at **26**. Virtues are often paired in asyndeton (cf. **20, 22, 26, 35**), as are vices (cf. **2, 4**) (for such pairs in Cicero, see XXVI.7.8.2).

Here we have a structural type, found also in Tacitus (and elsewhere), in which a unitary asyndeton bimembre (on my interpretation: see below) is followed by a generalisation, here introduced by *ceterasque*. Cf. in Sallust, **4**, and in Tacitus **3, 13, 15**. A variation on this structure is found at Sallust **22** (*aliasque*) and **38** (*et alia*) (cf. Tacitus **73**). *Omnis, totus* and *cunctus* are also found in such generalisations (see on Cicero **1**, where the difficulty of classifying such examples is noted, and also on Tacitus **100**). See further below, 3.3.3b, 4.2.4b, and particularly XVIII.6. This use of *ceterique* (etc.) may of course also follow longer asyndetic series, as at Cic. *Mur.* 15 *dignitatem generis integritatis industriae ceterorumque ornamentorum* *omnium* (cf. e.g. above, 2.2, 8 for *aliisque* in a passage of Cato). Sometimes on the other hand *ceteri* or other summarising terms are placed asyndetically at the end of a list (see below, 34, and also Dougan and Henry 1934: 180, Pease 1958: 1065, and 1066 on *reliqui*; also Leo 1960: 180 on *omnia, cuncta*). The addition of a coordinator, as in the present passage, perhaps tends to isolate the preceding asyndetic terms, which have a semantic unity and are precise rather than vague (see too Kühner and Stegmann 1955: II.154 on *ceteri*, coordinated and uncoordinated; note too Cicero 141, 142, where a generalisation linked to two pairs by a coordinator is clearly detached from the terms preceding). On the other hand words meaning 'all' may be asyndetic at the end of a list and still be semantically detached, as is clear from Tacitus 100 and the passages referred to ad loc. Note the problematic pair of similar Ciceronian examples discussed at Cicero 26, one of which I have numbered but the other not, an arbitrary decision reflecting the difficulty of classifying such sequences. I have usually chosen to classify as 'weak' asyndeta bimembria pairs with a distinct unity that are followed by a vague generalisation (see XVIII and particularly XVIII.6 on weak asyndeta bimembria), but am aware that others may prefer to see such structures as special types of tricola.

See also the commentary on Tacitus *Ann.* 2.73.3 (quoted after 70) (also 6.2c) for a structural similarity between the present passage and Tacitus 13.
Narrative.

(2) *Cat.* 10.4 *pro his superbiam crudelitatem, deos neglegere, omnia uenalia habere edocuit*, 'instead it taught men arrogance and cruelty, to neglect the gods and treat everything as for sale'.

The four objects of *edocuit* syntactically fall into two groups: first two nouns, uncoordinated, and then two infinitival clauses, also unconnected. The pattern of accumulation is typical of Sallust (see also above, 2.1 on Quadrigarius, 5), with a two-word asyndeton bimembre coming at the start of (or within) a longer sequence containing other forms of asyndeton, phrasal, clausal or with more single words than two (cf. e.g. 3, 27, 29, 35; also 3.3.3c, and for Tacitus, 4.2.4c, 5.2.3). *Crudelitas* is stronger than *superbia*.

This passage follows on immediately from 1. It is of the moralising, generalising type, in Sallust's own voice.
Narrative.

(4) *Cat.* 12.2 *rapere consumere, sua parui pendere, aliena cupere, pudorem pudicitiam, diuina atque humana promiscua ... habere*, 'they seized and wasted, valued their own property little and desired that of others,

considered purity and dishonour, divine and human matters as indistinguishable'.

There are two pairs of opposites (antonyms) after *cupere*. The first, alliterative, pair is an asyndeton, and the second has *atque* linking its members; for *atque* linking terms after an asyndeton bimembre in Sallust see below 3.3.3a, 6.2b (also XXIX.2.1.2 on Hor. *Sat.* 1.1.85, Wölfflin 1900: 32), and for cases as here where it is opposites (or virtual opposites) that are so linked, see 21, 29, 31, 32.

Pudor and *pudicitia* (a cognate pairing: cf. e.g. Plaut. *Trin.* 142 *fide et fiduciae*) can be virtual synonyms. Note for example Cic. *Har. resp.* 43, *Mil.* 77, where they occur together, in the latter passage probably as one pair in a sequence of pairs; cf. *Epist. Caes.* 2.7.8, p. 510 Ramsey *fides probitas pudor pudicitia*, where Sallust's imitator has picked up two phrases from Sallust (see above, 1 for *fides probitas*); further examples of *pudor pudicitia* are collected by Preuss (1881: 79) and Wölfflin (1933: 273) (for coordination note e.g. Cic. *Har. resp.* 9 *pudorem pudicitiamque*). They are taken as virtual synonyms here, for example, by Ramsey 2007: 91 ('virtually synonymous'). Woodman (2007) by contrast translates them as virtual opposites ('propriety and unchastity'), and such a rendering seems required by the context: if two things are treated 'indifferently', you do not expect them to be identical. *Pudicitia* is given only a favourable meaning by the *OLD*, but *pudor*, as well as having such a meaning, can also refer to a 'source of shame, dishonour, humiliation' (*OLD* s.v. 4a). It may indicate a sense of shame arising from a wrongdoing (see Cic. *Fam.* 14.3.2 for this meaning). The persons referred to by Sallust make no distinction between purity and the type of behaviour that ought to occasion a sense of shame: thus in effect honour versus dishonour. For opposites that are not quite explicit see XIII.5.5, and the present chapter, *passim*.

For *sua* and *aliena* (preceding *pudorem pudicitiam*) opposed in much the same sort of structure as that here see Tacitus 48.

Narrative: another moralising passage by Sallust.

(4) *Cat.* 13.3 *sed lubido stupri ganeae ceterique cultus non minor incesserat*, 'But the lust which had arisen for illicit sex and gluttony, and the other refinements, was no less' (Woodman 2007).

For *ganea* in an asyndeton bimembre, see Cicero 10, a passage in which gluttonous eating (*ganea*) and drinking are linked to sexual wrongdoing (cf. *stupri* here). For the structure (with *ceterique*) see above, 1. Again we see vices in asyndeton.

Narrative.

(5) *Cat.* 14.3 *omnes undique parricidae sacrilegi conuicti iudiciis*, 'everyone everywhere convicted of parricide or sacrilege by the courts'.
   A disjunctive asyndeton, expressing alternatives. Coordination would give the wrong meaning. The two terms are obviously members of a set (perpetrators of heinous crimes).
   Narrative.

(6, 7, 8, 9, 10) *Cat.* 20.7–8 *semper illis reges tetrarchae* (6) *uectigales esse, populi nationes* (7) *stipendia pendere; ceteri omnes, strenui boni* (8), *nobiles atque ignobiles, uolgus fuimus sine gratia sine auctoritate, iis obnoxii quibus, si res publica ualeret, formidini essemus. itaque omnis gratia potentia, honos diuitiae* (9, 10) *apud illos sunt aut ubi illi uolunt: nobis reliquere pericula repulsas iudicia egestatem*, 'it has always been to them that the dues of kings and tetrarchs go, that the taxes of peoples and nations are paid; all the rest of us – the committed and good, noble and ignoble – have been simply "the masses", denied favour, denied influence, beholden to those to whom, if the commonwealth thrived, we would be a source of fear. Hence all favour, power, honour and riches rest with them or are where they want them; to us they have left the dangers, rejection, lawsuits and destitution' (Woodman 2007, with slight modification).
   This passage is from the speech of Catiline. Here there are six nominal asyndeta bimembria (as well as a longer asyndeton with four members) in a rhetorical speech (I include the prepositional pair in this figure: see below, this paragraph). Two of them are in the first sentence (*reges tetrarchae*; *populi nationes*). The third (*strenui boni*), strictly adjectival but with the adjectives substantivised, precedes a pair of opposites joined by *atque* (see above on 3). Another asyndeton is prepositional (*sine gratia sine auctoritate*) and classified separately below, 85. All of these comprise near-synonyms or complementary terms (types of rulers, types of national groups: see Ramsey 2007: 84 for the distinction between *populi* and *nationes*), types of virtuous men, recipients of no favours). For the linking of tetrarchs and kings see Cic. *Dom.* 60 *tetrarcharum ac regum*; cf., for other forms of rule/rulers paired asyndetically, Cicero's *regna imperia* at 113, and also Sallust 28, 29 below. The asyndetic group of four *gratia potentia honos diuitiae* should probably be split into two pairs. For *gratia* with *potentia* see *TLL* VI.2.2212.56ff. (very common), and for *diuitiae* and *honor* together see *TLL* V.1.1633.67ff. The first pair denotes power, the second rewards, abstract and concrete, that fall to the influential.

For accumulations of asyndeta bimembria (usually juxtaposed) in a single passage see e.g. below, 18, 19, 31, 32, 35, 37, 41, 42, 44, 45, 47, 79, 80.

(? ?) *Cat.* 20.15 (speech of Catiline) <u>res tempus pericula egestas</u>, belli spolia magnifica magis quam oratio mea uos hortantur

Woodman (2007) translates the first five nouns/noun phrases as independent units ('The issue, the moment, the danger, the destitution, the magnificent spoils of war'), and that is no doubt right. The first pair might just be interpreted as an asyndetic hendiadys ('the circumstances of the time').

We have noted in 6–10 above six asyndeta bimembria from the speech of Catiline, and arguably a pair here could be added; there are also longer types. For an asyndetic pair of verbs in the speech see below, 68.

(11) *Cat.* 21.2 *tum Catilina polliceri tabulas nouas, proscriptionem locupletium, <u>magistratus sacerdotia</u>, rapinas, alia omnia quae bellum atque lubido uictorum fert*

Reynolds (OCT) omits the comma after *sacerdotia*, thereby introducing an asyndetic tricolon. Contrast (correctly, in my opinion) Wölfflin (1900: 32), and the translation of Woodman (2007): 'magistracies and priesthoods; and seizures and everything else . . .'. The pair occurs elsewhere (see XXII.7.2 and Livy 64), and belongs in the category of asyndeta describing officials/offices (see Tacitus 14, and also XXII.7.2; for an Umbrian asyndetic pair with the same meaning see XXII.4.7).
Narrative.

(12) *Cat.* 25.2 *haec mulier genere atque forma, praeterea <u>uiro liberis</u> satis fortunata fuit*

'Husband and children' belong to the category of pairs, whether syndetic or asyndetic, denoting family members, for which in general see XIV, with section 4 for this pairing. 'Wives and children' is more common (XIV.3).

Cf. also below Tacitus 97 for asyndeton in a pairing alluding to a family relationship, and note 14 below.

Here a phrase with *atque* precedes rather than follows the asyndeton bimembre.
Narrative.

(13) *Cat.* 51.1 *ab <u>odio amicitia</u>, ira atque misericordia uacuos esse decet*

Two pairs of opposites (the second equivalent to 'hostility/sympathy'), the second joined by *atque*. All nouns are dependent on a single preposition (see XXI, and on Tacitus 61, with cross references).
Speech of Caesar.

(14) *Cat.* 51.9 *rapi* uirgines pueros, *diuelli liberos a parentum conplexu*
This is from a speech by Caesar: a masculine + feminine opposition, girls and boys (cf. Plaut. *Epid.* 210). See XI.4.

(15) *Cat.* 51.9 caedem incendia *fieri*
Again from the speech of Caesar, and from the same sentence as that of 14; 16 is in the sentence too, which contains as well two pairs with the coordinator *atque*. The nouns are alliterative, and express different aspects of the savagery of war. They often occur together in Cicero (see Wölfflin 1933: 255: e.g. *Cat.* 3.15, where they are juxtaposed but in different phrases: *urbem incendiis, caede ciuis, Italiam bello liberassem, Cat.* 3.21, *Dom.* 89, *Sest.* 88; note also the juxtaposed verb phrases at *Cat.* 3.10: *caedem fieri atque urbem incendi placeret*), but in longer asyndeta (e.g. *Dom.* 89 *caedem incendia rapinas, Sest.* 88, same combination; at *Att.* 15.6.3 a letter of Hirtius is quoted containing the phrase *rapinis incendiis caedibus*; at *Cat.* 2.10 there is an asyndetic tricolon with anaphora, *nisi caedem, nisi incendia, nisi rapinas*). Cicero adds a coordinator when he uses the two on their own (e.g. *Cat.* 1.3 *caede atque incendiis,* 1.6 *caedis atque incendiorum, Dom.* 21 *caedis et incendiorum, Har. resp.* 6 *caede incendiisque,* 58, same phrase). The pairing was clearly well established (more examples in Wölfflin), but Cicero shows an unease about using it as an asyndeton bimembre. Note too Tac. *Ann.* 2.52.2 *incendia et caedes et terrorem.* Tacitus several times combines these nouns, but not in asyndeton (e.g. *Ann.* 14.26.1 *caedibus et incendiis*). At Livy 38.43.5 (*omnia exampla belli edita in se caedibus incendiis ruinis direptione urbis*) *caedibus incendiis* might possibly be one of two pairs, but see on Livy 23.

The sentence, as was noted above, has a massive accumulation of coordinated pairs, syndetic and asyndetic, and it is in accumulations in particular that pairs normally coordinated may be used asyndetically (see below, 5.2.4).

(16) *Cat.* 51.9 *postremo* armis cadaueribus, *cruore atque luctu omnia conpleri*
The sentence of Caesar again. Cf. *Jug.* 101.11 *telis armis cadaueribus.* Another asyndetic pair juxtaposed with a pair coordinated by *atque*: see the next passage. *Arma* is often in asyndetic pairs, in e.g. historians and Cicero: see below on Sallust 31.

(17) *Cat.* 52.3 (speech of Cato) patriae parentibus, *aris atque focis suis bellum parauere*, 'they prepared war against their fatherland and parents, altars and hearths'.

Aris atque focis is one unit (for which see on Cicero 16, and also Sallust 87), with the coordinator *atque* again, and the other two nouns are an alliterative asyndeton bimembre referring to parenthood in two different senses, metaphorical and physical. Both pairs contain complementary terms/express members of a set.

For *patria parentes* see also below, 46. It is a common collocation, sometimes in asyndeton bimembre, but also in longer asyndeta and with coordinators (for examples see Wölfflin 1933: 270, citing e.g. Livy 26.50.2 *patriam parentesque*, Goodyear 1981: 90 on Tac. *Ann.* 1.59.6 *si patriam parentes antiqua mallent quam dominos et colonias nouas*, which I take to be an asyndeton with three members, *TLL* X.1.764.2f. with cross references; also Cicero 105). According to Cicero, *Off.* 1.58, one's highest moral obligation is to *patria et parentes* (a similar obligation is expressed asyndetically at Sallust 87: *pro patria pro liberis*). Note too Lucil. 1337–8 *commoda praeterea patriai prima putare, | deinde parentum*. Cf. Cic. *Fam.* 1.9.18 *uim neque parenti nec patriae adferre oportet*. For the equivalent pair in Greek (in a longer sequence) see Xen. *An.* 3.1.3 πόθου πατρίδων γονέων, γυναικῶν παίδων, 'longing for native states and parents, wives and childrden' (see Huitink and Rood 2019: 73, with further examples).

(18, 19) *Cat.* 52.5 (speech of Cato) *qui semper <u>domos uillas</u>, <u>signa tabulas uostras</u> pluris quam rem publicam fecistis*, 'those of you who have always placed more value on your houses and villas, statues and pictures than on the state'.

Two juxtaposed asyndetic pairs, each with a semantic unity, the first embracing types of houses (opposites of a sort, based on the 'town/country' contrast, for which see below, Sallust 27), the second valuable contents of houses.

Domus and *uilla* are often paired, almost invariably with a coordinator (see *TLL* V.1.1965.58ff. for a long list of examples: e.g. *Epist. Caes.* 1.8.1, p. 494 Ramsey *nam domum aut uillam exstruere, eam <u>signis aulaeis</u>, aliisque operibus exornare* (note here again the presence of valuable contents, expressed asyndetically: statues, tapestries (see above, 2.2, 8)), Plin. *Epist.* 5.19.8 *rogo ergo scribas tuis, ut illi uilla, ut domus pateat*). Again we see a pair that is mainly coordinated used asyndetically in an accumulation, and in a speech (cf. on 15 above). For asyndeton see also Tacitus 104 *quod domos uillas id temporis quasi praedam diuisissent*.

For *signa* and *tabulae* in asyndeton bimembre see Cicero 22; see also above, 2.2, 8.

3 Sallust

(20) *Cat.* 54.5 *at Catoni studium* modestiae decoris, *sed maxume seueritatis erat*

There are contrasting sides to Cato's character, modesty and propriety on the one hand, but severity on the other. The first two nouns, indicating virtues (see above, on Sallust 1), go together, whereas the third is separated by *sed* and expresses a different personal attribute.
Narrative.

(21) *Cat.* 61.9 *uarie per omnem exercitum* laetitia maeror, *luctus atque gaudia agitabantur*, 'variously throughout the whole army there was gladness and sadness, grief and expressions of delight'.

This is the last sentence of the work. There are two pairs of opposites (antonyms), the first asyndetic, the second linked by *atque* again. The two pairs, expressing joy and sorrow, and then with a chiasmus sorrow and joy, are virtually equivalent. See above, Sallust 3 for two pairs of opposites juxtaposed, the second as here coordinated by *atque*.
Narrative.

(22) *Jug.* 1.3 probitatem industriam *aliasque artis bonas*

For this same combination but in the reverse order, see below, 35. Cf. e.g. Tac. *Hist.* 2.95.2 *probitate aut industria* and also *TLL* VII.1.1274.68, citing the present passage but no examples that are not mentioned here. The phrases that follow both here and at Sallust 35 are more diverse or comprehensive in character.

There is another asyndetic pair with *probitas* at Sallust 1 above (*fidem probitatem*). Particular words have a tendency to occur in asyndeta bimembria with a variety of other words (see e.g. above 16 on *arma* and below 25 on *gratia* and 30 on *uultus*). Another such is *domus* (see the next example). For further cases, in Cicero, see XXVI.7.8.2, final paragraph; also this chapter, below 3.3.2. The structure here, with the generalising *aliasque* attached, is much the same as the type with *ceterique* (on which see above, Sallust 1, with cross references); cf. also 38 (*et alia*).
Narrative.

(23) *Jug.* 14.11 *sicuti uidetis extorrem* patria domo, *inopem et coopertum miseriis effecit*, 'he made me, as you see, an exile from homeland and home, poverty stricken and covered in misery'.

An asyndeton bimembre with a semantic unity, indicating homeland and home. The same combination occurs in the same order in a very similar phrase at 24 below. The two nouns are in the reverse order in a prepositional asyndeton at Livy 22.39.13 *procul ab domo ab patria*. For the pair (in the latter order) with coordinator see Plaut. *Men.* 1069 *ea domus et*

patria est mihi. A passage of Gellius (2.12.1), translating Aristotle, overlaps lexically both with this and the next passage of Sallust: *is domo patria fortunisque omnibus careto, exul extorrisque esto.* See further Preuss (1881: 78), and cf. *patria parentes* at 17 above; contrast the interpretation of *urbe domo* in Virgil at XXIV.2.1.2, 16.
Speech.

(24) *Jug*.14.17 *nunc uero exul patria domo, solus atque omnium honestarum rerum egens*, 'But as it is, an exile from fatherland and home, alone and lacking in all honourable means' (Woodman 2007).

The idea of 'expulsion' from somewhere (note *exul* here and *extorris* in the previous example) often seems to evoke the use of asyndeta (see below on Sallust 52, and also Cicero 42, 71, Virgil 22 at XXIV.2.2, Livy 34; also E. *Med*. 255 ἐγὼ δ' ἔρημος ἄπολις οὖσ', with Mastronarde 2002 ad loc.). 24 is a phrasal asyndeton bimembre comprising first *exul patria domo* and then *solus* through to *egens*, with the two-word asyndeton bimembre embedded within the first member, a structure seen above at 2.1, 1 (Cato), with cross references (cf. e.g. 23 immediately above).
Speech.

(25) *Jug*. 15.2 *gratia uoce, denique omnibus modis... nitebantur*
This structure is of a type. There is first an asyndetic pair of complementary terms ('their influence, their powers of speech', Woodman 2007), and then a generalising summary introduced by an adverb. For *denique* in such a context see XVIII.6, Cicero 1, and below, Sallust 36, 37 (also Wölfflin 1900: 34), Tacitus 95, 96, 126. For *omnis* or *cunctus* in such a final element see again XVIII.6, with the next example, 26, and Tacitus 100 with cross references; also Sallust 1. *Gratia* was seen above, 6–10 = 85, in a different pairing (on which general phenomenon see above, 22, as well as the next example).
Narrative.

(26) *Jug*. 16.3 *perfecit uti fama fide, postremo omnibus suis rebus commodum regis anteferret*, '(he) ensured that the man put the king's advantage before his own reputation, his own credit – in short, all his own interests' (Woodman 2007).

Fides and *fama* are near-synonyms, and they are often together, either in longer asyndeta or joined by a coordinator (see Wölfflin 1933: 259, citing e.g. Cic. *Att*. 11.2.1 *fidem et famam*, but not quoting any examples of asyndeton bimembre). Cf. Tac. *Hist*. 1.30.2 *uestra fides famaque inlaesa ad hunc diem mansit*. The function of *postremo* is the same as that of *denique* at

25 above. In both passages the adverb is followed by a use of *omnibus*. For *postremo* see also Sallust 29, 86 (and Wölfflin 1900: 34), Tacitus 5. For *fides* in a different asyndetic pairing see above, Sallust 1.
Narrative.

(27) *Jug.* 20.8 *ceterum qua pergebat <u>urbis agros</u> uastare, praedas agere, suis animum hostibus terrorem augere*, 'Wherever he went, he devastated cities and countryside; drove away plunder; and magnified both the courage of his own men and the terror of the enemy' (Woodman 2007).
There are three clauses in asyndeton in this sentence, and within the first there is an embedded nominal asyndeton bimembre (for such embedding see 24 and the cross references). *Vrbis* and *agros* are opposites of the type 'town' versus 'country' (see XIII.5.1, and Cicero 19), a more specific manifestation of which, *domos uillas*, was seen at 18 above. For asyndeton see Plaut. *Am.* 226 *urbem agrum, aras focos* (two pairs: for *arae foci* see above, 17 and also Cicero 16). *Vrbs agri* occurs in a longer asyndeton at Livy 1.38.2 *urbem agros aquam terminos delubra utensilia diuina humanaque omnia*. For the pair with coordinators see Enn. *scen.* 137 Jocelyn *inter se sortiunt urbem atque agros*, Cic. *Pis.* 48 *ex agris urbibusque*, Hor. *Ars* 208 *coepit agros extendere uictor et urbes* | *latior amplecti murus*, Livy 4.21.6 *in urbe agrisque*, 5.25.6 *urbis atque agri capti*, 38.11.9 *cum urbe agrisque* (from an official document), 42.24.9 *urbem et agros*. The pairing occurs in the prayer for devoting an enemy city to destruction: Macr. 3.9.10 *in his locis regionibusque, agris urbibusque habitant*. Note too the opposition at Livy 34.13.6 *non agros inde populari sed urbium opes exhaurire licebit*. For a similar pair see Cicero 19 *agrorum oppidorum*.
Narrative.

(28) *Jug.* 31.9 *itaque postremo <u>leges maiestas</u> uostra, diuina et humana omnia hostibus tradita sunt*
The asyndetic pair is of a type, denoting instruments/forms of rule. See on 6 above and XXII.7.5, and note too the asyndetic tricolon in the next example. The pair that follows unusually for Sallust has *et* as the coordinator (see below, 6.2b).
Speech.

(29) *Jug.* 31.20 *quom <u>regna prouinciae</u>, leges iura iudicia, bella atque paces, postremo diuina et humana omnia penes paucos erant*
This long sequence consists of four groups, two asyndetic and two coordinated, each with a semantic unity. *Regna prouinciae* are types of states (for similar asyndeta see above, Sallust 6, 7), *leges iura iudicia* aspects

of legal systems (for two of the group paired see Cicero 7 *iudicia leges* (a pair in a longer sequence, mainly of phrases), *Dom.* 70 *legum iudiciorumque*). War and peace are opposites, as are things human and divine (both antonyms). For *regna* associated with *prouinciae*, usually in long sequences, see *TLL* X.2.2342.52ff. (note Sall. *Hist.* 3.15.6 Ramsey *aerarium exercitus regna prouincias occupauere* and also Tac. *Ann.* 1.11.4 *classes regna prouinciae*). The one asyndeton bimembre is right at the start, a typical position, *postremo* introduces the last unit (see above, 26), and the pair of opposites joined by *atque* comes after the asyndeta, again a typical position in Sallust for terms linked by *atque* (see 3).

The structure of this passage, with an asyndeton bimembre followed by an asyndetic tricolon and then two phrasal pairs in asyndeton with each other, is similar to that at Tacitus 16. See also below, Sallust 39.

Speech.

(30) *Jug.* 34.1 *terrebat eum <u>clamore uoltu</u>, saepe impetu atque aliis omnibus quae ira fieri amat*, '(the crowd) terrified him with shouting and expression, and often by charging and all the other acts that are usually motivated by anger'.

There are two pairs here, the first asyndetic, the second (separated from the first by *saepe*) consisting of a word and a phrase linked by *atque*. The two pairs are distinguished semantically, the first referring to non-violent aggression (conveyed by the voice and facial expression) and the second to aggression that might be violent. *Clamore uoltu* is similar to *uerba uultus* in Tacitus (58) and to comparable phrases in which *uultus* is combined with terms implying use of the voice (details at Tacitus 58; see also Cicero 162 on asyndetic terms to do with the making of a din, Sallust 39 below, and also 5.2.3). *Vultus* is another term that recurs in different asyndetic pairs, though not in Sallust himself (see above on 22 for this phenomenon; also 31 below).

Narrative.

(31, 32) *Jug.* 51.1 <u>arma tela</u>, <u>equi uiri</u>, *hostes atque ciues*

Three unitary pairs on my interpretation (see too Reynolds, OCT), the third with *atque*.

The first comprises inanimates, the tools of war, a commonplace combination, with and without asyndeton (Preuss 1881: 86–7, *TLL* II.591.45ff., and see also below 36). For asyndeton see Livy 36.18.1 *arma tela parant* (also 10.4.2 and 21), but Livy also often links the pair with *-que* (see 1.25.5, 22.48.2, 26.47.6) (see further Briscoe 1981: 248 on Livy 36.18.1, Oakley 2005b: 74 on 10.4.2; also id. 1997: 454 on 6.6.14). For other instances of *arma* in asyndeton bimembre see above, Sallust 16 *arma cadauera*, and

3 Sallust

below, Tacitus 20 *arma equi*, 99 *arma munimenta*, 102 *arma opes*, and also on Cicero 12.

The second comprises the animate fighting components of an army, horses and warriors (cf. *Jug.* 101.11 *equi atque uiri* for this pair coordinated). Tacitus at 101, 102 has a comparable group of two such pairs, *habui equos uiros, arma opes*, the first animate and identical to that here, the second inanimate. Also of note is Tacitus 110 *quo uoto equi uiri, cuncta [uicta] occidioni dantur. Arma, uiri* and *equi*, or two of the three, are constantly associated, either in asyndeton or explicitly linked (cf. Virg. *Aen.* 1.1 *arma uirumque cano*). See for example Preuss (1881: 91–2), above, 2.2, 18, and Adams (1970: 291–3 and the notes at 302), with material from the archive of the Thesaurus linguae Latinae.

Equi is combined with *armenta* at Tacitus 83 (but see the note on the text).

The third is a pair of animate opposites, the enemy and one's own citizens (outsiders and insiders, again with *atque*).

It has to be said that the analysis of the first four terms above is not straightforward. Note Livy 30.11.4 *equos arma tela* for an asyndetic tricolon with three of the four terms.

Narrative.

(33) *Jug.* 57.5 *in proxumos saxa uoluere, sudis pila, praeterea picem sulphure et taeda mixtam ardentia mittere*, '(they) rolled rocks onto those nearest and threw burning stakes and lances as well as pitch mixed with sulphur and pinewood' (Woodman 2007).

Three elements are objects of *mittere*, the first a unitary pair of near-synonyms (stakes and javelins, objects used as weapons: for a similar pair cf. Tacitus 11), and then an extended phrase denoting something different (pitch), introduced by an adverb (*praeterea*). *Saxa* is separate from *sudis pila*, in that it is object of a different verb, but cf. Sall. *Hist.* 2.74.2 Ramsey *saxa pila sudes iacere*, where the three nouns are object of the same verb. The same combination is at Livy 27.28.12 *saxis sudibus pilis absterrent hostem*; note too 34.15.5 *saxisque et sudibus et omni genere telorum*.

The problem of analysing phrase structure comes up again: is there an ascending tricolon, or are the first two terms semantically and structurally set apart from the final element? For *praeterea* as a divider following a unitary asyndetic pair, see XVIII.6, above 12 (where the placement of the asyndeton is unusual), below 34, 42, and Wölfflin (1900: 34). See also Cicero 105.

Narrative.

(34) *Jug.* 60.6 *lapides ignem, alia praeterea tela ingerunt*

Here again is an asyndetic pair of items used as weapons, and then follows a more general (summarising) phrase introduced by *praeterea*.
Narrative.

(35) *Jug.* 63.2 <u>*industria probitas*</u>, *militiae magna scientia, animus belli ingens domi modicus, lubidinis et diuitiarum uictor, tantummodo gloriae auidus*, '(he had) industry, probity, a great knowledge of soldiering, and a temperament which was remarkable in war but restrained at home, unconquered by cravings or riches, hungry only for glory' (Woodman 2007).

Another case of two uncoordinated single words at the start of a succession of phrases without coordinators (cf. e.g. Sallust 2, 29, 39, 58, 60, 64). Both terms denote conventional virtues, 'good arts'. For *probitas* in asyndeton bimembre see 1 and 22 (in this latter place with *industria* also). Tacitus several times has *industria* in asyndeton bimembre (see Tacitus 1, 4; also Cicero 193 *uirtutis industriae*, Plin. *Ep.* 1.14.7 *Aciliano uero ipsi plurimum uigoris industriae*). Again we see the tendency for particular terms to turn up in different asyndetic pairs.
Narrative.

(36, 37) *Jug.* 76.1 *quippe qui omnia,* <u>*arma tela*</u>, <u>*locos tempora*</u>, *denique naturam ipsam ceteris imperitantem industria uicerat*

The punctuation here with a comma after *omnia* (so Reynolds, OCT) is undoubtedly right (see below), and it is this punctuation that Woodman (2007) translates ('who by his industry had conquered everything – arms and weapons, place and time, in short Nature herself, the commander of all else').

Arma tela and *locos tempora* are both asyndetic formulae (for the first see above, 31). For *locus tempus* see Preuss (1881: 37); note Ter. *Eun.* 541 *locus tempus constitutumst*, Tacitus 6 *dum quaeritur tempus locus, quodque in re tali difficillimum est, prima uox*, *Ann.* 2.65.2 *nec diu dubitatum de tempore loco, dein condicionibus* (which I tentatively take to be a tricolon, with *dein* equivalent to a coordinator, though again there is an ambiguity to the structure). For the pair coordinated see *Jug.* 113.2 *tempore et loco*, Tac. *Ann.* 13.38.1 *tempus locumque*, 15.50.4 *de tempore ac loco*; cf. Livy 9.41.16 *prout loci natura tempusque patiebatur*.
Narrative.

(38) *Jug.* 85.41 <u>*sudorem puluerem*</u> *et alia talia relinquant nobis*, 'Let them leave sweat and dust, and other such to us.'

Sweat and dust go together (the sweat and dust caused by war: see for this passage *TLL* X.2.2630.50), and then there is a switch to a general expression (*et alia* . . .: for the type see on 1 above).

3 Sallust 567

Speech.

(39) *Jug.* 99.3 *ita cunctos* strepitu clamore, *nullo subueniente, nostris instantibus, tumultu formidine terrore quasi uecordia ceperat*
   Strepitu clamore are near-synonyms; *strepitus* may, but need not, imply use of the voice (see the three meanings listed by the *OLD* s.v.). For the combination in an asyndetic tricolon see *Rhet. Her.* 2.8 *strepitus clamor crepitus exauditus*; for coordinated pairs see Livy 4.41.5 *ex strepitu tamen et clamore,* Tac. *Ann.* 14.35.2 *ne strepitum quidem et clamorem tot milium ... perlaturos.* The two words occupy the usual position in a long sequence. They are followed by three uncoordinated units, the first two belonging together structurally in that both are ablative participial pairs. The third comprises an asyndetic tricolon. With this last cf. the prayer at Macr. *Sat.* 3.9.10 *fuga formidine terrore compleatis.*
   With *strepitu clamore* cf. *clamore uultu* at 30 above, with the two phrases illustrating again the tendency for particular words to occur in asyndeta bimembria with varying partners (for which tendency see also the next paragraph). Loud noise and commotion, shouting, lamentation and complaint seem to have motivated asyndetic pairs (see below, 5.2.3). It is likely that in speech a particular intonation suited to the meaning accompanied the omission of the coordinator. Not infrequently the terms also have repeated syllables. For further examples from this semantic category see on Cicero 162, and also Tacitus 58. Note too (XXIV.6.2, 5) Pac. *trag.* 263 Schierl *strepitus fremitus, clamor tonitruum et rudentum sibilus,* Plaut. *Am.* 1062 *strepitus crepitus, sonitus tonitrus* (two pairs: see XXIII.7.1).
   In this note we have seen *strepitus* juxtaposed with three different nouns.

(40) *Jug.* 101.9 dextra sinistra *omnibus occisis*
   I include *dextra* and *sinistra* among nominal uses here, though they could be classified as adverbial. Sallust does also have them coordinated (*Jug.* 50.4 *sinistra ac dextra*). These are a classic pair of opposites (directional), for which see XIII.5.4.
   Narrative.

(41, 42) *Jug.* 111.1–2 *quem si Romanis tradidisset, fore ut illi plurumum deberetur;* amicitiam foedus, *Numidiae partem quam nunc peteret tum ultro aduenturam. rex primo negitare:* cognationem adfinitatem, *praeterea foedus interuenisse,* 'if he handed him over to the Romans, he would be owed a very great deal: friendship, treaty, the part of Numidia which he now sought – all these would then come to him automatically. At first the king demurred: relations, in-laws, a treaty besides had passed between them' (Woodman 2007, slightly modified).

From *amicitiam* onwards and then from *cognationem* there are possibly two asyndetic tricola, with the third member of the first longer than the members preceding. But in both the first two words have a unity to them, being near-synonyms or closely related, and they may alternatively be taken as embedded asyndeta bimembria. The second pair, *cognationem adfinitatem*, is separated from the term that follows by *praeterea*, an isolating technique seen several times above in Sallust (see on 33). *Amicitia* may be a friendship between states (*OLD* s.v. 3), leading perhaps to a *foedus* (cf. Cic. *Balb*. 23 *quae est ista societas, quae amicitia, quod foedus*); *amicitia* is sometimes virtually equivalent to *foedus* (see Livy 38.38.2 *amicitia ... his legibus et condicionibus esto*, following §1 *foedus in haec fere uerba ... conscriptum est*).

With the other pairing (usually coordinated except in longer sequences) cf. *Lex Coloniae Genetiuae* (Crawford 1996: 1.407) XCV tabl. c.16–19 (p. 407) *cui ei, quae r(es) tum agetur, gener socer, uitricus priuignus, patron(us) lib(ertus), consobrinus <sit> propiusue eum ea cognatione atfinitate{m}ue contingat*, 'who <be> son-in-law or father-in-law to that person, whatever affair shall then be the subject of an action, or step-father or step-son, or patron or freedman, or cousin, or be closer to him than that *cognatio* or *adfinitas*' (p. 426). *Cognatio* was a technical term for relationships by blood; *adfinitas* was a less precise term for relationships by marriage (I am grateful to Wolfgang Ernst for information on this distinction). Note too *S. C. De Cn. Pisone patre* ed. Damon 77–8 *cognatione adfinitateue*, 79 *cognatus adfinisue* (translated as relationships by 'blood or marriage'). Cf. also e.g. Cic. *Verr*. 2.27 *cognatione adfinitate necessitudine*, and see further on Livy 6. Narrative.

(43) *Hist*. 4.60.16 Ramsey *magnas opes <u>uirorum armorum</u> et auri esse*

For the traditional triplet *arma uiri equi* and the asyndetic pairs derived from it see above on 31, 32. I take *uirorum armorum* to be an asyndetic pair semantically quite distinct from *auri*. Here is a place where in translation the 'Oxford comma' would be appropriate as setting apart the third item from the first two. Ramsey translates: 'you have great stocks of men, of arms and of gold', but one might modify slightly: 'great stocks of men and arms, and of gold'. For *arma uiri* itself see Preuss (1881: 74–5), a collocation also found with a coordinator (e.g. Livy 24.40.3 *uiris atque armis*).

Letter, in effect a speech.

(44, 45?) *Hist*. 4.60.17 Ramsey <u>*domum coniuges*</u>, <u>*agros imperium*</u>

3 Sallust

Of the Romans, who have 'possessed nothing except what they have stolen'. There are possibly two pairs here, the first expressing domestic possessions/responsibilities, the second ('lands and dominion') empire. 'House' and 'wife/husband' are sometimes connected (e.g. Virg. *Aen.* 2.579 *coniugiumque domumque*, where *coniugium* is for *coniugem*; for other similar combinations see *TLL* V.1.1981.31ff.). The pairing expresses aspects of a person's moral obligations, like *patria parentes* and *patria liberi* (see on Sallust 17, 87).
Letter.

(46) *Hist.* 4.60.17 Ramsey *conuenas olim sine patria parentibus*
For this pair see above, 17. Note too *Hist.* 2.79.3 Ramsey *ino<pes pa>triae parientumque*: is *parientum* right? It should surely be changed to *parentum*. For two (asyndetic) terms dependent on a single preposition see XXI, and on Sallust 13 and Tacitus 61, 63, 75, 91, 115.
Letter.

(47) *Hist.* 4.60.17 Ramsey *quibus non humana ulla neque diuina obstant quin socios amicos, procul iuxta sitos, inopes potentisque trahant excindant*, 'men who are prevented by nothing human or divine from plundering and destroying allies and friends – those situated far away or nearby, weak and powerful too –' (Ramsey).

For *socius* and *amicus* coordinated see e.g. Caes. *Civ.* 1.6.3 (from senatorial proceedings) *ut socius sit atque amicus*, Sall. *Cat.* 16.4 *amicis sociisque*, Cic. *Fin.* 5.65 *iis qui publice socii atque amici sunt*, Livy 38.11.2 *exercitum, qui aduersus socios amicosque eorum ducetur* (official context, from conditions of peace), 42.13.6 *socium atque amicum*. The asyndetic pair *amicitia societas* is found, of a relationship between states, in the *Lex de prouinciis praetoriis*, Cnidos copy, column III, ll. 16–21 (Crawford 1996: 1.249; the same asyndeton is in the Delphi fragment, same page): *quibus amicitia societas cum populo Romano est tributa*. Note too (with coordination) Livy 5.35.4 *nullum eis ius societatis amicitiaeue erat*, 42.6.8 *societas atque amicitia*. The two adjectives are found in longer asyndetic sequences (e.g. Cic. *Quinct.* 26 *amicum socium adfinem*; see also *TLL* I.1911.66ff.). See too XVIII.4.

For pairs to do with personal or interstate relationships, see Sallust 12, 41, 42, Tacitus 3, 10, 63, 72, 80 (another pair also containing *socius*), 97. Note too the Ciceronian pair *adfinitas societas* (1).

This pair is preceded by a pair of coordinated opposites, and followed by adverbial opposites in asyndeton (*procul iuxta*, 'near and far', antonyms, for which see 83; on pairs of adverbial opposites see XIII.5.4), and then by a pair of substantival opposites linked by *-que* (*inopes potentisque*, 'weak and powerful', antonyms again) and finally by a verbal asyndeton bimembre (expressing acts of violence: see above 2.1, 2 for this semantic type). The accumulation of pairs in a single passage is typical of Sallust (see 3.3.3c, d). This passage is striking, because the asyndeta are of different types, nominal, adverbial and verbal. For other such mixed combinations see e.g. Tacitus 4 *industria licentia, per uirtutes per uoluptates,* 66, 67 *plebes primores, iuuentus senes . . . incursant turbant,* 153 *temere prouisu, ob iram ob praedam* and Petron. 61.9 cited at 3.3.3e; see further 6.2. In *socios amicos* we have another pair which, though usually coordinated, is here used in asyndeton in an accumulation (see below, 5.2.4).

All the examples from 43 to 47 are in the same letter.

Several of the examples above have a pair followed by a generalising or other term introduced by e.g. *postremo, praeterea* or *denique* (cf. on 1, and also 25, 26, 33 and below, 3.3.3 (f)). Opinions may differ about the structure of such examples.

3.2.2 Adjectives

(48) *Cat.* 11.3 *ea (auaritia) semper <u>infinita insatiabilis</u> est, neque copia neque inopia minuitur*

Predicatives, two privative adjectives of ascending length and much the same semantic field. On the text here see below, 3.3.4. Note the contrast of opposites, coordinated, in the next clause. Neither Preuss (1881) nor Wölfflin (1933) cites examples of the combination *infinitus insatiabilis*. Cf. Lact. *Inst.* 4.26.12 *infinitae cupiditates . . . uel insatiabiles*.

Narrative.

(49) *Cat.* 11.5 *loca <u>amoena uoluptaria</u> facile in otio ferocis militum animos molliuerant,* 'Attractive and pleasurable localities had easily softened the defiant spirits of his soldiers during their periods of leisure' (Woodman 2007). Perhaps better, 'localities attractive, pleasurable'.

These attributive adjectives are loosely of the same semantic field, but the second is arguably stronger than the first.

Both 48 and 49 are in a moralising passage by Sallust (narrative).

(50) *Cat.* 18.4 *erat eodem tempore Cn. Piso, adulescens nobilis, summae audaciae, <u>egens factiosus</u>*

Adulescens has four epithets, but the final two form an asyndetic unit, with the second adjective possibly expressing a consequence of the first ('poverty stricken and (therefore) factious'). Or could there be an

adversative relationship: 'poverty stricken, but despite that (because of his *audacia*), factious'? For *egens* in asyndeta see below, 52.
Narrative.

(?) *Cat*. 19.1 *postea Piso in citeriorem Hispaniam quaestor pro praetore missus est adnitente Crasso, quod eum infestum inimicum Cn. Pompeio cognouerat*
These may be a pair of adjectives with the same prefix, but alternatively *inimicum* could be nominal.

(51) *Cat*. 25.2 *litteris Graecis [et] Latinis docta, psallere [et] saltare elegantius quam necesse est probae* (some manuscripts have *et* in both places).
This is the text as printed by Reynolds, OCT. Ramsey (2007) prints the first *et* but not that between the two verbs. He has no note on the text. If we were to take *docta* as both going with the ablatives *litteris Graecis/Latinis* and as governing the two infinitives *psallere/saltare* (on which possibility see Ramsey 2007: 133), a possible text would be *litteris Graecis Latinis docta, psallere et saltare elegantius quam*, with the asyndeton followed by a coordination. The adjectives are complements that constantly occur together. This is from a character sketch, from which another asyndeton bimembre is cited at 12 above. On the verbs here see Sallust 69.
Narrative.

(52) *Cat*. 33.1 *qui miseri egentes, uiolentia atque crudelitate faeneratorum plerique patriae, sed omnes fama atque fortunis expertes sumus*, 'we who, pitiful and needy, through the violence and cruelty of money-lenders are mostly lacking a fatherland, and are all lacking in fame and fortune'.
An asyndetic pair of adjectives with pathetic associations (secondary predicates, marked no doubt by a pause), followed by a much longer double-barrelled phrase dependent on *expertes*, which is a predicate with *sumus*. This is in the appeal of C. Manlius sent to Marcius Rex. *Egens* was seen above, 50 in asyndeton, and it is so used in Virgil (XXIV.2.1.1, 1 *ipse ignotus egens Libyae deserta peragro*) in a similar structure (in an asyndetic pair that follows a pronoun and is a secondary predicate in agreement with the subject of the verb). Cf. Ter. *Ph*. 751 *quae essem anus deserta egens ignota*, containing the same pair as in Virgil, and with the same reference to desolation (*deserta*), though it is expressed differently; and also Tac. *Ann*. 1.74.2 *egens ignotus inquies* (described by Goodyear 1981: 160 as an 'embarrassing echo' of Virgil, though it is just as likely, given the parallel in Terence, that this was a standard association of ideas; see further below). The combination in Sallust (*miseri egentes*) may be compared with that at

Ter. *Ph.* 357 (*egens relictast misera*), though there *misera* is probably attributive and *egens* predicative ('the poor girl's left penniless', Barsby, Loeb). In our passage the wretchedness is presumably caused by neediness, just as in 50 neediness may cause factiousness, though the placement of *egens* in relation to the juxtaposed adjective is different in the two passages.

Egens in asyndeta of varying length is not infrequently associated with expulsion from somewhere, as in the present passage, 52 (note *patriae . . . expertes*). Virgil 1 above is followed in the next line by *Europa atque Asia pulsus*. Note too Cic. *Quinct.* 62 *aliquem eiectum hominem, egentem litigiosum improbum*, *Fin.* 2.105 *expulsus egens, in palude demersus*, 5.84 *exsul orbus egens*, *Tusc.* 3.39 *Telamonem pulsum patria, exulantem atque egentem* (possibly a phrasal asyndeton bimembre, with the second member having its parts linked by *atque*; cf. Dougan and Henry 1934 ad loc.), Plautus *Rud.* 409 *timidas egentis eiectas exanimatas*, and Virgil (XXIV.2.2, 22) *eiectum litore, egentem*. On other such passages see Landgraf (1892), arguing for a connection with **exgens*. This suggestion is not convincing, but the contextual similarities between these various passages undermine Goodyear's idea that Tacitus specifically had Virgil in mind.

For *egens* see further on Cicero 41; also Lucretius (XXIV.7.2, 25) for *indigus*.

Speech.

(53) *Cat.* 39.2 *ipsi innoxii florentes, sine metu aetatem agere*, 'they themselves, unassailable, flourishing, lived a life free from dread'.

This is clearly an asyndeton bimembre, as the following phrase is the predicate with *aetatem agere*. Note the privative adjective in first position, a pattern found sometimes in Virgil (see 1 cited on 52 above, and also 15) and elsewhere. Again the adjectives, secondary predicates, are in agreement with the subject of the verb. The presence of *ipse* is also a feature shared by Virgil (see Virgil 1 again, and also 10 *ipse aeger anhelans* | *colla fouet*).

Narrative.

(?) *Cat.* 48.2 *incendium uero crudele inmoderatum ac sibi maxume calamitosum putabat*

Crudele 'cruel' is followed by a stronger word, *inmoderatum* 'excessive, going too far': 'they thought that burning was cruel – over the top'. Does *ac* introduce a new idea such that the first two adjectives are an embedded asyndeton bimembre, or should we see here end-of-list coordination? This looks like a tricolon with end-of-list coordination, the third member outdoing the other two ('and especially calamitous for themselves').

3 Sallust

Crudelis and *immoderatus* are juxtaposed in an asyndeton of three members at Cic. *Att.* 13.28.3 *superbum crudelem immoderatum fuisse*. For *immoderatus* in an asyndeton bimembre, though of different implication, see Livy 3.9.4 *immoderata infinita potestate* (in this example too the second adjective probably caps the first).
Narrative.

(?) *Cat.* 52.13 (speech of Cato) *malos ... loca taetra inculta, foeda atque formidulosa habere*, 'the wicked ... occupy places that are offensive, uncared for, foul and fearful'.

Opinions may again differ about the sequence of adjectives here. Is there a run of four, with coordination at the end, or are there two pairs? The typical structure of this group, with two words containing *atque* following the first two terms (see above, Sallust 3), may be thought to favour the idea that there is an asyndeton bimembre followed by a coordinated pair, but semantically there are not obviously two pairs (cf. Woodman 2007: 'places which are rotten, neglected, foul and fearful').

(54) *Jug.* 17.5 *mare saeuom importuosum; ager frugum fertilis, bonus pecori, arbori infecundus*

Two predicative adjectives without an expressed copula, the second a privative in *in-*. There follows an asyndetic phrasal tricolon, with a double chiasmus.
Narrative.

(55?) *Jug.* 18.2 *uagi palantes, quas nox coegerat sedes habebant*, translated by Woodman (2007) as 'wanderers and rovers, they took whatever abode night compelled them to have'.

This pair is discussed at II.3.2.2. Is there an asyndeton, as in the translation, or is the force perhaps 'wandering (*palantes*) aimless(ly) (*uagi*)'? In the latter case there would not be a true asyndeton. At *Jug.* 66.3 (*milites palantis inermos*) the adjective with *palantis* is predicative ('wandering unarmed'). Cf. e.g. *Jug.* 67.3 *intactus profugit* for this sort of predicative modifier. *Jug.* 66.3 (just quoted) along with Lucr. 5.973 (*nec plangore diem magno solemque per agros | quaerebant pauidi palantes noctis in umbris*, 'wandering in panic') suggests that *palantes* was prone to be used with a predicative complement, though there is an ambiguity here (see further II.3.2.2).
Narrative.

(56) *Jug.* 20.2 *ipse acer bellicosus*

Another predicative pair without copula, both terms of the same semantic field. Cf. Livy 21.16.3 *hostem acriorem bellicosioremque*, Sen. *Epist.* 83.22

acerrimas gentes bellicosasque. Bellicosus outdoes and is more specific than *acer*.
Narrative.

(57) *Jug.* 20.2 *at is quem petebat quietus inbellis, placido ingenio, opportunus iniuriae, metuens magis quam metuendus,* 'his target was peaceable, unwarlike, of placid disposition, vulnerable to wrongdoing, fearful rather than fearsome' (Woodman 2007).

A pair (of which the second term is more precise and stronger than the first) intended to contrast with those in the previous passage (56). The pair is similar to that in the next passage (and note the Tacitean parallels cited there). The asyndeton bimembre begins a longer sequence, and is followed by three asyndetic phrases (for this pattern cf. e.g. 35 with cross references, and 58).
Narrative.

(58) *Jug.* 44.1 *exercitus ei traditur a Sp. Albino proconsule iners inbellis, neque periculi neque laboris patiens, lingua quam manu promptior, praedator ex sociis et ipse praeda hostium, sine imperio et modestia habitus*

A long and varied phrasal asyndetic series, with, at the start, a single-word asyndeton bimembre, both of its terms privative adjectives. One of the definitions of *iners* given by the *TLL* VII.1.1309.1 is 'sine virtute bellica, ... imbellis', though this is not a meaning registered by the *OLD. Iners* can mean merely 'lazy'. *Inbellis* in our passage is climactic. A lazy army is one thing, whereas one unfit for war is out of line with the reason for its existence. There would in English be a pause between the two. *Iners inbellis* is not a pair noted either by Preuss (1881) or Wölfflin (1933). It does however occur with a coordinator at Livy 44.38.10 *iners atque imbellis*. Note too 57 above, where *inbellis* is in asyndeton with a different term, and also Hor. *Sat.* 2.7.39 *imbecillus iners* (XXIX.2.1.1) and Tacitus 82 *bellatorum imbellium*, 124 *imbelles inermes*. On 57 and 58 we see *imbellis* in asyndeton with four different terms.

Iners inbellis is postpositive, following both the noun in agreement and the verb. It is similar to secondary predicates in Virgil.
Narrative.

(59) *Jug.* 51.1 *facies totius negoti uaria incerta, foeda atque miserabilis*

A typical combination of two unitary pairs, the first asyndetic, the second with *atque*. The terms in asyndeton are virtual synonyms (compare 74.1 *uarius incertusque agitabat*; also Cic. *Div.* 2.128 *incidit in uisa uaria et incerta*), and semantically unlike the second pair. For *incertus*

in an asyndeton with a different word cf. Cicero 54 *cum alia omnia falsa incerta sint.*
Narrative.

(60) *Jug.* 89.5 *alia omnia uasta inculta, egentia aquae, infesta serpentibus*
Again the pattern whereby two uncoordinated single words are followed by asyndetic phrases. *Vasta* and *inculta* are vague terms of emptiness and neglect, whereas the two phrases are specific and about different dangers. For the association of ideas cf. Pac. *trag.* 232.2 Schierl *inculta uastitudine*, Sen. *Nat.* 1.praef.9 *inculta uastitas*. For *incultus* possibly in asyndeton with a different term, see *Cat.* 52.13 above (after 53).
Narrative.

(61) *Jug.* 91.7 *genus hominum mobile infidum, ante neque beneficio neque metu coercitum*
Mobilis is close in meaning to Eng. 'shifty' (see *OLD* s.v. 5 for some similar definitions), whereas *infidus* specifies the nature of the shiftiness: the referents let others down. Again the second term seems to strengthen the judgement. There follows a much longer phrase with a *neque . . . neque* construction, which introduces new elements to the characterisation. For asyndeta followed by *neque . . . neque* see above, 48, 58, and below, 70, 71. For the pairing cf. *Jug.* 46.3 *genus Numidarum infidum, ingenio mobili*. For *mobilis* in asyndeton with another term cf. Cicero 55 *caduca mobilia*.
Description.

(62?) *Hist.* 3.44.4 Ramsey *interdum lacerum corpus, semianimum omittentes*, 'by leaving in their wake mutilated, half-alive bodies' (Ramsey, Loeb).
The second adjective may express a consequence of the first (if we take the sense to be 'bodies mutilated, half-alive': predicative adjuncts). The order is discontinuous. Alternatively the two adjectives may differ in function, with the first attributive and the second predicative, 'leaving mutilated bodies half-alive'.
Narrative.

(63?) *Hist.* inc. 7 Ramsey (p. 402) *in nuda intecta corpora*
This is probably an asyndeton.
No context.

3.2.3 Verbs

(64) *Cat.* 6.5 *at Romani domi militiaeque intenti festinare parare, alius alium hortari, hostibus obuiam ire, libertatem patriam parentisque armis tegere*, 'But the Romans, at home and on campaign, concentrated on quickness,

preparation, mutual encouragement, confronting the enemy and protecting by arms their freedom and their fatherland and parents' (Woodman 2007).

A sequence of five infinitival constructions of ascending length dependent on *intenti*, with the first two verbs an asyndeton bimembre. For *festinare* in pairs in Sallust see below, 70 with cross references (also 3.3.2), and particularly 77 for this same combination. This pair expresses the general idea of hasty preparation, with *festinare* in effect a modifier (= *festinanter parare* or *festinantes parare*).

Libertatem patriam parentisque should not be interpreted as a tricolon with the structure ABCque. It is an asyndetic pair, [*libertatem*] + [*patriam parentisque*]. *Patria* and *parentes*, we have seen, are frequently paired (as at 17 and 46 above), with and without a coordinator, whereas liberty is an abstract concept and different in type. See further XVIII.4.

Narrative.

(65) *Cat.* 11.6 *ibi primum insueuit exercitus populi Romani* amare potare, *signa, tabulas pictas, uasa caelata mirari, ea priuatim et publice rapere, delubra spoliare, sacra profanaque omnia polluere*, 'that was the first time an army of the Roman people became accustomed to love-affairs and drink; to admire statues, paintings and engraved goblets; to seize them regardless of whether privately or publicly owned; to despoil shrines and to pollute everything sacred and profane alike' (Woodman 2007).

Amare potare falls into the semantic category labelled on Plautus XXIII.8.2 as 'decadent or depraved behaviour' (from the viewpoint of the speaker or writer). Various asyndeta (with two or more members) expressing whoring, drinking and eating are found in Plautus and elsewhere (see XXIII.8.2). The pair is also at 78 below, and at Plaut. *Poen.* 661, and it may have been an old expression of disapproval. Here it precedes four infinitival phrases also uncoordinated. For this type of accumulation see the preceding example, which is structurally the same: two dependent infinitives are followed by a series of asyndetic infinitival phrases, all dependent on the same term as the initial pair. Following *amare potare* is an asyndetic tricolon expressing items of luxury, for which type see above, 2.2, 8 on a passage of Cato.

Narrative.

(66) *Cat.* 12.2 rapere consumere, *sua parui pendere, aliena cupere, pudorem pudicitiam, diuina atque humana promiscua ... habere*

Another moralising passage. This too is typical of Sallust's structural use of asyndeton, containing as it does asyndetic pairs within a longer sequence

(see above, 3). Semantically the pair belongs to a type expressing forceful seizure of something followed by its use, misuse or destruction: cf. Sallust 68, 81 (quoted also below on 68).
Narrative.

(67) *Cat.* 16.3 *nihilo minus insontis sicuti sontis* circumuenire iugulare, 'he would nonetheless entrap and butcher the guiltless no differently from the guilty' (Woodman 2007).
A pair of asyndetic historic infinitives referring to actions in sequence. The pairing is semantically similar to that at 66, and to the others cited there; see also above on 2.1, 2.
Narrative.

(68) *Cat.* 20.12 *postremo omnibus modis pecuniam* trahunt uexant
A similar sequence again, 'they carry off and make inroads into money by every means at their disposal' (from the speech of Catiline, which, we saw, is full of asyndeta: see above, on 6–10, and also 3.3.1 below). For *traho* meaning 'take away illegally' see *OLD* s.v. 5a, and for *uexo* 'make inroads on', *OLD* s.v. 3b. They get hold of money that is not theirs and then waste it away (cf. 66). Sallust had a liking for this use of *traho* in asyndeta: cf. *Jug.* 41.5 *ducere trahere rapere* ('appropriated, looted and seized', Woodman 2007), and the fragment of the *Histories*, below 81 *trahant excindant*; cf. in an imitator, *Epist. Caes.* 2.3.4, p. 500 Ramsey *trahunt rapiunt*, with the same combination as in the *Jug.* above. Tac. *Ann.* 4.25.2 (*pecorum modo trahi occidi capi*) is quoted and discussed below on Sallust 76.

(69) *Cat.* 25.2 *litteris Graecis [et] Latinis docta,* psallere [et] saltare elegantius quam necesse est probae (some manuscripts have *et* in both places: see above on 51). On the difference between the two verbs see Ramsey (2007: 133): *psallere* means 'both to play a stringed instrument ... and to sing to this musical accompaniment, while *cantare* ... means simply "to sing"'. They are complementary, members of a set.
Narrative.

(70) *Cat.* 27.2 *dies noctisque* festinare uigilare, *neque insomniis neque labore fatigari,* 'Day and night he hurried and watched, and was exhausted by neither sleeplessness nor toil' (Woodman 2007).
Vigilare is picked up by *neque insomniis,* which has an adversative relationship to *uigilare* ('but was not exhausted by sleeplessness'), and *festinare* (loosely) by *neque labore fatigari,* which has the same adversative relationship to *festinare.* We refer to such patterns as 'correlative distribution' (see XVII). There is also a chiastic connection between the two initial

verbs and the following phrases (for this pattern cf. Tacitus *Annals* 159 with cross references). The verbs are not closely connected semantically, but both refer to relentless activity. See the next example for the function that such pairs may have in Sallust. Sallust, as remarked above, often uses *festino* in asyndeta bimembria (see 64, 71, 73, 77, 82: see 3.3.2), and indeed in the historic infinitive. For *neque . . . neque* constructions following an asyndeton bimembre see on 61 above, and the next passage.

For *uigilo* with a different verb in asyndeton, see below, 73.
Narrative.

(71) *Cat.* 31.2 *festinare trepidare, neque loco neque homini quoiquam satis credere, neque bellum gerere neque* . . ., 'People hurried and trembled; they did not quite trust any place or any individual; they were neither waging war nor . . .' (Woodman 2007).

The asyndeton bimembre is followed again by phrases with negative coordinators (*neque*), as in 70 and elsewhere. The two verbs seem to convey a single idea (that people were in a state of fearful haste), = *festinare trepidanter, trepide, trepidantes*.

For *festino* and *trepido* associated see e.g. the anaphoric construction at Plaut. *Cas.* 432 *ut ille trepidabat, ut festinabat miser* (see *TLL* VI.1.617.72ff.).
Narrative.

(72) *Cat.* 42.2 *nocturnis consiliis, armorum atque telorum portationibus, festinando agitando omnia plus timoris quam periculi effecerant*, 'by nighttime meetings, by moving arms and weapons about and by hurrying and general agitation, they had caused more fear than danger' (Woodman 2007).

Here an asyndeton bimembre with homoeoteleuton is contained within a long phrasal sequence. The second member *agitando* is extended (by *omnia*). The relation between the verbs is similar to that in 71 (= 'by hurrying in agitation'). For ablative gerunds in asyndeton, an old and persistent type, with assonance by definition, see XXIII.5.4. Woodman (2018: 71) remarks that Wölfflin (1900: 29–30) gives no example of an asyndetic pair of gerunds from Sallust.
Narrative.

(73) *Cat.* 54.4 *postremo Caesar in animum induxerat laborare uigilare; negotiis amicorum intentus sua neglegere, nihil denegare quod dono dignum esset*, 'Caesar, finally, had made up his mind to be hard-working and vigilant; devoted to the enterprises of his friends, he would neglect his own and refuse nothing that was worth giving' (Woodman 2007).

3 Sallust

This is a passage of characterisation. Following the asyndetic infinitives comes a pair of asyndetic clauses (cf. e.g. 64, 65, 66). There is a similarity to 70, with the two verbs in each case expressing a combination of watchfulness and activity (here = *laborare uigilanter*).
Narrative.

(74) *Jug.* 10.8 *colite obseruate talem hunc uirum, imitamini uirtutem et enitimini ne* . . . 'pay attention and respect to such a man as this; imitate his prowess and strive to ensure . . .' (Woodman 2007).

Four imperatives. The first two, in asyndeton, are near-synonyms (*colite* = 'cultivate', and *obseruo* can mean 'watch with admiration' (*OLD* 2d)). *Obseruo* and *colo* are often combined, with coordination: see *TLL* IX.2.212.48ff. (note Cic. *Fam.* 13.29.1 *obseruari coli diligi* for absence of coordination in a longer sequence). The next two imperatives are coordinated. They have the same ending, and are more diffuse in their semantics. The coordination here is by means of *et*, whereas Sallust usually uses *atque* in such an attached phrase (see 6.2b).

Imperatives in asyndeton are widespread from early Latin (see X, and XXIII.5.1).
Speech.

(75) *Jug.* 11.8 *ira et metu anxius moliri parare atque ea modo cum animo habere quibus Hiempsal per dolum caperetur,* 'under the strain of anger and dread, he laboured and prepared, and in his mind he considered only how Hiempsal might be seized by cunning' (Woodman 2007).

Moliri and *parare* are near-synonyms, and then there is an expansion introduced by *atque*, which is more specific. I take the first two verbs as an embedded asyndeton.
Narrative.

(76) *Jug.* 62.1 *multos mortalis captos occisos*
Either a temporal sequence or disjunctive (cf. *Jug.* 65.3 *si Iugurtha captus aut occisus foret*). This is part of a series of accusative + infinitive clauses uncoordinated (two before *captos occisos* and one after). For this pair of verbs associated see Enn. *Ann.* 289 Skutsch *summus ibi capitur meddix, occiditur alter*, and particularly Cicero 205 *multi occisi capti, reliqui dissipati*. In the order in this last example the two look disjunctive, but are not necessarily so: note (with the alliterative simplex *caesi* rather than *occisi*) Livy 4.61.6 *infra arcem caesi captique multi mortales* (there were many killings and captures); also Livy 23.37.6 *ad mille trecenti Carthaginiensium caesi et undesexaginta uiui capti*. For the association of these two terms (I do not make a distinction here between the simplex *caedo* and the compound

occido) see also Livy 38.23.5 *cecidere aut cepere*, 42.7.1 *septem milia Corsorum caesa, capti amplius mille et septingenti* (also e.g. 42.7.9). At Tac. *Ann.* 4.25.2 (*pecorum modo trahi occidi capi*) the translation (with coordination) 'they were dragged off, killed and captured' would not work. There is a varied relationship between the components. *Trahi* would be followed by a coordinator such as *et* if the group were filled out, but in the order *occidi capi* this pair is disjunctive: 'they were dragged off and killed or taken into captivity' (an asyndeton bimembre [*trahi*] [*occidi capi*], itself containing as its second member another asyndeton bimembre).

The original pair was presumably *caesus* (not *occisus*) + *captus*. See further below, 80.

Speech (indirect).

(77) *Jug.* 76.4 *contra haec oppidani festinare parare*, 'in response to these measures, the townsfolk lost no time in their preparations' (Woodman 2007).

I take it that *parare* is not dependent on *festinare*, but = 'made haste and prepared'. As we have seen, *festino* (as historic infinitive) is a favourite of Sallust's in such pairings (the same pair is at **64** above: = *festinanter parare*), and there are places where it cannot be interpreted as governing the infinitive that follows: note e.g. above, 70, 71.

Narrative.

(78) *Jug.* 85.41 *ament potent*
See above, **65**.
Speech.

(79, 80) *Jug.* 101.11 *sequi fugere, occidi capi*
Two juxtaposed asyndeta bimembria. The first is a pair of opposites ('pursuit and flight', converses here: see XIII.4.3), and the second a (disjunctive) formula (cf. **76**). For the association of *sequor* and *fugio* see Lucan 2.575 *non te fugiunt, me cuncta secuntur*, an association that according to *TLL* VI.1.1494.43f. is found often (no other examples cited). See also Tac. *Ann.* 6.35.1 *cum Parthus sequi uel fugere pari arte suetus distraheret turmas*.

Narrative.

(81) *Hist.* 4.60.17 Ramsey *inopes potentisque trahant excindant*
For *traho* in asyndeta see above, **68**. This same verb *excindo* is placed second in an asyndeton at Tacitus **133**.
Letter (direct address, = speech).

(82) *Hist.* inc. 9, p. 404 Ramsey *diu noctuque laborare festinare*

Festino in a modifying role again, = *laborare festinanter/festinantes*
No context.

3.2.4 Adverbs

(83) *Hist.* 4.60.17 Ramsey *socios amicos, procul iuxta sitos, inopes potentisque*
Opposites (antonyms). For a disjunctive role made explicit see Tac. *Hist.* 2.74.1 *procul uel iuxta*. This is one of those places where two asyndeta bimembria alongside each other are of different types: see on Sallust 47.
Letter = speech.

3.2.5 Prepositional Type

(84) *Cat.* 6.1 *genus hominum agreste, sine legibus sine imperio, liberum atque solutum*
Here again a coordinated pair follows, with the similar terms linked by *atque* (see above, 3). On the structure of this example and its relation to a passage of Tacitus, see 6.2a.
Narrative.

(85) *Cat.* 20.7 *uolgus fuimus sine gratia sine auctoritate*
See above, 6–10. For *gratia* in asyndeta see 25.
Speech.

(86) *Cat.* 47.1 *interrogatus de itinere de litteris, postremo quid aut qua de causa consili habuisset*
The structure is typical again (note *postremo*, and see above, 26).
Narrative.

(87) *Cat.* 59.5 *rogat ut meminerint se contra latrones inermos pro patria pro liberis, pro aris atque focis suis certare*
For asyndetic listing of one's highest moral obligations see also on 17 above. Note the following pair coordinated by *atque*, a combination found in this form also at 17.
Indirect speech.

(88) *Jug.* 10.1 *amisso patre, sine spe sine opibus in meum regnum accepi*
Speech.

(89) *Hist.* 4.60.21 Ramsey *exercitum sine frumento sine auxiliis*
Letter = speech.

3.3 Sallust: Conclusions

3.3.1 Contexts, Narrative versus Speech

Of the 89 numbered examples listed here, 2 are in such fragmentary contexts that it cannot be determined whether the passages contained narrative or a speech. Of the remaining 87, 33 are in speeches or the like, a substantial proportion (about 38 per cent). Moreover speeches tend to have accumulations of asyndeta bimembria. The speech of Catiline (*Cat.* 20) has seven such pairs (see on 10), and it also has other forms of asyndeton. Other clusters are in a speech by Caesar (13, 14, 15, 16), one by Cato (17, 18, 19, possibly *Cat.* 52.13, quoted after 53), that by Marius (38, 78), and in the letter of Mithridates in the *Histories*, which, as a form of direct address, is much the same as a speech (43–7, 83, 89). To Sallust asyndeton bimembre, particularly occurring in clusters, had a rhetorical character. Just as Catiline is given a particularly striking collection of asyndeta in his speech, so Cicero, as we have seen, at certain points of his own Catilinarians made conspicuous use of asyndeton (see Cicero 3, 4, and the conclusions, XXVI.7.6). In the late Republic accumulated asyndeton (bimembre, and also longer, as in Catiline's speech at *Cat.* 51) was certainly associated with orations delivered in dramatic political (or military) contexts.

3.3.2 Parts of Speech and Some Aspects of Uniformity

I have used the term 'narrative' to embrace contexts other than speeches, but it is not uniformly appropriate. Ash (2007: 87) says of one type (comprising historic infinitives) that it features 'especially in historians for rapid sequences of events', which may be true up to a point (see however V and XXXI.3.7), but in fact outside speeches asyndeton bimembre in Sallust is found particularly, not in narrative as such, but in moralising remarks or generalisations (e.g. 1, 2, 3, 22, 48) and character sketches (e.g. 12, 20, 34, 50, 51, 61). It is in line with this tendency that asyndetic pairs often denote virtues or vices (see on 1).

I have numbered above 47 asyndeta bimembria comprising nouns, 16 comprising adjectives and 19 comprising verbs. Wölfflin (1900: 30) states that asyndetic pairs of substantives are not particularly frequent in Sallust, but in fact they are the predominant type. Within these three categories a few addititional examples have been left unnumbered. The list is as complete as I could make it without reading the whole text again, and some examples may have been missed. In dealing with Sallust (but not other historians) I have been less than systematic in looking for adverbial pairs, and the single example given here may well only be part of the story.

3 Sallust

Within the three main categories (nouns, adjectives, verbs) there is a good deal of uniformity or repetitiveness. Structural aspects are dealt with later. Here I am only concerned with verbal uniformities.

The same noun tends to come up more than once, usually with different complements. *Pericula* occurs at *Cat.* 10.2 (quoted before 1), in the passage 6–10 in a tetracolon and at *Cat.* 20.15 quoted after 6–10. In both of the latter two sequences *egestas* also is found. *Probitas* and *industria* occur twice together (22, 35), and *probitas* is with another noun (*fides*) at 1. *Fides* also recurs, with a different noun (26). *Patria parentes* occurs twice (17, 46), as do *patria domus* (23, 24) and *arma tela* (31, 36). *Domus* occurs in other combinations at 18 and 45. *Arma* is also at 16 (with *cadauera*) and 43 (with *uiri*). *Gratia* is at 9 and 25, *clamor* at 30 and 39 and *ager* at 27 and 45. *Vir, uiri* are in various combinations (12, 32, 43). *Amicitia* is at 41 and *amicus* at 47.

Adjectives and particularly verbs also recur. Of adjectives, *egens* is at 50 and 52, *imbellis* at 57 and 59, *incultus* at *Cat.* 52.13 quoted after 53 and 60. For *festinare* see 64, 70, 71, 72, 77, 82 (at 64 and 77, *festinare parare*), for *parare* the last two examples and 75, for *amare potare* 65 and 78, for *uigilare* 70 and 73, for *occidi capi* 76 and 80, for *trahere* 68 and 81, and for *laborare* 73 and 82.

Some of the combinations are banal or formulaic, in that they occur in asyndeton, bimembre or longer, in other writers (3 *pudor pudicitia*, 14 *uirgines pueri*, 15 *caedes incendia*, 17 *patria parentes*, 18 *domus uillae*, 23 *patria domus*, 27 *urbs ager*, 31 *arma tela*, 32 *equi uiri*, 37 *locus tempus*, 40 *dextra sinistra*, 42 *cognatio adfinitas*, 43 *uiri arma*, 47 *socius amicus*, *Cat.* 48.2, quoted after 53, *crudelis immoderatus*, 59 *uarius incertus*, 65 *amare potare*, 74 *colere obseruare*, 76 *occidi capi*).

In the above list most of the pairs are nominal, with pairs of adjectives and verbs far less common. Similarly it is shown elsewhere (XXVI.7.7) that Cicero was more given to using banal asyndetic pairs of nouns than he was to using formulaic pairs of adjectives and verbs, and that pattern suggests that adjectives and verbs could more readily be juxtaposed off-the-cuff in new combinations. Was this a form of linguistic inventiveness current in the late Republic?

Nine of the sixteen numbered adjectival asyndeta contain at least one privative adjective (in *in*): 48, 53, 54, 57, 58, 59, 60, 61, 63. Two of these (48, 58) have a pair of privatives, and in all but one of the others the privative is in second place (the exception is 53). In this Sallust resembles Virgil and others. Two unnumbered sequences also have a privative in second place (both quoted after 53). Most of the pairs with privatives are either predicates with the verb 'to be' expressed or understood, or predicative adjuncts (the only exception is 63).

Nineteen pairs of verbs are numbered. Nine are historic infinitives: 66, 67, 70, 71, 75, 77, 79, 80, 82. There are also infinitives of other types: 64, 65, 69 (?), 73. Thirteen of the pairs consist of infinitives. On asyndetic pairs of historic infinitives see Wölfflin (1900: 28).

There are some recurrent usages with verbs. *Festino*, we saw above, occurs six times in asyndeta bimembria, in every case but one (82) preceding the other verb. Every example of *festino* is juxtaposed with another first conjugation verb, and homoeoteleuton is the result. *Festino* seems to colour the other verb, without having it as dependent: to hurry in one's toil or preparations, to be in a state of agitated haste, to be in a state of trembling haste, to be urgent in one's watchfulness. For other verbs recurring in asyndeton see above.

In a number of cases we have suggested that in pairs of verbs one acts as a modifier of the other (cf. in the last paragraph the comment on *festino*): 64, 71, 72, 73, 77, 82. This is a distinctive feature of Sallust's use of asyndeton of verbs. Much the same relationship between two terms in asyndeton has been seen elsewhere.

Some pairs belong to semantic categories that tend to generate asyndeta, and not only in Sallust. Pairs to do with exile and expulsion are often asyndetic (see 23, 24, 52), as are pairs of verbs expressing violent acts (67, 76, 80, 81) and of nouns denoting virtues or vices (see on 1). Asyndetic pairs to do with shouting, complaint, din are not uncommon (30, 39). Items of luxury or forms of behaviour deemed 'decadent' attract asyndeta (4, 19, 65, 78). One semantic category that occurs in Sallust but is not as common as in some writers is that consisting of pairs of opposites. See 3 *pudor pudicitia*, 13 *odium amicitia*, 14 *uirgines pueri*, 21 *laetitia maeror*, 27 *urbes agri*, 40 *dextra sinistra*, 79 *sequi fugere*, 83 *procul iuxta*.

3.3.3 Structural Patterns
I list here the main types.

(a) The asyndeton bimembre is followed (or occasionally preceded) by a pair linked by *atque*.

3, 8, 12 (the *atque*-phrase precedes), 13, 16, 17, 21, 28, 29 (with a separation), 30, 31, 32 (here the *atque*- phrase follows a double asyndeton bimembre), *Cat.* 52.13 quoted after 53, 59, 87. Occasionally the following pair is linked by *et*: 28, 74. A specific type is that in which *atque* links two terms that are not syntactically the same as the asyndetic pair (see 84). Roughly 20 per cent of

3 *Sallust*

the asyndeta bimembria in Sallust occur in this pattern (a). Cicero, for example, quite often has a coordinated pair after an asyndetic (XXVI.7.2.1, 7.3.1 (iii)), but what is distinctive about Sallust's usage is his taste for *atque* in this structure.

(b) *Ceterique* (or *aliique* or *et alii*) follows, introducing a generalisation.
1, 4, 22 (*aliasque*), 38 (*et alia*).

(c) The asyndeton bimembre is followed by different types of asyndeta (clausal, phrasal, tricola etc.) of varying number.
2, 27, 29, 35, 39, 57, 60, 64, 65, 66, 73.

(d) The asyndeton bimembre is preceded by different types of asyndeta.
3, 50, 72.

(e) There is an accumulation of asyndeta bimembria in the same sentence or short passage, sometimes comprising two examples, usually juxtaposed but sometimes separated (18, 19, 31, 32, 36, 37, 41, 42, 44, 45, 47, 51 (?), 69 (?), 79, 80), sometimes more examples (6, 7, 8, 85 [in the same passage as 6–8 and the following two], 9, 10, 47, the last with three different types of asyndeton bimembre, nominal, adverbial and verbal, all close together in the same clause).

Juxtaposed asyndeta bimembria are by no means confined to high literature. Note the pairs in curse tablets (including one such tablet in Oscan) cited by Adams (2016: 111), and also *per scutum per ocream egi aginaui* in a freedman's speech at Petron. 61.9.

(f) The asyndeton bimembre is followed by phrases introduced by *neque . . . neque*.
48, 58, 70, 71.

(g) The asyndeton bimembre is followed by *denique* introducing a more general phrase.
25, 36, 37. See Wölfflin (1900: 34).

(h) The asyndeton bimembre is followed by *postremo* introducing a more general phrase.
26, 29, 86. See Wölfflin (1900: 34).

(i) The asyndeton bimembre is followed by a phrase or term introduced by *praeterea*.
33, 34, 43. See Wölfflin (1900: 34).

It is difficult to compile statistics because there are overlapping categories above, but a very high proportion of examples of asyndeton bimembre of our type in Sallust occurs in certain structural patterns, usually marked by an accumulation of phrases of definable types. In the categories listed above at (a)–(e) there are more than 50 passages listed. Asyndeta bimembria may occur in isolation in unique contexts, but more often than not they are fitted into the patterns listed above.

3.3.4 Textual Matters

In the vast majority of cases where Reynolds (OCT) prints an asyndeton in his text of the *Catiline* and *Jugurtha* no textual variants are reported in his apparatus criticus. Where there are variants it is sometimes possible to support his text by reference to structural features of a passage. At 8 *strenui boni, nobiles atque ignobiles*, where *V* has *et* rather than *atque* between the second two terms, and has *atque* between *strenui* and *boni*, a distinctive Sallustian pattern would be eliminated by the changes. As for 48 *infinita insatiabilis*, Gellius 3.1.2 quotes the passage with *et* after *infinita*, but it would be unconvincing to remove a double privative asyndeton on such evidence, particularly since the pair is followed by a *neque . . . neque* construction, a pattern found elsewhere in Sallust (see above, 3.3.3f). Moreover at 58, as at 48, the pair followed by *neque . . . neque* consists of privative adjectives. In both 8 and 48 therefore the asyndeton is supported by structural features.

At 74 *colite obseruate* is given an *et* in some manuscripts and in Priscian, but the asyndetic pair, if it is accepted, is followed by a coordinated pair of imperatives, another accumulation of the type seen above. Asyndeton is particularly common in pairs of imperatives (see X).

At 70 *dies noctisque festinare uigilare* the omission of the *-que* in some manuscripts would produce juxtaposed asyndetic pairs of different parts of speech, a structure that does occur but is unusual in Sallust (see 47). The asyndeton is attested (see Preuss 1881: 33–4). 82, however (*diu noctuque laborare festinare*), gives support to the subordinator at 70.

In some other places I can see no other criterion for deciding between asyndeton and coordination than the relative reliability of manuscripts in the judgement of an editor: see 12 *uiro liberis* (with or without *atque*?), 40 *dextra sinistra* (or *sinistraque*?: Sallust elsewhere has the pair coordinated but asyndeton is well attested in this pair particularly in the early period), 51 and 69 (two pairs in the same sentence), *Cat.* 27.2 *uti semper intenti parati(que)* (see Wölfflin 1900: 30).

Punctuation of asyndetic sequences causes editors endless trouble, and consistency seems rarely achieved. I offer a few illustrations from the OCT. At 33 Reynolds prints *sudis pila, praeterea picem . . .*, with the asyndetic pair lacking a comma before another item introduced by *praeterea*. On the other hand the same structure at 42, *cognationem adfinitatem, praeterea foedus*, is given a comma within the asyndeton. At 34 (*lapides ignem, alia praeterea*) the Latin, as at 33, has an asyndetic pair of items used as weapons, followed by *praeterea* again, and here Reynolds inserts a comma within the pair.

At 1 (*fidem probitatem ceterasque artis bonas*) the first two abstracts are not separated by a comma. On the other hand at 22 two very similar abstracts (one of them *probitatem* again) are followed by an identical phrase introduced by *-que* (*probitatem industriam aliasque artis bonas*), and here Reynolds puts a comma between the abstracts.

At 30 *terrebat eum clamore uoltu* is followed by several more ablative phrases. Reynolds punctuates with a comma between *clamore* and *uoltu*. At 39 there are again two ablatives referring to a threatening din (*strepitu clamore*), and again ablative phrases and asyndeta follow, but here Reynolds does not put a comma between the initial ablative pair.

The two privative adjectives of ascending length, *infinita insatiabilis*, at 48 are both predicates with the verb 'to be', which follows. Reynolds does not insert a comma. The two adjectives of ascending length, *saeuom importuosum* (54), are also predicates with the verb 'to be' (understood), and the second of them is privative. Here Reynolds does insert a comma. He does so too at 57 (*quietus inbellis*), where the terms are once again predicates with the verb 'to be' understood. On the other hand at 61 (*genus hominum mobile infidum*), where yet again the second adjective is privative and the pair are predicates with 'to be' understood, no comma is used. By contrast 56 (*ipse acer bellicosus*), a sentence in itself without the copula expressed, is punctuated with a comma between the adjectives.

The two historic infinitives *festinare trepidare* at 71 are without a comma, whereas another such pair at 77, *festinare parare*, is given a comma. 66 (*rapere consumere*) and 67 (*circumuenire iugulare*) both express similar temporal sequences (seizure, entrapment followed by misuse/slaughter). The first is without a comma but the second has one.

4 Tacitus *Histories*

4.1 The Evidence

4.1.1 Nouns

(1, 2) *Hist.* 1.10.2 <u>luxuria industria</u>, <u>comitate adrogantia</u>, *malis bonisque artibus mixtus*, 'he had a mixture of luxury and industry, affability and arrogance, good and bad arts'

Three pairs of virtual opposites, the first two pairs asyndeta bimembria. In the third there is a coordinator, *-que*, which makes the structure similar to some in Sallust, with *atque* (see above on Sallust, 3.3.3a). For the coordinators in such added phrases in Tacitus, see below, 14, and for full details, 6.2b. By 'virtual' opposites I mean terms that are not explicitly opposites in one of the technical senses applied to 'opposites' in lexical semantics, but are nevertheless markedly contrastive and could be paraphrased with a real pair of opposites (see XIII.5.5). Tacitus in the *Histories* has juxtaposed asyndetic pairs of opposites (not infrequently inexplicit) at 4, 6, 7, 21, 22 as well as here (see also 4.2.3a, and for the *Annals*, 5.2.3).

For the threefold structure of the present example, with two unitary asyndeta bimembria followed by a third element showing coordination, cf. Sallust 31, 32 *arma tela, equi uiri, hostes atque ciues*. This third element also contains opposites (antonyms).

Although Sallust juxtaposes asyndetic opposites sometimes (3.3.2), and although he does juxtapose two asyndetic pairs (3.3.3e), he does not juxtapose two pairs of asyndetic opposites in this way. Sometimes however an asyndetic pair of opposites is followed by opposites linked by *atque* (see Sallust 3 with cross references).

The third element of the Tacitean passage above (*malis bonisque artibus*) has a distinctive structural feature. Whereas the first two elements comprise free-standing nouns that are opposed, in the third the opposed terms are adjectives dependent on a single noun, *artibus*, which continues the sequence of ablatival abstracts. The opposition in this case is embedded in the phrase instead of being free-standing and belonging to the same part of speech as the preceding ablatives. For this syntactic inconcinnity in Tacitus see on 72, and below, 6.2b. Sallust virtually never has such structures.

For *industria* in asyndeton bimembre combined with an opposite, see 4 below. Sallust also has *industria* in such asyndeta (22, 35).
Narrative.

(3) *Hist.* 1.22.1 <u>adulteria matrimonia</u> *ceterasque regnorum libidines*
Adultery and marriage are (virtual) opposites, illicit and licit liaisons, and then there is a generalisation introduced by *ceterasque*. Tacitus several times has this pattern. In view of the unity of the first pair I classify it as an asyndeton bimembre. For this structure (with *ceterasque*), see Sallust 1, with cross references, 3.3.3b and XVIII.6. For *adulteria* in an asyndeton bimembre see Tacitus 74.
Narrative.

(4) *Hist.* 2.5.2 *tribuni centurionesque et uolgus militum* <u>industria licentia</u>, *per uirtutes per uoluptates, ut cuique ingenium adsciscebantur*
'By industry or by licence, by virtues or by pleasures' is phraseology containing two disjunctive pairs each expressing virtual opposites (the first

4   *Tacitus* Histories   589

amounting to 'hard work' versus 'idleness', the second to 'virtue' versus 'addiction to vices').
   For the combining of an asyndetic pair with a pair showing repetition of a preposition cf. e.g. Sallust 8 *strenui boni, nobiles atque ignobiles, uolgus fuimus sine gratia sine auctoriate*, and for full details below, 6.2a. For an example outside high literature see Petron. 61.9 (freedman's speech) *per scutum per ocream egi aginaui*. The pattern is common in Cicero: see 48, 49, 79, 82, 87, 88, 155; note too Livy 42. See on Sallust 47 for other juxtaposed asyndeta bimembria of which the two pairs are of different types.
   Narrative.

(5) *Hist.* 2.29.2 *silentio patientia, postremo precibus ac lacrimis ueniam quaerebant*
   Two pairs, the first asyndetic, the second introduced by *postremo* and with members linked by *ac*. The two contrast with each other, the first expressing endurance in silence, the second noisy appeal. *Silentio* and *patientia* are near-synonyms, or the first may be interpreted as modifying the second (= 'silent endurance') (cf. on Cicero 56 *patiuntur tacent*). This relationship, modifier/modified, between two terms juxtaposed ('asyndetic hendiadys'), has recurred throughout this chapter: see (e.g.) 2.1, 6; cf. *intueri mirari* at 31 below, above, 3.2.2, second last paragraph, on Sallust, and also II.3.2.3.
   For *precibus ac lacrimis* cf. Livy 23.8.4 *uictusque patris precibus lacrimisque*.
   For the structure of our example, with at least one asyndeton bimembre followed by *postremo* introducing a final phrase of a different sort, see e.g. Sallust 26 along with 3.3.3h, and XVIII.6.
   Tacitus' use of *ac* here to coordinate *precibus* and *lacrimis* is as close as he gets to the Sallustian use of *atque* after an asyndetic pair (see 3.3.3a, 6.2b). For *ac* see below, 19 (though there the coordinated expression is attached to the asyndetic by *-que*), and for Tacitus' other coordinators in this position, below, 14, and 6.2b. Ash (2007: 156) takes the above sequence of nouns as a 'tricolon crescendo', but there are two distinct pairs, semantically distinguished, the first asyndetic, the second coordinated, a classic structure.
   One final point may be made about this passage. After the part quoted above there is at the end of the next sentence (§3) *gaudium miseratio fauor*. In Tacitus, as in Sallust, asyndetic sequences of different lengths tend to occur together in accumulations. See below, 16, with a parallel from Sallust, and 6.2d.
   Narrative.

(6) *Hist.* 2.80.1 *dum quaeritur tempus locus, quodque in re tali difficillimum est, prima uox*

The asyndetic combination 'time, place' is found in Sallust (see 37). The *-que* introducing a parenthetical explanatory clause seems to set the third term *prima uox* off from the first pair, which I treat as an embedded asyndeton bimembre. For *tempus* and *locus* coordinated, see the various passages quoted on Sallust 37.
Narrative.

(7, 8) *Hist.* 2.80.1 *dum animo spes timor, ratio casus obuersantur*

Two pairs of virtual opposites, hope and fear, i.e. optimism versus pessimism (a common juxtaposition, usually with a coordinator: for Tacitus see Gerber, Greef and John 1891–1903: 2.1536 s.v. *spes* a for a long list of passages with *spes* opposed to *metus*), and planning versus acceptance of chance. See also Tacitus 146 for 'fear/hope' in a phrasal asyndeton, and cf. *spes metus* at Livy 30.32.5 (text debated: Preuss 1881: 36).
Narrative.

(9) *Hist.* 2.86.2 *strenuus manu, sermone promptus, serendae in alios inuidiae artifex, discordiis et seditionibus potens, raptor largitor, pace pessimus, bello non spernendus*

A series of pairs (mostly phrasal), the last two, including *raptor largitor*, expressing opposites. *Raptor largitor* is a variant on the 'give/take' pairing, converses (see XIII.2). The final pair is phrasal, and contains a double opposition, 'peace/war', 'bad/quite good' (antonyms). The contrast *pessimus/non spernendus* illustrates vividly Tacitus' taste for inexplicit opposites.

For asyndeta bimembria preceded by phrasal asyndeta, as here, see, on Sallust, 3.3.3d; for Tacitus, see e.g. below, 31, and 4.2.4c (on phrasal asyndeta either preceding or following).
Narrative.

(10) *Hist.* 2.91.1 *pari libertorum amicorum socordia*

Nouns expressing some sort of personal relationship to the subject are not infrequently without coordinators (see Sallust 12, 47, Tacitus 63, 72; also 16, with an asyndetic tricolon of this semantic type). Sallust 47 combines *amicos* with *socios*: *amicus* is another word that occurs in asyndeton with various terms.
Narrative.

(11) *Hist.* 3.27.2 *dum e proximis agris ligones dolabras et alii falces scalasque conuectant*

There are two pairs of nouns here, the first asyndetic, the second (linked to the first by *et*: see on Tacitus 75 for this structure, with cross references;

4 *Tacitus* Histories 591

also below, 19, with *-que*, and for further details, below, 6.2g). Tacitus has truncated the usual *alii* ... *alii* construction by leaving out the first *alii*. For a comparable asyndetic pairing (tools/weapons listed: here *ligones* = 'mattocks', *dolabras* = 'picks') see Sallust 33 (*sudis pila*).
Narrative.

(12) *Hist*. 3.33.2 *utque exercitu uario linguis moribus*
Cf. Curt. 4.13.4 *hostes: discordis moribus linguis* (similar context). For *mores* in asyndetic pairings see below on Tacitus 78.
Narrative.

(13) *Hist*. 3.49.1 *felicitas in tali ingenio auaritiam superbiam ceteraque occulta mala patefecit*
A pair of vices, which I take to be in asyndeton, followed by a generalisation introduced by *ceteraque* (see above, Tacitus 3, with cross references) though some may prefer to see end-of-list coordination. Of nouns in asyndeton in the *Histories*, this is the only pair denoting vices. Otherwise Tacitus in the *Histories* has pairs of virtues and vices (1, 2, 4), and pairs of virtues (5, 17). See Sallust 1 and Cicero 17 and XXVI.7.8.2.
Narrative.

(14) *Hist*. 3.86.1 *consulatum sacerdotia, nomen locumque inter primores nulla sua industria, sed cuncta patris claritudine adeptus*
Two pairs, the second coordinated by *-que*. For this structure see *Annals* 158. Tacitus allows in such structures *ac* (see 5 with cross references), *-que*, as here, and in the *Annals*, *et* (see 59, 65, 80, 92, 108, 116, 164, and 6.2b). The first two nouns denote offices/honours (cf. Sallust 11 *magistratus sacerdotia*, and Tacitus 55 *consulatus triumphos*, and also Cic. *Rep.* 1.47 *ferunt enim suffragia, mandant imperia magistratus*, *ambiuntur rogantur*, Livy 64 *purpura uiri utemur, praetextati in magistratibus in sacerdotiis*), the coordinated pair high standing in general. There is not an unstructured colon with four members.
Narrative.

(15) *Hist*. 4.5.2 *potentiam nobilitatem ceteraque extra animum neque bonis neque malis adnumerant*
The type with *ceteraque* following. Again (cf. 14) the nouns express high standing. For *nobilitas* in asyndeton see Tacitus 108 (another term then that occurs in different asyndetic pairs). Note too the possible accumulation of three pairs at Cicero 113–15 *nam regna imperia, nobilitas honores, diuitiae opes*. For *potentia* in asyndeton see Cicero 153.
Narrative.

(16) *Hist.* 4.5.2 <u>ciuis senator</u>, *maritus gener amicus, cunctis uitae officiis aequabilis, opum contemptor, recti peruicax, constans aduersus metus*

Ciuis senator is one unit, and then there are three single nouns (all indicating categories of personal relationships: cf. Tacitus 10). The asyndeton *ciuis senator* expresses two formal roles of one person, and is not unlike the previous example but one, in which *consulatum sacerdotia* could readily be rewritten *consul sacerdos* in a context requiring instead the personal nouns of status. Note too Tacitus 55 cited there. Structurally cf. the similar accumulation to that here at Sallust 29 *quom regna prouinciae, leges iura iudicia, bella atque paces, postremo diuina et humana omnia penes paucos erant.* Another such accumulation is at Sallust 6–10, where one of the asyndeta refers to types of officials (*reges tetrarchae*). See too Cicero 122 *iudicibus magistratibus*.

Narrative.

(17) *Hist.* 4.8.3 *denique* <u>constantia fortitudine</u> *Catonibus et Brutis aequaretur Heluidius*

For this combination cf. Cic. *Fin.* 1.64 *e physicis et fortitudo sumitur contra mortis timorem et constantia contra metum religionis,* Tusc. 5.13 *constantia grauitas fortitudo sapientia,* Quint. 5.10.57 *fortitudo constantia continentia.*

Virtues in asyndeton again.

Speech (indirect).

(18) *Hist.* 4.52.1 *nam amicos* <u>tempore fortuna</u>, *cupidinibus aliquando aut erroribus imminui transferri desinere*

Two pairs of nouns, the second pair connected by *aut*. Each of the pairs has a loose unity. Circumstances and luck may not be controllable by humans, whereas desires and mistakes are part of human behaviour. Tacitean pairs, as we have seen, often lack a straightforward relationship. *Aliquando* has the effect of separating the coordinated pair from the asyndetic, ruling out end-of-list coordination. Of note is the asyndetic tricolon of verbs later in the same sentence. For *tempus* in another asyndetic pairing see Sallust 37, Tacitus 6.

For an asyndetic pair followed by a pair coordinated by *aut* see Tacitus 90; Tacitus 75 is similar, but the disjunctive phrase is attached to the asyndetic by *-que*.

Speech (indirect).

(19) *Hist.* 4.76.3 *redituram in animos* <u>formidinem fugam</u> *famemque ac totiens captis precariam uitam*

4 Tacitus Histories 593

Formidinem and *fugam* are semantically connected, as the first (emotion) motivates the second (action). *Famem* and *precariam uitam*, tacked on by *-que* and linked by *ac*, also belong together, as they have to do with lack of sustenance and precarious existence.

For *fuga* and *formido* juxtaposed (quite often) see on Cicero 5–7. Note particularly the prayer devoting a city to destruction, Macr. 3.9.10 *fuga formidine terrore compleatis* (quoted on Sallust 39). For a verbal asyndetic pair equivalent to the nominal, see Cicero 59 *pertimuit profugit*, and for this phenomenon, i.e. the coexistence of a nominal and a verbal pair matched semantically, see 5 above and the Ciceronian passage quoted in the first paragraph of the note there.

Tacitus rarely admits alliterative asyndeta bimembria in the *Histories*. In the examples collected in this section, this and 50 (*per uirtutes per uoluptates*) are the only cases (on the *Annals*, where such alliteration is a little more numerous, see 5.2.3).

For the use of *ac* here, see above, this section, 5, and also on 14. For the linking of the coordinated pair *famem* ... *ac* ... *uitam* to the asyndetic pair by a coordinator (here *-que*, i.e. *famemque*), a mannerism of Tacitus but not Sallust, see on 11 with cross reference.

Speech (indirect).

(20) Hist. 5.15.1 *cum praealtis paludibus arma equi haurirentur*

Arma and *equi* are often associated, with a coordinator (Livy 21.47.5, 29.1.5, 30.7.11) and without (Curt. 4.14.12 *equos arma distribui*), and with and without *uiri*. See on Sallust 31, 32.

Narrative.

4.1.2 Adjectives

(21, 22) Hist. 1.3.2 *prodigia et fulminum monitus et futurorum praesagia, laeta tristia, ambigua manifesta*

Two pairs of opposites (antonyms). I take them to be adjectival here. For two comparable pairs of (nominal) opposites in Sallust, but typically with the second pair linked by *atque*, see Sallust 21 *laetitia maeror, luctus atque gaudia*. For double pairs of opposites, see for Tacitus *Histories* the note on 1, 2, and also for the *Annals* 5.2.3.

Laetus is often opposed to *tristis*, but I have not found such an asyndeton. For the opposition see in Tacitus himself *Ann.* 1.7.1, 2.53.2 (*tristium laetorumque*) and also Cic. *Part.* 12 *laeta tristibus ... inteximus*, Livy 22.7.12 *laeta aut tristia*, Plin. *Epist.* 5.21.1 *partim laeta partim tristia continebant* (cf. Cic. *Fin.* 4.73, Livy 1.13.6, 35.32.13, Val. Max. 4.7.7). In the present passage

594   XXX   The Annalists, Sallust and Tacitus

then it is the structure (an accumulation) that inspires the asyndeton, not specifically the semantics of the pair (see 5.2.4).

This is the only passage cited at *TLL* I.1846.12 for the opposition of *ambiguus* and *manifestus*.

Narrative.

(23?) *Hist.* 1.56.1 <u>segnis pauidus</u> *et socordia innocens*, 'he was sluggish, frightened, and innocent because of his torpor'.

The first two seem to be a unit (cf. *Ann.* 16.25.2 *segnes et pauidos supremis suis secretum circumdare*), with the third phrase expressing a consequence of these two related characteristics. But should we classify the passage instead as having end-of-list coordination? This question arises in a succession of passages below. I have included them only tentatively with a question mark, usually on the grounds that the initial pair is semantically a unit and different in its semantics from the following term(s). Quite often Tacitus begins a long descriptive sequence with a pair of asyndetic single words with a unity, whereas the longer elements that follow take up new themes.

Narrative.

(24?) *Hist.* 2.11.3 *ante signa pedes ire,* <u>*horridus incomptus*</u> *famaeque dissimilis*, 'he went before the standards on foot, rough, unkempt, and the opposite of his reputation'.

Cf. Cic. *Att.* 2.1.1 *tua illa ... horridula mihi atque incompta uisa sunt*, Apul. *Met.* 5.28 *sed incompta et agrestia et horrida cuncta sint*, Aurel. Vict. *Caes.* 40.13 *cum sine his naturae bona quasi incompta aut etiam horrida despectui sint.*

Horridus and *incomptus* are near-synonyms, the second a privative adjective, and the phrase attached by *-que* summarises the impression created by the preceding characteristics.

Narrative.

(25?) *Hist.* 2.68.1 *apud Vitellium omnia* <u>*indisposita temulenta*</u>, *peruigiliis ac bacchanalibus quam disciplinae et castris propiora*, 'in the army of Vitellius everything was drunken disorder, more suited to all-night revels and bacchanalia than to the discipline of the camp'.

Indisposita and *temulenta* go together (possibly another asyndetic hendiadys), describing the character of Vitellius' army, and the next, long phrase passes judgement on that character.

Narrative.

(26?) *Hist.* 2.80.1 *in ipso nihil* <u>*tumidum adrogans*</u>, *aut in rebus nouis nouum fuit*, 'in him there was nothing puffed up, arrogant, or, in his new circumstances, anything new'.

4 Tacitus Histories

Tumidum and *adrogans* are near-synonyms. The following phrase is a generalisation not specifically related to arrogance.
Narrative.

(27) *Hist.* 3.39.2 <u>sanctus inturbidus</u>, *nullius repentini honoris, adeo non principatus adpetens, parum effugerat, ne dignus crederetur,* 'Honourable, opposed to revolution, moved by no desire for sudden honours, least of all for the principate, he could not escape being regarded as worthy of it' (Moore, Loeb).

Cf. Sallust 58 *exercitus ei traditur a Sp. Albino proconsule <u>iners inbellis</u>, neque periculi neque laboris patiens, lingua quam manu promptior, praedator ex sociis et ipse praeda hostium, sine imperio et modestia habitus.* In this latter passage two privative adjectives are followed by a double negative phrase. In the Tacitean passage an asyndetic pair with one privative adjective is followed by two negative phrases.
Narrative.

(28) *Hist.* 5.5.1 *cetera instituta, <u>sinistra foeda</u>, prauitate ualuere*
Two near-synonyms again ('baleful, foul'), predicative adjuncts.
Narrative.

4.1.3 Verbs

(29) *Hist.* 1.2.3 *cum . . . <u>agerent uerterent</u> cuncta odio et terrore,* 'when they were hounding and overthrowing everything with hatred and terror'.

Pairs of verbs loosely of the semantic field 'ravage' are not infrequently in asyndeton bimembre, as for example in Sallust (see above, 3.3.2, final paragraph), Cicero (see XXVI. 7.2.3) and Tacitus himself (*Hist.* 2.56.1, cited after 30, 35, below); note too above, 2.1, 2. Heubner (1963: 24) ad loc. cites various such examples. Note also Livy 3.37.7 *hi ferre agere plebem plebisque res* (on which phrase, which does not always refer to plundering, see Oakley 2005b: 360 on Livy 10.34.4).[1] Heubner also cites Cic. *Rep.* 3.45 *cum agunt rapiunt tenent dissipant quae uolunt* (but omitting the last two verbs). The pair in Tacitus above does not seem to be otherwise attested.

---

[1] This is translated by Foster (Loeb) as 'bullied the plebs and plundered their possessions', taking each verb as going with just one object (i.e. correlative distribution, with chiasmus), which looks in principle right, but the renderings of the verbs are inappropriate. *Ferre* means 'carry off' and goes with *res*, and *agere* means 'drive on', and goes with *plebem*. See Dover (1968: 129) on *Nub.* 241 ἄγομαι φέρομαι: 'One ἄγει the cattle and slaves of an enemy (and him too, for enslavement, if one can catch him), and one φέρει his portable goods.' For chiasmus combined with correlative distribution see on Tacitus 127, 128.

For the semantic category in Greek (of violent acts) see Mastronarde (2002: 92).
Narrative.

(30) *Hist.* 2.26.2 *formido fuit apud fugientes occursantes*
These are opposites ('among those who were fleeing and advancing there was fear': directional or reversives, if a single group was going in opposite directions). Cf. (with coordinator) Livy 22.15.7 *Numidae alii atque alii occursantes refugientesque*.
The participles here are substantival but I have placed them with verbs because they are so markedly verbal.
Narrative.

(?) *Hist.* 2.56.1 *dispersi per municipia et colonias Vitelliani spoliare rapere, ui et stupris polluere*
There is probably a tricolon here, consisting of historic infinitives, though it might just be argued that the first two are a unit (of robbery and removal, two verbs designating the same act of violent theft), with the pollution and sexual depravity of the third colon providing a new twist. It does however look possible that Tacitus picked up the association of *rapere*, *spoliare* and *polluere* from Sallust: cf. Sallust 65 *ibi primum insueuit exercitus populi Romani amare potare, signa tabulas pictas uasa caelata mirari, ea priuatim et publice rapere, delubra spoliare, sacra profanaque omnia polluere*.
Sallust several times has *rapere* in asyndeta: see 66 and *Jug.* 41.5 *ducere trahere rapere*.
For a similar use of *spoliare*, see below, 35.
Narrative.

(31) *Hist.* 2.70.3 *aggerem armorum, strues corporum intueri mirari*
Note the phrasal asyndeton with two members, followed by the single-word asyndeton bimembre. The two verbs come close to expressing a single idea, 'to look at in amazement'. Or perhaps a temporal sequence is intended, = 'to look at and consequently to be amazed'.
For the structure here (phrasal asyndeta preceding a single-word asyndeton), see, for Tacitus, above, 9 (with cross reference to Sallust).
Narrative.

(32?) *Hist.* 2.78.1 *post Muciani orationem ceteri audentius circumsistere hortari, responsa uatum et siderum motus referre*, 'after the speech of Mucianus, the others more boldly gathered around and encouraged him, and mentioned the responses of seers and the motions of the stars'.
This is another of those tricola that are hard to analyse (but see further below, on 33). The first two verbs are readily taken together, of gathering

4 Tacitus Histories 597

around to give encouragement (a temporal sequence), whereas the third verb phrase is a more specific expansion. The initial pair is a type of combination that occurs several times, with variations to the first verb that do not alter the meaning. Cf. Sall. *Jug.* 51.5, where a comparable pair of historic infinitives heads a longer sequence of more specific verb phrases: *circumire hortari renouare proelium, et ipse cum delectis temptare omnia, subuenire suis, hostibus dubiis instare, quos firmos cognouerat eminus pugnando retinere*, 'he circulated, encouraged, resumed the battle, and with picked men tried every possibility himself, helped his fellows, pressed enemy waverers, and by fighting at long range contained those whom he had learnt to be staunch' (Woodman 2007, slightly modified). I do not classify this as an asyndeton bimembre, because *renouare proelium* follows immediately without a coordinator, whereas the next verb phrases are attached by *et*, the presence of which makes the previous verbs and verb phrase look like a tricolon.

For much the same sequence as that of the two single verbs, but with a coordinator, see Caes. *Civ.* 2.41.2 *circumire ordines atque hortari incipit*. Tacitus has the same pair as that at Sallust *Jug.* 51.5 in asyndeton bimembre at **137** *Sabinus circumire hortari, ne*, and in a possible asyndetic pairing at **146** *gentium ductores circumire hortari, firmare animos minuendo metu, accendenda spe*. The structure of Sallust *Jug.* 51.5 and of Tacitus **32** and of the second Tacitean passage just quoted (**146**) is similar (with the initial pair followed by a longer verb phrase or phrases). Curtius 5.9.17 (*ille Persarum tabernacula circumire, hortari monere nunc singulos, nunc uniuersos non ante destitit* . . .) looks the same, but there *hortari* and *monere* form a unit and are separate from *circumire*.

Narrative.
Similar to **32** is the following:

(**33**?) *Hist.* 2.82.1 *ipse Vespasianus adire hortari, bonos laude, segnes exemplo incitare saepius quam coercere*

With this compare Tacitus **147** *simul suas legiones adire hortari; priorum admonere, nouam gloriam ostendere* (see also **136**). There is the same switch, from the general in *adire hortari* to specific forms of encouragement or action, as that commented above on **32**. In **147** just quoted the strong punctuation after *adire hortari* (semicolon) is adopted by Koestermann (Teubner), and it is justified by the fact that there is a change of construction thereafter: *nouam gloriam ostendere* cannot be construed directly with the accusative *suas legiones* that is object of *adire hortari*, but would require a dative (*suis legionibus*).

For the pairing of these verbs, but with a coordinator, cf. Livy 10.20.13 *ducem adeuntem ordines hortantemque inuadunt*.
The passages quoted in this note and those at 32 suggest that these pairs with *hortari* as the second element do tend to be units.
Narrative.

(?) *Hist.* 3.17.2 *ut cuique ingenium, spoliare capere, arma equosque abripere*
Similar to *Hist.* 2.56.1 above (quoted after 30): *spoliare capere* and *spoliare rapere* are followed by a longer and more specific verb phrase. Should the two initial verbs be taken as an embedded asyndeton bimembre? I opt here for an ascending tricolon, with *abripere* following on from *capere*.
Narrative.

(34?) *Hist.* 3.20.1 *duces prouidendo consultando, cunctatione saepius quam temeritate prodesse*, 'generals (he said) help by foresight and consultation, and more often by delaying than recklessness'. This pair has a nominal near-equivalent at 98 (*cura prouisu*).
For a verbal asyndeton bimembre followed by *saepius quam* in Tacitus see 33 above. Is this an ordinary ascending tricolon, or should we take the gerunds as an embedded pair?
Speech (indirect).

(35) *Hist.* 3.25.3 *nec eo segnius propinquos adfinis fratres trucidant spoliant*
Acts of violence again.
Narrative.

(36) *Hist.* 4.11.1 *ille unus ambiri coli*
Near-synonyms. Cf. Sallust 74 *colite obseruate*, Tacitus 145 *celebrari coli*. Note too Cic. *Rep.* 1.47 *ambiuntur rogantur* (for this pair but coordinated see Vitr. 6.praef.5 *rogant et ambiunt*, Tac. *Dial.* 9.3 *rogare ultro et ambire cogatur*).
Narrative.

(37) *Hist.* 4.77.3 *ite nuntiate* Vespasiano
For asyndetic imperatives see Sallust 74. This pair belongs to a very old type in Latin ('go' + another verb: see X.1.1 and particularly XXIII.5.1 for parallels to this pair).
Speech.

(38) *Hist.* 4.81.2 *Vespasianus primo inridere aspernari*
Near-synonyms, historic infinitives (see, for this type, this section, 31, 32, 33, 36, and also some unnumbered examples, and for Sallust, above, 3.3.2). *Inrideo* means 'laugh at, make fun of', whereas *aspernor* is stronger ('scorn, spurn').
Narrative.

4 Tacitus Histories

4.1.4 Adverbs
There are in Tacitus various asyndetic pairs of opposites:

(39–44) *Hist.* 1.40.1 *huc illuc* (so 1.76.1, 3.3, 3.73.1, 4.46.3, 5.20.1).
Directional opposites. All narrative except the last (indirect).

(45) *Hist.* 2.42.2 *non una pugnae facies: comminus eminus, cateruis et cuneis concurrebant*, 'there was not a single form of fighting: hand to hand and at a distance, and they charged in detachments and columns'.
A specialised variant on the 'near/far' opposition (cf. Sallust 47 *procul iuxta*, and XIII.4.3, 5.4), antonyms.
Narrative.

(46) *Hist.* 4.62.2 *fulgentibus hinc inde Gallorum uexillis*
Directional opposites again.
Narrative.

4.1.5 Prepositional Type

(47) *Hist.* 1.9.1 *superior exercitu legatum Hordeonium Flaccum spernebat, senecta ac debilitate pedum inualidum, sine constantia sine auctoritate*
Narrative.

(48) *Hist.* 1.52.2 *sine modo sine iudicio donaret sua, largiretur aliena*
The prepositional pair is followed by an asyndetic pair of verb phrases containing two verbs that are near-synonyms, and two substantivised adjectives that are opposites (complementarities). For *sua* and *aliena* opposed in two juxtaposed verb phrases, as here, see Sallust 3. For such verbs together in asyndeton cf. *Lex Coloniae Genetiuae* CXXXII.25 (Crawford 1996: I.417) *aliudue quit det largiatur, 30 aliutue quit dato donato largito*.
Speech, indirect.

(49) *Hist.* 1.54.1 *per principia per contubernia modo suas iniurias, modo uicinarum ciuitatium praemia . . . conquerentes*
Again the prepositional pair is followed by an asyndetic pair of phrases, this time with a double pair of non-explicit opposites.
Narrative.

(50) *Hist.* 2.5.2 *tribuni centurionesque et uolgus militum industria licentia per uirtutes per uoluptates, ut cuique ingenium adsciscebantur*
Notable here is the juxtaposition of two asyndeta bimembria of different types, on which phenomenon see on 4 above and Sallust 47.

600   XXX   The Annalists, Sallust and Tacitus

These are two disjunctive pairs of virtual opposites or at least markedly contrasted terms.
Narrative.

(51) *Hist.* 3.13.2 <u>sine proelio sine uolnere</u> uinctas manus et capta traderent arma
Speech, indirect.

(52) *Hist.* 3.68.1 *Romanum principem . . . relicta fortunae suae sede <u>per populum per urbem</u> exire de imperio*
Indirect speech, reporting the thoughts of observers of the event.

(53) *Hist.* 4.58.4 *tot bellorum uictores, <u>apud Geldubam apud Vetera</u>, fuso totiens hoste si pauetis aciem, indignum id quidem, sed est uallum murique*
Speech.

(54) *Hist.* 5.1.1 <u>in opere in agmine</u> gregario militi mixtus
Narrative.

4.2   *Tacitus* Histories: *Conclusions*

4.2.1   Narrative versus Speeches
The proportion of such asyndeta in the *Histories* found in speeches is lower than that in Sallust. There are just ten examples in speeches in the 54 numbered passages above, most indirect (17, 18, 19, 34, 37, 44, 48, 51, 52, 53; for direct speech see 37, 53), or about 18 per cent of the total (the percentage for Sallust is about 36: see 3.3.1). Four of the eight examples of the prepositional type are in speeches. Tacitus uses asyndeton bimembre in speeches more often in the *Annals*. One of the few certain asyndeta bimembria in Caes. *Civ.* is prepositional and in a direct speech (XXVIII.2.2, 14).

4.2.2   Parts of Speech and Other Features
Of the 54 pairs numbered above, 20, on the classifications adopted here, are pairs of nouns, 8 are adjectives, 10 are verbs, 8 are adverbs and 8 are of the prepositional type. As many as seventeen are followed by an additional member (or members), either with or without an introductory coordinator, which I have taken as detached in some way (3, 5, 6, 11, 13, 14, 15, 18, 19, 23, 24, 25, 26, 27, 32, 33, 34). If the initial pair has a marked unity not shared by what follows, I have treated it as an asyndeton bimembre within a longer sequence. An asyndeton bimembre can certainly be embedded within such sequences (see e.g. above,

4 Tacitus Histories

9, 16; the latter runs *ciuis sentator, maritus gener amicus* etc., where it is beyond doubt that there is a unified group of two, followed by a unified group of three, rather than a group of five undifferentiated nouns), but it is a subjective matter deciding whether to separate a pair from a later term or terms, and I am aware that others would be likely to treat (some of) these examples as tricola or longer sequences, with in some cases end-of-list coordination. But there are reasons for thinking that a pattern of the type ABC*que* in Latin need not necessarily be the same as the familiar English structure A, B and C (see XVIII.4).

The pairs of nouns never comprise miscellaneous terms, but are opposites, near-synonyms or complementary in some way.

Tacitus tends to use an asyndetic pair of adjectives, and then to add a longer summarising element. In only three of the adjectival pairs is there a privative adjective, two of which are after the other term (24, 27; cf. 25). In Sallust, as we saw (3.3.2), most of the adjectival pairs contain at least one privative.

4.2.3 Semantic Relationships
Here are just a few categories.

(a) Pairs of opposites.
1, 2, 3, 4, 7, 8, 9, 21, 22, 30, 39–44, 45, 46, 50

There are nineteen such examples, representing 35 per cent of the total number of asyndeta bimembria listed above from the *Histories*. We noted just eight pairs of opposites in Sallust (3.3.2), about 10 per cent of the total. In three cases in Tacitus two pairs of opposites are juxtaposed (1–2, 7–8, 21–2). It was noted that quite often Tacitus avoids the most direct expression of an opposition.

(b) Pairs denoting vices or virtues.
5, 13, 17

(c) Pairs in which the first seems to be a modifier of the second, or by which a single idea is conveyed.
5, 25, 31, 34 (perhaps).

4.2.4 Structural Patterns

(a) The asyndeton bimembre (there may alternatively be two such asyndeta) is followed by a pair linked by a coordinator (but not *atque*).
5 (*ac*), 11 (*-que*), 14 (*-que*), 18 (*aut*), 19 (*ac*)

(b) *Ceterique* follows, introducing a generalisation.
3, 13, 15

(c) The asyndeton bimembre is followed or preceded by phrasal asyndeta.
9 (with phrasal asyndeta both before and after), 27, 31, 33

(d) The asyndeton bimembre is followed by a longer asyndetic group of single words (and other asyndetic elements such as phrases).
16

(e) There is an accumulation of asyndeta bimembria in the same sentence or short passage (usually juxtaposed pairs of opposites).
1, 2, 4, 7, 8, 21, 22

(f) The asyndeton bimembre is followed by *postremo* introducing a more general phrase.
5

5 Tacitus *Annals*

5.1 The Evidence

5.1.1 Nouns

(55) *Ann.* 1.4.4 *congestos iuueni <u>consulatus triumphos</u>*
  For the type expressing public honours cf. Tacitus 14 *consulatum sacerdotia* with references. The implication of the asyndeton is that the benefits bestowed were virtually unlimited (an open-ended list).
  Indirect speech.

(56, 57) *Ann.* 1.7.1 *lacrimas gaudium, questus adulatione<m> miscebant.*
  Two pairs of inexplicit opposites. The ablative *adulatione* has been defended (see the apparatus of Koestermann 1965), but given the high frequency in Tacitus of such juxtaposed pairs, with all four terms in the same case, any such defence is perverse. For the double juxtaposition of a singular and plural cf. below, **66, 67** *plebes primores, iuuentus senes,* and also Sallust *Cat.* 20.15 (quoted after 10) *res tempus pericula egestas* (the latter with the singulars and plurals in the same order as those in our present passage). A plural *adulationes* (Divaeus: see Goodyear 1972: 138 ad loc.) would destroy the symmetry. There seems often in Tacitus to be some sort of symmetry of number in such juxtaposed pairs, whether two pairs of singulars (**6, 7**), two pairs of plurals (**21, 22, 68, 69, 84, 85, 101, 102**), or two singulars in one pair and two plurals in the other (**87, 88, 106, 107**; note also 113–15, with two pairs of singulars and then a pair of plurals).
  Cf. Sallust **21** *laetitia maeror, luctus atque gaudia,* in which both pairs are semantically much the same as *lacrimas gaudium*. For the association of

tears explicitly and joy cf. Juv. 10.51–2 *ridebat curas nec non et gaudia uolgi,* | *interdum et lacrimas* (see also *TLL* VI.2.1719.58ff.).
Narrative.

(58) *Ann.* 1.7.7 <u>uerba uultus</u> *in crimen detorquens recondebat*
For *uultus* associated in Tacitus with *uerba* or the near-synonym *uox*, either in asyndeton or with a coordinator, cf. *Hist.* 1.45.1 *auidum et minacem militum animum uoce uultuque temperans,* 3.58.3 *nec deerat ipse uultu uoce lacrimis misericordiam elicere,* (*Annals*) 77 *non temperante Tiberio quin premeret uoce uultu, Ann.* 2.28.2 *non uultu alienatus, non uerbis commotior,* 12.36.3 *non ... aut uultu demisso aut uerbis misericordiam requirens, Ann.* 15.55.2 *tanta uocis ac uultus securitate,* 15.61.2 *nihil triste in uerbis eius aut uultu deprensum confirmauit,* 16.29.1 *uoce uoltu oculis ardesceret.* Cf. Sallust 30 *clamore uoltu.* Note too Cic. *Dom.* 133 *oculi uultus uerba,* and particularly Cicero 112 <u>uoltus uoces</u>*, motus statusque,* where the first, asyndetic, pair is the same as that at Tacitus 77 (see above). Note too *Fam.* 13.6.4 *uerbis, uultu denique* (discussed after Cicero 192). See also Koestermann (1963: 90), with bibliography. For a coordinated pair see Virg. *Aen.* 4.4–5 *uultus uerbaque.*
The idea here is that one's words and looks tell a story. The terms are usually alliterative, but are not for the most part used in asyndeton bimembre.
Narrative.

(59) *Ann.* 1.21.2 *nihil reliqui faciunt quo minus* <u>inuidiam misericordiam</u>*, metum et iras permouerent*
Two pairs of virtual opposites, the first asyndetic (= hostility versus sympathy, antonyms), the second linked by *et.* For the structure in Tacitus (with *et* used thus) see 92 below, and 14 above, and also 4.2.4a. It is only in the *Annals* that he has *et* as the coordinator (see on 14). For Sallust (and *atque*) see 3.3.3a.
With the opposition *inuidia misericordia* cf. *Ann.* 2.37.4 *nec ad inuidiam ista, sed conciliandae misericordiae refero,* 3.17.3 *respondente nullo, miseratio quam inuidia augebatur.*
Narrative.

(60) *Ann.* 1.32.3 <u>uigilias stationes</u>*, et si qua alia praesens usus indixerat, ipsi partiebantur,* 'watches, pickets, and anything else which their immediate need indicated, were assigned by the men themselves' (Woodman 2004).
I have treated below (93) *stationes uigiliae* (in that order) as an asyndeton bimembre. For the two nouns together in a longer sequence cf. *Ann.* 1.28.4 *uigiliis stationibus custodiis.* For the pair coordinated, see Caes. *Civ.*

1.21.3 *perpetuis uigiliis stationibusque*. The same asyndeton bimembre is found in Livy (7 *stationibus uigiliis fessus* with some manuscript variation), but frequently in Livy the two terms are coordinated (e.g. 2.39.9, 3.28.4, 7.12.12, 9.13.9, 9.24.5, al.). In our passage there are the two precise terms that clearly belonged together, and then a generalisation that might embrace any other duties; there is also a change of syntax in this third element. This is a type of variation we will see again (see below 74, 77, 78). The specificity of the two nouns, together with the vagueness of the following clause and the syntactic change, seems to justify taking them as a unitary asyndeton bimembre within a longer sequence.

For generalisations coming after pairs taken as asyndeta bimembria in the *Annals*, see below, 73, 100, 103.

Narrative.

(61) *Ann.* 1.33.2 *mira comitas et diuersa a Tiberii sermone uultu, adrogantibus et obscuris*

The two plural adjectives agree with the two singular nouns, but form a separate colon. The Tacitean combination *sermo uultus* belongs in the same semantic category as *uerba uultus* and *uox uultus* seen above, 58. The two nouns are dependent on a single preposition. This pattern will come up again (see 63, 75, 91; cf. *Hist.* 3.63.2 *de numero seruorum, electione litorum loqui*). See also XXI.

For the two nouns coordinated see *Hist.* 4.8.2 *uoltus quoque ac sermones*, *Ann.* 4.54.1 *non uultu aut sermone*, 6.50.1 *sermone ac uultu*.

Narrative.

(62) *Ann.* 1.42.4 *infecta sanguine castra flumina*

This for once looks like a list (open-ended?) of unconnected items, not a stylised asyndeton.

Speech.

(63) *Ann.* 1.61.1 *ob propinquos amicos, denique ob casus bellorum et sortem hominum*

Two pairs, each with a semantic unity. The first refers to personal relationships (with a single preposition again). The second, with coordination and introduced by *denique*, refers to chance and fate. For the juxtaposition (either with coordination or in a longer asyndeton), cf. *B. Afr.* 56.2 *conspectum amicorum propinquorumque*, Sall. *Jug.* 14.15 *adfinis amicos propinquos ceteros meos*. Livy 3.26.11 *propinqui atque amici*, and see *TLL* I.1912.6ff. For terms of this semantic category together see Tacitus 10, with cross references, including 72 below, and 5.2.3 (on asyndetic pairs to do with personal or political relationships).

For this use of *denique* in Sallust see above, 3.3.3g.
Narrative.

(64) *Ann.* 1.67.2 *at uictoribus decus gloriam*
Near-synonyms. For the combination see *TLL* V.1.247.42ff., citing e.g. Plaut. *St.* 281 *potestas adipiscendist gloriam laudem decus*, Cic. *Fin.* 3.28 *ad decus et ad gloriam*, Sall. *Cat.* 20.14 *diuitiae decus gloria in oculis sita sunt* (same combination at 58.8). Cf. too 89 below for a comparable pair.
Indirect speech.

(65) *Ann.* 2.5.3 *fundi Germanos acie et iustis locis, iuuari siluis paludibus, breui aestate et praematura hieme*
The asyndetic pair is a unit, of terms designating features of the landscape that are an obstacle to movement (cf. Livy 5.53.9 *cum in his locis nihil praeter siluas paludesque esset*, 162 *per saltus per paludes*). This unit is followed by a phrasal pair denoting opposite seasons, coordinated by *et* (see above, 59, and for such a phrasal second pair, below, 108). Cf. Catull. 115.5 for a similar pair, *siluas saltusque: uno qui in saltu tot bona possideat,* | *prata arua, ingentes siluas saltusque, paludesque* (for the structure see XXVII.1.1).
Indirect speech, representing probably the thoughts of the referent.

(66, 67) *Ann.* 2.19.1 *plebes primores, iuuentus senes agmen Romanum repente incursant turbant*
Two pairs of opposites (the first expressing different social classes, low versus high (see XIII.5.3, and for a comparable opposition, below, 109), the second youth versus old age: antonyms). For the structure see above, 56, 57, with cross references. Then later in the sentence there is a pair of asyndetic verbs, of violence in two stages, a striking accumulation (for different types of asyndeton bimembre juxtaposed or in close proximity, see on Sallust 47); the two pairs in the present passage are immediately preceded by a phrasal asyndeton, *pugnam uolunt, arma rapiunt.*
Pleb(e)s is sometimes opposed to *patres* (Wölfflin 1933: 271), and the alliterative pair here is similar. Cf. Livy 4.1.3 *auferri a primoribus ad plebem summum imperium credebant*. The other opposition is conventional: cf. e.g. in Tacitus *Hist.* 2.48.1 *iuuenes auctoritate, senes precibus mouebat*.
For accumulations of asyndeta bimembria within a short space see 3.3.3e, 5.2.3.
Narrative.

(68, 69) *Ann.* 2.20.1 *nihil ex his Caesari incognitum: consilia locos, prompta occulta nouerat*

The first pair designates specific aspects of knowledge, the second opposites, of greater generality; on 'open/shut' as complementarities see XIII.2, but metaphorical uses such as these are gradable and thus antonyms (see too Cicero 173 *aperte tecte* and also 213). Tacitus often contrasts what is concealed (*occultus*) with what is open: e.g. *Hist.* 4.4.2 *inuidia in occulto, adulatio in aperto erant, Ann.* 1.49.1 *clamor uulnera sanguis palam, causa in occulto,* 16.5.2 *multis palam et pluribus occultis.* See particularly below, 85 *aperta secreta,* where the opposition 'open/concealed' is explicit rather than virtual as here.
Narrative.

(70) *Ann.* 2.60.3 <u>Libya Aethiopia</u> *Medisque et Persis et Bactriano ac Scytha potitum,* 'having gained control of Libya, Ethiopia, and the Medes and Persians, the Bactrian and Scythian' (Woodman 2004).

Three pairs, first an asyndetic, denoting countries, a second, denoting peoples in the plural, with members linked by *et,* and a last, with members linked by *ac,* denoting peoples in the collective singular. The second and third pairs are tacked on to the asyndeton by *-que* and then *et* (multiple coordination).
Indirect speech.

(?) *Ann.* 2.73.3 *quantum* <u>clementia temperantia</u>, *ceteris bonis artibus praestitisset*

I take this as an asyndetic tricolon because of the absence of a coordinator separating the third member from the other two: contrast e.g. Sallust 1 *namque auaritia fidem probitatem ceterasque artis bonas subuortit* (see the note ad loc.). '(The) other good arts' after terms designating virtues come up not only in these two passages but also at Sallust 22, and Tacitus possibly picked up the pattern from Sallust. At Tacitus 13 similarly (*felicitas in tali ingenio auaritiam superbiam ceteraque occulta mala patefecit*) two vices are followed in the same pattern by 'the other secret evils'.
Indirect speech.

(71) *Ann.* 2.82.1 *at Romae ...* <u>dolor ira</u>, *et erumpebant questus,* 'but at Rome ... there was pain and anger, and complaints burst out'.

See Goodyear (1981: 431) ad loc.: *erant* is understood with *dolor ira.* Tacitus also has this pair with a coordinator: *Ann.* 1.41.3 *isque ut erat recens dolore et ira* (cf. e.g. Cic. *Att.* 2.19.5 *ardet dolore et ira noster Pompeius, B. Afr.* 85.6 *ira et dolore incensi*; see also *TLL* V.1.1841.44ff.). Preuss (1881: 14) lists further examples of the asyndeton.
Narrative.

5 Tacitus Annals

(72) *Ann.* 3.1.4 *neque discerneres <u>proximos alienos</u>, uirorum feminarumue planctus*, 'nor could you distinguish relatives from the unrelated, the wailings of men or women'.

A pair of inexplicit opposites (complementarities, if translated as above), followed by another pair of male–female opposites (complementarities or antonyms?), linked by *-ue*, but these last two are dependent in the genitive plural on *planctus* and thus differ syntactically from the asyndetic pair in the accusative plural. For such types of syntactic variation in an additional pair of opposites, see below, **86**, **93** (also with *-ue*), **99** (with *uel*), and above, Tacitus **1**, **2**, with 6.2b.

For *proximi* of relatives, see *TLL* X.2.2040.45ff. For the opposition here see Cic. *Off.* 1.44 *in eo peccant, quod iniuriosi sunt in proximos; quas enim copias iis et suppeditari aequius est et relinqui, eas transferunt ad alienos*, Livy 7.4.3 *non magis in alienis quam in proximis*, Val. Max. 7.8.4 *et erant ab eo instituti heredes neque sanguine Regino pares neque proximi, sed alieni et humiles*.

For the type of semantic relationship in the first pair see above **63**, with cross references.

Narrative.

(73?) *Ann.* 3.2.2 *atrata plebes, trabeati equites pro opibus loci <u>uestem odores</u> aliaque funerum sollemnia cremabant*

For the structure here (with *aliaque* after juxtaposed terms) see on Sallust **1** with cross references, and 3.3.3b.

Narrative.

(74?) *Ann.* 3.22.1 *adiciebantur <u>adulteria uenena</u>, quaesitumque per Chaldaeos in domum Caesaris*, 'Also thrown in were charges of adulteries, poisonings, and that questions had been asked of the Chaldaeans concerning the family of Caesar' (Woodman 2004).

For *adulteria* in an asyndeton bimembre, see Tacitus **3**. There however the pairing is of different type; here the terms are an open-ended list.

After the pair of single words in asyndeton there is a change of construction (to acc. + inf.). Does that change justify taking the *quaesitum*-clause as separate from the first pair? For syntactic changes after an asyndeton bimembre, see above, **60**.

Narrative.

(75) *Ann.* 3.26.1 *uetustissimi mortalium, nulla adhuc mala libidine, <u>sine probro scelere</u> eoque sine poena aut coercitionibus agebant*, 'The most olden of mortals, with as yet no evil lust, lived without scandal and crime and thus without punishment or constraints' (Woodman 2004).

An asyndetic pair of near-synonyms (for this semantic category in an asyndetic pair cf. Cicero 17 *sceleribus flagitiis*), followed by another pair of terms introduced by *-que* and joined by *aut*. The second pair expresses a consequence of the first (for which relationship see e.g. below, 87, 92), as is made explicit by *eoque*, which also establishes the independence of *probro scelere* (as does the repetition of *sine*). For *aut* in a pair attached to an asyndeton bimembre see 90, and also Tacitus 18; cf. too *uel* at 99, this section, and *-ue* at 72 and 93.

For a coordinator (here *-que*) linking the second, coordinated, pair to the asyndetic first pair see, in the *Histories*, 11, 19, and the *Annals*, 70, 80; also 99. I have not noted this pattern in Sallust.

Here again a preposition governs two terms in asyndeton (see above, this section, 61).

Narrative.

(76) *Ann.* 3.33.4 *nunc uinclis exsolutis* domos fora, *iam et exercitus regerent*

Of women: with their bonds released they were ruling houses and fora, and now also armies. The first two nouns are opposites of the 'public/ private', 'inside/outside' type, for which pair and variants (e.g. *domesticus forensis*) see Cicero 107, with cross references. They also occur asyndetically at 166 below (*per fora per domus*). Note also Cic. *Phil.* 2.26 *foris potius quam domo*, translated by the Loeb as 'abroad rather than at home'.

Indirect speech.

(77) *Ann.* 3.67.2 *non temperante Tiberio quin premeret* uoce uultu, *eo quod ipse creberrime interrogabat*, 'Tiberius did not refrain from pressurising him by language, look, and from the fact of personally asking him very frequent questions.'

Again there is a change of construction after the asyndetic single words (see on 60 and 74). For the pair here (*uoce uultu*) see on 58, and also 61.

Narrative.

(78) *Ann.* 4.1.1 originem mores *et quo facinore dominationem raptum ierit expediam*

Another instance (cf. 77) in which the construction changes after the two asyndetic nouns, here with the additional element attached by a coordinator (cf. 74). *Originem* and *mores* allude to the background and character of the referent (cf. 12 for *mores* in an asyndeton bimembre, and also Cicero 86 *de omni statu P. Sesti, de genere uitae,* de natura de moribus, *de incredibili amore in bonos, de studio conseruandae salutis communis atque oti*, where the pair, like that here, is in a characterisation), whereas the *quo*-clause refers to

a specific crime. So at 74 the acc. + inf. refers to a specific charge after the unspecific charges contained in the single words.
Narrative.

(79) *Ann.* 4.36.3 <u>leues ignobiles</u> *poenis adficiebantur*, 'it was the lightweight, the ignoble who had punishments inflicted on them' (Woodman 2004).

The adjectives *leues* and *ignobiles* are here used substantivally. The same is so of *inlustres ignobiles* at 90 below. Note the privatives in *in-*. By contrast in Tacitus' *Histories* (see above, 4.2.2) privative adjectives are not a marked component of adjectival asyndeta bimembria. *Leues* and *ignobiles* are near-synonyms.
Narrative.

(80) *Ann.* 4.38.3 *proinde* <u>socios ciues</u> *et deos ipsos et deas precor*
Two pairs, the first comprising complementary terms or even opposites (friendly outsiders, insiders) and asyndetic, the second expressing a masculine + feminine opposition (embracing the totality of gods: see XI.2), linked to the first pair by *et* (see on 75 above), and themselves linked by *et* (see on 59).

For the first pair cf. Livy 28.13.5 *cum omni exercitu ciuium sociorum*, and with a coordinator, 9.16.16 *socios ciuesque* (see also Preuss 1881: 89). For pairs classifying persons according to their official status within a state or their relationship from outside to it, see Sallust 6 *reges tetrarchae*, 47 *socios amicos*, Tacitus 16 *ciuis senator*. *Socius* is used asyndetically with more than one term.
Speech.

(81) *Ann.* 4.43.3 *quod si* <u>uatum annalium</u> *ad testimonia uocentur*
A pair referring to different forms of narrative (in poetry versus prose) of early affairs. Earlier in the chapter (§1) the same contrast is presented syndetically in a slightly different way: *annalium memoria uatumque carminibus*. Cf. the Ciceronian asyndeton 102 *poema orationem*.
Indirect speech.

(82) *Ann.* 4.49.3 *cum ingens multitudo* <u>bellatorum imbellium</u> *uno reliquo fonte uterentur*
Opposites (antonyms), one with a privative prefix and both of the same root, though the second is not a straightforward negative of the first.

Here is a place where the omission of a comma would be ridiculous in a critical text, but I have followed my usual custom of not punctuating between items that in my view form an asyndeton bimembre. Absence of the comma might imply that *imbellium* was an adjective (as it usually is) modifying *bellatorum* (a type of oxymoron, 'unwarlike warriors'), but it is in reality substantival (Woodman translates 'combatants and noncombatants').

For the adjective in asyndeton bimembre see Sallust 57 *quietus inbellis*, 58 *iners inbellis*.

Narrative.

The next example follows very soon after this one.

(83) *Ann.* 4.49.3 *simul equi armenta, ut mos barbaris, iuxta clausa, egestate pabuli exanimari*

There follows *adiacere corpora hominum, quos uulnera, quos sitis peremerat; pollui cuncta sanie odore contactu*, within which we see again different types of asyndeton (first a pair with anaphora and then a tricolon) near an asyndeton bimembre (see 4.2.4c, d, 5.2.3).

The manuscript has *simul eque. Simulque* is one emendation. *Armenta* denotes the larger domesticated animals, cattle (*OLD* s.v. *armentum* 3). If *equi* is accepted, it would indicate animals of transport and combat, alongside the purely domestic (*armenta*). Exactly that asyndetic pairing (but with one term different), is found in Sisenna (above 2.1, 7 *iumenta pecuda*: = 'transport and farm animals'). Woodman (2018: 249) supports *simulque armenta* as expressing the idea that 'the Thracians were living alongside their animals', but 'living alongside' would not be well expressed by *iuxta clausa*. The verb implies that someone shut the animals up (together), and two groups of animals suit the verb phrase. The whole clause from *simul* to *exanimari* is about animals, in that the referents are killed by 'lack of fodder'. Humans are the subject of the next sentence, and their death is caused by 'wounds and thirst'.

Narrative.

(84, 85) *Ann.* 4.67.4 *miles nuntios introitus, aperta secreta uelut in annales referebat*, 'the soldiers recorded, as if in annals, their messengers, visits, disclosures and secrets'.

Two pairs, the second a pair of opposites (antonyms). Preuss (1881: 43) cites our (second) example among pairs of adjectival/participial opposites, referring to *clam palam* as a parallel (op. cit. 32–3; note especially 33 for other such asyndetic adverbial opposites of this semantic field, *palam secreto, aperte tecte*). *Nuntios* and *introitus* may refer either to outgoings and incomings (opposites, reversives), or to different types of incomings (complements). They could even be translated 'messengers (and) their visits', with the first virtually modifying the second (= 'messengers' visits'). The relationship between the two is left vague.

The combining of a complementary pair (if that is what the first is) with a pair of opposites was seen at **68, 69** above, and there the opposites (*prompta occulta*), also in the second position, are of the same meaning as those here, though not explicit opposites as these two are.
Narrative.

(86) *Ann.* 4.69.3 <u>congressus conloquia</u>, notae ignotaeque aures uitari

A pair of near-synonyms (or should we say that there is a temporal sequence, with the meeting preceding conferring?), and then a pair of positive–negative opposites linked by -*que*. The opposites are not free-standing but modifiers of *aures* (for the type see 6.2b). Or should we say that there is an asyndetic tricolon of ascending length? This is a familiar problem of classification when a sequence of three contains a distinctive pair as its first two elements, and it is an arbitrary matter to analyse the structure. See above, 3.2.1 on Sall. *Cat.* 10.2, quoted before 1. I am influenced in the present case by those structures seen at 6.2b below where a pair of coordinated opposites follows a unitary uncoordinated pair and in some cases is clearly divisible from the initial pair. Sall. *Cat.* 10.2 above on the other hand does not have opposites as the final member.

Congressus and *colloquia* are elsewhere paired but with a coordinator (e.g. Cic. *Phil.* 9.2 *cumque iam ad congressum colloquiumque eius peruenisset*, *Phil.* 12.26 *in Antoni congressum colloquiumque ueniendum est*), once in Tacitus himself: *Hist.* 4.64.1 *ut conloquia congressusque nostros arcerent* (cf. too Mela 1.47).

This passage (**86**) should be of interest to a textual critic. Anyone looking at the examples in the paragraph immediately before this, all with -*que* linking the same two nouns *congressus* and *colloquium*, might be tempted to think that -*que* has fallen out of Tacitus' text. But we know that Tacitus has used a particular structure, whereby an asyndeton bimembre is followed by a pair of opposites explicitly linked, but of different syntactic status from the terms in asyndeton. An asyndeton may be motivated by a structural pattern that a writer is adopting (see further below, 5.2.4).
Narrative.

(87, 88) *Ann.* 4.70.2 *quo intendisset oculos, quo uerba acciderent,* <u>fuga</u> <u>uastitas</u>, *deseri* <u>itinera fora</u>

Vastitas 'emptiness, desolation' is the consequence of *fuga*, and the two nouns thus have a relationship that is common in pairings, asyndetic or otherwise (cf. **75**, where two pairs have this relation to each other).

Cf. Cic. *Verr.* 4.114 *quae solitudo esset in agris, quae uastitas, quae fuga aratorum*, Livy 8.9.12 *fugam ac uastitatem late fecerunt*, Plin. *Pan.* 48.3 *nec salutationes tuas fuga et uastitas sequitur: remoramur resistimus ut in communi domo* (note in this last example the following pair of asyndetic verbs, of much the same meaning and with the same prefix).

Itinera and *fora* ('roads and public meeting places') are a complementary unit. Cf. Cicero 108–9 *forum fana, porticus uiae*.
Narrative.

(89) *Ann.* 6.8.4 *spectamus porro quae coram habentur, cui ex te opes honores, quis plurima iuuandi nocendiue potentia*, 'Further, we look only at what is held in front of us, to whom you dispense wealth and honors, who is possessed of the greatest power for aiding or harming' (Woodman 2004).

Opes and *honores* refer to honours/rewards, whereas the phrase in the next clause is different, referring to freedom of action of opposite types. For the first combination see Cic. *Phil.* 7.7 *hinc honores amplissimos, hinc mediocris opes ... consecuti sumus, Tusc.* 5.30 *diuitias honores opes contemnere* (from a much longer sequence), 5.45 *da diuitias honores imperia opes gloriam*, Val. Max. 4.7.7 *gratia honore abundantissimisque opibus fulgentem*.
For nouns of this type in asyndeton, see Cicero 114, 115, 153, Sallust 9, 10, Tacitus 64.
Speech.

(90) *Ann.* 6.19.2 *iacuit immensa strages, omnis sexus, omnis aetas, inlustres ignobiles, dispersi aut aggerati*, 'The wreckage stretched indefinitely – every sex, every age, illustrious, ignoble, scattered, or heaped' (Woodman 2004).

Opposites (antonyms), both with prefix *in-*, substantivised adjectives (see above on 79 *leues ignobiles*). This is part of an accumulation of asyndetic phrases (in apposition to *strages*), the last one too (*dispersi aut aggerati*) comprising opposites (antonyms) (for *aut* and equivalents in such pairs, see 75 with cross references). *Ignobilis* does occur in opposition to *illustris*, but not otherwise, it seems, in asyndeton without an anaphoric element. Cf. Sen. *Epist.* 66.33 *quae modo latior est, modo angustior, modo inlustris, modo ignobilis, modo ad multos pertinens, modo ad paucos* (three pairs of opposites with anaphora), Just. 25.5.6 *qui patriam certe suam angustam ignobilemque fama rerum gestarum et claritate nominis sui toto orbe inlustrem reddiderit* (see also *TLL* VII.1.299.71ff.). For *sexus* and *aetas* together, see below, 114.
Narrative.

(91) *Ann.* 11.5.3 *cuius de potentia et exitio in tempore memorabo*
This passage highlights the influence that editorial decisions may have on the corpus of asyndeta. The text above is that which editors print, but neither M nor L has *et*. M has *potentia exitio*, and L *potentiae exitio*. This is one of several places known to me where editors, faced with a single

5 Tacitus Annals 613

preposition and several dependent nouns, add a coordinator between the nouns if there is one missing, but without stating any principle leading them to the addition (cf. Livy 42.1.1, Vell.125.5, with XXI). But there is no reason why a coordinator should be added (or a second preposition, of the type *cuius de potentia, de exitio*). We have seen already in this section several passages where two nouns without a coordinator are dependent on a single preposition (see above, 61, 63, 75, and also Sallust 46; see too Tacitus 30 *formido fuit apud fugientes occursantes*). In our passage the two nouns are opposites (reversives), of the rise and fall of the referent, and it would be acceptable to punctuate *cuius de potentia, exitio in tempore memorabo*. In the passage of the *Histories* just cited too *fugientes* and *occursantes* are opposites of the directional/reversive type.
Narrative.

(92) *Ann*. 11.6.2 *nunc inimicitias accusationes, odia et iniurias foueri*
An asyndetic pair followed by a pair with *et* (see on 59). The relationship between the two members of each group is the same: the first (abstract), indicating a feeling, motivates the action expressed by the second (for this semantic relationship see above on 75). According to Malloch (2013: 99), citing Nipperdey and Andresen (1880) on *Ann*. 16.17.1, the structure seen here is more common in Livy, but that is open to doubt (see below, 6.2b for such patterns in Sallust and Tacitus).
Indirect speech.

(93) *Ann*. 11.18.3 *stationes uigiliae, diurna nocturnaue munia in armis agitabantur*
This is the structure whereby a pair of opposites coordinated (*diurna nocturnaue*) follows the asyndetic pair (for *stationes* + *uigiliae* see above, 60), but in which the opposites are modifiers of a noun and not of the same syntax as the pair in asyndeton (cf. 72, 86 with cross references).
Narrative.

(94) *Ann*. 11.24.2 *sed terrae gentes in nomen nostrum coalescerent*
For the combination see Cic. *Imp. Pomp*. 31 *omnes terrae gentes nationes*, Mart. 12.8.1 *terrarum dea gentiumque Roma*. *Terrae* and *gentes* are complements, in that different lands contain different peoples.
Speech.

(95?) *Ann*. 11.27 *discubitum inter conuiuas, oscula complexus, noctem denique actam licentia coniugali*
For *oscula complexus* as a unit see above, 2.1, 3 (Quadrigarius) and below, 140. For *denique* see the next passage, and Sallust 25 and 3.3.3g. This could

be taken as an ascending tricolon, but kissing/embracing are a single act and the pair may alternatively be treated as embedded. See Annalists 3.
Narrative.

(96?) *Ann.* 11.38.3 *ne secutis quidem diebus* odii gaudii irae tristitiae, *ullius denique humani affectus signa dedit*

Are the four nouns a tetracolon expressing mixed emotions, without falling into juxtaposed pairs, followed by a summarising member introduced by *denique* ('Not even during the following days did he give signs of hatred, joy, anger, sadness, or, in fine, of any human emotion', Woodman 2004)? There is arguably a correlative distribution (for which see XVII). The second term, 'joy', is the antonym of the fourth, 'sadness', and the first emotion, 'hatred', leads to the third, 'anger' (for this type of relationship between two terms see on 92 above). This relationship perhaps implies two interlocking pairs. The interpretation remains open to doubt.
Narrative.

(97) *Ann.* 12.2.1 *haudquaquam nouercalibus odiis uisura* Britannicum Octauiam, 'one who was by no means about to look on Britannicus, Octavia with stepmotherly hatred'.

The names are those of brother and sister. Similarly nouns for different family relationships may be juxtaposed in asyndeton (see Sallust 12 and XIV). A comma would be needed in a critical text.
Indirect speech.

(98) *Ann.* 12.12.1 *reuocare priscum morem, exercitare legiones,* cura prouisu *agere, ac si hostis ingrueret,* 'he revived the old-time conventions, exercised his legions, and acted with concern and foresight as if an enemy were closing in' (Woodman 2004).

Cura and *prouisus* are near-synonyms, or *cura* could be interpreted as a modifier of *prouisu*, 'with careful foresight'. There are three asyndetic clauses juxtaposed here, the third with an embedded single-word asyndeton bimembre. This pairing has a near-parallel in gerund form at Tacitus 34 (*prouidendo consultando*).
Narrative.

(99) *Ann.* 12.17.2 *cum* arma munimenta, *impediti uel eminentes loci, amnesque et urbes iuxta perrumperentur,* 'since arms and fortifications, impassable or lofty places, and rivers and cities alike were being broken through'.

Three pairs, the first asyndetic, the second with *uel*, and the third (tacked on by *-que*) with *et*. The variety of methods of coordination is matched by that at 70. For the attachment of the final pair by a coordinator, a Tacitean mannerism, see on 75. Note that in *impediti uel eminentes loci* the contrasting terms differ in syntax (because they modify *loci*) from the asyndetic pair (see 72 with cross references for this pattern).

Arma is often in asyndetic pairs: see above, 2.2, 18, Sallust 31, 36, 43, Tacitus 20, and also Cicero 12, 18.

Narrative.

(100) *Ann.* 12.33 *ut aditus abscessus, cuncta nobis importuna et suis in melius essent*, 'so that entry, exit, everything might be disadvantageous to us and to the advantage of his own men'.

A pair of opposites of the directional or reversive type (see XIII.2; for contrasting prefixes see below, 141), followed by a summarising generalisation introduced by *cuncta*, itself containing opposites, *importuna* and *in melius*, inexplicit antonyms (see the translation). Cf. for this use of *cuncta Ann.* 12.65.2 *ne quis ambigat decus pudorem corpus, cuncta regno uiliora habere*. The present passage (100) and the sentence just quoted contain an asyndetic dicolon and tricolon respectively, and then a summary. Cf. Cic. *Pis.* 37 *Achaia Thessalia Athenae, cuncta Graecia*, 'Achaea, Thessaly, Athens – the whole of Greece'. The absence of a coordinator or adverb separating *cuncta* from the preceding terms in all three of these passages does not alter the fact that the summary is set apart, and would probably in speech have been marked by a pause, but the analysis is not simple.

For the structure (with *cuncta*) cf. 110, 112 below. For *omnis* in such a context see Tacitus 103, 105, and Sallust 25, 26. See in general on Sallust 1 and XVIII.6.

Narrative.

(101, 102) *Ann.* 12.37.2 *habui equos uiros, arma opes*

Probably two pairs of loosely associated terms, the first designating animates, the second inanimates. Another possibility is that *equos uiros arma* go together, as elsewhere (see for bibliography Sallust 31, 32), in which case *opes* would be the fourth member of a single colon. I have however split *arma* and *equi uiri* into two cola at Sallust 31, 32, with good reason in the context.

Speech.

(103) *Ann.* 13.16.4 *dolorem caritatem, omnis adfectus abscondere didicerat*, 'she had learnt to hide pain, affection, every emotion'.

An asyndetic pair, then a general summarising third element, with *omnis* matching *cuncta* elsewhere (see 105 below, and also above, 100).

Dolor and *caritas* are a miscellaneous pair, but they do express contrasting emotions in a sense.
Narrative.

(104) *Ann.* 13.18.1 *quod domos uillas id temporis quasi praedam diuisissent*
For this pair in asyndeton see Sallust 18. The terms denote types of houses reflecting the opposition 'town/country' (see XIII.5.1).
Indirect speech.

(105?) *Ann.* 13.42.4 *crimen periculum, omnia potius toleraturum, quam ueterem ac diu partam dignationem subitae felicitati submitteret*
For the structure see above, 103. The second member of the asyndeton is stronger than the first, or may express a consequence of it.
Indirect speech.

(106, 107) *Ann.* 13.44.3 *ut adsolet in amore et ira, iurgia preces, exprobratio satisfactio, et pars tenebrarum libidini seposita*
The second pair expresses an inexplicit opposition equivalent to 'disapproval/approval' (antonyms). The first two terms mean 'abuse, entreaties'. They do not amount to virtual opposites, but denote very different modes of address, aggression versus pleading.
Narrative.

(108) *Ann.* 13.46.1 *sibi concessam dictitans nobilitatem pulchritudinem, uota omnium et gaudia felicium*, 'saying that nobility, beauty had been granted to him, things wished for by everyone and the delight of the fortunate'.
A pair of complements, and then in apposition a (phrasal) pair coordinated by *et*. For *nobilitas* elsewhere in Tacitus in asyndeton see 15.
Indirect speech.

(109) *Ann.* 13.48 *legationes, quas diuersas ordo plebs ad senatum miserant*, 'legations, . . . which the rank and plebs had sent separately to the senate'.
Ordo is the technical term for a local town-senate: Woodman (2004: 270 n. 95). The two nouns are opposites, expressing groups within society of contrasting status. Note the plural verb. For this type of pairing cf. Tacitus 66 *plebes primores*. One of the manuscripts, L, has *plebs et ordo*. A divergence such as this cannot be resolved unless greater weight is given to one manuscript than to the other.
The phrase should be punctuated with a comma in a critical text.
Narrative.

(110) *Ann.* 13.57.2 *quo uoto equi uiri, cuncta [uicta] occidioni dantur*

Another summarising use of *cuncta* (see 100). The other examples of this use of *cuncta* (see 100 and 112) are substantival, and *uicta* might have been introduced from *uictores* earlier in the sentence. The deletion is that of Becher. *Viua* has been suggested (Danesius) for *uicta*, and it makes good sense. *Cuncta uiua* would be an appositive supplement to the asyndeton.
On *equi uiri* see Sallust 32.
Narrative.

(111) *Ann.* 14.31.3 *exturbabant agris, captiuos seruos appellando*
A comma would be needed here in a critical text. *Seruos* is an intensification, even a correction, of *captiuos*, 'captives, nay slaves', the second term expressing a more permanent state.
Quoted words.

(112?) *Ann.* 15.19.2 *quod multa securitate, nullis oneribus gratiam honores, cuncta prompta et obuia haberent*, 'with considerable unconcern and no burdens, they had influence, honors, indeed everything, ready and waiting' (Woodman 2004).
Cuncta again. For *gratia* and *honor* associated see Cic. *Phil.* 3.39 *honores eis habeantur gratiaeque referantur*, Val. Max. 4.7.7 *gratia honore abundantissimisque opibus fulgentem* (cited above, 89). At Sallust 9, 10 *gratia* and *honos* are in juxtaposed asyndetic pairs. For *honores* in asyndeta bimembria see Cicero 114, Tacitus 89, and for *gratia* Sallust 25. But is there an asyndetic tricolon?
Gratiam honores is preceded by an asyndetic pair of phrasal near-opposites, a typical accumulation of different asyndeta.
Indirect speech.

(112a) *Ann.* 15.27.3 *castella eorum exscindit, plana edita, ualidos inualidosque pari metu complet*, 'he destroyed their forts and filled the flat and lofty places, the strong and the weak with equal fear'.
Two pairs of opposites, the second coordinated and explicit antonyms, the first asyndetic and inexplicit antonyms (in that *plana* 'flat, level' does not strictly mean 'low'). Cf. e.g. 90.
Narrative.

(113, 114, 115) *Ann.* 15.54.1 *sed mirum quam inter diuersi generis ordinis, aetatis sexus, dites pauperes taciturnitate omnia cohibita sint*
Three pairs, the first two composed of complementary terms, the third of opposites (antonyms). *Inter* preceding the first two pairs (in the genitive) has no expressed dependent words but such can be understood ('among

(those/people) of diverse ...'; see Ash 2018: 248). Then there is a switch into the accusative plural (*dites pauperes*), with these two terms directly dependent on *inter* (for the single preposition followed by asyndeton see Tacitus 61, 63, 75, 91).

'Rich' and 'poor' are often associated (see *TLL* V.1.1588.77ff.). For asyndeta see Hor. *Sat.* 2.1.59 *diues inops* (XXIX.2.1.1), and also Cicero 121; cf. Lucr. 1.455, discussed at XXIV.7.4. *Aetas* and *sexus* are not infrequently used together by Tacitus, for example in two asyndetic phrases at *Annals* 90. Cf. e.g. *Ann.* 1.56.3 *quod imbecillum aetate ac sexu*, 14.13.2 *per sexum et aetatem*; also Sen. *Oed.* 53.

Groups of three single-word asyndeta bimembria are rare. In Sallust I have noted no examples (though at 6–10 there are six pairs in close proximity, one of them not numbered in that citation). In Tacitus, 66–7 is a case of sorts, in that two nominal pairs (*plebes primores, iuuenes senes*) are followed four words later by a verbal pair, *incursant turbant*. See too 153 below.

Narrative.

5.1.2 Adjectives

(116) *Ann.* 1.13.1 *sed <u>diuitem promptum</u>, artibus egregiis et pari fama publice, suspectabat*, 'but he suspected him, as being rich and at the ready, and of exceptional qualities and with a matching reputation publicly'.

There are two pairs here, the first an asyndeton bimembre of single words (predicative adjuncts), the second phrasal with its two members linked by *et*. The second pair is semantically a unit, as *pari* is an explicit link to the first phrase. In the first pair the referent's 'readiness' may be a consequence of his wealth.

Narrative.

(117) *Ann.* 1.17.4 *militiam ipsam <u>grauem infructuosam</u>*, 'warfare itself was oppressive, unprofitable'.

The adjectives are predicates, and the second is privative and longer than the first.

Indirect speech.

(118) *Ann.* 2.48.1 *bona Aemiliae Musae, <u>locupletis intestatae</u> ... tradidit*, 'the goods of the wealthy but intestate Aemilia Musa ... he handed over ...'.

Translated by Woodman here (2004) as attributes, in an adversative asyndeton (see however I.2). Alternatively they may be taken as predicative adjuncts, conjunctive, 'the goods of Aemila Musa, (who was) rich, intestate'. See I.2.

5 *Tacitus* Annals 619

Narrative.

(119) *Ann.* 4.37.3 *ita per omnes prouincias effigie numinum sacra<ri> ambi-tiosum superbum*, 'to be consecrated throughout all the provinces by the likeness of divinities would be over-ambitious, nay arrogant'.
Another predicative pair probably pronounced with a pause between. *Superbus* expresses a harsher judgement than *ambitiosus*, which may simply mean 'eager for advancement, ambitious' (see *OLD* s.v. 4).
Speech.

(120?) *Ann.* 6.3.4 *Caesar <S>extium Paconianum praetorium perculit magno patrum gaudio, audacem maleficum, omnium secreta rimantem*, 'Caesar hit at Sextius Paconianus, a praetorian, to the great delight of the fathers, a man bold and noxious, who pried into everyone's secrets.'
Gerber, Greef and John (1891–1903) s.v. *maleficus* cite *audacem maleficum* with a comma between (implying that both are adjectives here). Woodman (2004) translates *maleficum* as a substantive, which is also possible. The *OLD* treats *maleficus* mainly as an adjective, but does have a separate lemma for the nominal use.
The first two terms seem to go closely together (on the interpretation adopted here), with the second capping the first, 'bold, (even) harmful', 'bold to the point of being harmful' (predicative adjuncts). Despite uncertainties of interpretation, the final element *omnium secreta rimantem* is more precise and strikes a different note from the other two terms. An embedded pair of predicative adjuncts, with another adjunct following after a pause.
Probably narrative.

(121) *Ann.* 6.8.4 *abditos principis sensus, et si quid occultius parat, exquirere inlicitum anceps*, 'to search out the hidden feelings of the princeps, and his still more concealed intentions, is unlawful, perilous' (Woodman 2004).
Anceps is here given meaning 8 in the *OLD* classification, with which it outdoes *inlicitus* semantically ('illegal and, worse, perilous').
Another predicative example, and again there is one privative adjective, but in first position.
Speech.

(122) *Ann.* 11.26.2 *se caelibem orbum, nuptiis et adoptando Britannico paratum*, 'he himself, celibate, childless, (was) prepared for marriage and for adopting Britannicus'.
The third element I take to be predicate, stating the consequences of the initial two adjectives, which I take to be secondary predicates (with

the second itself expressing a consequence, to date, of the first). For the pairing cf. Sen. *Phaedr.* 1215 *caelebs et orbus*, Amm. 14.6.22 and 28.4.22 *orbos et/uel caelibes* (further such examples may be found at *TLL* III.66.23, 25).
Indirect speech.

(123) *Ann.* 12.48.2 *poteretur Radamistus male partis, dum <u>inuisus infamis</u>*, 'let Radamistus possess his ill-gotten gains, provided he was hated and of ill repute'.

Near-synonyms, predicates at the end of a colon. Cf. Livy 25.3.13 *rem inuisam infamemque*, 27.20.11 *infamem inuisumque plebei Claudium fecerat*, Sen. *Contr.* 9.4.20 *erat inter infames maxime et inuisos homines Turdus*; cf. Cic. *Verr.* 2.168 *inuidiam atque infamiam* (see too *TLL* VII.1.1338.28).

For *infamis* with another adjective in *in-* in a longer sequence see *Ann.* 12.64.3 *utraque impudica infamis uiolenta haud minus uitiis aemulabantur*.
Indirect speech.

(124) *Ann.* 14.36.1 <u>*imbelles inermes*</u> *cessuros statim, ubi ferrum uirtutemque uincentium totiens fusi agnouissent*, 'unwarlike, unarmed, they would yield immediately when they recognized, after so many routs already, the steel and courage of their conquerors' (Woodman 2004, slightly modified).

Cf. Livy 9.4.13 *imbellis uidelicet atque inermis multitudo*, 28.23.2 *turbam feminarum puerorumque inbellem inermemque*. Note too Sallust 57 *quietus inbellis*, 58 *iners inbellis*.

Here again the adjectives are secondary predicates, in agreement with the (unexpressed) subject of the verb. See Sallust 53, 58 for privatives used as adjuncts, and also the next example.
Indirect speech.

(125) *Ann.* 16.26.3 *proinde <u>intemeratus impollutus</u>, quorum uestigiis et studiis uitam duxerit, eorum gloria peteret finem*, 'Accordingly, undefiled, unpolluted, in the glory of those whose footsteps and study had guided his life, let him seek his end' (Woodman 2004, slightly modified).

Again the (privative) adjuncts are in agreement with the unexpressed subject of the verb.
Indirect speech.

(?) *Ann.* 16.32.3 *auctoritatem Stoicae sectae praeferebat, habitu et ore ad exprimendam imaginem honesti exercitus, ceterum animo <u>perfidiosus subdolus</u>, auaritiam ac libidinem occultans*, 'he was parading the authority of the Stoic sect, trained to convey in demeanour and speech an image of honesty, but in reality (he was) treacherous, devious, and concealing his avarice and lust'.

Probably to be classified as an ascending tricolon, but the first two adjectives are virtual synonyms, conveying that the referent was given to deception, whereas the third element is more precise and syntactically different, referring to forms of his deception.
Narrative.

5.1.3 Verbs

(126?) *Ann.* 1.16.2 <u>lasciuire</u> *miles,* <u>discordare</u>, *pessimi cuiusque sermonibus praebere aures, denique luxum et otium cupere, disciplinam et laborem aspernari*
There are five historic infinitives in asyndetic clauses in this sentence. *Lasciuire* and *discordare* ('ran riot and engaged in disputes') both designate unruly behaviour in an imprecise way, and they are arguably a (discontinuous) unit distinct from the clauses that follow. The third clause is more precise (for the transition from the vague to the specific see e.g. the last example above, unnumbered), and the last two belong together, as they present a treble contrast (and are introduced by *denique*, which sets them apart from the rest of the sentence). *Cupere* and *aspernari* are opposites (antonyms). *Otium* and *laborem* (idleness and work) are antonyms or complemenarities. *Luxum* and *disciplinam* are also opposed, with self-control forming a contrast with abandonment to luxurious excess. If these last two are opposites, they are of the inexplicit type. In the clauses introduced by *denique* there is correlative distribution (for which in general see XVII).
Narrative.

(127, 128) *Ann.* 1.41.3 *orant obsistunt, rediret maneret*
Two pairs, both possibly consisting (loosely) of opposites. The first is translated by Woodman (2004) as 'They begged, they blocked the way', but *obsistunt* may be metaphorical (cf. *OLD* s.v. 4), forming an opposite to *orant*: 'they begged and resisted', i.e. they begged that something might be so, or resisted that something (else) might be so. Literally the meaning would be: 'they begged, they resisted: that she should go back, that she should remain'. On this view there would be a correlative distribution of the verbs, with chiasmus: 'they begged' would be picked up by *maneret*, and 'they resisted' by the juxtaposed *rediret*: = 'they begged that she should stay, they resisted that she should go back'. Both correlative pairs would have the same implication: she (Agrippina) should stay. The use of *obsistunt* would be elliptical, with *quominus* understood, or alternatively and more simply *ut* can be understood both with *orant* and with *obsistunt*: *ut*

rather than *quominus* (or *quin*) is sometimes used (at a later date) with verbs of preventing (see Kühner and Stegmann 1955: II.260–1). For chiasmus combined with correlative distribution see Sallust 70, Tacitus 141; see also Tacitus 29 with n. 1 on Livy 3.37.7.

The first pair is in the narrative, the second in indirect speech.

(129) *Ann.* 1.51.3 *pergerent properarent culpam in decus uertere*, 'they should proceed and press on with turning guilt into honor' (Woodman 2004).

These two verbs seem to convey a general idea, of proceeding with haste. The second could be replaced by an adverbial modifier or present participle (*pergerent propere/properantes*). It has been noted that pairs of verbs in Sallust containing *festino* sometimes have a similar relationship (see e.g. 71, 77). Whereas *propero* is in second position here, Sallust usually has *festino* first in such pairs (see 3.3.2 for a list of examples; 82 *laborare festinare* is an exception, and that too could be rewritten in much the same way as Tacitus 129: *laborare festinanter/festinantes*).

Indirect speech.

(130) *Ann.* 1.70.3 *iumenta sarcinae corpora exanima interfluunt occursant*, 'equines, packs, lifeless bodies flowed past or ran into them'.

This is a disjunctive asyndeton, of virtual opposites (of the 'hit/miss' type, difficult to classify).

Narrative.

(131) *Ann.* 2.14.3 *sine pudore flagitii, sine cura ducum abire fugere, pauidos aduersis, inter secunda non diuini, non humani iuris memores*, 'without shame at the outrage, without bothering about their leaders, they would depart and flee, panicking in adversity and amid prosperity not recalling either divine or human law'.

There are various ways of interpreting *abire* and *fugere*. They are near-synonyms, or there is a sequence of events ('leave and (then) flee') or alternatively the second is a modifier of the first, 'departed in flight', *abire fugientes* (cf. e.g. 129 above, and *Histories* 31 *intueri mirari* 'to look at in amazement', = *intueri mirantes*). For asyndetic pairs of verbs denoting departure see above, 2.1, 5 (Quadrigarius).

Note the asyndeton of prepositional phrases that precedes (for this pattern see below, 6.2a), and the asyndetic phrases that follow, containing pairs of antonyms (*aduersis/inter secunda, diuini/humani*): another striking accumulation.

Indirect speech.

5 Tacitus Annals

(132) *Ann.* 2.19.1 *plebes primores, iuuentus senes agmen Romanum repente incursant turbant*, 'plebs and rulers, young and old suddenly attacked and threw into confusion the Roman column'.

On this passage see above, 66, 67. The second verb describes a consequence of the first, or there may be simply a sequence of events. In Sallust too acts of violence are sometimes expressed by asyndetic pairs of verbs (see Sallust 67, 76, 80, 81); see too above, 2.1, 2, Cicero 67, and XXVI.7.2.3. Note also several of the examples below.
Narrative.

(133) *Ann.* 2.25.2 *populatur excindit non ausum congredi hostem*, 'he ravages and destroys the enemy not daring to engage'.

Two verbs of similar meaning, the second outdoing the first. For *excindo* as the second member of an asyndetic pair, cf. Sallust 81. For *populatur* in an asyndetic tricolon see Naevius 32 (quoted at XXIV.8).
Narrative.

(134) *Ann.* 2.67.1 *tribunique et centuriones monendo suadendo, et quanto longius abscedebatur, apertiore custodia, postremo gnarum necessitatis in urbem traxere*, 'and tribunes and centurions – by warnings, persuasion, and a form of custody the more obvious the farther away they were – dragged to the City a man who was now finally aware of the inevitable' (Woodman 2004).

The underlined verbs are a unit: the persuasion is a consequence of the warning. These two gerunds in a longer sequence are in Livy 4.48.11 *suadendo monendo pollicendoque gratum id singulis priuatim, gratum uniuerso senatui fore, sex ad intercessionem comparauere*. The third element in Tacitus (*apertiore custodia*) is introduced by *et*, and is separated from the pair by a clause as well, and is of a different part of speech. In the passage of Livy too *pollicendoque* is detached from the other two, not merely by *-que* but by the fact that it alone has a long dependent construction.

For asyndetic pairs of ablative gerunds see e.g. 136 below and Sallust 72 (with cross references).
Narrative.

(135) *Ann.* 3.33.4 *ab his negotia suscipi transigi*, 'business was undertaken and transacted'.

A sequence of events, the verbs inexplicit opposites, of starting and finishing (probably reversives; cf. *start/stop*, and see XIII.4 on *creat sepelit* at Pacuvius *trag.* 80 Schierl).
Indirect speech.

(136) *Ann.* 4.2.2 *inrepere paulatim militares animos <u>adeundo appellando</u>*
For *adire* + a verb of address forming an asyndeton see Tacitus 33, 147.
Narrative.

(?) *Ann.* 4.8.5 *Augusti pronepotes, clarissimis maioribus genitos, <u>suscipite regite</u>, uestram meamque uicem explete*, 'undertake, direct the great-grandsons of Augustus, begotten with the most brilliant ancestry; fulfill your own function and mine' (Woodman 2004).
Suscipite and *regite* may be taken together (note that Woodman has strong punctuation before the third element), but I have opted for a tricolon here.
Speech.

(137) *Ann.* 4.50.4 *cum Sabinus <u>circumire hortari</u>, ne* . . .
This pair is similar to those at 146 and particularly 33 and Sall. *Jug.* 51.5 quoted on Tacitus 32. The two verbs describe simultaneous acts.
Narrative.

(138?) *Ann.* 4.51.1 *eaque <u>prensare detrahere</u> et aduersum resistentis comminus niti*, 'those (bridges and ladders) they seized and dragged down, and they struggled hand to hand with those resisting'.
Two distinct actions are referred to, the first described by the pair *prensare detrahere* (grasping hold of and pulling), and the second (fighting off defenders in close combat) introduced by *et*. It seems justifiable to treat *prensare detrahere* as a unitary asyndeton bimembre, with the next clause conveying something different. Cf. e.g. above, 2.1, 3 for a similar combination of a pair + another element (though there with the pair at the end of the sequence). See also below, *Ann.* 6.35.2 (quoted after 144) *prensare detrudere*.
Narrative.

(139) *Ann.* 4.57.3 *idque Augusta <u>exprobrabat reposcebat</u>*, 'And that was the basis of Augusta's constant reproaches and demands for compensation' (Woodman 2004).
These are complementary acts.
Narrative.

(140) *Ann.* 4.63.1 *concursus ad exanimos <u>complectentium osculantium</u>*
For a similar combination cf. Tacitus 95 *discubitum inter conuiuas, oscula complexus, noctem denique actam licentia coniugali*. See Preuss (1881: 14), and above 2.1, 3 (Quadrigarius). I have chosen to put these two (substantival) participles among verbs rather than nouns.
Narrative.

(141) *Ann.* 5.7.1 *tunc singulos, ut cuique <u>adsistere adloqui</u> animus erat, retinens aut dimittens partem diei absumpsit*

Absistere ('stand back, withdraw') has been proposed for *adsistere*, and is accepted by Woodman (2004), who translates: 'Then he took up part of the day detaining or dismissing individuals, depending on whether each had a mind to withdraw or speak to him' (see also Woodman 2018: 70). That would produce a pair of opposites (reversives), picked up (in reverse order) by *retinens aut dimittens*, a form of correlative distribution (for the chiastic pattern cf. e.g. 127, 128 with cross references, 159). On the other hand it could be argued that approaching/standing around and addressing is an established asyndetic combination (cf. Tacitus 32, 33 with cross references). The pair of opposites is however better suited to the context, with the expression *ut cuique animus erat* implying contrasting forms of behaviour and thus suited to the disjunctive asyndeton *absistere adloqui*, and with the final participial pair echoing the main verbs. Here then a structure (chiastic correlative distribution) supports an emendation within an asyndeton. For the *ab-/ad-* contrast in an asyndeton, cf. Tacitus 100 *aditus abscessus*.

Narrative.

(142) *Ann.* 6.1.2 *praepositique serui, <qui con>quirerent pertraherent*

If the emendation is accepted the verbs are again sequential, searching out and dragging off, and in keeping with the use of asyndeton of acts of violence. For the simplex *traho* in asyndeta in Sallust, see Sallust 68, 81.

On emendations of the transmitted *quirerent* see Woodman (2018: 92).

Narrative.

(143) *Ann.* 6.24.1 *nisi quod Attii centurionis et Didymi liberti epistulae seruorum nomina praeferebant, ut quis egredientem cubiculo Drusum <u>pulsauerat exterruerat</u>*, 'except that the letters of the centurion Attius and of the freedman Didymus paraded the name of each slave who had beaten and terrorized Drusus as he left his bedroom' (Woodman 2004).

Acts of violence again. The terror follows on from the beating.

Narrative.

(144) *Ann.* 6.35.1 *corporibus et pulsu armorum <u>pellerent pellerentur</u>*, 'amid bodies and the smite of arms, men smote or were smitten' (Woodman 2004).

A distinctive type, with active and passive of the same verb juxtaposed, here probably disjunctive. This example and the phenomenon in general are discussed in VIII.

The pairing of active and passive forms of the same verb in Latin is far more common when there is a coordinator (see Wills 1996: 295–8 and above, VIII.1).

A Greek pairing that looks similar to **144** is Th. 7.71.4 νικῶντες κρατούμενοι, 'conquering, being conquered', but this I do not take to be a straightforward asyndetic coordination (see VIII.1).

Narrative.

(?) *Ann.* 6.35.2 *iamque et Albani Hiberique <u>prensare detrudere</u>, ancipitem pugnam hostibus facere*, 'And now the Albani and Iberians too grappled, dislodged, and presented the enemy with a twofold fight' (Woodman 2004).

The pair describes specific acts (of violence again) in a temporal sequence, with the seizing preceding the dislodging. The third member, a clause, is rather a generalisation about the nature of the fighting. The verb (*facere*) has an object, whereas *prensare* and *detrudere* are absolute. This passage is very similar to **138** above, where *prensare detrahere* is followed by another clause, though there with a coordinator attaching the third element. The structure here looks like a tricolon.

Narrative, which continues directly on from **144** above. There are asyndeta in successive sentences.

(**145**) *Ann.* 11.16.2 *atque eo, quod nullis discordiis imbutus pari in omnes studio ageret, <u>celebrari coli</u>*, 'and, because of the fact that he was not stained by any of their disaffections but acted with equal enthusiasm toward all, he was celebrated and courted' (Woodman 2004).

These are two (alliterative) synonyms. Cf. Sallust **74** *colite obseruate*, Tacitus **36** *ille unus ambiri coli*. Note that this last example and **145** both have the same verb as a passive historic infinitive in an asyndeton.

Narrative.

(**146?**) *Ann.* 12.34 *gentium ductores <u>circumire hortari</u>, firmare animos minuendo metu, accendenda spe*

The first two verbs occur elsewhere as an asyndeton bimembre (see Tacitus **137** and also on **32**). There follows an extended, more specific, verb phrase, with pairs of verbal (*minuendo, accendenda*) and nominal (*metu, spe*) opposites (the first reversive, the second – for which see Tacitus **7** – virtual antonyms). *Circumire hortari* I treat tentatively as a unitary asyndeton bimembre, within a tricolon. The structure here is similar to that at **147**.

Narrative.

(147) *Ann.* 15.12.3 *simul suas legiones adire hortari; priorum admonere, nouam gloriam ostendere*, 'at the same time he went to and encouraged his legions; he reminded them of what had gone before and held out the prospect of renewed glory'.

This is the punctuation of Koestermann (1965). For *adeo* with a verb of address in an asyndeton bimembre see Tacitus 33, 136. This pair is followed by a more specific phrasal pair containing virtual opposites (*priorum, nouam*, an inexplicit variant on the 'old/new' type): there is not a sequence of four elements of comparable status. On the syntax here see on 33.

Narrative.

(148) *Ann.* 15.55.1 *quae audiuerat coniectauerat, docet*, 'he revealed what he had heard or guessed'.

Probably disjunctive, virtually equivalent to 'heard/not heard'.

Narrative.

5.1.4 Adverbs

(149–152) *huc illuc*, which occurs at *Ann.* 1.56.5 (narrative), 4.5.4 (narrative), 12.34 (narrative; in a sentence following one with a verbal asyndeton bimembre), 15.50.4 (narrative).

Opposites, directional.

For the pair coordinated cf. 13.37.1 *hucque et illuc uolitans* (contrast 12.34 *huc illuc uolitans*), 15.38.3 *hucque et illuc flexis*.

(153) *Ann.* 12.39.2 *crebra hinc proelia, et saepius in modum latrocinii per saltus per paludes, ut cuique sors aut uirtus, temere prouiso, ob iram ob praedam, iussu et aliquando ignaris ducibus*, 'There were frequent battles after this, more often in the manner of banditry; through denes, through marshes; dependent on the lot or courage of each man; rashly or with foresight; for anger, for plunder; by order and sometimes even without the leaders' knowledge' (Woodman 2004).

A striking passage, with an accumulation of Tacitean mannerisms. *Temere prouisu* is an asyndeton bimembre comprising adverbial opposites (antonyms). In the same sentence there are two other asyndeta with two members, both prepositional (*per saltus per paludes, ob iram ob praedam*). A second pair of (inexplicit) opposites, this one with a coordinator, is *iussu et . . . ignaris ducibus*: equivalent to 'ordered/not ordered', complementarities. For the juxtaposition of a prepositional asyndeton with another asyndetic pair of different type, see 6.2a, Sallust 47 and also Cicero 79 *temere turbulente, per uim per furorem*, where there is the same order, adverbial pair + prepositional pair (and note *temere* again in asyndeton).

Narrative.

5.1.5 Prepositional Type

(154) *Ann.* 1.22.2 <u>cum osculis cum lacrimis</u> *dolorem meum impleuero*
Speech.

(155) *Ann.* 1.70.4 *pernoctauere* <u>sine utensilibus sine igni</u>
Narrative.

(156) *Ann.* 2.13.1 <u>per seria per iocos</u> *eundem animum laudibus ferrent*
Another pair of opposites (antonyms). See Cicero 101.
Indirect speech.

(157) *Ann.* 2.55.6 <u>in Agrippinam in Germanicum</u> *contumelias iacere*
Narrative.

(158) *Ann.* 3.15.2 *Tiberium* <u>sine miseratione sine ira</u> *obstinatum clausumque uidit*, 'he saw Tiberius, without pity, without anger, shut off and closed'.
Miseratio and *ira* are virtual opposites (of the type 'sympathy/hostility', antonyms). Then in juxtaposition to these Tacitus uses two near-synonyms, linked by *-que*.
Narrative.

(159) *Ann.* 4.60.2 *seu loqueretur seu taceret iuuenis, crimen* <u>ex silentio ex uoce</u>
Opposites, picking up chiastically two verbs of the same (opposite) meanings (speech versus silence) (complementarities or possibly antonyms): another case of chiastic correlative distribution: cf. Sallust 70, Tacitus 127, 128, 141.
Narrative.

(160) *Ann.* 6.7.3 *neque discerneres alienos a coniunctis, amicos ab ignotis, quid repens aut uetustate obscurum: perinde* <u>in foro in conuiuio</u>, *quaqua de re locuti incusabantur*
Virtual opposites, almost = 'in public/in private' (cf. Woodman 2017: 117). Note the three phrasal asyndeta preceding, all expressing opposites.
Narrative.

(161) *Ann.* 11.17.3 <u>per laeta per aduersa</u> *res Cheruscas adflictabat*
Virtual opposites (equivalent to 'favourable/unfavourable', antonyms).
Narrative.

(162–3) *Ann.* 12.39.2
There are two examples in this passage (*per saltus per paludes, ob iram ob praedam*), which is quoted in full in the previous section (153). For a similar pair to the first see Tacitus 65 *siluis paludibus*.

Narrative.

(164) *Ann.* 13.35.1 *satis constitit fuisse in eo exercitu ueteranos, qui* ... *uallum fossamque quasi noua et mira uiserent*, <u>*sine galeis sine loricis*</u>, *nitidi et quaestuosi, militia per oppida expleta*
Another asyndeton bimembre followed by coordinated pair.
Indirect statement.

(165) *Ann.* 13.35.4 *ipse cultu leui, capite intecto,* <u>*in agmine in laboribus*</u> *frequens adesse*
Narrative.

(166) *Ann.* 15.58.2 *uolitabantque* <u>*per fora per domus*</u>, *rura quoque et proxima municipiorum pedites equitesque*
For the pair *fora domus* see Tacitus 76. They are virtual opposites, = 'public/private'. Following the prepositional asyndeton there is a coordinated pair with the same preposition understood, and these two are opposites of a sort, = 'country/town'.
Narrative.

(167) *Ann.* 16.22.3 *diurna populi Romani* <u>*per prouincias per exercitus*</u> *curatius leguntur*
For this pair cf. Livy 38.35.7 *deque prouinciis et exercitibus*.
Speech.

5.2 Tacitus Annals: Conclusions

5.2.1 Distributions

The 113 numbered examples listed above are spread over the extant books of the *Annals* as follows:

Book	Number of examples
1	20
2	14
3	8
4	19
5–6	10
11	8
12	11
13	9
14	2
15	9
16	3

The usage is not evenly distributed. There is an obvious decline in the last three books. The fourteen examples there are fewer than than those in book 1 alone (20), yet books 14–16 in the Teubner text of Koestermann (1965) occupy 100 pages while book 1 occupies just 44 pages. Similarly the nineteen examples in book 4 occur in just 40 pages of text. The decline may start earlier, but the figures are hard to interpret. Books 1–4 have 61 examples, but 5/6–13 only 38. Books 1–4 however are slightly longer (167 pages) than 5/6–13 (126 pages). The dramatic decline is in the final three books.

A total of 80 of the 113 examples are in narrative, and 33 in speeches. The latter figure represents about 28 per cent of the total, a percentage just slightly lower than that for asyndeta in speeches in Sallust. In Tacitus' *Histories*, however, we saw a much lower percentage in speeches (see 5.2.1).

5.2.2 Types: Parts of Speech and Difficulties of Interpretation
Most asyndetic pairs comprise nouns or the like (62), which was also the case in the *Histories*. Ten pairs are adjectives, and 23 verbs. Adjectival pairs are proportionately fewer than in the *Histories*, verbal pairs about the same proportionately. There are five adverbial examples, and fourteen prepositional.

Quite a few of the pairs are followed by a further element or elements, coordinated or juxtaposed, and I have tried to state reasons why I have treated the first pair as unitary (though often putting a question mark against an example). The easiest examples to deal with are those with two pairs juxtaposed, each with its own semantic or structural unity. Less easy are those in which there is a single addition, perhaps attached by *et*. See 60, *Ann.* 2.73.3 quoted after 70, 73, 74, 76, 78, 95, 100, 103, 105, 110, 112, 120, 122, *Ann.* 16.32.3 quoted after 125, 134, *Ann.* 4.8.5 quoted after 136, *Ann.* 6.35.2 quoted after 144, 146. In quite a few of these a coherent pair is followed by a summarising term or phrase, or a generalisation (60, *Ann.* 2.73.3, 73, 100, 103, 105, 110, 112), sometimes introduced by *cunctus* or *omnis*. In some cases there is a change of construction or part of speech in the final element (60, 74, 77, 78, 95, 134, 147; on this last example see on 33). Sometimes there is a marked division before the final element, consisting of more than a mere coordinator (75). Or the members of the first pair may have a particularly close connection with each other, with the final element more explanatory, more precise, or expressing a consequence of the first two terms (122, 146). An element of formulaic expression is to be seen here, particularly in cases where a pair is followed by a summary.

5 Tacitus Annals

5.2.3 Semantic and Structural Features

Tacitus had a striking taste for pairs of opposites (or near-opposites): see 56, 57, 59, 66, 67, 69, 72, 76, 82, 85, 90, 91, 96, 100, 104, 107, 109, 112a, 115, 127, 128, 130, 135, 141, 144, 148, 149–52, 153, 156, 158, 159, 160, 161, 166. There are 37 examples listed here, representing about 32 per cent of the whole. This high percentage follows on from a similarly high percentage in the *Histories* (34 per cent: see 4.2.3a). We saw, for example, that in Cicero's speeches pairs of opposites are rare, whereas they are common in the philosophica but to a considerable extent determined by the subject matter. In the comments on the above examples in Tacitus it is often pointed out that his opposites are 'inexplicit' or 'virtual', that is variants on the most direct way of expressing a particular opposition. In the frequency of opposites and the way in which they are expressed we see a Tacitean mannerism verging on the mechanical. The term 'variatio' has long been used to describe a feature of Tacitus' style, and a non-explicit pair of opposites may be seen as a variant on the obvious way of stating a particular opposition. Sometimes two pairs of opposites are juxtaposed (56–7, 66–7, 127–8), or a pair of opposites is juxtaposed with a unitary pair of a different type (68–9, 84–5, 106–7, 113–15), or an asyndetic pair of opposites is followed by a coordinated pair of opposites (59, 72, 90, 112a, 141, 166).

Several pairs of opposites are of 'grammatical' types, with contrasting prefixes or a contrast of voice: 100 *aditus abscessus*, 141 *absistere adloqui*, 144 *pellerent pellerentur*.

It is not only pairs of opposites that are juxtaposed by Tacitus in the *Annals*. Asyndeton bimembre is something that tends to come in clusters in his work, with two pairs (of varying types) standing next to each other or scarcely separated. This is a structural feature that goes beyond semantics, a form of presentation (whether in narrative or speeches) based on the accumulation of striking contrasts. There are eleven such groupings of asyndeta bimembria, three indeed comprising three pairs (66–7 with 132, 113–15, 153 with 162–3): 56–7, 66–7 with 132, 68–9, 84–5, 87–8 (with a single-word interruption), 96, 101–2, 106–7, 113–15, 127–8, 153 with 162–3). This list has 24 asyndeta bimembria, none used on its own.

Moreover in other cases an asyndetic pair precedes a coordinated pair of single terms, or a coordinated pair of phrases: 59, 63 (coordinated phrases), 65 (phrases), 72 (the type in which the coordinated pair differs syntactically from the asyndetic pair, because the coordinated terms are dependent on another: here referred to as 'inconcinnity'), 75, 80, 86 (inconcinnity), 90, 92, 93 (inconcinnity), 99, 108 (phrases), 112a, 153, 158, 164 (the last two of a particular type, whereby a pair of the prepositional type is followed by a pair of coordinated adjectives). There are sixteen examples here. Those sequences marked by syntactic inconcinnity are quoted below, 6.2b.

Another manifestation of the tendency for asyndeta to occur in accumulations is the juxtaposition of a two-word asyndeton bimembre with phrasal or clausal asyndeta, or with a longer sequence of asyndetic single words, which elements may come before or after the asyndeton bimembre. See 126, 130, 131 (before and after; here, before *abire fugere* there occur the prepositional phrases *sine pudore flagitii, sine cura ducum*, an accumulation that may be compared with that at 153, where *temere prouisu* is preceded by *per saltus per paludes* and followed immediately by *ob iram ob praedam*: on such structures see below, 6.2a), 146, 147, 160 (three phrases occur before a prepositional asyndeton), 165.

It is clear that Tacitus displays a marked stylistic mannerism, in that he often has an asyndeton bimembre within a group containing other asyndeta bimembria or juxtaposed phrases of various types. It would not be good practice for an editor to add a coordinator (or follow a manuscript with a coordinator) when an asyndeton occurs within such a pattern. On the other hand it would be wrong to imply that such accumulations were particular to Tacitus. Accumulations in various forms go back to the earliest period (see e.g. XIX.1, XXIII.7).

Just ten pairs of adjectives are numbered above from the *Annals*. One formal feature of adjectives that stands out is the prefix *in-*. In three cases the pairing consists of two privatives (123, 124, 125), and in three other cases it has one privative (117, 118, 121), with privatives thus occurring in 60 per cent of the instances. The privatives that are in pairs are near-synonyms. By contrast we saw that in the *Histories* just two of the adjectival pairs have a privative adjective, whereas in Sallust the type is common. Note too (in the *Annals*) the substantivised privative pairs *leues ignobiles* (79), *bellatorum imbellium* (82) and *inlustres ignobiles* (90). There is nothing comparable in the *Histories*. Notable too are 124 and 125, both pairs of privative adjectives that are in agreement with the unspecified subject of the verb, a type we have seen for example in Virgil (predicative adjuncts).

Of verbs, several of the pairs have verbal similarities to types in Sallust (133, 137, 145). In about a quarter of cases the two verbs express acts of violence (132, 133, 138, 142, 143, 144, *Ann*. 6.35.2 quoted after 144; cf., in the *Histories*, 29, 35).

5 *Tacitus* Annals 633

Various semantic categories recur, or particular words turn up in more than one asyndetic combination.

At XXVI.7.8.2 it was noted that *domus* is not infrequently used in asyndetic pairs. It is found thus in Tacitus as well as Sallust. Note *domos uillas* (opposites) at Sallust 18 and Tacitus 104. Tacitus twice combines *domus* and *fora* (76, 166), and Sallust twice has *domus* with *patria* (23, 24).

Nouns (in particular, but also verbs) to do with the use of the voice especially in creating din, complaining, lamenting, were noted on Cicero 62 (*gemitus ploratus*), where similar phrases from Livy and elsewhere were cited (note Livy 33 *(clamor) dissonus impar*). So we saw Sallust 39 *strepitu clamore*, with different such pairs quoted from elsewhere, and Sallust 30 *clamore uultu* (again with additional material). See too Tacitus 58 *uerba uultus*, 61 *sermone uoltu*, 57 *questus adulationem* (cf. the passage of Livy referred to above for *questibus*), 77 *uoce uultu*, 106 *iurgia preces*, 159 *silentio uoce*. At 71 *dolor ira* leads to *questus*. The variability of these pairs shows that they were not mere fossilised formulae. That they belong, however, to the same semantic field suggests to me that there was a way that such pairs could be pronounced asyndetically (with a particular intonation?) that made asyndeton suitable to the meaning. Similarly asyndeton might have been appropriate for pairs of verbs of violence because of a potential intonation pattern.

Various Tacitean pairs are of military meaning, and those with two or more of the triad *arma equi uiri* were formulaic: see 60 *uigilias stationes*, 93 *stationes uigiliae*, 99 *arma munimenta*, 101, 102 *equos uiros, arma opes*, 110 *equi uiri*.

Another category consists of terms to do with personal or political relationships or social status: 63 *ob propinquos amicos*, 66 *plebes primores*, 72 *proximos alienos*, 79 *leues ignobiles*, 80 *socios ciues*, 90 *inlustres ignobiles*, 97 *Britannicum Octauiam*, 109 *ordo plebs*

I have noted fourteen pairs in the *Annals* that are alliterative: 58 *uerba uultus*, 66 *plebes primores*, 82 *bellatorum imbellium*, 86 *congressus conloquia*, 90 *inlustres ignobiles*, 100 *aditus abscessus*, 123 *inuisus infamis*, 124 *imbelles inermes*, 125 *intemeratus impollutus*, 129 *pergerent properarent*, 136 *adeundo appellando*, 141 *absistere adloqui*, 144 *pellerent pellerentur*, 145 *celebrari coli*. In six cases the two terms have the same prefix, and in four of these the prefix is *in-*. There are also two places where the alliterative but semantically opposite prefixes *ad-* and *ab-* are juxtaposed. The type with repeated fore-element is old (not least the sub-type with privative prefix). We saw that in the *Histories* (see on 19) Tacitus admits hardly any alliterative pairs. For such in Sallust see 3 *pudorem pudicitiam*, 15 *caedem incendia*, 17 *patriae*

634   XXX   The Annalists, Sallust and Tacitus

parentibus, 26 *fame fide*, 46 *patria parentibus*, 48 *infinita insatiabilis*, 58 *iners inbellis*, 76 *captos occisos*, 80 *occidi capi* (nine examples, with only two having a repeated fore-element, *in-*). Most of these look traditional or formulaic (3, 15, 17, 26, 46, 76, 78: seven of the nine). It should however be noted that it is very common at all periods for alliterative terms to be linked by *-que*: alliteration is not per se a determinant of asyndeton.

5.2.4   Some Textual Points
Some of the pairs that have come up in the *Annals* raise textual issues.

It is a contention of this book that it is not acceptable to emend away an asyndeton bimembre simply because other attestations of the pairing are always explicitly coordinated. This point may be illustrated from passage **86**: <u>*congressus conloquia*</u>, *notae ignotaeque aures uitari*. It was noted ad loc. that this combination is not uncommon, but the examples cited were all coordinated. Therefore, should an editor on the strength of the parallels add a coordinator? Emendation would not be justified, because the structure in which *congressus conloquia* is found here is significant. Not only is the asyndetic pair followed by a coordinated pair, a pattern favoured by Tacitus, but the coordinated pair (of opposites) is syntactically different from the first pair, in that the coordinated opposites are adjectives not nouns, hanging on *aures*. This syntactic 'inconcinnity' between an asyndetic pair and a coordinated pair that follows is a notable Tacitean pattern, which would be eliminated by emendation. It is not the pairing itself that determines the asyndeton, but the structure in which it is placed. An editor should always look at the structure in which a possible asyndeton occurs before considering emendation. For some other passages that raise similar issues see Sallust 18, 47, Tacitus 21.

At **91** (*de potentia exitio*) it was seen that the best manuscript, M, has no coordinator, but that editors usually add one. But the two terms are typical inexplicit reversives of a type found elsewhere in asyndeton in Tacitus, and Tacitus also uses asyndetic pairs dependent on a single preposition. Tacitean usage provides no grounds for the addition of a coordinator.

At **141** on the other hand (*tunc singulos, ut cuique* <u>*adsistere adloqui*</u> *animus erat, retinens aut dimittens partem diei absumpsit*) emendation, but of a different kind (of *adsistere* to *absistere*), is favoured by Tacitean usage (and by the general meaning of the sentence). The emendation introduces a pair of inexplicit opposites marked by the contrast of prefixes (a phenomenon that can be paralleled from elsewhere in the *Annals*), and also the

6 Conclusions: Sallust and Tacitus 635

following two phrases thereby are given a correlative relationship (with chiasmus) to the asyndetic terms, another pattern found elsewhere in Tacitus.

109 finally presents one of those manuscript variations between syndetic and asyndetic coordination which cannot be resolved by appeal to usage elsewhere. An editor here, as far as I can see, has nothing to go on apart from the relative reliability of the manuscripts.

6 Conclusions: Sallust and Tacitus

Despite some similarities between Sallust and Tacitus in the use of asyndeton, there are also differences, or partial differences, in that a phenomenon in Tacitus similar to something in Sallust may fall short of replication. In the following discussion I distinguish between verbal and structural similarities. A question hangs over the latter in particular. Do Sallust and Tacitus share certain structures because Tacitus was influenced by Sallust, or were those structures widespread in the literary language?

6.1 Lexical and Syntactic Similarities and Differences

Many words regularly occur together, whether coordinated or asyndetic, in the latter case in an asyndeton bimembre or longer sequences. The occurrence of the same asyndeton in two writers may therefore be due to the chance use by both of a traditional collocation (see e.g. Tacitus 6 on *tempus locus* and 64 on *decus gloria*).

But there are places where the similarity between two passages seems to go deeper. For example, the association of *spoliare, rapere* and *polluere* (see Tac. *Hist.* 2.26.2 cited after 30) may have been picked up from Sallust.

At Sall. *Jug.* 51.5 (on which see Tacitus 32) (*circumire hortari renouare proelium et ipse cum delectis temptare omnia, subuenire suis, hostibus dubiis instare, quos firmos cognouerat eminus pugnando retinere*) a pair of historic infinitives referring to two closely related actions (going around and encouraging) is at the head of a long sequence of more specific verb phrases containing some opposites. The opposites are *suis/hostibus, dubiis/firmos, instare/eminus pugnando*. Cf. Tacitus 146 *gentium ductores circumire hortari, firmare animos minuendo metu, accendenda spe*. There is the same expression *circumire hortari*, again with historic infinitives, and here too there is a more specific phrase following, expressed by means of twofold opposites (*minuendo/accendenda, metu/spe*; cf. too *firmos* in Sallust, *firmare* in Tacitus). The same expression *circumire hortari* occurs at *Annals* 137, with historic infinitives again. In the *Histories* (32) Tacitus has a slight variant, with a different compound in *circum-* (*circumsistere hortari*), and here too the verbs are in the historic infinitive and more specific phrases follow.

Circulating and giving encouragement are banal activities, particularly for a general before battle, but they do not have to be expressed either with asyndeton or in the historic infinitive, nor need any subsequent acts be conveyed by an accumulation of opposites.

Tacitus' use of pairs of verbs and that of Sallust have certain similarities, but they are not striking. Indeed several of the recurrent types we saw in Sallust (3.3.2: e.g. the frequent use of *festino* in asyndeton) are not to be found in Tacitus. Tacitus likes to combine verbs expressing acts of violence (see above, 5.2.3), and in this he has a resemblance to Sallust (see in Sallust 67, 76, 80, 81, and also the notes to Tacitus 29 and 132). Sallust (81) and Tacitus (133) both have such pairs of which the second verb is *excindo*. However, the point was made on Tacitus 29 that Cicero also has such combinations (see XXVI.7.2.3), and it is likely that an intonational feature of asyndetic verbs made the absence of a coordinator suitable when the verbs were of this semantic field (see above, 5.2.3).

Five of the 10 pairs in the *Histories* comprise historic infinitives (31, 32, 33, 36, 38), and six of the 20 in the *Annals* (126, 137, 138, 145, 146, 147). In Sallust the figure is nine of 19 (see 3.3.2). There is nothing of significance in these distributions to the relationship between Sallust and Tacitus; there is such a pair, for example, in the fragments of the annalists (2.1, 3).

Tacitus has some pairs of ablatival gerunds in a structure in which Sallust also has such a pair (see Tacitus 34, 134, 136; cf. Sallust 72). However, the type goes back to Plautus and is found in Cicero and elsewhere (see XXIII.5.4).

A sharp difference between Tacitus and Sallust lies in their use of pairs of opposites. Such pairs are extremely common both in the *Histories* and *Annals* (many of them inexplicit) (see 5.2.3), whereas their incidence in Sallust is far from striking (see 3.3.2). Here is a mannerism of Tacitus.

6.2 Some Structural Similarities and Differences

Asyndeta in Sallust and Tacitus often occur in sequences of pairs, with the other pairs varying in type. They may comprise for example other two-word asyndeta bimembria, phrasal asyndeta, or pairs that are linked by coordinators. I collect and discuss here various patterns. In this section full

6 Conclusions: Sallust and Tacitus

references to the texts are given, as well as the numbers used elsewhere in the chapter.

(a) Both Sallust and Tacitus sometimes combine pairs of asyndetic prepositional expressions (those in which a preposition is repeated) with other pairs (asyndetic or coordinated), which may have a significant semantic relationship. Particularly striking are the following two passages:

Sall. *Cat.* 6.1 (84) *genus hominum agreste, sine legibus sine imperio, liberum atque solutum*

Tac. *Ann.* 3.15.2 (158) *Tiberium sine miseratione sine ira, obstinatum clausumque uidit*

The structure of these passages is virtually identical. There is first a noun or noun phrase (*genus hominum agreste, Tiberium*). Then follow two asyndetic *sine*-phrases, each with a quasi-adjectival role in relation to the preceding noun/noun phrase. Finally, in agreement with the initial noun/noun phrase there is a pair of coordinated adjectives that are virtual synonyms. The one difference, which has come up already and will come up again, is that in the final phrase the coordinator is *atque* in Sallust but *-que* in Tacitus.

Note too the following, all of which also have an asyndetic pair of prepositional expressions associated with syndetic or asyndetic phrases or terms displaying significant semantic relationships either internally (i.e. of one member of the phrase or pair to the other) or externally (i.e. of one phrase with other juxtaposed phrases):

Sall. *Cat.* 20.7 (8 and 85) *ceteri omnes, strenui boni, nobiles atque ignobiles, uulgus fuimus sine gratia sine auctoritate*. Before *uulgus* there are two phrases, one asyndetic, the other with *atque* again, the first comprising complementary terms or near-synonyms, the second opposites.

Tac. *Hist.* 1.52.2 (48) *sine modo sine iudicio donaret sua, largiretur aliena*. Two clauses follow the prepositional expressions, with synonymous verbs and objects that are opposites.

Hist. 1.54.1 (49) *per principia per contubernia modo suas iniurias, modo uicinarum ciuitatium praemia . . . conquerentes*. Two phrases expressing a double opposition (*suas/uicinarum, iniurias/praemia*) follow the prepositional phrases.

Hist. 2.5.2 (50) *industria licentia, per uirtutes per uoluptates*. An asyndetic pair of opposites precedes the prepositional phrases.

Ann. 12.39.2 (**153, 162–3**) *temere prouisu, ob iram ob praedam, iussu et aliquando ignaris ducibus*. The prepositional asyndeton is between two pairs of opposites, the first comprising two asyndcetic adverbs, the second a term and expression coordinated. Before *temere* there is another asyndetic prepositional pair, followed by a clause with a disjunctive pair: *per saltus per paludes, ut cuique sors aut uirtus*.

Ann. 13.35.1 (**164**) *sine galeis sine loricis, nitidi et quaestuosi, militia per oppida expleta*. Woodman (2004) translates the coordinated pair that follows as 'sleek profiteers'. They are closely associated terms, as are the two nouns with *sine*. The structure of this passage is similar to that seen at the start of this section in the examples from Sallust (*Cat.* 6.1) and Tacitus (*Ann.* 3.15.2).

Note too *Ann.* 15.58.2 (**166**) *uolitabantque per fora per domus, rura quoque et proxima municipiorum pedites equitesque*. The following coordinated phrase is also dependent on *per*, and combines opposites.

It was pointed out on Tacitus 4 that the combining of an anaphoric prepositional asyndetic pair with another asyndeton is common in Cicero, and an example was also cited from a freedman's speech in Petronius (61.9 *per scutum per ocream egi aginaui*). Such structures may have been commonplace in rhetorical utterances, oratorical or conversational. They were certainly exploited particularly by Tacitus. The first two examples are structurally very similar, but need Tacitus have noticed the pattern solely in Sallust?

(b) The first two examples in the last section are particular manifestations of a general pattern that recurs in Sallust and Tacitus, where an asyndeton bimembre is followed immediately by a second, coordinated, pair. The coordinator is almost always *atque* in Sallust (the few other coordinators in Sallust are in bold below) but variable in Tacitus, and is never *atque* itself (though *ac* occurs):

Sall. *Cat.* 6.1 (**84**) *sine legibus sine imperio, liberum atque solutum*
Cat. 12.2 (**3**) *pudorem pudicitiam, diuina atque humana*
Cat. 20.7 (**8**) *strenui boni, nobiles atque ignobiles*
Cat. 47.1 (**84**) *interrogatus de itinere de litteris, postremo quid **aut** qua de causa consili habuisset*
Cat. 51.1 (**13**) *ab odio amicitia, ira atque misericordia uacuos esse decet*
Cat. 51.9 (**16**) *postremo armis cadaueribus, cruore atque luctu omnia conpleri*
Cat. 52.3 (**17**) *patriae parentibus, aris atque focis*
Cat. 52.13 (cited after 53) *loca taetra inculta, foeda atque formidulosa*
Cat. 59.5 (**87**) *rogat ut meminerint se contra latrones inermos pro patria pro liberis, pro aris atque focis suis certare*
Cat. 61.9 (**21**) *laetitia maeror, luctus atque gaudia*

6 Conclusions: Sallust and Tacitus 639

Jug. 10.8 (74) *colite obseruate talem hunc uirum, imitamini uirtutem* **et** *enitimini ne* ...
Jug. 31.9 (28) *itaque postremo leges maiestas uostra, diuina* **et** *humana omnia hostibus tradita sunt*
Jug. 31.20 (29) *quom regna prouinciae, leges iura iudicia, bella atque paces, postremo diuina* **et** *humana omnia penes paucos erant* (a more complex example, with two coordinated phrases, one with *atque* and the second with *et*).
Jug. 34.1 (30) *clamore uoltu, saepe impetu atque aliis omnibus*
Jug. 51.1 (31, 32) *arma tela, equi uiri, hostes atque ciues* (another complex example, with three pairs).
Jug. 51.1 (59) *uaria incerta, foeda atque miserabilis*

Tac. *Hist.* 2.29.2 (5) *silentio patientia, postremo precibus ac lacrimis ueniam quaerebant*
Hist. 3.86.1 (14) *consulatum sacerdotia, nomen locumque* ... *adeptus*
Hist. 4.52.1 (18) *tempore fortuna, cupidinibus aliquando aut erroribus*
Ann. 1.21.2 (59) *inuidiam misericordiam, metum et iras*
Ann. 2.5.3 (65) *siluis paludibus, breui aestate et praematura hieme*
Ann. 3.15.2 (158) *sine miseratione sine ira, obstinatum clausumque*
Ann. 6.19.2 (90) *inlustres ignobiles, dispersi aut aggerati*
Ann. 11.6.2 (92) *inimicitias accusationes, odia et iniurias foueri*
Ann. 12.39.2 (153, 163) *ob iram ob praedam, iussu et aliquando ignaris ducibus*
Ann. 13.35.1 (164) *sine galeis sine loricis, nitidi et quaestuosi*
Ann. 13.46.1 (108) *nobilitatem pulchritudinem, uota omnium et gaudia felicium*
Ann. 15.27.3 (112a) *plana edita, ualidos inualidosque*
Ann. 15.58.2 (166) *uolitabantque per fora per domus, rura quoque et proxima municipiorum*

Some of these passages contain two pairs of opposites or virtual opposites (*Cat.* 12.2 (3), 61.9 (21), *Ann.* 1.21.2 (59), 6.19.2 (90), 15.27.3 (112a)). Others have one pair of opposites, either in the asyndetic phrase (*Ann.* 3.15.2 (158)) or the coordinated phrase (*Cat.* 20.7 (8), *Ann.* 2.5.3 (65), 12.39.2 (153, 163); cf. *Jug.* 31.20 (29)).

Although this pattern is a marked presence in both writers (but with avoidance of *atque* as coordinator in Tacitus), and although Tacitus might have been vaguely influenced by Sallust, the pattern can be found elsewhere in literary language (for Cicero's speeches and philosophica see XXVI.7.2.1, 7.3.1(iii)). It is also attested in an old augural phrase in Plautus, and in a prayer in Cato (for details see XXIII.3). A specific connection between Sallust and Tacitus would be more plausible if Tacitus too had shown a preference for *atque*. As it is, both writers might independently have been using an old type of accumulation of different types of coordination.

Sometimes in Tacitus there is a variation on the type seen in most of the examples in the previous section. In this variant the members of the coordinated phrase are not of the same syntactic status as the asyndetic pair. Instead they are dependent on or modifiers of a noun that itself balances the two asyndetic terms. Thus for example in the second passage below *malis* and *bonis* are adjectives, whereas the asyndetic pairs comprise two nouns. Balancing these latter there is the noun *artibus*, which is modified by the two adjectives. In this structure the embedded pair in the phrase with coordination consists of opposites. The final pair could be rewritten as a nominal pair of opposites ('with luxury and industry, affability and arrogance, evil and good'). The only possible example I have noted in Sallust is the first below; this then looks like a Tacitean mannerism, typical of his taste for *variatio*. For comparable but not identical variation in Lucretius and Virgil see XXIV.2.2 on 26, 27.

Sall. *Cat.* 10.2 (quoted before 1) *labores pericula, dubias atque asperas res*

Tac. *Hist.* 1.10.2 (1, 2) *luxuria industria, comitate adrogantia, malis bonisque artibus mixtus*
Ann. 3.1.4 (72) *proximos alienos, uirorum feminarumue planctus* (note *-ue*, and cf. *aut* sometimes in passages in the previous section).
Ann. 4.69.3 (86) *congressus conloquia, notae ignotaeque aures*
Ann. 11.18.3 (93) *stationes uigiliae, diurna nocturnaue munia* (with *-ue* again).

(c) Note the following two passages:

Sall. *Cat.* 10.4 (1) *namque auaritia fidem probitatem ceterasque artis bonas subuortit*
Tac. *Ann.* 2.73.3 (quoted after 70) *quantum clementia temperantia, ceteris bonis artibus praestitisset*

In both there is a pair formed of two semantically overlapping abstract nouns, followed by a generalising expression *ceterae artes bonae*, in the appropriate case. At Tac. *Hist.* 3.49.1 (13) (*felicitas in tali ingenio auaritiam superbiam ceteraque occulta mala patefecit*) a very similar example to that of Sallust above is found, in which an abstract noun, personified (*felicitas*; cf. *auaritia* in Sallust), is subject of the verb of which two unitary abstract nouns are object. Moreover the clause introduced by *ceteraque* has a semantic connection with both the passages quoted at the start of this section, in that it contains the expression *occulta mala*, a near-opposite of the 'good arts' in the other two passages.

6 Conclusions: Sallust and Tacitus

(d) Another structure has an asyndeton bimembre followed by a unitary asyndetic tricolon comprising single words. The tricolon is followed by asyndetic phrases with significant semantic relationships, internally or externally. Note the following passages of Sallust and Tacitus:

Sall. *Jug.* 31.20 (**29**) *quom regna prouinciae, leges iura iudicia, bella atque paces, postremo diuina et humana omnia penes paucos erant*

Tac. *Hist.* 4.5.2 (**16**) *ciuis senator, maritus gener amicus, cunctis uitae officiis aequabilis, opum contemptor, recti peruicax, constans aduersus metus*

Regna prouinciae and *ciuis senator* both consist of complementary terms, as do the two tricola following. The two asyndetic phrases in Sallust after the tricolon have pairs of opposites within (war and peace, things divine and human), whereas the four asyndetic phrases in Tacitus may be classified into two pairs, with the two phrases forming each pair loosely opposed to each other (he was, in both groups, a supporter of what was right and despiser of what was wrong).

However, despite this similarity between the two writers, this is the pattern that I have elsewhere referred to as '2 + 3' (or, in reverse, '3 + 2'). It is not particular to Sallust and Tacitus (see e.g. XXVI.7.2.1, third point).

(e) I have made the point that single-word asyndeta bimembria are quite frequently followed by phrasal or clausal asyndeta (see 3.3.3c, 4.2.4c, 5.2.3). This is not the place to cite multiple examples, but note the following three passages, from Sallust and the *Annals*, in which there are strings of infinitives, the first two in each passage forming an asyndeton bimembre, while the rest (three in the first two passages, two in the third) are part of short asyndetic clauses or phrases):

Sall. *Cat.* 6.5 (**64**) *at Romani domi militiaeque intenti <u>festinare parare</u>, alius alium hortari, hostibus obuiam ire, libertatem patriam parentisque armis tegere*

Tac. *Ann.* 1.16.2 (**126**) <u>*lasciuire*</u> *miles,* <u>*discordare*</u>*, pessimi cuiusque sermonibus praebere aures, denique luxum et otium cupere, disciplinam et laborem aspernari*

Ann. 15.12.3 (**147**) *simul suas legiones* <u>*adire hortari;*</u> *priorum admonere, nouam gloriam ostendere.*

Here are a few further differences between Sallust and Tacitus.

(f) Tacitus often has two pairs of asyndeta bimembria juxtaposed, with the members of each pair opposites. Sallust does not have this structure. For Tacitus see:

Hist. 1.3.2 (**21, 22**) *laeta tristia, ambigua manifesta*
Hist. 1.10.2 (**1, 2**) *luxuria industria, comitate adrogantia*

Hist. 2.5.2 (4) *industria licentia, per uirtutes per uoluptates*
Hist. 2.80.1 (7, 8) *spes timor, ratio casus*
Ann. 1.7.1 (56, 57) *lacrimas gaudium, questus adulationem*
Ann. 1.41.3 (127, 128) *orant obsistunt, rediret maneret*
Ann. 2.19.1 (66, 67) *plebes primores, iuuentus senes*
Ann. 13.44.3 (106, 107) *iurgia preces, exprobratio satisfactio*

When Sallust juxtaposes asyndetic pairs, these are not both opposites but have a varied semantic relationship:

Cat. 25.2 (51, 69) *litteris Graecis [et] Latinis docta, psallere [et] saltare*
Jug. 51.1 (31, 32) *arma tela, equi uiri*
Jug. 76.1 (36, 37) *arma tela, locos tempora*
Jug. 101.11 (79, 80) *sequi fugere, occidi capi*

When Sallust does (occasionally) combine two pairs of opposites, the second pair has a coordinating element:

Cat. 12.2 (3) *pudorem pudicitiam, diuina atque humana*
Cat. 51.1 (13) *ab odio amicitia, ira atque misericordia uacuos esse decet*
Cat. 61.9 (21) *laetitia maeror, luctus atque gaudia*

Cf. too Sall. *Hist.* 4.60.17 Ramsey (47) *socios amicos, procul iuxta sitos, inopes potentisque*. This is a less straightforward example. The final coordinated elements, this time with *-que*, are virtual opposites. These are preceded by a phrase containing adverbial opposites in asyndeton (*procul iuxta*). At the beginning *socios amicos* is asyndetic, but the terms are complements not opposites.

(g) Tacitus sometimes links to an asyndeton bimembre another pair (whether asyndetic or coordinated), making the link by a coordinator rather than by mere juxtaposition. Sallust however adds further pairs only by juxtaposition. Here are the instances in Tacitus where the addition is made by a coordinator:

Hist. 4.76.3 (19) <u>*formidinem fugam*</u> *famemque ac totiens captis precariam uitam*
Ann. 2.60.3 (70) <u>*Libya Aethiopia*</u> *Medisque et Persis et Bactriano ac Scytha potitum*
Ann. 3.26.1 (75) *uetustissimi mortalium, nulla adhuc mala libidine,* <u>*sine probro*</u>
 <u>*scelere*</u> *eoque sine poena aut coercitionibus agebant*
Ann. 4.38.3 (80) *proinde* <u>*socios ciues*</u> *et deos ipsos et deas*
Ann. 12.17.2 (99) *cum* <u>*arma munimenta*</u>*, impediti uel eminentes loci, amnesque et urbes iuxta perrumperentur.*

(h) Asyndeta bimembria are more common proportionately in speeches in Sallust than in those of Tacitus *Histories*. The *Annals* however have a similar incidence in speeches to that in Sallust, but asyndeta are not so

6 Conclusions: Sallust and Tacitus

common in direct speeches in Tacitus. Sallust has notable clusters in some direct speeches.

In the use of asyndetic coordination the most distinctive feature of Tacitus' historical style is his combining of opposites, particularly by means of terms that are not the standard designations of the opposed ideas. In this he differs from Cicero in the philosophical works, who often has to express oppositions but uses basic terminology. Sallust does have some pairs of opposites, but such pairs are not an obtrusive mannerism of his style, as they are of Tacitus'. Tacitus' taste for varying the obvious means that there are few old formulaic asyndeta in his work (an exception being some pairs of adverbs), though he does tend to use asyndeta within certain semantic fields that attracted asyndetic coordination elsewhere, as for example when highlighting the violence of an action. As for features of Sallust, I would stress, first, the dense accumulations of asyndeta in certain speeches, as that of Catiline, accumulations that may well have been characteristic of impassioned delivery in late Republican politics. We noted that, just as Catiline is given such an accumulation, so Cicero at high points in his speeches against Catiline also resorted to accumulations. A second characteristic of Sallust is his use of *atque* to coordinate two unitary terms following an asyndeton bimembre. Tacitus has the same structure, but uses other coordinators. Both writers use asyndeton bimembre particularly in accumulations, and there are some structural parallels, but it is not only in historiography that such phenomena are found.

CHAPTER XXXI

Livy

1 Introduction

I have tried in this chapter to comment on every (possible) instance of asyndeton bimembre comprising two words in the following books of Livy: 4, 5, 9, 23, 30, 34, 38, 42. These books occupy about 697 pages of modern editions (OCTs and Teubners), which makes them collectively at least as long and probably longer than the whole of the *Histories* and *Annals* of Tacitus (see the conclusions below, 3.1). It will become clear that this type of asyndeton is rare in Livy. Quite a few of the examples numbered below are also open to doubt.

The examples are arranged according to parts of speech, with the anaphoric prepositional type treated separately. Consuls' names constantly occur together without a coordinator, but these are not dealt with separately in this book (see however XXII.9).

In the commentaries coordinated variants on the asyndetic pairs are regularly cited. A high proportion of the asyndeta bimembria in Livy (about 38 of the 66 examples below) have a variant with a coordinator, attested in Livy himself or other writers, or in Livy as well as others; one may add (e.g.) to the instances in this chapter *ferro igni(que)*, which, though found often in Livy with the coordinator, occurs once as well in asyndetic form, at 1.59.1 (see Oakley 1998: 299, and Cicero 182 for the type of pairing). It is rare to find in Latin a two-word asyndeton that is never varied by the addition of a coordinator, if one leaves aside a few old official or religious formulae, such as *patres conscripti* and (*Iuppiter*) *optimus maximus*, and even some of these (e.g. *sarta tecta, loca lautia*: see XXII.5.3, 5.4) sometimes have a coordinator. Conversely, any pair of words with some sort of semantic unity found usually with a coordinator may occasionally be converted by a writer into an asyndeton, for reasons that may sometimes be identified but are often unclear. If there is manuscript variation between asyndeton and coordination an editor may have

2   *Data*   645

reasons for regarding one manuscript as superior to another, but if there are no such reasons conventional distributional arguments for preferring one reading to the other are unlikely to be convincing. If A *et* B is attested four times in a writer and AB just once (cf. *ferro igni(que)* above), that is unlikely to be a good reason for changing the one instance of AB to A *et* B, given that in large numbers of pairs (and not only in Livy: the same point has been made in reference e.g. to Sallust and Tacitus) oscillation between coordination and asyndeton is well attested. A single asyndetic deviation from a normal coordination is perfectly possible. This is an issue that comes up several times below (and see 3.9 on some criteria for judging isolated asyndetic variants).

I have followed my usual practice of not punctuating with a comma pairs I consider to be asyndetic. That is merely my own convention for presenting this material: as I have argued elsewhere, there may be good reasons in particular cases for using a comma in a critical text. I have suggested on various examples below that there was probably a pause between the two terms (notably between *in*-privative adjectives), and an editor who feels that that must have been so in a certain case should mark the pause with punctuation.

Finally, I have adopted an inclusive policy here. Various examples that have troubled editors for good reason are included, usually with a question mark. I have also included some longer asyndetic sequences which I believe to contain 'embedded' pairs of asyndeta bimembria (see on 1 below).

2   Data

2.1   Nouns

(1) 4.3.12 *Ser. Tullium post hunc, captiua Corniculana natum, patre nullo, matre serua, ingenio uirtute regnum tenuisse?*, 'after him, did not Servius Tullius, born of a captive from Corniculum, with no father and his mother a slave, hold the royal power thanks to his innate ability and worth?'.

The asyndeton bimembre is preceded by an asyndetic phrasal tricolon, a not unusual type of accumulation, though the two groups here are not of the same syntactic status: the first three phrases modify *Ser. Tullium*, whereas *ingenio uirtute* is part of the verb phrase. For juxtaposed asyndeta of various types that differ in syntax see e.g. Sallust 3, 27, 39, Tacitus 48, 113–15, 153; see also below, 3, 4.

For the pair *ingenium uirtus* in a longer sequence see Livy 41.23.10 *genere materno, uirtute ingenio, fauore Macedonum longe praestitit Demetrius*, 'in his mother's family, his character and intellect, and in his support from the Macedonians, Demetrius far excelled (the other)'. This is a commonplace structure in which a unitary asyndetic pair is embedded within a longer sequence of coordinations, syndetic or asyndetic. The first and last phrases refer to external advantages that had befallen the referent, whereas the juxtaposed terms *uirtute ingenio* refer to personal qualities of his own. The two are also sometimes linked by coordinators, as at Cic. *Arch.* 25 *huius ingenium et uirtutem*, *Fam.* 2.3.2 *a summa uirtute summoque ingenio*: see *TLL* VII.1.1527.59f. and e.g. Cic. *Acad.* 2.3, *Rep.* 2.20, 2.46 (*uir ingenio et uirtute praestans*: cf. Livy 41.23.10 above), *Tusc.* 4.1. Pairs denoting virtues (or vices) and personal attributes are common in asyndeton in e.g. Sallust and Tacitus (see for example on Sallust 1 and Tacitus 13; also XXVI.7.8.2).

Virtus is often in asyndetic pairs with other words: see Cicero 8 *uirtus dignitas*, 193 *uirtutis industriae*, *Verr.* 3.154 *uirtutem eloquentiam*, Tacitus 50 *per uirtutes per uoluptates*. The tendency for some terms to be used asyndetically with a variety of other terms has been pointed out frequently in earlier chapters.

Speech.

(2) 4.4.2 <u>pontifices augures</u> *Romulo regnante nulli sunt*, 'in the reign of Romulus there were no pontiffs or augurs'.

Pairs denoting offices, honours or their holders are a recognisable type of asyndeton bimembre (cf. e.g. Cicero 122 *iudicibus magistratibus* and cross references, and also 4 below with cross references). *Pontifex* and *augur* are elsewhere associated in various ways, without necessarily being in asyndeton bimembre (e.g. Cic. *Leg. agr.* 2.96, Livy 6.41.9). They are however frequently juxtaposed in the *Lex Vrson.* (*CIL* II².5.1022), both in coordination and in asyndeton: note e.g. 66.34 <u>pontifices auguresque</u> *in pontificum augurum conlegio in ea colon(ia) sunto*, where the coordinated pair and the asyndetic are alongside each other (see further *TLL* X.1.2678.68ff.); see also XXII.7.2, where an asyndetic example is cited from the *Lex Coloniae Genetiuae*. Here is an asyndeton bimembre which, like many others, had a place in legal language (on this characteristic of legal Latin see Kalb 1912: 134–9, and XXII).

Speech.

(3, 4) 4.15.5 *sed tamen* <u>Claudios Cassios</u> <u>consulatibus decemuiratibus</u>, *suis maiorumque honoribus, splendore familiarum sustulisse animos, quo nefas fuerit*, 'but men like Claudius, Cassius raised their sights to forbidden heights because of consulships, decemvirates (their own honours and those of their ancestors: the splendour of their families)'.

2 Data

For single names in asyndeton, often listed *exempli gratia* rather than as a totality, see e.g. XXVI.2.2, 3.2, 4.2, 6.2, and also IV.3 (with some plurals of the type here; for which see also Cicero 212, from a letter of Caelius). *Consulatibus decemuiratibus* is also a selective list.

The next part of the sentence, to *sustulisse*, is not easy to analyse, but there seems to be an initial asyndeton bimembre (*consulatibus decemuiratibus*), with both terms referring to specific offices, followed by two appositions. The first appositional phrase explains *consulatibus decemuiratibus* ('= honours held by them and by their ancestors'), and the final phrase summarises what has gone before (= 'i.e. the splendour of their families'). For the type *consulatibus decemuiratibus* (and the variant showing officers rather than offices linked) see Sallust **6** *reges tetrarchae*, **11** *magistratus sacerdotia*, Tacitus **14** *consulatum sacerdotia*, **55** *consulatus triumphos*; also above, **2**, and below, **64** *in magistratibus in sacerdotiis*.

For an explanatory pair in apposition, see Cic. *Fam.* 3.6.4 (SB 69) *statuere multa, decernere iudicare*, with Shackleton Bailey's translation (Loeb): '(they were) making many decisions both administrative and judicial'.

Indirect speech.

(**5, 6**) 5.11.5 *qui amissis liberis fratribus, propinquis adfinibus lugubres domos habeant*, 'those who have houses in mourning for the loss of children and brothers, kinsmen and relations by marriage'.

I interpret the four nouns underlined as comprising two asyndetic pairs, each pair with a semantic unity. The first two terms express specific blood relationships ('children, brothers'). The second two are collectives, the first embracing relatives by blood or marriage or one category or the other (see below), and the second relationships by marriage. *Propinquitas* combines the ideas of *cognatio* (relationship by blood) and *adfinitas* (relationship by marriage). For the distinction see on Sallust **41, 42**, and see first *TLL* X.2.2013.51ff., on *propinquitas* of a relationship established by marriage, where it is equated with *adfinitas*; and second 67ff., on the same word of a blood relationship, where it is equated with *cognatio*. *Propinqui* in opposition to *adfines*, as in our passage, presumably refers only to a relationship by blood. There is a shift from the specific to the more general in the pairs. For a similar group of two asyndetic pairs see Cic. *Planc.* 29 *cum parente . . . cum patruo, cum adfinibus cum propinquis*. Here there is a digression after *cum parente*, and then Cicero resumes, making a transition from specific relatives to the same pair of plural collectives; cf. *Planc.* 27 *maximis uinculis et propinquitatis et adfinitatis coniunctus*. Cic.

Fam. 3.10.9 (SB 73) *opes ingenium liberi adfines propinqui* is translated by Shackleton Bailey (Loeb) as 'riches, talents, children, and relations by blood and marriage', with the last two terms rendered in the wrong order.

For *liberi* and *fratres* together in longer asyndetic groups, see Livy 22.60.1 *liberos fratres cognatos*, 34.3.7 *parentes uiri liberi fratres earum*.

Family members and relationships are often referred to in asyndeta bimembria (see XIV, Sallust **12**, **42**, Tacitus **97**, and in this chapter see below, **19**, **23** with cross references). Note too Tacitus **63** *propinquos amicos* (see the commentary), and Cicero **1** *adfinitas societas*.

The contrast between the two pairs here is admittedly by no means stark, as it is possible to cite asyndetic groups that combine members of both the suggested pairs. *Liberi* and *propinqui* are both used in conjunction with *amici* at Cic. *Fin*. 5.81, *Off*. 3.26 and 3.63. At Tacitus **35** the last three nouns in **5**, **6** are (in a different order) in an asyndetic group (*nec eo segnius propinquos adfinis fratres trucidant spoliant*). Nevertheless in the pairs above there is a movement from specific kinship terms to collectives, which I think justifies the punctuation proposed.

Like so many pairs sometimes used asyndetically, *adfinis* and *propinqui* may also be coordinated: e.g. Cic. *Verr*. 2.89 *adfinem atque propinquum*.

Indirect speech.

(7) 5.48.6 *Capitolinus exercitus, stationibus uigiliis fessus*, 'the Capitoline army, wearied by guard-duties, watches'.

The paradosis is asyndeton, with *et* (one MS of the π group) and *-que* (the editio princeps) conjectures. The same asyndeton occurs in Tacitus (**60**, **93**), and in Livy at 28.1.8 (*ea stationibus uigiliis, omni iusta militari custodia tuta et firma esse*) there is first the same asyndetic pair, and then a more comprehensive phrase embracing all types of military protection ('that this was kept safe and sound by pickets, watch patrols, every proper form of military protection'; here *stationes* and *uigiliae* are tending to be personalised, whereas at **7** they are more abstract). This tricolon is of a common type in historians. There is first what may be described as an embedded asyndeton bimembre comprising terms that have a unity and are semantically specific, and then a generalising or summarising phrase containing *omnis* or *cunctus* (see Sallust **1**, **25**, Tacitus **100** with cross references for this structure, with either *omnis* or *cunctus* in the final member; see too XVIII.6).

There is another reason for accepting the asyndeton, and that is because the two terms do not form a complete list: these were just two of the army's hardships, as the context makes clear. The translation of the Loeb (slightly modified) is: 'The army on the Capitol was worn out by guard-duties, watches; and though they had got the better of all human ills, yet was there one, and that was famine, which nature would not suffer to be overcome.' For asyndeton in selective pairs see e.g. on 4 above, and also IV.3.

Ogilvie (1965: 738), printing the lemma *stationibus uigiliis<que>*, describes the asyndeton at 7 as 'too harsh'. There is nothing harsh about it, as it is paralleled in Tacitus and belongs to a type, of terms that are near-synonyms or complementary, here expressing military duties of similar kinds (for military terms in asyndeton bimembre, a common category, see e.g. the conclusions below, 3.3, and also XXVI.7.8.2, XXX.5.2.3, Tacitus 99, 101, 102, 110).

Oakley (2005b: 570) argues that *uigiles* 'were the troops who guarded the rampart and that *uigiliae* is an abstract noun used to denote the activity of the *uigiles*'. The *statio* on the other hand (571) 'was the detachment that guarded the gate of the camp' (but a verbal meaning is needed for *stationibus* in 7, since it complements *fessus*).

The two terms often occur with an expressed coordinator (e.g. Caes. *Civ.* 1.21.3, Livy 2.39.9, 3.28.4, 4.27.11, 9.13.9, 28.24.10). This collection makes it clear that the two types of duties were closely connected, and that association gave the terms the potential to be used in asyndeton. It is of no relevance to textual criticism that coordination is more common in extant texts than asyndeton.

Narrative.

(8, 9) 9.6.6 *insignia sua consulibus, [fasces, lictores]*, arma equos, uestimenta commeatus *militibus benigne mittunt*, 'forthwith they ungrudgingly sent to the consuls their insignia, and arms and horses, garments and provisions to the soldiers'.

Arma equi is a pair found often elsewhere in asyndeton and with a coordinator (see on Sallust 31, 32). There seem to be two asyndetic pairs after *consulibus*, the first referring to fighting resources used by the soldiers (*arma equos*), the second to their personal necessities, clothing and provisions. The *TLL* (III.1823.55f.) says that *commeatus* is very often found with other things that soldiers use in war ('persaepe cum aliis rebus, quibus bello utuntur'), such as *arma* and *equi* (57ff.), but in the present passage there is a movement from combative resources to personal. *Vestimenta* and *commeatus* occur together with a coordinator at Livy 32.27.3 in a military context (*magni commeatus et uestimenta exercitui missa*). On the reasons for deleting *fasces, lictores* see Oakley (2005a: 99) ad loc., who does not comment on the asyndeton. He cites Val. Max. 5.1.ext.5 *protinusque consulibus insignia honoris, militibus uestem arma equos commeatus benignissime praestando* as 'lifted straight from' Livy (though Valerius has lost the

pairings). A pair semantically equivalent to *uestimenta commeatus* is Plaut. *Truc.* 137 *uestimento et cibo*. For *commeatus* in asyndeton see also below, 15.
Narrative.

(10, 11) 9.14.10–11 *caedunt pariter resistentes fusosque, inermes atque armatos, seruos liberos, puberes impubes, homines iumentaque*, 'they slaughtered alike those resisting and scattered, the unarmed and armed, slaves and free, adults and those prepubescent, men and quadrupeds'.

A series of five substantival opposites (antonyms and complementarities), two of them asyndetic, three syndetic (with two different coordinators). The oscillation between asyndeton and coordinators can be found elsewhere in such sequences: note Tacitus 70 *Libya Aethiopia Medisque et Persis et Bactriano ac Scytha potitum*. See also Sallust 31, 32 *arma tela, equi uiri, hostes atque ciues*, Tacitus 99, 153, Cicero 3, and see below, 20.

On Cic. *Nat.* 2.145 our example is cited by Pease (1958: 929, on *timidumque*) supposedly to show the use of -*que* connecting the final pair in a series of pairs, but there is no significance in that because -*que* also connects the first pair. It is the variation between different coordinators and asyndeton that is a mannerism here.

Compare the first two phrases, *resistentes fusosque* and *inermes atque armatos*, and also the preceding *caedunt pariter*, with 4.59.6 *caedes pariter fugientium ac resistentium, armatorum atque inermium*. For the opposition 'armed/unarmed', but in asyndeton, see below, 38.

With *seruos liberos* cf. Cic. *Cluent.* 148 *omnes uiri mulieres, liberi serui in iudicium uocantur*, B. *Afr.* 23.1 *expeditoque exercitu seruorum liberorum II milium numero*. *Liber* and *seruus* are constantly opposed (for coordinated examples see e.g. Caes. *Civ.* 3.14.3, 3.32.2, 3.80.3, Livy 29.29.3, 39.49.8, 45.14.7; also *TLL* VII.2.1280.67ff.). See also XIII.5.3.

The *TLL* s.v. *pubes* 2 does not seem to cite any other examples of the opposition above (for this passage see *TLL* X.2.2436.60).

Homines iumentaque is similar to a merism, not unlike Umbrian *dupursus/peturpursus* = 'bipeds, quadrupeds' (*Tab. Ig.* VIb.10–11) (see also West 2007: 100). In our passage the terms are a finite set, in that there would have been a specific number killed, whereas the merism, as that term seems to be used, would denote all living creatures (of the most common types).

Three (or more) asyndeta bimembria in a sentence are unusual. For a passage with six nominal pairs see Sallust 6–10. For such accumulations see below, 13, 14, 15, and also Tacitus 153.
Narrative.

(12) 9.25.5 *iuuentute armis Samnitem iuuisse*, 'they had helped the Samnites with men and arms'.

A variant on the commonplace *uiris armis*. For the terms in coordinations see Livy 28.37.4 *classis iuuentus armaque* (perhaps to be analysed *classis + iuuentus armaque*), 24.40.10 *iuuentutem Apolloniatium armaque et urbis uires*. Cf. Varro *Rust.* 2.10.1 *iuuentutem ... armatam* (and for similar expressions Livy 1.26.1, 23.40.3, 36.12.5, 40.30.2). Compare Tacitus' habit of varying asyndetic pairs of opposites by not using the normal explicit pairing. See XIII.5.5, and see Tacitus 1, 2, 9, 56, 57, 69, 72, 107, 135 and 5.2.3.
Indirect speech.

(13, 14, 15) 23.5.6 *legiones equitatus, arma signa, equi uirique, pecunia commeatus aut in acie aut binis postero die amissis castris perierunt*, 'legions and cavalry, arms and standards, horses and men, money and provisions perished either in battle or with the loss of two camps the next day'.
For *legio* and *equitatus/equites* opposed or juxtaposed, see Cic. *Phil.* 10.14 *nostrae sunt legiones, nostra leuis armatura, noster equitatus*, Caes. *Gall.* 5.8.2 *cum quinque legionibus et pari numero equitum*, *Civ.* 1.51.4 *cum omni equitatu tribusque legionibus*. A *legio* had some *equites* but presumably the point is that it was mainly composed of *pedites*.
For the (common) coordination of *arma* and *signa* see e.g. Caes. *Civ.* 3.21.5, 3.95.4, Livy 10.5.2, 30.30.8, Tac. *Hist.* 3.24.3, 3.47.2.
Equi uiri is a common asyndeton (see on Sallust 32), but the coordination here introduces typical variation into the accumulation.
For *pecunia* and *commeatus*, two necessities of an army, together see Tac. *Hist.* 3.2.2 *unde interim pecuniam et commeatus?*; also *TLL* III.1823.61.
Cf. Preuss (1881: 89) on *pedites equites*, but for coordination of such military pairs, XXVIII Appendix 2.
Another accumulation of pairs.
Speech.

(16) 23.12.4 *magnam uim frumenti pecuniae absumi*
After this at 23.12.5 the two are coordinated: *mittendam ... pecuniam frumentumque*. (*Pecuniae*)*que* is a conjecture in 16 (A[P]: see Briscoe 2016: xvi), but the coordinator is unnecessary. The asyndeton is similar to *pecunia commeatus* in 15 above.
Cf. too 23.12.14 *frumentum et pecuniam date*, Tac. *Hist.* 3.50.3 *nec frumentum aut pecuniam prouiderant*, and the examples at *TLL* III.1823.67ff.
Indirect speech.

(17?) 34.1.6 *nam etiam ex oppidis conciliabulis conueniebant*
There is manuscript variation in this prepositional expression ('from towns, communities/meeting places'). The Bamberg MS (B) lacks

a coordinator and the Italian MSS (χ) have *conciliabulisque*. Briscoe in his Teubner prints *conciliabulisque* but leans towards ('forte recte') the asyndeton both in his apparatus (see below on 25) and commentary (1981: 11, 45). *Oppida* and *conciliabula* do occur in several laws in longer asyndetic sequences (see *TLL* IV.39.1ff.), including one cited by Briscoe (1981: 45), though they are not juxtaposed. I have not found them in an asyndeton bimembre, though that does not rule out asyndeton here, as they clearly had an association (on the meaning of *conciliabula* see Briscoe 2008: 269). Nevertheless the case for asyndeton is no stronger here than it is at 26 below, in which asyndeton is ruled out by Briscoe.

This example raises a familiar syntactic question: should an asyndeton bimembre be allowed (in Livy) if two nouns are dependent on a single preposition? I return to this question at 25, but see also 18, 22, 29, and the conclusions, 3.9. See also the Appendix to this chapter for a collection of passages showing the different patterns attested in Livy when a single preposition has two nominal dependents.

For Caesar's practice see XXVIII Appendix 1, and for Cicero, Cicero 15. For the historians, Sallust 13, Tacitus 61 with cross references. See also XXI.

Narrative.

(18) 34.5.12 *in rebus ad omnes pariter uiros feminas pertinentibus*, 'in matters that concern them all alike, men and women'.

Feminasque χ, *feminas* B. Briscoe (1981: 11) says that it is 'more or less certain that B should be followed' (note that the two nouns are again dependent on a single preposition). Cf. Cic. *Cluent.* 148 *omnes uiri mulieres, liberi serui in iudicium uocantur* and the various passages cited by Preuss (1881: 93) and Briscoe (1981: 57) ad loc., including Livy 45.24.11 *quidquid Rhodiorum uirorum feminarum est*. The pair is also found with coordination, as at Livy 27.51.9 *a uiris feminisque* (see Preuss 1881: 93). For the type of asyndeton see XI.3, where a reason is given for accepting asyndeton here.

Direct speech.

(19) 34.35.7 *liberos coniuges restitueret*
Both B and χ have asyndeton.

Coniuges and *liberi* often occur together, in asyndeton (see below, 23; this latter example occurs in phraseology almost identical to that of a passage of Caesar; cf. also Livy 4.28.5 *domos parentes coniuges liberos*: could this group be divided into two pairs?) or, with coordinator, e.g. 5.38.5 *ad coniuges ac liberos*, Cic. *Off.* 3.48 *coniugibus et liberis*. Cf. also Cicero 158

cum uxore cum liberis. Further details can be found at XIV.2.3, above on 5, 6 and at Preuss (1881: 92).
This is in a statement of conditions of peace, and is thus a quotation, akin to speech.

(20?) 34.38.3 *erant autem Romanorum sociorumque, simul peditum equitum, simul terrestrium ac naualium copiarum, ad quinquaginta milia hominum*, 'but there were, of Romans and allies, infantry and cavalry, land and naval forces, about fifty thousand men'.

B has *equitum* not *equitumque*, and if the asyndeton is allowed (for asyndeton in B, see above on 17 and 18 and below on 22; also Briscoe 1981: 11) the three pairs would be connected in different ways (one by *-que*, another by asyndetic coordination and the third by *ac*). For *pedites equites* in asyndeton see 27.13.9 *ut . . . omnes pedites equites armati adessent edixit*, 'he ordered that . . . they should all, infantry and cavalry, present themselves under arms' (and also the asyndetic phrases at 35.2.4 and 37.50.11), and Preuss (1881: 89); they are also coordinated, as at Livy 28.13.5 *cum omni exercitu ciuium sociorum, peditum equitumque quinque et quadraginta milibus* (an asyndetic pair, *ciuium sociorum*, for which see Tacitus 80, followed by the coordinated pair: see e.g. XXX.6.2b).

For alternation in sequences of pairs, some asyndetic, some syndetic, see above 10, 11 (*-que* and *atque* alternating with asyndeton). An asyndeton would suit the context in 20, in that it would introduce a typical variation in an accumulation of pairs. I discuss the structure of this passage again at 3.7 and 3.9 below, where arguments for accepting *peditum equitum* will be stated.
Narrative.

(21?) 34.52.4 *arma tela signaque aerea et marmorea transtulit*, 'it carried past arms and spears, and statues of bronze and marble'.

I take it that there is an asyndeton bimembre *arma tela*, and then a separate phrase attached by *-que*; this is not the use of *signa* = 'standards' that may be combined with *arma* (see 14), but a non-military use semantically unconnected. *Arma tela* is a common pair (see on Sallust 31, 32, with Preuss 1881: 86–7, and also Oakley 1997: 454, 2005b: 74), found for example elsewhere in Livy (36.18.1 *arma tela parant*, with Briscoe 1981: 248 on the text; cf. 10.4.2; note too the legal text *Dig*. 48.6.1 *quia arma tela domi suae agroue inue uilla praeter usum uenationis uel itineris uel nauigationis coegerit*). For coordinated examples, see *OLD* s.v. *telum* 1b. See XXII.3.4 for *arma telaque* in a prayer.

If there is end-of-list coordination, it is still the case that the first pair is a unit, and distinct from the third element semantically.
Narrative.

(22?) 34.61.5 *in circulis conuiuiis celebrata sermonibus res est*, 'the affair was discussed at social gatherings and dinners' (*conuiuiisque* χ, *conuiuiis* B).
For these terms associated see Cic. *Att.* 2.18.2 *sermo in circulis dumtaxat et in conuiuiis est liberior* (note that here as in the passage of Livy *sermo* takes place in such gatherings), *Balb.* 57 *in conuiuiis rodunt, in circulis uellicant*, Livy 32.20.3 *in conuiuiis et circulis* (with Briscoe 1973: 204 ad loc.), Tac. *Ann* 3.54.1 *nec ignoro in conuiuiis et circulis incusari ista* (with Woodman and Martin 1996: 390 ad loc., listing various other pairings of the two terms).
For a similar pair in asyndeton see Tacitus **86** *congressus conloquia*.
The fact that *circuli conuiuia* is a common (alliterative) pair of semantically overlapping terms means that it may well sometimes have been used in asyndeton, like various other pairs also used with coordinators. The text adopted must depend on the weight an editor is prepared to attach to B (see above, **19**, where Briscoe follows B in printing an asyndeton), and also on the editor's view of asyndetic pairs dependent on a single preposition in this author. I return to this issue below, **25**, and at 3.9; see also the Appendix.
Narrative.

(23) 38.43.6 *coniuges liberos in seruitium abstractos*
There is an almost identical clause in Caesar: *Gall.* 7.14.10 *liberos coniuges in seruitutem abstrahi* (cf. Sallust **12** for 'husband, children'). On the present pair see above on **19**.
Indirect speech, in which this pair follows on from the asyndetic sequence *caedibus incendiis ruinis direptione urbis*, which I do not take as comprising two pairs. It is true that *caedes incendia* is a common pair, in asyndeton or coordinated (see Sallust **15**), but it is also the case that *incendium ruina* and *ruina incendium* are found in asyndeton in legal Latin (see Kalb 1912: 137), and it would be artificial to separate *ruinis* here from *incendiis*.

(24) 38.48.4 *quo libertatem immunitatem ciuitatibus datis*, 'with which you bestow freedom, immunity on states'.
For the two terms together, usually coordinated (e.g. Cic. *Font.* 27), see *TLL* VII.1.507.51ff. Later in the same sentence there are two juxtaposed pairs of opposites (**49, 50**). This pair falls into the class of legal terms. Cf. Cicero **20** for *immunitas* in another asyndetic pair of legal type.
Direct speech.

2   *Data*   655

(25?) 42.1.1 L. *Postumius Albinus M. Popilius Laenas cum omnium primum de prouinciis exercitibus ad senatum rettulissent*
V omits *et* before *exercitibus*, the addition of which is an emendation of Vahlen. Briscoe prints the emendation with *et*, and states (2012: 152): 'V's asyndeton is unparalleled and would be very strange in an expression of this sort.' He does not specify of what sort (see below). The asyndeton is not strange: for this pair in asyndeton see Tacitus 167 *diurna populi Romani per prouincias per exercitus curatius leguntur*. *Prouinciae* and *exercitus* were often associated: see e.g. 38.35.7 *de re publica deque prouinciis et exercitibus senatum consuluerunt*, a similar context to that at 25, and with the consuls' names preceding, though not in asyndeton (also 27.5.1, 35.24.2, 37.57.3, and Cic. *Phil*. 3.38 *eae prouinciae eique exercitus*, Caes. *Civ*. 2.22.1 *auxiliis prouinciarum et exercituum desperatis*). See too *TLL* V.2.1392.23ff. (further coordinated pairs) and Briscoe's note (with some examples). Any coordinated pair may sometimes be used in asyndeton, as has been stressed constantly, and one cannot rule out an asyndeton simply by quoting cases with a coordinator (see the Introduction above and penultimate paragraph below). The present context is official, describing a referral to the senate, with the names of the consuls in the official manner in asyndeton. We have seen above various pairs of official terms in asyndeton (e.g. 2, 4), and others will come up below (26, 28, 52). On the other hand the context at 38.35.7 above could be taken to support coordination in 25. Here is a place where the original text seems not to be recoverable with any certainty.

For asyndeta bimembria in motions in the senate, which provide a similar context to that here, see the numerous examples from Cic. *Phil*.: Cicero 25, 75, 76, 77, 78; cf. also 90.

Both ablatives are dependent on a single preposition. Can *et* (or -*que*) be left out under these circumstances?

Briscoe defends an asyndeton in one such prepositional expression (without commenting on the syntax): 34.5.12 *ad omnes pariter uiros feminas* (above, 18). Similarly at 34.1.6 (17), though he prints *ex oppidis conciliabulisque* (χ), in his apparatus he says of *conciliabulis* (B), 'forte recte'. Another example in Livy (where the text seems certain) is discussed below (3.7) in a different connection: 8.33.20 *propter Q. Fabium ciuitatem in laetitia uictoria, supplicationibus ac gratulationibus esse*. In official (legal) language this type of asyndeton occurs. See XXI.4; also Kalb (1912: 137) cites several such expressions: *Dig*. 5.1.80 *si in iudicis nomine praenomine erratum est*, 37.11.8.2 *sed et cum in praenomine cognomine erratum est*. Asyndeta bimembria dependent on one preposition are in Sallust and Tacitus, Cicero and others (see XXI). Two nouns dependent on the same preposition do not need a coordinator, at least in some writers (Caesar, we have seen, is an exception: see XXI.3, XXVIII.2.1), though coordinators are far more common than asyndeton (see the Appendix to the present chapter), just as coordinated pairs of other structures are far more common than asyndetic. However, the question ought to be faced to what extent Livy himself admits this structure, in passages that are not open to textual uncertainties (see below, 3.9).

If there is manuscript variation in such phrases, the textual problem thereby raised may be insoluble. There is no point in citing a few parallels either for coordination or asyndeton. Nor are semantic factors necessarily helpful. *Circulis conuiuiis* at 22 is alliterative and comprises two near-synonyms, both of which features are typical of asyndeta bimembria, but they are also typical of pairs linked by *-que*. Structural patterns may however be significant (see XXI.2). At Cic. *Prov. cons.* 15 (*bellum cum maximis Syriae gentibus <et> tyrannis consulari exercitu imperioque confectum*) editors add a coordinator (this is the text of Peterson, OCT), no doubt rightly: a long phrase *maximis Syriae gentibus* with a single noun tacked on has the elements in the wrong order for an asyndeton.

A referral to the senate, and thus reported speech.

(26) 42.3.7 *cui sarta tecta exigere sacris publicis et loca<re> tuenda more maiorum traditum esset*, '(the magistrate) to whom had been entrusted, in the manner of the ancestors, the duty of enforcing a good state of repair, below and on top, for public temples and of contracting for their maintenance'.

See XXII.5.3 on this passage and on the legal pair *sarta tecta*. On the textual problem here (*loca*), which is irrelevant to our purposes, see Briscoe (2012: 162). Verbs of maintaining are several times used with *sarta tecta* as object (see XXII.5.3), and *loca<re> tuenda* looks right.

Indirect speech.

(27?) 42.12.4 *celebratas esse utrasque nuptias gratulatione donis innumerabilium legationum*, 'both marriages had been celebrated with congratulations, gifts from innumerable embassies'.

Donis V, with *et* before *donis* a conjecture (Hertz). Briscoe (2012: 190) says: 'asyndeton is unlikely', and prints <et>. For *donis* as the second member of what looks like a semantically and structurally similar asyndeton bimembre, also with an abstract noun preceding, see Livy 8.33.21 *arae ... honore donis cumulentur*. The implication of an asyndeton would be that other benefits bestowed could also have been listed. In both cases

the abstract noun, in the singular, is longer than the plural *donis*. An asyndeton would certainly be acceptable.
Indirect speech.

(28) 42.26.5 *ut ex instituto loca lautia acciperent*, 'so that they might receive, in accordance with the custom, lodging, hospitality'.
On this old official phrase see XXII.5.4. It is taken to refer to the lodging and official entertainment/hospitality accorded envoys.
Indirect speech.

(29?) 42.31.8 *commeatus classi legionibusque ut ex Sicilia Sardinia subueherentur*, 'so that provisions might be conveyed to the fleet and legions from Sicily and Sardinia'.
Briscoe, along with other editors, adds *-que* to *Sardinia* (see Briscoe 2012: 256; *Sardinia* V), noting that there are several other places in Livy where the two place names are linked by *-que*.
This is an official context, recording a vote (and thus indirect speech). For two asyndetic proper names dependent on a preposition see Cicero 32 (personal names) and Caes. *Civ.* 3.4.3 *<ex> Creta Lacedaemone* discussed at XXVIII.2.1. However, neither of these cases is an exact parallel for the present example because special factors are at work, and also Livy's method of coordinating place names dependent on a preposition elsewhere has to be taken into account (see the Appendix). I would not print an asyndeton.
Indirect speech.

(30) 42.54.3 *oppidanos, diem noctem eosdem tuentes moenia, ... labor conficiebat*, 'the toil was wearing out the townsmen, who, unchanged, were defending the walls day and night'.
Briscoe (2012: 345) cites 8.34.10 *nec discernatur interdiu nocte, aequo iniquo loco, <iussu> iniussu imperatoris pungent* (an asyndetic accumulation of opposites). For the accusative see Cic. *Div.* 2.59 *quasi uero quicquam intersit mures diem noctem aliquid rodentes scuta an cribra corroserint*. Cf., with coordinator, Tac. *Hist.* 3.26.2 *per diem noctemque* (see Preuss 1881: 33–4). On this old Indo-European pair see Gonda (1959: 337–8).
Narrative.

2.2 Adjectives

(31) 4.2.8 *Iuppiter optimus maximus*
I list here and below without comment the various examples of this religious phrase (discussed at IV.4).
Indirect speech.

(32) 4.28.4 *'hic praebituri,' inquit, 'uos telis hostium estis indefensi inulti?',* "'Are you," he said, "going to offer yourselves here to the weapons of the enemy, undefended, unavenged?"'

Indefensi inulti is a postpositive predicative adjunct consisting of two terms with the prefix *in-*, agreeing with the subject of the verb, a common type (see VI.2.2 and below, 3.4). *Indefensus* and *inultus* are near-synonyms (see *TLL* VII.1.1130.23ff., VII.2.241.28ff.).

In the same speech note the longer asyndeton at §5: *qui uisuri domos parentes coniuges liberos estis.*

Further instances of *in-*privative adjectives in asyndeton will be seen below. Note too 35.34.7 *singulos uniuersosque obtestantes ne insontem indemnatum consenescere in exsilio sinerent* (with which cf. Cicero 42) and also 35 below, where another such pair from outside the books considered is quoted.

Direct speech.

(33) 4.37.9 (*clamor*) *ab Romanis dissonus impar, segnius saepe iteratus* [*incerto clamore*] *prodidit pauorem animorum.* 'The shouting of the Romans, dissonant and uneven, constantly repeated more slowly, betrayed feelings of panic.'

On the textual problem here (*incerto clamore*) see Ogilvie (1965: 593) ad loc.

There is a difference of function between, on the one hand, the pair *dissonus impar* (for a similar pair, one with the prefix *dis-* and the other with *in-*, see below on 35, where 40.28.2 is cited, and see particularly VI.4.2 on the present passage for negative adjectives with different prefixes paired, and also 34 below), and, on the other, the next phrase: the shouting, dissonant, uneven (predicative adjunct/secondary predicate) (was) constantly repeated more slowly (predicate).

Narrative.

(34) 5.30.6 (*orare* ... *coepere*) *ne exsulem extorrem populum Romanum* ... *in hostium urbem agerent*, '(they began to beg them) not to drive the Roman people, exiled, banished ... into the city of the enemy'.

The two adjectives have the same prefix, and are of a semantic field found commonly in asyndeta (see Sallust 24, 52 with cross references). Cf. Livy 2.6.2 *extorrem egentem*, 37.53.21 *extorris expulsus*. At Tac. *Hist.* 5.24.2 the same pair occurs with a coordinator: *exulem eum et extorrem*. Ogilvie (1965: 693) describes the phrase *exsulem, extorrem* as a 'legal tag', referring the reader to 2.6.2, where his note (1965: 249) on *extorrem egentem* has nothing to justify this claim. The latter note does however have useful material on terms of this semantic field in asyndeton. Such pairs often have pathetic associations, expressing rejection and abandonment (see on Sallust 52). They are also typically, as here, predicative adjuncts. They would almost certainly have been uttered with an intonation or pause that brought out the pathos.

For negative adjectives with the prefix *ex-* in asyndeta see XXIII.6 on Plaut. *Cas.* 550, and also VI.4.2 with VI.7, final paragraph.

Indirect speech.

(35) 5.45.4 (*urbis*) *oppressae ab hoste inuisitato inaudito*, 'a city, crushed by an enemy, unseen, unheard of'.

This pair occurs several times in Livy, with coordinators: see 4.33.1 *noua erumpit acies, inaudita ante id tempus inuisitataque*, and particularly 5.37.2 *inuisitato atque inaudito hoste ab Oceano terrarumque ultimis oris bellum ciente* ('an unseen, unheard of enemy was stirring up war from the ocean and the remotest shores of the world'). Here the adjectives accompany the same noun as in **35** and in a similar context. However, in 5.37.2 the adjectives precede the noun and have a coordinator (and seem to be attributes), whereas at **35** they are postponed and in the common (predicative) adjunct position. Cf. above, **32**, for a pair of privative adjectives in this position. In **35** the Budé editor Bayet (1954) deletes *inaudito*, without justification (see the comments of Williams in the review referred to in the next paragraph). Cf., for the near-synonymy of such words, Cic. *Fin.* 3.15 *si enim Zenoni licuit, cum rem aliquam inuenisset inusitatam, inauditum quoque ei rei nomen imponere*.

Ogilvie (1965: 730) says of our example: 'The asyndeton of near-synonyms is solemn (cf. 27.43.7, 40.28.2) and is here particularly appropriate since it is almost sacral and the words bear a special emphasis (G. W. Williams *JRS* 45 (1955), 228).' There are no grounds for use of the word 'sacral'. Nor is 'solemn' appropriate, as near-synonyms in asyndeton are commonplace. The two examples cited by Ogilvie are, however, in other ways interesting. At 27.43.7 (*audendum aliquid improuisum inopinatum*) there are again two *in*-privative adjectives in final position. At 40.28.2 (*dispersi inordinati exibant*) the adjectives are in agreement with the unexpressed subject of the verb (on which feature see below, 3.4; both pairs are predicative adjuncts). One member of the second pair is an *in*-privative, and the other has the prefix *dis-*, a structure seen above at **33**, *dissonus impar*. *Dispersi* and *inordinati* are in an explicit contrast with an earlier pair (40.28.1 *omnes compositi et instructi*) (the troops were now drunk), and it is possible that the asyndeton would have highlighted the antithesis.

Narrative.

(36, 37) 5.50.4 *Iuppiter optimus maximus*; also 5.51.9.

The first of these is in an indirect speech, the second in a direct.

(38, 39) 9.3.3 <u>armati inermes</u>, <u>fortes ignaui</u>, *pariter omnes capti atque uicti sumus*, 'we are all alike – armed and unarmed, brave and cowardly – captured and defeated'.

Two pairs of opposites, the first probably complementarities, the second antonyms (in agreement with the unexpressed subject of the verb: predicative adjuncts), misleadingly punctuated in the OCT with four commas. For the association of *uicti* and *capti* see Livy 9.4.3, in the reverse order. Cf. above, 10, 11, where 4.59.6 (*fugientium ac resistentium, armatorum atque inermium*) is cited: it has two pairs of opposites, one the same as that here, but both with coordinators. For *armatus* opposed (in various ways, and not necessarily asyndetic; often in antitheses) to *inermis* see *TLL* II.620.70ff. *Inermus* (*-is*) is in another asyndetic pair, *imbelles inermos*, at Tacitus 124 (see also below, 41). *Fortis* is in asyndeton with *ignauus* at Cic. *Nat.* 2.145 in a protracted sequence of pairs of opposites, mostly asyndetic but the last with *-que*: *nam et uirtutes et uitia cognoscunt, iratum propitium, laetantem dolentem, <u>fortem ignauum</u>, audacem timidumque cognoscunt*. For this pair with a coordinator see Tac. *Hist.* 3.27.1 *ut discretus labor fortes ignauosque distingueret*.

Speech.

(40?) 9.34.15 *ne degeneraueris a familia <u>imperiosissima superbissima</u>*, 'do not fall away from a family most imperious, most proud'.

ΠΛ have *et*, whereas M has no coordinator; these witnesses are of equal weight. Walters and Conway (OCT) delete *superbissima*, pointlessly. At §24 the addressee (Appius Claudius) has the characteristic *superbia*. The pair may possibly be a postponed asyndetic adjunct, comprising superlatives denoting features of those with supreme power, presumably (if the text is right) articulated with a pause between. *Superbia* was the 'characteristic *par excellence* of the patrician Claudii' (Oakley 2005a: 444). The structure is the same as that of *ab hoste inuisitato inaudito* at 35 above. It cannot be determined with certainty what Livy wrote, but asyndeton is at least a possibility, with the deletion above ill-founded. See however the conclusions, 3.4 below, for a feature of this pair which would make it the odd one out among adjectival asyndeta bimembria in our eight books. Oakley accepts *et*.

Speech.

2 Data

(41) 23.3.2 *clausos omnes in curia accipite, solos inermos*, 'take them all, shut up as they are in the senate house, alone, unarmed'.
A postponed predicative adjunct, with the negative adjective in second position. For *inermis* see above, 38.
Direct speech.

(42) 23.27.5 *ut quisque arma ceperat, sine imperio sine signo, incompositi inordinati in proelium ruunt*, 'as each man took up arms, without command, without signal, they rushed into battle, lacking order, lacking formation'.
The two adjectives are in agreement with the unexpressed subject of the verb. They follow an asyndetic prepositional expression (see on 61 below; for different types of asyndeton bimembre together, see the conclusions, 3.7, final paragraph, and also on Sallust 47, Tacitus 4, with cross references to Cicero, and see too XXX.3.3.3c–e; similar accumulations are cited in the commentary on 54 below). For *sine*-expressions juxtaposed with *in*-privatives and behaving as alternative privatives see on Cicero 44.
The adjectives are near-synonyms. For the pair in Livy (otherwise with a coordinator) see 22.50.8 *qui inordinati atque incompositi obstrepunt portis* (Preuss 1881: 114).
Narrative.

(43, 44) 42.20.3 *Ioui optimo maximo* (indirect speech); also 28.8 (oratio obliqua: decree of senate).

Finally, I note for completeness that at 4.40.8 (*deserta castra, relictos saucios milites*) the Loeb translates 'a deserted camp and wounded and forsaken soldiers', but it is as likely that the second phrase means 'wounded soldiers abandoned', with the two modifiers differing in rank (= [*relictos*] [*saucios milites*]).

2.3 Verbs

(45?) 4.48.11 *suadendo monendo pollicendoque*
On this passage see on Tacitus 134. The first two gerunds are arguably a pair, with the third detached from them.
Narrative.

(46) 9.24.9 *defendite, ite*, 'defend, go'.
For pairs of imperatives used asyndetically see X. *I(te)* or *abi* often comes first. Here the order is reversed, on which reversal see X.1.3.
Speech.

(47) 23.11.10 *magistrum equitum ... fusum fugatum*, 'the master of the horse ... had been routed, put to flight'.

Esse is understood. For this pair ('scattered, put to flight'; here in 47 the first verb is closer to 'routed': see *OLD* s.v. *fundo* 11b for these meanings), found a number of times in Livy with and without a coordinator (Preuss 1881: 96–7; it often has *-que*, as e.g. at 34.20.6), see 51, below. Note too Fronto p. 7.8 van den Hout *cuius causa tot legiones funduntur fugantur*; also Livy 4.43.2 *turpi fuga funduntur*. Dispersing is the start of putting an army fully to flight: the second verb has a finality to it. See also VII.1, penultimate paragraph, on Livy 40.52.6.

Indirect speech.

(48) 34.7.4 *sed in purpura, quae teritur absumitur, iniustam quidem sed aliquam tamen causam tenacitatis uideo*, 'but in the case of purple, which is rubbed away, destroyed, I see some reason, unjust to be sure but nevertheless a reason, for niggardliness'.

The second verb expresses a consequence of the first, = 'worn away to destruction'. Alternatively, since *teritur* could be replaced by *terendo*, the first verb could be described as modifying *absumitur*. For verbs of destruction or the like in second position in an asyndetic pair see XXX.2.1, 2, with cross references.

Direct speech.

(49, 50) 38.48.4 *regna augetis minuitis, donatis adimitis*, 'you increase and diminish kingdoms, you present them and take them away'.

Two pairs of opposites (reversives), which should be brought out by punctuation with a single comma as here.

With the first pair cf. Vitr. 1.4.6 *augendo aut minuendo*, Manil. 1.519 *quae nec longa dies auget minuitque senectus*, Scrib. Larg. 16 *augetur minuiturque numerus coclearium*, Frontin. *Aq.* 104.1 *neque augeri placere nec minui <numerum> publicorum salientium* (examples taken from *TLL* s.v. *augeo*, where more such are to be found). The opposition was standard. I have not found an asyndeton bimembre, but note the tricolon at Cic. *Nat.* 1.35 *quae causas gignendi augendi minuendi habeat*.

For the similar (reversive) opposition 'give/take away', in asyndeton, with coordinators and in other antitheses, see e.g. Cic. *Agr.* 3.6 *imbibit illis legibus spem non nullam cui ademptum est, aliquem scrupulum cui datum est, Mil.* 73 *qui regna dedit ademit* (note that the object of the asyndetic pair is the same as that in Livy above), Hor. *Sat.* 2.3.288 *Iuppiter, ingentis qui das adimisque dolores*, Ovid *Met.* 8.615 *si dant adimuntque figuras*, Tac. *Ann.* 13.56.1 *ut arbitrium penes Romanos maneret, quid darent quid adimerent* (a

type of asyndeton, with anaphora). See also Preuss (1881: 39). Note too Cicero 138, 140 for a similar asyndetic pair of opposites (but converses in this case), *dare/accipere*.
Direct speech. The same sentence contains another asyndeton (see 24).

(51) 38.53.2 *quattuor exercitus fudit fugauit* (with some textual variation), 'he scattered and put to flight four armies'.
On the text see Briscoe (2008: 187). Cf. 47 above for asyndeton.
Direct speech.

(52) 38.54.3 *fuit autem rogatio talis: uelitis iubeatis, Quirites, quae pecunia capta ablata coacta ab rege Antiocho est quique sub imperio eius fuerunt, quod eius in publicum relatum non est, uti de ea re Ser. Sulpicius praetor urb<an>us ad senatum referat, quem eam rem uelit senatus quaerere de iis qui praetores nunc sunt*
Velitis iubeatis is an asyndetic formula 'used by the magistrate presiding over an assembly when taking a vote' (Briscoe 1973: 70 on 31.6.1). On the syntax of the formula (and for a translation of the above) see XXII.5.2.
Direct speech.

(53?) 42.45.7 *classem instructam ornatam*, 'the fleet drawn up and decked out'.
Ornatam<que> Fr. 1 (Editio Frobeniana 1531), *ortanam* V. See Briscoe (2012: 308): 'asyndeton cannot be excluded'. He adds that there is no parallel, but for the pair coordinated see Cic. *Pis.* 5 *prouinciam Galliam ... exercitu et pecunia instructam et ornatam*; cf. Livy 30.3.4 *classem paratam instructamque*. Often, as I have stressed, the parallel for an asyndetic pair is an example of the pair explicitly, as distinct from asyndetically, coordinated. However, for additional doubts about this asyndeton see below, 3.5.
Narrative.

2.4 Adverbs

(54) 23.3.3 *nec quicquam raptim aut forte temere egeritis*, 'nor do anything in a rush, or accidentally, heedlessly'.
This is not the only asyndeton bimembre that we have noted from this speech (see 41). The two pairs are in adjacent sentences.
See Preuss (1881: 54–5), stating several times that the terms may express a single notion, but this is one of those phrases in which the second term outdoes the first. *Forte* 'by chance' does not in itself imply thoughtless

behaviour, as *temere* does. This was a formulaic pair: cf. Ter. *Ph.* 757 *quam saepe forte temere | eueniunt*, Cic. *Div.* 2.141 *nisi ista casu non numquam forte temere concurrerent* (see further Pease 1963: 570 and Briscoe 2008: 276 for five examples from Livy himself). For the type of opposition see Cic. *Sull.* 13 *atque haec inter nos partitio defensionis non est fortuito, iudices, nec temere facta*, a passage which implies a contrast between the two adverbs.

For *temere* in other asyndetic pairs see Cicero 79 temere turbulente, per uim per furorem (where *turbulente* is the stronger word; for the accumulation, cf. 42 above), Tacitus 153 *crebra hinc proelia, et saepius in modum latrocinii per saltus per paludes, ut cuique sors aut uirtus, temere prouiso, ob iram ob praedam* (opposites: 'rashly, with foresight'; another similar accumulation).

Direct speech.

2.5 Prepositional Type

(55) 5.4.6 *patiatur se ab domo ab re familiari, cui grauis inpensa non est, paulo diutius abesse*, 'let him therefore put up with it that he is away a little longer from house and property, which does not suffer heavy charges'.

Many manuscripts have the text printed here (but *ac* is in Ver. for the second *ab*). The old OCT of Conway and Walters deletes *ab domo*, needlessly (not so that of Ogilvie). Asyndeton bimembre with a repeated preposition is not uncommon in Livy, as will be shown in this section (further examples may be found, under a different heading, in Oakley 1997: 729, 1998: 58, 2005a: 276). Of *ac (re familiari)* Ogilvie (1965: 637) on 5.4.6 says: '*ac* (Ver.) is confirmed by 2.4 which passage also disposes of any reasons for deleting *ab domo* as a gloss'. *Ac* is not confirmed by 2.4. On this latter (following the lemma *ac domus ac res*) Ogilvie (1965: 633) states: 'the first *ac* links *cedere* and *invisere*, the second *domus* and *res* (cf. 4.6 n.)'. Here is implied the argument that if *domus* and *res* (not, be it noted, *res familiaris* as at 4.6, but *res ... suas*) are linked by *ac* in one place, so they must be linked by *ac* elsewhere. This argument is unconvincing: the evidence is massive that the same pairs of words are linked by a diversity of coordinators (or left unlinked) in case after case, in Livy as in other writers. Since Livy has asyndeta bimembria with a repeated preposition (and not least when the two terms are connected semantically), it is reasonable to print the anaphoric construction here.

Domus is often in asyndetic pairs: see XXVI.7.8.2 on Cicero, Sallust 18, 23, 44, Tacitus 76, 104, 166. For the juxtaposition here cf. Plaut. *Bac.* 458 *rem familiarem curat, custodit domum*.

Direct speech.

(56) 9.9.12 *cum senatu cum populo* de pace ac foedere agere, 'to deal with senate, with people, over peace and a treaty'.

For *senatus* in asyndetic anaphoric prepositional pairs see Cicero 49 *cum senatu cum bonis omnibus*, 187 *sine senatu sine magistratibus*, 186 (same combination, discontinuous, with the elements in the reverse order).
Speech.

(57, 58) 9.19.3 *quaterni quinique exercitus saepe per eos annos in Etruria in Umbria, Gallis hostibus adiunctis, in Samnio in Lucanis gerebant bellum*, 'often in those years four or five armies at a time would wage war in Etruria, in Umbria (with the Gauls also added as an enemy), in Samnium, among the Lucanians'.

The four prepositional expressions form a tetracolon, but they do seem to fall into two pairs, separated by the intrusive *Gallis hostibus adiunctis*. For an intrusive element splitting a sequence of four terms (proper names, adjectives) into two groups see Cicero 166, 167 and also Caesar 2, 3 (c); see too Cicero 127.

This sentence is followed immediately (§4) by an extended prepositional expression with a single preposition (and variations of coordinators): *Latium deinde omne cum Sabinis et Volscis et Aequis et omni Campania et parte Vmbriae Etruriaeque et Picentibus et Marsis Paelignisque ac Vestinis atque Apulis*. Livy has varied the prepositional construction between the two sentences.
Narrative.

(59) 9.37.10 *ad castra ad siluas* diuersi tendebant, 'they made their way in different directions, to the camp, to the woods'.

These are imprecise opposites (denoting a human habitation and uninhabited places).
Narrative.

(60) 9.39.8 ut ... *per arma per corpora* euaserint, 'that they passed over arms, over bodies'. Cf. Sall. *Cat.* 51.9 *armis cadaueribus*.
Narrative.

(61) 23.27.5 ut quisque arma ceperat, *sine imperio sine signo*, incompositi inordinati in proelium ruunt (see above, 42).

Cf. Sallust 84 *sine legibus sine imperio*, a pair that is followed by two coordinated adjectives, in much the same way as the present pair is followed by two uncoordinated adjectives.
Narrative.

(62?) 30.20.9 *centum milibus armatorum <u>ad Trasumennum ad Cannas</u> caesis*, 'after a hundred thousand armed men had been slain at Trasumennus, at Cannae'.
There are manuscript variants (*aut Cannas, et Cannas*).
Indirect speech.

(63) 30.30.12 *quod ego fui <u>ad Trasumennum ad Cannas</u>, id tu hodie es*, 'what I was at Trasumennus, at Cannae, that you are today'.
Speech.

(64) 34.7.2 *purpura uiri utemur, praetextati <u>in magistratibus in sacerdotiis</u>*, 'shall we men wear purple, and, if holding offices, priesthoods, be clad in the toga praetexta?'
Here again an asyndetic pair comprises terms for public office(r)s. Cf. 2, 4 above, with cross references, and particularly Sallust 11 *magistratus sacerdotia*. Note too Sall. *Cat.* 21.2 *tum Catilina polliceri . . . magistratus sacerdotia rapinas*, Livy 34.7.8 *non magistratus nec sacerdotia nec triumphi nec insignia . . . iis contingere possunt*.
Speech.

(65) 38.10.3 *<u>per legatos per litteras</u> Dolopas Amphilochosque et Athamaniam erepta sibi querens*, 'through legates, through letters, complaining that the Dolopians, the Amphilochians and Athamania had been snatched from him'.
Legati and *litterae* are paired (with *-que*) at Cic. *Deiot.* 11 (Wölfflin 1933: 264). For *litterae* in asyndetic prepositional pairings see Cicero 208, Sallust 86.
Narrative.

(66) 38.23.1 *ruunt caeci <u>per uias per inuia</u>; nulla praecipitia saxa, nullae rupes obstant*, 'they ran blindly along paths, along pathless places; no steep rocks, no cliffs held them back'.
Opposites, of the positive–negative type. Cf. 23.17.6 *per uias inuiaque*, and contrast the oxymoron *uia . . . inuia* at Virg. *Aen.* 3.383 (see II.2.4).
Narrative.

There are also some instances in this book where the second member is phrasal:
5.41.4 *sine ira, sine ardore animorum*. Narrative.
5.44.6 *sine munimento, sine stationibus ac custodiis*. Narrative.
5.51.9 *ad deos, ad sedem Iouis optimi maximi*. Direct speech.

3 Conclusions

3.1 Incidence

Oakley (1998: 736) remarks that '*asyndeton bimembre* is quite regular in the historians' (for the passage in book 8 on which he was commenting see above, 28), but it has to be added that asyndeton bimembre of the type that is the main subject of this book is far less frequent in Livy than in Sallust or Tacitus. As was stated at the start, the eight books of Livy considered here comprise roughly 697 pages in the editions used (OCTs for the earlier books to 30, and Teubners for books 34, 38 and 42). I say 'roughly' 697 pages because pages are not numbered in earlier OCT texts and I have had to count them one by one. The total of 66 asyndeta bimembria (some of them moreover questionable or even explicitly rejected above) in 697 pages is roughly one instance per ten pages. The complete historical works of Tacitus (*Histories* and *Annals*) occupy about 630 pages in the Teubner editions that I have used, and they contain 167 instances of asyndeton bimembre, which is roughly one case every 3.7 pages. In the OCT of Sallust the *Catiline*, *Jugurtha* and fragments of the *Histories* that are included in it fill about 200 pages. These have 89 instances of asyndeton bimembre, or roughly one every 2.2 pages. These figures are merely a guide, because the number of words per page in the various editions is bound to vary. Nevertheless the conclusion is obvious that asyndeton bimembre is admitted much more sparingly by Livy than by Tacitus and particularly Sallust, and the difference would be even more striking if we removed from the figure of 66 above the dubious or rejected examples. A related question is: did Livy use asyndeton differently in other ways as well, compared with the other two?

3.2 Speeches versus Narrative

Another feature of asyndeton bimembre in Livy is that it seems disproportionately frequent in speeches, direct and indirect. A total of 43 of the 66 examples are in speeches, a proportion of about 64 per cent. This figure is higher than that for Sallust and Tacitus, though both do have a tendency to put such asyndeton into speeches (Tacitus mainly in the *Annals*). In Sallust and Tacitus' *Annals* speeches account for about 30 per cent of examples of asyndeton bimembre (in Tacitus' *Histories* the figure is 16 per cent) (see for details XXX.3.2.1, 5.2.1, 6.2 (h)). There are some notable accumulations in single speeches in Sallust, particularly that of Catiline (see on Sallust 10, 11, with cross references).

The significance of these proportions is difficult to evaluate, because it would be very hard to determine what proportion of any historical work consisted of narrative and what of speeches. Direct speeches are easy to identify, but indirect speech may be embedded in the narrative and is difficult to quantify. Nevertheless the figure of 64 per cent looks high, and it is put into some perspective by the lower percentages for Sallust and Tacitus.

It might be tempting to conclude from this distribution in Livy that asyndeton bimembre had a 'colloquial' character. There are indeed scattered non-standard usages in speeches in Livy (see Adams 2016: 697, index s.v. 'Livy' and most of the references there; *abi nuntia* twice in short direct utterances in book 22 perhaps was slangy in tone: see XXIII.5.1). This explanation does not, however, fit asyndeton bimembre in general, because in speeches it is constantly in legal, official, religious and other formal phrases (see 3.3 below for details). Asyndeton bimembre, at least of certain types and particularly in accumulations, seems to have had a powerful rhetorical impact in the classical period: it occurs for example at dramatic points in some of Cicero's speeches, and in letters to addressees on whom Cicero wanted to make some sort of impression (see Cicero 3, 4, 193, XXVI.7.1, 7.5.3, 7.6). The only instance of asyndeton bimembre in a prepositional expression in Caesar's *Bellum Ciuile* is in a direct speech (see XXVIII.2.2, 14). It was shown (XXVIII Appendix 1) that otherwise in the work Caesar has 61 prepositional phrases with coordination. It was almost certainly the speech context that motivated the asyndeton (with anaphora). Quintilian's comments on rhetorical *amplificatio* at 8.4.26–7 are of interest, though not specifically to do with asyndeton. An 'accumulation' (*congeries*) of words and sentences having the same meaning (*congeries quoque uerborum ac sententiarum idem significantium*) is a form of amplification, he says. Asyndeton, as we have seen *passim*, often has near-synonyms paired (e.g. **22** *circulis conuiuiis*, **32** *indefensi inulti*, **35** *inuisitato inaudito*, **42** *incompositi inordinati*). Quintilian also goes on to say (27) that 'accumulation also often shows a rising pattern, when every word marks a step in an ascending series' (Russell, Loeb). So in asyndeton bimembre the second word is often stronger than the first (e.g. **40** *imperiosissima superbissima*, **48** *teritur absumitur*, **52** *uelitis iubeatis*).

3.3 Nouns

Of the 31 numbered pairs of nouns, 20 are in speeches (1–6, 12–16, 18, 19, 23–29), a proportion of about 64 per cent.

3 Conclusions

The 31 pairs belong mainly to a small number of categories. Two types predominate.

First, there are pairs that may be described as 'official', that is related to public life, administration and the law: 2 *pontifices augures*, 4 *consulatibus decemuiratibus*, 5, 6 *liberis fratribus, propinquis adfinibus*, 11 *seruos liberos* (classifications of persons by status), 19 *liberos coniuges*, 23 *coniuges liberos*, 24 *libertatem immunitatem*, 25 (?) *de prouinciis exercitibus*, 26 *sarta tecta*, 27 (?) *gratulatione donis*, 28 *loca lautia*, 64 *in magistratibus in sacerdotiis*. It is clear from examples 26 and 28, which are old, and e.g. from the expression *patres conscripti*, that the 'shorthand' asyndetic manner of linking closely related terms had long had a place in official/legal language (see XXII). It continued to be found in legal language well into the Empire (see Kalb 1912: 134–9). All the examples just listed are in speeches or the like. Livy was not making a show of official language in his own narrative, but putting it into the mouths of characters in appropriate contexts. A combination of factors has determined the choice of asyndetic coordination: the speech context, and the official character of the phrase.

Second, a related category consists of pairs with a military connection; military language may be described as a branch of official language: 7 *stationibus uigiliis*, 8 *arma equos*, 9 *uestimenta commeatus*, 12 *iuuentute armis*, 13 *legiones equitatus*, 14 *arma signa*, 15 *pecunia commeatus*, 16 *frumenti pecuniae*, 20 (?) *peditum equitum*, 21 *arma tela*. There are ten examples here, five of them in speeches (12, 13, 14, 15, 16).

Next, there are several pairs expressing family relationships: 5 *liberis fratribus*, 6 *propinquis adfinibus*, 19, 23 *liberi coniuges*, 10 *seruos liberos*. Three of these six are in speeches (5, 6, 23). Such pairs also have an official character, and some have been listed above in the first category as well.

The frequency of these various types in speeches suggests that it was not simply their semantic features that determined the asyndeta, but Livy's feeling that asyndeton had a place in formal speech.

3.4 Adjectives

There are fourteen adjectival pairs listed above (31–44). Five of these (31, 36, 37, 43, 44) are in the old and invariable religious formula *Iuppiter optimus maximus*, about which I will say nothing more here. For clarity I set out the other nine in a few groups:

(32) 'hic praebituri,' inquit, 'uos telis hostium estis <u>indefensi inulti?</u>'
(38, 39) <u>armati inermes, fortes ignaui</u>, pariter omnes capti atque uicti sumus

(41) *clausos omnes in curia accipite,* <u>*solos inermos*</u>
(42) *ut quisque arma ceperat, sine imperio sine signo,* <u>*incompositi inordinati*</u>
in proelium ruunt

(33) *(clamor) ab Romanis* <u>*dissonus impar,*</u> *segnius saepe iteratus [incerto clamore] prodidit pauorem animorum*
(35) *(urbis) oppressae ab hoste* <u>*inuisitato inaudito*</u>
(40) *ne degeneraueris a familia* <u>*imperiosissima superbissima*</u>

(34) *ne* <u>*exsulem extorrem*</u> *populum Romanum . . . in hostium urbem agerent.*

There are some patterns here. First, in seven cases the pair has at least one *in*-privative adjective (I leave out 40 *imperiosissima*, where the prefix has a different function). In three pairs both members are *in-* adjectives. When there is just one such adjective, it invariably is in second position (four times). Those pairs with at least one privative adjective are almost always placed at the end of their clause/colon; 42 is the only exception, but arguably *incompositi inordinati* forms a colon of its own, probably with a pause both between the terms and after the second (predicative adjuncts: see the next paragraph).

The first example may be used to illustrate a feature of quite a few of the examples: 'Are you about to offer yourselves here to the weapons of the enemy, undefended, unavenged?' *Indefensi inulti* is in agreement with no expressed noun (or pronoun) in the sentence, and that is a reflection of the fact that Latin is a language that does not have to have a subject pronoun. Traditionally we would say that *indefensi* and *inulti* are in agreement with the unexpressed subject of the verb. They are predicative, and have a detachment (part of the English translation could be rewritten as 'are you, who are (or 'being') undefended, unavenged, going to . . .?', or with a concessive, 'are you, though undefended'). The term 'predicative adjunct' has been used here, or 'secondary predicate'.

The two pairs 38, 39 have this same function, as does 42. Two of the other examples (41 *solos inermos*, 34 *exsulem extorrem*) are much the same. They are both in the accusative, but again are predicative (34 for example refers to driving the Roman people into the city of the enemy '(so that) they are exiled, banished'). 33, 35, 40 have adjectives that could be classified as attributive, but they are all postponed and again appear detached.

As well as the four pairs with the prefix *in-*, there is 34, where again the two terms have the same fore-element, this time *ex-*, which also has a negative implication. With the exception of 40, every pair thus has either at least one privative adjective, or consists of terms with the same fore-element. Some may feel that this exceptional feature of 40 requires an

3   Conclusions   671

editor to print the pair with a coordinator. On the other hand it is structurally the same as the two examples grouped with it, and thus poses a problem for an editor.

Livy's use of adjectival asyndeta bimembria can be paralleled in other writers, for example Sallust, Tacitus' *Annals* and Virgil, not only in the high incidence of *in*-privatives, but also in their placement and status as predicative adjuncts. For Sallust see XXX.3.3.2, for Tacitus' *Annals*, XXX.5.2.3, and for Virgil, e.g. XXIV.2.2.1, 2. See also IV.4.

3.5   Verbs

Nine pairs of verbs are listed, of which seven are in speeches. Most are of formulaic or recognisable types. Formulaic are 47 *fusum fugatum*, 51 *fudit fugauit*, 52 *uelitis iubeatis*, in all of which the second verb arguably caps the first. 46 is of an old and standard type, a pair of imperatives, though it has an unusual order. 48 *teritur absumitur* is an established semantic type, with a verb of destruction in second place. 49 and 50 are juxtaposed pairs of opposites (reversives), a commonplace accumulation with parallels e.g. in Cicero and Tacitus. 45, if it is accepted as a pair, is a familiar morphological type (pair of ablative gerunds). The odd one out is 53 *instructam ornatam*, over which there are textual doubts. Again we see Livy's habit of admitting formulae and formulaic patterns particularly in speeches. This last possible example, 53, is in the narrative and a case could be made for emendation.

3.6   Pairs of Opposites

There are about nine pairs of opposites in the eight books (10, 11 *seruos liberos, puberes impubes*, 30 *diem noctem*, 38, 39 *armata inermes, fortes ignaui*, 49, 50 *augetis minuitis, donati adimitis*, 59 *ad castra ad siluas*, 66 *per uias per inuia*), about 13 per cent of the 66 asyndeta. In three places there are two pairs juxtaposed. Livy is halfway between Sallust and Tacitus in the frequency with which he admits opposites in asyndeton. Sallust has only eight such pairs, or 9 per cent of the total (XXX.3.3.2, final paragraph). Tacitus in the *Histories* has 19 (= 35 per cent) (XXX.4.2.3a), and in the *Annals* 36 (= 32 per cent) (XXX.5.2.3). These figures bring out above all a distinctive feature of the style of Tacitus.

There is a difference between Sallust on the one hand and Livy and Tacitus on the other that is worth noting. Livy and Tacitus both juxtapose two pairs of opposites, but Sallust does not do so.

3.7 Some Other Features of Distribution and Structure

Of the three juxtaposed pairs of opposites, two are in direct speeches (38 and 39, 49 and 50). The second of these speeches has in the same sentence the pair *libertatem immunitatem* (24). Speeches have other accumulations. At 3 and 4 there are the juxtaposed pairs *Claudios Cassios* and *consulatibus decemuiratibus*. *Coniuges liberos* at 23 follows *caedibus incendiis ruinis direptione*, which I did not take as containing two asyndeta bimembria, but the case could be made that it does. *Solos inermos* (41) and *forte temere* (54) are in the same direct speech. Another such accumulation is in a direct speech at 34.7 (48 *teritur absumitur*, 64 *in magistratibus in sacerdotiis*). A final accumulation, this time in narrative, is at 57, 58, showing two instances of the prepositional type in the same sentence.

There are about eight accumulations referred to here, of which six are in speeches. An examination of these speeches would probably reveal other types of asyndeton as well, such as phrasal and clausal. Sallust too piles up asyndeta bimembria in speeches, for example by Catiline (see e.g. Sallust 6–10), Caesar (13–16) and Cato (17–19). In the late Republic and Augustan period an obtrusive use of asyndeton was it seems associated (at least partly) with rhetorical style.

There are a few other structural features shared with Sallust and/or Tacitus, but these are not very marked. It is easier to find similarities between Sallust and Tacitus, whereas Livy's use of asyndeton bimembre can more readily be associated with legal and military Latin (and oratory).

On 20 it was noted that at 28.13.5 an asyndetic pair is immediately followed by a pair coordinated with *-que* (*ciuium sociorum, peditum equitumque*). It is a mannerism of Sallust and Tacitus that an asyndetic pair is often followed by a coordinated pair (see XXX.6.2b), a structure that is not however confined to historians (see e.g. XIX, and XXVI.7.2.1 on Cicero; also e.g. Cato *Agr.* 140.2 *utique tu fruges frumenta, uineta uirgultaque grandire beneque euenire siris* for an instance in a prayer).

This is a pattern that does not seem to have been favoured by Livy, despite the example quoted above. In the eight books examined here I have found no straightforward examples. 10, 11 (*caedunt pariter resistentes fusosque, inermes atque armatos, seruos liberos, puberes impubes, homines iumentaque*) is superficially of this type, in that *pubes impubes* is followed by *homines iumentaque*, but there are two asyndeta bimembria, not one in the manner of Sallust and Tacitus, preceding the coordinated pair.

I note however in passing that some other books have cases of a particular manifestation of this Sallustian/Tacitean structure (with *ac*

3 Conclusions

the coordinator). Note 8.33.20 *quam conueniens esse propter Q. Fabium ciuitatem in laetitia uictoria, supplicationibus ac gratulationibus esse* (my punctuation). Oakley (1998: 734), punctuating with a comma after *laetitia* as well, sees here a 'pattern of asyndeton followed by *ac*' (i.e., I take it, ABC *ac* D, end-of-list coordination), citing also 7.30.23 *salutem uictoriam, lucem ac libertatem* (see his note ad loc., 1998: 301, where by contrast no commas are used in the quotation). In fact there are two pairs, with the structure AB, C *ac* D, which is also found at Tacitus 5: *silentio patientia, postremo precibus ac lacrimis ueniam quaerebant*; here *postremo* makes the separation of the two pairs explicit. At 8.33.20 above *supplicationibus* and *gratulationibus* (with a five-syllable homoeoteleuton) go closely together, both denoting festivities in honour of the gods ('supplications and thanksgivings'). *Laetitia* and *uictoria* are a classic pair of closely related terms expressing a single idea, with one acting as a modifier of the other (= 'joyful victory' or 'the joy of victory'; for the association of ideas cf. Nep. *Timoth*. 2.2 *quae uictoria tantae fuit Atticis laetitiae*). For this type of relationship see e.g. XXX.2.1, 6 with cross references. The Loeb translator (Foster) also interpreted the passage as containing two pairs ('How proper was it that because of Quintus Fabius the citizens should <u>exult in victory, with thanksgivings and rejoicings</u>' (alternatively, and more literally, 'how proper it was that ... the state was given over to the joy of victory, to supplications and thanksgivings').

At 7.30.23 above both pairs can be analysed in the same way as *laetitia uictoria* ('the safety of victory, the light of liberty'). Oakley notes (1997: 539) that *libertas* and *lux* are elsewhere paired, as e.g. at Cic. *Verr*. 5.160. A comma should be placed after *uictoriam*.

I move on to a slightly different pattern, with Tacitean parallels. On 20 it was suggested that the asyndeton *peditum equitum* can be supported against the variant reading *peditum equitumque*. This pair is followed by an interesting pair of opposites, coordinated: *terrestrium ac naualium copiarum*. What is distinctive here is that *terrestrium* and *naualium* are adjectives, not nouns like the preceding pair *peditum equitum*. This is a type of syntactic switch that is found particularly in Tacitus in juxtaposed pairs: the second pair modifies the word (here *copiarum*) that continues the syntax of the (asyndetic) pair before. See XXX.6.2b for the Tacitean examples, and a possible one from Sallust. It might be argued that in 20 the reading *peditum equitum* is supported by the structure of the following phrase. The question however remains whether this pattern is common in other books of Livy, and whether it is a feature of historiography, or rather of the literary language in general.

Livy occasionally juxtaposes asyndeta bimembria of different types (3, 4 *Claudios Cassios, consulatibus decemuiratibus* (the difference here is only of case), 42, 61 *sine imperio sine signo, incompositi inordinati*). A striking example of such varied accumulation is at Sallust 47, where three different types of asyndeton bimembre are in the same sentence. In the note to that passage twofold accumulations are cited from Tacitus' *Histories* and *Annals*, several of which, as in Livy 42, 61, have the prepositional type alongside another type. This pattern is not however peculiar to historiography, as we saw above in the note to Livy 61.

3.8 Contextual Factors and Other Determinants

Asyndeton (of different types) has a reputation for being suited to 'rapid narrative', 'battle narrative' and the like. Ash (2007: 87) for example, says of one type (comprising historic infinitives) that it features 'especially in historians for rapid sequences of events'. See further V.1 for such judgements.

There are some asyndeta in the context of battles in Livy (e.g. 10, 11, 13, 14, 15, 33, 42), but rapidity is not necessarily the issue. 10–11, for example, is a catalogue of victims, expressed by pairs of opposites. 13–15 similarly is a catalogue of losses, again expressed by a series of pairs. The contexts in which asyndeta occur are varied. 1, for example, is a statement about the background of Servius Tullius and his character and achievements (for asyndeton in character sketches see on Sallust at XXX.3.3.2, and also Oakley 2005a: 179), 2 is about an administrative feature of the distant past, 3 and 4 are about the honours achieved by various persons and their motivating power, 5 and 6 list in pairs the loss of family members, 7 refers to the causes of the present physical state of an army, 8 and 9 are a catalogue of the equipment of an army, 16 lists military resources, 19 lists family members and 20 is a catalogue of men. There is no need to go on (but see further V).

In our eight books of Livy there are no asyndetic pairs of historic infinitives at all, and I have not been able to find this pattern elsewhere in Livy. Here is a difference between Livy and both Sallust and Tacitus. We have seen that in Sallust nine of 19 asyndetic pairs of verbs are historic infinitives (XXX.3.3.2), in Tacitus *Histories* five of 10, and in the *Annals* six of 20 (see XXX.6.1 on Tacitus). On pairs of verbs in Livy see above, 3.5. In any case historic infinitives overlap in function with the imperfect tense, and may refer to prolonged or repeated actions rather than rapid events.

3   Conclusions   675

We have already in these conclusions referred to factors that influenced Livy in his use of asyndeta bimembria, even if they did not fully 'determine' this form of coordination. Such asyndeton was felt to be appropriate in speeches (3.2), and in accumulations therein (3.7). A substantial number of his asyndeta, particularly those comprising nouns, had an official or military flavour. He was happy to use, it seems, old asyndetic pairs from varieties of official language. It is impossible in the state of the evidence to establish just how many of his pairs were old, but one can offer some guesses, with varying degrees of plausibility. Here is a list of possibilities: 2 *pontifices augures*, 5 *liberi fratres*, 6 *propinqui adfines*, 8 *arma equi*, 19, 23 *liberi coniuges*, 10 *serui liberi*, 14 *arma signa*, 18 *uiri feminae*, 20 *pedites equites*, 21 *arma tela*, 24 *libertas immunitas*, 26 *sarta tecta*, 28 *loca lautia*, 30 *dies nox*, 31, 36, 37 *(Iuppiter) optimus maximus*, 34 *exsul extorris*, 38 *armatus inermis*, 46 *defendite, ite* (structure: see note), 47, 51 *fundo fugo*, 50 *donare adimere*, 52 *uelitis iubeatis*, 64 *magistratus sacerdotia*. There are 26 examples here, to which could be added other pairs with a military or quasi-official flavour. It is also the case that Livy's six adjectival asyndeta containing at least one privative in *in-* belong to an ancient type with parallels in e.g. Greek and Italic. Livy was a conservative, not an inventive user of asyndeton bimembre.

Although asyndeta bimembria may be used in isolation, Livy shares with Sallust and Tacitus (and others) a liking for juxtaposed asyndetic and syndetic pairs, phrasal, clausal or single-word, expressing contrasts and oppositions, which are a manifestation of the rhetorical taste for antitheses (I am not referring here to the type comprising just an asyndetic pair + a coordinated, which, it was noted in the previous section, is not found in our books). Such accumulations seem to have been a particular feature of higher-style Latin (such as e.g. the later speeches of Cicero). Here are the relevant examples in the sample of Livy: 1, 3, 4, 5, 6, 8, 9, 10, 11, 13, 14, 15, 20, 38, 39, 42 (61), 49, 50, 57, 58. In one of the passages within this list (13–15) Livy has three asyndeta bimembria juxtaposed or in close proximity to one another (and in juxtaposition also with coordinated pairs).

3.9   Asyndeton Bimembre and Textual Criticism

The point was made in the Introduction and several times thereafter that pairs found in coordination may occasionally appear in asyndeton, and that this variation may cause problems for an editor attempting to establish a text. Should an isolated asyndeton be accepted in a text if there is not uniformity in the manuscript readings? This type of textual problem was referred to in six cases above, in four of which the problematic pair was dependent on a preposition: 7 *stationibus uigiliis*, 17 *ex oppidis conciliabulis*, 18 *ad ... uiros feminas*, 20 *peditum equitum*, 22 *in circulis conuiuiis*, 40 *a familia imperiosissima superbissima*. In several other places there is little or no manuscript support for coordination, but editors have been bothered by the asyndeton: 16 *frumenti pecuniae*, 25 *de prouinciis exercitibus*, 27 *gratulatione donis*, 29 *ex Sardina Sicilia*, 53 *instructam ornatam*. Are there any criteria that might be used to determine whether an asyndeton is right?

There are criteria that can sometimes be used. First, if a pair is attested in asyndeton elsewhere, a possible asyndetic example in Livy might have more weight than it would if the pair were otherwise attested only with coordination, but this on its own is a very weak criterion. Second, I argue in the chapter on Sallust and Tacitus and that on Caesar that structural factors were a major determinant of asyndeta bimembria: that is, asyndeta were favoured within certain verbal patterns. Are any of the problematic asyndeta in Livy found in structures in which asyndeton is likely to have been admitted? Third, there may be semantic or other features of a pair that recur in asyndeta bimembria. This criterion would rarely be decisive on its own, because the semantic or other features of asyndetic pairs are usually shared by coordinated pairs. Nevertheless it is a factor that could add support to other arguments. Fourth, on the negative side there may be stylistic or other features of a pair that make asyndeton unlikely.

The first criterion above gives some, but by no means decisive, support to 7 *stationibus uigiliis*, 18 *ad ... uiros feminas*, 20 *peditum equitum*, 25 *de prouinciis exercitibus*. 27 *gratulatione donis* might be added to this list, because it is paralleled by a very similar asyndetic pair in Livy.

Of these examples, 20 receives further (twofold) support of a structural kind (the second criterion above). First, if *peditum* and *equitum* are printed as asyndetic, they become one of a group of three pairs, each with a different form of coordination, syndetic or asyndetic. An asyndeton bimembre is not infrequently one member of a series of pairs, which may have varying coordination. Second, it was shown above (3.6) that *peditum equitum(que)* is followed by a structure (*terrestrium ac naualium copiarum*: two contrasting adjectives connected by *ac*) of a type found in Tacitus and possibly once in Sallust after an asyndeton bimembre; moreover the *simul ... simul* construction by which the two phrases are introduced sets them apart from the preceding *Romanorum sociorumque*. Our third criterion is also relevant to this example: the phrase *peditum equitum* is military, and military pairs are one of the most prominent groups of

3   Conclusions

nominal asyndeta bimembria in Livy (3.3). The case for *peditum equitum* is strong.

B has *peditum equitum* as an asyndeton, and it is B that has several of the other possible asyndeta above: 17 *ex oppidis conciliabulis*, 18 *ad . . . uiros feminas* and 22 *in circulis conuiuiis*. To the second of these pairs (18) the first of our criteria above is applicable, in that the pair is well attested as an asyndeton. That feature too it shares with *peditum equitum*. It is also in a direct speech, and speeches, as we saw (3.1), are a favoured location for asyndeta bimembria.

Given that B looks right in preserving asyndeton in 20, the onus should be on an editor to find explicit fault with the Latinity of the other three asyndeta in B above (17, 18 and 22), if they too are not to be accepted. They look plausible as asyndeta, 18 for the reasons stated in the last paragraph, and the other two in that they are pairs of near-synonyms, one of them alliterative. However, all three pairs are dependent on a single preposition, and in the whole of our eight books we have found only five examples of this type (25, 29 in addition to the above three), and in every one of these cases there is either manuscript variation or editorial uncertainty for other reasons. On 25 there was cited an example of preposition + asyndeton that seems textually certain from another book (8.33.20), but ideally there should be a far more systematic search of Livy to determine whether asyndeta bimembria dependent on a single preposition are unambiguously attested and in reasonable quantities; see the Appendix below. 25 itself (*de prouinciis exercitibus*) does however satisfy our first criterion and is also in a formal context.

Stationibus uigiliis (7), it was noted above, is one of those asyndeta that are attested elsewhere. It can be added that it is a military expression, and Livy, as we saw, had a taste for asyndeton in military phrases.

I offer a negative comment on another of the prepositional examples, 29 *ex Sardinia Sicilia*. It will become clear in the Appendix below that *-que* is particularly favoured in Livy when a pair of proper names is dependent on a single preposition. There is a double uncertainty hanging over this asyndeton, arising from its prepositional structure and the nature of its components.

Finally, doubts were hinted at, above 3.5, about 53 *instructam ornatam*. Other asyndetic pairs of verbs in the sample of Livy are in formulae or formulaic patterns, but this would be an ad hoc asyndeton. It would have had more in its favour if it had been in a speech, but it is in narrative.

Appendix: Prepositions with Two Dependent Nouns in Selected Books

In this Appendix I have listed from books 5, 30 and 34 all cases (some may have been missed, but the precise details are of little consequence) of prepositions with two single-word dependent nouns. There would be many more examples listed if I had included dependent phrases as well as dependent single words. The aim has been merely to put in perspective the two types of prepositional asyndeta bimembria that appear in the collection of 66 asyndeta in the main part of this chapter. The asyndetic types comprise, first, the five instances in which a preposition may be followed by two nouns without coordination, three from book 34 (**17, 18, 22**) and two from book 42 (**25, 29**), and, second, twelve instances with repeated preposition of the type *cum senatu cum populo*, only four of which are from the books considered for the material below in this Appendix. These twelve instances are at 2.5 above. We have noted that of the five instances of an asyndeton dependent on a single preposition, all have been subject either to manuscript variation or editorial conjecture. In the lists that follow from books 5, 30 and 34 I have not quoted the examples of the two asyndetic types just described and listed.

Book 5
19.7 *cum Faliscis et Capenatibus*
23.12 *a Volscis et Aequis*
27.11 *in foro et curia*

2.4 *ab urbe et ab re publica*
52.13 *de sacris loquimur et de templis*
27.15 *et ab hostibus et a ciuibus*

6.3 *in montes siluasque*
11.4 *in Sergium Verginiumque*
11.6 *in Sergio Verginioque*
12.8 *ab Sergiis Verginiisque*
25.9 *ad sacra ludosque*
30.1 *pro aris focisque*
33.6 *inter Appenninum Alpesque*
39.9 *in arcem Capitoliumque*
44.5 *ex arce Capitolioque*
47.11 *inter Veios Romamque*

2.7 *in opere ac labore*
2.11 *in domos ac tecta*

Appendix: Prepositions with Two Dependent Nouns

6.3 *per niues ac pruinas*
15.4 *in stationibus ac custodiis*
19.9 *inter murum ac uallum*
35.2 *inter Padum atque Alpes*
38.5 *ad coniuges ac liberos*
39.3 *inter Romam atque Anienem*
39.9 *cum coniugibus ac liberis*
43.1 *inter incendia ac ruinas captae urbis*
43.4 *per uim atque arma*

Book 30
3.2   *ex Sicilia quoque et Hispania*
6.2   *inter caedem et uulnera*
16.10   *ex Italia et Gallia*
17.8   *sine metu et certamine*

24.5 *et ab hoste et ab tempestatibus*

1.5 *ab natura fortunaque*
2.7 *cum exercitibus imperioque*
3.9 *extra fossam etiam uallumque*
4.7 *apud Poenos Numidamque*
4.12 *ad Syphacem Hasdrubalemque*
7.8 *in urbe agrisque*
8.1 *ad Syphacem Carthaginiensesque*
24.10 *ex oculis manibusque*
24.11 *per litora portusque*
30.25 *inter Africam Italiamque*
33.3 *in dextram laeuamque*
38.5 *ex Sicilia Sardiniaque*

1.7 *in Etruria ac Liguribus*
4.7 *ex mentione ac spe pacis*
10.3 *pro aggere ac pontibus*
10.20 *inter adsiduas clades ac lacrimas*
16.10 *inter Italiam atque Africam*
35.9 *cum fessis ac sauciis*
36.1 *ad mare ac naues*

Book 34
2.12 *per uias et compita*
4.9 *de donis et muneribus*
7.13 *in manu et tutela*
32.5 *ab Iaso et Bargyliis*
34.4 *in machinationes et tormenta*
43.3 *in Hispania et Macedonia*
56.10 *cum caedibus et incendiis*

4.3 *in Graeciam Asiamque*
19.8 *ex agris castellisque*
21.7 *ex ferrariis argentariisque*
22.4 *in Italia Hispaniaque*
24.6 *de Romanis Aetolisque*
46.7 *ad uallum castraque*
50.2 *in pectora animosque*
56.13 *in oppidis agrisque*

14.11 *in uirtute ac uiribus*
28.3 *cum equitibus atque expeditis*
28.3 *in terrorem ac tumultum*
35.10 *in fidem ac dicionem*
45.7 *sine oculis ac naso*
50.10 *per Thessaliam atque Epirum*
51.1 *ab Oreo atque Eretria*
51.5 *per seditionem ac tumultum*
57.5 *ex dignitate atque utilitate populi Romani*
57.8 *in pacem atque amicitiam.*

Here are some statistics taken from the above lists. There are 14 pairs with *et*, 30 with *-que* and 28 with *ac/atque*. Since we only found five possible asyndeta after a preposition in the whole of the eight books, clearly it was not a favoured construction.

The figures for pairs of proper names dependent on a preposition are of some interest. A total of 15 of the 30 pairs linked by *-que* are proper names (50 per cent). Only 6 of the 28 linked by *ac/atque* are proper names. The proportion for *et* is higher (6 of 14). The single example of a possible asyndeton comprising proper names (*ex Sardinia Sicilia*) looks doubtful, with *Siciliaque* the most convincing alternative.

Addendum

For *spes metus* possibly at Livy 30.32.5 see p. 590.

PART 6

Conclusions

CHAPTER XXXII

Asyndeton in Latin

1 Some Types of Asyndeton Bimembre

Asyndeton bimembre was old (see e.g. III.1, XIX.1), but I have resisted the idea that it was 'undoubtedly older' than explicit coordination of pairs (III.1). *-Que* and its root were ancient too, and I would prefer with e.g. Dunkel (1982) to leave open the matter of relative antiquity and to assume a long coexistence (III.1). From the very beginning in Latin asyndeton bimembre was diverse in its types and in their stylistic level. It has however been exposed to snap judgements derived from a failure to look at the distribution of its forms in a range of genres. For example, at XXIV.5.1.1, 8 (cf. 5.1.1, 1) Skutsch is quoted as saying that two adjectives with one noun are characteristic of ritual language. Asyndetic pairs of adjectives are common in many writers, some of them working in mundane genres (see below, this section), and indeed one type (consisting of pairs of judgemental adjectives in open-ended lists placed at the end of cola) we have related speculatively to a pattern of speech (see IV.4; cf. V.2, and also below, this section). Or again, Ogilvie (1965: 730), commenting on Livy 35, describes a pair of privatives (*inuisitato inaudito*) as 'almost sacral'. Privatives in asyndeton, whether two together or one juxtaposed with a different type of adjective, are so widespread in a variety of genres, e.g. oratory, historiography, Horace's *Satires*, that a whole chapter has been devoted to them (VI). Similarly Jocelyn (1967: 175) on Enn. *trag.* 9 *pugnant proeliant* refers to the 'official language', but while some pairs of verbs belonged to legal language this is not one of them, and asyndetic pairs of verbs fall into diverse categories (see below, this section).

Asyndeton certainly had a place in contrived genres, such as the language of law. Old legal and religious formulae in Latin are pointed out in various places, as at XXII.5, 6 and XXIII.3. A legal accumulation containing *usus fructus* identical in structure to some late legal accumulations was noted already in Plautus, and an augural formula in Plautus was shown to be related to one in Umbrian, both of them having asyndeton of a similar sort (XXIII.3). The formula must have gone a long way back in Italy. There are other such legal/religious pairs in Plautus, which are collected at XXIII.3. Several chapters deal with artificial types or patterns of asyndeton bimembre, such as VII, on simplex + compound verb (found particularly in curse tablets), IX, on pairs of verbs of different tense or mood (mainly legal), XI.5, on masculine + feminine pairs in legal contexts, and XVII, on correlative distribution (in various stylised genres). An artificial type used mainly in republican Latin consists of pairs (or longer sequences) of long suffixal derivatives or compounds, often coinages, which seem to be employed (by e.g. Plautus and Lucilius) with humorous or abusive intent (see XXIII.4) (see further below, 4).

But asyndeton bimembre was by no means only artificial or confined to high-style writing. A freedman in Petronius uses an accumulation (61.9 *per scutum per ocream egi aginaui*) containing a verbal pair that has now turned up in asyndeton again in some curse tablets from Mainz (see below, 3.3, and also XIX.1, and for other asyndetic pairs in curse tablets see Adams 2016: 114, 250–1). The adjectival pair *saluus sanus* appears in a soldier's letter from Qasr Ibrim in Egypt (*P. Rainer Cent.* 164), and is also attested in another Egyptian text (a receipt) from Puluinos (*ChLA* 3.204 = *CEL* 156) (see Adams 2016: 200). Freedmen in Petronius also use other pairs, of revealing types. At 71.11 there is a positive–negative pair of opposites, *uelit nolit* (see VI.6, 7), which is included in a list of proverbial pairs by Donatus (see VI.6). For a (discontinuous) adjectival pair of judgemental terms in a freedman's speech see 43.3 *durae buccae fuit, linguosus, discordia non homo* (predicates, with the third element an explanatory addition). 37.7 (*est sicca sobria, bonorum consiliorum*) is a tricolon, but embedded within is a pair of synonymous alliterative judgemental adjectives that are again predicates; the third member differs in meaning. Another discontinuous pair, of nouns this time, is at 76.8: *uenalicia coemo, iumenta* (slaves, animals, a variant on the pairing of humans and animals: see XXIV.7.1.2, 6, and West 2007: 100 on the 'two-footed, four-footed' pairing; for the discontinuous structure in a pair denoting miscellaneous creatures see Men. *Samia* 14–15 quoted on Cicero 150). For open-ended lists (for which in general see IV.3) see 38.15 *solebat sic cenare quomodo rex: apros gausapatos, opera pistoria, auis, . . . cocos pistores* (stressing the former wealth of the referent; the last two terms are an embedded unitary pair), 46.2 *inueniemus quod manducemus, pullum oua* (incomplete list of foodstuffs, at the end of a colon; the same asyndetic pair is at Hor. *Ep.* 2.2.163, for which see XXIX.3.2). These Petronian instances, judgemental adjectives,

1 Some Types of Asyndeton Bimembre 685

discontinuous pairs, incomplete lists and some formulae, seem to have been commonplace types of asyndetic pairs.

Elsewhere in the novel Petronius has other examples of asyndeta of common types, such as a pair of adverbial opposites, *huc illuc*, at 114.3 (for the type see XIII.5.4). Notable are some uses of adjectives (or equivalents). At 15.4 (*nescio quis ex cocionibus, caluus, tuberosissimae frontis*) we have predicative adjuncts, postponed, at the end of a colon, referring to physical defects, a type sometimes in Lucilius (XXV.1.1.4); note the extended length of the second member, for which see XXIV.2.2. See too 81.3 *ut inter <tot> audaciae nomina mendicus exul, in deuersorio Graecae urbis iacerem desertus*. These are predicative adjuncts again, substantival this time, here alluding to abandonment, a constant theme of asyndetic pairs (see below, 3.4). Notably, they accompany the unexpressed subject of the verb *iacerem*, which is elsewhere used in association with asyndetic pairs of adjuncts: see XXIV.2.2 on Virgil 21, XXIV.7.2 on Lucretius 25. In the passage of Petronius the verb has a predicate (*desertus*) as well as the asyndetic pair of secondary predicates (*mendicus exul*), as is the case in the passage of Lucretius (25) just referred to: 5.223 *tum porro puer* . . . | . . . *nudus humi iacet, infans, indigus omni | uitali auxilio* (*nudus* is predicate with *iacet*, and *infans, indigus* . . . are secondary predicates/adjuncts). At 107.5 (*in conspectu uestro supplices iacent iuuenes, ingenui honesti*) again the verb is *iaceo*, and again it has a predicate, *supplices*, and an asyndetic pair of secondary predicates, though the order is different here, with the adjuncts at the end.

The structures seen here, with asyndetic adjectives or the like, often postponed, used as adjuncts and expressing pathos or judgements of some sort, are found in Latin of diverse types (see e.g. IV.4, V.2, XXIII Appendix on Plautus, XXV.1.1.4 on Lucilius, Cicero 42, 48, 172, XXVII.1.2 on Catullus, Sallust 52, 53, 58, XXIV.2.1.1 after 15 on Virgil, Livy 32, 34, 38, 39, 42, Tacitus 21, 22, 124, 125; see also the examples from Seneca listed by Axelson 1987: 170).

Another banal asyndetic type is that consisting of pairs of imperatives, usually addressed to slaves or subordinates of other types (see X). Asyndetic pairs of verbs are readily classifiable into a variety of types: they are not a unity subject to simplistic generalisations. At one extreme are pairs made up of an active and a passive form of the same verb, such as *amant amantur* (see VIII). These are extremely rare in Latin, and tend to be in elaborate writing. They seem in part too to be semantically determined, in that they were used particularly to express mutual love. Various other artificial types with generic restrictions were referred to above: e.g. repetition of a single verb, with the second member of the pair in a different tense or mood from that of the first member (IX); simple verb followed by its compound, with the second often an intensification of the first (VII). Some asyndetic pairs of verbs are marked by assonance, and these too were presumably regarded as stylised. In this category are for example pairs of ablative gerunds, a type found in varieties of high literature and also comedy (see XXIII.5.4). Pairs of verbs with repeated prefix also exploit sound effects (see e.g. XXIII.7.1, XXVI.7.2.3). A run-of-the-mill verbal pairing identified in Plautus consists of a verb of motion followed by another verb, the type mirroring in non-imperatival form the commonplace imperatival structure 'go do something' (XXIII.5.3). Different again is a structural pattern found in Cicero (XXVI.7.2.3), in which a sentence is followed (without any explicit connection) by two asyndetic verbs that explain it. Pairs of verbs expressing acts of violence, with the second outdoing the first, are a classic case of rising emphasis, and it is suggested below (3.4) that the asyndeton in these may have reflected an intonation pattern of expressive speech. I mention finally a pair of verbs, *alit* + *auget*, which are often alongside each other in different writers either with a coordinator or in asyndetic sequences with more than two members. These are also found in asyndeton under the influence of the structure in which they are located (see below, 3.1).

Pairs of adjectives with at least one privative are distributed over a diversity of genres, such as at one generic extreme Horace's *Satires* and at the other philosophy (see in general V.2, VI.2.2; see XXIX.2.1.5 on Horace's *Satires*, where all adjectival pairs have at least one privative, and most are semantically unelevated).

The aim of this section has been to show that asyndeton bimembre is diverse in distribution and stylistic level, and that its character cannot be captured by single labels. This diversity has been stressed in places in literary chapters, as on Plautus (XXIII.9, and also XXIII.2–4), Lucilius (the whole of XXV.1) and Catullus (note the contrasting examples at XXVII.1.1).

2 Asyndetic Tricola (and Longer), versus Asyndeton Bimembre

An asyndetic tricolon at Varro *Ling.* 7.8 (*inter ea conregione conspicione cortumione*) in a passage on the taking of the auspices is stylised in the sense that the terms have repeated endings and a repetition of the prefix *con-*, but it is not stylised merely because it has three asyndetic members. Nor do its features of assonance tie it specifically to religious language. In a good deal of Latin literature even of unpretentious type asyndeton is the norm in

3 *Some Determinants of Asyndeton Bimembre* 687

sequences of three or more. Varro in the *Res rusticae* coordinates pairs but uses asyndeton for groups of three (see Adams 2016: 81–3). In recipes Apicius likewise coordinates pairs of ingredients but lists longer groups asyndetically (see IV.2). The medical author Scribonius Largus writing under Tiberius has many dozens of asyndeta with 3+ members, and many pairs with coordination, but comparatively few asyndeta bimembria (see below, 4). For details of the incidence of asyndeton versus end-of-list coordination and multiple coordination in selected works of Cicero, Livy and Cato in sequences of three or more members see XVIII.2, and also I.4. Asyndeton is favoured. As for any supposed special association of the assonance above with sacral or archaic style, note e.g. at I.4 Cic. *S. Rosc.* 110 *hortatore auctore intercessore* (from an early speech considered to be in undeveloped style); at XVIII.2.2.1 the asyndetic tricola from *Off.* 1 with members having repeated endings; at XXIII.6 the tricola and longer sequences of privatives in Plautus; and at XXV.7 another comparable Ciceronian tricolon. Gellius (1.5.3) quotes an offensive remark addressed to L. Torquatus by Hortensius in which the point of the abuse is expressed by a Greek asyndetic tricolon with assonance: *tum uoce molli atque demissa Hortensius 'Dionysia' inquit 'Dionysia malo equidem esse quam quod tu, Torquate,* ἄμουσος, ἀναφρόδιτος, ἀπροσδιόνυσος. In Horace's *Satires* asyndetic tricola and longer series are semantically run-of-the-mill (XXIX.3.1), as they are in the second book of the *Epistles* (XXIX.3.2.1; e.g. shopping lists). For the greater frequency of asyndetic tricola as compared with dicola in several classical prose works see I.4.

In a tricolon then in classical prose we would expect often or usually to find asyndeton, whereas asyndeta bimembria are comparatively rare, indeed exceptional, such that their determinants have to be considered. In poetry too coordinated pairs far outnumber asyndetic. See XXVII.3 on coordinated pairs in Catullus, which are a marked feature of his style and have a much higher incidence than asyndetic; also XXIX.4.1 on Horace, and XXIV.9 (Appendix) on coordinated pairs in Lucretius and Virgil.

3 **Some Determinants of Asyndeton Bimembre**

3.1 Accumulations and Structures

It has been shown throughout this book that asyndeton bimembre occurs with particular frequency in accumulations (for statistics see XIX.2). In the two philosophical works of Cicero examined earlier about 63 per cent of pairs are in accumulations (XXVI.7.3.1). The most striking feature of pairs of opposites is that they are often in accumulations (see XIII.6; also XIII.4). An accumulation may be described as a determinant of an asyndeton in a general sense, in that it is a feature of accumulations that they contain a mixture of methods of coordination, and asyndeta are bound to appear in juxtaposition with coordinated groups. There is also a more specific sense in which such structures motivated switches from an expected coordination to asyndeton. Quite a few pairs which are attested in prose either with a coordinator, or in asyndeton if they are in a sequence with more than two members (on the significance of the length of the sequence see the last section), turn up occasionally in asyndeton bimembre, but only if they are located in an accumulation (see XXIV.6.3, 6–8 for *alit auget* in an accumulation in Cicero, compared with 7.1.3, 12 for Ciceronian examples with either coordination or placement in a longer sequence; also Sallust 15 on *caedes incendia*, 47 on *socii amici*; see too on Sallust 19, 27). In Tacitus an opposition *laeta tristia* is used asyndetically in an accumulation (22), but elsewhere I have found *laetus/tristis* only coordinated. See also Tacitus 86 on *congressus colloquia*, 90 on *illustris ignobilis*, 123 on *inuisus infamis*, Livy 49 on *augeo minuo*.

The role of accumulations with certain structures in sanctioning asyndeton bimembre is nowhere clearer than in Caesar, *Civ.*, where definite asyndeta bimembria hardly occur, except in accumulations (see XIX.2, XXVII.2). In the *Lex Antonia de Termessibus* various pairs of verbs with what might seem to be unexpected coordination (the participles *usei fructeiue* and variants) on closer inspection turn out to be in the second part of an accumulation consisting of an asyndetic pair and then a coordinated pair. In this case it is the coordination that is determined by the structure (see XXII.2.2). At XXII.5.7, 8 it is shown that *emptio uenditio* and *locatio conductio* are pairs that are usually coordinated, except in accumulations: thus *emptio et uenditio* but *emptio uenditio, locatio conductio*.

3.2 Genre

The types of texts that are the prime location for asyndeta bimembria are laws and other legal/official works. We saw one law in which asyndeta outnumber explicitly coordinated pairs (XXII.2.1). Changes of fashion occurred in legal drafting (see e.g. XXII.2.3), but even in late legal texts asyndeton remained common. The persistent formulaic asyndeta in such works seem to reflect a matter-of-fact legal shorthand. Pairs of verbs of different tense or mood (see above, 1) are almost exclusively a feature of

3 Some Determinants of Asyndeton Bimembre 689

legal language (IX; see too XII). Asyndetic pairs denoting family members, and particularly kinship terms consisting of a masculine + feminine noun, are mainly in legal texts (see XIII.3 and also XIII.2.5 and above, 1; also XII). In the books of Cicero's *Philippics* examined here there are various asyndetic pairs from motions in the senate (see 23, 24, 25, 76, 77, 78). For the frequency of legal/official asyndetic pairs in Cicero see XXVI.7.8.1 (42 of 209 asyndetic pairs in the sample are of this type), and in Livy, XXXI.3.3, 3.8 (listing 26 such pairs). Pairs denoting types of officials or offices belong in this same category: see e.g. Cicero 122 with cross references, Livy 2, 4, 64, Sallust 11, Tacitus 14.

Variations in the incidence (and types) of asyndeton bimembre occur from genre to genre. In the works of Horace such variation is particularly noticeable (see XXIX.5). Commonplace types, such as adjectives with at least one privative member and pairs of imperatives, are found in the *Satires*, but asyndeton bimembre of whatever type is almost non-existent in the *Odes*. In the latter Horace may have had in mind the practice of certain Greek poets (see XXIX.4.1.8, 4.5), whereas the *Satires* drew on speech.

One difference between Cicero's philosophical works and speeches is that he hardly uses pairs of opposites in the speeches, but has them often in the philosophica (see XV). They were presumably suited to the presentation of philosophical ideas. See particularly XXVI.7.3.1 for distinctions between the philosophica and speeches.

See also in general III.3.

3.3 Formulae versus ad hoc Asyndetic Pairs Reflecting Intonation Patterns (?)

A distinction should be made between fossilised asyndetic pairs and ad hoc pairings, some of the latter probably determined by the way in which the pair was pronounced, with a pause for emphasis. Formulae, particularly legal, came up at XXII.5, 6. *Patres conscripti* (XXII.5.1), for instance, partly reflects the constant use of asyndeton in legal/official language, but there may in this case have been a special historical reason for the lack of coordinator, namely the manner in which a summons into the senate was originally expressed, with the *patres* called first, and then, after a gap, the *conscripti*, with no need for a coordinator when the second group were summoned. Such pairs had a long history: see for example *usus fructus* at Plaut. *Merc*. 834 (XXIII.3, and above, 1). They tended to acquire a coordinator, particularly if used outside legal contexts, metaphorically or informally. See for example Cicero 163 on *aequi boni*, XXII.5.3 on *sarta tecta*, and XXII.9 on pairs of consuls' names, which came to be coordinated particularly when only a single name was used for each referent (i.e. when there was an absence of formality to the naming). Not all formulaic asyndetic pairs, however, were legal (or religious). A verbal pair found in a freedman's speech in Petronius (61.9 *egi aginaui*) has, it was noted above, 1, now surfaced several times in Mainz curse tablets of the second half of the first century AD (see Adams 2016: 249, citing Blänsdorf 2010: 172, 173–5), and it was presumably in formulaic use. A formulaic pair might denote a single entity, even something as pedestrian as a game (*par impar*: see XXIX.2.1.1). Pairs of adverbial opposites in particular were often fossilised, a process facilitated by the fixed form of most adverbs (see in general XIII.5.4; the type also comes up in various literary chapters). Though Horace in the *Odes* hardly ever admitted asyndeton bimembre, at 2.3.26 he uses the asyndetic adverbial opposites *serius ocius* (see XXIX.2.3). Donatus on Ter. *Hec.* 315 refers to asyndetic opposites of this type as proverbial (XIII.5.4).

Coordinators were probably omitted ad hoc sometimes in speech for dramatic effects. In a written text, particularly if the writing system is largely unpunctuated, intonation patterns and emphases cannot easily be conveyed, but that does not mean that written asyndeta were never intended to reflect aspects of pronunciation. Take for example the asyndetic tricolon of approval at Hor. *Ars* 428 *clamabit enim 'pulchre! bene! recte!'* (see XXIX.3.4). This must be a quotation, and it is reasonable to think that the three terms were uttered emphatically and with pauses. The insertion of coordinators would convert the words from a dramatic cry to a mundane description of what was said. Asyndeton may be functional in the sense that it is meant to suggest aspects of intonation. The writer decides on occasions to make an omission off-the-cuff with speech patterns in mind (see also XV).

A theme of this book has been the frequency of pairs of adjectives, pejorative, pathetic or judgemental, placed at the end of cola and often secondary predicates, with the second tending to cap the first semantically (see above, 1). These are not usually in formulae but are created to suit the context, though one structural type recurs, that with a privative prefix (see e.g. VI.2.2; also e.g. XXIX.2.1.5). Sometimes nouns are used instead in the same way, e.g. pejoratively in identifications (see the first example below). Such pairs are open-ended, in the sense that the list could be further extended if a stronger term could be found (see IV.4; also V.2). Both Catullus and Horace allude to this open-endedness. See Catull. 42.13 *non assis facit? o lutum lupanar,* | *aut si perditius potest quid esse!* (XXVII.1.1). The female referent is identified with mud, with a brothel, and then Catullus generalises ('or if anything can be more depraved than that'), implying that it might be possible to outdo the pair. Cf. Hor. *Sat.* 2.7.39 *nasum nidore supinor,* | *imbecillus iners, si quid uis, adde, popino* (see XXIX.2.1.1). First Horace uses a pejorative asyndetic pair of privatives, and then suggests that the pair could be added to, which he demonstrates by adding a stronger term himself. For a similar passage see Cicero's comment on a phrase of Lucilius at *Fin.* 2.25, quoted and discussed at XXV.6 in a note on Lucilius 1122–3.

Judgemental adjectival pairs in asyndeton do not belong to mechanical writing but are functional, in that they almost certainly imply a pattern of pronunciation. 'Breathless action' does not come into it, but rather slowed-down delivery.

3.4 A Few Semantic Types

Might semantics sometimes have determined a use of asyndetic coordination instead of syndetic? It is certainly the case that many asyndetic pairs are classifiable into semantic categories. I have listed such categories in various places in this book (XV, XXIII.8, XXIV.2.1.1 after 15, XXVI.7.8.1, 2, XXX.5.2.3), and will not restate them all here. It seems unlikely though that the semantic character of a pair was the sole determinant of an asyndeton. In Horace, for example, there are many coordinated pairs that semantically belong to categories in which asyndeton is thought to be common (see XXIX.4.1, and especially 4.1.8); see also XXVII.3 on this phenomenon.

Nevertheless it is remarkable how widespread a few semantic types are in asyndeton, such as terms (mainly adjectives) expressing exclusion, expulsion, abandonment and its pathos (cf. above, 1 on Petron. 81.3). The adjective *egens* occurs in such pairs constantly. For examples of the type see Cicero 41 (with *egens*), 42, 71, Sallust 24, 50 (*egens*), 52 (*egens*), Virgil 1 (*egens*), 22 (*egens*), Livy 32, 34. It is possible that the pathos of the abandonment could be highlighted by a pronunciation with absence of a coordinator, a factor that was mentioned in the last section. The asyndetic coordination would have a point, in representing a speech characteristic used to bring out the emotion in the situation. Asyndeton in pairs of verbs expressing violent acts (with the second outdoing the first) might also have implied an intonation pattern suited to the meaning (for which type see e.g. XV, XXVI.7.2.3, 7.8.2, XXX.2.1, 2, 3.3.2, 5.2.3). The writer could leave out the coordinator if he wanted to suggest an intonation pattern. Semantics goes hand in hand with pronunciation (see also XV).

3.5 Personal Taste

The use and frequency of asyndeton bimembre in a writer was influenced by personal preference, and preferences were not fixed but changeable. A change of taste is vividly represented in the distribution of asyndetic pairs in Tacitus' *Annals*: see XXX.5.2.1. A sharp decline in the incidence of asyndeton occurs in the last three books, 14–16. This is a typical Tacitean change of taste, which tells us nothing about the state of the language. Or again, Tacitus shows a marked liking for asyndetic pairs of opposites in both the *Histories* and *Annals* (see XXX.5.2.3), whereas in Sallust such pairs of opposites are relatively infrequent (see XXX.3.3.2, last paragraph). Livy uses asyndetic pairs far less frequently than both Tacitus and Sallust (see XXXI.3.1). Sallust and Tacitus quite often juxtapose asyndetic pairs with coordinated, but only Sallust uses the coordinator *atque* in such structures (see XXX.6.2b). Livy by contrast did not favour the structure (see XXXI.3.7). Clearly these variations (and others that have come up in the relevant chapters) have nothing to do with the genre historiography, but were determined by the individual writers' views of asyndetic forms of coordination.

In Virgil asyndetic pairs of verbs do not occur (see XXIV.2.1.4), whereas the type does occur both in Ennius (XXIV.5.1.4, 5.2.4) and Lucretius (XXIV.7.1.3). Does that mean that the language had changed? Of course not. Pairs of verbs are well attested in many classical genres and writers, such as Cicero and history (see above, 1). Virgil's own taste and influences (notably that of Homer) are reflected in this avoidance (and also in his readiness to use adjectival asyndeta).

Or again, asyndeton bimembre is found in the first book of Horace's *Epistles*, but not in the second (see XXIX.2.2.1).

3.6 Addressees, Contexts, Circumstances

Cicero uses asyndeton bimembre in letters to Atticus sparingly (XXVI.7.1), whereas in letters to certain addressees in the *Ad familiares* there are accumulations of asyndeta (see Cicero 193, 194 on letters to Appius Pulcher, with whom Cicero's relations were correct but cool, and 197, 198 on a letter to the consul Crassus, which is marked by 'insincerity': so Shackleton Bailey). It looks as if asyndeton in accumulations had a formality to it, which might make it suitable as a rhetorical ploy or distancing device (see XXVI.7.5.3).

In the speeches of Cicero the incidence of asyndeton bimembre varies, with its frequency greatest at political highpoints (see XXVI.7.6 on such variations), presumably because, with the pauses I have assumed asyndeton reflects in speech, it was capable of expressing strong emotion. See for example Cicero 3, 4 on the dramatic opening of the third speech against Catiline, with its asyndetic accumulation. Similarly there is a marked accumulation of asyndetic pairs in the speech that Sallust puts into the mouth of Catiline (seven pairs: see Sallust 6–10, and *Cat.* 20.15 quoted after 10 and 68; also XXX.3.3.1). This similarity between the two speeches by different composers but related to the same historical events is suggestive of the rhetorical role of asyndeton bimembre in public life in the late Republic (see also XXXI.3.2). It is also a fact that the one instance of asyndeton bimembre in Caesar's *Bellum ciuile* that is outside an accumulation is in a direct speech (XXVIII.2.2, 14). In Livy 64 per cent of the asyndeta bimembria in our sample books are in speeches. Livy's speeches also have accumulations of asyndeta (see XXXI.3.7).

4 Asyndeton and Latin Literature

Languages do not change regularly over time such that one can readily set up a 'chronology' of the language. The attempt to divide Latin into periods with chronological divisions raises many problems. One should not expect to identify a clear chronology in the use of asyndeton versus coordination, as changes of fashion come into it as well as language change or development (cf. 3.5). For example, we did find what looks like a decline in the frequency over time of asyndeton in a group of three legal texts (see XXII.2.1–3), but it was pointed out (XXII.1) that in a decree (of 189 BC) that antedates all three only coordination is found, and indeed in a pairing that much later turns up with asyndeton. The three texts do not straightforwardly reflect changing practice even in the language of law. Various phrase types given their own chapters show a particular frequency of asyndeton in legal documents, whatever their date (e.g. IX, XI.5 and XIV.3). Asyndetic naming of the two consuls for a year may recede in favour of explicit coordination (see XXII.9), but a thorough study of later texts and laws would show that asyndeton of this type was still persistent, for example in historians such as Livy and Tacitus. As for prayers, in the corpus examined at XXII.3 asyndeton bimembre is far outnumbered by coordination, but we did elsewhere see some old religious asyndeta, such as an augural formula with a near-parallel in Umbrian (see XXII.6.3), and some pairs in Plautus (see XXIII.3, and above, 1), Cicero (see 4, 16, 160) and miscellaneous sources (XXII.6). Again, it is possible that changes of fashion were taking place from time to time.

I turn to some further aspects of change and diversity. The theme has come up already in this chapter, for example in the discussion of the inadequacy of using single descriptive terms meant to characterise asyndeton bimembre (see above, 1, first paragraph), and in the remarks about genre as a possible determinant of the phenomenon (see 3.2).

One type that seems to be early republican consists of at least one compound or suffixal derivative, often apparently a coinage, juxtaposed either with another such or with a word or words of different type. These are dealt with at XXIII.4 (with cross references), and alluded to above, 1, second paragraph). A classic example is Pacuvius' *repandirostrum incuruiceruicum* (see XXIV.6.1, 3). Lucilius 540 (XXV.1.1.1, 1) combines two Greek compound terms, *calliplocamon callisphyron*. At Petron. 55.6 Trimalchio recites a poem that he attributes to Publilius, which has *pietaticultrix gracilipes crotalistria* (see XXIII.4). There are quite a few such terms in Plautus, some of them abusive (e.g. *Mo.* 356 *plagipatidae ferritribaces*), others possibly technical terms to do for example with fashion trades. It would not do, given the Plautine evidence, merely to label such terms as 'tragic' (but see Sommerstein 2019: 303 for accumulations of such compounds in Aeschylus). They probably reflect the readiness of early writers to form compounds or suffixal derivatives as a means of establishing a 'literary' register, although some suffixal derivatives perhaps belonged to technical language. The presence of pairs of this type in Plautus alongside on the one hand religious/legal pairs, and on the other pairs of imperatives addressed to slaves brings out the diversity of asyndeton bimembre in early literature.

At XXIV.4 it was pointed out that Virgil has similarities to Homer in his use of adjectival asyndeta, but it was suggested that the significance of these needed to be assessed by comparing Virgil with Ennius. If Virgil's practice resembled that of Ennius too the possibility of direct Homeric influence on Virgil would recede. But at XXIV.5.3 it is shown that Virgil and Ennius are different in their use of asyndeton. Ennius hardly in the extant fragments has asyndetic adjectival pairs that are uncontroversial, and Virgil for his part, unlike Ennius, does not admit pairs of verbs (see above, 3.5). The few adjectival pairs that there are in Ennius differ in type from the Virgilian. At XXIV.7 it is shown that Lucretius is aligned with Ennius and Pacuvius in the use of asyndeton, and that Virgil, differing from all three, resembles

4 Asyndeton and Latin Literature 695

Homer (on which subject see also XXIV.9). The other three writers have similarities to Plautus (for a similarity between Ennius and Plautus see XXIV.5.2.1, 14; also XXIV.5.3), and their usage may reflect coordinating conventions of the earlier period. Both Plautus and the three early high-style writers employ commonplace and functional forms of asyndeton bimembre, as well as more artificial (see XXIV.9). Here we see the state of the literary language hinted at. It is all too easy to come up with false generalisations about early Latin by fixating on one high-style and much studied writer, such as Ennius: see XXIV.5.3 for the similarities between Plautus and Ennius.

The near absence of asyndeton bimembre in Caesar's *Bellum ciuile* may represent a change. The genre is that of a military report, and asyndeta did have a place in military reports and language (see Adams 2005: 76 for instances from the *Bellum Africum*, Plautus and a letter of Vatinius at Cic. *Fam.* 5.10b). Examples from the *Bellum Africum* are collected by Wölfflin and Miodoński (1889: 258), though there tend to be textual variants, and a modern critical edition of the work is needed. A letter of Caelius quoted in the chapter on Cicero (numbered 205) has the pair *occisi capti* in what is in effect a military report. Asyndetic military pairs turn up often in earlier chapters: see e.g. Sallust 31, 32 on pairs extracted from the triad *arma uiri equi*, and on Livy 7 and 47 with cross references. If the textual tradition of the *Bellum ciuile* is to be regarded as fairly reliable (and there is now a good critical edition), Caesar must have made a decision to exclude asyndeton bimembre except in a special context (a direct speech) and in certain structures. Is it possible that there was developing a feeling during the late Republic that an over-mechanical use of this form of coordination was inappropriate? In Virgil, for example, asyndeton bimembre is infrequent, and it is even more so in Ovid's *Metamorphoses*. I have not dealt with Ovid in this work, but have read four books of the *Met.* and found virtually nothing of relevance. Note however:

Met. 3.407 *fons erat inlimis, nitidis argenteus undis* (one member of extended length).
3.433 *quod amas, auertere perdes*
4.261 *sedit humo nuda, nudis incompta capillis* (of interest here is the privative adjective in the longer member).
4.73 *ter quater exegit repetita per ilia ferrum* (for the type see XXIX.2.2 on Hor. *Ep.* 1.1.58).

There is also an apparent decline in the incidence of asyndeton bimembre during the Republic in another genre, agricultural writing. (I have to stress here that any figures given in the rest of this chapter from authors not dealt with systematically in earlier chapters are provisional, in that manuscript evidence has not been considered.) I have collected the evidence from Cato *Agr.* at Adams (2016: 78–80) (asyndeton) and (2016: 76–7) (coordination), and from Varro *Rust.* at (2016: 81–3). Cato has eighteen nouns in asyndetic pairs, nineteen adjectives and eight verbs, a quite substantial total of 45 instances. The figures are also given for nouns coordinated by *et* (about 85 examples) and by *-que* (25 examples). *Et* is the normal coordinator in pairs of nouns, but asyndeton is almost as frequent as *-que*. By contrast Varro has just one pair of nouns in asyndeton (Adams 2016: 81), 3.9.14 *e capite e collo*, the anaphoric type. Nouns are paired by coordinators (for examples see Adams 82). Just one possible pair of asyndetic verbs is cited (Adams 83), but doubts are raised about its status as an asyndeton. There are about nine instances of adjectives in asyndeton (Adams 82–3), most of them postponed in some sense. The total of about ten asyndetic pairs in the whole work (of about 150 pages) is a good deal lower than that for Cato. As was noted earlier (see above, 2), Varro does use asyndetic tricola freely. There is further evidence here that asyndetic adjectives, particularly if postponed, had something of an everyday character (see e.g. V.2 and above, 2 on Petronius).

Cato incidentally also made some use of asyndeton bimembre in his historical work (see XXXI.2.4). On asyndeton in his speeches see Norden (1897: 33).

However, despite the apparent insignificance of asyndeton bimembre in Varro's agricultural work, it would be a mistake to generalise by asserting that asyndeton bimembre was in decline in technical writing. The medical writer Scribonius Largus (c. AD 1–50), though for the most part coordinating pairs and using asyndeton in sequences of three or more members (e.g. 22 *deinde adicitur sarcocolla glaucium opium tragacanthum*), does admit asyndeton bimembre. I have noted 24 examples in 100 pages of text, an incidence of one every four pages, which is quite high. Almost all of these fall into one of three distinct groups, pairs of nouns, not infrequently in the genitive, pairs of passive verbs, and pairs of passive participles (see below, where the examples are arranged accordingly). Coordination is more common in such contexts, and indeed linking some of the same word forms as in the asyndetic pairs, but clearly Scribonius was keen to introduce some variation into what was a repetitive presentation. Personal choice comes into play again, and it is that which determines the asyndeta, not the state of the language. There are also some accumulations in evidence. The passive verbs incidentally are that stylised use of the passive

4 Asyndeton and Latin Literature   697

expressing directives, and they are equivalent to imperatives. Here are the asyndeta:

22 *abstinentia dico, sanguinis detractione*
95 *ad stomach inflationem grauedinem*
96 *purgat etiam interaneas* <u>*uomicas suppurationes*</u>
140 <u>*alium*</u> *quam plurimum edat* <u>*et betaceos, caseum mollem*</u>
173 *ad coli inflationem,* <u>*iocineris pectoris*</u> *dolorem, tussientes, aduersus mala medicamenta omnia* (the asyndetic genitives are embedded in an accumulation; two other coordinated *ad*-expressions precede the first here).
183 *uentris infert* <u>*grauitatem inflammationem*</u>*, postea dolorem cum urinae difficili exitu* (*postea* seems to separate the first two objects from the third).
206 *adiuuat* <u>*coeliacos torminosos*</u> *uentri toto circumdatum, item uesicae tumenti prodest* (the list is not complete, and continues).
206 *punctus* <u>*neruorum musculorum*</u> *. . . sanat* (again, genitives).
208 *facit . . . proprie autem ad* <u>*neruorum musculorum*</u> *punctus,* <u>*contusiones luxa*</u>*, et in totum tumorem non patitur fieri* (an accumulation, with first two genitives again, and then a second asyndetic pair, with which compare the next example).
209 *ad punctus neruorum et ad musculorum, item* <u>*ad contusum luxum*</u>*, praecipue ad ossa fracta* (an accumulation, with the asyndetic pair preceded by a coordinated pair).
260 *ad praecordiorum tensionem,* <u>*uentris stomachi*</u> *duritiem cum dolore*
265 *praeterea ad* <u>*iocineris praecordiorum*</u> *duritiem uel dolorem bene facit* (in this and the previous passage there are two further pairs of asyndetic genitives).

32 *aqua pluuiali commiscentur teruntur*
71 *haec omnia in unum tunduntur cribrantur*
87 *contunditur crocum, percribratur* (discontinuous).
92 *folia rosae* <u>*contunduntur cribrantur*</u>*, myrrha teritur, opium aqua maceratur* (accumulation).
255 *arida quae sunt* <u>*contunduntur cribrantur*</u> (cf. 88, 106 *contunduntur et cribrantur*).

60 *cortex sole arefacta, et contusa cribrata* (cf. 61, 128 *contusa et cribrata*).
119 *haec omnia* <u>*contusa cribrata*</u> *. . . miscentur*
131 *pridie maceratum, deinde* <u>*tritum contusum*</u> *ceteris miscetur*
232 *bene facit et cinis ex sarmentis* <u>*cribrata aspersa*</u> (an accumulation: see on the next example).
232 *alumen* <u>*fissum tritum*</u> *bene et eodem modo* <u>*aspersum*</u> *atque intestino repositum* (this follows on directly from the last passage; the asyndetic participles (if they are genuinely asyndetic) are separated by *et eodem modo* from a coordinated pair of participles).

140 *ad taenias* <u>*necandas eiciendas*</u>.

There are also phrasal and clausal asyndetic pairs, which I have not collected systematically: e.g. 67 *Syriacum, aqua dilutum, crassius per pinnam faucibus adhibitum*, 153 *urinam detrahit, lapidem extenuate*.

The part played by individual taste is also shown by a comparison of Scribonius' practice with that of another technical writer of the period, Vitruvius (Augustan). In books 1–2 of the *De architectura* (about 60 pages of text) I have found only the following asyndeta bimembria:

1.1.10 *ad ambitum stillicidiorum et cloacarum luminum* (if a comma is to be placed after *cloacarum* with editors, there is an asyndeton comprising first a coordinated pair and then a single word).
1.5.4 *quae erunt dextra sinistra* (this pair has a coordinator 44 times in the work, but cf. 5.6.3 *qui erunt dextra sinistra*; it is unclear why Vitruvius might have found asyndeton appropriate in this construction).
1.6.13 *signandum dextra sinistra* (cf. 9.7.4, identical phrase).
2.6.5 *trans Apenninum uero . . . item Achaia Asia, omnino trans mare* (cf. Cicero 166, 167 for pairs of place names in a list).
2.9.4 *efficiunt inanes eas, uitiosas* (discontinuous adjectives, at the end of a sentence, an established type).

In addition, in references to points on a diagram indicated by letters of the alphabet Vitruvius switches between coordination and asyndeton in stating the pairs of letters: 1.6.13 *in quibus litterae LM* (elsewhere in the same passage e.g. *litterae N et O*); also *ubi erunt litterae GH*. 'Asyndeton' of this type might be better referred to as abbreviation.

In the classical poetry considered in this book asyndeton bimembre is not frequent. On Marx's numbering of the fragments of Lucilius there are about 1,375 lines, and from these I have collected about 33 instances of asyndeton bimembre (XXV.1), one every 41 lines. There is a decline after Lucilius. It has already been remarked that such asyndeton is infrequent in Virgil, and even more so in Ovid's *Metamorphoses*. Lucretius' poem has 7,416 lines, and from these I have numbered (XXIV.7.1) just 30 pairs (not all of them certain), or one every 247 lines. In the whole corpus of Catullus only eleven instances of asyndeta bimembria in the strictest sense were found (see XXVII.1.6). The two books of Horace's *Satires* have 2,113 lines, and in these only 22 examples were noted (XXIX.2.1.5), or one about every 96 lines. Asyndeton bimembre was a styleme not much exploited in classical poetry. In Horace's *Odes*, as we saw, it is almost entirely avoided (XXIX.3.3.1). It was shown that Horace's methods of coordination in the *Odes* were not unlike those in a sample of Pindar (XXIX.4.5). In the late Republic and early Empire asyndeton bimembre belonged particularly to certain types of high-style prose, oratorical and political, and historiographical (a genre with a political content, in which also orations were included), and also to a few technical genres (legal, philosophical) in which oppositions were frequently expressed. Caesar seems to have had little use for asyndeton bimembre in the spare style of the *Bellum ciuile*, except in special contexts.

I conclude that, despite apparent fading of asyndeton bimembre in this or that genre, it was a form of coordination that continued to be available and was exploited by some. It had a prominent place in legal language and a rhetorical potential in public discourse in the late Republic. Personal taste emerges as a major factor in its use or avoidance. It was open to individual writers to use it to suit their purposes, as is clear from the distinctive if restricted ways in which it was employed by Scribonius, one of whose patterns (pairs of passive verbs conveying instructions) is a stylised replacement for pairs of asyndetic imperatives. Whereas one writer may all but avoid asyndeton bimembre, another will use it extensively even in a genre in which it had not been particularly common. Pliny the Younger for example is said to have made frequent use of it in letters (see Norden 1897: 34), though, if that is so, it is for some reason all but non-existent in the correspondence between Pliny and Trajan in *Ep.* 10. I have noted just one instance with prepositional anaphora (and an extended second member), and one adjectival adversative instance, also with an extended second member: 10.22.2 *solent et ad balineum, ad purgationes cloacarum, item munitiones uiarum et uicorum dari*, 10.70.1 *domus, ut audio, pulchra, nunc deformis ruinis*. Potentially interesting questions are whether Pliny departed from his usual practice when writing to the emperor, and if so why, but these could not be answered without a substantial review of the correspondence.

Asyndeton bimembre is not absent from late Latin (see e.g. Norden 1897: 34 with n. 3 on Arnobius). I have not dealt specifically with late Latin in this book, but for a detailed account of asyndeton in one late text, the *Historia Augusta*, see Tidner (1922), Chap. II.

Bibliography

ADAMS, J. N. (1970), *A Philological Commentary on Tacitus, Annals 14, 1–54* (Thesis submitted for the Degree of Doctor of Philosophy, Oxford July 1970).
ADAMS, J. N. (1995a), 'The language of the Vindolanda writing tablets: an interim report', *JRS* 85, 86–134.
ADAMS, J. N. (1995b), *Pelagonius and Latin Veterinary Terminology in the Roman Empire* (Leiden).
ADAMS, J. N. (2003), *Bilingualism and the Latin Language* (Cambridge).
ADAMS, J. N. (2005), 'The *Bellum Africum*', in Reinhardt, Lapidge and Adams (2005), 73–96.
ADAMS, J. N. (2013), *Social Variation and the Latin Language* (Cambridge).
ADAMS, J. N. (2016), *An Anthology of Informal Latin 200 BC – AD 900: Fifty Texts with Translations and Linguistic Commentary* (Cambridge).
ADAMS, J. N., CHAHOUD, A. and PEZZINI, G. eds (forthcoming), *Early Latin: Constructs, Diversity, Reception* (Cambridge).
ADAMS, J. N. and MAYER, R. G. eds (1999), *Aspects of the Language of Latin Poetry* (Oxford).
ADAMS, J. N. and NIKITINA, V. (forthcoming), 'Early Latin prayers and aspects of coordination', in Adams, Chahoud and Pezzini (forthcoming).
ALLAN, W. (2008), *Euripides: Helen* (Cambridge).
ANDERSON, W. B. (1928), *Livy Book IX*, 3rd edn (Cambridge).
ANDRÉ, J. (1949), *Étude sur les termes de couleur dans la langue latine* (Paris).
ARNOTT, W. G. (1996), *Alexis, the Fragments: A Commentary* (Cambridge).
ARNOTT, W. G. (1996–2000), *Menander*, 3 vols (Cambridge, Mass. and London).
ASH, R. (2007), *Tacitus Histories Book II* (Cambridge).
ASH, R. (2018), *Tacitus Annals Book XV* (Cambridge).
AUDOLLENT, A. (1904), *Defixionum tabellae* (Paris).
AUSTIN, R. G. (1955), *P. Vergili Maronis Aeneidos Liber quartus* (Oxford).
AUSTIN, R. G. (1964), *P. Vergili Maronis Aeneidos Liber secundus* (Oxford).
AUSTIN, R. G. (1971), *P. Vergili Maronis Aeneidos Liber primus* (Oxford).
AUSTIN, R. G. (1977), *P. Vergili Maronis Aeneidos Liber sextus* (Oxford).
AXELSON, B. (1987), *Kleine Schriften zur lateinischen Philologie*, ed. A. Önnerfors and C. Schaar (Lund).
BADER, F. (1962), *La formation des composés nominaux du latin* (Paris).

Bibliography 701

BAILEY, C. (1947), *Titi Lucreti Cari De rerum natura libri sex*, 3 vols (Oxford).
BALDI, P. and CUZZOLIN, P. eds (2009), *New Perspectives on Historical Latin Syntax* 1: *Syntax of the Sentence* (Berlin and New York).
BALDI, P. and CUZZOLIN, P. eds (2010), *New Perspectives on Historical Latin Syntax* 2: *Constituent Syntax: Adverbial Phrase, Adverbs, Mood, Tense* (Berlin and New York).
BANNON, C. J. (2013), 'Pipes and property in the sale of real estate (*D* 19.1.38.2)', in P. J. du Plessis ed., *Law and Society in the Roman World* (Edinburgh), 207–23.
BARRETT, W. S. (1964), *Euripides: Hippolytos* (Oxford).
BARSBY, J. (1999), *Terence: Eunuchus* (Cambridge).
BARSBY, J. (2001), *Terence*, 2 vols (Cambridge, Mass. and London).
BATE, J. and RASMUSSEN, E. (2007), *The RSC Shakespeare: William Shakespeare, Complete Works* (Basingstoke).
BATTEZZATO, L. (2018), *Euripides: Hecuba* (Cambridge).
BATTEZZATO, L. and RODDA, M. A. (2018), 'Particelle e asindeto nel Greco classico', *Glotta* 94, 3–37.
BAUER, B. L. M. (2017), *Nominal Apposition in Indo-European: Its Forms and Functions, and its Evolution in Latin-Romance* (Berlin and Boston).
BAUER, L. (2009), 'Typology of compounds', in Lieber and Stekauer (2009), 343–56.
BAUER, W., ARNDT, W. F. and GINGRICH, F. W. (1952), *A Greek–English Lexicon of the New Testament and Other Early Christian Literature*, 4th edn (Chicago).
BAYET, J. (1954), *Tite-Live, Histoire romaine*, tome v, livre v, with translation by G. Baillet (Paris).
BENNETT, C. E. (1910–14), *Syntax of Early Latin*, 2 vols (Boston).
BERRY, D. (1996), *Cicero: Pro P. Sulla oratio* (Cambridge).
BIDDAU, F. (2008), *Q. Terentii Scauri De orthographia* (Hildesheim).
BLÄNSDORF, J. (2010), 'The defixiones from the sanctuary of Isis and Mater Magna in Mainz', in Gordon and Simón (2010), 141–89.
BLOOMFIELD, L. (1935), *Language*, 2nd edn (London).
BOCCOTTI, G. (1975), 'L'asindeto e il τρίκωλον nella retorica classica', *Bollettino dell'Istituto di filologia greca, Università di Padova* 2, 34–59.
BOWIE, A. (2019), *Homer: Iliad Book III* (Cambridge).
BRASWELL, B. K. (1988), *A Commentary on the Fourth Pythian Ode of Pindar* (Berlin and New York).
BREED, B. W., KEITEL, E. and WALLACE, R. eds (2018), *Lucilius and Satire in Second-Century BC Rome* (Cambridge).
BRIGGS, W. W. (1983), *Concordantia in Catonis Librum de agri cultura* (Hildesheim, Zurich and New York).
BRINK, C. O. (1971), *Horace on Poetry* (Cambridge).
BRISCOE, J. (1973), *A Commentary on Livy Books XXXI–XXXIII* (Oxford).
BRISCOE, J. (1981), *A Commentary on Livy Books XXXIV–XXXVII* (Oxford).
BRISCOE, J. (1986), *Titi Liui Ab urbe condita libri XLI–XLV* (Stuttgart).
BRISCOE, J. (2008), *A Commentary on Livy Books 38–40* (Oxford).

BRISCOE, J. (2012), *A Commentary on Livy Books 41–45* (Oxford).
BRISCOE, J. (2016), *Titi Liui Ab urbe condita* (Oxford).
BRISCOE, J. and HORNBLOWER, S. eds (2020), *Livy Ab urbe condita Book XXII* (Cambridge).
BRIX, J. and NIEMEYER, M. (1907), *Ausgewählte Komödien des T. Maccius Plautus* I: *Trinummus*, 5th edn (Leipzig and Berlin).
BROTHERS, A. J. (2000), *Terence: The Eunuch* (Warminster).
BROWN, R. D. (1987), *Lucretius on Love and Sex: A Commentary on De rerum natura IV, 1030–1287 with Prolegomena, Text, and Translation* (Leiden, New York, Copenhagen and Cologne).
BUCK, C. D. (1904), *A Grammar of Oscan and Umbrian* (Boston).
BUCK, C. D. (1933), *Comparative Grammar of Greek and Latin* (Chicago).
BUCKLAND, W. W. (1921) *A Text-Book of Roman Law from Augustus to Justinian* (Cambridge).
BUTLER, H. E. and CARY, M. (1924), *M. Tulli Ciceronis De provinciis consularibus oratio ad senatum* (Oxford).
CALBOLI, G. (1993), *Rhetorica ad C. Herennium* (Bologna).
CALBOLI, G. (1997a), 'Asindeto e polisindeto', *Enciclopedia Oraziana* (Rome), 2.799–803.
CALBOLI, G. (1997b), 'Ossimoro', *Enciclopedia Oraziana* (Rome), 2.933–5.
CARDINALETTI, A. and GIUSTI, G. (2001), '"Semi-lexical" motion verbs in Romance and Germanic', in N. Corver and H. Van Riemsdijk eds, *Semi-Lexical Categories: On the Function of Content Words and the Content of Function Words* (Berlin), 371–414.
CHAHOUD, A. (1998), *C. Lucilii reliquiarum concordantiae* (Hildesheim, Zurich and New York).
CHAHOUD, A. (2018), 'Verbal mosaics: speech patterns and generic stylization in Lucilius', in Breed, Keitel and Wallace (2018), 132–161.
CHANTRAINE, P. (1953), 'Un tour archaïque chez Pindare (*Ol*. VI, 78; *Pyth*. IV, 217)', *RPh* 27, 16–20.
CHAPOT, F. and LAUROT, B. (2001), *Corpus de prières grecques et romaines* (Turnhout).
CHRISTENSEN, H. (1908), 'Que – que bei den römischen Hexametrikern (bis etwa 500 n. Chr.)', *ALL* 15, 165–221.
CHRISTENSON, D. M. (2000), *Plautus: Amphitruo* (Cambridge).
COLEMAN, R. G. G. (1999), 'Poetic diction, poetic discourse and the poetic register', in Adams and Mayer (1999), 21–93.
COLLARD, C. (1975), *Euripides: Supplices* 2 (Groningen).
COLLINGE, N. E. (1985), *The Laws of Indo-European* (Amsterdam and Philadelphia).
COLSON, F. H. (1942), *Cicero: Pro Milone* (London).
CORNELL, T. J. (1995), *The Beginnings of Rome: Italy and Rome from the Bronze Age to the Punic Wars c. 1000–264 BC* (London and New York).
COULON, V. and VAN DAELE, H. (1977), *Aristophane* III: *Les oiseaux, Lysistrata* (Paris).

COURTNEY, E. (1991), *The Poems of Petronius* (Atlanta, Ga).
COURTNEY, E. (1993), *The Fragmentary Latin Poets* (Oxford).
COURTNEY, E. (1999), *Archaic Latin Prose* (Atlanta, Ga).
CRAWFORD, M. H. ed. (1996), *Roman Statutes*, 2 vols (Bulletin of the Institute of Classical Studies Supplement 64) (London).
CRUSCHINA, S. (2018), 'The "go for" construction in Sicilian', in R. D'Alessandro and D. Pescarini eds, *Advances in Italian Dialectology: Sketches of Italo-Romance Grammars* (Leiden), 292–320.
CRUSE, D. A. (1986), *Lexical Semantics* (Cambridge).
CURBERA, J. B., SIERRA DELAGE, M. and VELÁZQUEZ, I. (1999), 'A bilingual curse tablet from Barchín del Hoyo (Cuenca, Spain)', *ZPE* 125, 279–83.
DALBY, A. (1998), *Cato on Farming: De agricultura* (Exeter).
DAMON, C. ed. (2015a), *C. Iuli Caesaris Commentariorum Libri III De bello ciuili* (Oxford).
DAMON, C. (2015b), *Studies on the Text of Caesar's Bellum civile* (Oxford).
DANIEL, R. W. and MALTOMINI, F. eds (1990–2), *Supplementum magicum*, 2 vols (Opladen).
DAUBE, D. (1956), *Forms of Roman Legislation* (Oxford).
DE MELO, W. (2019), *Varro: De lingua Latina*, 2 vols (Oxford).
DE MEO, C. (1983), *Lingue tecniche del latino* (Bologna).
DE VAAN, M. (2008), *Etymological Dictionary of Latin and the Other Italic Languages* (Leiden and Boston).
DE ZULUETA, F. (1945), *The Roman Law of Sale* (Oxford).
DE ZULUETA, F. (1946), *The Institutes of Gaius* 1 (Oxford).
DELAMARRE, X. (2003), *Dictionnaire de le langue gauloise*, 2nd edn (Paris).
DELBRÜCK, B. (1900), *Vergleichende Syntax der indogermanischen Sprachen* 3 (Strassburg) (= K. Brugmann and B. Delbrück, *Grundriss der vergleichenden Grammatik der indogermanischen Sprachen* 5).
DENNISTON, J. D. (1934), *The Greek Particles* (Oxford).
DENNISTON, J. D. (1952), *Greek Prose Style* (Oxford).
DEUFERT, M. (2017), *Prolegomena zur Editio Teubneriana des Lukrez* (Berlin and Boston).
DEUFERT, M. (2018), *Kritischer Kommentar zu Lukrezens De rerum natura* (Berlin and Boston).
DEUFERT, M. (2019), *Titus Lucretius Carus De rerum natura libri VI* (Berlin and Boston).
DEVINE, A. M. and STEPHENS, L. D. (2006), *Latin Word Order: Structured Meaning and Information* (New York).
DI NAPOLI, M. (2011), *Velii Longi De orthographia* (Hildesheim).
DICKEY, E. (2012), *The Colloquia of the Hermeneumata Pseudodositheana* 1: *Colloquia Monacensia-Einsidlensia, Leidense-Stephani, and Stephani* (Cambridge).
DICKEY, E. (2015), *The Colloquia of the Hermeneumata Pseudodositheana* 2: *Colloquium Harleianum, Colloquium Montepessulanum, Colloquium Celtis, and Fragments*(Cambridge).

DIEHL, E. (1911), *Poetarum Romanorum veterum reliquiae* (Bonn).
DIGGLE, J. (1994), *Euripidea: Collected Essays* (Oxford).
DIGGLE, J. (2004), *Theophrastus: Characters* (Cambridge).
DIK, S. C. (1968), *Coordination: its Implications for the Theory of General Linguistics* (Amsterdam).
DOUGAN, T. W. (1905), *M. Tulli Ciceronis Tusculanarum disputationum libri quinque* 1: *Books I and II* (Cambridge).
DOUGAN, T. W. and HENRY, R. M. (1934), *M. Tulli Ciceronis Tusculanarum disputationum libri quinque* 2: *Books III–V* (Cambridge).
DOVER, K. J. (1968), *Aristophanes: Clouds* (Oxford).
DOVER, K. J. (1993), *Aristophanes: Frogs* (Oxford).
DUNKEL, G. (1982), 'The original syntax of *-k^{w}e*', *Die Sprache* 28, 129–43.
DURANTE, M. (1976), *Sulla preistoria della tradizione poetica greca* 2: *Risultanze della comparazione indoeuropea* (Rome).
DYCK, A. R. (2004), *A Commentary on Cicero, De legibus* (Ann Arbor).
DYCK, A. R. (2008), *Cicero: Catilinarians* (Cambridge).
DYCK, A. R. (2010), *Cicero: Pro Sexto Roscio* (Cambridge).
EISENHUT, W. (1983), *Catulli Veronensis liber* (Leipzig).
ELLIS, R. (1889), *A Commentary on Catullus*, 2nd edn (Oxford).
ENK, P. J. (1932), *Plauti Mercator, cum prolegomenis, notis criticis, commentario exegetico*, 2 vols (Leiden).
ERNOUT, A. (1935), *Plaute Bacchides: commentaire exégétique et critique* (Paris).
ERNOUT, A. (1946), *Philologica* (Paris) (the first of what were to be three volumes).
FEDELI, P. (1980), *Sesto Properzio: il primo libro delle Elegie* (Florence).
FEHLING, D. (1969), *Die Wiederholungsfiguren und ihr Gebrauch bei den Griechen vor Gorgias* (Berlin).
FERRERO, M. G. (1976), 'L'asindeto in Menandro', *Dioniso* 47, 82–106.
FINGLASS, P. J. (2007), *Sophocles: Electra* (Cambridge).
FINGLASS, P. J. (2011), *Sophocles: Ajax* (Cambridge).
FORDYCE, C. J. (1961), *Catullus: A Commentary* (Oxford).
FRAENKEL, E. (1950), *Aeschylus: Agamemnon*, 3 vols (Oxford).
FRAENKEL, E. (1960), *Elementi Plautini in Plauto* (Florence).
FRAENKEL, E. (2007), *Plautine Elements in Plautus (Plautinisches im Plautus)*, translated by T. Drevikovsky and F. Muecke (Oxford).
GERBER, A., GREEF, A. and JOHN, C. (1891–1903), *Lexicon Taciteum*, 2 vols (Leipzig).
GOLDBERG, S. M. and MANUWALD, G. (2018), *Fragmentary Republican Latin: Ennius*, 2 vols (Cambridge, Mass. and London).
GOMME, A. W. and SANDBACH, F. H. (1973), *Menander, a Commentary* (Oxford).
GONDA, J. (1959), *Stylistic Repetition in the Veda* (Amsterdam).
GOODY, J. (1977), *The Domestication of the Savage Mind* (Cambridge).
GOODYEAR, F. R. D. (1972), *The Annals of Tacitus* 1: *Annals 1.1–54* (Cambridge).

GOODYEAR, F. R. D. (1981), *The Annals of Tacitus 2: Annals 1.55–81 and Annals 2* (Cambridge).
GORDON, R. L. and SIMÓN, F. M. eds (2010), *Magical Practice in the Latin West: Papers from the International Conference held at the University of Zaragoza 30 Sept.–1 Oct. 2005* (Leiden and Boston).
GRATWICK, A. S. (1993), *Plautus: Menaechmi* (Cambridge).
GRAY, C. (2015), *Jerome, Vita Malchi: Introduction, Text, Translation, and Commentary* (Oxford).
GREEN, J. (2010), *Green's Dictionary of Slang*, 3 vols (London).
GRIFFIN, J. (1995), *Homer: Iliad Book Nine* (Oxford).
GRIFFITH, M. (1983), *Aeschylus: Prometheus Bound* (Cambridge).
GRIFFITHS, E. (2018), *If not Critical*, ed. F. Johnston (Oxford).
GRILLO, L. (2015), *Cicero's De provinciis consularibus oratio* (New York).
HALLA-AHO, H. (2009), *The Non-Literary Latin Letters: A Study of their Syntax and Pragmatics* (Helsinki).
HALM, C. (1863), *Rhetores Latini minores* (Leipzig).
HARRISON, S. J. (1991), *Vergil: Aeneid 10* (Oxford).
HASPELMATH, M. ed. (2004a), *Coordinating Constructions* (Amsterdam and Philadelphia).
HASPELMATH, M. (2004b), 'Coordinating constructions: an overview', in Haspelmath (2004a), 3–39.
HEUBNER, H. (1963), *P. Cornelius Tacitus, Die Historien 1: Erstes Buch* (Heidelberg).
HEYCOCK, C. and PETERSEN, H. P. (2012), 'Pseudo-coordinations in Faroese', in K. Braunmüller and C. Gabriel eds, *Multilingual Individuals and Multilingual Societies* (Hamburg Studies on Multilingualism 13) (Amsterdam), 259–80.
HICKSON, F. V. (1993), *Roman Prayer Language: Livy and the Aneid* [sic] *of Vergil* (Stuttgart).
HOFMANN, J. B. (1951), *Lateinische Umgangssprache*, 3rd edn (Heidelberg).
HOFMANN, J. B. and RICOTTILLI, L. (2003), *La lingua d'uso latina*, 3rd edn (translation with supplements of Hofmann 1951 by L. R.) (Bologna).
HOFMANN, J. B. and SZANTYR, A. (1965), *Lateinische Syntax und Stilistik* (Munich).
HORNBLOWER, S. (2008), *A Commentary on Thucydides 3: Books 5.25–8.109* (Oxford).
HORNBLOWER, S. (2015), *Lykophron: Alexandra* (Oxford).
HORSFALL, N. (2000), *Virgil, Aeneid 7: A Commentary* (Leiden, Boston and Cologne).
HORSFALL, N. (2006), *Virgil, Aeneid 3: A Commentary* (Leiden and Boston).
HORSFALL, N. (2008), *Virgil, Aeneid 2: A Commentary* (Leiden and Boston).
HORSFALL, N. (2013), *Virgil, Aeneid 6: A Commentary*, 2 vols (Berlin and Boston).
HUDDLESTON, R. (2002), 'Syntactic overview', in Huddleston and Pullum (2002), 43–69.

HUDDLESTON, R., PAYNE, J. and PETERSON, P. (2002), 'Coordination and supplementation', in Huddleston and Pullum (2002), 1273–1362.
HUDDLESTON, R. and PULLUM, G. K. eds (2002), *The Cambridge Grammar of the English Language* (Cambridge).
HUITINK, L. and ROOD, T. (2019), *Xenophon: Anabasis Book III* (Cambridge).
INSLER, S. (1998), '*mitrā́váruṇā* or *mitrā́ váruṇā?*' in J. Jasanoff, H. C. Melchert, L. Olivier eds, *Mír Curad: Studies in Honor of Calvert Watkins* (Innsbruck), 285–90.
JAMISON, S. W. and BRERETON, J. P. (2014), *The Rigveda: The Earliest Religious Poetry of India*, 3 vols (Oxford and New York).
JESPERSEN, O. (1924), *The Philosophy of Grammar* (London).
JOCELYN, H. D. (1967), *The Tragedies of Ennius* (Cambridge).
JOHANSEN, H. F. and WHITTLE, E. W. (1980), *Aeschylus: The Suppliants*, 3 vols (Hofbogtrykkeri).
KALB, W. (1888), *Das Juristenlatein: Versuch einer Charakteristik auf Grundlage der Digesten*, 2nd edn (Nuremberg).
KALB, W. (1912), *Wegweiser in die römische Rechtssprache, mit Übersetzungsbeispielen aus dem Gebiete des römischen Rechts* (Leipzig).
KASTER, R. A. (1977), 'A note on Catullus, c. 71.4', *Philologus* 121, 308–12.
KASTER, R. A. (2006), *Marcus Tullius Cicero: Speech on Behalf of Publius Sestius* (Oxford).
KASTER, R. A. (2011), *Macrobius, Saturnalia: Books 3–5* (Cambridge, Mass. and London).
KASTOVSKY, D. (2009), 'Diachronic Perspectives', in Lieber and Stekauer (2009), 323–40.
KAUER, R. and LINDSAY, W. M. (1926), *P. Terenti Afri comoediae* (Oxford).
KAY, N. M. (2020), *Venantius Fortunatus: Vita Sancti Martini: Prologue and Books I–II* (Cambridge).
KIPARSKY, P. (2010), 'Dvandvas, blocking, and the associative: the bumpy ride from phrase to word', *Language* 88, 302–31.
KLEINKNECHT, H. (1937), *Die Gebetsparodie in der Antike* (Stuttgart and Berlin).
KOESTERMANN, E. (1963), *Cornelius Tacitus, Annalen* I: *Buch 1–3* (Heidelberg).
KOESTERMANN, E. (1965), *Cornelii Taciti Libri qui supersunt* I: *Ab excessu divi Augusti* (Leipzig).
KOESTERMANN, E. (1967), *Cornelius Tacitus, Annalen* III: *Buch 11–13* (Heidelberg).
KOESTERMANN, E. (1968), *Cornelius Tacitus, Annalen* IV: *Buch 14–16* (Heidelberg).
KÖHM, J. (1905), *Altlateinische Forschungen* (Leipzig).
KRENKEL, W. (1970), *Lucilius: Satiren*, 2 vols (Leiden).
KROLL, W. (1924), *Studien zum Verständnis der römischen Literatur* (Stuttgart).
KROLL, W. (1929), *C. Valerius Catullus*, 2nd edn, 1st edn 1922, reprinted with addenda 1968.
KROPP, A. (2008a), *Defixiones: Ein aktuelles Corpus lateinischer Fluchtafeln* (Speyer).

KROPP, A. (2008b), *Magische Sprachverwendung in vulgärlateinischen Fluchtafeln (defixiones)* (Tübingen).
KRUSCHWITZ, P. (2002), *Carmina saturnia epigraphica: Einleitung, Text und Kommentar zu den saturnischen Versinschriften* (Stuttgart).
KÜHNER, R. and GERTH B. (1898–1904), *Ausführliche Grammatik der griechischen Sprache*, 2 vols (Hanover and Leipzig).
KÜHNER, R. and STEGMANN, C. (1955), *Ausführliche Grammatik der lateinischen Sprache: Satzlehre*, 3rd edn revised by A. Thierfelder, 2 vols (Leverkusen).
LANDGRAF, G. (1892), '*Egens = exgens*', *ALL* 7, 275–7.
LANDGRAF, G. (1914), *Kommentar zu Ciceros Rede Pro Sex. Roscio Amerino*, 2nd edn (Leipzig and Berlin).
LANGSLOW, D. (2009), *Jacob Wackernagel, Lectures on Syntax, with Special Reference to Greek, Latin, and Germanic* (Oxford).
LAUSBERG, H. (1960), *Handbuch der literarischen Rhetorik: Eine Grundlegung der Literaturwissenschaft* (Munich).
LAUSBERG, H. (1998), *Handbook of Literary Rhetoric: A Foundation for Literary Study*, translated by M. T. Bliss, A. Jansen and D. E. Horton, edited by D. E. Horton and R. D. Anderson (Leiden, Boston and Cologne).
LEDGEWAY, A. (1997), 'Asyndetic complementation in Neapolitan dialect', *The Italianist* 17, 231–73.
LEDGEWAY, A. (2009), *Grammatica diacronica del napoletano* (Tübingen).
LEDGEWAY, A. (2016), 'From coordination to subordination: the grammaticalization of progressive and andative aspect in the dialects of Salento', in A. Cardoso, A. M. Martins, S. Pereira, C. Pinto and F. Pratas eds, *Coordination and Subordination, Form and Meaning: Selected Papers from CSI Lisbon 2014* (Newcastle), 157–84.
LEE, G. (1991), *The Poems of Catullus* (Oxford and New York).
LENAGHAN, J. O. (1969), *A Commentary on Cicero's Oration De haruspicum responso* (The Hague and Paris).
LEO, F. (1898), 'Sub divo columine', *ALL* 10, 273–8.
LEO, F. (1912), *Plautinische Forschungen*, 2nd edn (Berlin).
LEO, F. (1960), *Ausgewählte kleine Schriften* I: *Zur römischen Literatur des Zeitalters der Republik*, ed. E. Fraenkel (Rome).
LEUMANN, M. (1977), *Lateinische Laut- und Formenlehre*, 6th edn (Munich).
LIEBER, R. and STEKAUER, P. eds (2009), *The Oxford Handbook of Compounding* (Oxford).
LINDERSKI, J. (1986), 'The augural law', *ANRW* 2.16.3, 2146–2312 (Berlin and New York).
LINDHOLM, E. (1931), *Stilistische Studien: Zur Erweiterung der Satzglieder im Lateinischen* (Lund).
LINDNER, T. (2002), *Lateinische Komposita: Morphologische, historische und lexikalische Studien* (Innsbruck).
LINDSAY, W. M. (1900), *The Captivi of Plautus* (London).
LINDSAY, W. M. (1907), *Syntax of Plautus* (Oxford).

LODGE, G. (1924–33), *Lexicon Plautinum*, 2 vols (Leipzig).
LÖFSTEDT, E. (1911), *Philologischer Kommentar zur Peregrinatio Aetheriae* (Uppsala).
LÖFSTEDT, E. (1956), *Syntactica: Studien und Beiträge zur historischen Syntax des Lateins* I, 2nd edn, 2 (Lund).
LUISELLI, B. (1969), *Il problema della più antica prosa latina* (Cagliari).
LUNELLI, A. (1980), *La lingua poetica latina: saggi di Wilhelm Kroll, Hendrikus H. Janssen, Manu Leumann* (Bologna).
LYONS, J. (1968), *Introduction to Theoretical Linguistics* (Cambridge).
LYONS, J. (1977), *Semantics* 1 (Cambridge).
MACRAE, D. E. (2018), 'The freedman's story: an accusation of witchcraft in the social world of early imperial Roman Italy (*CIL* 11.4639 = *ILS* 3001)', *JRS* 108, 53–73.
MADVIG, N. (1876), *M. Tullii Ciceronis De finibus bonorum et malorum libri quinque* (Copenhagen).
MAEHLER, H. (2000), 'Beobachtungen zum Gebrauch des Satz-Asyndetons bei Bakchylides und Pindar', in *Poesia e religione in Grecia: Studi in onore di G. Aurelio Privitera* (Naples), 421–30.
MAEHLER, H. (2004), *Bacchylides: A Selection* (Cambridge).
MAGNI, E. (2010), 'Mood and modality', in Baldi and Cuzzolin (2010), 193–275.
MAGUINNESS, W. S. (1965), 'The language of Lucretius', in D. R. Dudley ed., *Lucretius* (London).
MALHERBE, A. J. (1984), '"In season and out of season": 2 Timothy 4:2', *Journal of Biblical Literature* 103, 235–43.
MALLOCH, S. J. V. (2013), *The Annals of Tacitus: Book 11* (Cambridge).
MANUWALD, G. (2007), *Cicero, Philippics 3–9* 2: *Commentary* (Berlin and New York).
MANUWALD, G. (2018), *Cicero: Agrarian Speeches, Introduction, Text, Translation, and Commentary* (Oxford).
MARIOTTI, S. (1951), *Lezioni su Ennio* (Pesaro).
MARIOTTI, S. (1952), *Livio Andronico e la traduzione artistica* (Milan).
MAROUZEAU, J. (1962), *Traité de stylistique latine*, 4th edn (Paris).
MARTIN, R. H. (1976), *Terence: Adelphoe* (Cambridge).
MARX, F. (1904–5), *C. Lucilii Carminum reliquiae*, 2 vols (Leipzig).
MASTRONARDE, D. J. (2002), *Euripides: Medea* (Cambridge).
MATTHEWS, P. H. (2014), *The Positions of Adjectives in English* (Oxford).
MAURACH, G. (1988), *Der Poenulus des Plautus* (Heidelberg).
MAURACH, G. (1995), *Lateinische Dichtersprache* (Darmstadt).
MEYER-LÜBKE, W. (1900), *Grammaire des langues romanes* 3: *Syntaxe* (Traduction française, by A. Doutrepont and G. Doutrepont) (Paris).
MONTANARI, F. (1995), *Vocabolario della lingua greca* (Turin).
MOREL, W. (1927), *Fragmenta poetarum Latinorum epicorum et lyricorum praeter Ennium et Lucilium*, 2nd edn (Stuttgart).

Bibliography 709

MUNRO, H. A. J. (1886), *T. Lucreti Cari De rerum natura libri sex*, 4th edn, 3 vols (London).
MYNORS, R. A. B. (1990), *Virgil: Georgics* (Oxford).
NICHOLAS, B. (1962), *An Introduction to Roman Law* (Oxford).
NIPPERDEY, K. and ANDRESEN, G. (1880), *Cornelius Tacitus 2: Ab excessu divi Augusti XI–XVI*, 4th edn (Berlin).
NISBET, R. G. (1939), *M. Tulli Ciceronis De domo sua ad pontifices oratio* (Oxford).
NISBET, R. G. M. (1961), *M. Tulli Ciceronis In L. Calpurnium Pisonem oratio* (Oxford).
NISBET, R. G. M. (1978), 'Notes on the text of Catullus', *PCPhS* 24, 92–115.
NISBET, R. G. M. and HUBBARD, M. (1978), *A Commentary on Horace: Odes Book II* (Oxford).
NISBET, R. G. M. and RUDD, N. (2004), *A Commentary on Horace: Odes Book III* (Oxford).
NORDEN, E. (1897), *De Minucii Felicis aetate et genere dicendi* (Greifswald).
NORDEN, E. (1939), *Aus altrömischen Priesterbüchern* (Lund and Leipzig).
NORDEN, E. (1957), *P. Vergilius Maro: Aeneis Buch VI*, 4th edn (Darmstadt).
NORDEN, E. (1958), *Die antike Kunstprosa vom VI. Jahrhundert v. Chr. bis in die Zeit der Renaissance*, 5th edn (Stuttgart).
OAKLEY, S. P. (1997), *A Commentary on Livy Books VI–X 1: Introduction and Book VI* (Oxford).
OAKLEY, S. P. (1998), *A Commentary on Livy Books VI–X 2: Books VII and VIII* (Oxford).
OAKLEY, S. P. (2005a), *A Commentary on Livy Books VI–X 3: Book IX* (Oxford).
OAKLEY, S. P. (2005b), *A Commentary on Livy Books VI–X 4: Book X* (Oxford).
OGILVIE, R. M. (1965), *A Commentary on Livy Books 1–5* (Oxford).
OLSON, S. D. (2002), *Aristophanes Acharnians* (Oxford).
ONIGA, R. (1988), *I compositi nominali latini* (Bologna).
OTTO, A. (1890), *Die Sprichwörter und sprichwörtlichen Redensarten der Römer* (Leipzig).
PANAYOTAKIS, C. (2010), *Decimus Laberius: The Fragments* (Cambridge).
PARKER, L. P. E. (2007), *Euripides: Alcestis* (Oxford).
PEASE, A. S. (1955), *M. Tulli Ciceronis De natura deorum libri III: Liber primus* (Cambridge, Mass.).
PEASE, A. S. (1958), *M. Tulli Ciceronis De natura deorum libri III: Libri secundus et tertius* (Cambridge, Mass.).
PEASE, A. S. (1963), *M. Tulli Ciceronis De divinatione libri duo* (Darmstadt) (reprint: originally published in two volumes with different pagination in *University of Illinois Studies in Language and Literature* [6], 1920 and [8], 1923).
PENNEY, J. H. W. (2005), 'Connections in archaic Latin prose', in Reinhardt, Lapidge and Adams (2005), 37–51.
PETERSMANN, H. (1973), *T. Maccius Plautus: Stichus* (Heidelberg).

PINKSTER, H. (1969), 'A B & C coordination in Latin', *Mnem.* ser. 4, 22, 458–67.
PINKSTER, H. (1990), 'La coordination', *L'information grammaticale* 46, 8–13.
PINKSTER, H. (2015), *The Oxford Latin Syntax* 1 (Oxford).
PINKSTER, H. (forthcoming), *The Oxford Latin Syntax* 2.
POCCETTI, P. (2018), 'Another image of literary Latin: language variation and the aims of Lucilius' Satires', in Breed, Keitel and Wallace (2018), 81–131.
POTTER, D. S. and DAMON, C. (1999), 'The *Senatus consultum de Cn. Pisone patre*', *AJP* 120 1 (Special Issue: The *Senatus consultum de Cn. Pisone patre*), 13–41.
POULTNEY, J. W. (1959), *The Bronze Tablets of Iguvium* (Philological Monographs Published by the American Philological Association, 18).
POWELL, J. G. F. (1988), *Cicero: Cato Maior de senectute* (Cambridge).
POWELL, J. G. F. (2005), 'Cicero's adaptation of legal Latin in the *De legibus*', in Reinhardt, Lapidge and Adams (2005), 117–50.
PREMINGER, A. and BROGAN, T. V. F. eds (1993), *The New Princeton Encyclopedia of Poetry and Poetics* (Princeton, N.J.).
PREUSS, S. (1881), *De bimembris dissoluti apud scriptores Romanos usu sollemni* (Edenkoben).
PUTTFARKEN, W. (1914), *Das Asyndeton bei den römischen Dichtern der archaischen und klassischen Zeit* (Kiel).
QUIRK, R., GREENBAUM, S., LEECH, G. and SVARTVIK, J. (1972), *A Grammar of Contemporary English* (London).
QUIRK, R. and WRENN, C. L. (1957), *An Old English Grammar*, 2nd edn (London).
RADERMACHER, L. (1954), *Aristophanes' 'Frösche': Einleitung, Text und Kommentar*, 2nd edn, revised by W. Kraus (Vienna).
RAMSEY, J. T. (2007), *Sallust's Bellum Catilinae*, 2nd edn (Oxford).
RAMSEY, J. T. (2015), *Sallust 2: Fragments of the Histories; Letters to Caesar* (Loeb Classical Library) (Cambridge, Mass. and London).
RANSTRAND, G. (1951), *Querolusstudien* (Stockholm).
REID, J. S. (1885), *M. Tulli Ciceronis Academica* (London).
REID, J. S. (1925), *M. Tulli Ciceronis De finibus bonorum et malorum libri I, II* (Cambridge).
REINHARDT, T. (2003), *Cicero's Topica* (Oxford).
REINHARDT, T., LAPIDGE, M. and ADAMS, J. N. eds (2005), *Aspects of the Language of Latin Prose* (Oxford).
RENEHAN, R. (1976), *Studies in Greek Texts: Critical Observations to Homer, Plato, Euripides, Aristophanes and other Authors* (Göttingen).
RENEHAN, R. (1977), 'Compound-simplex verbal iteration in Plautus', *CP* 72, 243–8.
REYNOLDS, L. D. ed. (1998), *M. Tulli Ciceronis De finibus bonorum et malorum libri quinque* (Oxford).
RIBBECK, O. (1871), *Scaenicae Romanorum poesis fragmenta* 1: *Tragicorum Romanorum fragmenta*, 2nd edn (Leipzig).

RICCOBONO, S. (1968), *Fontes iuris Romani antejustiniani* Pars prima: *Leges*, 2nd edn (Florence).
RICHARDSON, N. (2010), *Three Homeric Hymns, to Apollo, Hermes, and Aphrodite (Hymns 3, 4 and 5)* (Cambridge).
RIX, H. (2002), *Sabellische Texte: Die Texte des Oskischen, Umbrischen und Südpikenischen* (Heidelberg).
ROBY, H. J. (1884), *An Introduction to the Study of Justinian's Digest* (Cambridge).
ROSS, D. O. (1969), *Style and Tradition in Catullus* (Cambridge, Mass.).
RUCKDESCHEL, F. (1910), *Archaismen und Vulgarismen in der Sprache des Horaz* (Munich).
RUSSELL, D. A. (2001), *Quintilian: The Orator's Education*, 5 vols (Cambridge, Mass. and London).
RUTHERFORD, R. B. (2012), *Greek Tragic Style: Form, Language and Interpretation* (Oxford).
SCALISI, S. and BISETTO, A. (2009), 'The classification of compounds', in Lieber and Stekauer (2009), 34–53.
SCHEID, J. (1998), *Commentarii Fratrum Arvalium qui supersunt: Les copies épigraphiques des protocoles annuels de la Confrérie Arvale (21 AV. – 304 AP. J.-C.)* (Rome).
SCHIERL, P. (2006), *Die Tragödien des Pacuvius: Ein Kommentar zu den Fragmenten mit Einleitung, Text und Übersetzung* (Berlin and New York).
SCHMELING, G. (2011), *A Commentary on the Satyrica of Petronius* (Oxford).
SCHMIDT, E. G. (1975), 'Philosophische und poetische Elemente bei Lukrez', in Urushadze and Gordeziani (1975), 175–99.
SCHWYZER, E. (1950), *Griechische Grammatik auf der Grundlage von Karl Brugmanns Griechischer Grammatik 2: Syntax und syntaktische Stilistik*, completed and edited by A. Debrunner, 4th edn (Munich).
SHACKLETON BAILEY, D. R. (1965–70), *Cicero's Letters to Atticus*, 7 vols (Cambridge).
SHACKLETON BAILEY, D. R. (1977), *Cicero: Epistulae ad familiares*, 2 vols (Cambridge).
SHACKLETON BAILEY, D. R. (1991), *Cicero, back from Exile: Six Speeches upon his Return* (Atlanta).
SHERK, R. K. (1969), *Roman Documents from the Greek East: Senatus consulta and epistulae to the Age of Augustus* (Baltimore, Md.).
SJÖGREN, H. (1900), *De particulis copulatiuis apud Plautum et Terentium quaestiones selectae* (Uppsala).
SKARD, E. (1933), *Ennius und Sallustius* (Oslo).
SKUTSCH, O. (1985), *The Annals of Quintus Ennius* (Oxford).
SMITH, M. F. (1992), *Lucretius: De rerum natura*, revised version of the edition of W. H. D. Rouse (Cambridge, Mass. and London).
SOMMERSTEIN, A. H. (1987), *Aristophanes: Birds* (Warminster).
SOMMERSTEIN, A. H. (1989), *Aeschylus: Eumenides* (Cambridge).
SOMMERSTEIN, A. H. (2019), *Aeschylus: Suppliants* (Cambridge).

SPAL, A. (2016), *Poesie – Erotik – Witz: Humorvoll-spöttische Versinschriften zu Liebe und Körperlichkeit in Pompeji und Umgebung* (Berlin and Boston).
STANFORD, W. B. (1963), *Aristophanes: The Frogs*, 2nd edn (London).
STEVENS, P. T. (1971), *Euripides: Andromache* (Oxford).
STRZELECKI, W. (1964), *Cn. Naevii Belli Punici carmen* (Leipzig).
TARRANT, R. (2012), *Virgil: Aeneid Book XII* (Cambridge).
TAYLOR, B. (forthcoming), 'Lucretius and early Latin', in Adams, Chahoud and Pezzini (forthcoming).
THOMAS, R. T. (2011), *Horace: Odes Book IV and Carmen saeculare* (Cambridge).
THOMSON, D. F. S. (1997), *Catullus: edited with a Textual and Interpretative Commentary* (Toronto, Buffalo and London).
TIDNER, E. (1922), *De particulis copulatiuis apud Scriptores Historiae Augustae quaestiones selectae* (Uppsala).
TIMPANARO, S. (1954), review of O. Skutsch, *The Annals of Quintus Ennius* (An inaugural lecture delivered at University College, London, 29th November, 1951) (London, 1953), *JRS* 44, 155–7.
TIMPANARO, S. (1967), 'Note a interpreti Virgiliani antichi', *RFIC* (95), 428–45.
TIMPANARO, S. (1978), *Contributi di filologia e di storia della lingua latina* (Rome).
TIMPANARO, S. (1994), 'Alcuni tipi di sinonimi in asindeto in latino arcaico e in età classica repubblicana', in id., *Nuovi contributi di filologia e storia della lingua latina* (Bologna), 1–74.
TOMLIN, R. S. O. (2016), 'Inscriptions', *Britannia* 47, 389–415.
TORREGO, M. Esperanza (2009), 'Coordination', in Baldi and Cuzzolin (2009), 443–87.
UNTERMANN, J. (2000), *Wörterbuch des Oskisch-Umbrischen* (Heidelberg).
URUSHADZE, A. V. and GORDEZIANI, R. V. eds (1975), *Problems in Ancient Culture* (Tbilisi).
USHER, R. G. (1978), *Euripides: Cyclops, Introduction and Commentary* (Rome).
VAHLEN, J. (1903), *Ennianae poesis reliquiae*, 2nd edn (Leipzig).
VAN DEN HOUT, M. P. J. ed. (1988) *M. Cornelii Frontonis Epistulae* (Leipzig).
VAN RENGEN, W. (1984), 'Deux défixions contre les bleus à Apamée (VIe siècle apr. J.-C.', in J. Balty ed., *Apamée de Syrie. Bilan des recherches archéologiques 1973–1979: Aspects d'architecture domestique d'Apamée* (Actes du colloque tenu à Bruxelles les 29, 30 et 31 mai 1980) (Brussels), 213–33.
WACHTER, R. (1987), *Altlateinische Inschriften: Sprachliche und epigraphische Untersuchungen zu den Dokumenten bis etwa 150 v. Chr.* (Bern).
WACKERNAGEL, J. (1905), *Altindische Grammatik* 2.1: *Einleitung zur Wortlehre, Nominalkomposition* (Göttingen).
WACKERNAGEL, J. (1969), *Kleine Schriften*, 2nd edn, 2 vols. (Göttingen).
WALBANK, F. W. (1979), *A Historical Commentary on Polybius* 3: *Commentary on Books XIX–XL* (Oxford).

WALTHER, H. (1967), *Carmina medii aevi posterioris Latina* II/5: *Lateinische Sprichwörter und Sentenzen des Mittelalters in alphabetischer Anordnung* 5: *Sim–Z* (Göttingen).
WALTHER, H. (1969), *Carmina medii aevi posterioris Latina* II/6: *Lateinische Sprichwörter und Sentenzen des Mittelalters in alphabetischer Anordnung* 6: *Register der Namen, Sachen und Wörter zu Teil 1–5* (Göttingen).
WARMINGTON, E. H. (1936), *Remains of Old Latin* 2: *Livius Andronicus, Naevius, Pacuvius and Accius* (London and Cambridge, Mass.).
WARMINGTON, E. H. (1961), *Remains of Old Latin* 1: *Ennius and Caecilius*, 3rd edn (London and Cambridge, Mass.).
WARMINGTON, E. H. (1967), *Remains of Old Latin* 3: *Lucilius, The Twelve Tables*, 2nd edn (London and Cambridge, Mass.).
WATKINS, C. (1967), 'An Indo-European construction in Greek and Latin', *HSCP* 71, 115–19.
WATKINS, C. (1995), *How to Kill a Dragon: Aspects of Indo-European Poetics* (Oxford).
WATSON, A. (1967), *The Law of Persons in the Later Roman Republic* (Oxford).
WATSON, A. (1968), *The Law of Property in the Later Roman Republic* (Oxford).
WATSON, A. (1971), *Roman Private Law around 200 BC* (Edinburgh).
WEST, M. L. (1966), *Hesiod: Theogony* (Oxford).
WEST, M. L. (1978), *Hesiod: Works and Days* (Oxford).
WEST, M. L. (1988), 'The rise of the Greek epic', *JHS* 108, 151–72.
WEST, M. L. (2007), *Indo-European Poetry and Myth* (Oxford).
WILKINSON, L. P. (1963), *Golden Latin Artistry* (Cambridge).
WILLIAMS, G. (1968), *Tradition and Originality in Roman Poetry* (Oxford).
WILLIAMS, R. D. (1960), *P. Vergili Maronis Aeneidos liber quintus* (Oxford).
WILLS, J. (1996), *Repetition in Latin Poetry: Figures of Allusion* (Oxford).
WINTERBOTTOM, M. (1970), *Problems in Quintilian* (Institute of Classical Studies, Bulletin Supplement No. 25) (London).
WINTERBOTTOM, M. (1984), *The Minor Declamations ascribed to Quintilian* (Berlin and New York).
WINTERBOTTOM, M. ed. (1994), *M. Tulli Ciceronis De officiis* (Oxford).
WÖLFFLIN, E. (1900), 'Zum Asyndeton bei Sallust', *ALL* 11, 27–35.
WÖLFFLIN, E. (1933), *Ausgewählte Schriften*, edited by G. Meyer (Leipzig).
WÖLFFLIN, E. and MIODOŃSKI (1889), *C. Asini Polionis De bello Africo commentarius* (Leipzig).
WOODCOCK, E. C. (1959), *A New Latin Syntax* (London).
WOODMAN, A. J. (1977), *Velleius Paterculus: The Tiberian Narrative (2.94–131)* (Cambridge).
WOODMAN, A. J. (1983), *Velleius Paterculus: The Caesarian and Augustan Narrative (2.41–93)* (Cambridge).
WOODMAN, A. J. (2004), *Tacitus, the Annals* (Indianapolis, IN and Cambridge, Mass.).
WOODMAN, A. J. (2007), *Sallust: Cataline's War, The Jugurthine War, Histories* (London).

WOODMAN, A. J. (2017), *The Annals of Tacitus: Books 5 and 6* (Cambridge).
WOODMAN, A. J. (2018), *The Annals of Tacitus Book 4* (Cambridge).
WOODMAN, A. J. with KRAUS, C. S. (2014), *Tacitus Agricola* (Cambridge).
WOODMAN, A. J. and MARTIN, R. H. (1996), *The Annals of Tacitus Book 3* (Cambridge).
WOYTEK, E. (1982), *T. Maccius Plautus, Persa: Einleitung, Text und Kommentar* (Vienna).
YOUTIE, H. C. (1982), *Scriptiunculae posteriores* 2 (Bonn).
YOUTIE, H. C. and BONNER, C. (1937), 'Two curse tablets from Beisan', *TAPA* 68, 43–77 (= Youtie 1982: 609–77).
ZAGO, A. (2017), *Pompeii Commentum in Artis Donati partem tertiam*, 2 vols (Hildesheim).
ZIMMERMANN, R. (1996), *The Law of Obligations: Roman Foundations of the Civilian Tradition* (Oxford and New York).

Subject Index

This index is necessarily highly selective, because many of the topics that are listed here come up constantly in the presentation of texts in the literary chapters. The topics dealt with in the book are catalogued in detail in the table of contents.

acclamations, cries of approval 527
'accumulations' of asyndeta/coordinations
 and textual criticism 217, 500, 501, 611
 antiquity of 212
 classified by type 463–4 see Chap. XIX
 containing adverbs 164
 containing opposites 156–61, 292–3, 430–1
 containing verbs 466
 in Aeschylus 279
 in Cicero 466–7, 467–70
 in curse tablets 116, 214, 684
 in Ennius 334–5, 340
 in Greek 215–16, 694
 in Horace 515–16
 in Livy 672
 in Oscan 214
 in Petronius 214, 684
 in Plautus 278
 in prayers and religious contexts 213, 242, 243
 in Sallust 585
 in Umbrian 213, 246–52, 250
 motivating an asyndeton 260–1
 of 1 + 2 + 2/3 elements 119, 375
 of 2 + 3 elements 252 (in Umbrian) 412, 515
 of 2 + 2 + 1 elements 483, 515
 of 2 + 2 + 3 elements 430
 of 2 + 4 elements 391
 of 3 +2 elements 100, 366–7, 375–6, 394, 526
 of compounds, e.g. on the same verbal root 116, 117 (in Greek) 279, 285
 prolonged 407, 434, 557, 627, 653
 statistics 464, 467–70 see also structures
active, passive verbs see verbs, asyndetic
adjectives
 agreeing with unexpressed subject of verb 314, 317, 661, 670
 and 'rank' 34–5, 36–7

asyndetic pairs of, supposedly avoided by poets 41, 330, 336, 363–4
 at start of line of verse 314, 317, 323, 330
 attributive, predicative, secondary predicates/ predicative adjuncts see Chap. II
 combined with participle 314, 315, 316, 321, 331
 'genitival' 36, 40, 42–3
 in Cicero, statistics 465, 473
 in Livy 669–71
 in Virgil, adjectival asyndeton most prominent type 323
 judgemental, often at end of colon/postponed 73, 74–5, 80–1, 311, 381, 389, 690–1
 pairs offering difficulties of interpretation see Chap. II
 positive + negative 102–8
 postpositive 315, 317, 328, 359
 privative/negative 289–9, 317, 329, 345, 377, 389–91, 513–14, 519 see Chap. VI *passim*
 separation of in asyndeton allegedly feature of 'early Latin' 37–41, 44, 323–4
 'stacking, layering' of 34–5, 41, 43, 44
adverbs
 adverbs modifying adverbs 290 n. 4, 311, 486
 gemination of, asyndetic *see* gemination, of adverbs
 opposites in pairs 163–4, 485–6, 522, 581, 599
agricultural works 695–6
alliteration 243, 244, 401
ancient classifications/discussions of asyndeton 10–13, 78–9
antiquity of asyndeton versus coordination 55–7
Apicius 69
apposition, distinguished from asyndetic coordination 318
ascending length, rule of *see* Behaghel's law
assonance *see also* alliteration

715

Subject Index

assonance (cont.)
  in compound coinages 279
  in general 119, 549–50
  in sequences of verbs 283–6
  with repeated prefix and/or suffix 285
asyndeton
  adjectival, with second member of extended length 320–3
  adversative 9–10, 18, 22–6 (clausal)
  causal (explanatory, explicative) 27–9
  clausal 20–7, 135–6
  clausal, of subordinate clauses 22
  comprising different parts of speech 293–4, 336, 375, 417–18, 674
  dependent on a single preposition *see* prepositional expressions
  determinants of *see* determinants of asyndeton
  discontinuous *see* discontinuous asyndeton
  'embedded' 295–6, 366, 376, 428, 431, 432 (?) 433, 445, 578
  expressing reciprocal actions 121
  false/pseudo-'asyndeton' *see* Chap. II, *passim*
  in direct speech 506, 507
  long versus short 14–16
  occupying whole line or more 328, 329, 351, 359, 377, 392, 395, 524, 526
  of imperatives 114, 128–37 280–2
  of names 229, 385–6, 394, 416–17, 437–8, 517
  of single word + extended phrase, or the reverse 19–20, 320–3, 518–19
  phrasal 17–19, 251 (in Umbrian)
  'prepositional' type *see* asyndeton with anaphora
  with one term possibly a modifier of the other 49–53, 255, 425, 546, 547, 573, 578, 580, 581, 589, 596, 622, 662 *see also* compounds: quasi-compounds; hendiadys, asyndetic
  with second/final term semantically stronger 172, 255, 342, 545
  with syntactic inconcinnity 322
asyndeton with anaphora, particularly prepositional
  in general 29–30, 249 (in Umbrian), 296 (in Greek), 296–7, 319–20 (in Virgil) 358, 387, 442–3, 450–2, 581, 628–9
  combined with asyndeton of different part of speech or type 293–4, 427, 588–9, 599, 627, 637–8
  sine ... sine combined with or acting as *in*-privatives 91, 92, 93, 97, 289, 519, 661
augury, 'augural language' *see* formulae

Behaghel's 'law' 177–87, 323, 400
  exceptions to 179
'bitter-sweet' structures in Latin? 459–60
'boys, girls' 141
'brother, sister' 168

Caelius and asyndeton 458–61
Caesar *see* Chap. XXVIII
ueni uidi uici 11, 77–8
carmina 323, 376–7
circumlocutions, poetic 35–6, 37–8, 43
clausulae, as influencing coordination/asyndeton 125, 221, 427
coinages *see* compounds
colon dividers 203–4, 375, 379, 411, 412–13, 421, 438, 500, 515, 665
  between asyndetic pair and syndetic pair 410
colon structure *see* phrase structure
compounds
  adjective + participle 41
  alliterative 277
  appositional 44–6
  compound coinages 272–3, 276–80, 348, 378, 390, 694
  compound + simplex 285, 350 *see also* Chap. VII
  dvandva 57–61
  Greek terms, in Latin 374, 390
  quasi-compounds 48, 49–52, 316
  simplex + compound *see* Chap. VII
conjunct hyperbaton 220–1
  comprising merisms 220–1
  comprising opposites 220
  in Greek 221
  influenced by clausula 221
  of names 447, 455
  with 'weak' separating term 220
consuls, named, with and without asyndeton 16–17, 270
coordination(s) (coordinated pairs or sequences)
  accumulations of 242, 243, 245, 528
  alliterative, with assonance 401–2, 493, 531
  antiquity of 56–7
  expressing opposites 530
  in Horace (far outnumbering asyndetic pairs) 528–32
  in Lucretius 368–72
  in religious texts 245, 246
  in Virgil 368–72
  multiple 362–3 (in Lucretius), 399–400 (in Lucilius), 535–40 (in Horace), 606 (in Tacitus)
  of pairs matching asyndetic types 529–31
  versus asyndeton 55–7, 61–5, 477–9, 492–4, 503 (in military pairs in Caesar), 504, 511

Subject Index 717

(military pairs again), 528–32 (in Horace), 539–40, 542–3 (genre-related in Horace), 644– (in Livy)
correlative distribution 188–91, 577–8, 614, 621, 625, 628
curse tablets 116, 117

determinants of/influences on asyndeton 687–93
   accumulations 156–61, 166, 407, 687–8
   addressees 454, 456, 473–4 692–3
   formulae 154, 371, 689–91
   genre and context 64, 116, 125–7, 144–5, 166, 172, 474–5, 531, 542–3 (in Horace) 582, 688–9, 692–3, 693–9
   influence of Homer on Virgil 694–5 see Virgil: and Homer *and* Homer
   intonation/manner of articulation 6, 79–81, 82–3, 371–2, 689–91
   parts of speech (notably imperatives) 371
   personal taste 692, 699
   rhetorical effect 532, 668, 693
   semantic 372 see semantic categories
   structures 407, 512, 625 see particularly Chap. XXVIII
discontinuous asyndeton 39, 221–4, 335, 353, 358, 393, 456
   comprising opposites 222
   in Homer 223
   in Horace 516
   in Lucilius 376, 388
   in Menander 224
   in Petronius 684
   judgemental terms in 223
   with stronger term second 223, 449
dvandva compounds see compounds: dvandva

'eat/drink' 287
'effects' of asyndeton
   rapidity? 76–9, 219
   to imply 'pauses for thought' 79–81, 483
   end-of-list coordination 15, 192–210
   false/open to different interpretations 200–4, 244
   frequency of 193–8
   in Catullus 491
   in Greek 210
   in Horace 532–4
   in Lucilius 398–9
   in Lucretius 362
   in prayers 197, 205, 242
English 111–12
Epitaphium super Vergilium 189

'father, mother' 167–8

'fore-elements', repeated see prefixes (or 'fore-elements')
formulae
   augural 247, 264–5, 331–2, 333
   fetial 154, 265
   imperatival 128–9, 130–1
   in prayers 248
   legal 168, 169–70, 252–63, 274–6, 445, 479–80, 656, 663
   name of game 106, 514
   of betrothal 276
   of divorce 276
   official 130–1, 265–6, 657
   old, later becoming coordinated 256, 257, 258
   old, used metaphorically 257
   religious 263–5, 268, 274–6, 409, 413, 444, 479–80

gemination, of adverbs 319, 486
genre(s) see determinants of/influences on asyndeton
gerunds, in the ablative, asyndetic 285–6, 598
'go' (and) do something 128–35, 281
'gods, goddesses' 138–9
Greek
   and Latin compared 109–11, 136–7, 144, 273
   influencing Latin 111, 144, 540–3

haruspices, books of 245–6
hendiadys, asyndetic 54, 263, 412, 414, 445, 449, 546, 596
Homer
   asyndeton in 324–30
   influence on Virgil? 326, 329, 330–1
Horace
   and Pindar 540–3
   asyndeton rare in *Odes* 523, 527, 529
hyperbaton see conjunct hyperbaton

imperatives, asyndetic see Chap. X
   addressed to slaves in comedy 128–30, 685
   in Catullus 487–8
   in Greek New Comedy 136–7, 281–2
   in later Latin and Romance 132–5
   paired, with extended second member 129–30
   'intensification' of simple verb by compound 115, 116
intonation, articulation 6, 78–80

kinship terms 169–70

laws, legal/official texts see Chap. XXII
   changes of fashion in 234, 240, 269–70
   legal/official expressions 113, 126–7, 141–2, 168, 188, 189, 252–63, 265–8

laws, legal/official texts (cont.)
  used metaphorically 256
  pairs of different tense or mood 126–7, 265–6
lictor, addressed 130–1
lists
  as totalities 66–71
  length of and coordination 69–70
  menus, dinner lists 67–8, 525
  of grammatical type 71, 380, 395
  of names 69, 70, 72, 416–17
  of weapons, threatening objects 394
  open-ended, selective, illustrative 71–5, 379–80, 386, 395, 396, 417, 432, 524, 525
  recipes 68
  shopping lists 69, 526
longer term second *see* Behaghel's 'law'
Lucilius
  and early high-style poetry 403
  compared with Horace 388, 403
Lucretius, compared with Ennius, Pacuvius and Virgil 363

masculine + feminine pairs 138–42, 304–5, 516, 652
Medieval Latin verse 189
'men, women' 140–1
menus *see* lists
merisms 55, 249, 431, 650
multiple coordinations *see* coordination(s)

name-lines 541–2
names
  and textual problems 447, 455, 497–501
  in general in asyndetic pairs, cited *exempli gratia* 229, 517, 647
  in the plural 646
  of brother and sister 168
  of consuls 270
  of places 394, 497–501, 606, 665, 666
negatives other than *in-* in asyndeta 97, 98–9, 351, 358, 378, 390, 391, 419, 513, 658, 659

opposites *see* Chap. VI *passim*
  adverbial 163–4
  antipodals 153–4
  antonyms 150–1, 385
  complementarities 150
  converses 122, 151–2, 155, 546
  directional 123, 152
  in conjunct hyperbaton 220
  in Horace 518
  in Livy 671
  in Lucretius 354–5, 363
  in philosophy 431
  in Plautus 303–4

in Tacitus 631, 642
inexplicit type 158–9, 165–6, 602, 603, 616, 628, 665
middle term(s) expressed or implied 153–4
of social status 162–3
pairs of, juxtaposed or in longer sequences
  430–1, 587–8, 590, 593, 605, 650, 660, 662
  with asyndeton and coordination both represented 650
positive-negative type 155
reversives 425, 426
semantic illogicality of some pairs 106, 318–19, 482
structural patterns 156–61
Ovid 695
oxymoron 37

pairs forming a unit 16–17
parataxis 4
'parent, children' 169
Petronius 133, 279, 684–5
phrase structure, problems of interpretation 419, 477, 546, 625
Plautus
  and early high-style poetry 272–3, 277–9, 306, 367–8
  and Umbrian 247, 264, 274
  compared with Menander (or vice versa) 288, 300, 301, 302 306
  features of asyndeton in 306–7
  positive + negative pairs 102–8, 482–3
  prayers 139, 212, 215 (favouring coordination) 275
  see Chap. XXII
predicates, mainly secondary
  in general 33–4, 49
predicative adjuncts *see* predicates, mainly secondary
prefixes (or 'fore-elements')
  different, but with similar function 326, 351
  different, on same root 285
  mixed verbal prefixes in asyndetic sequences 116
  opposites in meaning 104, 164, 615
  privative *see* Chap. VI *passim*
  repeated in asyndeton, in pairs and longer sequences (*see also above*, 'privative') 108–9, 243, 326, 328, 341, 366–7, 369, 449
  repeated in coordinations 401
  with negative function but not *in-*privative 106–8, 658 *see also* negatives other than *in-* in asyndeta
prepositional expressions
  asyndetic with anaphora of the preposition *see* asyndeton with anaphora
  in distinctive structures 225, 227

Subject Index 719

that are opposites 229
  with asyndeton emended away 227, 229
  with two terms dependent on a single preposition 413, 508–10, 558, 612–13, 655–6, 677, 678–80 *see* Chap. XXI
present participles in asyndeton 288
privative adjectives *see* adjectives: privative/negative
pronunciation *see* intonation, articulation
Propertius 23–4
proverbial expressions 163, 166
'public, private' 162, 608
punctuation, problems and inconsistencies of 475–7, 586–7

'sacral language' 348–9, 687
Sallust and Tacitus compared 588, 590, 595, 596, 635–43
Scribonius Largus 687, 696–7
semantic categories found often in asyndeton 171–3
  acts of violence 99, 171, 172, 424, 425, 545, 559, 595, 596, 598, 625, 626, 691
  alliance, friendship *see below*, family
  animals, of different domestic types 386, 547–8, 610
  animals, wild versus domestic 442, 443
  approaching and encouraging, verbs of 596–7, 597–8, 626, 627, 635–6
  athletic pursuits 301–2, 396
  banishment, exclusion, abandonment, rejection 91, 93, 171, 321, 441, 481, 562, 571, 659, 685, 691
  components of the world/universe 361–2
  decadent behaviour 299, 576
  destruction, preceded e.g. by capture 545, 576–7, 579–80, 623
  eating/drinking 300, 556
  expressing judgements 381, 382, 383
  family and other close relationships 167–70, 171, 304, 388, 406, 506, 517, 558, 567, 569, 590, 604, 647–8, 652–3, 654
  female adornment 171, 297–9, 393, 551
  food lists 301
  'goods and chattels' 408
  grief and lamentation 444–5, 481
  home/homeland 560, 561, 562, 568, 569
  luxury 278, 356, 393, 415, 526, 548–9, 560
  military terms 412–13, 458, 481, 648, 649, 653, 662, 669
  numerical approximations 294, 302–3, 520–1

offices, officials, official terms, honours, status 266–7, 415, 416, 436, 463, 591, 592, 602, 612, 616, 617, 633, 646, 666, 669, 675
old age, decrepitude 171, 302
opposites *see* opposites
parts of the body, complementary 304
'pathetic', of adjectives 172, 318
pejorative terms 99, 381
precious metals 301, 340 414, 436, 545
'rich'/'poor' 618
shouting, din, complaint 564, 567, 633
threatening objects, weapons 450, 565, 590–1
tools of war 564–5, 566, 568, 593, 614, 653
types of administration, administrators 266–8, 563
virtue and vice 171, 300–1, 411, 414 416, 433, 444, 455, 463, 480, 554, 561, 566, 591, 592, 601, 606
senatorial proposals 265–6, 655
separation, of adjectives in asyndeton *see* discontinuous asyndeton
slaves, addressed with imperatives 128–30
speeches in historians 557, 559, 582, 600, 642–3, 667–8
structures
  adjectives, at start of line of verse 314, 324, 325, 326
  adjectives, postpositive 73, 74–5, 325
  and problems of interpretation 625
  and textual criticism 217, 611
  asyndetic pair + anaphoric asyndeton 440, 467
  asyndetic pair + coordinator + another pair 642–3
  asyndetic pair followed by a summarising or generalising element 206–9, 406–7, 415–16, 437, 441, 554–5, 585, 615, 617, 630
  asyndetic pair followed by longer asyndetic sequence 420, 463–4, 547, 564, 575, 592, 602, 641
  asyndetic pair followed by multiple coordinations 500, 501
  asyndetic pair followed by *neque ... neque* or other forms of negatives 585, 595
  asyndetic pair juxtaposed with syndetic 159, 212, 218, 225, 227, 247, 294–5, 378, 408, 410, 411, 415, 435, 483, 499–500, 506, 507, 513, 515, 558, 559, 561, 584–5, 589, 601, 605, 609, 611, 638–40, 672–3
  with syndetic pair containing *ac* 227, 408, 513, 589
  with syndetic pair containing *atque* 159, 515, 558, 559, 561, 584–5
  with syndetic pair containing *aut* 612

structures (cont.)
  with syndetic pair containing *et* 435, 601, 605, 613
  with syndetic pair containing -*que* 91, 159, 204
  asyndetic pair or pairs embedded in a sequence of coordinations or longer asyndeta 160, 376, 407, 409, 428, 431, 433, 445, 483, 502, 523, 578, 579, 646, 653
  asyndetic pair preceded or followed by phrasal/clausal asyndeta 464, 547, 602, 641, 645
  asyndetic pair separated from asyndetic pair by colon divider/coordinator 379, 421
  coordinated pair + single term, uncoordinated 550
  in Cicero, classified 466, 467–70, 472
  juxtaposed asyndetic pairs 119, 156–8, 160–1, 212, 213, 292–4, 412, 420, 422, 435, 463, 651
  juxtaposed pairs of different parts of speech 214–15, 250 (in Umbrian) 293–4
  juxtaposed pairs with syntactic imbalance/inconcinnity 505, 607, 613, 640, 673
  pairs of opposites juxtaposed with other pairs of opposites, asyndetic or syndetic 292–3, 430–1, 641–2, 650, 660, 662 *see also* opposites
  patterns shared by Sallust and Tacitus 637–41
  semantically stronger term second *see* asyndeton, with second/final term semantically stronger

Tacitus
  changing style 629–30
  in comparison with Sallust *see* Sallust and Tacitus compared
textual criticism and problems
  criteria open to editors 63–5, 228
  in general 119, 127, 129, 140, 218, 227, 228, 229–30, 244, 264, 290 n. 4, 311, 383, 384, 391, 393, 396, 409, 414, 419, 442, 443–4, 447, 448–9, 453–4, 455–6, 477, 484, 586–7, 602, 610, 612–13, 616, 625, 634–5, 648–9, 651–2, 654, 655–6, 660, 663, 664, 675–7 *see* Chap. XXVIII *passim*
  manuscripts as a factor 63, 616
  punctuation, inconsistencies of 475–7, 586–7
  punctuation, to reflect special or structural factors 609–10
  relevance of semantics to the authenticity of an asyndeton 65
  relevance of structural patterns to the authenticity of an asyndeton 63–4, 676

totalities 66–71, 138
'town' versus 'country' 161–2, 414, 432, 451, 457, 563, 616
tricola and longer sequences, asyndetic and coordinated 14–16, 67–9, 686–7

Umbrian 103, 164, 246–52

Vedic 91–2, 104–5, 140
Venantius Fortunatus 189
verbs, asyndetic
  active + passive 121–4, 123 (in Greek) 488, 489, 625–6
  expressing acts of violence *see* semantic categories
  expressing reciprocal actions 121
  historic infinitives 621, 636, 674
  imperatives 128–37, 384, 685–6
  in Cicero, structures and types 465–6, 471
  in Ennius 346
  in laws 235–6, 238, 240
  in Menander 288
  in Pacuvius 352
  in Plautus 280–8
  in Umbrian 248–9, 250
  juxtaposed, expressing changes of mind 123
  of different tense and mood juxtaposed 125–7, 427 *see* Chap. IX
  pairs of, avoided by Virgil 319
  pairs with one a modifier of the other 5–6, 422 *see also* asyndeton: with one term possibly a modifier of the other
  present participles 448
  simplex + compound or the reverse 113–20
  subjunctives, in pairs, comparable to imperatives 282, 397
  with repeated prefix *see* prefixes
versus rapportati 188
Virgil
  and Homer 326–7, 329, 330–1, 367, 694–5
  borrowing from Lucretius 322
  Ennius and Virgil compared 345–7
  privatives in 317
  structural features of asyndeton in 317–18
Vitruvius 698

'weak' asyndeton bimembre 206–9, 406, 630
'women/wives, children' 168–9
word order
  determinant of exceptions to Behaghel's law 179, 184–6
  interlocking 315, 333, 353
  reversals of the norm 131–2

Index Mainly of Selected Pairs and Longer Sequences

The word forms used in this index are often the base-form (e.g. first person present tense for verbs, nominative singular for nouns), but I have not followed that practice without variation. Some formulaic pairs, for example, are used only or mainly in a particular form. The point of a pair of ablative gerunds would be missed if the pair were quoted in the first person present. Pairs from poetry are often kept in the form that they have in the text, and many of the Greek examples fall into this category. Single-word entries are largely, but not entirely, excluded, but it is easy enough to identify words that occur in several combinations from the following list. There are indeed many words that occur in a variety of different pairs. It should be stressed that not all the pairs listed here are interpreted in the text as asyndetic.

Included in this index are a lot of sequences, short and long, showing assonance of one kind or another, such as repeated prefixes, suffixes or inflections.

Quite a few pairs are in both orders. I have not listed all of these twice.

Latin
ab acia et acu 56
abdo apscondo 285
abduco duco 117
abeo fugio 622
abi, actutum redi 304
abi deprome 280
abi nuntia 281
abi prae, nuntia 281
abi quaere 280
abiit, apstulit mulierem 282
abiit, operuit fores 283
abnuo negito 287
absisto adloquor 190, 625
acer bellicosus 573
ad pingendum fingendum 413
ad praedam ad gloriam 506
adeamus appellemus 282
adeo adduco 283
adeo hortor 597, 627
adeo perquiro 283
adeundo appellando 109, 286, 624
adfinitas societas 207–8, 406
adfirmat ... adiurat 108, 223, 449
aditus abscessus 104, 164, 615

adsideo subduco 450
adsisto adloquor 109
adsum defendo 421–2
adulteria matrimonia 588
adulteria uenena 607
aedificia oppida 238
aeger anhelans 50, 97–8, 316
aegram indignantem 315, 317
aequom bonum 275, 445, 690
aequus facilis 439
aequus iniquus 105
aetas sexus 226, 617
age + imperative 135–6
ager locus 228, 237–8
agite icite uoluite rapite 283
agnoscis agnosceris 122
ago agino 684, 690
ago uerto 595
agri oppida 414
agricola accola 303
alba, solo recubans 321
algor error pauor 277
alienus maestus 382
alligo deligo 116
alo augeo 160, 190, 213, 349

amant amantur 121, 488
ambiguus manifestus 158, 268, 593
ambio colo 598
ambitiosus superbus 81, 619
ambitus iudicia 268, 451
ambulo sedeo 156, 439
amici amicae 142
amicitia foedus 267, 567–8
amicitia societas 267
amicus affinis 304
amicus amator 396
amicus socius *see* socius amicus
amisso exfundato 545
amo poto 576, 580
amoenus uoluptarius 570
anademata mitrae 356, 393
ancillae penum 298
ancillae pueri 379
ancillae serui *see* serui ancillae
animo formo 160, 190, 213, 349
ante post 164
antiquum ingens 316
aperta secreta 160, 610
aperte tecte 165, 448, 459–60
apsterreo abigo 285
arae foci 160, 268, 275, 303, 413
arbor olea 46
arma cadauera 559
arma corpora 665
arma equi 649
arma munimenta 614
arma opes 615
arma signa 651
arma tela 564, 566, 653
armatus inermis 105, 150, 660
armipotens, praeses belli 323
asper, acerba sonans 19, 322
asper, acerba tuens 19, 322, 359
aspernor repello 26, 185, 441, 466
assiduitas indulgitas 53, 547
attribuerunt attribuerint 126
auaritia superbia 591
auarus libidinosus 80
audax improbus 209
audax maleficus 619
audax proteruus 438
aude incipe 521
audio coniecto 627
auerto perdo 695
augeo minuo 158, 186, 662
aurea, perpetua semper dignissima uita 359
auream . . . pulcram 366
aureaque . . . fulgentia mala 40–1
aurum argentum 185, 209, 301, 414, 436
aurum ebur 301, 340

aurum ornamenta 298
ausculto iubeo 281
ausculto opseruo 287
auus auia 168
auxilia equitatus 63, 502

bellator imbellis 106, 609
bellicosam . . . gentem feram 40
bellum pax 518
bene ac prospere 56, 275
benigne lepide 311
bibite pergraecamini 281, 287, 299
bibitur estur 215, 287
bibo edo 287
bini terni 294, 302
bis ter 521
bona fortunae 407–8
bonus malus 157, 158 (reversed)

caducus mobilis 421
caede . . . urgue 384
caedes incendia 8, 429, 559
caedo capio 579–80
caedo concido 118
caelatus laqueatus 340
caelebs orbus 619
calliplocamon callisphyron 277, 374, 403, 694
calx caementa 228
candida longa recta 490
canes equi 442
cantrices cistellatrices 278
capio occido 579–80
capruginus aprugnus 67
captiui serui 617
castra flumina 604
castra siluae 665
catapultas pila sarisas 394
celebro colo 626
cenat dormit lauat 394
circuli conuiuia 654
circumcido amputo 439
circumeo hortor 53, 186, 624, 626
circumsisto hortor 179, 596
circumuenio iugulo 577
ciues urbs 515, 517
ciuis senator 267, 592
clam furtim 311
clam inprouiso 5, 385
clamat parturit 288
clamor concursus 412
clamor uoltus 564, 603
clarus obscurus 430
clementia temperantia 606
cocus pistor 430, 684

Index Mainly of Selected Pairs and Longer Sequences 723

coeliacus torminosus 697
cognatio adfinitas 169, 567–8
cognitus incognitus 105
coiit coierit 126
colligo ligo 116
collum caput 696
colo obseruo 579
comedim congraecem 284
comesum expotum 109, 287
comitas adrogantia 587
comminus eminus 164, 599
commisceo tero 697
complector osculor 624
concesserunt concesserint 126
concurso coeo 202
conducendo locando 441
conduco loco 158, 185, 226, 440–1
conficto cano 350
confidens tumidus 390, 515
confirmo excito 448
congressus conloquia 109, 186, 611
coniuges liberi 168, 654
conquiro pertraho 625
conregione conspicione cortumione 686
conscribo comparo 108, 426
conscribo decurio 426
consilia loci 160
constans perpetuus 420
constantia fortitudo 592
consulatus decemuiratus 266
consulatus sacerdotia 266, 591
consulatus triumphi 266, 602
consusurro confero 285
contemno admiror 430
contemplo conspicio 292
contundo cribro 697
conueniam orabo 283
conuenit conuenerit 126
coquite facite festinate 283
cor cogitatum 214
coruos parra 56, 264, 274
creo sepelio 160, 190, 212, 349
cribro aspergo 697
crimen periculum 73, 610
crispus cincinnatus 295
crispus incanus 291
crudelis inmoderatus 98, 572
crudelissimus saeuissimus 74, 81
culter securis 293
cum osculis cum lacrimis 628
cum senatu cum populo 665
cupio fastidio 430
cura prouisu 614
curans cogitans 288
curo educo 286

dando accipiendo 123, 285, 439–40
darent adsignarent 126, 266
dati adsignati 126, 266
de ambitu de iudiciis 451
de flammis de ferro 450
de natura de moribus 429
de sedibus de focis 428
deamo depereo 284
debetur dabo 304
decalauticare ... despeculassere 378
decerno statuo 236 n. 2
decus gloria 605
defendant defenderint 125, 427
defendite ite 132, 661
delectat ductat 178–9, 342
deminui ... recreari 222, 358
depugis nasuta 513, 518
deruncinatus deartuatus 284
desidia inertia 97, 411
deteriores repulsos 245
deuotos defixos 214
deuotum defictum 214
dextra sinistra 164, 567, 698
di deae(que) 56, 139
dic, impera mi 281
dicenda tacenda 108, 521
dico edico 115
dico rogo 236 n. 2
dicto imperio 274
dies nox 657
differor difflagitor 284
differt dissupat 108, 341
difficilis querulus 523
dignus indignus 104, 106, 303, 318
diripiebatur ardebat 424
diruo aedifico 82, 152, 222, 425, 521
discedo abeo 356
disco exerceor 450
dispereo pereo 117, 285
dispersi inordinati 99
dissicis dispulueras 366–7
dissonus impar 98, 514, 658
distraho diripio 212
disturbo diripio 108, 424
disturbo uerto 424–5
dites pauperes 226
diues inops 106, 514, 518
diues pauper 430, 617
diues promptus 618
diuitiae opes 435
diuitiae paupertas 150, 158, 185, 436
dixit dixerit 126
do accipio 159, 160, 184, 440
do adsigno 184, 427
do attribuo 240

724 Index Mainly of Selected Pairs and Longer Sequences

do deuoueo 244
do dono 295, 299, 305
do facio 185, 441
do paro 287
do praebeo 238
do subdo 236
docendo discendo 160, 285, 440
doceo educo 285
docilitas memoria 433
dolor caritas 71, 615
dolor ira 606
dolus perfidia 300
domesticus forensis 158, 162, 456, 457
domus coniux 568–9
domus fora 162, 608, 629
domus patria *see* patria domus
domus, res familiaris 664
domus sedes 428
domus uilla 415, 560, 616
dono adimo 158
duco ago 238 n. 3
ductando amando 285
dulcis amarus 157, 185, 215, 430
duplex triplex 294, 302
durus mollis 161

eburatus auratus 301
edax furax fugax 277
egens 691
egens factiosus 81, 570
egentem, probatum suis 14, 19, 418
egi ago uel axim 127
eiectum litore, egentem 321
eiulans ... maerens 288
elogia historiae 548
emo uendo 226, 441
emptio uenditio 259–62
eo redeo 152, 184, 426
equi armenta 610
equi canes 442
equi leones 443
equi uiri 564, 615, 616–17
equus musimo 386
est erit 127
este effercite uos 281, 287
estur bibitur *see* bibitur estur
euinco uinco 116
euiscerata inanima 97, 351
ex silentio ex uoce 190
excludo reuoco 518
excordem caecum incogitabilem 291
exeo proficiscor 423
exoro aufero 286
expello relego 425–6
exprobratio satisfactio 165, 616

exprobro reposco 624
exsul extorris 109, 658
exterritus amens 316, 338
extorris egens 658
extorris expulsus 658
exunctum elotum 293

fabula rumor 458
facies sura 515
facio curo 53
facite fingite inuenite efficite 283
facta dicta 225, 435, 455
facta transacta 287
factum non factum 107, 157
faeceos mores, turbidos 39, 222–3
falsiloquom falsificum falsiiurium 109, 279
falsus incertus 97, 421
fama fides 562
fames frigus 213, 305, 376
familiaris necessaries 506
fana luci 268, 444
fandus nefandus 107, 482
fas nefas 104
fateor patior 284
fauebant gaudebant 52, 209, 425
fecit fecerit 126
femina mas 46
ferae pecudes 151, 202, 354, 442
fero feruenti 359–60
feror differor 119, 212, 285
ferrareae argentifodinae 545
ferrum faces 190, 226, 412
ferrum flamma 450
festinando agitando 285, 578
festino paro 52, 575–6, 580, 641
festino trepido 52, 578
festino uigilo 190, 577
fides probitas 554
fidicinae tibicinae 299
fiduciae mandata 226, 436–7
filius filia 168, 170
flabelliferae sandaligerulae 278
flagro ardeo 426, 465
flentes plorantes lacrumantes obtestantes 344
fletus questus 445
flexibilis durus 430
forensis domesticus *see* domesticus forensis
foris intus 163
formido fuga 592–3
formosus fortis 383
forte temere 663–4
fortis ignauus 660
fortis inuictus 97
fortuna ferro 341
fortuna fors 374

Index Mainly of Selected Pairs and Longer Sequences 725

forum conuiuium 628
forum domus 629 *see* domus fora *and* per fora per
 domos
forum fana 434
foueo foueor 122
frater pater 380, 521
frater soror 168
fremo queror 445, 449
frigus fames 433
fruges frumenta 56, 212, 242
frugum inopia, fames 409
frumentum pecunia 203, 651
fuga formido 244 (with third element *terrore*) 409
 (with third element *discordia*)
fuga uastitas 611
fugio occurso 229, 596
fugo ago 295
fulgente tonante 178
fundis sagittis 506
fundo confundo 119
fundo fugo 119, 662, 663
fur trifurcifer 300
furiosus furiosa 142
furtiuam abductam 51
fustitudinas ferricrepinas 2

gemitus ploratus 444–5
gener socer 169
genus ordo 226, 617
gesta sunt geruntur postque gerentur 127
gignendo educando 185, 285, 442
gracila... pernix 376
gradarius optimus 382
Graecus Latinus 457, 571
Graius homo, rex 338
gratia honores 617
gratia potentia 557, 591
gratia uox 562
gratulatio dona 656
grauis acutus 430
grauis infructuosus 99, 618
grauitas inflammatio 697

habeo possideo 127, 189, 238
hac illac 163
harioli haruspices 275
hinc illinc 165, 485
hinc inde 165, 186, 599
honestus locuples 80
honestus turpis 430
honos diuitiae 557
horrendum ingens 81, 315
horridus incomptus 99, 594
hospes cliens 452
huc illuc 82, 165, 599, 627

humilis supplex 316

i (following imperative) 131–2
i arcesse 129
i, lictor 130–1
i pete 130, 522
i sequere 130
i uise 130
Ianuario Februario 417
ibo adducam 283
ibo alloquar 283
ibo orabo 283
ibo ornabor 283
ibo uisam 283
iecur pectus 697
iecur praecordia 697
ignarus inuitus 92, 420
ignauus improbus 91
ignotus egens 98, 314
imbecillus caducus 421
imbecillus iners 513, 691
imbellis inermis 93, 620
immanem intolerandum uesanum 291
immunde insulse indecore 101
immundus instrenuos 300
immunitas uectigal 414
impedio prohibeo 461
imperator, consul designatus 16, 265, 415,
 416
imperia magistratus 266
imperio dicto 274
imperiosissimus superbissimus 661
impetritum inauguratumst 95, 264, 275
improbus edentulus 290, 302
improbus ineptus 383
improuisus inopinatus 93
impudens impurus inuerecundissimus 291
impudicus scelestus 290 300
impure inhoneste iniure inlex 101, 291
impurus auarus 291
imus uenimus uidemus 78
in foro, domi 162, 434
in foro in conuiuio 165
in usu, experiundo 286
inamabilis illepidus 91, 289
inanis imparatus 96, 447–8
inanis uitiosus 698
inauditus nouus 97, 421
inberbi androgyni, barbati moechocinaedi
 389–90
incompositus inordinatus 93, 661
incurso turbo 623
indecore inique inmodeste 101
indefensus inultus 81, 93, 658
indemnatus innocens 91, 418

726   *Index Mainly of Selected Pairs and Longer Sequences*

indispositus temulentus 594
indoctae immemori insipienti 101, 291
indomito, pleno amoris ac lasciuiae 291
indomitus ferox 291
indomitus incogitatus 91, 289
industria licentia 165, 215
industria probitas 566
iners inbellis 81, 92, 574, 595
infans, indigus omni uitali auxilio 96, 359, 685
infans minutulus 291
infelix, aeuo confectus 322
infelix miser 290
infestus inimicus 571
infinitus insatiabilis 92, 570
ingenium uirtus 646
ingens arboreum 316, 317
ingentes alites 347
ingenuus honestus 685
inimicitiae accusationes 613
inimicus atrox 98, 317
iniudicatus incondemnatus 91, 93
inlicitus anceps 81, 99, 619
inlustris ignobilis 96, 612
inluuie inbalnitie inperfundi<ti>e incuria 391
innoxius florens 97, 572
inops infamis 34
inpudens inpurus inuerecundissumus 101
inrideo aspernor 82, 598
insania adrogatio 97, 416
insignite inique 290
insipientia iniustitia 432
insons indemnatus 93
insperatus opportunus 291
intercedo impedio 461
instituta ornata 287
insulsus inutilis 289
intemeratus impollutus 93, 620
inter sacrum saxumque 56
interfluo occurso 622
intestabilis infandus 93
intro foras 163
intueor miror 53, 186, 596
inuideo faueo 430
inuidia misericordia 165, 603
inuidiosus detestabilis 421
inuisitatus inauditus 92, 93, 659
inuisus infamis 96, 320
inutile turpe inhonestum 397
ioca seria 432, 628
iocose lepide 486
iocur pectus *see* iecur pectus
iocus ludus 305–6
irascatur ... mitigetur 222
ite, concinite in modum 488
ite nuntiate 281, 598

ite sequimini 487
itinera actus 188
itinera fora 611
iudices magistratus 266, 436
iudicia leges 409
iudicia suffragia 434
iudicia recuperationes 237
iumenta pecuda 547
iurauit iurauerit 126
iurgia preces 165, 616
ius cerei 437
ius iniuria 157
iussa uetita 161
iustus iniustus 104, 105, 158, 303
iuuentus arma 651
iuuentus senes 154, 158, 186, 605

labitur liquitur 285
labores pericula 503–4, 554
laboro festino 52, 580–1
laboro uigilo 578
lacer semianimus 575
lacrimae gaudium 602
laeta tristia 151, 158, 268, 593
laetitia maeror 151, 561
laetitia uictoria 53, 159, 227, 673
laetor doleo 430
laetus lubens 275
lana, opus omne 387
lapides ignis 565
lapis silex 45
laqueis manicis pedicis 396
lasciuire ... discordare 223, 621, 641
latus angustus 430
lauando eluendo 119, 285
laudo culpo 385
legati litterae 666
legationes priuati 444
leges imperium 268, 581
leges iura 434
leges maiestas 563
legiones equitatus 651
lego sublego 215, 235
lemnisci corollae 298
lenis mitis 73, 80
leuis asper 157, 185, 215, 430
leuis ignobilis 99, 609
liberi coniuges 207, 652
liberi fratres 169, 647
liberi parentes 169
libertas immunitas 267, 654
libertinus tricorius 377
libertus amicus 590
libidinosus proteruus 438
ligo dolabra 590

Index Mainly of Selected Pairs and Longer Sequences 727

ligo obligo 116
linguae mores 591
loca lautia 64, 257–8, 657
loca templa sacra urbs 201, 241
locatio conductio 259–62
locuples intestatus 10, 618
locus tempus 566
longa ... infinita 97, 223–4, 315, 353
longa nomina contorplicata 38, 44
longus breuis 430
luce palam 428
lucrifugas damnicupidos 278
lucto delucto 116
luctus gemitus 445
lupus femina 46
lurcones comedones 375
lustratus piatus 381
lutum lupanar 483, 691
luxuria industria 165, 587

madidus sobrius 34
maerore errore macore 283
maestus sordidatus 420
magis magis 319, 486
magistratus sacerdotia 266, 558, 666
magistratus senatus 451
magnae gentes opulentae 39, 222, 335–6
magnum ... uix credibile 514, 516
magnus minutus 303
magnus paruus 430
magnus pulcher pisculentus 550
malacas capularias 278
maledictum contumelia 429
malignus largus 158, 303
malus bonus 303
malus periurus 291
manus copiae 410
mater cognata 170, 304, 379
mater cognati 517
mater pater 168
matrona ancilla 229, 518
medicina tonstrina 296
meliorem ... pudentiorem 223, 456
melius peius 158
mendicus exul 685
mentem memoriam 214
metus formido obliuio 241
mihi fidei magistratuique meo 244
minimis maximis mediocribus 153
mirabilis innumerabilis 97
mirifice apte 486
miser egens 571–2
misere male 311
mitis indulgens 73, 80, 81
mobilis infidus 98, 575

modestia decor 561
modo hoc modo illoc 486
modo huc modo illuc 30, 486
modo sursum modo deorsum 387
molior paro 82, 579
monendo suadendo 286, 623
muginamur molimur subducimur 395
multa minax 339, 484
multa pauca 430
multiloquos gloriosus 289
mundus elegans 430
municipia coloniae 184, 266, 415

nasutus macellus 381
neco eicio 697
nepos neptis 168, 170
nerui musculi 697
nobilitas honores 435
nobilitas pulchritudo 616
nolens uolens 103
nolo uolo 107
nomen praenomen 228, 655
nomino creo 236 n. 2
non curo ... uolo 390
notus ignotus 105, 303
nudus intectus 575
nuntii introitus 160, 610
nuntii renuntii 304
nutans, distorquens oculos 288, 519
nuto nicto 292

obligo perobligo 116
occido capio 160, 458, 579, 580
occido concido 119
occurram in triuiis, deducam 518
odi diligo 430
odium amicitia 558
opaca ingens 314, 315
opera consilium 454
opera labor 305
opes honores 612
opes potentia 442
oportet oportebit 126
oppida conciliabula 651–2
oppressa uindicata 422
opsigno consigno 116, 284
opsto opsisto 284
optumus maxumus 14, 74, 75, 418, 420, 421, 657, 661
opulentus inclutus 74
opus labor 305
ordo plebs 267, 616
origo mores 608
oro obsecro 276, 294
oro obsisto 621

oscula complexus 546, 613
ostrea peloris 67

palam secreto 46, 264, 459–60
pallor tineae 387
palmipedalis 60
palmipes 60
par impar 106, 518
parentes patria 200–1, 229, 433
parerent obseruarent 179, 338
parricida sacrilegus 557
parricida sicarius 407
patagiarii indusiarii 277
patefacta inlustrata 422
pater rex 190, 268, 337
paterent darentur 188, 215
patior taceo 422, 465
patres conscripti 252–4, 303, 689
patria domus 561, 562
patria liberi 581
patria parentes 200, 559–60, 569
patronus patrona 142
patruelis matruelis 168
pauidi palantes 360–1
pecudes armenta feraeque 202, 322
pecunia commeatus 651
pedibus manibus/manibus pedibus (cf. (laqueis) manicis pedicis) 304
pedites equites 653
pellerent pellerentur 121, 123, 184, 625
peloridas sphondylos 67
per damna per caedes 523
per fora per domos 608, 629
per laeta per aduersa 186, 628
per latrones per seruos 429
per medium per non medium 107, 358
per scutum per ocream 214, 684
per seria per iocos 161, 628
per tela per hostis 319
per tela per ignis 319
per uias per inuia 106, 666
per uim per furorem 215, 428
per uirtutes per uoluptates 215
pereo intereo 285
pereo pertimeo 284
perfer obdura 487
perfidia iniustitia 291
perfidiosus subdolus 620
perge aude 131
perge excrucia 131, 281
perge, ne remorare 487
pergo propero 53, 622
perspicue palam 311
pertimesco profugio 184, 423
peruersus perperuersus 116

pes et palmus 60
petis pipas 384
pietaticultrix gracilipes crotalistria 694
pingendum fingendum 226
pingo fingo 212, 285
piscor uenor 521
pistillum mortarium 293
plagipatidae ferritribaces 278, 694
planus editus 617
plebes primores 158, 163, 186, 605
plorans eiulans 288
plorans opsecrans 288
poema oratio 432
poema pictura 443
polio expolio 119, 212, 285
pontifex, pro praetore 265, 416
pontifices augures 267, 646
populi nationes 267, 557
populor excindo 172, 186, 623
populus Romanus Quirites 262–3
porticus uiae 434
possum audio 423
potens gratiosus 80
potentia exitium 229, 612
potentia nobilitas 591
poto amo 299
praecantrix coniectrix 278
praefuit praefuerit 127
praenomen cognomen 655
prandet potat 287
prandi potaui 287, 299
prandium cena 297
pransum paratum cohortatum 549
prata arua 483
prenso detraho 624
prenso detrudo 626
prima postrema 154, 265
prisci casci (?) 336
pro patria pro liberis 581
probitas industria 561
probrum scelus 225, 227, 607
procax rapax trahax 277
procul iuxta 159, 164, 215, 581
prodigium ... portentum 348
prodo oppugno 423
proelia pugnas 355
prognariter ... prudens 336–7
prompta occulta 160, 605
promulgo fero 184
prope longe 157, 164, 215, 430
propera, abi domum 281
propere celeriter 312
propinquus adfinis 169, 647
propinquus amicus 225, 304, 604
prosit obsit 104, 158, 164

Index Mainly of Selected Pairs and Longer Sequences 729

proteruus iracundus 289
prouidendo consultando 286, 598
prouinciae exercitus 629, 655
prouinciae iudicia 429
proximus alienus 159, 607
puberes impubes 105, 650
publicus priuatus 158, 162, 456, 458
pudor constantia 434
pudor pudicitia 434, 555–6
pueri/puellae 141, 516
pueri/uirgines 141, 305, 559
pugno proelio 341–2
pugnus calx 304
pulcer praepes 331–4
pulla purpurea ampla 365
pullus oua 526, 684
pulso exterreo 625
pupillus pupilla 142
purus putus 171, 339–40

quadratus longus 157, 215, 430
quae bona quae mala 388
quae sint, quae futura sint 126
quae uolt quae neuolt 107
questus adulatio 602
quid cauendum . . . quid uitandum 387
quid sumam quid non 387
quid uelint, quid non uelint 107
quid utile quid non 107
quietus inbellis 98, 574
quindecim 58
quod fuit, quod non fuit 106, 107

rador subuellor desquamor pumicor ornor
 expilor <ex>pingor 394–5
rapax . . . fraudulentus 300
rapio consumo 576
raptor largitor 152, 590
ratio casus 590
recta honesta 68, 431
redemptor redemptores 235 n. 1
redeo maneo 621
reges tetrarchae 267, 557
regna imperia 267, 435
regna prouinciae 267, 563
religio caerimoniae 226, 411
remiges gubernatores 502–3
remissus fatigatus 80
renuntiauit renuntiauerit 126
repandirostrum incuruiceruicum 277, 347–8, 694
repente . . . subito 311
reppuli reieci 284
repressi redii 285
res urbanae, prouinciae 162, 451

respuo uermino 546
restitando retinendo 285
retineo teneo 117, 350
retundo redigo 285
rumor fama 459
rursum (-s) prorsum (-s) 163, 341
rursum uorsum 311
ruta caesa 64, 258

sacer scelestus 300
sacres sinceri 265, 275
saeuus importuosus 98, 573
sagittarios funditores 504–5
salsis locis . . . pisculentis 37, 44
saltatores citharistae 415–16
saltus paludes 628
salus uictoria 53
salutat respondemus 288, 304
saluus sanus 203, 684
sanctus inturbidus 99, 595
sanguineam ingentem 315, 317
sarta tecta 64, 256–7, 274, 656
satur supinus 36, 484–5
sauior amplexo(r) 546
saxa pila sudes 565
saxosusque sonans 50
scelestus falsidicus 300
scelus flagitium 414
sciens . . . infidus 49
sciens lubenter 5
scio nescio 107, 123
scrupea saxea 347
segnis . . . indignus 514, 516
segnis pauidus 594
senatus consulta, edicta 458
senatus consultum, lex 267
senatus, equites Romani 409
senatus magistratus 267, 451
senatus populus 267, 665
sentio nosco 449
sequor fugio 160, 580
sequor subsequor 118
seria ioci 161, 432 see per seria per iocos
serius ocius 522
sermo uultus 229, 604
serui ancillae 142, 304, 305
serui liberi 162, 650
serui pastores 503
seruoli ancillae 304
sessio accubito 157, 435
sex septem 302, 520
si deus si dea 29, 139
siccus inanis 514
siccus sobrius 684
signa statuae 548–9

signa tabulae 414–15, 560
silentium patientia 54, 589
silentium uox 628
siluae paludes 605
sine constantia sine auctoritate 599
sine galeis sine loricis 629
sine gratia sine auctoritate 557, 581
sine imperio sine signo 665
sine legibus sine imperio 30, 637
sine miseratione sine ira 637
sine modo sine iudicio 599
sine proelio sine uolnere 600
sine sensu sine fauore 428
sine spe sine opibus 581
sinister foedus 595
sint fiant 238
socius amicus 9, 159, 215, 267, 569
socius ciuis 267, 609
sol, aura aduersa 386
sol luna 356
sola ... maerens 50, 315
solus inermus 99
sonitus tonitrus 292
spero metuo 430
spes metus 590
spes timor 590
spolio capio 598
spolio rapio 596
stadium gymnasium 396
stationes uigiliae 603, 613, 648
status condictus 275
status incessus 157, 435
stimulus lammina 295
sto moueo 157, 215, 430
stolidus combardus 300
strenuus bonus 557
strepitus clamor 567
strepitus clamor crepitus 212
strepitus crepitus 212, 292
strepitus fremitus 212, 283, 349
studia beneficia 452
studia instituta 455
stuprum dedecus 300
stuprum ganea 556
sub di(u)o columine 263–4
subat ardet 357
subblanditur palpatur 37
subiecto adfligo 350
sublimas subices umidas 38, 44
subpilo pullo premo 396
sudes pila 565
sudo palleo 426, 465
sudor puluis 566
suffuror suppilo 285
summis saxis ... asperis 38, 44

summus adprimus 364
summus infimus 106, 154, 457
sumo consumo 113
sumo habeo 236
sunt erunt/fuerunt 127
suouetaurilia 58, 60
superbia crudelitas 555
superbiter contemtim 365
superi inferi 159
supersitiosa ... saeua 40
supplicabo exopsecrabo 294
supra infra 164, 165
supremus optumus 74, 365
supremus ualidus uiripotens 74
surgamus eamus agamus 397
surge ... duc te 384
surge ... i domum 130
sursum deorsum 163, 388
suscipio rego 624
suscipio transigo 623

taeter incultus 98, 573
taeterrimus crudelissimus fallacissimus 74
taetros anguimanus 354
tarda ... uoluentia 49
tardo ... pingui 516
tardus inhumanus 419
temere prouiso 160, 627
temere turbulente 215, 427
templa delubra 268, 408–9
templum tescumque 56
tempus fortuna 592
tempus locus 590
tenebrae latebrae 215
tenuia ... minuta 354
tenuis libertinus 418
ter quater 302–3, 695
tero contundo 697
teror absumor 52, 662
terra mare caelum 344, 356
terrae gentes 613
terriculas Lamias 387
tollenda dimolienda 240
tonante fulgurante 264
topper citi 365–6
traho excindo 172, 580
traho exhaurio 287
traho occido capio 198–9
traho uexo 577
tristis difficilis 382
tristis iracundus 300
trucido spolio 598
tumidus adrogans 594–5
turbatus inermis 98, 314
turbo misceo 287

Index Mainly of Selected Pairs and Longer Sequences 731

turdus asparagi 67
tutantur seruantur 284
tutela societas 226, 436

uacuum . . . inane 223, 353
uade, dic illi 133
uade uale 487 522
uade uoca 133
uagi palantes 51, 573
ualeat uiuat 487
ualete abite 487
uarius incertus 98, 574
uastus incultus 98, 575
uates annales 609
ubertas agrorum, frugum copia 409
uelim nolim 107
uelis nolis 104
uelit nolit 684
uelitis iubeatis 64, 254–5, 424, 663
uenalicia . . . iumenta 684
uendendo emendo 285, 441
uendo emo 158, 185, 440–1
ueni uidi uici 11, 77–8
uenio accedo 547
uenter stomachus 697
uentus turbo 46
uerba uultus 452, 603
uerbera compedes 296
uerbum entymema locus 395
uestem . . . ancillas 516
uestimenta commeatus 649
uetulus claudus 302
uetulus decrepitus 302
uetulus edentulus 302
uetus decrepitus 302
uetus, restibus aptus 382
ui pugnando 5, 286
uia inuia 37
uiator praeco 215, 235, 236
uicini . . . noti 515
uicos urbem 517
uicti tristes 316
uictus cultus 274
uigiliae stationes 603
uineta uirgetaque 212
uineta uirgultaque 56, 212
uinnulus uenestulus 295
uinum ganea 204, 411
uir liberi 169, 558
uires uirtutes 214
uiri arma 203, 568
uiri feminae 140, 141, 652
uiri fortes, magni homines 17
uiri mulieres 140

uirtus dignitas 227, 410, 444
uirtus eloquentia 411, 475
uirtus industria 453
uirtus uoluptas 599
uis arma 53, 412, 414
uis manus 53, 429
uita mors 150, 158, 185, 436
uitricus priuignus 169
uiuo floreo 457–8
uiuo regno 450
uiuo ualeo 305, 487, 521
ultro citro 82
unanimans fidens 278
unguentarii saltatores 73
uolens propitius 34, 46–9, 275
uolitat furit 52, 449
uolo nolo 107
uomica suppuratio 697
uox uultus 435, 603, 608
urbanus prouincialis 158, 162, 457, 458
urbanus rusticus 162, 432
urbs ager 160, 303, 563, 274 486
urbs domus 318
uro aduro 116
usus auctoritas 263
usus fructus 258–9, 274, 689
utilis inutilis 105
utor fruor 238, 259
uultus uox 434–5

Greek

ἀγαθός κακός 104, 215, 431
ἄγαμον ἀδάματον 89
ἄγαμον ἄπαιδα ἄοικον 100
ἄγε + imperative 135
ἀδέρκτως ἀφώνως ἀλόγως 100
ἄθεος ἄνομος ἄχαρις 100
αἴθωνες μεγάλοι 325
αἴρεσθε τοῦτον, εἰσφέρετε 136, 281–2
ἄϊστος ἄπυστος 89, 327
ἀκέραιος ἀνεπίπληκτος 90
ἄκλαυτος ἄθαπτος 88
ἄκλαυτος ἄϊστος 89
ἄκλαυτος ἀστένακτος 90
ἄκλαυτος ἄταφος 90
ἄκλαυτος ἄφιλος ἀνυμέναιος 100
ἄκληρος ἄμοιρος 89
ἄκοιτον ἄϋπνον 90
ἄκων ἕκων 107
ἀλώμενος, ἄλγεα πάσχων 328
ἄμαχον ἀδάματον ἀπόλεμον 100
ἄμαχον ἀπόλεμον 101
ἄμουσος ἀναφρόδιτος ἀπροσδιόνυσος 687
ἀνάπηρον ὄντα, χωλόν 224, 302

Index Mainly of Selected Pairs and Longer Sequences

ἀνδρεία δειλία 104
ἄνδρες γυναῖκες 140
ἄνω κάτω 165
ἄπαις ἄτεκνος 90
ἀπέδικες ἀπέταμες 108
ἄπηρος ... ἄνουσος, ἀπαθὴς κακῶν 100, 216
ἄπιστον ἄλογον δεινόν 102
ἀπριάτην ἀνάποινον 88, 324
ἀπρόσδεικτος οἰόφρων 216
ἀργῆτι φαεινῷ 51
ἄρρεν θῆλυ 104, 431
ἄσιτος, ἄπαστος ἐδητύος ἠδὲ ποτῆτος 89
ἀσπαίροντας, θυμοῦ δευομένους 328
ἀστραπὴ βροντή 178
ἄτακτα ἀδιόρθωτα ἀόρισθ' 101
ἄφθιτον ἀκαμάταν 90
ἀφνειὸς ἀμύμων 95, 327
ἀφρήτωρ ἀθέμιστος ἀνέστιος 100
ἄφυλλος ἄτεκνος 89
ἄχορον ἀκίθαριν δακρυογόνον 89, 178

βαθύσχοινον λεχεποίην 327
βατράχων κύκνων 44–5, 46
βοῶν ἀπειλῶν 288
βώλοις λίθοις 394

γλυκὺς πικρός 215
γυνή, θυγάτηρ 169

δάκνειν δάκνεσθαι 123
δεξιὸν ἀριστερόν 104, 431
δήσατε καταδήσατε 116
δῆσον κατάδησον 116
διαλέγου πρέσβευσον 137, 282
δίδου μεταδίδου 113–14
δίκαιον ἄδικον 104
δίπλακα μαρμαρέην 325
δύστηνον ὀδυρόμενον 51–2

ἐγγυῶ δίδωμι 83, 276
εἰλίποδας ἕλικας 327
ἔλεγχ' ἐλέγχου 123
ἕν πλῆθος 104, 431
ἔπαιον ἐπαίοντο 123
ἔρημος ἄπολις 96, 562
εὔβοτος εὔμηλος 216
εὐκαίρως ἀκαίρως 104, 216
εὐθὺ καμπύλον 104, 431
εὔπαις εὐηδής 216
εὐσεβὲς ἀσεβές 104
ἐφίλει περιέβ[α]λλ' 546
ἔχω λαμβάνω στέργω 83

ἑώθουν ἐμάχοντο, ἀπέκτεινον ἀπέθνησκον 12
ἑώθουν ἐωθοῦντο, ἔπαιον ἐπαίοντο 123

Ζεῦ κύδιστε μέγιστε 329

ἠγάπησά σε, [ἀγ]απῶ 125
ἦλθον ἀπήντησα ἑδεόμην 78
ἠρεμοῦν κινούμενον 104, 431
ἤφριζον εἰσέβαλλον 178

θέλει(ς) οὐ θέλει(ς) 107
θέλεος ἀθέλεος 103

ἱδρὼς ἀπορία 96
ἴθι/ἴτε + imperative 131

καλῇ χρυσείῃ 326
καλὸν δαιδάλεον 326
καλὸν νηγάτεον 324
κάμηλον ἀμνόν 45, 46
κατὰ φῦλα, κατὰ φρήτρας 330
κάτεχε σαυτόν, καρτέρει 127, 282
κελαινεφές, αἰθέρι ναίων 74
κλαίοντες οἰκτίροντες 288
κλάων ἀντιβολῶν 52, 288
κοίτας φέρονται, στραμνί' 224
κρεμὰς γυπιάς 216
κύδιστε μέγιστε 74, 75, 329
κύνας γὰρ ἔτρεφέ μοι, / [ἵππο]υς 442

λευκὸς μέλας 215, 431

μέγας μικρός 216, 431
μεῖνον ἀνάμεινον 117–18

ναῦται ... κύνες 45, 46
νικῶντες κρατούμενοι 123, 626

οἰνοπληθὴς πολύπυρος 216
Ὀλυμπίοις ... Ὀλυμπίασι 138–9, 221, 276
ὄτριχας οἰέτεας 325
ὄχλος ..., φλυάρου μεστός 80
ὄψιμον ὀψιτέλεστον 108, 324

παῖδας γυναῖκας 169
πανταρκὴς ἀκάκας ἄμαχος 102
πᾶσι πάσαις 138–9, 221
πέρας ἄπειρον 103, 431
περιττὸν ἄρτιον 103–4, 431
πίνωμεν ἐμπίνωμεν 113, 117
πίονα πεντάετηρον 325
πλέον πλέον 486

Index Mainly of Selected Pairs and Longer Sequences 733

πολυκτήμων πολυλήϊος 108, 326
πολύρρηνες πολυβοῦται 108, 327
(χλαῖναν) πορφυρέην οὔλην 365
πρωτοπαγεῖς νεοτευχέες 325
πωλεῖν ἀγοράζειν 158

σωφροσύνη μανία 104

τετράγωνον ἑτερόμηκες 104, 431
τυφέτω καιέτω 137

ὕπαγε φώνησον 133
ὑπάκουσον ἄκουσον 117

φῶς σκότος 104, 431

χαλεπανεῖ, κεκράξεται 288
χαλεποί . . . ἄγριοι 223
χαμαιτύπη . . . ὄλεθρος 80, 300
χόρευε συνεπίβαινε 136, 179, 282

ὤτρυνον, εἰσέβαλλον εἰς ἕρκη κακά 178

Umbrian
aṙeper arves 246
aṙpeltu statitatu 250
arsmahamo caterahamo 248–9
asamaṙ ereçlamaṙ 249

berva frehtef 250

dupursus peturpursus 56, 249

endendu pelsatu 248

fasio ficla 247
fato fito 249
fertuta aituta 250
fons pacer 49, 248

hostatir anostatir 103, 213

mefa uestisia 247

ocriper fisiu totaper iiouina 249

parfa curnase . . . peiqu peica 56, 247
pernaies pusnaes 164
perne postne 250
preplotatu preuilatu 250

sakre uvem 247
sepse sarsite 249, 250
sihitir ansìhitir 103, 213
sim kaprum 247
snata asnata 103, 248
strusla ficla 247

uesticatu atripursatu 248
vinu pune 29, 247
uiro pequo 247
uirseto auirseto 103, 248

Oscan
fakinss. fangvam biass. biítam 214

Selective Index Locorum

The references in this index are mainly to asyndetic pairs and to passages of which the interpretation is problematic. The literary chapters have many lists of coordinations of different types and of longer asyndeta, and it would not have been practical to index every component of these lists.

Latin
Ammianus
22.15.30 51

Anthologia Latina
800 189

M. Antonius
ap. Quint. 3.6.45 105, 107, 157–8

Apicius
2.3.2 69
3.4.1 69
7.4.1 69
7.4.3 69
7.5.2 69
7.6.6 69
9.7 69

Aquila
41 11

Bellum Africum
23.1 650
36.4 5
89.2 203

Caelius
ap. Cic. *Fam.*
8.1.1 458
8.1.4 10, 46, 459–60
8.8.6 461
8.8.7 459
8.11.2 459
8.16.1 199, 461

Caesar

Civ.
1.2.7 16
1.4.3 505
1.24.2 503
1.26.1 37, 506
1.26.3 506
1.29.3 502
1.30.4 37, 228
1.38.3 498, 499
1.39.3 510
1.74.4 503
1.80.4 503
2.1.1 206
2.4.1 502
2.39.3 506
3.3.2 498, 501
3.4.3 227–8, 394, 498, 500, 510
3.4.6 394, 497, 501
3.5.2 498, 499
3.12.4 498, 499
3.26.1 497
3.44.6 504
3.53.4 503
3.91.3 220
Gall.
7.14.10 168

Cato
Agr.
14.5 228
18.3 45
134.2 47
135.6–7 60–1
139 47, 139
140.2 672
141.1–3 242
141.2 56, 212

Selective Index Locorum

157.3 228
FRH 5
F76 548–9
F97 549
F99 550
F104 550
F109 550–1
F111 550
F116 545
F138 551
ORF
XII.73 142, 305

Catullus
1.1 36–7, 484
3.9 7, 30, 485
4.14 492
5.4 492
6.9 492
8.11 487
9.7 490
12.5 221
12.8–9 220
14.18–19 490
14.21 487
17.21 30, 488
28.9 221
32.10 484–5
36.10 34, 486
38.3 486
42.13 483, 489, 513
45.20 121, 488, 489
46.11 48
61.38–9 488
61.47 122
61.116 488
61.193 487
63.19 487
63.59 490
63.60 205
63.63 30
63.85–6 491
64.197 491
64.274 486, 489
64.405 106, 107, 482, 489
65.21 485
66.58 189
68.133 485, 489
71.4 486
86.1 490
112.2 221
115.5 483, 489, 515
115.8 484, 489

Charisius

p. 37.5 257

Cicero
Ac.
1.16 22–3
2.29 105
2.39 23
2.103 23
2.125 164
Att.
1.14.3 450
1.14.4 448
1.16.8 448
1.18.1 448
1.18.3 268, 451
2.2.3 23
2.20.2 108, 223, 449
2.22.1 52, 449
2.23.3 227, 443–4
4.2.6 268, 444
4.5.1 449
4.15.7 449
4.16.2 446
4.17.5 446
5.13.1 444
5.14.3 126
5.16.2 444–5
5.20.6 450
5.21.9 394, 446
5.21.12 450
6.1.4 446
6.1.13 447
6.1.24 162, 451
6.3.4 220, 451
6.3.5 447
7.7.4 445
7.9.2 22
7.11.4 451
7.13.1 267, 451
7.20.1 447–8
7.21.3 447
7.26.1 451
8.2.3 224, 447
8.12.5 452
9.10.2 101
Cat.
1.11 205
1.20 422
1.32 219, 422
2.1 422
2.6 184, 423
2.14 418
2.22 208, 407
3.1 407–8
3.2 268, 408–9

Cat (cont.)
3.16 423
4.1 204
4.18 428
Clu.
148 126, 140, 265
De or.
2.226 258
Div.
2.42 264
2.141 664
Dom.
14 420
17 409–10
23 227, 410
34 24
35 229, 416
44 424
47 30, 424
55 410
68 215, 427, 428
70 184, 424
80 255
113 108, 424
114 424
121 226, 411
137 152, 222, 425
138 267, 428
139 420
143 428
Fam.
2.10.3 458
2.13.4 457
3.12.1 453–4
3.13.1 115, 454–5
5.8.5 153, 158, 162, 227, 452, 456
7.5.1 452
7.5.3 223, 456
7.18.1 220
7.32.3 458
8.16.1 199
13.6.4 452–3
14.4.5 457–8
15.2.4 199
15.4.7 455
15.4.12 457
15.9.1 455
16.4.3 158, 162, 457, 458
Fin.
1.27 429
1.42 221
1.51 221
1.57 205

1.61 438
2.12 223
2.23 220, 430
2.31 25
2.36 157, 164, 185, 215, 430
2.62 437
2.76 431
2.77 162, 432
2.80 220
2.85 432
2.107 432
2.109 184–5, 442
2.111 220
3.58 220
3.63 30
3.67 220
4.3 437
4.25 220–1
4.37 442
4.49 208, 437
4.54 220
4.69 433
5.7 203–4
5.15 220
5.36 436, 433
5.38 442
5.39 220, 439
5.47 157, 439
5.52 200–1, 433
5.62 434, 438
5.73 442
5.89 5, 162, 434
Har. resp.
20 212, 245
28 220
Leg.
3.10 161
Leg. agr.
2.64 456
Mil.
73 662
87 168
Mur.
15 15
20 221
Nat.
1.17 107
1.95 221
2.65 178
2.145 660
2.150 226, 500
3.34 153
Off.

Selective Index Locorum 737

1.9 442–3
1.12 207
1.22 123, 160, 184, 439–40
1.38 443
1.43 438
1.50 160, 440, 443
1.53 434
1.56 159, 184, 440
1.102 434
1.114 438
1.115 267, 435
1.126 157, 225, 435
1.128 157, 435
1.150 208
1.158 29
2.11 436
2.37 150, 158, 185, 436
2.40 158, 185, 440
2.59 438
2.64 261, 439, 441
2.67 266, 436
2.87 443
3.15 443
3.66 441
3.70 185, 226, 268, 436, 441
2.87 443
3.99 168, 443
3.119 26, 441
Orat.
131 222
Phil.
1.24 429
1.26 53, 414
1.33 421
2.35 414
2.37 16
2.62 209, 414
2.82 26
2.84 426
2.89 152, 184, 426
2.109 414–15
3.37 415
3.38 184, 266
4.13 421
5.15 208, 415–16
5.29 20, 416
5.36 108, 416, 426
5.46 125, 265, 416, 427
5.53 126, 266, 427
6.9 28
6.18 208, 266, 416
13.28 254
Pis.
37 208

59 426
64 429
Prov. cons.
8 23, 221
14 414
19 417
25 221
37 417
Quinct.
48 207–8, 406–7
75 421–2
Rab. perd.
13 130
Red. Quir.
13 409
Red. sen.
5 26
10 423
14 289, 419, 428, 513
18 424
29 21
30 420
Rep.
1.47 266
S. Rosc.
19 418
110 687
131 418
152 14, 19, 418
Sest.
1 420
5 429
20 204, 411
21 52, 209, 425
22 411
29 425
33 16, 266, 417
34 426, 429
40 412
56 220
83 428
85 53, 412, 421
88 190, 226, 412–13, 500
90 268, 413
129 421
135 266, 417
139 209
143 17
Top.
23 263
66 445
Tusc.
2.21 131
5.114 105

Verr.
1.128 256
1.131 256
3.154 118, 475
3.155 118, 475

CIL
VI.101 139
VI.32323 47

Claudius Quadrigarius *FRH* 24
F4 551
F37 551
F40 546
F46 552
F49 546
F84 379, 547

Coelius *FRH* 15
F24 551
F38 552
F41 552
F44 545

Coll. Mon.-Eins. ed Dickey (2012)
9n 133

Digest
2.4.4.1 169
2.14.7.1 260
2.14.58 260
3.1.1.11 142, 169
5.1.80 228
18.1.9.2 261
19.4.1.2 261
37.11.8.2 228
38.10.1.4 168
38.10.1.5 168
38.10.10.16 169–70
46.3.80 261
48.9.1 168
50.16.19 261

Donatus
Ter. *Ad.* 990 104, 48
Hec. 315 163

Ennius
Ann.
22 336
35 338
86 331–3
141 39, 222, 335–6
192 5, 336–7
279–81 334–5
294–6 179, 338
367–8 339
385–6 334
446–7 339
457 333–4
591 190, 268, 337
620 339, 484
trag.
3–4 37, 38, 44
9 341–2
65 339–40
89–90 340
91 340
116 341
117 108, 341
166 341
237 343
239 343
296 38, 44
303 178–9, 342

Festus
p. 304.24–30 253
p. 482 366

Fronto
p. 205.28–9 51

Gellius
1.5.3 687
1.12.14 262
7.5.1 172
10.24.3 262

Historia Augusta
Tyr. Trig.
9.9 116

Horace
Ars
96 188
121 527
172 523
314 254
428 527
Carm.
2.3.26 522
3.14.17 130, 522
3.25.7 527
3.30.16 48
4.4.59 523
Ep.
1.1.38 525
1.1.58 520
1.1.100 152, 521

Selective Index Locorum 739

1.1.106–7 525
1.2.15 526
1.2.16 220
1.2.40–1 521
1.4.10 526
1.6.54 521
1.6.57–8 521, 526
1.6.67 487, 521
1.7.72 108, 521
1.13.10 526
1.13.19 487, 522
1.16.75–6 526
2.1.121 526
2.1.192 526
2.1.211–12 526
2.2.56 526
2.2.180–1 526
2.2.203–4 526–7
Epodes
2.61–6 534
Saec.
59 29
Sat.
1.1.39 523
1.1.74 524
1.1.77 524
1.1.85 515, 516
1.2.1–2 524
1.2.63 229, 518
1.2.93 381, 513, 518
1.2.98 524
1.3.2–3 390
1.3.58 516
1.4.15 524
1.6.31–3 515
1.6.34 515
1.7.6–8 390, 515–16
1.8.18 221
1.9.13 517
1.9.26–7 517
1.9.52 514, 516
1.9.59 518
1.9.64–5 288, 519
2.1.59 106, 514, 518
2.2.14 514
2.3.12 517
2.3.57–8 524
2.3.94–5 524
2.3.97 524
2.3.127 524
2.3.215 516
2.3.227–9 524
2.3.236 514, 516
2.3.248 106, 514, 518
2.3.255 525

2.3.264 518
2.3.267–8 518
2.3.325 141, 516
2.5.28 519
2.7.39 483, 513, 691
2.8.9–10 525
2.8.27 525

ILS
5050 47

Justinian *Inst.*
3.22 260
3.23 261

Laberius
18.2 521

Lex agraria
27 228
32 228

Lex Antonia de Termessibus
See pp. 237–40
I.7 200

Lex Coloniae Genetiuae
LXX.14 113
LXXIX tabl. b.5–6 189
LXXIX tabl. b.1–7 234
XCV.16–18 169
CXXVIII.12–13 53

Lex Cornelia de XX quaestoribus
See pp. 234–7
I.41 113
II.15–18 215
II.29 189

Lex Quinctia
13 228

Livius Andronicus
Od.
10 (11) 364
26 (28) 365
30 365

Livy
1.16.3 48
1.24.7 154, 265
1.26.7 130
1.26.11 130
2.6.2 658
2.32.7 105

Livy (cont.)
3.48.3 130
4.2.8 657
4.3.12 645
4.4.2 267, 646
4.15.5 266, 646
4.28.4 658
4.37.9 658
5.4.6 664
5.11.5 169, 647
5.30.6 109, 658
5.45.4 659
5.48.6 648
5.50.2 205
5.51.8 202–3
7.26.4 48
7.30.23 53, 673
8.8.16 220
8.10.4 199
8.13.1 199–200
8.33.20 53, 227, 673, 677
8.34.10 104
9.3.3 105, 150, 660
9.4.16 131
9.6.6 649
9.9.12 267, 665
9.11.13 130
9.14.11 105, 162, 650
9.18.9 25
9.19.3 665
9.24.9 132, 661
9.25.5 650
9.34.15 660
9.37.10 665
9.39.8 665
22.3.13 281
22.10.2 254
22.49.10 281
23.3.2 663
23.3.3 661
23.5.6 651
23.11.10 662
23.12.4 651
23.27.5 215, 665
24.21.10 48
24.38.8 47–8
27.28.12 565
27.43.7 93
28.39.19 257
29.14.13 48
29.27.2 127
30.20.3 201–2
30.20.9 666
30.28.1 30
30.30.12 666
30.32.5 590
34.1.6 651–2
34.5.12 140, 652
34.7.2 266, 666
34.7.4 52, 662
34.34.7 201
34.35.7 168, 652
34.38.3 653
34.45.7 30
34.52.4 653
34.61.5 654
35.23.11 258
35.34.7 418, 658
37.53.2 658
38.10.3 666
38.23.1 666
38.43.6 168, 654
38.48.4 158, 186, 654, 662
38.53.2 663
38.54.3 254, 663
40.28.2 99
40.52.6 119
41.10.7 274
42.1.1 655
42.3.7 256, 656
42.12.4 656
42.19.7 16
42.20.3 661
42.22.5 16
42.26.5 257, 657
42.31.8 657
42.45.7 663
42.54.3 657
45.24.11 140

Lucilius
19–22 375
65 381
75 375
88–91 385
102–4 375–6, 394
112–13 386
219 394
242 381
245 394
256 386
256 386
264–5 394–5
292 386
293 382
294 395

Selective Index Locorum 741

296–7 376
312 395
347 395
352–4 380
358–61 380
365–6 395
385 390
387 107 387
409–10 393–4
445 37
447 374
476 382
484–5 387
515–16 395
520 387
540 277, 374
582 400
593 390
596 390
599–600 213, 376, 391
641 396
600 101
609 387
615–16 386
629 390
641 302
669 377
679 119
680 391
681 378
682–3 378, 391
703 163, 387
794 387
813 382
816 384
837–9 400
843 384
882–3 378–9
902 396
967 396
978–9 382
982 400
990 396
994 379
995 387
1021 385
1026 383
1034 387
1056–7 379
1058 389
1060 382
1065–6 383
1070 34
1092 397

1113 397
1121 383
1157 161
1195 393
1197 397
1225–6 397
1249 384
1293 400
1320 5, 385
1329–30 388, 390, 397

Lucretius
1.14 151, 202
1.15 354
1.163 202
1.258 36
1.454 355
1.491 359–60
1.523 223, 353
1.557–8 223–4, 353
1.680 356
1.873 357
1.1075 107, 358
2.7–8 360
2.77 355
2.118 355–6
2.505 42
2.517 151
2.921 202
3.395 360
3.13 359
3.395 202
3.405 43
4.313–15 43
4.570 359
4.623–4 353
4.1129 356, 393
4.1165 360
4.1199 357
5.13 41, 44
5.24–5 41, 43
5.32–3 40–1, 359
5.223 359
5.228 202
5.257 357
5.323 222, 358
5.418 356
5.972–3 360–1
5.1302 354
6.48 358
6.387–8 36
6.1188 354

Macrobius

Sat.
3.9.7 29, 201
3.9.7–8 241–2
3.9.11 244
3.13.12 67–8

Naevius
Bellum Punicum
17 365
25.3 366
32 366
37 365
58 367
com.
57 366–7

Ovid
Met.
3.353–5 141
3.407 19, 695
3.433 695
4.73 695
4.261 19, 695
Tr.
3.12.5 141

P. Rainer Cent.
164 684

Pacuvius *trag.* ed. Schierl
3.3 351
17 283
76 348
80 160, 190, 213, 349
101 351
171 347
199.8 117, 350
205.1 43–4
217 127
221 347
238 277, 347–8
239.6 50
240.2 350
255.1 350
262.4 351
263 212, 283

Paul. Fest.
p. 6.24–30 253
p. 443.2–3 383

Petronius
7.11 684
15.4 685
37.7 684

38.2 28
38.6–7 28
38.15 684
43.3 684
46.2 684
55.6 279, 694
57.9 133
61.9 68
76.8 684
80.4 133
81.3 685
107.5 685
114.9 133

Phaedrus
2.2.2 122

Plautus
Am.
226 160, 292, 303
551 118
650–1 294
898 300
923 276
923–4 294
928 487
991 274
1001 34
1012 295
1012–13 296
1062 292
1132 275
As.
34 277
169 285
222–3 295
245–6 294
247 104, 303
259–60 56, 264, 274, 295
340 302
475–6 100
548–9 295
555 5
562 5
Aul.
95 293
318 288
346–7 283
453 283
509 277
512 278
513 278
693 288
727 288
764–5 115

Selective Index Locorum 743

Bac.
380 295, 304
400–1 105, 158, 303
612–14 289, 293
615 295
784 300
901 130
935 116, 285
1080 295
Capt.
114 29, 163
502–3 285
617 56
648 295
Cas.
521 142
550 290, 302
642 206
970 56
Cist.
208 119, 212, 285, 293
216–17 295
512 153
521 304
Cur.
5 275
74 206
89 47, 275
280 105, 303
647 46
Epid.
198 296
210 141, 294, 305
211 302, 520
226 298
666 302
Men.
174 206
290 265, 275
339 142, 304
476 287, 299
801 298
863 291
974–5 296
Merc.
7 107
47 291
50 287
55 287
192 285
291 302
314 302
360 116
618 131
678 203

681 117, 285
832 259, 274, 293
834 689
948 168
988 296
Mil.
191 109, 279
201 288
252 287
373 170
413 35
420 282
544 291
693 295
864 304
1055 278
1127 298
Mo.
22 287, 299
22–4 293
64–5 287, 293, 299
105–6 290, 293, 300
152 302
235 287, 295
275 302
356 278
765 264
1031 285
1118 304
Per.
168 101, 291
408 101, 291
410 277
522 51
686–7 291
707–8 38–9, 44
Poen.
219–23 119
221 212, 285, 292
223 285
290 45
653 288, 304
661 299
791 275
819 294, 304
835 215, 292
1099–1100 22
Ps.
64–5 296
580 294, 300, 302
676 287
794 289 293
844 304
1133 278
1265 295, 298

Rud.
125 291
194 101
346 220
567 130
616 303
652 291
664–5 295
882 276
907 37–8, 44
993 46
1020 294
1097 290
St.
227 278
304 291
Trin.
142 201
251–4a 278, 293
254 304
289 293
299 39, 222–3
317 257
360 107
361 107
406 109, 287, 293
689 34
799 142
821 275
826 291
832 274
1021 279
Truc.
318 207
435 278
583 131

Pliny the Elder *Nat.*
28.87 93
37.201 141
Pliny the Younger
Ep.
1.15.2 68
10.22.2 699
10.70.1 699
Pan.
21.4 122

Pompeius
GL V.304.29–30 204–5

Porcius Licinius
1 40

Propertius
1.5.11–2 23–4
1.12.11 28

Quadrigarius *see* Claudius Quadrigarius

Querolus
41.17 122

Quintilian
9.3.50 12
9.4.23 13
Decl. min.
254.21 80
257.12 80
267.10 80
328.14 73, 80
329.9 74

Rhetorica ad Herennium
2.8 212
4.41 12

Sallust
Cat.
2.2 191
6.1 268, 581, 637
6.5 52, 200, 575–6
10.2 554
10.4 206, 554, 555
11.3 570
11.5 570
11.6 576
12.2 21–2, 555–6, 576
13.3 556
14.3 9
16.3 577
18.4 570
19.1 571
20.7–8 267, 557, 581, 637
20.12 577
20.15 558
21.2 266, 558
25.2 169, 558, 577
27.2 190, 577
31.2 52, 578
33.1 571–2
39.2 572
42.2 578
47.1 581
48.2 572
51.1 558
51.9 8, 141, 559

Selective Index Locorum   745

52.3 559–60
52.5 560
52.13 573
54.4 578
54.5 561
59.5 581
61.9 151, 159, 561
Hist.
2.77 36
3.44.4 575
4.60.16 203, 568
4.60.17 9, 159, 164, 172, 215, 229, 267, 568–70, 580, 581
4.60.21 581
inc.
7 575
9 52, 580
Iug.
1.3 561
10.1 581
10.8 579
11.8 579
14.11 561
14.17 562
15.2 208, 562
16.3 209, 562
18.2 51, 573
20.2 573, 574
20.8 563
31.9 563
34.1 564
44.1 574
51.1 564, 574
57.5 565
60.6 207, 565
62.1 579
63.2 566
76.1 566
76.4 52, 580
79.2 222
85.41 207, 566, 580
89.5 575
91.7 575
99.3 567
101.9 164, 567
101.11 160, 580
111.1–2 267, 567–8

ps.-Sall. *Rep.*
2.4.2 141

SCC De aquaeductibus
125 188, 215

Scribonius Largus
22 697
32 697
60 697
67 697
71 697
87 697
92 697
95 697
96 697
119 697
131 697
140 697
153 697
173 697
183 697
206 697
208 697
209 697
232 697
255 697
260 697
265 697

Seneca
Dial.
6.17.1 168

Servius
Aen. 2.707 135
Sisenna *FRH* 26
F19 53, 547
F50 552
F56 551
F82 547
F102 21, 552

Suetonius
Aug.
71.4 106
Caes.
37.2 11

Tabula Heracleensis
74 259
106 253
115 215

Tacitus
Agr.
3.1 25
12.3 25
18.4 26

Ann.
1.4.4 602
1.7.1 158, 602
1.7.7 603
1.13.1 618
1.16.2 223, 621
1.17.4 618
1.21.2 165, 603
1.22.2 628
1.32.3 207, 603–4
1.33.2 229, 604
1.41.3 621
1.42.4 604
1.51.3 53, 622
1.61.1 225, 604
1.67.2 605
1.70.3 622
1.70.4 628
2.5.3 605
2.13.1 161
2.14.3 622
2.19.1 154, 158, 163, 605, 623
2.20.1 160, 605–6
2.25.2 172, 186, 623
2.26.2 229
2.29.1 186
2.48.1 10, 618
2.55.6 628
2.60.3 606
2.67.1 623
2.73.3 206, 606
2.82.1 606
3.1.4 159, 607
3.2.2 207, 607
3.15.2 628, 637
3.22.1 607
3.26.1 225–6, 607–9
3.33.4 162, 608, 623
3.67.2 608
4.1.1 608
4.2.2 109, 624
4.8.5 624
4.25.2 198
4.36.3 609
4.37.3 619
4.38.3 267, 609
4.43.3 609
4.49.3 106, 609, 610
4.50.4 53, 186, 624
4.51.1 201, 624
4.57.3 624
4.60.2 190, 628
4.63.1 624
4.67.4 160, 610
4.69.3 109, 186, 611

4.70.2 611
5.7.1 109, 190, 625
6.1.2 625
6.3.4 619
6.7.3 165, 628
6.8.4 612, 619
6.19.2 612
6.24.1 625
6.28.4 25
6.35.1 121, 625–6
6.35.2 626
11.5.3 229, 612–13
11.6.2 613
11.16.2 626
11.17.3 186, 628
11.24.2 613
11.26.2 619
11.27 208, 613
11.38.3 208, 614
12.2.1 168, 614
12.12.1 614
12.33 152, 164, 208, 615
12.34 626
12.37.2 615
12.39.2 627, 628, 638
13.16.4 208, 615
13.18.1 616
13.35.1 629, 638
13.35.4 629
13.42.4 208, 616
13.44.3 165, 616
13.46.1 616
13.48.2 267, 616, 620
13.57.2 616–17
14.31.3 617
14.36.1 620
15.12.3 20
15.19.2 208, 617
15.27.3 617
15.37.4 106
15.54.1 226, 617
15.55.1 627
15.58.2 162, 629
16.22.3 629
16.26.3 620
16.32.3 620
Hist.
1.2.3 595
1.3.2 151, 158, 593
1.9.1 599
1.10.2 165, 587–8
1.22.1 588
1.40.1 599
1.52.2 599, 637
1.54.1 599, 637

Selective Index Locorum 747

1.56.1 594
2.4 164
2.5.2 165, 215, 588–9, 599, 637
2.11.3 594
2.26.2 596
2.29.2 54, 589
2.42.2 599
2.56.1 596
2.68.1 594
2.70.3 53, 596
2.78.1 179, 596–7
2.80.1 590, 594
2.82.1 597
2.86.2 152, 158, 590
2.91.1 590
3.13.2 600
3.17.2 598
3.20.1 598
3.25.3 598
3.27.2 590
3.33.2 591
3.39.2 595
3.49.1 207, 591
3.68.1 600
3.86.1 266, 591
4.5.2 267, 591, 592
4.8.3 592
4.11.1 598
4.52.1 592
4.58.4 600
4.62.2 599
4.76.3 592–3
4.77.3 133, 281, 598
4.81.2 598
5.1.1 600
5.5.1 595

Terence
Ad.
846 223
990 105
An.
248 275, 287
676 304
889 487
Eun.
278 163
332 302
624 129
818 107, 123
962 115
1079 223
Hau.
142 142
643 158

810 139
1061 223
Hec.
315 163
Ph.
488 288
556 158
687 159
757 664
777 281
950 107

Tertullian
Val. 10.3 46

trag. inc. inc. Ribbeck
19 40
74–5 40

Tubero
FRH 38
F12 163

Varro
Ling.
7.8 56, 686
9.104 258
Rust.
1.2.20 46
3.9.14 696

Venantius Fortunatus
Vita S. Martini
2.79 189
2.412 189

Virgil
Aen.
1.384 314
1.531 320
1.600 318
1.753 135
2.67–8 314
2.358 319
2.542–3 42
2.664 319
3.383 37
3.392 321
3.618–19 314
3.658 314
4.32 50, 315
4.179–81 315
4.373 321
5.24 42
6.113–14 321

Aen (cont.)
6.237–8 321
6.283 315
6.458–9 320
6.531 135
6.552 33–4
8.621–2 315
8.392 50
8.559 50
9.424 316
9.793–4 19
10.696 50
10.837 50, 316
11.85 322
11.483 323
12.363 542
12.707–9 323
12.811 106, 318
12.888 316
12.902 50
12.930 316
Ecl.
9.5 316
Georg.
1.163 49
1.328 42
1.407 317
2.182–3 50
2.377 50
3.28–9 50
3.149 19
4.311 319
4.370 50

Vitruvius
1.1.10 698
1.5.4 698
1.6.13 698
2.6.5 698
2.9.4 6987
5.6.3 698

Greek
Aeschylus
Ag.
769 101
1410 108
Cho. 54 100
Pers.
855 102
Supp.
143=153 89
681–2 89, 178
794–6 216
862 103

Alexis
fr. 25.4 K 113

Antiphanes
146 (148K) 117

Aristophanes
Av.
1559 45
Eum.
352 89
565 89
785 89
Nub.
1287 319, 486
Pax
404 169
Ran.
157 140
207 44–5
587 169
857 123
861 123

Aristotle
Metaph.
1.5.6 (986a.23) 103–4, 431
1.5.7 (986a.32) 215, 431
Rh.
1413b.29–30 10
1414a.2–3 13

Arrian
Epict.
3.3.3 107
3.9.16 107

Bacchylides
19.23 90

Demetrius *Eloc.*
61 13
63 11
64 11
194 11
268 12–13

Demosthenes
4.36 101
5.2 221
5.6 221
21.72 12–13

Euripides
Alc.

Selective Index Locorum 749

173 90
399 117
400 117
Cyc.
659 137
661 137
Hec.
30 90
314 282
387 130
Hipp.
591–5 27–8
IT
1406 486
Med.
255 97
765–7 29
1252 117
Or.
950 288
Supp.
966 966

Herodotus
1.32 100, 216
3.86 178

Hesiod
Th. 28 48

Homer
Il.
1.98 88, 324
1.210 135
1.544 190
2.42 324
2.54 42
2.308–10 328
2.324–5 108, 324
2.331 135
2.362 330
2.403–4 325
2.467 36
2.667 328
2.671–3 13
2.765 325
2.825 328
2.839 325
3.125–6 325
3.293–4 328
3.298 329
3.324 108
3.330–1 328

3.419 51
4.281–2 329
4.339 330
4.383 327
5.9 327
5.193 326
5.613 325
9.63 100
9.154 108, 327
9.466 327
22.386 88–9, 529
Od.
1.55 51–2
1.130–1 326
1.136–7 366
1.198–9 223
1.242 89, 327
3.110 364
4.788 89
10.251–2 12
15.406 216
19.225 365

Longinus
19.1 12
19.2 12
20.1–2 12–13

Lycophron *Alexandra*
1291 45

Menander
Asp.
88 223
239–40 224
415 102
255 169
Dysk.
448 224, 287
524 208, 416
579–80 302
662 224, 302
762–3 276
818 113–14
921 140, 305
946 302
954 136, 179, 282
960 136
963–4 224
Epit.
297 288
527 221
878 117

Epit (cont.)
908–10 90
Georg.
78 221
Heros
72 96
Kith.
fr. 1.3 165, 306
Kolax
fr. 1 138–9, 221, 276
E230 288
Mis.
7 165
50–2 178
696 52, 288
708–9 125
712 300
803 102, 224
Pk.
155–6 546
509–10 137
Sam.
14–15 224
70 288
327 127, 282
348 224, 300
549 288
606–7 288
703 288
717–18 218
Sik.
96 288
150 223
269–70 288, 306

New Testament
Jo 4.16 133
2 Tim. 4.2 104, 216

Pindar
Nem.
3.60–2 541
3.72 541
3.84 541
4.9–11 541
4.25–7 541
4.52 540
4.75 541
5.19 541
6.1 540
6.43–4 541
7.2–3 540
7.19 542

7.92 541
8.2 529
8.33 541
9.4 542
9.29 542
10.47–8 542
10.71 541

Plato
Euthphr.
4d 433
Phdr.
240a.5 100

Sophocles
Ajax
60 178
Ant.
1079 140
Electra
719 178
OC
130 100

Suppl. Mag.
II.53.12–13 116
II.57.34–5 116

Thucydides
7.71.4 123, 626

Xenophon
Cyr.
7.1.38 123
Mem.
1.1.16 104

Umbrian
Tab. Ig.
Ia.1–2 164
Ib. 32–3 246
IIa.19 248
IIa.25–6 29, 250
IIa.31–2 250
IIa.40 247
IIb.1 247
III.8–9 247
III.12–13 250
IV.6 249
VIa.1 56, 247
VIa.23 49
VIa.42 42, 248
VIa.50 42

VIa.51–2 251
VIa.52 247
VIa.53–4 249
VIa.59 247
VIb.10–11 249–50
VIb.15–16 248
VIb.17 247

VIb.30 248
VIb.40 248
VIb.44 247
VIb.51 251
VIb.56 248
VIb.59–60 213, 250